A GLOSSARY
OF THE
TRIBES AND CASTES
OF THE
PUNJAB AND NORTH-WEST
FRONTIER PROVINCE

A GLOSSARY
OF THE
TRIBES AND CASTES
OF THE
PANJAB AND NORTH-WEST FRONTIER PROVINCE

Based on the Census Report for the Punjab, 1883, by the late
Sir Denzil Ibbetson, K.C.S.I.,
and the Census Report for the
Punjab, 1892, by
Sir EDWARD MACLAGAN, K.C.I.E. C.S.I.,
and compiled by
H. A. Rose.
of the Indian Civil Service

VOL. I.

Published by

Gyan Publishing House
5, Ansari Road
Daryaganj, New Delhi-110002
Phone: 011-47034999, 9811692060
E-mail: books@gyanbooks.com

Distribution Network
gyanbooks.com
India, USA, Canada, UK, Australia, France

ISBN : 978-81-212-3437-5 (Set)
ISBN : 978-81-212-4840-2 (PB)
First Published, 1919

2nd Impression 2020

Printed at: Gyan Press, Delhi.

A Glossary of the Tribes and Castes of the Punjab and North-West Frontier Province
Author: Sir Denzil Ibbetson

A GLOSSARY

OF THE

TRIBES AND CASTES

OF THE

Punjab and North-West Frontier Province.

Based on the Census Report for the Punjab, 1883, by the late
Sir DENZIL IBBETSON, K.C.S.I.,
and the Census Report for the
Punjab, 1892, by
Sir EDWARD MACLAGAN, K.C.I.E., C.S.I.,
and compiled by
H. A. ROSE,
of the Indian Civil Service.

VOL. I

Lahore :

PRINTED BY THE SUPERINTENDENT, GOVERNMENT PRINTING, PUNJAB.

1919.

Revised List of Agents for the Sale of Punjab Government Publications.

In the United Kingdom.

Constable & Co., 10, Orange Street, Leicester Square, London, W. C.

Kegan Paul, Trench, Trübner & Co., Limited, 68-74, Carter Lane, E.C., and 25, Museum Street, London, W.C.

Bernard Quaritch, 11, Grafton Street, New Bond Street, London, W.

T. Fisher Unwin, Limited, No. 1, Adelphi Terrace, London, W.C.

P. S. King & Son, 2 & 4, Great Smith Street, Westminster, London, S. W.

H. S. King & Co., 65, Cornhill, and 9, Pall Mall, London.

Grindlay & Co., 54, Parliament Street, London, S. W.

W. Thacker & Co., 2, Creed Lane, London, E. C.

Luzac & Co., 46, Great Russell Street, London, W. C.

B. H. Blackwell, 50 and 51, Broad Street, Oxford.

Deighton Bell & Co., Limited, Cambridge.

Oliver & Boyd, Tweeddale Court, Edinburgh.

E. Ponsonby, Limited, 116, Grafton Street, Dublin.

William Wesley & Son, 28, Essex Street, Strand, London.

On the Continent.

Ernest Leroux, 28, Rue Bonaparte, Paris, France.

Martinus Nijhoff, The Hague, Holland.

In India.

The Manager, Imperial Book Depôt, Delhi.

Gulab Singh & Sons, Mufid-i-'Am Press, Lahore.

Manager, Punjab Law Book Depôt, Anarkali Bazar, Lahore.

Rama Krishna & Sons, Book-sellers and News Agents, Anarkali Street, Lahore.

Honorary Secretary, Punjab Religious Book Society, Anarkali, Lahore.

N. B. Mathur, Superintendent and Proprietor, Nazir Kanun Hind Press, Allahabad.

D. B. Taraporevala, Son & Co., Bombay.

Thacker Spink & Co., Calcutta and Simla.

Newman & Co., Calcutta.

R. Cambray & Co., Calcutta.

Thacker & Co., Bombay.

Higginbothams, Limited, Madras.

T. Fisher Unwin, Calcutta.

V. Kalyanaram Iyer & Co., 189, Esplanade Row, Madras.

G. A. Natesan & Co., Madras.

Superintendent, American Baptist Mission Press, Rangoon.

PREFACE.

The compilation of this the 1st volume of the Glossary of Tribes and Castes of the Punjab and North-West Frontier Province has occupied my leisure since the year 1903 when the Ethnographic Survey of India was inaugurated by the late Sir Herbert Risley. Fourteen years may appear a long time to have spent on this compilation, but the leisure of an official in India is necessarily limited and I feel that another four or five years might with advantage have been devoted to arranging my material better and completing various lines of enquiry. I may for instance cite the section on Hinduism, especially on Hinduism in the Himalayas, which seems to me to be painfully incomplete and is probably inaccurate. The enquiries made by Mr. H. W. Emerson, I.C.S., in the Bashahr State show that many primitive customs which have been more or less worked into the various forms of Hinduism survive in that part of the Himalayas and I have no doubt whatever that similar survivals could be discovered by keen-witted officers in Kulu, Chamba and elsewhere. Officers who are gifted with *flair* often discover matters of historical and ethnographical importance which their less-talented predecessors have overlooked, despite all their efforts to add to our knowledge. Mr. G. C. L. Howell, I.C.S., has, for example, unearthed some valuable historical facts regarding the ancient kingdom of Makarása in Kulu and the old Tibetan trade-routes in that valley. He has shown that these trade-routes have left their influence on the ethnical constituents of that part of the Himalayas and I have no doubt that facts of equal interest await sagacious investigators in other parts of these Provinces. But too often during the fourteen years that I have been occupied in my enquiries I have felt that as an official my leisure was entirely inadequate to do justice to them, and I have also felt that other officers also had little or no leisure to supplement my materials. I feel that one of the greatest perils which awaits an investigator in India is the temptation to overlook points which come within his personal observation and to shirk personal inquiry, because it involves personal responsibility. One always likes to have 'authority' to cite for a fact or its explanation. But I have also felt the truth that there is in India 'neither collaborator nor substitute in official life,' as Mr. J. C. Jack, I.C.S., and temporarily of the Royal Field Artillery, expresses the isolation which an investigator must always feel in India. Hence I trust that the present volume will be acceptable not as a work on the religious and social observance of the Punjab people so much as a compilation of raw material on which fuller and more systematic investigations may be based. This volume has been pieced together as material came to hand and as new books and writings came to my notice. For example in writing on Jainism I laboured under the great disadvantage of not having Mrs. Sinclair Stevenson's work *The Heart of Jainism* to refer to before that section had been printed. That valuable work only appeared in 1915. The section on Islam is to my great regret very incomplete, because when I began to compile it I had no conception of the wealth of material which existed to throw light on the continuity of Islamic thought and tradition from mediæval times down to the present day. An Indian friend has proposed to translate this section into Urdu and publish it separately with a view to the collection of additional material and the correction of the numerous errors into which I must have fallen. I hope that this proposal will materialise and that some day an Indian scholar with a competent knowledge of Arabic and Islamic religious literature will write a work which will altogether supersede the fragment which I have been able to compile. Hinduism is so vast a subject that I do not think any one inquirer could do justice to it. It appears to me for example that a thoroughly scientific study of the worship of Devi would be of immense interest and importance not only as a contribution to the history of Hinduism but also as a chapter in the evolution of human thought. The excellent series of booklets on the religious life of India inaugurated by the Right Revd. Dr. Whitehead, Bishop of Madras, in *The Village Gods of South India*, will provide an investigator with materials for such studies, but in the history of such cults as those of Devi a vast deal remains to be done and the same remark will doubtless apply to the forthcoming studies on Vaishnavism, the Shaiva Siddhanta and kindred topics. It is understood that Dr. J. P. Vogel is taking up the study of Nága-worship which fully merits scientific examination and analysis. I for one do not regard Nága-deities as the idols of a primitive or degraded superstition. Just as Islam has its unseen world, so pre-Buddhist India had evolved a belief in an under-world of spiritual or immaterial beings who manifested themselves in two main things that came from the earth, the serpent and the stream. Both are associated with fertility, as the earth is the mother of vegetation and the sun its father.[1] But on this simple basis of metaphorically explained fact metaphysical thought has built up endless theories which find expression in an infinite range of popular beliefs as well as in philosophic literature. The only way in which the mazes of Hindu thought can ever be made intelligible to the Western mind will be by a scientific systematization of each phase of that thought.

I have not attempted to write an introductory essay on caste, but I may commend to the reader's notice the valuable chapter so entitled in the late Mr. R. V. Russell's work on *The Tribes and Castes of the Central Provinces of India*. The more one studies castes in the works of Nesfield, Ibbetson, Risley and other writers the more one sees, I think, that caste like law may be defined as a function of economics. In the lower groups of Indian society this function is easily recognised and it is practically the only function which caste expresses. In the higher castes the function is not so transparently clear but examination seldom fails to reveal that it is the dominant function and always the originating function. But the history of caste closely resembles the history of law. Human society begins by organising itself in the manner most effective to produce material results and defend itself against its enemies. Thus caste in its inception embodies, as Sister Nivedita has pointed out, the conception of national duty. But duty carries with it certain privileges. The man who does his duty to society is justly entitled to his reward. The tenant-in-chief who held land in feudal England under the King held his lands as a reward for and as a condition of the military service which he was bound to render to the State in time of need. But a right contingent on the performance of a duty always seems to tend to become an absolute and unconditioned privilege. The feudal right or tenure passes into an indefeasible right of property which belongs to the holder adversely to the State as well as to his fellow-subjects. It appears to me that the history of caste has followed a very similar line of development. Caste privileges begin as a reward for services rendered or due to be rendered. In course of time the obliga-

[1] To cite one of the scores of parallels which might be cited Athena born by the waters of Trito was at first a water-goddess and then a goddess of irrigation. Associated with the Erichthonios snake, she finds her prototype in the snake-goddess of the shrine-depository of the Minoan palace of Knossos in Crete, so that the principle on which her cult is founded is of great antiquity: Kainos Smith, *Greek Art and National Life*, 1914, *p.* 190.

tion to render service is forgotten, or at any rate less keenly felt than it was originally, and so by degrees privileges are established without any corresponding obligations. I do not think that any novelty can be claimed for this view, but I think that the parallel suggested is a new one. I will not attempt to work it out in any detail, but I may give an instance of its practical working. The Hon'ble Mr. H. J. Maynard, I.C.S., has pointed out in a paper read before the Punjab Historical Society that Indian Rájás used caste and the governing bodies of caste as administrative agents. Not only did they do so but in all probability they created governing bodies within the caste for administrative purposes. They probably used what lay to hand, but where they found no agency ready to hand they created or developed new institutions on existing and customary lines. The result was that new castes could be created, old castes promoted and existing castes sub-divided by the creation of privileged sub-castes within them. But the political conditions of India being what they are the privileges thus bestowed seem to have remained, when the justification for their existence had long been forgotten. In a small State like Kahlúr the Rájá probably promoted the outcaste Koli to a recognised status within the pale of caste because he needed his services as a soldier: whereas the Katoch Rájá refused to remove the ban on the Kolís of a tract like Rájgiri, where the clan is pretty numerous because he had no need of their services in a military capacity.[1] Where the Rájá was autocratic or powerful and above all where he had a divine power behind him, he could bestow the thread of caste, even it would seem, on individuals; and doubtless he could, in extreme cases, resume his grant. But it is characteristic of the East, just as it was of the West, that privileges tend to become hereditary even where they are not conferred expressly in tail or remainders and we rarely, if ever, hear of degradation from caste being made by royal authority. Within itself caste is democratic and intensely jealous of its privileges. It is no doubt ever ready to expel offending members, especially women who offend against its moral code, and to split itself up into sub-castes which observe its canons with greater or less rigour. But nearly all the forces at work combine to maintain privileges rather than enforce duties. And by a very

[1] The late Sir James Lyall says the negotiations have always fallen through 'because the bribe offered was not sufficient.' We may conjecture that in earlier times military necessity might have even compelled the Katoch Rájá to adopt as liberal a policy as was imposed on Kahlúr.

similar process law degenerates into legalism, which preaches the values of individual rights and ignores the countervailing duties of the citizen to the State.

The history of the Brahman 'caste'—which is by a current and invincible fallacy regarded as the highest of all—illustrates both the processes. Beyond all question the title or status of a Brahman was originally to be earned by scholarship or a holy life, but when the status became hereditary all inducement to attain its qualifications disappeared.

The result has been that the Brahman, when unable to make a living by begging alms, enters domestic service, especially as a cook.[1] Yet we do not hear that the abandonment of learning by the Brahmans as a caste ever brought upon them any ruler's displeasure or involved them in forfeiture of the privileges bestowed on them. No doubt we find very many instances of Brahmans whose status is mediocre or even debased. But the degradation is always due to economic necessity or the acceptance of contaminating functions. The cultivating Brahmans of Kángra and the Jumna valley have been driven to the plough by the pressure of want and the Mahá Brahman has been compelled by hunger to accept offerings which are at once unclean and uncanny. But the higher groups of the caste still retain all their sanctity, inviolability and other privileges which as individuals few of them would have earned by their attainments.

The latest writer[2] on the origin of caste contends that the system must have been found in existence when the Aryan immigrants made their irruption into India and proceeded with their conquests He also surmises that at the outset the system had for its object the due adjustment of sexual relations, that the measures adopted with this view were found to promote economy, benevolence, and morality and have accordingly been adopted by the Hindu religious authorities and been strengthened by religious ceremonial. It is not improbable that the pre-Aryan races of India had evolved the rudiments of a caste system,[3] but such

[1] Punjab Census Report, 1902, p. 371. But the progressive Muhial Brahmans, who have eschewed all priestly functions, are not hampered by any prejudices against similar employment and thrive in the professions and in Government service.

[2] Mr. A. H. Benton, I.C.S. (Retired), in *Indian Moral Instruction and Caste Problems*, 1917, pp. 20 and 17.

[3] *Ib.*, pp. 18, 20 and 21. It can hardly be denied that the Dravidians had class distinctions even if they had not 'castes' in the Hindu sense. Indeed, the difficulty is to find any society which has not such distinctions and does not enforce restrictions on marriage on their basis,

Dravidian or Kolarian tribes as exhibit such rudiments seem to have failed signally in legislating against immorality in sexual matters In the most highly developed and organised castes it may be that the rules regulating marriage within the caste but prescribing all kinds of exogamous, isogamous, and hypogamous restrictions in unions between the various sections and groups into which the caste has divided itself were intended to adjust sexual or connubial relations. But if that was their intention they have proved remarkably unsuccessful in practice, and they seem to afford a remarkable proof of the theorem suggested that rules which human society devises for its protection and conservation soon become fetters which hamper its development and ensure its degeneration. If Hindu social reformers framed regulations designed to promote sexual relations which would be socially wholesome and eugenically effective they must have been disappointed to find that they only created the institution of Kulinism, not only in Bengal but in the Punjab and not only among Brahmans but among Khatrís, Siál Rájpúts, and other castes, over-producing brides in one group and not leaving enough to meet the demand in another. But to write :—"The basis and starting point of the whole system are obviously the fact that the community consists of sections, the members of which are under agreement to exchange brides with each other on certain customary conditions. These sections have not been formed by priests or rulers but solely by the members among themselves, either subsisting from of old or varied from time to time of fresh consent. Priests and rulers, if they were ever so anxious, could not produce such associations. The need for brides was one that had to be met somehow, if the existence of the community was to be continued. If we scan the benefits, which are derived from the caste system, as above set forth, we shall not find a single one, which would compel people to bestir themselves and take action to secure it, save this one. They were, however, obliged by necessity to undertake the solution of the problem—How to find brides when wanted?"[1]—seems to postulate the division of the community into groups before any social problems affecting inter-marriage arose. The simplest solution of the matrimonial difficulties which exist under the caste system and mostly in consequence of its complexities would be its abolition. As a matter of fact exchanges of brides are far from universal and their purchase

[1] Mr. A. H. Benton, I.C.S (Retired), in *Indian Moral Instruction and Caste Problems*, 1917, pp. 17-18.

is by far the most prevalent rule, at any rate in the Punjab. The purchase of a bride is an economic need as well as a social necessity, and her price tends more and more to be regulated by the laws of supply and demand. It can hardly be imagined that the original division into a few castes was based on anything but function. It is singularly unfortunate that we do not know what were the 'eighteen elements of the State' of the Kashmír and Chamba inscriptions,[1] whether they were occupational groups or tribes, but they can hardly have been anything but functional groups. But the origin of caste is a matter of academic interest rather than of pressing importance when we are considering its utility. Let it be assumed that unequal matrimonial transactions are the exception and exchanges of brides on equal terms the rule, how can it be said that the restrictions on the free choice of a bride operate for good under modern conditions? The restraints seem to have been imposed in order to ensure purity of blood by a conquering race or a succession of invading tribes. But once the fashion was set it became capable of endless amplification and capricious modification. Society fell a victim to its rules, just as it is sacrificed to legal formulæ which when they were forged made for progress but which under changed conditions and altered ideals rivet obsolete institutions on generations which had no say in their designing. Moreover the rules of caste seem to go far beyond the necessities of the case, if they were designed to facilitate the wife-supply. The rules restricting smoking and eating with and taking food and water from the hands of a lower caste seem entirely superfluous if child-marriage presents any individual selection of a partner for life, and they can only accentuate and embitter a cleavage which is already sufficiently marked. Whatever the origins of caste may have been and however expedient its codes of rules and restrictions may once have been, its apologist can hardly deny that they now regard man as made for caste and not caste as made for man.

A very striking example of the sanctity which once attached to caste is also cited by Mr. Benton. Diodorus says that the whole agricultural class was sacred and inviolable, insomuch that they could carry on their operations in perfect security, while hostile armies were contending in their immediate neighbourhood : neither side dared to molest or to

[1] The system extended as far east as Kulu for a proverb says : 'All the 18 castes are in Nagar :' Diack, *Kuluhi Dialect*, p. 38.

damage agricultural property.[1] Such a rule seems to have been based on an instinctive or far-sighted view that the destruction of the food-supply, even in the hands of an enemy, would recoil on the destroyer's own head. The economic importance of the cultivator made his function semi sacred – but only for a time. The rule did not become permanent nor was it apparently observed universally even in India. So rules however humane and foreseeing are not always adopted, but a rule once adopted may flourish like a green *banyan* tree and encumber the ground. It seems at least as difficult for the East to eliminate the waste products of its thought as it is for the West. 'It is a historical fact that human thinking has been enormously improved by the invention of logical rules in the past.' But we have outgrown some of them and 'Aristotle's formal syllogistic scheme seems to us now so poor and clumsy that any insistence upon it is a hindrance rather than a furtherance to Thought.'[2]

I have not thought it desirable to deal with such latter-day movements as the Arya Samaj or the Ahmadiyas The literature on these topics is already voluminous. Scholars like Dr. H. Griswold have discussed the Arya Samaj in *The Encyclopædia of Religion and Ethics*, and *The Arya Samaj, an account of its aims, doctrines and activities* by Lajpat Rai adds many details that merit profound study. But the object of the Ethnographic Survey was not the discussion of modernist or up-lift movements so much as the rescue from oblivion of much that must else have perished before it was brought to record. To the ethnographer the principal interest in a work like the one just cited lies in its attitude towards the *niyoga*, a custom of immense antiquity which has a certain sociological value. It is defensible on the ground that the continuity of the family is so essential that the need to ensure it should override individual jealousies or inclinations. It is also interesting to the student as illustrating the impossibility of escape from national temperament. Just as character is fate, so racial temperament seems, when all is said and done, to influence the forms of its social institutions. A strongly individualistic race would not produce women willing to accept certain forms of the *niyoga* or other institutions which lower their social value. But the Indian tendency to merge the individual in the

[1] *Op. cit.*, p. 28, citing Mc'Crindle's *Ancient India*, p. 38.

[2] Graham Wallas, *The Great Society*, 1914, p 226.

group is just as inevitable, given a country exposed to incessant invasion, as the evolution of a caste system from economic needs.

Inquiries into religious beliefs, social usages and custom too often ignore what is already known and start with the supposition that the field of investigation is still virgin soil. It is of the highest importance to an investigator to find out first what work has been done and to build on that, instead of starting afresh. For example, several very full and apparently exhaustive accounts of customs in Kulu have reached me, but a reference to Sir Alexander Diack's *Kulúhi Dialect of Hindi* shows that many usages and institutions must have existed and may still survive in that sub-division which my correspondents do not mention. The glossary in that work tells us that cross-betrothal[1] exists under the name of *dori desi* (p. 60) and that a cash payment called *badophri* (p. 48) is by the parents of the older *fiancée* to compensate for the excess of her age over that of the younger. The system of working for a bride exists, as to earn a wife by labouring for her father is *ghálná* (p. 62). Old maids are not unknown, as land set aside for an unmarried female of a family is called *pharogal* (p. 84). No term for a best man is traceable, but a bridesmaid is *balhari* (p. 49). It is common for a bride to stipulate that her husband shall not marry a rival wife (*saukan*) (p. 89) except under certain circumstances, such as her proving barren, and when a husband takes a second wife he has to pay her compensation called *bhor pit* (p. 52).[2] Married women hold private property called *chheti* (p. 56). Adultery was mulcted in a fine, *rand* (p. 86,, payable to the injured husband. Abduction of a married woman was of two kinds or possibly degrees, for the seducer who eloped with his neighbour's wife and settled the matter with him was not obliged to cross the border and was called *niau kaṛu* (p. 80), while he who absconded with her across the border was *dhuál kaṛu* (p. 59). Legitimacy was a question of degree.

[1] Apparently limited to cases where a brother and sister are betrothed to a sister and brother.

[2] Such an agreement would probably be void under section 26 of the Indian Contract Act which is taken from the draft Civil Code of New York. Literally construed it has been taken to void all agreements in restraint of polygamy: see Pollock and Mulla's Ed. 1918, p. 166. The history of the section and the construction placed upon it are pregnant with warning.

FINAL LIST OF ADDENDA, CORRIGENDA AND CROSS-REFERENCES.

Vol. II, Page 1—

Add under ABDÁL:

See also Vol. I, p. 524 *supra.*

Page 3, *insert* :—

ADREH. Formerly a powerful clan but almost annihilated by the Gakkhars, the Adra or Adreh hold 7 villages in tahsil Gujar Khan: Cracroft's Ráwalpindi *Sett. Rep.*, § 318.

AGHORI : the word is variously derived (1) from Sanskr. *ghor*, hideous and is really *ghori*: or (2) from *aghor*, 'without fear,' an epithet of Shiva.[1] These cannibal *faqírs* are also called Aghorpanthi, and appear to be sometimes confused with the Oghar. See under Jogi, at p. 404, Vol. II, also.

Page 9—

Add under AKÁLI :—

For the Bibeki Akális see Vol. I, p. 729 *supra.*

Page 12—

ANDARYA, a body-servant: Mandi *Gazetteer*, App. VII, p. 16.

Page 12—

ARDASIA, a Sikh title:

ARGHÚN : see Tarkhán (2) in Vol. III. Argun, the offspring of a Cháhzang by a Lohár woman. Should a Cháhzang take a woman of that caste into his house he will be considered as having done wrong, but other Cháhzangs will eat from his hand. An Argun will marry with a Lohár: Kulu *Gazetteer*, 1883-84, p. 120.

Page 24—

ATÍT, a sect of Jogis who considered themselves released from worldly restraints: Macauliffe, *Sikh Religion*, I., p. 162.

ATRI, see under SOTWI.

Page 31—

BABLA (2) a section of the Sirkikhel. See under Hathi Khel, and on p. 330 read Tobla for Tohla, and Babla for Bahla: Bannu *Gazetteer*, 1907, p. 56.

[1] P. N. Q., I., §§ 875, 365 and 41. In P. N. Q., III., § 205, an account of their origin is given, but it does not appear to be known in the Punjab.

Page 33—

Insert after BAGHUR :—

Bagiál (Janjúa)—see Bugiál.

Insert after BÁGRI :—

Bagshi or Bagsi=*kaith* in the Simla Hills except in Bashahr and Kumbársain : P. Tika Ram Joshi, *Dicty. of Pahári* in J. A. S. B., 1911, p. 184. The term seems a corruption of *bakhshi*.

Page 35—

BAI, see under Hathikhel.

Page 36—

Under BAIRÁGI add :—

Thedi Singh, Rájá of Kulu, c. 1753, granted lands to militant Bairágis : Lyall, Kángṛa *S. R.*, § 82.

Page 39—

BAKHSHÍSH *sádhs*, a term applied to two Sikh sects, the Ajít Mal and Dakhní Rai *sádhs*, because their founders received the *bakhsh* or gift of apostleship from the Gurú (which Gurú?). The followers of Ajít Mal, who was a *masand* or tax-gatherer, have a *gaddi* at Fatehpur. Those of Dakhni Rái, a Sodhi, have a *gaddí* described to be at *Gharancho* or *Dhilman ád nag'án vichh*.

BAKKAR, see under Háthikhel.

Page 40—

BAKKA KHEL, probably the most criminal tribe on the Bannu border. A branch of the Utmánzai Darwesh Khel Wazírs, they have three main sections, Takhti, Narmi and Sardi. The first are both the most numerous and wealthy, possessing extensive settlements in Shawál. The Mahsuds are encroaching year by year on the hill territory of the tribe and driving them to the plains, in which their settlements lie about the month of the Tochi Pass. Much impoverished of late by fines etc. Bannu *Gazetteer*, 1907, p. 57.

Page 56—

Add under BALOCH :—

The Baloch of the Sandal Bár are mainly Jatoi, but at some places there are Chaddrars, Gadgors and even Kharrals who, from working with camels, are called Baloch. The Baloch almost always form their *rahná* as a square facing inward, the mosque and common kitchen being in the middle.

In Muzaffargaṛh the Gopángs, Chándias (two of the principal tribes), Ghazlánis and Sarbánis have the worst of characters, but are no worse than the neighbouring Jáṭs : *Gazetteer*, 1908, p. 65.

Page 56—

BANDA-PANTHÍ. The followers of Banda Bairágí are said to form a sect in the south-west of the Punjab: Cunningham's *Hist. of the Sikhs*, p. 378.

Page 57—

Under BANGÁLI add:—The Bangáli septs include Banbi, Gharo, Lodar, Ma(n)dahár, Qalandar, Kharechar and Teli. The Bangális also affect Baba Kálu of Pachnangal, the saint of the Jhíwars.

Tradition has it that Bába Goda's son Ishar went to Bengal and there married Ligao, a Bengali woman—so he was outcasted: *Hand-book of Criminal Tribes*, pp. 34-5.

Page 62—

Under BANJÁRA insert:—

The Banjáras are, Briggs observes, first mentioned in Muhammadan history in Niámat-ulla's *Tárikh-i-Khán-Jahán-Lodi* under the year 1505 A. D. [when their non-arrival compelled Sultán Sikandar to send out Azam Humáyún to bring in supplies,] as purveyors to the army of Sultán Sikandar in Rajputáná: E. H. I., V., p. 100.

The feminine is Banjáran or Banjárí, *i.q.* Vanjáran, Vanjárí.

BANOTÁ, BANAUTÁ, a commission agent.

BÁNS-PHOR,-tor, s. m. The name of a caste who work in bamboos.

BÁNTH, a scullion: Mandi *Gazetteer*, App. VII.

BÁNWAYYÁ, s. m. a manufacturer.

Page 64—

To Bar add:—See under Tharána, *Handbook of Crim. Tribes*, p. 123.

Page 65—

BARARAKKI.

See *Legends of the Punjab*, II, p. 134.

Add under BARÁRÁ. In Kulúhi the form is Bárrá or Bárḍa: Diack, *Kulúhi Dialect of Hindi*, p. 47.

BARETA, *bareṭha, fem. bareṭhan*: a washerman or fuller: Platts' *Hindustáni Dicty.*, p. 151.

The Barhai or drummer of Lyall's Káṅgṛa *Sett. Rep.*, p. 34, should probably be Bharai, while the Barhai of p. 33 is the sawyer as there given.

Page 66—

Insert after BARLÁS :—

Barora, the offspring of a Saniási, who broke his vow of celibacy : in Kumáuṇ the descendants of a Dakhani Bháṭ who married the daughter of a Hill Brahman : *Report on Hindu and Buddhist Monuments*, p. 194.

Page 69—

Add to :—

BASHGALI (not -áli). Their seats are the valleys of the Bashgal river and its tributaries but their settlements extend to Bírkot on the Chitrál stream : J. A. S. B., 1911, p. 1.

Page 70—

Insert : —

BATWÁL—see Barwála. In Mandi the *batwál* is one who puts weights in the scale when salt is being weighed : *Gazetteer*, p. 51.

Page 79—

Add : BED (2), in Láhul the *beds* or physicians hold land called *man-sing*, rent free : see under Jodsi.

Add under BEḌA :—

Diack describes the Beḍa as a dancing caste in Kulu : *Kulúhi Dialect*, p. 50. A. H. Francke places the Bheda (='difference' in Sanskrit) as a caste below the Mons who may be descended from their servants : *Hist. of Western Tibet*, p. 78.

Page 80—

BELEMA, a half mythical race of gigantic men, whose mighty bones and great earthen vessels are even now said to be discovered beneath the sand-hills in the Thal of Miánwáli. They are apparently the Bahlím Rájputs.

BEOPÁRI, see QASSÁB.

Insert before BETU :—

Beṭhú, baiṭhú, a Dági attendant on a Kanet family : Diack, *Kulúhi Dialect*, p. 51. Members of a *beṭhú* family have the sole right of performing ceremonial functions.

Cf. paikhu.

BHAKREL, a tribe of Muhammadan Jáṭs, found in Gujrát. It claims descent from Ghalla, a Janjúa Rájput, who had three sons, Bhakári, its eponym, Natha (founder of the Nathiál), and Kanjúh (founder of the Kanjiál).

Page 83—

BHAINSWÁL, a Jáṭ tribe or *got* (from *bhains*, buffalo) which is found in the Dádri tahsil of Jínd.

Page 84—

Add to BHANWÁLA : This *got* claims to be descended from Bhaun, its eponym. It is found in Jínd tahsil where it has been settled for 24 generations.

Page 101—

Add to Bhátra: Lyall in Kángra *Sett., Rep.* § 69, p. 65, speaks of the Bhátra as the most numerous among first grade Brahmans. But Bhátra here appears to be a mistake for Batehru. The Bhátra clan is described as inhabiting the Tira and Mahl Mori *iláqas*.

Page 83—

Bhandári, a keeper of a store-house or treasury (*bhandár*), *e. g.* in Mandi. *Cf.* Bhandári.

Bhandh, an officer in charge of *dharmarth*: an almoner: Mandi *Gazetteer*, App. VII.

Page 84—

Bhanjiera (*sic*)—an important and industrious class in Mandi. It makes useful articles of bamboo at very low rates: See *Gazetteer*, p. 53, where a proverb is quoted.

Page 101—

Add to note*: For a Bhattia Rája (ally of Jaipál) see Briggs' *Ferishta*, p. 9.

Page 100—

Bhau: for an account of this Rájput tribe see the forthcoming *Gazetteer* of Sialkot by Mr. D. J. Boyd, C.S.

Bhaun, a tribe of Jáṭs, found in Kapurthala, whither it migrated from Delhi: *Cf.* Bhanwálá, *supra.*

Page 90—

Insert after Bharoi:—

Bharoṭu, in Kulu, *bhárṭu* in Outer Saráj, a porter, fr. *bhár*, a load: Diack, *Kulúhi Dialect*, p. 29: *Cf.* p. 52 (-ṭú).

Page 106—

Bhátu, a Brahman in charge of the materials of worship: Mandi *Gazetteer*, App. VII.

Add under Bheda: a Jáṭ tribe of this name, said to be derived from *bheda*, a wolf or sheep, is also found in tahsils Sangrur and Dadri of Jínd.

Page 114—

Insert after Bishnoi:—

Bisht = *wazír*, Diack, *Kulúhi Dialect*, p. 53. *Cf.* Basíth under Megh. In Kanaur the form is *bishtang*.

Page 115—

Bohár, a sweeper of the palace: Mandi *Gazetteer*, App. VII.

Bisan Khel, one of the 5 sections of the Ahmadzai Darvesh Khel Wazírs, with 3 sub-divisions, the Daulat, Iso and Umar Khán in the plains, and a 4th, the Mughal Khel, in the hills. Settled on the left bank of the Kurram in Bannu. The Painda Khel is a cognate clan: Bannu *Gazetteer*, 1907, p. 57.

Add under Bohra :—

In Bashahr their customs are looser and they marry Kanet girls. They came from the Deccan with Rájá Sher Chand—their ancestor being his *wazír :* Simla Hill States *Gazetteer*, Bashahr, p. 19.

Page 116—

Boti, a cook : Mandi *Gazetteer*, App. VII.

Boza, one of the main divisions of the Umarzai.

Bangera, see Wangrígar.

Page 121—

For Dablijiya read Dahlijia,—which suggests a connection with *dahlíz*, 'portico.'

For Bhibhal read Bhimwál, or after Bhibhál read 'or Bhimwál.'

Page 142—

Insert after Budh :—

Budhál, a clan found in Gujar Khán and Kahúta tahsils : like the Bhakrál in origin and customs they claim descent from Prophet's son-in-law : Ráwalpindi *Gazetteer*, 1893-94, p. 111.

Page 146—

Add under Cháhng :—Changar was one of the two provinces of Katoch—Pálam being the other. It comprised the broken hilly country to the south of Pálam and round Jawálamukhi.

Chákha, a taster : Mandi, App. VII.

Page 151—

Insert after Chamang :—

Chamiál—a Rájput sept to which Pípa Bhagat belonged : P. N. Q., III, § 125.

Page 159—

Add as a footnote :—

The Lún country is the Salt Range. The only Nakodar known is in Jullundur. The Chatti-Painti—' 35 and 36 '—is a tract now unknown by that name, as is the Diniar-des. The latter can hardly be the Dhani.

Page 160—

Chaksi :—see under Káng-chumpo.

Page 152—

Add under Chandar :—Sáhibán was betrothed in the Chardar tribe : *Legends of the Punjab, III, p.* 20.

Page 170—

The Chilásis claim descent from Rája Chanderas, a son of Rája Risálu : Neve, *Thirty Years in Kashmir*, p. 132. *Cf.* pp. 166-7.

Page 181—

CHOBA, a hereditary astrologer, in Spiti.[1] The word is probably derived from Chau-ved, one learned in the 4 Vedas.

Page 2?0—

Add to DAHIMA: These Brahmans appear to be much on a level with the Khandelwál. They are fed on the 13th day after death and take neither black offerings nor *grahn kı dán*. Hissar *Gazetteer*, 1904, p. 78. (2) There is also a Dahíma clan of Rájputs, as to which see TAHIM, and note* on p. 238 in this volume.

Page 221—

DAHRIA, a Persian term, denoting atheist.

DÁHRU, a head orderly: Mandi *Gazetteer*, App. VII.

Page 222—

Add to ḌAMMAR. They are found in the south of Muzaffargarh. The name suggests a connection with the Dámaras of Kashmir, whose rise dates from c. 700 A. D.

Page 235—

DHANOTR, a Jáṭ tribe, found near Kínjhir in Muzaffargarh.

DHER KHARRAL, see under Valána. *The Hand-book of Crim. Tribes*, p. 120, refers to *Áín-i-Akbari* on Kharrals.

Page 238—

Add to DHILLON. The Dhillon of Dhillon, a village in Khalra *thána*, Lahore, are proclaimed under the Criminal Tribes Act.

Page 240—

In Dhúnd for Khalára read Khalúra.

Page 242—

DIWÁLA, a Jáṭ tribe found in the centre of Muzaffargarh.

Page 247—

The DOSÁLI is also found in Mandi: *Gazetteer*, App. VII.

Page 247—

DOTAL, see under Ránki-dotal.

Page 249—

DUDHIA, a caste of milkmen found in Ambala Cantonment: P. N. Q., III, § 119.

Page 272—

GÁDRI, one of the principal Jáṭ *gots* in Gurdaspur: found in Batála tahsil.

[1] Kulu *Gazetteer*, 1883-4, p. 132.

Page 274—

GAHLAUR, see Katkhar.

Page 278—

GANGA-JÁLI, one who keeps drinking-water: Mandi *Gazetteer*, App. VII.

Page 279—

GANI, a prostitute.

Under GÁR: After Rája in line 4 insert Pál.

Page 280—

GÁRA, GERA, said to be a distinct caste in Spiti, where an agriculturist cannot take a Gára woman to wife without becoming a Gára himself.

GARWÁL, a branch of the Janjua: Ráwalpindi *Gazetteer*, 1893-4, p. 111.

Page 282—

Under GELUKPA add: see Kádamb a in List of Addenda, Vol. I.

Page 283—

Add to GHANGHAS: In Karnál the Ghanghas claim descent from Badkál, whom they still worship. He has a shrine at Púthar. They hold the *thápa* of Mandi and say they came from Dhanana near Bhiwáni in Hissar.

Page 284—

GHARÍBDÁSÍ, 'a modern sect of the KABÍRPANTHÍS': I. N. Q., IV § 245. But see under SÁDHU. According to the Punjab *Census Rep.*, 1912, § 189, they are a declining branch of the Dádupanthis.

Page 285—

The GHAZLÁNI are described as a Baloch tribe in Muzaffargarh *Gazetteer*, 1908, p. 65.

Page 297—

GHOTAKHOR, diver: see Toba.

Page 301—

GILGAR, -KAR or -SAZ, a worker in clay; see under Kumhár.

Page 302—

GORAKHPANTHI, a Jogi who is a follower of Guru Gorakhn Punjab C. R., 1912, § 150.

Page 303—

Gorkun,-kand, a grave-digger : said to be generally a Kumhár.

Gulbli, fem. -an, a wandering tribe, generally known as Bázígar or Naṭ.-The name may be derived from *gulel*, a sling. In the Baháwalpur *Gazetteer*, 1904, p. 340, it appears as Gilail.

Page 420—

Kádamba, a Lamaistic sect, founded by Atiça, Dípankara-Sri-Jnáná who was born in Bengal in 980 and died in 1053 A. D. Domton or Tomton (Hbromsston) and Marpa re-united his followers into a sect and founded Radeng : Milloué, *Bod-youl ou Tibet*, 1906, p. 177.

Page 435—

Add : Maheb is a synonym of Kahár in Gurdáspur, *Gazetteer*, 1891-2, p. 62.

Page 438—

Kaladhari, followers of the Bairági *mahants* of that designation in Hoshiárpur. Pb. C. R., 1912, § 196.

Page 476—

Kárgyut-pa, a Lamaistic sect, see under Sakyapa.

Vol. III., page 25—

Insert after Laliána :—For the Lalji see Shahpur *Gazetteer*, p. 83.

Page 39—

Insert after Lunghere :—

Lumba, a maker of toys, huqqa stems, caps etc.: also keep donkey-stallions : in Zafarwál tahsil, Siálkot.

Page 57—

Add under Malang :—

For the Malangs in Kurram, see Vol. I, p. 586.

Page 66—

Insert after Mangal Khel :—

Mangala-mukhi, a title of musicians, Turi, in the Simla Hills. P. Tika Ram Joshi, *Dicty. of Pahári* in J. A. S. B., 1911, p. 203.

Page 72—

Add under Masand :—

G. C. Narang derives the terms from *masnad-i-ali*=' Excellency.' They were appointed to the 22 provinces or sees and apparently still survive among the Banda-panthís, but by them are called Bhais : *Transformation of Sikhism*, pp. 35 and 23.

Page 73—

Insert after Matu :—

For the Mulasanti see Shahpur *Gazetteer*, p. 84.

Page 75—

Add under *Mávi* :—

Máwí was the old name of Akbar's *khidmatias* : *Aín-i-Akbari*, I, p. 252, cited in Russell's *Tribes and Castes of the Central Provinces*, IV, p. 338.

Page 77—

Add under MEGH :—

Basíth is from Sanskr. Washisht, 'one who resides at a court.' *Cf.* Bisht in Diack's *Kulúhi Dialect of Hindi*, p. 53.

Page 86—

Add under MEOṚA (not -RA) :—

The definition should be 'a Guru's messenger' not 'priest.' The *meorás* were natives of Mewát, famous as runners, and excellent spies : they could perform the most intricate duties : *Aín-i-Akbari*, I, p. 252. For the *dák-meorás* of Kháfi Khán, *cf.* I, p. 243.

Page 128—

Add under MON :—

Manchaḍ . . . . the religion of which is akin to that of Kanaur : A. H. Francke, *Antiquities of Indian Tibet.*

Page 139—

Nagálu, a basket-maker, in Simla Hills (*Gazetteer*, Bashahr, p. 17) : Nagálí according to P. Tika Rám Joshi, *Dicty. of Pahári* in J. A. S. B., 1911, p. 209.

Page 155—

The Nánakshâhi are described as descendants of Sri Chand, founder of the Udásís, by S. Muhammad Latíf, *Hist. of Lahore*, p. 150.

Page 176—

Add after OMARA :—

Oṭ, fem.-*ni*, a carpenter = Báḍhí, in Bashahr : *Dicty. of Pahári*, in J. A. S. B., 1911, p. 214.

Page 193—

Insert after PAHULIA :—

Paikhu, a low caste attendant, a Ḍági, employed at death ceremonies : Diack, *Kulúhi Dialect of Hindi*, p. 81.

Page 193—

Insert after PAINDA KHEL :—

Pajori, an assistant to a NEGI or *pálerá* : Diack, *op. cit.*, pp. 81-2.

Page 194—

Insert after PALLEDÁR :—

Pálerá, = *negi* : Diack, *op. cit.*, p. 81.

Page 194—

Add to PÁNDA :—'a Brahman who receives donations at an eclipse' : *Dicty. of Paháṛi* in J. A. S. B., 1911, p. 217.

Page 203—

Insert after PÁRNAMI :—

Paroha, a supplier of water at the wayside : Diack, *Kulúhi Dialect*, p. 82.

Page 205—

Add to footnote—

Sir Richard Burton says Paṭhán is supposed to be a corruption of Ar. Fat'hán, 'conquerors,' or to be derived from Hindi *paithná*, 'to penetrate' (hostile ranks). The synonym Sulaimáni recalls the phrase 'Sulaimáni Zárámi, the Sulaimánis are ruffians in Arabic : *Pilgrimage to Al-Madina*, I, p. 45.

Page 206 —

For Wdyána read Udyána, and in footnote.‡

Page 216—

For Khitali read Khilchi under Ghilzai.

Page 234—

After PHÁNHERE insert :—

Phandári (? Bh-), a priest : Diack, *Kulúhi Dialect*, p. 83.

Page 237—

After PRAHU, insert :—

Prámú from *pram-*, 'masonry' ; a mason, assistant to the *thávi* or carpenter : Diack, *Kulúhi Dialect*, p. 85.

After PRÍT-PÁLA insert :—

Puhál, Palhál, a shepherd, Diack, *op. cit.*, p. 85.

Page 264—

For 'him' in 3rd para. read 'them.'

Page 266—

After 'temple' in 4th line read 'to pay.'

Page 273—Under A add :—

1.	Jammál	from	Jammu.
1.	Samiál	,,	Sámba.
2.	Chárak	,,	Chakri.
3.	Kátil	,,	Katli.
2.	Salária	,,	(Chak) Salár[1] : Lunda Satár in Shakargarh.
2.	Manhás	,,	Máhú, eponym.
	Bára Manga	,,	12 villages in Shakargarh.
3.	Lahotra	,,	Lalhi in Jammu.
2.	Jaggi	,,	Jagiain in ,,

[1] In Zafarwál.

3. { Kadiál from, Punni „, Kadía „ } Intermarry with Kátil now on equal terms.

2 are Thakkars.

Page 275—

Add a footnote :—

Mr. D. J. Boyd, C. S., writes.—'Three or four years ago the *saildár* of Charwa, Moti Singh, a Chárak Rájput, called a meeting of Cháraks, Salehrias and others of about the same grade and presuaded them to agree to *dohra* marriages and to refuse brides to the more lofty *gots*. The Manhás people would not touch the proposal and have great difficulty in getting brides in consequence. The Cháraks and Salehrias have scored. I am told that the Maháraja of Jammu held an opposition meeting later to try to break the compact but it remains in force with, of course, many qualifications.'

Page 322—

Add under Ranghar :—

The term Ranghar used to be more widely used. Thus Khazán Singh writes of the Ranghars about Morinda and Bághánwála in Ambála and round Sathiála and Batála in Gurdáspur : *Philosophic Hist.* of *Sikhism*, I, pp. 211 and 240 : they were also known in Sirmúr : *Gazetteer*, p. 46.

Page 334—

After Rongar add :—

Rono, fr. Rajauri—a tribe or class found in Gilgit.

Page 351—

Insert after San :—

Sanauri, an enameller : M. Latifi, *Industrial Punjab*, p. 276.

Vol. III, page 398—

Prefix to art. SHAHID:—Among Muhammadans the term Shahíd, from the same root as *sháhid*, 'witness,' is applied to a martyr who dies for the faith and extended to anyone who is killed or executed, provided he does not speak after receiving his death-stroke.[1] In popular hagiolatry the term is frequently confused with Sayyid.[2] Many shrines in northern India are undoubtedly tombs of Moslem warriors who were killed in the Muhammadan invasions and wars, and occasionally such shrines are styled Mashhad or 'place of martyrdom.' Thus an Imám Nasír-ud-dín is said to have met his death at a spot in the Mashhad quarter of Sonepat town, near Delhi.[3] But more commonly the term Ganj Shahídán or 'enclosure of the martyrs' is applied to traditional cemeteries containing such graves, but these are not regarded as shrines or worshipped. A Ganj Shahídán at Súnám in Patiála probably commemorates those who fell when that fortress was taken by Tímúr in 1398 A. D.[4] The Shahíds do not appear to have belonged to any of the Muhammadan orders nor do their shrines seem to be affected by any particular order or sect. They are often minor shrines, representing the militant side of Islám, not its mystical or Súfiistic tendencies. Such are the shrines of Makki and Kháki Shah, Shahíds at Pinjaur in Patiála, at which food and sweets are offered on Thursdays.[5] Shádna Shahíd at Multán has a *naugaza* or tomb 9 yards in length, but as a rule *naugazas* are not tenanted by Shahíds. Shádna Shahíd had a mother who tempted the saint Baháwal Haqq and then accused him falsely, as Potiphar's wife did Joseph, but the child, then only 10 months old, gave miraculous evidence against her and when done to death by her was restored to life by that saint. He is now invoked by anyone who wants a thing done in a great hurry.[6]

But other Shahíds have a less exalted origin. Thus in Baháwalpur State the roofless shrine of Khandu Shahíd commemorates a Rájpút who was killed by the kinsmen of a Ját woman who had fallen in love with him. Another Jamál or Jamáldi Shahíd is presented with offerings after marriage both by Hindus and Muhammadans.[7] Other shrines of the same clan commemorate chieftains who fell in a tribal feud, and vows are made at them, especially by their clansmen.

[1] P. N. Q., I., § 517.

[2] Ibbetson, § 226. For an account of how one of these 'Sayyids' met his death see Ibbetson, Karnal Sett. Rep., § 376. A Hindu Rájá used to exact the *droit de seigneur* from virgin brides, and the father of a Brahman girl thus outraged appealed to a Sayyid, Mírán Sáhib, for redress. He raised a Moslem host and the Sayyid shrines in the neighbourhood towards Delhi are the graves of those who fell in the campaign against the tyrant. Lamps are lit at them on Thursdays, but offerings are seldom made except in illness or in fulfilment of a vow. They take the form of a fowl or goat, and especially, a goat's head, and are the perquisite of Muhammadan *faqírs*. Sayyids are very fond of blue flags and a favourite prescription in illness is to build a shrine to one with an imaginary name or even no name at all. A *kos minár* or imperial mile-stone near Karnál town has been converted into a Sayyid's shrine. Mírán Sáhib himself went on fighting without his head, but before he died he exclaimed *haqq! haqq! ib.*, § 331: and so apparently he is not himself a Shahíd.

[3] Delhi *Gazetteer*, p. 218.

[4] Phulkián States *Gazetteer*, p 82: for another Ganj Shahídán, at Kaliána in Jind, see p. 262. The Ganj Shahíd at Lahore is the burial-place of Sikhs who were executed by a Hindu governor under the later Mughals: Muhammad Latif, *History of Lahore*, p. 161.

[5] *Ib.*, p. 81.

[6] Sir E. D. Maclagan, Multán *Gazetteer*, pp. 347 and 348.

[7] Baháwalpur *Gazetteer*, p. 178.

Apparently, it will be observed, most of these shrines are old, but that of Músa Pák Shahíd, a well-known shrine at Multán, is almost modern. Shaikh Abulhassan Músa Pák was a descendant of Abdul Qádir Giláni, born at Uch in 1545. *Post* 1600 he was killed in a skirmish and in 1616 his body was brought to Multán. It is said that it was not at all decomposed and that it was carried in sitting on a horse. The shrine is largely affected by Paṭhans and has a small *mela* on Thursday evenings.[1]

All over the eastern Punjab small shrines exist to what are popularly called Sayyids. These shrines are Muhammadan in form, and the offerings, which are made on Thursdays, are taken by Muhammadan *faqirs*. Very often however the name of the Sayyid is unknown, and diviners will even invent a Sayyid hitherto not heard of as the author of a disease, and a shrine will be built to him accordingly. The Sayyids are exceedingly malevolent and often cause illness and even death. Boils are especially due to them and they make cattle miscarry. One Sayyid, Bhúra, of Bari in the Kaithal tahsíl of Karnál District, shares with Mansa Deví of Mani Májira in Ambála the honour of being the patron saint of thieves in the eastern Punjab.[2] Thus the Sayyid has annexed many of the functions of Deví, both as a godling of disease and as the prototype of the martyr who immolates himself for the tribal weal. This theory would also account for the curious tradition that the saint Nizám-ud-dín Aulía was a patron of thieves alluded to above on p. 493. It is no doubt possible that *ṭhags* elected to regard him as their protector, just as thieves in Europe chose to affect St. Nicholas,[3] the patron saint of Eton College. But a change of creed does not necessarily involve a change in moral principles, and just as Muhammadan thieves transferred their allegiance from Mansa Deví to Sayyid Bhúra so the Muhammadan *ṭhags* seem to have transferred them from Bhawáni Deví to Nizám-ud-dín. The parallel is complete.

Among Hindus the term Shahíd has a similar meaning. Thus Rám Mal, a Jáṭ chieftain, is known as Buddha Shahíd, because he was murdered by some Jáṭs of the Chima tribe into which he had married with the connivance of eldest son. When wounded he begged for wine but he died before it could be given him and so his kinsmen sprinkled some over his shrine, and to this day same wine is sprinkled over it at the rite of *bhog bharna*[4] and the rest given to the tribal bards *mirásís* to drink.

[1] Multán *Gazetteer*, p. 346.

[2] Ibbetson, *loc. cit.*, § 226.

[3] St. Nicholas was a great patron of mariners, and also of thieves who long rejoiced in the appellation of his clerks: *cf.* Shakespear, I, Henry IV, Act II, i, 67. Cervantes' story of Sancho's detecting a sum of money in a swindler's matting is merely the Spanish version of a 'Lay of St. Nicholas': *Ingoldsby Legends*, Ed. 1903, p. 193. St. Nicholas took over one of the functions of Hermes, who was known at Pellene as *dolios* and became the patron god of thieves, liars and defrauders. For a discussion of the origins of such attributes see Farnell, *Cults of the Greek States*, V, pp. 23-5.

[4] This rite is observed at the close of the period after child birth during which the mother avoids the use of collyrium for her eyes, henna for her hands, the cent of flowers, and contact with dyed thread. All these things are then offered at Buddha Shahíd's shrine and the restriction on their use is thus removed. It must be observed on a Monday in the bright half of any month.

Page 689, line 24, *for* "explusion" *read* "expulsion."
„ 690, line 6, *for* "states" *read* "States."
„ 692, line 6, *for* "states" *read* "States."
„ 693, lines 5, 22, *for* "states" *read* "States."
„ 702, line 23, *for* "proclamied" *read* "proclaimed."
„ 703, line 25, *for* "Fatih" *read* "Fateh."
„ 704, note[1], *for* 'Cunninghan" *read* "Cunningham."
„ 70[illegible], note[1], *for* "*pule*" *read* "*pulé*."
„ 712, line 1, *for* "*kacha*" *read* "*kachha*."
„ 712, lines 33, 39, *for* "*gur-wára*" *read* "*gurudwára*."
„ 719, line 26, *for* "*sacha*" *read* "*sachha*."
„ 731, in heading *for* "Rights" *read* "Rites."
„ 739, line 2, *for* "*un-ginat*" *read* "*anginnat*."
„ 739, line 15, *for* "planels" *read* "planets."
„ 743, line 4 from bottom, *for* "Gayathri" *read* "Gayatri."
„ 750, line 11, *for* "*kasunbha*" *read* "*kusumbha*."
„ 751, note[2], *for* "struck" *read* "stuck."
„ 757, line 13, *for* "Uarna" *read* "Varna."
„ 769, line 10, *for* "*maleda*" *read* "*malída*."
„ 771, line 16, *for* "*chhila*" *read* "*chihla*."
„ 778, line 53, *for* "tribunal" *read* "tribal."
„ 784, line 12, *for* "Phalgani" *read* "Phálguni."
„ 795, line 7, *insert* "bargain" *after* "pecuniary."
„ 801, line 4, *for* "conscientiousness" *read* "consciousness."
„ 803, line 34, *for* "*máshháta*" *read* "*mashháta*."
„ 805, line 2 from bottom, *for* "Syyid" *read* "Sayyid."
„ 808, line 32, *for* "Id-ul-fiter" *read* Idu'l-Fitr."
„ 832, line 39, *for* "ridegroom" *read* "bridegroom."
„ 840, line 2, *for* "Garúr" *read* "Garur."
„ 840, line 18, *for* "*tilanjáli*" *read* "*tilanjali*."
„ 855, line 27, *for* "*chhoná*" *read* "*chhorná*."
„ 857, line 18, *for* "Garúr" *read* "Garur."
„ 866, line 30, *for* "nose" *read* "noose."
„ 878, line 10, *for* "chain" *read* "chin."
„ 888, line 9, *for* "*qulk-hwáni*" *read* "*qul-khwáni*."
„ 888, line 13, *for* "*fatiha*" *read* "*fátiha*" and so on next page.
„ 890, lines 18, 28, 31, 34, *for* "*kul*-or *kul-khwáni*" *read* "*qul-khwáni*."
„ 903, note[4], *for* "Ambergine" *read* "Aubergine."
„ 907, note[2], *for* "*Taskira-i-Gulistán*" *read* "*Taskira*." and *for* "Muhk" *read* "Mulk."
„ 909, the article on Caste and Sectarial Marks is continued from p. 909 on pp. 921-23.

Erratta.

Page 14, line 36, *for* " Elliott " *read* " Elliot."

„ 22, footnote[6], line 2, *for* " Partar " *read* " Tartar."

„ 23, line 8, *delete* " the."

„ 33, lines 17, 21, 29, *for* " Appolonius " *read* " Apollonius."

„ 43, line 6, *for* " views " *read* " wives."

„ 45, line 2, *for* " called " *read* " culled."

„ 46, line 11, *for* " Kanishke " *read* " Kanishka " ; *for* " Avistic " *read* " Avestic."

„ 54, line 4, *for* " Mahábhárta " *read* " Mahábhárata."

„ 56, line 45, *for* " cuaiously " *read* " curiously."

„ 57, line 16, *for* " Zu'l-akar " *read* " Zú'l-fiqar."

„ 58, footnote, *for* " Barrett " *read* " Barnett."

„ 66, line 4, *for* " Macauliff " *read* " Mucauliffe."

„ 68, line 22, *for* " Budha " *read* " Buddha."

„ 69, line 26, *for* " abbotts " *read* " abbots."

„ 71, line 29, *for* " pratégé " *read* " protégé."

„ 76, line 12, *for* " abbott " *read* " abbot."

„ 84, line 6, *for* " abbott " *read* " abbot."

„ 126, line 34, *for* " Chalya " *read* " Ahalya."

„ 135, note[3], *add* in blank 138 : *after* " Mahadeo " 267.

„ 137, line 19, *insert* 212 after " page —"

„ 174, note[1], line 7, *read* " slave."

„ 182, line 29, *for* " Langs " *read* " Lang."

„ 183, line 19, *for* " shráda " *read* " shráddha."

„ 200, note[6], line 3, *for* " Duryodhara " *read* " Duryodhana."

„ 218, note[1], line 9, *for* " Elliott " *read* " Elliot."

„ 317, note[2], line 2, *for* " Goraknáth " *read* " Gorakhnáth."

„ 338, line 47, *for* " operation " *read* " apparition."

„ 369, line 42, *for* " Budha " *read* " Buddha."

„ 420, line 16, *for* " Bhát " *read* " Bhút."

„ 422, line 40, *read* " is a Bhardawáj Brahman."

„ 511, line 28, *for* " Oraiisi " *read* " Oraisi."

„ 547, line 20, *for* " Neh " *read* " Uch."

„ 645, line 10, *for* " phathic " *read* " phallic."

„ 646 line 18, *for* " repitition " *read* " repetition."

CHAPTER I.

PART I.—BRIEF DESCRIPTION OF THE PUNJAB AND NORTH-WEST FRONTIER PROVINCES.

1. HISTORICAL AND POLITICAL IMPORTANCE OF THE PROVINCES.— Ibbetson, § 1.
The Punjab with its feudatory States and the North-West Frontier Province with its Agencies and Tribal Areas cover an area of 175, 248 square miles and include a population of 28,006,777 souls, or one-tenth of the whole area and one-eleventh of the total population of the Indian Empire. They number among their inhabitants one-fourth of the Muhammadan, one-twentieth of the Hindu, and eleven-twelfths of the Sikh subjects of the King. Occupying the angle where the Himálayas, which shut in the peninsula to the north, meet the Sulaimáns which bound it on the west, and lying between Hindustán and the passes by which alone access from the great Asian continent is possible, the old Punjab Province was, in a very special sense, the Frontier Province of India and guarded the gateway of that Empire of which it was the last portion to be won. This description now applies with even greater accuracy to the North-West Frontier Province which was carved out of the Punjab in 1901, its area being increased by the addition of the protected territories which form the Political Agency of Dír, Swát and Chitrál. This new Province is thus bounded on the north by the Hindu Kush mountains, which shut it off from the Pámírs, and on the east by the territories of the Maháraja of Kashmír and by the Punjab; in the south it is bounded by the Dera Ghâzi Khán District of the Punjab, and on the west by the kingdom of Afghánistán. Ethnologically indeed it includes the eastern part of the Afghánistán or 'land of the Afgháns,' and it is essentially a Paṭhán or Afghán country. It falls into three main divisions—(*i*) the cis-Indus District of Hazára, and the trans-Indus territories of Dír, Swát and Chitrál* : (*ii*) the comparatively narrow strip between the Indus and the Afghán hills which forms the districts of Pesháwar, Kohát, Bannu and Dera Ismail Khán : and (*iii*) the rugged mountainous regions on the west between those districts and the border of Afghánistán which form the Political Agencies of Wazíristán, Southern and Northern, the Kurram and the Khyber. The North-West Frontier Province is ethnologically of great interest and importance to the student of the races of the Punjab, but the materials for its history are scanty and uncertain as compared with those which, imperfect as they are, exist in the case of the Punjab.

Historically the Punjab is of equal importance to the student of Indian ethnology. The great Aryan and Scythian swarms which in successive waves of migration left their arid plateaux for the fruitful plains of

*See the article Chitráli in Volume II. An article on the Káfirs of Káfiristán will also be found in that volume as the Káfirs appear to represent the aboriginal population of the Indus Kohistán and the mountainous territories of Dír, Swát and Chitrál. The Káfirs offer many points of resemblance and more of contrast to the Muhammadanised races which have supplanted or converted them.

India, the conquering armies of Alexander, the peaceful Chinese pilgrims in search of the sacred scriptures of their faith, the Muhammadan invaders who came, driven by lust of territory and pride of creed, to found one of the greatest Muhammadan empires the world has ever seen, the devastating hordes led successively by Qutlugh, Tímúr, Nádir Sháh, and Ahmad Sháh, the armies of Bábur and of Humáyún,—all alike entered India across the wide plains of the five rivers from which the Province of the Punjab takes its name. The great central watershed which constitutes the eastern portion of the Punjab has ever been the battle-field of India. Its eastern valley west of the Jumna was in pre-historic times the scene of that conflict which, described in the Mahábhárata, forms the main incident of one of the oldest epics in existence; while in later days it witnessed the struggles which first gave India to the Muhammadans, which in turn transferred the empire of Hindustán from the Lodi Afghán to the Mughal dynasty and from the Mughals to the Mahrattas, which shook the power of the Mahrattas at Pánípat, which finally crushed it at Dehli and made the British masters of Northern India, and which saved the Indian Empire in the terrible outbreak of 1857. Within the limits of the Punjab the Hindu religion had its birth and the most ancient sacred literature in the world was written; and of the two great quietist movements which had their rise in the intolerable nature of the burden laid by the Brahmans upon men's shoulders, Sikhism was born, developed into a military and political organisation, and after a period of decline now flourishes again within that Province; while, if the followers of Buddha are now represented in the Punjab only by a few thousands of ignorant hill-men, it was from the Punjab that sprang the founder of the Gupta dynasty, under whose grandson Asoka the Buddhist religion attained, there as elsewhere, a supremacy such as it never enjoyed either before or since in India.

Ibbetson, § 2. 2. Interest of the Provinces to the Ethnologist.—And if the Punjab is historically one of the most important parts of that great eastern empire which has fallen in so strange a manner into the hands of a western race, it yields to no other Province in present interest and variety. Consisting for the most part of the great plains of the five rivers and including some of the most and some of the least fertile tracts of our Indian territories, it stretches up to and beyond the peaks of the Central Himálayas and embraces the Tibetan valleys of Láhul and Spiti; and while on the east it included the Mughal capital of Delhi and the western borders of Hindustán and on the south encroaches on the great desert of Rájpútána, on the west it embraces, in its trans-Jhelum territory, a tract which except in respect of geographical position can hardly be said to belong to India. Nor are its inhabitants less diverse than its physical aspects. It does not indeed contain any of the aboriginal tribes of India, at least in their primitive barbarism; and its people, in common with those of neighbouring Provinces, include the peaceful descendants of the old Rájpút rulers of the country, the sturdy Jáṭ peasantry which forms the backbone of the village population of North-Western India, and the various races which are allied to them. But the nomad and still semi-civilised tribes of its great central grazing grounds, the Baloches of its frontier, so distinct from all Indian races, the Khatris, Aroras, Súds, Bhábras and Paráchas who conduct its commerce, and the Dogras, the Kanets, the Ṭhákurs and Ghirths of its hills, are almost peculiar to the Province; while the Gakkhars, the Awáns, the Kharrals, Káṭhias, Khaṭṭars and many other tribes of the Ráwalpindi and Multán Divisions present a series of problems sufficiently intricate to satisfy the most ardent ethnologist. Within the confines of the Province three distinct varieties of the great Hindi family of languages are to be found, two of them peculiar to the Punjab; while Balochi, Kashmíri, Pashtu, and many of those curious hill dialects which are often not separate languages only because each is confined to the valleys of a single stream, have their homes within its borders, and Tibetan is spoken in the far mountains of Spiti.

3. INTEREST OF THE PROVINCES TO THE SOCIOLOGIST.—To the student of religion and sociology the Provinces present features of peculiar interest. In the earliest days of Hinduism the people of the Punjab Proper were a bye-word in the mouths of the worshippers of Brahma, and Brahmanism has always been weaker there than perhaps in any other part of India. Neither Islám nor the Hindu religion has ever been able to expel from the lives of the people the customs and superstitions which they brought with them from the homes of their ancestors; and the worship of godlings unknown to the Hindu pantheon, the social customs which still survive in full force among the majority of the nominal adherents of either religion, and the peculiar cults of the inferior and outcast races, offer for investigation an almost virgin field full of the richest promise. In the Punjab hills the Hindu religion and the caste-system to which it gave birth are to be found free in a very unusual degree from alteration by external influences, though doubtless much deteriorated by decay from within. Sikhism must be studied in the Punjab if at all, and among the Bishnois of the Hariána is to be found a curious offshoot from the national religion which is peculiar to them alone. For the inquiry into primitive institutions and the early growth of property in land the Punjab and North-West Frontier Provinces afford material of singular completeness and importance. Tribal organisation and tenures are to be found nowhere in India in such primitive integrity as on the western frontier of the latter Province, while in the eastern plains of the Punjab the village communities are typically perfect in their development. Between the two extremes every step in the gradation from one form to the other is exemplified, while in the hills of Kángra and Simla community of rights, whether based on the tribe or on the village, is unknown. Ibbetson, § 3.

The Punjab can show no vast cities to rival Calcutta and Bombay; no great factories, no varied mineral wealth; but the occupations of its people are still not without an interest of their own. The husbandmen of the Punjab furnish to the English market supplies of wheat. The pursuits of the nomad pastoral tribes of the western *doábs* and of the river populations of the Indus and Sutlej, the POWINDAH traffic of Dera Gházi Khán and the salt mines of Jhelum are all well worthy of investigation and description; while the silk and *pashm* fabrics and embroideries of Delhi, Ludhiána and Amritsar, the enamels of Multán, the damascening of Siálkot and Gujrát, the pottery of Multán, and the beautiful jewellery and miniature painting of Delhi, have acquired a fame extending far beyond the limits of the Province.

Ibbetson, § 4. 4. BOUNDARIES AND ADMINISTRATIVE DIVISIONS.—The Punjab Province, together with Kashmír which lies to its north and the North-West Frontier Province on its west, occupies the extreme north-western corner of India. Along its northern borders run the Himálayas which divide it from Kashmír. On its west lies the North-West Frontier Province from which it is separated, broadly speaking, by the Indus river. To its south lies the great Rájpútána desert, in which indeed is included a large part of Baháwalpur; while to the east the river Jumna divides it from the United Provinces of Agra and Oudh.

In shape the two Provinces are something between a dice-box and an hour-glass, the axes crossing at Lahore and the longer axis running nearly E. by S. The constriction in the middle is due to the fact that the northern boundary runs up into the hills of Chamba and Kulu in the east and of Hazára in the west; while to the south the Punjab stretches down the fertile banks of the Jumna to the east and the Indus to the west, between which two rivers the arid desert of Rájpútána extends northward to within a hundred miles of Lahore.

Ibbetson, § 5. 5. The Punjab includes two classes of territory; that belonging to the British Crown, and that in the possession of the thirty-six feudatory chiefs of the Province, almost all of whom pay tribute in some form or other, and all of whom are subject to a more or less stringent control exercised by the Punjab Government. The area of British territory is 99,779 square miles and its population 19,974,956; the corresponding figures for the collective Native States are 36,551 and 4,212,794. British territory is divided into 29 districts which are grouped under 5 divisions, and each of which, except the sanitarium of Simla, comprises as large an area and population as can conveniently be controlled from its head-quarters. The dominions of the thirty-six native chiefs vary in size from the principalities of Patiála and Baháwalpur, with areas of 6,000 and 15,000 square miles and populations of 1,407,659 and 780,641 respectively, and ruled over by chiefs subject only to the most general supervision, to the tiny State of Dádhi, with an area of 25 square miles and a total population of 244 souls whose ruler is independent in little more than name.

Ibbetson, § 6. 6. THE HIMALAYAN TRACT.—Along the eastern portion of our northern border, and within the great net-work of mountain ranges which fringe the central system of the Himálayas, are situated the States of Chamba, Mandi and Suket, with Bashahr and the twenty smaller states which are under the charge of the Superintendent of Hill States at Simla and Sirmúr, while among them lie the hill station of Simla and the great Kángra District, the latter including the Kulu Valley which stretches up to the mighty range of the mid-Himálayas, and the cantons of Láhul and Spiti which, situated beyond the mid-Himálayas, belong geographically to Ladákh and Tibet rather than to India. This mountainous tract includes an area of some 19,840 square miles, much of which is wholly uninhabited, and a scanty population of about 1,539,000 souls living scattered about the remaining area in tiny hamlets perched on the hill-sides or nestling in the valleys, each surrounded by its small patches of terraced cultivation, irrigated from the streams which run down every gulley or fertilised by the abundant rainfall of the hills.

The people chiefly consist of hill Rájpúts, including Ṭhákurs, Ráṭhis and Ráwats, and of Kanets, Ghirths, Brahmans and the Kolis or Dágis who are menials of the hills. They are, either by origin or by long isolation from their neighbours of the plains, very distinct from the latter in most respects; and they speak dialects peculiar to the hills, though belonging to the Hindi group except in the trans-Himálayan cantons where Tibetan is spoken. They are almost exclusively Hindus, but curiously strict as regards some and lax as regards others of the ordinances of their religion. The nature of the country prevents the growth of large towns, trade is confined to the little that crosses the high passes which lead into Tibet, and the people are almost wholly rural, supplementing the yield of their fields by the produce of numerous flocks of sheep and goats, and by rude home manufactures with which they occupy themselves during the long winter evenings. They keep very much to themselves, migration being almost confined to the neighbouring mountains and low hills.

7. The Ethnography of the Eastern Hills.—In many respects the most interesting part of the Punjab is that which forms its north-eastern corner. In this, the eastern hills, are included the Himálayan area and the Siwálik range which separates it from the plains between the Beas and the Jhelum. Throughout this tract of low hills with wide dales and lofty mountains with deep and remote valleys the ascendency of a type of Rájpút society is well marked, and this part of the Province might almost be called ethnographically the Rájpútána of the Punjab, as it has called its Switzerland from its physical characteristics. The hill Rájpúts with their subordinate grades, the Ránás, Miáns, Ráṭhis and Ṭhákurs, are probably those among all the peoples of the Punjab who have retained their independence longest; and probably a still older element in its population is represented by the Kañets and Kolis, the Gaddis, Ghirths and Cháhngs or Bahtis who form the mass of its agricultural classes. The Brahman is found disseminated all through this wide tract, and in many parts of the Himálayan area, for instance, in Kángra, Kulu, Chamba and the Simla Hills he forms a well defined cultivating caste, distinct both from his namesakes who exercise sacerdotal or professional functions on the one hand and from the secular castes on the other. He is not however by any means rigidly endogamous, and the Hindu population of this tract is singularly homogeneous, owing to the fact that hypergamy is the normal rule among and between all the castes which can be regarded as within the pale of Hinduism. The ethnical character of the tract is due to its inaccessibility and remoteness from the lines which foreign inroads into India have always taken. Often invaded, often defeated, the Rájás of the Kángra Hills succumbed for a short period to the Mughals in the reign of Sháh Jahán, but they soon threw off the imperial yoke, and it was reserved to

Ranjít Singh to annex to his dominions the most ancient principalities in Northern India, and to penetrate into the remoter valley of Kulu. Thus the Kángra Hills are that portion of the Punjab which is most wholly Hindu, not merely by the proportion which the number of real or nominal Hindus bears to the total population, but still more because there has never been any long-sustained Musalmán domination, which should either loosen the bonds of caste by introducing among the converted people the absolute freedom of Islám in its purity, or tighten them by throwing the still Hindu population, deprived of their Rájpút rulers, more wholly into the hands of their priests. It is here then that we might expect to find caste existing most nearly in the same state as that in which the first Muhammadan invaders found it when they entered the Punjab, but it is difficult to say with certainty, as Ibbetson wrote, that here the Brahman and the Kshatriya occupy positions most nearly resembling those assigned them by Manu. One is almost tempted to believe that the type of Hindu society still found in this tract preserves an even more archaic organisation than anything described by Manu. The Khatri is indeed found among the Gaddis of Kángra, but he is, if tradition is to be credited, a refugee from the plains, whence he fled to escape Muhammadan persecution. The type of society found in the eastern hills no doubt bears many resemblances to that feudal Rájpút system which was evolved, as far as can be seen at present, after the downfall of the Kshatriya domination in the plains of India, but it differs from it in several respects. In this tract we do not find a distinct Rájpút caste which disdains all marriage with the cultivating classes, but a Rájpút class itself divided into two or three quite distinct grades, the lowest of which accepts brides from the Kanet or Ghirth. The constitution of Rájpút society in the Kángra Hills will be found fully described in the article on Rájpúts.

The Himálayan canton of Spiti is purely Tibetan by race and Buddhist by religion, while the cantons of British Láhul, Chamba-Láhul, and Kanur in Bashahr are half Indian and half Tibetan, Buddhistic in creed with an ever-thickening varnish of Hinduism.

Ibbetson, § 7. 8. From the borders of Chamba, the westernmost portion of the tract, to the river Jhelum, the frontier between Kashmír and the Punjab lies immediately at the foot of the mountains, which are wholly included in the former; and the eastern hills are the only mountainous portion of the latter Province with the exception of the Salt Range and the country beyond it which adjoins the North-West Frontier Province.

Ibbetson, § 8. 9. The Submontane Tract.—Skirting the base of the hills, and including the low outlying range of the Siwáliks, runs a narrow submontane zone which includes the four northern tahsils of Ambála with the Kalsia State, the whole of the Hoshiárpur District, the three northern tahsils of Gurdáspur, tahsils Zafarwál and Siálkot of the Siálkot District, and the northern portion of Gujrát. This submontane tract, secure in an ample rainfall and traversed by streams from the neighbouring hills, comprises some 6680 square miles of the most fertile and thickly-peopled portions of the Province, and is inhabited by a population of about 3,040,000 souls who differ little in race, religion, or language from their neighbours of the plains proper described below in paragraphs 17 to 20. The tract has only one town, Siálkot, of more than 60,000 inhabitants,* its trade and manufactures are insignificant, and its population is almost entirely agricultural and in the low hills pastoral.

10. THE ETHNOGRAPHY OF THE EASTERN SUBMONTANE.—All along the foot of the Siwáliks from Ambála to Gurdáspur the dominant population is Rájpút and Jáṭ, interspersed with numerous foreign elements, such as Patháns, a few Mughals, Shaikhs, Awáns, Khokhars, and many others. Of these elements all are modern, except the Rájpúts and possibly some Jáṭ tribes. But in the eastern part of the Ambála submontane the Jáṭ is certainly a recent invader; and he owes his position in this tract to the Sikh inroads, which once carried the arms of the Khálsa across the Jumna, but only succeeded in permanently establishing a single Jáṭ state of any importance, *viz.* that of Kalsia in the Ambála District which owes its name to one of the Sikh *misls* or companies. In this tract the Jáṭ to some extent displaced the Rájpút whose most ancient tribes, the Chauhán and Taoni, were dominant in it down to the Mughal period. How old their settlements in this tract may be it is impossible to say, but the Chauhán at least were probably firmly established in the Ambála submontane before the Muhammadan invasions.

Further north beyond the Sutlej the Hoshiárpur submontane is held by Hindu Rájpút tribes or Rájpút tribes partly converted to Islám. Their settlements undoubtedly owe their origin to feudal grants made by the Hill Rájás to military families under their own leaders as a condition of service against Muhammadan invaders from the plains. They may thus be regarded as outliers of the Hindu Rájpút system of the Himálayas. As a counterbalance to their power the Muhammadan emperors planted Paṭhán colonies at a distance of 4 or 5 miles from the Siwáliks in a line stretching from the town of Hariána to the border of the Garhshankar tahsil, and the place-names of the district still mark a considerable number of these settlements, such as Urmur-Tánda, Jahán-Khelan, and Ghilzián.

Upon these irregular lines of opposing forces the Sikh movement launched Jáṭ tribes, but not in any great numbers. The Kanhya and Ramgaṛhia *misls* obtained large tracts in the north, but in the earlier period of the Sikh risings the Rájpút states of the hills often afforded an asylum to the Sikh *gurus* and their followers. At one time the *gurus*, who had sought refuge in the Hill States of Sirmúr, Mandi and Nálagarh, might well have hoped to convert their Rájás to the Sikh faith, but as the Sikh power grew in strength the *gurus* visited the Hill States less frequently and were content to establish strongholds at Una and Anandpur in the Jaswán Dún. The Jáṭ movement however did not even penetrate the barrier of the Siwálik, and their subsequent encroachments under Sikh chiefs had little permanent effect. The Jáṭs, whose villages lie scattered all along the foot of the hills from Ambála to Gurdáspur,

*This includes the Cantonment population.

are not separated by any definite line of demarcation from the Sikh Jáṭs of the Central Punjab to the south-west or from the Jáṭs of the western submontane to the west. Perhaps the only tangible distinction is that the Jáṭs of the eastern submontane are, broadly speaking, Hindus, while those of the western submontane are Muhammadans, and those of the central districts Sikhs, but followers of all these religions are to be found in almost every tribe. In character and position there is nothing to distinguish the three groups, save that those of the eastern submontane never enjoyed the political importance which distinguished the Sikh Jáṭs under the Khálsa. The Jáṭ of this tract cannot be regarded as in any sense *under* the Rájpút. The Jáṭ communities are independent of his influence and stand aloof from him. They have no aspirations to be called Rájpút or to form matrimonial alliances with men of that caste. Some of the Manj Rájpúts of Gurdáspur have no doubt become Jáṭs by status or are called Jáṭs by others, but as a rule the distinction between the two castes is rigidly fixed.

11. The Ethnography of the western submontane.—Along the western part of the northern border of Gurdáspur, and all along the Jammu border in Siálkot, Gujránwála and Gujrát, the conditions closely resemble those found in the eastern submontane, but the line of demarcation between Jáṭ and Rájpút is fainter. The true Jáṭs, such as the Chíma, Varaich and Tárar, are mainly confined to Siálkot and Gujránwála. The typical Rájpút tribes are found close under the Jammu Hills and include such interesting communities as the Bajju Rájpúts and the Chibhs, with many minor clans towards Gurdáspur. The Jáṭ looks to the south for his affinities in religion and marriage, but the Rájpút regards the Jammu Hills with their ancient principalities of Bhimbar, Rajauri and Jammu as his ancient home. And from Jammu and Kashmír the lower castes are also reinforced. Of the Jáṭs of the western submontane Sir Denzil Ibbetson wrote:—

Ibbetson, § 431.

"The most extraordinary thing about the group of Jáṭ tribes found in Siálkot is the large number of customs still retained by them which are, so far as I know, not shared by any other people. They will be found described in Mr. Roe's translation of Amin Chand's *History of Siálkot*,* and I shall notice one or two of them. Nothing could be more instructive than an examination of the origin, practice, and limits of this group of customs. They would seem to point to aboriginal descent. Another point worthy of remark is the frequent recurrence of an ancestor Mal, which may perhaps connect this group of tribes with the ancient Malli of Multán. Some of their traditions point to Sindh, while others are connected with the hills of Jammu. The whole group strikes me as being one of exceeding interest, and I much regret that I have no time to treat it more fully." Further investigation has shown that their customs are more widespread than Sir Denzil Ibbetson thought, not only among the Jáṭs, but among such castes as the Khatris.

Ibbetson, § 9.

12. The Eastern Plains.—The remainder of the Punjab, with the exception of the tract cut off by the Salt Range which will be described presently, consists of one vast plain, unbroken save by the wide eroded

* A work of great value, despite its countless typographical errors.

valleys within which the great Punjab rivers ever shift their beds, and by the insignificant spur of the Aravalli mountain system which runs through the Gurgaon District and the south of Delhi and re-appears in the low hills of Chiniot and Kirána in Jhang. A meridian through the city of Lahore divides this wide expanse into two very dissimilar tracts which may be distinguished as the Eastern and the Western Plains. East of Lahore the rainfall is everywhere so far sufficient that cultivation is possible without irrigation in fairly favourable seasons; but over the greater portion of the area the margin is so slight that, save where the crops are protected by artificial irrigation, any material reduction in the supply entails distress if not actual famine; and while the Eastern Plains, comprising only a quarter of the area of the Province, include half its cultivation, nearly half its population, and almost all its most fertile portions, they also include all those parts which, by very virtue of the possibility of unirrigated cultivation, are peculiarly liable to disastrous failure of crops.

13. PHYSICAL DIVISIONS OF THE EASTERN PLAINS.—A broad strip parallel to the submontane zone partakes in a lower degree of its ample rainfall. It is traversed by the upper Sutlej, the Beás, the Rávi, the Bári Doáb Canal, and many smaller streams which bring down with them and deposit fertilising loam from the lower hills, irrigation from wells is everywhere easy, and the tract is even superior in fertility, security of produce, and populousness to the submontane zone itself. It includes tahsil Ambála and the Thánesar tahsil now in the Karnál district, the northern portions of Patiála and Nábha, the whole of the Ludhiána, Jullundur and Amritsar Districts and of the Kapúrthala State, and so much of the Gurdáspur and Siálkot Districts as is not included in the submontane zone. Its area is some 8600 square miles and the population about 4,004,207 souls. Ibbetson, § 10.

14. The next fertile strip is that running along the eastern border of the Province parallel to the river Jumna. It enjoys a fair average rainfall, it includes the low riverain tract along the Jumna itself where well irrigation is easy, the Saraswati and its tributaries inundate a considerable area, and much of it is watered by the Agra and Western Jumna Canals, so that it is for the most part well protected against famine. It comprises the whole of the Delhi Division with the exception of the Kaithal and Rewári tahsils of Karnál and Gurgáon, together with the small state of Pataudi and the Gohána and Sámpla tahsils of the Rohtak District: its area is about 4870 square miles, and its population some 1,727,431 souls. Ibbetson, § 11

15. Along the southern border of the tract runs the Hissár District with the small states of Dujána and Lohárn, the Muktsar tahsil of Ferozepur, the Rohtak and Jhajjar tahsils of the Rohtak District, the Rewári tahsil of Gurgáon, and some outlying portions of Patiála, Jínd and Nábha. This is the most unfertile portion of the tract. A large part of it skirts the great Rájpútána desert, the soil is often inferior, the rainfall always scanty and precarious, while, except in the south-eastern corner, where alone wells can be profitably worked, irrigation is almost unknown save where the Western Jumna Canal Ibbetson, § 1

enters Hissar and the Sutlej borders the Ferozepur District[1]. The area is about 11,570 square miles, and the population about 1,889,000. This and the central portion next to be described are the parts of the Punjab where famine is most to be dreaded[2].

Ibbetson, § 13. 16. The remaining or great central portion of the tract includes the greater part of the states of Patiála, Nábha and Jínd, the Kaithal tahsil of Karnál, the three northern tahsils of Ferozepur, the two eastern tahsils of Lahore, and the states of Farídkot and Máler Kotla. Its area is some 9930 square miles and its population about 2,735,630. It occupies an intermediate position in respect of fertility between the two preceding tracts, the rainfall generally being highest and the soil best to the east, west and north in the direction of the Jumna, the Sutlej and the hills, and lowest and worst in the centre and south, while to the north-east the Ghaggar system of hill streams inundates a certain area, and well irrigation is practised along the Sutlej and the northern border.

Ibbetson, § 14. 17. ETHNOGRAPHY OF THE EASTERN PLAINS.—The plains east of Lahore have thus been split up into zones of varying fertility by lines running for the most part parallel to the hills. But the boundaries which separate religion, race and language are somewhat different from these. A meridian through the town of Sihrind or Sirhind, nearly due north of Patiála and once the capital of a Mughal *Suba*, but razed to the ground by the victorious Sikhs in 1763 in revenge for the assassination of the children of Guru Govind Singh which had taken place there some 60 years before, roughly divides the Punjab Proper from Hindustán and the Panjábi from the Hindi language, and forms the eastern boundary of the Sikh religion. So much of the Punjab plains as lies east of that line, namely, the Delhi, Gurgáon, Karnál, Ambála and Rohtak Districts, and the States of Kalsia, Jínd and Pataudi, differs little if at all in the character of its population from the western districts of the United Provinces. Except in the Rohtak District, Jáṭs form a smaller and Rájpúts a larger proportion of the population than in the tract immediately to the west; while Kambohs, Rors and Gújars are numerous in Ambála and Karnál, Tagás in Karnál and Delhi, Ahírs in Rohtak, Delhi and Gurgáon, and Meos and Khánzádas in Gurgáon.

Ibbetson, § 15 The Hissár District to the south of the tract differs from the districts just mentioned chiefly in that, lying as it does on the confines of Bíkáner, the dialect and people are more akin to those of Rájpútána than to those of Hindustán, Rájpúts being very numerous, and there being a considerable Ahír population. The religion is still Hindu, with a certain admixture of a curious sect called Bishnoi. The Sirsa tract which forms the western portion of the southern border of the tract was all but uninhabited till it came under English rule; and it has drawn its settlers pretty equally from Hindu and Hindi-

[1] A certain area is also inundated by the precarious floods of the lower Ghaggar.

[2] But the Sirhind Canal opened in 1882 protects a large part of the central and some portion of the southern tract.

speaking Hissár and Rájpútána and from the Sikh and Panjábi-speaking Jáṭ state of Patiála, while its western portion is occupied by Muhammadan immigrants from the lower Sutlej.

In all the remainder of the tract Panjábi is the language of the people. Immediately below the hills Sikhism has obtained but little hold, and the Hindu element, strong in Hoshiárpur, gradually gives way to the Musalmán as we pass westwards through Gurdáspur till it fades into comparative insignificance in Siálkot. But all the centre of the tract, the great Phúlkián States of Patiála, Jínd and Nábha, the States of Farídkot and Máler Kotla, and the Districts of Ludhiána, Ferozepur, Lahore and Amritsar, and in a less degree of Jullundur and Kapúrthala, form the very centre and stronghold of the Punjab Sikhs Even here however a very large proportion of the population is Musalmán, a proportion constantly increasing from east to west; and it is the Hindu element alone which is displaced by the Sikh. In the matter of race the population of this portion of the tract is very uniform, Rájpúts, Jáṭs, Gújars, and their allied tribes forming the staple of the agricultural population, largely supplemented by their attendant menials. Among the Siwáliks and immediately under the hills Jáṭs are few and Rájpúts and Ghirths numerous, while somewhat further south the proportion of Jáṭs increases and Gújars, Sainis and Aráins, and in Kapúrthala Kambohs, Mahtons (Mahtams), and Dogras, become important elements in the population. In the Lahore Division, Farídkot, and the Phúlkián States the mass of the population is Jáṭ; though in Lahore, Ferozepur and Farídkot Kambohs and Mahtams, and in Ferozepur Dogras, hold large areas, while in Patiála, Jínd and Nábha there is a considerable admixture of Ahírs. The Changars and Sánsis of Amritsar and the surrounding districts, the Báwarias of the upper Sutlej, the Ráwals of the northern districts and Lahore, and the Aheris of the Delhi Division are curious outcast tribes, some of them probably aboriginal; and as we pass westwards and northwards from Hindustán and Rájpútána into the Province, the Bánia of the Delhi territory gives place to the Khatri of the central, the Súd of the northern, and the Aroṛa of the western Punjab. Ibbetson, § 16.

The tract includes all the most fertile, wealthy and populous portions of the Province, and may be called the granary of the Punjab. Within it lie the three great cities of Delhi, Amritsar, and Lahore, besides a very large proportion of the larger towns; and the population is by comparison with that of the western Punjab largely urban. Trade and manufactures flourish, while with the exception of the south-westward portions where flocks and herds still pasture in extensive jungles, the greater part of the cultivable area is under the plough. Ibbetson, §

18. The three most distinctive elements in the population of the eastern plains are the Sikh Jaṭs of the central districts, the Jáṭs, mainly Hindu, of the south-eastern districts, and the Rájpúts of the country to the west of the Jumna. The so-called Jaṭs of the Salt Range and the Western Punjab possess well marked characterstics of their own, but directly we leave the Salt Range behind us and

enter the tract which is under the influence of Lahore and Amritsar, directly in fact we come within the circle of Sikh religious influence as distinguished from the more political influence of the Sikhs, we find the line between Jáṭ and Rájpút sufficiently clearly marked. The Jaṭ indeed, here as elsewhere, claims for himself Rájpút origin, but a Varaich for instance does not say that he is still a Rájpút. He is a Jaṭ and content to be so The fact is that within the pale of Sikhism Rájpúts were at a discount. The equality of all men preached by Guru Govind disgusted the haughty Rájpúts, and they refused to join his standard. They soon paid the penalty of their pride. The Jaṭs who composed the great mass of the Khálsa rose to absolute power, and the Rájpút who had despised them was the peculiar object of their hatred. Their general policy led them to cut off such poppy-heads as had not sprung from their own seed, and their personal feeling led them to treat the Rájpút, who as a native-born leader of the people should have joined them, and who would if he had done so have been a very important element of additional strength to the cause, with especial harshness. The old Settlement Reports are full of remarks upon the decadence, if not the virtual disappearance, of the Rájpút gentry in those districts where Sikh sway was most absolute. Thus the Jats we are considering are far more clearly marked off from the Rájpúts than are those of the western plains where everybody is a Jaṭ, or of the Salt Range Tract where everybody who is not an Arab or a Mughal calls himself a Rájpút; indeed there is if anything a tendency here to call those Jaṭs who are admitted to be Rájpúts further west. Only on the edge of the group, on the common border line of the Sikh tract, the Salt Range, and the great plains, do the Mekan, Gondal, Ránjha and Tárar claim some to be Jaṭs and some to be Rájpúts. The first two were described by Sir Denzil Ibbetson under Rájpúts, the last under Jaṭs, but this was more as a matter of convenience than of ethnic classification. The Jaṭ tribes of the Sikh tract are, except perhaps on the confines of the Gujránwála Bár, essentially agricultural, and occupy the same social position as do those of the eastern plains, whom indeed they resemble in all respects. The Jaṭs of the Sikh tract are the typical Jats of the Punjab, including all those great Sikh Jaṭ tribes who have made the race so renowned in recent history. They occupy the central districts of the Punjab, the upper Sutlej and the great Sikh States of the eastern plains. All that has been said regarding the absence of any wish on the part of the Jaṭs of the Khálsa to be aught but Jaṭs, applies here with still greater force. A Sidhu claims indeed Rájpút origin, and apparently with good reason. But he is now a Sidhu Jaṭ, and holds that to be a prouder title than Bhaṭṭi Rájpút. The only tribe among this group of which any considerable numbers return themselves as Rájpúts are the Virk; and among them this has happened only in Gujránwála, on the extreme outskirts of the tract. These men are the backbone of the Punjab by character and physique as well as by locality. They are stalwart, sturdy yeomen of great independence, industry and agricultural skill, and collectively form perhaps the finest peasantry in India. The Jaṭs of the Sikh tract are essentially husbandmen, and the standard of agricultural practice among those at any rate of the more fertile northern districts is as high

Ibbetson, § 431.

Ibbetson, § 434.

as is reached in any portion of the Province. Special attention may be called to the curious traditions of the Bhular, Mán, and Her tribes, which claim to be the original nucleus of the Jaṭ caste.

19. THE JÁTS OF THE SOUTH-EASTERN PLAINS.—The group of Jáṭ tribes, which occupies the Jumna Districts with Jínd, Rohtak and Hissár, call themslves Jáṭ not Jaṭ,* and are the same people in every respect as the Jáṭs of the Jumna-Ganges Doáb and the lower Jumna valley, differing however in little save religion from the great Sikh Jaṭ tribes of the Málwa; though perhaps the latter, inhabiting as they do the wide unirrigated plains of the central states, are of slightly finer physique than their neighbours of the damper riverain. The eastern Játs are almost without exception Hindu, the few among them who are Musalmán being known as Múla or "unfortunate," and dating their conversion almost without exception from an ancestor who was taken as a hostage to Delhi and there forcibly circumcised. Indeed these men were not unfrequently received back into caste on their return from captivity, and their descendants are in this case Hindus, though still known as Múla. Their traditions show them to have come up either from Bíkáner and Rájpútána, or northwards along the Jumna valley, and very few of them appear to have come from the Punjab to the Jumna. The Jáṭ of Gurgáon indeed still look upon the Rájá of Bhartpur as their natural leader, and the fall of Bhartpur made such an impression on their minds that old men still refer to it as the era from which they date events. Ibbetson, § 489.

The Jáṭ of these parts is, if anything, even a better cultivator than the Sikh Jaṭ; and that chiefly because his women assist him so largely in the field, performing all sorts of agricultural labour, whether light or heavy, except ploughing, for which they have not sufficient strength, and sowing, which is under all circumstances a prerogative strictly confine to the male sex. Directly we leave the south-eastern districts and pass into the Sikh tract, women cease to perform the harder kinds of field-work, even among the Jaṭs; while in Musalmán districts they do not work at all in the fields. So essentially is the Jáṭ a husbandman, and so especially is he *the* husbandman of these parts, that when asked his caste he will quite as often reply *zamíndár* as Jáṭ, the two names being in that sense used as synonymous. The social standing of the Jáṭ is that which the Gújar, Ahír, and Ror enjoy; in fact these four castes eat and smoke together. They stand at the head of the castes who practise *karewa* or widow-marriage, a good deal below the Rájpút, but far above the castes who grow vegetables, such as Aráin and Máli. If the social scale is regulated by the rules of the Hindu religion they come below Bánias who are admittedly better Hindus. But the manly Jáṭ despises the money-grubbing Bánia, and all other castes and tribes agree with him.

*Or, more accurately, Jaṭṭ, the double *ṭṭ* compensating for the loss of the long *á*. The difference is purely dialectical and to speak of Jáṭs and Jaṭṭs are racially distinct, as is done in E. H. I. IV, p. 240, is absurd and misleading The Muhammadan peasantry of the Punjab are not necessarily Jets or Jats though many Jáṭs and Jaṭṭs are Muhammadans

In the extreme south-eastern corner of the Punjab the Játs who have come in from the north and west, from Rájpútána and the Punjab, are known as Dhe, to distinguish them from the original Jáṭ tribes of the neighbourhood who are collectively called Hele, the two sections abstaining from intermarriage and having in some respects different customs. In Sirsa again, that meeting place of races, where the Bágri Jáṭ from the Bíkáner prairies, the Sikh Jaṭ from the Málwa, and the Musalmán Jaṭ from the Sutlej valley, meet the Jáṭ of Hissár, the last are distinguished as Desi and the Musalmán Jaṭs as Pachháde or western; but these terms appear to be unknown to the people in their respective homes. There the superiority of the Sikh and Desi Jaṭ over the stunted Bágri and the indolent enervated Jáṭ of the Sutlej is most strikingly apparent.

There is an extraordinary division of the Jáṭs of Delhi, Rohtak, and Karnál, and indeed of the other land-owning castes who have for the most part taken the one side or the other, into two factions known as Dehia and Haulánia. The following passage from Sir Denzil Ibbetson's *Settlement Report* of Karnál and Pánipat describes these factions :—

"The Dehias are called after a Jáṭ tribe of that name, with its head-quarters about Bhatgánw in Sunpat, having originally come from the Bawána near Delhi. The Haulánia faction is headed by the Ghatwál or Malak Jáṭs, whose head-quarters are Dher-ka-Ahulána in Gohána, and who were, owing to their successful opposition to the Rájpúts, the accepted heads of the Jáṭs in these parts Some one of the emperors called them in to assist him in coercing the Mandahár Rájpúts, and thus the old enmity was strengthened. The Dehia Játs, growing powerful, became jealous of the supremacy of the Ghatwáls and joined the Mandahárs against them. Thus the country-side was divided into two factions; the Gújars and Tagas of the tract, the Jáglán Jáṭs of *thapa* Naultha, and the Látmár Jáṭs of Rohtak joining the Dehias, and the Hudá Jáṭs of Rohtak and most of the Jáṭs of the tract except the Jágláns joining the Haulánias. In the Mutiny, disturbances took place in the Rohtak District between these two factions, and the Mandahárs of the Nardak ravaged the Haulánias in the south of the tract. And in framing my *zails* I had to alter my proposed division so as to separate a Dehia village which I had included with Haulánias, and which objected in consequence. The Dehia is also called the Jáṭ, and occasionally the Mandahár faction. Even Sir H. Elliott seems to have been unaware of the existence of these factions. The Jáṭs and Rájpúts seem independently of these divisions, to consider each other, tribally speaking, as natural enemies; and I have often been assured by Jáṭs, though I do not believe it, that they would not dare to go into a Rájpút village at night."

Mr. Maconachie quoted a Delhi tradition which makes two brothers from Rájpútána called Mom and Som the respective ancestors of the Haulánia Rájpúts of the Doáb and the Haulánia Jáṭs of Rohtak.

Here again, in the south-eastern districts the distinction between Jáṭ and Rájpút is definite and well-marked, the Jáṭ nearly always practising and the Rájpút almost always abstaining from *karewa;* though Ibbetson did not think that here a family could raise itself from the former to the latter caste by discontinuing the custom, as would appear to be possible elsewhere.

20. THE RAJPUT OF THE EASTERN DISTRICTS.—The Rájpút tribes of this tract are divided into two groups. All but the last four are almost confined to the Delhi territory, at least as Rájpúts proper, and are roughly arranged in order from north to south down the Jumna valley, and then westwards through Rohtak and Hissar. The last four tribes carry on the series through Patiála, Ferozepur and Gujránwála, and connect the Rájpúts of the eastern with those of the western plains. The first group belongs chiefly to the great royal families of the Rájpúts who, occupying the Delhi territory, have not as a rule superseded their old tribal designation by a local name, as has been so often the case in the west of the Punjab. The great majority of them are descendants of the Túnwar and Chauhán dynasties of Delhi. Their local distribution is fairly well marked, the Túnwar lying to the north-west of the first group, and shutting off the Jáṭ tribes of the central plains from the Rájpúts of the Delhi territory, their line being broken only by the Chauhán colony on the Ghaggar of the Hissár border. Next to them come the Chauhán, Mandahár and Pundír of the Kurukshetr, and the Ráwat, Gaurwa, Bargújar and Jádu of Delhi and Gurgáon followed by the Játu, themselves Túnwar, and the Bágri of Hissár. The Punwár colony of Rohtak is an off-shoot of the Punwárs of the western plains. The Jáṭs of this tract are very largely if not wholly true Jáṭs, who preserve strong traditions as to the Rájpút tribes from which they claim to be descended. The Rájpút of these parts is a true Rájpút. Living in the shadow of Delhi, the capital of his ancestral dynasties, he clings to the traditions of his caste. He cultivates largely, for little other occupation is left him; but he cultivates badly, for his women are more or less strictly secluded and never work in the fields, while he considers it degrading to actually follow the plough, and will always employ hired ploughmen if he can possibly afford it. He is a great cattle-grazier and as great a cattle-thief. His tribal feeling is strong, and the heads of the village or local group of villages have great influence. He is proud, lazy, sometimes turbulent, but generally with something more of the gentleman about him than we find in the more rustic Jáṭ. Ibbetson, § 444.

21. THE WESTERN PLAINS.—The great plains lying to the west of the Lahore meridian present a striking contrast to those to the east of that line. They form the common terminus of the two Indian monsoons, which have exhausted themselves of their vapour before they reach their goal; and the rainfall, heaviest in the north and east and decreasing towards the west and south, is everywhere so scanty that cultivation without irrigation is absolutely impossible. But in this very circumstance they find their security against famine or distress from drought; for their cultivation is almost independent of rain, a failure of which means little worse than a scarcity of grass, in itself a sufficiently serious calamity[1]. In many parts, indeed, more danger is to be anticipated from excessive floods than from deficient rainfall. The tract is traversed throughout its length by five great rivers, the Sutlej, Rávi, Chenáb, Jhelum and Ibbetson, § 18.

[1] Rain, of course, is needed here as elsewhere. But its absence means only a diminished yield, and not none at all; and so little is sufficient if the fall comes at the right time, and absolute drought occurs so seldom, that the crops may be said never to fail from this cause.

Indus; and along either side of each of these runs at a distance of a few miles a more or less distinctly marked bank, which defines the excursions of the river within recent times as it has shifted from side to side in its course. These banks include between them strips of low-lying land which are periodically inundated by the rising floods as the winter snows of the Himálayas melt under the summer sun, or in which the nearness of the sub-soil water makes well-irrigation easy. All outside these narrow boundaries is a high arid plain. Beyond the Indus, and between the Sutlej and the Jhelum and its continuation in the Chenáb, it consists of soil which, wherever water is available, is sufficiently fertile save where north of the Sutlej that saline efflorescence which has so puzzled geologists clothes the surface for miles together like a recent fall of snow. But between the Indus and the Jhelum-Chenáb and south of the Sutlej it is covered by great parallel lines of rolling sand separated by narrow hollows in which the original soil is exposed.

Ibbetson, § 19 The Gújránwála and Wazírábád tahsils of the Gújránwála District[1] secure a fair amount of rain by their vicinity to the hills. Numerous streams, for the most part of intermittent flow, which run down from the Sulaimán mountains to join the Indus, and innumerable small inundation canals carried out from the Sutlej, the Lower Chenáb, the Upper Jhelum, and the Lower Indus across the zone of well-irrigation into the edges of the central steppes render cultivation possible along their courses; while wells sunk in the long hollows of the Thal or sandy desert and the drainage of the Bár or stiff loam uplands collected in local depressions perform a similar office. But though some of the finest wheat in the world is grown on the wells of the western Thal, the proportion of the area thus brought under the plough is wholly insignificant. The remainder of the tract is covered by low stunted bush and salsolaceous plants and with short grass in good seasons. Over this range great herds of camels which thrive on the saline herbage, and of cattle, sheep and goats. They are tended by a nomad population which moves with its flocks from place to place as the grass is consumed and the scanty supply of water afforded by the local hollows exhausted, or in search of that change of diet which camels love and the varying local floras afford. The tract includes the whole of the Multán Division and the State of Baháwalpur, the Districts of Sháhpur and Gujránwála, the greater part of Gujrát, and the two western tahsils of Lahore[1]. Its area is some 60,870 square miles or more than two-fifths of that of the whole Province, while its population, numbering about 4,885,000 souls, includes little more than one-fifth of the people of the Punjab, and it comprises not one-quarter of the total cultivated area.

[1] In physical characteristics parts of Gujránwála, Gujrát and Lahore belong rather to the northern portion of the eastern plains; but as they lie west of the Lahore meridian and their area is small, they have been included in this tract of which they form the north-eastern corner.

22. NATURAL DIVISIONS OF THE WESTERN PUNJAB.—It is the fashion to describe the Punjab Proper as marked off by its rivers into six great Doábs which constitute the natural divisions of the Province. This description is true in a sense; but the sense in which it is true possesses but little significance, and its chief merit seems to be that it can easily be verified by reference to a map. To the east of the Lahore meridian such rivers as there are lie close together, the whole of the country between and beyond them is comparatively populous, and there are no natural boundaries of any great importance. But west of that meridian, or throughout the greater portion of the Punjab Proper, the real obstacles to inter-communication, the real barriers which separate the peoples one from another are, not the rivers easily crossed at any time and often fordable, in the cold weather, but the great arid steppes which lie between those rivers. The advance of the agricultural tribes has followed almost invariably the courses of the great rivers, the new-comers having crept along both banks of the streams and driven the nomads from either side into the intermediate Doábs, where they have occupied the portions nearest the river lands from which they had been ejected, leaving the median area of greatest aridity as an intangible but very effectual line of separation. Ibbetson, § 20.

23. ETHNOGRAPHY OF THE WESTERN PLAINS.—Between the Sulaimáns and the great sandy deserts of Baháwalpur and the Sindh-Ságar Doáb[1] the dominant race is Baloch. Descending from the hills this Iranian people overcame a miscellaneous collection of tribes which, still forming a very large proportion of the population, have been included by their conquerors under the semi-contemptuous term of Jáṭ—here an occupational as much as an ethnological designation—till they have themselves almost forgotten their original race. In the remainder of the tract the divisions of the people are rather tribal than racial, the great majority of them being Jáṭs and Rájpúts, or belonging to races, perhaps in some cases of aboriginal origin, which can now no longer be distinguished from them. In Gújrát the importance of the Gújar element is indicated by the name of the district, while Sayyids are numerous to the south-west. The number of clans into which the people of these great plains are divided is enormous. The Dáúdpotra, Joiya, Wattu, Dogar and Mahtam of the Sutlej, the Kharral and Káthia of the Rávi, the Siál and Khokhar of the Chenáb, and the Khokhar and Tiwána of the Jhelum, are some of the most important. The curious river-tribes of the Sutlej and Indus, the Jhabel, Kehal and Kutána, also present many interesting features. The Indus Paṭháns and a certain proportion of the Baloches speak their national Pashtu and Balochi. The remaining population of Dera Ghází Khán, Muzaffargarh, Multán and Baháwalpur speak Jaṭki, a language holding an intermediate position between Panjábi and Sindhi. Panjábi is the speech of the remainder of the tract. The population is essentially Muhammadan, the proportion being largest on the west and smallest to the east and south. Multán is the only town of just upon 100,000 inhabitants, and the population is very markedly rural. There is no manufacture of importance, and the important POWINDAH traffic between India and the countries to the west only passes through the tract Ibbetson, § 21.

[1] The Sindh-Ságar Doáb lies between the Indus and the Jhelum and Chenáb.

on its way to the commercial centres of Hindustán. Pastoral pursuits occupy a more important position than in the rest of the Punjab, agricultural produce being largely supplemented by clarified butter, wool, hides and barilla.

bbetson, § 22. 24. THE SALT RANGE TRACT.—There still remains to be described the north-western corner of the Punjab. Situated in the angle occupied by the Salt Range and separated from the rest of the Province by the upper Jhelum, it includes the Districts of Attock, Ráwalpindi and Jhelum. It presents in almost every respect the strongest possible contrast with the Punjab Proper, and indeed, as has already been remarked, can hardly be said to belong to India save by mere geographical position. The outer Himálayas, crossing the Jhelum, run up the eastern boundary of the Ráwalpindi District and cut off the Murree and part of the Kabúta tahsils. There they and the mid-Himálaya meet on the banks of the Indus in a confused mass of mountains. The curved ranges which connect the extremities of the mid-Himálayas with the Safed Koh by the Salt Range which, starting from opposite the point where the mid-Himálayas abut upon the Jhelum, runs along the right bank of the river through the south of the Jhelum and the north of the Sháhpur District, crosses the Indus in the north of Miánwáli, and turning down the right bank of the Indus through the latter District, enters the North-West Frontier Province and follows the boundary between Bannu and Dera Ismáil Khan till it joins the Sulaimáns. Rising abruptly from the river and the great desert which lie to the south of it, the Salt Range of Jhelum and Sháhpur falls away imperceptibly to the north into a great table-land enclosed by the range itself, the Hazára hills, and the river Indus, crossed in every direction by chains of low hills, and cut up by the streams which issue [illegible] m them into innumerable ravines. It is this table-land which constitutes the Districts of Jhelum and Ráwalpindi.

PART II.—HISTORICAL NOTES.

No attempt will be made in this compilation to give a history of the Punjab in the ordinary sense of that term, but the following notes are intended to sum up from the imperfect and fragmentary data at present available, all that is known of the ancient political and ethnic conditions of the Punjab and North-West Frontier :—

PRE-HISTORY.

In the domain of pre-history nothing has been done for the Punjab and probably very little will ever be found possible of achievement. Its plains were formed of vast alluvial deposits which must have concealed all pre-historic remains beyond hope of recovery, save by some lucky accident, and the physical features of the hills are rarely favourable to their preservation.

The Stone Age has left its traces in India, but palæolithic relics are mostly localised in the South, while the neolithic artifacts are much more widely spread. The distribution of the latter is naturally influenced by the prevalence of rocks suitable for their manufacture. Neolithic implements are found over the greater part of Southern India, but instances of their occurrence in the Punjab, Rájpútána, and Sind, except at Rohṛi, are rare. Some finds of pre-historic pottery in Balochistán are tentatively considered to be neolithic.

The first use of iron in Northern India must be carried back to a very remote antiquity. The literary evidence indicates its introduction into the North-West subsequently to the composition of the *Rig Veda* but before the *Atharva Veda* was written and the latter work is not later than 1000 B.C. Before that date copper occupied the place of iron. All the Indian implements discovered are certainly of extreme antiquity and must be dated back to before 1000 B. C.

At two sites in Balochistán implements of practically pure copper have been found. At Mathura, east of the Jumna, Cunningham excavated a flat copper celt and copper harpoon heads are said to have been frequently found in its vicinity. At Kohistán Hill and Tank, probably not very far from Gwadar, in Western Balochistán, copper arrow heads have been discovered. These and other finds in Northern India carry the range of copper implements all over that area from the Hugli on the east to the Indus on the west, and from the foot of the Himalayas to the Cawnpore district, but no specimens from the Punjab have been recorded.

Thus India as a whole had no Bronze Age.[1] In Southern India the neolithic period passed directly into that of iron, but in Northern India a Copper Age intervened between the neolithic period and the Iron Age. The South was severed from all intercourse with the North, and in 700 B C. Panini, who was born at Salatura, (Lahor) in the Peshawar valley, knew nothing of the South, but about that time the intrusive northern races began to penetrate the broad and nearly impassable barrier of forest which then covered the natural defences of the Vindhyans and their associated races.

[1]This is also Canon Greenwell's conclusion : see Vincent Smith, *The Copper Age and Prehistoric Bronze Implements of India*, *Ind. Ant.*, 1907, p. 53.

The Dravidian element.

Is there any Dravidian element in Northern India? The problem is a difficult one. A Dravidian speech survives among the Bráhúi of Balochistán, but none is traceable in the Punjab. The question not only remains insoluble but raises further and larger questions. Sten Konow has detected some resembles between Dravidian and the remains of the Etruscan language,[1] but Prof. Jules Martha, the latest writer on this subject, says nothing of this theory and regards Etruscan as a branch of the Finno-Ugrian group of languages.

The antiquity of the Vedic culture.

Scholars are divided in opinion as to the probable date of the rise or introduction of the Vedic culture into India, and the Aryan invasions may date back to a period as remote as 3000 B. C. or even earlier, but it is certain that the 15th century B. C. saw chiefs in northern Mesopotamia bearing Aryan names or worshipping Vedic deities, and this fact lends some support to Kennedy's view that the Aryan conquest of the Punjab can scarcely have taken place before 1700 B. C. and may well have been a century or two later.[2] Sten Konow accepts this view and points out that it is consistent with the linguistic evidence.

The Iranian Dominion.

As we shall see presently the great Persian empire which was overthrown by Alexander the Great had established its power on the confines of the Western Punjab and deputed a Greek to explore or survey the Indus. These facts point to a strong Iranian influence over India centuries after the pre-historic Aryan invasions, and Farishta's *History of the Muhammadans in India* preserves many traditional details of the Iranian dominion over the North-West Frontier of India and the Punjab and the present writer wishes to invite special attention to his *Chapter on the Hindoos*. What Farishta tells us has not received the attention it deserves. He is a careful historian and his statements appear to be founded on authorities, lost to us, but trustworthy, and to be handled by him in a critical spirit. For instance he is quite sound in his account of the origin of the Rájpúts.[3] As he says the Brahman and Kshatriya existed from time immemorial, but the Rájpúts are only known since the beginning of the Kaliyuga. They attained power after Vikramajít's demise, something more than 1600 years ago (when he wrote) and he derives their origin from the children of *rájás* by female slaves, the sons of Rájá Súraj being the first to bear the title of Rájpút.

The history of Rájá Súraj is closely connected by him with that of Persia. He makes Krishna,[4] elected king by the people of Behár, contemporary with Tahmorasp[5] of Persia. Krishna's eldest son Mahrájá

[1] J. R. A. S., 1904, p. 2, and *La Langue Étrusque*, reviewed in *Athenæum*, Jany. 1914.

[2] J. R. A. S., 1909, pp. 1119 and 1108.

[3] Pp. lxiii—iv of Briggs' Translation.

[4] Farishta is careful to point out that this is not the Krishna of Mathra.

[5] Apparently the Talamurs, called the Dev-band or Magician-binder, of Malcolm's *History of Persia*, I, p. 14. He ruled Persia for 30 years and was succeeded by the famous Jamshíd, who fell before Zuhák.

succeeded him and divided the people of India into tribes (? castes). He named the [Rájpút] tribes Rahtor, Chauhán, Punwár, Bais etc. after the chiefs of each. He kept up a friendly intercourse with Persia, but his nephew Dongur Sain sought refuge with Farídún of Persia and the latter king despatched a force under his son Kúrshasp[1] to invade the Punjab, and Mahrája was compelled to cede a part of his kingdom—doubtless a part or the whole of the Punjab—to Dongur Sain. Passing by the interesting statement that the islands of Acheen, Malacca, Pegu and the Malabar coast broke away from his empire, Farishta tells us that it was simultaneously threatened by an attack on its north-west frontier and that Mahrája was compelled to send his lieutenant Mál Chand of Málwa[2] to defend the Punjab but was obliged to cede it to Persia. Some writers, adds Farishta, say that Farídún even possessed the Punjab and that the descendants of his son Kúrshasp held it together with Kábul, Tibet, Sind and Nímroz down to the time of Rústúm, *i. e.* for four generations.

Farishta's account may have to be supplemented from the *Tabaqát-i-Násiri*. When Farídún had deposed the sorcerer Zuhák he despatched an army to dispossess Bustám who held the dominion of Hindustán at the hand of Zuhák whose descendant he was, and Bustám retreated into Shignán and Bamián and eventually devoted his energies to the colonization of the mountains of Ghor. He made peace with Farídún and the Arab tribes akin to Zuhák took up their abode in those mountainous tracts, and from him Muhammad of Ghor claimed descent.

Mahrája, after a reign of 700 years, was succeeded by Kesu Rái who invoked the aid of Manúchahr against the Rájás of southern India. Sám[3], son of Narímán, was sent to his assistance and they joined forces at Jálandhar in the Punjab. The allies compelled the recalcitrant rulers to pay homage to Kesú Rái. Manír Rái, son of Kesu Rái, succeeded him in Oudh, but he forgot his debt to Persia and when the

[1] Farishta distinctly speaks of Gurshasp as the son of Farídún. But—

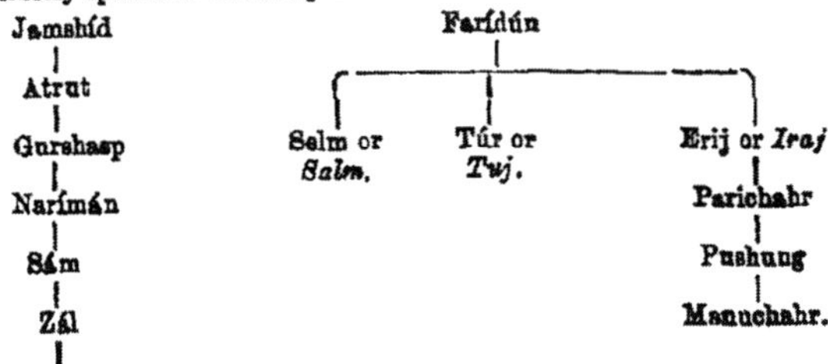

are the pedigrees given in Malcolm, pp. 24 and 21. The *Tabaqát-i-Násiri* gives the sons of Farídún as italicised and says that Iraj held Iráq with Hind and Sind, while the *Rauzat-ut-Táhirin* says he held Khorásán with only a portion of Hind and Sind: *T. N.*, I, p. 308.

[2] Farishta expressly says that it derives its name from Mál Chand. It appears to be the Málwa of Central India, not the tract in the Punjab.

[3] Hereditary prince of Seistán, according to Malcolm, p. 24.

Turk, Afrasiáb, king of Turán, invaded that kingdom, he wrested the Punjab from Zál,[1] the son of Sám, and made Jálandhar his capital. He acknowledged fealty to Afrasiáb and it remained in his possession till Kaikobád deputed Rústúm, son of Zál, to reconquer it. Rústúm expelled Manír Rái and placed Suraj, a Hindu chief, on the throne. He gave his sister's daughter to Rústúm, and died after a reign of 250 years ! Of his 35 sons Bhai Rájá, the eldest, succeeded, and some say that he invested his brothers with the title of Rájpút. But he abandoned the regulations established by Mahrája and incurred the enmity of Kidár, a Brahman of the Siwálik mountains. Here Farishta or his translator must be alluding to the Siwálik kingdom—Sapádalaksha. Kidár defeated him and took his kingdom, but had to pay tribute to his contemporaries Kai-Kaús[2] and Kai-Khúsrau.

Farishta's account now becomes confused. Afrasiáb re-appears on the scene. He confers the government of India on Rohat, son of Sankal Rájá[3] of Lakhnauti or Gaur in Bengál, but Rohat dying without issue Mahrája II, a Kachwáhá Rájpút of Márwár, places himself on the throne and his nephew Kidár wrests the Punjab from Rústúm's descendants. He lived for some time in Behera (? Bhera), but built the fortress of Jammu where he left Durga, the Búlhás[4], one of his kinsmen, in charge, but Durga allied himself with the Khokars[5] and Chaubea[6], 'the ancient Zamíndárs of the Punjab,' and with the hill people between Kábul and Kandhár and expelled Kidár Rája from the Punjab.

[1] Zál-i-zar—Zál of the golden hair—held the city of Zábul, which gave its name to Zábulistán. It was also called the city of Zuhák, and Vigne—(*Ghásni, Kábul and Afghánistán*, p. 109)—described its position thus :—'On the continuation of the even-topped ridge of the Sar-i-Koh [which Raverty—*Notes on Afghánistán*, p. 507—says is the crest of the great range of Mihtar Sulaimán, bounding the Ghazni state on the east] are to be seen, as I was informed, the ruins of a large city, called Zohaka, after the king who reigned there before the time of the Mussalmen.' The ruins of Zábul appear to lie in the Máidán-i-Rustam according to Raverty (*op. cit.*, p. 456). For a note on Zábulistán see the Appendix to this Part.

[2] Son of Kaikobád.

[3] Sankal Rájá, according to Farishta, founded Lakhnauti in Bengal, after usurping Kidár's throne. He maintained a vast army and refused to pay tribute to Afrasiáb, and Píran-Wisa, the *wazír* of Afrasiáb, was sent against him with 50,000 Turki horse, but compelled to retreat. Afrasiáb however joined him with 100,000 horse and carried off Sankal Rájá to Túrán, where he was eventually killed in action by Rústúm. Malcolm is completely silent as to this episode. Possibly this is the Shankal 'King of Sind' who supplied Bahrám Gor with 12,000 or 1000 sweet-voiced minstrels from his kingdom. They became the ancestors of the present Lúri or Lúli, the musician gypsy tribe, of modern Persia : A. C. Woolner in Punjab Historical Society's *Journal*, II, p. 120. Local tradition in Saháranpur preserves the name of a 'Muhammadan tyrant,' named Afrásá, who burnt down the sacred grave in Kankhal near Hardwár : *Calcutta Review*, 1874, p. 194.

[4] "Which tribe has inhabited that country ever since," adds Farishta.

[5] Farishta says Gakhars, but he always confuses them with the Khokhars and the latter must be meant.

[6] The name Chaubea is extremely puzzling. Conjecturally it is misreading of Joiya but this is very uncertain. We find Chaubín as a Partar name (Malcolm I, p. 51, note). But Bahrám who took possession of the Persian throne in 590 A. D.—at a much later period—was also called Chaubin, or the 'stick-like,' probably from his appearance : (*ibid* p. 152, note 2).

These tribes, hitherto separate, now formed a single powerful state and Farishta imagined them to be those now called Afgháns, though he quotes no authority for his theory. After Kidár's death Jai Chand usurped the throne. He was contemporaneous with Bahman and Dáráb. Dahla his brother[1] usurped the throne and founded Dehli. He was however attacked by P'húr, a Rája of Kumaun,[2] and taken prisoner. P'húr refused to pay the Persian tribute and opposed the inroad of Alexander, according to the 'the Brahminical and other historians.' After P'húr's death Sansár Chand (Chandra Gupta) made himself master of India, but sent tribute to Gúdarz,[3] king of Persia, until Júna, nephew of P'húr, regained the throne. He was a contemporary of Ardashir Bábegán[4] who invaded India but was induced by Júna's presents of gold and elephants to stay his advance on the frontier. Júna reigned at Kanauj and was succeeded by his son Kalián Chand.

Farishta now turns to the history of Málwa. He makes Vikramajít Punwár also a contemporary of Ardashír Bábegán[5], but notes that others make him contemporary with Shapúr.[6] He lost his life in a battle with Shálivahana, a Rája of the Deccan, and from his death the Hindus date one of their eras.

Málwa then fell to Rája Bhoj, also a Punwár, while one Vásdeo (Vásudeva) seized the 'province' of Kanauj. During his reign Bairámgor,[7] king of Persia, visited Kanauj in disguise,[8] but was recognised by the Indian ambassador who had carried tribute to Persia, and so Vásudeva seated Bairámgor on his throne, gave him his daughter in marriage and escorted him back to Persia. Vásudeva left 32 sons, but his throne was usurped by Rámdeo Rahtor, who expelled the Kachwáhás from Márwár and established the Rahtors in that province. He also extorted tribute from the *rájas* of Siwalik, after subduing the Rája of Kumaun, and plundered Nagarkot Thence he marched on Jammu, and though its Rája opposed him in the woods he was eventually defeated. The fort of Jammu fell and Rámdeo secured a daughter of the Rája[9] for one of his sons.

Rámdeo, says Farishta, was contemporary with the Sassanian Firoz,[10] and to him and his son Kaikobád[11] tribute was paid by India. After

[1] Uncle of his infant son and so doubtless Jai Chand's brother.

[2] Farishta did not get this statement from a Persian source: *cf.* Malcolm, *op. cit.*, p. 77.

[3] Gudurz is the only one of the Ashkanian kings mentioned by Farishta, p. 87, and he must have reigned long after Chandra Gupta's time. There were possibly two kings of this name, Bahram Gudurz the third of the Arsacides, who reigned after Christ, and Gudurz, son of Pellas: Malcolm *op. cit.*, pp 85-87.

[4] Artaxerxes, the Sassanian, 226-240 A. D., p. 93.

[5] Ardeshir II (acc. 381 A. D.) has clearly been confused here with Ardeshir Bábegán.

[6] Shapur III, acc. 385 A. D., Malcolm, p 112.

[7] Bahrám V, acc. 421 A. D.

[8] This tale is also noticed by Malcolm, *op. cit.* I, p. 118.

[9] Rámdeo then reached Shivkot Pindi, situated at a small distance on the top of the neighbouring hill at Nagarkot. There he summoned the Rája to meet him at the temple of Durga, which goddess he venerated. The Rája bestowed a daughter on one of Rámdeo's sons—in acknowledgment no doubt of his suzerainty.

[10] Acc. 458 A. D.

[11] Acc. 488 A. D.

Rámdeo's death civil war again ensued, and his general, Partáb Chand, a Sisodia, seized the throne. He refused the Persian tribute and Naushírwán's ambassador returned empty-handed,[1] so Persian troops invaded Multán and the Punjab. Partáb Chand submitted and paid the annual tribute thenceforth without demur. After his death each of his generals seized a province. Of these Anand Deo, a Bais Rájput, was the most powerful, but his power did not extend apparently over the Punjab.[2] He lived in the era of Khusrau Parvís[3] and died after a reign of 16 years. At this time, says Farishta, a Hindu, named Máldeo, collected a force in the Doáb and seized Delhi and Kanauj, but he left no son fit to succeed him and civil war ensued everywhere on his death. After him no single *rája* ruled over India, and Mahmúd of Ghazni found it divided thus:—

Kanauj, held by Kúwar Rai.
Mírath, held by Hardat Rai.
Mahávan,[4] held by Gúlchandr Rai.
Lahore, held by Jaipál, son of Hatpál.

In 1079 Ibrahím bin Masá'ud I Ghaznavi having extended his conquests to Ajudhan (now Pák Pattan) returned to Rudpál—a fort on the summit of a steep hill. Thence he marched to Dera, whose inhabitants had originally come from Khorassán, having been banished thence for frequent rebellions. They had formed themselves into a small independent state, and cut off by nearly impassable mountains from intercourse with their neighbours, had preserved their ancient customs and rites, by not intermarrying with any other people. Dera was well fortified and remarkable for a fine fort about a parasang and a half in circumference. The Muhammadans took it and carried off 100,000 persons into captivity.[5]

This closes Farishta's account, but in this connection Mr. Vincent Smith may be quoted. After the decay of the Kushán power, as he points out, coins of Vásudeva continued to be struck long after he had passed away, and ultimately present the royal figure clad in the garb of Persia and manifestly imitated from the effigy of Sapor (Sháhpur I), the Sassanian monarch who ruled Persia from 238 to 269 A. D. Bahrám (Varahrán) II is also known to have conducted a campaign in Sístán between 277 and 294; and 'two great paramount dynasties, the Kushán in Northern India and the Andhra in the Deccan tableland, disappear together almost at the moment when the Arsakidan dynasty of Persia was superseded by the Sassanian. It is impossible to avoid hazarding the conjecture that the three events were in some way connected, and that the Persianizing of the Kushán coinage of Northern India should be

[1] Acc. 531 A. D.

[2] Malcolm says that the emperors of India and China courted Naushírwán's friendship, and he describes the magnificent presents sent by the former (*op. cit.*, p. 144). The tribute was, however, refused to his unworthy successor (p. 151). Naushírwán's power, it is implied, only extended to the Indus (p. 150).

[3] A. D. 591-628.

According to the *Raghsvansa* Raghu carried his arms into Persia: *Indian Shipping*, p. 65

[4] Mahávan, says Briggs, is supposed to be a village on the left bank of the Jumna about 10 miles below Mathra. Gúlchandr must be the 'Kool Chand,' Rája of Mahávan, attacked by Mahmúd of Ghasni in or about 1017 A. D.: Briggs, *op. cit.*, p. 58.

[5] Briggs, I, pp. 189-40.

explained by the occurrence of an unrecorded Persian invasion.'[1] But Farishta appears to preserve the records of the revival of Persian influence during the period which elapsed between the overthrow of the Kushán power and the Muhammadan inroads.

The theory of the predominance of the Iranian element in North-western India is confirmed by the thesis advanced by Sten Konow that in Bashgali, which may be taken as the type of the language of the Siáhposh Káfirs of Northern Káfiristán, we have a dialect derived from an ancient Iranian dialect which had retained the Aryan *s* and not changed it to *h*. We also know of the existence of such a language, spoken by tribes who in the 14th century B. C., worshipped gods such as Mitra, Varuna, Indra and the Násatyas.[2]

The latest view is that the Kambojas were an Iranian tribe. Both Brahmanic and Buddhistic literature refers to their fine breed of horses. The Nepalese tradition may be due to the fact that the early Tibetan mode (or one of the Tibetan modes) of disposing of the dead was similar to the Iranian, but exposure of the dead to be devoured by birds is a fairly widespread practice and does not prove identity of race in those who practise it. The Kambojas seem to have esteemed it a sacred duty to destroy noxious or Ahramanic creatures, as did the Iranians, but such a belief would not be proof of racial identity. The Iranian affinities of the Kamboja are however accepted by Kuhn, G. K. Nariman and Zimmer.[3]

But however strong may have been the Iranian element in the population of the Hindu Kush and on the north-western frontier many indications show that it was not advanced in civilisation. The tribes which occupied the modern Káfiristán, Gilgit and Chitrál were called Pisácha or 'eaters of raw flesh,' and traditions of ritual cannibalism still survive among the Shíns of Gilgit, the Wai and Bashgal Káfirs and in Dardistán.[4] Indeed the Dards of Gilgit had a reputation among the Kashmiris for cannibalism as late as 1866. It must, however, be pointed out that very similar legends of ritual cannibalism are very common all the world over and that cannibalism was supposed to exist in Muzaffargarh as late as 1850. The Romasa or shaggy and the Sringi-nara or horned men are mentioned in the *Mahábhárata* as if they occupied the same seats as the Madrakas and Pahlavas,[5] and if so they must have been settled in the plains or at least in the sub-montane.

On the other hand the Iranian element may have been a highly civilising influence, bringing Zoroastrian ideas into the Punjab plains and the hills on their western frontier, but unable to penetrate the Indus Kohistán and Hindu Kush to their north. In the present state of our knowledge the evidence is accumulating but it is at present fragmentary and conflicting. The question of Zoroastrian influences on Indian religions and religious art is now being raised for the first time and is noticed briefly below.

[1] *Early History of India*, pp. 254-5. For the countries which appear on Vásudeva's coins, see the Appendix to this Part.

[2] J. R. A. S., 1911, pp. 1 and 46.

[3] See J. R. A. S., 1912, pp. 255-7, and references there given.

[4] *Ib.* 1905, pp. 285-8. Grierson says that a connexion between Pisácha and the Pashai Káfirs is phonetically possible, but Pashai is not the name of a sept. It is the name of a valley.

[5] J. R. A. S., 1909, p. 140.

SUMMARY.

It is now necessary to hark back and discuss the condition of the Punjab prior to and after the episode of Alexander's invasion.

Of the sixteen States of Northern India enumerated in the most ancient literary traditions[1] at least four and possibly five lay, in whole or in part, within the modern Punjab or on its frontiers. These were—

(*i*) Gandhára,[2] which included the modern Districts of Peshá-war, Attock and Ráwalpindi. It appears to have derived its name from the Gandhára tribe which is mentioned as holding with the Yavanas the Kábul valley and the regions still further west. The Persian satrapy of Gandaria was distinct from those of India, Arachosia (Kandáhar) and Aría (Herát). It comprised the North-Western Punjab. Its capital was at one time Takshasila, but at others Pushkalávati.

(*ii*) Kamboja, which adjoined Gandhára, and lay in the extreme north-west, with Dwáraka as its capital.[3] Mr. Vincent Smith however points out that Kambojadesa is the name applied in Nepalese tradition to Tibet.[4] Dwáraka may be the Dárva of Dárvábhisára, *i.e.* Dárva and Abhisára, the whole tract of the lower and middle hills between the Jhelum and the Chenáb, including the modern Rajauri. But this would make Kamboja too far to the east to be in agreement with Rhys Davids' view.

(*iii*) Kurú, held by the Kurús, with its capital at Indraprastha, close to Delhi.

(*iv*) South of the Kurús and west of the Jumna lay the Matsya or Macchas, possibly represented by the modern Meos of the Mewát.

(*v*) The Súrasenás, whose capital Madhura (doubtless Mathra) was in the Jumna valley and who thus lay immediately north-west[5] of the Macchas and west of the Jumna.

In addition to the great cities mentioned above we find Ságala, probably the modern Siálkot, described as the capital of the Maddas.

Professor Rhys Davids has called attention to the fact that the earliest Buddhist records reveal the existence, side by side with more or less powerful monarchies, of small aristocratic republics, with either complete or modified independence, in the 6th and 7th centuries B. C. When Buddhism arose there was no paramount sovereign in India, but four great monarchies existed in north-east India. None of these however included, or even adjoined, the Punjab, and the countries held by

[1] *E. g.* the *Anguttara,* and *Vinaya Texts.*—See *Buddhist India,* p. 333.

[2] *Not* Kandahár (as Professor Rhys Davids thinks): *op. cit.,* p. 28—See Vincent Smith, *Early History of India,* pp. 34, 35, 25 and 27: also pp. 297 and 300. The kingdom of Gandhára was overwhelmed by the Huns in 500 A D. and regained by Mihiragula, the Hun, from its ruler, perhaps himself a Hun, about 530.

[3] *Op. cit.,* p. 28:—See also the map at the end of that work. *Cf.* also Vincent Smith, *op. cit.,* p. 55.

[4] *Op. cit.,* p. 173.

[5] Clearly not *south*-west as in *Buddhist India,* p. 27.

the Kurús, Matsyas and Súrasenás did not apparently form kingdoms, but were doubtless rather tribal confederacies, loosely organised and with ever-changing boundaries, like the Mewát or Bhattiána of more recent times. At the time of Alexander's invasion these conditions had undergone little change, though the tendency to form kingdoms had become more marked. The Macedonian invaders found the Indus the boundary between India and the Persian empire.

Somewhat later Persian influence began to make itself felt in the north-west frontiers of India, and in 516 B. C. Skylax, a Carian Greek, explored the Indus under Darius' orders. Sailing from Kaspapyros[1], a city of the Gandhárians, in the *Paktuiké gé* (the land of the Paktyes) he made his way down that river to the ocean, and his surveys enabled Darius to annex the Indus valley. The Persians formed the conquered territory into an Indian satrapy, which extended from Kálábágh to the sea, and perhaps included territories on the east bank of the Indus. It certainly excluded Gandaria and Arachosia (Kandahár).

Elsewhere, in the territories not included in the Indian satrapy, the conditions described above had undergone little change, though the tendency to crystallise into organised monarchies had become decidedly more marked in the northern or submontane tracts of the Punjab. Peukalaotis (Pushkalávati, the capital of Gandhára), the capital of a tract (also so called after it), which corresponds to the present Yúsufzai country, was overrun by Alexander's generals, who were accompanied by Omphis 'Taxiles,' the king or feudatory chief of 'Taxila'.[2] Alexander himself advanced from near Jalálábád into Bájaur by the Kúnar valley. In Bájaur he encountered the powerful Aspasians, and took Nysa, a town and hill-state which probably lay on the lower spurs of the Koh-i-Mor. Thence he crossed the Gouraios (Panjkora) and attacked Massaga, perhaps Manglaur, the old capital of Swát, in Assakenian territory. This was followed by the capture of Aornos.[3]

Although no part of these Provinces has, as far as can be learnt from historical records, undergone less change than the hill tracts to the north of Pesháwar, hardly a certain trace of Alexander's conquests remains. The tribes mentioned in the histories of his invasion have disappeared, and the cities he captured cannot, in any one case, be identified with any certainty. Yet the social system remains much the same—a loose congeries of tribes under nominal chiefs who are known by territorial names.

Crossing the Indus, probably at or near Und or Ohind, Alexander advanced to Taxila, whose ruler was then at war with Abisáres, the ruler of Dárva and Abhisára, the whole tract of the lower and middle hills, lying between the Jhelum and the Chenáb, and which included Rajauri.

[1] Or Kaspatyros: possibly Kasyapapura (Multán), which was, we must conjecture, a dependency of Gandhára.

[2] Just as Ámbi (Omphis) assumed the title of Taxiles on his accession to the throne of Taxila, so Arsakes, the ruler of Urasha, would appear to have taken his name from his realm and the Pathán chiefs of the present day in Dir and Swát have a precisely similar system. In much the same way tribes like the Katoch and Dogra derive their names from the territories which they occupy or in which they are dominant.

[3] Not Mahában—See Stein, Report of Archæological Survey work in the North-West Frontier Province for 1904-05.

Abisáres indeed sent convoys to Alexander, but he was in secret league with Poros, the Paurava,[1] who ruled between the Jhelum and the Chenáb. After defeating his forces in a great battle probably on the Karri plain, just above Jhelum, Alexander crossed the Chenab to attack another Poros, nephew of the former and ruler of Gandaris, which may have corresponded to the modern Gondal Bár. Poros was not however absolute ruler of this tract for it was partly held by independent tribes, and adjacent to it lay the Glausai or Glaukanikoi.

Similarly on the east bank of the Rávi lay the Kathaioi,[2] and still further east, on the Beás, the Oxydrakai (Kshudrakas), while to their south-west, along the lower course of the Rávi below Lahore were the warlike Malloi. These tribes formed a loosely knit confederacy, but the Kathaioi were attacked before the Malloi could reinforce them, and while only supported by the minor clans in their immediate neighbourhood. Thus Alexander was able, after crossing the Rávi and receiving the surrender of Pimprama from the Adraistai, to invest Sangala into which the Kathaioi had thrown themselves. After its fall Alexander advanced to the Beás which he probably reached just below its southward bend below Paṭhánkoṭ. Indeed if speculation be admissible we may conjecture that Pimprama was Paithán and that the Kathaioi are represented by the Katoch. However this may be, Alexander appointed Poros king of all the conquered territories between the Beás and the Rávi, then occupied by the Glausai, Kathaioi and 5 other nations, and comprising no less than 2000 townships. Taxiles was confirmed in his sovereignty, formerly somewhat shadowy, over all the territory between the Jhelum and the Indus. Lastly, he made Abisáres satrap of Bhimbhar and Rajauri, together with the overlordship of Urasa.

On his return march Alexander reached the Jhelum, having first secured control of the southern part of the Salt Range which formed the kingdom of Sophytes (Saubhúti). Near the confluence of the Chenáb and Beás, then probably close to Jhang, Alexander landed troops from his flotilla to forestall an attempt by the Siboi and Agalassoi to join the Malloi, who lay lower down the river. The Siboi, a rude tribe clad in skins and armed with clubs, submitted, but the Agalassoi mustered 40,000 foot and 3000 horse to resist the invader and were apparently exterminated. Both their principal towns were taken, but the capture of the second cost the Macedonians many lives. It is clear from this account that the tract round Jhang was then highly fertile and densely populated, partly by a backward race (the Siboi), partly by a well-organised nation, the Agalassoi, which possessed fortified towns. The citadel of their second town escaped destruction, and was garrisoned by a detachment from the Macedonian army.

The Malloi still remained unconquered. It appears certain that they held an extensive and fertile tract, along both banks of the lower Rávi, and that they were in ordinary times at feud with the Oxydrakai.

[1] 'The guess that Poros might be Paurava,' says Mr. Vincent Smith, 'is not very convincing': *op. cit.*, p. 56. In the Sassanian chronicles the name appears as Fúr.

[2] The Kathaioi have been identified with the modern Káthiás who settled in the Montgomery district about 11 generations ago from Kathiáwár. The Káthiás never had any settlements east of the Rávi according to their own traditions.—See Montgomery *Gazetteer*, 1899, pp. 82-3.

But in this emergency the two tribes formed an alliance, cemented by a wholesale exchange of brides, and endeavoured to combine against the invaders. But Alexander acted too promptly to allow their forces, which united would have formed an army of 100,000 men, including 10,000 horse, with 700 or 900 chariots, to collect. Crossing the Bár, even at that period a waterless steppe, between the Chenáb and Rávi, he surprised the Malloi in their fields. Those who escaped were shut up in the fortified towns, one of which, with a citadel situated on a commanding height, was stormed and 2000 of its garrison slain. Pushing on Alexander caught up the flying Malloi at a ford across the Rávi, and inflicted further severe loss upon them; and, crossing the river into the Montgomery district, he took a Brahman stronghold, perhaps Shorkot, the ancient Shor.[1]

The Malloi too had still another stronghold in a small town 80 or 90 miles north-east of Multán. This offered a desperate resistance. Alexander was wounded in the assault: in revenge all its inhabitants were massacred. At the confluence of the five rivers with the Indus, or possibly at their confluence with the Hakrá, Alexander founded a city. In its neighbourhood lay the independent tribes styled Abastanoi, Xathroi (Oxathroi, ? Kshatriya) and Ossadioi by Arrian. Curtius, however, says that Alexander came to a second nation called Malli and then to the Sabarcae,[2] a powerful democratic tribe without a king, who numbered 66,000 warriors with 500 chariots. Further south the extremity of the modern State of Baháwalpur lay within the dominions of Mousikanos.

Thus the political conditions in the Punjab were, as we shall always find them, strongly marked and deeply contrasted. In the Punjab Proper ruled dominant tribal democracies,[3] the tribes or tribal confederacies of the Malloi, Oxydrakai, Kathaioi, the precursors of the Sikh commonwealth; while the hills which encircled them were held by petty chiefs, Saubhúti, Ambhi of Taxila, Abisares, Arsakes and the two chieftains or kinglets designated Poros. Sind then, as often later, formed a kingdom or group of principalities.

Of the states in the north-west Punjab few were of any great extent. The dominions of the elder Poros between the Jhelum and Chenáb only comprised 300 townships,[4] whereas the country from the former

[1] Shor was identified by Cunningham with Alexandria Soriana, but Dr. Vogel has shown that its ancient name was Shibipura. Shibi was a tribal name, often mentioned in Sanskrit literature, and Chinese Buddhist tradition places a Shibi-rája in the Upper Swát valley.—*Journal of the Punjab Historical Society, I, p.* 174.

[2] Diodorus calls these Sambastai, and adds that the Sodrai and Massanoi occupied both banks of the river (? Indus).

[3] "The Kathaians were not ruled by kings like the tribes which lay nearer the Indus (in the Salt Range and other hills), but were autonomous, *each of the communities into which they were divided being self-governed:*" McCrindle's *Ancient India*, p. 37, n., in which the words in italics are apparently the editor's own deduction. No authority is cited, and from Note L, to his *Invasion of India*, p. 347, it would appear that the note is based on Arrian, who speaks of the Kathaians and other tribes of independent Indians, which does not necessarily imply that the Kathaians were *autonomoi* at all. Strabo indeed expressly says that they chose as king the handsomest man, probably meaning that no one physically deformed could succeed to the kingship. But in any event the rule of a king would be quite consistent with the existence of 'autonomous' village communities.

[4] *Ancient India*, p. 35, § 39 (Strabo).

river to the Beás was held by no less than nine nations with 5000[1] townships, though the latter number may be exaggerated.

The state of civilisation then existing in the Punjab is described with some detail in the Greek histories.

Under the Mauryan dynasty[2] the Punjab became a mere province of the empire, and with Kashmír, Sind and the territories west of the Indus formed a viceroyalty governed from Taxila. Yet few traces of the Buddhist code imposed on its people remain. Again from the time of Demetrios (190 B. C.) to the overthrow of Hermaios (c. 56 A. D.)—a period of two centuries and a half - the Punjab was dominated by Greek or Græco-Bactrian influences which have left still fewer traces, although it was signalised by the reign of Menander (Milinda in Prákrit), the king whose brilliant capital was at Ságala (Siálkot) and who was converted to Buddhism. Ságala lay in Maddarattha, the country of the Maddas, the Madras or Madrakas of Sanskrit literature. With the Madras and the people of Ságala, the Kshudrakas and Málavas were all included in the general term Báhíka[3], and the inhabitants of Ságala itself formed a class of the Báhíka called Jártika. The Græco-Buddhist civilisation was destroyed by the Parthians, and they in turn fell before the Indo-Scythian dynasty, whose greatest ruler, Kanishka, also became a convert to Buddhism. But the Buddhism of his time was that of the Maháyana or Great Vehicle,[4] 'largely of foreign origin and developed as the result of the complex interaction of Indian, Zoroastrian, Christian, Gnostic and Hellenic elements,' chiefly made possible by the unification of the Roman world under the earlier emperors.[5] The centre of the Indo-Scythian power lay in Gandhára and Kashmír, and Kanishka's capital was Purashapura (Pesháwar), but his great Buddhist council sat at the Kuvana monastery at Jálandhar, and in Kashmír.[6] Sir John Marshall is now in possession of proof that Kozoulo-Kadphises (I) was reigning in 79 A. D. so that Kanishka was reigning in the 2nd century of our era. This should settle the controversy regarding Kanishka's dates.

From Kanishka's time date the Gandhára sculptures, many of whose characteristic features are due to the cosmopolitan Græco-Roman influence.

[1] *Ancient India*, pp. 9 and 40: but in the *Invasion of India*, p. 112, the number is given as 500—clearly an error, for Strabo *twice* says 5000.

[2] Dr. D. B. Spooner regards Mauryan as equivalent to Mervian and observes that the founder of the dynasty, Chandragupta, was certainly not a Buddhist: J. R. A. S., 1915, pp. 414 and 416.

[3] References to the Báhika, Báhlika or Váhlika are frequent in Sanskrit literature, but it is difficult to locate them with precision. Cunningham (A. S. R., I, p. 148) placed the Báhika country, which was named after Báhi and Hika, two demons of the Beas river, in the Jálandhar Doab, while Lassen, on the authority of the *Trikanda Sesha*, says the Báhika are the same as the people of Trigartta. Cunningham apparently followed the authority of the *Mahábhárata*, but that poem also describes the Madra as also called Báhika and Jártika, *ib.* V., p. 195. They must not be confused with the Pahlava or Pallava as has been done by a writer in J. R. A. S., 1912, p. 256. It is tempting to suggest that they are represented by the modern Bhaos of Siálkot.

[4] Or Northern School, which still prevails in Japan, China and Tibet, in Spiti and, in very impure form, in Láhul and Kanáwar.

[5] Vincent Smith, *op. cit.*, p. 283.

[6] *Early History of India*, p. 234: it probably sat at Jálandhar in the cold weather and in Kashmír in the hot season (*cf.* p. 229 for the treatment of the Chinese hostages).

The Kushán power in the rest of India undoubtedly decayed under Vásudeva, whose name shows how thoroughly Indianised the invaders had become; but in the Punjab and Kábul they held their own until they were overthrown in the 5th century by the Ephthalites or White Huns. But about the middle of the 3rd century the Kushán coinage became Persianised, and possibly this is to be ascribed to the unrecorded Persian invasion, discussed above, pp. 24-5.

During the Gupta ascendancy the Punjab, with Eastern Rájputána and Málwa, was for the most part in the possession of tribal democracies, or confederacies, which had subsisted through all the dynastic changes and invasions of the preceding centuries. The Madrakas still held the Central Punjab, but a new tribe, the Yaudheyas (Joiyas), now appear as occupying both banks of the Sutlej, while the Abhíras with the Málavas held part of Eastern Rájputána. The Kusháns, eventually confined to Gandhára and Kábul, maintained diplomatic relations with Samudragupta, but neither their territories, nor the Punjab as a whole, was much influenced by the Hindu renaissance of the Gupta period[1].

The White Huns assailed the kingdom of Kábul and thence poured into India in 455-484 A. D. Ten years later they overwhelmed Gandhára under the leadership of Toramána, whose son Mihirakula made Ságala (Siálkot) his capital. His reign was chiefly remarkable, as far as the Punjab is concerned, for his persecution of the Buddhists, and a great massacre of the people of Gandhára on the banks of the Indus, the king being a bigoted worshipper of Shiva, his patron deity. But he died soon after, in 540, and his kingdom did not long survive him, for in 563-7 the Turks and Persians overthrew the White Huns in the Oxus Valley, and thus destroyed the root of their power in India. For nearly 500 years India now enjoyed almost absolute immunity from invasion of her North-Western Frontier, but during this long opportunity she failed to create any organised State powerful enough to protect her when the tide of invasion once more flowed in upon her. Nothing is known of Punjab history in the latter half of the 6th century, but by 604 A. D. we find a powerful kingdom established at Thánesar (Sthánvísvara) in the holy circuit of the Kurukshetra. Here, towards the end of the 6th century, Prabhákara-vardhana had raised himself to eminence by successful wars against the Hun settlements of the North-West Punjab and the clans of Gurjara (Gujrát). His son Harsha, who reigned from 606 to 648, established a great kingdom over Northern India from the Himalaya to the Narmada, but its administration compares unfavourably with that of the Guptas. Violent crime was rare, but the pilgrim Hiuen Tsang was more than once robbed by brigands.

Imprisonment of the cruel Tibetan type was now the ordinary penalty, the prisoners being left to live or die, but mutilation was often inflicted for serious offences—such as filial impiety—though it was sometimes commuted into banishment. Ordeals were much in vogue. Nevertheless the civil administration was founded on benign principles. The rent of the crown lands, fixed in theory at $\frac{1}{6}$th of the produce, was the

[1] Kartripura, a place which gave its name to a kingdom embracing Kumaon, Almora, Garhwál and Kángra, is identified by Fleet with Kartárpur, but that town appears to owe its origin to the Sikhs. Hutchison mentions Brahmapura as a more ancient kingdom comprising British Garhwál and Kumaon: Chamba *Gazetteer*, p. 69.

principal source of revenue, taxes were light and compulsory labour was paid for. Moderate personal service was exacted and liberal provision made for religious communities. Officials were remunerated by grants of land. Education was widely diffused especially among the Brahmans and Buddhist monks, and records of public events were kept. Harsha's court was the centre of an accomplished literary circle, which included Búna, the Brahman who composed the *Harsha-charita*, or 'Deeds of Harsha,' still extant. The religious position was however confused. In his latter days Harsha favoured the Buddhist doctrines, first in their Hínayána, then in the Maháyána, form, but he also worshipped Siva and the Sun. Near Multán he also built a vast monastery of timber in which he entertained strange teachers, apparently Zoroastrians for a time; but finally he set fire to the structure in which 12,000 followers of the outlandish system, with all their books, perished. For a century this holocaust restricted the religion of the Persians and Sakas to very narrow limits. Such is the tradition preserved by Táranáth, but according to Hiuen Tsang about 644 Multán was a province where the Sun-god was held in special honour and formed, like Po-fa-to which lay to its north-east, a dependency of Tseh-kia, a kingdom which comprised the greater part of the country between the Indus and Beás, and had its capital close to Ságala. Kashmír, which was then the predominant power in the north, had reduced Taxila and Singhapura (the Salt Range), with the Urash plain, Púnch and Rajauri to the rank of feudatories

The pilgrim returned, after a month's stay at Jálandhar, to China, penetrating the defiles of the Salt Range with difficulty, crossing the Indus, and following the route over the Pamírs and through Khotan in 646 A. D.

The connection of India with China at this period was indeed close. Harsha sent a Brahman envoy to the imperial court of China, and in return a mission was sent which only reached India after Harsha's death. To go back to the first half of the 6th century China had then lost Kashgár, but in the 7th and 8th centuries she made great efforts to recover her lost ground, and in 661-65 she enjoyed unparalleled prestige. Kapisa, the country to the north of the Kábul river, was a province of the empire, and at its court were ambassadors from Udyána (Swát) and all the countries from Persia to Korea. After some vicissitudes her activity revived in 713 against the Arabs, who had blocked the roads over the Hindu Kush, and the Tibetans. In 719 the Arabs sought alliances amid the petty states on the Indian borderland, but the Chinese raised the chiefs of Udyána, Khottal (most of Badakhshán), Chitrál, Yasín, Zábulistán (Ghazní)[1], Kapisa and Kashmír to the rank of kings, in her attempts to form a bulwark of states against Arabs and Tibetans alike. In 651 however the Arabs, aided by the Karluk tribes, overthrew the Chinese and direct contact between the politics of India and China ceased for more than twelve centuries.

It is convenient now to consider what influences the almost incessant political changes of the foregoing centuries had brought to bear upon India, and what racial elements they had introduced. From the earliest period apart from the pre-historic Aryan inroads, the only Indo-European elements supplied by the invasions were Iranian and Greek, if the latter

[1] See the appendix to this part.

term can be justly applied to the heterogeneous mass which is called Græco-Bactrian.

The Parthian influence.

Closely connected with the migrations of the Sakas and allied nomad tribes was the development of the Parthian or Persian power under the Arsakidan kings. Mithradates I (174 to 136 B. C.), king of Bactria, had extended his power as far as the Indus and possibly to the east of that river, and the Saka chiefs of Taxila and Mathura took the title of satrap, presumably because they had become feudatories of the Parthian monarchy. About 120 B. C. Maues[1] or Mauas attained power in the Kábul valley and the Punjab. The most famous of his successors was Gondophares, and the coins of his nephew Abdagases are found in the Punjab only, but those of his successor Orthagnes are more widely spread. The Indo-Parthian princes were however expelled from the Punjab by the Yueh-chi by the end of the first century A. D. Towards the close of that century Appollonius of Tyana visited Taxila and found it the capital of a sovereign who ruled over what was of old the kingdom of Porus. He bore the name of Phraotes,[2] apparently a Parthian name, but was an Indian king, who had been educated by Brahmans and married the daughter of a king beyond the Beás. Appollonius was the bearer of a letter from the Parthian king Bardanes at Babylon, and this he presented to the satrap of the Indus at its crossing, and he, although no officer of the Parthian king, supplied them with boats and a guide to the Rávi out of regard for him. It thus appears that the Parthian power did not then extend even to the Indus at Attock Appollonius' object was to study the rites and doctrines of the Sramans and Brahmans, and he found many monuments of Alexander's invasion and considerable traces of Greek influence.[3]

The account of Appollonius' visit to India does not come to us at first hand, but it is confirmed indirectly by the fact that Hermaios, the last Greek ruler of Kábul and possibly other territories adjoining it, was not overthrown by the Kusháns till about 50 A. D., and even his downfall was gradual, for Kadphises I at first struck coins in their joint names, and then replaced the bust of Hermaios by the effigy of the Roman emperor Augustus, showing that he acknowledged a shadowy suzerainty in Rome through his immediate overlord, the Parthian monarch.

The Central Asian inroads.

While the earlier invaders of India appear to have been Aryan, Iranian, or Greek, the first or second century B. C. brought down upon India a torrent of Central Asian[4] peoples which only

[1] It might be tempting to suggest some connection between Maues and the Máwis of the Simla hills if the former name did not appear as Moga.

[2] *Cf.* Phraates, a Parthian name.

[3] *India and Rome*, by Priaulx, pp. 11-12 etc.

[4] The term Indo-Scythian, which appears to the present writer wholly unjustifiable and misleading, appears to be due to the fact that, as Herodotus records, the Persians termed all Scythian nomads Sakai. But the Saka originally held territory to the west of the Wu-sun horde, apparently situated between the Oliu and the Jaxartes (Syr Darya) rivers to the north or south of the Alexander mountains. From those seats they were expelled by the Yueh-chi. Moreover, as Dr. D E. Spooner has now pointed out, even Herodotus used the term Sakai in more than one application and for long periods Shákа denoted Iranians, not Scythians at all. As Dr. Fleet has contended there were no Scythians in the north of India in early times and Shákyamuni should be translated 'Iranian sage.'

ended with the Mughal invasions. The earliest of these invaders were the Sakas[1] who overran the valley of the Helmund and gave their name to that country, so that it became known as Sakasténé or Sístán after them, some time after 130 B. C. Other branches of the horde, penetrating the Indian passes, established satrapies at Taxila and Mathura, which were closely connected. Very little is known about the Saka civilization. They adopted, it would appear, the religion of the Persians, presumably Zoroastrianism, for according to Táranáth,[2] Harsha of Thánesar in the 7th century A. D. built the great monastery of timber near Multán, but eventually set fire to it and burnt all its heretical denizens as already described.[3] But as a ruling race the Sakas probably disappeared from the Punjab before the great Yueh-chi invasion under Kadphises I, who was chief of the Kushán section of that tribe. He probably conquered Kábul about 60 A. D. and his successor, Kadphises II, finally extinguished the Indo-Parthian power in the Punjab and Indus valley.

Thus these nomads, who may have been a Mongolian or Turk stock or a mixed race known as the Yueh-chi, had established themselves in Kipin, probably north-eastern Afghánistán if not Kashmír, and in the Kábul territory by 60 A. D., and the kingdom of Kadphises I doubtless included all modern Afghánistán and extended to the Indus. Between 90 and 100 A. D. the Yueh-chi dominion was extended all over north-western India, and the Kushán dynasty lasted till 225, a period of nearly two centuries. But the Turki Shahiyas of Kábul were, or at least claimed to be, descended from Kanishka, the Kushán, so that the Turki element apparently held its own at Kábul from A. D. 60 to c. 900.

As a race the Yueh-chi were not snub-nosed Mongols, but big men with pink complexions and large noses, resembling in manners and customs the Hiung-nu, a tribe of Turki nomads of the same stock.[4] They came originally from the province of Kan-suh in north-western China and must have comprised, at the time of their defeat by the Hiung-nu, about 500,000 or 1,000,000 souls with 100,000 to 200,000 bowmen. What were the numbers which accompanied Kadphises I and Kadphises II into the Punjab we have no means of knowing. All that is known is that their great successor, Kanishka, wielded a military power so vast that he was able to wrest Kashgár, Yarkand and Khotan from China. He embraced the Buddhist faith and founded at Peshàwar, his capital, the Kanik-chaitya which Alberúní alluded to as late as 1030 A. D. But though Kanishka was a Buddhist the coins of the Kusháns continued to bear images of Zoroastrian deities, such as Mithra, the Sun-, Váta, the Wind-, and the War-gods. But other coins bore the names and figures of non-Iranian gods, and those of

[1]Mr Vincent Smith speaks of this as an Indo-Parthian dynasty and some of them bear Iranic names, *e.g.* Onones. But Maues and Azes are believed to be Scythic names and Prof. D.R Bhandarkar would regard them as Sakas, some of whom assumed Iranic names just as Greeks took Buddhist and even Hindu names: *Ind. Ant.*, 1911, p. 13, n. 15.

[2]The Tibetan historian of Buddhism.

[3]P. 32 *supra*. See *Early Hist. of India*, p. 298. The text gives a very imperfect idea of the probable extent of Zoroastrian influences during this period. Reference can only be made to Dr. D. B. Spooner's valuable paper on *The Zoroastrian Period of Indian History* in J. R. A S., 1915, page 405 *f*

[4]*Early Hist. of India*, p. 217. The Hiung-nu were not Huns or Ephthalites.

Vásudeva are restricted in their types to the more or less barbarous representations of a few non-Zoroastrian deities. Almost all the coins of this Kushán, like those of Kadphises II, exhibit the figure of Shiva with the bull Nandi.

CHINESE AND TIBETAN INFLUENCES.

As has already been shown China exercised at least for a time an important influence in the extreme north-west of India in the 7th and 8th centuries. When her power decayed that of the Tibetans increased and in 747 A. D they (and *not* the Chinese, according to Waddell[1]) invaded north-eastern India, but apparently did not extend their inroads to any part of the modern Punjab. The population of Western Tibet, says the Revd. A. H. Francke, is the result of a long process of blending of at least three stocks, two Aryan, *viz.* the Mons of North India and the Dards of Gilgit, and the third, and most numerous, Mongolian which is the Tibetan nation.

Of the Mons little is known as they were overlaid by the Dard migrations, except in Zangskar, even before the Central Tibetans overwhelmed them. In Zangskar all Indians, Kashmiris or Dogras are called Mon and Mr. Francke thinks that the ancient Mons were an Indian tribe, but it is not necessary to assume this. The *kiang*, the wild sheep and the wild yak had their feeding grounds much further to the west[2] than they are now-a-days and though Tibetan nomads may have extended as far as Gilgit as far back as the time of Herodotus, it appears more probable that the Mons came not from India or the south but from the west and represent a stream of direct Aryan migration rather than one which had filtered through Kashmir from India. However this may be the Mons had some connection with pre-Lámaist Buddhism, as imposing remains of ancient Buddhist art are found among the ruins of their settlements in Zangskar and Ladákh. Of the Dards a good deal more is known, but though their influence in Western Tibet must have been enormous they cannot have affected the population of the Punjab or more than very slightly that of the Indus Kohistán.

About 800 A. D however Chamba was subdued by a race of foreigners called Kíra who were probably Tibetans, while Kulu seems to have often been liable to Tibetan inroads and for centuries it remained tributary to Ladákh. Kashmir and Kishtwár had also a later period of Tibetan rule[3].

THE HUN AND TURKISH ELEMENTS.

If historical material for the third century A. D is lacking very little is available for the history of the second half of the sixth century, but after the golden age of the Guptas, which had lasted from 370 to 455 A. D., the Huns must have poured into India in ever-increasing numbers. These White Huns or Ephthalites held a comparatively short lived supremacy over Northern India, for the Turkish tribes

[1] J. R. A. S., 1911, p 208, and A. Q. R., Jany. 1911. The introduction of Buddhism into Tibet was probably the result of the invasion of 747.

[2] The existence of the wild sheep in Lahul, where it has been extinct for centuries, is proved from rock-carvings in that canton: *A History of Western Tibet*, pp. 13, 18, 19, 20, 65, 188.

[3] *Ibid*, p. 65.

in alliance with the Persian king destroyed them between 563 and 567 in the Oxus valley and the Turks were soon able to extend their power as far southwards as Kapisa and annex all the countries once included in the Hun empire.[1] But soon after the Huns came the Gurjaras who may indeed have come along with them, though the Gurjaras are never heard of until near the end of the 6th century, as the records frequently bracket them with the Hunas. Recent investigation has shown that the Pratihára (Parihár) clan of the Rájputs was really only a section of the Gújars and this fact raises a strong presumption that the other 'fire-born' Rájput clans, the Solanki (Chalukya), Punwár (Paramára) and Chauhán (Chahámána) must also be of Gurjara origin.[2] The Túnwars (Tomaras) must be assigned a similar origin.[3] The Gurjara empire was of great extent. At the beginning of the 9th century it included or dominated the Bhoja, Matsya, Madra, Kuru, Yadu, Yavana, Gandhára, and Kira kingdoms, practically the whole Punjab. It certainly comprised the modern district of Karnál and extended to a point below Jullundur.[4] The Gurjaras gave dynasties to Kanauj, Ajmer, and other states and from their ruling clans are descended the mass of the modern Rájput clans.

The nomadic Gújars, on the other hand, colonised a line running from Mewát (the 'Gujarát' of Alberúni) up both sides of the Jumna valley, and thence following the foot of the Punjab Himalaya, right up to the Indus.[5] Now it is undoubtedly true that the Gújar is one of the few great 'castes' or races of northern India which has retained its own dialect. Even in the extreme north-west, amongst Pisácha-speaking peoples in Swát and Kashmir the nomadic Gújar graziers and shepherds speak a language which closely resembles the Rájasthání of Mewát and Jaipur. In Kashmir this dialect is called Primu. In the north-western hills and indeed in the Punjab generally the Gújar has not amalgamated largely with the other tribes indigenous or immigrant and in Attock it is 'remarkable how much they are disliked and despised by other tribes. Though good cultivators and often well off, they seem to be looked upon as little better than menials, and the appointment of a Gújar to any place of authority over any other tribe is always the signal for disturbance. They are good landlords and among the best cultivators in the district, and in physique of the same type as the Ját whom in many ways they much resemble' Prone to thieving, when circumstances permit, 'quarrelling and intriguing are blots on their character, but not much more evil can be said of them. They differ entirely in character from the idle, thievish and cowardly Gújars of the southern Punjab'—and it is a great grievance that the army is closed to them, but a good many find their way into it by assuming another tribal name.[6] That some of the great Rájput tribes then may have been formed from Gurjara elements is by no means inconceivable, but if the Rájputs as a body are Gujars by origin it is difficult to account for the above account of the esteem in which they are held. Moreover to be perfectly frank, the present writer is not quite as convinced as he was

1 Vincent Smith, *op cit.* p 278.
2 J. R. A. S, 1909, p. 53.
3 *Ib.*, pp. 253, 260.
4 *Ib.*, pp. 264, 267, 268.
5 Grierson in J. R. A. S., 1912, p. 1084.
6 Attock *Gazetteer*, 1907, p. 91.

of 'the Gujar origin of the Rájputs.'[1] Assuming that *pratihára* means 'durward' that surname may have been adopted by *a* Gurjara family which attained to Rájput or gentle rank, but it would not follow that all Pratiháras were Gurjaras and still less need it be assumed that all the Rájput clans were Gurjaras.

Further the theory leads almost of necessity, to other theories still more difficult of acceptance. It follows that if the Rájputs were Gurjaras all tribes of Rájput origin must be Gurjara too. For example the Kanets would be Gujars by blood, but Sir George Grierson[2] would restrict that origin to the Ráo (Rahu) Kanets and assign to the Khash or Khasia a Khasha descent The Khashas are frequently mentioned as a northern tribe addicted to cannibalism like the Pisáchas, in the *Mahábhárata* and many later works. They appear to have been once settled in Western Tibet, but in historical times they were restricted to a comparatively limited region, the valleys lying immediately south of the Pir Panjál range between the middle Jhelum and Kishtwár, all now in Kashmir territory. That they spread further eastward over the hills of Chamba and Kángra into the Kulu valley can only be conjectured from the similarity of their name to that of the Khash Kanets. The different groups among the Kanets have no traditions of different descent, indeed their divisions appear to be sectarian by origin. This is at least true of the Kuran Kanets of the Simla hills. The Khakhas of the Jhelum valley are almost certainly the modern representatives of the Khashas, but if the Khash Kanets are to be identified with them it would appear equally probable that the Khashai or Khakhai Paṭhans. progenitors of the Yúsafzai, Tarklani and other Paṭhan tribes, are Khash also.

In the eastern hills the Gurjara strain may have amalgamated much more readily with the indigenous tribes Grierson indeed suggests that the earliest known Indo-Aryan or Aryan inhabitants of the Himálaya tract, known as the Sapádalaksha, were the Khashas who spoke a language akin to the Pisácha languages of the Hindú Kush These are now represented by the Khas clan of the Kanets. Later on the Khashas were conquered by the Gurjaras, who are now represented by the Rájputs, and also by the Ráo (Rahu) clan of the Kanets which represents those Gurjaras who did not take to warlike pursuits but remained cultivators—whence their claim to be of impure Rájput descent. Over the whole of Sapádalaksha Gurjaras and Khashas amalgamated gradually and they now speak a language mainly Gurjari, but also bearing traces of the original Khasha population.[3]

As will be seen later many of these Gurjaras of Sapádalaksha invaded Rájputána and there developed the Rájasthání tongue. Subsequently there was constant communication between Rájputána and Sapádalaksha and under the pressure of the Mughal domination[4] there ultimately set in a considerable tide of emigration back from Rájputána into Sapádalaksha This great swirl of population appears

[1] Accepted in Vol. III, p. 300 *infra*.
[2] *The Pahari Language*, in *Ind. Ant.*, 1915.
[3] J. R. A. S 1912, p. 1088-4.
[4] So Grierson, but it is suggested that the tide set in much earlier, in the time of the earliest Moslem inroads.

to the present writer to have extended right round the Punjab, Grierson suggests that during the period in which Rájput rule became extended over the Punjab the Rájput (Gurjara) fighting men were accompanied by their humbler pastoral brethren.

The Kuran Kanets appear to be looked down on by both the Khash and Rahu Kanets on religious grounds as will appear from the following valuable note by Mr. H. W. Emerson :—

The Kurans are looked down upon by other branches of the Kanets and as they can neither take nor give wives outside their own group, they are forced to intermarry among themselves So great are the difficulties thus created that several villages but little larger than hamlets have divided their houses into three or more sub-divisions, intermarriage being permitted inside the village but not within the sub-division. The main grounds on which the Kurans are looked down upon are three in number. In the first place they summon no Brahman at death or other ceremonies. Secondly they erect in honour of the dead at a local spring or cistern an image which consists of the head only, not of the whole body. Thirdly, they ill-treat their gods. The gods of the tract are five in number, and all of them came from Kashmir with Mahásu when that deity chased Chasrálu, his immortal enemy, across the mountains. The fugitive at last slipped into a deep but narrow cleft where none was bold enough to follow him and there he still lurks, watched by the five gods whom Mahásu sent to watch him. But he is still associated in worship with his warders and his cavern is the scene of strange rites. But for four months in the year he sleeps and his gaolers need not keep strict watch over him. Each year they go to sleep when snow begins to fall on the mountains and do not wake until their worshippers arouse them. This is the occasion for the great festival of the Kurans and it is held at each of the five temples of their gods at the full moon in Phágan. In each temple is a small open window let into the outer wall. Below this inside the building is placed an image of the god and two bands, each of from 8 to 11 men, are chosen from his worshippers. These men fast for some days before the festival One represents the god's defenders, and the other side attacks them. Both are armed with snow-balls The defenders station themselves close to the window and try to beat off the attacking party whose object is not to hit them back, but to arouse the god by their missiles. If they fail to do this before their supply is exhausted they are fined several rams, but if they succeed in hitting him on the head it is peculiarly auspicious and then they dance and leap for joy, shouting that the god has risen from his sleep. The defenders on their part revile them for the sacrilege, hurl stones at them and chase them through the village, firing shots over their heads. When a truce is called the god's opinion is asked through a diviner in an ecstacy, but while he invariably commends his defenders for their zeal he thanks their assailants for awaking him, and joins in the festival which lasts for several days.

Where the Gujars settled in the plains they lost their own language, but as we enter the lower hills we invariably come upon a dialect locally known as Gujari. All this is pre-eminently true, but to the present writer it appears that the Rájput-Gujars and the Gujar settlements of the modern Punjab may owe their origin to administrative or military colonisation of the Punjab and its eastern hills by the great Gujar empire, whose rulers found the Punjab difficult to hold and had constantly to enfief Rájput or Gujar condottieri with allodial fiefs held on condition of military service.

The Huns.—The first recorded invasion of India by the Huns is ascribed to the reign of Skandagupta, and must have occurred between 455 and 457 A. D. It was repulsed by their decisive defeat, but this first incursion must have been made by a comparatively weak body since about 500 A. D. the nomads appeared in greater force and overwhelmed Gandhára. From this new base they penetrated into the Gangetic provinces and overthrew the Gupta empire. Indeed Toramána, their leader, was actually established as ruler of Málwá in Central India prior to 500 A. D. and on his death in 510 A. D his empire passed to his son Mihiragula whose capital was at Ságala in the Punjab. Song-Yun, the Chinese envoy, also found a Hun king ruling over Gandhára in 520, though whether this king was Mihiragula or not is uncertain and unimportant.

Again in 547 A. D. Cosmas Indicopleustes describes Golles, a White Hun king, as lord of India. Mihiragula probably died in 540, but even after his death it is certain that all the states of the Gangetic plain suffered severely from the ravages of the Huns during the second half of the 6th century and it was in that period that the Rája of Thánesar gained renown by his successful wars against the Hun settlements in the north-west Punjab. In 604 his eldest son had advanced into the hills against them, but he was recalled by his father's death and we have no record of any final destruction of these Hun settlements. Harsha's conquests lay in other directions. The Hun invasion thus began in 455 and we still find the tribe established on the north-west frontier in 604—150 years later.

In later Sanskrit literature the term Húna is employed in a very indeterminate sense to denote a foreigner from the north-west, just as Yávana had been employed in ancient times, and one of the thirty-six so-called royal Rájput clans was actually given the name of Húna.[1] This designation may however quite possibly have been its real name and denote its real descent from the Huns, a tribe or dynasty of that race having, we may assume, established itself in India and, as a conquering or dominant race, acquired Rájput status.

[1] Vincent Smith, *op. cit.*, pp. 278-8.

A NOTE ON ZABULISTAN.

On coins of Vásudeva occur the names of three countries, Takan, Jáulistán and Sapardalakshan. The latter is the later Siwálik.

Tukan or Takan was according to Stein the name of the province which lay between the Indus and Beás and it was known as early as the 8th century A. D.[1]

Bhandarkar suggests that Takan should be Ṭák=Ṭakka, and Ṭáq was apparently a town which lay in Zábulistán. But *ṭák* or *ṭáq* meant an arch and the place-name Tánk would appear to be derived from it and not from Ṭák or Ṭakka.

The name Zábulistán or Záwulistán would appear to mean the 'land of Zábul' and it was also so called, but strictly speaking Zábul was its capital. Its situation has already been described. Cunningham's identification of Jáulistán with Jábulistán is incontrovertible and Bhandarkar takes that to be Zábulistán, an equation which appears hardly open to dispute. It is equally probable that the Jávula Toramána of the Pehewa inscription derived his title from Zábul, but beyond that it appears unsafe to go. The coins of the Sháhi Javúvla or Jabula, the Toramána Sháhi Jaúvla of the Kura inscription from the Salt Range, must be those of this king, but it does not follow, as Hoernle says, that there was a Jávula tribe.[2] Still less does it follow that the Jávulas were Gurjaras: or that, as Vincent Smith implies, the title Jáula was a Hun title[3]

It would be out of place here to discuss the extent or history of Zábulistán, but one or two points may be noted. It did not correspond to Seistán, but it included the Sigiz or Sigizi range whence Rustam derived his name of 'the Sigizi' and which may have given its name to Seistán,[4] and the towns of Baihaq or Mukir, Táq and apparently Uk of Sijistán,[5] which was afterwards called Rám Shahristán.[6] Zábulistán lay north-west and south-west of Ghazni, but did not include that city[7]. Le Strange says the high-lands of the Kandahár country, along the upper waters of the Helmund, were known as Zábulistán.[8]

[1] *Rajatarangini* I, p. 205, note 150. Grierson suggests that Tákri is the script of the Takkas: *J. R. A. S.* 1911, p. 802.
[2] J. R. A. S., 1905, p. 3.
[3] *Ib.* 1909, p. 268.
[4] *Tabaqát-i-Násiri*, I, p. 184.
[5] *Ib.*, pp. 67, 355-6, and II, p. 1120.
[6] *Ib.*, II, p. 1122.
[7] *Ib.*, I, p. 71, and II, p. 1020.
[8] *The Lands of the Eastern Caliphate*, p. 334: *cf.* p. 349. For Ṭáq in Seistán see p. 343: for Ṭáq in Daylam, p. 374 and for Ṭáq-i-Bustán, p. 187.

PART III.—THE ELEMENTS OF THE PUNJAB PEOPLE.

THE MUTABILITY OF CASTE.

Before attempting to give any history of the modern Punjab tribes it will be well to attempt a sketch of the foreign elements in the Hindu population of India generally as determined by recent scholarship. Professor D. R Bhandarkar[1] has pointed out that the orthodox theory of Hindu society as once split up into four distinct castes is untenable. The Vedic castes were not absolutely distinct from one another. A Kshatriya, a Vaisya, even a man of the lowliest origin, could aspire to Brahman-hood. Vishvámitra, a Kshatriya, founded a Brahman family. The sage Vasishtha was born of a harlot, but became a Brahman by religious austerities. 'Training of the mind,' says the verse of the *Mahábharata*, 'is the cause of it' The reputed compiler of that epic, Vyása, was born of a fisherman and Paráhara, the sage, of a Chaṇḍála woman. 'Many others, who were originally not twice-born, became Bráhmaṇas.' So in the Punjab of the present day we find that it is function which determines caste, and not birth Two of the old royal and essentially Rájput families in the Kangra hills, those of Kotlehr and Bangáhal, are said to be Brahmans by original stock.[2] So too is the ruling family of Jubbal. Its founder was Bhir Bháṭ and his son by his wife, who was of his own caste, became the *parohit* or spiritual guide of his two half-brothers, sons of his father by the widowed Ráni of Sirmúr, and also of his uterine brother, her son by its Rájá.[3]

Not only was it possible for men of humble origin to attain to Brahman-hood, but marriage between the castes was frequent. Kshatriyas married with Brahmans on equal terms.[4] But the son of a Brahman by a Sudra woman was a Nisháḍi and numerous instances might be given of new 'castes' formed by similar mixed marriages. But such unions did not by any means always produce new castes On the contrary by a process very analogous to what goes on in the Punjab at the present day among the Asht-bans Brahmans,[5] the *female* issue of a mixed marriage could by degrees

[1] *Ind. Ant.*, 1911, January.—What follows is practically taken from this invaluable paper with details and illustrations added to emphasise the applicability of Professor Bhandarkar's thesis to these Provinces. That the present writer is in entire accord with them will be apparent from his paper in *Man*, Vol. VIII, July 1908, No. 52. Mr. W. Crooke's important paper on *the Stability of Caste and Tribal Groups in India* (Journal of the Anthropological Institute, 1914, Vol XLIV, p. 270 ff.) may also be consulted with advantage.

[2] The ruling family of Koti, a feudatory of Keonthal State, in the Simla Hills, is a branch of the Kotlehr Rájás. Its *gôt* is said to be Kaundinia, and the children of its founder Rám Pál, being of a Rájput wife, became Rájputs. Simla Hill States *Gazetteer*, Koti, p. 5.

[3] *Ibid*, Jubbal, p. 4. The legend is of much interest as showing the absence of prejudice against widow re-marriage also.

[4] See Vol. II, post., p. 501.

[5] Vol. II, p. 127.

regain their place. Thus if a woman born to a Bráhmaṇa of a Sudra wife married a Brahman her issue would rank lower than a Brahman, but if her daughter again married a Brahman and their daughter again did so, the issue of the 'sixth female offspring' would, even if a son, be regarded as a pure Brahman.[1] In other words the Sudra taint would be eliminated in seven generations, or as a verse of the *Manu-smriti* says: 'If (a female) sprung from a Bráhmaṇa and a Súdra female, bear (*female*[2] children) to one of the highest caste, the inferior (tribe) attains the highest caste within the seventh generation.' This is not, strictly speaking, paralleled in British Láhul at the present day. In that remote canton the Ṭhákurs take to wife Kanet women as *srújat*,[3] but not as *lahri* or full wife; and though the sons of such women are not at first considered pure Ṭhákurs, yet in a few generations they become equal always, we must assume, on condition that they can find Ṭhákur brides.[4] Very similarly Brahmans also have Kanet women in their houses, and the sons of such women succeed as if legitimate. Their fathers, however, will not eat from their hands, though they will smoke with them. They are known as *gurú* and marry Kanets or women of mixed caste, if they can find any. There are many of these *gurús* in Láhul, but they call themselves Brahmans and are probably accepted as Brahmans in a few generations. In fact no new 'caste' of *gurús* appears to have been formed. Here we see in operation a principle by which the *male* descendants of a mixed marriage eventually regained their father's caste. By an analogous principle women of lower castes could aspire to marriage with men of the highest castes, but not in a single generation. It takes the Ghirth woman seven generations to become a queen, but the Ráthi's daughter can aspire to that dignity in five. In other words, by successive marriages in a higher grade a Ghirthni's daughter, daughter's daughter, and so on, is in seven generations eligible to become the bride of a Rája. An exact parallel to the *Mitákshara* rule is not found in the modern Punjab, but the analogies with and resemblances to it are striking. It would also appear that in ancient times a Brahman's male descendants by a Shúdra woman would in time regain Brahmanical status, just as they seem to do in modern Láhul, for Manu ordained that "if a Párashava, the son of a Brahman and a Shúdra female, marries a most excellent Párashava female, who possesses a good moral character and other virtues, and if his descendants do the same, the child born in the sixth generation will be a Brahmaṇa." Here we have a new 'caste,' the Párashava originating in a mixed marriage, but never developing, it would seem, into a caste, because its members could by avoiding further *mésalliances* and rigidly marrying *inter se* regain their ancestral status.

[1] This rule comes from the *Mitákshara*.

[2] Cap. X, v. 64. It is suggested that by children, *female* children must be meant. It is not clear that *male* offspring could regain the full status of a Brahman.

[3] *Srújat* is equivalent to the Panjabi *surat*, Pashtu *suratat*. Such women are in Láhul termed *chanmá* or workers.

[4] Kángra *Gazetteer*, Parts II to IV, 1899, p. 26 of Part III, Láhul. It is not stated that any such condition is in force, but judging by analogies it is highly probable that it exists.

In ancient times, however, the effect of an union between two different castes was ordinarily the formation of a new 'caste'. No doubt the intermarriage of two castes of more or less equal status had not such a result[1] or at least it only resulted in forming a new group of much the same status. For instance the Bráhmana Harichandra, surnamed Rohilladhi,[2] had two views, a Brahman and a Kshatriya. His children by both were called Pratihára,[3] but the sons of the former were Bráhmana Pratiháras and those of the latter Kshatriya Pratiháras. And the Pratiháras, in spite of their Gujar origin, became a Rájpút clan, one of the four Agnikulas. But when the disparity between the contracting parties was great, or when by what was termed a *pratiloma* marriage a man espoused a woman of *higher* caste than his own, a new caste was generally formed. Numerous instances of such new castes could be cited from Colebrooke's *Essays*. The late Sir Denzil Ibbetson excerpted the following note from Colebrooke's work :—

"It would seem that the offspring of marriage and of illicit intercourse between different castes were called by the same name; but this is open to some question (p. 272). Those begotten by a higher or a lower are distinguished from those begotten by a lower or a higher class (p. 273). The third is sprung from inter-marriages of the first and second set; the fourth from different classes of the second; the fifth from the second and third, and the sixth from the second and fourth. Manu adds to these tribes four sons of outcastes. The *Tantrá* named many other castes (the above are apparently got from the *Puránas*): (p. 274). Except the mixed classes named by Manú, the rest are terms for profession rather than tribes; and they should be considered as denoting companies of artisans rather than distinct races. The mention of mixed classes and professions of artisans in the *Amara Sinha* supports this conjecture (p. 274). The *Játimálá* mentions 262 mixed castes of the second set (above). They, like other mixed classes, are included in Súdrá; but they are considered most abject; and most of them now experience the same contemptuous treatment as the abject mixed classes mentioned by Manu (p. 275). The *Tantra* says, 'avoid the touch of the Chandála and other abject classes; and of them who eat cow flesh, often utter forbidden words, and omit the prescribed ceremonies.' They are called Mlechhá, and going to the region of 'Yavana have become Yávanas.' Again: 'These seven, the *Rajaka* (? mason), *Karmakára* (smith), *Naṭa* (dancer, actor!), *Barada* (? *tárútsás*!), *Kaivarta* (fisherman), *Medabhilla*[4] are the last tribes' and pollute by contact, mediate or immediate. A man should make oblations for, but should not dally with, women of Naṭa, Kapála, Rajaká,

[1] The son of a Brahman who married a Kshatriya woman by *anuloma* was apparently himself a Brahman.

[2] This surname surely points to a northern origin.

[3] 'Chamberlain,' *lit.* door-keeper. This is, however, doubted by Professor Bhandarkar. The Pratiháras are represented in the modern Punjab by the Parihár Jáṭs in Dera Ghází Khán. Pratihára is the Sanskritised form of Paḍihár. For the office of *pratihára*, see Vogel's *Antiquities of Chamba*, pp. 135 and 284.

[4] Or rather 'Meds and Bhíls.' Colebrooke does not explain all these names. Rajaka is not traceable. Platts gives *biraẓait* as a bard or bowman, but it can hardly = powder-maker.

Nápita (barber) castes, and prostitutes. Besides their special occupation, each mixed class may follow the special occupation of his *mother's* class; at any rate if he belongs to the first set (above). They may also follow any of the Súdrá occupations, menial service, handicraft, commerce, agriculture."

Indeed so firmly established was this principle that a marked *mésalliance* or a *pratiloma* marriage founded a new caste, that it apparently became customary to define the status of a caste of lowly origin, aboriginal descent or degraded functions in the terms of an assumed or fictitious mixed marriage. Thus in order to express adequately the utter degradation of the Chanḍála he must be described as the issue of a Shúdra man, begotten of a Brahman woman,[1] just as the uncleanness of the Ḍakaut Brahmans can only be brought out by saying that they are descended from the *rishi* Ḍaka by a Shúdra woman.[2]

The formation of new castes on the principles set forth above was a very easy matter, so easy indeed that new castes might have been multiplied to infinity. But new factors came in to check their unrestricted creation. One of these factors was occupation, another was social usage. These were the two determining factors. Thus a Rájpút who married a Jáṭ wife did not necessarily sink to Jáṭ status, but if his descendants tolerated widow re-marriage he certainly did so, and if they took to cultivating the soil with their own hands they probably did so in time, and having lost their status as Rájpúts adopted widow re-marriage as a natural corollary. Countless Jáṭ tribes claim, doubtless with good right, to be descended from Rájpút ancestors who fell by marrying Jáṭ women, or Gujars or others of like status. For a converse instance of promotion by marrying a woman of higher status see the case of the Dodái Baloch at p. 43, Vol. II.

Professor Bhandarkar arrives at the conclusion that even in the highest castes purity of blood is not universal, and he goes on to show how foreign elements were absorbed into the Hindu population. This appears to have been effected by a two-fold process. The descendants of invaders or immigrants were admitted into the pale of Hinduism according to their degree. The priestly Magian became a Brahman and the warrior a Kshatriya, precisely as in modern Láhul the Ṭhákurs or gentry and *quondam* rulers have begun to assert a Rájpút origin, though more or less pure Mongolians by blood, just as the Kanets, at any rate in the valleys of Gára and Rangloi, are pure Botias[3] or Mongolians. The second process was intermarriage.

[1] See Vol. II, p. 151, *s. v.* Chanál.

[2] Vol. II, p. 136. *Cf.* the foot-note* on p. 139 as to the origin of the Sáwani Brahmans.

[3] The real Kanets of Patan who are Hindus look down upon the Kanets of Gára and Rangloi and call them Botzát and regard them as of inferior caste. But this may be due to the fact that they are Buddhists; see Kángra, *Gazetteer*, 1897, Parts II to IV, Part III, p. 25, compared with the top of p 21. Crooke, *op. cit.*, p. 271, accepts the present writer's view that Sir T. H. Holland's conclusions, referred to at p. 456. Vol. II *infra*, regarding the Kanets are vitiated by his failure to distinguish between the mixed and unmixed groups of the Kanets in Láhul.

Professor Bhandarkar illustrates the first-named process by some very interesting historical facts, culled from all parts of India. He cites the recently discovered inscription at Besnagar in Gwálior[1] for an instance of a Greek ambassador, a Yavana-duta, with the Greek name of Heliodorus, erecting a *garudu* column to Vasudeva, god of gods, not as a mere compliment but because he was a *Bhagavata* of the god and therefore fairly to be described as a Vaishnava and a Hindu. The Yavana men however were oftener Buddhists than Hindus. They were succeeded by the Sakas, also a foreign tribe, whose dynasty ruled Afghánistán and the Punjab. Some of their *kshatrapas* or satraps were Buddhists, but others affected the Brahmanic religion, as did also many private individuals among the Sakas. At about the same period came the Abhíras, the modern Ahírs, described as bandits and foreigners, but undoubtedly Hindus. One of their sub-castes is closely associated with the cult of Krishna and claims descent from his foster-father Nanda.[2] Abhíra Brahmans are found in Rájpútána and elsewhere, but not apparently in the Punjab. After the Sakas came the Kushanas, whose kings had Turki names and Mongolian features. After the Buddhist Kanishka the Kushán kings did homage to Shiva and other deities of the Brahmanic pantheon.

Of more special interest, however, are the Maga or Shákadvípi Brahmans who must be assigned to about this period. They were undoubtedly Magi, and were brought into Jambudvípa by the son of Krishna Sámba, who was suffering from white leprosy and was advised by Nárada to build a temple to Surya on the Chenab. This temple was erected at Multán or Sambapura, one of its earlier names.[3] The Magas were also called Bhojakas and wore an *avyanga* or girdle which was originally the skin of the serpent-god Vásuki, and Professor Bhandarkar points out that the name of their originator, Jarashasta, bears a close resemblance to that of Zoroaster,[4] and he is informed that the *pujárís* of the temples of Jagadísha and Jawálámukhi[5] (in Kángra)

[1] J. R. A. S., 1909, p. 1089.

[2] See Vol. II, p. 5. Are we to take it that the Nand-bansi Ahírs are descended from Abhíras who adopted the cult of Krishna, while the Jádubansi are descended from those who took Yádava wives, *i.e.* intermarried with the indigenous races? The legend goes that Arjuna, after cremating Krishna and Balaráma, was marching through the Punjab to Mathura with the Yádava widows, when he was waylaid by the Abhíras and robbed of his treasures and beautiful women.

[3] This agrees with Abu Rihán-al-Beruni, who says that the names of Multán were Kasht-, Hans-, Bag and finally Sánb-pur. Múlisthán was the name of the idol and from it is derived the modern name of the town. The temple of the Sun was styled Aditya. Below it was a vault for storing gold. See Raverty in J. A. S. B., 1892, Part I, pp. 191 *et seqq.* Elliot's translations in his *History of India*, I, pp. 14, 15, 35, were incorrect.

[4] The sage Rijihva, of the Mihira *gotra*.

Súrya, the Sun × Nakshubhá.

Jarashasta or Jarashabda — equated to Jaratusta or Zoroaster.

Mihira is the Sanskritized form of the Old Persian *mihr*.

[5] If Professor Bhandarkar's information is correct the derivation of Bhojki suggested on p. 107 of Vol. II is untenable and the Bhojkis of Kángra are the Magas or Bhojakas.

are Sákadvípi Brahmans, as are the Sewak or Bhojak, most of whom are religious dependants of the Oswál Srávaks (Saraogís) in Jodhpur. These Sewaks keep images of Súrya in their houses, and worship him on Sunday when they eat rice only. They used to wear a necklace resembling the cast-off skin of a serpent. The Paráshari Brahmans of Pushkar were also originally known as Sewaks and Sákadvípí Brahmans. About 505 A. D. we find the Magas spoken of as the proper persons to consecrate images of Suryá, and c. 550 it is complained that in the Kaliyuga the Magas would rank as Brahmans. In all probability then the Magas came into India about the middle of the 5th century or earlier with Kanishka as his Avistic priests. It may be of interest to add that the presence of the Magian fire-worshippers in the Punjab would explain a curious passage in the *Zafarnáma*, which states that Tímúr found the inhabitants of Sámána, Kaithal and Asandi to be mostly fire-worshippers. The people of Tughlikpur, 6 *kos* from Asandi, belonged to the religion of the Magi (*sanawíya*) and believed in the two gods Yazdán and Ahrimán of the Zoroastrians. The people of this place were also called Sálún.[1]

After the power of the Kushanas was overthrown and that of the Guptas established, India enjoyed respite for about two centuries. During the first half of the 6th century the Húnas penetrated into India with the allied tribes of Gurjaras, Maitrakas and so forth, eclipsed the Gupta power and occupied northern and central India. The Húna sovereign Mihirakula, in spite of his Persian name,[2] became a Hindu and his coins bear the bull—an emblem of Shiva—on the reverse. The Húnas, undoubtedly the White Ephthalites, or Húns, had come to be regarded as Kshatriyas as early as the 11th century, and became so thoroughly Hinduised that they are looked upon as one of the 36 Rájpút families believed to be genuine and pure. The name is still found as a sub-division of the Rahbári caste.[3] The Gújar, Sanskritised as Gurjara, were undoubtedly another foreign horde, yet as early as the first half of the 7th century they had become Hindus, and some of them at least had actually acquired the rank of Kshatriyas, being commonly styled the imperial Pratihára dynasty. One inscription speaks of the Gurjara-Pratiháras. Among the 36 royal families of the 'real' Rájpúts again we find the BADGÚJAR, who represent an aristocracy of Gújar descent and of Rájpút status. The Gújar-Gaur Brahmans are also, in all probability, Brahmans of Gújar-race from the tract round Thánesar. The late Sir James Campbell identified the Gújars with the Khazars who occupied a very prominent position on the borderland of Europe and Asia, especially in the 6th century, and who are described as "a fair-skinned, black-haired race of a

[1] E. H. I., III, p. 494, *cf.* p. 481.

[2] Mihirakula is the Sanskritised form of Mihrgul, 'Rose of the Sun.'

[3] Professor Bhandarkar says that Húna is now-a-days found as a family name in the Punjab, but the present writer has not come across it. He is, however, in entire agreement with Professor Bhandarkar's view that the Rájpút Húnás are Húns by origin, see *Man*, 1908, p. 100.

remarkable beauty and stature. Their women indeed were sought as wives equally at Byzantium and Baghdad."[1]

Another Rájput tribe, which is in all probability of Gújar origin, is the Chálukya or Chaulukya. Two branches of this tribe migrated from northern India. One, called Chálukya, descended from the Siwálik hills in the last quarter of the 6th century and penetrated far into southern India. The other, the Chaulukya or Solanki, left Kanauj about 950 A.D. and occupied Guzerat, but Solanki Rájputs are still to be found in the Punjab in Hoshiárpur and in the tracts bordering on Rájputána in the south-east of the Province. Like the Paḍihárs they are regarded as Agnikulas.

The Cháhamánas, the third Agnikulá tribe, are now the Chauháns. Professor Bhandarkar would attribute to them a Sassanian origin and read Cháhamána for Vahmana on the coins of Vásudeva, who reigned at Multán over Ṭakka, Zábulistán and Sapádalaksha or the Siwálik kingdom. Vásudeva's nationality is disputed. Cunningham thought him a later Húṇa, Professor Rapson would regard him as a Sassanian and Professor Bhandarkar as probably a Khazar and so a Gurjara. However this may be, the Cháhamánas were undoubtedly of foreign origin, and they were known as the Sapádalakshía-Cháhamánas or Chauháns of the country of the 125,000 hills, which included not only the Siwálik range, but a territory in the plains which included Nágaur on the west as well as the Punjab Siwáliks and the submontane tracts as far as Chamba[2] and Ṭakka or Ṭák, the province between the Indus and the Beas.

The Maitraka tribe probably entered India with the Húns. Their name appears to be derived from *mitra*, the sun, a synonym of *mihira*, and to be preserved in Mer, *Mair*, and it may be suggested Med, unless the latter term means boatman, *cf.* Balochi Metha.

Closely associated with the Maitrakas were the Nágar Brahmans whose origin Professor Bhandarkar would assign to Nagarkoṭ, the modern Kángṛa. One of their *sharmans* or name-endings was Mitra. But into the Nágar Brahmans other castes appear to have been incor-

[1] This theory leaves unexplained the dislike and contempt in which the Gújars are held by other tribes. Even when, as in Attock, good cultivators and well-to-do, they seem to be looked upon as little better than menials, and the appointment of a Gújar to any place of authority over any other tribe is always the signal for disturbance: Attock *Gazetteer*, 1907, p. 91.

[2] To the references given by Professor Bhandarkar may be added Raverty's *Tabaqát i-Násiri*, pp. 110, 200, etc. 'Nágaur of Siwálikh' was spoken of in early Muhammadan times The tract from the Sutlej to the Ganges extending as far south as Hánsi was called the Siwálikh, and some native writers include the whole of the Alpine Punjab below the higher ranges from the Ganges to Kashmír under the name of Koh-i-Siwálikh, *ibid*, p. 468[4]. As to the Ahichhatra, which Jaina works also mention as the capital of Jángala, placed in the *Mahábharata* near Mádreya, it appears to be the modern Arura in Ludhiána, identified with Ahichatta by the late Sir Atar Singh of Bhadaur. But Hatur was also called Aichata Nagri, as well as Arhatpur. Cunningham identified Bhadaur with Arhatpur: Ludhiána *Gazetteer*, 1904, pp. 14 and 227.

porated, and among others the Vaisya name-suffix Datta is found as a *sharman* of the Nágar Brahman, just as it is among the Muhiál Brahmans.[1] On the other hand, the Nágra Jáṭs probably derive their name from Nagar, a place described as not far from Ahichchhatra, which was either the Ahichhatra now represented by Arura (or possibly by Hatúr) or a place in the Siwálik hills.[2]

The Aborigines of the Punjab.

It has long been the practice to speak of aboriginal tribes in the Punjab, but it is very difficult to say precisely what tribes or elements in its population are aboriginal. Both these Provinces are on the whole poor in early historical remains, and both are singularly destitute of relics of pre-history. In the Thal or steppe of Míánwáli local tradition attributes the first possession of the country to a half mythical race of gigantic men, called Belemas, whose mighty bones and great earthen vessels are even now said to be discovered beneath the sand hills. But the Belemas can hardly be other than the Bahlíms, a tribe still extant as a Rájput sept. It was established on the Indus previous to the Seers (Siars) and Mackenzie mentions it as extinct, but not apparently as a very ancient race : Leia and Bhakkar *Sett. Rep.* 1865, § 32.

Thorburn records that the Marwat plain was sparsely inhabited by a race which has left us nothing but its name, Pothi, and this race appears to have been found in Marwat so late as three or four centuries ago when the Niázís overran it from Tánk.[3]

Raverty also notes that the Budli or Budni, who consisted of several tribes and held a large tract of country extending from Nangrahár to the Indus, were displaced by the Afgháns when they first entered Bangash, the modern Kurram.[4] He deprecates any hasty conjecture that they were Buddhists, as the Akhund Darveza says they were Káfirs, that is, non-Mussalmáns, but he does not say they were Buddhists. Raverty adds that the Budlis were expelled from Nangrahár by Sultán Bahrám, ruler of Píoh and Lamghán.

[1] Vol. II, p. 121.

[2] Professor Bhandarkar postulates at least three Ahichchhatras, one in the United Provinces, about 22 miles north of Badáun, a second not located and a third in the Himálayas in the Jángala country near Mádreya, which was situated between the Chenab and Sutlej. If the Mádreya is to be identified with the Madra Des the Jángala would certainly appear to be the modern Jangal tract of the Málwa country, south of the present Sutlej valley, and Arura lies in this tract. Probably there were two Ahichchhatras in the Punjab, to wit, Arúra, and one in the Himalaya, possibly in Kángra, in which District Chhatt is still the name of a village. But a Chhatt is also found near Banúr in Patiála territory. And the place-name may be connected with the institution of *chhat* and *makán* among the Rájputs.

[3] *Bannu or our Afghan Frontier*, p. 14. Pothi suggests a connection with Pothohár or wár,—a region lying between the Jhelum river and the Indus. 'But strictly speaking, the limits of Pothwár are confined to the four ancient *parganas* of the *Aín-i-Akbari*, *viz.*, Fatehpur Báori, now Rawalpindi, Akbarábád Tarkhpari, Dángali and Pharwála or Pharhála.'—*J. G. Delmerick in* P. N. Q. I., § 617.

[4] *Notes on Afghánistán*, pp. 380-81.

Thence they fled eastwards, according to the Akhúnd, and there found others of their race. Raverty hazards a conjecture that the Awáns, Kaṭhars and Gakhars were some of the Budli or Budni tribes who crossed the Indus into the Sindh-Ságar Doáb.

In the Peshâwar valley we find the Khands, but it is doubtful whether they can be regarded as even very early settlers in that tract, though it is tempting to connect their name with the Gandhára.

In the Central Punjab Murray[1] describes the Káthis as "a pastoral tribe, and as Jún, their other name denotes, they live an erratic life." But Sir Alexander Cunningham correctly describes the Júns as distinct from the Káthis, though he says that both tribes are tall, comely and long-lived races, who feed vast herds of camels and black cattle which provide them with their loved libations of milk. Cunningham however appears to be speaking of the Jan, 'a wild and lawless tribe' of the southern Bári Doáb, which has apparently disappeared as completely as the Jún, though Capt. J. D. Cunningham, writing in 1849, speaks of the Jans as being, like the Bhattis, Siáls, Karrals, Kathis and other Tribes, both pastoral and predatory: see his *History of the Sikhs*, p. 7.

In the northern Punjab tradition assigns the whole of the modern Siálkot district to the Yahars or Yeers, who lived in *juns* (*jans*,) or rude mud huts. The Yeers also held the Jech and Sindh-Ságar Doábs, and were known as Jhuns and Puchedas in the Rechna Doáb, and in the Bári Doáb as Bhular, Mán and Her, the three original tribes of the great Ját 'caste'. The Shoon Dul were also recorded as the most powerful tribe in the Punjab in the time of Bikramajit.[2] It is impossible to say whence these traditions were obtained or what substratum of truth there may be in them. The Jhúns, Júns or Jans thus appear to have left a widespread tradition, yet they are unknown to history, unless we may conjecture that they preserve the name of Yona or Yavanas, the territory of the Græco-Bactrian King Milinda whose capital was Ságala.[3]

The aborigines of Láhul were the Mon or Mon-pas, and Cunningham thought that the ancient sub-Himalayan people were the Mon or as they are called in Tibetan, Molán.

Tribal areas and tribal names.

The Punjab is studded with tracts of very varying size, which derive their names from the tribes which now, or at some recent period, held sway therein. Along its northern border lie the Khattár,[4] Kahutáni and Bála Gheb tracts in Ráwalpindi. The Bálá Gheb or

1 *History of the Punjab*, p. 38.
2 Prinsep's Siálkot *Settlement Report*, 1865, p. 38-9.
3 Cunningham's *Ancient Geography of India*, p. 186.
4 From the Khattar tribe, according to the Ráwalpindi *Gazetteer*, 1883-84, but the name appears to be obsolete as applied to the tract held by this tribe.

Gahep, literally Upper Gheb, derives its name from the Ghebas. It is held by Ghebas calling themselves Rewals of Mughal descent.[1] The Ghebas also gave their name to Pindi Gheb, a township now held by the Jodhras. According to Raverty, Chakkawál, now Chakwál, was one of the principal places in "the Dhani Gahep"—Dhani being the name of the tract, and Gahep a great Ját tribe. But the Gahep cannot be other than the GHEBA and they do not now hold the Dhani, 'west Chakwál' tahsil. The name Dhani appears to give their name to the DHANIAL Rájputs and to be so called from *dhan*, 'wealth,' owing to its fertility.[2] The Kahúts have given their name to the Kahútáni tract in Chakwál tahsil and the Kahúta hills and town preserve memories of their former seats. The Bugiál tract, described by Cunningham as lying on the bank of the Jhelum under Bálnáth, is also called Báisgrám or the 22 villages. Cunningham says it derives its name from the Bugiál branch of the Janjúas, but as there is also a Gakkhar sept of that name he suggests that the Bugiál septs in both those tribes derive their name from the locality—a not improbable conjecture.[3] The Awáns hold the Awánkári in the Salt Range and a smaller tract in the Jullundur District bears the same name.

In the District of Gujrát, a name which itself denotes the territory of the Gujars,[4] lie the Herát and Jatátar. The latter clearly means the Ját realm, but the derivation of Herát is obscure. It is popularly derived from Herát in Afghánistán, but this derivation is hardly tenable. Cunningham[5] derived Hairát, which he says is the original name of the city of Gujrát, as Hairát-des was of the district, from the Araṭṭa. But tempting as the derivation is, it is difficult to accept it. The Araṭṭa appear to be identical with the Sanskrit Aráshtraka, 'the king-less,'[6] which name is well preserved in Justin's Arestæ, Arrian's Adraistæ, and the Andrestæ of Diodorus. But Araṭṭa was also equivalent to Madra, Járttikka, and the 'thieving Báhíka' of the *Mahábhárata*, as the Kathæi of Sangala (? Siálkot) are stigmatized in that poem[7]. The term king-less might well have been applied to the democratic Punjab tribes of that period, but it is doubtful if the Her Jáṭ tribe derives its name from Araṭṭa. The

[1] Ráwalpindi *Gazetteer*, 1893-94, p. 57. Rewal is apparently a mistake. Ráwal can hardly be meant.

[2] The statement that the Dhaniál give their name to the Dhani, on p. 235 of Vol. II, is made on Ibbetson's authority: *Census Rep.* 1881, § 453. The Dhani is very variously defined. One writer says it is the same as Pothowár: P. N. Q. I., § 380. The eastern Dhani was a lake which was only drained under Bábar's orders. It was held by Gujar graziers from whom the Kahúts collected revenue to remit to Delhi: Jhelum *Gazetteer* 1904, p. 109. It was called Balú ki Dhan from Bal, ancestor of the Kassars or Maluki Dhan from the Janjúa chief Mal of Malot: *ib.*, pp. 107-09. Lastly *dhan* appears to mean a pool or lake.

[3] A. S. R. II, p. 27. For the Bugiál *mandis*, see p. 267 of Vol. II, *infra*.

[4] Gujrát denotes the Gujar *tract*; Gujránwála the Gujars' *village*: a distinction overlooked in Baden Powell's *Indian Village Community*.

[5] *Ancient Geography of India*, p. 179.

[6] According to Grierson this is a doubtful explanation: *The Pahari Language*, p. 4, note 27, in *Ind. Ant.*, 1915.

[7] Cunningham, *op. cit.*, p. 215.

modern Jatátar does not quite correspond to the ancient country of the Jártikas whose capital Sákala lay on the Apagá (now the Aik) to the west of the Rávi, if we are to understand that the Jártikas did not extend to the west of the Chenab. But the Madra country or Madra-des is said by some to extend as far west as the Jhelum, though others say it only extends to the Chenab, so that the modern Jatátar may well represent a Jártika tract of the Madr-des, if we may assume that the term Jártika was strictly only applicable to the western tribes of the Madr-des[1]: Cunningham also records that in the Chaj or Chinhat Doáb we find a Ránja Des, so called from the Ránjha tribe, and a Tárar *tappa*, while in the Rachna Doab we have a Chíma Des, to the south and west of Siálkot. The two latter names are derived from the Jáṭ tribes which predominate in those tracts, but all three appear to be obsolescent if not obsolete.[2]

Further east, in Siálkot, lies the Bajwát[3] or territory of the Báju Rájputs, whom it is tempting to identify with the Báhíkas of Sákala or Ságala. In Gurdáspur the Riár Jáṭs give their name to the Riárki tract.

In Jullundur the Manj ki Dardhak or Dárdhak, which appears as a *mahal* in the *Áín-i-Akbari*, included the modern tahsil of Ráhon with parts of Phillaur and Phagwára. The Manj or Manjki tract, on the other hand, includes the western part of the Phillaur tahsíl and a large part of Nakodar. The modern Grand Trunk Road separates the Manj tract from the Dardhak It is, however, doubtful whether either tract derives its name from the Manj tribe. Quite possibly the Manj or Manjki is named from the tribe which held it, but it is not impossible that the tribe takes its name from the soil or the situation of the tract.

In Hoshiárpur the Khokhars hold the Khokharain, a tract on the Kapúrthala border. And the Jaswán Dún[4] is named from, or more probably gives its name to, the Jaswál Rájputs.

The Gaddis of Chamba and Kángra occupy the Gadderan, a tract which lies across the Dhaola Dhár.

It is very doubtful if the name Kulu can be derived from the Koli tribe, but in the Simla Hills the Ṭhákurs gave their name to the Ṭhákurain[5].

In the Simla Hills the Mangal Kanets give their name to the Mángal tract, while the petty fief of Rawahin or Rawain is probably so named from the Rao or Ráhu Kanets. In Hissár the Punwár Rájputs held a Punwárwati.

[1] *Ibid.*, p. 185.

[2] A. S. R. II, p. 56 He also mentions Miáni Gondal but that is only a village.

[3] Prinsep (Siálkot *Settlement Report*, 1865, p. 39) gives the form Bajwant. This would appear to be the older form of the word: *e.g. cf.* Paṭhánti and Nádaunti. The former appears to be the country round Paṭhánkot, the latter the tract round the town of Nádaun. Cunningham, however, calls the country round Paṭhánkot Pathâwat, a name now apparently obsolete: *op. cit.*, p. 144.

[4] It is possible that the ancient form of the name was Jaswant: *cf.* Bajwant and Nádaunti.

[5] In Kulu the *ṭhákurain* was the period of the Ṭhákurs' rule.

In the extreme south-east of the Province lies part of the Mewát, so called after the Meos, but in its turn it gives its name to the Mewátis, or people of the Mewát. The Mewát further comprises the Dhangalwati, Naiwára and Pahatwára, three tracts named after the *páls* of the Meos which hold them. The Jáṭ country round Palwal[1] is also called the Jatiyát, and the Ahír country round Rewári, the Ahírwati. But the latter term is apparently only used by the Ahírs themselves, as the Meos call the country west of Rewári the Ráth or Bíghauta. The Ráth is also said to be distinct from Bíghauta and to be one of the four tracts held by the Alanot Chauháns. It was the largest of those tracts, lying for the most part in Alwar, but including the town of Nárnaul, which was also named Narráshtra.[2] Narráshtra must, however, be the name of a tract, not a city, and it is suggested that Ráth is derived from Narráshtra. The Ráth is said to have lain to the south of Bíghauta, which tract followed the course of the Kasáoti river stretching southwards along the west of the modern tahsil of Rewári in Gurgaon. The Dhandoti tract lay between Bíghauta and Hariána. It was a sandy stretch of country running from east to west across the centre of the Jhajjar tahsil.—P. N. Q. I., §§ 133, 370, 618.

The Bhaṭṭís give their name to at least two tracts, the Bhaṭṭiána which comprised the valley of the Ghaggar from Fatehábád in Hissár to Bhatner in the Bíkáner State, together with part of the dry country stretching north-west of the Ghaggar towards the old bank of the Sutlej: and also to the Bhaṭṭiora, a considerable tract in Jhang lying between the Sháh Jiwana villages in the west and the Láli country in the east. The Bhaṭṭiora is thus in the Chinioṭ tahsil, north of the Chenab. Numerous place-names, such as Bhaṭner, which Cunningham appears to identify with Bhaṭistala,[3] Pindi Bhaṭṭián and Bhaṭiot, are called after this tribe. According to Dr. J. Ph. Vogel, the Bhaṭṭiyát in Chamba is probably also named from the Bhaṭṭi caste, but it does not appear that any such caste was ever settled in Chamba. Bhaṭṭiyát appears to be a modern form, and Dr Vogel thinks its termination is a Persian plural. It has lately been introduced into official documents, and it is often indicated by the name Bára Bhaṭṭián, which points to its having once consisted of 12 *parganas*. Geographically nearly the whole of this territory belongs to the Kángra valley, and it is noted as the recruiting ground for the Chamba army.[4] It is suggested that its name is derived from *bhaṭa*, a soldier, and that it means 'the 12 fiefs held on a military tenure' or simply 'the 12 military *parganas*.'

[1] It is suggested that Palwal may be the Upaplavya of the *Mahábhárata*. It was the capital of the king of Matsya who brought mountain chiefs in his train. Pargiter suggests that the Matsyas must have come from the northern part of the Aravalli hills, but it is suggested that they are the modern Meos. Palwal is now-a-days said to mean 'countersign.'

[2] Phulkián States *Gazetteer*, 1904, p. 197. For the folk-etymologies of Nárnaul see G. Yazdani's paper in J. A. S. B., 1907, p. 581.

[3] The derivation of Bhaṭinda from the tribal name Bhaṭṭi, put forward in Vol. II, p. 101, must be abandoned. Its ancient name was Tabarhindh or possibly Batrind. But the latter name can hardly be derived from Bhaṭṭi. See Phulkian States *Gazetteer*, 1904, p. 189.

[4] *The Antiquities of Chamba State*, I, pp. 4 and 18.

The Gondal Jáṭs give their name to the Gondal Bár, the length of which is some 30 *kos* from north-east to south-west, with a breadth of 20 *kos*. It is difficult to accept Cunningham's identification of this tract with the Gandaris of Strabo, which was subject to the younger Porus, and it is not correct to speak of the Gundal- or Gundar- Bár *Doáb*, as this Bár never gave its name to the tract between the Jhelum and the Chenab, nor does its upper portion now form the Gujrát district. The people of Gandaris, the Gandaridæ, are also said to have been subjects of Sophytes. Gandaris therefore appears to have stretched right across the Chenab from the Jhelum to the Ravi, its western portion being held by Sophytes, while its eastern part was subject to the younger Porus.

In the North-West Frontier Province the Paṭhán tribes give their names to many tracts, such as Yusufzai, Razzar, Marwat as well as to numerous villages. Instances of other tribes giving names to tracts are however rare, though in Dera Ismail Khan there is another Jatátar.

The whole question of these tribal areas is one of considerable interest and corresponding difficulty. The system under which a tract is named after the tribe which holds it or is dominant in it must be one of great antiquity, as indeed we know it to have been in other parts of India. Yet in the Punjab the only tribal tract-name of any antiquity seems to be Gujrát. In Kashmír the Khashas gave their name to the valley of Khaśálaya, now Khaishál, which leads from the Marbal Pass down to Kishtwár. But with hardly an exception the ancient tribal names of the Punjab have disappeared. Thus Varáhamihira writes: 'In North-East, Mount Meru, the kingdom of those who have lost caste, the nomads (Pashupálas, possibly worshippers of Pashupati, or more probably cattle-owners), the Kíras, Káshmíras, Abhisáras, Daradas (Dards), Tanganas, Kulútas (people. of Kulu), Sairindhras (who may possibly be 'people of Sihrind'[1]), Forest men, Brahmapuras (of the ancient kingdom whose name survives in Bharmaur in Chamba), Ḍámaras (a Kashmír tribe, but ḌAMMARS are also found on the Indus), Foresters, Kirátas, Chínas (doubtless the Shíns of Gilgit, but we still find CHHINA and Chína Jáṭs in the Punjab plains), Kauṇindas, Bhallas (still the name of a Khatri section), Paṭolas (unidentified), Jaṭásuras (? Jaṭṭs, or Jáṭ heroes or warriors), Kunaṭas, Khashas, Ghoshas and Kuchikas'. Here we have not only tribal names but also occupational terms and Ghosha and Kuchika recall the *goshfandwál* or sheep-folk and *kuchis* or nomads of Dera Ismáil Khán. There are difficulties in nearly every identification suggested, as for instance in deriving Kanet from Kunaṭa or Kuṇinda (Kauṇinda), as Grierson points out, the more so in that the Kulú people are already mentioned once as Kulútas and we should have to identify the Kunindas with the Kanets of the hills excluding Kulu[2]. But it is

[1] Sir George Grierson writes: 'I never saw the equation Sairindhra from Sihrind. It looks most enticing.'

[2] Sir George Grierson writes in a private communication: 'As regards Kanet having derived from Kanishṭa [junior or cadet] the derivation is phonetically possible, but only possible and also improbable. From Kanishṭha, we should ordinarily expect some such word as *Kanéṭh*, with a cerebral ṭ aspirated, whereas Kanét has a dental t unaspirated. There are isolated instances of such changes, but they are rare. I have a memory of a class of village messengers in Bihar called *kanait* (bowman, I think, from *kán*, 'arrow'). Perhaps Kanet may have a similar origin. That is, however, a matter of history.'

not necessary to find a racial term in every name. If we insist on doing so the number of tribes becomes bewildering.

To the above several names may be added from various works. Thus the ***Mahábhárta*** classes the Madras, Gandháras, Vasátis, Sindhús and Sauvíras (two tribes dwelling on the Indus) with the despicable Báhíkas. We have still a Jáṭ tribe called SINDHÚ and its name can only be derived from Sindh or the Indus, but no trace exists of the Madras, Vasátis and Sauvíras. To this list remain to be added the Prasthalas whose name suggests some connection with ***pratisṭhána*** and who may have been the people settled round Paṭhánkot or akin to the Paṭhán. Then we have the Kankas, Páradas (apparently associated with the Daradas), Tukháras, all from the north-west[1] and Ambashṭhanas,[2] who were close to the Madras, besides tribes like the Araṭṭas already mentioned.

Why should these tribes have nearly all disappeared, leaving no certain trace even in place-names? The answer appears to be that they were non-Brahmanical in creed and foreigners by race. 'When shall I next sing the songs of the Báhíkas in this Ságala town', says the poet of the ***Mahábhárata***, 'after having feasted on cow's flesh and drunk strong wine? When shall I again, dressed in fine garments in the company of fair-complexioned, large-sized women, eat much mutton, pork, beef and the flesh of fowls, asses and camels?' The Báhíkas can only be the Báhlíka tribe which came from Balkh (Báhlíka) and in close connexion with them we find the Mágadhas, the warrior class of Shákadwípa or Persia, spoken of contemptuously. The Báhíkas had no ***Veda*** and were without knowledge. They ate any kind of food from filthy vessels, drank the milk of sheep, camels and asses and had many bastards. The Araṭṭas in whose region they lived occupied the country where the six rivers emerge from the low hills, *i.e.* the sub-montane from Rúpar to Attock, yet they are described as the offspring of two Pisháchas who dwelt on the Beas. But the value of such a pedigree is well described by Mr. J. Kennedy[4]. As he says, 'primitive men

[1] Grierson says the Khashas and Tukháras were Iranian inhabitants of Balkh and Badakhshán, the Tokháristan of Muhammadan writers: see his valuable introduction to the volume of the Linguistic Survey dealing with the Pahaṛi languages published in *Ind. Ant.*, 1915.

[2] With the Kaikeyas the Ambasṭhas inhabited the Ráwalpindi country and Gandhára in the days of Alexander according to J. Kennedy in J. R. A. S., 1915, p. 512. Possibly Amb in the Salt-Range may commemorate their name and locality. A discursive foot-note might be written on the name of Ambasṭha. An Amtaṭṭha-rája appears in a Páli legend about the origin of the Shákiya and Koliya family: *ibid.*, p. 439. He had five wives, of whom three bore astronomical names. He disinherited his sons by his senior wife and they migrated to found a new colony. Does this mean that the Ambasṭhas were an offshoot of the fire-worshipping Iranians who settling in the Punjab were compelled to intermarry so closely that they were reputed to espouse their own sisters? Then again we have Ambashṭa = Vaidya, 'physician': Colebrooke's *Essays*, II, p. 160.

[3] If the Jártikas, a clan of the Báhíkas, be the modern Jáṭs, the latter term may be after all Iranian and the nucleus of the Jáṭ 'caste' Iranian by blood, a far less difficult hypothesis than the Indo-Scythian theory. Grierson says Báhíka = 'outsider' (*op. cit.*, p. 4) but is this anywhere stated? It would be quite natural for Brahmanical writers to style Báhlíkas punningly Báhíkas.

[4] J. R. A. S., 1915, pp. 511-2.

rarely, perhaps never, conceive of a great country, the Punjab for instance, as a whole; they name a tract after the people who inhabit it or they give it a descriptive title'. And some of its tribes may in turn derive their names from those descriptive titles. 'It is only in a more advanced stage that they arrive at the conception of a country inhabited by various peoples, as a unity, and give it a common name, and when they do they invent for it and its inhabitants a common ancestor. This is the eponymous ancestor. A felt community of interests is only conceivable as a community of blood'. The Punjab furnishes an excellent illustration of this. Anu is the progenitor of all the Punjab tribes. Eighth in descent from him we have:—

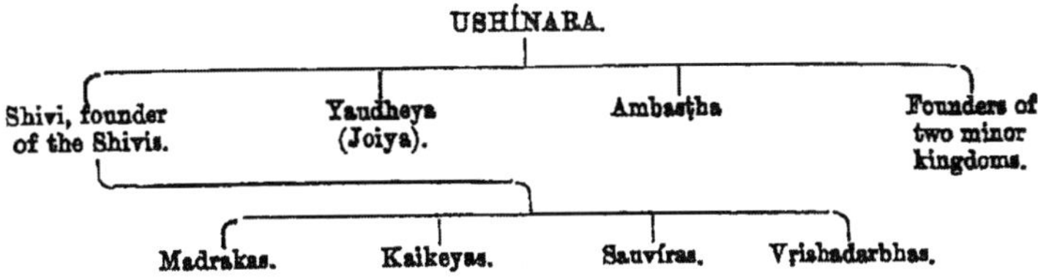

But the Shivis and Ushínaras are as old as the Anus. All that the pedigree indicates is a growing sense of national unity cemented by the fiction or revival of racial kinship.

Local legends in the Punjab itself rarely throw much light on its history or ethnology, but on the North-West Frontier legendary history though hopelessly inaccurate is sometimes interesting.

"The following" writes Mr. U. P. Barton, C. S., "is the legendary history of Kurram as related at the present day. The aboriginal inhabitants were *deos* or demons who lived under the domination of their king, known as the Sufed Deo, or white devil. This mythical kingdom was finally broken up by two equally mythical personages styled Shudáni and Budáni who are said to have been brothers. They came with a great army from the north and after fierce fighting overthrew the armies of the demons. The legend gives full details of the last great battle in which the *deos* finally succumbed, but it is hardly worth while to repeat them. I may mention that a Dúm resident in Zerán claims to be a descendant of the victorious brothers. Having completed the conquest of Kurram the invaders settled in the valley, where their descendants held sway for many centuries, until displaced by fresh immigrations from the north. There may be a grain of truth in the legend implying, as seems to be the case, the extinction of the aborigines by an invading horde of Aryas.

I have not been able to trace any other legend of local origin. It is true that the people delight in legendary lore, but the stories most recounted are almost invariably the common property of the Afghans generally. Doubtless the 'Dúms' are largely responsible for the wide range of these tales of the people. I give the following of those most frequently heard:—

Once upon a time there was a king of the fairies named Nimbulla. He had a friend named Timbulla. The two friends often made visits to far off countries together. On one occasion they were travelling through the Swát valley, when they met a girl named Begam Ján. She was very beautiful and Nimbulla fell in love with her. This Begám Ján was the daughter of a Khán of the Swát valley. Nimbulla took invisible possession of his inamorata to the great consternation of the Khán, her father, and his court. Every effort was made by the *mullas* or priests from far and near to exorcise the spirit but in vain. At length a famous *mulla*, Bahádur by name, appeared on the scene, and promised to expel the fairy's soul from the girl, on condition that the girl herself should be the reward of his efforts. The Khán promised his daughter to the priest who after great exercise of prayer succeeded in exorcising the spirit which together with that of Nimbullah he confined in an earthen pot. Both fairies were then burnt, despite the entreaties of the seven sisters of the captives. The *mulla* was then united with the rescued fair one. But he had incurred the enmity of the fairy tribe by his treatment of the two friends, and in an unwary moment was seized by the *deos* and ignominiously hanged. This is a very favourite legend and the Dúms frequently sing metrical versions of it at weddings and other occasions of rejoicing.

Yet another legend of Yúsufzai origin is often recited by the Kurram Dúms. It enshrines the lives of Músa Khán and Gúlmakai, their quarrels and final reconciliation. It is very well-known I believe on the Pesháwar side, and has probably been already recorded.

The legend of Fath Khán and Bíbi Rabia is of Kandahári origin. Here a male friend named Karami shares the affections of the husband, an irregularity which leads to the estrangement of Bíbi Rabia from her spouse. Meanwhile the Kandahári's attack general Shams-u-Dín, one of the Mughal emperor Akbar's leading soldiers, on his way to India *viâ* Ghuzni. The Kandahári's are defeated and Fath Khán mortally injured. On his death-bed he is reconciled with his wife who remains faithful to his memory after his death, refusing to remarry. This also is a very common legend among the Afgháns."

Colonel H. P. P. Leigh writes as follows:—'Close to Kirmán is a peculiar mushroom shaped stone, which is the subject of a curious legend:—

At this spot, Hamza, son of Mír Hamza, nephew of the Imám Ali, is said to have given battle to the armies of Langahúr and Soghar, Káfirs, in the time gone by. They were defeated and Hamza is said to have erected this stone to commemorate his victory. It is a time-worn block of granite, with a thin vein of quartz running through it, which is looked upon as the mark of Hamza's sword. It is stated that colossal bones are found occasionally in the vicinity, and cuaiously enough, not many yards from the spot is a line of three enormous graves, each six paces in length; the head and heel stones are blocks of granite, deeply sunk in the earth, and the intermediate spaces filled in with earth and smaller stones. They have an ancient look, and are confidently pointed out as the graves of Káfirs. Close by is another block of granite, with a perfect bowl hollowed in it, apparently by water action. This is said to be Hamza's *kachkol* or *faqír's* dish. On the edge of the cliff some way up the torrent, which dashes down from the Pára Chakmauni hills, are the ruins of a village, which is still known as Langahúr, and which are put down as having been a Káfir's habitation. Coins have been found there, of which however none are forthcoming, but from the description of the figure with Persian cap and flowing skirts, would be probably those of Kadphises, king of Kábul in about 100 A. D'

On the west frontier of Upper Bangash is the *kot* of Matah-i-Zakhmi, or Matah the wounded, so called from a legend that the Khalífa, Ali, killed an infidel, Matah, with his sword Zu'l-akar at this spot.[1]

Thus an investigation of the traditional aborigines of the Punjab yields results nearly as negative and barren as those given by a study of the historical data. From a very early period it was usual to define status in terms of race. The lower functional groups thus became defined by names denoting impure descent, or by names which connoted unnatural unions. Thus the lowest outcast who performed worse than menial functions was defined as the son of a Brahman woman by a Sudra, and called a Chandál.[2] Conversely any man who rose in the social scale became a Jáṭ or yeoman, a Rájput or Sáhu, *i.e.* 'gentle', and so on. If a Rájput family lost its status it became Jáṭ or Kanet, and so on. But it does not follow that it did not adopt a racial or tribal name. Thus, while we may be certain that Rajput was never a racial name and that it is absurd to speak of a 'Rájput race' we cannot be at all sure that there never was a Jáṭ race or tribe. All that we can say is that when the *Dabistán* was written more than two centuries ago its author was aware that the term Jáṭ meant a villager, a rustic *par excellence* as opposed to one engaged in trade or handicraft, and it was only when the Jaṭṭs of Lahore and the Jáṭs of the Jumna acquired power that the term became restricted and was but still only occasionally employed to mean simply one of that particular race.[3]

But however uncertain may be any of the current identifications of modern Punjab tribes with those mentioned in history we may accept without misgivings the theory first propounded by Hoernle and supported by the weighty authority of Sir George Grierson. According to this theory there were two series of invasions of India by the so-called Aryans, a name which was probably itself not racial in its origin. The first series of their invasions took place at a time when the regions stretching from the heart of Persia to the western marches of India were still fairly well watered and fertile. Some early 'Aryan' tribes—

[1] This seems a different place to the one mentioned in Colonel Leigh's note.

[2] Vol. II, p. 151.

[3] Capt. J. D. Cunningham, *Hist. of the Sikhs*, p. 5. n.

tribes, that is, of superior culture—parting from their Iranian kinsmen, slowly moved on foot and in waggons with their women, flocks and herds over those regions, perhaps by the Kábul valley, but also very possibly by other passes to its south, entered India on the north-western border and established themselves in the Punjab, where most of the *Rig-Veda* took shape. As they had brought their own women with them and generally avoided union with the aboriginal races, at any rate among their upper classes, they were able to keep their blood comparatively pure; and hence we find to this day in the Punjab a physical type predominating which in many respects resembles that of certain European races, and is radically different from the typical characteristics of the other Indian stocks, although the Punjab has been for thousands of years the gate of Hindustan, and wave after wave of invasion has swept through it to break on the plains beyond.

After these Aryas had passed on into the Punjab, the same thing happened on the north-western marches as has taken place in Turkestán. The rivers and streams slowly dried up, and the desert laid a dead hand upon the once fertile lands. The road was now closed for ever closed to slow migrations of families; it could be traversed only by swiftly moving troops. Henceforth the successive waves of foreign invasion, though for a time they might overwhelm Hindustan, could not leave any deep and lasting change in the racial characteristics of the Indian peoples; for the desert forbade the invaders to bring with them enough women to make a colony of their own race.[1]

To the type of this second series of migrations belong all the invasions which have poured over the Punjab in more recent times. The Afghán has made remarkably little impression upon its population east of the Indus. Scattered Paṭhán families, hardly forming septs, exist all over the Punjab in places where Pathán garrisons were located by the later Mughals or where Paṭhán soldiers of fortune obtained grants on feudal tenures from the Muhammadan emperors. Moreover the Paṭhán tribes, as we know them, are by no means ancient and their earliest settlements in the Pesháwar valley and other tracts now pre-eminently Paṭhán do not go back much farther than the 14th century. The Mughals have left remarkably slight traces on the population compared with the mass and power of their invasions, and no one who reads the histories of their inroads can fail to be struck with their ephemeral devastating character. Few Mughal villages exist, because they never founded colonies. Traces of their domination are perhaps strongest in Hazára, but in the Punjab itself they have never amalgamated with the rest of the Muhammadan population though the Chughattai *gót's*, or sections, found in certain artizan castes may owe their origin to guilds of Mughal artificers incorporated in those castes. To go a little further back the Gakkhars are probably a tribe of Turki origin whose founders were given fiefs in the Ráwalpindi hills by Tímúr's earlier descendants. They are certainly distinct from the Khokhars who if not demonstrably indigenous were probably allies of the earlier Muhammadan invaders, like the Awáns. Working backwards in this way it is not difficult to form some idea of the way in which the modern Punjab population has been formed. The Paṭhán or Iranian

[1] Taken almost *verbatim*; from Dr. Lionel Barrett's *Antiquities of India*, p. 8.

element is slight, the Mughal or Turki still slighter, while the Arab element is practically negligible. Behind the Arab and the later Muhammadan invasions which began under Mahmúd of Ghazni we have dim traditions of Persian overlordship, but we cannot assign an Iranian origin to any one tribe with certainty. A gap of centuries separates the Getæ and Yuechi from the earliest allusion to the Jáṭs by the Muhammadan historians of India

We may think with Lassen that the Jáṭs are the Jártikas of the *Mahábhárata* and it is doubtless quite possible that the term Jártika meant originally yeoman or land-holder as opposed to a trader or artizan, or was the name of a tribe which had reached the agricultural stage, and that it was then adopted by a mass of tribes which owned land or tilled it and had come to look down upon the more backward pastoral tribes. The modern Khatri is undoubtedly the ancient Kshatrya, though he had taken, like the Lombard, to trade so thoroughly that Cunningham speaks of him as the Katri or grain-seller as if his name were derived from *katra* or market ![1]

Appendix to Part III—A note on the people of Chilás by Col. Ommaney.

The inhabitants of Chilás are known generally as Bhúltai, so called from Bhúlta, a son of Karrár, an Arab, who came from Kashíral (Kashmír) where an ancestor of his first settled. The descendants of Karrar are called by the inhabitants themselves Shín: the Paṭháns called them Ráná. Four classes now reside in Chilás:

Shín = rána

Yashkun ?

Kamín.

Dúm.

The Shín do not give their female relations in marriage to the inferior classes, though they can take women from them · the same principle is observed by the inferior classes towards one another.

The Shín are divided into 4 classes,[2] as it were, who divided the country into 4 equal shares and apparently each class gave a portion to the Yashkún class who perhaps helped the Shín class to conquer the country. The Yashkúns appear to have more rights in land than the other two classes who only hold small plots by purchase on condition of service, but a Yashkún cannot sell or mortgage his land without the

[1] A. S. R. II, p. 8.

[2] Kotannai.
Bíchwai.
Baitaramai.
Shaitingai.

consent of the Shin proprietary body nor even leave it without permission.

The residents of Chilás are also called Dards, but can give no reason for it. The Chilási tribe in Darrial (or-el) north of the Indus shave the head leaving a lock of hair on top but they do not shave the upper lip.

PART IV.—RELIGIONS.

SECTION 1.—THE RELIGION OF THE BON IN TIBET.

It is difficult to say what the primitive religion of the Punjab or North-West corner of India must have been, but easy to conjecture its general outlines. It was doubtless a form of Nature-worship, combined with magic, whose object was to attain power over the material universe generally and in particular to get children, ensure good harvests, and destroy enemies or at least secure immunity from their onslaughts. A type of this primitive religion may have long survived the Vedic period in the Bon-chos or religion of the Bon-pos. The Bon-chos was also called Lha-chos, or 'spirit cult', and in the gLing-chos of Ladákh we have probably the earliest type of it.[1]

Unfortunately it is almost impossible to say what was the principle of this Bon[2] cult as its literature is relatively modern and an imitation of that of the Buddhists and the only ancient authorities on it which we possess are open to grave suspicion as being Buddhist works treating of the struggles which that religion had to sustain against that of the Bon. But it is generally agreed that it must have been a kind of rude *shaman*-ism, that is to say an animistic and at the same time fetishistic adoration of natural forces and of good and evil spirits, generally ill-disposed or rather perhaps benevolent or the reverse according as they were satisfied or discontented with the cult vouchsafed to them by means of prayers and incantations, sacrifices of victims and sacred dances—a form of religion close enough to the popular Táoism of the Chinese which indeed the Bon-pos themselves claim to have founded.

According to the Bon-pos' tradition their religion has gone through three phases called the Jola-Bon, Kyar-Bon and Gyúr-Bon, the last synchronising with the king Thisrong Detsan and his grandson Langdarma and having for its principal characteristic a number of ideas and practices adopted from Buddhism as well some elements borrowed from Indian philosophy, and the Tántric doctrine of the Sakti.

The gods of the Bon religion were those of the red meadow (the earth), of the sun, of heaven, King Kesar and his mother Gog-bzang lha-mo.[3] But at least as primitive were the *pho-lha* and *mo-lha* or deities of 'the male and female principle.[4] Sun-worship must have been important as the cult was also called gYung-drung-bon' or the *swástika-bon*.[5]

But the Bon-pos also recognise the existence of a supreme being Kúntú-bzang-po corresponding to Brahma, the universal soul of the Brahmans, and to the Adi-Buddha of the Buddists, the creator according to some, but only the spectator according to others, of a

[1] A. H. Francke, *Antiquities of Indian Tibet*, Calcutta, 1914, p. 21.

[2] Pronounced Pon according to Sarat Chandra Das (*Journal* of the Buddhist Texts Society of India, 1893, Appendix, cited by Milloué, *Bod-Youl ou Tibet*, Annales du Musée Guimet, Paris, 1906, p. 155), or Peun with the French *eu*.

[3] Francke, *op. cit.* pp. 2 and 65.

[4] *Ib.*, p. 21

[5] *Ib.*, p. 93. For some further details see Francke, *A History of Western Tibet*, pp. 52-7.

spontaneous creation issuing from the eternal void. When the functions of a creator are attributed to him he is assigned a spouse or *yúm*, literally 'mother,' representing his active energy with which he engenders gods, men and all beings. Beneath him come Kyúng, the chief spirit of chaos, under the form of a blue eagle, 18 great gods and goddesses, 70,000 secondary gods, innumerable genii and a score of principal saints all eager to fight for mankind against the demons.[1]

But the most important personage of the Bon pantheon, more worshipped perhaps than Kúntú-bangpo, himself, is the prophet Senrab-Mibo, held to be an incarnation of the Buddha and believed to have been himself reincarnated in China in the philosopher Lao-Tseu, the patron of Táoism. To him is attributed the mystic prayer, *Om! ma-trihmou-ye'-sa lah-dú* which in the Bon takes the place of the Buddhist invocation *Om! mani padme-húm* and whose eight syllables represent Kúntú-bzangpo, his Sakti, the gods, genii, men, animals, demons and hell, as well as the sacred dance called that of the white demon, the different kinds of rosaries corresponding to the different degrees of meditation, the offerings of alcoholic liquors made to propitiate the spirits and in brief almost all the necromantic rites relating to funerals, to exorcism and to the means of averting the effects of evil omens. During his long religious career he was served by Vúgúpa, a demon with nine heads, whom he had overcome by his exorcisms and converted by his eloquence. The practices inculcated by him form almost all that we know about the actual worship of the Bon-pos who, according to the Lámas, have also borrowed a part of the mystic and magic ritual from Lámaistic Buddhism. The Bon in its animism and demonolatry is very like the cults of the Mongolian and Siberian *shámans* in which dances (or sacred dramas acted by mimes), offerings, the drinking of intoxicating liquors, and animal sacrifices, especially those of sheep, play a considerable part. They also immolate birds to the spirits of the dead and fowls to demons.

As in all animistic religions the Bon priest is above all a sorcerer. His principal functions are to propitiate by his prayers and sacrifices the genii who are ready to be benevolent, to put to flight or destroy by exorcism those whose malevolence causes devastating storms, floods, drought, epidemic disease, accidents and even the countless little privations of daily life. As an astrologer he reads the sky and draws up horoscopes of birth, marriage and death—for one must ascertain the posthumous fate of those one loved—and teaches means of averting evil omens. As a diviner he discloses the secrets of the future, discovers hidden treasures, traces thieves by inspection of the shoulder-blades of sheep, by cards, dice, the flight of birds or opening a sacred book at random. As a doctor he treats men and animals with simples but more often with charms and incantations, an obvious proceeding, since all sickness is the work of demons. In a word, as depository of all knowledge sacred and profane he teaches children a little reading, writing and arithmetic, but above all the precepts of religion.

[1] Milloué, *op. cit.*, p. 155.

The Bon priesthood is trained by ascetic exercises, the study of the sacred books, magic and sorcery and to submit itself to certain rules of monastic discipline, celibacy included, though that does not seem to be an absolute obligation. Their morals are said to be lax, and their conduct anything but exemplary. They live in monasteries, often very large and wealthy, called *bon-ling*, under the direction of an elected superior But it is also said that some of these superiors of certain large monasteries are perpetual incarnations of Senrab-Mibo or other gods. There are also nunneries of women who are called Bon-mos.

Bon ethics, eschatology and metaphysics are closely allied to those of Buddhism, but less regard is paid to the principle of *ahinsa* or the preservation of all life. The Lámas indeed accuse the Bon-pos of plagiarising from their books and they have certainly borrowed from Buddhism the story that a synod or council was held in the land of Mangkar, at which sages and religious teachers attended from India, Persia and China to collaborate with the Tibetan Bon-pos in the editing or compilation of the 84,000 *gomos* or treatises which form their canon.

The Bon-pos or some of them at least accept the Indian dogma of the metempsychosis, but appear to restrict it to those who blinded by ignorance (*avidyá*) have failed to grasp the eternal verity of the Bon-Kú (emptiness, unreality, vanity, mutability of mundane things composed of different elements and therefore perishable), and remain subject to the law of *karma* or consequences of one's own deeds, whereas the wise freed from earthly bonds and enlightened by the splendour of the *bon-kú* (which has some analogies with the *bodhi* or knowledge) go to be absorbed into the pure essence of the *san* or spiritual immutability, composed of pure light and absolute knowledge which constitutes the subtle body of Kúntú Bzang-po. Two parallel and inseparable ways lead to this state of abstraction or of the absolute, which is the supreme aim of the Bon-pos—*viz. darshana* (active, will and perhaps action) and *gom*[1] or meditation. This latter, probably an imitation of the Buddhist *dhyána*, has three stages, the *thún-gom*, *nang-gom* and *lang-gom*,[2] not four as in Buddhism, and is the one really efficacious, though it should be accompanied or preceded by *darshana* apparently. In the *thún-gom*, which is practised by a devotee initiated by a spiritual guide, *i.e.* a *láma*, by counting the beads of a rosary and chanting the merits of *bon-kú*, the mind should not be absorbed in the particular object of meditation. But in the second degree absorption and meditation are equal, the mind is filled with light and then, entering into profound meditation (*yoga*), it is completely abstracted and finally is void even of meditation itself. The moment of *lang-gom* commences when all kinds of *vidya* (consciousness) have been acquired and the real object has been seen, when meditation has ended and the mind has ceased to think of acquiring the essence of *sunyata*. At this moment all sins, evil thoughts, &c., are changed into perfect wisdom (*jñána*), all matter visible and invisible enters into the pure region of *súnyatá* or *bon-kú* and then transmigratory existences and those emancipated, good and evil, attachment and separation, etc., all become one

[1] Apparently *gyána*.

[2] Or *long-gom*.

and the same. To attain to the perfect meditation of the *lang gom* the Bon-po has nine roads, vehicles (*yána*) or methods called *bon-drang* open to him of which the first four, the *p'va-sen*, *nang-sen*, *thúl-sen* and *srid-sen* are called the 'causative vehicles'; the next four, the *gen-yen*, *ákar*, *túh-srúng* and *ye'-sen* 'the resulting vehicles'; and the ninth contains the essence of the other eight. The *p'va-sen* comprises 360 questions and 84,000 proofs or tests. The *nang-sen* contains four *gyer-gom* and 42 *tah-rag* or divisions of meditative science. The *thúl-sen* teaches miracle-working. The *srid-sen* deals with the 360 forms of death and with funeral rites, of the four kinds of disposing of the dead and of 81 methods of destroying evil spirits. The *gen yen* sets forth aphorisms relating to bodies, animal life, their development and maturity. The *ákar* gives numerous mystical demonstrations. In the *ye'-sen* are described mental demonstrations, and in the *khyad-par*, the ninth, the five classes of *upadesa* or instruction. The *tang-srúng* describes the different kinds of *búm* or monuments destined to the preservation of relics. The *khyad par* alone can achieve that which the other eight methods can only effect collectively. Moreover the four *gyer-bon* secure the enjoyment of four *bhúmis* (degrees of perfection) of honourable action during several ages. The *gen-yen* and *tong-srúng*, after having protected the *sattvam* (animal nature) for three *kalpas* lead it on to emancipation. The *ákar* and the *ye'-sen* can procure for the *sattvam* freedom of the existence after its first birth and the *khyad-par* can ensure it even in this life Bon temples (*bon-k'ang*) exist besides the monasteries and though the Bon has long been in conflict with *láma*-ism it has survived in strength in eastern Tibet and tends more and more to become fused with the doctrines of the adepts of the Nyigma-pa sect or red *lámas*.[1]

M. deMilloué, whose account of the Bon faith is based on that of Sarat Chandra Das,[2] speaks of it as '*assez obscur*', but it is strange that no one has hitherto compared or contrasted its teachings with those of Jainism. A. H. Francke's notices of the Bon-chos, fragmentary as they are, show that he was dealing with its earlier phases as the following notes show:—

Human sacrifice was probably a leading feature of this primitive creed. Oaths at important treaties were made binding by human as well as animal sacrifices, new houses were consecrated by immuring human beings in their walls, and a person was killed when one was first inhabited.[3] Dr. Francke mentions a *láma* in the Sutlej valley who had recently beheaded his father while asleep in order to render his new house habitable.[4] The old were apparently put to death, a custom toned down in modern times to a rule which

[1] "There is an error prevalent regarding the dress of Lámas, *viz.* that the dress of Lámas of the 'red' persuasion is red, and that of the 'yellow' persuasion yellow. The dress of both is red, with the exception of the one special order of the Geldanpa who, to my knowledge, only exist in Zangskar, whose dress is also yellow. But Lámas of the 'red' persuasion also wear red caps and red scarves round their waist, whilst in the case of the 'yellow' Lámas *these* and these *only* are 'yellow':" K. Marx, quoted in *Hist. of Western Tibet*, pp. 23-4.

[2] In J. A. S. B., 1881, p. 203 *f*.

[3] Francke, *op. cit.*, p. 21.

[4] *Ib.*, p. 22.

relegates a father to a small house when his son marries and a grandfather to a still smaller one.

The ibex was worshipped for fertility and figures of it often carved on rocks. Now a-days 'flour ibex' are offered by neighbours to the parents of a new-born child[1] Kesar'aBruguma and other pre-Buddhistic divinities are still invoked to grant children,[2] but it does not follow that this was their real or principal function in the Bon-chos. The *swástika* was already a symbol of the sun and the *yoni* of the female principle.[3] The dead were buried, burnt, exposed to the air or cast into the waters as might seem appropriate. Thus people who had died of dropsy were cast into a stream.[4] Even so in recent times the people of Kanaur[5] used to practise immersion of the dead in water (*dúbant*), eating (*bhakhant*) and cremation as well as burial. Corpses were also cut into pieces and packed into clay pots.[6]

Spirits also played a great rôle for good or ill. That of the Miru monastery was carried off even in Buddhist times to Hemis in a bundle of twigs.[7] When the country suffered from violent gales the spirits of the wind were caught in a pot, and stored up in a *stúpa* which had already been built over the home of an evil spirit.[8]

1 *Ib.*, pp. 96 and 105.

2 *Ib.*, p. 105.

3 *Ib.*, pp. 105 and 107.

4 *Ib.*, p. 23.

5 Pandit Tika Ram Joshi, *Ethnography of the Bashahr State*, J. A. S. Bengal, 1911, p. 536.

6 Francke, *op. cit.*, pp. 65, 72 and 74.

7 *Ib.*, p. 65.

8 *Ib.*, p. 81.

SECTION 2—BUDDHISM.

The study of Buddhism is of more practical importance for the Punjab than its present restriction to a few semi-Tibetan cantons of the Himalayas would indicate. The ideas underlying Sikhism find some prototypes in Buddhism and Macauliff did not hesitate to speak of the 'Gautamist predecessors' of the Sikh *gurus* although no proof exists that Sikh teaching was directly derived from Buddhistic teachings or traditions. Buddhism, however, did not disappear from Northern India until the Muhammadan invasions and it is difficult to think that its traditions are rapidly forgotten. The interval between its final disappearance about the 10th or 11th century and the birth of Nának in 1469 was not great, as time goes when religious traditions are in question. In the Himalayas Nága-worship maintained its footing and obscure though its connection with latter-day Buddhism may be the Nág cults certainly preserve a phase of Buddhism.

Writing in 1882 Ibbetson expressed a very unfavourable opinion of Tibetan Buddhism as the following paragraphs show :—

Ibbetson, § 249. **Rise of Buddhism.** It is not my intention to attempt any description of tenets of the Buddhist faith. They can be studied in the books mentioned in the first paragraph of this chapter. Gautama Buddha was brought up in the strictest sect of the Hindus, he scrupulously followed their hardest precepts, he endured long-continued mortification and penance without finding peace of mind; and in the end his soul revolted against the sore burdens with which the Brahmans would oppress him and the artificial paths by which they would lead him. He proclaimed that their gods were false; that the Almighty was everywhere and everything; that each man must endure the consequences of his own acts, of which prayer and sacrifice were unavailing to relieve him; that all evil sprang from the lusts and longings of the flesh and of the fleshly mind; that peace consisted in final release from the bonds of incarnation and in absorption into the absolute, and that it was to be obtained only by the extinction of desire. "Buddhism is no religion at all, and certainly no theology; but rather a system of duty, morality, benevolence, without real deity, prayer, or priest." But unlike Hinduism, it gave its followers a man to revere and imitate whose personal character was holy and beautiful; and for the first time in the religious experience of India it called upon its hearers to change their lives with their faith, and introduced them to the new ideas of proselytism and conversion. The new doctrine was the *ne plus ultra* of quietism; and though now infinitely corrupted and defiled, at any rate in the northern school, by the admixture of other and less pure cults, it still retains many of its original characteristics. Above all things it recognises no hereditary priesthood, and, teaching that all men are equal, admits no distinctions of caste, at least in the countries in which it is now professed; though how far this could now have been said of it had it remained the religion of India, is perhaps a doubtful question[1]. The story of how it gradually spread over Northern India, apparently obscuring for a time the Brahminism against which it was a protest, how it attained perhaps its highest pitch under Asoka, how it gradually spread into Tibet, China, Burma, and Ceylon, how it was followed in its victorious advance beyond the confines of Indian peninsula by the resurgent Brahminism, which finally succeeded in expelling it from the country of its birth, or perhaps more really in so absorbing it that it can no longer be traced save in its effect on some of the esoteric doctrines of the Hindu faith, and how it now flourishes as a separate religion only in the foreign realms which it has conquered, is matter of history in its broad outlines and of the uncertainty of ignorance as to its minor details. Buddha preached about 600 540 B C.[2], Asoka lived about three centuries after him, and Buddhism first became the state religion[3] of China in the 4th century of our era, while it disappeared from India some 4 to 5 centuries later. The first Buddhist king of Tibet is said to have reigned in the beginning of the 7th century, but Ladákh, the part of Tibet which borders on the Punjab, would seem to have been converted by missionaries sent by Asoka

Buddhism as it is in the Punjab.—The Buddhist doctrines were early divided into two great schools, the northern which prevails in Tibet, China, and Japan, and the southern to which belong Ceylon, Burma and Siam.[4] The latter retains the teachings of its founder almost unchanged; but the former soon substituted the final beatitude of the Hindus for the ultimate absorption of Buddha, and developed an elaborate and extravagant system of incarnate saints and demi-gods of different degrees which has obscured and almost superseded the original Gautamic legend. The Buddhism of Spiti and of the higher parts of Pángi in Chamba, the only portions of the Punjab whose inhabitants return themselves as Buddhists, is the Lámaism of Tibet, perhaps the most utterly corrupt form of the religion of Gautama. We shall see how largely, so soon as we enter the Himalayas, the Hinduism of the plains becomes impregnated with the demonology of the mountain tribes. A similar fate befell Buddhism in the mountain ranges of Central Asia. To the mysticism, with which the northern school had already clothed the original simple creed, have

Ibbetson, § 250.

1 The attitude assumed towards caste by Gautama is elaborately discussed by Dr. Wilson at pp. 278 *et seq.* of the first volume of his work on Indian Caste. His teaching would seem to be not very widely removed from that of Bába Nának, to be described presently. He recognised existing social distinctions, but held that they were the results of good or evil deeds in a previous life, and, unlike the Brahmans, taught that *all* castes should be admitted equally to the privileges of religion and were equally capable of obtaining salvation. Dr Wilson thus sums the early Buddhist practice on the subject: "Though it is evident, both from the testimony of the Buddhists themselves and of their enemies the Brahmans, that they opposed caste as far as they were able according to the exigencies of the times in which they lived, they actually, as a matter of policy, often winked at its existence in Indian society. While it was not carried by them into foreign countries, it was tolerated, though disparaged by them wherever they found that they had been preceded by Aryan rule." (See also Barth's *Religions of India*, p. 125*f*)

2 Rhys Davids and Barth put this date nearly a century later.

3 Recent research shows that it survived till a much later period.

4 These two schools are commonly known as the great and the little Vehicle, perhaps because the exoteric and esoteric doctrines to which these names seem originally to have been applied have respectively become predominant in the one and the other.

been added the magic and devil-worship of the *Tántras* and the impure cult of the female principle or Sakti, till the existing system is a superstition rather than a religion.

In the northern school Buddha is still reverenced, but only as one of many, and not so much as some; while the objects of worship recognised by the most esoteric doctrine include gods and demi-gods, though they stand lower in order of honour than the beatified saints. But Lamaic Buddhism has gone further than this:—"As in India the Brahmans have declared all the ancient village Thákurs and Devis to be only so many different forms of Mahádeo and Párbati, so in Tibet the *lámas* have craftily grafted into their system all the ancient gods and spirits of the former inhabitants. Hence, though Buddhism is the prevailing religion of the country, yet the poor people still make their offerings to their old divinities, the gods of the hills, the woods, and the dales. The following are some of the classes of deities which are worshipped under distinct Tibetan names:—Mountain Gods, River Gods, Tree Gods, Family Gods, Field Gods, and House Gods. The mystical system of the Tántrists has been engrafted on the Buddhism of Nepal and Tibet, and the pictures of the prevailing sects are filled with representations of the three-eyed destroying Iswara and of his blood-drinking spouse,[1] while the esoteric docrines include the filthy system of Budha Saktis, or female energies of the Pancha Dhyáni Buddhas, in which the *yoni* or female symbol plays a prominent part."—(General Cunningham).

The wrath of Káli is daily deprecated in the religious service of the temples,[2] trumpets made of human thigh-bones are used, and offerings are made to the Buddhas in which even meat is included, though one of the precepts most rigidly insisted on by Gautama was a regard for animal life. The priests "foretell events, determine lucky and unlucky times, and pretend to regulate the future destiny of the dying, threatening the niggard with hell, and promising heaven, or even eventually the glory of a Buddha, to the liberal. Their great hold upon the people is thus derived from their gross ignorance, their superstitions, and their fears; they are fully imbued with a belief in the efficacy of enchantments, in the existence of malevolent spirits, and in the superhuman sanctity of the Lámas as their only protection against them. The Lámas are therefore constantly exorcists and magicians, sharing no doubt very often the credulity of the people, but frequently assisting faith in their superhuman faculties by jugglery and fraud."—(Wilson's *Religions of the Hindus.*)

Ibbetson, § 251.

Prayer has been reduced to a mechanical operation, and the praying-wheel is a triumph of the Tibetan genius.[3] It consists

[1] The image of Iswara has a snake round his waist, carries a thunderbolt or a sword in his right hand, and is trampling human beings beneath his feet. He is represented as frantic with anger, his eyes staring, his nostrils dilated, his mouth wide open, and his whole body surrounded by flames. His spouse is of a blood-red colour, and wears a necklace of skulls; in her right hand is a sceptre surmounted by skulls and the holy thunderbolt, while with her left she carries a cup of blood to her mouth. A circle of flames surrounds her body. D. I.

[2] This service is described at length in Chapter XIII of Cunningham's *Ladák*; it bears no little resemblance to the ceremonies of the Roman Catholic Church.

[3] The praying wheel is peculiar to Tibet, where it was generally used at least as early as 400 A. D.

of a cylinder turning on an axis and containing sacred texts and prayers, or sometimes gibberish whose only merit is that it has a sort of rhythm. It is made of all sizes, from the pocket wheel to be turned in the hand as one walks along, to the common wheel of the village which is turned by water and prays for the community in general. Each revolution is equivalent to a recital of the prayer contained in the cylinder. Flags inscribed with prayers are fixed at the corners of the houses, and answer a similar purpose as they flap in the wind. Every village has its *mani* or stone dyke, sometimes nearly half a mile long, on which are flung small pieces of slate inscribed with mystic formulæ—"These slabs are votive offerings from all classes of people for the attainment of some particular object. Does a childless man wish for a son, or a merchant about to travel hope for a safe return; does a husbandman look for a good harvest, or a shepherd for the safety of his flocks during the severity of the winter; each goes to a Láma and purchases a slate, which he deposits carefully on the village *mani* and returns home in full confidence that his prayer will be heard."

These *manis* must always be left on the right hand, and people will make considerable detours in order to do so. Small shrines are erected in the fields to propitiate the deities and obtain an abundant harvest. The dead are sometimes burnt and the ashes preserved, in the case of great men, in a cenotaph; but corpses are often "exposed on the hills to be eaten by wild beasts, or cut into small pieces and thrown to dogs and birds according to the custom of Great Tibet, where these beneficient methods are philosophically preferred as most likely to be pleasing to the Heavenly Powers." In some of the monasteries the abbotts are, like the Hindu Sanyásis, buried in a sitting posture and in full canonicals within the building. The people eat the flesh of dead animals, but will not kill for food.

Caste distinctions are said not to obtain in Spiti; but the people are divided into three classes who do not intermarry, the landowners, the artisan menials, and the minstrel beggars; and the remarks of Mr. A. Anderson quoted below seem to show a state of things which can scarcely be distinguished from caste in a very lax condition. Caste restrictions grow weaker and weaker as we go farther into the hills, as I shall show in my chapter on Caste; and I suspect that there is at least as much difference in this respect between Kángra and Láhul as there is between Láhul and Spiti. Mr. A. Anderson wrote thus:—"In Spiti there are three classes: Cháhzang, Lohár or Zoho, and Hensi or Betha, but caste is unknown. A Cháhzang will eat from a Lohár's hand. It is considered no social crime to eat with the lower classes, but marriage is not permitted. A Cháhzang will marry a Cháhzang, but having regard to relationship; that is, they will not intermarry within the same clan (*rus* or *haddi*). This is the rule also with Lohárs and Hensis. Should a Cháhzang take a Lohár woman into his house he will be considered as having done wrong, but other Cháhzangs will still eat from his hand. The offspring of such a marriage is called Argun, and an Argun will marry with a Lohár. It is said that it is not common for a Cháhzang to eat with a Hensi, but should the latter touch the food it is not thereby defiled.[1] It is common among Bots (or Tibetans) generally to consider all the body below the waist as polluted, and if the skirt or foot of a Bot should touch the food or water, it is defiled and thrown away. It is enough if the skirts pass over the food. I was told that when the Spiti people saw the Láhul enumerators stepping across the water which ran to the Spiti encamping ground, they refused to take the water and went higher up the stream for it. This idea is found among Hindus also, but it is not so strictly acted on."

As we have already seen Buddhism found established in Tibet a strongly organised religion in the Bon-chos, which as we now know it has been systematised and purified by contact with Buddhism itself. It must have been a crude animism in its primitive form The Tibetans assign a very ancient date to the importation of Buddhism into Tibet, but the Chinese annals place it under the reign of the emperor Taï-Tsúng, 627-650 A. D., though possibly a Buddhist monastery had been erected on the sacred Kailâsa mountain in 137 B. C. If any such monastery was founded however it must have been shortlived. Lamaistic tradition indeed declares that about the middle of the 5th century B. C., when Tibet was plunged in profound barbarism, an Indian prince named Nyahthi-Tsanpo,[2] a descendant of Sákyamúni himself according to some but according to others an exiled son of Prasenajit king of Kosala, made himself recognised as king of Tibet, introduced Buddhism and civilisation and founded the royal Tibetan family. But his efforts failed and as soon as he was dead Buddhism disappeared completely. Nevertheless the Tibetans date the Ngadar or period of primitive Buddhism from his reign.

Under his 37th descendant or successor Lha Thothori Nyantsan[3] in 331 A. D. four objects of unknown use fell on the roof of the royal palace and the king was warned to preserve them piously as pledges of the future prosperity of Tibet whose meaning would be revealed in due course to one of his successors. This and the tradition of a monastery in Kailasa doubtless mean that Buddhism gained a footing in Tibet long before it became the state religion.

However this may be, in the reign of Srongtsan-Gampo—617 to 698—the first authentic ruler of Tibet, Buddhism met with a royal patron The king had married two princesses, one Chinese, the other a daughter of Ansúvarman of Nepal The latter at any rate was a devout Buddhist and the king was induced to send his chief minister Thúmi or Thonmi Sambhota to search for Buddhist books and preachers in India. He returned in 650 A. D. with a certain number of books and an alphabet adapted to the translation of Sanskrit texts into Tibetan. About 644 the king had built at Lhasa the famous temple of Rasa called later Lhasei-tso-khang or Jovo-khang to receive the sacred images of Akchobhya and Sákyamúni brought from Nepal and China by his queens who

[1] So Sir J. B. Lyall wrote: "All other classes avoid eating food cooked by the Bethas who are with reason treated as a very low and disreputable set of people. So again, they would not admit them to the equality conferred by the common use of the same pipe, or by dipping the hand in the same dish."

[2] Ngah-K'ri-bTsan-po. The name may preserve the suffix-sthamba.

[3] Lha-Tho-thori *g*Nyan-*b*tsan.

are also said to have built the monasteries of Labrang and Ramoche. But the earliest monastery in Tibet would appear to have been that of Samyé built a full century later.

It is clear that if Buddhism was not officially introduced or recognised in Tibet until the middle of the 7th century A. D. the form then adopted as the state religion can hardly have been the pure uncontaminated creed preached by Buddha and his immediate successors. This supposition is borne out by what followed. Srongtsan Gampo was a warlike ruler, yet he was deified as an incarnation of the Dhiáni Bodhisattva Chanresi[1] or Avalokitesvara, a personification of charity and the love of one's neighbour and the patron deity of Tibet, while his queens also received divine honours as incarnations of the goddess Dolma or Tára, the Nepalese lady under the name of the Green Tára[2] and the Chinese as the White Tára.[3] Proof of their divine nature was discerned in their barrenness.

Under Srongtsan Gampo's four successors Buddhism, at grips with the Bon-pos, made no progress and may have been completely driven out of Tibet, and it was not until the reign of Thisrong Detsan —728-786— that it became definitely the state religion, in spite of the opposition of the prime minister and the queen, herself a devout Bon-po. Thisrong Detsan in 744 sent a monk into India to retain Sánta Rakshita, superior of the *vihára* at Nálanda near Buddha-Gaya, whose services were secured in 747. Raised to the dignity of high priest of Tibet Sánta Rak-shita had no easy task. The gods, genii and demons of the country raised up storms, inundations and sicknesses of all kinds against him and he was compelled to ask for the assistance of his brother-in-law the Achárya Padma Sambhava, who was accordingly brought from India by the king's orders. Padma Sambhava was a native of Udyána,[4] a *protégé* of Indrabodhi, the blind king of that realm, and skilled in magic. All along the road into Tibet he engaged in combats and overcame by the power of his magic charms the numerous demons who had sought to stay him and as soon as he arrived at the king's palace he hastened to convene on the hill Magro the full array of the gods, genii and local demons whom he compelled to take oath that they would henceforth defend Buddhism, promising them in return a share in the cult and in the offerings of the faithful.

By this judicious compromise Buddhism became the dominant creed of Tibet, but its subjects retained their own religion as a submissive faith—a phenomenon often noticed under such circumstances. Padma Sambhava thus secured against opposition initiated a few chosen disciples into the mystic doctrine and magic practices of the *Tántrás* of the Yogáchára school, while Sánta Rak-shita taught the discipline and philosophy of the Mádhyamika school. In 749 Padma Sambhava founded the Samyé monastery some 30 miles from Lhasa on the model of

[1] Spyan-ras-gzigs. 'The Lord that looks down from on high': fr. *avalokita* (looking on) and *isvara* (lord)

[2] Doljang (Sgrol-ljang).

Dolkar (Sgrol-dkar).

[4] Milloué says Dardistán, but it also included Swát.

the one at Udantapura with 20 Indian monks and 7 Tibetan initiates. Padma Sambhava did not stay long in Tibet. He is said to have returned miraculously to India and to have left concealed in rocks many treatises on esoteric and magic learning to be discovered by sinless saints when human intelligence should have developed sufficiently to understand them—a belief fruitful in sectarianism. Nevertheless the Bonchos was not extinct, for the progress in Tibet of the mystic Mahá-yána also met with great obstacles in the existence of other Buddhist sects professing various doctrines. To combat a Chinese monk named Mahâyána, who preached a doctrine of quietism and inaction, Thisrong Detsan called in a disciple of Santa Rak-shita named Kamala Síla from Magadha who defeated the schismatic in debate. Under that king's son and especially under his grandson Ralpachan, who brought the Achárya Jína Mitra and many other *pandits* from India, Buddhism made progress and by 899 in which year Ralpachan was assassinated by his brother Langdarma the translation of the 108 tomes of the *Kan-júr* and of most of the 250 of the *Tan-júr* had been completed. Langdarma, however, placed an interdict on Buddhism and tried to eradicate its doctrines from his kingdom until he was assassinated by the *láma* Paldorje in 902.

Thus ended the era of the Nga-dar or primitive Buddhism and began that which Tibetans call the Ch'yi-dar or 'later Buddhism,' styled by Europeans Lámaism.

Lamaism.

By Lámaism, says de Milloué, must not be understood merely the religion of Tibet. In reality, like Hinduism, it embraces both its social and religious systems crowned by the absolute theocracy which has governed it for upwards of three centuries. While Lamaism professes to follow the doctrine of the Maháyána or idealistic school of northern Buddhism it has exaggerated it to such an extent and introduced into it so many modifications in its fundamentals, so many local beliefs and practices that it has hardly more of Buddhism than the name. Hence, like Hinduism, it can only be studied in its sects and orders. These will be described in their historical order.

The Kádampa order owes its origin to Atisa who was born in Bengal in 980 A. D. Educated as a Brahman he was converted to Buddhism and initiated into the Maháyána doctrine at Krisnnagiri. At the age of 19 he took the vows at Udantapuri under the famous Síla Rak-shita with the religious name of Dípankara-Sri-Jnána and was ordained at 31. Nominated superior of the Vikrama-Síla monastery by the king of Magadha and recognised as hierarch by the Maháyánists of that kingdom, he was invited by Lha-lama in 1038 to undertake reforms in Tibet, but only yielded to the instances of Lha-tsún-pa when he had reached the age of 60. Arriving in Tibet in 1040 he was given as residence the monastery of Tho-ling and devoted his energies to purifying Tibetan Buddhism of the gross and immoral practices imported into it by the Bon-po shamanism allied with mysticism of Tántric teaching. Before he died in 1058 at Ngethang he had gathered round him a number of disciples who formed a sect called Kadampa[1] under Marpa and Domton or Bromton[2] in the monastery at Raseng or Radeng. This sect or order has counted 3000 eminent *lámas* in its ranks since its foundation and some writers regard it as a restoration of the ancient teaching of Thúmi Sambhota. It affected especially the *Vinóya* with its views of chastity, imposed respect for and worship of the Buddhas and of Sákyamúni in particular, charity and love for all creatures, and practised fervent meditation. It professed the exoteric doctrine of the Void (*sunyáta*) and without entirely rejecting mysticism and the *Tántra* adheres strictly to the teachings of the *Kan júr* in regard to them. This sect has lost much of its importance since the reforms of Tsong-khapa and has to a great extent merged in the Geluk-pa order or sect.

The Nyigmapa order, incorrectly called Ningmapa in Vol. III, page 171 *infra*, owes its origin to dissent from Atisa's reforms. The great majority of the *lámas* continued their attachment to the lax doctrines of Padma Sambhava and his successors, called themselves *Rnyig-ma-pa* or 'ancients,' of the old school. Their doctrines were based entirely on the Tántras and the treatises and commentaries of Padma Sambhava and his school, and are saturated with the shamanism of the Bon-chos. As Padma Sambhava had professed to draw upon books written and hidden by Nágárjúna which he had discovered by a miraculous revelation from that saint, so the principal Nyigmapa apostles attributed their lucubrations to Padma Sambhava, pretending to discover the writings hidden by him as already described. These books, styled *Ter-ma*, contain many extravagances and obscenities, some recommending unbridled license as the surest way of attaining salvation.

The Nyigmapa neglect as a rule all the restraints of Buddhist discipline, especially in regard to celibacy, abstinence from flesh and liquor. Many are married and almost all given to drunkenness. Their supreme divinity is the mystic Buddha, Kúntu Zangpo, the Sanskrit Samantabhadra but in preference to the Buddhas generally adored by other sects they affect tutelary demons called Si-Yidam-kyi-lhá, 'benevolent protectors' and P'ro-Yidam-kyi-lhá, 'terrible protectors,' represented in the Tántric way as each holding their *yúm*[3] or *sakti* in a close embrace. The former belong to the class of Buddhas, the latter to that of the Shiva istic deities. The Si-Yidam of the sect is called Vajra-p'úrba and the P'ro-Yidam Dúppa-Kágye.' They have also a guardian demon called Gúrgon, a monster with two heads, and they worship Padma Sambhava under various forms, human, divine and demoniac. The cult, which is essentially one of propitiation, which they offer to these divinities, consists in magic rites of all kinds, and in these flesh, fermented liquors and blood offered in human skulls form the principal ingredients. Their numerous sub-sects, separated by insignificant shades of choice between a special *Tántra* or *Terma* and another or of a special tutelary deity are scattered all over Tibet as are their monasteries, some of which are renowned. Among them are those at Samyé, the metropolis of the order, Morú, Ramoché and

[1] *Bkah-g dams-pa.*

[2] *H broms-s ton.*

[3] Lit. 'mother', a tern applied to a goddess or any lady of quality.

Karmakhya, the last three having colleges for the study of astrology, exorcism, magic and divination.

All the Nyigmapas however did not approve of the licentious and dangerous doctrines of the Tertons as the discoverers or inventors of hidden treatises were called and a certain number of them protesting against their pretended revelations constituted under the name of the Sarma school an independent group which while preserving the mystic and Tántric tradition which had become imbedded in religious morals, imposed on itself a strict physical and moral discipline, the rigorous observance of monastic rules as to celibacy, abstinence, obedience and the renunciation of the world, the practice of universal charity and the exercise of meditation. To this group belong the Karmapa, Bhrikhúngpa[1] and Dúgpa[2] sub-orders. It possesses the important monasteries of Mindoling,[3] Dorjedak,[4] Karthok,[5] Khamtathag and Sich'en-tsogch'en, each the seat of an independent sub-sect.

The Kargyút-pa and Sakya-pa sects or orders.—If the revolt of conscience which resulted in the formation of the Sarma school was, as is believed, anterior to the reforms of Atisa and Bromton and in consequence independent of them, their preachings and efforts did not fail to exercise a certain influence on the Nyigmapas and contributed to form new or half-reformed groups which have played an important part in the religious history of Tibet. Of these the most important are the Kargyút-pa[6] and Sakya pa.[7]

Among Bromton's disciples was a monk named Marpa who remained attached to the Nyigmapa doctrines in spite of all because their toleration appeared to him particularly suited to the Tibetan temperament. He undertook to correct them by mingling the excessive fondness of the Nyigmapas for mystical and magical practices with the excessive severity of the Kádampas and towards the end of the 11th century he founded an order which he called the Kargyútpa or 'those who follow several teachings.' In this he was powerfully aided by his principal disciple and successor, Milarapa. This order or sect professes to follow a doctrine revealed by the supreme Buddha Dorje'chang or, in Sanskrit, Vajradhara, to the Indian sage Telopa and transmitted to Marpa by the Pandit Náro of the Nálanda monastery. His doctrine, called the *mannyag* or Náro'chorug, imparts constant meditation on the nature of the Buddhas and the means of acquiring it, charity, adoration of the Adi-Buddha, the absolute renunciation of the world, life in solitude and by preference in a hermitage in order to restrain action and desire, the rigorous observance of the rules of the *Vináya*, the study of Tántric metaphysic and of the philosophy of the Madhyamika School, and the practice of *yoga*. It addresses its worship especially to the tutelary

[1] Or Dikúngpa.

[2] Brug-pa: this sub-order is scattered all over the south of Tibet, especially in Bhutan and Sikkim.

[3] Smin-grol-*g*ling.

[4] *R*do-rje-brag.

[5] Garthok.

[6] *B*kah-brgyud-pa

[7] Sa-*s*kya-pa.

Yi-dam Dem-chog and to his Shakti Dorje-p'agmo, the Sanskrit Vajravaráhi, the goddess with three heads, one of which is that of a wild sow and it venerates as its principal saints and patrons Telopa, Náro, Marpa and Milarapa. Once it boasted many followers and its monks had a great name for learning and holiness, but it has now-a-days fallen into decay.

The Sakyapa sect or rather order will be found described in Vol. III, pp. 346-7.

The Nyigmapa *lámas* and the orders which have sprung from it are generally designated 'red *lámas*' or more precisely 'red caps'—*sa-mar* owing to the colour of their costume.[1] But the Kadampa *lámas* wear the *sa-ser* or yellow bonnet of the orthodox Gelukpa sect.

The Gelukpa order.—At the very moment when the Sakyapa sect was about to attain the zenith of its power in 1355 a miraculous child, an incarnation of the Bodhisattva Manjúsri, or perhaps even of the Dhiáni-Buddha Amitábha, was born in eastern Tibet. His intelligence and religious vocation were so precociously developed that the *láma* Rolpa'idorje of the Kármapa sect initiated him at the age of 3, and at the age of 8 he was first ordained by a *láma* named Tondúo-Rinchen and assumed as his new name the style of Lozang-tagpa or Sumatikirti. Tradition avers that he received instruction from a western monk, possibly a Christian and if so probably a Nestorian. However this may be, Tsongkha-pa—as he is generally called from the place of his birth—soon acquired such a name for piety and learning that he attracted numerous disciples in spite of the severity of his discipline, especially in what concerned the vows of chastity. He recalled his disciples to the inflexible rules of the 253 canons of the *Vináya*, to the liturgy and ritual traditions of the primitive Maháyána. He imposed upon them the yellow garb of the Hindu mendicant to recall by its shape the clothing of the Indian *bhikshus* and distinguish them from the red-clad *lámas* and gave them the name of Gelukpa[2] or 'observers of virtue.' In 1409 he founded the monastery of Galdan,[3] the centre of the sect, and after some years those of Sera and Depúng. At Galdan he died in 1417 or 1419, leaving the pontificate of the sect to his nephew and chief disciple, Gedún Grúb. His soul ascended to the heaven Túshita, residence of the Bodhisattvas, where he reigns with Nágárjúna at the side of the future Buddha Maitreya, an ascension commemorated by the feast of lamps from October 20th to 25th. He is also the object of a cult as Jámpál Nying-po and his relics are worshipped at Galdan. To him is attributed the authorship of numerous treatises, the canons of the Gelúg-pa order, the four principal being the *Bodhimúr*, the *Tarnimmúr*, the *Altánárke* and the *Lámrim*. In spite of his great renown he never held in his lifetime any higher official title than that of abbott of Galdan which

[1] Ramsay gives the following as 'Red-cap' sects:—

1. Rnikmápa.	5. Skarmápa.
2. Urgiúpa.	6. Drigong-pa.
3. Saskiápa.	7. Stagbunpa.
4. Kárgiootpa.	8. Hlondrukpa.

Ramsay: Western Tibetan Dicty., p. 18, *cf.* pp. 79-85.

[2] *Dge-lags-pa.* The sect is also called Galdan-pa.

[3] *Dgah-ldan.*

his successor also bore until his elevation in 1439 to the rank of Grand Láma. The latter's pontificate was remarkable for the foundation of the monastery of Tashilhúm po in 1445 and the enunciation of the dogma of the incarnation of the Grand Lámas of the Gelúg-pa order by which his successor Gedún-Gröb-Gyetso was the first beneficiary. It appears however that the only incarnation believed in at that epoch was that of the spirit of the first Grand Láma, not that of a god, and that the only purpose of this tenet, from which the sect has drawn such advantages, was to create for these eminent personages a kind of spiritual heirship in imitation of (or improvement on) the rule of natural heredity observed by the rival sect of the Sakyapa. Nevertheless the office of abbott at Galdan is elective. Apart from the adoption of the title of Gyetso,[1] which means 'Ocean of Majesty' and is equivalent to the Mongolian Talé, Europeanised as Dalai, and the transfer of the head see to Depúng, the sect had no history except one of rapid and continued progress during the pontificates of Gedún-Grúb Gyetso (born in 1475, died in 1543), Sodnam-Gyetso (1543-1589) and Yontan-Gyetso (1589-1617). Je-Ngavang-Lozang-Thúbtan-Jigsmed-Gyetso (1617-1682) however was able to raise the Kochot Mongols against the king of Tibet and make the victors do homage to himself. He thus united the spiritual and temporal authority under the protection of China in the hands of the Dalai Lámas who succeeded him. He is also said to have devised the doctrine of the perpetual re-incarnation of the Dhiáni-Boddhisattva Chanresí (the Sanskrit Avalokiteswara) in the Dalai Lámas which was extended retrospectively to his four predecessors. He also created the dignity of Panchen-Rinpotche, an incarnation of the Buddha Odpagmed (Sanskrit Amitábha, the spiritual father of Avalokiteswara) for his old preceptor the abbott of Galdan whom he also appointed to be the independent pontiff of Táshilhúmpo. The Gelúgpa have preserved a well-merited reputation for learning. They admit the validity of the magic and sorcery inculcated in the *Gyút*, the 7th section of the *Kan-júr*, but in all other respects follow scrupulously the canon of the primitive Maháyána as the Kádampa sect had received it from Atisa. But contrary to its doctrine they admit the existence of the soul though it is not conceived of by them in the same way as it is in Europe. They regard it as immortal or rather as endowed with an indefinite existence and perhaps even as eternal in its essence In its inception this soul is a light imprisoned in a material body endowed with an individuality which subsists, though to a limited extent, in its transmigrations and permits it to undergo the good or evil effects of its *karma*. Eventually the corporal envelope wears thin and finally disappears when the man becomes Buddha and enters Nirvána. Nirvána is neither annihilation nor its opposite. It can be attained by three roads, that of the inferior, intermediate and superior beings. For the first named Nirvána is a repose of nothingness. For the superior it is to reach the perfect-state of Buddha. In it the individuality of a being melts into a kind of confluence: like Sákyamúni himself it is confounded with the other Buddhas. Nevertheless its personality is not totally destroyed, for if it cannot re-appear in the world

[1] Bgya-mts'o.

under a form perceptible by the senses it can manifest itself spiritually, to those who have faith. It is in themselves then that they see it.

The Gelúgpas worship all the deities of the Tibetan pantheons, but they especially affect the supreme Buddha Dorjechang, the future Buddha Maitreya who inspires their teaching, the Yidams Dorjejigje,[1] Demchog[2] and Sangdus[3] and the *gon-po* or demoniac genie Tamdin.[4] The ceremonies consecrated to the three latter have a magical character and are accompanied by Tántric rites.

No theology of Lamaism, as a whole, can be said to exist. Each sect has its own pantheon and that of the Gelúgpas is typical of all the others This sect divides the celestial world into nine groups, the Buddhas, Yidam or tutelary deities, the Lhag-lha or those above the gods, the Boddhisattvas, the Arhats or saints, the Dákkinis, the Dharmapálas or 'protectors of the law', the Yul lhá or Devas, who are terrestial deities and the Sa-bdag, local deities or those of the soil. The clue to this multiplication of divine being must be sought in the Lamaistic conception of the Buddhas. Incapable of reincarnation, plunged in the beatitude of the Nirvána, they can no longer intervene in the affairs of men. At most they have power to inspire and sustain the saints who are devoted to the salvation of human beings. In a sense the Buddhas are dead gods, while the living, active gods are the Boddhisattvas.

I.—The Buddhas form the class of higher beings perfect in excellence, presided over by Dorjechang (Vajradhara), the Adi-Buddha of Indian Buddhism, who is the external, all-powerful, omniscient Buddha, an abstract being imitated from the Brahma or universal soul of the Brahmans, though he does not apparently fulfil all his functions. He is often confounded with Dorjesempa (Vajrasattva though it may be that the two conceptions are distinct, the former being exclusively meditative, the latter active. They are depicted as seated with the legs crossed in the attitude of imperturbable meditation, adorned with rich jewels and crowned with a five-gemmed crown. But while Dorjechang makes the gesture of perfection, with the index-fingers and thumbs of both hands joined and raised to the level of the chest, Dorjesempa has his hands crossed on his breast and holds the thunderbolt (*dorje* or *vajra*) and the sacred bell. Several sects, including the orthodox sect of the Gelúgpas, do not however acknowledge their supremacy but regard them merely as celestial Boddhisattvas, emanations of Akchobhya, and attribute the supreme rank to Vairochana.

The class of the Buddhas is divided into 5 groups: (*i*) the Jínas or Dhiáni-Buddhas, (*ii*) the seven Buddhas of the past, (*iii*) the 35 Buddhas of confession, (*iv*) the Tathágata physicians, and (*v*) the 1000 Buddhas. (*i*) The Jínas are five abstract personages who represent the virtues, intelligences and powers of Dorjechang, from whom they emanate. They are protectors of the 5 cardinal points, the zenith, east, south etc., and personifications of the 5 elements, the ether, air, fire etc., and probably also of the 5 senses. But they are neither

1 Sanskrit Vajrabhairava.
2 Sanskrit Samvara.
3 Sanskrit Guhya Kála: ? Grihya Kála.
4 Sanskrit Hayagríva.

creators nor do they interfere in material phenomena or in the affairs of the world. They preside over the protection and expansion of the Buddhist faith and each by an emanation of his essence procreates a spiritual son, a Dhiáni-Boddhisattva, who is charged with the active supervision of the universe, while at the same time they inspire and sustain the saints who aspire to attain Buddha-hood. Hence we have five Triads each composed of a Dhiáni-Buddha, of a Dhiáni-Boddhisattva and of a Mánúshi-Buddha or human Buddha These five Dhiánis are named Vairochana,[1] Akchobhya,[2] Ratna-Sámbhava,[3] Amitábha[4] and Amoghasiddhi.[5] By a phenomenon as interesting as it is unusual they assume three different forms, natural, mystic and tantric according to the parts which they are made to play. In their natural form they resemble all other Buddhas and can only be recognised by their gestures[6] and by the attributes sometimes assigned to them. Thus Vairochana is in the attitude of 'turning the wheel of the Law',[7] Akchobhya in that of 'taking to witness',[8] Ratna-Sámbhava in that of charity,[9] Amitábha in that of meditation[10] and Amoghasiddhi of intrepidity[11] In their mystic forms they are assigned a crown with 5 gems, and adorned with necklaces, girdles and precious bracelets, which makes them resemble Boddhisattvas of the usual type. Under these aspects Akchobhya changes his name to Chakdor[12] and Amitábha to Amitáyus.[13] And the latter becomes 'infinite life' instead of 'infinite light.' Finally in their tantric forms they are each united to a goddess and often given a number of arms, each charged with a weapon or magic attribute.

(*iii*). The 'Seven Buddhas of the Past,' also called Tathágatas, comprise Sákyamúni and the six human Buddhas who preceded him on earth. They also are to be distinguished by their attitudes. They are Vipásyin,[14] who combines the attitudes of testimony and imperturbability, Sikhin[15] (charity and imperturbability), Visvábhu[16] (meditation), Krákuchanda[17] (protection and imperturbability), Kánákámuni[18] (preaching and imperturbability), Kásyapa (charity and resolution) and Sákyamúni (preaching and imperturbability). Like the Dhiánis the seven Buddhas can on occasion assume mystic and above all tantric forms when they fulfil the functions of a tutelary god of a monastery, tribe or family.

1 Rnam-par-snáng-mzad.

2 Mi-bskyod-dpah.

3 Rin-hbyung.

4 Od-dpag-med.

5 Don-hgrub.

6 Or attitudes, *pyag-rgya*, Sankr. *mudra*.

7 The right index-finger touching the fingers of the left hand.

8 The right hand hanging and resting on the right knee.

9 The right arm extended and the open hand directed towards the earth as if to attract beings to it.

10 Both hands resting one on the other, palms upwards.

11 The arm raised, the hand presented open, the fingers pointed upwards.

12 P'yag-na-rdor.

13 Tse-dpag-med.

14 Rnam-gzigs.

15 Gtsug-gtor-can

16 Ta'm-c'ad-skyob.

17 Ko'r-va-hjigs.

18 Gser-t'ubpa

(*iii*). The 35 Buddhas of Confession are divine personages addressed to obtain the remission of sins or at least mitigation of punishments. They include the 5 Dhiánis, the 7 Buddhas of the Past, the 5 physicians and 19 other Buddhas who appear to personify abstractions. They are frequently invoked and fervently worshipped on account of their functions as redeemers.

(*iv*). The Tathágata physicians form a group of 8 Buddhas including Sákyamúni as president. The principal, Be-du-ryai Od-kvi-rgyál-po, holds a cup of ambrosia and a fruit or medicinal plant and his colour is indigo blue But the others are only distinguished by their attitudes and complexions, three being red, one yellow, one pale yellow and another reddish yellow. They are addressed for the cure of physical as well as spiritual maladies.

(*v*). The last group consists simply of Buddhas and includes 1,000 imaginary Buddhas believed to be living or to have lived in the '3000 great thousands of worlds' which constitute the universe. Among them the most venerated are the Pratyeka Buddhas generally cited anonymously in the Buddhist scripture.

II.—In the Yidams we find the most fantastic conceptions of the Buddhist theology, resulting from the introduction into it of Hindu Tantrism. Absolute perfection to the Indian mind consists in the absence of all passion, of all desire and movement, in a word in absolute inaction. Hence a god acting as creator or preserver is no longer a god since such acts presuppose passion, or the desire to act, and the movement to accomplish the object of that desire. To reconcile this conception of divine perfection with the deeds ascribed to the gods by myth and legend, mystic Brahmanism hit on the idea of a doubling of the god, considered primitively as androgynous, in an inert, purely meditative personality, which is the god properly so called, and an acting personality which is his active energy. To the former they gave the masculine, to the latter the feminine form. The latter is the goddess or Shakti, a companion of every god. De Milloué says that these conceptions were introduced into Buddhism towards the 5th century of our era, and applied not only to the gods, active servitors of the Buddhas, but also to the Buddhas themselves so that they came to be regarded not indeed as creators but as the efficient causes of creation The Buddha, source and essence of all, is thus a generator and as such regarded as bound to interest himself in the creatures begotten by him and above all to protect them against the demons, the great and abiding terror of the Tibetans. In all representations the Yidam is characterised by the Yúm which he holds in his embrace, and this characteristic leads to the most incongruous unions. The Yidams of the highest rank are the tantric manifestations of the Dhiánis, of some other Buddhas and Boddhisattvas. But apart from the addition of the Yúm they all preserve their traditional figures, a few Yidam-Boddhisattvas excepted who assume for the nonce terrifying expressions—calculated, we may presume, to complete the rout of the demons which they have to combat. Only the most active Boddhisattvas are depicted standing. The Boddhisattva Yidam Chakdor, a tantric manifestation of Vajrapani, may be considered the most characteristic type of this series. He is represented as making frightful grimaces, the eyes flashing anger, with a wide mouth armed with fangs, flames instead of hair and a human skull in his left hand, while the right brandishes a thunderbolt, and trampling under foot the corpses of his conquered enemies. He is the implacable destroyer of demons. Although he is a form of Indra or Vishnu the legend which explains why he shows such special hatred for the demons is in part borrowed from the myth of Shiva. When the gods had drunk the *amrit* produced by the churning of the ocean they entrusted to Vajrapáni's care the vase containing the rest of the precious liquid of immortality, but profiting by a moment of carelessness the demon Rahu drank it all and replaced it by an unnameable fluid whose exhalations would certainly have poisoned the world. To avert this danger and punish Vajrapáni for his negligence the gods condemned him to drink the frightful liquid and by the effect of the poison his golden tint turned to black, a misfortune which he never forgave the demons.

The superior Yidams are not numerous, the great majority being formed of Hindu gods, principally forms of Shiva, transformed into secondary Buddhist divinities. It is generally they who are the patrons of sects, monasteris and families, and in this last capacity they also protect herds and crops They too have frightful visages and are depicted with many arms, animals' heads, and all kinds of weapons, including the thunderbolt and the sacred bell which scares demons. They also carry a human skull in which they drink their enemies' blood and which serves as a vessel in their temples for offerings, libations of the blood of victims and fermented liquors. The Yúms of these Yidams are generally agreeable to look at, but sometimes have demon features or several heads and generally many arms with hands laden with weapons and the inevitable skull.

III.—The term Boddhisattva[1] in orthodox Buddhism means a perfect being who has acquired in previous existences prodigious merits which he renounces in order to devote them in love and compassion to the salvation of other beings, who makes a vow in order to attain *bodhi* and is designed to become a Buddha in a future worldly existence. It is in fact the title which Sákyamúni bears in the Túshita heaven and on earth until he becomes Buddha. With it he consecrates Maitreya, his successor, before incarnating himself for the last time. It seems then that at that time there was only one Boddhisattva in Heaven as there was only one Buddha on earth, but the Maháyána by multiplying the number of the Buddhas also multiplied that of the Boddhisattvas infinitely, applying that venerable title to abstract personifications of intelligences, virtues, forces, phenomena and ideas, and at the same time to saints destined to become Buddhas. Hence this group includes personages of very different nature and origin.

First come the Dhiani-Boddhisattvas, emanations of the 5 Dhiáni-Buddhas personifying their active energies and named Samantabhadra,[2] Vajrapáni,[3] Ratnapáni,[4] Avalokiteswara or Padmapáni[5] and Vis-

[1] Byang-C'ub-Sems-dpah.

[2] Kun-tu-bzang-po.

[3] P'yag-rdor.

[4] Pyag-rin-chen.

[5] Spyan-ras-gzigs: pron. Chanresi.

wapáni.[1] Three of these are merely nominal divinities, although much prayed to. Only the second and fourth fulfil very important rôles both in religious legend and in popular tradition. Vajrapáni enjoys more propitiation than genuine adoration, if we understand by that a feeling of gratitude and love, probably because of his demon-like appearance in his Tantric form. On the other hand Padmapáni, 'the lotus-handed' or 'he who holds the lotus in his hands,' is above all the beloved being, venerated, adored, besought in all circumstances in preference to the greatest Buddhas themselves, including even his spiritual father Amitábha.

Many reasons explain the special devotion which Avalokiteswara enjoys. He presided at the formation of the actual universe, and is charged to protect it against the enterprises of the demons and to develop in it the beneficent action of the Good Law. Then he personifies charity, compassion, love of one's neighbour: more than any other he is helpful, and in his infinite kindliness has manifested and still manifests himself in the world in incarnations whenever there is a danger to avert, a misdeed of the demons to repair, or a wretch to save. Lastly he presides, seated at Amitábha's right hand, over the paradise of Sukhávati whose portals he opens to all who invoke him with devotion, love and faith. He might almost be called the redeemer, if the idea of redemption were not irreconcilable with the Buddhist dogma of personal responsibility and the fatal consequences of one's own acts. As protector and saver as well as in remembrance of his repeated incarnations Avalokiteswara assumes, according to the part attributed to him, very different forms corresponding to his 33 principal incarnations. Generally he is represented seated (or standing to signify action) as a handsome youth, crowned and richly attired. Very rarely he is given a feminine aspect. At other times he has several heads and arms. His most celebrated image has 11 heads, arranged in a pyramid, and 22 arms. In this form he is the recognised patron of Tibet. In his mystic and Tantric cult he has as Shakti the goddess Dolma,[2] a benevolent form of the Shivaistic Kálí, styled in India Tárá the helper. Besides this special office Tárá forms one of the celestial Boddhisattvas in twenty-one transformations, each the object of a fervent cult, for the Maháyána assigns a great place in its pantheon to the feminine element—in opposition to the Hinayána.

Below the Dhiáni Boddhisattvas functions the numerous class of beings also called Boddhisttvas or would-be Buddhas, some purely imaginary, personifications of virtues or even books, others who lived or pass for having lived, canonized saints, some of whom may be regarded as having had a historical existence, such as the king Srong-tsan Gampo and his two wives who are regarded as incarnations of Tárá under the names of the White and Green Tárá.[3] At the head of this class stands Manjúsri,[4] occupying a place

[1] P'yag-na-t'sog.

[2] Sgrol-ma.

[3] Sgrol-ma dkar-po and ljangs ku.

[4] Hjam-pai-dbyangs-pa: pron. Jam-jang. His sword of great understanding cut the darkness of ignorance.

so high that he is often ranked as a Dhiáni-Boddhisattva, who personifies the transcendant knowledge or wisdom of Buddhism. He is recognised by his flaming sword, held in his right hand, while a book supported by a lotus stalk figures on his left. He is always seated on a lotus or on a lion who rests on a lotus. Among the principal Boddhisattvas also stands Maitreya[1] the future Buddha, who is seated like a European. Then come the 21 Tárás, saviours and compassionate, Shaktis of Avalokiteswara; and finally the female Boddhisattva Od-zer-chan-ma more usually called rDorje-p'ag-mo, who is perpetually incarnated in the abbess of Palti and who may be recognised by her three heads, one that of a sow. Speaking generally the Boddhisattvas are intermediaries and intercessors between men and the Buddhas.

IV.—*The* lámas.—By *láma* the Buddhists translate the Sanskrit *gurú*. The *lámas* as a body include very diverse elements. They have attained *nirvána*, but not the absolute *parinirvána*, which would preclude them from re-appearing on earth or interesting themselves in worldly affairs, even in the progress of religion and so on. In the first rank are the 12 *grúbchen* or wizards, imitated from the Vedic *rishis*, having acquired sanctity and supernatural power by austerities, mortifications of the flesh and, above all, by magical practices. Then come the 16 *arhats* or chief disciples of the Buddha, the 18 *sthaviras*, his patriarchal successors or heads of the principal sects, the Indian or Tibetan *pandits* who introduced, spread or restored Buddhism in Tibet, the founders of the schools of philosophy, religious sects and great monasteries, and in brief all the dignitaries regarded as perpetual incarnations of Buddhas, Boddhisattvas, saints or gods who are on this account styled 'living' or 'incarnated' Buddhas. At the head of this group the Gelugpas naturally place Tsong-kha-pa, their founder, and the Dalai-lámas from Gedún-grúb downwards. It begins chronologically with Nágárjuna and his disciple Aryadeva, the founder and propagator of the Maháyána in India, Padma Sambhava and Santa-Rákshita who introduced it into Tibet, and Atisa its reformer Then come Brom-ton, founder of the Kadampas, Saskya Pandita (13th century), and others.

V.—*The Dákkinis.*—The Maháyána, having borrowed most of its inferior divinities from Shivaism, especially Tantric Shivaism which makes the cult of the Shaktis predominant over that of the god himself, was compelled to give the Dákkinis precedence over the male gods. Sometimes they are represented as beautiful young women, adorned like queens, but more often with fearful visages, with animal heads crowned with flaming hair, and so on, either to indicate that they can torment and ruin those who neglect their worship, or more probably to signify their power to destroy the demons whom it is their mission to combat. Nevertheless all have a twofold character, benevolent and demoniac or maleficent. They are the Yúms of the Yidams, Buddhas etc., but also play most important personal parts. Many monasteries, even among those of the orthodox sect, are consecrated to one of them as tutelary patron, as are many Tibetan families. First in

[1] Byams-pa: pron. Chaupa or Jampa.

rank stands Lha-mo (Mahá-Kálí), 'mother of the gods'. She is represented in 15 different forms, but especially as a woman of frightful aspect holding a club with a dead man's head at its end, a skull for cap, and riding on a steed harnessed with human hide—said to be that of her own son killed by her for the sins of his father. Another important group is that of the six Mka'-hgro-ma, of whom the powerful Seng-gei-gdong-c'an has a lion's head and dances naked on the bodies of men and animals.

VI.—The Choï-chong[1] or Drag-gseds include almost all the gods of Hinduism, represented as Yidams and Dákkinis under a demoniacal aspect, although they are the recognised defenders of the Law and the universe against the demons. The most venerated are Yáma,[2] judge of the dead, and Kuvera,[3] god of wealth.

VII.—*The Yul-lha or terrestrial gods.*—This group includes the various deities appointed to guard the world. It comprises a good many Hindu gods, such as Brahma, Indra, Chandr, Garúda etc., reduced to the status of inferior divinities, servitors and henchmen of the Buddhas and Boddhisattvas, as well as a number of gods, probably Tibetan by origin, such as Pihar or Behar, the patron of monasteries in general, Dala,[4] god of war, a kind of Hercules usually accompanied by a black dog who above all makes war on demons, and Me-lha, god of fire and also of the domestic hearth.

VIII.—The Sa-bdag or local gods are of purely Tibetan origin and are charged with the protection of the land, hills, rivers etc., etc. They are very numerous and as each locality has its special protector they cannot be named or even numbered, but one, Nang-lha, god of the house, who is represented with the head of a hog or wild boar, is worshipped throughout Tibet But while he protects the house he is also a tyrant for if he chooses to dwell on the hearth the cooking fire must be carried elsewhere, under penalty of his wrath, and so on. He changes his abode about once every two months. The family gods are in reality ancestors for whom special ceremonies are observed at each change of season.

IX.—The Gegs or demons are a perpetual source of terror to the Tibetans who attribute to them every material ill from which the country may suffer as well as such trivial annoyances of daily life as milk boiling over. They are styled collectively *gegs* or 'enemies' and the most dreaded are the *lha-ma-yin*, corresponding to the *asúras*, the *dúd-po*, phantoms, spectres and ghosts, and above all the Sin-dje, henchmen of the god of death. All the demons are the object of practices, magical ceremonies and offerings designed to propitiate them, and of exorcisms for which the *lámas* must be resorted to and out of which they make a good part of their income.

[1] Ch'os-skyong.

[2] Sin-dje.

[3] Dzam-bha-la.

[4] Dgra-lha.

The Lamaistic clergy.

The term *láma* is applied indiscriminately to the clergy of Tibet, but strictly speaking it should only be applied to high dignitaries who only acquire it after having given proofs of profound knowledge. In reality the clergy is composed of 5 distinct classes, the *genyen*[1] or listener, the *getsúl*[2] or novice, the *gelong*[3] or ordained priest, the *láma* or superior priest and the *khanpo*[4] or overseer (abbott or bishop). Above this hierarchy in which promotion is earned by merit and holiness are two higher ranks conferred by birth, those of *khúbilgan*, the incarnation of a Tibetan saint, and of *khútúktú*, that of a Hindu saint. Finally the edifice is crowned by the two sublime dignitaries, the Panchen Rinpoche and the Dalai Láma.

The attractions of the priesthood are many, but they are strengthened by a law or usage[5] which compels every family to vow one of its sons, ordinarily the eldest, to the priesthood. The boy is presented at the age of 7 or 8 by his father, mother or guardian in a monastery. After a cursory examination of the family's standing[6] he is medically examined as any deformity, epilepsy, leprosy or phthisis would disqualify him. The boy is then entrusted to some kinsman in the monastery or to an aged monk who is charged with his literary and religious education. He keeps his lay garb and his hair and can be visited by his kinsmen every week. After two or three years of study, legally two suffice, his *gegan* or religious instructor asks for his admission as a *genyen* or catechumen, which necessitates a rigid examination of his conduct and attainments.

At the age of not less than 15 the *genyen* can solicit admission to the novitiate. Aided by his preceptor he presents himself before the chapter of the monastery and answers the questions prescribed by the *Vindya* as to his person and condition, and undergoes a severe examination in dogma. If he fails he is sent back to his family and his preceptor is fined. If he succeeds he is made to take the vows of *pravajya* or quitting his house, his head is shaved, he is dressed in the red or yellow robe of his order and given the regulative utensils. He thus becomes a *getsúl* and can attend all religious functions, without taking an active part in them.

At 20 after further study of theology, he may ask to be ordained. This requires a fresh examination, lasting three days and a series of debates on religious topics, tests so difficult that the unhappy candidate is allowed three tries. If he fails he is definitely expelled the order, but generally proceeds to exercise irregular functions as a sorcerer

[1] Dge-bangen, corr. to Sanskr. *upásaka*.

[2] Dge-tsul, corr. to S. *sramanera*.

[3] Dge-slong, corr. to S. *sramana*.

[4] Mkan-po, corr. to S. *sthavira*.

[5] Called *btsun-gral*.

[6] Certain monasteries only admit candidates of high rank in which case the investigation is very searching.

lámas in the villages. If he passes he is invested with all rights and powers of the finished cleric.

Once invested with the character of holiness the *gelong* is qualified to act in all the rites of the cult and may even become, by election, head of a minor monastery. So the majority go no further, but the more ambitious or those devoted to learning go to continue their studies in the great university-monasteries such as Depúng, Sera, Galdan, Garmakhya and Morú. The two last teach especially astrology, magic and other occult sciences as well as theology and mathematics. After difficult and costly examinations the successful candidate can obtain the degree of *geses*[1] or licentiate, with which most are contented, of *rabjampa*[2] or *lharamba*, 'doctor in theology.' Adepts in occult science take the special title of *choi-chong*.[3] The holder of any of these degrees is entitled to be styled *láma*. Another honorific title *choi-je*[4] is awarded by the Dalai Láma or the Panchen Rinpoche to clerics distinguished by sanctity, but it confers no right to exercise the superior functions which the *geses* and *lharambas* can perform. Among the former are chosen the superiors of the monasteries of middling importance, some being elected by the chapters, others being nominated by the Dalai Láma or Panchen Rinpoche. The latter supply the *khanpos* who are promoted by those two hierarchs to form his entourage with the title of Councillor or *Tsanit*. They thus correspond to the cardinals of the Roman church fulfilling various functions, such as abbotts of the great monasteries, with an ecclesiastical jurisdiction like that of bishop, coadjutor of the incarnate Lámas, governors of provinces and occasionally generals of the army.

The *khubilgans* are very numerous, but enjoy a purely local influence, confined to the district of their own monasteries, whereas the *khútúktú*, fewer in number, receive a greater veneration and their spiritual authority almost independent is exercised over wide areas. They include such dignitaries as the Dev or Depa-rája, the spiritual and temporal sovereign of Bhutan.

Another high dignitary in the Lamaic church is the grand Láma of the sect and monastery of Sakya who, though not an incarnation, is the hereditary successor[5] of Matidvaja, nephew of the celebrated Sakya Pandita P'agspa who converted Mongolia and on whom the emperor Khúbilái Khán conferred in 1270 spiritual authority over all Tibet. In spite of the predominance of the orthodox Gelúgpa order, the State church, his authority is still very great and is acknowledged, at least nominally, by all the sects of 'red' *lámas* who are opposed to that of the Dalai Láma. Tibetan politics centre round the position of the Dalai Láma whose authority is more nominal than real. Even his

[1] Dge-ses.

[2] Rabs hbyams-pa.

[3] C'os-skyong

[4] C'os-rje, *lit.* 'noble of the Law.'

[5] The 'red' *lámas* of the Sakya order are permitted to marry.

spiritual and doctrinal authority is frequently disputed by dissenting sects, which nevertheless regard him as chief of the religion and revere him as a true incarnation of Chanresi and his representative on earth.

The *lámas* only distantly resemble the *bhikshús* of early Buddhism. Wool has naturally replaced cotton in their garb, but in order to observe the canon which required a monk in the presence of a superior or of the *sangha* or in the temple to wear a mantle draped over the left shoulder so as to expose the right shoulder and arm, the Tibetan monk during the offices wears a mantle or large scarf (*lagoi*) over his other vestments. This scarf is, like the robe, yellow for the orthodox sect and red for the unreformed or Nyigmapá sects. Instead of going bareheaded the *lámas* wear caps or hats, red or yellow, of felt or silk, to indicate not only the sect but the rank of the wearer; and for use during the offices they have a choir cap, always red or yellow, which is a kind of stiff Phrygian cap surmounted sometimes by a crest of *chenille* which gives it a curious resemblance to the Grecian helmets of the Homeric age.

Like the *bhikshu* the Tibetan monk must have certain utensils, *viz.* a bowl to receive alms in, a razor and a needle-case, as well as a rosary, a praying-wheel, a small gourd for holy water enclosed in a kind of bag of cloth, silk or velvet, a tinder-box and a knife. Generally the begging bowl as useless is replaced by a wooden tea-cup of the common type. The bowl is the less necessary as daily begging has been suppressed, the monks being supported by the vast resources of the monasteries which are continually being increased by voluntary gifts or by imposts of all kinds levied on the pious superstitions of the faithful laity. The canon has also been greatly relaxed as regards abstinence and diet generally. The fasts are less frequent and severe, being restricted to the rainy season (*vassa*)—or rather to the corresponding period in the calendar, for there is no monsoon in Tibet. The end of the time during which it falls in India is observed as a rigid fast for four days and by certain solemn ceremonies for which the community prepares by fasts of two, three or four days. Exemptions can however be obtained in case of illness or weakness, and the fasts are also sensibly mitigated by the consumption of tea which is only deemed to break the fast of the fourth day of the *nyúngpar*, 'to continue the abstinence', a ceremony during which it is forbidden even to swallow one's saliva. The canon does not interdict such austerities and mortifications of the flesh, however severe, as the devout may wish to impose on themselves, but in theory the assent of one's superiors should be obtained unless one belongs to the class, by no means numerous, of the hermit ascetics who are not dependent on any monastery. The only dietary rule incumbent on the *bhikshús* was to avoid eating more than one meal a day and this rule is observed in Tibet but mitigated by the absorption of many cups of tea (eight or ten during the exercises and offices) and two or three cups of tea-gruel, a mixture of tea, milk and butter, every morning and evening. While the principal meal is taken in the common refectory or separately in the cells these collation of tea or gruel are served in the hall of the monastery or even in the temple during suspensions of the office arranged for the purpose.

The modifications which Buddhism has undergone have changed the daily life of the monks profoundly. While the *bhikshú* of its early phase had no occupations save to take his turn at begging, to listen to the Master's teaching, meditate on the truths of the Law and endeavour to spread them, the institution of a cult which has become more and more complex created for the priest-monk new and absorbing duties, in Tibet more than elsewhere, looking to the eminently sacerdotal character which it assumed there. Without describing the studies, serious and difficult enough, which candidates must undergo, the daily life in the cloisters of the lamaist monk is in reality very minutely occupied A little before dawn the tinkling of the bell or the resonant call of the conch summons the denizens of the monastery who as soon as they awake mutter a prayer, make hasty ablutions and recite on their rosaries the prayers specially consecrated to their tutelary deities of whom each chooses one as his patron saint. At a fresh signal from bell or trumpet monks and novices, dressed in choral mantle and hat, go in procession to the temple and in profound silence take their seats according to their rank. There, after some prayers, tea is served and then they perform the ritual in honour of the Boddhisattva Chanresi, of the holy disciples of Buddha and of the Yidams and for the welfare of dead commended to their prayers. Then they take a repast of tea and gruel and after an invocation to the Sun withdraw to their cells for private devotions. Towards 9 A.M. the community re-assembles in the temple for a service in honour of the divinities who guard against the demons. At midday a new convention is followed by the chief meal of the day. Then they are free till [illegible] P.M. when they re-assemble to make offerings at the temple, to teach novices, to debate questions of dogma, discipline and philosophy. Finally at 7 P.M. they gather together for the last time to do the service of acts of grace, followed by the daily examination of the tasks of the novices and candidates. During each sitting tea is served thrice.

But these do not exhaust a *láma's* functions. In Tibet he is not merely a priest. He is teacher, scholar, physician, writer, and artist, wizard, and he should devote himself in the moments of freedom, which the sacred offices leave him, to the branch of occupation which he has chosen. In the monasteries all or nearly all the monks are charged with the education of boys destined to the priesthood, and in the villages, where there are no schools, it is the resident *láma*, generally one of the failures of the nearest monastery, who fulfils the functions of schoolmaster and teaches children to read, write and cypher well enough to use the ready-reckoner. It is noteworthy that even in the tents of the nomad shepherds men and women possess the rudiments of education. As writers and calligraphists many *lámas* devote themselves to re-copying the sacred writings or reprinting them by means of wooden blocks. While lay artists are not unknown, especially at Lhása, the works of monkish artists are preferred on account of the sanctity which attaches to their works. These include illuminated manuscripts, paintings on silk, cloth and paper, frescoes, charms, amulets and metal-work, usually of a religious character.

The practice of medicine is entirely in the hands of the *lámas* who, if indifferent surgeons, are skilled in the use of simples and learned in the secular lore of plants. They are also the only persons qualified to expel demons to whose maleficence all ills are ascribed. Exorcism is thus their chief source of income. As a science it is practised by all, even by those of the orthodox sect. Even in a temple it finds a place as the demons of evil must be expelled from it before the office is begun. Another important function of the *lámas* is the prediction of the future by astrology. But those of the orthodox sect to their credit refuse as far as possible to lend themselves to these practices, which Tsong-khapa and the teachers of the sect condemned, though they are often obliged to perform them in order to satisfy the wishes of their faithful laymen.

Besides the monks there are communities of nuns, instituted on the model of the Indian Bhikshúnis. To such foundations Buddha only assented with reluctance. The nuns in Tibet are subject to the same obligations as the monks, wear the same garb, though the robe is slightly longer, and have to sacrifice their hair. But their discipline is stricter. They must obey 258 rules of conduct instead of 250 as the monks do. They owe respect and obedience to the monks whatever their rank, and all their convents, even if there be an abbess, are subject to the spiritual and disciplinary direction of an aged monk from the nearest monastery who presides even at the general confession of the Pratimoksha. At one time nuns were numerous in Tibet, but now-a-days their numbers have diminished. Their principal order has its seat in the monastery at Samding and its abbess is a perpetual incarnation of the goddess or feminine Boddhisattva, Dorje P'agmo,[1] who is represented with three heads, one a sow's.

Om mani padme húm.—This formula we are now able to explain. It has hitherto been explained as meaning: 'Oh, thou jewel in the lotus!' But it is clear that Manipadme is the vocative of Manipadmá, the deity of the jewel lotus, the *shakti* of Manipadma who must be identical with Padmapáni or Avalokiteswara. The formula goes back to the times of Sron-btsan-sgam-po.[2]

Ibbetson, § 253.

The Hindu-Buddhists of Lahul.—I have said that Spiti is the only portion of British Territory whose inhabitants have returned themselves as Buddhists. But though the Census figures shown in the margin would draw a line of the sharpest and most definite kind between the religions of Hinduism and Buddhism where they meet in the mountains of the Kulu sub-division, yet the actual line of demarcation is by no means so clearly marked. On this subject Mr. Alex. Anderson, the officer in charge of Kulu, writes:—"In Kulu including Waziri Rupi and outer and inner Seoraj, the population is Hindu with scarcely an exception. In Spiti the only religion is Buddhism. In Láhul there is a mixture of Hinduism and Buddhism. Since the last Census, Hinduism in Láhul has advanced, and Buddhism

[1] Sanskr. Vajravárári, 'sow of diamond.'

[2] A. H. Francke in J. R. A. S., 1915, pp. 402-3.

retreated.[1] In the valley of the Chandra Bhága, Hinduism has always existed, and is now the prevailing religion. No doubt some Buddhist observances still exist, modifying Hinduism more or less ; and in secret the people may observe some Buddhist customs more than they will publicly admit. But they are brought by trade into close intercourse with the people of Kulu, and find it to heir advantage, from the social point of view, to prefer Hinduism. In the separate valleys of the Chandra and the Bhága, Buddhism has a much stronger hold than in the valley of the united rivers. But here again Hinduism is advancing. The people declare that they are Hindu Kanets, though they are probably more Buddhist than Hindu ; and the Moravian missionaries at Kailang state that caste distinctions, which do not exist among pure Buddhists, are becoming more marked. The Lámas of Láhul[2] will not eat with a European, while the Lámas of Tibet have no objection to doing so. This advance of Hinduism is ascribed in part to the influence of the Thákurs or Barons of Láhul ; but it is, apart from such influence, which no doubt has its effect, inevitable and natural. These two valleys (the separate valleys of the Chandra and Bhága) are best described as a margin or debateable land between the two religions, though at present they are more Buddhist than Hindu. The people were once Buddhists and are so now to a great degree. But they have accepted caste and respect Brahmans to some extent, and though it is known that many of their religious observances are of a Buddhist character, still they are accepted in Hindu Kulu as Hindus."

Mr. Heyde, the Moravian missionary, puts the case rather more strongly for Buddhism. He writes :—" Buddhism is the dominant religion throughout the separate valleys of the Bhága and Chandra. The professors of it in these parts seem to prefer to call themselves Hindu, but this is a mere pretension. They are Buddhists, and the majority wish at present to be nothing else. However, in speaking of the now prevailing religions of Láhul, one must not forget that both Brahmanism and Buddhism are still to a great extent pervaded by the demon worship which no doubt alone prevailed in Láhul in early times"

[1] In an account of the religion of Láhul written for Mr. Lyall in 1868 by Rev. Mr. Heyde, whose long residence among the people, by whom he is invariably respected, and great knowledge of their language and customs ensured its accuracy, that gentleman described the religion of Láhul as "essentially Buddhism," and stated that pure Hindus were found in only a few villages and were a low set of Brahmans and that those of the remaining population who were not pure Buddhists "leaned more strongly towards Buddhism than Brahmanism." They maintained Buddhists monasteries, abjured beef, and "in case of severe illness, &c., would call in both Lámas and Brahmans who performed their respective rites at one and the same time."—D. I.

[2] Mr. Anderson says elsewhere : "In Láhul I do not consider that all are Hindus. There are Lámas who ought certainly to have been shown as Buddhists, but there is a tendency to ignore Buddhism in Láhul." These Lámas must have returned themselves as Hindus unless there was some error in the compilation of our figures. The papers were in an unknown character and tongue, and had to be translated orally : but there could hardly have been any confusion about such a plain entry as that of religion; and if there had been, it is difficult to see why it should have been confined to the figures of Láhul and to the Buddhists only, and should not have affected those of Spiti and of other religions in Láhul also. There appear to have been only seven of these Lámas in Láhul in 1872, though there were also 110 cultivating land-holders who had taken Lamaic vows but "had very little of the monk about them."—D. I.

Ibbetson § 254.

Even the transition from Hindu to nominal Buddhist and back again seems to be possible. Mr. Anderson writes in another place :—" A Kanet (a Hindu caste) cuts his scalp-lock and becomes the disciple of some Láma, and this may even be after marriage. The Lámas of Láhul may marry, the sons belonging to their father's original caste. Lámas sometimes cease to belong to the priesthood, allow their scalp-locks to grow, and are again received as Kanets. These facts show how intimately Hinduism and Buddhism are connected in Láhul. It is still common for both Brahmans and Lámas to be present at weddings and funerals."

It would appear that there is little of Buddhism about the Láhul Lámas save their title. Even in small things the progress of Hinduism is visible. When Dr. Aitchison visited Láhul the people would not as a rule kill an animal, eating only those which died naturally. But when the craving for the fleshpots grew too strong, several combined in the slaughter in order to diminish the crime of each by distributing it over many. Now-a-days sheep and goats are commonly slaughtered without any scruple. Even in 1868 the so-called pure Buddhists freely sacrificed sheep and goats to the *lhas* or local genii, employed Brahmans in many of their ceremonies, and shared in all the superstitions and beliefs in witches and magic of their Hindu brethren. The same change which has taken place in Láhul has apparently been going on in Upper Kanaur, for in 1829, when Captain Gerard visited it, the religion of this tract was most certainly an impure Buddhism, while in the present Census the State of Bashahr returns only one Buddhist among its inhabitants. In the Census of 1868 all the inhabitants of both Láhul and Spiti were returned as Hindus, though Buddhists were separately shown for other districts; and in 1872 Mr. Lyall wrote thus on the subject :—The people of Láhul have now-a-days so much traffic with Hindus that they cannot afford to be out of the pale, and are rapidly adopting all Hindu ideas and prejudices. The process has been going on in some degree ever since the Rájás of Kulu annexed the country, but it has been greatly accelerated of late years by the notice taken by our Government of the Láhulis and their headmen, and by their contact with Hindus more orthodox and exclusive than those of Kulu and Chamba. The force of attraction which Hindu exclusiveness brings to bear upon outlying tribes is enormous, and seems to be in no way weakened by the fact that the Government is in the hands of Christians. That fact of political subjection leaves the Hindus no other vent for their pride of race but this exclusiveness, and therefore heightens its value. Moreover, the consolidation of many Hindu races into one great empire increases the power which Hinduism has always had of drawing outsiders into its circle, for in social matters the empire is Hindu, and as Hindus the Láhulis are free citizens, while as Buddhists and Botias (Tibetans) they would be left out in the cold. The Láhuli now looks upon the name of Boti as a term of reproach. One of the headmen, when in my camp on the borders of Ladákh, met his own brother-in-law, a Boti of Ladákh, and refused to eat with him for fear that my Hindu servants might tell tales against him in Kulu and Kángra.

LAHUL AND ITS PRE-BUDDHIST RELIGIONS.

The three dialects of Láhul are Bunan, Manchat and Tinan. Their relationship to the Mundari languages is exactly the same as that of Kanauri though they possess a Tibetan vocabulary which preserves a phonetic stage of that language much more archaic than any known dialect of Tibetan.

Manchat is also the name of a tract which has preserved an ancient custom, probably Mundari. A slab of stone is put up by the roadside in memory of a deceased person and on many of them is a rock-carving of a human figure in the centre or a portrait of the deceased in relief. Those erected recently have a spot smeared with oil in the centre. In the village temples stone slabs are also found on which are carved rows of figures, often exceeding ten in number. These too are well bathed in oil. At irregular intervals rich families which have lost a member continue to feast the whole village and a slab with these portraits of the dead is placed in the temple in recognition of this. The older slabs represent the ancient costume of Láhul—a frock reaching from the loins to the knees, with a head-dress of feathers for the chiefs similar to that of the North American Indians. In this costume a rock-carving near Kyelang depicts a man hunting the wild sheep.

The most ancient religions of Láhul were probably phallus and snake worship—the cults of the fertilising powers of sun and water. The original phallus was a raw stone, set up in a small grove or near a temple door. It was smeared with oil or butter. The polished stones found in Manchat owe their origin to the introduction of modern Hinduism into the valley—from the Chamba side in the 11th century A. D. The village temples are small huts with a sloping gable roof of shingles and a ram's head, also a symbol of creative power, at the end of the topmost beam. They preserve the oldest type of habitation in Láhul—which was probably evolved when the country was better timbered than it is now.

Human sacrifice at Kyelang was performed to benefit the fields. The peasants had to find a victim in turn—and probably slaves were kept for this purpose. One year a widow's only son was to be sacrificed as she had no servants, but a wandering hermit offered to take his place if he were well fed till the day of execution. On the appointed day he was led with much noise to the wooden idol of the god of the fields whom he challenged to take his life. But the god failed to respond and so the hermit smote him with the executioner's axe and cast the fragments of the idol into the river which carried them down to Gugti where they were caught and put up again. Another version, however, makes the god of the field a rose-tree which was borne down to Gugti by the water and there replanted. Since then the god has had to be content with the sacrifice of a goat and mention of the courageous *láma's* name suffices to terrify him.

In Manchat the last human sacrifice was that of the queen, Rúpi *ráni*, who was buried alive. With her last breath she cursed the name so that no one now lives to a greater age than she had attained when she was immolated.

Between 600 and 1000 A. D. the decline of Buddhism in Kashmír deprived its monks of their revenues and drove many of them to settle in Ladákh and Western Tibet. The destruction of the monastery at Nálanda in the 9th century was its culminating disaster. Lotsava Rinchen-bzango (c. 954) settled in Ladákh and the Kashmíri monks first settled at Sanid in Zangskar and built the Kanika monastery.[1]

Buddhism seems to have entered Láhul from India in the 8th century A. D. The famous Buddhist missionary, Padma Sambhava, is mentioned in connection with its oldest Buddhist monasteries as well as Hindu places of worship in adjacent provinces. He visited Zahor (Mandi) and Gazha (= Garzha). Three such temples are known, *viz.* Gandola at the confluence of the Chandra and Bhága, Kangani in Manchat, and Triloknáth in Pángi-Láhul. They are wooden structures with pyramidal roofs and interesting old wood carvings.

Lamaistic Buddhism entered Láhul in the 11th or 12th century and from about 1150 to 1647 Láhul formed in a loose way part of the Ladákhi empire. The monasteries of this latter type are distinguished by their flat roofs.[2]

The Buddhism of Kanaur.

An account of the form of Buddhism found in Kanaur is given in Vol. III, pp. 447-454, *infra*. To it the following list of the Tibetan gods popularly accepted in Kanaur, in theory if not in practice, may be added, together with a note on divination[3] :—

The Tibetan deities and their mantras *with explanations.*

(1) *Nám-chhrá* (God) or Náráyan : is said to be of white complexion with two hands (holding an umbrella in the right, and with the left a mungoose vomiting diamonds), and riding on a lion called Singé. The *mantra* is :—*Om behi-sharmaṇé swáhá.* 'May God bless us.'

(2) *Láṇgán-darsé* or *Chhog-dak :* the deity Ganesha, the remover of obstacles. He is represented as crimson in colour with an elephant head having a human body with four hands, holding respectively a hook used in driving elephants, a noose as a weapon of war, a boon and a lotus, and having only one tusk. The *mantra* is :—*Om zambálá zálindáé swáká.* 'May God cast away all obstacles and bestow upon us wealth.'

(3) *Táremá* or *Chheringmá :* the goddess of wealth or long life, equivalent to Lakshmí or Mahálakshmí. She is represented as of golden colour, with two hands, holding in the right a spear, and in the left a diamond cup full of jewels, riding on horse-back. The *mantra* is :—*Om birúnákhe choozam dukhé húm hirá háng táre dukhé bishúmáte bimayé swáhá.* 'O thou mother of the world, be pleased to grant us prosperity and long life.'

[1] The monks of Kanika wear the red robe which shews that the yellow robe of such Zangskar monasteries as that at Gargya was not introduced by monks from Kashmir : A. H Francke, *A Hist. of Western Tibet*, p 51.

[2] *Ib.*, pp. 181-191.

[3] Furnished by P. Tika Ram Joshi.

(4) *Dukar*, the Indian Trinity, equivalent to Dattátreya-muni, is represented as of white complexion, with three heads, yellow, white and blue in colour, and eight hands, holding respectively an image of the deity *Hopámed*, an arrow, a thunderbolt, and a boon in the four right hands; in the four left hands, *abhaya*, a noose, a bow and a nectar-cup respectively, and seated in the Padmásana attitude. The *mantra* is:— *Óm shrí panmá latitá bájrá todá hulu hulu húm phat swáhá.* 'O thou reverend sage, promote our welfare, and destroy our enemies.'

(5) *Páldan-lámó*, the supreme goddess, equivalent to Mahákáli, is represented as of dark blue colour with three eyes (one in her forehead) and four hands (holding in the right a naked sword and a human skull full of blood, and in the left a lotus and a long trident), wearing a garland of human heads and a snake of green colour as her sacred thread, riding on a mule, with a green snake for a bridle and a saddle of human skin, and with a crown of five human head-bones with a streak of moon in the centre. Her fierce teeth are exposed as is her tongue, and her eyes are full of indignation. The *mantra* is:— *Óm húm shriyá debá káli káli mahá-kali húm zó.* 'O supreme goddess, keep us from all evil.'

(6) *Dolmá*, a goddess or *devi*, is described as of white complexion, with two hands, offering a boon in the right, and the left in the Abhaya position. She is dressed in a splendid robe wearing many ornaments and much jewellery; seated on a lotus. The *mantra* is:—*Óm táré tu táré turé swáhá.* 'O goddess, thou, who art the remover of worldly troubles, bestowest upon us blessings.'

(7) *Ningmet-chhebe*, the deity of health and long life. The following is a *mantra* of this deity, used by the Tibetans and Kanaur people for securing a long, prosperous and healthy life. It is found in the scripture called *Chhoos*. They believe that whosoever repeats it daily as many times as possible, will enjoy a happy life for 100 years:—

Ó Ningmet-chhebé darzen-chang-rási,
dingmet-khembe wángbó-jámbe-yang,
dudpung málú chomdan-sángwe-dakk,
gásáng-gábe chung-gyán-chung gáfá,
lobzang-dák-párá shyábláswowánde.

(8) (*a*) *Ganbó chhág-du-gbá*, the goddess Tárá, or Tárá-Deví, is described as of blue colour like the forget-me-not, with six hands, a fat short body, three eyes and wearing a lionskin. The *mantra* is:—*Óm shhá húm phat.* 'Turn away enemies.'

(*b*) *Ganbó-chhág-jibá*, Tárá-Deví, has four hands.

(*c*) *Ganbó-chhág-nibá*, Tárá-Deví, has only two hands. In other respects these two are like *Ganbó-chhág-dugbá*, and the *mantras* are the same.

(d) *Gónkar-chhág-ḍugbá,* Tárá-Deví, is said to be of white complexion, but in other respects is like *Ganbó-chhág-ḍughá.* The *mantra* is :—*Óm shum mánî chum maṇi húm phaṭ swáhá.*

(e) *Gaabo-pening chhog-jibá sil-sibá,* Tárá-Deví, is of white complexion, having four heads and four arms and wearing a garland of human heads, but resembling in other respects *Ganbo chhag-dughá.* The *mantra* is :—*Griháṇa payah griháṇa payah, húm phaṭ swáhá, hánáhó bhagawáná bájrá binderánsá húm pháṭ swáhá,* 'O goddess, be pleased to accept this milk, and shower down upon us thy blessings.'

The following is a chant or *mantra,* found in the *chhoss,* to be repeated daily for the success of any business or transaction :—

> *Óm bájrá sáto sámáyá manú pálá ṭinúpá, ṭita ṭitó mewáwá, supkháyó mewawáaná rajá mewáryá, sarbá siddhi mewaryáng, súdang michió dang, hyáryá húm húm phoṭ swáhá.*

The following six chants or *mantras* of the Tibetan scriptures, written in the Tibetan character called Bhúmí, are repeated many times (often more than a hundred) by the Lámas to cure a man suffering from the influence of an evil-spirit, ghost, demon &c. :—

(1) *Óm yámá rájá sádhó méyá,*
yámé darú náyó dáyá,
yadáyó nírá yakkháyá,
chhaní rámá húm húm phaṭ phaṭ swáhá.

(2) *Óm ṭán-gya riká húm phaṭ.*

(3) *Óm dekhyá rátí húm phaṭ.*

(4) *Óm danṭá riká húm phaṭ.*

(5) *Óm bajrá rátí húm pháṭ.*

(6) *Óm muwá ratí húm pháṭ.*

Divination.

Divination by a series of 50 picture cards is practised in Kanaur, as well as in Tibet. The full description of it is too long to be reproduced here, but many of the cards are pictures of gods etc. which are of considerable interest.

For example :—

1. *Pák-pá-jam-pal :* the deity Dharmaráj or Dharamarájá means :—'You will succeed by worshipping your deity.'

2. *Chung-mong-bu-theng-má padminip :* a lady with her son :—'You will get many sons and be successful in your affairs ; any trouble can be averted by adoration of your deity.'

3. *Sán-gyá-mallá,* Ashwini-kumára : the celestial physician :—'You are to attain long life and always succeed, but keep your mind firmly fixed on God.'

4. *Dug-dul* Nága Sheshanága: the cobra :—' This forebodes no good but loss of money, corn and animals, and but danger of illness; by worship of your deity, a little relief may be obtained.'

5. *Sergá-sáji* : the golden hill, Sumeru-parvata :—' You will achieve success ; and if there is fear of illness, it can be removed by worship of your deity.'

6. *Ták sám-shing* : the Celestial tree which grants everything desired :—' You are welcome everywhere ; your desires will be fulfilled but with some delay ; if there is any risk of sickness recovery is to be gained by adoration of your deity.'

7. *Sál-lá-mo* ; the goddess Deví Bhagavati :—' You are to obtain prosperity of every kind ; the king will be pleased with you ; but in the attainment of your object there will be quarrels ; a woman is troublesome to you, but should you agree with her you will be successful.'

8. *Sán-gyá-tán-bá* : the deity Buddha Shákya Singha :—' The king is greatly pleased with you ; your desire will be achieved ; but if you fear illness, then worship your deity steadfastly.'

9. *Gyál-bo* : the king of ghosts, Brahma-rakshasa :—' You will be unsuccessful in every way ; your friends have turned against you ; an evil spirit pursues you ; better engage in God's service, or make a pilgrimage to your deity, then your fate will be all right.'

10. *Nám-gyál-bum-bá* : the nectar-pot, *Amrita-kalasha* :—' The auspices are excellent ; if you are suffering from any illness, worship of your deity will soon restore you to health.'

11. *Rál-di* : a *dodhára-khádga* :—' All your desires will be fulfilled ; you will be blessed with an heir ; you are to receive wealth from the king ; if there is any trouble, it is on account of your kinsmen, and can be only removed by agreeing with them.'

12. *Ḍimo-ḍá-ják* : a female evil spirit, *ḍákini* or *ḍáyan* : —' You are to lose wealth and suffer great trouble ; your relatives are against you ; there is no remedy but to worship your deity steadfastly, and that will indeed give a little relief.'

13. *Dar-se-gyá ḍum* : the thunder-bolt, *basra* :—' He is your enemy whom you take for a friend ; there is some fear from the king, perhaps you may be fined ; your object will not be gained, so it is better for you to adore your deity.'

14. *Yu-ḍon-má* : a goddess, *deví* :—' You are devoted to everyone's welfare, but there is a doubt as to the accomplishment of your desire ; you will be successful but only after great delay ; if you ask about anyone's sickness it is due to the anger of your deity, whose worship will of course remove the trouble.'

15. *Ni-má* : the sun, Surya :—' You earn much, but it is all spent ; your friends and relatives are ungrateful ; at first you will suffer great trouble, but at last you will succeed ; if there is anyone indisposed, then it is owing to the lack of worship of your deity, whose adoration will certainly remove the sickness.'

16. *Dug :* thunder of the cloud, *Megha garjaná :*—'You are welcome to everybody ; you are to be blessed with prosperity ; if there is anyone ill in the family, it is due to his defiling a water-spring, which should be well cleaned, then he will recover.'

17. *Du-chi-mum-bá :* a golden pot, *swarna-kalasha :*—' You are always happy, and your desires will be fulfilled ; should you be suffering from illness ask the help of a physician and worship your deity heartily, then you will be in perfect health.'

18. *Ser-nyá-yu-nyá :* of fish, *mína-yuga :*—' You will get much wealth and many sons, the king will hold you in esteem ; your desire will be fulfilled with but little delay ; if there is anyone sick in the family, then have the worship of your deity duly performed and he will be restored to health.'

19. *Pán-chhenlá :* the king of the Bhlis, *Bhilla-rája :*—' You have great fear of your enemy, but be assured that he will be destroyed ; the king will be pleased with you, and all will love you ; if there is someone ill he should devote some time to the worship of his deity, which will restore him to perfect health.'

20. *Chhu-láng :* a she-buffalo, *Mahishi :*—' You have a quarrel with your kinsmen ; you are to suffer from some discease ; there is no remedy save worship of your deity, by which a little relief may be obtained.'

21. *Sin-morál-chán-má :* a she-cannibal, *Manushya-bhakshiká :*—' You are to lose health and prosperity ; your offspring will never live ; if you ask about anyone's sickness that is due to failure to worship your deity, but if you will heartily adore him there will be some relief.'

22. *Sstpá-Sán-ji :* the golden mountain, *swarṇa parvata :*—' All have enmity with you, even your relatives are against you and you are fond of quarrels ; there is also fear of illness, which is due to your troubling a woman ; should you agree with her, there will be no fear of it.'

23. *Sál-lámó* (2nd) : Baṭuka-Bhairava, the deity Bháírava :—' You have prosperity, servants, and quadrupeds ; your desire will be fulfilled ; should there be anyone sick in the family, it is due to his committing some sin in a temple, and that can be removed by the worship of your deity.'

24. *Mai-khá-ne-cho :* a parrot, *totá* or *súwá :*—' There will be a quarrel ; you will have to suffer much by sickness, which is due to your impurity in the god's service : you should worship your deity steadfastly, then you will get some relief.'

25. *Gi-ling-tá :* a steed :—' You are to lose wealth ; you frequent the society of the wicked, spend money in bad ways ; there is no remedy but to worship your deity, without whose favour you will not be successful.'

26. *Nyán-bá-ḍu-thok :* a mariner or sailor :—' You will fail in your business and have no hope of success at all ; there is risk to health, but if you worship your deity you will get a little relief.'

27. *Shyá-bá-khyi :* a hunting-dog :—'The king is against you ; your friends act like enemies ; should there be someone ill, he will have to suffer much, and for this there is no remedy but to worship your deity, by which you will get a little relief.'

28. *Mám-zá-pyá :* the peacock, *mayúra* :—'You have a dispute with your kinsmen ; your mind is full of anxiety ; loss of money and honour is impending ; all are against you, so it will be well for you to worship your deity heartily.'

29. *Chháng-ná-dar-zé :* the deity Kála-bhairava :—'Fortune is to smile on you ; you will reap a good harvest, get good servants and quadrupeds ; if there is anyone ill in the family, then he will be restored to perfect health by worship of his deity.

30. *Dár-zé :* the thunderbolt, *bajra* :—'All your desires will be fulfilled ; you will be blessed with many sons ; the king will favour you, and your enemies will not succeed in troubling you.'

31. *Dung :* conch-shell : *shaṅkha* :—

32. *Chá-rok :* a crow, *káka, kawwá* :—

33. *Gán-kár-bó :* the Mánas-lake, Mána-sarovara :—
all three of good omen.

34. *Cháng-tak :* the lion, *siṅha* :—a bad omen.

35. *Má-páng-yum-chhó :* a sacred lake, Mána-talái:—a good omen.

36. *Chhok-ten-nák-pó :* a black temple ; *Kálá-mandira* :—a bad omen.

37. *Chá-khyung :* the vehicle of Vishṇu, *garura*, Vishṇu-*ratha* :—
a good omen.

38. *Ṭsú :* a monkey, *bandar, vánara* :—

39. *Yung-rung :* a wheel, *chakra* :—

40. *Chhokten-kárbó :* the temple of the man-lion, *Nrisiṅha mandir* :—
all three good omens.

41. *Chyáng-kú-ro-janmá :* a lion, *siṅha* :—

42. *Nád-pá :* disease, *rogávádha* :—
both bad omens.

43. *Siṅghé :* a lion :—a good one.

44. *Bong-bú :* a camel, *usṭrah, úṅt* :—a very bad one.

45. *Chhot-kang :* A small temple to the Buddhas made on the roof of the home :—a good omen.

46. *Chhumit :* a cascade, *jaladhárá* :—a fairly good one.

47. *Nar-bú* ; the fire, Agní :—a very good one.

48. *Meri-nàk-pó :* the smoke, *dhúmah, dhúwán* :—a bad one.

49. *Dhan-jyut-gibá :* a cow, *gáya, gauh* :—

50. *Rubó :* a ram, *mésha, khárú* :—
both good omens.

The ruling family of Bashahr is, according to the *Shástras,* held to be of divine origin, and the Lamaic theory is that each Rájá of Bashahr is at his death re-incarnated as the Gurú Láma or Gurú of the Lámas, who is understood to be the Dalai Láma of Tibet. There is also another curious legend attached to the Bashahr family. For 61 generations each Rájá had only one son and it used to be the custom for the boy to be sent away to a village and not be seen by his father until his hair was cut for the first time in his sixth year. The idea that the first-born son is peculiarly dangerous to his father's life is not confined to Bashahr. Both these legends originate in the doctrine of the metempsychosis, which is prevalent in the hills of the North-East Punjab and indeed throughout these Provinces.

Section 3.—Jainism.

The following paragraphs are reproduced from Sir Denzil Ibbetson's Census Report of 1883 because they illustrate the position of Jainism at that time. Like Sikhism it was rapidly falling into the position of a mere sect of Hinduism. Like the Sikh, the orthodox Jain intermarries with Hindus, especially with the Vaishnavas,[1] and apparently he does so on equal terms, there being no tendency to form a hypergamous Jain group taking brides from Vaishnavas or other Hindus but not giving their daughters in return, on the model of the Kesdhári Sikhs described in Vol. II, p. 353 *infra* :—

The affinities of the Jain Religion.—The position which the Jain religion occupies with reference to Hinduism and Buddhism has much exercised the minds and pens of scholars, some looking upon it as a relic of Buddhism, while other and I believe far weightier authorities class it as a Hindu sect. In favour of this latter view we have, among others, the deliberate opinions of Horace Wilson and H. T. Colebrooke, who fully discuss the question and the arguments on either side. The latter concludes that the Jains 'constitute a sect of Hindus, differing indeed from the rest in some very important tenets, but following in other respects a similar practice, and maintaining like opinions and observances.'[2] The question of the origin of the religion and of its affinities with the esoteric doctrines of the two rival creeds may be left to scholars. We have seen how much of Hindu belief and practice has been intermingled with the teachings of Buddha as represented by the northern school of his followers; and it is probable that, had Buddhism survived as a distinct religion in India side by side with Brahminism, the admixture would have been infinitely greater. On the other hand, modern Hinduism has probably borrowed much of its esoteric doctrines from Buddhism. It is certain that Jainism, while Hindu in its main outlines, includes many doctrines which lean towards those of Buddha; and it may be that it represents a compromise which sprang into existence during the struggle between Hinduism and Buddhism and the decay of the latter, and that as Rhys Davids says 'the few Buddhists who were left in India at the Muhammadan conquest of Kashmír in the 12th century preserved an ignoble existence by joining the Jain sect, and by adopting the principal tenets as to caste and ceremonial observations of the ascendant Hindu creeds.' Ibbetson, § 255.

But as to its present position, as practised in the Punjab at least, with reference to the two faiths in their existing shape, I conceive that

[1] Speaking roughly the mixed group may be said to be the Bhábras or the main body of that caste in Hoshiárpur. The present writer is now inclined to think that the account of the Bhábras alluded to on page 81 of Vol. II gives a clue to the history of the caste. The Bhábras were originally Jains, recruited from Oswál and Khandilwál Bánias. They were reinforced by *Sikhs* or Saraogis from the Aggarwáls. As a title of some dignity and antiquity Bhábra came to be applied to and assumed by the Oswál, Khandilwál, Aggarwál and any other Bánia group whether orthodox Jains or unorthodox, or not Jains at all but Vaishnavas.

[2] Dr. Buchanan, in his account of the Jains of Canara, one of their present head-quarters, taken from the mouth of their high priest, says: "The Jains are frequently confounded by the Brahmans who follow the Vedas with the worshippers of Buddha, but this arises from the pride of ignorance. So far are the Jains from acknowledging Buddha as their teacher, that they do not think that he is now even a devata, but allege that he is undergoing various low metamorphoses as a punishment for his errors."

there can be no manner of doubt. I believe that Jainism is now as near akin to Hinduism as is the creed of the Sikhs, and that both can scarcely be said to be more than varieties of the parent Hindu faith; probably wider departures from the original type than are Vaishnavism and Saivism, but not so wide as many other sects which, being small and unimportant, are not generally regarded as separate religions. As a fact the Punjab Jains strenuously insist upon their being good Hindus. I have testimony to this effect from the Bhábras of two districts in which every single Bhábra is returned as a Jain; and an Agarwál Bánia, an Extra Assistant Commissioner and a leading member of the Jain Community in Dehli, the Punjab head-quarters of the religion, writes: 'Jains (Saráogis) are a branch of Hindus, and only differ in some religious observances. They are not Buddhists.' Indeed the very word Buddhist is unknown to the great part even of the educated natives of the Province, who are seldom aware of the existence of such a religion.

I think the fact that, till the disputes regarding the Saráogi procession at Dehli stirred up ill-feeling between the two parties, the Hindu (Vaishnava) and Jain (Saráogi) Bánias used to intermarry freely in that great centre of the Jain faith, and still do intermarry in other districts, is practically decisive as to the light in which the people themselves regard the affinities of the two religions. I cannot believe that the members of a caste which, like the Bánias, is more than ordinarily strict in its observance of all caste rules and distinctions and of the social and ceremonial restrictions which Hinduism imposes upon them, standing indeed in this respect second only to the Brahmans themselves, would allow their daughters to marry the followers of a religion which they looked upon as alien to their own. I have already explained how elastic the Hindu religion is, and what wide diversity it admits of under the cloak of sect; and I shall presently show that Sikhism is no bar to intermarriage. But Sikhism is only saved from being a Hindu sect by its political history and importance; while Buddhism is so utterly repugnant to Hinduism in all its leading characteristics, that any approach to it, at any rate in the direction of its social or sacerdotal institutions, would render communion impossible. Even in Láhul, where, as we have seen, Hinduism and Buddhism are so intermingled that it is difficult to say where the one begins and the other ends, intermarriage is unheard of. I shall briefly describe the leading tenets and practices of the Jains; and I think the description will of itself almost suffice to show that Jainism is, if not purely a Hindu sect, at any rate nearer to that religion than to the creed of Buddha.[1]

[1] It is true that in Rájpútána considerable animosity prevails between the Hindus and the Jains. There is a saying that "it is better to jump into a well than to pass a Jain ascetic on the road;" and another: "A Hindu had better be overtaken by a wild elephant than take refuge in a Jain temple; and he may not run through the shadow of it, even to escape a tiger." So too, many of the later Vaishnava scriptures are very bitter against the errors of the Jains. But hatred of the fiercest kind between the rival sects of the same faith is not unknown to history; and at one time Jainism was the dominant belief over a considerable part of India. In Gújarát (Bombay), on the other hand, "the partition between Hindu and Jain is of the very narrowest description, and cases are not uncommon in which intermarriage between the two sections takes place. The bride, when with her Jain husband, performs the household ceremonies according to the ritual of that form of religion, and on the frequent occasions when she has to make a temporary sojourn at the paternal abode, she reverts to the rites of her ancestors, as performed before her marriage."—*Bombay Census Report.*

The tenets of the Jains.—The chief objects of Jain reverence are twenty-four beatified saints called Arhats or Tirthankárs, who correspond with the Buddhas of the northern Buddhists and of Vedantic Hinduism, but are based upon the final beatitude of the Hindus rather than upon the final absorption preached by Buddha, and are wholly unconnected with the Gautamic legend, of even the broad outlines of which the Punjab Jains are entirely ignorant. Of these saints, the first, Rishabnáth, the twenty-third, Párasnáth, and the twenty-fourth, Mahávír, are the only ones of whom we hear much; while of these three again Párasnáth is chiefly venerated. Rishabnáth is supposed to be an incarnation of Vishnu, and is worshipped in that capacity at his temple in the south-west of Mewár by Hindus and Jains in common.[1] But besides these saints, the Jains, unlike the Buddhists, recognise the whole Hindu Pantheon, including the Puranic heroes, as divine and fit objects of worship, though in subordination to the great saints already mentioned, and place their images in their temples side by side with those of their Arhats. They have indeed added to the absurdities of the Hindu Olympus, and recognise 64 Indras and 22 Devís. They revere serpents and the *lingam* or Priapus, and in many parts ordinarily worship in Hindu temples as well as in their own.[2] Like the Buddhists they deny the divine origin of the Hindu Vedas; but unlike them they recognise the authority of those writings, rejecting only such portions of them as prescribe sacrifice and the sacred fire, both of which institutions they condemn as being inimical to animal life. Like the Buddhists they deny the Hindu doctrine of purification from sin by alms and ceremonies, and reject the Hindu worship of the Sun and of fire except at weddings, initiations, and similar ceremonies, where they subordinate their objections to the necessity of employing Brahmans as ministrants. The monastic system and celibate priesthood of the Buddhists are wholly unknown to them, and they have, like the Hindus, a regular order of ascetic devotees who perform no priestly functions; while their *parohits* or family priests, and the ministrants who officiate in their temples and conduct the ceremonial of their weddings, funerals, and the like, must necessarily be Brahmans, and, since Jain Brahmans are practically unknown, are always Hindus.[3] The idols of the Jain saints are not daily bathed, dressed, and fed, as are the Hindu idols; and if fruits are presented to them it is not as food, but as an offering and mark of

Ibbetson, § 255.

[1] Gautama Buddha is also said by the Hindus to be an incarnation of Vishnu who came to delude the wicked; but the Buddhists of course strenuously deny the assertion.

[2] "In Upper India the ritual in use is often intermixed with formulæ from the Tantras, and belonging more properly to the Saiva and Sákta worship. Images of the Bhairavas and Bhairavis, the fierce attendants on Siva and Káli, take their place in Jain temples; and at suitable seasons the Jains equally with the Hindus address their adoration to Sarasvati and Devi." At Mount Abu several of the ancient Jain inscriptions begin with invocations to Siva. (Wilson's *Hindu Sects.*)

[3] Horace Wilson observes that this fact "is the natural consequence of the doctrine and example of the Arhats, who performed no rites, either vicariously or for themselves, and gave no instructions as to their observance. It shows also the true character of this form of faith, that it was a departure from established practices, the observance of which was held by the Jain teachers to be matter of indifference, and which none of any credit would consent to regulate; the laity were therefore left to their former priesthood as far as outward ceremonies were concerned."

respect. The Jains, unlike the Buddhists, observe in theory the twelve Sanskáras or ceremonies of purification prescribed by the Hindu creed from the birth to the death of a male, though in both religions many of them are commonly omitted; but they reject the Hindu Sráddhas or rites for the repose of the spirit Their ceremonial at weddings and their disposal of the dead are identical with those of the Hindus and differ from those of the Buddhists; and, unlike the latter, they follow the Hindu law of inheritance, calling in learned Brahmans as its exponents in case of disputes.[1] The Jains observe with the greatest strictness all the rules and distinctions of caste which are so repugnant to Buddhism, and many if not all wear the Brahminical thread; in the Punjab the religion is practically confined to the mercantile or Vaisya castes, and considerable difficulty is made about admitting members of other castes as proselytes. Their rules about intermarriage and the remarriage of widows are no less strict than those of their Hindu brethren, with whom they marry freely. The extravagant reverence for relics which is so marked a feature of Buddhism is wholly unknown to the Jains, who agree with the Hindus in their veneration for the cow. They carry the reverence for animal life, which is taught by the Hindu and practised by the Buddhist, to an absurd extent; their devotees carry a brush with which they sweep their path, are forbidden to move about or eat when the sun is down or to drink water without straining, and many of them wear a cloth over their mouths, lest they should tread upon, swallow, or inhale an insect or other living thing.[2] Indeed some of them extend the objection to taking life to plants and flowers. 'To abstain from slaughter is the highest perfection; to kill any living thing is sin.' The Jains, unlike the Buddhists, observe all the Hindu fasts and attend the Hindu places of pilgrimage; though they also have holy places of their own, the most important being the mountain of Samet near Pachete in the hills between Bengal and Behar, which was the scene of Párasnáth's liberation from earthly life, the village of Pápauri, also in Behar, where the Arhat Vardhamána departed from this world, and the great Jain temples on Mount Abu in Rájpútána and Mount Girinár in Káthiawár. In no case do they make pilgrimages to the holy places of Buddhism.

I have been able to collect but little information about the actual practice of the Jain religion by the mass of its modern followers, as distinguished from its doctrines and ceremonials set forth in the scriptures of the faith. The Jains, and particularly the orthodox or Digambara sect, are singularly reticent in the matter; while the religion being almost wholly confined to the trading classes, and very largely to cities, has not come under the observation of the Settlement Officers to whom we are indebted for so large a part of our knowledge of the people. But the Jains are the most generally educated class in the Punjab, and it is probable that the religion has preserved its original form comparatively unaltered. Horace Wilson, however, says of the Jain *Jatis* or

[1] See Bombay High Court rulings *Bhagwan Das Tejmal* v. *Rajmal*, X (1873), pp. 241 *et seq.*, and rulings there quoted. But see also Privy Council case *Sheo Singh Lal* v *Dakho and Marori*, Indian Law Reports, I, Allahabad (1876-78), pp. 688 *et seq.*

[2] Elphinstone says that the Buddhist priests also observe all these precautions; but I think the statement must be mistaken.

ascetics :—'Some of them may be simple enthusiasts; many of them, however, are knaves, and the reputation which they enjoy all over India as skilful magicians is not very favourable to their general character; they are in fact not unfrequently charlatans, pretending to skill in palmistry and necromancy, dealing in empirical therapeutics and dabbling in chemical or rather alchemical manipulations.'

Since these paragraphs were written not only has a great deal more knowledge of Jainism and its teaching been acquired by European scholarship, but the Jains themselve have in the last two or three decades displayed considerable intellectual activity. Whatever the causes of this may be, and one of them at least has been the stimulus of contact with western inquiry and thought, it has resulted in the formation of new groups or the revival of old groups under new names or the adaptation of old names to new ideals. The attempt to describe the Jains as a caste and to unravel their sects made in Vol. III, pp. 340-9 *infra*, fails because Jainism, like all other living creeds, is in a state of flux. Recently the Sthánakwási group has come to the front. In 1901 the term Thánakwási was returned as a mere synonym of *sadh-márgi* or Dhúndia, an ascetic of extreme orthodoxy.[1] But the Sthánakwásis now number 22 per cent. of the Jain population of the Punjab, and are classed by Pandit Hari Kishan Kaul, C. I. E., as a branch of the Swetámbaras quite distinct from the Dhúndias.[2] Ibbetson, who does not allude to the Sthánakwási, thus describes the Dhúndias :—"A more modern sect is the Dhúndia, so called because its followers were persecuted by the orthodox and compelled to take refuge in ruins or *dhúnd*. It was with these ascetics that the practice of hanging a cloth or *patti* before the mouth originated; and the Terahpanthis and Dhúndias[3] carry their regard for animals to extremes, teaching that no living thing should be interfered with, that a cat should be permitted to catch a mouse, or a snake to enter the cradle of a child. It would appear that the Dhúndias are wholly celibate ascetics, and include no laity. They altogether renounce idols, and call those who venerate them *pujári* or 'worshippers.' They are, I believe, confined to the Swetámbara section, the Digambaras laughing at the cloth, as breeding more insects in the mouth than it prevents from entering it." By *pujári* may have been meant *pujera*. The priests of the Dhúndias are called *puj* or *sri puj*.

Classification of the Jain sects and orders.

Sir Edward Maclagan suggested the following classification of the Jain sects :—

Digambara	...	Tera-panthi Bis-panthi Swetámbara	Mandirpanthi or Pujári.
Swetámbara	...	Dhúndia Baístola Tera-panthi	Dhúndia.

[1] Vol. III, p. 343 *infra*.
[2] Pb. Census Rep., 1911, § 229.
[3] This should read "Tera-panthi sect of the Dhúndias."

But, putting aside the non-idolatrous Sthánakwásis and Dhúndias,[1] the idol-worshipping Jains may be tentatively classified as follows :—

I. Digambara, 'sky-clad' or naked, or perhaps tawny clothed. This, according to Ibbetson, is the orthodox sect, and has preserved the religion in more of its original purity than have the Swetámbara. The idols of the Digambara are naked, their ascetics are supposed to reject clothing, though now-a-days they wear coloured raiment, only throwing it aside when they receive or eat food, and they hold that no woman can attain salvation.

The Digambaras include two great sub-sects :—

(*i*) The Bíspanthi, who worship standing before naked idols, and refuse to burn lamps before them. It is not quite clear what is the difference between this distinction and that into Digambaras and Swetámbaras. Horace Wilson notes that the Bíspanthis are said by some to be the orthodox Digambaras, of whom the Terahpanthis are a dissenting branch.[2]

(*ii*) The Terapanthi, who clothe their idols, worship seated, burn lamps before them, but present no flowers or fresh fruit to them, holding it to be a sin to take away even vegetable life, though they will eat vegetables if anybody will give them ready cut and prepared for cooking.

II. The Swetámbara or white-clothed, whose idols are clothed in white, as are their ascetics, except perhaps in the last stage which few if any attain, and women are capable of beatitude; indeed they believe the 19th Arhat to have been a woman, and so represent her in many of their temples.

The Swetámbara have no recognised sub-sects, but their ascetics generally known as *sádhus* appear to have a special sub-division called Sambegi or Samegi. The *sádhus* form a superior order or the superior degree in an order, the *jatis* being an inferior order or novitiates in the order in which the *sádhu* holds the higher degree.[3]

The Digambaras also have ascetics, called *muni*[4] who appear to be identical with the *sádhus*, described in Vol. III, p. 344 *infra*. In both of these main sects the laity is or ought to be called Saráogi,[5] the more

[1] Including (*i*) the Tera-panthi sect which will not interfere with anything living, but not interfere with a cat catching a mouse, and so on; and (*ii*) the Baistola who go a step further and will interfere to protect one animal against another.

[2] Mr. Fagan also affirms that the Bíspanthi are the more orthodox. They are divided into 4 sub-sects—Nandi, Sain, Singh and Bir called after the names of their *rishis*—according to him: Pb. *Census Report*, 1892, § 123. But these may be sub-*orders*. The Bíspanthi reverence the *gurú*, the 24 Arhats and the *Shástras*.

On the other hand the Tera-panthis allow the Arhats and *Shástras*, but refuse to acknowledge that there is any *gurú* other than the *Shástras* themselves, a doctrine which reminds us of the orthodox Sikh teaching after Gurú Gobind Singh's installation of the sacred *Granth* as the *gurú* of the Sikhs.

[3] *Cf.* Vol. III, pp. 341-2.

[4] Maclagan, § 122.

[5] Ibbetson translates Saráwak by 'laity.' *Cf.* Maclagan, § 122.

honorific term Bhábra being reserved for laymen of higher spiritual standing or priority of conversion.

The Jain caste system.

The doctrines which divide the Digambara from the Swetámbara are abstruse and as yet not fully understood, but the former hold that the Arhats were saints from birth and so their images should be naked and unadorned, while the Swetámbara hold that they only attained sanctity on reaching manhood and so should be clothed and decked with jewels.[1] The disruption of the Jain community will be intelligible, though far from fully explained, when we come to consider their philosophy, but before doing so a brief note on the caste-system of the Jains may be usefully interpolated.

According to Sir Denzil Ibbetson "nearly 99 per cent. of the Jains in the Punjab belong to the trading classes and almost exclusively to the Bánia and Bhábra castes, the latter being chiefly confined to the northern Divisions. I believe that Oswál Bánias are almost without an exception Swetámbara Jains, and that such of the Kandelwal Bánias and Bhábras as are Jains also belong to this sect. The Agarwál Bánias, on the other hand, are, I understand, invariably Digambaras. The Mahesri Bánias are seldom if ever Jains.[2] Mr. Lawrence Assistant Agent to the Governor-General at Mount Abu, to whose kindness I am indebted for much information collected on the spot at Ajmer, the great centre of Jainism in those parts, tells me that there the Jains are divided into two sects, the Digambaras or Saráogis, and the Swetámbaras or Oswáls, and he confirms the assertion after repeating his inquiries at my request There is no doubt whatever that 'Oswál' is a tribal and not a sectarian name, and is quite independent of religion; and that the term Saráogi properly applies to the whole of the Jain laity of whatever sect. But the fact that Oswál and Swetámbara are in Ajmer used as synonymous shews how strictly the tribe adheres to its sect. This erroneous use of the words apparently extends to some parts of the Punjab The Bhábras of Hushyárpur, who are of course Swetámbaras, state distinctly that all Jains are Saráogis, themselves included; but a Bhábra of Gurdáspur emphasized his assertion that no Agarwál could become a Bhábra by pointing out that the former were all Saráogis. On the other hand Mr Wilson writes that in Sirsa, on the Rájputána border, the words Oswál and Saráogi, which according to Mr. Lawrence express in Ajmer the two poles of Jainism, are 'used as almost convertible terms.' The matter seems to need clearing up. The real fact seems to be that Agarwáls belong so invariably to the Digambara and Oswáls to the Swetámbara sect, that the term Oswal is used for the latter while Saráogi is applied to the former and more orthodox sect only.[3] There is a local tradition that Párasnáth, the probable founder of the Swetámbara sect, was an Oswál of Osia or Osnagar in Jodhpur, Ibbetson, § 259.

[1] Maclagan, § 122.

[2] The very term Mahesri denotes that they are Vaishnava *Hindus*: H. A. R.

[3] So in Sindh and Gújarát the tribal name Mahesri is used to distinguish Hindu from Jain Bánias.

the place from which the Oswáls take their name; but the Jain scriptures say that he was born at Benáres and died in Behar."

The same authority points out that the Swetámbara and Digambara do not intermarry, and the Bhábras do not intermarry with Saráogis.[1] But the Swetámbara and Dhúndia are said to intermarry.[2] These restrictions are purely sectarian, but they may well be accentuated by tribal distinctions. However this may be the sectarianism of the Jains does not appear to have relaxed their caste system but to have introduced into it new restrictions on intermarriage. The Jain tenets have however had other important social consequences. Not only is monogamy the general rule, but the survivor of a married couple should not marry again and this ideal is followed to some extent by Hindus in the whole south-eastern Punjab. Women also hold a better position in Jainism than they do in most Hindu castes.

The Jain philosophy.

Jainism, like Buddhism, is a monastic religion which denies the authority of the Vedas and is regarded by the Brahmans as heretical. The Jains comprise a laity and a monastic order, and are also divided into two great sub-sects, the Swetámbaras or 'White-robes', and the Digambaras or 'Sky-clad' as the monks of the latter went about naked until the Muhammadans compelled them to adopt a loin cloth. Their dogmatic differences are trivial, and they differ more in conduct.

Jainism goes back to a very remote period and to those primitive currents of religious and metaphysical speculation which gav rise to the oldest philosophies of the Sankhya and Yoga, and also to Buddhism, but while it shares in the theoretical pessimism of those systems and in liberation, their practical ideal, it realises their principles in a different way. Life in the world, perpetuated by the transmigration of the soul, is regarded as essentially bad and painful, and our aim must be to put an end to it. This will be attained when we attain to right knowledge. Like Sankhya and Yoga, Jainism recognises a dualism of matter and soul. Souls are principally all alike substances (monads) characterized by intelligence, connexion with matter causing the differences actually in them. Matter is a something capable of becoming anything, as in the Sankhya. But Jainism has worked out these general metaphysical principles on its own lines, upon animistic ideas and popular notions of a cruder and more primitive character than the Sankhya, which adopted Brahmanical ideas. Jainism being like Buddhism originally an order of monks outside the pale of Brahmanism has often been confounded with it, but it rejects the Buddhist views that all things are transitory and that there is no absolute or permanent Being. It is at least as old as Buddhism, for the canons of the latter sect speak of the rival sect under its old name of Niganthas[3] and of Nátaputta, an epithet of the last Jain prophet, Vardhamána Mahávíra, its leader in Buddha's time. Mahavíra indeed was probably somewhat older than Buddha. He was not however the founder of the sect, and no such traditions as make

[1] Vol. II, p. 81 *infra*.

[2] *Ib.*, p. 349.

[3] Sanskr. Nirgrantha. For what follows Jacobi's art. in the *Encyclopadia of Religion and Ethics* has been freely drawn upon.

Buddha the author of a new religion are preserved of him He followed an established faith, became a monk and in twelve years attained perfect knowledge (*kevala*). His predecessor Párshva, the last but one of the Tirthankaras, has better claims to be considered the founder of Jainism. He died 250 years before Mahávíra. His predecessor, Arishtanemi, is said to have died 84,000 years before the latter's *nirvána* and so can hardly be regarded as a historical personage. He was the 22nd Tírthankara and is connected with Krishna by relationship in the legend.

Jain philosophy is abstruse. It is based on the theory of the 'Indefiniteness of Being' which is upheld by a very strange dialectical method called *Syádváda* to which the Jains attach so much importance that it is frequently used as a synonym for the Jain system itself.

Supplementary to this is the doctrine of the *nayas* or ways of expressing the nature of things. All these are one-sided and contain but a part of the truth.

Metaphysically all things, *dravya* or substances, are divided into 'lifeless,' *ajívakáya*, and 'lives' or 'souls,' *jíva*. The former comprise space, *akása*, two subtle substances, *dharma* and *adharma*, and matter, *pudgala*. Space affords room for souls and matter to subsist, *dharma* enables then to move or be moved, *adharma* to rest. In primitive speculation the two latter terms seem to have denoted the two invisible fluids which cause sin (*pápa*) and merits (*púnya*), respectively Space again is divided into *lokákása*, occupied by the world of things and its negative, the absolute void. *Dharma* and *adharma* are co-extensive with the world, and so no soul or atom can get beyond the world as outside it neither could move or rest without their aid. Matter is eternal and consists of atoms, but it is indeterminate in its nature and may become anything, as earth, fire etc.

Different from matter are the souls, which are infinite in number. The whole world is literally filled with them. They are substances and, as such, eternal, but are not of definite size, contracting or expanding according to the dimensions of the body in which they are incorporated for the time being. Their characteristic is intelligence which may be obscured but never destroyed. They are of two kinds, mundane (*samsárin*) and liberated (*mukta*). The former are still subject to the cycle of birth, the latter have accomplished absolute purity, will be embodied no more, dwell in perfection at the top of the universe and have no more to do with worldly affairs. They have reached *nirvána*, *nirvriti* or *mukti*.

A cardinal doctrine of Jainism is the evil influence of *karma*. Matter is of two kinds, gross which we can perceive, and subtle, beyond the ken of our senses. The latter, for instance, is that matter which is transformed into the different forms of *karma*. Subtle matter ready to be transformed into *karma* pours into the soul by influx (*ásrava*). A soul harbours passions (*kasháya*), which like a viscous substance retain this subtle matter, and combines with it, by *bandha* (combination). This subtle matter in such combination is transformed into the 8 kinds of *karma* and forms a kind of subtle body, *karmanasharíra*, which clings to the soul in all its future births and determines its individual lot. But as it has been caused, so *karma* in its turn causes painful or pleasant conditions and events which the individual must undergo. Having thus produced its due effect, the *karma* matter is purged from the soul by *nirjará* or 'purging off.' The *bandha* and *nirjará* processes go on simultaneously, and thereby the soul is forced to continue its mundane existence. After death it goes, with its *karmanasharira*, straightway to the place of its new birth and assumes its new body, contracting or expanding according to its size.

Embodied souls are living beings, and their classification is of great practical as well as theoretical interest to the Jains. Their highest duty, *parama dharma*, being not to kill any living beings, *ahinsa*, they must learn the various forms which life may possess. The highest have five senses, and such are the vertebrates. Others may have fewer, and the lowest have only the sense of touch. Most insects have two, *e.g.* bees have the senses of touch and sight The higher animals, men, denizens of heaven, and the gods possess in addition an internal organ or mind (*manas*) and are therefore rational (*samjnin*), while the lower animals are *asamjnin*. The Jain notions about beings with only one organ are in part peculiar to themselves. As the four elements are animated by souls, so particles of earth, water etc., are the body of souls called earth-lives, water-lives and so on. These elementary lives live, die and are re-born, in the same or another elementary body. They may be gross or subtle, and the latter are invisible. The last class of one-organed lives are plants; in some species each plant is the body of one soul only, but of other species each plant is an aggregation of embodied souls which have all functions of life, such as nutrition and respiration, in common. That plants have souls is a belief shared by other Indian philsophies, but the Jains have developed this theory in a remarkable way. Plants in which only one soul is embodied are always gross, and can only exist in the habitable world; but those of which each is a colony of plant-lives may also be subtle and, being invisible, may be distributed all over the world. Such plants are called *nigoda*, and are composed of an infinite number of souls forming a very small cluster, have respiration and nutrition in common, and experience the most exquisite pains. Innumerable *nigodas* form a globule, and with them the whole space of the world is closely packed, as a box is filled with powder. The *nigodas* furnish the supply of souls in place of those who have reached *nirvána*. But an infinitesimal fraction of a single *nigoda* has sufficed to replace all the souls liberated since the beginningless past down to the present, so the *sansára* will never be empty of living beings.

Mundane beings are also divided or cross-divided into four grades (*gati*), *viz*. denizens of hell, animals, men and gods, into which beings are born according to their merits or demerits.

The theory of *karma* being the key-stone of the Jain system merits fuller explanation. The natural qualities of soul are *jnána* (= *gyán*, profound reflection) or perfect knowledge, intuition or faith (*darshana*), highest bliss and all kinds of perfections, but these inborn qualities are obscured in mundane souls by the *karma*-matter. When it has penetrated the soul it is transformed into 8 kinds (*prakriti*) of *karma* singly or severally which form the *kármanasharíra*, just as food is transformed by digestion. These 8 kinds include *gotra*, *i.e.*, that which determines the race, caste, family, social standing &c. of the individual: *áyuska*, which determines his length of life as a hell-being, man, god or animal; and *náma*, which produces the various elements which collectively make up an individual existence, *e.g.* the body with its general and special faculties etc. Each kind of *karma* has also predestined limits of time within which it must take effect and be purged off. Connected with this theory of *karma*-working is that of the six *leshyás*. The totality of *karma* amalgamated by a soul induces on it a transcendental colour, which our eyes cannot perceive. This is called *leshyá*, and it may be black, blue or grey, which are bad, and yellow, red or white, which are good 'characters' morally.[1]

The individual state of the soul is produced by its inborn nature and the vitiating action of *karma*, and this is its developmental or *párinámika* state. But there are other states which refer only to the behaviour of the *karma*. Ordinarily *karma* takes effect and produces its proper results: then the soul is in the *audayika* state. But by proper efforts *karma* may be neutralized (*úpashamita*) for a time, though it is still present, then the soul is in the *aupashamika* state. When it is annihilated, the soul is in the *kshapita* state, which is necessary for reaching *nirvána*. The *ksháyika* and *aupashamika* are the states of holy men, but ordinary good men are in a *ksháyopashamika* in which some *karma* is annihilated, some neutral, and some still active. This doctrine has an important bearing on practical Jain ethics. The whole apparatus of monastic conduct is required to prevent the formation of new *karma*, and it is also stopped by austerities (*tapas*) which, moreover, annihilate old *karma* speedily.

Jain ethics has for its end the realisation of *nirvána* or *moksha*, and to attain it the possession of the three jewels of right faith, knowledge and conduct is essential. Of first importance are the 5 vows (*vratas*), not to kill, lie, steal, indulge in sexual intercourse, and to renounce all interest in worldly things, especially to keep no property These are the 5 great vows (*mahávrata*) taken by every monk on entering the order, or, as it is called, taking *díkshá*. Laymen should also observe them as far as conditions permit, but if they were to observe all of them they could not go about their business. So they may observe the small vows (*anuvrata*) and refrain from intentionally killing living things for food, pleasure or gain and so on. A layman may, however, take one of the following particular vows (*shílavrata*) :—he may limit the distance to which he will go in any direction (*digvirati*) ; abstain from engaging in anything that does not strictly concern him ; set a measure to his food, drink and anything he enjoys, besides avoiding grosser pleasures (these 3 vows are called *gunavrata*) ; he may also reduce the area in which he may move (*deshavirata*) ; give up, by sitting motionless and meditating on holy

[1] Jacobi points out that the belief in colours of the soul seems to be very old as evidenced by the expressions, 'a black soul,' 'a bright soul' which were apparently understood in a literal sense.

things, all sinful actions at stated times (*sámáyika*); live as a monk on the 8th, 11th or 15th day of the lunar fortnight at least once a month (*paushadhopavása*); and provide for monks. These 4 last vows are called *shikshávrata* or disciplinary. Eating by night is forbidden to all Jains, monks or laymen, as are certain kinds of food. The rules for a voluntary death have a similar end in view, *viz.* to enable laymen to participate in the merits of monastic life without absolutely renouncing the world. Jainism differed from early Buddhism in that it regarded the lay state as preliminary to, and in many cases a preparation for, the monastic life, instead of regarding the laity as outsiders. But in modern times a change seems to have come about in this respect as the monastic order is now recruited chiefly from novices entering it at an early age, not from laymen in general. Nevertheless the principle that the duties of the laity differ only in degree, not in kind, from those of the monks, has contributed greatly to the stability of Jainism. Monastic discipline is elaborate[1] but not as a rule severe or grotesque. In Jain asceticism *yoga* means the activity of body, speech and mind through which *karma*-matter pours into the soul and to prevent this *ásrava* it is necessary to regulate those activities by the 3 *guptis* or guardings of the mind etc. The monk must also observe the 5 *samitis*, *i.e.* he must be cautious in walking etc., lest he kill or hurt any living thing. He must avoid vices and endure discomfort and hardship without flinching. The last item in his curriculum is *tapas* or asceticism, but it must be practised in the right way and with right intentions for there are also 'austerities of fools,' *bálatapas*, through which temporary or temporal merits, such as supernatural powers, birth as a god etc., may indeed be acquired, but the highest good can never be attained. *Tapas* is one of the most important institutions in Jainism, and it is either external or internal. Among the former austerities fasting is the most conspicuous and it has been developed into a fine art. Its usual form is to eat only one meal every 2nd, 3rd, and 4th day and so on down to half a year. Another form is to starve oneself to death. Other forms of abstinence are also practised and to the same category belong also sitting in secluded spots for meditation and the postures taken up during it. Internal austerities include confession and repentance. Greater sins must be confessed to a superior (*álochaná*) and repented of. In less serious cases penance consists in standing erect in a certain position for a given time (*káyotsarga*), but for graver transgressions the superiors prescribe the penance and in the worst cases a new ordination of the guilty monk. Contemplation (*dhyána*) is the most important spiritual exercise. Contemplation may be evil or good and the latter is of two kinds, religious (*dharma*) and pure (*shukla*). The former leads to intuitive cognition not only of religious truths but of other things hidden from common mortals, and the accuracy of knowledge in all kinds of science claimed in the sacred books and later treatises is to be ascribed in great measure to this intuition. Pure contemplation leads through four stages to final emancipation, and at the last stage when the wordly existence is drawing rapidly to its close the remaining *karma* may be suddenly consumed by a kind of explosion called *samudghâta*. Then in the last

[1] For the *Kalpa-Sutra*, an old collection of disciplinary rules for Jaina monks, see *Ind. Ant.*, 1910, p. 257 f.

stage all *karma* being annihilated and all activities having ceased the soul leaves the body and ascends to the top of the universe where the liberated souls stay for ever. Pure contemplation however is not by itself a means of attaining liberation but only the last link in a long chain of preparation and only *kevalins*, 'those who have reached omniscience', can enter into the last two stages which lead directly to liberation. The last man to attain *kevala* was Jambúsvámin, the disciple of Mahávira's disciple Sudharman, and he was liberated on his death. Hence during the rest of the present Avasarpini period no body will be born who will reach *nirvána* in the same existence though *nirvána* is necessarily preceded by twelve years of self-mortification of the flesh which should be the closing act of a monk's career. The Jains also attach great importance to the doctrine of the fourteen *gunasthánas* or fourteen steps which lead from total ignorance and wrong belief to absolute purity of the soul and final liberation.

The terms *ásrava* or pouring in and *samvara* or stoppage are as old as Jainism, and from it the Buddhists must have borrowed the former term. But they use it in a different sense and instead of *ásrava* they employ the term *ásravakshaya* or 'destruction of the *ásrava* for they do not regard the *karma* as subtle matter and deny the existence of a soul into which it could have influx. In Buddhism *samvara* denotes 'restraint,' as in *sílasamvara* 'restraint under the moral law.' This seems to prove that Jainism is considerably older than Buddhism.

The monk's outfit is restricted to bare necessities, clothes, a blanket, and alms-bowl, a stick, a broom to sweep the ground, a piece of cloth to cover the mouth when speaking lest insects should enter it. The man's outfit is the same but they have additional clothes. The Digambara uses peacock's feathers instead of a broom. Monks shave the head, or preferably remove the hair by plucking it, a rite peculiar to the Jains and necessary at particular times. Originally the monks had to lead a wandering life except during the monsoon when they recessed at one place—compare the Buddhist *vassa*. But this ordinance has been modified owing to the institution of convents, *upáshraya*, corresponding to the Buddhist *viháras*. The Swetámbara as a rule only visit places where there are such *upásrayas* and in them the monks preach to laymen. A monk's duties are arduous, *e.g.* he should only sleep 3 hours in the night and devote the rest of the day to repentance of sins, study, begging, the removal of insects from his clothes etc. and meditation. When the novice (*shaiksha*) is initiated he takes the vows (*vratádana*), renounces the world (*pravarajyá*) and takes *díksha*. The most important rite at his initiation is the shaving or pulling out of the hair under a tree. He may then rise to the degrees of *upádhyáya*, *ácharya*, *váchaka*, *ganin* etc. according to his qualifications and functions as a teacher and superior.

The Jain cosmography differs widely from that of the Brahmans, especially with regard to the upper spheres or heavens. The world has in time neither beginning nor end. In space the Universe occupies the part called Lokákásha as distinguished from the absolute void. It is figured as a spindle resting on half of another, or as a woman with her arms akimbo. Older still is the comparison with a man: the earth's disk is in the lower part of the middle and forms the man's waist, below it are the hells and above it the upper regions. These regions are too numerous to be detailed here, but in the centre of the earth itself towers Mt. Meru, 100,000 *yojanas* high, round which revolve suns, moons and stars. Immediately above its summit begins the threefold system of heavenly regions called Vimanas, the abodes of the Vaimánika gods, which number 26 in all. In Ishatprágbhára, the highest, dwell the souls in liberation.[1]

As the soul by itself has an upward gravity and will, if cleansed of all *karma*, rise in a straight line to this heaven on leaving the body, the Jains permit religious suicide in two cases, though they condemn *bálamarana* or 'unwise death' and recommend *panditamarana* or a 'wise death.' In the first case if a Jain contracts a mortal disease or is in danger of certain death he may resort to self-starvation and a monk should do so rather than break the rules of his order or when he cannot sustain the austerities prescribed. In the second a pious layman may go through a regular course of religious life, the phases of which are the 11 standards (*pratimá*), the first being observed for one month, the second for two, and so on. In the last standard, which he must observe for 11 months, he becomes practically a monk and at its end abstains from all food and devotes himself to self-mortification, patiently awaiting death which will ensue within a month. In the case of a monk the period of self-mortification lasts 12 years instead of as many months, but during it he should try to ward off premature death. At the end of this period he should abstain from all food and the severance of the soul from the body may be brought about by three different methods in two of which the movements of the limbs are restricted.[2]

A system of theology and mythology so rich in ideas naturally produced an equal variety of religious symbolism in art and Jain iconography is as highly developed as Buddhist. But the subject has not yet been fully studied. Some notes on it are given by Prof. D. R. Bhandarkar,[3] but complete explanations are lacking. It appears however that a *kevalin's* place in heaven is represented on earth by a *samavasarana*, a shrine with three ramparts, the innermost of gems with battlements of rubies, constructed by the Vaimánikas, the second of gold with battlement of gems, constructed by the Jyotiskas or gods of Sun, Moon, stars etc. and the outer of silver with battlements of gold, built by Bhavanapatis.[3] All the elaborate architecture and art lavished on such a building have their meanings, as have the processional entries and ritual Animals, it should be noted, appear to be admitted to the shrine, though not to its inmost rampart.[4] The whole picture of such a shrine drawn in the manuals used by Jain artists is an extraordinarily comprehensive one of all nature joining in the worship of one who has attained to perfect knowledge and listening to his teaching.

[1] E. R. E, Vol. 4, pp. 160-1, *Jain Cosmography* by H. Jacobi.

[2] *Ib.*, 4, pp. 484-5.

[3] *Ind. Ant.*, 1911, p. 125 f. and p. 153 f.

[4] *Ib.*, pp. 157-8. It may be conjectured that these are the higher animals.

The doctrine of *karma* lent itself equally to the construction of countless tales which pointed a moral, inculcating reverence for life in all its forms and the need for self-purification. These tales were embodied in stone reliefs whose interpretation is being slowly worked out by the aid of such Jain scriptures as the *Tírthakalpa* just as the Buddhist sculptures are being translated with the help of the *Játakas*. The story of the princess who was born a kite for the slaughter of a snake resembling a fowl but was reborn as a princess as a reward for her kindness to a tired Jaina nun in her last incarnation but one will be found in an article on *Jaina Iconography* by Prof. Bhandarkar.[1]

The history of the Jain sects.—Like Buddhism Jainism will have to be studied in its sects. Quite apart from the various schools and orders into which it has been divided it has been rent by no less than eight schisms (*nihvana*) according to the Swetámbaras. Of these the first was originated by Maháviras's son-in-law Jamáli and the last in 83 A. D. gave rise to the Digambara sect.[2] But the last-named know nothing of the earlier schisms and say that under Bhadrabáhu rose the Ardhaphálaka sect which in 80 A D. developed into the Swetámbara sect. This is the more remarkable in that doctrinal differences are not acute. The Digambaras[3] hold that *kevalins*, such as the Tírthankaras, live without food, that Máhávíra's embryo was not removed from Devánanda's womb to that of Trishalá, that a monk who owns any property, even clothes, and a woman, cannot reach *nirvána*. While the Digambaras disown the canonical books of the Swetámbaras, holding that they were lost after Mahávíra's *nirvána*, they recognise one at least of the most authoritative Swetámbara *sutras*. Nevertheless in consequence of their early separation they have an ecclesiastical as well as literary history of their own and their religious ceremonies especially in regard to the laity differ from those of their rivals. With them their list of the patriarchs only agrees in respect of the 1st, Jambu, and the 6th Bhadrabáhu. The latter, they say, migrated to the south at the head of the true monks and from him dates the loss of their sacred literature. According to their modern tradition the main church (*múla-sangha*) split into four *ganas*—Nandi, Sena, Simha and Deva—about the close of the 1st century A. D.[3]

The list of Swetámbara patriarchs begins with Mahávíra's disciple Sudharman and ends with the 33rd, Sándilya or Skandila. In some cases the names of the disciples of each patriarch, and of the schools and branches (or orders) styled *gana*, *kula* or *shákha*, founded by or originating with him are preserved. After the 6th, Bhadrabáhu, a great expansion of Jainism took place in the north and north-west of India. In later times *gachchas* or schools were founded by individual teachers, theoretically 84 in number and differing only in minute details of conduct. Of these the most important is the Kharatara which has split up into many minor *gachchas*, the Tapá, Anchelá &c. and the most interesting is the Upakesa *gachcha*, 'known as the Oswál Jains,'

[1] A. S. R., 1905-6, p. 141 *f*.

[2] Also called Digvasanas : E. R. E, Vol. 4, p. 704. Another Swetámbara version is that in 83 A. D. Shivabhúti started the heretical sect of the Botikas or Digambaras : *ib*.

[3] For details of these four 'orders' see Vol. II, *infra*, p. 348.

who begin their descent from Párśva, Maháv́ira's predecessor.[1] Down to the 9th century A. D. much uncertainty prevails as to Jain history and the legend that the first patron king of the sect was Asoka's grandson Samprati is very doubtful.

Modern Jain temples.

The Jain temple at Zira is called after the name of Sri Paras Náth, who was its founder. After the completion of the *mandir* all persons of the Jain sect gathered together and adored Sri Krab Dev, one of the 24 incarnations, on the *shudi ikádshi* in Maghar Sambat 1948 (7th April 1887). On that day an annual fair is held and the banner of the temple is carried through the town in a great procession. This is called *rath játra.* The temple contains many images made of metal. Of these, the image of Paras Náth, the finest, is 3¾ feet high. The *vedi* on which the image is installed is also handsome and decorated with gold. The administration is carried on by the Jain community, but *pujáris* are employed as servants, their duties being to open the *mandir,* clean it and supply fresh water for the washing of the images &c. Worship is generally performed by Jains, but in their absence it is performed by the temple servants who are Brahmans. As a rule, the *pujári* must bear a good character and avoid eating flesh, drinking wine &c. It is of little importance whether he be celibate or not. The *pujári* is not hereditary and is dismissed on infringement of any of the above rules. No special reverence is paid to the chief priest. The usage of *charas* is forbidden. Sweetmeat is used as *bhog,* but anything else may also be offered as such to the image. It is important to light the sacred lamp and burn *dhúp* and incense in the temple. Cash offerings are deposited in its treasury, and are only spent on its upkeep. No other shrines are connected with this. Many pictures of certain gods are hung on the temple walls.

At the *mandir* of the Saraogis at Tehl in Karnál an annual fair, called Kalsá Jal, is held on the 14th of the light half of Bhádon, and at this the image of Maháráj is carried The fair was first held in S. 1942, though the temple was founded in S. 1901. It contains marble images of Paras Náth, Mahábíri and Ajat Náth, each 1¼ feet high. Its administration is carried on by the Saraogi community, each member taking duty in turn. No special reverence is paid to the *pujári* on duty and there is no ritual or sacred lamp.

[1] The above, from H. Jacobi's account in E. R. E., Vol. 7, p 473, differs a good deal from that given *infra* in Vol. II, pp. 346-7.

Section 4.—The Hindus of the Punjab.

The elasticity of Hinduism.—What is Hinduism—not the Hinduism of the Vedas, which was a clearly defined cult followed by a select society of a superior race living among despised barbarians of the lowest type, but the Hinduism of to-day, the religion of the masses of India, which has to struggle for existence against the inroads of other and perhaps higher forms of belief? The difficulty of answering this question springs chiefly from the marvellous catholicity and elasticity of the Hindu religion. It is in the first place essentially a cosmogony, rather than a code of ethics. The esoteric teaching of the higher forms of Hinduism does doubtless include ethical doctrines, but they have been added to rather than sprung from the religion itself. Indeed it seems to me that a polytheistic creed must, from the very nature of things, be devoid of all ethical significance. The aspects of Nature and the manifestations of physical force are manifold, and can reasonably be allotted to a multiplicity of gods, each supreme in his separate province; but only one rule of conduct, one standard of right and wrong is possible, and it cannot conveniently be either formulated or enforced by a Divine Committee. In many respects this separation of religion from ethics is doubtless an advantage, for it permits of a healthy development of the rules of conduct as the ethical perceptions of the race advance. When the god has once spoken, his worshippers can only advance by modifying their interpretation of his commands; and no greater misfortune could befall a people than that their religion should lend all the sanctions of its hopes and terrors to a precise code of right and wrong, formulated while the conscience of the nation was yet young and its knowledge imperfect. Ibbetson, § 210.

But if the non-ethical nature of the Hindu religion is in some respects an advantage to its followers, it has also greatly increased the difficulty of preserving that religion in its original purity. The old Aryans, who worshipped the gods of the Vedas, were surrounded by races whose deities differed from their own in little but name, for both were but personifications of the forces of Nature. What more natural than that, as the two peoples intermingled, their gods should gradually become associated in a joint Pantheon. If the gods of the Vedas were mightier, the gods of the country might still be mighty. If malevolent, it was well to propitiate them; if benevolent, some benefits might perhaps be had from them. In either case it was but adding the worship of a few new gods to that of many old ones; for since neither these nor those laid down any immutable rules of conduct or belief, no change of life, no supersession of the one by the other was necessary. The evils the Hindus feared from their deities were physical; the help they hoped for material and not spiritual. Their gods were offended, not by disbelief and sin, but by neglect; they were to be propitiated, not by repentance and a new life, but by sacrifice and ceremonial observance; and so long as their dues were discharged they would not grudge offerings made to others as an additional insurance against evil.[1] The members of the Hindu Pantheon had many ranks and degrees, and, among the superior gods at any rate, each worshipper selected for himself that one which he would chiefly venerate. Thus it was easy to add on at the bottom of the list without derogating from the dignity of those at the top; while the relative honour in which each was held presently became a matter for the individual to decide for himself. And so we find that the gates of the Hindu Olympus have ever stood open to the strange gods of the neighbourhood, and that wherever Hindus have come into contact with worship other than their own they have combined the two, and even have not unseldom given the former precedence over the latter. The Hindu of the plains worships the saints of his Musalmán neighbours, and calls his own original gods by Muhammadan names unknown to an Indian tongue; the Hindu of the hills worships the devils and deities of the aborigines, and selects for special honour that one of his own proper divinities whose nature is most akin to theirs; both mollify by offerings innumerable agencies, animal, human, demoniacal, or semi-divine, who are not perhaps ranked with the greater gods of the temples, but who may do harm, and to propitiate whom is therefore a wise precaution.

Ibbetson, § 211.

BRAHMANISM THE DISTINGUISHING FEATURE OF HINDUISM.—But through all these diversities there does run a common element, the clue to which is to be found in the extraordinary predominance which the priestly class have obtained in India, as the explanation of the diversity itself is largely to be found in the greed of that class. In polytheistic Europe the separation of ethics from religion was no less complete than in India; but while in the latter the study of the two was combined, in Europe Greece developed religion into philosophy, while Rome formulated practical ethics in the shape of law, and each was content to receive at the hands of the other the branch which that other had made her own. When Christianity swept away the relics of the old gods, the separation had become too complete to be ever wholly obliterated; and though the priests of the new monotheism struggled fiercely, and with no small measure of success, to recombine the two and to substitute the canon for the civil law, yet there ever existed by the side of, but distinct from the clergy, a lay body of educated lawyers who shared with them the learning of the day and the power which that learning conferred. If then under such circumstances the political power of the Church in Europe was for centuries so immense for good or evil as we know it to have been, it may be conceived how wholly all authority was concentrated in the hands of the Brahmans and with what tyranny they exercised that power in India, where all learning of every sort and kind

[1] "I suspect that in many cases the strictly territorial nature of the aboriginal gods facilitated their inclusion in the Hindu worship. It would be less difficult to recognise a deity who did not even claim authority beyond certain set bounds, or pretend to rival the Vedic gods in their limitless power; and it would seem especially reasonable on entering a territory to propitiate the local powers who might be offended by the intrusion. The gods of the hills were, and many of them are still, undoubtedly territorial—see *supra*, Hinduism in the Himalayas. It would be interesting to discover whether the aboriginal gods of the plains presented the same characteristic. With them the limits of the tribe would probably define the territory, in the absence of any impassable physical boundaries such as are afforded by mountain ranges." [Ibbetson.]

was absolutely confined to the priestly class.[1] The result was that Hinduism early degenerated from a religion into a sacerdotalism, and would, in its present form, be far better described as Brahmanism than by any other single word; and it is this abject subjection to and veneration for the Brahman which forms the connecting link that runs through and binds together the diverse forms of worship and belief of which I have spoken.

It is in this predominance of the priesthood, moreover, that Ibbetson, we may find an explanation at once of the catholicity and of the exclu- § 212. siveness which characterise the Hindu religion. If to give to a Brahman is to worship God, the larger the circle of worshippers the better for the Brahman; and if new worshippers will not leave their gods behind them, it would be foolish to exclude them on that account, as there is ample room for all. On the other hand, as the Levitical body so increased in numbers that a portion of them was necessarily illiterate, the Brahmans were compelled to fall back upon hereditary virtue as the only possible foundation for the power of their class. Here they found in the tribal divisions of the people, and in the theory of the hereditary nature of occupations which had sprung from them, an institution suited to their purpose and ready to their hands; and this they developed into that complex web of caste-restrictions and disabilities which envelopes a high-caste Hindu from his mother's womb. And so the special power and sanctity of the Brahman came to depend for its very existence upon the stringency with which caste-distinctions were maintained, the act of worship was subordinated to the idea of ceremonial purity, and for a definite creed was substituted the domination of a priestly class, itself divided into a thousand sects and holding a thousand varieties of doctrine. To the aborigine who, with his gods on his back, sought admission within the pale of Hinduism, these restrictions presented no obstacle. They were but developments of the system which obtains in all primitive forms of society: and so far as they differed from the rules which he already observed, they tended to raise him in the social scale by hedging him round with an exclusiveness which was flattering if inconvenient. But to the outcast, whose hereditary habits or occupation rendered him impure from the birth, admission was impossible, at least to the full privileges of Hinduism.[2]

The sacerdotal despotism has now altogether over-shadowed Ibbetson, the religious element; and the caste-system has thrust its roots so deep § 213. into the whole social fabric that its sanction is social rather than religious. A man may disbelieve in the Hindu Trinity, he may invent new gods of his own, however foul and impure, he may worship them with the most revolting orgies, he may even abandon all belief in supernal powers, and yet remain a Hindu. But he must reverence and feed the Brahman, he must abide by caste rules and restrictions, he

[1] The position of the Brahmans with respect to religion in India seems to have been closely analogous to that which the lawyers formerly held with respect to law in England. The language in which religious rites were conducted was scrupulously kept from the knowledge of the people, while the procedure was extremely technical, and any error in form, however minute, destroyed the efficacy of the ceremony.

[2] I had, after repeated warnings, to fine severely one of my Hindu compilers, a man in a good position, and of education and intelligence, but who positively refused to include scavengers who returned themselves as Hindus in the figures for that religion.

must preserve himself from ceremonial pollution and from contact and communion with the unclean on pain of becoming Anathema Maranatha. With individuals indeed even these restrictions are relaxed, on the condition that they affect a personal sanctity which, by encouraging superstition and exciting terror, shall tend to the glorification of the priesthood; and the filthy Aghori, smeared with human ordure and feeding on carrion and even on human carrion,[1] is still a Hindu. But the masses must observe the rules; and any who should, like Buddha or Bába Nának, propose to admit the body of the laity to share in a license which is permitted to the naked ascetic, would at once be disavowed. The Christian and Buddhist recognise no distinction of caste, nor does the Musalmán save where influenced by the example of those whom he has so bitterly persecuted, while all three profess to disregard the Brahman; and for this reason, and not because they worship a different god, the Hindu holds their touch to be pollution. The Sikh has fallen away from his original faith; in his reverence for the Brahman and his observance of caste-rules he differs only in degree from his Hindu neighbour; and I shall presently show how difficult it is to draw the line between the two religions. The Jain I take to be little more than a Hindu sect.

VEDIC CULTS.

At a census when a man is asked to say what deity he specially affects, he will often say that he worships all the gods alike. But whatever gods he may name they are not as a rule those of the *Vedas* or *Puranas*. Nevertheless the worship of Brahma is still to be found in the Punjab. Thus Adi Brahma is worshipped at Tiri in Kulu. At his festival he is personated by a villager seated in a high-backed sedan chair, with eight masks of metal silvered and gilt at the back. About the chair are stuck tufts of barley and peacock's feathers and everyone present wears a bunch of young barley in his cap. The man who acts the god affects to answer questions, and his replies often cause much merriment.[2] Adi Brahma also seems to have a temple at Khokhan Dera in Kulu where he is worshipped at four festivals, one held on the 1st of Baisákh, Sáwan and Asuj and on the full moon day of Maghar, each lasting four days. Brahman *deota* also has a temple at a place called Darewa-i-Dhara in Kothi Tárápur where he is worshipped yearly from Sunday to Thursday in the dark halves of Sáwan, Maghar and Phágan.

In Saráj a *deota* Brahma is worshipped. The story goes that a villager once saw a Brahman sitting in a lonely forest, so he asked what had brought him there. The Brahman replied that he was a god and that if the people made an image of him and worshipped it, they would obtain their heart's desire, and further that any questions put to him through his *gur* or disciple would be answered. So saying the Brahman disappeared beneath the earth. The temple is said to have been founded in the Dwápar Yúg. It is of stone and contains a black stone image, 3 feet high and 2 broad. Its administration is carried on

[1] An Aghori was caught by the police in the Rohtak district about 1881 in the act of devouring a newly buried child which he had dug up for the purpose. For other instances of *aghorbidya*, which seems to be a term for their ritual cannibalism, see Russell's *Tribes and Castes of the Central Provinces*, II, p. 15. Also Oman's *Mystics, Ascetics and Saints of India*, pp. 164-5, there cited.

[2] N.I.N.Q., I., § 431, citing Moorcroft and Trebeck's *Journey to Ladakh*, I, p. 176.

by a *kárdár*, a Kanet of the Káshab *got*. He is married. A Sársut Brahman *pujári* is also employed for worship. He is a Gautam by *got*. He too is married. Both these posts are purely hereditary. Seven other shrines are connected with this one. Brahma is not worshipped in Chamba, nor are there any temples to him so far as Dr. Hutchison can ascertain.

In Ambála the shrine of Brahma is a stone under a *bargat*, 'banyan,' tree, and offerings are made to it to cure fevers and recover lost property.[1]

Brahm himself is returned by some, but a man who returns himself as a worshipper of Brahm[2] generally means little more than that he worships the Supreme God, —*Parmeshar ko mántá hai*, or *Khudá ko mántá hai*,—an assertion in which almost all Hindus would join. The term Brahm-panthí may refer in some cases to Brahmos, but there appears to be a sect of this name with special doctrines of its own. It is found in Hazára, and was started by a man called Gautam Raghi, and its holy book is termed the *Nyáyak Granth*.[3] It worships one God only: its members are recruited from all castes, and they partake of animal food; their object is to associate freely with both Hindus and Musalmáns and they are consequently looked on with disfavour by both religions. Maclagan, § 46.

The other two members of the Hindu Triad—Shiva and Vishnú—are more frequently before the minds of the modern Hindu than Brahm, and their respective worships represent two distinct forms of belief and practice regarding which I shall be speaking presently. Omitting for the present Rám Chandra and Krishn, whose cult is closely connected with that of Vishnú, the most popular of the minor deities are Ganesh and Hanúmán and Bhairon. Ganesh is the well-known elephant deity, the "obviator of difficulties and impediments," and as such is invoked at the commencement of a journey or of work of any kind. He is worshipped, first of all the gods in holy rites; women are particularly devoted to his worship; and his followers fast in his name on the 19th of each month, more especially in Mágh. He is also known as the Sangat-deota.

The worship of Hanumán or Mahábír, the monkey-god, is closely connected with that of Rám, in whose aid Hanúmán fought against the demons of Lanká. He is represented as a red-coloured monkey with a long tail and is worshipped by all castes. He is supposed, however, to be the particular patron of the wandering acrobats of the

[1] Wynyard's *Ambála Settlement Rep.*, § 419.

[2] Strictly speaking Brahm is pure spirit or *átma* in the pantheistic sense—pervading all space. Brahma is the manifestation of spirit, and so a distinction should be drawn: Brahm is impersonal, and Brahma conveys the conception of personality.

[3] During his residence in the Himalayas Gautama founded the Nyáyak sect: S. C. R., II, p. 480. But the Gautam Raghi of the text may be the Gautama Rikhi, author of the *Nyáya* or dialectical philosophy described in Colebrooke's *Essays*, I, p. 280 *ff*. Gautama was also called Akshapáda or Akshacharana and his followers Ashapádáh, but no trace of such a school is now to be found in this Province, unless it is represented by the modern Brahm-panthís. A scandalous legend about this Gautama *rishi* will be found on p. 126 *infra*. The term *nyáya* has many meanings, but its most usual one is 'logic'; Platts' *Hindustani Dicty.*, p. 1164. It is not confined to Hinduism, the *Nyáyavatara* of Siddha Sena Divakara being the earliest Jain work on pure logic.

Hissar district, the Bádís of the Bágar and the Nats of the Jangal or Des. A small shrine to Hanúmán is often erected near the site of a new well which is under construction, in order to prevent accidents during the process, and also to ensure that the water shall turn out sweet. He is respected for his generosity and chivalry. His followers fast of a Tuesday, and on that day distribute sweetmeats.

At Gurkhri, four miles from Kángra town, there is a temple to Anjana, wife of Kesari and mother of Hanúmán, whom Anjana bore to Váyu or Pavana, the wind, not to her husband Kesari, a monkey. Hence Hanúmán obtained his metronym of Anjaneya. A fair is held in her honour in October and many years ago a man attending this fair disturbed a bees' nest and a song was composed to celebrate the event.[1]

Bhairon or Bhairava is described *infra*.

Maclagan, § 40.

Early saints and heroes.—Along with the gods themselves we may notice the names of demigods and *rishis* to whom special reverence is paid. There are the five Pándavas, the heroes of the *Mahábhárat*, favourite objects of worship in the east, and sometimes addressed as the Panj-Pír Many are the legends current about these heroes and they are localised at quite a number of places. The hill of Mokshpuri, just above Dunga Gali, has an elevation of 9232 ft. Its name means 'hill of salvation' and on its summit is a *Pándúán da Sthán*, or 'place of the Pánduas,' where it is said they were visited and tempted by *apsaras* who still frequent the place. Such *sthâns* are not uncommon in the Himalayas. They are also known as Pánch Pándu and often consist of a small square enclosure: in this stands a tree, on which rags are hung. At every *sankránt* a kind of fair is held for the benefit of those in charge. It is believed that any attempt to build on the site would fail.[2] Another hero is Shámji, the Chauhán Rájá of Garh Dadna, who gave his head to Krishna and Arjan on condition that he should be allowed to see the fight between the Kauravas and Pándavas.[3] And there is Dhanwantar or Dhanwánú, the old physician, who is still looked up to by the Hindu members of the profession. And there is Daruna, the Acháraj, the *gurú* of the Pándavas, from whom the Acháraj clan, the Brahmans who accept gifts at deaths and conduct the funerals of the dead, trace their descent. The Kumhárs in the same way reverence their prototype Prajápati, whether this implies some human or semi-human progenitor, or refers to Brahm, the Lord of Creatures, the Great Potter who shapes the plastic world Similarly the northern branch of the Káisths revere their semi-divine ancestor Chatargupt, the watcher of good and bad actions, who sits with his great register before him in the audit office of the nether world. So also Biásji, the sage Vyása, and a hundred others are still looked up to with respect, and most of the Hindu tribes, and not a few of the Musalmáns, claim descent from one or other of these heroes and saints of early Hinduism.

[1] *Calc. Rev.*, 1882, p. 58, or *Selections from the C. R.*, *VII*, 1896, p. 449. See also p. 129 *infra*.

[2] *Ib.*, VIII, p. 128.

[3] This Shámji has his shrine at Kotla in the Jaipur State.

Pándu the pale accompanied by his two wives, Mádri and Kunti or Pritha, retired to the Himalayas. There they bore the five Pándavas, sons of various gods but acknowledged by him as his own.[1]

The interesting rock-temples at Mukeshwar on the Rávi, five miles above Sháhpur in Gurdáspur, are said to date back to the Pándavas, and to have been visited by Arjan and Párbati. A long cleft in the rock a little way up the river is known as Arjan's *chula* or hearth.[2] Shiv as Achleswar Maháráj has a temple at Achal a few miles from Batála. It lies in a tank and is ascribed to the same mythical period.[3]

Tradition says that once Báwan of Lanká (Ceylon) went to Shiva at the Kailása hill and begged him to visit his island kingdom. Shiva accepted on condition that Báwan would not set him on the ground throughout the journey. Báwan agreeing took him on his shoulder, but when he reached the place where this temple stands, he felt a call of nature and, forgetting the condition, put Shiva down on the ground. On his return he tried his utmost to lift Shiva up again, but could not and so had to leave him there. Hence the place is called Achchal from Achleshahr, incapable of moving further.

The temple contains 101 stone images, each 1½ feet high. Marble images of Ganesh, Durga, Bishnú and Súraj Bhagwán stand in the four corners of the temple. Each is 3 feet high. Besides these, there is a marble image of Gauri Shankar. Annual fairs are held on 1st Baisákh, the *naumi* and *dasmi* in Kátak, on every *amáwas* and on the *chetar chaudas* (14th of the light half of Chet).

The worship of Nature.

The chief characteristic of the Vedic mythology is that it is a worship of nature in all its aspects. In the modern Punjab that mythology has disappeared almost completely, but the worship of nature is still a living force in popular religion. Nature is reverenced or propitiated, coerced or bargained with in many diverse ways, but through all the rites with which she can be influenced runs the pantheistic idea. As God is in all Nature so He speaks through all Nature. Everything, living or inanimate, can speak as His mouthpiece with equal authority. Nothing is silent or without its lesson and meaning for mankind—if man has but the wit and knowledge necessary to comprehend its speech or its signification. To the initiated in the varied lore of divination the slightest hints are full of meaning. The flight of birds southwards in autumn is a sign of the approach of winter. In a sense then it 'predicts' the coming of winter. Nature supplies countless similar 'predictions' to people who are of necessity in close contact with her. But man's speculative and rational faculties develop more rapidly than his capacity for accurate observation and

[1] *S. C. R.*, VIII, p. 126. He appears to be identical with or confused with Gúga, Chauhán, of Garh Darera. In the Himalayas Panjpiri is often regarded as a single personage and identified with Záhir Pír or Gúga, but the distinction of personages is also recognised in their representation by five stones placed under a *pípal* and smeared with red lead. P. N. Q., III., § 139. See also p. 186 *infra*.

[2] Gurdáspur *Gazetteer*, 1914, p. 26.

[3] *Ib.*, p. 31.

logical control of intuition. Upon the firm and safe basis that nature provides auguries which are a certain indication of coming events, man has hurried to the conclusion that everything in nature is a portent, forgetting that the happening of such events as the southward flight of birds is explained by readily ascertainable facts which could have no other results and are therefore significant of their causes, but that other events can have no such significance. We who know the causes of an eclipse and can theorise on the cause of earthquakes, are under no temptation to attribute them to supernatural agencies, but to the primitive philosopher or metaphysician it is self-evident that all phenomena in nature, whether trivial or impressive, are due to the working of a force which is immanent in all things. From this theory a whole series of primitive sciences and applied rituals was evolved. Astrology is based upon its application to the stars, and other branches of the science of omens on its application to various natural phenomena of the body or external world. Hence we shall find a science of divination from respiration, sneezing, twitching of the eyelids and the like: from the movements of animals and birds, especially such as are intelligent or uncanny; and from the most trivial accidents in the happenings of daily life. All is eloquent of the world-soul animating it from within, and if from this assumption there arises a mass of pseudo-science which has only come down to us in fragments, we may recollect that as a compensation the worship of nature taught that all life is one, and from this teaching arose much curiously beautiful lore about trees and animals which all found rank, as well as place, a definite relationship to a godhead, a function, as it were, in the spiritual world, and a kind of individuality in addition to their general claim upon man's mercy.

Had primitive speculation rested there it could have done nothing but good and, by forming a firm basis for the closer study of nature, it would have facilitated progress. But just as divination in the hands of the Roman State authorities became formalised into a set of rules for ascertaining the good-will of the gods and obtaining their sanction for the operations of the community, but which had no scientific basis whatever, no relation to truth and fact,[1] so in the hands of the professional classes which practised divination and codified its laws in verse the promising sciences with which it was pregnant were atrophied and distorted into useless and barren arts.[2]

Ibbetson, § 219.

First among the pure and benevolent gods comes *Súraj Devata*, or *the Sun godling*. The Sun was of course one of the great Vedic deities; but his worship has apparently in a great measure dropped out of the higher Hinduism, and the peasant calls

[1] Ihering's fanciful theory that the study of the flight of birds was prompted by the desire to get information about mountain passes and the course of great rivers during the Aryan migration is unnecessary. A much simpler explanation is suggested. But once started on the path of science by observation of the facts of bird-life, the signs of the weather and the like, man inevitably proceeds to see predictions in everything, even on the shoulder-blade of a sheep, like the Baloch, or in the exta of red puppies which had been sacrificed.—*Cf.* Warde Fowler, *Religious Experiences of the Roman People*, pp. 298 *et seqq.*

[2] *Op. cit.*, p. 295.

him, not Deva but Devata, a godling, not a god.[1] No shrine is ever built to him, but on Sunday the people abstain from salt, and they do not set their milk as usual to make butter from, but make rice milk of it and give a portion to the Brahmans. After each harvest, and occasionally between whiles, Brahmans are fed in his honour; and he is each morning saluted with an invocation as the good man steps out of his house. He is *par excellence* the great god of the villager, who will always name him first of all his deities. After him comes, at least in the east of the Province, *Jamna Jí*, or *Lady Jamna*. She is bathed in periodically. Brahmans are fed in her honour, and the waters of the canal which is fed from her stream are held in such respect by the villagers that they describe the terrible evils which they work in the land as springing "from Lady Jamna's friendship." *Dharti Máta*, or *Mother Earth*, holds the next place of honour. The pious man does obeisance to and invokes her as he rises from his bed in the morning, and even the indifferent follows his example when he begins to plough or to sow. When a cow or she-buffalo is first bought or when she first gives milk after calving, the first five streams of milk drawn from her are allowed to fall on the ground in honour of the deity; and at every time of milking the first stream is so treated. So, when medicine is taken, a little is sprinkled in her honour.

The Sun is still widely worshipped in Karnál. Sunday is sacred to him and on that day no salt is eaten, and no milk set for *ghi*, but it is made into rice milk, part of which goes to a Brahman in honour of the Sun. A lamp is always lit to him on Sundays and Brahmans fed now and then on that day, especially on the 1st Sunday after Asarh 15th when the harvest has been got in. Before the daily bath water is always cast towards him (*argha*).[2]

The Legends of Raja Rasalu.

Rájá Rasálú, or Rásálú according to Cunningham,[3] is even more important in Punjab folklore than Gúga. According to that authority his legend belongs essentially to the Poṭhwár, between the Jhelum

[1] The sun-god, however, certainly had temples in India in ancient times. There was one at Taxila: *Arch. Survey Reports*, II, p. 114; and at Multán; *ibid.* V, pp. 115 and 120. Farishta says the Hindus used to worship the Sun and Stars, like the Persians, until King Suraj (*sic*) taught them idolatry: Briggs, *Ferishta*, I, p. lxviii. But in later times images of Surya or Aditya were rare: *A. S. R.*, XIII, p. 68. For the absence of temples to the Sun see *infra*.

[2] This should also be done to the new moon also, on the evening of her appearance: Karnál *S. R.*, p. 147. According to Maclagan (§ 48) the worshippers of the sun, according to the manuals, are termed Sauras or Saurapatias, and constitute one of the main sects of Hinduism. The old constitutional god Surya is, however, little attended to now except in the south and east, where Súraj Narain is almost the sole orthodox deity of the Hindu pantheon who finds a place in the common religion of the peasants.

[3] A. S. R. II, p. 153. The meaning of the name is not at all certain. *Rasál* is a present to a friend: *Panjabi Dicty.*, p. 957. The present writer is inclined to think that Rasálú is derived from *risála* 'a troop of horse,' and that Rasálú means the rider, the charioteer of the sun. But *risála* is a Persian word, not Sanskrit or even Hindi. "The people in Chamba pronounce the name Rasálu. Cunningham identified Rásálu with Sálavahana, but I see they are supposed to have been father and son. To me it is a tempting supposition that they were identical and that Rasálu is simply Rái Sálu. Sála is found in the *Rájatarang* as short for Sáláváhana—as the name ought to be spelt—not Sálivahana. The change of the terminal á to u is very common in Indian names. In olden times the title *Rái* was in common use for Rájá *e.g.* Rái Pithora of Delhi, and I could give many other examples" (Hutchison).

and Indus, but is also well-known at Ambá Kapi, near Lahore, the legendary residence of Rájá Sir-kap. Ambá Kapi is the general name for seven places named after three brothers, Rájás Sir-kap, Sir-sukh and Ambá and their four sisters Kápi, Kalpi, Munda and Mandehi. All seven are also described as *rákshasas* whom Rasálú destroys. Sir-kap is a gambler and his stakes are human heads which he invariably wins until overcome by Rasálú. Past Ambá Kapi flows the Bágh-bacha stream and Cunningham connects this with the story of Budha's offering of his body to appease the seven tiger cubs.

Tradition also localises Rasálú's legend at Mánikpur or Udinagar where the seven *rákshasas* lived. Every day he devoured a man until Rasálú destroyed all of them except Thera (possibly *tera*, the 'roarer') whose bellowings are still to be heard in a cavern of the Gandghar hills, north of Attock. Mánikpur is said to lie 'west of the Jhelum' and may be Manikiála.

His pedigree is :—

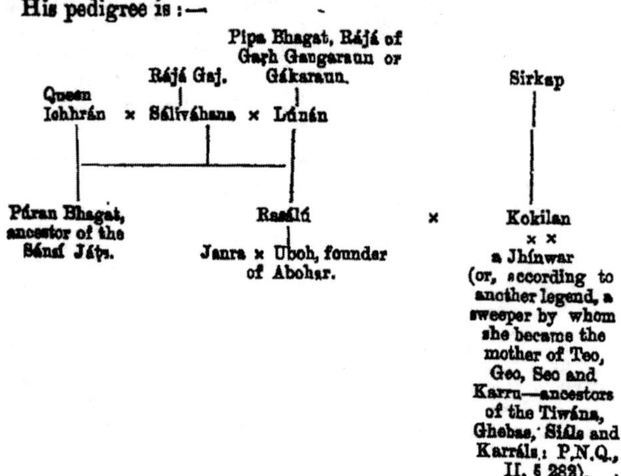

It is however much more likely that Rasálú is a solar deity by origin, and that round his original myth nearly all the folk lore of the province has gathered.

Sir R. C. Temple on the other hand protests strongly against this view and regards Rasálú as a historical personage, to be identified with the Ranbal of the Muhammadan historians, a Hindu prince who opposed the Moslem invaders in what is now Afghánistán between A. D. 700 and 870. But hitherto no coins or inscriptions bearing the names of Rasálú and the legendary personages connected with him have been discovered. He writes in the *Calcutta Review*, 1884, p. 380[1] :—

"King Rasálú, it is asserted, was a solar myth. No one at all acquainted with the science of comparative mythology can, we are told, for a

[1] Or *N O. R.*, 1896, p. 188.

moment, doubt it. Thus, as the sun in his course rests not in toiling and travelling, so Rasálú's destiny forbade him to tarry in one place. And as the sun, after a battle, however tremendous, with the elements, shines forth clear and victorious, so Rasálú, after a series of magical thunderbolts hurled at him by the giants, is found, shortly after, standing calm and undaunted. Hence Rasálú is considered as merely another form of the fables of Indra, Savitar, Woden, Sisyphus, Hercules, Samson, Apollo, Theseus, Sigurd, Arthur, Tristram, and a host of other heroes, with one or other of whom every country, civilised and uncivilized, is familiar. Again, one large class of the old nature myths relates to the fortunes of 'fatal children,' in whose lives the destruction of their parents is involved—even as the rising sun destroys his parent the darkness, from which he springs. These children are almost invariably the subject of prophecy, and though exposed and made to suffer in infancy, invariably grow up beautiful, brave and generous. Thus, Perseus, who kills Akrisius : Œdipus, who smites his father Laius ; and Rasálú, whose destiny it was to slay Salvahn his father. Again, like the early ideal of Samson, and like the later ideal of Arthur, Rasálú is the king of spotless purity. Moreover, as the sun dies in the west but rises again, so Rasálú, in common with King Arthur, is expected to appear once more.

"Then, Rájá Rasálú has a wonderful horse, who at a crisis warns his master not to touch him with whip or spur. In like manner, in the sun-myth of Phaeton, that hero is charged not to touch with his whip the horses of Helios. To take one more instance, the legend of Mír Shikári is, as the author has remarked, the story of Orpheus, of Amphion and of Pan; but it is also the story of Hermes, Sigurd, Volker, Tristram, and many others; all of whom were pre-emiently harpers, surpassing all men ; or, in other words, they were impersonations of the action and the power of air in motion.

"There are many other remarkable points in these singular legends of Rasálú, pointing them to a common origin with the ancient solar myths of all countries; but we have said enough to enable our readers to understand the principles, at least, which lead the Westminster Reviewer, and other students of comparative mythology, to regard the sun as the original fount at which story-tellers of all ages have refreshed their listeners' thirst for recitals of a heroic nature."

Púran Bhagat, also called Gyánsarúpa or Purakh Siddh Chauranjwenáth, or Chaurangi Náth, is one of the *gurús* or hierarchs of the Kanephatta Jogis. Legend makes him a son of Sáliváhana by Ráni Achhrán and Rája Rasálú's elder brother. He is beloved by his step-mother Ráni Lúnán[1] and is calumniated by her and has his feet and hands cut off. Thrown into a well at Kallowál near Siálkot by his father he is rescued by Gorakhnáth, who has his ears bored and makes him his disciple. He revisits Siálkot and makes the deserted garden bloom again. He restores his mother's sight, which she lost from weeping for him, and promises Ráni Sundrán a son, giving her a grain of rice to eat, and returns to Gorakhnáth. One version of the story makes Gorakhnáth first send Púran to Ráni Sundrán of Sangaldíp[2] to beg alms of her. She would fain make him her husband, but he refuses to rule and even when bidden to accept

[1] One variant makes Ráni Lúndán, a Chamár woman. Subsequently Rasálú, seeing the evils of marrying women of low caste fixed limits within which each caste should marry.

[2] Temple (*Legends of the Punjab*, II, p. 276) would identify Sangaldíp with Sákala-dvípa or Sháka-dvípa in the northern Punjab. It would be the country round Siálkot.

her kingdom by Goraknáth he disobeys his *gurú* and becomes a Jogi, while Sundrán casts herself down and kills herself.[1]

As Chaurangi Náth Púran visited the Bohar monastery of the Jogis in Rohtak, but was refused food until he brought fodder for their cattle. He obeyed but cursed the place which fell into ruins, only the Kálá Mahál remaining intact, but no religious rites are performed in that building which is a small arched room with walls 4½ feet thick. It is said to have belonged to the PAGAL PANTH of the Jogis. When Chaurangi Náth revisited the place he established his fire or *dhúni* and worshipped there for 12 years. Once a Banjára passing by said his load of sugar was salt. Salt it became, but as he repented of his falsehood, the saint made it sugar again and in gratitude he built a monument over the *dhúni*. This building contains no wood, its walls are 7½ feet thick and its shape suggests layers of sugar sacks. In it a lamp is kept burning day and night.[2]

Bisáde is said to have been a disciple of Púran Bhagat, and he has a very old temple at Baliána in Rohtak. *Gharbari*, non-celibate Jogis, take the offerings. Milk is offered on the 14th *sudi* of the month and a fair held on that day in Mágh.

MOON-WORSHIP.—The worship or propitiation of the moon takes various forms. At first sight of a new moon Hindus take seven threads from the end of their turbans[3] and present them to her. Then throwing the end of the turban round their necks they say: *Chandaná, bhági bhayá thanḍ wartáin, te roṭi kapra bahut devín.* 'O moon, make us prosperous and happy, and grant us bread and clothes in plenty.' Then they exchange with one another the salutation 'Rám, Rám!' and the younger of both sexes bow to their elders, while newly-married people get 'Moon gifts' from their parents-in-law, or in their absence from near relatives. If Hindus see a new moon in Bhádon, a day called *patharchauth* or day of stones, they consider it so unlucky that they fear misfortune or a false accusation, and to avert it they will throw stones into their neighbours' houses in order to cause them to abuse them in return, in which case they will suffer in their stead.[4]

The Moon became enamoured of Chalya, wife of Gautama Rishi, and visited her in her husband's form. The Rishi discovered this and cursed his wife, who turned into a stone. He also cast his shoe at the Moon and it left a black mark upon him.[5] This occurred at Goindar in Pánipat tahsíl where Gautama also gave Indra his 1000 eyes.[6]

Maclagan, § 48.

PLANET WORSHIP.—Our Census returns show a number of persons who are said to worship Saníchar, or the planet Saturn, known also as Chhanchan *deota*. These persons are Ḍakaut Brahmans, who are clients of this malignant divinity, and who beg in his name and receive from the

[1] For details see Temple, *op. cit.*, II, pp. 375 (*The Legend of Púran Bhagat*), I, p. 2 etc. Also P. N. Q., II, § 390.

[2] Rohtak *Gazetteer*, 1910, pp. 63-4. A similar tale is told of the Ghaibi Pír (*ib.*, p. 63), and a song sung to Báwa Farid has the same theme.

[3] Muhammadans do this and then throw the shreds to the right. They also toss a coin into the air. P. N. Q., II., § 254.

[4] P. N. Q., II, §§ 255-256.

[5] N. I. N. Q., I, § 87. It will be noticed that here the Moon is male.

[6] *Ib.*, § 862.

faithful gifts of oil and iron. Saníchar is the god after whom Saturday is named and the Ḍakauts receive their offerings on that day.

Those returned as Budh-worshippers may possibly be men with a reverence for Buddha, but more probably they refer to the planet Mercury, from whom Budhwár, or Wednesday, is named.[1] Mangal (Mars) is held sacred in the same way, as an auspicious planet; and in many minor matters, as in commencing a house, the nine planets are invoked together.

During an eclipse Hindus bathe in a sacred stream so as to be pure enough to repeat the *mantras* which will release the Sun or Moon from Ráhu and Ketu's persecutions.[2] The husband of a wife pregnant for the first time should not look on any eclipse or his child will be deformed in some way and is peculiarly liable to hare-lip.[3]

In Gilgit portents are generally supposed to foreshadow political events. Thus heavy rain forebodes invasion from Yasín, and many kites hovering over Gilgit one from Nagar. If packs of wolves assail the flock an attack from Hunza is expected and an unusually good harvest one by the Puniál chiefs.[4]

In Gilgit Grahn is a giant and a lover of the moon whom he seizes on the 14th of the lunar month when she is in her full beauty leaving untouched only the part which contains a fig tree. At such times the people beat iron pans and cry aloud to make Grahn leave the moon. In the meantime the (threatened) eclipse ends and they rejoice at their success.[5] Grahn also becomes angry at the sun whenever a good king dies or is banished his country, and he then darkens the whole or a part of the sun's face.

In Siálkot storms which proceed from the north or south-east are generally accompanied by lightning. They prevail during the rains. If they occur in December damage is done by the lightning to such crops as gram, *másur*, *alsí* and *til*, which are called *phúl-sak* or *lirhkmár* in consequence. The electricity passing over the flowers is said to make them all fall off, the seed is lost and the crops seldom ripen. To counteract this evil the cultivator never sows gram till the first appearance of the moon, a light is placed on the seed which is prepared for sowing, and as the moon appears it is cast over the field, and always at night, the popular belief being that in this way the electric current will pass over the crop.[6]

Astrology plays a large part in all the affairs of life, and may even be used to foretell natural events. The chief exponents of the science are Sahdeo and his spouse Bhandli, Bhaddali or Bhádali, whose couplets are usually addressed to each other turn and turn about.[7]

[1] Or, in Gurgaon at any rate they may refer to the worshippers of the small-pox goddess under her name of Budho.

[2] N. I. N. Q., I, § 103.

[3] Ghulam Muhammad: *On the Festivals and Folklore of Gilgit*, Monographs, Asiatic Society of Bengal, I, § 691.

[4] *Ib.*, p. 107.

[5] *Ib.*, p. 107. Apparently this is done once in every lunar month, not only at a lunar eclipse.

[6] Prinsep's Siálkot *Sett. Rep.*, §§ 128-9. Probably the people have no conception of any electric current at all.

[7] See p. 134 of Vol. II.

Thus clouds and lightning on the 1st of the light half (*sudi pritham*) of Baisákh presage an abundant harvest as does the concurrence of Thursday and the asterism Rohini in the *akhaitij* or *akhtij* the 1st Baisákh, on which date the accounts of the last harvest are settled.

If the asterisms Múl and Kárh or Akhára coincide with the first of Jeṭh on a Wednesday there will be an earthquake. And if the 10th of the dark half of Jeṭh fall on a Saturday there will be no rain, and but a few will live.

If the full moon, *púrnáma* (*púranmási*) of Chait fall on a Monday, Thursday or Wednesday there will be rejoicing in every house.

The rest of Sahdeo's couplets are a systematic meteorological forecast. For example: if Kritka be seen for an hour in Rohini *i.e.* if Kritka overlap Rohini (in June) crowds with potsherds in their hands will beg from door to door; in other words, there will be famine. The prognostications are generally gloomy and only occasionally reassuring as in the couplet:

Aswani gale, Bharni gale, gale Jeṣtha Múl,
Púrbá Khúd dharúkia upje sáton chúl.

If Aswani and Bharni, which fall in May, Jeṣtha and Múl, at the end of December and in January, all be wet and Púrváshádha in January be cloudy, the seven grains will flourish.[1]

The following story about Venus or Shukar comes from Siálkot:—The Rikhi Prigugi had a son called Shukar and a disciple (*sewak*) named Bala Rájá. Bala worshipped God so fervently that He promised to appear before him and receive the *pirthi dán* (the earth in alms) at his hands. Shukar then told Rájá Bal that God was the greatest deceiver that had ever existed on earth and that he should not believe what He said about His incarnation, but Rájá Bal put no faith in what Shukar told him, and when God appeared he took up a *loṭa* to throw water on His hands and gave Him three *kadams* of land in alms. Shukar then became a tiny creature and seated himself in the spout of the *loṭa* so that the water stopped running through the spout. But God had a twig in His hand, and this He thrust into the spout, making Shukar blind in his right eye. Shukar then ran away and the water flowed out freely. God was so displeased at Shukar's act that He gave him a *sráp*, turned him into a star and cursed him, saying that no women should come before his face or at his right hand and that his setting would be very baneful. So when this star is set a newly married Hindu bride does not go to her father's or husband's house if she chances to be in her husband's or father's house. She prefers to go to her husband's or father's house when the star is up and on her left hand. If she acts against these rules she is believed to suffer. To reach her father's or husband's house when it is set or on her right hand she must start when it is up or on her left and stay a night outside the village in which she happens to be. As on account of this star wives thus spend a night outside the village it is also called the 'wives' star' (*wauṭián dá tára*). It appears sometimes in the west, sometimes in the east and at other times not at all.

[1] P. N. Q., II, §§ 856 and 706.

Meteors are hot coals cast from heaven at the devil who is always trying to ascend to it. This appears to be a Muhammadan belief.[1]

A comet, *púchhalwála tára* or *dumdár sitára*, will bring epidemics or famine and if one appears subscriptions are raised to feed Brahmans and *faqírs*.[2]

Lightning is attracted by black, so red stripes are inserted in blankets of that colour. Bell metal is also held to be a great conductor.

But the worst attraction is afforded by an uncle and his sister's son sitting together because the lightning was once born as the daughter of Devki, niece of Kansa, and was struck by her uncle, who cast her to the ground against a stone. She flew up to heaven, but has ever since borne enmity to all maternal uncles.[3]

The whirlwind contains an evil spirit and to avoid meeting one you should say:—*Hanumán Jodha, terí kár*—'O warrior Hanúmán! thy charmed circle (protect me).' Hanúmán is invoked in the same words said seven times if you meet a *bhút*, who should be seized firmly by the top-knot. If it is then tied into a noose the spirit will obey you. Do not let him go till he has sworn thrice by Hanúmán Jodha to serve you in difficulties.[4]

Dust-storms are avoided by invoking Hazrat Sulaimán thrice, pointing the while with the fourth finger to the direction you wish the storm to take.[5]

The East wind or *purwá* comes over the sea and is harmful to mankind, though it brings more rain than the *pachhwá* or west wind which is land-borne.[6]

When the earth is worshipped as Dharti Máta at the first season's ploughing the prayer in common use is: 'keep our rulers and bankers contented and grant a plentiful yield: so shall we pay our revenue and satisfy our money-lender.'[7] The year's ploughing must not be begun on a Monday or a Saturday. A curious form of earth-worship is performed by dacoits, or apparently by any one in desperate case. When they are at bay they take up a little earth and scatter it on their heads.[8]

Natural features are almost always ascribed to supernatural or heroic agency. This is especially the case in the Himalayas For example, in Kanaur the Raldang mountain is said to be a chip of the true Kailás brought down to Sángla by the wishes of an ancient king

[1] P. N. Q., III, § 53.

[2] I. N. Q., IV, § 424.

[3] *Ib.*, §§ 36, 37. For shrines of the Máma-Bhánja or Uncle and his Sister's Son, see *infra*, under ISLÁM.

[4] *Ib.*, §§ 38, 39. A variant is *Bhái Pherú, terí kár*, Bhái Pheru the names in the small whirlwinds so common in the Punjab. He is the husband of Deví and is represented as a disciple of Sakhi Sarwar. See *Legends of the Punjab*, III, p. 301, and II, pp. 104 and 106

[5] P. N Q., III, § 685.

[6] I. N. Q., IV, § 349.

[7] Karnál *S. R.* p. 168.

[8] For a parallel in Europe see Whitehead's *Gaspard de Coligny*. p. 218. The German foot chose the moment of advance to mutiny for pay at Moncontour in 1568. When pacified they kissed the ground and swore to die with honour.

and penitent. It is meritorious to circumambulate the hill, keeping it always on one's right.[1] The Kailás *kunḍ* or lake is still held sacred because it afforded an asylum to Vásuki when surprised by his enemy Garuda. The Kailás peak at the source of the Sutlej and the peak of Munh Mahesh, at the head of the Rávi, are both regarded as the home of Shiva[2], and the GADDIS' land is Shivbhúmi.

EARTH-WORSHIP.—On the 14th of the light half of Kátik is held the *surgṭukri* or feast of lamps. Very early in the morning men and women go out to bathe and the women set afloat mats of rushes or reeds on each side of which they place seven lamps alight, singing :—

> 'My lamp before : my soul behind.
> With my lamp before me, Rám will carry me across.'

Then in an adjoining field they set up a hut made of clods and worship in it a *ghi*-fed lamp. After this they return home, having performed a good work leading to heaven.[3]

About 5 miles from Ráwalpindi at the Chir Paháṛ there is a cleft which tradition says was caused by Rájá Rasálú's sword when he clove a demon in twain. The mark of his horse's hoof is also there.[4]

About 10 miles north of Ráwalpindi is a famous Rámkunḍ or Ráma's pool, with a Hanúmán *kunḍ*, a Lachhman *kunḍ*, a Súraj *kunḍ* and a Síta *kunḍ*, but in the last-named no Hindu will bathe though bathing in all the others is meritorious on any holy day and more especially on the 1st of Baisákh at the *sankránt*.[5] Two miles to the east of it is a Gupt-Ganga or silent pool in a running stream, which is also a *tírath*. Such pools are looked upon as sacred to the penance of some *rishi* or saint throughout the Himalayas. Two miles to the south of Rámkunḍ is Núrpur Sháhán, where a Muhammadan fair is held on the 1st Thursday after Baisákh 15th. Ecstasy and frenzy (*hál*) are not unknown on this occasion. The fair begins on the arrival of an offering of every kind of fruit in season from Peshåwar and cannot commence without it. It is held in honour of Sháh-i-Latíf Barri or Barri Sultán, said to have been a pupil of Sayyid Hayát-ul-Nur, Qádria. Barri Sultán used to be supplied daily with milk by a Gujar, but the buffalo which gave the milk always used to die on the day it was milked for the saint. At last the Gujar was reduced to a bull, but the saint bade him milk it too. It also died, and the Gujar only recovered his cattle from the spring to see them all turned into stones, where they stand to this day, because he disobeyed the saint's behest not to look back when he called out their names one by one at the spring.[6]

[1] P. N. Q. I., § 199. Baldang-Mahádeo.

[2] *Ib.*, III, § 78.

[3] *Ib.*, III, § 482.

[4] *Ib.*, I, § 561.

[5] Visvamitra is said to have done penance at Rámkunḍ, but the orthodox accounts of his penance do not mention the place. Another folk-tale associates it with Rájá Mán Singh of Amber, but it is opposed to all history, though it contains much of interest as folk-lore; S. C. R., VIII, pp 119-21.

[6] S. C. R., VIII, pp. 121-2.

At the western summit of the Sakesar hill are some rugged rocks called the Virgins—Kunwári, whose origin is thus described:—In the time of Muhammad Sháh Tughlaq, the country was infested by bands of *ghásis* or *jihádis* who used to carry off booty and village maidens to their fastnesses in Afghánistán. Some of them visited Bágh, 'the garden,' a village whose ruins are still traceable, held by the Tarer, a tribe now apparently extinct, and the Tarer put some of their daughters to death to prevent their falling into the bandits' hands, while others sought refuge among the rocks which rent in twain at their prayers and swallowed them up. The Tarers then scattered among the neighbouring villages.[1] Ranithrod in Ráwalpindi owes its name to the legend that the Rájpút women cast themselves over the precipice in the belief that their husbands had been defeated by the Moslems, and that their husbands on their return followed suit.[2]

How much real but forgotten history is preserved in such legends it is impossible to say, but it appears certain that they often preserve relics of ancient creeds or religious organizations. Thus Gurgaon derives its name from the tradition that it was granted to Drona Achárya, *gurú* of Yudishthira.[3] But the best exemplar of this is furnished by the Kurukshetr, an account of which will be found in Cunningham's *Arch. Survey Reports*.

Attock (Aṭak) on the Indus means a stoppage, and various modern legends attach to it from Sikh times.[4] Koṭ Bithaur in the hills nearby was Rájá Sir kap's fortress, and by an ingenious suspension bridge he used to cross the Indus to visit a Fair Rosamund until fate overtook him and he fell into the river.[5]

The name Jálandhar, which is found in Kurram and in Kulu as well as in the plains city of that name, appears to preserve the memory of a time when lake formations were much commoner than they are now in North-West India. Various legends are connected with it. In the Páṇḍavas' time Jálandhara, who reigned from the Sutlej to the Kángṛa hills, founded it, but it was destroyed and refounded by a *faqír* Jálandharnáth, in the days of Vikramaditya.[6] Many myths are attached to it and its tanks, named Gúpha and Brahmkuṇḍ. Ráhon was originally Raghupur, and possesses a Surajkund or sun-pool, and an old Hindu temple, while Núrmahal was once a Rájpút fort called Koṭ Kahlúr or Ghalúr. It has a sacred well called Ganga.[7]

Another account makes Trigartta, *Sankr.* for 'three forts,' the country between the Sutlej, Beás and Rávi, while Jálandhara was the portion of the *hills* over which Shiva threw Jálandhara to the

1 P. N. Q., I., § 697. The Tarer are probably the modern criminal tribe called Tarh; see Vol. III, p. 456 *infra*.

2 *Ib.*, III, § 101.

3 *Ib.*, I, § 1058.

4 *Ib.*, I, § 1029.

5 *Ib.* I, § 102.

6 *Ib.*, II, § 298.

7 *Ib.*, § 276.

daityas and its seat of government was Kángra.[1] Tradition also has it that Jálandhar was overwhelmed by a great flood in A. D. 1843.

Bhágsu, near Dharmsála, is so called because of the following legend. When Vásuki (Básak) Nág, king of the serpents, robbed Shiva of the bowl which contained the water of immortality Shiva taxed him with the theft, and in his flight Vásuki turned the bowl upside down, and caused the water to flow out. This happened at Bhágsu, which is named from Vásuki's flight (*bhág*).[2]

Illiterate Hindus believe that sleeping with feet to the north is an insult to the *deotas* as well as to the ancestors (*pitrs*), as they reside in that quarter. Literate Hindus have the same belief, on the theory that the attractive influence of the North is dangerous.[3]

Good Hindus will not sleep with their feet to the east out of respect for the Ganges (or because that would be an omen that their ashes would soon be carried to the sacred river), which flows to the east; or to the North, out of respect for Deví.[4]

Another version is that Hindus should sleep with their *heads* to the east because that will bring prosperity and learning, or to the south because that is respectful to Jampuri, the city of the lower world, while to sleep with one's head to the west brings trouble, and to the north disease and death.[5]

Bánias sometimes keep off rain by giving an unwed girl some oil which she pours on the ground, saying:—

'If I pour not out the oil, mine the sin,
If thou disperse not the clouds, thine the sin.'

Another prescription is to put a 1¼ *sers* of rain water into a new *ghara* and bury it at a spot on to which a roof spout discharges. This will stop the rain at once.[6]

During scarcity petty shopkeepers wishing to maintain high prices and keep off rain fill lamps with *ghi* and set light to them when clouds collect. After a while the light is blown out—and then of

[1] P. N. Q., II, § 222. But Dr. Hutchison writes:—

"Trigarta—as it should be spelt—cannot bear the meaning of 'three forts.' It is a case of confusing the word *gaṛ* with *gṛh*. The latter means 'fort', but *gaṛ* means a small stream or river. According to Cunningham the three rivers referred to were the Sutlej, Beis and Rávi. Vogel says that *gaṛ* cannot properly be used to indicate a big river, and that Trigarta more probably refers to the Bánganga, Kuráli and Nayagul—the principal rivers of Kángra—which unite at Siba fort and flow into the Biás under the name of Trigadh which is the same as Trigar. The final *ta* means country or region, and is often found in hill names *e.g.* Kuluta."

[2] P. N. Q., I, § 960.—Oldham records a legend which makes Bhágsu Nág originally a serpent *deota* whose temple has now, under Brahmanical influence, become sacred to Shiva and changed its name to Bhágsu Náth. The old stone figure of the snake still remains under a tree close by, but Shiva, *i.e.* a *linga*, occupies the temple.

[3] N. I. N. Q., I, § 107.—For the pre-Christian belief that the North was under the prince of the Power of the Air, see Durandus' *Symbolism of Churches*, p. xcv.

[4] I. N. Q., IV, § 192.

[5] *Ib.*, IV., § 419, § 48.

[6] P. N. Q., III, § 514.

course the clouds dispel.[1] Another and unsavoury method of frightening away clouds is practised by Hindu grain-dealers who have been speculating for a rise. When clouds appear they take a loaf into the fields or place rice, sugar etc. at a cross-road, and then *hique consedens supra panem album exonerant.* Or they lay in wait for people on a dark night and *stercore advenientes conspuicant: necnon asinorum terga eodem purgamine onerant.* These practices are said to be common in the Mánjha and to occur in Ambála.[2]

In Gilgit sacred springs are used on a similar principle. Sacrifices are offered to them, but if owing to drought heavy rain is wanted the people used to get a foreigner to throw an unclean thing, such as the bone of a dog, into the spring and then it rained until the thing was taken out. For this service the foreigner received a large quantity of grain as the people themselves believed in the power of the spring to inflict harm.[3]

On the other hand, rain may be caused by throwing a pot of filth over the threshold of an old woman with a bad temper. If she is annoyed and expresses her feelings rain will come down, but the rite may fail and the crone, keeping her wrath to herself, retaliate in kind.[4] To bring rain girls also pour water in which cowdung has been dissolved on an old woman, or she is made to sit just under the spout of the roof.[5] In Kulu the *deotas* are directed by the Rájá to send it and they are fined if it does not fall in the time allowed.[6]

To Hindus the rainbow is Rám Chandra's bow: to Muhammadans that of Bába Adam.[7] But in the Punjab it is generally called *pígh,* the swing or the old woman's swing, and in Multáni the *píngh* of Bíbi Bai who is very plausibly identified with Sakhi Sarwar's wife.[8] In Pashtu it is called the 'old woman's swing,' but in the Marwat it is called the bowl (*kásah*) and in Balochi *drín,* a word of unknown significance.

The Milky Way is in Multáni *bera da ghas,* 'the path of (Noah's) boat,' but is also called Akás Ganga, or the heavenly Ganges, the 'white garland,' the 'gate of heaven' and 'Bhagwán's court-house.'[9]

Wells disused and forgotten are believed to be revealed in dreams—at least to dreamers gifted with a special faculty for their discovery.[10]

1 P. N. Q., I, § 539.

2 *Ib.*, §§ 578, 833. Ibbetson's explanation, that the use of *ghí* instead of the cheaper oil and the waste of the food are intended to show the rain-god that there is no scarcity, is undoubtedly correct. The god is supposed to be withholding the rain of set purpose and the idea is to show him that he has failed in it—so he might as well send it.

3 Ghulam Muhammad, *On the Festivals and Folklore of Gilgit,* Asiatic Society of Bengal, Monograph I, pp. 112-13.

4 P. N. Q., I, § 791.

5 N. I. N. Q., I, § 572.

6 P. N. Q., II, § 249.

7 I. N. Q., IV, § 401. In Sanskrit it was either Sakrachápa, or Indrachápa, 'Indra's bow,' and so on. P. N. Q., I, § 1053.

8 P. N. Q., II, § 305.

9 *Ib.*, §§ 1027, 308, 610, (519), 528.

10 P. N. Q., I, § 695.

Goats have a reputation as well-finders, and a herd is believed to lie down in a circle round an old well even when filled up and overgrown by jungle. No goat, it is said, will walk over a hidden well: it will turn aside.[1] Goats will not lie down over an old well, and are said to detect it by stamping with their feet.[2] *Faqírs* are occasionally said to have the same power.

A goat is also a peace-offering, at least in Ríwalpindi, when the offering must apparently be accepted when tendered by one who wishes to close a feud. At Buria in Ambála, near Jagádhri, is or was a sacred well, but its efficacy has departed. The Ganga at Núrmahal has already been noticed.

Earthquakes are believed to be due to a fever in the earth's interior, causing ague. This is said to be a doctrine of the Yunáni school of medicine. Wells act as safety-valves for the trembling, however, so earthquakes are common in Persia and Kashmír, where wells are scarce, and rare in the Punjab.[3] Earthquakes are also said to be caused by the Earth Mother's anger at the prevalence of sin.[4] But many Hindus believe that the sacred bull which supports the world, first on one horn, then on the other, causes it to shake when he shifts it.[5]

If a shock is felt when the doors are open *i.e.* by day, it is auspicious, but if it occurs at or after midnight it is the reverse.[6]

Thunder is supposed to destroy chickens in the shell if it occur a day or two before they should be hatched. Every care is also taken to prevent children suffering from small-pox hearing thunder, and its noise is drowned by plying a hand-mill.[7]

Worship of the Ganges is distinctive of the APAPANTHIS, but it is not confined to them. Under the name of Bhagírathi it is worshipped very often, and principally by the ODS who claim descent from Bhagíratha, the Puranic hero who brought the Ganges down from heaven.[8]

Yáma, the god of death, is supposed to live in rivers. He is propitiated by making an image of gold according to one's means. This is worshipped and then given to a Brahman

The worship of the Beás is hardly distinguishable from that of the Rishi Vyása[9] whose shrine is at or near Bashist on the Beás

[1] P. N. Q., I, §§ 117, 118, 119, 344, 345, 694.

[2] *Ib.*, I, § 18.

[3] *Ib.*, III, § 183.

[4] I. N. Q., IV., § 199.

[5] *Ib.*, § 489.

[6] N. I. N. Q., I., § 591.

[7] P. N. Q., III, §§ 180, 179.

[8] Maclagan says the O*ds* often wear a black blanket, either because the Ganges has not flowed to the place where their ancestors' bones repose and so they wear mourning till it does so, or because Bhagíratha's *father* had sworn never to drink twice out of the same well, but one day he dug very deep and was buried by the well falling in on him—so they wear black blankets and bury their dead: Punjab *Census Rep.*, 1892, p. 105. For a charming picture of Bhagíratha with Shiva and Párvati, see Coomaraswamy's *Arts and Crafts of India and Ceylon*, Plate 76 and p. 98.

[9] Arranger of the *Vedas* and composer of the *Puránas*.

in Kulu where Moorcroft and Trebeck[1] found his image, about 1½ feet high, standing against the wall nearest the rock of a temple built a few feet in front of it. Its walls of loose stone form three sides of a quadrangle, the side next the stream being open so as to leave access to it free for its presiding genius, Vyása. By its side stood a smaller figure. Both images were much worn. The Rishi lived, however, at Vyás Asthal (now Bastali) in the Kurukshetr, and there the Ganges flowed underground to save him the trouble of going to bathe in that river, bringing too his *lota* and loin-cloth which he had left there to convince him that the water was really that of the Ganges.[2]

In the same way the Sarsuti or Saraswati river is not always to be distinguished from Saraswati, the goddess of learning, but only the former is at all extensively worshipped and then only locally. The Márkanda is confused in the same way with the Rishi of that name. The most noticeable river cult, however, is that of the Indus—see SEWAK DARYA—and that of Khwája Khizr is also important.

Dr. J. Hutchison regards the *minjrán ká mela* held in Chamba as probably a survival of the aboriginal worship of the river-god, but it is possibly connected with the cult of Mahádeo, to whom are offered ears (*minjrán*) of basil.[3] This *mela* is held on the third Sunday in Sáwan. In its main features it is peculiar to Chamba, though the name is known, and some of the ceremonies are observed in other parts of the hills. The essential part of the *mela* consists in the throwing into the Rávi of a male buffalo as a sacrifice to the river god. A week before the time comes round each person has a silk tassel made which is attached to some art of the dress and worn. This is called a *minjar*. On the day appointed, the Rájá and his court proceed to the spot, where the *mela* has been held from time immemorial. There a great concourse of people assembles. The Rájá gives the signal by throwing into the river a cocoanut, a rupee, *drub* grass, and some flowers, and thereupon the live buffalo is pushed into the flood. The Rájá throws his *minjar* in after the buffalo and all the people follow his example. The animal is then closely watched, as its fate is believed to foreshadow prosperity or adversity for the coming year to the reigning family and the State. If carried away and drowned, the event is regarded as propitious, the sacrifice having been accepted. If it crosses the river and gets out on the other bank, this also is propitious—the sins of the town having been transferred to the other side of the river. But if it emerges on the same side, coming evil is portended to the State. Being a devoted thing, the animal, if it escapes, is retained till the following year, doing no work, and is then cast in again, and so on till finally carried away and drowned. The buffalo is provided at the expense of the State. This *mela* is probably of aboriginal origin, and connected with the earth-worship which was prevalent among the aborigines of the hills. It was probably intended to secure good rains and a bountiful harvest.

TREE AND ANIMAL WORSHIP.—Traces of tree worship are still common. Most members of the Fig tribe, and especially the *pípal* Ibbetson, § 233.

[1] Journey to Ladákh, I, p. 190.

[2] N. I. N. Q., I, § 862.

[3] Chamba *Gazetteer*, 1904, p. 191: see page *infra*, and also under cult of Mahádeo.

and *baṛ* (*Ficus religiosa* and *Bengalensis*) are sacred; and only in the direst extremities of famine will their leaves be cut for the cattle. Sacred groves are found in most villages from which no one may cut wood or pick fruit. The *jaṇḍ* (*Prosopis spicigera*) is reverenced very generally, more especially in the parts where it forms a chief feature in the larger flora of the great arid grazing grounds; it is commonly selected to mark the abode or to shelter the shrine of a deity, it is to it as a rule that rags are affixed as offerings, and it is employed in the marriage ceremonies of many tribes. In some parts of Kángṛa, if a betrothed but as yet unmarried girl can succeed in performing the marriage ceremony with the object of her choice round a fire made in the jungles with certain wild plants, her betrothal is annulled and the marriage holds good. Marriage with trees is not uncommon, whether as the third wife elsewhere alluded to, or by prostitutes in order to enjoy the privileges of a married woman without the inconvenience of a human husband. The *deodár* worship of Kulu has been described. Several of the Jáṭ tribes revere certain plants. Some will not burn the wood of the cotton plant, the women of others veil their faces before the *ním* (*Melia Indica*) as if in the presence of a husband's elder relative, while others pray to the tiger grass (*Saccharum spontaneum*) for offspring under the belief that the spirit of the ancestor inhabits it. These customs are probably in many cases totemic rather than strictly religious (as for example among the Rájpúts). The Bishnoi also objects to cutting a tree by a pool or to pruning or lopping a *jaṇḍi* (the female of the *jaṇḍ*) as its cutting would lead to bloodshed. The *jaṇḍ* and *pípal* should be watered in Baisákh. *Tíraths* or holy pools are greatly believed in, the merit of bathing in each being expressed in terms of cows, as equal to that of feeding so many. Some of these pools are famous places of pilgrimage. The Hindu peasant venerates the cow, and proves it by leaving her to starve in a ditch when useless rather than kill her comfortably. Yet if he be so unfortunate as to kill a cow by mishap, he has to go to the Ganges, there to be purified at considerable expense; and on the road he bears aloft the cow's tail tied to a stick, that all may know that he is impure and must not enter a village, and may avoid his touch and send out food to him. His regard for animal life in general forbids him to kill any animal; though he will sometimes make an exception in favour of owls and even of snakes, and he seldom has any objection to anybody else destroying the wild animals which injure his crops. In the east he will not eat meat; but I believe that in the Punjab proper the prohibition extends to women only. The monkey and peacock are specially sacred.

Trees also have a kind of social precedence among themselves. Thus the *pípal* is regarded as the Brahman among trees, while the *siras* is regarded as the *sirdár* or head of all save the *pípal* by Jáṭs, and by some Muhammadans as the Sayyid—and this is said to be the reason why a bunch of its leaves is hung up over the door of a room in which a male child has been born.[1]

[1] P. N. Q., II, § 1060. The *pípal* is also worshipped as the abode of the Panjpíri and Nár Singh, and where there is no *pípal* the *baṛ* or banyan is substituted: *ib.*, III, § 169.

The indigo plant is by caste a *mehtar* or sweeper and so orthodox Hindus have a strong dislike to blue clothes and to growing indigo.[1] It was a disgraceful punishment to have one's face smeared with it whence the proverb: *níl ká ṭíká mujhe mat lagwáná:* 'may I never be anointed with indigo.'

But in Chamba tree worship is by no means distinctive: indeed it is doubtful if any tree but the *pípal* is really worshipped. As this tree does not grow much above an elevation of 3,000 feet its worship is prevalent only in the lower and outer valleys of the State. The Nág and Deví temples are frequently found in cedar groves and the *Cedrus deodara* is then regarded as sacred, and may not be cut down. The tree itself, however, is not worshipped, nor is it looked upon as sacred unless it is close to a temple. The same is true of other trees which are believed to be the abode of malevolent spirits, such as the *kainth,* fig, pomegranate etc. The tree is not worshipped, only the spirit residing in it. Even the shadow of these trees is injurious. But though many of the forest trees are believed to be the abodes of evil spirits the Banbirs—see page —also dwell in certain trees.

Tree worship is practised in several ways. Thus at domestic festivals many Brahmans and Khatris perform rites to the *jaṇḍ* (*Prosopis spicigera*). Some families never put on their children clothes made at home, but only those begged off friends, and the ceremony of putting on a child's first clothes is observed when it is three years old. It is then taken to a *jaṇḍ* from which a twig is cut and planted at its foot. A *swástika* made of rice-flour is made before it, and it is also offered sugar. Nine threads are then cut into lengths and one of them is tied round the twig in Shiva's or Krishna's distinctive knot, while another is tied round a piece of dried *gur* and put on the *swástika*. *Mantras* from the *Yájur Veda* appear to be recited the while, and finally sugar and rice are given to all the women and children present, for besides the Brahman celebrant no other adult males may be present. The Brahman then puts on the child his first clothes, impressing on them the mark of his hand in saffron, and ties a thread, to which is fastened the purse, which contained his fee, round its loins. In front this thread has a small triangle of red silk lined with *sálu*—like the only garment of very small girls. This may be done in order to disguise the boy as a girl, and the custom is said to refer to the extermination of the Kshatria boys by Paras Ráma.[2]

The *ámla* (*emblica officinalis*) is worshipped in Kátik as propitious and chaste, Brahmans being fed under it, threads tied round it and seven circumambulations made round it. As the pennate leaves of the *jaṇḍ* and its galls make it resemble the *ámla* it too is worshipped in the same way.[3] At weddings its worship is widely practised, and in Muzaffargarh Hindu bridegrooms generally and a few Muhammadans cut off a small branch of it and bury it before marriage. Offerings are also made to the tree by relatives of Hindus suffering from small-pox.[4]

The chichra (*butea frondosa*) is sacred because of its use for funeral pyres[5]

[1] P. N. Q., III, § 581, § 715.
[2] *Ib.*, II, § 344.
[3] P. N. Q., II, § 449.
[4] Muzaffargarh *Gazetteer*, 1883-84, p. 22.

The *tulsi* is worshipped among women by placing a lamp made of flour at its root and saying: *Tulsi díva bália, Mainún mardi nún sambhália:* 'I have lit a lamp for Tulsi and she will take care of me when I die.' The *pípal* is worshipped in the same way with the rhyme:—

Patte pátte Govind baiṭha, ṭahni ṭahni Deota,
Muḍh te Sri Kishan baiṭhá, dhan Brahma Deota.

'Govind sits on every leaf, and a god on every branch.
And on the trunk holy Krishna: glory to Brahma *devata*.'[1]

And the worship of the *pípal* is believed to be equal to that of the above gods. A *tulsi* plant is kept in an orthodox Hindu house partly because it is Vishnu's plant, partly because it is sweet-scented and a deodoriser. Much the same ideas prevail regarding the sandal-wood tree. The tendrils of the *pípal* make a cooling medicine for children, and its leaves are a powerful charm in fever.[2]

The *kíkar* tree also has magical powers. For fever take a cotton thread and wind it in hanks of seven threads from your left big toe round your head. Then tie these hanks round a *kíkar* and embrace its trunks seven times. This propitiates the tree, and it will cause the fever to leave you. Such hanks are often seen round *kíkar* trees.[3]

When a wealthy Hindu is sonless he will marry a Brahman to a *tulsi* plant which is regarded as a nymph metamorphosed by Krishna. The ceremonies are solemnised in full and at some expense. The *tulsi* is then formally made over to the Brahman who is regarded as the donor's son-in-law for the rest of his life, because he has received his bride at his fictitious father-in-law's hands.[4]

See also under Mahádeo, note 1 *infra*, and at p. 121 note, *supra*, under Panjpiri.[5]

Trees also play important rôles at weddings and in connection with marriage.[6]

A *babúl* (*Acacia Arabica*) or *lasúra* (*Cordia myxa*) planted near a house will ruin the dwellers in it.[7] Orthodox Hindus too will not sleep under a *babúl* for it causes sickness. Indeed it is regarded as a very Chamár among trees and its wood is disliked even for burning corpses. But Chamárs themselves use it freely.[8] On the other hand, the shade of a *ním* is very lucky.

Both plantain and mango leaves are sacred among Hindus and used on all auspicious occasions, and when any sacred book is read it is often placed between small posts covered with those leaves.[9]

In Karnál the leaves of the *siraṣ* are especially powerful and after them those of the mango. They are hung in garlands with an inscription on a platter in the middle, and the whole is called a *ṭoṭka*. The *jaṇḍ* is also a very sacred tree.[10]

1 P. N. Q., III, § 556.
2 *Ib.*, III, §§ 718-14.
3 P. N. Q., I, § 852.
4 *Ib.*, II, § 816.
5 *Ib.*, III, § 159.
6 P. N. Q., III, § 90.
7 *Ib.*, III, § 182.
8 *Ib.*, III, § 208.
9 I. N. Q., IV, § 118.
10 *Sett. Rep.*, p. 154.

Besides the *babúl* and *lasúra* the *beri* and *arand* (castor-oil plant) are haunted by evil spirits. The *pípal* too is said to be so haunted and the *kíkar* unlucky.[1]

The egg-plant, *baingan*, is unlucky and not eaten because its seed remains in the stomach for a year, and if the eater die within that term he will go to hell. But another version makes the egg-plant[2] a forbidden vegetable because once a number of fairies were eating its fruit and one of them got caught in its thorns The Rájá asked her what she wished and she said: 'I wish to be released: to-day is the *ikádshi* (a fast day), bring me a person who has fasted.' But the only person who had fasted that day was a little girl who had refused to eat her breakfast, and so the Rájá made her give up to the fairy all the benefits she had derived from her fast, and then the *baingan* released its captive. Fasting on the *ikádshi* was then unknown. The *baingan* is also said to be objected to for a prudish idea.[3] It is also likened in a catch to a Malang, a *faqír*, with green cap and purple face.[4]

After sunset trees sleep and so it is a great sin to pluck even a leaf from one during the night, as it will awaken the sleeper. *Rákshasas* also inhabit trees after nightfall.[5]

The *dál* of *masúr* or pulse is objected to because it resembles drops of blood and the carrot, turnip and other vegetables for prudish reasons. Jogis collect the herb called *jari-búti* from the Dhángir hill near Paṭhánkot and mix it with the ashes of an unmarried Hindu. If the mixture is given to an enemy he will be bewitched, and can only be cured by another Jogí's incantations.[6]

Wood-cutting and kiln-burning are unlucky occupations as they both involve the destruction of life in living trees and of the insects in the earth while it is being burnt. The sin is punished in each case by a shortened life. Another unlucky occupation is that of the Bhaṛbhunja or Bhujwá who are *mahápápi*, 'great sinners,' butchering the grain they parch. Indigo too is full of insects which are killed while it is rotting in the vat,[7] and they will retaliate on the workers in the next birth.[8]

Dyers attribute the accidental spoiling of their dyes to some sin of their own, but it can be transferred to those who have reviled them by telling some incredible tale which will cause their hearers to speak ill of them and thus relieve the dye of its burden.[9] Potters too are very wicked for they make vessels with necks and thus impiously imitate Brahma's handiwork. They also cut the throats of their vessels.[10]

The cow is worshipped on the 8th of the light half of Kátik, on the Gopíshtami, or 'cow's eighth.' At evening men and women go to the cows and worship them, garlanding their horns with flowers. Each cow is then fed with kneaded flour-balls (*perá*), her feet dusted and obeisance done to her with the prayer: 'O cow, our

[1] I. N. Q., IV., §§ 42, 180.
[2] P. N. Q., III, § 449.
[3] *Ib.*, III, § 776.
[4] I. N. Q., IV, § 68 (13).
[5] P. N. Q., II, § 738.
[6] N. I. N. Q., I, § 117.
[7] P. N. Q., III, §§ 566, 792.
[8] *Ib.*, § 715.
[9] I. N. Q., IV, § 120.
[10] *Ib.*, § 426.

mother, keep us happy.' A woman thus worshipping the cow marks her own forehead also with sandal-wood and red lead[1] A song sung on this occasion runs :—'O ploughman, thou of the yoke, I recall to thy memory, eat thine own earnings, and credit mine to Hari's account.'

To let a cow die with a rope round its neck is a heinous sin : its value must be given to Brahmans and a pilgrimage made to the Ganges. A cow when ill is at once let loose.[2]

Bulls are let loose as scape-goats, the sins of their deliverers' forefathers being transferred to them. They are called Brahmani.[3]

No Hindu will ride on a bull as it is sacred, nor on a mare in foal as it injures the foal whenever conceived.[4]

No bullock can be worked on an *ikádshi*—11th of a lunar fortnight—nor can any corn be eaten on such a date.

A bullock with a small fleshy growth, called *jíbh* or tongue, in the corner of its eye or on its head or back must not be yoked by any Hindu, in Gurgaon, under pain of excommunication. Such an animal is called *nádia*,[5] and must be given to a Jogí who takes him about with trappings and strings of couries on him when begging to excite reverence by exhibition of the sacred mark.[6]

Cholera can be got rid of by painting a young he-buffalo with red lead and driving it on to the next village As the goddess of cholera likes this she will leave you also.[7]

The horse is commonly given the title of Gházi Mard or Ghází Mián—Conquering hero.[8]

Horses were created before any other animals, and elephants next, so they never give a false omen. Both can smell danger from a distance and warn their riders of it.[9]

The scars on horses' legs mark where they once had wings. God took away their wings when they flew from heaven to earth for the use of man when He made Adam.[10]

When leopards roar at night *deotas* are believed to be riding them in Kulu. The leopardess always has three cubs, but one of them is always stunted and only grows up into the leopard cat.[11]

[1] P. N. Q., III, §§ 480, 887.

[2] I. N. Q., IV, § 492.

[3] *Ib.*, IV, § 891.

[4] N. I. N. Q., I, § 866.

[5] The derivation suggested there is from *nandi*. the sacred bull of Shiva, but the word *nádia* may come from *nádh*, a whistle, which is worn by Jogis probably as an emblem of Shiva,—II, § 126. Nandia Jogis are found in the Central Provinces (Russell, *op. cit.*, III, p. 252), but not in the Punjab apparently For the *nád* of the Jogis see Vol. II, pp. 390, 399, *infra*.

[6] P. N. Q., I, § 6

[7] I. N. Q., IV, § 196.

[8] P. N. Q., II, § 1068.

[9] I. N. Q., IV, § 188.

[10] P. N. Q., III, § 290.

[11] N, I. N. Q., I, § 558.

It is a heinous sin to kill a cat, for it is a Brahmani, and its killing is punished by the slayer's becoming a cat in his next birth. To avert this fate a cat made of gold should be given to a Brahman.[1]

Do not abuse your house rats, for then they will not injure your chattels.[2] If poison is mentioned they will understand and not touch it, so when mixing it people say they are cooking food for neighbours.[3]

A camel's right hoof is a potent charm against rats and will clear a house of them.[4]

If a camel's bones be placed in a crop of sugarcane no ants will attack it: if buried at the entrance of a house no evil spirit will enter in.[5]

Pious Hindus consider it a duty to release caged birds, especially on holidays like the *amáwas* and *ikádshi* of each month.[6]

The peacock is sacred to Hindus as being the vehicle of Saraswati,[7] the goddess of learning. A curious belief is said to exist that pea-fowl do not mate: the hen is impregnated by the tears of the male![8]

Thunder can be heard by the peacock 100 *kos* away, and their cry portends rain.[9]

The *garuda*—adjutant crane—is Vishnu's vehicle, and one should manage to catch a sight of it on the Dasahra.[10]

If a crow picks up a woman's kerchief and drops it she will at once give it to a beggar.[11]

Grain is also scattered for crows to eat and the birds are netted for sale to pious people who let them go again. The chief purchasers are Bánias' wives who are believed to be specially liable to metempsychosis into crows, so the trappers hold up a crow in front of each Bánia's shop and cry: 'Behold so-and-so's wife.' This compels the wife to buy the bird and she immediately releases it.[12]

The kite, crow, kingfisher, owl and snake are all believed to live 1000 years.[13]

The young of the kite do not open their eyes until an article of gold is shown to them. Hence kites carry off gold ornaments. And the best cure for weak eyes is *surma* mixed with the contents of their eggs and applied to the eyes.[14]

The parrot is called Ganga Rám by Hindus, and Míán Mitthu by Muhammadans.[15]

A *chakor* (partridge) is often kept to ward off evil, as it takes upon itself all its owner's misfortunes.[16]

The partridge, both the *titar* and *chakor*, are averters of the evil eye. They eat fire at the full moon.[17]

1 P. N. Q., III, § 279.
2 N. I. N. Q., I, § 97.
3 *Ib.*, § 658.
4 *Ib.*, I, § 244.
5 I. N. Q., IV, § 497.
6 N. I. N. Q., I, § 648.
7 P. N. Q., III, § 479.
8 I. N. Q., IV, § 496.
9 *Ib.*, IV, § 194.
10 N. I. N. Q., I., § 112.
11 *Ib.*, I., § 104.
12 *Arch. S. Rep.*, V, p. 136.
13 I. N. Q., IV, § 358.
14 P. N. Q., III, §§ 880-1.
15 *Ib.*, III, § 888, and I. N. Q., IV, § 472. For the cult of Míán Mitthu in Gurdáspur see *infra*.
16 P. N. Q., III, § 289.
17 I. N. Q., IV, § 495.

The dove is said never to mate twice, and if one of a pair dies its mate pines to death.[1]

The *papíha*, or black and white crested cuckoo, is a bird which sings in the rainy season and is said to have a hole in its throat.[2]

The feathers of the blue-jay are supposed to be soothing to babies that cry, and one tied round neck of a child that gnashes its teeth in sleep[3]—a portent of death to one of its parents—will cure it of that habit.[4] Yet in Muzaffargarh it is a bad omen to see the blue-jay or *chánh*.

Killing a pigeon is considered unlawful among the Kheshgi Paṭháns of Kasúr. Some Muhammadans regard it as a Sayyid among birds, and therefore it is a sin to kill it—though it is lawful food.[5]

The *mahára* is a bird which causes *múnhkhur*,[6] foot-and-mouth disease, in Multán.

The *malálı*, butcher-bird or shrike, is ill-omened if seen in flight.[7]

The heron standing on one leg is the type of a sanctimonious hypocrite, so it is styled *bagla bhagat*.[8]

Locusts go off to the east, when they die of eating salt earth (*reh*).[9]

The large glow-worm which comes out in the rains is in the Murree hills called the *honwála kíra* because it was in its former life a *faqír* who refused fire to Behmáta or Bidhi Máta, the goddess who records a child's future at birth, and was condemned by her to carry a light for ever. *Hon* is the 'light' in the tail—*fr. hon* = *havan*—apparently.[10]

The many-hued grass-hopper which feeds on the *ak* is called Rámji ki-gáo or Rám's cow in Hariána.[11] The little Indian squirrel is similarly called Rám Chandr ká bhagat because when that god was bridging the sea 'twixt India and Lanka the squirrel helped by shaking dust from its body on to the bridge. The black lines in its body are the marks of his fingers.[12]

Ants are fed in Kángṛa with five articles, called *panjíri* or *gullar*, for luck.[13]

Sir James Lyall noticed that the practice of beating pots and pans to induce bees to settle in a swarm previous to hiving prevails in Kulu, as it did or does in English country places. The Kulu men at the same time tell the queen-bee and her subjects :—*Besh, Mahárání, besh, aur tobí agge jási, Mahárání ri drohí osi ;* "Be seated, great queen, be seated, and (turning to the bees) an appeal has been made to the queen against your going any further."

The *chhapáki* is an ash-coloured bird, the size of a dove. If you kill one and then touch a person afflicted with itch he will be cured.[14]

Owls and goat suckers, *ghugh*, *ullán*, and *huk*, are all birds of ill-omen, especially the *ghugh*, which is called the *Kiṛakku shinh* or

[1] I. N. Q., IV, § 177.
[2] P. N. Q., III, § 600, p. 142, *cf.* p. 151.
[3] *Ib.*, III, § 585.
[4] *Ib.*, III, § 780.
[5] N. I. N. Q., I, §§ 75, 440.
[6] *Panjabi Dicty.* p. 698.
[7] Muzaffargarh *Gazetteer*, 1883-4, p. 29
[8] P. N. Q., II, § 855.
[9] Sirsa *S. R.*, p. 255.
[10] P. N. Q., I, § 14.
[11] *Ib.*, III, § 40.
[12] *Ib.*, III, § 231.
[13] *Ib.*, III, § 273.
[14] Muzaffargarh *Gazetteer*, 1883-4, p. 30.

'Kirárs' tiger,' from the superstitious dread in which that caste holds it.[1] The *chikri* or button owl is equally unlucky, apparently on account of its ugliness.

In Muzaffargarh the kite, *hil* (Hindi *chil*), is supposed to be male for 6 months in the year and female during the other half. In much the same way the popular belief on the banks of the Indus is that if *methra* or fenugreek (*trigonelle, foenum graecum*) be sown before noon *methra* will grow, if after noon *assún* (*brassica eruca*). Under certain circumstances *morhi* (*Ervum lens*) turns into a seed called *rári*.[2]

The king crow, *kal-kalichi,-kariche* or-*karohki* is revered by the Shias because it brought water to the dying Imám, Hassan, and also because it is always astir early. Its note is said to be: *utth sohágan, chakki pí*, 'get up, good wife, and grind corn.'[3]

The *galei* is a larger lizard than the house lizard. If a woman touch one before she makes butter it will be abundant.[4]

The *khan* is a black and white lizard with a bluish tinge about which many tales are told. It is found full grown in the belly of a snake, and not born. Though harmless it is supposed to be most deadly. The flesh of another lizard, the *sáhndu*, is credited with restorative powers.[5]

SNAKE WORSHIP AND THE CULT OF GUGA.

Various superstitions attach to the snake. For example: After her young are born (? hatched) the female snake makes a circle round them. Those that crawl out of it survive, but those that stay in it she devours.[6] If you see a snake on a Sunday you will see it for 8 successive Sundays.[7]

When a snake is seen, say Sayyids and other Musalmáns of high class, one should say *bel, bel, bel*, and it will become blind. The shadow of a pregnant woman falling upon it has the same effect.[8]

A curious belief exists regarding the *man* or snake-stone. It is sometimes said to be a fine silky filament spat out by a snake 1000 years old on a dark night when it wants to see. It is luminous. The way to get hold of it is to cast a piece of cow-dung upon it, and its possession insures immunity from all evil and the realisation of every wish. It protects its owner from drowning, parting the waters for him on either side.[9]

Still stronger is the belief that lightning will strike a tree if it have a snake's hole (*barmi*) under it. Lightning invariably falls where there are black snakes and it is peculiarly fatal to snakes of that colour as it attracts the lightning.[10]

The *Singhs*, or *Snake gods*, occupy an intermediate place between the two classes into which I have divided the minor deities. They are males, and though they cause fever are not very malevolent, often taking away pain. They have great power over milch cattle, the milk of the

Ibbetson § 216

1 Muzaffargarh *Gazetteer*, 1883-4 p. 29.
2 *Ib.*, p. 95.
3 *Multáni Glossary*.
4 Muzaffargarh *Gazetteer* p. 32.
5 *Ib.*, p. 32.
6 N. I. N. Q., I, § 671.
7 N. I. N. Q., I, § 256.
8 P. N. Q., I, § 122. A snake should be called *sher*, 'tiger,' or *rassi*, 'rope,' never by its proper name.
9 P. N. Q., I., § 607.
10 *Ib.*, I., § 927.

eleventh day after calving is sacred to them, and libations of milk are always acceptable. They are generally distinguished by some colour, the most commonly worshipped being Káli, Hari, and Bhúri Singh, or black, green, and grey. But the diviner will often declare a fever to be caused by some Singh whom no one has even heard of before, but to whom a shrine must be built; and so they multiply in the most perplexing manner. Dead men also have a way of becoming snakes, a fact which is revealed in a dream, when again a shrine must be built. If a peasant sees a snake he will salute it; and if it bite him, he or his heirs, as the case may be, will build a shrine on the spot to prevent a repetition of the occurrence. They are the servants of Rájá Básak Nág, king of Patál or Tartarus; and their worship is most certainly connected in the minds of the people with that of the *pitr* or ancestors, though it is difficult to say exactly in what the connection lies. Sunday is their day, and Brahmans do not object to be fed at their shrines, though they will not take the offerings which are generally of an impure nature. The snake is the common ornament on almost all the minor Hindu shrines.

Mrs. F. A. Steel vouches for the following account of snake-worship:—During nine days in Bhádon the snake is worshipped by all castes and religions, but at the end of Sáwan Mirási women of the 'snake' tribe make a snake of flour, paint it red and black, and place it on a winnowing basket with its head poised like a cobra's. This basket they carry round the village singing verses invoking Alláh and Gúga Pír. Every one should give them a small cake and some butter, but generally only a little flour or grain is given, though in houses where there is a newly married bride Re. 1-4-0 and some clothes are given, and this gift is also made if a son has been born. Finally the flour snake is buried and a small grave built over it, at which the women worship during the nine days of Bhádon. The night before they set curds, but next morning instead of churning it they take it to the snake's grave and offer a small portion, kneeling and touching the ground with their foreheads. They then divide the curds amongst their children. No butter is made or eaten on that day. Where snakes abound this rite is performed in jungles where they are known to be.[1]

That certain persons are believed to be immune from snake-bite is undeniable. Thus in Kángra a man has been known to allow himself to be bitten by a poisonous snake once a year in the rains. First bitten by a cobra he was cured by prayers at a shrine to Gúga called Kútiári dá Gúga. Such persons are said to give out a peculiar odour and to feel a kind of intoxication when the time for getting bitten, which they cannot escape, comes round. They recover in a few days. Some people believe that the snake that bites

[1] P. N. Q., II, § 555. Mrs. Steel also declares that the Snake *zát* or tribe is not uncommon, and that they are Muhammadans of Kasúr. They observe all these rites also every morning after a new moon, and further every Monday and Thursday cook rice and milk for the snake, never making or using butter in those days. They are immune from snake-bite and if they find a dead snake give it a regular funeral. Possibly a sect of this kind exists. The Bangális claim the power of recognising disguised snakes—for a snake changes its form and must do so every 100 years when it becomes a man or a bull—and follow them to their holes, where they ask to be shown where treasure is hidden. This snakes will do in return for a drop of blood from the little finger of a first-born son. But see also III, § 418.

is a female and so they recover,[1] but arsenic taken repeatedly is probably an effective prophylactic.[2]

That snakes hibernate appears to be recognised by the following custom: after the Diwáli in Kángra a festival, called Nág-ká-pújá, is held in November to say good-bye to the snakes. At this an image of the Nág made of cow-dung is worshipped, but any snake seen after it is called *nisúgrá* or ungrateful and killed forthwith.[3] Many Hindus take a lamp used at the Diwáli to their houses to scare snakes away from them for the next six months[4]; and the *chhhri-saresh* or *churi-saroj*, the fragrant *Artemisia elegans*, is also kept in houses to frighten them away.[5] A curious by-product of snake-worship is the prohibition against giving milk to a dying man, as it will make him a serpent at his next birth[6]

The existence of a two headed snake (*domúnha*) is believed in and any person once bitten by such a snake will be regularly sought out and bitten by it every year afterwards.[7] Such an experience confers immunity even from poisonous snakes though insensibility ensues.[8] Certain simples are used to cure snake-bite, but a purely magic rite consists in taking a handful of shoots and, while praising the snake's ancestors, fanning the wound with them. This is called *dáli hálná* and is done in Kángra.[9] Pouring water and milk down a snake's hole is a preventive of snake-bite.[10]

In primitive speculation the snake was supposed to renew its youth when it cast its skin and so to be immortal.[11]

[1] P. N. Q., II, § 995

[2] *Ib.*, III, § 175.

Ib., III, § 353.

[4] *Ib.*, III, § 176.

[5] *Ib.*, III, § 177.

[6] *Ib.*, III, § 584.

[7] *Ib.*, III, § 291.

[8] *Ib.*, III, § 452.

[9] *Ib.*, III. § 788.

[10] *Ib.*, II, § 672.

[11] See Sir J. G. Frazer's valuable article on *The Serpent and the Tree of Life* in *Essays presented to William Ridgeway*, Cambridge, 1914, p. 418 *ff*. Support to his theory will be found in the following account of a primitive Nág cult in the Simla Hills recently thus described by Mr. H. W. Emerson :—" In the remote tract called Tikrál, which lies near the source of the Pabur, the people were warlike and ferocious down to a century ago. Their country is subject to a confederacy of five gods, called the Pánch Nágs, who hibernate during the winter, going to sleep at the first fall of snow and only waking up again at the Phag, the festival which corresponds to the Holi in the plains, when they are aroused by their worshippers. Each temple has a small aperture cut through an outer wall of the second storey and opening into the chamber where the god's couch is laid. A miniature image is placed below the window inside the room. A few days previous to the full moon two parties are chosen from the subjects of the god, each composed of from 8 to 10 men. One party represents the god's defenders, the other his awakeners; but the members of both have to prepare themselves for their sacred duties by fasting until the appointed day arrives. On that day they arm themselves with a large supply of snow-balls, the snow being brought from the hills above, if, as rarely happens, it has melted from round the homesteads. The assailants stand about 20 paces from the window, while the rest take up their position immediately below it. All hold their snow-balls ready in the skirts of their long coats and at a given signal go into action, but whereas the god's support-

Another rain god of serpent origin in the Simla Hills is Basheru. Once a woman was cutting grass when her sickle struck a three-faced image of gold. She took it home and placed it in her cow shed, hoping that her herds would multiply. But next morning the shed was full of water and the cattle all drowned. So she gave it to a Brahman who put it in his granary. But next morning it too was filled with water and so he set the people to build the image a temple a mile or two away whence the god still controls the weather according to the wishes of his votaries. As he had no village green he drained a lake by coming down in spate one night and cutting a deep channel. On the sward his festivals are now held. At the one in early spring the god is rejuvenated by being carried to his birth-place and there laid on his side so that he may be recharged as it were with the divine essence which still emanates from his natal soil. This process takes 6 or 7 hours, during which his bearers lie prostrate and his worshippers keep strict silence, but his musicians play—to assist the ascent or transmission of the divine spirit, as well as to relieve the tedium of the god's inactivity. No sacrifices are offered.

On the Upper Sutlej a snake goddess gave birth to seven sons, the territorial gods of as many valleys. They had no father, or at least his name is not known. Her own home is a spring situate in a forest glade dedicated to her use, and there her watchman, Gunga, the dumb man, keeps guard over her sanctuary from a holly bush. Should any one cut down a tree or defile the sacred spring he curses him with dropsy. Not even the sons can approach their mother without

ers pelt his adversaries they are themselves safe from attack and the other party must aim at the open window Should no ball fall into the room where the deity reclines before the stock of ammunition is exhausted the throwers have to pay a fine of several rams, since their indifferent skill has then defeated the very object of the mimic battle. The god sleeps on unconscious of the efforts made to break his slumber and other means are taken to rouse him from his lethargy. Men creep up the staircase carrying trumpets and conch shells and when all are ready blow a mighty blast in unison. Others bang the door and rattle its massive chains shouting to the god to bestir himself. This at best is but a poor way of awakening the Nág, as annoying to the worshippers as to the god. The latter would fain sleep on, but if he has to wake—and wake he must—he would rather have a snow-ball hit him, cold and painful though the awakening be, than have his dreams disturbed by an unseemly din outside his chamber door. So if the throwers succeed as they usually do in placing a missile through the window the omen is considered most auspicious. They then leap and dance with joy, shouting that the god has risen from his bed. The *fidei defensores*, on the other hand, feign to be horror-stricken at the sacrilege, and pursue the culprits with a running fire of snow, clods, stones, abuse and even gun shots. The chase continues through and round the village until at length a truce is called Both parties agree to accept the ruling of the god and repairing to his temple consult the oracle. The spirit, refreshed and invigorated by the winter's rest, descends upon the diviner, who shakes and shouts under the full force of the divine afflatus. Having explained the situation to his master he interprets the divine decision. This is always to the same effect. The Nág, while commending his supporters for their spirited defence, thanks his assailants for their kindly thought in rousing him now that the time of winter cold has passed and the season of spring time is at hand. Thus every one is pleased and the assembly prepare to listen to the further sayings of their god. The god will tell the story of his journey from Kashmir and the many incidents which happened on the way. Then he foretells the future, prophesying what fortune will attend the rules of the neighbouring States, which crops will flourish and which fail, whether the herds and flocks will multiply, what domestic sorrows will befall his subjects, and in general whether the year will be a good or evil one. The announcement of harvest prospects and the interpretation of omens is a special feature of the oracles which often continue for many hours. On its completion the audience commence a feast which lasts for several days. Drinking, dancing and singing are its main features, and the god as usual joins heart and soul in the merriment."

his leave. If one of them has lost his vigour his followers bring him to Gunga, and having obtained his consent, carry the god to the spring and lay him there in his litter, prone on his side. Such energy oozes from the fountain that in a hour or two he is reinvigorated for several years and can bestow blessings on his people until his strength runs down again. Some say that the snake herself appears in serpent form and men have seen her licking the suppliant's face. (*Pioneer*, January 14th, 1916.) For the sacred serpent licking a patient's sores see Richard Caton's *The Temples and Ritual of Asklepios*, London, 1900, p. 30.

The Nag cults in Chamba.

Dr. J. Hutchison describes the Nág and Deví cults as the oldest in the Chamba hills, and Dr. Vogel regards the Nágas as water spirits, typifying the alternately beneficial and destructive power of water. This theory, however, does not adequately explain how the Nágas of Brahmanic and Buddhist literature and the Nágs of the Himalayan valleys came to be regarded as snake gods. Brigade Surgeon C. F. Oldham's theory[1] that the so-called snake-gods and *devís* are the deified rulers of the people has little to commend it, and is based on the assumption that the hooded snake was the racial emblem of the ruled. It is safer to regard both the Nágs and the *devís* as emblems of the powers of fertility and reproduction.

The Nág shrines in Chamba are very numerous, and there are also Nágni shrines, but the latter are not common. The image in these shrines is usually of stone in human form, with the figure of a snake entwined around it and a serpent canopy over head. The shrine also contains figures of snakes in stone and iron, with a *tirsúl* or trident, a lamp, an incense holder, a *gurj* or weapon like a sword, and finally the iron chain or *sangal* with which the *chela* scourges himself. This is said to be an exact copy of that shown in the hand of the Egyptian god Osiris. Springs of water are believed to be under the control of these snake godlings, and, in some parts of the hills, to such a degree are springs and wells associated with snake influence in the minds of the people that Nág is the name in common use for a spring of cool and refreshing water. A spring will usually be found in proximity to a Nág temple. Many of the Nága godlings are believed to have the power to grant rain, and in times of drought they are diligently propitiated. *Jágras* or vigils are held in connection with the temples, incense is burnt and sheep and goats are offered in sacrifice. The *pujára* gets the head and the *chela* the shoulder, while the low caste musicians are given the entrails and cooked food. The rest of the animal is taken away and consumed by the offerer and his family or friends. Money offered is equally divided between the *pujára* and *chela*; also dry grain. If people belonging to a low caste offer cooked food, which is not often done, it is given back to them after being presented to the Nág. A *jágra* or vigil is always held at the time of a *mela*, which as a rule takes place once a year at each shrine.

The Nág and Devi temples are all erected on much the same plan and are usually situated in a clump of cedar trees near a village. Such

[1] The Sun and the Serpent.

trees around a temple may not be cut down, and are regarded as the property of the deity in their midst. Sometimes a temple is erected within the interior of a forest or in some mountain ravine, standing quite alone. The usual pattern is a square resting on a raised platform of stone. The building itself may be entirely of wood, or of the wood and stone style of architecture so common in the hills. It generally consists of a central *cella* with an open verandah around it and a small door in front. The whole is covered in with a pent-roof of wood which either slopes on two sides from a central ridge, or on four sides from a surmounting cap or ball. This roof is supported on cross beams resting on wooden, or wood and stone, pillars one at each corner of the platform, with intermediate supports if necessary. Sometimes the verandah is entirely closed in, with only a doorway opposite the door of the *cella*. The *cella* remains the same from age to age, and is not renewed unless it becomes ruinous, but the roof is frequently renewed as a mark of respect to the deity within. This, however, is not now done as often as was the custom in former times, and in many cases repairs are carried out only when absolutely necessary. The wood-work of the verandah is covered in parts with carvings of a grotesque character, while hanging around are the horns of animals which have been offered in sacrifice, with bells suspended over the doorway, and sometimes a pole in front, called *dhuj*. The image is inside the *cella*. The temples have probably remained much the same in shape and structure since the earliest times. Occasionally they consist of a small *cella* only of the simplest kind, with no verandah. Often too the image may be seen resting in the open, under a cedar tree, with little to indicate its character except the paint and oily appearance from the *ghi* with which it is besmeared.

The rites of worship are similar at both Nág and Deví temples. Bloody sacrifice holds the foremost place. On ordinary occasions incense is burned, and circumambulation of the *cella* within the verandah is performed by the priest. There is also the ringing of bells, and the sounding of the conch shell, accompanied by the beating of drums. A *mela* is usually held once a year at each temple, when a great concourse of people takes place on the green near the shrine, and all are seated in prescribed order according to ancient custom—a special place being reserved for the officials of the *pargana* in which the temple is situated. Music and dancing, and often drinking, play an important part at these *melas*. Each temple has a *pujára* or priest, who may be of any caste, and a *chela* who is usually a low caste man. The god or goddess is supposed to speak through the *chela*, who is believed to become inspired by the deity. Seated at the door of the temple, he inhales the fumes of burning cedar wood from a vessel held before him, while he is fanned by a man standing near. The drums are beaten furiously; soon he begins to quiver and tremble, and this trembling increases till the entire body shares in the incessant motion, this being the recognised sign of the god having entered into him. Continuing to work himself into a frenzy, he springs to his feet and dances madly, scourging himself all the time with the *sangal* or *tirsúl* which he holds in his hand, sometimes with such severity as to draw blood. The harsh and discordant music gets louder and wilder, and others join in the dance, forming a circle with the *chela* in their midst. A goat is then brought forward and presented to the god, and water is thrown upon it and put into its ear to make it tremble, this being the sign that the victim has been accepted. Forthwith the head is struck off and presented to the god, and in some cases the *chela* drinks the warm blood as it flows from the quivering carcase. The dancing proceeds more wildly than ever till at last the *chela* calls out that the god has come. All are then silent and questions are asked by the people and answered by the *chela*, as the mouthpiece of the god. Having done this part, the *chela* sinks on the ground exhausted, and is brought round by fanning and sprinkling of water on his face and chest. The people then disperse to their homes.

The temples may be visited in times of drought and famine, or pestilence in men or beast, also by individuals on account of any special circumstances such as sickness or for any family or personal reason. These are called *játra*, and on the way to the temple round marks are made with rice water on the stones by the wayside, probably to indicate that the pilgrimage has been performed. Only special Nágs have the reputation of being able to give rain, and in time of drought those shrines are much frequented, the same procedure being adopted as that already described. Sheep and goats are freely offered at such times. If rain falls too abundantly the Nág shrine is again resorted to with offerings, to constrain the god to stay his hand.

There are many traditions current in the hills which point to human sacrifices having been frequent at Nág and Deví temples in former times. In Pángi and other parts of the Chandra-Bhága Valley a singular custom obtains in connection with Nág worship. For a fixed time every year in the month of Sáwan, and sometimes for the whole of that month all the milk of the village is devoted to the local Nág and is then said to be *suchcha* (pure).

The villagers do not use it themselves, that is, they do not drink it, and they are very unwilling to supply milk to travellers during the period. The milk is churned as usual, and *ghi* is made from it, the butter-milk being stored and used up at feasts held on certain days during the month. Every few days any offering of milk and sweet bread is made to the Nág, some of the milk being sprinkled over it. It is also smeared with *ghi*. A final feast is held at the end of the month. In Pángi only 15 days are observed, and this only in the lower part of the valley.

Generally speaking, the foundation of the Nág *and* Deví temples is ascribed to the era of Rájá Músha Varma, A. D. 820–40, but most of them probably are of much older date. Three temples, two of Mahal Nág and one of Jamun Nág at Baini, are said to have been built in the time of Báná Beddha.[1]

Further the *pujáras* and *chelas* are most commonly Ráthis by caste, but, in a good many cases, only the *pujára* is a Ráthi, the *chela* being a Háli, as in the temples of Kálú Nág and Manovar Nág at Bháráram, Mahal Nág at Báthula, Nandyásar Nág at Puddhra, Tarewan Nág at Lunkh, Him Nág at Bharawin, Mahal Nág at Bairi and Bairo, Muthal Nág at Gulera, Nandalu Nág at Sirha, Suána Nág at Bharoga, Khul

[1] A famous Báná of the olden time who lived in Barnota *pargana*, date unknown.

Nág at Nabi-Bhuta, Parha Nág at Singaki Bani and Charas Nág at Tikri.

Priests and *chelas.*

In some cases the *pujára* is a Háli, *e. g.* at the temples of Bhudhu Nág at Lambota, Parbhut Nág at Andwás, Sri Nág Stulji at Sudlaj, Thainang Nág at Gung Rás, Kalan Nág at Khalandar. At Sri Potir Nág's temple at Bhinan the *pujára* and *chela* are both Kolis; at Kalan Nág's temple at Chilli they are both Bhachhra Gaddis; at Handol Nág's temple at Chandrola both are Battan Gaddis; at Sagta Nág's at Bani Sagwari both are Sapahi Gaddis.

Brahmans are incumbents of the following temples:—

Mahal Nág's at Bani (Brahmans of the Paddha *gôt,* with Háli *chelas*), Thainang Nág's at Dirog and Mahr Nág's at Manglana (of the Kalián *gôt,* also *chelas*), Mahal Nág's at Jamohar (of the Kalián with Háli *chelas*), at Thainang Nág's temple at Kharont (of the Ratan Pál *gôt* with Ráthi *chelas*), at Thainang Nág's temple at Bahnota (of the Kalián *gôt* also *chelas*), at Ham Nág's at Talhána (of the Káshab *gôt,* also *chelas*): at Nág Belodar's and Mahal Nág's at Jangal Bani (of the Kalian *gôt,* also *chelas*): at Sindhu Nág's at Sundhár (Gaur Brahmans, also *chelas*), at Bajog Nág's at Sirba (Gaur Brahmans, also *chelas*), at Balodar's at Baldruni the *pujára* is a Kandu Brahman, at Mahal Nág's at Talai he is a Tharatu Brahman, at Karangar Nág's in Sanaur he is a Lecha Brahman, with a Ráthi *chela,* at Sudhun Nág's in Suri a Kalián, also with a Ráthi *chela,* at Sar Nág's in Sarsara he is a Káshab, at Jamun Nág's at Bari Jamuhár he is a Kalián with a Ráthi *chela,* and at Ráh Nág's temple in Rah he is a Káshab with a Háli *chela.*

In Pángi Brahman *pujáras* officiate at the shrines of Mindhal Kantu Nág at Re, and Markula Deví at Tindi and Udaipur: Ránás are the *pujáras* at Kilár and Sálhi, and Ráthis with Háli *chelas* at all the other shrines.

The following is a list of the principal Nágs worshipped in Churáh and the northern portion of the Sadr *wizárat,* with the name of the village in which each has a shrine:—

Name.	Village.	*Pargana.*	Name.	Village.	*Pargana.*
Balodar ...	Nabi Bani ...		Thainang ...	Dirog ...	
Malun ...	Alwas ...		Kalang ...	Manglana ...	
Satohi ...	Bakuud ...		Mahal ...	Sáru ...	
Dakhla ...	Chhampa ...		Sarwál ...	Mundál ...	
Kálu ...	Sarnagrí ...		Tarewan ..	Lunkh ...	Lohtikri.
Kálu, Kaluth	Dhár ...	Tiss.	Him ...	Mohwa ...	
Greater ...	Gupha ...		Him-Nág ...	Bhararwin ...	
Mahal	Jangal Bhunjreru.		Kalu ...	Baráhara ...	
Bhujgar			Bhandári ...	Batrundi ...	
Kálang ...	Jangal Kal-kundi.		Sri Budhu	Lamhota ...	
Mahal			Bwátir ...	Bhiwan ...	
Jaman			Balodar ...	Gámbhir ...	
Jamori			Larhasan ...	Shalai ...	
Chhalasar unsar	Bani ...	Barnota.	Chhalasar ...	Sahu ...	Himgarin.
Khandwál			Kálan ...	Chilli ...	
			Mandol ...	Chandrola ...	
			Sthul Nág	Khángu ...	

Name.	Village.	*Pargana.*	Name.	Village.	*Pargana.*
Parbhut	Andwás	Himgari	Thainang	Ghari	Sai.
Sthulji	Sudla		Do.	Gurwán	
Deotán	Deotán		Sungal	Gulela	Diur.
Mahr	Manglana	Lohtíkri	Mahal	Khandi	
Kálu	Bharárá		Kalan	Bani Kálandal	Juhnd.
Manovar			Sagta	Sagwári	
Mahal	Bahnota		Sar	Sarsara	
Nandayásur	Paddhra		Do.	Bani Saroi	
Bujir	Junth	Sai	Sur Mer	Jassu	Bhándal.
Thing	Satun		Mahal	Bhavadan	
Thainang	Gungyás		Karwár	Choted	
Mahal	Bhorás		Marar	Charetar	
Do.	Bairu	Baira	Suana	Bharoga	Kihár.
Thainang	Degarán		Mahal	Chakhutar	
Muthal	Gulara	Jasaur	Khul	Bani Bhuthan	Manjír.
Kálú	Barálu		Parhu	Sangaki Bani	
Thainang	Kharonth		Charas	Tikri	
Pardhan	Kundiára		Do.	Siru	
Thainang	Bahnota		Guldhan	Manjír	
Him	Talháná		Do.	Bahi Salon	
Mandolu	Sirha		Thainang	Chakhra	Bhándal.
Peju	Bajonth	Kohál	Tundi	Uthluga	Baghai.
Mahal	Do.		Jammu	Jamuhár	Panjla.
Balodar	Jangal Bani		Do.	Bari do.	
Mahal	Do.		Malundu	Malund	
Sindhu	Sundhár	Tariod	Khallar	Khallru	
Tono	Pukhri		Dittu	Khaddar	
Bajog	Sirha	Rajnagar.	Surju	Gudda	
Balodar	Baldrani	Kharont.	Rah	Rah	
Mahal	Taláí	Dhund.	Jammu	Bhala	Sahu.
Barar	Barráni		Darobi	Chalai	
Karangar	Sinúr	Gudiál.	Durbdu	Bhidhar	
Sudhun	Súi		Budhu	Langera	Bhándal.
Bhedu	Ghat	Bhalei.			
Do.	Gand				
Mahal	Jamchár	Band-Bagor.			

Legends.

The following are some of the legends associated with special Nágs and Devís in different parts of the States—

Básak Nág was brought from Bhadrawáh 100 years ago, because disease was prevalent among the cattle of the State. Básan Nág and Nágni were also brought from Bhadrawáh on a similar occasion, and Digghu Nág from Pángi.

Indru Nág derives his name from Indra.[1] Tradition says that aRáná from Suket came to Kanyára in Kángra, thence to Korási, and thence to Sámrá, the Nág and his *pujára* accompanying the Ráná. The Nág's disciple, Dhanda, was drowned in Dalnág, and his idol was also cracked in its temple. In one of its hands it holds a trident, in the other a chain, with which the *chelas* beat themselves.

Kalihár Nág, his original name, now better known as Kelang, came from British Láhul 15 or 16 generations ago when cattle disease was prevalent at Kugti, and the people of that village had vowed to hold a fair if it abated. Tradition says that Kelang, in the form of a serpent, rode on the horns of a ram from Láhul, and stopped at Dúghi two miles

[1] Indru Nág has a temple in Kángra also—see *infra* p. 154.

from the present temple. Remaining there for three generations, he went to Darún at the source of a stream, a cold place difficult of access, so the people petitioned his *chela* to remove lower down, and the Nág, through his *chela*, told them to cast a *bháná*[1] from the place, and to build a new temple at the spot where it stopped. By digging the foundations they found a three-headed image of stone, and on removing it a stream gushed forth. This was many generations ago. This image is in the Padmásan attitude.[2] Rájá Sri Singh presented a second image of eight metals (*ashtdhát*) which stands upright, holding a *láthi* or pole in its right hand. Its head is covered with figures of serpents, and it wears a necklace of *chaklas* with a *janeo* and *taragi* or waistbelt or *pasab* (loin cloth), all of serpents. This temple is closed from Mágh 1st to Báisakh 1st. At other times worship is performed every Sunday, but only sheep and goats are accepted as offerings.

The following is a list of the Nágs worshipped in the various villages of Brahmaur and the southern portion of the Sadr *wizárat* with the dates of the fairs and vigils held at each, the castes to which the *pujáras* and *chelas* belong, and the Rájás in whose reigns the worship is said to have been introduced:—

Name.	Village.	*Pargana.*	Date of Fair.	*Pujáras* and *chelas*	Founded in the reign of
Badyála Nág	Auráh ...	Brahmaur	Siwan 5th	Kurets Gaddis	Lachhmi, Varma.
Básak Nág	Dhár or Báskaher.	Sámrá ...	Baisákh 4th and 5th	Suláhi Sarsuts	Ráj Singh.
Básaki Nág	Ser	Lil ...	Baisákh 4th, 5th.	Shipnste Brahmans, Hális.	Músh Varma.
Básan Nág	Dhár or Báskaher.	Sámrá ...	Baisákh 4th, 5th (Jágrá on 1st of Baisákh).	Sársuts, Hális	Músh Varma.
Bijku Nág	Mahlá ...	Mahlá ...	Daljátra ...	...	Músh Varma.
Bujúru Nág	Trehtá ...	Trehta ...	...	Swahí Brahmans.	Sáhil Varma.
Dighanpál Nág.	Benghlá ...	Mahlá ...	Jágrá on 10th of Siwan.	Frangete Gaddis.	Músh Varma.
Dhanchohú Nág.	Ghrehar ...	Brahmaur	...	Banetu Gaddis	Sáhil Varma.
Digghu Nág	Bargrán ...	Brahmaur	Nág Panchmi in Hár or Sáwan.	Paráhan Gaddis.	Umed Singh.
Guldhár Nag	Púlni ...	Brahmaur	...	Káletu Gaddis	Sáhil Varma.
Indru Nág	Sámrá ...	Kothi Ranhú	Bhádon 1st	Bhogelu Brahmans, Ráthis.	Músh Varma.
Indru Nág	Urai ...	Kothi Ranhú	...	Tiláru Brahmans.	Músh Varma.
Indru Nág	Sunáo ...	Chanotá ...	Bhadon 1st Asáuj.	Bhat Brahmans.	Músh Varma.
Indru Nág	Lámu ...	Chanotá ...	Bhádon 1st	Luntelu Brahmans.	Músh Varma.
Indru Nág	Kuwársi ...	Chanotá ...	Bhádon 1st & Asauj 1st.	Pranghálu Gaddis, Hális.	...
Indru Nág	Thonklá ...	Kothi Ranhú	Do.	Jesu Brahmans.	...

[1] A musical instrument like a plate of metal, which is struck with a stick.
[2] Sitting cross-legged in the attitude of devotion, like representations of Buddha.

Name	Village.	*Pargana.*	Date of Fair.	*Pujáras* and *chelas.*	Founded in the reign of
Indru Nág	Sulákhar ...	Brahmaur	...	Kharauhtu Brahmans.	Yugákar Varma.
Kalihár or Kelang Nág.	Kugti ...	Brahmaur	..	Sassi (Dhattatreya gotra) Brahmans.	New.
Kutherhu Nág.	Chobbiá ...	Brahmaur	...	Sánghrantu Brahmans.	Sáhil Varma.
Kelang Nág	Kugti ..	Brahmaur	Asauj 2nd	Sassi Brahmans.	Sáhil Varma
Kelang Nág	Kaláh ...	Trehtá ...	...	Kaláhi Gaddis	..
Kutherhu Nág.	Pálni ...	Brahmaur	Jágrá on Maghar 1st	Pálnal Gaddis	Sáhil Varma.
Latu Nág ...	Panjsai ...	Brahmaur	Bhádon 1st	Auren Gaddis	Sáhil Varma.
Mehal Nág	Ráchná ...	Lil ...	Nág Panchmi of Hár or Sáwan.	Bhresán Gaddis.	...
Mehal Nág	Bhúniáh ...	Mahlá ...	Baisákh 1st	...	Músh Varma.
Mehal Nág	Kulwára ...	Bakán ...	Hár 10th-13th	Ráthis ...	Músh Varma.
Prohal Nág	Bhámal ...	Lil ...	...	Jhalánu Brahmans.	Músh Varma.
Punu or Indru Nág	Sutkar ...	Trehtá	Asauj 2nd	Padlu Brahmans.	Músh Varma.
Sandhola Nág	Gawari ...	Brahmaur	...	Barán Gaddis	Yugákar Varma.
Hamási Nág	Bagrá ...	Mahla ...	Jágrá on Bhádon 15th	Khátelu ...	Músh Varma.
Sehrá Nág	Siner ...	Sámri ...	Asárh 3rd	Ránás ...	Músh Varma,
Satuhar Nág	Tur ...	Basu ...	Baisákh 15th-16th.	Chhinghwána Gaddis.	Músh Varma.
Khugehar Nág.	Kundi ...	Basu ...	Baisákh 9th	Mukwáu Brahmans.	Músh Varma.
Sátúhar Nág	Shikroná ...	Lil ...	Bhádon 1st	Chate Gaddis	Músh Varma.
Sátúhar Nág	Bandlá ...	Lil ...	..	Ghukán Gaddis.	Músh Varma.
Uman Nág	Kalaudredibaui.	Kalandrá	Daljátrá in Bhádon or Asauj.	Phigas Brahman, Ráthis.	Músh Varma.

The following is a list of the Nágs in Pángi:—

Name.	Village.	*Pargana.*	Name.	Village.	*Pargana.*
Danti Nág			Chanir Nág	Parmaur ...	
Kasir Nág	Darwas ...	Darwás.	Bamba Nág	Shor ...	Sách.
Besir Nág ...			Kidaru Nág		
Banek Deo	Surál ...		Mindhal Deví	Mindhal ...	
Det Nág ...	Kilár ...	Kilár.	Mirkula Deví		
Jagesar Nág	Sach ...		Kálka Deví		
Pror Nág ...			Sítla Deví	Tindí ...	
Mal Nág ...	Helor ...		Mihl Nág		
Jeryun Nág	Kutal ...		Arwas Nág		
Digal Panihár Nág.	Gisal ...		Niletu Nág		Láhul.
Kutásan Nág		Sách	Mahl Nág	Bajun ...	
Biru Nág ...	Sálhi ...		Bhani Nág	Silgráon ...	
Jatrun Nág			Bharsi Nág		
Dosar Nág	Machim ...		Rásher Nág	Margráon ...	
Kuru Nág	Helu ...		Nisar Nág	Tunde ...	
Kantu Nág	Re ...				

The legend of Det Nág at Kilár is that he was originally located in Láhul, and human victims were offered to him. The lot had fallen on the only remaining son of a poor widow, and she was bewailing her misfortune when a Gaddi passed by, and, hearing the tale of woe, offered to take her son's place. He, however, stipulated that the Nág should be allowed to devour him, and on his presenting several parts of his body in succession without any result he got angry and threw the Nág into the Chandrabhága. It got out of the river at Kilár and being found by a cowherd was carried up to the site of the present temple, when it fell from his back with the face on the ground. A shrine was erected and the image set up with its face looking inwards: and a clump of cedar trees at once grew up around the shrine.

Kathura Nág is a godling associated with pulse just as Sandhola Nág is with barley. The offerings to a Nág are an iron mace (*khanda*) a crooked iron stick (*kundi*), both of which are left at the shrine, a sheep and cakes, which are shared by the priest, the *chela* and the worshipper and eaten.[1]

The Nág cults in Kángra.

In Kángra where snake-worship is not uncommon Nág temples are rare, but the following is one :—

Name.	Date of fair.	Ritual.
Indrú Nág founded by a Rána of Ghaniára. The idol is that of his family god.	Jeth 1st ..	The image of a snake is engraved on a slab. A *yag* or a *jagra* is celebrated at each harvest and the poor are fed. A *nagdeha* is also observed at each harvest, and 16 goats are sacrificed at the Rabi and 18 at Kharíf, *siddhás* and *faqírs* being entertained. The ritual of sacrifice is conducted according to the behests of the *chelas* who go into trances and manifest the gods concerned. The *Durga páth* is recited during the *Naurátra* festivals. The popular belief is that the prosperity of the harvests depends on this god whose displeasure is said to cause hail and drought.

In *thána* Ránítál is a shrine to Nág Jamwálan or 'Nág of the Jamwál tribe' (or possibly 'the people of Jammu'). At this snake-bite is cured and goats etc. are sacrificed.[2] Besides Shesh Nág, who supports the world on his head, there are 7 Nágs, *viz.* Takshak, Básuki, Bajr Danshan, Karkotak, Hemmalli, Sankhu and Kali Nág. The Nág Takolak plays an important part in the *Mahábhárata* and Vásuki is also well known in Hindu mythology. Kali and Sankhu Nágs are found in Kulu. Vajra-damchána may be the Sanskrit form of Bajr

[1] See Vol. II, p. 271 *infra*, for offerings to Nágs. Kailung Nág is also noticed on p. 215 *infra*.

[2] P. N. Q., II, § 120.

Danshan and if so his name means 'he whose bite is like lightning.' Sankhu is also called Dudhia, the milky snake. He and Káli Nág are worshipped on Tuesdays, especially in Háṛ and Sáwan: they protect crops from white-ants and rats and are offered milk, honey, he-goats etc.[1]

At the *mandir* of Naga Baṛi in Chatroli no fair is held. The temple was founded by Rána Kalás of Núrpur some 150 years ago, but was afterwards built by Rájá Jagat Tani. He enshrined in it a stone image of a snake. It is managed by a Brahman *pujári* whose *gót* is Sapule. Fruit etc. is offered as *bhog* morning and evening after worship and a lamp is lit every evening.

The Nág cults in the Simla Hills.

The *deota* Nág[2] in *pargana* Kandaru.—Nág is one of the most powerful *deotas* in the Simla hills. He appeared some 1500 years ago, at a time when three *deotas* held the part of the country which is now the Nág's dominion. These were Dadru in *pargana* Kandaru, Bathindlu in *pargana* Chadára in Keunthal, Malánshar in Madhán State (at Kiári), but their history is no longer remembered. The States of Madhán, Keunthal and Kumhársain had already established themselves when Nág appeared and there was a State called Koti or Rajána, apparently in Kandaru *pargana*, whose rulers belonged to the family of Sirmúr. Some people say that the Bain Ṭhákur family of Madhán having died out, a prince of Kahlúr (Biláspur), ancestor of the present chief, was brought in to rule over Madhán soon after Nág appeared. Nág's history is that five Brahman brothers named Kálú, Gájan, Moel, Chánd and Chánan once lived at Bharána, a village now in Madhán. Kálú, the eldest, was a hermit. Once a *sádhu* came to Bharána and put his *ásan* under a *kelo* tree, cooked some food and asked Kálú to eat it with him. He gave Kálú four loaves, of which he ate two and kept the other two in his pocket. At the *sádhu's* invitation Kálú stayed the night with him, and at midnight saw carpets spread before the *sádhu's ásan*, torches lighted and *parís*, Rájá Indra's dancing girls, come and dance before the *sádhu*. Kálú watched this with amaze, but before day-break the *sádhu* and all had disappeared Kálú returned home, but was intent on finding the *sádhu* again, as he believed him to be Rájá Bhartari himself. He climbed to the top of Tikkar hill where his brothers grazed their sheep, but they could tell him nothing and bade him return home and fetch food. When he reached home Kálú found his daughter-in-law at work, and on his asking her to give him some flour she said that she was in a hurry to milk the cows and so he returned to Tikkar empty-handed. In his disappointment and from love for the *sádhu* he fled like a mad man leaving his cap, *topa*, on the Tikkar peak, and throwing his two remaining loaves which had turned into black stones, to the shepherds While roaming far and wide in search of the *sádhu* Kálú flung away his clothes and everything he had on him one by one

[1] Kángra *Gazetteer*, 1904, p. 103.

[2] *Deota Nág*. 'This combination,' writes Dr. Hutchison, 'must be wrong. The first name may be Diuta or some such word, but it cannot be *deota*. The Devtas and Devís are quite distinct from the Nágs. A Nág therefore cannot be called a *deota* or *devta*.'

at different places, and at last died. It is believed by the people that when he gave his brothers the stones, they and the sheep also turned into stones and that Kálú when he died became a *sareli* (a big snake).[1]

This *sareli* devoured men and lived on Tikkar hill. It would wander all over Chadára, Madhán and Kandaru—the then Koṭi State,[2] until the people begged the *deotas* Dodru, Bathindlu and Malánshar for protection, but they declared weeping that they could not subdue the Nág that had appeared in the form of a *sareli*. Such a terror to the countryside had he become that he would draw people into his mouth from afar with his breath. Háṛtú fort was then in possession of Sirmúr and its officer sent 32 men to Ruper to fetch supplies. On their return they saw a cave where they intended to halt, but found themselves in the monster's mouth. Four Silu brothers, Kaláls, of Kelti village, volunteered to kill the *sareli* and collected people for the enterprize. They found it sleeping in a Nálá, with its head at Kelti and its tail at Khingshá, a distance of over 5 miles. It was arranged that one of the Kaláls should enter its mouth with an iron *jamdaṛ* or spear in his hand, so that if the *sareli* shut its mouth the *jamdaṛ* would keep its jaws open, and another man might enter its throat and thrust his *jamdaṛ* through its neck, while others mounting its back might see the spear head and avoiding that spot hack at the serpent on every other side until it was cut to pieces. Led by the Kaláls the people acted as arranged and the monster was killed, the escort[3] from Haṛtú emerging alive from its stomach. In the monster's huge head were found two images of Múl Nág, as the *deota* had said. This image is jet black with a *singhásan* on which the Nág reposes, two Bhagwati Devís sitting on either side with hands clasped and also on each side a tiger watching. One of the images in the temple is at Dhar village and the other is at Jadun temple in Chadára *pargana*. Some say three images were found. Hundreds of people collected and Brahmans who carried the images fell into a trance and the Nág spirit spoke through them saying that he claimed the dominion of the three *deotas* and should be carried first to Kiári.[4] Besides others Pargi of Kelti, Moel Brahman of Bhrana, Faqír Pujára of Jadun and Sadi Rám Pujára of Dhar (Kandaru) accompanied the Nág to Kiári and asked Dhonklu Chand, Ṭhákur of Madhán, and his brother Kela to accept this new *deota*. The Ṭhákur said that none but Malánshar was his god and that the image was nothing but a *newa* or *páp* and so he hesitated to treat the Nág as a god. The people said that the Nág would strike like lightning. The Nág then left Kiári, but rested in a cave called Shungra near it until some three months later a man named Gori of Kharal gave him *dhúpdip* and *ghi* and thus encouraged Nág soared to the skies and a bolt from the blue destroyed Malánshar *deota's* temple. The Ṭhákur's Ráni was distressed in many ways, his sons while sleeping were overturned in their bed and

[1] *Sareli*. In Chamba the word is *sarál* with the same meaning.

[2] This Koṭi State should not be confounded with the present Koṭi State near Simla.

[3] Some say that the Haṛtu men were not *Bárá Bísh, i.e.* 12 + 20 = 32, but *Bárá Bíshi, i.e.* 12 × 20 = 240 men. Haṛtu is more commonly called Haṛatu or Hattu.

[4] Kiári was then the capital of the chiefs of Madhán State, Dharampur being chosen ater on.

rolled down to the *obra* (cowshed), serpents appeared in the milk and worms in the food served to the family. *Deota* Malánshar confessed that he had no power to check the Nág and the Ṭhákur of Madhán was compelled to acknowledge him as his family god instead of Malánshar who fled to Pujarli where a temple was subsequently built for him. Nág became *chaurikádeo, i.e.* god of the *gaddi* and *chaur*. Some people say that it was after this time that the Bain family of Madhán was succeeded by a Kahlúr prince. When acknowledged as *gaddi deota* of Madhán, Nág returned to Chadára and asked the people to build him a temple at a place shown by ants. Jadun was indicated and here the Nág's temple stands. It is said that Nág is not fond of gold ornaments, so he never accepts gold, but the two loaves turned into stones were placed in the temple. Bathindlu *deota* was also forced to abandon his dominions to Nág and he took up his abode at Chotha in Bhajji. Besides the Jadun temple Nág wanted a temple at the spot where the *sádhu* had appeared and Kálú had received the two loaves, so there, too, a temple was built and in its enclosure stands the *kelon* tree beneath which there was the dance. A fourth temple to Nág was built at Dhar in Kandaru. Dodru *deota's* temple which stood below Kamali village was destroyed by lightning. Dodru fled to Madhán and Dobra is named after him. A Ṭhákur of the Sirmúr family ruled Koṭi in Kandaru, and his family god was Narotu, a *deota* which had come with him from Sirmúr. Mul, commonly called Padoi, had also accompanied this prince from Chunjar Malána *revar* (?cave) near Mathiána. This Ṭhákur was hard pressed by the Rájá of Kulu who was building a fort on Tikkar, so he invoked the Nág for help. A small *deori* (temple)[1] had already been built at Tikkar for Nág close to where the fort was being built by the Rájá of Kulu, and Nág performed miracles which deterred him from building the fort. The *negi* of Kulu used to go to sleep at Tikkar and awake to find himself at Malag, 5 miles away in Bhajji. For some time a mysterious spirit carried him to Malag every night and at last when sitting on a plank at Tikkar he found it sticking to his back Dismayed at the power of Nág *deota* the Rájá's camp left Tikkar and returned to Sultánpur in Kulu, the plank still sticking to his *negi's* back. Distressed at this sight the Rájá begged Nág to pardon his *negi*, promising to present him with an image and copper *nakáras* and also to sacrifice goats to him wherever he himself or any of his *negis* passed through the Nág's dominions. As soon as this vow was made the plank fell from the *negi's* back. When anything clings to a man the proverb goes *Kalwa Nág re jae takhti*, "like the plank of Kalwa Nág." The Kulu Rájá sent a pair of copper *nakáras* and an image still kept in Dhár temple called Mán Singh (presumably the Rájá's name). When the Kulu *negi* left Tikkar the Ṭhákur of Koṭi affected Nág more than ever and gave him a *jágír* in several villages. The name of this Ṭhakur was Deva Singh, but whether he was the Dothainya[2] who came from Sirmúr or a descendant of the Sirmúr Dothainya is not known.

[1] Apparently this word should be *deoṛhí*, but that would mean a porch, not a temple. But both *deoṛí* and *dewra* are said to mean 'temple.' The rest of this account is far from lucid. We are not told the Kulu Nág's name. Kalwa derives his name from Kálu, Brahman, apparently.

[2] For Dothainya (= heir-apparent) see Vol. III, p 11. It is the Sanskr. Dwisaniya (cadet).

Deota Nág has the following *bhárs* (servants), and certain Bhagwatis are his companions :—

(1) Bhors (as he is commonly called).—It is said that Kálu, Brahman, in his wanderings tore a hair out of his head and threw it away at a place called Loli (hair). It became a spirit and joined Nág when he appeared from the *sareli's* head. He acts as a watchman and is given a loaf by the people: when there is a *khin* at Loli he is given a *khadu* or sheep.

(2) Khoru.—This *bhár* appeared from Khoru *thách* (a plain near Ránipur, two miles to the east of Tikkar hill). Kálu had left something at this *thách,* and it too turned into a spirit and joined Nág when he appeared. This *bhár* protects cattle, and is given an iron nail or ring called *kanaila* as an offering by the people.

(3) Shakta.—This *bhár* appeared from Shiwa or Shabhog the place where the *sareli* had his tail. Some indeed say that its tail became a spirit called Shakta. He is offered a loaf by the people for protecting goats and shepherds.

(4) Sharpál is considered a low class *bhár* and worshipped by Kolis etc.; his spirit does not come into a Kanet or *pujára,* but a Koli is inspired by him and speaks. His function is to drive away evil spirits, *bhút, paret* etc. Nág does not go into the house of any low caste man and so Sharpál is sent in his place, Nág's *harqi* (iron staff) accompanying him. A loaf is given for him. When returning the Nág's *harqi*[1] is purified by sprinkling on it milk and cow's urine. This is called *shajherna* (making pure).

(5) Gungi is considered a female *bhár* and her abode is at Dya above Dhár village. Every third year on an auspicious day (*mahúrat*) fixed by a Brahman Nág goes to Dya. A goat is sacrificed to Nág and a *cheli* or kid to Gungi. She appeared at Dya from a hair which fell from Kálu or from his sweat and joined Nág. She protects people from pestilence.

(6) Than is also a *bhár* : he originated at Kiári and came with Nág when he was acknowledged by the Madhán *gaddi.* He also drives away *bhút, paret* etc.

These are the six *bhárs,* but the other companions of Nág rank above them in degree. These are the Bhagwatis—

(1) Bhagwati Rechi.—A few years before the Gurkha invasion Ranji[2] of Bashahr came to Jadun and Dhár and plundered Deota Nág's treasury, some of whose images he took to Bashahr. Deota Nág punished him by his power and he found his ribs sticking out of his sides and the milk that he drank coming out through the holes. One of the Láma Gurús told him that his spoliation of Nág's treasury was the direct cause of his complaint, so he returned all what he had taken from the temple. Bhíma Káli of Saráhan in Bashahr also gave Nág a pair of *chamba* wood *ḍhols* and a *karnál* together with a *káls*[3] shut up in one of

[1] No such word as *hargi* is traceable in Tika Rám's *Dicty. of Pahaṛi Dialects,* J. A. S. B., 1911. He gives *scherna* : to purify. *Sharijherná* = *rstar karná.*

[2] Ranjít *wazír* commonly called Ranji and great-grandfather of Rám Bahádur, *wazír* of Bashahr, who conquered Dodra Kowar.

[3] *Karnál* = A long straight trumpet fluted at the mouth. *Kál* or *káli* = A small drum shaped like an hour-glass.

the *dhols*. When the instruments were put in Nág's temple they played of themselves at the dead of night. When people asked Nág the reason he said that the Káli sent by Bhíma Káli sounded them. The Káli of Bashahr, however, could do no further mischief as she was subdued by Nág and bidden to dwell at Rechi, the hill above Sandhu, on the Hindustan-Tibet Road, where a *chauntra* (platform) was built for her. She is a kind of subordinate companion to Nág and protects women in child-birth.

(2) Nichi is a Bhagwati. She dwells at Roni in Chadára in a small *deora* (small temple) and lives with Jharoshra Kolis, but her spirit speaks through a Turi. Her duty is to guard Nág's musical instruments, *nishán* (flag) etc. If a Koli touches any instrument a goat is taken from him as a punishment.

(3) Jal Mátri Bhagwati has her temple at Kingsha. She appeared near the water where the *sareli* was killed and is a goddess of water.

(4) Karmechri Bhagwati came out of a piece of the *sareli's* flesh and her *deora* is close to that of Nág at Jadun. She also drives away evil spirits and can tell all about the *lagabhaga* (?)—the kind of spirit that causes trouble.

(5) Dhinchai Bhagwati preserves stores of milk and *ghi*. People invoke her for plenty of milk and *ghi* in their houses.

(6) Devi Bajhshi Bhagwati appeared from Ránipur where something fell from Kálu and became this Bhagwati. She protects people from famine and pestilence.

(7) Bhagwati Tikkar lives with Nág at Tikkar. Tikkar Nág is the same as Jadun and Dhár Nág. This same Nág has separate images at Jadun, Kiári, Bharána, Dhár and Tikkar. As generations have passed away, people now think each a separate and not the same Nág. The different *parganas* each worship the Nág of their own *pargana*. People say that Kálu left his *topa* at Tikkar and that it turned into this Nág. Dhár Nág calls Nág of Tikkar his *guru*. Jadun Nág calls Dhár Nág his *dáda* or elder brother. Dhár Nág calls Jadun Nág his *bhái* or younger brother, and Bharána Nág is called by him *bahadru* or brother. From this it may be inferred that Tikkar Nág is the central spirit of the other Nágs, because it was here that Kálu became the *sareli* and his shepherd brothers with the sheep and the two loaves all turned into stones. There are two temples on the top of Tikkar.[1] On the following *teohárs* which are celebrated on Tikkar people collect at *melas*: (*i*) the Salokri in Baisákh : (*ii*) the Jathenjo in Jeṭh, when all the Nágs stay there at night and all the residents of the countryside bring a big loaf and *ghi* and divide them amongst the people. This loaf is called *saond*: (*iii*) at the Riháli, when 11 images called the 11 *múls* are brought, the shepherds also bringing their sheep and returning to Dhár at night. The *pujáras* feast the people and next day two images (*kanarti*) go to Kamáli village to receive their dues and two

[1] This is the ridge which is seen from Simla to the north and from which the Sháli peak rises. The ridge stretches north-east from the Sháli and between the two temples lies the boundary line, the southern valley being shared between Madhán and Keonthal and the northern between Bhajji and Kumhársain. The boundaries of four States meet here.

images go to Neori village for the same purpose. These two images are the Deo ká Mohrá and that of Mán Singh of Kulu: (*iv*) at the Nág Panchmi in Bhádon the observances resemble those at the Salokri: (*v*) at the Mágh or Makkar Shankránt when three goats are sacrificed, one given by Kumhársain State, one by the *zamíndárs* and a third by the villagers of Loli. Deota also gives alms. One of the temples at Tikkar belongs to the Kandaru people and the other to those of Jadun and Madhán.

It may be noted here that there is also a Nág Deota at Kandi *kothi*, in Suket, who is an offshoot of the Deota Kalwa Nág. The legend is that a Brahman of Bharána village went to Charag, a village in Suket, and asked women who were husking rice to give him some for his idol of the Nág as *bhog* (food): the women scornfully declined to give him any, so the image stuck to the *ukhal* and warned by this miracle they gave it some rice. At this time a *bhút* which dwelt in a large stone used to devour human beings and cattle so the people called on the Nág for help, and he in the guise of lightning broke the stone in pieces and killed the *bhút*. The people built the Nág a temple which had 11 rooms. Another Nág's temple stands at Hemri in Bhajji. Crows destroyed the crops in this village and so a Bharána Brahman brought an image of Nág and established it at Hemri. Dum Deota, who also lives there, made friends with the Nág. The place where they live is called Deothán.[1] At Neori village Dhai Nág slew a *bhút* who used to kill cattle. It lived in a stone close behind the village and a Neori woman secretly worshipped it, but Kalwa Nág destroyed the stone with the devil inside it and overwhelmed the house of the woman who was killed together with her three sheep. When the Nág goes to his village he sits on the spot and speaks to the people. Every third year the Nág goes to Bharána and there drinks milk from a vessel. In Kelo, a village in Bhajji, there lived an old man and his wife who had no son, so they asked the Nág for one, and he told them to sit there one Sunday at a place which had been purified by cow's dung and urine, and thereon present a goat for sacrifice and think of him. This they did, and the Nág appeared in the sky in the form of a large eagle. Descending to the place he placed in the woman's lap a male child and took away the goat. The old woman found her breasts full of milk and nursed the baby. This family is now called the Ludi Parwar or eagle's family. This miracle is said to have occurred 700 years or 17 generations ago. Another miracle is thus described:—

Some people of Dhár who were returning from the plains through Kunhiár State halted at Kunhiár for the night. As they were singing the *bár* (songs) of the Nág, he as usual appeared in one of the men, who began to talk about state affairs in Kunhiár. The Ráná asked them about their *deota* and his powers and they said that their Nág Deota could work miracles. So the old Ráná asked the Nág for a son and heir (*tikka*) and vowed that if by the Nág's blessing he had a *tikka* he would invite the Deota to Kunhiár. The Ràna was blessed with an

[1] Deo, *i.e.* Deota and *sthán* a place, *i.e.* the Deota's place.

heir, but he forgot his vow and the boy fell sick. When all hope of his life was lost, the Brahmans said that some *deota* has caused his illness as a punishment for some ingratitude. The Ráná was thus reminded of his vow and invited the Nág to Kunhiár and it is said that one man from every house in his dominions accompanied the Nág to Kunhiár; and the Ráná afraid to entertain so large an assemblage soon permitted the *deota* to return home saying that he would not invite him again as he was only a petty chief, but presented him with 11 idols to be distributed among his temples. These images are called the *kanartu mohras*.

Padoi Deota is the Nág's adoptive brother and Shari Devi of Mathiána is his adoptive sister. The *deota* Manan is also his adoptive brother, but this tie has only lately been created.

The Jadun *deota* sometimes goes to bathe at Maláwan, a stream close to Jadun village, and he considers the Shungra cave, where the Nág goes and stays at night, his *tírath* (place of pilgrimage).

Deota Nág of Dhár holds from Kumhársain a *jágír* in Kandaru *pargana* worth Rs. 76-6-3.

Ḍúm Deota has a small temple at Kamáli in Kandaru. A man from Gathri brought him to Kamáli. The Kamáli villagers alone accept Ḍúm Deota as their family god, though they respect the Nág seeing that they live in his dominions.

Deota Nág of Dhali in *pargana* Chebishi.

Not more than 500 years ago there was a temple in a forest at Tilku, where the *zamíndárs* of Dhali had broken up some land for cultivation. A *deota* there harassed them and the Brahmans said that he was a Nág, so they began to worship him and he was pleased: they then brought his image to Shailla village and built him a temple. When Padoi Deota passed through this village a leper was cured by him and the people of Shailla began to worship him, so the Nág left the village and Padoi took possession of his temple there. But the people of Dhali took the Nág to their own village and placed him in a temple. Padoi is now the family god of the Shailla people and the Dhali men regard Nág as their family god. The Nág's image is jet black and a Bhagwati lives with him. A *ḍhol* and a *nakára* are his instruments of music and he also has a *jagunth* or small staff. He visits his old place at Tilku every year on the Nág Panchmi day. He is only given *dhúpdip* once a month on the Shankránt day. The Brahmans of Barog, which lies in another *pargana*, worship him, as they once lived at Khecheru near Tilku. This Nág has no *bhor* and holds no *jágír* from the State. He has no connection with Kalwa Nág, the Nág of Kandaru.

Deota Nág of Dhanal in Chebishi.

Another Nág Deota is he at Dhanal in Chebishi *pargana*. Nearly 500 years ago he appeared in a field at Nago-thána, a place near Pati Jubar on the Shangri State border, where there was an old temple. A man of Dhanal village was ploughing his field near Nago-thána when he found a black image. He took it home, but some days afterwards it began to persecute him and the Brahmans said that it was the Nág who wished to be worshipped. So the Dhanal people began to affect him. This *deota* too has a *ḍhol* and *karnál* but no *jagunth*. No *khin* is given him The Dhanal people regard Malendi as their family god yet they worship Nág too in their village, thinking that he protects cattle and gives plenty of milk etc. He has no *bhor* and holds no *jágír* from the State. The people of Kandaru think that these Nágs in Dhanal and Dhali are the same as Kalwa Nág. The spirits came here also, but the Chebishi men do not admit the fact. This Nág has really no connection with Kalwa Nág of Kandaru.

Deota Nág of Ghunda.

Ghunda, a village in Chagaon *pargana* of Kumhársain, is inhabited by Rájpúts, 'Mians', who trace their ancestry to the old Bairat family which once held the *ráj* of Sirmúr. When their ancestor came from Sirmúr they brought with them an image (probably of their family god at that time) and made a temple for him at Ghunda. Nág, another *deota* at Ghunda, also resides with this *deota* of Sirmúr. This *deota* is called Shirgul. The history of Deota Nág is as follows :—

Many generations ago there lived in village Charoli (Kot Khái) a Brahman whose wife gave birth to a serpent. This serpent used to come from a great distance to the Naga Nali forest in Kumhársain and loved to play in a *maidán* near Kothi (in Kumhársain). Cows grazed in the *maidán* and the serpent sucked the milk from them. The cowherd was duly reprimanded by the people for his carelessness, but at last he found how the serpent used to suck the milk. A *faqír* in Kothi village then determined to kill the serpent, so he came to the *maidán* at noon tide, and cut the serpent into three pieces, but was burnt alive whilst killing it. Some days later a woman who was digging clay found images into which the three pieces of the serpent had turned. One of these images was brought by Brahmans to Ghunda village, another was taken to Bági (a village in Chajoli, in Kumhársain) and the third was taken by the Brahmans of Bhamraṛa, a village in Ubdesh *pargana* of Kumhársain. Temples were built to Nág in these villages. The Ghunda Nág (though Nág is usually *dudhadhári*) is not *dudhadhári* and goats are sacrificed to him. Every third year a *baltipaja mela* is held, but no annual fair is held. The people of Ghunda, Charhayayna, Kotla, Koṭhi and Katali, especially the Kolis, worship him. Nág Deota has a grant of land worth Rs. 2-2-6 a year from Kumhársain.

Sharvan and Chathla Nágs.

Sharvan Nág of Shoshan is called Sharvan after the village of Shoshan. The following tale is told of the Nág of Chathla :—

A woman named Bhuri of Machroti, a village in the Kot Khái *iláqa*, gave birth to a snake (*nág*). She was terrified but the snake told her not to be afraid but to go and live in the upper storey leaving the lower one to him and to give him milk through a hole. She did as the snake told her, and after six months he had grown so large that he filled the whole room. He then told her of his intention to quit her house for good, and said she would get something for her maintenance, if she brushed his body with a broom when he moved. This she did, whereupon gold fell from his body but when she saw it, thinking to keep the wonderful reptile, she caught hold of its tail and pulled it towards her The serpent, however, gave a jerk and threw her into the air, so that she fell on a rock at Máhon in Kumhársain and was killed. She is worshipped there to this day. The snake afterwards settled in a ravine in Kothi, a village in Kumhársain, and lived on the milk of the cows which came there to drink. When the *samíndárs* of Kothi saw how their milk went, they cut the snake in three pieces with a sword. One piece fell in Chathla village, where it was at once changed into an image, another fell in Ghunda, in Kumhársain, and the third in Pál, a village in Balsan, and they have all been worshipped ever since.

THE NÁG GOLI OF KOT KHÁI.

This Nág originally dwelt in Kulu where for generations he sent rain and sunshine in due season. But suddenly he began to send nothing but rain, so his followers one day cast his idol, images and litter into the Sutlej, as a hint that they were no longer satisfied with his rule. Some days later however one of his images was washed up on the river's bank and there a villager from Farog found it on his return from a trip to Kulu. Thinking he had only found an ornament, he passed through a hamlet where a *jag* was being held in honour of the goddess and joined in the merry-making. The sacrificial victims however would not shiver, even when sprinkled with water, in token that they were acceptable to the goddess, and when the priests consulted the oracle they were told by the goddess that a greater than she had cast a spell upon them. She also revealed the stranger's possession of the Nág and when a goat was sacrificed to him he lifted the spell which lay upon the animals and they were duly sacrificed. The villager then went on his way home, where he was constant in worship of the Nág but he kept his possession of the image secret. In those days the goddess was worshipped through all the countryside, but when the villager got home she was away on tour collecting her usual offerings, and when on her return journey she reached a deep ravine the rain began to pour in torrents and in the middle of the stream the goddess and her escort were swept away by a sudden spate. She was never seen again, and her escort also perished. The deluge too continued, causing ruin of harvests and landslides until the people through the diviners discovered the Nág's presence in their midst. Him they installed in the Devi's old temple and now he only occasionally turns summer into winter or brings rain at harvest time. For long his fame extended no further than the adjoining villages and once a large serpent dammed up a narrow torrent during the rains, until its pent-up waters threatened to overwhelm a Ṭhákur's castle and township though perched high above them. The villagers' own god, pre occupied with the preservation of his own shrine, was powerless to save them, so they invoked the aid of Nág, promising him grants of land and an annual festival. Already the waters had invaded their own god's temple and his idol had fallen on its face, when Goli Nág flew to the rescue. A ball of fire smote the serpent, rent it into a thousand pieces, and released the stream. Goli Nág also became the patron deity of the Ránás of Kot Khái by a similar feat. One of them was attacked by the ruler of Kulu who besieged him in his fort. In this desperate strait he sent for the priests of all the neighbouring gods and pledged himself to serve him whose priest could eat two loaves, each containing half a maund of barley flour. Goli Nág's Brahman at once passed the test and him the Ráná sent to plead his cause with the Nág. In answer to his prayers a great thunder cloud fell on the Kulu Rájá's camp and a flash of lightning blew up his magazine. As his men fled the Nág pursued them with thunderbolts and drowned many by rain spouts or the swollen torrents which overwhelmed them. So Kot Khái fort still stands on its isolated rock, a monument to Goli Nág's power. But the late adherence of these two states to his cult gives his first worshippers precedence over them and so when he patronises their festivals he only sends his smaller images, carried in a miniature palki, while his tours among his senior votaries are regal progresses in which he rides in a palinquin decked with a full panoply of images and trappings. Once a Ṭhákur made him and his escort prisoners and mockingly challenged him to fill a huge vessel with water in the drought of May. Not only did the Nág achieve this, but the rain changed to sleet and then to snow, until the hills around were capped with it. In vain the Ṭhákur tried to appease him with gifts. The Nág cursed his line and his territories were annexed to another state. But descendants of its former subjects assert that the Ṭhákur was forgiven and that his gifts were accepted, as they still hang on the walls of the Nág's temple in token of his victory.[1]

THE SNAKES OF BRUA.

Brua is a hamlet on the Baspa, a tributary of the Sutlej, and the story goes that once upon a time a man took to wife a girl from Paunda. When she went to visit her mother the latter noticed that the girl looked thin and ill, and learnt from her that Brua, which is perched a thousand feet above the river, was so far from any stream that the women had to fetch all the water for the village from the Baspa. So she captured some snakes and put them in a basket which she handed to her daughter with injunctions not to peep inside the basket on her way back and to place the snakes in a corner of her lower storey. Just before she reached the village however curiosity overcame her and she opened the basket. One snake slipped out there and before she got home two more escaped in a similar way. At each place streams gushed forth, and to this day refresh the wayfarer. At the corner of the room where she placed the basket on her arrival at the village a fountain sprang up so that she no longer had to fetch water from the Baspa. When the other housewives of the village noticed that she no longer went to the river to bring water they asked her why she did not go with them. Then she told them all that her mother had done, and how that in the lower storey of her house a never-failing spring was flowing. But an ill-natured hag became jealous that a stranger should be spared the toil of her sisters, cursed her with an evil eye and hatched a plan to bring misfortune upon her. She bade her offer incense to the sacred snakes which had caused

[1] Condensed from the *Pioneer* of July 6th, 1913.

the springs to flow and told her to mix filth with oil and earth and burn it at the fountain. This she did and as the smoke ascended the snakes swelled out in anger, growing to huge serpents, and darted to the door by which she was standing. In fear for her life she slashed at the nearest and cut it into fragments, thereby committing a grievous sin, for the *lámás* say when a snake is killed the world of serpents is plunged in mourning for the next 8 days, and none will taste of food. As a punishment the spring disappeared, but to this day grass grows in the corner of the cattle-shed. The three other snakes escaped unhurt. One crossed the pass to Pekián where it became warder of the god Chasrálu. The second made its way to a neighbouring village of which it became the god, but the third elected to remain at Brua. The girl picked up the remnants of the fourth and cast them down a precipice where they re-united. This Nág, now of fabulous dimensions, climbed up the slopes behind the village until it reached a plateau where it made for itself a lake in which it now dwells. To this lake the local deities are sometimes carried and then the Nág reveals his god-head by entering into one of the god's diviners who becomes as if possessed. The Nág of Pekián is a mere lieutenant of Mahásu, and not long ago the people of a hamlet close to Brua took their god to pay him a ceremonial visit. Having exchanged greetings the visitor returned across the pass in the great central chain of the Himalayas which separates Kanaur from the territory in which Mahásu's cult predominates. After his return this god's diviner manifested all the symptoms of divine afflatus, and declared himself to be possessed by Mahásu who had returned with the party and demanded a welcome and a shrine. This incident is paralleled in the hills by the popular belief that a powerful deity can accompany his female votaries to their married homes, and the adhesion of a god to a brother deity appears to be a mere variation of this belief. Indeed so frequently does it occur that a god attaches himself as it were to the party which carries a brother deity back from a place of pilgrimage that this habit has led to certain pilgrimages being discontinued. In the midst of the lofty peaks which border on Garhwál and Tibet is a sacred sheet of water that has given birth to many gods, and during the summer months it used to be a place of pilgrimage for them. The votaries of any snake gods that had emanated from the lake used to visit it and bathe their deity therein. But on several occasions it happened that when the pilgrims returned to their own villages they found that the strange divinity had become incarnate in the person of the temple oracle who invariably insisted that an alien spirit from the lake had attached himself to his companion. As the intrusion of a new divinity in a village involves the erection of a new shrine to house him and heavy expense upon the villagers, there is considerable reluctance now to take gods to this lake for bathing as of yore. To this rule however the men of Sangla, a large village in the Baspa valley, are an exception, for they still take their deity every 3rd or 4th year to his native lake and the visit invariably results in the supernatural seizure of his diviner. Indeed the people are now so used to this visitation that they halt half-way on their return and there after the diviner has ascertained the nature and needs of their self-invited guest they propitiate him with sacrifices and then beg him courteously but firmly to return whence he came. This lack of hospitality is justified, for the temple is already endowed with so many godlings that they could not afford to entertain another. As a rule the new god recognises the reasonableness of their request and goes in peace, but sometimes he refuses to do so, and then the people make a gift of him to some neighbouring hamlet Several temples thus owe a minor deity to the Sangla pilgrimage, but the villagers have usually made it a condition of acceptance that the new-comer should remain subordinate to the family god, that is to say to the existing incumbent of their village temple. But new deities, especially gods of position like Mahásu, are sometimes unwilling to accept a second place, and so the people of Kanaur, in a vain attempt to check the progress of that god, are only too likely to ostracize the only community which acknowledges him within their borders. This ostracism may take the form of refusing to take wives from the villages in which the new god has been installed. But the difficulties of limiting the jurisdiction of an enterprising deity are increased by yet another method. Since an article once dedicated to a god's service remains his property for ever, it follows that if a sacred vessel be removed by theft or ignorance to another village the god goes with it and once having gained a footing in it he soon discovers a means of making it his permanent abode. (Condensed from the *Pioneer* of June 12th, 1913).

The Nágs in Kulu.

In the Saráj or highlands of Kulu we find Chamaun Nág worshipped at Bhunga. Once, it is said, a Brahman went to bathe in a hill-stream. As he bathed a huge snake came towards him, raised its head and declared itself to be Ses Nág, promising happiness and prosperity to any who might worship it. Its temple was built in the *dwápar yuga* and contains an idol of stone 3½ feet high by 2½ in breadth. Its manager is a Kanet of the Káshel *gót*, but its *pujári* is a Gautama Sársut Brahman. This Nág seems distinct from Chamaun.

Badi Nágan has a *mandir* with a Sársut Brahman *pujári*. It was built in the *treta yuga*. Once a shepherd went forth to graze his sheep and found a large tank whose existence he had never before heard of. It was revealed to him in a vision that the Nágan had come from *Patál* and that the folk should worship her.

At Balugohar is a temple to Balú Nág and the following is the legend of its foundation:—Once a Brahman of Chatarká went to Mandi to buy salt and on his road he found a child but four months old, who bade him follow it. The Brahman took it up and travelling all night reached Balú forest. There the child bade him dig and he did so, finding a black stone image in the sand or *bálu*. Then the child disappeared, but in the morning a Kumhár came to graze his sheep in the forest and to him the Brahman told his tale. In a trance the Kumhár declared that he was himself the Nág, but the Brahman declared that he could not believe him unless the Nág bestowed a son upon him. The temple, founded in the *dwápar yuga*, contains the black *pindi* or idol dug up by the Brahman and is ministered to by a Sársut Brahman of the Gautama *gót*. The appearance of the Kumhár (Shiva) points to a Shiva origin of the cult or an attempt to affiliate it to Shiva teaching.

Kirtná Nág has a *mandir* at Shiuli. He is called after the name of the village of Kirthá which had a tank to which thirsty kine used to resort, but in it lived a snake which used to suck the cows dry. When the owner went to kill it, it declared it was a Nág and should be worshipped in order to earn blessings for the people. The people pay more respect to its *chela* or *gur* than they do its Brahman *pujári*.

Járu, the deaf Nág of Pháti Túnan, has a curious legend. This god was born at Surápá in Bashar, the chief of which place had a daughter who was sent out one day to graze his sheep. She found a beautiful tank with nine flowers floating on its surface and, tempted by their beauty, gathered them all. But no sooner had she done so than she became unconscious and so remained nine days in the forest. Subsequently she gave birth to nine gods, called Nágs, and bringing them home kept them in a basket. One day when she was sent out with food for the labourers in the fields, she warned her mother not to touch the basket, but when she had gone her mother's curiosity overcame her and she opened it, only to find the nine Nágs which in her fright she caste into the fire. All escaped unhurt, save one whose ear was burnt so that it became deaf. The injured Nág fled first to Tárápur and thence to Khargha where a Ráná's cow stopped to give it milk. Then it went to Deohri Dhár where cows again yielded it their milk. The people of both places then began to worship it as a god. Its idol is of black stone, sunk in the ground and standing two feet high. Its *pujári* is a Kanet, and its *gur* is specially reverenced because in his trances he gives oracles. Two fairs are held annually on the *púran máshi* and *naurátras* in Chet. The former is held at Khirgá and the latter at Deohri Dhár. At these 14 he-goats are sacrificed and visitors are fed free. Another fair, held on the 10th and 11th of Jeṭh, is frequented mostly by people from the surrounding States.

Sharshái, the Nág of Sharshá, has the following tradition :—Once four women went to draw water from a spring called Nái. Three returned home safely, but the fourth could not recover her pitcher which had sunk in the spring. At its edge was a black stone image to which she made a vow for the recovery of her pitcher. It was at once restored to her, but she forgot her vow and it rained heavily for seven days. Then she told the people and they brought the idol to the village and founded a temple in the *treta yuga*. The idol is 2¼ feet high and masks of gold and silver adorn its chariot. The temple walls are painted with pictures. Its *pujári* is a Bhárdwáj Brahman and only a Brahman is allowed to worship the god, whose *gur* answers all questions put to the Nágs and is more respected than the *pujári* himself.

Danwi Nág of Danw, a village in Manjhadesh *pháti*, Kothi Naráingaṛh, is a brother of Sarshái Nág. Both have Kanet *pujáris* according to another account.

Pane Nág is also called Punúṇ and Kungash. Once a Ráni, Bir Nán, wife of the Ṭhákur of Ráníkot, was told in a vision that she would be blessed with a son if she built a temple to the Nág at the corner of a tank called Punúṇ. In the morning the Ṭhákur saw a snake swimming on the surface of the tank and it told him that it had come from he Krukshetr, being of the Kaurava and Pándava race. So the Ṭhákur built a temple in which the Nág appeared of his own accord in the form of a *pinḍi* of stone which still stands in it. This occurred in the *dwápur yuga*. The *pujári* is a Sársut Brahman.[1]

The Nág Kui Kanḍha has several temples.[2] Sri Chand, Ṭhákur of Srigaṛh, had a cow which used to graze at Kanḍha, but was sucked dry by a snake. The Ṭhákur pursued it, but from its hole a *pinḍi* appeared and told him that it was a Nág, promising that if worshipped it would no longer suck the cow's milk. So a temple was built to the Nág whose image is the metal figure of a man, one foot high. Its fair at Kui Kanḍha is held every third year on a day fixed by the votaries. At Srigaṛh it is held every year on a similar date, and at Kotá Dhár on any auspicious day in Jeṭh. It also has a temple at Kanár or Sriwálsar.[3] Its *pujári* is a Bhárdawáj Brahman. This Nág also appears to be worshipped as Kui Kanḍha in Shiogi. Its temple was founded by a Ṭhákur of Katabar, regarding whom a similar legend is told. The *pujári* however is a Bhárdawáj Brahman and its *gur* is selected by the god himself who nods his assent to his appointment.

Chamaun Nág has a temple at Kalíwan Deora. The story goes that once a *ṭhákur*, named Dablá, was a votary of Hansnú. He went to bathe at that place of pilgrimage, and while bathing he saw an image emerge from the water. It directed him that it should be installed at the place inhabited only by Brahmans and blessed by the presence of *kelo* trees. Accordingly it was brought to Kalíwan where a temple was built. Religious importance also attaches to the water from which the image emerged. The date of foundation is not known. The temple contains the stone *pinḍi* of the god. Its affairs are managed by a *kárdár*, by caste a Kanet. The *pujári* is a Gauṛ

[1] The following are the dates of the fairs of the Nág *deotas* in Saráj not given in the text :—

Chamaun Nág	...	Annual fairs are held in Chet, during the *naurátras* in Baisákh on the *bíáspúja* in Háṛ, on the *nág panchmí* in Bhádon, and in Mágh and Phágan. The practice is to choose auspicious days for the fairs.
Baḍi Nágan	...	A fair is held annually on 7th Baisákh and 15th Jeṭh.
Balú Nág	...	The fairs are held on 20th Baisákh and on the *púranmáshi* in Bhádon every year.
Kirtha Nág	...	One fair lasts from 15th Poh to 2nd Mágh, another is held on 1st Phágan and the third on 20th Sáwan. These fairs are held annually.
Sharahái Nág	...	The annual fairs are held on 2nd and 3rd Asauj and at the Dewáli.
Paneo Nág	...	The annual fairs are held on 2nd and 12th Asauj and on 10th Maghar.
Kui Kanḍha Nág	...	The fairs are held annually on the *sankránts* of Jeṭh and Bhádon at the Diwáli.
Shankhú Nág	...	The two fairs are held, one on 1st Bhádon and the other on 1st Phágan.
Takrasi Nág	...	The annual fairs are held on 1st Jeṭh, 10th and 12th Sáwan and on 1st Poh.

[2] Temples of Kui Kanḍha Nág are at :—
Tandi (in Plehi *pháṭi*), Nataunda in Phaṭi Lot, Himri, and Rama below Katehi, and Plehi Dhár in Plehi *pháṭi* : as well as at Shiogi in Plehi *pháṭi*, at Shagogi, Kotadhar, Srigarh Madheṛh, in Siungul *pháṭi*; and at Kui Kanḍha in Himri—Common to two *koṭhis*.

[3] Sriwálsar is in Jalauri *koṭhi* and there is no temple there : Kui Kanḍha Nág used to go there, but does not now do so.

Brahman of the Bhardawáj *gót*. They are not celibate. A *bhog* of milk, rice &c. is offered every morning. A Brahmbhog or free distribution of food is also held in Baisákh. No other shrine is connected with this one. The annual fairs are held on 8th Baisákh, 1st Hár and on an auspicious day in Sawan.

Shankhú Nág or the Nág of the conch has temples at Keoli Ban, Rahwáli and Rupá. Once a *sádhú*, who was engaged in meditation in the Keoli forest, blew his conch and placed it on the ground. Out of it crept a snake and told the *sádhú* that he should be worshipped as a Nág. The conch forthwith turned into an idol of stone. The idols in Keoli Ban are two, one of stone 3 feet high, the other a stone *pindi* only one foot high.

The Nág Takrasi of Takrasi cursed a Thákur, so that he died. The Thákur's cow used to yield its milk to a stone image and when he went to break it, a snake sprang out to defend it. The Thákur went home only to die, but his cowherd worshipped the image and a temple is built to it. Connected with this is the shrine at Mitharsi.

Chatri Nág was originally worshipped by the Thákur Sadhu of Shudá who heard a strange cry coming from a forest and going into it found a stone image which he brought home to worship. Its *pujári* is a Kanet.

Snake-worship in Kulu.

In Batáhar village, Kothí Nagar, there is a snake deity called Bású Nág (*basná*=to dwell). The story is that the *deota* Bású Nág had a wife Nágani, who, when near her delivery, took refuge in an unbaked earthen vessel. A Kumhár came and lighted a fire underneath it, whereupon seven young ones were born, who ran all over the country. Nágani then became a woman with the tail of a snake. The seven sons were (1) Shirgan Nág or Sargun, who came out first (? head foremost, from *sir*, head), and went to Jagatsukh, as did (2) Phál Nág, who lives now near the Phál Nálá; (3) Gosháli Nág, lives at Goshál, he is also called *andhá* or blind because he lost an eye in the fire, his other name is Gautam-Rikhi; (4) Káli Nág, who got blackened, went to Raison Kothí; and (5) Piúli (Píli) Nág, the 'yellow' snake,[1] was the smallest of all, and went to a village near Batáhar; (6) Sogu Nág went to the Sagu Khol, a precipice near Ralha; and (7) Dhunbal Nág (Dhum Rikhi), so called because he came out of the spout in the jar from which smoke came, and went to Halan. It will be noticed that the most of these have distinct names, while the rest have only the names of the places in which they now live, and though Gosháli Nág is also called *andhá*, the latter name seems little used now. The proverb in Kulu runs: *Athára Nág,' athára Nárain*, so that there are in theory ten other snake temples in Kulu. Básu Nág's temple is at Narain-di-dera, which looks as if Nág were only another name for Narain. On the other hand Sir James Lyall described Káli Nág as leaving a standing feud with Nárain, with whose sister the Nág ran away in olden days. So whenever a fair is held in honour of Káli Nág the enemies fight on the mountain top and the ridge on the right bank of the Beás and the *deodar* grove at Aramag in the Sarwari valley are found strewn with their iron arrows.

[1] Pingala, the yellow one, was another name for Nakula, the mongoose, the favourite son of Kubera by Háríti: A. Q. R., 1912, p. 147.

Báski Nág appears to be distinct from Básu Nág. He too had seven sons, by Devi Bhotanti, his second *ráni*. Of these six were slain by Bhágbati and the seventh escaped to Kiáni where he has a temple and is called Kiáni Nág.

Báski Nág had a brother, Turu Nág, who has a cave upon a high hill. Like his brother this Nág gives rain and prevents lightning. He also gives oracles as to rain, and when rain is about to fail water flows from his cave.

Other[1] Nágs in Kulu are Káli Nág Shiṛar, Bhalogu, Phahal, Ramnún, and Shukli. Another Nág is Bhalogu Nág at Dera Bhalogi Bhal. In Jalse Jalsú Nág is worshipped with Jamlú on the 2nd and 3rd of Sáwan.

In Suket Máha Nág, the 'bee' Nág, got his name by resuming Rájá Sham Singh in the form of a bee : *Gazetteer,* 1904, p. 11. Other Nágs in Manḍi are Kumaru whose stone idol at Sáchan goes back to Panḍva times. It is said to avert epidemics. Barnág is important in Saner : Manḍi *Gaò*, p. 40.

The Nág generally appears to be conceived of as a harmless snake, as distinguished from the *sámp* or poisonous one, in the Punjab hills, where every householder is said to have a Nág's image which he worships in his house. It is given charge of his homestead and held responsible that no poisonous snake enter it. No image of any such snake is ever made for worship.[2]

Nágs in Gilgit.

Traces of Nág-worship exist in Gilgit in the Nagis. One of these goddesses was Nagi Suchemi who had at Nangan in Astor a stone altar at the fort of Nágishi hill. A person accused of theft could take an oath of compurgation here. The ritual had some curious features. For instance, the men who attended it returned home by night and were not allowed to appear 'in daylight' before others of the village under penalty of making good the loss. The case awaited the Nagi's decision 'for some days' and if during that period the suspect incurred a loss of

[1] The following are the dates of the fairs held at the temples of some of these Nágs :—

Bású Nág ...	Nine days on the *ikádshi* of Phágan, one day on the 1st Chet, four days on the new year's Baisákh, one day in Asauj.
Pahal Nág at Bharka Dera ...	10th of the lunar month of Baisákh.
Káli Nág at Dera Kal Nág ...	1st to 14th Asauj and Maghar, and on the 3rd, 5th and 7th of the light half of Sáwan and Bhádon.
Káli Nág at Matiora in K. Har Khándi...	4th Baisákh, besides a *yag* on 7th Bhádon
Káli Nág Shiṛar at Kat Kali Nág ...	(1) 1st of *nauráta* in the light half of Chet, (2) light half of Jeṭh, (3) a *yag* (Narmedh) is performed every third year in the light half of Sáwan (4) 1st of Mágh, (5) 1st of Phágan, (6) 1st of Chet.
Phúli Nág at Batáhar Dera in K. Nagar...	1st of Phágan, 1st day of Phágan and 1st of Chet, four days in the light half of Chet at the beginning of the new year
Sargun Nág ...	31st Bhadon to 2nd Asauj.
Ramnún Nág at Kehli Aga ...	1st to 3rd Chet, 31st Sáwan to 3rd Bhádon and 1st to 3rd Asauj.
Shukli Nág at Nandla Dera ...	1st to 3rd Asauj and for two days from full moon day of Maghar.

[2] P. N. Q., III, § 477.

any kind he was adjudged guilty.[1] Nagi Sochemi's sister is Sri Kun and she lived at Shankank near Godai in Astor. To her the villagers used to present goats and pray for the supply of their wants, but her followers were forbidden to keep cows or drink their milk under penalty of loss of flock, herd or crop.[2]

Nág-worship was also known in ancient Buner. Hiüan-Tsang mentions the 'dragon lake' on the mountain Lan-po-lo—which probably lay 4 or 5 miles north of Manglaur.[3] Legend connected it with a saint Sákya who married the dragon or Nág's daughter and founded an ex-royal house of Udyána.[4]

Near Manglaur also lay a lake worshipped as the habitation of a miracle-working Nága King, in whom must be recognised the Nága Apalála, tutelary deity of Udyána, and whose legend is connected with the source of the Swát river.[5]

GÚGA AS A SNAKE-GOD.

Under serpent-worship may be classed the cult of Gúga but for no better reason than that he has a peculiar power of curing snake-bite. Of him Ibbetson[6] wrote as Gúga Pír, also called Záhir Pír the 'Saint Apparent,' or Bágarwála, he of the Bágar, from the fact that his grave is near Dadrewa in Bíkáner, and that he is said to have ruled over the northern part of the Bágar or great prairies of Northern Rájpútána. He flourished about the middle of the 12th century. He is really a Hindu, and his proper name is Gúga Bír or Gúga the Hero (*cf. vir* Latin). But Musalmáns also flock to his shrine, and his name has been altered to Gúga Pír or Saint Gúga, while he himself has become a Muhammadan in the opinion of the people. He is to the Hindus of the Eastern Punjab the greatest of the snake kings, having been found in the cradle sucking a live cobra's head; and his *chhari* or switch, consisting of a long bamboo surmounted by peacock feathers, a cocoanut, some fans, and a blue flag, may be seen at certain times of the year as the Jogís or sweepers who have local charge of it take it round and ask for alms. His worship extends throughout the Province, except perhaps on the frontier itself. It is probably weakest in the Western Plains; but all over the eastern districts his shrines, of a peculiar shape and name, may be seen in almost every large village, and he is universally worshipped throughout the sub-montane tract and the Kángra hills. There is a famous equestrian statue of him on the rock of Mandor, the ancient capital of Jodhpur.

In Hissár he appears to be also worshipped, at Karangánwáli and Kagdána, under the name of Rám Dewa. Fairs are held at those places on Mágh 10th. The legend is that Rám Dewa, a Bágari, disappeared into the earth alive seated on his horse and he is still depicted on horse back. His cult, once confined to the Bágris, has now been adopted by the Játs, and Brahmans and the *pujáris* at these two temples belong to those castes respectively.

[1] Ghulam Muhammad, *On the Festivals and Folklore of Gilgit*, Asiatic Society of Bengal's Monographs, I, p. 103. The account is a little vague. Suchemi or Sochemi may derive her name from *sach*, 'true', or 'truth disclosing.'

[2] *Ib.*, p. 111.

[3] Sir Harold Deane, *Notes on Udyána*, I. L. A. S., 1896, p. 661; the Saidgai is probably meant.

[4] Sir Auriel Stein, *Serindia*, p. 176.

[5] *Ib.*, p. 13.

[6] *Ib.*, § 238.

THE CULT OF GÚGA IN NORTH-WESTERN INDIA.

A vast body of folklore has clustered round Gúga, but the main outlines of the story can still be traced, and will be made clearer by the following table of his descent and family :—

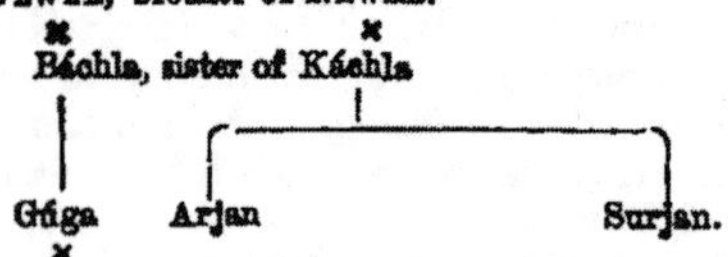

In the following notes an attempt is made to summarise all the legends concerning the cult of Gúga already published. To these summaries are appended some variants, not hitherto published.

THE STORY OF GÚGA ANALYSED.

Two legends of Gúga have been published, both in the *Legends of the Punjab*, by Sir R. C. Temple. The first is found at page 121 of volume I of that work, and may be analysed as follows :—

1.—*Analysis of the miracle play of Gúga, the Rájpút of the Bágar country.*

Beginning with an invocation to Sárad or Saraswatí this play opens with a dialogue between Jewar and his queen Báchhal, who lament that they have no children. Their family priest, Pandit Rangachár, consoles them, saying they will have three sons, a prophecy which is not apparently fulfilled, as will be seen later. Meanwhile the gardener announces the arrival of Gorakhnáth, the saint, and Jewar goes to see him, while Báchhal sends her maid to find out what has caused all the excitement. The maid, Híra Deí, hears that it is due to the arrival of Gorakhnáth from the door-keeper, and takes Báchhal to visit the saint.

The plot here is obscure. Báchhal begs the saint to vouchsafe her a son, but he makes no promise, and the scene changes abruptly. Káchhal, who is undoubtedly Báchhal's sister, enters and conspires with her slave-girl to visit the saint too. But when she goes to Gorakhnáth, he detects her evil heart, and refuses her request for a son.

According to the published text Káchhal, however, persists in her prayer, to which the saint assents, but I take it that Báchhal is meant—on page 136 of the text. However this may be, Báchhal again comes to the saint (see page 137) and he appears to tell her that she is not destined to have a son. But all this part (up to page 138) is very obscure, and only intelligible in the light of other versions. To resume—

Káchhal appears on the scene, and is promised two sons, which she will bear if she eat two seeds, according to the ordinary version, but in this text (page 139) the saint merely gives her two flowers.

Again the scene changes so abruptly as to suggest that the text is very incomplete, and Báchhal appears and receives a promise that she too shall have a son, but the saint curses Káchhal for her deceit, and declares that she shall die at the birth of her twins, and that they shall only live 12 years. Káchhal now appears on the scene no more, and it may be convenient to pause here and note what other versions say about her.

Sir Richard Temple's text assumes that Káchhal is Báchhal's co-wife, and this appears to be by far the commonest version. But in another account I find Káchhal represented as the wife of Newar, brother of Jewar. This idea I believe to be a late addition to the story, but that is a point for further discussion.

Káchhal's conduct is much more lucidly set forth in other versions. According to them she learns that the saint has given Báchhal an appointment for the evening, at midnight one at least says, and she manages to borrow her sister's clothes, on some pretext not explained, and personates her before the saint, receiving his gift of the twins. Various other details are added, as that Báchhal serves the saint for six months before she can induce him to promise her a son, and so on.

To return now to our published text. We find (page 148) that Jewar's sister, Sabír Deí, by name, makes mischief. She poisons Jewar's mind against his wife, and eventually he sends her away to her father's house at Ghazní.[1] On the road the cart, in which Báchhal is riding, is halted for the midday rest, and the oxen are taken out, whereupon a snake bites them both and they die. This introduces snakes into the drama.

Gúga now makes himself heard, and his power over snakes felt, though he has yet to be born. Báchhal weeping at the loss of the oxen falls asleep, and in a dream Gúga directs her to cut a branch from a *ním* tree, and calling on Gorakhnáth to heal the oxen. On awaking Báchhal does so, prays to Gorakhnáth, repeats the charms for the 8 kinds of snakes and sings the praises of the charmer. The oxen are forthwith cured and come to life again.

In our present text Báchhal goes on to Gajní Fort, as Ghazní is called on page 155, and falls into her mother's arms. She tells her all her story, and adds the curious detail that though 12 months have elapsed, Gúga is not yet born. Gúga again speaks, and protests that he will be for ever disgraced if he is born in his maternal grandfather's house, an idea which is quite new to me. In the Punjab it is the rule, at least in certain parts, for a wife to go to her parents' home for her first confinement.[2] He implores them to show his father some great miracle in order that he may take back his mother.

[1] Gájni or Gájnipur, the ancient name of Ráwalpindi, may be indicated; not Ghazni—which was then Muhammadan.

[2] Dr. Hutchison notes:—"The explanation probably is that from ancient times till quite recently no Rájpút maiden after marriage might ever again return to her father's home. And under no circumstances might she or her husband be in any way indebted to his hospitality—not even for a cup of cold water. This custom was abandoned within the last 10 or 15 years chiefly, I believe, on the initiative of the Mahárája of Kashmír. Even at the wedding in November 1915 the Mahárája had all supplies for himself and his special attendants—even to their drinking water—sent from Jammu. The bridegroom and his friends were of course the guests of the Chamba State as well as the general company of wedding guests."

Again we have an abrupt change of scene, and find ourselves back in Jewar's palace. Jewar laments his harshness towards Báchhal, and his *wazír* advises him to depute him to fetch her back. The *wazír* sets out to Gajní, where he is met by the king Chandarbhán, who, we thus learn, is Báchhal's father, and Jewar takes Báchhal back with him without any miracle or fuss of any kind, an instance of the playwright's entire lack of literary skill.

On their return to Jewar's capital, a place called Gard Daréra later on in the poem, Gúga is at last born at midnight on the 8th-9th of Bhádon. Pandit Rangachár thinks this an auspicious date, and avers that Gúga's votaries will use fans of flowers and blue flags, which they of course do, and all the land of Bágar rejoiced. Rájá Jewar bids his *wazír* acknowledge Gúga as his heir by putting on him the sign of royalty, although Káchhal's twins had presumably been born before Gúga. However this may be, I take it that by putting on the sign of royalty can only be meant the mark which would make Gúga the *tíka* or heir-apparent to Jewar. But it is important to note that Jewar for some reason or other hesitates to make this order, and after Gúga's birth two months elapse before he is thus recognized.

A considerable period, nearly 12 years at least, now elapses, and in the next scene we find Gúga out hunting. Tortured by the heat he rides up to a well and asks a Brahman woman to give him some water to drink, but she refuses on the ground that her pitcher is an earthen one and would be defiled, apparently, if he were to drink from it. Gúga, vexed at her refusal, invokes Gorakhnáth and shoots an arrow, wherewith he breaks both the Brahman woman's pitchers, so that the water drenches her body.[1] Weeping, she curses Gúga, and his children, but Báchhal endeavours to atone for the insult. Why the insult was such an inexpiable one is not clear.

Again the scene changes and we see Rájá Sanjá send out a priest to find a match for his daughter Chhariyál or Siriál as she is more usually called. This priest, Gunman by name, comes to Jewar's city and solicits Gúga's hand in due form, which is bestowed on Chhariyál. But at this point Báchhal breaks in with a lament for the ill-timed death of Jewar, and on hearing of that event Rájá Sanjá, in alarm at evil omen, breaks off the engagement

Báchhal is greatly distressed at this breach of faith, and on learning the cause of her grief Gúga goes to the forest, and there sings the mode of defiance and war. His flute-playing charms the beasts and birds of the forest. Básak Nág, the king of the Snakes, sends his servant Tátig Nág to see who it is.

[1] Whether this is a rain-charm or not I am unable to say. A similar but expanded version of the rite occurs in the legend of Rájá Rasálú, who first breaks the pitchers of the women of the city with stones. They complain to Sáliváhan who bids them use pitchers of iron, but these he breaks with his iron-tipped arrows.—*Legends of the Panjab, I*, pp. 6-7. Apparently a fertility charm is hinted at. Possibly a man who could succeed in breaking a jar of water poised on a woman's head once acquired a right over her. According to Aryan usage a slave might be manumitted by his owner pouring over his head a pot of water, with gram and flowers, and the custom of pouring out water was observed in all ceremonies accompanying the transfer of property; for instance it took place when land was sold, and when a father handed over his daughter to her husband. Witnesses too were examined before a fire and a jar of water. See Barnett's *Antiquities of India*, pp. 128 and 126. We find the custom again in the Dúm legend—see *infra*—current in the Simla Hills,

Gúga informs Tátig Nág that he is the grandson of Rájá Amar, and that his village is Gard Daréra: he adds his name of Gúga was given him by Gorakhnáth, but says nothing about its popular form *gúgal*, bdellium, a-plant commonly used for incense. He tells, however, of the broken betrothal, and Básak places Tátig Nág's services at his disposal.

Gúga accordingly sends Tátig Nág to Dhúpnagar, a place across 7 rivers, where Siriál, as she is now called, lives in the country of Kárú, whose patron goddess is Kamachhya, and whose people are great wizards. At Dhúpnagar Tátig Nág finds Siriál in her garden, and, assuming the guise of a Brahman, he gains access to her, then suddenly resuming his own form of a snake he bites her, while she is bathing in the tank. But it is perhaps important to note that he only succeeds at his second attempt, for on first resuming his snake's form he climbs a tree and thence attempts to bite Siriál, but is detected by her before he can effect his object.

A maid hastens to inform Sánja of his daughter's peril, and Tatig Nág, again taking the form of a Brahman, goes to the palace, where he asks the *panhári* (or female water-carrier) who appears to be the maid-of-all-work there, what has happened. She tells him and he sends her to tell the Rájá that a snake-charmer has come When ushered into the Rájá's presence, Tátig Nág exacts a promise in writing that the betrothal shall be carried out if Siriál recovers, and then cures her, taking a branch of the *ním* tree, and using charms, but showing practical ability by sucking all the poison down into her big toe. Sánja does not openly repudiate his promise, but fixes the wedding 7 days ahead, yet in spite of the shortness of the time Gúga is miraculously transported to Dhúpnagar in time for the nuptials, with an immense retinue which it almost ruins Sánja to entertain. Siriál takes a tender farewell of her mother and on reaching Gard Daréra is presented to Báchhal by Gorakhnáth.

We now come to the last act in the drama. Gúga goes to see his twin cousins, Arjan and Surjan, the sons of Káchhal. They, however, demand a moiety of the property, but Gúga objects to any partition. Then they persuade Gúga to go out hunting with them, and treacherously attack him, but Gúga slays them both, and returns home with their heads tied to his horse's saddle. He then returns home and shows the heads to Báchhal, who upbraids him for his deed, and says:—'See me no more, nor let me see you again.' Gúga takes her at her word, and appeals to the Earth mother to swallow him up. But the Earth refused on the curious ground that he is a Hindu and should be burnt, only Muhammadans being buried. So she advises him to go to Rattan Hájí and learn of him the creed of Islám. Now Hájí Rattan was a Muhammadan of Bhaṭinda, but the Earth is made to direct Gúga to Ajmer. Thither Gúga goes, meets the Hájí and Khwája Khizr, the Muhammadan water-spirit, and from the former learns the Musalmán creed. He then returns to Gard Daréra where the Earth receives him. This ends the play.

The song of Gúga given in Volume III of the *Legends of the Punjab* purports to be a historical poem, though its history is somewhat mixed. It plunges *in medias res,* commencing with a fuller and very interesting account of the quarrel between Gúga and his twin cousins.

In the first place, we notice that Báchhal has adopted Arjan and Surjan, who ask:—'Are we to call thee Mother or Aunt? Thou art our *dharm kí mán, i. e.* adoptive mother.'[1] Do the cousins base their claim to a moiety of the property on this adoptive relationship? I think the answer must be 'yes.' Báchhal urges Gúga to make them his land-brothers,[2] but describes them as her sister's sons. Gúga retorts that they are not the sons of his father's brother, a statement which is quite irreconcilable with the idea that they are the sons of Newar, Jewar's brother, alluded to above. It seems clear that for some reason or other the twins are of doubtful or extraneous paternity.

The twins, however, are bent on enforcing their claim, and they set out for Delhi. In response to their appeal, the emperor Firoz Sháh takes a large force to reduce his contumacious feudatory to obedience. Gúga, taunted by Siriál, goes forth to fight, with all the ceremony of a Rájpút warrior. But, interesting as this passage is, we need not dwell upon it, as it does not affect the development of the plot. After a Homeric combat, Gúga slays the sons of his mother's sister, defeats Firoz Sháh, and returns to his palace. There Báchhal meets him and demands news of the twins. Gúga says he has no news, but eventually shows her their heads tied to his horse's saddle, whereupon she bids him show his face no more.

A third version is current in the Bijnor District of the United Provinces, and was published in the *Indian Antiquary.*

THE BIJNOR VERSION.

Under Prithví Rájá, Chauhán, of Delhi, there ruled in Márú-désa, now called the Bágar, a king named Nár Singh or Már Singh (called Amar Singh further on), whose family stood thus:

Amar Singh — Kánwar Pál of Sirsa Patan in Bijnor.
| |
Jewar — Báchhal.
Gúga.

As he had no son Jewar practised austerities in the forest, while Báchhal fasted and so on at home. Gorakhnáth, accompanied by Kání Pawá, his senior disciple, came to her palace, and was about to depart when Kání Pawá warns Báchhal that she may waylay him. Achhal, her sister, overhears this, and with her face veiled, stops Gorakhnáth when about to start, and receives from him two barley-corns, which she is to wash and eat at once. When Báchhal appears on the scene,

[1] Yet, we are assured, the phrase *dharm báp* is never used for adoptive father.

[2] For the *bhúm bhái* or earth brother in Karnál see *infra,* under fictitious kinship. A stranger might be adopted as a *bhúm bhái,* but by so doing he lost all rights in his natural family—Karnál *Gazetteer,* 1890, p. 138. The story points to a conflict between the agnatic and cognatic principles.

Gorakh has her beaten, but Kání Pawá protests, and induces Gorakh to go to Bhagwán, who says that Báchhal is not destined to bear a son. Gorakh replies that he is well aware of that, and that is just why he has come. So Bhagwán rubs some of the dirt out of his head, and Báchhal divides it into four parts, giving one to a Brahmaní, one to a sweeper's wife, a third to a gray mare, and keeping the fourth for herself. All four females, hitherto barren, now become fruitful.[1]

Amar Singh's mind is now set against Báchhal, and he sends her to Kumár Pál (Kanwar Pál ?) At the end of seven months Gúga complains that he will be called Nanwar, if he is born in his maternal grandfather's house, so he tells Báchhal to make the crippled carpenter build her a cart, which is achieved.

On the road back to Jewar's capital, Gúga makes Rájá Vásúki acknowledge his power by performing *kandúri*, a form of worship to Fátima.[2] Finally in due course, Gúga is born as Záhir Pír, simultaneously with Nara Sínha Pánre to the Brahmaní, Patiyá Chamár to the sweepress, and Bachrá, the colt, to the mare.

One day Gúga goes to Búndí and finds Surail, king Sanjai's daughter, in the garden. He plays dice with her and finally wins her. But when Sanjai sends the signs of betrothal Arjan and Surjan object that, owing to an old feud with Búndí, it cannot be accepted. In this Amar Singh agrees, but Gúga insists on its acceptance, and eventually says the wedding procession will start on the 9th of Bhádon *badí*. Meanwhile as Amar Singh will not go, Báchhal tries to get her father to attend the wedding, but he declines. It appears that by this time Jewar is dead, and so Gúga falls back on Gorakh, who calls him 'Kání Pawá's brother, Záhir Pír,' an unexplained title.

After his marriage, while out hunting one day, Gúga shoots a deer, but Arjan and Surjan claim it. Then they say that half the kingdom is theirs, *because their mother and Gúga's were sisters!* They also claim Surail *because to them Búndí had sent the signs of betrothal*, and not to Gúga, a fact not stated before. They then complain to Pirthví Rájá, and he sends an army to help them, but Gúga kills Surjan with an arrow, *whereupon Arjan cries like a child*, and so Gúga kills him too. On his return Gúga tries to put his mother off, but at last he shows her the heads and challenges her to say which is which. Reproached by her Gúga makes for the forest. In Sáwan, when newly-wed brides dress up in their best and swing, Surail weeps, and Gúga says to his steed:—"Let us go and see thy brother's wife, who is weeping for thy brother." [3]

[1] This scene vividly recalls the piece of Græco-Buddhist sculpture in the Lahore Museum which formed the subject of Dr. Vogel's paper in the *Journal of the Panjab Historical Society*, I, pp. 135-40. There we have the mare with her foal, the woman with her child, and the groom with some horses' heads. The simultaneous birth by similar miraculous power of a prince, his brothers and attendants, and even the animals who serve him is a stock incident in folk lore which would appear to be derived from the Buddhist teaching that all life has a common origin. An instance of its occurrence will be found in the legend of Magneshwar from the Simla Hills—*infra*.

[2] In which males have no part.

[3] If the steed was Bachrá, he was in a sense Gúga's (half) brother, so by 'thy brother' Gúga means himself.

But the guard refuses him admittance. Surail dreams that he has come, and lets him in, but he jumps his horse over the roof. At last one day Báchhal comes in and before her Gúga *veils his face.* As he rides off Surail overtakes him and seizes the reins of his horse. Then at last Záhir Díwán bethinks him of Gorakh, and descends below the earth, at *Záhir Díwán ke náná ká ujará khérá,* "the deserted mound of the *maternal* grandfather of Záhir Díwán," which lies 9 *kós* from Núr and 27 from Hissár.

The Rájpútána version.

According to Tod[1] Gúga was the son of Vachá Chauhán, Rájá of Jangal Des, which stretched from the Sutlej to Hariána, and whose capital was at Mehera, or Gúga ká Mairí, on the Sutlej. Gúga, with his 45 sons and 60 nephews, fell in defence of his capital on Sunday, the 9th of the month.[2] Oaths are sworn on his *sáká.* His steed, Javádiá, was born of one of the two barley-corns which Gúga gave his queen. The name is now a favourite one for horses.

A variant from Sirsa.

Another account from Sirsa gives the following as Gúga's pedigree :—

Umar (*sic*), Chauhán, a chieftain of Bágar in Bíkáner.
|
Jhewar × Báchhal.
|
Ugdí-Gúga, who was born at Dadréra, in Bíkáner, about 50 miles from Sirsa, and who flourished as late as the time of Aurangzeb (1658—1707).

Báchhal served Gorakhnáth for 12 years, but Káchhal, her sister, by deceit obtained the gift of twins, so Gorakh gave Báchhal some *gúgal* as a special mark of his favour. Káchhal's sons demanded a share of the inheritance, and Aurangzeb sent a force to aid them, but Gúga compelled them to retreat to Bharera in Bíkáner. Thence they raided Gúga's cattle, and the herdsman Mohan's wife tells Báchha. She rouses Gúga from his siesta, and he goes forth to seek revenge. He slays Arjan with his lance, Surjan with his sword. Javádiá, when cut in two, is put together again. On his return home Báchhal withholds water from him, until thirst compels him to confess that he has killed his cousins. Báchhal then curses him (which seems very unfair, seeing that she sent him out to punish the raiders). Gúga then turns Muhammadan, and sinks into the earth at Mori, 24 miles from Sirsa. At this place and at Dadrera fairs are held on Bhádon 8th-9th. Gúga was faithful to his wife for 12 years, and visited her nightly, until his mother caught him and upbraided him for lack of filial affection!

A variant from the Nábha State.

According to a version of the legend current in Nábha, Gúga was born at Daréra in Bíkáner territory; and was the son of Rájá Jiwar, a

[1] Rájasthán, II, 418. For further data from Tod see p. 16 *post.*

[2] A day held sacred to the *manes* of Gúga throughout Rájpútána, especially in the desert, a portion of which is still called Gúga-ka-thal.

Chauhán Rájpút. The story runs that Gorakhnáth came to the Rájá's garden, where he lit a fire and subsequently bade his disciple Ogar take some *bhabút* (ashes) from his wallet and scatter them over the trees and plants which had all dried up. The ashes caused them to bloom again. Jíwar's queen Báchhal seeing this begged the saint to bestow children upon her. But after serving him for 12 years, on the very day that her prayer was to be granted, Achhal borrowed her clothes and went to Gorakhnáth from whom she received two barley-corns. She gave birth to twins in due course, but meanwhile Báchhal had to serve the saint for yet another 12 years, after which period he went in search of a son for her. With Shiva he went to Rájá Básak, who had 101 sons, and asked him for one of them, but his queen refused to give up a single one of them. This incensed the Rájá who foamed at the mouth, and Gorakhnáth promptly saturated some *gúgal* in the saliva. This *gúgal* he gave to Báchhal, and she ate some of it herself and gave the rest to her Brahman's and sweeper's wives, and a little to her mare. Báchhal in due course gave birth to Gúga, the Brahmaní to Nársingh, the sweepress to Bhajú, and the mare to a blue colt.

When Gúga grew up, the sons of his mother's sister claimed a share of his father's estate, but this he refused them. They appealed to the court, and a force was sent against Gúga. In the fight which ensued, Nársingh and Bhajú were both killed, but Gúga cut off the twins' heads and took them to his mother. She drove him from her presence and he went 12 *kos* into the jungle, and dismounting from his horse found an elevated spot, whence he prayed to the earth to swallow him up. She replied that as he was a Hindu she could not do so. Instantly the saints, Khwája Muhí ud-dín, Ratn Hájí and Míran Sáhib, appeared and converted him to Islám. Gúga then recited the *kalima* and hid himself in the earth. His tomb is shown on the spot and an annual fair is held there on the 9th *badi* Bhádon. Its guardians are Muhammadan Rájpúts, but Muhammadans are said not to believe that Gúga was a Muhammadan, though some low-caste Muhammadan tribes believe in him too. Many people worship him as king of the snakes, and sweepers recite his story in verse. It is said that Hindus are not burnt but buried after death within a radius of 12 *kos* from his shrine.[1] Close by it is the tomb of Nársingh at which libations of liquor are made: and that of Bhajú, to whom gram and he-buffaloes are offered.

A NEW VERSION FROM GURGAON.

At Darúherá in the Hissár District lived Jewar, a Chauhán Rájpút of the middle class.[2] He and Báchla his wife had to lament that they had no son, and for 12 long years Báchla served Sada Nand, a disciple of Gorakhnáth, without reward. Then Sada Nand left the village and Gorakhnáth himself came there, whereon Jewar's garden,

1 Mr. Longworth Dames suggests that the prevalence of burial among the Bishnois who are found in the very tract, the Bágar, referred to in the legends of Gúga, must be connected with the legend.

2 Other accounts make Jewar a king who ruled at Dardrera. A few miles distant from his capital lay the Dhaulí Dhartí or 'grey land,' a dreary forest, in which Gúga is said to have spent his days.

in which the trees and flowers had died of drought, bloomed again. Báchla hearing of this miracle went to visit the Jogí who seeing a woman coming closed his eyes and remained silent. Sada Nand, however, was in his train and told her of his Gurú's power. At last Báchla contrived to touch the bell which hung in his tent rope, whereupon the Jogí opened his eyes and asked why she had waited upon him. In reply to her petition he declared that she was not destined to have a son. Despite her disappointment Báchla served him for 12 full years.

Báchla's sister, Káchla, was not on good terms with her so she disguised herself in her sister's clothes, and appeared before the Jogí to pray for a son. Gorakhnáth pierced her disguise, but nevertheless gave her two barley-corns to eat, as a reward for her long service, and promised her two sons. Káchla now returned in triumph to her sister and told her that the Jogí was about to depart, whereupon Báchla hastened to see him and stopped him on his way. He declared that he had already granted her prayer, and thus Báchla learnt that her sister had supplanted her. Recognising her innocence the Jogí now gave her a piece of *gúgal* out of his wallet, saying she would attain her desire by eating it.

At the end of seven months Sawerai, Jewar's sister, discerned her pregnancy and complained to him of her suspected infidelity. Jewar would have killed her, but for the entreaties of her maid, Sawaldah, who vouched for her innocence. Nevertheless Jewar beat her and drove her from his house. Báchla then went in a cart to her parents' house at Sirsa, but on the way she passed a serpent's hole wherein dwelt Básak, the Snake King. Hearing the cart rattle by, Básak told his queen that in the womb of the woman sitting in the cart lay his enemy. At her behest he bade his *parohit* (?) bring Astik, his grandson, and him Básak commissioned to bite Báchla. But as he raised his head over the cart Báchla struck him down with her fist. Astik, however, succeeded in biting one of her oxen who drew the cart at the midday halt. Báchla cried herself to sleep at this misfortune, but in a dream a boy bade her tie the *dárá* on her head to the head of the dead ox. She did so, and this brought the animal to life again.

Báchla soon reached her parents' house in safety, but there she again saw in a dream a boy who bade her return to her husband's house, otherwise her child's birth would be a disgrace to her and her family. So to Darúhera she returned, and there Jewar gave her a ruined hut to live in and bade his servant not to help her.

At midnight[1] on Bhádon 8th Gúga was born, and at his birth the dark house was illumined and the old blind midwife regained her sight. Jewar celebrated the event, and gave presents to all his menials. Gúga, it is said, in a dream bade his mother make the impression of a hand, *tháp*, on the door of the hut to avert all evil.

When he had grown up Gúga married Seral. His twin cousins did all they could to prevent this match, but Nársingh *bír* and Kaila

[1] On Tuesday, the 9th of Bhádon, in Sambat 363, Vikramajít, in the reign of Rai Pithóra.

bír[1] assisted him. Another version is that the twins attempted to trick Rájá Sindha into giving Seral to them instead of to Gúga. One day on his return from hunting he saw Narú, the wife of his *parohit*, drawing water from a well, and, as he was thirsty, he bade her give him some to drink. Thinking he spoke in jest she was going away without doing so, when he shot an arrow at her pitcher, which was broken and all her clothes drenched with the water.

Eager to revenge this insult the *parohit* demanded a whole village as his fee for services at Gúga's wedding. This Gúga refused, as he had already given the Brahman 101 cows, and on his persisting in the demand Gúga struck him with his wooden shoes. Thereupon the Brahman went to Gúga's cousins and urged them to demand a partition of the joint estate. Gúga told them they could have full enjoyment of the whole property, but at a sign from the Brahman they persisted in their demand for its division. Gúga accordingly bade Nársingh *bír*, his familiar, seize the twins and re-cast them into prison, but at his mother's intercession they were released.[2] Instigated, however, by the Brahman they went to lay their suit before Pirthí Ráj, king of Delhi, and he deputed his officer, Ganga Rám, to effect the partition. But Gúga having had Ganga Rám beaten and his face blackened turned him out of the city.

This brought Pirthí Ráj on to the scene with an army, but when he bade the *parohit* summon Gúga that mischief-maker advised the king to seize Gúga's cows and detain them till nightfall. Seeing that his kine did not return at evening Gúga mounted his horse and attacked the king. His forces comprised the men of 22 neighbouring villages together with Gorakhnáth's invisible array. Presenting himself before the king Gúga offered to surrender all he had, if any one could pull his spear out of the ground. No champion, however, accepted this challenge, and so the battle began. Gúga smote off both his cousins' heads and tied them to his saddle. He then drove the defeated king's army into Hissár town, and though the gates were closed against him he forced a way in, whereupon the king submitted and sued for pardon.

On his return home Báchla asked which side had won, but Gúga, parched with thirst, only replied by casting his cousins' heads at her feet. At this sight Báchla bade him not show her his face again. In his distress Gúga stood beneath a *champa* tree and prayed the Earth to swallow him up, but it bade him learn *yog* of Ratn Náth,[3] Jogí at Bhatinda, or else accept the *kalima*. On the way thither he met Gorakhnáth who taught him *yog*, and in the Dhaulí Dhartí the earth then answered his prayer, engulfing him with his horse and arms, on the 14th *badi* of Asauj.

A shepherd, who had witnessed Gúga's disappearance, brought the news to Báchla, who with his wife went to the spot. But they found no trace of Gúga and returned home. That night Gúga's wife cried herself to sleep and in a dream saw her husband, on horseback with his

[1] Two of the 360 disciples who accompanied Gorakhnáth.

[2] According to one account Káchla, their own mother, is said to have died, whereupon Báchla adopted them both *as her own sons*.

[3] Bábá Ratn Hájí Sáhib of Bhaṭinḍa, more correctly called Hájí Abul Razá Ratn Tabrindí or Tabarhindí.

spear. Next morning she told her old nurse, Sandal, of the dream and was advised by her to pass the rest of her life in devotion. As a reward her prayers were heard and the Almighty bade Gúga visit his wife every night at midnight. Gúga obeyed, but stipulated that his mother should not hear of his visits. Once, however, at the *tij* festival in Sáwan all the women, dressed in their finest clothes, went to Báchla to ask her to permit Gúga's wife join in the festivities, and Báchla sent a maid to call her. She came, putting off all her ornaments, &c.—which she was wearing in anticipation of Gúga's visit,—but the girl told Báchla what she had seen. Báchla, suspecting her daughter-in-law's fidelity to Gúga's memory, urged her to tell her all, and when she refused to reveal the truth, beat her. Under the lash she disclosed Gúga's visits, but still Báchla was incredulous and exacted a promise that she should herself see Gúga. Next night Gúga came as usual, and Báchla ran to seize his horse's bridle, but Gúga cast his mantle on the ground and bade her pick it up. As she stooped to do so, he put spurs to his horse, reminding her of her own command that he should show his face to her no more, and disappeared.

Thus ends the legend of Gúga. It is added that when Muhammad of Ghor reached Darúhera on his way to Delhi, the drums of his army ceased to sound. And hearing the tale of Gúga the invader vowed to raise a temple to him on the spot if he returned victorious. Accordingly the present *mári* at Darúhera was erected by the king.

In his *Custom and Myth* Mr. Andrew Lang remarks that there are two types of the Cupid, Psyche, and the 'Sun-Frog' myths, one that of the woman who is forbidden to see or to name her husband; the other that of the man with the vanished fairy bride. To these must now be added a third variant, that of the son who is forbidden to see his mother's face, because he has offended in some way. Again Mr. Langs would explain the separation of the lovers as the result of breaking a taboo, or law of etiquette, binding among men and women, as well as between men and fairies. But in the third type of these myths this explanation appears to be quite inadequate, as the command to Gúga that he shall see his mother's face no more must, I think, be based upon some much stronger feeling than mere etiquette.

Gúga in Kulu.

Gúga was killed by the *dains.* He will re-appear in the fold of a cow-herd, who is warned that the cattle will be frightened at his re-appearance, and that he must not use his mace of 20 maunds. When he appears, however, the cattle are terrified and the cow-herd knocks him on the head with his mace. Hence Gúga only emerges half-way from the earth. His upper half is called Záhir Pír and his lower Lakhdáta. The former is worshipped by Muhammadans and the latter by Hindus.

Gúga's pedigree in Kulu is given thus :—

Báchla, sister to Káchla.

- Gúga
- Gugri
- Jaur
- Jareta.[1]

[1] Doubtless a diminutive of Jaúr.

The two brothers looted a cow, called Gogo, which belonged to Brahma and this led to their fight with Gúga. In Gúga's temple (*makán*) at Sultánpur which belongs to Chamárs Gúga and his *wazír* Tribal are mounted on horses and Gogri on a mare while Nar Singh, Kaila Bír and Gorakhnáth are on foot.

The cult of Mundlíkh.

The deified hero of the Mundlíkh cult in Chamba is doubtless the valiant Rájpút champion, Gúga. Chauhán[1] who lived at Gaṛh Dandera, near Bindraban, in the time of Pirthví Ráj, the last Hindu King of Delhi, A. D. 1170—93. Gúga is said to have fought many battles with the Muhammadans, and in the last his head was severed from his body, hence the name *Mundlíkh* from *munda* head, and *líkh* a line. He is said to have continued fighting without the head, and by some to have disappeared in the ground, only the point of his spear remaining visible. The legend is sung to the accompaniment of music by the hill bards, and with such pathos that their audiences are often moved to tears. Mundlíkh's death is supposed to have taken place on the ninth day of the dark half of the moon in Bhádon, and from that date for eight days his *shráda*, called Guggnaih, is yearly observed at his shrines. He is represented by a stone figure of a man on horseback, accompanied by similar figures of his sister Guggari, a deified heroine, his *wazír*, Kailu, and others. The rites of worship are much the same as at Devi temples.

Mundlíkh has a *mandar* at Gaṛh in *pargana* Tísa, another at Palewar in Sahu, and Gugga Mundlíkh-Siddha has one at Shálu in Himgari. The temples are of wood and stone.

The images are of stone, but vary in size and number, that at Gaṛh being about a foot high, and that of Palewar containing four idols mounted on horseback, while at Shálu, Gugga Mundlíkh is represented by the statue of a body of twelve. There are no incumbents at Gaṛh, but at Palewar the *chela* and *pujára* are weavers, in whose families the offices are hereditary. Gúga's *chela* and *pujára* are Chamárs, and their offices are also hereditary. The Mundlíkh of Gaṛh goes on tour for eight days after the Janam Ashṭami in Bhádon. He of Palewar goes on tour for three days after, and Gúga's chain and umbrella (*chhatar*) are paraded through the villages for the eight days after the Janam Ashṭami.

Ráná Mundlíkh, otherwise called Gúga Chauhán, was a Rájpút Chief whose kingdom called Gaṛh Dadner is said to have been near Bindraban. His father's name was Devi Chand and his mother's Báchila. His parents had been married a good many years, but no son had been born to them, and this was a cause of grief, especially to the wife. One day while using the looking glass Báchila noticed that her hair was becoming grey, and overcome with sadness she burst into tears. Her husband coming in at the moment asked her the reason of her grief, and she told him that all hope of offspring had died out in

[1] *Vide* Archæological Survey Reports, Vol. xiv, pp. 81-84, and xvii, p. 159. Jaya Chandra, the last Rájá of Kanauj, was also called Mundlíkh by the Chauhán bards. He fell in battle with the Muhammadans, A. D. 1194. *Vide* also Kángra *Gazetteer*, p. 102.

heart. If no one was born while she was young how could she expect now that age was stealing over her. The husband tried to comfort her, but she refused to be comforted, and insisted on leaving the palace and retiring into the jungles to practise *tapas* or self-mortification, in the hope of thereby having a son. Thus 12 years went past and Báchila was reduced to a shadow of herself by her austerities. One day a visitor came to her hut and announced himself as Jogí Gorakhnáth. He asked why she was undergoing such self-denial and she replied that he might judge for himself as to the cause of her distress. As the wife of a Rájpút chief she had all things—money, jewellery and position—but all these were held in light esteem for no son had come to bless their name. He replied that her *tapas* had earned its reward, and that she should return to her home and come to him in three days when the boon she craved would be granted. Báchila then went back to her palace and told her story which caused much rejoicing. Now Báchila had a sister name Káchila, the wife of the Rájá of Gaṛh Málwá, and she too was childless. On hearing of her sister's return Káchila at once came to visit her and on learning of the promised boon from Gorakhnáth she determined to secure it for herself, by personating her sister. Having purloined Báchila's clothes and jewellery she on the following day—one day before the appointed time—presented herself before the saint and demanded the boon. He found fault with her for coming before the time, but she said she could not wait longer, and that he must give what he had to give now. Accordingly he handed to her two barley seeds and told her to go home and eat them and two sons would be born to her. This she did, and in due time her sons—Arjan and Surjan—were born.

On the day fixed by the Jogí, Báchila presented herself before him and craved the boon promised. Gorakhnáth, not knowing of the deceit practised on him, blamed her for coming again, after having already received what she asked. Being annoyed at his answer and thinking he was disinclined to fulfil his promise, she turned away and went back to the jungle where she resumed her *tapas* and continued it for 12 years more. At the end of that time Gorakhnáth again came to her and promised that she should have her reward. He then put some ashes into her hand and told her to keep them, but being annoyed at the form of the gift she threw them away and from them sprung Nurya Siddh and Gurya Siddh, who began to worship the Gurú. Gorakhnáth then said "Why did you throw away the boon? You have done wrong, but in consideration of your great *tapas* it will begin a second time." He then gave more ashes and told her to take them home and swallow them. She, however, ate the ashes on the spot and at once her belly swelled up, from which she knew that she had conceived. On returning home, Devi Chand, her husband, seeing her belly swollen, said "You have brought a bastard from the Jogís or Gosáíns." She remained silent, and vexed at her reception and ordering a bullock-cart started for her parents' home. Now her father was Rájá Kripál of Ajmer, and on the way to his palace the oxen stopped and refused to go on. Then a voice came from her womb saying.—"Return to your home or I will remain unborn 12 years." On turning the cart the oxen at once started off towards Gaṛh Dadner and Báchila resumed her place in.

the palace. In due time her son was born, and when he was 7 years old his father abdicated and he became Rāná. A daughter named Gugeri was also born to Báchila. Mundlíkh's birth took place on the first Sunday in Mágh, and in the morning. Báchila had a brother whose name was Pithoria (Prithwi Rájá).

The next event of importance was Mundlíkh's betrothal, and this was arranged through a Brahman, with Surjila, the daughter of the Rájá of Bangála. Now Surjila had already been betrothed to Básak Nág, king of the Nágs. In due time Mundlíkh set out for Gaur Bangála with a large retinue to celebrate his nuptials. In his train were 52 *Bírs*, including Kailu Bír, his Kotwál, and Hanúmán Bír with an army of 9 lakhs of men. In the course of their journey they encamped on the bank of a river, and great deal of smoke was observed on the other side indicating another large encampment. Thereupon Mundlíkh called for a *Bír* to cross and ascertain the reason for such a gathering. Kailu Bír volunteered for this duty. Mounting his steed Aganduáriya he struck it once, and at one bound was transported across the river. Dismounting Kailu left his horse in concealment and assuming the disguise of a Brahman, with a book in his hand, he entered the encampment, and encountered the principal officer. On enquiry he was told that Básak Nág on hearing of Mundlíkh's betrothal had come with an immense army to contest his claim to Surjila, who had in the first instance been betrothed to himself. Kalihár said to Kailu Bír: "He will destroy Mundlíkh's army, and first of all Kailu Bír, his *kotwál*, shall be killed." On this Kailu's anger was kindled, but pretending to help he said: "Conceal yourselves in the tall grass and attack Mundlíkh's army as it marches past. This they did, and then Kailu throwing off his disguise mounted his horse, which came running towards him. He struck it once and it pranced and reared. At the second stroke sparks came from its hoofs and set fire to the grass in which the Nág army was concealed and all were completely destroyed. At the third stroke he was transported across the river into Mundlíkh's camp where he related all that had happened.

The wedding party then went on to Bangála and on arriving at Gaur Mundlíkh was met by a sorceress sent by Surjila to cast a spell over them so that the Rāná might not wish to return to Garh Dadner (the reason of this presumably was that Surjila did not wish to leave her home). The sorceress cast a garland of beautiful flowers round Mundlíkh's neck so as to work the enchantment: but Hanúmán Bír—who alone seems to have understood the real object—gave a cry and the garland snapped and fell off. This was done thrice, and on the third occasion not only did the garland break but the sorceress's nether garment became loose, leaving her naked. She complained bitterly to Mundlíkh at being thus put to shame, and Hanúmán was reproved for acting like a monkey. At this Hanúmán took offence and said he would return to Garh Dadner, but that it would be the worse for Mundlíkh who would have to remain in Bangála for 12 years. Hanúmán then departed and Mundlíkh entered the palace, and the marriage ceremony was performed and a spell cast on him and his company. Mundlíkh was overcome by love of his wife and became indifferent to everything, while his followers being also under a spell were led away and distributed as servants etc. all through Bangála, and there they remained for 12 years.

While Mundlíkh and his army were thus held in bondage great distress befell Gaṛh Dadner. His cousins, Arjan and Surjan, having been born through the efficacy of the boon granted to Báchila, regarded themselves as in a sense Báchila's sons, and therefore entitled to a share in the kingdom of Dadner. Just then too a wonderful calf[1] called Panch Kaliyáni was born in Gaṛh Dadner. This they wanted to possess, and hearing of Mundlíkh's absence and captivity they thought it a good time to invade the country. They therefore sent to invite Mahmúd of Ghazni to help them in their invasion, and he came with a great army. All the military leaders and fighting men being absent with Mundlíkh the conquest was easily effected and the town was captured with much looting and great slaughter of the inhabitants. But the fort or palace, in which were Báchila and her daughter, Gugeri, still held out. Looking from the ramparts Gugeri saw the town in ruins, and frantic with anguish she roamed about the palace bewailing their lot and calling Mundlíkh. Just then a letter came from Mahmúd demanding the surrender of the fort and promising life and safety to all on condition that Gugeri became a Muhammadan and entered his harem, otherwise the place would be taken by assault and all would be massacred. In her despair Gugeri went from room to room and at last entered Mundlíkh's chamber, which was just as he had left it. His sword in the scabbard was lying on the bed and his *pagri* lying near. Invoking her brother's name the sword came to her hand, and donning his *pagri* she ordered the gate to be opened. Then alone and single-handed she attacked the enemy and routed them with great slaughter.

On her return to the fort Gugeri bethought her of a friend and champion of her brother's named Ajia Pál, who lived on his estate not far away. To him she sent a message, imploring him to seek and bring back Mundlíkh. Ajia Pál had for some time been practising *tapas*, and in his dreams had seen Mundlíkh fighting without a head. On receiving Gugeri's message he started for Bangála, accompanied by 5 *Bírs* among whom were Nársingh Bír and Káli Bír and two other *Bírs*. On arriving in Gaur they went from door to door as mendicants, singing the songs of Gaṛh Dadner, in the hope that Mundlíkh would hear them. He was still under the influence of the spell, and never left his wife or the palace. One day singing was heard in the palace which excited him. Surjila tried to soothe him into apathy, but he insisted on seeing the singers, and at once recognised Ajia Pál. The spell was now broken, and on hearing of the disasters at Gaṛh Dadner Mundlíkh determined to return. The retinue of *Bírs* etc. were all brought out and set free, and accompanied by his Rání, Surjila, Mundlíkh returned to Dadner and resumed his place as Rána.

Mundlíkh is said to have fought many battles, some say 13, with the Muhammadans, and carried the Guggiána *duhái* to Kábul. In the last of these battles his head was severed from his body by a *chakra* or

[1] More probably 'foal.' The term *panch kaliyáni* is applied to horses.

discus which came from above, but the head remained in position, only the line of the *chakra* being visible, hence the name Mundlíkh, from *munda* head and neck and *likha*, a line. Seated on his horse Níla-rath he went on fighting, and behind him was Ajia Pál, who watched to see what would happen, having recalled the dream he had had before starting for Bangála. It was believed that if the head remained in its place for 2½ *gharis* Mundlíkh would survive, and 2 *gharis* had gone. Just then four kites appeared in mid-air saying "Behold what wonderful warfare is this! Mundlíkh is fighting without his head." Hearing these words Mundlíkh put up his hand to his *pagri* and looked back towards Ajia Pál, whereupon his head lost its balance and rolled off and he too fell dead from his horse. His death took place on the 9th day of the dark half of the moon in Bhádon, and during that month and from that date for eight days his *shrádha* is observed at his shrine every year.

An addition to the legend is that Surjila after her husband's death refused to put off her jewellery etc. and don a widow's garb, averring that Mundlíkh was alive and visited her every night. On one occasion Gugeri was allowed to stay concealed in the room in which Surjila was waiting, and at midnight a horse's tramp was heard and Gugga dismounted and came into the rooms. Gugeri then quickly withdrew, and on reaching the court found the horse Níla standing waiting for his master. Clasping him round the neck she remained in this position for some distance after Mundlíkh had remounted and ridden off. At last he detected her presence and told her that having been seen by her he could not come again.

The above version of the Gugga legend is current in the Chamba hills, and it is noteworthy that in it there is no mention of Gugga having become a Muhammadan or of his having any intercourse with Muhammadans: it may therefore be assumed to represent the older version of the legend. As to the historical facts underlying the legends it seems not improbable that by Gugga is indicated one of the Rájpút kings of the time of Muhammad of Ghor. The mention of Rái Pithor, or Prithwi Rájá, the last Hindu Rájá of Delhi, makes this probable. He reigned from A. D. 1170 to 1193. The name Mundlíkh was probably a title given to Rájpút warriors who distinguished themselves in the wars of the time. There were five Rájpúts who bore this title among the Chudásama princes of Girnár in Káthiáwár, the first of whom joined Bhíma-deva of Gujrát in the pursuit of Mahmúd of Ghazni in A. D. 1023.

From the Chauhán bards, who were his enemies, we learn that Jáya Chandra Ráthor, the last Rájá of Kanauj (killed in A. D. 1194), also bore this title. He had taken a leading part in the wars with the Muhammadans, whom he again and again defeated, or drove them back across the Indus. But at last enraged with Prithwi Rájá of Delhi he invited Muhammad of Ghor to invade the Punjab, with the result that both Delhi and Kanauj were overthrown and the Muhammadans triumphed. Jai Chand was drowned in the Ganges in attempting to escape.

Tod[1] says that Goga or Chuhán Goga was son of Vacha Rájá who acquired renown by his defence of his realm against Mahmúd's invasion. It lay on the Sutlej and its capital was Chibera. In the defence of it he perished with his 45 sons and 60 nephews. Briggs notes that Behera (? Bhera) was a town in (on) the Gára (Sutlej) often mentioned in early history : it belonged at the first Moslem invasion to Goga Chauhán.[2]

The shrines of Gúga are called *mári* and it seems very usual for them to have one small shrine on the right dedicated to Nár Singh and another on the left to Gorakhnáth, whose disciple Gúga was. Nár Singh was Gúga's minister or *díwán*. But in some cases the two subordinate shrines are ascribed to Káli Singh and Bhúri Singh, Nár Singh being a synonym of one or both of these. In a picture on a well parapet in a Ját village Gúga appears seated on a horse and starting for the Bágar, while his mother stands in front trying to stop his departure. In his hands he holds a long staff, *bhála*, as a mark of dignity and over his head meet the hoods of two snakes, one coiling round the staff. His standard, *chhari*, covered with peacock's feathers is carried about from house to house in Bhádon by Hindu and Muhammadan Jogís who take the offerings made to him, though some small share in them is given to Chúhras.[3]

In Karnál and Ambála Jaur Singh is also worshipped along with Gúga, Nár Singh, and the two snake gods. He is explained to be Jewar, the Rájá who was Gúga's father, but the name may be derived from *jora*, twin, as Arjan and Surjan are also worshipped under the name of Jaur.[4] A man bitten by a snake is supposed to have neglected Gúga.

By listening at night to the story of Gúga during the Díwáli a Hindu prevents snakes from entering his house.[5]

The following table gives some details of two Gúga temples in Kángra :—

Name.	*Pujári.*	Dates of fairs.	Ritual etc.
The *mandir* of Gúga in Saloh, Pálampur *thána*. Gúga manifested himself in 1899 S., and the temple was founded in 1900 S.	Girth ...	Besides small fairs held every Sunday, a fair on the *janam-ashtmi* in Bhádon.	The temple contains images of Gúga, Gúgri, and Gurú Gorakhnáth, each 3 feet high and mounted on a horse. A *bhog* of water and earth is distributed among the votaries.

[1] Rájasthán II, p. 447.

[2] Briggs' *Ferishta*, p. lxxii.

[3] P. N. Q., I., § 3. Hanúmán and Bhairon's shrines are occasionally found together on one side, and Gorakhnáth's on the other : *ibid.*, § 212.

[4] *Ib.*, I, § 3.

[5] *Ib.*, IV, § 178.

Name.	Pujári.	Dates of fairs.	Ritual etc.
Mandir Shibo dá Thán in Barmar, in Kotla *thána*. Some 500 years ago Shibo, a barber, used to worship Gúga, who, pleased with his devotion, directed him to build a temple. So he erected a *mandir* in which was enshrined the god's image. Next Gúga conferred on him power to cure snake-bite, saying that whoever drank the water, with which the image had been washed, would be cured. The cure is instantaneous. The descendants of Shibo have similar powers.	Barber ...	Each Sunday in Sáwan.	The temple contains 6 stone carvings of men on horses, height ranging from 1 to 3 feet, and 11 stone *pindis* whose height is from 1 to 2 inches. The *pindi* of Shiva is a foot high and the carving of a cow 2 feet.

In this district Gúga not only cures snake-bite, but also brings illness, bestows sons and good fortune. His offerings are first-fruits, goats, cakes etc. At Thán Shibo the worship of Gúga appears to have been displaced by that of Bába Shibo himself for the *faqír* in charge lays the sufferer from snake-bite in the shrine, says over him prayers in the name of Bába Shibo and makes him drink of the water in which the idol has been washed. He also makes him eat of the sacred earth of the place and rubs some of it on the bite. Pilgrims also take away some of this earth as a protection.[1] The legend also varies somewhat from those already given. The Rájá's name is Deoráj and Kachla has a daughter named Gugri. Gúga is brought up with the foal and taking it with him goes to woo a beautiful maiden with whom he lives, being transformed into a sheep by day and visiting her by night. In his absence a pretender arises who is refused admittance by a blind door-keeper who declares that on Gúga's return his sight will be restored. Hard pressed Gugri sends a Brahman to Bangáhal to fetch Gúga and escaping the hands of sorcery he mounts his steed, also rejuvenated by the Brahman's aid, and arrives home. The door-keeper's sight is restored and Gúga and Gugri perform prodigies of value, the former fighting even after he has lost his head. He is venerated as a god, always represented on horse-back, and his temples are curious sheds not seen elsewhere.[2]

In Rohtak Gúga's shrine is distinguished by its square shape with minarets and domed roof and is always known as a *mári* and not as a *thán*. Monday is his day, the 9th his date, and Bhádon 9th the special festival. It is generally the lower castes who worship the Gúga Pír. Rice cooked in milk and flour and *gur* cakes are prepared and given to a few invited friends or to a Jogi. The most typical shrine in this district is that at Gubhána, erected by a Lohár whose family takes the offerings. Inside the *mári* is a tomb and on the wall a fine *bas relief* of the Pír on horseback, lance in hand. Inside the courtyard is a little

[1] P. N. Q., II, § 120.

[2] Kangra *Gazetteer*, 1904, pp. 102-3. Guruknáth on p. 102 should clearly be Gorakhnáth.

thán for the worship of Nársingh, one of the Pír's followers, and outside the wall a socket for the reception of a bamboo with peacock's feathers on the top. At Babrah one Sheo Lál, Rájpút, has lately fulfilled a vow for a son bestowed in his old age and built a shrine to Gúga Pír, facing of course the east, with a shrine to Gorakhnáth facing east, and one to Nársingh Dás (*sic*) west towards the Bágar.

In Gurgaon fairs to Gúga are held at many places, generally if not invariably on Bhádon *badi* 9th. His temple often consists of nothing but a *maṇḍh* or platform which is said to cover a grave. The *pujári* may be a Brahman who lights a lamp daily at the temple or a Jogí who does the same. Offerings consist of grain or, at the fair, of *patáshas* and *púras*. At Islámpur the temple is a building erected by a Brahman whose house kept falling down as fast as he built it until Gúga possessed him and bade him first erect the temple and then make his own house. These temples to Gúga contain no images.

But in Ludhiána at Ráikot, where there is a *mári*[1] to Gúga, a great fair is held on last day but one (*anant chaudas*) of Bhádon. This fair, however, is said to be really held in honour of Gúga's cousins. North of the town lies a tank, called Ratloána, at which ever since its foundation a mud hill has been built on that date and Gúga worshipped—owing, it is said, to the fact that a grove full of serpents existed there. The temple was built in fulfilment of a vow for recovery from fever. Once a snake appeared on the mud hill and at the same time a girl was possessed by Gúga and exhorted the people to build him a temple. Its *pujáris* are Brahmans who take the offerings. But the temple fell into ruins and the fair has been eclipsed by that at Chhapár. The latter, also called the Sudlakhan fair, is also held on the *anant chaudas* or 14th Bhádon *sudi*. At a pond near the *mári* people scoop out earth 7 times. Cattle are brought to be blessed and kept for a night at the shrine[2] as a protection against snakes. Snake-bite can also be cured by laying the patient beside the shrine. The offerings in cash (about Rs. 300 a year) go to the Brahman managers of the shrine, but Mírásis and Chuhrás take all edibles offered by Muhammadans and Hindus respectively.

A very interesting explanation[3] of Gúga's origin makes him the god of an ancient creed reduced to the position of a godling subordinate to Vishnu. A *gana* (Dwárapála) of Mahá Lakshmi was embodied as *gúgal*

[1] Said to be derived from Pers. *már*, snake.

[2] Called *chauki bharwáná*.

[3] By Pandit Hem Raj, Government High School, Jhelum, who also writes :—

"Folk-etymology makes Gúga a compound of *gu* (earth) and *ga* (to go), and says he was converted into gum and reappeared as a man with the power of converting himself into any shape. When his wife saw that his eyes did not move, she asked him his caste and then he disappeared. Some people fast in memory of different forms of Gúga and consider the *anant chaudas* and *nágpanchami* holy." This may explain why the day after the *janamashtmi* Hindus of Pind Dádan Khán tie a yellow thread on their right leg and during Sáwan fast for one day in honour of Gúga. In the rainy season Hindu women in Jhang prepare *chúri*, grated bread mixed with sugar and butter, fill a dish with it and, putting some *gur* thereon, go to the Chenab On an old *beri* (*jujube vulgaris*) bush on its bank they sprinkle water and place some *chúri* and raw thread at its roots with the following incantation: —"Oh Gúga, king of serpents, enter not our homes nor come near our beds." When they go home they take with them a cup of water and sprinkle it over their children and others of the family who come in contact with them.

(the gum of a tree), and reappeared as Shesh Nág by the auspicious glances of Gorakhnáth, who is known to have the power of controlling Gúga. Gúga is believed to guard hidden treasures. People sometimes offer milk and *sharbat* when he appears at their houses as he is believed to dwell in the sea of milk so when he thinks that Vishnu, Lord of the Khír Samundar, approaches he quits the place. He is known by nine names:—Anant, Wásuki, Shesh, Padm, Nabh, Kambal, Shankhpal, Dharatrashtar, Takhi and Kali.

Some believe that he who recites these names morning and evening is immune from snake-bite and prospers wherever he goes.

The classical story of Shesh Nág is well-known, but it is strange to learn that Gúga in the Satyug, Lachhman in the Treta, Baldeva in the Dwápur and Gorakhnáth in the Kalyug are all forms of the same god. This accords with Dr. Vogel's suggestion that Baladeva was developed from a Nága. The Bhágaratas, like the Buddhists before them, sought to adapt the popular worship of the Nágas to their new religion.[1]

Sir Richard Temple regards Gugga as "a Rájpút hero who stemmed the invasions of Mahmúd of Ghazni and died, like a true Rájpút, in defence of his country, but by the strange irony of fate he is now a saint, worshipped by all the lower castes, and is as much Musalmán as Hindu. About Kángra there are many small shrines in his honour, and the custom is, on the fulfilment of any vow made to him, for the maker thereof to collect as many people as he or she can afford, for a small pilgrimage to the shrine, where the party is entertained for some days. Such women as are in search of a holiday frequently make use of this custom to get one: witness the following:—

> Come, let us make a little pilgrimage to Gugga:
>
> Come, let us make a little pilgrimage to Gugga,
>
> Sitting by the roadside and meeting half the nation
>
> Let us sooth our hearts with a little conversation,
>
> Come, let us make a little pilgrimage to Gugga.[2]"

The Jain version of Gúga.

In the time of Nandibraham who reigned 2431 years ago Chandkosia, a huge venomous snake, lived in a forest near Kankhal. Whatsoever he looked at was burnt to ashes so that not even a straw was to be seen within 12 miles of his hole, and no passer-by escaped with his life. When the 24th Autár Mahábír Swámi turned mendicant, he passed by Chandkosia's hole disregarding all warnings, and though the serpent bit his foot thrice he was not injured. Mahábír asked him:—"What excuse will you give to God for your ruthless deeds?" Chandkosia on this repented and drawing his head into his hole only exposed the rest of his body so that the way should be safe for travellers. Thenceforth he was regarded as a snake-god and wayfarers and milkwomen sprinkled *ghi*, milk, oilseeds, rice and *lassi* (watered milk) when they

[1] A. S. R., 1908-09, p. 162.

[2] S. C. R., VII, pp. 428-9.

passed that way. The ants too assembled and wounded his whole body, but the serpent did not even turn on his side lest they might be crushed. He now became known as Gúga.

According to the *Sri Mat Bhágwat* the *rishi* Kapp had two wives, Kadro and Benta. Kadro gave birth to a snake and Benta to a *garur* which is the vehicle of Bhagwán. The snake, who could transform himself into a man at will, was called Gúga. So Hindus regard both the *garur* and snake as sacred.

SPIRIT WORSHIP.

Maclagan, § 42.

VENERATION OF THE HOMESTEAD AND ANCESTORS.—The earth (Prithi) is a common object of worship in the south-east of the province; but it usually appears in the form of Bhúmia, or the god of the homestead, whose shrine in the village consists either of a small building with a domed roof or of nothing more than a masonry platform. This deity is more especially adored at the return of a marriage procession to the village. A similar deity is the Khera Deota, or Chanwand, who is often confused with Bhúmia, but who is said to be the wife of Bhúmia and has sometimes a shrine in a village in addition to that of Bhúmia and is worshipped on Sunday only. In the centre of the province the most conspicuous object of worship of this kind among the peasants is the *jathera* or ancestral mound; and the *jathera* represents either the common ancestor of the village or the common ancestor of the tribe or caste. One of the most celebrated of these *jatheras* is Kála Mahar, the ancestor of the Sindhu Jats, who has peculiar influence over cows, and to whom the first milk of every cow is offered. The place of the *jathera* is, however, often taken by the *theh* or mound which marks the site of the original village of the tribe.

Ibbetson, § 218.

The four deities *Suraj-Deota*,[1] *Jamna Ji*, *Dharti Mátá* and *Khwája Khizr* are the only ones to whom no temples are built. To the rest of the village godlings a small brick shrine from 1 to 2 feet cube, with a bulbous head and perhaps an iron spike as a finial, is erected, and in the interior lamps are burnt and offerings placed. It never contains idols, which are found only in the temples of the greater gods. The Hindu shrine must always face the east, while the Musalmán shrine is in form of a grave and faces the south. This sometimes gives rise to delicate questions In one village a section of the community had become Muhammadans. The shrine of the common ancestor needed rebuilding, and there was much dispute as to its shape and aspect. They solved the difficulty by building a Musalmán grave facing south, and over it a Hindu shrine facing east. In another village an imperial trooper was once burnt alive by the shed in which he was sleeping catching fire, and it was thought well to propitiate him by a shrine, or his ghost might become troublesome. He was by religion a Musalmán; but he had been burnt and not buried, which seemed to make him a Hindu. After much discussion the latter opinion prevailed, and a Hindu shrine with an eastern aspect now stands to his memory. The most honoured of the village deities proper is Bhúmia or the god of the homestead, often called Khera (a village). The erection of his shrine is the first formal act by which the proposed site of a new village is consecrated; and where two villages have combined their homesteads for greater security against the marauders of former days, the people of the one which moved still worship at the Bhúmia of the deserted site. Bhúmia is worshipped after the harvests, at marriages, and on the birth of a male

[1] The sun-god, however, certainly had temples in India in ancient times. There was one at Taxila: *Arch. Survey Reports*, II, p 114; and at Multán; *ibid.* V, pp. 115 and 120. Farishta says the Hindus used to worship the Sun and Stars, like the Persians, until King Suraj (*sic*) taught them idolatry: Briggs *Ferishta*, I, p. lxviii. But in later times images of Surya or Aditya were rare: *A. S. R.*, XIII, p. 68. For the absence of roofs to temples to the Sun, see *infra* under ISLAM, hypæthral shrines.

child, and Brahmans are commonly fed in his name. Women often take their children to the shrine on Sundays; and the first milk of a cow or buffalo is always offered there.

The above paragraphs are reproduced here as they stand, but the present writer's information appears to justify some modifications in them. The Bhúmia is hardly the god of the homestead. He is the godling of the village. And it is very doubtful whether the *jaṭhera* is ever the common ancestor of the village. He is essentially the tribal ancestor or at least a prominent member of the tribe. The worship of the *jaṭhera* is a striking feature of the Jáṭs' religion, though it is not suggested that it is confined to them. A full account of it will be found in Vol. II, p 374, *post*. The following details are of more general application:—

In Gurgaon the Bhúmia[1] is generally one of the founders of the village, or in one instance at least the Brahman of the original settlers. The special day for offerings is the *chaudas* or 14th of the month. Some Bhúmias are said to grant their votaries' prayers, and to punish those who offend them. Some are easy and good-tempered, but they are neglected in comparison with those who are revengeful or malignant. To these offerings are often made. A somewhat similar local deity is Chanwand, or Khera *deota*. Sometimes described as the wife of Bhúmia, other villages seem to place her or him in his place, but Chanwand is worshipped on Sundays and his shrine is often found in addition to that of Bhúmia in the same village.[2]

Among the minor deities of the village in Rohtak the Bhaiyon is by far the most important. The shrine of the god of the homestead is built at the first foundation of a village, two or three bricks often being taken from the Bhaiyon of the parent estate to secure a continuity of the god's blessing. It is placed at the outside of the village though often a village as it expands gradually encircles it. A man who builds a fine new house, especially a two-storeyed one, will sometimes add a second storey to the Bhaiyon, as at Badli, or whitewash it or build a new subsidiary shrine to the god. Every Sunday evening the house-wives of the village, Muhammadans included, set a lamp in the shrine. A little milk from the first flow of a buffalo will be offered here, and the women will take a few reeds of the *gandar* grass and sweep the shrine,

[1] Bhúmia should, by his name, be the god of the land and not of the homestead. But he is most certainly the latter, and is almost as often called Khera as Bhúmia. There is also a village god called Khetrpál or the field nourisher, and also known as Bhairon; but he is not often found. In some places however Khera *Devata* or godling of the village site is also called Chanwand and alleged to be the wife of Bhúmia (Channing's Gurgaon *Settlement Report*, p. 34; see also Alwar *Gazetteer*, p. 70). It is a curious fact that among the Gonds and Bhíls the word Bhúmia means priest or medicine man, while among the Korkús, another Kolian tribe, Bhúmka stands for high priest. It is also said to mean a village bull somewhere. For Kala Mohar see p. 238 *infra*.

[2] Chanwand appears to be also found in Sirmúr under the name of Chawind. The local legend current in that State runs thus:—A girl of Manon, a village in Sirmúr, was married in Keonthal State. Returning when pregnant to her father's house on the occasion of some festivity, she was seized with the pains of labour while crossing the Giri and gave birth to two serpents, which fell into the stream. For some hours the serpents remained in each other's embrace and then separated, one going to Tarhech, in Keonthal and the other to Dháíla Deothi in Sirmúr where it died shortly afterwards. It is now worshipped as Chawind *deota*, and a temple was erected at Deothi, which means a 'place dedicated to a god,' or 'the abode of a god.'

and then praying to be kept clean and straight as they have swept the shrine, will fix them to its face with a lump of mud or cow-dung. Women who hope for a child will make a vow at the shrine, and if blessed with an answer to the prayer, fulfil the vow. At Lohárheri vows for success in law-suits are also made here. The Bhaiyon is the same as the Bhúmian or Bhonpál of adjacent districts. Bhonpál is said to have been a Jáṭ whom Ishar could not make into a Brahman, but to whom he promised that he should be worshipped of all men.

Each village has its Panchpír in addition to its Bhaiyon. Often this is no more than a mud pillar with a flag on the top or similarly marked spot, and generally seems to be near a tank or under a *jal* tree and away from the village, but at Asauda it is much more like a Bhaiyon in appearance. In Naiabás it is said that the *first* man to die in a village after its foundation becomes Panchpír, the second Bhaiyon. Little seems to be known of the worship of this deity.

In Gurgaon the Saiyid-ká-thán or Saiyad's place is to the Muhammadan village what Bhaiyon is to the Hindus, but Hindu residents in the village reverence it, just as Muhammadans do the Bhaiyon. Though built in the form of a tomb it is erected whenever a village is founded.

The spirit of a Saiyid like that of a *bhút* must not touch the ground. Sometimes two bricks are stuck up on end or two tent pegs driven into the ground in front of his shrine for the spirit to rest on.

In Gurgaon the Búndela is a godling who is only worshipped in times of sickness, especially cholera. In the last century cholera is said to have broken out in Lord Hastings' army shortly after some kine had been slaughtered in a grove where lie the ashes of Hardaul Lála, 'a Bundelkhanḍ chief.'[1] The epidemic was attributed to his wrath, and his dominion over cholera being thus established, he is in many villages given a small shrine and prayed to avert pestilence when it visits the village.

Ancestor-worship is very common in the hills, at least in Chamba where it takes several beautiful forms. The root-idea seems to be that the living acquire *pun* or merit by enabling the dead to rejoin their forefathers. The commonest form of the worship is the placing of a stone or board, called *pitr*, in a small hut beside a spring. On it is cut a rough effigy of the deceased. This is accompanied by certain religious rites and a feast to friends. Sometimes the board has a hole in it with a spout for the water, and it is then set up in the stream. Other forms of this worship are the erection of wayside seats or of wooden enclosures in the villages for the elders, bearing in each case a roughly cut effigy of the deceased. One of the commonest forms, especially in the Chandrabhága valley, is the erection of a *dhaji* or monolith near a village, with a rough figure of the deceased cut on it, and a circular stone fixed on the top. Many such stones may be seen near villages. Some are neatly carved, but as a rule they are very crude. Their erection is accompanied by

[1] Sleeman places this event in Bundelkhanḍ and says it occurred in 1817. He speaks of Hardáwal Lála as the new god, and says that his temples sprang up as far as Lahore: *Rambles*, I, p. 210-11. His worship is common in the United Provinces: for his songs see N. I. N. Q., V., § 458. He is also called Hardaur or Harda Lála: I. N. Q., IV, § 798.

religious rites and feasting on a great scale, involving much expense. These rites are repeated from time to time.

This custom also prevails in Kulu, Manḍi and Suket, but is restricted to the royal families of those states and regarded as an exclusive privilege. It must however be of ancient date, for it is found in one at least of the Ráná families whose ancestors held rule in Kulu before the Rájás obtained supreme power. Mr. G. C. L. Howell mentions one such family, that of Nawáni, which still observes this custom; and we may conclude that it was observed by this family when in independent possession of their lands. I have not seen the Kulu and Suket stones which are said to be near the respective capitals of those States. The Manḍi monoliths are probably the most ornate of any in the hills. It is possible that such monoliths also exist in Biláspur and other Hill States of the Simla group.[1]

Sir Alexander Cunningham thus described the Manḍi monoliths:—"The *sati* pillars of the Manḍi Rájás and their families stand in a group on a plot of ground on the left bank of the Suketi Nála, a little way outside Manḍi town, on the road to Suket. Some of them are 6 and 7 feet high and all are carved with figures of the Rájás and of the women who became *sati* with them. Each Rájá is represented as seated above with a row of *ránís* or queens, also seated, immediately below: still lower are standing figures of *khwásis* or concubines and *rakhális* or slave girls. The inscription records the name of the Rájá and the date of his death, as also the number of queens, concubines and slave girls who were burnt with him. The monuments are valuable for chronological purposes as fixing with certainty the date of each Rájá's decease and the accession of his successor from Hari Sen A. D. 1637 down to the present time." The number has been added to since Cunningham's visit, though no *satis* have taken place since the annexation of the Punjab or rather since 1846, when Manḍi came under British control after the First Sikh War. These pillars therefore are not pure *sati* pillars, but are rather of the nature of monoliths in memory of the death similar to those of Pángi, and are probably consecrated with similar rites. At Nagar in Kulu similar monoliths are found which are described as follows by Colonel Harcourt in *Kooloo, Lahoul and Spiti*, page 357:—"There is a curious collection of what resemble tombstones that are to be found just below Nagar Castle. They are inserted into the ground in four rows, rising one over the other on the hillside; and in all I have counted 141 of these, each ornamented with rude carvings of chiefs of Kulu, their wives and concubines being portrayed either beside them or in lines below. One Rájá is mounted on a horse, and holds a sword in his hand, the animal he bestrides being covered with housings just as might be a crusader's charger. A very similar figure to this is carved in wood over the porch of the Dúngri temple. The report is that these stones were placed in position at the death of every reigning sovereign of Kulu, the female figures being the effigies of such wives or mistresses who may have performed *sati* at their lord's demise. If this be the true state of the case then the human sacrifices must have been very great in some instances, for it is not uncommon to find 40 and 50 female figures crowd-

[1] This and the following paragraph are by Dr. J. Hutchison.

ing the crumbling and worn surface of the stones. At the death of the late Rái Gyán Singh, the representative of a once powerful family, his servants executed a rude effigy of him, and this will take its place beside the other funeral relics of his ancestors. The Buddhist wheel appears in several of the stones, but the people about Nagar positively declare that none of these rough sculpturings are over 200 years of age. Here however I think they are mistaken and they know so very little about the history of their own country that anything they say that refers to dates must be received with great caution." There can be no doubt that Colonel Harcourt was right in believing that these stones date back to a remote past and are the *sati* pillars of the Kulu Rájás. It would be interesting to have an account of the Suket monoliths.

In the Himalayas is to be found a variety of shrines and heaps of stones erected by the road-side in fields and on the mountain passes. Their purposes are as varied as their structures. First of importance are those erected in honour of the dead, and the memorial tablets placed by the side of a stream or fountain have proved of considerable archæological value owing to the inscriptions on them. In the Simla Hills inscriptions are rare and the memorials are usually in the form of small slabs of slate or stone on which the figure of the deceased is rigidly carved. The rites which attend their erection vary. Thus the soul of a man who has died away from home or been killed by accident without administration of the last rites will require elaborate ceremonies to lay it at rest and many, but not all, the memorial stones commemorate such a death. The ideas underlying them appear to be twofold. In the first place when the tablet is merely attached to a cistern or well the disembodied spirit seems to acquire merit from the act of charity performed by the dead man's descendants. Secondly it is believed that the spirit by being provided with a resting place on the edge of a spring will be able to quench its thirst whenever it wishes. The attributes assigned to serpents as creators and protectors of springs suggest that the selection of a spring as the site for a memorial tablet may be connected with Nág worship. But in the Simla Hills at any rate the Nágs are not now propitiated generally in connection with funeral rites. Nor is it believed in these hills that snakes which visit houses are the incarnations of former members of the family. The snake's incarnation is only assigned to the exceptional case of a miser who during his life-time had buried treasure and returns to it as a serpent to guard it after death. This idea is of course not peculiar to the Himalayas. In the Simla Hills the peasant cares little for the living reptile beyond drawing omens from its appearances. If for instance a snake crosses his path and goes down-hill the omen is auspicious, but if it goes uphill the reverse. Should a poisonous snake enter his house it is welcomed as a harbinger of good fortune but if it is killed inside it, its body must be taken out through the window and not by the door.

Some ghosts are more persistent than others in frequenting their former haunts. Such for instance are the souls of men who have died without a son and whose property has gone to collaterals or strangers. The heirs anticipating trouble will often build a shrine in a field close to the village where the deceased was wont to walk and look upon his crops.

These shrines are unpretentious structures with low walls of stones piled one upon another and sloping roofs of slates. They are open in front and a small recess is left in one of the walls in which earthen lamps are lighted at each full moon by pious or timid heirs. Similar are the buildings often seen in fields at a distance from the village, but these are usually involuntary memorials to departed spirits extorted from reluctant peasants by a kind of spiritual blackmail. It sometimes happens that a man marries a second wife during the life-time of the first without obtaining her permission and the latter in a fit of jealousy takes poison or throws herself down a precipice. Then soon after her death the husband becomes ill with boils or other painful eruptions, proving beyond doubt that a malignant spirit has taken up its abode in his body. Brahmans have many means of searching out a mischief-making spirit of this kind and the following may be recommended for its simplicity. The peasant chooses a boy and girl both too young to be tutored by the Brahman who plays the chief part in the ceremony of exorcism. They are taken to the peasant's house and there squat on the floor, each being covered with a sheet. The Brahman brings with him a brazen vessel in which he puts a coin or two and on top of which he places a metal cover. On this improvised drum he beats continously with a stick whilst he drones his incantations. Sometimes this goes on for hours before the boy or girl manifests any sign, but as a rule one or the other is soon seized with trembling, an indication that the desired spirit has appeared and assumed possession. If the boy trembles first the ghost is certainly a male, but if the girl is first affected it must be a female spirit. When questioned the medium reveals the identity of the possessor, which usually turns out to be the spirit of the suicide. A process of barter ensues in which the injured wife details the deeds of expiation necessary to appease the spirit whilst the husband bargains for terms less onerous to himself. The matter ends in a compromise. The husband vows to build a shrine to house the spirit and to make offerings there on certain days in every month. He may also promise to dedicate a field to her and hence these ghostly dwelling-places are often situated in barren strips of land because no plough may be used on a field so consecrated. When the shrine stands on uncultivated land a piece of quartz may glisten from its roof or one of its walls may be painted white. Such a building serves a double purpose. Not only is the unsubstantial spirit kept from inconvenient roaming, but the gleam of white also attracts the envious glances of passers-by and so saves the crops from being withered up. (Condensed from the *Pioneer* of 16th August 1913.)

Ancestor-worship also takes the form of building a bridge over a stream in the deceased's name, or making a new road, or improving an old one, or by cutting steps in the rock.[1] In each case the rough outline of a foot or a pair of feet is carved near the spot to show that the work was a memorial act. In former times the worship took the form of erecting a *panihár* or cistern. In its simplest form this consisted of a slab with a rough figure of the deceased carved on it and a hole in the lower part, with a spout, through which the stream flowed. The board above des-

[1] See the *Antiquities of Chamba*, I, fig. 8 on p. 21 for an illustration of such steps.

cribed is clearly a degenerate modern form of these cisterns. Sometimes the slab was of large size and covered with beautiful carvings, but for a description of these reference must be made to Dr. Vogel's work.[1] That writer describes their purpose. Their erection was regarded less as a work of public utility than as an act of merit designed to secure future bliss to the founder and his relatives. The deceased, either wife or husband, for whose sake the stone was set up, is often named in the inscriptions. The slab itself is invariably designated Varuna-deva, for the obvious reason that Varuna, patron of the waters, is usually carved on it. This name is no longer remembered. Such stones are called *naun* in Pángi, *naur* in Láhul and *panhiyár* or 'fountain' in the Rávi valley.

Far otherwise is it in Sirmúr, where the cult of the dead is sometimes due to a fear of their ill-will. Thus in the Pachhád and Rainká tahsíls of that State when an old man is not cared for and dies aggrieved at the hands of his descendants, his *pápra* or curse[2] is usually supposed to cling to the family. Whenever subsequently there is illness in the family, or any other calamity visits it, the family Brahman is consulted and he declares the cause. If the cause is found to be the displeasure of the deceased, his image is put in the house and worshipped. If the curse affects a field, a portion of it is dedicated to the deceased. If this worship is discontinued, leprosy, violent death, an epidemic or other similar calamities overtake the family. Its cattle do not give milk or they die, or children are not born in the house. Indeed the *pápra* appears to be actually personified as a ghost which causes barrenness or disease, and if any one is thus afflicted a Bhát is consulted, and he makes an astrological calculation with dice thrown on a board (*sánchi*). There the sufferer summons all the members of the family, who sound a tray (*tháli*) at night, saying '*O páp kisi upar utar á,*'[3]—'O soul descend on some one,' and (though not before the third or fourth day) the *pápra* or imp takes possession of a child, who begins to nod its head, and when questioned explains whose ghost the *pápra* is, and shows that the patient's affliction is due to some injury done by him or his forefather to the ghost, and that its wrongs must be redressed or a certain house or place given up to a certain person or abandoned. The patient acts as thus directed. The costliness of ancestor-worship is illustrated by the cult of Pálu in Sirmúr. He was the ancestor of the Hámbi Kanets of Hábon and other villages, and is worshipped at Pálu with great pomp. His image, which is of metal, is richly ornamented.

The spirits of *young* men who die childless are also supposed to haunt the village in Gurgaon, as are those of any man who dies discontented and unwilling to leave his home. Such spirits are termed *pita*, 'father,' euphemistically, but they generally bear the character of being vindictive and require much attention. A little shrine, very much like a *chulha* or fire-place, is generally constructed in their honour near a tank and at it offerings are made. Sometimes a *pita* descends on a person and he then becomes inspired, shakes his head, rolls his eyes

[1] *Op. cit.*, pp. 29-35.

Lit. 'sin.'

[3] *Páp* is of course 'sin.' *Pápra* would appear to be a diminutive.

and reveals the *pita's* will. This is called *khelan* or playing, as in the Himalayas. Occasionally too a Brahman can interpret a *pita's* will.[1]

In Chamba a person[2] dying childless is believed to become a *bhút* or *autar*[3] and to harass his surviving relations unless appeased. For this purpose a *jantra* is worn by adults, consisting of a small case of silver or copper containing a scroll supplied by a Brahman. An *autar* necklet of silver, with a human figure cut on it, is also commonly worn. Another form is the *nád,* of silver or copper, and shaped like an hour-glass. An *autar* must also be propitiated by a goat-sacrifice, and the deceased's clothes are worn for a time by a member of the family: a soap-nut kernel is also worn hanging from a string round the neck.

The Bhábṛas have a custom which, to judge from many parallels, is a relic of ancestor-worship. Many of them will not marry a son until he has been taken to the tomb of Bábá Gajju, a progenitor of the Bar Bhábṛas, at Pípnákh in Gujránwála, and gone round the tomb by way of adoration.[4]

Ibbetson, § 220

THE WORSHIP OF THE SAINTED DEAD.—The worship of the dead is universal, and they again may be divided into the sainted and the malevolent dead. First among the sainted dead are the *pitr* or 'ancestors.' Tiny shrines to these will be found all over the fields, while there will often be a larger one to the common ancestor of the clan. Villagers who have migrated will periodically make long pilgrimages to worship at the original shrine of their ancestor; or, if the distance is too great, will bring away a brick from the original shrine, and use it as the foundation of a new local shrine which will answer all purposes. In the Punjab proper these larger shrines are called *jaṭher,*[5] or 'ancestor,' but in the Dehli Territory the *sati* takes their place in every respect and is supposed to mark the spot where a widow was burnt with her husband's corpse. The 15th of the month is sacred to the *pitr*, and on that day the cattle do no work and Brahmans are fed. But besides this veneration of ancestors, saints of widespread renown occupy a very important place in the worship of the peasantry. No one of them is, I believe, malevolent, and in a way their good nature is rewarded by a certain loss of respect. *Gúga beṭa na dega, tau kuchh na chhín lega*—"If Gúga doesn't give me a son, at least he will take nothing away from me." They are generally Muhammadan, but are worshipped by Hindus and Musalmáns alike with the most absolute impartiality. There are three saints who are pre-eminently great in the Punjab,

[1] Gurgaon *Gazetteer*, p. 67, *cf.* p. 69.

[2] Doubtless a male is meant: Chamba *Gazetteer*, 1904, p. 195. See also Vol. II, p. 270, *infra.*

[3] Fr. *aputara*, souless.

[4] P. N Q., III, § 89. No mention of the Bar Bhábṛas will be found in Vol. II, pp. 80-82. Pípnákh has a curious legend. Its Rájá is said to have been Pilpá, the Chamiál (Rájput ?), whose daughter Lúnán was sought in marriage by Sálbáhan of Siálkot. When Pilpá refused the match his city was destroyed, and it has been called Pípnákh ever since. Pilpá appears to be Pípa, the Bhagat.

[5] *Jaṭhera* is clearly derived from *jeṭh*, an elder, especially a husband's elder brother and the phrase *dadera jaṭhera* means 'ancestors on the father's side.' The classical type of the widow *sati* is Gandhári, wife of Dhritaráshtra and mother of Duryodhana. When her husband was consumed by the force of his *yoga* at Saptasrotra, near Hardwár, she too sprang into the flames, and the god gave her this boon, that she should be worshipped as the protector of children and the goddess of small-pox: N. I. N. Q., IV, § 454.

and thousands of worshippers of both religions flock yearly to their shrines.

But the *sati* was only a particular case of a general idea—the idea of devotion and fidelity transcending the love of life. Men who sacrificed themselves were called *satú*, and cases of such self-immolation are recorded in North Rájpútána. Generally ladies of rank were attended on the funeral pyre by attached female slaves, as occurred at the cremation of Mahárája Ranjít Singh. But the highest grade of all was attained by the *má-sati* or mother-*sati* who had immolated herself with her son.[1] These *má-satis* were of all classes from the potter-woman to the princess. At Paṭaudi the most conspicuous cenotaph is that of a Jaisalmír Mahárání who had come to her father's house accompanied by her young son. He was thrown from his horse and killed, and she insisted on ascending the pyre with him.[2] It is also said that occasionally when the widow shrank from the flames the mother would take her place.

No doubt *sati* worship is very prevalent in the Delhi territory, but it is also found elsewhere, especially among tribes which appear to have a Rájpút origin or at least claim it, such is the Mahton. It is rare among Jáṭs. In Gurgáon the *sati* is often propitiated as a possibly malignant spirit. Thus in the village of Rojkar Gujjar there is the shrine of a Gujarni *sati* who has constituted herself the patroness of the Brahman priests of the village, and unless *they* are properly looked after she gets angry and sends things into the offenders' bodies, causing pain; and then on the first day of the moon the Brahmans have to be collected and fed at her shrine.

The child is also depicted in the case of a *má-sati*. Cunningham noted that *sati* monuments were almost invariably if not always placed to the west of a stream or tank but that they faced east.[3] In Karnál the monument appears not to be a slab, but a regular shrine larger indeed than any other kind, being 3 or 4 feet square. Lamps are lit and Brahmans fed at them on the 11th or 15th of Kátik. The shrines are also regarded as tutelary guardians of the village. Thus in one case some Tagás who had migrated from their old village used to go 40 miles to make annual offerings at their old *sati*, but eventually they carried away a brick from her original shrine and used it for the foundation of a new one in their present village.[4]

In the Chamba hills if a man falls over a precipice or is accidently killed on a journey in such a way that his body cannot be recovered a pile of wood is gathered on or near the spot and each passer-by adds a stick to it as if it were funeral pyre. In the case of one of the Rájás who was killed along with his brother by his own officials, the spot on which the assassination took place has remained uncultivated since A. D. 1720. As both brothers died childless they were regarded as

[1] The form *má-sati* appears to be used, but *mahásati* is perhaps commoner.

[2] I.N. Q., IV, § 158, and N. I. N. Q., II, § 726.

[3] A. S. R., XXI, p. 101.

[4] *Sati* monuments are ordinarily slabs of stone stuck in the ground with the figure of the *satti* carved on them, either sitting or standing.

autars. And a temple was erected near the place. Chamba *Gaz.*, p. 95.

In Kángra the people bear the name of Kirpál Chand in reverential memory. He appears to have been childless, and to have devised the construction of the canal called after him as a means of perpetuating his name. His liberality to the people employed was munificent. To each labourer was given six *sers* of rice, half a *ser* of *dál*, and the usual condiments; and to every pregnant woman employed, he gave an additional half allowance in consideration of the offspring in her womb. The people believe that he still exercises a fostering influence over his canal; and some time ago, when a landslip took place, and large boulders which no human effort could remove choked up its bed the people one and all exclaimed that no one but Kirpál Chand could surmount the obstacles. They separated for the night, and next morning when they assembled to work, the boulders had considerately removed themselves to the sides, and left the water course clear and unencumbered ![1]

Ibbetson, § 226.

THE WORSHIP OF THE MALEVOLENT DEAD.—Far different from the beneficent are the malevolent dead. From them nothing is to be hoped, but everything is to be feared. Foremost among them are the *gyáls* or sonless dead. When a man has died without male issue he becomes spiteful, especially seeking the lives of the young sons of others. In almost every village small platforms may be seen with rows of small hemispherical depressions into which milk and Ganges water are poured, and by which lamps are lit and Brahmans fed to assuage the *gyáls*,[2] while the careful mother will always dedicate a rupee to them, and hang it round her child's neck till he grows up.

The jealousy of a deceased wife is peculiarly apt to affect her husband if he takes a new one. She is still called *saukan* or co-wife and at the wedding of her successor oil, milk, spices and sugar are poured on her grave. The *saukan mora* or rival wife's image is put on by the new wife at marriage and worn till death. It is a small plate of silver worn round the neck, and all presents given by the husband to his new wife are first laid upon it with the prayer that the deceased will accept the clothes &c. offered and permit her slave to wear her cast off garments, and so on. In the Himalayas if one of two wives dies and her *churel* or spirit makes the surviving wife ill an image (*muhra*) of the deceased is made of stone and worshipped. A silver plate, stamped with a human image, called *chauki*, is also placed round the haunted survivor's neck.[3]

Another thing that is certain to lead to trouble is the decease of anybody by violence or sudden death. In such cases it is necessary to

[1] *Selections from Punjab Public Corr.*, No. VIII, cited by Barnes, Kangra *Sett. Rep.*, § 166.

[2] I believe them to be identical in purpose, as they certainly are in shape, with the cup-marks which have lately exercised the antiquaries. They are called *bhorka* in the Delhi Territory.

[3] P. N.Q., III, § 200.—The *mora* appears to be a *murat*, 'image,' or possibly *mahurat*, 'omen.' According to Mrs. F. A. Steel Muhammadans also propitiate the deceased *saukan*: *ib.* § 113.

propitiate the departed by a shrine, as in the case of the trooper already mentioned. The most curious result of this belief is the existence all over the Eastern Punjab of small shrines to what are popularly known as Sayyids. The real word is *shahíd* or martyr, which, being unknown to the peasantry, has been corrupted into the more familiar Sayyid. One story showing how these Sayyids met their death will be found in § 376 of the Karnál *Settlement Report*. But the diviners will often invent a Sayyid hitherto unheard of as the author of a disease, and a shrine will be built to him accordingly. The shrines are Muhammadan in form and the offerings are made on Thursday, and taken by Musalmán *faqírs*. Very often the name even of the Sayyid is unknown. The Sayyids are exceedingly malevolent, and often cause illness and death. Boils are especially due to them, and they make cattle miscarry. One Sayyid Bhrúa, of Bari in Kaithal, shares with Mansa Deví of Mani Májra in Ambála the honour of being the great patron of thieves in the Eastern Punjab. But Jain Sayyid in Ferozepur is a bestower of wealth and sons and an aid in difficulty. Offerings vowed to him are presented on a Sunday or on the first Sunday of the Muhammadan month. He also possesses women, and one so possessed is in much request by women to perform a *baiṭhak* or *chauki* on their behalf. She first bathes in clear water, perfumes and oils her hair, dons red clothes and dyes her hands and feet with henna. Then, seated in a Mírásan's house who sings songs in Jain Sháh's honour and thereby pleases him, she begins to shake her head violently. While she is thus possessed the suppliants make their offerings and proclaim their needs. These the medium grants through the Mírásan, mentioning the probable time of fulfilment. She also foretells fortunes. The Mírásan takes the offerings. The efficacy of a Sayyid's curse is illustrated by the legend of Abohar. It was held by Rájá Abram Chand and the Sayyids of Uch carried off his horses, so his daughter carried out a counter-raid as he had no son and the Sayyids came to Abohar where they formed a *mela* or assembly and threatened to curse the raiders unless the spoil was surrendered. But the Rájá held out and the Sayyid ladies came from Uch to seek their lords who thereupon called down curses upon all around including themselves. The tomb of the women in the cemetery and that of the holy men in the sand-hill still exist. Sirsa *Settlement Report*, page 195.[1]

Many of those who have died violent deaths have acquired very widespread fame; indeed Gúga Pír might be numbered amongst them, though he most certainly is not malevolent; witness the proverb quoted anent him. A very famous hero of this sort is Teja, a Jáṭ of Mewár, who was taking milk to his aged mother when a snake caught him by the nose. He begged to be allowed first to take the milk to the old lady, and then came back to be properly bitten and killed. And on a certain evening in the early autumn the boys of the Delhi territory come round with a sort of box with the side out, inside which is an image of Teja brilliantly illuminated, and ask you to 'remember the grotto.' Another case is that of Harda Lála, brother of the Rájá of

[1] N. I. N. Q., I., § 763.

Urchar in Bundhelkhand. He and Teja are generally represented on horseback. So again Harshu Brahman, who died while sitting *dharna*,[1] is worshipped everywhere east of Lahore.

Ibbetson, § 227. But even though a man has not died sonless or by violence, you are not quite safe from him. His disembodied spirit travels about for 12 months as a *paret*, and even in that state is apt to be troublesome. But if, at the end of that time, he does not settle down to a respectable second life, he becomes a *bhút*, or, if a female, a *churel*, and as such is a terror to the whole country, his principal object then being to give as much trouble as may be to his old friends, possessing them, and producing fever and other malignant diseases. Low-caste men, such as scavengers, are singularly liable to give trouble in this way, and are therefore always buried or burnt face downwards to prevent the spirit escaping; and riots have taken place and the Magistrates have been appealed to to prevent a Chúhra being buried face upwards. These ghosts are most to be feared by women and children, and especially immediately after taking sweets so that if you treat a school to sweetmeats the sweet-seller will also bring salt, of which he will give a pinch to each boy to take the sweet taste out of his mouth. They also have a way of going down your throat when you yawn, so that you should always put your hand to your mouth, and had also better say 'Nárain!' afterwards. Ghosts cannot set foot on the ground, and you will sometimes see two bricks or pegs stuck up in front of the shrine for the spirit to rest on. Hence when going on a pilgrimage or with ashes to the Ganges, you must sleep on the ground all the way there so as to avoid them; while the ashes must not rest on the ground, but must be hung up in a tree so that their late owner may be able to visit them. So in places haunted by spirits, and in the vicinity of shrines, you should sleep on the earth, and not on a bedstead. So again, a woman, when about to be delivered, is placed on the ground, as is every one when about to die. Closely allied to the ghosts are the *súris* or fairies. They attack women only, especially on moonlight nights, catching them by the throat, half-choking them, and knocking them down (? hysteria). Children, on the other hand, they protect. They are Musalmán, and are propitiated accordingly; and are apparently identical with the Parind or Peri with whom Moore has made us familiar. They are also known as *sháhpuri*, but resent being so called; and no woman would dare to mention the word.

[1] If a Brahman asks aught of you and you refuse it, he will sit at your door and abstain from food till he gain his request. If he dies meanwhile, his blood is on your head. This is called sitting *dharna*. Or he may cut himself with a knife and then you will be guilty of Brahmhatia or Brahman-murder. A Brahman who commits suicide may become a Deo in the Simla Hills,—see p. 445 *infra*. *Per contra* when the use of a house has been forbidden in those hills by a *sádhu* or Brahman, the latter can remove his ban by sprinkling some of his own blood on the place: Simla Hill States *Gazetteer*, Bashahr, p. 84. Another instance is Tiru of Junga—p. 447 *infra*. But a Brahman does not always attain Deoship by such a suicide. Thus Kulu Brahman of Barog regarding himself as oppressed by a Rána of Baghat cut off his own head, and it cost the State a good deal to put matters right. The suicide need not be a Brahman—see for instance the account of Gambhir Deo at p. 467 *infra*. A great deal of information regarding suicide by Bháts and Chárans will be found in the late Mr. R. V. Russell's *Tribes and Castes of the Central Provinces*, Aghoris, II, pp. 14-5, 164, 175, 256. It is known as *chandi* or *trága* which term is used in the Punjab in a different sense.

Malevolent deities are appeased by building them new shrines or by offerings at old ones. Very often the grain to be offered is placed the night before on the sufferer's head. This is called *orra*. Or the patient may eat some and bury the rest at the sacred spot; or the offering may be waved over his head; or on some night while the moon is waxing he may place it with a lamp lit on it at a cross-road. This is called *langri* or *nagdi*. Sometimes it suffices to tie a flag on the sacred tree to roll in front of the shrine or rub one's neck with its dust. To malevolent or impure gods *kachhi roti*, generally consisting of *chúrma* or stale bread broken up and rolled into balls with *gur* and *ghi*, is offered. Brahmans will not take such offerings.[1]

Resuscitation from death is believed to occur, and people who have come to life say they went to Yamaráj, the kingdom of the dead, and found they had been mistaken for some one else, so they were allowed to return.[2] The ashes of great personages are carefully watched till the 4th day to prevent a magician's tampering with them, as he can restore the dead to life and retain power over him thereafter.[3] Illiterate Hindus believe that the soul is in appearance like a black bee. It can leave the body during sleep.[4]

Spirits are of many kinds and degrees. A *Bramh rákhas* is the ghost of a Brahman who has died *kumaut* and is a very powerful demon, malignant or the reverse.[5] *Hadal* is a spirit that gets into the bones and cannot be exorcised.[6]

It is difficult to define a *bhút*. It is sometimes equated with *pret* as the spirit of one who dies an ill death, *kumaut*, *i.e.* by violence or an accident.[7] But it is also said that every man dying on a bed becomes a *bhút* and every woman so dying a *churel*.[8] In Kángra a *bhút* is also called a *baital* or 'demon' and he may be charmed into servitude, for once a Brahman's *chela* by his magic made a *bhút* cultivate his land for him, feeding him on ordure and the scum found on rivers the while. But one day in his absence his womenfolk fed the slave on festival food, which so annoyed him that he went and sat on the inscribed stone at Kaniára and devoured every living thing that came his way. On the Brahman's return he nailed him to the stone with a charm whose words form the inscription, and it is called *bhút sila* or 'ghost-stone' to this day.[9]

Bhúts have no temples, but are propitiated by offerings in sickness or misfortune, a basket of food, fruit and flowers being passed round the patient's head and then carried out after dark and placed on the road leading to the house or village, to appease their anger. The sickness will seize on any one who tampers with the basket.[10] *Bhúts*

[1] Karnal *Sett. Rep.*, §§ 362, 360, pp. 146—145. To the benevolent gods or ancestors only *pakki roti*, *i.e.* cakes or sweets, fried in *ghi*, may be offered.

[2] N. I. N. Q., I., § 227.

[3] *Ib.*, § 221.

[4] P. N. Q., III, §§ 678-9.

[5] *Ib.*, III, § 196.

[6] *Ib.*, III, § 197.

[7] *Ib.*, II, § 657.

[8] To die at your own time is *maut marna*: P. N. Q., III, § 190

[9] P. N. Q., I, § 680.

[10] *Ib.*, III, § 245.

live just like human beings, but do everything by night. They rear families, and the whole earth is strictly parcelled out among them. A *bhút* casts no shadow as he moves, and ceremonial purity is the only safeguard against his attacks.[1] On the other hand, *bhúts* are said to cook at noon, as well as at evening; so women should not leave their houses at those times lest they be molested by *bhúts* over whose food they have passed.[2]

In Gurdáspur and the adjacent parts of Jammu *bhúts* and witches (*ḍain*) are believed to haunt the living and victimise the weak. Every imaginable disease is attributed to witches, and any woman can become one by learning a charm of 2½ letters. *Chelas* are exorcists of these witches, and they cure a patient by placing some ashes on his forehead and making him swallow the rest, or in serious cases water is used instead. Each *chela* has his *thán*, a raised spot in the corner of the house sacred to the *deota* by whose power he overcomes witches and *bhúts*.[3]

Churels are of two classes—(1) the ghosts of women dying while pregnant or on the very day of the child's birth; (2) those of women dying within 40 days[4] of the birth. But the worst *churel* of all is the ghost of a pregnant woman dying during the Diwáli. *Churels* are always malignant, especially towards members of their own family, though they assume the form of a beautiful woman when they waylay men returning from the fields at nightfall and call them by their names. Immediate harm may be averted by not answering their call, but no one long survives the sight of a *churel*.

To prevent a woman's becoming a *churel* small round-headed nails, specially made, are driven through her finger-nails, while the thumbs and big toes are welded together with iron rings. The ground on which she died is carefully scraped and the earth removed. Then the spot is sown with mustard seed, which is also sprinkled on the road by which the body is carried out for burning or burial, and it is also sown on the grave in the latter case. The mustard blooms in the world of the dead and its scent keeps the *churel* content, and again, when she rises at nightfall and seeks her home, she stops to gather up the mustard seed and is thus delayed till cock-crow when she must return to her grave. In her real shape the *churel* has her feet set backwards and is hideous to behold.[5]

In Kángra the *churel* is believed to long for her child, but to be a curse to all others. On the way to the burning-ground a sorcerer nails her spirit down and the mustard seed is scattered along the road to make her forget it.[6]

[1] I. N. Q., IV, §§ 189-190.

[2] P. N. Q., II, § 500.

[3] *Ib.*, III, § 192.

[4] Or 10 days in Kángra.

[5] P. N. Q., II, § 905.

[6] *Ib.*, § 994. Mustard seed is said to be often scattered about a magistrate's court to conciliate his sympathies: III, § 104.

The *churel* of a dead co-wife sometimes haunts her surviving rival and makes her ill, in which case an image of the deceased should be made of stone and worshipped, and a silver plate, stamped with a human image, called *chauki*, is also worn by the sick survivor round her neck.[1]

Jinns have a right to share in the fruits of the earth, and if they do not get it the crop will be worthless. Once a *jinn* employed a mortal as a teacher and in reward promised to exempt his grain from this tax —so that land now yields four times what it used to do.[2] *jinns* have no bones in their arms and only four fingers and no thumb.[3]

Archæology records instances of people being buried as 'guardians of the gate,' because it was believed the spirit would survive and do watch and ward over the city wall or the entrance through it. A similar belief led to a custom recorded by Martyn Clarke. When the country was unsettled valuables were very commonly buried and when they were at all considerable, misers were in the habit of burying a child alive with them, in the belief that its *bhút* or spirit would protect them. On an auspicious day the miser dug a pit to which was fitted a tight-shutting wooden lid. A child was then decoyed, sometimes from a considerable distance. He had to be a male, aged 6 or 7, healthy and handsome, and he was well fed and kindly treated until the night, fixed by consulting the stars, arrived for burying the treasure. Then he was purified, dressed in white, and made to acknowledge the miser as his master. He was then lowered into the pit with the treasure and a lamp, a *loṭa* of milk and a basket of sweets placed beside him. Finally the lid was fastened down and the boy left to his fate. As a result of this practice, or of the belief that it existed, finders of treasure trove often will not touch it, fearing lest the *bhút* in charge would do them some evil.[4] This idea of the guardian-spirit may explain many folk-tales in which the artificer is rewarded by being sacrificed by his patron, ostensibly to prevent his skill being employed by a rival. The legends that Gugga, the workman who built the temples at Brahmaur in Chamba, was rewarded by having his right hand cut off by the Ráná whose house he had built and then accidentally killed by a fall from the temple porch after he had all but completed the building, are doubtless further examples of this type.[5]

Evil spirits are very fond of fresh milk, and if a Punjabi mother has to leave her child soon after she has given it any she puts salt or ashes in its mouth to take away the smell.[6].

They are also fond of the scent of flowers, and it is dangerous for children to smell them as the spirits, always on the look out for children, will draw them away through the flowers.[7]

[1] P. N. Q., III, § 200.

[2] N. I. N. Q., I, § 668.

[3] *Ib.*, I, § 678.

[4] P. N. Q., II, § 251. Similar beliefs are very common among the Sclavonic peoples; *cf.* Ralston's *Songs of the Russian People*, pp. 126-8. The game called 'London Bridge' is based on the same idea. See also p. 268 *infra*.

[5] Chamba *Gazetteer*, p. 296.

[6] I. N. Q., IV, § 198.

[7] *Ib.*, IV, § 352.

During prairie fires and at dead of night lonely herdsmen in Sirsa used to hear the cries of those who had been killed in old forays and people used to be afraid to travel save in large parties for fear of encountering these supernatural enemies.[1]

In order to avoid becoming *bhúts* after death some Hindus are said to perform their own funeral rites during life.[2] In Chamba two modern cases of suicide were preceded by their performance. If you see the ghost of a dead kinsman give alms in his name, or he will do his best to make you join him.[3]

Any demon can be exorcised by placing red paint (*roli*), red lead, incense, sweetmeat, flesh, fish, spirits, betel-nut and rice on a tray, with a lamp alight, under a *pípal*, at a tank or cross-roads, or on a burning-ground, but only if a man does so, not a woman The man must have been sprinkled first with holy water and then worship the offering. If it be placed under a *pípal* 1, 5, 11 or 21 nails should be driven into the tree and after the rite a string with 3, 5, 7, 11 or 21 knots should be worn until it drops off. Hair from the head buried in a bottle will also drive away spirits.[4]

Witchcraft.—Recitation of 2½ (*i. e.* 3) verses of the Qurán backward enables a witch to take out a child's liver and eat it, and in order to do this more effectively she must first catch a *tark*, a wild animal not larger than a dog, feed it with sugar and *ghi* and ride on it repeating the charm 100 times. A witch cannot die until she has taught this charm to another woman, or failing her to a tree.[5] It makes a witch powerless to extract her two upper front teeth.[6]

Sorcerers write charms or spells on a bit of paper and drop ink on it. Flowers are then placed in a young child's hands and he is bidden to look into the ink and call the four guardians. When he says he sees them he is told to ask them to clean the place and summon their king who is supposed to answer questions through him, but no one else sees or hears the spirits. This is called *hazrat*.[7]

Virgins are in special request for the performance of all spells and charms. If an iron platter be thrown by a young girl out of the house it will cause a hailstorm to cease.[8]

Some witches are liver-eaters—*jigar-khor*. But when one has succeeded in extracting a liver she will not eat it for 2½ days and even after that she can be compelled by an exorcisor to replace it by an animal's liver.[9]

[1] Sirsa *Sett. Rep.*, p. 32.
[2] N. I. N. Q., I, § 44.
[3] *Ib.*, I, § 118.
[4] P. N. Q., III, §§ 198, 199.
[5] *Ib.*, III, § 31.
[6] *Ib.*, III, § 30.
[7] N. I. N. Q., I, § 564.
[8] P. N. Q., III, § 532.
[9] N. I. N. Q., I, § 88.

Sickness and death.—In Chamba sacrifice is often made for the sick in the belief that a life being given, his life will be preserved. Nails are driven into the ground near a corpse and its hands and feet fastened to them with a cord, to prevent the body from stretching and becoming a *bhút* or evil spirit. Sometimes too a thorn is put at the crematorium lest the spirit of the deceased return and trouble the living. The spirit returns to its abode on the 10th, or 13th, day after death, any unusual noise indicating its presence. If a child die the mother has water poured over her through a sieve above its grave, to secure offspring. The water used must be from a well or stream whose name is of the masculine gender.

If a woman's children die she must beg *áṭá* or flour from seven houses, and when her next child is born this *áṭá* is baked into a large cake, from which the centre is cut out, leaving only a circular rim. Through this hole the infant is passed seven times to ensure its living. Similarly a new-born child may be passed seven times through the *chulha*, or fire-place. With the same object is the nostril pierced immediately after birth and an iron nose-ring inserted. Or the infant is given to a poor person, and then taken back to break the continuity of the ill luck. Another curious recipe for this purpose is this :—Take the bark of 7 trees and water from 7 springs all with masculine names. Boil the bark in the water and after dark let it be poured over the woman at a cross-roads. She must then change her clothes and give away those she had on at the ceremony, and the evil influence will go with them.

Two places, in Tariod *pargana* and Hubár, have a curious reputation. When a woman, owing to an evil influence, called *parchháva*, has no children or they die, she visits one of these places, and after certain rites or ceremonies creeps thrice through a hole artificially made in a stone, and only just large enough to admit an adult, and then bathes, leaving one garment at the spot. This is believed to free her from the influence. Sunday morning is the proper time for this and Bhádon and Mágh are the best months. At Hubár the woman bathes besides a Muhammadan *nau-gaza* (nine yards long) grave.

The evil eye.—The evil eye is the subject of various beliefs, which cannot be described here in full, though it is too important a factor in popular usage to be passed over in silence. The term 'evil eye' is generally accepted as a translation of *nazar*, but that word denotes a good deal more than the evil effects of an 'ill-wishing' person's gaze. It connotes the subjective effect of the gaze of any one, however benevolent or well-disposed, when that gaze has induced complete satisfaction in the mind with the object observed, whether animate or inanimate.[1] Thus low-caste persons may cast *nazar* upon a man of higher caste, not because they are of low caste but because of the envy of him which they are supposed to feel. Children are peculiarly subject to *nazar* because they may induce a feeling of pride or satisfaction in those who gaze on them, and for this reason their faces are left unwashed for six

[1] P. N. Q., I, § 864.

years, among the poorer classes.[1] To avert it the Gujars of Hazára use amulets of *batkar* wood (? *Celtis Australis*) and they are also tied round the necks of cattle.

On the same principle anything beautiful or charming, when looked upon by a person bent on mischief, prompts him to do harm, while anything ugly in itself is safe from the evil eye. Hence anything beautiful is daubed with black so that the eye may fall on the daub and not on the thing itself. Accordingly an iron vessel is hung up when a house is abuilding as a *nazar-wattu* or averter of *nazar*, or a blackened pitcher will serve equally well. Such pitchers are often hung permanently on a conspicuous part of a completed house also. The pattern on ornamental clothes is spoilt by introducing a marked irregularity somewhere for the same reason.[2] Iron is not in itself a protection against *nazar*, unless it is black, and the efficacy of arms as prophylactics against spirits appears to be based on the idea that an armed man or woman should have no fear of anything.[3] To avert the evil-eye a small black stone with a hole in it is often worn on the shoulder or round the neck and to this the term *nazar-wattu* is specially applied.[4]

Ibbetson, § 229. The evil eye is firmly believed in, and iron is the sovereign safeguard against it. While a house is being built, an iron pot (or an earthen vessel painted black is near enough to deceive the evil eye, and is less expensive) is always kept on the works; and when it is finished the young daughter of the owner ties to the lintel a charm, used on other occasions also, the principal virtue of which lies in a small iron ring. Mr. Channing thus described the theory of the evil eye:—

"When a child is born an invisible spirit is sometimes born with it; and unless the "mother keeps one breast tied up for forty days while she feeds the child from the other, "in which case the spirit dies of hunger, the child grows up with the endowment of the "evil eye, and whenever a person so endowed looks at anything constantly, something "evil will happen to it. Amulets worn for protection against the evil eye seem to be of "two classes; the first, objects which apparently resist the influence by a superior innate "strength, such as tigers' claws; the second, of a worthless character, such as cowries, "which may catch the eye of their beholder, and thus prevent the covetous look."

A father was once asked, "Why don't you wash that pretty child's face?" and replied "A little black is good to keep off the evil eye." If so, most Punjabi children should be safe enough. It is bad manners to admire a child, or comment upon its healthy appearance. The theory of the scapegoat obtains; and in times of great sickness goats will be marked after certain ceremonies, and let loose in the jungle or killed and buried in the centre of the village. Men commonly wear round their necks amulets, consisting of small silver lockets containing sentences, or something which looks like a sentence, written by a *faqír*. The leaves of the *siras* (*albizzia lebbek*) and of the mango (*mangifera Indica*) are also powerful for good; and a garland of them hung across the village gate with a mystic inscription on an earthen platter in the middle, and a plough beam buried

[1] P. N. Q., II., § 253.

[2] *Ib.*, I., § 597.

[3] *Ib.*, I., § 599.

[4] *Ib.*, I., § 557. In slang a *nazar-wattu* is a worthless fellow—of no use except to keep off the evil eye.

in the gateway with the handle sticking out, show that cattle-plague has visited or was dreaded in the village, and that the cattle have been driven under the charm on some Sunday on which no fire was lighted on any hearth. An inscription made by a *faqír* on an earthen platter, and then washed off into water which is drunk by the patient, is a useful remedy in illness; and in protracted labour the washings of a brick from the *chakahu* (*chakra bhyu*) fort of Amin, where the 'arrayed army' of the Pándus assembled before their final defeat, are potent; or if anybody knows how to draw a ground plan of the fort, the water into which the picture is washed off will be equally effective.[1] When a beast gets lame, an oval mark with a cross in it, or Solomon's seal, or Siva's trident, or the old mark of the Aryan need-fire[2], in general shape like the Manx arms, is branded on the limb affected; or a piece of the coloured thread used by the Brahman in religious ceremonies is tied round it.

In Sirmúr a person endowed with the evil eye is called *dág*[3] or *dágni*, and to avert his influence seven kinds of grain are mixed with cow-dung and plastered on the house door, an obscure *mantra* being recited. *Dains* are witches or the spirits of women, which inflict injury in unknown ways. To avert their influence a charm is written on a sheet of paper which is held over burning incense and then tied round the arm or neck of the person possessed. These charms also contain pictures of Bhairon or Mahánbír (Hanúmán) with a charm inscribed in a circle. Another method of averting the influence of a *dág* or *ḍain* is to call in a Bhát or Dhaki who has a reputation for skill in such matters. He first cooks a loaf which is placed on the patient's head. Then a lamp of *ghi* with four wicks is lighted and certain *mantrás* recited thrice, the loaf being waved round the patient's head meantime, and finally placed on the ground. A he-goat is then decapitated and the blood caught in a *túmbá*, which, with the goat's head, is also waved round the patient's head. Lastly, the loaf, the lamp, and *túmbá* with the blood and goat's head are all placed by night at a spot where four roads meet.

In Jubbal the *ḍákan* is a witch and in former days if so adjudged she was banished from the State. Only a Brahman can detect a *ḍákan* and he judges by marks on her face. A popular way of detecting one was to tie her up hand and foot and cast her into a pond. If she floated she was proved to be a witch.[4]

In Chamba belief in evil spirits exerts a powerful influence on the popular imagination. Evil spirits and fairies are believed to have a special liking for fair-complexioned children, and so a black mark is put on a child's forehead to keep them away, and also to protect it from

[1] The virtue of the fort is due to its standing on the edge of a pond in which the Sun was born, and where women who wish for sons go and bathe on Sunday.

[2] The sign is often drawn at the door of a house or shop to keep off the evil eye.

[3] The *dág* is also a spirit or witch. In the Simla Hills the evil eye is called *dág*: Simla Hill States *Gazetteer*, Kumhársain, p. 12. But the term is also applied to ghosts connected with fields from which they are supposed to filch the crops: Simla District *Gazetteer*, p. 42 The *ḍain* makes Bhádon unhealthy because she thirsts for blood in that month and to avert its evil days Brahmans give their flock threads on the Rakhri or Salono day. On Asauj 1st or Sáer is the fête day which marks the close of the bad month: Manḍi *Gazetteer*, p. 35: see also *infra*.

[4] Simla Hill States *Gazetteer*, Jubbal, p. 14.

the evil eye. The idea seems to be that malign influences affect beauty more than ugliness; charms are also used to avert *bhúts* or evil spirits and the evil eye. These are made of leopards' and bears' claws, and the teeth of pigs, in the belief that as they belong to fierce animals they will frighten away anything harmful. A cowrie, a shell or the bone of a crab has the same virtue. For the same reason brass anklets, called *rehâru,* are put on children. A person dying sonless becomes a *bhút* or *autar-aputra* (sonless), and troubles his surviving relatives, unless duly appeased: so adults wear a *jantra,* a small silver or copper case containing a scroll supplied by a Brahman. An *autar* or silver necklet with a human figure cut on it is also worn. Another form is the *nád,* of silver or copper and shaped like an hour-glass. An *autar* must also be propitiated with the sacrifice of a goat, and for a time his clothes are worn by one of the family—a soapnut kernel is also carried on a string round the neck. Iron about the person protects one from evil spirits. A woman outside her house should be careful not to bathe quite naked, as she is liable to come under the shadow of an evil spirit. A child whose *jattu* or first hair has not been cut, must not be taken to a *mela,* as the fairies who go to fairs may exert an evil influence. A piece of netted thread hung above the doorway will keep out evil spirits during labour or sickness.

Asá Hará is a godling in Gurdáspur to whom cairns are erected in large uninhabited jungles.

Bahro is a male spirit, ugly in form, who causes disease and must be appeased.[1]

Banásat, a female spirit who lives in forests and on high mountain slopes. As a guardian of the cattle she is propitiated when the herds are sent to the summer grazing grounds. She also presides over quarries and cuttings and must be propitiated before work is commenced. A goat must be killed over a lime-kiln before it is lit, an offering made to her before a tree is felled in the forests, and grain cannot be ground at the water-mill without her consent. She is apparently a Jogini, and much the same as the Rákshani.[2]

The Banbírs are deified heroes or champions of the olden times. They are said to live in the pomegranate, lime, *tun,* fig, *kainth, simbal* and walnut trees. They also haunt precipices, waterfalls and cross-roads and are propitiated on special occasions at those spots. They can cause sickness, especially in women, and some of them, such as Kála Bír and Nársingh, visit women in their husbands' absence. If the husband returns while the Bir is in human form he is sure to die unless a sacrifice is offered.[3]

The *banshira bhút* of the Simla Hills is doubtless the *binsira* or headless demon, so common in folk-tales. He haunts the jungles whose king he is supposed to be.[4] But he also haunts old buildings, valleys and mountains, and like a ghost is propitiated in some places, by sacrifices of goats and in others of earth or gravel.[5]

[1] Chamba *Gazetteer*, 1904, p. 192
[2] *Ib.*, p. 191.
[3] *Ib.*, p. 191.
[4] Simla Hill States *Gazetteer*, Kumhársain. p, 12.
[5] *Ib.*, pp. 48-9.

Bír Batál is a water-sprite whose habitat is in every river and stream. His ancient name was Varuna, but he now bears also the name of Khwája Khizr. *Khicheri*, sodden Indian corn, 3 balls of moss, 3 of ashes, 3 measures of water, a pumpkin or a flour-sheep are offered to him. The Minjarán ká mela is held in his honour. A bridge is likely to be unsafe unless a sacrifice be made in his honour, and the opening of a water-course requires one also.[1]

Chungu is the male demon found in walnut and mulberry trees and under the *karangora* shrub. He is worshipped or propitiated. He is under the control of a sorcerer whose messenger he is.[2]

In the Simla Hills he brings things to him and also drinks the milk of cows, to whose owners too he brings milk, *ghí* etc.[3]

In Chamba sorcery and witchcraft are still very commonly believed in. Various diseases are caused by witches, either directly by incantations, or indirectly through the malevolent spirits under their control. Cattle disease is also ascribed to witchcraft, and even the ravages of wild animals such as leopards. Formerly when witchcraft was suspected the relatives of the person affected complained to a court or to the Rájá. An order was then issued to a *chela* who was reputed to have the power of detecting witches. Accompanied by a musician and a drummer he went to the place. A pot of water (*kumbh*) was first set over some grain sprinkled on the ground and on this was put a lighted lamp. Ropes were also laid besides the *kumbh*. The musicians played, and when the *chela* had worked himself into a state of afflatus, he asked the people standing by if they wished the witch to be caught, warning them that she might be one of their own relatives. They would, however, assent. This went on for three days, and on the third the *chela* standing by the *kumbh* would call out the witch's name and order his attendants to seize her. Picking up the ropes they would at once execute his order and she would be seized and bound. In olden times witches were cruelly tortured to get confessions of guilt. One of the methods was that once customary in Europe. The witch was dipped in a pool, the belief being that, if guilty, she would rise to the surface, but would sink if innocent. Guilt being proved, she was banished, and sometimes her nose was cut off. The *chela* received a fee of Rs. 12, part of which went to the State. *Chelas* can also exorcise evil spirits by making the person afflicted inhale the smoke of certain herbs. Though the belief in witchcraft still survives, the detection of witches and all the cruel practices associated with it are now illegal, and have been entirely discontinued.

The list of hobgoblins and spirits in Chamba is endless, for there is hardly anything the hillman does or attempts to do which is not

[1] Chamba *Gazetteer*, p. 191, and *supra*, p. 135. Also *infra* p. 267.

[2] *Ib.*, p. 192, and Vol. II, p. 270 *infra* for the offerings made to him.

[3] I. A. S. B., 1911, p. 145.

under the control of one or other of the presiding genii of the mountains, without whose good will and favour all his efforts will be attended with failure; while the neglect of the customary offering may bring disaster on himself and his family. When sickness or calamity is believed to have been caused by any of these malevolent spirits the sick person, or some one for him, goes to the local *chela* who tells them which spirit ought to be appeased, and acts as the medium of cure. This he professes to do with the help of the godling whose *chela* he happens to be. All such diseases are called *opari,* that is, from supernatural influences—as distinct from those that are *sarīri,* or connected with the body.

Gunga is the disease-spirit of cows, and also their protector within the village cattle-shed, just as Banásat is on the high pastures.[1]

Gwála was a holy man in Kángra. His legend runs thus:— One day as he was sitting in a lofty hill near Baroh, a wedding procession passed by and he said to the bride: 'Thorns on this side and on that: she who wears the red veil is my wife.' The bridegroom challenged him to jump down from the hill and he did so, but was killed. The bride then took his head in her lap and said to the bridegroom: 'You gave me to him; I burn on the pyre with him.' This resolve she carried out, and the cairns erected in memory of Gwála's bravery exist to this day.[2]

Jakh.

In Chamba *jakh* is a godling under whose control are the products of the cow. Each cow has her own *jakh,* and when buying one it is necessary to ask its name so that its demands may be properly met.

In the Síbá *jágír* of Kángra the *jakhs* are local deities to whom first fruits are offered symbolically. The offerings actually made consist of milk, curds and clarified butter made from the milk of the animal to whom a male calf has been born. If a female buffalo-calf be born a young he-goat is also presented. Clarified butter is never sold before the first fruits have been offered, but in the case of milk and curds the usage has broken down. Moreover, the Rájá leases out the right to collect the offerings to the *jakhs,* but the bids seldom exceed Rs. 25 a year. He also leases out the right to dispense music at festivals, weddings and the like.[3]

Joginis, rock spirits, as they seem to be in Chamba, may be identical with the *banásats* or *rákshinis.*[4] But in Kulu the *jogini* is a fairy of the woods and seemingly ranks as high as any *deota.* Some *joginis* exercise wide powers Thus at Phangni *jogini's* command smoking, wearing leather and the use of bedsteads are forbidden in the Sarwari

[1] *Chamba Gazetteer,* p. 192: for an account of his propitiation see Vol. II, p. 270, *infra.*

[2] P. N. Q., III, § 15.

[3] Chamba *Gazetteer,* p. 192, and P. N. Q., III, § 257. *Jakh* is the Sanskr. *Yaksa*' ogre,

[4] For the offerings made to them, see Vol. II, p. 270, *infra.*

valley, and the order is obeyed.[1] But other *joginis* appear to be merely malignant spirits which haunt water-falls and hill-tops, as well as woods, so that the gray moss which floats from the branches of trees in the higher forests is called '*the jogini's* hair.' Some of these spirits resemble the Nágs in function, for she of the Chúl, a peak in the Jalauri range, sends hail to destroy the crops if the villagers below fail to make a pilgrimage to her peak and sacrifice sheep on the appointed day.[2]

The Jaljogans inhabit wells, springs and streams. They cast spells over women and children, causing sickness and even death.[3]

Kailu or Kailu Bír is the *numen* of abortion. His elaborate worship during pregnancy will be found described at p. 270 of Vol. II *infra*.

To him are offered a red cap, an iron mace and a kid, the cap and part of the kid go to the priest, the rest to the worshipper. He is worshipped on Thursdays. He lives on the mountain slopes and when unappeased rolls landships down into the valleys.[4]

Kailung is a Nág and father of all the Nágs. He is worshipped only on Sundays, whereas other Nágs are worshipped on Thursdays also. Like Shiv he is worshipped under the form of the *darát* or sickle.

He is associated with wheat.

His offerings are a mace, a goat and a red cap.[5]

The god Koilo has in some villages a platform, and it is believed that snake-bite can be cured by lying down on it. Koilo

Masán or *mashán* is a goblin who haunts burning-places, at any rate in the Simla Hills, and *chirkhu-masán* is a male spirit which swings—whence its name—and haunts cross-roads, frightening passers-by, in Chamba.[6]

Rákshasas appear to be quite distinct from the *rákshanis* mentioned above (p. 213). In Chamba they are also called *ráksis* and as spirits of the mountain are all dread realities to the hillman. In his disordered fancy every peak and pass is the abode of these demons, and they

[1] Lyall, Kangra *Sett Rep.*, § 94. Phugni in Maṇḍi is a *devi* : *Gazetteer*, p. 40. The *joginis* will be discussed further *infra*, p. 248. As the *ḍains* render all Bhádon unhealthy (p. 211, *supra*), so the *joginis* of the four points of the compass make the 16th of that month a very critical day. On that night they meet the *deotas* in fight on the Kambogir, a ridge in Maṇḍi, and if victorious famine may be expected. On that night too cattle are brought down from the ridge lest the *joginis* kill them and Hindus distribute rape-seed to avert their influence : Maṇḍi *Gazetteer*, p. 41.

[2] Kangra *Gazetteer*, Pt. II, Kulu, pp. 46, 47.

[3] Chamba *Gazetteer*, p. 192.

[4] *Ib.*, pp. 155 and 191.

[5] *Ib.*, pp. 151, 155.

[6] J. A. S. B., 1911, p. 143. Like *shyána* and *rákshas*—also names for goblins—*masán* gives its name to a Kanet sept—see pp. 73, 305 and 417 of Vol. III *infra*. *Masáni*, a wasting disease of children in Sirmúr (*Gazetteer*, p. 25), may be derived from it. It is said to be a corruption of Sanskrit *shamshán* by Maya Singh, *Panjabi Dicty.*, p. 733. For *masán* or ashes as a disease and the cure for it see p. 104 *supra*.

control the winds and the storms. When the tempest rages on the mountain summit he believes the *rákas* are contending with one another, the falling rock and the avalanche or the weapons of their wrath. In ascending a snowy pass the coolies often refrain from all noise till they reach the top, lest they should inadvertently offend the spirit of the mountain, and bring destruction on themselves; and no Gaddi would think of crossing a pass without first propitiating the pass-deity to secure fair weather, and a safe passage for flocks. A cairn with flags hanging from twigs fixed on the top is found on the summit of almost every pass and represents the pass-deity.[1]

'Marmot' records a curious rite practised during an eclipse of the moon in Pángi. The Pángwáls stood in a circle on one leg, holding each a big stone poised on the right shoulder while with the other hand they pinched the left ear. This was done to propitiate the *rákshasas*, and the posture was maintained until the eclipse was over.[2]

Elsewhere not only do *rákshasas* inhabit trees, as we have seen (p. 189 *supra*) but it is also wise to halt at sunset when on a journey lest they lead you astray during the night. Further, if you are eating by lamp-light and the light goes out you should cover your food with your hands to prevent them from carrying it off in the dark.[3] Like the *prets* or ghosts they dwell to the south. In the earlier mythology the *rákshasas* seem to have been giants and it was they who snatched the book of learning from Saraswati's hands when she came down from the hills to beyond Thánesar and made her in shame become a river which sank into the earth and go to join the Ganges.[4]

In Kulu the *jalpari* are of two kinds:—*jal jogni* and *batáli* or *churel*. The influences of the former are averted by offering flowers and a lamb by the side of a water-course. The former is said to meet humankind very seldom: but when she does get hold of a man she takes him to her lodging and at night cohabits with him: if he will not obey her wishes she will kill him but otherwise she does no harm to him. There is no means of opposing her influence. The *nahas pari* are offered rice to get rid of them. Women are apt to be influenced by them because they are generally weak minded.

As the *jogni* are supposed to live on mountains and the *churel* in ravines the use of red clothes is avoided on both, especially on the mountains.

In the Simla Hills, besides the gods, spirits of various kinds are believed in and propitiated. Such are the *bhúts* or ghosts, *parís*, especially the *jal-parís* or water-sprites, also called *jal-mátris*, the *chhidras*,[5]

[1] Chamba *Gazetteer*, p. 191

[2] P. N. Q., II, § 121.

[3] *Ib.*, II, § 788.

[4] *Ib.*, III, pp. 215, § 196.

[5] *Chhiddar*, Sanskr. *chhidra*, means 'hole': J. A. S. B., 1911, p. 141. But *dáis*, a synonym of *ḍág*, does not appear to be connected with *ḍais*, *ḍaisí*, a den or large hole in a rock: *ib.*, p. 147. In Kulu *chhidra* seems to mean an oath or obligation and to be a synonym of *chhea*.

and *banshira*. The *bhût* is the ghost of the cremating ground. *Pret* is the term applied to the ghost for one year after the death of the deceased: *rishet*[1] its name from the end of that year to the fourth. *Jal-paris* are conceived of as female forms, some benevolent, others malevolent. To propitiate the former a sacrifice is required. The *chhidra* is conceived of as a terrifying spirit which must be propitiated by incense of mustard seed. The *banshira* haunts old buildings, valleys and peaks. It is propitiated by sacrifices of goats, or in some places by offerings of dust or gravel. In lieu of sacrifice a *púja*, called *kunjham*, is offered to Káli and to *parís* or *mátrís*. A tract of hill or forest is set apart as the place of this worship, and even if the rest of the forest is cut down the part consecrated to the goddess or spirit is preserved for her worship, none of the trees in it being cut, or their boughs or even leaves removed. *Ḍágs* are the demons specially associated with fields. If the crop yields less than the estimated amount of produce it is believed that the difference has been taken by the *ḍág*. The *dúdádhári* or *mánashári* spirit is one which haunts burning *ghâṭs* and is averted by wearing a silver picture round one's neck. If possessed by the former one should abstain from meat. Ghaṭialú or Gaṭerú is a demon known in Dhámi. He is said to possess people and is propitiated by the sacrifice of a *khaḍhú* (ram). He is embodied in a stone which is kept in the house and worshipped to protect the cattle from harm. He is said to have come from Bhajji State[2] The fair of the *gásián* or fairies at Bamsan in Nádaun (Kángṛa) is held on the first Tuesday in Háṛ and on all Tuesdays in other months. Only women attend the fair to worship the *parís* who inflict boils on children. The fair has been in existence from time immemorial, but the special worship on Tuesdays dates from the birth of Rája Bhím Chand's son

Baháwalpur is equally rich in spirits. There in addition to the *paret*, *bhût*, *dît* (? *datt*), *rákhash*, *ḍain*, *churel* and *pari*, we find the *pashâj*,[3] *dákan*, *shákan* and *deo*. To these are mostly ascribed diseases of the brain and womb in women, but they occasionally possess men too. Khetrpál's temple at Uch is a famous place for casting out spirits. Many of the disorders of children are ascribed to demons, such as the *umm-us-sabián* or 'mother of children,' who causes convulsions. Such diseases are believed to be connected in some way with low castes, and so Bhangís and Chúhṛás are employed to exorcise them.[4] If anything goes bad it is believed to be bewitched (*bándhná*) by an enemy, apparently through the agency of a spirit, and those skilled in combating magic by charms are generally called in to undo the mischief, but sometimes it can be remedied without such aid. Thus a dyer whose indigo has got spoilt can make it regain its colour by relating some gossip he has heard in a highly coloured form.

[1] Fr. *rishi*, a sage.

[2] In that State *gaṭeṛa* is said to mean ghost: J. A. S. B., 1911, p. 168. In Sirmúr Ghaṭriáli is a goddess – see p. 300 *infra*.

[3] Clearly the *pisácha* or cannibal demon. The word *deo* has had a long and interesting history. It is curious to find it used here of an *evil* spirit, apparently, because in the Punjab Himalayas *deo*=*deota*.

[4] Baháwalpur *Gazetteer*, p. 187. Sometimes a *labána*, a kind of insect, is tied round the neck of a child suffering from convulsions. This may be done because the Labánas is a low caste: but *cf.* p. 4, Vol. III, *infra*. The *labána* is also said to be used to cure warts.

In the hands of one who has by fasting etc. attained to *bidya* mustard seeds are very potent and can be used to kill a healthy enemy, cure a sick friend or recover stolen property. For the latter the recipe is: take a gourd and some mustard seeds, rub them between four fingers, repeat charms over them and throw them at the gourd. It will then float away in the air to the spot where the booty is concealed.

Ibbetson, § 224.

AGRICULTURAL SUPERSTITIONS.—The superstitions connected with cattle and agriculture are endless. No horned cattle or anything appertaining to them, such as butter or leather, must be bought or sold on Saturday or Sunday; and if one die on either of those days it is buried instead of being given to the menials. So the first beast that dies of cattle-plague is buried. Cattle-plague can be cast out across the border of one village into the one which adjoins it in the east. All field-work, cutting of grass, grinding of corn and cooking of food, are stopped on Saturday morning; and on Sunday night a solemn procession conducts a buffalo skull, a lamb, *siras* sticks, butter-milk, fire, and sacred grass to the boundary, over which they are thrown, while a gun is fired three times to frighten away the disease. Last year a man was killed in an affray resulting from an attempt to transfer the plague in this manner. A villager in Gurgaon once captured the cattle-plague in its material shape, and wouldn't let it go till it promised never to remain where he or his descendants were present; and his progeny are still sent for when murrain has fastened on a village, to walk round it and call on the plague to fulfil its contract. The sugar-press must be started, and a well begun on a Sunday. On Saturday night little bowls of water are set out round the proposed site, and the one which dries up least marks the exact spot for the well. The circumference is then marked, and they begin to dig, leaving the central lump of earth intact. They cut out this clod, call it Khwája Jí (appealing to Khwája Khizr) and worship it and feed Brahmans. If it breaks it is a bad omen, and a new site will be chosen a week later. The year's ploughing or sowing is best begun on a Wednesday: it must not be begun on a Monday or on a Saturday, or on the 1st or 11th of any month; and on the 15th of each month the cattle must rest from work. So weeding should be done once, twice, thrice or five times: it is unlucky to weed four times. Reaping must be begun on a Tuesday and finished on a Wednesday, the last bit of crop being left standing till then. When the grain is ready to be divided, the most extraordinary precautions are observed to prevent the evil eye from reducing the yield. Times and seasons are observed, perfect silence is enjoined, and above all, all audible counting of the measures of grain is avoided.[1] When sugarcane is first sown, sweet-

[1] You cannot measure grain without all kinds of precautions. It must not be measured at all on a new or full moon (*parúa*) day, and Saturday is bad. Begin at dawn, midday, sunset, or midnight, when the spirits are busy. Let 4 men go inside an enclosing line with an earthen vessel—and no one else till they have finished. Let them face the north. Keep silence during the measuring and avoid counting the number aloud, tallies being kept by putting down small heaps of grain called *bohali*. Once the grain is measured it is safe from the evil eye. The measuring is made systematically, doubtless to avoid confusion and cheating or quarrelling. See p. 173, §§ 485-6 of Ibbetson's Karnál Sett. Report, and pages 194 *ff* and 236 *ff* of Vol. I. of Elliott's *Races of the North-Western Provinces.*

ened rice is brought to the field and with it women smear the outside of the vessel. It is then given to the labourers. Next morning or when it is planted out a woman puts on a necklace and walks round the field, winding thread on to a spindle[1]; and when it is cut the first fruits are offered on an altar called *makál* built close to the press, and sacred to the sugarcane god, whose name is unknown unless it too be *makál* and then given to Brahmans. When the women begin to pick the cotton they go round the field eating rice-milk, the first mouthful of which they spit on to the field toward the west; and the first cotton picked is exchanged at the village shop for its weight in salt, which is prayed over and kept in the house till the picking is over.

When the fields are being sown they sing:—

'A share for the birds and fowls, a share for wayfarers and travellers:
A share for the passers-by, a share for the poor and mendicant.'[2]

On the 9th of the light half of Kátik both men and women walk round a town early in the morning, re-entering it by the same gate that they left it by. During this circumambulation they sing hymns while the women scatter *satnája* by the way, saying:—

'Friend husbandman, take thy share,
Our share we write down to God.'[3]

To protect gram from lightning it should be sown with wheat—at least this is believed to be the case in Kángra apart from the benefits of a mixed crop.[4]

The threshing floor is naturally of considerable importance in folk-religion. From the time the grain is cut until it is formally weighed it is exposed to the rapacity of demons and *bhúts*. But they are only of mediocre intelligence and can easily be imposed upon It is only necessary to draw a magic circle round the heap and place a sickle on top of it to keep them off.[5] Or in Montgomery and the other parts of the south-west the village *mulwána* or holy man writes a charm which is stuck in a cleft stick in the heap. For this a fixed fee, called *rasúl-wáhi*, is paid. Special care has to be taken when the winnowing begins. Friday being the goblins' holiday should be avoided, or the grain will vanish. At a fit time the workers go to the spot and a couple of men are posted to prevent any living thing from approaching. Winnowing is carried on in silence. If by evening it is not finished the charm is left on one heap and the other is pressed down with the winnowing basket. Goblins sleep at night, but a somnambulist can do harm if this plan is not adopted. The same precautions are observed in dividing the produce.[6]

The agricultural superstitions in Baháwalpur are of special interest because in that state disease is personified and even trees become anthropomorphised.

[1] Karnál *S. R.*, p. 181. This custom is falling into disuse.
[2] P. N. Q., IV, § 85.
[3] *Ib.*, III, § 481.
[4] *Ib.*, II, § 477.
[5] N. I. N. Q., IV, § 598.
[6] Purser, Montgomery *S. R.*, p. 100.

Charms for crops and cattle.

If a crop of wheat, gram or maize be attacked by insects (*kungi* or *tela*) a charm (*kalám*) is recited to avert injury, or a camel's bone burnt so that the smoke may drift over the crop, a *kalám* being also read. The following charms are in use:—

Kungi, Kíra, Múla, Bakhra cháre bhain bhira,
Hukm Khuda de nál ái hawá ate gaí udá.

"*Kungi, Kíra, Múla*, and *Bakhra* are brothers and sisters (of the same family); by the command of God a wind blew and drove them all away." This is spoken over sand, which is then sprinkled over the crop. The following verse is recited and blown over the diseased crops:—

Kungi, Kíra, Bakhra tariye bhain bhira.
Roṭí be nimáz dí gaí wá udá.

"*Kungi, Kíra, Bakhra* are all three brothers and sisters. The bread of one who does not pray (*nimáz*) was carried away by the wind." Meanwhile the owner walks round the field, eating fried wheat. If he meets any one while so doing he gives him the wheat, but must not speak to him. When grain has all been threshed out by the cattle the owner digs round it a trench (*kara*), which he fills with water. No one may enter this circle, which protects the crop from evil spirits. Blight is averted by hanging up a pot, on a long stick, in the field, the pot being filled with earth from a saint's tomb. In selecting a place for a stack of corn, a pit is first dug and the earth excavated from it put back again. If it exactly fills the pit, the place is unpropitious and another place is chosen. But if some earth remains over the corn is stacked and the grain winnowed there Many cultivators set up a plough in a heap of corn, and draw a line round it with a knife to prevent genii from eating the grain. If when corn has been winnowed the grain appears less than the husks, it is believed that some evil genii has got into the heap and stolen the grain and a ram or he-goat is killed and eaten jointly by the farmers to expel it. Such genii assume the shape of ants or other insects, and so, when the husks have been separated from the grain, the ground around the heap is swept and no insect allowed to get into it. When cattle &c. are diseased they are commonly taken to a shrine, and in a dream the owner is told what means will effect a cure: or the *mujáwar* of the shrine hears a voice from the tomb or the cattle get frightened at night and run away, in either of which cases it is expected that they will recover. In the Ubha the following *mantar* is used in cases of foot and mouth disease:—

Suranjít de tre beṭe, Dar, Dathar, Buhára,
Bíwi Bái de páp ḍubban je dhan wich kare pasára.

"Suranjít had three sons, Dar, Dathar and Buhára. The sins of Bíwi Bái shall sink her down (*i.e.*, she will be annihilated) if she lives at all in this world."

In the Lamma this disease is called *muhára* and to cure it the shrine of Jeṭha Bhuṭṭa is much resorted to. If grass does not agree with the cattle the following *mantar* is recited 7 or 11 times and the *mulláh* blows into each animal's ear :—

Kála paṭhṭha pabbar wannán.
Zimín wich hik salu upannán,
Na kar paṭhṭha eḍa mánán ;
Maiṇ bhí terí sát pachhúnáṇ.
Ant nagri, ant gor,
Mare paṭhṭha te jíwe ḍhor.

On the other hand Sawant appears to be a benevolent spirit who casts out diseases. 'Bantari gave birth to Sawant beyond the river, whereby ulcers, abscesses, tooth-aches, ophthalmia and swellings of the breast departed', runs the couplet. If the right breast be swollen the left is exorcised and *vice versá.* In a somewhat similar way scorpion-bite is cured by proxy. A man goes on the patient's behalf to the exorciser who blows a spell on the water which the proxy drinks, and then the sufferer recovers.[1]

If a young tree is peculiarly flourishing or vigorous, it is dedicated to a *pír* or even called after his name, and offerings are made to it. Villagers often visit such a tree in small groups. Gradually the tree is supposed to be the saint himself and to distinguish it a flag is fastened to it. The *pír* chosen in such cases is the one most implicitly believed in by the villagers.[2]

MINOR SUPERSTITIONS.—Good and bad omens are innumerable. Black is unlucky, and if a man go to build a house and turn up charcoal at the first stroke of the spade, he will abandon the site. A mantis is the horse of Rám, is very auspicious, and always saluted when seen. Owls portend desolate homes; and the *koil* (*Eudynamys orientalis*) is also especially unlucky. Chief among good omens is the *dogar*, or two water-pots one on top of the other. This should be left to the right, as should the crow, the black buck, and the mantis; but the snake to the left. To sneeze is auspicious, as you cannot die for some little time after. So when a man sneezes his friends grow enthusiastic and congratulate him, saying 'live a hundred years'! On the other hand it is said that sneezing is *always* a bad omen among Hindus and a sneeze from any one near him will always prevent a Hindu's starting on a journey or any important business. He will sit down for a while before recommencing and if he should fail even then he will attribute it to the sneeze.[3] But after sneezing you may eat, drink or sleep, only you must not go on a visit.[4] Odd numbers are lucky :—'*Numero Deus impari gaudet.*' But three and thirteen are unlucky, because

[1] Bahawalpur *Gazetteer*, pp. 188-89.

[2] For the spell, which is an invocation of the Name (of God), see *ib.*, p 187. Some believe that the Prophet permitted the practice of hanging rags (on the Pilgrims' tree) and explained the peculiar name of the expedition called *Zát-ul-riká's* (place of shreds of cloth) by supposing it to be a term for a tree to which the Moslems hung their *ex-voto* rags. The *Tárikh-i-Tabari* mentions it as a practice of the pagan Arabs and talks of evil spirits residing in the date-tree: Burton's *Al Madina*, (1906), I, p. 155.

[3] *Ib.*, I, § 776. The Buddhist idea is the same and a Tibetan proverb often said when a man sneezes runs—

Chhering námmet Funchung shokh,
Lorgyá thung-sang tongyá thukh,
Tondá débará sorbá thukh.
'May God prolong your life, and avert the evil omen'.

[4] *Ib.*, I, § 949.

they are the bad days after death; and *terah tín* is equivalent to 'all anyhow'. So if a man, not content with two wives, wish to marry again, he will first marry a tree, so that the new wife may be the fourth and not the third. The number five and its aliquot parts run through most religious and ceremonial customs. The shrine to Bhúmia is made of five bricks; five culms of the sacred grass are offered to him after child-birth; five sticks of sugarcane are offered; with the first fruits of the juice, to the god of the sugar-press, and so on without end; while offerings to Brahmans are always 1¼, 2½, 5, 7½, whether rupees or *sers* of grain. The dimensions of wells and well-gear on the other hand are always fixed in so many *and three quarter* cubits; and no carpenter would make or labourer dig you any portion of a well in round numbers of cubit. In Siálkot *wáhde* (apparently fr. *wadhan*, to increase) is always used in counting for *tín*. Elsewhere in counting *bahut* is used for it and the *shísham* with its 3 leaves is a type of utter failure. 12, on the contrary, is peculiarly lucky, and complete success is called *pao bára*. 52 also appears to be a happy number, and appears in Buddhism as the number of 'the divisions of thought, word, and deed.... all the immaterial qualities and capabilities which go to make up the individual'[1]. Both 12 and 52 occupy a conspicuous place in the organisation of caste. A *baiya*, or group of 22 villages, is, like *bára* and *báwan* or groups of 12 and 52, respectively, a favourite term for a tribal settlement containing *about* that number of villages. So too 32 is in Buddhism the number of 'the bodily marks of a great man' (Sacred Books of the East, Vol. XXXV, p. 116). But indeed all the twos, 22, 32, 42 etc. are favourite numbers. On the other hand 8 does not appear to be a lucky number, though it is the number of prostrations made in the worship of the Bhagat-panthís. The 8th child is unlucky.

Council of three unlucky.

But for three persons to act together as a council or committee is unlucky, at any rate in Baháwalpur. *Trehoṅ janiáṅ dí majlis khoṭi*, *i.e.* a committee consisting of three members is unlucky (lit. counterfeit). On the other hand to be five in council is thrice blessed, for the proverb goes: *pánchoṅ meṅ pír, panj pardhán* or *panjo meṅ parmeshar*, there is god in the 5 leaders, or in 5, *i.e.* their decision is final. But *panch* may mean that you will have to go to the authorities (*panchâyat*) for redress, and *sat* is an omen of *sath*, a quarrel, so transactions of the 5th and 7th are put down as of the 4th and 6th

Amongst Hindus the 9th year is *angint*, or without a number, and is so called, but there is no objection to returning it at a Census under that name. Again in the case of boys the 8th[2] and 12th years are unlucky and also called *angint*. The unlucky numbers, however, do not appear to be unlucky at all when used of ages. Thus 9 is neither lucky nor unlucky, though it is a multiple of 3 which is quite disastrously unlucky. 5 is very lucky and 1, 5, 7, 11, 13, 15, 17, 21, 25, 31, 41.

[1] Rhys-David, *American Lectures on Buddhism*, p. 156. But in the hills 2 is distinctly unlucky and a *dásilla*, two ears of wheat, barley or maize in one, is ill omened, while in any calculation if 2 be the balance it is unlucky and called *páshi*, lit. 'hanging', J. A. S. B., 1911, pp. 156, 219. In ancient India 13 was not ill-omened: J. R. A. S., 1916, p. 350 *ff*.

[2] Just as the 8th month of pregnancy is unlucky.

51, or 101 are fortunate as indeed are all odd numbers (except 3),[1] but in the Kurram 3, 13 and 16 are peculiarly unlucky.

For an interesting account of numbers in Punjab folklore see Temple's *Legends of the Punjab*, preface to Vol. I, pp. xviii—iv : 2, 4, 8, 16, 3 and 7 are common, but 12 is the commonest of all : 6, 18, 24, 36, 48 and 9 also occur. 5 is also frequent, while there are instances of 13, 14, 19, 20, 21 and 22, while 60, 70 and the old Indian magic number 84 are also found. See also pref. to Vol. II, pp. xix and xx, for some further details. In religion we have the 33 crores of gods, the 84 Sidhs, the 9 Náths, the 64 Jognís, the 52 Víras (Bírs), the 6 Jatis—or, among the Jains, 7 Trumpp's *Translation of the Adi-Granth*, Introd., p. xlix

Besides sneezing other bodily affections are ominous. Thus a movement of the right eyelid or a singing in the right ear means joy; of the left, grief[2] : a movement of the flesh in the right upper arm or shoulder means that you will soon embrace a friend, but one in the left portends a debilitating sickness. A tingling in the right palm means a gain of 2 or 3 rupees at least : in the left it means money to be paid away. In the sole of either foot tingling denotes a journey or that you will put your feet in the mud—a serious calamity.[3] Shaking one's leg while sitting on a chair or couch means loss of money.[4] Yawning is very unlucky and to avert evil Muhammadans say *lá hauld wa lá quwata illá billáh*.[5] Biting one's tongue means that some one is telling tales against one.[6]

Twitching (*sank*) of the right eye is a lucky omen in Kángra, and the general science of its omens is summed up in the lines :—

> 'If the lower left lip twitch, know there will be a blot on the happiness.
> If the upper lid twitch, say all will be delight and pleasure.
> If the outer lids, it will be wealth and gain : but if the inner, loss.
> For the right it will be the reverse.'[7]

Omens.—A large number of omens are naturally connected with the horse, probably because he is both a valuable animal and used to be the representative or vehicle of the Sun-god. His actions, colour and form therefore are all full of significance. If you go to buy a horse and he shakes his head it is a warning to you against purchasing him, but the reverse if he paws the ground in welcome.[8] The normal points of a horse are not regarded, or rather his 'points' consist in the numerous marks and signs on him which are auspicious or the reverse. The classical work on this science is the *Farasnáma-i-Rangín* or treatise by

[1] P. N. Q., I., § 127.

[2] According to another account twitching of the right *upper* eyelid *in a man* portends good, but in the *lower* it is just the opposite, and in a woman twitching of the left eyelid is a sure source of joy : P. N. Q., I, § 927.

[3] *Ib.*, § 849.

[4] *Ib.*, III, § 27.

[5] *Ib.*, III. § 683.

[6] *Ib.*, III, § 781.

[7] *Ib.*, III, § 111.

[8] *Ib.*, I, § 458.

Unlucky horses.

Rangín (Sa'ádat Yár Khan) who regards the horse as one of a captive yet god-like race.[1] The matter is of grave practical importance as it seriously affects the selling value of a horse Thus in Baháwalpur the following horses are unlucky:—

(*a*) A horse or mare, with a white spot, small enough to be covered by the thumb, on the forehead Such a horse is called *tára-peshóni*, or starred on the forehead.

(*b*) A horse or mare with three feet of one colour and the fourth of another. A white blaze on the forehead, however, counteracts this evil sign. Such an animal is called *arjal*.

(*c*) A horse with a black palate (*Siáh kám asp* in Persian).

(*d*) A horse with both hind feet and the off forefoot white. But a white *near* forefoot is a good omen, as in the Persian couplet:—

Do páish sufed-o-yake dast-i-chap,
Buwad láiq-i-sháh-i-áli nasab.
"A horse with two white (hind) feet and a white near forefoot is worthy to be ridden by a king"

(*e*) A horse or mare which is wall-eyed (*mánki*) or which has an eye like that of a human being, is called *táki* and is ill-starred.[2]

[1] Translated by Lt.-Col. D. C. Phillott, Quaritch, 1912. After describing the horse Rangín proceeds to enumerate the five grand defects of the horse. First and worst of these, transcending spavin, exceeding malformation, and even ill manners (which last are looked upon by Rangín as inherent) are placed 'The Feathers.' 'The Feathers' are those whorls where the different currents of hair meet, to them the first section of the book is given, and the pre-eminence is one of which they are certainly worthy considering that their influences are momentous, predestined, and to a large extent sinister. It is a science akin, in its minuteness and intricacy, to palmistry; it is also exact as becomes a table of laws from which there is no appeal. If there be only one feather in the centre of the forehead it is not to be regarded as an ill-mark; but if there be two on the forehead avoid that horse and do not dream of buying it. If there be 3, 4 or 5 feathers on the forehead Persians will not even look at the horse; others call it a ram, saying 'it will butt you to misfortune.' The battle of the good and evil feathers continues from head to tail. A feather low down on the forearm, if it points downward, is called 'Driver-in-of the Peg' and is lucky, but if it points upward is called 'Up-rooter-of-the-Peg' and is baleful. A feather under the girth is lucky and is called 'width of the Ganges.' A feather under the saddle is unlucky: "Buy not a horse with such a feather. Do not even keep him in your village" (Strange that in Ireland also there are turns of the hair that are accounted fortunate, both in horses and in cattle). The colours are doomful and precise in their augury as the feathers themselves:—"If there are in the blaze hairs the colour of the rest of the body, shun the horse; experts call that horse a scorpion. A white spot on the forehead, sufficiently small to be concealed by the tip of the thumb, is called a star. This mark is sinister and ill omened unless there is also some white on the legs. If a horse has either the near or off hind white, it is defective and is called *arjal*. If the seller says to you, 'Oh but there is white on the forehead too,' do not give ear to his specious words, for the Prophet has said that an *arjal* is bad: what else then is there to be said?" The best colour for a horse is bay, the second *khákí* dun, the third a dun with a black mane and tail, called *samand*. This last would, with the addition of a black strip down the back, be identical with an Irish 'shan buie' and of an Irish 'shan buie' it has been said (in illustration of his adroitness and agility) that he 'would tend a slater.' We are with Rangín in his high estimation of the *samand*. Low on the list comes the grey; many on this side of the world would give him (and preferably her) a higher place, and it is not long since that an Irish dealer of exhaustive experience averred that his fancy was for greys and that he had seldom had a bad grey horse and never a bad grey mare:. *Times Literary Supplement*, 1912, p. 71.

[2] *Baháwalpur Gazetteer*, p. 184.

But the *panch-kalián* or horse with 5 white blazes, one on the forehead and one on each foot, is apparently lucky, and the hero's horse is often named Panchkaliáni or-a in folk-tales.

So too when buying a buffalo, cow or bullock it is a good sign if it defecate, but do not buy if it urinate. If a buffalo lows (*ríngdi*) it is a good omen, but the reverse if a by-stander sneezes [1]

If an owl hoot thrice on a man's house he must quit it for 3, 7 or 11 days, placing thorns at its door and feasting Brahmans, sacrificing a goat and offering a broken cocoanut before he re-enters it.[2]

A kite settling on the roof of a house is unlucky.[3]

Dogs are peculiarly gifted for they can see evil spirits moving about and so their howling is a portent of evil. If out hunting a dog rolls on its back game will be plentiful, but if it lies quietly on its back in the house it is praying for help and some calamity is imminent.[4] When out shooting it is very lucky to meet a *garúr*, a name applied in the Punjab to a small king-fisher with bright blue plumage, which is let out of its cage at the Dasehra as a sacred bird.[5] A cat or a crow throwing water over itself denotes a coming guest.[6]

The perils of travel have led to the development of something like a science of augury in regard to it. Before starting on an important journey a Hindu will consult a Brahman as to what day will be propitious and if he cannot start on that day he will send on a *paitra*, a small bundle of necessaries, to some place near the gate by which he intends going, and start himself within the next two days.[7]

When starting on a journey if a Brahman or Dúmna is met, or any one carrying an empty pot (*ghaṛa*) or basket (*kilṭa*), the omen is unfavourable, and the traveller turns back. If a child is met or a person carrying full *ghaṛa* the omen is favourable. For a journey or any work of importance a Brahman is consulted to ascertain the *sat* or lucky moment, and if the person is unable to start on the day and at the time fixed, his walking stick or bundle is put outside the door, and this is looked upon as equivalent to his departure.

After seeing a bier or touching a scavenger good Hindus will bathe, and the scavenger must also wash his clothes himself.[8]

If when setting out on any purpose you meet a person carrying an empty *ghara* it is an ill omen, but good if the water-pot is behind you. So too it is unpropitious to meet a person carrying wood, but the reverse if he comes behind you.[9] It is unlucky to meet a widow but a good omen to meet a woman with a male child.[10]

In Dera Gházi Khán it is lucky to meet a man at starting, but a

1 P. N. Q., II, § 490.
2 *Ib.*, III, § 113.
3 *Ib.*, II, § 179.
4 *Ib.*, I, § 703.
5 *Ib.*, I, § 864.
6 *Ib.*, I, § 854.
Ib., I, § 1016.
7 *Ib.*, IV, § 41.
8 *Ib.*, I, § 610.
9 *Ib.* I, § 855.

woman forebodes failure in your purpose. So too it is unlucky to encounter a shrike[1] on the left hand, and Baloch calls this *chhapi* or 'sinister', turning back to make a fresh start. But to meet one on the right is propitious. The neighing of a horse or the braying of a he-ass is a favourable omen. In this district auguries are also taken by kicking one's shoe into the air while walking If it falls on its sole it is a good, but if it turns over, a bad sign.[2]

In Dera Ismáíl Khán the Muhammadan Jáṭs and Baloch have the following omens :—

To meet a woman when starting on a journey is a bad omen. For any one to recall a man as he starts is also a bad omen. *Shikáris* consider it unlucky to meet a jackal when they start. If a man who is ill and is setting out to obtain treatment, meets a snake it is a bad omen if he fails to kill it but a good one if he succeeds in doing so If a she-jackal (*pavi*) call behind the house of a sick man he is certain to die—

Ráthi bulde kukr	"By night if the cock,
Te dehen bulde shighar[3]	By day the jackal calls
Ekki badli Sáhibi[4]	A king changes
Te ekki ponda kál	Famine befalls"

If a sick man hears a stallion neigh at night it portends his recovery. A smut or dirt in the left eye is ill, in the right, good luck.

It is unlucky to drink water before starting, but auspicious to eat sugar in any form.

But in spite, it would seem, of all omens, prosperity in travel may be secured by saying :—

Sítá Raghúpat Rám ke tamak bándhlo háth,
Áge áge Har chale, píchhe Har ká sáth

'Join hands in praise of Sítá and Rám
And God will precede you, and you will follow God.'[5]

To see a partridge on one's right is lucky provided that one is going to a field, to meet a friend or homewards: *Khet, mít, ghar ahane*; but *bánwan banij beopár, i.e.* it is better to meet it on the left when one is going on business. On a journey homewards again or to meet a friend it is auspicious to meet a *Bhangan* or any woman of very low caste, or one with two *gharas* on her head.[6] But it is always unlucky to meet a load of wood or a Brahman, and if one meets the latter one should try and pass to the left, letting him pass on the right.[7]

To meet a Chúhṛa is lucky, the more so if he has a basket or broom in hand.[8]

[1] In Jaṭki speech *malháa*, in Balochi *gyánokh*: P. N. Q., I, § 1019.
[2] *Ib.*, § 1020.
[3] *Shighar* is the male jackal.
[4] *Sáhibi*—" ruler."
[5] P. N. Q., II, § 670.
[6] This omen may be connected with the superstition referred to in the account of Gúga.
[7] P. N. Q., II, § 150.
[8] *Ib.*, II, § 849.

Never proceed on a journey begun if you are called back at starting. So strongly is this believed to be unlucky that relations will send things accidentally left after a traveller rather than call him back.[1]

If when going anywhere with an object you meet a jackal it is a good omen, but two are better: provided the animal does not cross your path—when your object will be frustrated.[2]

To hear a jackal barking is, in Dera Gházi Khán, most unlucky. It is known as *bhúnkári*[3] In Rohtak it is lucky to hear a jackal howling on the left, but not on the right,[4] and the jackal should not be spoken of by his proper name as *gídar*, but as Jambu.[5]

In Baháwalpur to hear a donkey bray behind when one is starting on a journey, or a partridge call on the left is an omen that the journey will fail in its object. But a partridge calling on the right is lucky. Also it is fortunate to meet a sweeper carrying filth, or a coffin, when setting out on business It is a good omen to see the bird, called *malháła*, on the right hand early in the day and later on the left, and *vice versá*. If a thief, when going to steal, hear a pheasant on the left he considers it a bad omen and returns. If a *maina* or a *láli* be heard warbling on the roof, the women reply, *áṭá píhá piá he, ja mimhán kon lið.* "The flour is ready ground, go, fetch the guest," *i.e.* a guest is expected. The bird's note is supposed to be *pího pího*, the imperative of *píhná* (*písna*), to grind. If a man sneezes when starting on a journey, the journey will be unsuccessful. Similarly it is a bad omen for a marriage procession to hear the roar of thunder or meet with a gale of wind on their way to the bride's house. Any additions to a house are made by the Hindus in front of, or in line with, the buildings that exist, not in their rear. A new building at the back of the house is calculated to bring some calamity on the owner's head. A crow on the coping of the house-wall denotes that a relation is coming on a visit, or at least that news from one will soon arrive. On the other hand, if a woman gets hurt she will put it down to having heard a crow cawing on the coping. A kite sitting on the house is unlucky, so a black *hándi* or scare-crow is usually hung on the loftiest part of the roof. Omens.

In Kángra it is also lucky to meet a married woman, a pot full of water, a corpse in a *doli*, flesh, fish, a cow with calf, a mongoose, ox, the sound of music, a wild parrot perching on your body, a blue jay, a peacock, a *kirla* (lizard) or a *chipkali* (white lizard). But it is unlucky to meet an ass, a bull-buffalo, a sweeper with refuse, any one carrying salt or earth, a potter, a Brahman bare-headed or one who does not return your greeting, a widow, an empty pot, a blind or wall-eyed man, a *bairági* or a *faqír* smeared with ashes, an oil-crusher (? a Teli) with his pot, a crow, a jackal or a cat

[1] P. N. Q., IV. § 270

[2] *Ib.*, § 608.

[3] *Ib.*, § 1019.

[4] *Ib.*, § 150.

[5] *Ib.*, § 151.

[6] P. N Q. III, §§ 109, 110. In Attock it is unlucky to meet any man with a bare head, any Brahman or a *mullah*, any one weeping or smoking, or fire, a crow flying towards one, a widow, any one carrying a broken pot, a gardener with an empty basket, a cat, a goat, a cow, or any black animal, a snake or an empty vessel if carried. To hear the sound of weeping or a person sneeze while on a journey is most unfortunate, and the latter omen will almost always occasion a delay at any rate: *Gazetteer*, p. 107.

Eat curds, and go where you please, but do not eat pickle or anything sour when going to visit an official, or you will either fail to see him or not gain your purpose. Success on a journey to pay such a visit or for any important business may be assured by observing the simple rules:—

Jo sur châle, wohi pag dîje,
Pothî patra kabhî na lîje,

i.e. if you find that your right nostril breathes more quickly than your left start with you right foot, and *vice versâ*: 'never mind books and almanacs.' Should you chance to see a noseless man or a barren woman do not let them cross you or you will fail in your undertakings.[1]

The study of omens from crows alone is almost a science:—

"When going on a journey if a crow caw to the left,
Know for certain that you will prosper.
If (a crow) on a journey go before you cawing;
I tell you the crow is saying that you will get a wife.
If a crow caw to the right and go cawing to the left,
I tell you it is telling you that you will lose your wealth.
If it caw first to the left and go cawing to the right,
The crow is bringing you wealth and honour above all.
If a crow caw to the left and go upward,
Your journey is stayed, and you should stop at home.
If a crow caw to the left and turn its back upon you,
It is bringing grief and trouble upon you.
If a crow stand on one leg with its back to the sun
And preen its wings, some great man will die.
If, when you are eating in the field, a crow caw,
You will obtain riches out of the earth.
If a crow flutter both its wings on high,
Though you try a thousand plans you will suffer loss.
If a cawing crow sit on the back of a buffalo,
You will surely be successful in your labours.
If a crow pick up a bone from the ground and throw it into water,
Know that in a few days you will be beneath the sod.
If a crow lower its head towards the north,
It is bringing on a disturbance and lightning.
If crow lower its head to the north and preen its wings,
It is exiling you from your country.
If a crow keep on cawing, I tell you what will happen:
He is calling a guest from a foreign land.
If on a journey a crow caw with a piece of meat in its mouth,
Trouble is over, and you will enjoy the fruit of happiness."

[1] P. N. Q., II, § 815. [2] P. N. Q., II, § 801. These verses are attributed to one Jai Singh

Crows always pray for more children in the world as they get sweets from them.[1]

In Kángṛa it is lucky to meet a Brahman telling his beads or saluting you with his *tilak* (sectarial mark) on.[2]

'If you meet one Sudra, and as many Bánias, three Brahmans, and four Chhattris—nine women coming in front—don't go on: I give you this omen.'[3]

If on the road you meet milk and fish, two Brahmans with books, 'tis a good omen and all wishes will be granted you.[4]

Quarrels are caused by mixing fire from two houses, standing a broom in a corner or allowing a child to turn over a dirty ladle,[5] or by clattering scissors.[6]

The loan of a comb or kerchief causes enmity.[7]

If while kneading flour a bit of the dough gets loose, a guest is coming.[8]

If unleavened bread rise while being baked on an iron plate it means that the person for whom it is being made is hungry.[9]

Finding gold is unlucky at any time, and metal found on a Saturday, when it is unlucky to find anything, is given to a Ḍakaut or Mahá-Brahman. No real Brahman takes alms on that day.[10]

Put the fingers of both hands to your forehead and look down to where the wrists join the hands: if they appear to slip from the wrists your death is near.[11]

It is lucky to have one's crop trodden down by a superior, as it will yield the more.[12]

If, when one is thinking of a person or wishes to see him, he turns up it forebodes long life to him.[13]

A change of garment will change one's luck, and it is sufficient to change the right shoe to the left foot and *vice versâ*, to secure good sport.[14]

[1] P. N. Q., III, § 451.

[2] *Ib.*, III, § 109: The omens in this district are very numerous, *cf. ib.* §§ 110, 111, 112, 113, 114.

[3] N. I. N. Q., I, § 238.

[4] *Ib.*, § 239.

[5] P. N. Q., II, § 1089.

[6] *Ib.*, II, § 798.

[7] *Ib.*, III, § 682.

[8] *Ib.*, III, § 779.

[9] *Ib.*, III, § 29.

[10] *Ib.*, IV, § 493.

[11] *Ib.*, IV, § 34.

[12] *Ib.*, II, § 740.

[13] *Ib.*, III, § 504.

[14] *Ib.*, I, § 15.

Tabus.—Eating the leavings of another's food causes 100 generations to burn, and is nearly as bad as back-biting which condemns countless generations to the flames.[1]

Muhammadans object to beating a brass tray as the dead might be awakened, thinking the Last Day had arrived.[2]

Some Hindus will not wear a white turban as long as their father is alive.[3]

Red food is said to be avoided by Hindu Bánias as it resembles flesh; P. N. Q., IV, § 193.

It is sometimes said that Hindus consider it unlawful to eat food cooked by an unmarried person.[4]

However, this may be some *tabus* are clearly based upon delicacy of feeling. Such is the prohibition which, regarding it as a great sin to accept any help from a daughter or to make any use of her property, *tabus* even a drink of water from her well or a rest under the shade of the tree among high-caste Hindus. Brahmans will often not even drink water in a son-in-law's village. And among high class Khatri families such as the Seṭh, Khanna, Kapúr and Mihrotra sections of Ḍháighar status a mother will not even use her daughter's fan.[5] Among Brahmans and Khatris a daughter invariably receives a present at a festival. An elder brother too going to visit a married sister will not accept food or water from her. If he does not take them with him he must pay for them, in addition to the usual gift which he is bound to make to her.[6]

Among the Rájpúts in Karnál the village into which a girl is married is utterly *tabu'd* to her father, elder brother and all near elder relatives, and even the more distant elder relatives will not eat or drink from her husband's house, though they do not *tabu* the whole village. The boy's father in turn can only go to the girl's village by her father's leave.[7]

The *tabu* on new vessels of metal among Hindus may be removed by letting a horse eat out of them. Some orthodox Hindus will also, after this, rub them with ashes to purify them from the touch of their low-caste makers.[8] The horse is here probably symbolical of the Sun-god.

Among Brahmans and other high-caste Hindus no food that has been in the house during an eclipse of the sun or moon can be eaten and it must be given away. But to avoid this necessity *halwáis* keep some *kusa* or *dúb* grass, *cynodon dactylon*, in the baskets of sweet stuff during an eclipse.[9]

A widespread *tabu* is that placed upon buildings of burnt brick or stone.[10]

1 N. I. N. Q., I, § 242.
2 *Ib.*, I., § 114.
3 *Ib.* I, § 519.
4 P. N. Q., I, § 670.
5 *Ib.*, I, § 1002.
6 N. I. N. Q., I, § 25.
7 Karnál *Sett. Rep.*, p. 184.
8 P. N. Q., II, § 887.
9 *Ib.*, I, § 705.
10 *Ib.*, I, § 755.

In the plains milk should not be churned on a Thursday by either Hindus or Muhammadans as that day is held sacred to the Muhammadan saints. Part of that day's milk is used, and the rest given away to mendicants.[1]

The *Gazetteer* of the Simla Hill States thus describes the *tabu* on the use of milk which is found among the Kanets:—'Amongst Kanets the belief is universal that if a man drinks the milk of his own cow or gives it to others to drink he will incur the displeasure of his *deota* in a practical form.[1] But no evil consequences attach to the making and selling or eating of *ghí* from this milk. As a consequence of this idea those who arrange for supplies to visitors have to get milk from Kolis as it is said that although the milk of a Koli's cow may not be drunk by the owner himself, it may be safely given to other people. Sceptics say that Kanets have often been compelled to furnish milk for distinguished visitors when Kolis' milk was not available, and that no evil has resulted. They call the story of the god's wrath a convenient fiction designed to ensure owners of cattle the full benefit of the profitable industry of *ghi* making and to protect them from exaction.'

Following up this clue Mr. H. W. Emerson has elicited the following data regarding this interesting and important *tabu*:—

"Now the custom is so widespread and presents such interesting features that a fuller account of it may free the hill-folk from the aspersions cast upon their sense of hospitality. In the first place the belief is far from universal amongst Kanets. The restriction in fact depends upon the dispensations and dispositions of various gods. Some there are who insist on their full rights and forbid the use of milk in any other form than *ghí*. Others content themselves with a formal recognition of their prerogative, whilst not a few allow their worshippers both to drink themselves and give to others.

As an instance of the autocratic despot we may cite the case of Dúm, a god who exercises sway around Nárkanda. He will not permit his devotees to deal in any way with pure milk or curds and even the *ghí* must be properly clarified. Cases have occurred in which a new-born child whose mother has died in childbirth has had to wait hungry until a milch cow could be brought from Kulu or some other district where the local god imposed no veto. For it is an old feature of the superstition that prohibition or freedom to use the milk are dependent on the origin and lineage of the animal that gives it. A cow imported from the jurisdiction of an alien deity remains subject to the rules and regulations of its ancestral god. Neither she nor her offspring can acquire the liberties or incur the disabilities as the case may be, of naturalised subjects of the new divinity. The principle is indeed applied to objects other than the sacred cow, for if the offerings made to certain deities pass from their spheres of influence the gods go with them and thus often gain a footing in villages which have neither known them in the past nor want them in the future. "The god holds what the god has

[1] I. N. Q., IV, § 351. Very different ideas prevail elsewhere. Thus the Brahúí and Baloch nomads of Peshín will give milk in exchange for other commodities, but deem it a disgrace to make money by it, and among the Badami in Arabia *labbán* or 'milk-seller' is a term of disgrace: Burton's *Al-Madina*, I, p. 246.

held" is the motto of celestial beings in the hills. Dúm, like the majority of interdicting deities, is a fearsome deity of whom the peasants stand in awe. Originally he was a human being, born to a childless peasant by the mercy of the goddess Devi, but on his death his spirit showed a strange perversity. It would not rest in peace, but liked to vex the people. So in despair they defied it and popt him fairly quiet He still retains however some traces of his ghostly devilry and if his worshippers transgress his orders, calamity will surely fall upon them. The udders of their cows dry up, the crops are blighted, and their children die, until at length they expiate their sin by generous sacrifices.

Passing to the next type of supernatural beings who play the rôle of benevolent monarchs we find that such are satisfied with a mere acknowledgment of their supposititious rights. They exact only the performance of the following ceremonies from their worshippers. When a calf is born the mother is not milked until the fourth day after birth. The milk is then placed in a vessel and left to curdle. When firmly set it forms part of a sacrifice offered to the animal's ancestral god. *Ghí*, curds and milk are poured upon the idol's head; incense, flowers and sweetened bread are laid before it. The owner offers up a prayer that the cow and calf may prosper and asks the god's permission to use the produce of the former. The bread is eaten by the suppliant and after he has sacrificed a goat he may assume that the deity has vouchsafed the liberty to use the *ghí* and milk as he deems fit. Since the cattle are mostly of local breed the rites are usually performed within the village temple. But this is not invariably the case, for where the cow or her progenitors have been imported a pile of stones is built to represent her family god. There the goat is slaughtered and the votive offerings paid. Sometimes when the local temple is at a distance the offerings are poured over the horns of the cow itself, and this is always done if, though the animal is known to be of alien stock, all record of its god has been forgotten.

The third class of democratic deities who impose no terms upon their clients are not uncommon, but they can grant no privileges for beasts other than their hereditary property. For example milk from the progeny of any cow, once owned by a worshipper of Dúm, has the same pains and penalties attaching to its use as though it lived within his jurisdiction. And this is so although its present owner lives far outside the limits of Dúm's sway and the original stock was imported several generations back.

With reference to the Kolis the issues are obscured to some extent by the fact that a number of the caste cannot afford the luxury of either milk or *ghí*. Also in the olden days it was the policy of the rulers to depress their menials and if the noise of churning was heard within the Koli's house, he was assuredly fined. This much seems certain that the superstition is not so general among Kolis as it is amongst Kanets. Where it applies the cause can usually be attributed to the worship of some deity adopted from the pantheon of the superior caste. Where both castes worship the same god, the nature of the veto is the same for both. Sometimes in a village the Kolis are under the disability whilst the Kanets are free; more often the reverse is found to be the case. The custom does not appear to be aboriginal; the Kolis have learnt it from the Kanets and not the Kanets from the Kolis."

Dr. J. Hutchison has found that similar customs prevail as far north as the Tibetan border, but are said not to exist in Ladákh or Eastern Tibet. He writes :—

In the Rávi Valley the procedure is somewhat as follows :—After calving the calf is allowed to drink all the milk for three days. This seems to be the period most generally allowed. After the third day a certain quantity of milk—usually one half—is put aside for the calf and the rest is put into a vessel called *dudhár* after each milking. When the vessel is full the milk is churned and butter is made which is also stored and when enough has been accumulated it is made into *ghí*. The milk is not drunk by the family and is said to be *suchcha*—that is forbidden. This period may last from a few days to three, six or even more months if the cow goes on giving milk according to the will of the owner. During this time butter is made at regular intervals and then converted into *ghí*, which is stored for the merchants who come round to purchase it, but none of it is used by the family until certain ceremonies have been performed. The impression is general that the procedure is observed purely for financial reasons, there being a brisk trade in *ghí* all through the Rávi Valley. Caste seems to make no difference and the custom prevails among high and low, rich and poor. When the period which may range from the 9th day to the 9th month has expired, the owner of the cow makes an offering to the local *deota* Nág or Deví, under whose special protection the cow is considered to be and who is called *jakh*, after which the milk ceases to be *suchcha* and may be used by the family. Nowhere did I hear of any instance in which the owner was entirely debarred from using the milk of his own cow, except during the period I have indicated. The offering made to the *jakh* consists of curds, milk, butter and *ghí*, which are generally rubbed on the face of the image. Incense is also burnt and sweet bread is also presented and if it is a first calf a goat is sacrificed.

The custom is almost certainly of aboriginal origin and has come down from a time long anterior to the appearance of the Rájás on the scene. I am inclined to agree with what seems to be the general belief among the people around us that the custom is practised for profit only. One need not call it mercenary, for it is simply in keeping with the ordinary trade practices in these hills.

The above description applies chiefly to the Rávi Valley and the outer mountains. In the Chandra Bhága Valley, especially in Pádar, Pángi and Láhul the milk is kept *suchcha* after calving only for 9 to 12 days. Then an offering is made to the Nau grah and local deity in much the same way as in Chamba, except that instead of a live goat the imitation of one in *áṭa* is offered presumably to save expense. The milk is then freely used.

There is, however, another interesting custom which seems to be peculiar to those regions. In Pádar for the whole month of Sáwan, and in Pángi for 15 days in that month, all the milk of the valley is regarded as *suchcha* or devoted to the local Nág or Deví. The cows are milked as usual and the milk accumulates in the special receptacle called [illegible].

It is churned at intervals and the butter so procured is made into *ghí* which is stored up, while the buttermilk is drunk at special gatherings. On special days also some of the curds, milk and *ghí* are offered to the Nág. All this is done when the cattle are up in the *puháli* or high mountain pastures. At the end of the period special offerings are made and a sheep is sacrificed for the whole village and then the milk becomes common again. On such occasions it is hard for travellers to procure milk as the people are very unwilling to give it. This custom does not prevail in Láhul. The object probably is to lay in a yearly supply of *ghí* at the time of year which is most convenient to themselves and where the pasture is at its richest and the milk consequently most abundant and of good quality. In Láhul the cattle remain in the village all the year round and are not sent to a *puháli* or mountain pasture. The *ghí* made in the Chandra Bhága valley is for domestic use only.

Omens.—To return to the topic of omens, it is even less easy to explain many of them than it is to account for *tabus*. Thus in Attock meeting water when starting on a journey is lucky, because water is much prized, and sweepers may be good omens as they are humble, honest and useful. But if Brahmans and *mulláhs* are seldom met without their asking for alms it might be supposed that their blessing would outweigh the loss of the money bestowed on them.[1]

Good and bad omens are much regarded in Chamba. If a *chakor* (Greek partridge) cackles on the roof, it forebodes death to one of the family. An owl or kite settling on the roof, or on a tree close by, portends calamity. Bad omens also affect cattle. If a cow lies down while being milked, or blood comes from her teats the animal must be sent away. A poisonous snake entering a house portends good, and the Nág is regarded as specially auspicious. If killed in the house a snake must be removed by the window and not by the door, or one of the family will die. If a cock crow in the evening it should be killed at once lest it should crow thrice, portending death to some one in the family. Twin calves are unlucky. A white spot on a horse's forehead is called *tára* and is unlucky to its purchaser. Hair growing the wrong way on a horse's neck is a bad omen called *putha bál*, as is also a tuft of hair anywhere on the animal. White hair near the hoofs or on the forehead, called *panjkalyáni*, is considered auspicious.[2]

On maize 4 or 5 cobs on one stalk are a bad omen. If a snake crawls past a heap of grain it must be given away. An injury to any one at the burning *ghát* is ominous, and an offering must be made to avert calamity. An adult sneezing at the commencement of any work or when starting on a journey is ominous, but good in the case of a young girl. The sight of a centipede means that some one is speaking evil of the person who sees it. A sudden tremor of one part of the body points to impending disease, and the side is touched with a shoe to avert it. Itching in the right palm indicates coming wealth, and in the sole of the foot that a journey is near. Singing in the right ear means pleasant news in prospect, but bad news if it is in the left. If hiccup is slight some relative is thinking of you: if troublesome, some one is abusing you. If the eyelid quivers grief is near. A spider on the body means good clothing or a friend in prospect.

[1] Attock *Gazetteer*, p. 107.

[2] See p. 225 *supra*.

Dreams.—If a person dreams in the early morning the dream will come true. If in a dream a dead relative appears and mentions a date on which the person dreaming will die, some measures are taken to defeat this evil influence. A *chela* is called on the date mentioned, who dances, and he and the friends try in many ways to divert the man's attention till the critical time is past. The omen is inauspicious if in a dream copper or iron is given to the person dreaming. A dog coming towards the person to bite him is also ominous, and is called *grah*. An elephant in a dream means that Ganesh is angry and must be appeased. If a little child appears saying pleasant things Káli is benignant, but if something unpleasant is said Káli needs to be appeased. If a boy appears Mahádev is signified. A snake coming towards the dreamer to bite him is a bad omen. If some one is seen to leave the house the person dreaming will die, but if a living relative is seen dying he or she will recover. Crossing a stream in a dream points to some coming difficulty.

A dream should never be mentioned to any one as it is most unlucky to do so, but to dream during the afternoon or at noon is harmless however bad the dream may be.[1]

Dreams naturally are often ominous, for good or evil. To see one's self riding on a male camel, ass or buffalo means death, which is imminent if one sees one's self climbing a tree to gather fruit—probably because the ashes of a burnt corpse are hung on a tree. To see raw meat portends sickness, and to be falling from a hill or rock calamity as well. To swim in clear water and gain the shore predicts recovery from a long illness. To see smoke, rain, mud or dirty water or to laugh in one's sleep means grief. To dance and sing means calamity as well. To see ashes, bones or cowries portends grief and loss. To be attacked by a snake or scorpion on the left side means loss, and to see the bed of a dried-up pond or river, loss of salary. To climb to a hill-top means profit, and to see one's self or another eating meat or curds or to be attacked by a snake or scorpion on the right side, wealth. To ride on an elephant or a white horse means promotion and to be in prison is to be soon a ruler, while to see one's head cut off - or the sun or moon rising is to be soon a king. A naked sword or a road portends an unexpected journey. The happiness of one's ancestors is assured by the vision of a *faqír* or *sádhu*.[2] A dream during the latter part of the night is however auspicious as it is then that the gods are roaming and you are sure of gain.[3] Dreams may be cured by reciting a common invocation to Hanúmán.

Shoes lying over each other are a sign of travel and if you see a broom upside down put it right way up or you will suffer somehow. It is lucky to find silver but not gold, and on a journey it is lucky to meet a sweeper, a snake or a corpse, but the reverse if one meets a Brahman, a village headman or a washerman.[4]

Divination, Possession, Exorcism and Charms—Such being the varied choice in the matter of malevolent spirits offered to Ibbetson, § 228.

[1] P. N. Q., III, §§ 680-1.
[2] *Ib.*, I., § 769.
[3] *Ib.*, I., § 780.
[4] *Ib.*, I., §§ 789-90.

the Punjab peasant by the belief of the countryside, it may be supposed that divination and exorcism are practised widely, and possession and the virtue of charms firmly believed in. Of witchcraft proper one hears but little, and it is, I believe, chiefly confined to the lowest castes; though some wizards are commonly credited with the power of causing a woman to die if they can obtain a lock of her hair, and then bringing her to life again for their carnal enjoyment.[1] Illness is generally attributed to the malignant influence of a deity, or to possession by a spirit; and recourse is had to the soothsayer to decide who is to be appeased, and in what manner. The diviners are called 'devotees' (*bhagat*)[2] or 'wise men' (*syána*), and they generally work under the inspiration of a snake-god, though sometimes under that of a Saiyad (see above). The power of divination is generally confined to the lower and menial (? aboriginal) castes, is often hereditary, and is rarely possessed by women. Inspiration is shown by the man's head beginning to wag; and he then builds a shrine to his familiar, before which he dances, or, as it is called by the people, 'sports' (*khelná, khel kúdna*). He is consulted at night, the inquirer providing tobacco and music. The former is waved over the body of the invalid and given to the wise man to smoke. A butter-lamp is lighted, the music plays, the diviner sometimes lashes himself with a whip, and he is at last seized by the afflatus, and in a paroxysm of dancing and head-wagging declares the name of the malignant influence, the manner in which it is to be propitiated, and the time when the disease may be expected to abate. Or the diviner waves wheat over the patient's body, by preference on Saturday or Sunday: he then counts out the grains one by one into heaps, one heap for each god who is likely to be at the bottom of the mischief, and the deity on whose heap the last grain falls is the one to be propitiated. The malignant spirit is appeased by building him a new shrine, or by making offerings at the old one. Very often the offering is first placed by the patient's head for a night or waved over his body, or he is made to eat a part of it; and it is sometimes exposed on a moonlight night while the moon is still on the wax, together with a lighted lamp, at a place where four cross-roads meet. Sometimes it is enough to tie a rag taken from the patient's body on to the sacred tree—generally a *jaṇḍ* (*prosopis spicigera*)—beneath which the shrine stands, and such trees may often be seen covered with the remnants of those offerings, blue being the predominating colour if the shrine be Musalmán, and red if it be Hindu.

The Jáṭs and Baloch of Dera Ismáíl Khán and Miánwáli are firm believers in magic:—

A useful charm is to get 4 men to write out at the same time but at separate places, the Muhammadán creed. The whole is worn as an amulet. It is said to be of general efficacy, and to safeguard the wearer from hurt, though Husain Khán, Baloch, who told me, got a sword-cut all the same from a Wazír near Pezu in Edwardes' time. Passing a hut in Multán an old woman came out and cried *Áhi all*

[1] In the hills, however, magic is said to be common; and in the plains certain men can charm the livers out of children, and so cause them to pine away and die. Englishmen are often credited with this power.

[2] The term Bhagat, I believe, properly applies only to the devotees of the goddess Deví. But it is locally used by the villagers for any wise man or diviner.

ádmí! níl ádmí! "Oh blue man, blue man—what shall I give my child for the cough?" I did not know the answer and foolishly promised some medicine. She told me I ought to have bid her steal something from a neighbour's field or house, as that would have cured the cough There are many other spells of this class but people will not own to any knowledge of them.

Earth taken from a sweeper's grave or from a Hindu burning place, moulded into the shape of an enemy and the *Surat Yasín* read over it, is supposed to be fatal to him. To call up the devil himself it is only necessary to repeat the creed backwards. Within the memory of several men whom I know a Sayyid from Multán who could control the *jinns* appeared at Leia and Bhakkar in Miánwáli. He produced cooked food from the air, pomegranates out of season, pots of *ghí* and at the instigation of a Leia money-lender, rupees. It is admitted that a man who possesses a full knowledge of the great names (*ism*) of the Deity, who knows how to combine them and the demons affected by each, can render them obedient to himself or to the ring on his little finger. But only the learned and scrupulously pure can attain to this knowledge. Certain of the *isms* repeated before going into court or before a *hákim* are certain to gain favour for the sayer. Black magic.

Amulets are much used. A headman to prevent the anger of a justly incensed *hákim* from falling on him sat with an amulet tied conspicuously on his *sáfa*. He admitted the reason when asked. Amulets.

Whereas possession by the god is, as a rule, invoked, possession by evil spirits is dreaded, and various remedies resorted to for their expulsion. Such spirits are known by various names, but Bhairon and Kális are also believed to cause demoniacal possession. When a man becomes thus possessed, the *pandit* ascertains by astrology whether the possession is really due to evil spirits, and if this appears certain, he takes the man to the abode of the god. The people assemble and invoke the god with incessant cries, the *pujári* remaining still and silent for a time. Soon he begins to tremble and nod his head. He then asks the god to cure the sufferer. Casting rice at the people he curses them until in terror they offer to propitiate the god with sacrifices of goats etc., whereupon he advises that sacrifice be made. He then offers rice to the god and says that the evil spirit will depart. *Dhúp* is not offered, nor is music played, and as a rule, no *mantrás* are read, but in rare cases Káli is thus invoked:— Demoniacal possession.

Káli chari char chari kát kát,
Dehi ko khái,
Páni bahi samundar ká, bhút,
Churel bhasam ho jái.

"Káli has arisen and devours the sacrifice. Let the ocean flow, let ghost and demon turn into ashes."

Fasts and Festivals.—Religious festivals play a great part in the life of the peasant; indeed they form his chief holidays, and on these occasions men, and still more women and children, don their best Ibbetson, § 235.

clothes and collect in great numbers, and after the offering has been made enjoy the excitement of looking at one another. The great Hindu festivals have been described in numberless books, and I need not notice them here. But besides these, every shrine, Hindu and Musalmán, small and great, has its fairs held at fixed dates which attract worshippers more or less numerous according to its renown. Some of these fairs, such as those at Thánesar on the occasion of an eclipse, those of Bába Faríd at Pák Pattan, and of Sakhi Sarwar at Nigáha are attended by very many thousands of people, and elaborate police arrangements are made for their regulation. There are two festivals peculiar to the villages, not observed in the towns, and therefore not described in the books, which I will briefly notice. The ordinary Díwáli or feast of lamps of the Hindus, which falls on Kátik, 11th, is called by the villagers the little Díwáli. On this night the *pitr* or ancestors visit the house, which is fresh plastered throughout for the occasion, and the family light lamps and sit up all night to receive them. Next morning the housewife takes all the sweepings and old clothes in a dust-pan and turns them out on to the dunghill, saying, *daladr*[1] *dúr ho:* 'May thriftlessness and poverty be far from us!' Meanwhile they prepare for the celebration of the great or Gobardhan Díwáli, on which Krishna is worshipped in his capacity of a cowherd, and which all owners of cattle should observe. The women make a Gobardhan of cow-dung, which consists of Krishna lying on his back surrounded by little cottage loaves of dung to represent mountains, in which are stuck stems of grass with tufts of cotton or rag on the top for trees, and by little dung-balls for cattle, watched by dung-men dressed in bits of rag. Another opinion is that the cottage loaves are cattle and the dung-balls calves. On this are put the churn-staff and five whole sugarcanes, and some parched rice and a lighted lamp in the middle. The cowherds are then called in and they salute the whole and are fed with rice and sweets. The Brahman then takes the sugarcane and eats a bit; and till then no one must cut, press, or eat cane. Rice-milk is then given to the Brahmans, and the bullocks have their horns dyed and get extra well fed. Four days before the Díwáli, *i.e.* on Kátik 11th, is the *Devuthni Gyáras* on which the gods awake from their four months' sleep, which began on Hár 11th. On the night of the *devuthni* the children run about the village with lighted sticks and torches. During these four months it is forbidden to marry, to cut sugarcane, or to put new string on a bedstead on pain of a snake biting the sleeper. On the 15th and 11th of Phágan the villagers worship the *aonla* tree, or *phyllanthus emblica*, mentioned by Huen Tsang as being so abundant beyond Delhi. This tree is the emblic myrobolus, a representation of the fruit of which is used for the finial of Buddhist temples. Its worship is now connected with that of Shiv: Brahmans will not take the offerings. The people circumambulate the tree from left to right (*prikamma*), pour libations, eat the leaves and make offerings, which are taken by the Kanphate Jogis. Fasts are not much observed by the villagers, except the great annual fasts; and not even those by the young man who works in the fields and cannot afford to go hungry. But sugar, butter, milk, fruits and wild seeds, and anything that is not technically 'grain' may be eaten, so that the abstinence is not very severe.

[1] *Daladr* = 'thriftless, lazy', and so 'poor'.

The south is a quarter to be especially avoided, as the spirits of the dead live there. Therefore your cooking hearth must not face the south, nor must you sleep or lie with your feet in that direction except in your last moments. The demon of the four quarters, Diásul, lives in the east on Monday and Saturday, in the north on Tuesday and Wednesday, in the west on Friday and Sunday, and in the south on Thursday; and a prudent man will not make a journey or even plough in those directions on those days. So when *Shukr* or Venus is in declension, brides do not go to their husbands' homes, nor return thence to visit their fathers' houses. On the Biloch frontier each man is held to have a star, and he must not journey in certain directions when his star is in given positions. But when his duty compels him to do so he will bury his star, *i.e.* a piece of cloth cut out in that shape, so that it may not see what he is doing.[1] It is well not to have your name made too free use of, especially for children. They are often not named at all for some little time; and if named are generally addressed as *buja* or *buji*, 'Baby,' according to sex. If a man is rich enough to have his son's horoscope drawn a few days after his birth, the name then fixed will be carefully concealed till the boy is eight or ten years old and out of danger; and even then it will not be commonly used, the everyday name of a Hindu, at least among the better classes, being quite distinct from his real name, which is only used at formal ceremonies such as marriage. Superiors are always addressed in the third person; and a clerk, when reading a paper in which your name occurs, will omit it and explain that it is your name that he omits. A Hindu peasant will not eat, and often will not grow onions or turnips, as they taste strong like meat which is forbidden to him. Nor will he grow indigo, for simple blue is the Musalmán colour and an abomination to him. He will also refuse to eat oil or black sesame if formally offered him by another, for if he do he will serve the other in the next life. A common retort when asked to do something unreasonable is *kyá, main ne tere kále til chábe hain?*: 'What, have I eaten your black sesame?' The shop-keeper must have cash for his first transaction in the morning; and will not book anything till he has taken money. Ibbetson, §§ 231-36.

The months of Chet, Poh and Mágh are regarded as unlucky, and are called *kále mahíne* or black months. The people like to hear the name of Chét first from the lips of Dumnas, and the name of Mágh is best heard from a class of Brahmans called Basbara, who come during that month from the plains to sing and beg. An infant should not be taken outside for the first time in these months, this being unlucky. If a cow has a calf in Bhádon, both it and the calf must be given away to avert misfortune. Sunday, Tuesday and Saturday are unlucky days for celebrating a marriage, for if a marriage takes place on Sunday the couple will not agree with one another, if on Tuseday, the husband will soon die; if on Saturday, there will be much sickness in the family. Unlucky months, days and names in Chamba.

[1] But it would appear that there is a unanimity in the motions of these stars which reduces the rule to one of dates. Thus, on the 1st, 2nd, 11th, and 12th journeys must not be made towards one quarter; on the 3rd, 4th, 13th, and 14th towards another; on the 5th, 6th, 15th, and 16th towards a third, and on the 7th, 8th, 17th, and 18th towards the fourth. On the 9th, 10th, 19th, 20th, 29th, and 30th the traveller is free to face as he pleases.

A woman must not wash her head on a Friday, or her brother will become sick. This is called *gal lagdi.* Cowdung should not be offered to any one on a Friday, or the cow will become sick and its milk will dry up. On Wednesday and birthdays nothing should be given away unless in the form of *dán*, otherwise good luck will cease. A journey should not be begun on Sunday, Tuesday or Friday, but Monday, Wednesday and Thursday are lucky days for such a purpose, especially Wednesday. Sunday is good for entering on anything requiring haste.

Saturn being a planet of bad omen, no oil should be put on the head on Saturday. On that day a little oil—enough to see one's face in—is put into the palm of the hand and then given to a Brahman. Some diseases are believed to be due to the malign influence of the planet Saturn, and to remove them *kichari* (a mixture of *dál* and rice with spices) is cooked and passed round the sick person's head and then given away, the idea being that the disease is thus transferred to the person who eats the *kichari*.

Again a woman should not wash her head on a Saturday, or her husband will become sick. There are five days in each month called *panchak*, which are unlucky, and on them no work should be done. If work is in progress a holiday should be given, and no new work should be commenced on any of these days, or it will be attended with loss. If any one dies on one of the days of *panchak* cloth dolls, corresponding in number to the days still remaining, are made up and laid alongside the corpse and burnt with it, otherwise more members of the family will die. This custom is called *panchak shánti.* If a buffalo calves on a Wednesday it is unlucky, and the calf must be given away. A child born on a Tuesday will be attended with misfortune in the marriage state in after life. There is also a special day in each year, called *gúrbúr*, usually a birthday, on which no work must be done; the special day is indicated by a *pandit*.

Every Saturday the Bánias of Multán pour oil and gram over small raised spots where streets cross. This is done in honour of Sani or Saturn.[1]

On Sundays and Tuesdays salt should never be eaten. By refraining the gods are propitiated and will supply all wants.[1]

In some parts of the Punjab salt is not eaten on a Sunday. At Multán all Hindu shops were closed on Sundays.[2]

Friday is an unlucky day for sport in Ráwalpindi.

Saturday, Sunday and Tuesday are all unlucky days for the sale of cattle or *ghi*, lending or borrowing money, and shaving. The last-named leads to one's own death or that of a son. Tuesday is also a very unfortunate day on which to return home from a journey.[3]

Sáwan ghori, Bhádon gái,
Mágh más jo bhains bijáe,
Jí se-jáe, khasmon kháe.

"The mare that foals in Sáwan, the cow that calves in Bhádon and the buffalo in Mágh, will either die or kill her owner."[4]

[1] P. N. Q., IV, § 496.
[2] *Ib.*, III, § 499.
[3] *Ib.*, II, §§ 739-744.
[4] *Ib.*, III, § 21.

A mare foaling in the day-time too is unlucky. In Baháwalpur to avert the evil effects the ear of colt or filly is bored or the tip cut off. But strangest of all is the idea prevalent in the hills north of Gurdáspur that the character of the monsoon can be forecasted from the number of kittens born in a litter during the preceding cold weather: thus, if the usual number is 4 or more the rains will be ample; if 2 it will only rain for 2 months; if one, then the monsoon will fail utterly.[1]

It is in the Deraját unlucky to give away money on a Sunday, and Hindus will not even pay wages on that day. Travelling in any direction on a Wednesday is regarded as very unlucky, but the objection to travel north etc. on certain other days is not much regarded.[2]

Lucky and unlucky days of the week.

Lucky days appear to depend largely on the state of the moon, but this does not explain the various and often conflicting beliefs regarding days of the week. Thus in Attock some cultivators will not begin ploughing on a Sunday or Tuesday, while others consider the latter the best day because Adam began to plough on that day. Both days too are considered most lucky for beginning legal proceedings. It is unlucky to set out on a journey northwards on Tuesday or Wednesday[3] but lucky on Monday or Friday. To start southwards on Thursday is bad, but on Wednesday good. Do not go east on Monday or Saturday or west on a Sunday or Thursday, but choose Sunday or Tuesday to go eastward or Monday or Saturday to go west.[4]

The Paṭháns of Kohát have few beliefs about unlucky days. Saturday is *kháli*, *i.e.* devoid of all blessings: one should not shave on a Sunday: or begin a journey on a Friday, because it is a day of public prayer and the journey will be unsuccessful. But if compelled to start on an unlucky day a Paṭhán notable will have his travelling bag sent beforehand out of the house on a lucky day to the village shrine in the direction of his journey. This is called *parasthán*.[5]

Sunday.

As a rule, in Dera Ismail Khán, both ploughing and harvesting are always begun on a Sunday. It is however unwise to cross the

[1] Gurdáspur *Gazetteer*, 1914, p. 63. It might be suggested that some instinctive anticipation of a sufficient food-supply increases prolificness, but statistical evidence is wanting. Such an anticipation is credited to the *tatíri* or plover who is said to build its nest low down by the stream when the monsoon will fail but high above it if the rains are to be good. The beliefs noted on the text are fairly general but in Attock it is also considered very unlucky for a cat to kitten in Jeṭh, donkey to have a foal in Sáwan, a camel to have young in Baisákh, a goat in Poh or a dog in Chet. Probably at one time a complete pseudo-science of this kind existed. In Attock a Brahman or a *mullah* is consulted as to what should be done to avert these omens: *Gazetteer*, p. 107.

[2] P. N. Q., II, §§ 987, 988.

[3] *Mangal Budh na jáiye paháṛ*

Jíti bázi diye hár.

'Go not north on Tuesday or Wednesday,

Even if you win, it will cause you loss.'

[4] Attock *Gazetteer*, p. 106.

[5] Lit. 'living elsewhere': cf *pastána* in Dera Ghází Khán.

Indus on that day:

Aj Itwár, ná langen pár,

Matte jitta áwen hár.

"To-day is Sunday, do not cross,

Or you will lose what you have won."

Monday. Monday and Thursday are the best days to begin making new clothes, which should be worn for the first time on a Wednesday or Friday and in the morning rather than in the evening. For shaving, depilation or cutting the nails Monday is good, but Hindus prefer Sunday and Muhammadans, Friday. Like Tuesday, Wednesday and Thursday are unlucky for these acts.

Tuesday. As we have seen, Tuesday is an unlucky day, and inauspicious for beginning a new work or starting on a journey—

Budh, Sanichar kapra, gahna Aitwár,

Je sukh sutta loryen manji unin Somwár.

"Put on new clothes on Wednesday and Saturday, and jewellery on a Sunday;

If thou desirest happy sleep weave thy couch on a Monday."

On the other hand many acts are lucky if done on certain days. Thus on Sunday eat betel (*pán*) and go which way you will, you will get what you wish. On Monday look at your face in the glass and you will prosper. On Tuesday eat a clove and good fortune will attend you when you set out on business. On Wednesday eat sweet stuff, and on Thursday drink curds—a *chiṭák* will suffice. On Friday eat new bread and on Saturday white salt. By eating thus you will always reach your goal in safety.[1]

Cock-crowing at noon is very unlucky and Muhammadans will always kill one that does so.

The early morning is a risky time for various things if done by particular persons. Thus it is then unlucky for a tailor to mend clothes, for a *halwái* to sell *baṭáshas* (sugar-drops), for a *bazáz* or clothier to sell red cloth (*qand*), for a Bánia to sell *ghí*, a *pansári* paper, a Kasera zinc, or for a Sarráf to deal in gold.[2]

Midday and evening are bad times to begin a new work or start on a journey.

Just as every day has its good and bad times so the day itself is unlucky for certain events, such as hearing a horse neigh. A child born at noontide is also unfortunate.[3] How far these ideas are based on astrology it is difficult to say.

[1] P. N. Q., II, § 20.

[2] *Ib.*, III, §§ 711-12.

[3] *Attock Gazetteer*, p. 107.

BELIEFS AND SUPERSTITIONS CONNECTED WITH UNLUCKY DAYS.

Both Hindus and Muhammadans believe in the *jogniáṇ* or *chihil abdál.*[1] The *chihil abdál* are forty saints who live in different directions on various dates. Their number is invariably forty. If one of them dies, a new saint takes his place. To undertake a journey in any direction on the dates when the saints are in that direction is unlucky. Agriculturists also do not reap a crop facing in the direction in which the saints are. The following figure shows the different dates when the saints are believed to be in each direction:—

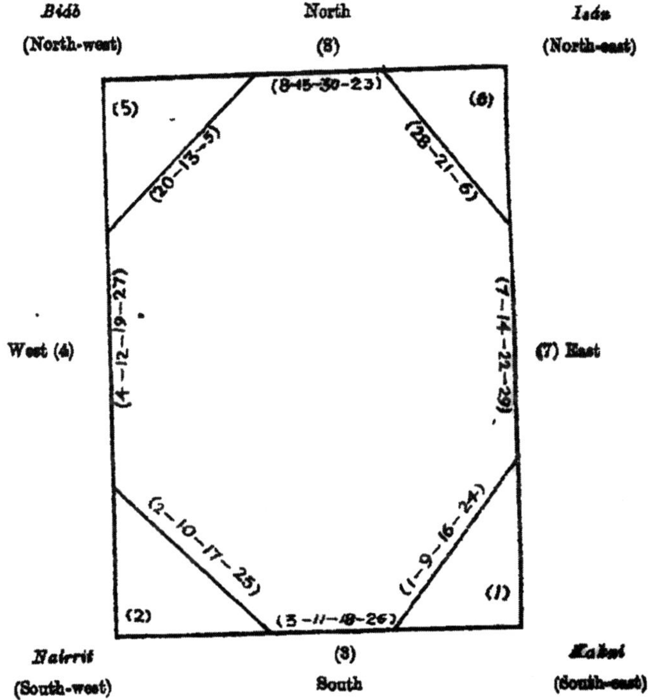

Note.—The numbers within brackets inside the square denote dates, while those on the corners and within the brackets outside the square signify directions.

[1] There is a 'sect' of Muhammadan *faqírs* in Kángra called Abdálí who appear to be bards to the Hindu chiefs. They are also said to be found in Chamba. It is just possible that there is some connection.

The following lines give the dates on which the *chihil abdál* are in the different directions :—

Pahli, nánwin, solán, chawwi, kakani[1] *wich pehchán.*
Do, dah, satárá, panjhi, nairat[2] *shak na án.*
Tarai, chhabbí, athára, gyára wich janúbe *ján,*
Chár, bárá, satáwí, áni, maghrib *shak na án,*
Panj, tera, wíh, turaí dikáre, baib[3] *de wich ján,*
Chhe, ikkí, atháwí sach much wich Isán[4] *pechhán,*
Sat, chauda, unattirí, báwí mashraq *gaib rijal,*
Ath, pandra, tarih, trewí rehnde wich shimál.

That is, the *chihil abdál* occupy *kakani* (*kakni*) on the 1st, 9th, 16th and 24th, the *nairat* on the 2nd, 10th, 17th and 25th, the south (*janúb*) on the 3rd, 26th, 18th and 11th, the west (*maghrib*) on the 4th, 12th, 27th and 19th, the *baib* on three dates, *viz.* the 5th, 13th and 20th, the *isán* on the 6th, 21st and 28th, the east (*mashriq*) on the 7th, 14th, 29th and 22nd, the north (*shamál*) on the 8th, 15th, 30th and 23rd.

It is asserted that the *chihil abdáls* were originally saintly persons whose prayers were acceptable to God, but that credulous Moslems have by degrees identified them with the Hindu *jognián*. But it must be confessed that the *joginís* are said to be 64 in number,[5] whereas the *abdál* are generally said to be 40 in number though some accounts make them 7 or 70.

The following tradition, which is said to be only oral, ascribes the origin of the 40 *abdáls* to the Prophet himself. One Dayá-Kalbí had no children, and on his plaint the Prophet for 40 days gave him a daily charm, which he in his ignorance of their use kept, until all the 40 had been given him. Then he washed them and gave them to his wife, who in due course bore 40 sons. Appalled at this event Dayá-Kalbí exposed 39 of the children in the desert, but on his return home he missed the 40th also, so he went back to the desert and there found all the 40. Seeing that they were inseparable he kept them, and they lived under a dome not built by human hands. Presently a plague smote Medína, and it was revealed to the Prophet that it was caused by the 40 *abdáls*, but on his announcing himself as Muhammad they refused to discuss matter with one so proud, and only when he proclaimed himself as

[1] *Kakni* is not explained.

[2] Nairrit, Sanskr : fr. *nir-riti* = south-western : Platts, 1166. It is also said to mean red, originally, and hence south-west.

[3] *Baib* is said to be derived fr. *ba* or *wa*, wind, and to mean the corner whence the wind comes = Sanskr. *váyú-kaun* or *váyú kon* (Platts), the wind corner or N.-W. (In Hind *baib* = 'at a distance, a far off.')

[4] *Ishan* is said to mean 'rising' in Sanskr.; hence = 'north-east.' It is also a name of Siva : (Platts, p. 113).

[5] *E.g.* in the *Granth*, *cf.* Macauliffe, *Life of Gurú Nának* (p. 32.) For the legend among the Gujars of Hazára etc. *cf.* P. N. Q., II, §§ 1071 : also § 1071, and 1120.

Muhammad the Poor, would they acknowledge him. He then gave them a piece of illuminated cloth, from which each made a girdle without diminishing its size, and they all entered Medína. The disease promptly escaped in the shape of the goat, which the *abdáls* caught and devoured, all except the tail. This this they threw skywards, judging that men would forget God if there were no diseases. So now the tail revolves round the earth, and wherever it chances to be disease breaks out. But the 40 *abdáls* now plundered Medína and evoked the Prophet's curse, under which they wander round the world, occupying certain regions at fixed times, on specified dates of the lunar months.

The orthodox Hindu belief in the *jogistán* is based on astrology. They are believed to occupy the following points of the compass on the *tithś* or lunar dates specified :—

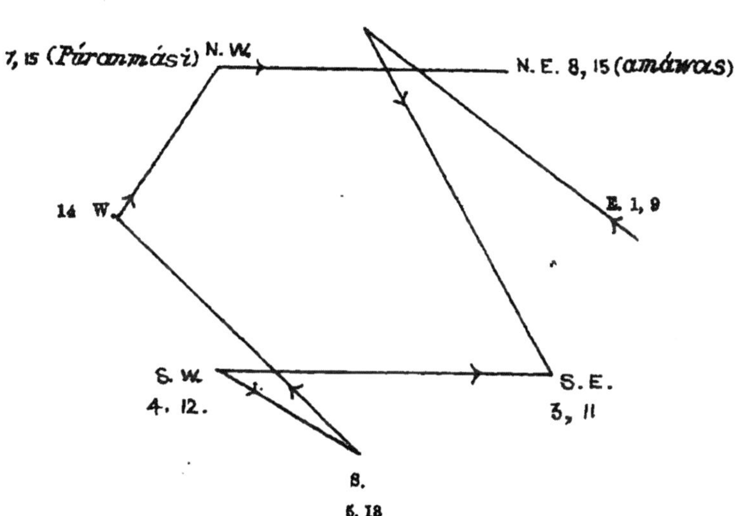

That is to say they start from the E. on the 1st, and reach the N-E. on the 8th. On the 9th they again start from the E. Or, as an account from Ambála puts it, they go from E. to N., S.-E., S.-W., S., W., N.-W., and N.-E., on the *prithemá* to the *ashtami*, and again from the *naumi* to the *purimá* and *amáwas*.

It is unlucky to travel in the direction in which the *joginís* are on any given day, but this omen may be evaded by the device called *pastáná* [1] in Dera Ghazi Khán. This consists in throwing salt, or one of

[1] *Cf. parasthán* in Kohát.

the things to be taken with one, in the direction of the intended route on a day prior to that fixed for starting, and when the *joginis* are in a different direction. Hindus also throw rice, sugar etc. with a pice, tied up in red cloth.

The *dikshul* or point at which a spear is hanging is as follows :—

			Chihil Abdál.
On Sunday in the E.	...	...	W.
„ Monday in the W.	...	...	E.
„ Tuesday and Wednesday in the N.		...	N.
„ Thursday in the S.	...	...	S.
„ Friday in the E.	...	...	W.
„ Staturday in the W.	...	...	E.

For facility of comparison the directions in which, according to a Persian quatrain,[1] the *chihil abdál*, or *rajal-ul-ghaib*, are found are also given Their E. and W. day are the converse of those assigned to the Hindu *dikshul*. It is auspicious, when on a journey, to one's wealth to have the *chihil abdál* on the left hand, and if they are behind one all enemies will be destroyed. But if on the right they augur loss of property, and if facing one risk to life. This is in precise accord with the Hindu quatrain saying regarding the *jogan* which runs :—

Agge jogan kadí na rás.
Pichhe jogan paunche ás,
Dákne jogan yás dhare,
Báṇhweṇ jogan ás dhare.

" If the *jogan* be in front it is evil, but if it be at your back there is hope ; if it be on the right, you will be disappointed, but if on the left you may hope."

[1] Of which one version runs :—

Ba yakshamab-o-Júmah maghrab marau,
Ba doshambah-shamb ah-mashraq marau
Ba sihshmbah-o-charshambah shamál
Janubi taraf panjshambah wabál.

This is rendered in the Western Panjábi of Dera Ghási Khán thus :—

Chanchhan Som na jáwín mashriq,
Adit Juma gurab :
Mangal Budh shamál do no wanjín
Khámis junáb.

But in Dera Ismaíl Khán both the Baloch and Jáṭs say :—

Khámis dí diháṛí lamme na wanjan,
Mangul, Budh ubhe na wanjan :
Adit wa jumá dilár na wanjan,
Suhar te Chanchan dibárte na wanjan.

The *joginián* are 64 in number, but only 8 of them are of importance. The following diagram shows their names and the directions in which they stay :—

Isán N. E. — East — Agni Kon S. E.

(8) *yogni*	(1) *Shákni*	(2) *Dákni*
(7) *Baitál Kámni*	EARTH	(3) *Kákni*
(6) *yákni*	(5) *Rákni*	(4) *Hákni*

North (left) — South (right)

Wáyú Kon N.W. — West — Nairrit

The *joginián* (or *jogs*) play an important part in astrology and are of much help to astrologers in forecasting the results of games, epidemics, rains, storms, fires, earthquakes etc.

This belief is illustrated by the following instances :—

(1) The *jogini*, by name *Yoga* or *Jogeshri*, along with the Moon, completes its revolution round the earth in 2½ hours or 60 *gharís*. If during its revolution it joins with *Chandramáṇ* (Moon), *Budh* (Mercury), *Shukra* (Venus) and *Brihaspati* (Jupiter) in a *Jal-ráshi*, *i.e.* in one of the signs—*Kirk* (Cancer), *Min* (Pisces), *Kumb* (Aquarius) or *Makar* (Capricornus)—the result is rain ; if with the *Súrya* (Sun) and *Mangal* (Mars) in an *Agni-ráshi*, *i.e.* in one of the signs—*Mekh* (Aries), *Singh* (Leo) or *Brichhak* (Scorpio)—the result is fire ; if with *Chandramáṇ* (Moon) and *Shanichar* (Saturn) in a *Váyú-ráshi*, *i.e.* in one of the signs—*Tula* (Libra)

or *Dhan* (Sagitarius)—the result is a storm. And if with *Ráhu* (a planet) and *Sanichar* (Saturn) in a *Prithvi-rási, i.e.* in one of the signs—*Kanyá* (Virgo), *Mithan* (Gemini) or *Brikh* (Taurus)—the result is an earthquake.

(2) The *jogini* known as *Shárdúl* also completes its revolution in 60 *gharis*. If it is facing the hunter while out hunting, he (or she) is likely to sustain an injury, but if it is behind or on his right he will make a bag.

(3) The *jogini* called *Vijaiy* or *Pakhsh* completes its revolution in 15 days. In the bright lunar half it travels towards the east and *Agni Kon* (south-east) but in the dark half in the opposite direction, *viz. Isán* (north-east) etc. Its situation is observed when proceeding on an expedition in war. It is unlucky while it is facing one, but otherwise it is auspicious.

Similarly, there are other *Joginís*, such as *Bálá, Shávid, Sankránti, Grah, Lagni* etc. of minor importance which are believed to control or affect the success or failure of all human enterprises and undertakings.

According to the belief in Kángra the *joginís'* head-quarters are in the—

East in the month of *Kátak*.

South-east in the months of *Jeth* and *Maghar*.

South in the month of *Sáwan*.

South-west in the months of *Hár* and *Phágan*.

West in the month of *Bhádon*.

North-west in the months of *Chet* and *Mágh*.

North in the month of *Assú*.

North-east in the months of *Baisákh* and *Poh*.

The Moon too like the *Joginís, Dishásúl* or *Ráhu Chakra* has good or evil effects on earthly bodies during her revolution. She also plays an important part in astrology and her situation is ascertained when fixing lucky hours and days for journeys, voyages, enterprises, expeditions or ceremonies.

The Moon completes her revolution round the Sun in a month, taking 2½ days to pass through each of the twelve signs of the Zodiac, as is apparent from the following diagram :—

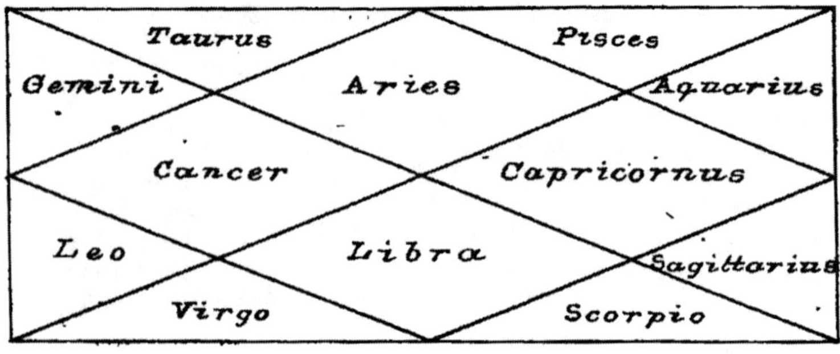

The Moon while revolving in four directions passes through the following signs of the Zodiac :—

	Direction.		*Signs.*
(*a*)	East ...	...	Aries, Leo, and Sagittarius.
(*b*)	South ...	...	Taurus, Virgo and Capricornus.
(*c*)	West ...	...	Libra, Aquarius and Gemini.
(*d*)	North ...	...	Cancer, Scorpio and Pisces.

Since the Moon takes 2¼ days to travel through each sign she takes 125 *ghaṛís* in all to revolve in the eight directions as will appear from the diagram below :—

Isán — East — Agnikon

14 Ghaṛís	16 Ghaṛís	15 Ghaṛís
15 Ghaṛís	EARTH	21 Ghaṛís
19 Ghaṛís	18 Ghaṛís	16 Ghaṛís

North. (left) — South. (right)

Báib — West. — Nairrit

If the Moon is in front of or facing one, hope is fulfilled; if on the right, it gives health and wealth; if behind, there is likelihood of loss of life; and if on the left, loss to property. It is a strong belief that while proceeding on a journey if the Moon is facing one all the evil effects whatsoever of the *joginián*, *dishásh úl*, *kál-chakra* etc., are fully counteracted.

Like the *joginián* and the Moon, the *nakshatras*, which are 28 in number, also play an essential part in astrology. They too have good or evil effects, in their movements, on earthly bodies. But as educated people of the present day are losing faith in these beliefs, the *nakshatras* are losing ground, as compared with the *jogs* and the Moon. Still people even now pay some regard to them in ascertaining lucky or unlucky days. The following diagram will throw some light on the *nakshatras* :—

Sammat (Direction).	*Nakshatra.*			*Tith.*		Day.			REMARKS.
East ...	*Múl*	*Sharavan.*	*Jeshta*	(1st) *Parva.*	(9th) *Naumi.*	Saturday...	Monday ...	...	It is quite unlucky to undertake journey in the directions on the days and *thiths* and under the *nakshatras* shown in this statement.
West ...	*Rohni*	*Push*	...	(6th) *Chhat.*	(14th) *Chaudas*	Tuesday ...	Sunday ...	Friday...	
South ...	*Purva Bhadr Pad.*	*Ashwani*	*Dhauvishta.*	(5th) *Panchmi.*	(13th) *Taras.*	Thursday	...	...	
North ...	*Hast*	*Utra Phalgan.*	...	(2nd) *Duj.*	(10th *Dashmi.*	Wednesday	Sunday ...	Tuesday	
Isán (N.-E.) ...	...	...	...	...	...	Do.	Saturday...	...	
Agni (S.-E.) ...	...	...	...	...	...	Thursday	Monday...	...	
Báih (N.-W.) ...	...	...	...	...	...	Tuesday ...	...	...	
Nairrit (S.-W.)	...	...	...	...	...	Friday ...	Sunday ...	...	

To avert the evil effects of *dishdshúl*, one should on the following days take the things noted against each, before proceeding on a journey :—

Sunday	... ...	*Ghí* (clarified butter).
Monday	... ...	Milk.
Tuesday	... ...	Jaggery.
Wednesday	... ...	Sesamum.
Thursday	... ...	Curd.
Friday	... ...	Barley.
Saturday	... ...	Urd (*másh*).

In a month five Sundays forecast epidemic.

„ „ „ „ Tuesdays „ terror and fear.

„ „ „ „ Saturdays „ famine or drought.

Each month has been divided into—

(1) the *sudi* (bright lunar half) and (*b*) *badi* (dark lunar half).

During the *bdi* the days from the *parva* (1st) to *panchmi* (5th) are lucky and from the *panchmi* (5th) to the *amávas* (15th) mediocre or middling. Those from the *ekam* (1st) (of the bright half) to the *panchmi* are deemed unlucky, from the *panchmi* to the *dashmi* (10th) mediocre, and from the *dashmi* to the *púranmáshi* (15th) lucky.

Like the *Disháshúl*, Ráhú Chakra or Kál Chakra has its evil influences. Hence it is essential to ascertain its situation also while going on a journey. The belief is that Kál Chakra while in front or on the right is very inauspicious and dangerous, but otherwise propitious. The following diagram shows its situation on different days of the week :—

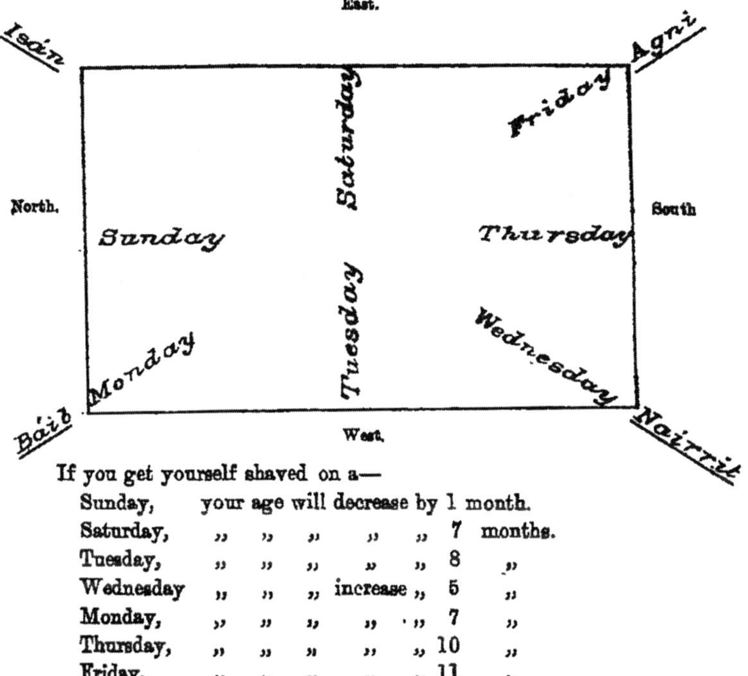

If you get yourself shaved on a—

Sunday,	your age will decrease by 1 month.						
Saturday,	„	„	„	„	„	7	months.
Tuesday,	„	„	„	„	„	8	„
Wednesday	„	„	„	increase	„	5	„
Monday,	„	„	„	„	„	7	„
Thursday,	„	„	„	„	„	10	„
Friday,	„	„	„	„	„	11	„

Certain hours of the days of the week are also considered lucky. These are termed *sakki*[1] *or chaugharia-mahúrat.* The following lines

[1] The Indian day (and night) has four degrees of auspiciousness :—(*i*) *sakki* A., good ; (*ii*) *bain* A., intermediate ; (*iii*) *rih*, air ; and (*iv*) *ihráq* A., burning. Of these the effects of *rih* are ephemeral, passing by like the air : and those of *ihráq* are most baneful. The following is the scheme :—

		1	2	3	4	5	6	7	8
Saturday	(night)	Rih	Zakki	Zakki	Bain	Ihráq	Ihráq	Bain	Rih.
„	(day)	Bain	Rih	Bain	Ihráq	Do.	Bain	Zakki	Zakki.
Sunday	(night)	Do.	Ihráq	Zakki	Zakki	Bain	Rih	Ihráq	Ihráq.
„	(day)	Do.	Do.	Ihráq	Bain	Rih	Zakki	Zakki	Bain.
Monday	(night)	Ihráq	Do.	Bain	Rih	Zakki	Do.	Ihráq	Do.
„	(day)	Do.	Do.	Do.	Do.	Do.	Do.	Bain	Ihráq.
Tuesday	(night)	Bain	Rih	Zakki	Zakki	Bain	Ihráq	Ihráq	Rih.
„	(day)	Rih	Zakki	Do.	Bain	Ihráq	Do.	Rih	Bain.
Wednesday	(night)	Zakki	Do.	Rih	Ihráq	Rih	Bain	Ihráq	Zakki.
„	(day)	Do.	Do.	Do.	Do.	Ihráq	Rih	Bain	Do.
Thursday	(night)	Rih	Rih	Ihráq	Zakki	Zakki	Bain	Rih	Bain.
„	(day)	Bain	Ihráq	Do.	Rih	Bain	Zakki	Zakki	Do.
Friday	(night)	Ihráq	Do.	Bain	Zakki	Zakki	Rih	Ihráq	Do.
„	(day)	Bain	Do.	Ihráq	Rih	Do.	Zakki	Bain	Rih.

give the lucky hours of the various days :—

> *Zakki, Ait (or Sunday), Jumma, Khamis pahr dhayan pichhchhe.*
> *Adhe pahr thin pichchhe Chhanchhan*[1] *jo koi zakki puchchhe.*
> *Deḍh pahr thin pichchhe zakki Mangal bujh Sawár.*
> *Awwal sárá ákhar adhá zakki hai Budhwár.*

The *sakki* hours on Sunday, Friday, and Thursday begin at 2½ *pahrs* after sunrise (a *pahr*=3 hours) ; on Saturday, half a *pahr* after sunrise ; on Tuesday and Monday 1½ *pahrs* after it ; and on Wednesday the whole first *pahr* and half the last *pahr* are *zakki*.

The hours other than those mentioned are considered unlucky. Works undertaken in the hours given in the above lines are believed to end satisfactorily and well.

THE EARTH SLEEPS.

Another superstition is that the earth sleeps for 7 days in each lunar month, and so anything done on those days would turn out badly :—

> *Sankrát miti din pánchweṇ náṇweṇ sátweṇ so*
> *Das ikkis chaubis din, khat din prithwí so*

"On the 1st, 5th, 7th, 9th, 10th, 21st and 24th days of every lunar month the earth sleeps."[2]

In those days ploughing or sowing should not be begun, though once begun they may go on.[2]

In Chamba town the names of certain places are regarded as unlucky and must not be mentioned in the morning. These are Núrpur, Basohli and Jammu. This prejudice doubtless arose in consequence of the frequent wars with these States in olden times. If it is necessary to refer to Núrpur, the phrase Sapparwála Shahr or the 'rocky town' is used, while Basohli and Jammu are spoken of as *párlá mulk*, that is 'the country across the Rávi.' This superstition is very common in all the north-eastern Punjab, *e.g.* in Hoshiárpur, where it is also ascribed to the fact that some of these unlucky places were the sites of Sikh toll-posts and so on. But the new name, which must be used before breakfast, is not always more auspicious than the old. Thus Talwára where Goler and Núrpur used to meet Dáda Síba and Datárpur in fight is styled Kaliádh or the place of the fight, *kalha*, or Barapind, the 'big village,' or Chandrapind, the 'unlucky' one.[3]

Wasting diseases are often attributed to a form of witchcraft called *sáyá* or *masán*. A woman will collect ashes from a *masán* or

[1] Chhanchhan in the south-west Punjab = Saníchar, Saturn or Saturday.

[2] A Jullundur version is :—

> *Sankránt mitti din pánchwen, nánwen, sátwen le,*
> *Das, ikki, chaubíswen, khat din pirthawí swne :—*

that is on the *sankránt* 5th, 7th, 9th, 10th, 21st and 24th, *six khat* days, the earth sleeps : according to Purser *S. R.*, § 15.

[3] Hoshiárpur *Gazetteer*, 1904, p. 74. *Kalha* does not appear in the *Panjabi Dicty.* but it may be connected with the word *ghalha-ghara*—s. v., p. 379.

burning-ground and cast them over an enemy's child, causing it to waste away, while her own child thrives. Hence the proverb: *Sáhukar ko kasán, bálak ko masán*—'the banker battens on the peasant, like a child on ashes.'[1] To ascertain if a child is suffering from *sáyá*, take a new earthenware pot and fill it with water from 7 wells, bury it under the threshold and dig it up after 7 days. If the water has dried up, the child is afflicted by *sáyá*. This affliction is also called *Aseb* and can be cured by passing the child seven times under a vessel filled with well-water, which should be thrown away on waste land as it would destroy any crop.[2]

Hiccoughing (*hirki*) is attributed to recollection on the part of some relative or friend who, if mentally identified at the time, can stop the affliction.[3] To cure it then it is only necessary to go through the names of them all and it will cease when you hit on the one who is thinking about you.

Hiccough may also be cured by shock—by thinking of something that disturbs the mind.[5]

Closely connected with the healing properties of many quaint and often unwholesome edibles are the magic properties possessed by articles of various kinds. Thus the jackal's horn, *siál sing* or *gídar sing* possesses the power of conferring invisibility. It is also said to be the tiny horn carried by the jackal that leads their howls and when worn prevents any one scolding its wearer from being scolded, for which reason it is much sought after by Government servants. It sells for Rs. 50 or even Rs. 100, and is a recognised article of commerce among *shikáris*.[6]

The white or pink rock salt of Kálabágh is believed to cause impotence, so the black Kohát salt or that of the Sambar Lake is preferred.[7]

When a goat kills a snake it devours it and then ruminates, after which it spits out a bead (*manka*) which applied to a snake-bite absorbs the poison and swells. Dropped then into milk it is squeezed and the poison drips out. This cures the patient. If not put into milk, the *manka* will burst.[8]

Among other quaint remedies for sickness are pea-fowls' legs, for fever and ear-ache: soup made from the white paddy-bird (*bagla*), for asthma[9]: the tip of an ibex horn soaked in boiling water, which is then drunk for rheumatism.[10]

Piles can be cured by winding a thread of 5 colours, white, red, green, yellow and black, thrice around the thumb, and then putting it round the big toe at night, for a fortnight ending on a Tuesday, the day sacred to Hanúmán.[11]

[1] P. N. Q., III, § 992. For Kisán see Kusán, Vol. II, p. 572 *infra*. In Sirmúr *masáni* is a wasting disease the cures for which are described in the *Gazetteer* of that State, p. 25.

[2] *Ib.*, IV, §§ 110, 109. *Aseb* is not traceable in the *Punjabi Dicty*.

[3] *Ib.*, II, § 564.

[4] P. N. Q., II, § 805.

[5] *Ib.*, III, § 778.

[6] *Ib.*, I, § 702.

[7] *Ib.*, II, § 27.

[8] N. I. N. Q., I, § 102.

[9] P. N. Q., 1, §§ 700-01.

[10] *Ib.*, I, § 7[illegible].

[11] *Ib.*, II, § 1088.

Tiger's flesh has magical qualities. Khatrís always keep a little by them dried and when a child is attacked by small-pox they burn a little near him to propitiate the goddess. Hence when that disease is raging in a town the house of a Hindu who has tiger's flesh is frequented by people begging for small pieces of it.

Hare's blood in a lump of cotton is used in many ailments, the cotton being soaked in water and the blood extracted given to the sick. It is said to be most efficacious in fits of various sorts.[1]

Owl's flesh, particularly the heart, is a potent love-philter, making the recipient fall violently in love with the giver. Nothing can destroy the affection thus engendered.[2] Every owl has in its body a bone which will empower its possessor to make others subservient to his will. Keep an owl wide awake for two days and a night and it will tell you where this bone is to be found.[3]

For spleen use the flesh of the *ugga* or peewit, a bird which, it is believed in the Mánjha, will cause the death of any animal if it fly round it seven times, unless the following charm be used: its owner must strip himself naked and draw a line of cowdung round the animal and then setting fire to some grass run round it quickly with the burning grass in his hand, calling on his landlord, headman and king against his plunderer.[4]

Epilepsy is cured by administering a snuff made from dried worms snorted out by male camels during the rutting season, and which are believed to live on the animals' brain.[5]

In the hills a curious belief exists regarding the *akás-bel* or 'heavenly creeper,' as it is called in Punjabi.[6] Crows are said to pluck twigs of the *Cuscuta reflexa*[7] and *anguina* and drop them into water, when they turn into snakes and so furnish the crows with food. The possession of the root of this plant is also believed to confer invisibility.

Blindness, provided it is not congenital, may be cured by antimony, applied for 8 days. Antimony is obtained at the Karangli hill near Pind Dádan Khán. Once a *faqír* turned that hill into gold, but the people feared lest it should lead to wars for the sake of the gold, so he turned it all into antimony which still exists on its inaccessible summit and is washed down by the rains.

Scorpion-sting may be cured in various ways by simple remedies, but charms are also used. Draw a pentathlon in ink thrice over the wound at intervals of 5 minutes and the pains will disappear: or hang a scorpion's sting up in the house where children are playing and they will never be stung. Indra and Gaurja Devi are also invoked in a rhyme which will send the poison into the Kumbhi, the lowest hell.[9]

[1] P. N. Q., II, § 262.
[2] *Ib.*, I, § 699
[3] *Ib.*, III, § 451.
[4] *Ib.*, II, § 888.
[5] *Ib.*, II, § 900, where Millett suggests that as epilepsy is attributed to erotic causes in the *Dár-ush-shafa* this cure is probably explicable (on the principle that 'like cures like').
[6] *Punjabi Dic'y.*, p. 20.
[7] Or air-plant known in Balochi as *homo*—P. N. Q. II, § 406.
[8] P. N. Q., IV, § 38.
[9] *Ib.*, III, § 870.

To cure obstinate sores a little curdled milk is put over them and a dog allowed to lick them. They will be cured in two or three days afterwards. This has led to a belief that English men kill dogs for their tongues which contain *amrit* or ambrosia, a cure for sores of long standing.[1]

Remittent fever may be cured by taking a spinning-wheel and placing it on a cot in the sun.[2] The wheel, doubtless represents the sun.

For tertian ague take a saucepan lid and stick on to a wall with dough, saying: 'Don't come out of it.'

For ague take a spider, cover it with cotton and tie it round your neck. You will be cured when you forget all about it.

To cure lumbago it is only necessary to have the painful part touched with the right foot of one who was born feet foremost. And if that fails, to get it touched thrice with the peg to which a she-buffalo is usually tied.[3] A whitlow can be cured by any *siána* or wise man. Place the hand on the ground palm downwards and keep it as steady as possible while the *siána* sits before you and hits the ground hard with a shoe, muttering a charm and calling on the demon of the whitlow with implications to withdraw. If your hand moves in spite of you, the disease will be cured.[4] To cure ague take a grass stalk of your own height and cast it into a well some hours before the next attack is due, and this will stave it off. For tertian fever take five shreds from a scavenger's tomb on a Sunday and tie them round the patient's neck. Another cure consists in putting juice of the *madár* (*asclepias gigantea*) on his finger-nails, secretly, so that no one else sees it done and on a moonless (*nichanda*) Sunday. For a quartan fever tie a thread seven times round a *kikár* tree early only on a Tuesday morning and then let the patient embrace the tree once. But for a woman it suffices to cover up her spinning wheel with a cloth and remove her to another house.[5]

To cure sore-throat get a person whose right little finger and fore-finger will meet over the backs of his two middle fingers to rub your throat with them in that position: or take a piece of salt to a potter and get him to stroke your throat with it seven times, and then bury the lump of salt under an unbaked earthen pot. As the salt melts your sore-throat will go.[6]

A strange cure for tertian fever is to make a pretence of burying your village headmen, or, if you have only one in your village, those of adjacent villages. Very small graves suffice, but they must be smooth and neat, a place about half a mile from your house being chosen, and no one should see you going or coming.[7]

To stay tertian fever get a *mantra* written on a *pípal* leaf, wash it and drink the water.[8]

[1] P. N. Q., I, § 1024.
[2] *Ib.*, III, § 288.
[3] *Ib.*, I, § 866.
[4] *Ib.*, I, § 867.
[5] P. N. Q., I, § 988.
[6] *Ib.*, I, § 861.
[7] *Ib.*, II, § 261.
[8] *Ib.*, I, § 598.

Hydropathy is practised throughout the Punjab Himalayas. Young children are placed under small artificial cascades, so that the water may fall on the brain. This is done for several hours in the hot weather and less in the cold. Children not so treated are said to generally die, and this *nála* or hydropathy is alleged to cause steady bowels, healthy eyes, free action of the throat and a less inclination to small-pox.[1]

Another instance of treatment by shock is furnished by the Bánias who in a case of lingering sickness recite the *kalima* or Muhammadan creed to the patient. The shock is said to accelerate his departure from this world[2]; but probably it is believed to bring about his recovery. The Christian creed is also said to be recited at the death-bed of a *bhagat sáis* or groom.

Lingering labour may be relieved by giving the school-boys in the village a holiday,[3] or by administering water in which the *azárband* or girdle of a Rájá or holy personage has been washed.[4]

In cases of lingering illness Hindus recite the *Bhagavad Gita* or *Vishnu Sahasranáma* to the patient for 3, 4 or 7 consecutive days. Sikhs recite the *Adi Granth* instead. The patient ought to die or recover on one of these days.[5]

Relief from sickness, or at least a painless death, can be obtained by performing *tuládán*, in which rite the rich sufferer is weighed against silver and the seven kinds of grain called *satnája*, while the poor may be weighed against copper and coarse grain. The coins and grain go to the Ḍakauts. It is also well to break a cocoanut that rattles over the *satnája*, so that its milk may be sprinkled all over it.[6]

Bathing in the Rávi is regarded by Hindus in Lahore as a sure cure for obstinate dyspepsia, that river being very sacred.[7]

Sayyids and Paṭháns feed fishes when any one in the household is ill, especially if it be the master of the house or any one of importance. Every member of it makes a pill of bread in which is placed a charm, generally one of the 99 names of God. The women throw these pills into the nearest tank or river.[8]

To cure toothache, which is due to a weevil, take a bit of paper and write on it 786, the numerical value of the invocation *Bismilláhi'-r-rahími-r-Rahmán* and under the figures write the charm *Yá sahaq luná* 'O Changer of colour':—all in Arabic. Fix the paper to any tree except the sacred *pípal* and banyan (*boṛ*) by a nail through the *qáf* in *sahaq*. This causes instant cure if done first thing in the morning.[9]

Just as trees have castes, so have fevers, and the first step in their cure is to ascertain the caste of the disorder. Some fevers are scavengers (*mihtar*), some farmers, others Gújars or cowherds, and so on. A Gújar

[1] P. N. Q., I, § 584.

[2] *Ib.*, II, § 342. This recitation is apparently called *an kahni* or inappropriate saying.

[3] *Ib.*, III, § 37.

[4] *Ib.*, IV, § 40. *Cf.* II, § 666.

[5] P. N. Q., II, § 882.

[6] *Ib.*, II, § 934, and III, § 201.

[7] *Ib.*, IV, § 82.

[8] Mrs. F. A. Steel in P. N. Q., I, § 538.

[9] P. N. Q., II, § 814.

fever is cured by giving plenty of milk. If it is a *mihtar*, make the patient sweep the floor; if '*zamíndár*, let him plough; and so on. If the fever spirit be a thief, go at midnight to the graveyard and get a clod of earth, put it to sleep with the patient and next morning hung it on a *kíkar* tree. This is an infallible remedy as it hangs the fever-thief. This caste of fever comes stealthily by night But if the night-fever be not of this caste, a good plan is to put the dirty spoon out of the cooking-pot on the patient's pillow, as that will disgust him, so that he will not sleep with the patient. Among Muhammadans a light may be lit and taken to the mosque at night by the patient who pretends to be looking for something until an inquisitive passer-by asks what he is looking for. Then the sufferer should throw down the lamp and reply: 'find it yourself.' The fever will then leave the patient and go to the passer-by.[1]

A stye can be got rid of in a very similar way. Go at nightfall and knock at a neighbour's door. At the cry, 'Who is there?' reply that you have given and they have taken the disorder. When the inmates rush out to abuse you, you must escape their pursuit.[2]

Vaccination is also objected to by some Muhammadans because it is believed that the Imám Mahdi will be born with milk in his veins, and vaccination would reveal this child by puncturing its arm.[3]

The causes and cures of disease in animals differ only in detail and not in principle from those of disease in men. In the Dehli District branding Chamárs on the back has been resorted to as a means to extirpate cattle-disease. The victim appears to be entitled to a fee. He must turn his face away from the village and not look back. This should be done on a Saturday.[4] It may also be got rid of by volley firing near the animals affected.[5]

Transference of cattle-disease is effected by a rite called *rorá dálná* or *nikálná*, *rorá* being the articles carried in procession to the boundary of the infected village and thrown into the confines of the one adjacent to it. In one case under a *jogí's* advice they consisted of a buffalo's skull, a small lamb or pig (carried by a sweeper), vessels of butter and milk, fire in a pan, wisps of grass, and sticks of *siras* (*acacia speciosa*).[6] This must be done on a Sunday and on that day and the preceding Saturday no field work must be done, grass cut, corn ground, food cooked or fire lighted. The village to which the murrain is transferred must lie to the east of that which transfers it. A Brahman should be present and a gun fired off three times.[7] A simpler method is to get a *faqír* to write a charm on a wooden label, hang inside a pot like the clapper of a bell and hang it over the village gate. It will ring when the wind blows and stay the disease.[8]

[1] Mrs. F. A. Steel in P. N. Q., I, § 352.

[2] P. N. Q., II, 774.

[3] *Ib.*, II, § 939, and I, § 1012.

[4] *Ib.*, I, § 227, I, § 596.

[5] *Ib.*, I, § 228.

[6] P. N. Q., I, § 760. Saturday and Sunday are in some way sacred to horned cattle, for cattle, leather and *ghi* must not be bought or sold on those days. And all cattle dying on those days are buried, not eaten by the village menials: *ib.* I, § 1015.

[7] *Ib.*, I, § 532. A similar rite is performed in cases of cholera epidemic: *ib.*, II, § 25.

Should a bull die of murrain, it should be wrapped in a cotton and buried in a road leading to the village over which the sick cattle will pass. This will stay the disease.

Túna or *tona* is the generic name for physical prayers of this character. A murrain may be stayed by getting a *faqír* to bless a long string by reciting passages from the sacred books over it and attaching to it potsherds and bits of red rag on which charms have been written. It is then hung up across the village-gate, and the cattle passing under it will be cured.

For the disease called *sat* it suffices to tie up one of the stricken cattle outside a shrine.[1] But in Hazára a more elaborate rite is used by the Gújars against cattle-plague. The infected animals are placed in a circle and a *mulláh* or some person of saintly descent goes round them thrice. Each animal is then passed under a long piece of cloth in which a Qurán has been wrapped. The bones of dead animals are occasionally buried in another stable to which it is hoped to transfer the disease.[2] Elsewhere a *kár* or circle is drawn round the herd and a holy man rides round it, sprinkling water and repeating the creed.[3]

A galled bullock may be cured by applying the ashes of a lizard killed on a Sunday and burnt.[4]

The disease of horses called *simuk* is cured by killing a goat or fowl and letting its blood flow into the horse's mouth, or if this cannot be done quickly, it is sufficient for a naked man to strike the horse's forehead 7 times with his shoe.[5]

When the pods open and cotton is ripe for picking women go round the field eating rice-milk, the first mouthful of which is spat on the field towards the west. This is called *pharakná*. The first cotton picked is exchanged for its weight in salt which is prayed over and kept in the house till the picking is over.[6]

Catarrh in horses is cured by burning blue cloth in a *loṭa* and making him smell it.[7]

Múla or blight may be expelled from a crop by enticing a Hindu named Múl Chand or Múlráj into the field and thence kicking him out or driving him away with blows.[8]

Madness in dogs is ascribed to their eating bones on which a kite has dropped its excreta.[9]

Sikhs believe that recitation of the words *om sat nám* will cure rheumatism, cough and billiousness. They procure salvation in the next world and safety in this. Recited after meals they help digestion and bring good luck.[10]

[1] P. N. Q., I, § 1015.
[2] *Ib.*, II, § 278.
[3] *Ib.*, II, § 800.
[4] *Ib.*, III, § 796.
[5] *Sirsa Sett. Rep.*, p. 207.
[6] *Sirsa Sett. Rep.*, p. 183.
[7] Montgomery *S. R.* (Purser), p. 82.
[8] P. N. Q., III, § 539.
[9] *Ib.*, II, § 246.
[10] N. I. N. Q., I, § 184. *Cf.* § 309.

Modern Hinduism.

Shaivas and Vaishnavas —The grand distinction in actual practice between Shaivas (including Shaktís) on the one hand and Vaishnavas on the other does not lie in any of the numerous theoretical differences noted in the books written on the subject so much as in the fact that the former have not, generally speaking, any objection to the eating of meat, while the latter have. "In Hindustán," as the author of that very curious book, the *Dábistán*, puts it, "it is known that whoever abstains from meat and hurting animals is esteemed a Vaishnava without regard to the doctrine." The Shaiva may worship Vishnu, and the Vaishnava Shiv, but the Vaishnava will not taste meat, while the Shaiva may partake of meat and drink spirits. It is sometimes said that the worshippers of Deví are of two classes,--those who worship Vishnu-Deví and who are in every respect Vaishnavas being in the one class, while those who worship Kálí-Deví and to whom the term of Shiv is more applicable constitute the other. Of antagonism between the Vaishnavas and the Shaivas we hear very little in the Punjab; and the distinction here is less one of religion or of the god worshipped than of practice and ceremony and the manner of food eaten. Outwardly the main distinction lies in the *tilak* or forehead marks: those of the Vaishnavas being generally speaking upright, while those of the Shaivas are horizontal. The rosaries of the one sect will be of *tulsí* bead; those of the other of the *rudráksh* plant. The Vaishnavas worship in the Ṭhákurdwáras where Rám or Síta or Lachman is enthroned: the Shaivas in Shiválas or Shivdwálas where the *ling* is the central object of worship. There is more gladness and comprehensiveness in the ideas of the former: more mystery and exclusiveness in those of the latter. The Bánia is almost always a Vaishnava; the Brahman, unless he belongs to a clan which has Bánias for patrons[1] (*jajmáns*), is generally a Shaiva.

The Shaivas.

The terms Shaiva and Shakti.—A worshipper of Shiv is not necessarily, in the ordinary sense of the term, a Shaiva by sect, nor is a person necessarily to be termed a Shaktí by sect because he worships Deví. The term Shaiva is generally applied, not to any worshipper of Shiv, but to those only who are more or less exclusively devoted to his worship or who perform certain ceremonies or adopt certain customs which may or may not be specifically connected with the worship of this deity, but which are at any rate in strong contrast to those which are followed by the Vaishnavas. Similarly, the word Shaktí, though applicable in the wide sense of the term to all worshippers of Deví, is in its narrower meaning applied only to those who have been initiated in, and have been allowed to witness and partake in, the more secret worship of the goddess; but as these more mysterious ceremonies are in popular estimation of a somewhat disreputable character, there is a certain bad odour about the term Sháktik, which induces many true members of the cult to return themselves merely as Deví worshippers.

[1] I have changed 'clients' here to 'patrons;' the term *jajmán* means, literally, 'he who gets a sacrifice performed.'—H. A. R.

Maclagan, § 46.

Shiv.—The wonderful mingling of attributes in the great deity Shiv, the strange coalescence of death and mystery, and lust and life, is forcibly described in one of the most powerful of Sir Alfred Lyall's poems. The god is reverenced under each of his many characters and many attributes. To some he is the great primeval cause, the origin of creation, the "Sadá Shiv," the god that ever was and ever will be. His worshippers, following the Musalmán terminology, sometimes term him Bábá Adam. To others he appears as the pattern ascetic: powerful by his austerities and terrible in his curses: he feeds on flesh and drinks strong drinks: he lives on *bhang;* he takes one-and-a-quarter maunds of *bhang* every day. To a great part of his worshippers he appears less as a god than as a strenuous devotee, all-powerful with the gods. To another part he is an unseen influence, personified in the *ling* or conical stone, which in its origin represents the regenerative power of nature, but which to nine-tenths of its present adorers has probably no meaning whatever beyond the fact that it is a representation of Shiv. In the plains the *ling* forms the central object of worship within the dark, narrow cell which constitutes the ordinary Shivála or Shiv temple: and it is only in the hills that it is commonly to be seen outside or by itself; but in the Punjab, generally speaking, the worship of the *ling* is not so prevalent or prominent as in Benáres and other places, where the worship of Shiv is in greater force.

Shiv has 100 names, but the commonest of all is Mahádeo, or the Great God, under which name he was most frequently designated by his followers at the Census. They also termed him Maheshí,—Mahesh-wara, the Great Lord, and Shambú, the Venerable One. They call him also Sheonarain, and his following is known as Sheo-mat, Sheo-dharm, or Sheomarg. His strongholds are mostly outside these provinces, at Benáres, Rámeswar, Kidárnáth, Somnáth, Baijnáth etc. The Ganges, which flowed from his matted hair, is specially sacred to his followers. Their chief scriptures are the *Shiv Purán* and *Uttam Purán.* They worship at the Shivála with offerings of flowers and water and leaves, with the ringing of bells, and the singing of hymns. Their sectarian marks are horizontal across the forehead, and they will often wear necklaces of the *rudrákhsa.*

All castes are worshippers of Shiv; but he is not a popular favourite in the same way as Vishnu or Krishna. It has been before pointed out that the worship of Shiv is mainly a Brahman worship, and it is undoubtedly most prevalent where the Brahmans have most power—a fact which conflicts somewhat with the theory sometimes put forward that Shaivism is a remnant of the aboriginal religions of the country. The following of Shiv is in these provinces confined mainly to the high class Brahmans and Khatrís, and the example of the latter is followed by the Sunárs, or goldsmiths, and the Ṭhaṭheras, or copper-workers; the *Mahesri* Bániás are also his devotees: but among the ordinary agricultural community the worship of Shiv is uncommon and the Shiválas in the villages of the plains are almost always the product of the piety of money-lenders and traders, not of the agriculturists themselves

Rose, § 28.

In the Himalayas Shiv is worshipped extensively, especially by all the lower castes. The home of Shiv is believed to be the peak of Khaskar in *pargana* Takpa of Bashahr, and music is at times heard on its summit. Old men say that on the smallest of its peaks, visible from Chíni, is a pool surrounded by mountains amongst which lie Shiv's temple and the homes of the other *deotas*. Many years ago a holy *faqír* came to this mountain to worship Shiva and accomplished his pilgrimage, but by returning to ask some favour of the god, incurred his displeasure and was turned into a rock which can be seen from Kailás north of Chíni. This rock has a white tint at sunrise, a red at mid-day, and a green at sunset. Kailás itself is the abode of the dead.

On Sri Khanḍ, a peak 18,626 feet above sea-level, is a stone image of Shiv, called Sri Khanḍ Mahádeva, which is worshipped by placing a cup of *charas* in front of it and burning the drug to ashes. Everything offered to the god is placed under a stone. Six miles further on, in Kulu, is Níl Kanṭh Mahádeva, a peak visited by *sádhús* only on account of its inaccessibility. It has a spring of red water. Barmaur again is a Shiva-bhúmi or 'territory of Shiva,' and hence, it is said, the Gaddís of Chamba are Shaivas.

The prevalence of Shaivism in the Himalayas may be gauged by the following note by Dr. Vogel:—"There are no less than 49 places of worship (44 being temples proper) in Manḍi, and of these 24 are Çivalayas, 8 Deví temples and 2 are dedicated to Çivaistic deities. This shows the preponderance of Çivaism in Manḍi. Ṭhe number of Ṭhákurdwáras (Vishnu shrines) is *seven* only. Among the çivalayas most are Linga-temples, but the oldest are dedicated to Çiva Pancavaktva (*i.e.* the five-faced) whose curious images are remarkably numerous in Manḍi." Writing of Káŋgṛa, Dr. Vogel says:—"Though Çivaism no doubt prevails everywhere and all the principal temples and *tírthas* are dedicated to Mahádeo or Deví under various names, there seems to have been a great deal of Vishnu (or Krishna) worship among the Rájás. At least I found this with regard to those of Káŋgṛa and Núrpur, who may be considered to have been the more important ones. It seems that while the popular religion was the grosser Sivaism, the Rájás took to the higher form of Vishnuism. This seems to be the most obvious explanation, though it is quite possible that there were other causes and the Rájás perhaps introduced Vishnuism from the plains It is curious that a Krishna image in the Fort at Núrpur is said to have been brought from Udaipur in Rájpútána."

Similarly, in Kulu, Ṭhákur Gopál, the cow-herd (Krishna), is worshipped by the former Gurús of the Rájás, though Sivaism is prevalent in the Kulu Valley, and in the Simla Hills the cult of Vishnú is said to be entirely confined to immigrants from the plains, the indigenous population being wholly Shaivas or Shaktaks.

The following are accounts of some Shiva temples in Káŋgṛa:—

The Shrine of Bálak Rúpi, near Sujánpur in Káŋgra.—One Ganesha Brahman, a *parohit* of the Jaswál Rájas, gave up his office and took up his abode in Dhár Bálak Rúpi, whence he repaired to Hár where the temple of Bábá Bálak Rúpi now stands. His grandson, Jogu, when he was about 10 or 12 years old, one day went to his fields with a plough on his shoulder. In the jungle he met a young Gosáín[1]

[1] He is so called because the Bábá manifested himself while yet a child (*bálak*).

who asked him if he would serve him. Jogu consented, whereupon the Gosáín instructed him not to tell anybody what had passed between them. Leaving the Gosáín Jogu went to the fields where other men were working, and on his arrival there began to dance involuntarily, saying that he did not know where he had left his plough. The men rejoined that the plough was on his shoulder and asked what was the matter with him. Jogu told them the whole story, but when he had finished telling it he became mad. Ganesha, his father, thereupon took some cotton-thread and went to a Gosáín, by name Kanthar Náth, who recited some *mantras*, blew on the thread, and told him to put it round the neck of Jogu, who on wearing it was partially cured. Kanthar Náth then advised Ganesha to take the lad to Bábá Lál Púri, a good Mahátma who lived in the village of Ganyar Ganjhar, which he did. Lál Púri let him depart, telling him that he would follow him. He also declared that the Gosáín whom the mad lad had met was Bábá Bálak Rúpi, and that he had been afflicted because he had betrayed the Bábá. Ganesha went his way home, but Bábá Lál Púri reached Hár before him. Thereafter both Bábá Lál Púri and Jogi Kanthar Náth began to search for Bábá Bálak Rúpi. At that time, on the site where Bálak Rúpi's temple now stands, was a temple of Gugga, and close to it was a rose-bush. Bábá Lál Púri told Ganesha to cut down the bush and to dig beneath it. When he had dug to a depth of 4 or 5 cubits he discovered a flat stone (*pindi*) against which the spade, with which he was digging, struck (the mark caused by the stroke is still visible) and blood began to ooze from it till the whole pit was filled with gore. But after a short time the blood stopped and milk began to flow out of it. Next came a stream of saffron which was followed by a flame (*jot*) of incense (*dhúp*) and finally by a current of water. Bábá Lál Púri said that all these were signs of Bábá Bálak Rúpi. He then took the idol (*pindi*) to Neogal Nadi or Kund in order to bathe it, whereupon milk again began to issue from it. The idol was then taken back to its former place. While on the road near Bhochar Kund (a tank near the temple on the roadside) the idol of itself moved from the palanquin, in which it was being carried, and went into the tank. Bábá Lál Púri and Kanthar Náth recovered it and brought it back to the place where it had first appeared. During the night it was revealed to Bábá Lál Púri in a vision that Gugga's temple must be demolished and its remains cast into the Negal Kund or used in building a temple to Bálak Rúpi on the same site. This can only mean that the cult of Bálak Rúpi is, or was, hostile to that of Gugga. Accordingly the idol was stationed on the place pointed out. Bába Lál Púri said that Jogu's eldest son and his descendants should have the right to worship the idol, while the out-door duties would be performed by Kanthar Jogi's descendants. At that time Sasrám Chand Katoch was the Rájá of that territory. Rájá Abhi Chand was the first to make a vow at the temple of Bábá Bálak Rúpi in order that he might be blessed with a son. When he begot a child, the Bábá began to be resorted to more eagerly.

A Patiál Rájpút girl was once told by her brother's wife to graze cattle, and on her refusing, the latter said:—'Yes, it is beneath your dignity to graze cattle because you are a Ráni; be sure you will not be married to a Rájá.' The girl in distress at this taunt untied the cattle and led them to the jungle. At that time Bába Bálak Rúpi had again become manifest. The girl supplicated him and said that she would not believe him to be really Bálak Rúpi unless she married a Rájá, adding that if her desire were fulfilled, she would offer a bullock[1] of copper at his temple. Five or seven days had not elapsed when a Rájá of the Katoch dynasty chanced to pass by where the girl was herding cattle, and seeing her he bade her to be taken to his seraglio, where he married her. Unfortunately the girl forgot to fulfil her vow, and so a short time after all the Ránís in the seraglio began to nod their heads (*khelná*), as if under the influence of a spirit, and continued doing so day and night. The Rájá summoned all the *sádhús* and *chelas*. One of the latter said that the cause of the Ránís' being possessed by spirits was that a vow to Bába Bálak Rúpi had not been fulfilled. The Rájá replied that if all the Ránís recovered, he would take all his family to the temple and present the promised offering. The *chela* then prepared a thread in the name of the Bába and when this was put round the neck of the persons possessed they recovered. This all happened on a Saturday in Jeṭh. Thereafter a bullock was made of copper, and the Rájá also erected a temple. When the bullock was offered (*jíb-dán*), the artist who had made it died forthwith.[2]

Whenever any misfortune is about to befall the Katoch dynasty the copper bullock is affected as if by fear This occurred on the 29th of Háṛ Sambat 1902 and Rájá Partáb Chand died on the 15th of Sáwan in that year. On that day Bábá Bálak Rúpi's idol also perspired. For these reasons the bullock is worshipped and vows are made to it.

The *játrís* (offerers) who make vows at the temple of the bullock on the fulfilment of their desires offer *jopu topu* and *boṭna* and rub the bullock with the offering. They also put a bell round his neck. These offerings are taken by the Jogi on duty, there being several Jogís who attend by turn.

Four fairs, lasting eight days, are held in Bálak Rúpi's honour on every Saturday in Jeṭh and Háṛ. Those who have vowed to offer he-goats present them alive, while those who have vowed to sacrifice he-goats slaughter them at a fixed spot within the temple precincts. The head, fore-legs and skin are given to the Jogi on duty, and some rice and a pice are also paid to him as compensation for ancestor-worship. The he-goats brought to be slaughtered are killed at Neoga Kunḍ, and also cooked and eaten there. But sometimes the people take the cooked meat home and distribute it as a holy thing.

The ceremony of *jamwálu* (or shaving the hair of a child for the first time) is usually performed in Bálak Rúpi's temple and the hair is then offered at the temple. Even those who observe the ceremony at home often come to the temple and offer the hair. An additional present, the amount of which varies from two pice to any sum that one's means allow, is also made. All these offerings are taken by the Jogi on duty. *Játrís* who make offerings (*e.g.* of a human being such as

[1] Clearly the bull (*beil*) of Shiva.

[2] *Cf.* the story on p. 207 *supra*.

a child, or of a buffalo, cow, horse etc. according to their vow), give it, if an animal, to the Jogi on duty, but in the case of a child its price is paid to the Jogi and it is taken back. Besides these, cash, curds, umbrellas, cocoanuts and *ghí* are also offered. The offerings are preserved in the *bhanḍár* (store-house).

The people living in the vicinity of the temple, within a distance of 15 or 20 *kos*, do not eat fresh corn (termed *nawan*, lit. 'new') unless they have offered some of it at Bálak Púri's temple. Fairs are held on each Saturday in Jeṭh and Háṛ.

There is another temple to Bálak Rúpi at Nagroṭa, but no fair is held there. It has been in existence for about 13 generations, and contains a marble image of Mahádeo, 4 fingers high. A Gosáín *pujári* manages it. His caste is Puri and *got* Úsab. He may marry, but a *chela* always succeeds his *gurú*. Worship is performed morning and evening, fried gram in the morning and bread in the evening being offered as *bhog*. *Ártí* is also performed in the evening and a sacred lamp lit.

In Manḍi Bálak Rúpi is described as another famous temple of Shiva in Bangáhal. He is worshipped in severe illness and is also supposed to remove ailments of all kinds [1] As a Siddh he has a shrine at Bálak-Rúpi in Kamlá, and a smaller one at Hatli, both visited for the cure of diseases.[2] Bálak Náth, the son of Shiva, appears to be quite distinct from Bálak Rúpi.[3]

The shrine of Siddh Bairág Lok near Pálampur.—The founder of the shrine, when a boy, when herding cattle, once met a Gosáín who told him never to disclose the fact of their friendship or he would no longer remain in his place. Keeping the secret, however, made him ill, and so at last he told his parents all about the Gosáín. They gave him *sattu* for the holy man, but when about to cook it the boy complained that he had no water, whereupon the Gosáín struck the ground with his *gaja* (an iron stick) and a spring appeared, which still exists. The Gosáín did not eat the food, saying his hunger was satisfied by its smell. The boy then caught the Gosáín by the arm, upon which the latter struck him with his hand and turned him into stone. The Gosáín himself disappeared in the earth. The boy's parents searched for him for 5 days, until one night the secret was revealed to one of his family who was directed to erect a temple a little above the spring. Another story is that a few days later a Bhát Brahman became possessed and saw all that had occurred. So a temple was erected and the place called Bairág (Gosáín) Lok, from *alop*, disappearance. As Bairág Lok had been a herdsman, he became peculiarly the god of cattle and fulfils vows made regarding cattle. The fair is held on Háṛ 3rd. He-goats and corn are offered. In this temple there is also an image of Gorakhnáth, placed therein by a Goleria Mián in Sikh times. The stone idol of the boy has disappeared. The followers of the shrine regard the Gosáín as Gorakh-

[1] Manḍi *Gazetteer*, p. 41.

[2] *Ib.*, p. 40.

[3] *Ib.*, p. 38; see *infra* under Hinduism in the Himálayas, for the cults of Shiva in Manḍi.

náth himself. The keepers of the shrine are Gir Gosáíns and Bhát Brahmans.[1]

If in the above examples Shiva is disguised almost beyond recognition, those tabulated below are often connected with Shiva by the slenderest of ties, such as the mere presence of his image in the fane:—

Place and name of temple.	*Pujári.*	Dates of fairs.	Ritual.
Bhaniár-Shivji Gandhurb in the only remaining bastion of the Gandhurb fort which was destroyed in the Sikh times.	Brahman, *got* Samkariye and *gotar* Atri.	*Shibrát* on Phágan *badi chaudas*. Vows are made for relief from periodic fevers and *rot* offered.	*Bhat* in the morning and soaked gram in the evening.
Dudahu-Shivji, founded in Sikh times by a Rájput.	A Brahman is employed under the Rájpút *pujári*.	None, but on 14th Phágan *sudi* people assemble to look at the idol of Shiva which is a span high and seated on a *jalahri*.	Fruit.
The *mandir* of Baij Náth at Pálampur. The story in that Ráwan meditated here and consequently obtained success in every undertaking.	Bhojki and Brahman. The *pujári* is a Brahman, caste Samlú, *got* Koudal.	A fair lasting 4 days on the *chaudas* in Phágan.	It contains a stone *ling* of Shiva, which is one foot high above the ground. A sacred lamp is kept lit day and night. Connected with this are the shrines of Lachmi Naráin and Sidh Náth.

[1] For other Siddh shrines see p. 278 *infra*.

Place and name of temple.	*Pujári.*	Dates of fairs.	Ritual.
Súraj Kuṇḍ *mandir*. The main tank is called Súraj Kuṇḍ. Near it are three small tanks, called the Rám Kuṇḍ, Síta Kuṇḍ and Lachhman Kuṇḍ. These buildings and tanks have been in existence about 550 years or from the time of Jahángír.	A Giri Gosáín, *got* Atlas.	None ...	The largest building contains a stone *pindi* of Shiva, one span high; also an image of Man Mahesh seated by its side, ½ cubit high. The place is one of great sanctity and people come to bathe and pay devotions here. Worship is performed twice a day, morning and evening. Fruit in the morning, rice at noon and bread in the evening form the *bhog*.
The *mandir* or Thákurdwára of Gupt Ganga. The tank here is fed underground from the Manikarn spring and so it is called Gupt Ganga. Two other *kuṇḍs* to its north and east are called the Shiv Kuṇḍ and Gauri Kuṇḍ, respectively. The temple was founded in S. 1923.	Brahman, Lagwál, *got* Gárg.	None	The temple contains images of Shiva, Ganga and Narbada made of marble. That of Shiva is 4 fingers high and that of Ganga one cubit. Both are adorned with gold and silver ornaments. Fruit is offered as *bhog* morning and evening.
The *mandir* of Kapáli Bhairon in Kángra town. At the *jag* celebrated by Parjapati, his daughter, Shiva's wife, being insulted, committed suicide. Her *kapál* or brain fell from above and Bhairon, an attribute of Shiva, standing below caught it on this spot. Hence the *mandir* was called Kapáli Bhairon.	A Jogi, *got* Alakh	None.	

Place and name of temple.	*Pujári.*	Dates of fairs.	Ritual.
The *mandir* of Bir Bhadar Shúr, the subordinate god of Shiva, was founded in the Sat Yúg. It is held in great sanctity.	A Brahman, caste Bhoda, *got* Bhárdawáj.	None... ...	It contains a black stone image of Shiva seated on a *jalher* and one span high.
The *mandir* of Chakar Kuṇḍ: the disc or *chakar* which killed the *rakkhasa* Jálandar fell on this spot; hence it was called Chakar Kuṇḍ.	A Gosáín, caste Púri, *got* Bhoru.	None	The temple contains a stone *pinḍi* of Shiva, one span high. The Púskar temple is connected with it.

THE CULT OF MAHÁDEO.

Mahádeva is the originator or creator of many castes, generally of the lower grades, Brahma being the progenitor of the higher castes, such as the pure Brahmans, while Mahádev created such castes as the Bháṭs and the Chárans. He created the former to attend his lion and bull, but they would not prevent the lion from killing the bull which vexed Mahádev as he had to create new ones. He therefore formed the Cháran, equal in devotion to the Bháṭ, but of a bolder spirit, and placed him in charge of his favourite animals. Thenceforth no bull was ever destroyed by the lion.[1]

Sleeman relates a story of an informant who naively declared that the British Government was nothing but a multiplied incarnation of Shiva. The god himself had so declared through his oracles and had announced that his purpose was to give his people impartial Government and prevent internecine warfare.[2] The flattery was not so gross as it might appear.

To Mahádeo are offered daily leaves of the *bel, Ægle marmelos,* called *bil-patri,* and *tulsí kí minjarán* or ears of the sacred basil,[3] while ambergris is also burnt before him daily. To him in particular is sacred the *pipal,* though Shiva is found in its branches together with Brahma and Vishnu. The banyan tree is similarly sacred to Vishnu and the *nim* to Devi as Káli Bhiwáni.

[1] Malcolm's *Central India,* II, p. 109.

[2] Sleeman's *Rambles,* II, p. 241, quoted in P. N. Q. III, § 401. The story recalls the one told to Sir G. Robertson when he asked if Yush, the chief of the devils, resembled himself, and was informed that he did not, but that he was like the English private soldier, *i.e.* of a reddish colour.

[3] Dr. Hutchison connects the *minjarán ká mela* of the hills with the cult of a river-god: see p. 213 *supra.*

Cult names of Mahádeo are numerous. In the Simla Hills he is called Bhoteshar, from Bhothi, the name of a village in which his temple[1] is situated.

The cult of Mahádeo is not only deeply seated in Kángra, but it is also varied in form, Mahádeo being worshipped under various names. At Jawáli he appears as Kamteshar,[2] as Kalishar in Kuthiára,[3] as Narbadeshar in Sujánpur,[4] as Bilikeshar[5] in Sapṛa (Nádaun), as Tameshar in Nádaun,[6] and so on.

The real history of the shrine of Bába Baroh Mahádeo, near Jawála Mukhi, is not known, but the story goes that under a *banyan* or *bari* tree (whence the name *baroh*) appeared an idol of stone still to be seen in Danaya, by name Kálí Náth, whose merits Bába Lál Púri preached. In 1740 S. Dhián Singh, *wazír* of Goler, was imprisoned at Koṭla and a soldier at the fort, a native of Danáya, persuaded him to make a vow to Bába Baroh, in consequence of which he was released. The *wazír* however forgot his vow and so fell ill, until he made a large pecuniary offering to the shrine. In that year the small old temple was replaced by the present larger one under Bába Lál Púri. The followers of Bába Baroh keep a *jholi* (cloth bag), an iron chain, *khaṛáwán* (sandals), and a *choli* or shirt, in their houses. Grain is usually offered at the shrine, with flour, *ghi* and *gur* for the bullock (there appears to be an image of a bullock also). If a he-goat is sacrificed, the skin and a hind-leg are offered up, the rest being eaten by the *játri* on his way home. Sometimes a *kudhú* or living he-goat is offered, as the substitute for a life in case of sickness, or by one who is childless. Women can enter the shrine.[7]

Gowála was a holy man in Kángṛa. His legend runs thus :—

One day as he was sitting on a lofty hill near Baroh a wedding procession passed by and he said to the bride: 'Thorns on this side and on that: she who wears the red veil is my wife.' The bridegroom challenged him to jump down from the hill and he did so but was killed. The bride then took his head in her lap and said to the bridegroom: 'You gave me to him; I burn on the pyre with him.'

[1] A temple to Mahádeo may owe its foundation to a trivial cause, *e.g.* the image of Mahádeva of Purag was found in a field named Majhoni. It resembled Shiv in appearance and hence it was called Mahádeva.

[2] Ascribed to the time of the Pánḍavas, this temple contains a stone image called Gang Mahádeo, one span high.

[3] Also ascribed to the time of the Pánḍavas. Before that Káli performed austerities at this spot.

[4] Called after a conical stone or *ling* brought from the Narbada, the temple was founded by Ráni Pansan Devi, wife of Rájá Sansár Chand of Kángṛa. Founded in S. 1870 it was completed in S. 1882. On each side of it are 4 small shrines: a sun temple, containing an image of a man on seven-headed horse, 2½ ft high; a Ganesh temple; one Chatarbhuji Devi; and one to Lachhmi Náráin. Each of these contains a stone image 3 ft. high. *Bhog* is offered five times a day, *misri*, milk, *koṛáh*, gram etc. being given.

[5] Said to be called 'after the Biás and the Kanah.' It is said that 10,000 years ago the Pánḍas or gods began to erect the temple by night. This was noticed by some men and so the gods left it half-built. It was finished by Rájá Bhom Chand.

[6] Founded by Rájá Abhi Chand (date not known). It contains a stone *ling* 4½ cubits high. Connected with it is a temple of Sítala containing 4 images.

[7] This shrine seems independent of the cairns near Baroh.

This resolve she carried out, and the cairns erected in memory of Gowála's bravery exist to this day.

The following is a list of temples in this district to Mahádeo:—

1	2	3	4
Place.	*Pujári.*	Date of fair.	Ritual offerings &c.
The *mandir* of Gang Bhairo Mahádeo, in Achi, dates from the Satyug when Ganga came and sat down to rest. A few cows were grazing here and the cowherd called to one of them whose name was also Ganga. Ganga thinking she had been recognized by the man disappeared, leaving the marks of her hoofs on a stone, which is held in great reverence and people worship it. Formerly an image of Mahádeo stood at the foot of a *pípal* tree.	Giri Gosáín, *got* Atlas.	*Shivrátri* ...	The temple contains a carving of Gang Bhairo Mahádeo on a black stone, 1 span high and 4 in circumference.
The *mandir* of Tapteshar Mahádeo in Baranj. A hot spring near the temple is attributed to the power of the god. It was founded by a Goler Rájá.	Brahman Gosáín, *got* Lash.	*Shivrátri* ...	It contains an image of Shiva, of white stone and 1 foot high. Worship is performed morning and evening when fruit or food cooked by the *pujári* is offered to the god.
Chiri—Srí Soba Náth. There is a smaller *mandir* in the verandah of the temple. It is said that Soba Chand, Ráná of Chiri founded the small temple and named it after himself, but eventually it came to be called Soba Náth.	Brahman Bhojki. The manager of the endowment is a Giri Gosáín by *got* a Rátash, who is celibate	*Shivrátri* ..	Rice in the morning only. The temple contains a black stone image (*pindí*) of Shiva, 4 ft. in circumference and ½ ft high. It is held sacred and worshipped largely by the people of Rihlu.

1	2	3	4
Place.	*Pujári.*	Date of fair.	Ritual, offerings &c.
The *mandir* of Kunjesar Mahádeo in Pálampur was once the site of a grove of *bel* trees amidst which a crane made its nest. From its nest sprang Mahádeo and manifested himself. He was named Kunj after the crane. One night it was revealed to Rájá Diláwar Chand of Kángra then childless, that if he built a temple in honour of Shiva, he would be blessed with a son. Accordingly he made a search for the *pindi* of Shiva in the *bel* forest and it was found among the trees where the temple was built. It was not long before the Rájá begot four sons. In fulfilment of his vow he celebrated a great fair.	A party of *pándas* who attend the temple in turns. Their *got* is Kondal. The *pujári* is always chosen from the *pándas*.	*Shivrátri* in Phágan.	*Bhog* of *dál*, bread and rice etc. is offered in morning. In the evening soaked gram is offered and distributed only among the low caste people, such as Chamárs, Juláhás etc. But these low castes are not allowed to make offerings to the temple, nor are they admitted into it.
The *mandir* of Indar Shúr Mahádeo in Kángra town. Once Rájá Indar in a procession passed Durbale Rishi who offered him a garland which the Rájá, considering it beneath his dignity to wear, put on his elephant. The devotee in anger at this cursed him and ere long the Rájá was utterly ruined. So he resorted to the devotee and begged him to restore his lost blessings. He recommended him to worship Deví Barashwari and she pleased with his devotion restored his fortunes.	A Bráhman, caste Sándal *got* Koshal.	None ...	The temple contains a black stone *pindi* of Shiva 4 fingers high and 3 cubits in circumference; and two images of Páras Náth (*sic*).

1	2	3	4
Place.	*Pujári.*	Date of fair.	Ritual, offerings &c.
The *mandir* of Nandi Kashúr Mahádeo in Jadrágal is situate on the bank of the Ban Ganga river. It is said that Nandi-ji practised devotional exercises here and enshrined an image of Shiva whence the temple is called Nandi Kashúr. It is said to have been founded by a Suket Rání.	Its affairs are managed by a *pujári* and a supervisor, both Giri Gosáins, *got* Atlas. One is celibate and the other not; so succession is governed both by natural and spiritual relationship.	A fair is annually held on the *Shivrátri* in Phágan.	The temple contains a stone image of Shiva seated on a *jalheri* and 1¼ spans high. It is said that above this image (without any support) hung the image of Nandi, whom the Rání once visited to do it homage. Seeing the miraculous suspension of the image, she hesitated to enter the temple, lest it should fall on her. So she built a supporting wall before she entered it. It is held in great sanctity by the Hindus.
Bindi—Juṛ Mahádeo ...	A Bhaṭṭi Jogi, *got* Maríchh.	No fair, but people gather on the *Shivrátri* to look at the image.	The temple contains a stone *pinḍi* of Shiv-ji. It is a cubit high and a foot in circumference. It stands on a *jalheri*. Either *guṛ* or soaked gram is used as *bhog* in the morning. In the evening only *árti* is performed.
Gúga Mahádeo and Indarshur Mahádeo at Chitru founded by the same Rájpút who founded Kidár Náth's temple at Shuráh.	A Gosáin of the Sándash *got*.	Jeṭh 13th ...	Sugar or fruit is offered as *bhog* in the morning and evening. The image of Indar Shúr is a cone of stone ½ cubit high and a foot in circumference. Gúga is mounted on a horse.
Ghaniára—Mahádeo, Indeshar, founded by a Bharthi Gosáin in time of Ranjít Singh, some 200 years ago (!)	A Bharthi Gosáin who is elected from the *chelas*.	None ...	The temple contains a white stone image, 4 fingers high, brought from the Narbada.

1	2	3	4
Place.	*Pujári.*	Date of fair.	Ritual, offerings &c.
Dal Kareri—Mahádeo Ghanbheria: no temple.	A Jogi, by *gotar* Alakh.	Though there is no temple, a *pindi* of Shiva exists, and though no fair is held, people resort to the place for bathing on the *ashtmi* of the *Shúkal pachh* in Bhádon when the hill is clear of snow. The place is called after the image.	*Rot* is offered and he-goats etc. sacrificed in *bhog.*
At Dharmsála—Warweshwar Mahádeo.	A Giri Gosáín ...	*Sudi ashtmi* in Bhádon.	*Bhog* is offered twice a day, rice or bread in the morning and soaked gram in the evening.
At Dharmsála Mahádeo Bhágsu Náth: called by the Gaddis Bhágsu Nág, by others Bhágsu Náth, his real name is Bhageshar.	A Giri Gosáín by *gotar* Atarsan, who is celibate.	Durga-ashtmi, *sudi* Bhádon. On the day of the fair, offerings of curd, *ghí*, milk or grain are made. Thread is also offered in lieu of a *janeo* or sacred thread.	Worship is performed twice a day morning and evening. Something cooked is offered as *bhog* at noon. The black stone *pindi* of Mahádeo, 2 spans high, is said to have created itself. On the birth of a calf, people offer milk, curd and *ghí* which are called *fakh.* A young goat is also sacrificed, its head and loins being taken by the *pujári* as his perquisite.
At the *mandir* of Mahán Kál in Pálampur the god Kál performed devotions. The fair is celebrated on the date on which the building was completed. It has been in existence for 100 years and was founded by Sáh Chand, a Katoch.	Brahman, *got* Bhodah.	*Nirjalá ikádshí* in Jeth.	The temple contains a stone *ling* of Shiva, ½ foot above the ground. *Bhog* is offered at noon and evening, and then distributed among *faqírs*, the *pujári* etc. The temple is held in great sanctity and the dead of the adjacent towns and villages are brought to be cremated here.

The cult of Shiva being so widespread in the Himalayas, it is interesting to find that in the remote tract of Saráj in Kulu few temples of Mahádeo are reported to exist. At Shángri Ishar Mahádeo has a temple which came to be founded in this wise: One Chandi, a Kanet, went on a pilgrimage. On the way he met a *faqír* who joined him. When evening came on they halted for the night in Dhamoli where there were no houses, but only a few deodár trees. The *faqír* told the Kanet that he had meditated there in the Duápar Yug. Meanwhile a Brahman had joined them, and they asked him to dig at a certain spot where a *pindi* would be found. It was found accordingly and the *faqír* then disappeared. The temple was built at this spot and the *pindi* installed therein. The *pujárís* are Sársut Brahmans.

Shamsheri Mahádeo derives his name from Shamsher, a village where he has five temples. A stone *ling*, resembling Shiva, appeared beneath some *drub* grass and was brought to a village by the Brahman who founded the temple in which it is enshrined. Four fairs are held here, the Bhonḍa in Poh, the Shánd on an auspicious day in Maghar, the Jal on the *amáwas* in Phágan and the Parbat on Chet 8th. At the first-named two 400 he-goats must be sacrificed, but at the last two 40 suffice. Three of the five temples are built of stone and two of wood. There are ten stone idols, each 6 feet high, and a stone ox also. A few masks of brass representing human faces are also used in decorating the god.

Bini Mahádeo similarly derives his name from Bin, the village in which his temple stands It is called Bindehra. Legend has it that in Bin lived two Ṭhákars, named Jaún and Tadashú. A dispute arose between them and they fought at Malgidográ, until a *mahant* or saint came out of the stream and bade them cease. Ṭhákar Jaún asked him whence he had come and whither he was going. The saint replied that he had come from the land of the Kaurús and Páṇḍavás. The Ṭhákar begged him to settle the quarrel and when he had done so he and Jaún started for the Biás. On the road they were annoyed by a man at Sholad, so the saint cursed the people of that village, and it was burnt. Next day they reached a spring and the saint vanished in the water. At night a voice was heard saying that a temple must be built in the village which should be named Bin after him. So the temple was built and a *ling* of Mahádeo appeared in it of its own accord.

Jagesar Mahádeo has two temples in Saráj, one at Dalásh on the Sutlej and one at Rohru. The Shánd is celebrated every 30 years at Dalásh, and there are annual fairs at each temple. The story is that in the Duápar Yug a devotee, Jagad Rishi, came down from Kailás and meditated here. A black stone idol soon manifested itself to him, and he was so overjoyed at its sight that he became its votary. One night it was revealed to him in a vision that it was Mahádeo himself, who was born on the 5th of Bhádon. In the morning the *rishi* found that he was blind, so he made a vow to Mahádeo, and as his sigh was restored, he built the temple and fixed the date of its fair. Th other temple at Rohṛú was built later. The temple is managed by Jhínwar *kárdár*, but the *pujári* is a Sársut Brahman. Special reverenc is only paid to the *gur* or disciple of the god, because he goes into trances and answers all questions put to the god.

Buḍá Mahádeo has a temple at Netar Ḍera. The story of its foundation is that Kapál Díp, an aged devotee, meditated at its site for many years. At length he disappeared beneath the earth and thenceforth he was known as Buḍá Mahádeo. Once Rájá Parichat pitched his tent on the site of the temple. Next morning he found himself blind in both eyes. In reply to his supplications he was told of Kapál Muni (*sic*) and he sought his aid. When his sight was restored he built this temple which was called Netar Ḍera or the 'place of the eye.' The annual fair lasts from the end of Sáwan to the 15th Bhádon. *Prabs*, a kind of fair, are also held in Chet, Phágan, Jeṭh, Sáwan, Bhádon, Asuj and Poh. Low caste people are not allowed to make offerings.

Bashehar Mahádeo[1] has a temple at Nirmanḍ on the Sutlej. A cow was observed to yield her milk to a *pinḍi* hidden in long grass and so it was woshipped and a temple eventually built over it. The people of Nirmanḍ use no milk or *ghí* till it has been offered to the *pinḍi*.

The temple of Bongṛu Mahádeo and Deví Haṛwá in Pháti Chanúl is known by many names, such as Gashwálá Deorá, Deori Deorá, and Shiglí. Annuál fairs are held on the Shivrátri in Phágan, lasting for 15 days; during the three days after the Holi; on the Naurátrás in Chet and Asúj; on the 9th and 12th Baisákh; the 20th and 25th Háṛ; on the Puniyá in Sáwan; the 2nd, 4th and 5th Asúj; the 16th Kátak; and on the 5th Maghar.

The story of its origin is that a Ráná when hunting reached the summit of a hill, and found a *yogi* deep in meditation, who told him that he came from Shivpuri and was Shivá himself. At the Ráná's prayer the *jogi* accompanied him to his home at Kahá where he asked the Ráná to build him a temple, but when it was built he would not sit in it and took from his pocket a small box out of which sprang a beautiful maid called Haṛwá Devi. He then desired that a temple should be erected for this goddess also, and so a shrine was built in her honour.

Kulchhetar Mahádeo has a temple at Alwá, a village founded by Paras Rám after he had extirpated the Khatrís. A few Brahmans settled in it, and to them he gave a metal *kals* for worship. It was enshrined in a temple, and stands three cubits high.

At the temple of Bhanáh Mahádeo fairs are held at every Diwáli and on the 1st Baisákh. The Bhunḍa is celebrated every 40 years, and is said to be followed by a Shánḍ which is held every 12 years. The story of its origin is that a Ṭhákur, Raghú, had a cow which was grazed by a blind boy on the further side of the river. A snake sucked the

[1] The temple of Bashehar, Sanskr. Vishveshvara, Mahádeo at Bajaurá in the Kulu valley appears to give its name to that place. It probably dates from the 17th century when the Rájás of Kulu vigorously promoted the worship of Krishna and Ráma: *Arch. Survey Rep.* 1909-10, p. 20. It is suggested that the promotion of this worship was connected with the importation into Kulu of the militant Bairágis recorded by Lyall: Kangra *Sett. Rep.*, §§ 82 and 94, on p. 85 as having been made under Rájá Thedi Singh, *flor. c.* 1758.

cow's milk for many days, until, to the cowherd's great joy, when he reached the other side of the river, his sight was restored. The news reached the Ṭhákur's ears. The snake was found, but ere long it disappeared under the ground whence rose a metal image which said that it was Mahádeo himself. The Ṭhákur then built a temple in which it was enshrined. The *pujári* is a Gauṛ Bráhman.

In Kulu proper Mahádeo has some ten temples. His cult names are Bijli Mahádeo or Bijleshar, the lightning god, at Malthán Dera, Jawanu, Larain or Larani at Laran, Manglishar, Siáli, Sangam and Shibrhárach, besides Gauri Shankar and Nílkanth :—

Deota Mahádeo ...	Chohki Ḍera ...	9th of the light half of Maghar.
Deota Bijli Mahádeo or Bijlishar Mahádeo.	Malthán Ḍera ...	1st of Chet and 1st of Hár, 1st to 7th Asúj, five fairs from 1st to 5th Baisákh. Pípal Játra for 12 days at Sultánpur, 18th Baisákh and 19th Baisákh.
Deota Gauri Shankar Mahádeo.	Dawala Washál Waugar	Shivrátri in the dark half of the month of Phágan for 2 days.
Deota Jawanu Mahádeo.	Ḍera Jawánu Mahádeo ...	1st and 2nd Chet, during the same month in the light half of Parwa and Dutia, 1st to 3rd Baisákh, 1st and 2nd Sáwan and 1st to 3rd Bhádon.
Deota Larain Mahádeo.	Laran Ḍera ...	In Phágan, 2nd Chet, new year's day 1st Baisákh, 1st Jeṭh, 1st Bhádon, Janam-ashṭmi and 1st Asúj.
Deota Manglishar Mahádeo.	Chhanwar Ḍera ...	6th Baisákh and a *yag* every 2nd year from 1st to 4th Sáwan.
Nílkanth Mahádeoji	Known by the name of its deity.	On the Shivrátri, the 4th of the dark half of Phágan and Kálí Púja from 1st to 4th of Jeṭh.
Sangam Mahádeo ...	...	No fair, but two festivals called Tára Rátri and Shiv Rátri.
Deota Siali Mahádeo	Ḍera Siali Mahádeo ...	26th of Phágan on the Shivrátri, 12th and 13th of Chet.
Deota Shibrhárach ...	Ḍera ...	1st of Phágan.

In Manḍi Nangol Mahádeo in Lad has countless natural idols of Shiva. A Gaddi who had incurred his wrath was also turned into stone.[1]

[1] Manḍi *Gazetteer*, p. 41.

Koṭ Ishwar.—Koṭ Ishwar Mahádeo (Shiva) originated from the temple of Durga at Hát Koṭi. (Durga's own history goes back to the times of the Mahábhárata.) When Koṭ Ishwar Mahádeo began to oppress the people in Hát Koṭi the Brahmans thought that the god had become a *rákshasa* (devil), and two Brahmans, Obu and Shobu, by magic shut him up in a *tumbi* and corked up its mouth. The *tumbi* with the god and goddesses and two *mátris* in it they intended to throw into the Sutlej 40 miles from Hát Koṭi, which lies on the banks of the Pabar. When they reached Paroi Bíl, two miles from the Sutlej, the Brahman who was holding the *tumbi* stumbled and let it fall. As it broke in pieces the imprisoned god, with the two *mátris*, escaped. Koṭ Ishwar Mahádeo took shelter among the *bana* and *bhekhal* bushes: one of the *mátris* soared to the top of the Tikkar hill, now called Kecheṛi, where she took up her abode in the *kail* trees; and the other flew across the Sutlej halting at Khekhsu. Koṭ Ishwar again began to trouble the people in the form of a serpent. He would suck milk from the cows and they blamed the cow-boy who was much alarmed, when one day he saw a serpent suck milk from his cows. He told the owners of the cattle, and a Brahman of Bataṛa, a village near Kumhársain, went to the spot and called on the serpent to appear if he were a god, threatening to burn him by magic as an evil spirit or devil, if he did not. So the god walked into his presence and the Brahman bowing before Koṭ Ishwar invited him to his village where he lived for 12 years. No Rájá then ruled this part of the hills which were held by the *mawannas* or *máwis*. Sunu, a powerful *mawanna*, heard of the god's miracles and began to worship him. Once he dreamed that the god did not wish to live at Mathana Jubaṛ where a temple was proposed for him, but would prefer Pichla-tiba, now called Koṭi; so a temple was built there for him. Long after, his present temple was built on a larger scale at Madholi. At first he was represented by a single *ashṭ dhát* idol, but subsequently some 15 more idols of mixed metal were added as its companions. A *rath* (palanquin) was also made and the god seated in it at *melas*. Bhuṛa, another contemporary *mawanna*, came to a *mela* organised in honour of the god by Sunu *mawanna*. He was dressed in ape skins. But Sunu did not allow Bhuṛa to come before the god or touch his *rath*, so Bhuṛa returned to his home at Bhuṛa, scarcely 3 miles from Madholi, in disgust. One day after his return, when breaking up new land he found a gold image, and for this he made a *rath*. Seated in it this *deota* was brought to Madholi as he desired to live there with Koṭ Ishwar, and Sunu and Bhuṛa abandoned their feud. Koṭ Ishwar was a terror to the countryside. He would kill any *mawanna* who did not obey him. Some indeed say that the gold image which Bhuṛa found was Koṭ Ishwar himself in a new form, and that Bhuṛa was killed by him. When the Brahmans of Hát Koṭi learnt that Koṭ Ishwar had become a good spirit and was displaying miracles at Madholi, two of them came to Lathi village, where they have been settled now for 77 generations. Bhuṛa *deota* appeared about the same time as Koṭ Ishwar. His worshippers offer him only gold or *masru* cloth while Koṭ Ishwar can accept anything. Goats are usually sacrificed. The following *melas* called *jágrás* are held in honour of these *deotas*:—

(1) Bharaṛa on the 1st Jeṭh; (2) Madhauni on the Rakhṛi Punia in Bhádon; (3) Madholi on the *Púranmáshi* day in Bhádon; (4) Pati Jubaṛ on the 6th or 7th Asáṛ; but at several places the *jágrás* are held in Baisákh and Sáwan on any day that may be fixed.

Koṭ Ishwar ruled this part of the hills before the Geṛu or Giáṛu family settled at Karangla. Some time later the Geṛu brothers quarrelled over the partition of the kingdom, and so a cow-girl divided it into two parts, *viz.*, Karangla and Kumhársain.[1] When the first Ṭhákur came to Kumhársain the country was made over to him by Koṭ Ishwar, who showed him favour so that State has given him a *jágír* worth Rs. 506, and pays the expenses of his *jágrás*. Six generations ago Ṭhákur Rám Singh of Kumhársain fought with Ráná Pirthi Singh of Keonthal and the Ṭhákur gained a victory by his aid. Every third year the *deota's chari* or staff is taken to all the *básas*, and when a new Ráná ascends the *gaddi* the *deota* himself tours the country in a *rath*. Every house presents 4 *pathas* of grain. Koṭ Ishwar is the *Kula Deo* or *Kul deota* (family god) of the chief of Kumhársain.

MAHÁDEO IN GURGAON.

The *deota* Sherkot of Kumhársain has his temple in the palace at Kumhársain. He is none other than Koṭ Ishwar himself, but is called Sherkoṭ. None but members of the Ráná's family and the State *parohits*, who are called Sherkoṭu Brahmans, can go into his temple. It is said that the original idol of Koṭ Ishwar is kept here, and that the image at Mandholi is only a duplicate.

The temple of Bindeshwar Mahádeo at Fírozpur-Jhirka in Gurgaon is peculiarly interesting because its administration vests in 4 Hindu and as many Muhammadan Jogi families, appointed by the Hindus of the town. Their duty is to keep it clean and watch it by night. The offerings are taken by all the Jogis according to their shares, but they are distributed by the Hindus, Muhammadans not being allowed to touch them. There is no *mahant*. The Muhammadan Jogis are Bar-Gújars by tribe and 'Ismáíl' (*sic*) by *panth* or sect. They can enter the temple, but may not touch the image and take no part in the worship, doing only menial duties. All the Jogis are at liberty to marry. The image came out of the hill 1000 years ago. West of the image stands a minaret.

The fair of Swámi Dyál is held at Swámíká in tahsíl Núh on Kátak *súdi* 13th and 14th. An old man, Swámi Dás by name, used to worship here, so when he died a temple was built and called after him. The village was founded afterwards and was named after the temple. Its management vests in the Hindu Khatrís who keep the place clean and take the offerings. Their *got* is Jángar. Another temple connected with this stands inside the village, but its administration vests in the Muhammadan land-holders of the village and they take the offerings. In the time of the Nawáb of Hathín some thieves robbed people at the

[1] Her decision is said to have been:—Jis Kepu tis Kanár, Jis Khekhar tis Dalár—"He who gets Kepu will get Kanár and he who takes Khekhar shall have Dalár." (Kepu and Khekhar are villages on the banks of the Sutlej and Kanár and Dalár are villages high up the valley. A stream, the Sawári Khad, divides the country.)

fair held at the temple outside and so this small temple was built in the village. The fair is now held there. A drum is beaten on every Sunday and lamps are lit. At the fair a *chádar* or piece of cloth is offered on the grave, and offerings of cows and cash are also made. These are taken by the Muhammadan Rájpúts who also take a share of the offerings to the outer temple. The courtyard of the inner temple has a grave at each of the four corners. The offerings on all these are taken by the Muhammadans.

At the temple of Bábáji, situate in Bajhere, a fair is held from Kátak *súdi* 14th to Mangsir *badi* 1st, lasting 3 days. It begins at Swámíká whence the people come to Bajhere. The temple was built 119 years ago by the Rájá of Bhartpur. It contains no image and has no *pujári*, but there are 4 bedsteads, one in each corner of the temple, and offerings are made upon them. Its administration is carried on by the Hindu Ṭhákurs of the village whose *got* is Khajúri. A *chirágh* is lit by a Gaur Brahman every evening at each bedstead and the offerings consist of pice, sweets and other eatables Some 6000 or 7000 people visit the fair. They are mostly Chamárs, but they only come to see the sights and make no offerings. The four bedsteads represent the four Bábájis or *faqírs*. The eldest was the *swámi*, the next his son, the other two his grandsons.

At the temple of Mahádeo at Núh a fair, called the Jal Jhálni, is held on 11th Bháden for 4 *gharís* in the evening from 4 P. M. The temple was built by Rúṛa, a Gauṛ Brahman, 10 years ago. Before that the fair was held at a tank close by. The offerings are taken bye Jogi.

The Siddhs.—A cult of very great antiquity is that of the Siddhs. In the *Mahábhárata* they are seemingly associated with sister-marriage and Pársi funeral rites which might indicate a Zoroastrian origin.[1] They are described by Monier Williams as semi-divine supposed to possess purity. They probably represent deified ascetics of ancient times. They are propitiated in the same manner as the Nágs and Devís.

In Chamba there are temples to Siddhs at Chhatri, in *pargana* Kohal, at Alla in Pichhla Diur, at Ghorni in Kihar, at Jharoli and Saroga in Kihar, at Siddhkadera in Pángi, and to Nanga Siddh at Rájnagar and at Mua in that *pargana*. It will be seen that all but the latter are nameless Siddhs. The temple at Chhatri is a square building one storey high, built of wood and roofed with slates, and is said to have been built in the reign of Músha Varma. It contains three images of stone, each the miniature of a man, riding a horse of stone. The hereditary *chela* and *pujára* are Ráthís by caste. The temple contains 10 iron chains and 3 maces, which are taken from village to village during the 8 days after the *janam-ashṭami*. The god is supposed to make a tour during this period, and villagers, who are under a vow, then make offerings which serve as his *bhog* throughout the year. *Bhog* is offered to the god, and he is worshipped once a day. The other Siddh temples resemble that at Chhatri in construction, and all are said to date from the time of Músha Varma. Their images are precisely

[1] J. R. A. S., 1915, p. 440. This description refers to Uttara Kuru.

the same in character, but vary in number, there being 4 at Alla, 2 at Ghorni, 5 at Sabil, 2 at Jharoli and Saroga, 1 at Rájnagar, and 3 at Mua (Moa). The *chelas* and *pujáras* are hereditary, but of different castes, being Chamárs at Alla, Ráthís at Ghorni, Sabil Brahmans at Jharoli, Ráthís at Saroga and Rájnagar, and Hálís at Moa. In only one instance it will be seen are they Brahmans. The Siddhs of these places also go on tour precisely like the Siddh of Chhatri and at the same period. In some cases the *chela* and *pujára* divide the cash offerings, reserving those in kind for the Siddh.[1]

Dewat Siddh.—The Siddhs of the Himalayas do not appear to be connected with the Jogís, though they may be spiritual relations of Gorakhnáth, as the following account of Dewat Siddh shows:—

Bába Bálak Náth was born in the house of a Gaur Brahman at Girnár Parbat, a famous place of pilgrimage for a sect of *faqirs*[2] in Káthiáwár. He was the disciple of Ridgir Saniási, and wandered to Changar Talai in Biláspur where he became the cowherd of a woman of the Lohár caste. Some Jogis[3] attempted to convert him and pierce his ears by force, but he refused to abandon his faith and called aloud, whereupon a rock close by split open and he disappeared into the cleft, in which he is supposed to be still alive, though he was born 300 years ago. A sacred fire (*dhúni*)[4] is kept burning in the cave, which was made by enlarging the cleft and reached by a ladder placed against the cliff. The priests are Giri Gosáíns who are celibate, and Brahmans, who receive ⅓nd of the income while the rest goes to the Gosáín chief priest. The itinerant *chelas* collect offerings in kind, such as flour, out of which *rot* or large loaves are made for the other Siddhs. The followers of Dewat Siddh carry a small wallet (*jholi*) and a Jogi's crutch (*phaori*). Hindus, Muhammadans and low-caste people alike offer sacrifice: for example Bangáli snake-charmers offer cocks, and Hindus a goat which must shake itself to show that the sacrifice is accepted. Adherents of the sect (for such they may be called) should visit it every third year, and Sundays, especially the first in the month, are the best days for worship. Women cannot[5] enter the cave, but they may make offerings to the lesser images of the Siddh at the foot of the ladder. In the cave itself are three images of the Siddh, one of stone, said to be the oldest and about a foot high, one of white marble, and a very small one of gold. The cliff is covered with carvings of Hindu gods etc. Connected with this shrine are those of the brothers

[1] Chamba *Gazetteer*, 1904, p. 183. For the offerings to a Siddh among the Gaddís, see Vol. II, p. 269 *infra*. They clearly denote their character, being suitable to wandering devotees.

[2] They are 'akin to the Jogís' (*Punjab Census Report*, 1892, § 46, p. 107).

[3] Another story is that a party of Gosáíns tried to persuade him to join their sect because they saw his sleeping form overshadowed by a cloud while the rest of the land was exposed to the sun. But he fled and when pursued disappeared in the earth. At the spot a Brahman and a Ját afterwards found a lamp burning: whence his name of Dewat. The cave is reached by a flight of 16 steps and a platform on which some 200 people can just stand.

[4] On this the *bhog* or food of the Siddh is cooked.

[5] Another account says they can. Probably they cannot enter if ceremonially impure.

of Dewaṭ, Bálak Rúpi near Sujánpur and Baroh Mahádeo near Jawála Mukhi, in Kángṛa; and other Siddh shrines have been founded at Banga, in Jullundur, and in Manḍi, as the cult is spreading and its popularity increasing. The legend points to some old dissension between the Jogi worshippers of Shiva and those of Bhairava, the earth god, and the fact that a cave is used as the temple also points to earthworship. In Hoshiárpur Dewaṭ Siddh is said to have sucked milk from an uncalved cow (doubtless a form of parthenogenesis) and his shrine is consulted for sick children or cattle.

But the accounts of the Siddh's origin are so discrepant that nothing certain can be predicated of his cult. The fact that his fair is held annually on the *Gúgá Naumi*, the day after the *Janam-ashṭmi* in Bhádon, points to some connection with Gúga. Again it is said that only men of good caste are permitted to worship at the cave, and that the Siddh changed his abode and appeared in five different places during a recent famine, but returned at length to his first home.

Dewaṭ Siddh must not be confused with Siddh Deota who, according to Oldham, has numerous small altars and slabs of stone in the Kángṛa valley. On these are sculptured foot-prints of Buddha, known as Siddh-pát, and they are often seen decked with flowers. Oldham identified Siddh Deota with the Boddhisattwa Manjusri and speaks of images of Siddh or Buddha at Baijnáth and another temple to Shiva, as well as of a Siddh *deota* of Siddh Koṭ, a very ancient and popular cult.[1] The sign of a Siddh in Chamba also is a pair of foot-prints and to him a pair of sandals are offered.[2] But the correctness of Oldham's deductions is open to question. He describes a *new* image of Buddha which its priest, an orthodox Brahman, called Siddh *deota*. It is doubtful if the image was one of Buddha if new, though an old image might be revered as that of a Siddh. In Hoshiárpur, where there are 10 or 12 Siddhs and the one at Baratri is of some importance, the cult is said to be a branch of Shiv worship, and as local divinities of the outer Himalayas all their shrines are found on the tops of the green hills[3]

At the Shivála known as Sidh-Singhwála in Moga a fair is held at the Shivrátri. This temple was built in S. 1934 by Sidh Singh, Jáṭ. It contains an image of Shiva made of stone. Its administration is carried on by a Saniási *sádhu* who is celibate The *pujári* washes the *ling* or symbol of Shiva twice a day and performs *árti* morning and evening.

Rosaries.—The Hindu rosary in the Punjab is called *japmála* and contains 108 beads, excluding the sumer or head bead, but each sect has its special type of bead, as the following table shows:—

Shaivas	. *rudráksha*	the dark brown seeds of the *rudráksha*=*clæocarpus ganitrus*.

[1] P. N. Q., III, § 253.

[2] *Ib.*, § 163. According to the Simla Hill States *Gazetteer*, Biláspur, p. 11, a favourite offering to Dewaṭ Siddh is a small pair of wooden sandals, and stones so marked are his commonest symbol.

[3] Hoshiárpur *Gazetteer*, 1904, p. 68. For Siddh Bairág Lok, see p. 111 *supra*.

Shaivas ...	*bhadráksha* ..	the brown seeds of the *bhadráksha.*
Vaishnavas ...	*tulsímála* ...	the white seeds of the *tulsi*=*ocymum sacrum.*
Do. ...	*chandanmála* ...	sandal-wood stained red.
Shåktas ...	*naridrásh* ..	yellow beads made of turmeric root.
All Hindus ...	*kadam ki mála* ..	of white beads made of *kadamba*=*nauclea cadamba wood.*
Rájputs ...	*pramál* ...	red coral.
Wealthy Brahmans, Khatrís and Bánias	*muktamála* ...	white pearls.
Bánias and lower castes ...	*kamaldodi ki mála*	the black seeds of the *kamal dáda* (?)

TRIBAL DEITIES.

Most of the tribal deities appear to be forms of Shiv or semi-mythical ancestors equated to Shiv.

Bájwa.—Apparently Bába Báz (or Báj) was an ancestor of the Bajus. He was a very holy *faqír* who worshipped on the bank of the Chenáb at Chak Khoja, near Phuklían. Ishwar in the shape of Lakhmanji appeared to him out of the river. So did the Jal Pír. Then he became a Siddh (*i.e.* a famous saint). When he died he was buried, not burned, and his *samádh* is there. Near it is a temple or *ṭhákurdwára* of Raghonáthji. The principal *múrat* in it is one of Ṭhákurji, but there are smaller *múrats* of Shiv, Vishnu, Krishan and Deví, Lakhmanjí, Rám Chandar and others. When Báz was recognized by the gods and became a Siddh the Bajus all put on necklaces of *tulsi* in token that they were followers of Báz.[1]

Cháhil.—At the *mandir* called Jogi Pír at Kuli Cháhilán in tahsíl Moga a fair is held on the 4th *naurátra* in Chet. This temple is called after a Cháhil Jáṭ. It contains no image, and the worship is only offered to Jogi Pír. A *faqír* keeps it clean, but the offerings go to a Ṭhákur Brahman in whose family this office is hereditary.[2]

Gil.—At the temple of Rájá Pír in Rajiána, tahsíl Moga, in Firozpur two fairs are held, one on the *chaudas* of Chet, the other on 1st

[1] The Bájwas have a curious rhyme:—

> *Unche pinḍon ái Mihr Dádu Dia:*
> "*Tujhe Mának, Manga, Nár Singh, Naráin dia,*
> *Aur bhi dia, aur bhi dia.*"
> "*Bas?*" "*Bas bhi dia.*"

Mihr Dádu Dia, a Mírási, came from Unche Pinḍ and said to the ancestor of the Bájwas:—"Naráin has given you Mának, Manga and Nár Singh." The Bájwa said:—'*Bas?*.' "He has given you *Bas* also"—Bas being a daughter of the Bájwa. Hindus of the clan may not say *bas* and after a meal they say *anand hogayá.*

[2] Jogi Pír is alluded to in the article on the Cháhil in Vol. II, p. 146 *infra.*

Baisákh. Rájá was a Jáṭ.[1] The date of its foundation is not known, but it is said to have existed before the settlement of the village. It contains no image, only a platform of burnt brick. Its administration is carried on by the Gil Jáṭs, its votaries. They bring a Gil Jáṭ *chela* to officiate at the fair and he takes the offerings. *Chúri* or *karáh parshád* is offered, but only by Gil Jáṭs. No sacred lamp is lit. At the fair both men and women dance before the sanctuary.

Gorá ya.—In Rupána, a village in Muktsar tahsíl, lived one Bála Dín, a Muhammadan and a Goráya by tribe. He was a *faqír* who used to make charms etc. and was very popular, so the fair held there was called Goráya after his tribe. On his death on 20th Phágan S. 1953 a brick platform was raised on which his tomb rests. It contains no image. The administration vests in a *darwesh* who lights lamps at the tomb. The fair is held on 20th Phágan and sweetmeats etc. are offered.[2]

Mallhi.—At the temple known as Mári Lachhman at Pabbián in Ludhiána a large fair is held annually on the day after the Chet *chaudas*. The villagers who are Jáṭs of the Mallhi *got* thus describe its origin:—At Charkh in the Kalsia State a large fair is held on this date, and as the Mallhi Jáṭs are entitled to the offerings made there, those of Pabbián claimed a share in them, but the Mallhis of Charkh refused it. So about 300 years ago the Mallhis of Pabián sent Sháman, their *mírási*, to Charkh to bring two bricks and two oil lamps belonging to the *mári* from that place clandestinely. With the bricks the foundation of the *mári* at Pabián was laid in the time of Rái Qarar of Talwandi, and the fair which now attracts about 10,000 people every year was inaugurated. The *mári* is a large dome-shaped building of brick, 22 feet square and about 43 feet in height. It is two storeyed with an open court-yard on all sides which with the *mári* building occupies 12 *biswas* of land in all. Inside the *mári* is a platform of 10 bricks, 4 feet 9 inches long and 3 feet 8 inches wide, but no image of any sort. Several hundred *bighas* of uncultivated land are attached to the *mári* for holding the fair, and no one uses any wood standing on this land for his own purposes. There is no *mahant* or manager, but the Mallhi Jáṭs collectively take the offerings. The only form of worship is that men and women of the village gather there every Thursday and distribute sugar in fulfilment of vows. At the fair people from a distance also offer presents which they had vowed to present, if by the grace of the Máriwála Pír their desires have been fulfilled. People also bring cattle to get them cured by a night's stay at the *mári*. Inside the *mári* is another but smaller dome known as the temple of Bhairon. He, it is said, was a devotee of Lachhman by whose name the *mári* is known.[3]

This fair is clearly connected with the one thus described:—At the temple of Lachman Siddh at Mári village in Moga tahsíl a fair is held annually on 14th Chet. Lachman was a Mallhi Jáṭ. The temple

[1] He was a Gil and so specially affected by the Wairsi Gils: Vol. II, p. 300, *infra*.

[2] This fair is not alluded to on p. 303, Vol. II, *infra*, and is not apparently a tribal one.

[3] In the article on the Mallhi Jáṭs (Vol. III, p. 68, *infra*) this *mári* is described as that of Tilak Rái, ancestor of the clan.

contains no image. Only a round platform which is kept covered with a sheet. A lamp is lit every evening by a Mallhi Jáṭ of Mári. No *pujári* is employed, but one of the tribe is chosen to officiate at the fair and he takes the offerings.

Sindhu.—At the place called Kálá Paisa or Kálá Mohar[1] in Kohar-Singhwála in Firozpur tahsíl no fair is held Tradition says that Kála, a Sindhu Jáṭ of Rájá Jang in Lahore, was a cattle thief who ravaged all the countryside between Farídkoṭ and Koṭ Kapúra, until he met 5 saints to whom he gave milk to drink. They named him Kálá Paisa. A few days after this, he died and was burnt at this spot which is held sacred. His descendants founded many villages named after them, such as Kohar-Singhwála, Jhok Thel Singh etc. The custom of the Sindhu Jáṭs is to lay one brick on this spot when any of them visits it. A bride and bridegroom also do obeisance to it and offer *gur* etc. Kohar-Singhwála village was only founded some 60 years ago. A *mírási* lives at the place, and the Sindhu Jáṭs make offerings of *gur* etc. which are taken by him. At the *mári* or tomb of Mana Singh, *zaildár*, a fair is held on the Baisákhi every year. He was a Hindu Mahtam who died some 20 years ago, and his descendants built him a *máṛi* of brick. The fair is attended by 1000 or 2000 people, the *Granth* being recited and *kaṛáh parshád* distributed among the visitors. Lamps are lit at the Baisákhi, Diwáli and *Amávas.*

According to a legend current in Siálkoṭ Kála Pír came from Ghazni in Central India, and settled in the Punjab. As his eyes were never closed when he slept, people thought he was always awake. He had two servants (*lágís*) a Brahman and Mirási, who were with him day and night. His enemies first asked the Mirási when he slept, and he replied that he never slept. Then they asked the Brahman who betrayed the truth that he slept with his eyes open. So with the Brahman's connivance they came and killed him, and his head fell at the spot where he was slain, but his body continued fighting sword in hand until some women met it and said one to another:—"Look! a headless body is fighting." Then it fell to the ground and Kála Pír declared that his offspring would never trust Brahmans. So wherever Sindhu Jáṭs live they build a place to Kála Pír in their village according to their means, and at a wedding bring the bride and bridegroom there to *salám*. They also give a goat, a rupee and other gifts according to their means to the Mirási.

How these tribal deities come to be regarded as emanations or manifestations of Shiva cannot as yet be explained. Possibly some light on the problem could be obtained from Professor Chatterjee's work on Shaivism in Kashmír, but despite repeated efforts no copy of that work has come into the compiler's hands.

It is, in this connection, curious to note that Sir Denzil Ibbetson said:—"Shiválas are not at all uncommon in the villages, built almost without exception by Bánias. The priests are *gosáíns* or *jogís*, generally of the *kanphaṭe* or ear-pierced clan, and they take the offerings. No Brahmans can partake of the offerings to Shiv, or be priests in his tem-

[1] 'Black pice' or 'Black *mohar*,' literally. No explanation of this curious name is given. It appears on p. 425 of Vol. III as Kálá Mihr, but Kálá Mohar must be more correct as Kálá Paisa is its synonym.

ple, though they will worship him and sometimes assist in the ceremonies, thus deviating from the strict rule of the original cult. On the Sheorátris on the 13th of Sáwan and Phágan such people as have fasted will go to the Shivála; but it is seldom entered on any other days.[1]" The Bánias are essentially a caste of the south-east Punjab. On the other hand, the cult of Sakhi Sarwar, "chiefly worshipped by the Gujars and Rájpúts," is apparently dissociated from Shaivism, for its great festival is held on the Salono, in the south-east of the Province[2], and this festival falls on the 15th of the light half of Sáwan, a day not apparently devoted to Siva, for it is auspicious for the consecration of amulets, or *rakhis*, which are then put on. Brahmans and Bairágís take the offerings to Vishnu, and there would not appear to be any Shaiva Brahmans in this part of India, though they exist elsewhere, one of their number having founded the Jangam sect.

It appears to be impossible to reduce the ritual of any cult to hard and fast rules, but that of Shiva in Karnál offers most varied features. Thus the *shivála* at Kirmach Chak is visited on the *badi ashṭami* in Bhádon, while that of Jagan Náth is visited on the *tarostís* in Sáwan and Phágan, and the *chabútra* or platform of Shiva in Dáúdpura only on the *tarosti* in Phágan. This last only contains a stone image of Shiva, one foot high. A Jogi only attends at the fair and he takes all the offerings. No *pujári* is employed and no scared lamp is lit. On the other hand, the temple at Kirmach contains 15 stone images of Sálig Rám and 4 brass images of Lál Ji, while an image of Hanúmán stands in a small temple to Ṭhákar in the precincts of the main *mandir*. Its administration is carried on by a Bairágí. That of Jagan Náth contains a stone image of Shiva 15 inches high, one of Párbati 13 inches high and an effigy of Hanúmán is painted in vermillion on the wall. Its administration vests in a Brahman. Occasionally it is said of a *mandir* that its *pujári* must be a Brahman, but he may generally be a Gosáín or a Jogi and may celebrate all the offices of the temple like a Brahman. A *pujári* may be hereditary or elected, or his office may go by spiritual descent if it vests in any order. But a Brahman *pujári* is generally hereditary.[3] The greatest differences are found too regarding the *bhog*, the use of a scared lamp and the maintenance of fire. How far all or any of these divergences in ritual are due to the various deities associated with Shiva it is impossible to say, but the gods and godlings found in his temple vary infinitely. For example, at the *Shivála* of Ek Onkár at Karnál the annual fair, held on the *dhuj sudi* Bhádon, is frequented both by Hindus and Muhammadans who pay their devotions alike. Founded by Báwa Kirpál at the charges of Mahárája Ranjít Singh, in S. 1873, it contains a stone image of Mahádeo, 1½ feet high and 2 feet thick, a stone image of that god only 6 inches high, and one of Síta 1½ feet high: also stone images of Párbati (9 inches high), of Lachhman (1½ feet), one in red stone of Ashṭ-bhuji (10 inches high),

[1] Karnál *Sett. Rep.*, 1883, § 364.

[2] *Ibid.*, § 382.

[3] That is to say, a Brahman if appointed *pujári* would transmit his office to his descendants. This may seem incompatible with Ibbetson's view, but probably a Brahman who becomes a Jogi or Gosáín is eligible for appointment in a Shiva temple as he loses his Brahmanhood by entering one of those orders and yet retains his hereditary sanctity.

and small stone images of Sálig Rám, Ganesh and Gomti. A clay image of Hanúmán stands in its outer wall. The *pujári*, who is always selected from the Gosáíns, is held in great respect, and performs all the rites of worship. The use of *charas* is ceremonial and all the *sádhús* are provided with it. *Bhog* is offered morning and evening A *dhúni* or sacred fire is always kept burning and votaries also light lamps at the temple.

The *matt* of the Gir Gosáíns at Karnál is said to have been in existence for 800 years. It contains stone images of Deví and Shiva. *Bhog* is offered in the morning, and a sacred lamp lit in the evening is kept burning all night.

The *astal* or *mandir* of the Bairágís at Karnál is visited on the *Janamashtmi* in Bhádon. It is said to be 500 years old and contains images of Krishna and Rádhika made of brass; a copper image of Hanúmán and a stone image of Sálig Rám; and another image of Hanúmán made of clay and set on a wall. Its administration vests in a Bairági *pujári*, by sect a Mímánadi and by *got* a Rájpút. He is celibate and held in great respect. He performs all the rites. *Bhog* is offered on the *janamashtmi* in Bhádon and distributed among all the visitors. A sacred lamp is lit every evening. No distinction is made in the offerings of different Hindu castes

At the *matt* of Gosáín Báwa Bhagwángir no fair is held, but the place is visited on each Monday in Sáwan and on the *Shivchaudas* in Phágan; on which occasions offerings of water are made. Said to be 400 years old, it contains 4 stone *pindís* of Shiva, varying in height from 4 to 6 inches and 3 stone images of Deví, each 2 inches high. The Gosáín *pujári* is held in great respect and as such is styled *mahant*. He performs all the rites of worship. The use of *charas* is not ceremonial. *Bhog* is offered in the morning Sacred fire is kept burning. No distinction is made in the offerings of different Hindu castes. Connected with this is the Gosáín *dhera* in Pansána.

At the *asthal* of the Bairágís no fair is held, but the place is visited by people who fast on the *badi ashtmi* in Bhádon and make offerings of water The story is that Vishnu dwelt here for some time and after his departure a cow lived on the same spot and in her honour the temple was eventually built. It has been in existence for 200 years, and contains a brass image of Krishna, with two brass images of Bálmokand Jí, all 4 inches high, while that of Deví is 6 inches in height. Three brass images of Naráin each 2½ inches high stand under a canopy. The height of a brass image of Hanúmán is 2½ inches. There are also small oval-shaped stones which are called Sálig Rám. The administration is carried on by a Bairági who is a Vaishnava. He is celibate and the senior *chela* or disciple always succeeds his *gurú*. The *mahant* is held in great respect and performs all the rites. The use of *charas* is ceremonial. *Bhog* is first offered to the images in the morning and evening and then distributed among all present at the shrine. Sacred fire is always kept burning but a lamp is lit in the evening only. No distinction is made in the offerings of different Hindu castes. Connected with this is the *dhera* in Parthali. The *samádh* or *asthal* of Devi Dás Bairági has existed since the settlement of the village, 100 years ago. It contains brass images of Hanúmán, Sálig Rám, Khaniyá, Rádhika and Shivji. The administration is carried on by a Bairági.

Another Gosáín *mandir* is that of Bába Sáhib Mohini in Barota who died in S. 1893. Founded in S. 1901 it has no fair, but it is built of brick and contains his tomb with a few brass and stone idols placed round it. Sacred fire is always kept burning. No distinction is made in the offerings of different Hindu castes. A *Shiválа* is connected with it.

The *akhára* of Báwa Sehjgir in Halka Uncha Sewana was erected in commemoration of the Báwa after whom it is called. It contains the tombs of many saints, and has a *shivála* in its precincts containing a stone image of Gaurán Párbati and one of Sálig Rám, both 1¼ feet high. A sacred lamp and fire are both kept burning in the temple. No distinction is made in the offerings of different Hindu castes. Connected with this is the *akhára* of the same Báwa in Karnál.

A shrine of obscure origin is the *maṛri* of Saidúl Singh in Karnál. No fair is held here, and nothing is known of its history. It contains no image. Its administration vests in a celibate Jogi. No *bhog* is offered, but lamps are lit on Tuesdays and Thursdays.

The *samádhs* of Bábas Sítal Puri and Bál Puri at Kaithal date from the Mughal times. The place is visited on the Dasehra and *púranmáshi* in Phágan, when sweets are distributed among the visitors. The *mahant* is a Gosáín. Connected with these are 5 *shiválas*:—

(*i*) called Gobha, a very old building, containing a black stone image of Mahádeo:

(*ii*) of Nanda Mal, which contains the *ling* of Mahádeo, also of black stone:

(*iii*) of Dáni Rái, which also contains a black stone *ling* of Mahádeo and a white stone image of Vishnu which is 3 feet high, with an image of Ganesh 1 foot in height:

(*iv*) of Janta Mal Chaudhri:

(*v*) of Bhái Sher Singh.

These two last are modern, being only about 60 or 70 years old. They contain similar *lings*.

Other Puri shrines are:—

(*i*) the Ḍera of Brij Lál Puri at Kaithal which contains an image of Bishan Bhagwán and a *ling* of Shiva. The priest is a Gosáín who is in special request at weddings and funerals. Connected with it are:-

(*a*) two *mandirs* of Ṭhákar Jí, each containing stone images of Rádha and Krishna 1 cubit high:

(*b*) two small *shiválas*, each containing a stone *ling* of Shiva; and

(*c*) a *mandir* of Deví Káli which contains an image of the goddess, 1 cubit high.

(*ii*) the *samádh* of Bába Ráj Puri where an annual fair is held on the *ikádshi* in Asauj.

The shrines or *samádhs* of Rámthali are of some interest. The original *samádhs* are those of Bashisth-puri Saniási and his disciple Darbár-puri, but Bashisth-puri does not seem to have founded the succession, for we are told that at Kaithal and Delhi are the *samádhs* of Sítal-puri who was the spiritual forerunner of Darbár-puri: in Agondh is the *samádh* of Lál-puri, the spiritual great-grandfather of Darbár-puri: in Kheri Ghulám Ali is that of Deo-puri his disciple; while at Baram, Bhúna, Chika Nábha are *samádhs* of other disciples of his. In several villages of Patiála also *samádhs* of his disciples are to be found. Nothing seems to be known of Bashisth-puri or Darbár-puri's other predecessors, but he himself is said to have been a Káyasth by caste and a grandee of Sháh Jahán's court about 350 years ago. He resigned his *wazirship* and was offered 12 villages in *muáfi*, but only accepted one, Rámthali, to which place he brought the remains of Bashisth-puri from Pasawal,[1] a village some miles away. Here Darbári Lál, as his name was, settled down as the ascetic Darbár-puri, his fame gaining him thousands of followers. The *Dewal* or brick building over the *samádh* was built in the time of Mahant Nirbha-puri about 100 years ago. It is an octagon facing east and about 40 feet high, surmounted by a guilt *kalas*. Its interior is 12 feet square and contains the *samádhs* of Bashisth-puri and Darbár-puri. It opens to the north where there are *samádhs* of Anpúrna, the sister of Darbár-puri and of his wife. No images exist. The *samádhs* are all circular, standing about 4 feet high above a platform and some 6 feet in circumference. Numerous other *samádhs* stand on the platform. Five smaller *dewals* stand on the east and south of the larger one and a temple to Sivaji (Mahádeo) is situated on the platform to the south of it. Two fairs are held, one on the *phag*, the day after the Holi, commemorating the day of Bashisth-puri's demise; the other, the *bhandara* on the 7th of Sáwan *badi* the date of Darbár-puri's death. The administration is carried on by a *mahant* who is the spiritual head of the sect, elected by the other *mahants* and members of the brotherhood. No Brahmans are employed. A supervisor (*kárbári*) looks to the cultivation of the land and other matters not directly under the management of the *sádhús*. Another man is in charge of the stores and is called *kothar*. But it is the *pujári's* duty to look after everything that appertains to the *dewal*. The whole of this administration is carried on by the *mahant* and under his supervision—external affairs he manages with the consent of his *kárbári* and others fitted to advise him. The position of the chief *mahant* is that of the manager of a Hindu joint family. As the spiritual head of the sect he is the only man who can admit disciples, do worship at the *phag* and on Sáwan *badi satmi* and perform the *hawan* on Chet *sudi ashtami*.

The ritual is as follows:—The whole of the *dewal* and the platform is washed daily at 4 A. M. at all seasons. The *samádhs* are also washed and clothed. At 8 o'clock *chandan* and *dhúp* are offered to all the shrines and to Mahádeo. *Bhog* is offered first to the *samádh* and then the *langar* is declared open at noon. At 4 P. M. *dhúp* is offered to all

[1] But the same account also says that Darbár-puri obtained a grant of villages originally granted to Sítal-puri of Kaithal. This was about 350 years ago. The institution then appears to have been originally at Kaithal.

the *samádhs*. . *Árti* begins at sunset, *bhog* is offered at 8 P. M. and then the doors are closed. The ceremonial offering of *bhang* at the *samádhs* is in vogue, but there is no ceremonial use of *charas* or any other intoxicant in the sect. In Phágan on the *phag* day as well as in Sáwan on the 7th *badi* a special *bhog* is offered to the *samádhs* which consists of fried gram and *rotra* (flour and sugar) and this is offered as *prasád* to any one that worships the *samádhs*. A sacred lamp is kept lit day and night throughout the year A special feature at Rámthali is that the doors of the *langar* are not closed against any body, equality being the guiding rule, the *mahant* and men of the highest caste taking the same food as the lowest, excepting Chamárs and sweepers who are not allowed to ascend the platform but may worship from the ground. Offerings are not accepted from a Dúm, Bharái, Chuhrá or Biás. The shrines at Kaithal, Agondh, Baran, Kherí Ghulám Ali, Bahúna Chika, Mansa, Kishangarh, Khandepat, Radhrana, Masinghan in Patiála, Nábha town, Delhi town and Chhota Darieba are all connected with this shrine.

Panipat. The *asthal* of the Bairágís in Trikhú is connected with the Trikhu bathing fair founded by Bairági Sohlu Rám, a great devotee: it has been in existence for 500 years. It contains stone images of Krishna, Rádhika and Bal Deo, 1½ spans high and all set on a small square. Below them stand brass idols of Rádhika and Krishna, each 1 span high. There are also 4 brass images of Bála Jí, each a span high, just before which are seated 6 brass idols of Gopál Jí. A few stone idols of Sálig Rám also stand in front of them. The Bairági in charge is by caste Niyáwat and by *got* an Úchat. A *bhog* of milk or sweetmeat is offered morning and evening, but the sacred lamp is lit only in the evening. *Árti* is performed morning and evening when all the images are washed and dried. No distinction is made in the offerings of different Hindu castes. Connected with this are the shrines in Dáher, Lotha, Rehr, Brahmanmájra, Alupur, Tárá, Lohari, Gangtha and Mondhlawá in Rohtak and Hát in Jínd. These are all governed by the *mahant* whose disciples are appointed to each temple. He goes on tour and examines all the accounts of income. At the election of a new *mahant* a free distribution of food or *bhandár* is celebrated.

The Trikhú Tírath at Pánípat is visited on the *somti-amáwas*, a bathing fair, to which great religious importance attaches. Trikhú means 'three-sided,' but its other meaning is 'to wash away the sins of all those who bathe in the tank.' The Tírath dates from the time of the Mahábhárata. West of it is the temple of Jakash which is very old. It contains the images of Jakhash and his spouse Jakhashni.

Karnal. At the *mandir* of Tírath Parálsar in Balopura fair is held every year on the *ikádshi*. In the desert, where this temple now stands, Palsra Rishi used to meditate. After his death the place was depopulated, but the pond dug by him was frequented by the people. The temple has only been in existence for 80 years. In the precincts of the main building are 3 smaller *mandirs* and a tank. The image of Shiva is of stone, one span high. Of those of Ráma and Síta, Sálig Rám, Gopál, Durga and Hanúmán, the first five are of metal and each is a cubit high. The last named is of clay. The administration is carried on by a Gosáín, by caste a Bhingam and *got* Atras. The use of *charas* is ceremonial. *Bhog* is offered and then distributed among those present. Sacred fire is kept burning but a lamp lit only in the evening. No distinction is made in the offerings of different Hindu castes. Connected with this are the *dehras* of the Gosáíns at Hardwár and Karnál.

The *mandir* of Jugal Kishor in Guli is old having been in existence for 400 years. It contains 145 metal images of Rádha, Krishn and Sálig Rám, each 1½ feet high. Its administration vests in a Bairági *pujári*, a Vaishnava, by *got* Achtar. The use of *charas* is ceremonial. *Bhog* is offered and then distributed among all those present. The sacred lamp is lit in the evening. Connected with this are the shrines in Sari, Purána, Karnál, Japrúli, Gangu, Nismali and in Tabirá.

The Katás fountain is a Tírath. Of the temple built round it the oldest is the one called Raghúnáth jí ká Mandar. Here the Katas Ráj fair is held on 1st Baisákh, and the neighbouring villagers bathe on the *somawati amáwasya* and at solar and lunar eclipses. Katas is derived from *katakh*, 'an eye', because at the creation water fell from the eye of Shiva at this spot and formed the spring. When the Pándus reached it all but Yudhishtara drank its water and became senseless, but he sprinkled some of the water on them and restored their senses. Hence it is also called Amarkund. On the north-west the water is very deep and is believed to be fathomless, so Katás is also called Dharti ká netri or 'the eye of earth.' Stone images of Rám Chandar, Lakshman, Síta and Hanúmán stand in the Raghúnáth *mandar*. They are 5 ft high. The temple is in charge of Bairágís who recite Raghúnáth's *mantra*. Other temples have been built by Rájás and private persons and *shiválas* are attached to them. The *pujáris* are Brahmans.

Tilla Jogian. The peak in Jhelum called Tilla is 25 miles south-west of the town of that name. Gurú Gorakhnáth settled at Tilla in the *Tretayug* after Rámchandar and adopted Bal Náth as his disciple. Bal Náth underwent penance on Tilla hence it was called Bal Náth's Tilla after him. Rájá Bhartari, a disciple of Gurú Gorakhnáth, also learnt to practise penance from Bal Náth at Tilla and a cave at Tilla is named after him to this day. It is said that owing to a dispute between the Rájá and his fellow disciples he cut off part of Tilla and carried it to Jhang where it forms the Kirána hill. Tilla is the head-quarters of the Jogís and from a remote period all the other places of the Jogís in the Punjab have been under it. The ancient *mandirs* on this hill were all destroyed during the Muhammadan inroads, and the existing temples were all built in the reign of Rájá Mán. A fair is held here on the *shivrátri*, but as the road is a difficult one and the water bad, people do not attend it in great numbers. Most of the Jogís visit the place on a *shivrátri* in order to see the cave, and laymen go too there. Food is supplied by the *gaddínashín* but some people use their own. A lamp has been kept burning in one of the temples for a very long time. It consumes a *ser* of oil in 24 hours. Jogís chant a *mantra* when they go to see it, but this *mantra* is not disclosed to any one but a Jogi. It is transmitted by one Jogi to another.

Kohát town possesses a *thán* Jogíán which is visited by Hindus from Kohát and Tíráh. Its *pírs* dress in red and have their ears torn.

Near Bawanna are the shrines of Barnáth and Lachi Rám. At the former Hindus assemble to bathe at the Baisákhi instead of going to Khushhálgarh. At the latter gatherings take pl·ce several times a year.

The *mandirs* of Nagar Jí and Gopál Náth Jí in tahsíl Dera Ismail Khán were founded nearly 500 years ago, by Agú Jí Brahman. After his death his son went to Sindh where he became the disciple of a Gosáín and acquired power to work miracles. On his return home he brought with him an image of Sri Gopál Náth which he enshrined in the temple in S. 1600. The temples were once washed away by the Indus, but the images were afterwards recovered and enshrined in new temples in the town. One of the temples contains a brass image of Nagar Jí, 1 foot high, seated on a throne. The other temple contains a similar image of Gopi Náth. Nagar Jí's temple is managed by Gosáíns and Gopi Náth's by a person employed by them. A Brahman is employed in each temple to perform worship etc. *Bhog* of sweetmeat, fruits and milk with sugar is offered thrice a day. A sacred lamp or *jot* is only kept burning in the *mandir* of Nagar Jí. Twelve *mandirs* and *shiválas* are connected with these.

The thela *or wallet of Kewal Rám.*—Kewal Rám left Dera Ghází Khán for Dera Ismail to become a devotee There he dwelt in a secluded corner of Gopi Náth's *mandir*, and spread out his wallet on which he sat absorbed in meditation. This *thela* (wallet) has been worshiped for 400 years. Hindus have their children's hair cut here and make offerings in fulfilment of vows. The *chola* is also performed here. The Brahman officiating at the temple takes all the offerings except the sugar which is first offered to the wallet and then thrown amongst the gathering to be carried away. The sugar thus taken is considered sacred. The place is visited on the Baisákhi, in Chet and in Bhádon.

SAIVA CULTS IN THE HILLS.

THE CULT OF SHIRIGUL OR SHRIGUL IN SIRMÚR.

Siva is not extensively worshipped under that name in the Punjab Himalayas, but two cults, those of Shirigul and Maháśú, appear to be derivatives of Saivism. That of Shirigul is especially interesting and is described below. The home of this god is on the Chaúr[1] (Chúr) Peak which is visible from Simla. But he is worshipped chiefly in Sirmúr, from which State comes the following account of his myth, temples and cult :—

Shirigul (or Sargul,[2] fancifully derived from *sard* cold) has special power over cold, and, according to one account, is propitiated by a fair in order to avert cold and jaundice. In some dim way this attribute appears to be connected with the following version of the Shirigul legend :—Shirigul's expeditions to Delhi were made in quest of the colossal vessels of brass which the Muhammadans had taken away. On his return his mother's sister-in-law brought him *sattu* (porridge) to eat, and, as he had no water, it gushed out near a field at Shaya, a village in the Karli

[1] See article in the Imperial Gazetteer of India.

[2] The name is probably a corruption of Srí Gúru.

iláqa. Having washed he was about to eat the *sattu* when suddenly he saw some insects in it and at once refused to eat it. After rescuing his kinsmen from the snake he went again to Delhi and attacked the Turks single-handed, killing great numbers of them, but suddenly seeing a stone tied to a *bor*, or banyan tree, he knew that it had been sent by the wife of his servant (*bhúr*), by name Churú, as a signal of distress. Shirigul at once returned and found that all the members of Churú's family, except his wife, had been transformed into one body by the serpents, and even to this day any branched stone is supposed to be Churú's family and is much venerated.

The following is another legend which is current regarding the origin of the cult:—One Bhakarú, a Rájpút, of Sháyá, had no offspring, and desiring a son he journeyed to Kashmír where dwelt Pánún, a *pandit*, whose house he visited in order to consult him. The *pandit's* wife, however, told Bhakarú that he was sleeping, and that he used to remain asleep for six months at a stretch.

Bhakarú was disappointed at not being able to consult the *pandit*, but being himself endowed with spiritual power, he created a cat which scratched the *pandit* and awoke him. Learning that Bhakarú had thus had power to disturb his sleep, the *pandit* admitted him and told him he was childless, because he had committed Brahm-hatiá, or Bráhman-murder, and that he should in atonement marry a Brahman girl, by whom he would become the father of an incarnation. Bhakarú accordingly married a Bhát girl of high degree and to her were born two sons, Shirigul and Chandésar, both the parents dying soon after their birth. The boys then went to their maternal uncle's house and Shirigul was employed in grazing his sheep, while Chandésar tended the cows. But one day their uncle's wife in malice mixed flies and spiders with Shirigul's *sattu* or porridge, and when he discovered this, Shirigul threw away the food and fled to the forest, whereupon the *sattu* turned into a swarm of wasps which attacked and killed the uncle's wife. Shirigul took up his abode in the Chúr Dhár, whence one day he saw Delhi, and, being seized with a desire to visit it, he left Churú, a Bhór[1] Kanét by caste, in charge of his dwelling, collected a number of gifts and set out for the city. Halting near Jhíl Rain-ká, "the lake of Rainká", his followers were attacked by a tiger which he overcame, but spared on condition that it should not again attack men. Again, at Kólar in the Kiárda Dún, he subdued a dragon which he spared on the same terms. Reaching Delhi he went to a trader's shop who weighed the gifts he had brought, but by his magic powers made their weight appear only just equal to the *pasang* or difference between the scales, but Shirigul in return sold him a skein of silk which he miraculously made to outweigh all that the trader possessed. The trader hastened to the Mughal emperor for redress and Shirigul was arrested while cooking his food on his feet, because in digging out a *chulá* he had found a bone in the soil. In the struggle to arrest Shirigul his cooking vessel was overturned and the food flowed out in a burning torrent which destroyed half the city.

[1]Probably *bhúr*, 'servant,' is meant, and, if so, we should read "Churú, the *bhúr*, a Kanet by caste."

Eventually Shirigul was taken before the emperor who cast him into prison, but Shirigul could not be fettered, so the emperor, in order to defile him, had a cow killed and pinioned him with the thong of its hide. Upon this Shirigul wrote a letter to Gúgá Pír of the Bágar in Bikánér and sent it to him by a crow. The Pír advanced with his army, defeated the emperor, and released Shirigul, whose bonds he severed with his teeth. Shirigul then returned to the Chúr Peak.

During his absence the demon Asur Dánún had attacked Churú, completely defeating him and taking possession of half the peak. Shirigul thereupon cursed Churú who was turned into a stone still to be seen on the spot, and assailed Asur Dánún, but without success, so he appealed to Indra, who sent lightning to his aid and expelled Asur Dánún from the Chúr. The demon in his flight struck his head against a hill in Jubbal, and went right through it; the Ul cave still exists to testify to this. Thence he passed through the Sanj Nadí and across the Dhárla into the Tons river, by which he reached the ocean. The Dhárla ravine still remains to prove the truth of the legend.[1]

Another account says nothing of Shirigul's visit to Delhi, but makes Bhakarú the Rána of Sháyá. It further says that Shirigul became a *bhagat* or devotee, who left his home to live on the Chúr Peak upon which Siva dwelt. Gaining greater spiritual power from Siva, Shirigul caused all the boys of the neighbourhood to be afflicted with worms while he himself assumed the form of a Bhát and wandered from village to village, proclaiming that if the boys' parents built him a temple on the Dhár he would cure them all. The temple was built on the Chúr Peak and Shirigul began to be considered a separate deity.

The temple of Shirigul at Churidhár is square and faces east. It has but one storey, nine feet in height, with a verandah, and its roof consists of a gable, the topmost beam (*khinwar*) of which is adorned with brass vessels (*anda*) fixed to it by pegs. Outside the temple is hung a necklace (*málá*) of small pieces of wood (*kharóri*). There is only one door, on which figures etc. have been carved. Inside this temple is another smaller temple also of *deodár*, shaped like a dome, and in this is kept the *ling* which is six inches high and four inches in circumference. It is made of stone and is placed in a *jalahri* or vessel of water, which, too, is of stone. No clothes or ornaments are placed on the *ling*.

[1] An instance of the countless legends which explain natural features by tales of Sivá's prowess, or attribute them to his emanations. Below is one attributed to Shirigul himself. The Sikan ká Páni legend says that in the old times an inhabitant of Jhojar village went to Shirigul at the Chúr Peak and asked the *deotá* to give him a canal in his village. He stayed three days at the peak and did not eat or drink anything. Shirigul appeared in a monk's garb and gave him a *tumbá* full of water, which the god covered with a leaf telling the man not to open it on his way home, but at the place where he wanted the canal to run. On reaching Sikan the man opened the *tumbá* and found in it a snake which sprang out and ran away. Water flowed behind the snake, and a small canal still flows in Sikan and waters several villages. Being thus disappointed, the man again went to the Chúr and the god again gave him a *tumbá*, telling him to throw the water and say, *Niche Jhojar, Upar Jhajal*—'Jhojar village below and a waterfall above it,' and he should have plenty of water. But the man again forgot and said *Upar Jhojar, Niche Jhajal*—Jhojar above and the waterfall below.' This mistake caused the water to flow below the village and that only in a small quantity.

A worshipper brings with him his own Bháṭ, who acts as *pujári.* The Bháṭ must not eat until he has performed the worship and made the offerings. He first bathes in the adjacent spring, puts on clean clothes and lights a lamp, burning *ghí*, not oil, before the idol. Then he takes a brass *loṭá* of fresh water, and sprinkles it over the idol and the floor of the temple with a branch of the *chikhon* or *chhánbar* shrub. He next fills a spoon with fire, *ghí*, and the leaves of the *katharchál* and *láhṣrí* odoriferous plants found on the Dhár, and burns them before the idol, holding the spoon in his right hand, while he rings a bell with his left, and repeats the names of *tíraths* and *avatárs* only. After this office he blows a conch, terminating it with a prostration to the idol. It may be performed at any time. The *játrí* or worshipper now bathes, puts on clean clothes, and prostrates himself before the idol. After this he may make the offerings which consist of a *ratti*[1] of gold or silver, money, *ghí* (but not more than two *chhitáks*), a pice or two, small vessels, *andas* of pewter or copper, which are hung on the temple, and a he-goat. The benefits sought are secular, not spiritual, and the worship is expected to ward off evil.

Jága or uninterrupted worship for a whole night can only be performed at the temple, as the *ling* must not be removed from it. A lamp in which *ghí*, not oil, is burnt, is placed all night before the *ling*, and in the course of the night three offices are performed, one at evening, another at midnight, and the third at morn. At this last the *pujári* feeds the god; water is poured over the back of a he-goat, and if the animal shivers, it is believed that the god has accepted the offering and the goat is killed. The head is offered to the god and taken by the *pujári* on his behalf, the remainder being cooked and eaten. Or the goat is not killed but let loose, and it then becomes the property of the Dewa.[2]

Another account says the two men, a *pujári* and a Dewa, accompany the worshipper, the former receiving the goat's head, and the latter the other offerings.[3]

Other temples to Shirigul.

1.—*At Mánal.*

Shirigul has also a temple at Mánal, which was built by Ulga and Jojra, Déwás, as the following legend tells :—

In order to enhance his sanctity Shirigul made an effigy. This he

[1] *Ratti* is a weight equal to eight grains of rice or 1¼ of a grain (Eng. weight).

[2] The Déwás are a class of Kanets or Bháṭs, held to be peculiarly the men of the god.

[3] The *pujári* kindles fire on a stone and offers incense, made of *ghí*, *páji* and *katarchár* leaves, while he recites the following *mantra* :—Ao aur wanaspaió punarwar binó mákuto, Sarb such, soji . . . . barchhas bha uang, nom, uam, gani sagnam, chára hotí, narsaugnun, namo nami janto, masinó, jiyá bhamón, nandar nóu, odarkas tari gaure, mari masni, miyá sagain, bhagain, jainar, jsanuar, bhósnó jamandwár, nioas hár, parbúm, parchandu, nashu puari, parbarsái, korsanui, suáman shanti, nesh kóli, deóua shántí, bhorátari, pátri jharí, kárú dauéle, sargal deotá kí kárú dabéle, Bijal. Bijái kí káru dabéle chár, wa mur wa Dilígadh káru dabéle. Chár bhái Mahásbó, kárú dabéle, Ganga, Hardwár, Badrí Kidár kárú dabéle, pátri jharí.

placed with some lamps in a basin which he floated on the Jalal stream in Bhádon. The basin reached Shakohal village in Pachhád tahsíl, and there a Rájpút of the Sapála (= *sapéla* or snake charmer) family of Chanálag saw it. Struck with amazement, he challenged it to float on if a demon, but if a deity to come to the bank. The basin came to the bank where he was standing, and the Rájpút took it to his home. Some days later it was revealed to him that the image was that of Shirigul, that it would never be revered by the Rájpúts who were ignorant of the mode of worship, and that it should be taken to Bakhuta where it was duly worshipped, and hence a Dewa, Bidan by name, stole it and brought it to Mánal.

A fair is held on the Hariálí,[1] and another on any three days of Sáwan at Gelyon, a small plateau in the lands of Nahra, at a *kós* from Mánal. Men and women here dance the *gí*, a hill dance, and people exchange *mora* (wheat parched or boiled), maize, rice &c.

The temple at Mánal is square, 24 cubits high, with three storeys, each provided with a stair to give access to the one above it. The property of the god is kept in the middle storey. Outside the door there is a wooden verandah, on which figures are carved and which is furnished with fringes of wooden pegs, *andas* are also fixed on to it. The highest storey contains the idol, and has the *khinwar* or gable like the Chur temple. The whole of the woodwork is stained with *gurú*. The temple faces south-west.

The temple contains 12 images of Shirigul, all placed on wooden shelves (*gambar*) in the wall, and the principal of these is the idol brought by Bidan. This is made of *asht-dhát*[2] (bell-metal), and is five fingers high by two fingers broad with a human face. It is clothed in *masrú* or silk cloth, with a piece of broad-cloth, studded with 100 rupees and 11 gold *mohars* round its neck. The remaining 11 images are of brass, and are of two classes, four of them being a span in height and 9 fingers wide, with a piece of *masrú* round the neck: the other seven are 10 fingers high and 7 broad. The images are thus arranged :—

3, 3, 3, 3 2, 2, 1 2, 2 3, 3, 3,

the original image being in a silver *chauki* (throne), with a small umbrella over it.

2.—*At Deona and Bandal.*

The temples at Deona (Dabóna) and Bandal are similar to the one at Mánal. Each has a *bhandár* or store-room, in charge of a *bhandári* or store-keeper. These *bhandárs* are rich, and from them the *pujáris*, *bájgís*, and *bhandáris* are paid, and pilgrims and *sádhús* are fed. The Dewás also are maintained from the *bhandárs*.

The second class images of the Mánal and Deona temples can be taken home by a worshipper for the performance of a *jágá*, as can the

[1] Hariálí is the last day of Hár, and the Sankránt of Sáwan, and derives its name from *hárá*, 'green.'

[2] *I.e.* eight metals.

first class image from that of Bandal. The image is conveyed in a copper coffer borne by a bare-footed *pujári* on his back, and followed by 10 or 12 Dewás, of whom one waves a *chauri* over the coffer. The procession is accompanied by musicians and two flags of the god.

On arrival at the worshipper's house, the place where the image is to be placed is purified, being sprinkled with Ganges water. The image is removed from the coffer inside the house and placed on a heap of wheat or *mandwa*. The arrival should be timed for the evening. The *jágá* ritual is that already described. Next day the god is fed and taken back to his temple. The worshipper has to pay to the *pujári* and *bájgi* each Re. 1, to the *bhanḍári* annas 4, and to the Déwá Rs. 2 or Rs. 3.

3.—*At Jámná.*

There is also a temple of Shirigul and Jámná in Bhoj Mast. Here the god is worshipped twice daily, in the morning and evening. The *pujári* is a Bhát, who, with the *bájgi*, receives the offerings. When a he-goat is offered, the *pujári* takes the head, the *bájgi* a thigh, while the rest is taken by the *játri* himself. The temple is like an ordinary hill-house, having two storeys, in the upper of which the god lives. The door of the upper stôrey faces west and that of the lower eastward. There is also a courtyard, 15 feet long by 10 feet wide, on this side. The forefathers of the people in Jámná, Pobhár, Kándon, Cháwag and Thána villages brought a stone from Chúr Dhár and built this temple as a protection against disease. It contains an image which was obtained from Junga, and is furnished with a palanquin, canopy, *singhásan* or throne and an *amrati* or vessel used for water in the ritual. The Bisu fair is held here from the 1st to the 5th of Baisákh, and both sexes attend. It is celebrated by songs, dancing, and the *thoda* or mock combat with bows and arrows.

4.—*In the Páontá Tahsíl.*

Shirigul has no special *mandar* in Páontá Tahsíl, but he has several small *mandars* in villages. These contain images of stone or a mixture of lead or copper. He is worshipped to the sound of conches and drums; leaves, flowers and water being also offered daily, with the following *mantra*:—

Namón ád álá, namon brahm balá.
Namón ad Náthí, namón shankha chakra
Gadá padam dhárí.
Namón machh kachh baráh awatári
Namón Náhar Singh kurb kí dharí.
Namón asht ashtengí, namón chhait kárí
Namón Srí Suraj deotá, namon namskárá.

'I salute thee who wert in the beginning, who art great and supreme Brahma, who wert Lord of all that was in the beginning, who holdest the conch, mace, quoit and lotus (in thy four hands), who revealest thyself in the forms of a fish, a tortoise, a bear, and a man-lion, who hast eight forms and who art beneficient. I also salute thee, O Sun! thou art worthy of adoration.'

5.—*At Naoni.*

There is another temple of Shirigul at Naoni village in the *tahsíl* of Náhan. A fair is held here on the day of Hariálí or first of Sáwan. He-goats, *halwa* or *ghí* are offered. The people dread him greatly.

6.—*At Sangláhan.*

There is also a *deothali* or 'place of the god,' Shirigul, at Sangláhan. The *pujári* is a Brahman and the mode of worship and offerings are similar to those at Jawála Mukhi's temple. Goats are, however, not sacrificed here, only *halwa* being offered. The fair is held on the Gyas day, the Katik *sudí ikádshi* of the lunar year, and the 30th of Kátik in the solar year. Only men and old women, not young girls, attend this fair.

In Jaitak also there is a temple of this god.

The Story of Sri Gul Deota of Churi Dhar in Jubbal.

In the Jubbal State, which lies to the north and east of the Chaur Peak, a variant of the Shirigul legend is current. This variant is of special interest, and it appears worth recording in full :—

In the Dwápar Yuga Krishna manifested himself, and, after killing the *rákshasás*, disappeared. Some of them, however, begged for pardon, and so Krishna forgave them and bade them dwell in the northern hills, without molesting god or man. This order they all obeyed, except one who dwelt at Chawkhat, some seven miles north of Churi Dhár. In the beginning of the present age, the Kalí Yuga, he harassed both men and cattle, while another demon, Neshíra, also plundered the subjects of Bhokrú,[1] chief of Shádgá, in the State of Sirmúr. The former *asur* also raided the States of Jubbal, Taroch, Balsan, Theog, Ghond etc. The people of these places invoked divine protection, while Bhokrú himself was compelled to flee to Kashmír, and being without heirs, he made over his kingdom to his minister Déví Rám. For twelve years Bhokrú and his queen devoted themselves to religious meditation, and then, directed by a celestial voice, they returned home and performed the *aswamedha*, or great horse sacrifice. The voice also promised Bhokrú two sons who should extirpate the demons, the elder becoming as mighty as Siva, and the younger like Chandéshwar and saving all men from suffering. Ten months after their return, Bhokrú's queen gave birth to a son, who was named Srí Gul. Two years later Chandéshwar[2] was

[1] The Bhakrú of the Sirmúr version. Shádgá and Shíyá would appear to be one and the same place.

[2] The Chandésar of the Sirmúr variant.

born. When the boys were aged 12 and 9½, respectively, the Rájá resolved to spend the evening of his life in pilgrimage and went to Hardwár. On his way back he fell sick and died, his queen succumbing to her grief, at his loss, three days later. Srí Gul proceeded to Hardwár to perform his father's funeral rites, and crossed the Chúri Dhar, the lofty ranges of which made a great impression on his mind, so much so that he resolved to make over his kingdom to his younger brother and take up his abode on the peak. On his return journey he found a man worshipping on the hill, and learnt from him that Siva, whose dwelling it was, had directed him to do so. Hearing this, Srí Gul begged Chúhrú—for this was the name of Sivá's devotee—to wait his return, as he too intended to live there. He then went to Shádgá and would have made his kingdom to Chandéshwar, but for the remonstrances of his minister, who advised him to only give his brother Nahula village, *i.e.* only a part of his kingdom and not the whole, because if he did so, his subjects would certainly revolt. To this Srí Gul assented, making Déví Rám regent of Shádgá during his own absence.

Srí Gul then set out for Delhi, where he arrived and put up at a Bhábṛá's shop. The city was then under Muhammadan rule, and once when Srí Gul went to bathe in the Jamna, a butcher passed by driving a cow to slaughter. Srí Gul remonstrated with the man but in vain, and so he cut him in two. The emperor sent to arrest him, but Srí Gul killed all the soldiers sent to take him, and at length the emperor himself went to see a man of such daring. When the emperor saw him he kissed his feet, promised never again to kill a cow in the presence of a Hindu. So Srí Gul forgave him. He was about to return to the shop when he heard from Chúhrú that a demon was about to pollute the Chúr Peak, so that it could not become the abode of a god. Srí Gul thereupon created a horse, named Shanalwi, and, mounted on it, set out for Chúri Chandhrí. In the evening he reached Búriya, near Jagádhri, next day at noon Ṣirmúr, and in the evening Shádgá, his capital. On the following day he arrived at his destination by way of Bhil-Kharí, where he whetted his sword on a rock which still bears the marks. Thence he rode through Bhairóg in Jubbal, and halting at Kálábágh, a place north of Chúri Choṭí, he took some grains of rice, and, reciting incantations, threw them on the horse's back, thereby turning it into a stone, which to this day stands on the spot. Srí Gul then went out to Chúri Choṭi and there he heard of the demon's doings. Next morning the demon came with a cow's tail in his hand to pollute the Peak, but Chúhrú saw him and told Srí Gul, who killed him on the spot with a stone. The stone fell in an erect position, so the place is called Aurípotlí [1] to this day. It lies eight miles from the Chúr Peak. After the demon had been killed, the remainder of his army advanced from Chawkhat, to attack Srí Gul, but he destroyed them all. Then he told Chúhrú to choose a place for both of them to live in, and he chose a spot between Chúri Choṭí and Kálábágh. Srí Gul then sent for Déví Rám and his

1 *Aurí* means an erect stone, *potlí*, the hide of a cow or buffalo. It is also said that the cow's hide which the demon had in his hand, as well as the stone which Srí Gul threw at him, are still to be seen on the spot.

(the minister's) two sons from Shádgá, and divided his kingdom among them, thus :—To Déví Rám he gave, *i.e.* assigned, the State with the village of Kárlí[1] ; to the elder son Rabbu he gave Jorna, the *pargana* of Bháhal, Jalkhólí in Jubbal State, Balsan, Theog, Ghond and Ratesh States, and *pargana* Pajhóta in Sirmúr, and to Chhínú, the younger son, he allotted Saráhan, with the following *parganas* : Hámil, Chhatta, Chandlóg, Chándná, Satótha, Panótra, Néwal, Shák, Chánju, Bargáon, Sunthá, in Jubbal State, and Taróch, with Ládá and Kángra, in the Sirmúr State, as far as that part of Jaunsár which is now British territory. Déví Rám and his two sons built a temple to Srí Gul between Chótí Chúri and Kálábágh ; which is still in existence, and the younger brother also built a *baolí*, which held no water until Srí Gul filled it.

When the three new rulers had finished building their *ráj-dhanís*[2] Srí Gul sent for them and bade them govern their territories well, and he made the people swear allegiance to them. On Déví Rám's death, his third son, by his second wife, succeeded to his State. Srí Gul bade the three rulers instal, when he should have disappeared, an image of himself in the temple at each of their capitals, and side by side with them to erect smaller temples to Chúhrú. He also directed that their descendants should take with them his image wherever they went and to whatever State they might found, and there instal it in a temple. With these instructions he dismissed the ministers and their subjects. After a reign of 150 years, Srí Gul disappeared with Chúhrú, who became known as Chúhrú Bír, while Srí Gul was called Srí Gul Deóta.

Two centuries later, when the descendants of Rabbú and Chínú had greatly multiplied, those of them who held Jorna migrated to Mánal in the Bharmaur *iláqa*, where they built a temple for Srí Gul's image. The Rájá of Sirmúr assigned half the land of the *pargana* for its maintenance. Some of Chínú's descendants settled in Deóna, a village in Sirmúr, where they, too, built a temple.

According to this *quási*-historical legend Srí Gul was a king, who was, we may conjecture, supplanted in his kingdom by his chief minister's family. This minister's sons divided the kingdom into three parts, each of them ruling one part—precisely what happened about a century ago in State of Bashahr. The old capitals of Jorna,[3] Saráhan[4] (in Jubbal State), and Shádgá (apparently in Sirmur) are, with Deóná, to this day the centres at which the grain collected on behalf of the god is stored. A *patha*[5] is collected from every house.

[1] Should probably read :—To Déví Rám he assigned his own State of Shádgá with the addition of Kárli ; to Rabbú, Jorná, as his capital, with Bháhal etc., and to Chhínú Saráhan as his capital, with etc.

[2] Royal residence or capital.

[3] The god in Jorna is called Góvánú, from *gos*, 'sky' in the Paháṛi dialect. He has one eye turned towards the sky, and hence is so named.

[4] The god in Saráhan is called Bijat.

[5] The *patha* is a basket-like measure made of iron or brass and holding some two *sére* of grain.

Every year the descendants of Rabbú and Chínú who settled in Sirmúr take the god's image from Saráhan or Jorna in Jubbal to their own villages, in which temples have been built to him. Some 50 *kárdárs* (officials) and *begáris* (*corvée* labourers) accompany the god, and each house offers him Re. 1 and a *patha* of grain, but if any one desires to offer a gold coin, he must give the *kárdárs*, musicians and *pujáris* Rs. 6, Rs. 12, or even Rs 25. Anyone who refuses to make a *dhiánkra* or offering will, it is believed, meet with ill luck.

Like many other gods in the hills, Srí Gul exercises civil and criminal jurisdiction. Anyone doing wrong in his capital has to take the god to Hardwar, or, for a petty offence, pay him a gold coin. Oaths are also taken on the god's image at Saráhan and Jorna, in cases in which enquiry has failed to elicit the truth, by parties to cases in the States of Jubbal, Balsan, Taróch and Sirmúr. The god reserves judgment for three or six months, during which period the party who is in the wrong is punished by some calamity.

Connected with the cult of Shirigul is that of the dual god Bijat and his sister Bijái.

The cult of Bijat.

The legend of Bijat, the lightning god, which is connected with that of Shirigul, relates that when the Asur Agyasur, the great demons who were hostile to the gods, assailed the Chúr Peak and the temple of Shirigul thereon, the god fell upon them in the form of lightning, whence an image fell to earth at Saráhan in Jubbal, and at that place a temple was built for the image, which was placed, with other images, in it. From Saráhan a Dewa, the ancestor of the present Déwás of Deona, brought a stone idol of Bijat to Deona, and this is now the principal image in the temple, and is considered to possess the most power.[1] There are 27 other images, all of brass.

The stone idol is to the left of all the minor images, and is never clothed or ornamented. Of the rest four are covered with old silk (*masrú*), and have pieces of woollen stuff round their necks, studded with 80 rupees, and 15 gold *mohars*. The remaining 23 have no clothes or ornaments. All have human faces.

The fair of Bijat is held on any three days between Baisákh 1st and the end of Jeṭh. It is called Bisu, because it is usually held in Baisákh, and is held annually in Deona, and every third or fourth year in Chokar, Sanej and Andheri villages. It resembles the fair at Mánal, and the *thoda* game is played.

The temple of Bijat at Bándal was founded in this wise. The Déwás at Deona multiplied, and so one of them came to Bándal with a brass image of Bijat from the temple there, and built a separate temple. There are now 52 images of Bijat in the Bándal temple. All

[1] *Precedence of deities in a temple.*—The presiding image is that which is the most powerful and is placed in the centre, the others being placed on either side of it in the order of their powers, the more powerful being seated near the presiding image, and the others further from it. Dependants occupy lower seats in front. All the images face *to the west* n the high hills.

are of brass, with human faces. Only the five primary images are clothed, and these have garments studded with rupees and gold *mohars*. They are considered to possess more power than the remaining 47, and the principal of them, the one brought from Deona, is placed in the centre and reposes in a silver *chauki*.

Bijai, as a goddess, has a temple, seven storeys high, at Batroli where the image is of brass and has a woman's face. It is clothed in silk and ornamented. The Bháṭs, but not the Kanets, serve as *pujáris*. A pilgrim to the temple is fed once on behalf of the god. When a he-goat is sacrificed the blood is sprinkled over the temple. For a *jágá* the idol is taken to a worshipper's house where a he-goat is killed and the flesh distributed among those present. The ritual resembles that of Shirigul, but there is no fair.

Closely connected with the cult of Bijat is that of the goddess Ghatriáli,[1] who has a temple at Panjáhan in Rainká tahsíl, similar to that of Bijat at Batrol. The ritual is also the same, and no fair is held. The legend regarding this temple avers that a certain Kanet chieftain, Bíja by name, of Tathwa village, once sallied forth with eighteen of his followers to attack his enemies in Dáhar. When the assailants reached Dáhar they were seized with a sudden panic and fled homeward, but on reaching Bholná, a mile from Dáhar, they met some women bearing pitchers. On asking who they were, they were told that the women belonged to Jam-log, a village at which a *jágá* in honour of Bijat was being celebrated, and that they had come to fetch water. Bíja asked if he and his companions could see the *jágá*, and was told that they could come and see it, but must show no fear of what they saw even when offered seats of serpents and scorpions by the people of Jam-log. The women also said they would be offered grains of iron to eat and gave them rice which they could eat instead, concealing the iron Lastly, the women said that if they were desired to take the image to their house for the celebration of a *jágá*, they should seize it and flee with it, but must on no account look back. Accordingly Bíja and his men went to Jam-log where they found three images being worshipped with great pomp, and were told that the finest image to which the greatest reverence was paid was that of Bijat, the second that of Báiji, and the third that of Ghatriáli. Bíja, on the pretence that he desired to worship the images, was allowed to draw near with his companions, and they then seized the images and fled. The men of Jam-log pursued them without success, but Bíja's eighteen companions looked back and perished. Bíja, however, reached his house in safety, and concealed the image in his granary, which was nearly empty. When he opened the granary in the morning it was full to overflowing. Bíja fell senseless at this portent, and was only revived by the sacrifice of eighteen he-goats over him. Then one of the three gods took possession of a man, who began to nod his head, saying he was Bijat, the god, and could not remain in Tathwa, as it was not becoming for him to live with his sisters, so the image of Bijat was sent to Saráhan in Jubbal where it still remains. The people of Tathwa then separated, dividing their property, some going to settle in Káṇḍí

[1] In Dhámi Ghatiálu is a ghost : see p. 217 *supra*.

and the others remaining in Tathwa. The image of the goddess Bijái fell to the men of Kánḍi, and is now at Batrol of Dasákná *bhoj*, while Ghatriáli remained at Tathwa and her temple was established at Panjáhan in Thakri *bhoj*.

Every year Bijat gives his sister Bijái a rupee for sweetmeats, and whenever either of them goes to visit the other, the host entertains the guest with a he-goat, and gives him or her a rupee. Bijat always gives Bijái twice as much as she gives him.

Relations of Bijat and Bijái

It is not expressly stated that Bijat and Bijái are twin deities, but there is a similar pair in Bhur Singh and his sister, and Bhur Singh appears to be identifiable with Búre Singh and Bhúri Singh the twin of Káli Singh.

The twin-god Bhur Singh.

At Pejarlí in Sirmúr is a temple dedicated to Bhur Singh and his sister Debi (Devi), the children of a Bháṭ of Pánwáh village. When their mother died the Bháṭ married again, and their step-mother during his absence from home used to treat them harshly. Once she sent Bhur Singh to tend cattle in the forest, and as on his return home in the evening one of the calves was missing, she sent him back to find it by hook or by crook. When the Bháṭ reached home he found his son had not returned, and in going to search for him found him and the lost calf both lying dead at the spot where the shrine now stands. Meanwhile Debi, who had been given in marriage to a one-eyed man, was, in her mortification, returning home; she passed the place where Bhur Singh lay dead, and stricken with grief threw herself from her *ḍoli* over the cliff. The brother and sister are now worshipped together as Bhur Singh. There are two temples, one at Pejarlí, the other on the high hill known as Bhur Singh kí dhár. The *pujáris* are two Bháṭs, one for Bhur Singh and one for Debi, and at the fair, on the Kátik *sudi ikádshi*, no one dances save the *pujári* of Debi, and he dances by night in the temple so that the people may not see him, and at midnight coming out of the shrine leaps on to a great rock above a high cliff. Standing there for a few moments he gives one oracle, and no more, in answer to a question. On returning to the temple he swoons, but is speedily and completely revived by rubbing. Meanwhile, when the secret dancing begins the men of the Panál family form a line across the door of the temple, and those of the Kathár temple rushing upon them with great violence break the line and enter the temple, but leave it again after touching the idol. As Bhur Singh is known to live on nothing but milk, animals are never sacrificed.

In Karnál and Ambála Jaur Singh is worshipped with Gugga, Nár Singh, Kála Singh and Búre Singh. He is said to be Rájá Jemar, the usual name of Gugga's father, but the twin *jora*) brothers of Gugga, Arjan and Surjan, are also worshipped as Jaur.

Káli Singh and Bhúri Singh sometimes have twin shrines and Nár Singh is said to be another name for one or both of them.

(B)—The cult of Mahásu in Sirmúr.

The head-quarters of this god are at Sion, a village in Rainka tahsíl, where he has a temple on a small hillock, at the foot of which flows the Girí. It is close to the village and shaped like a hill-house with two storeys only. The ground floor has a door facing to the north, while the upper storey has no door, and one ascends by small steps through the first storey. It is only lighted by sky-lights. The gods are kept on a *gambar* or wooden shelf. There is one large brass idol and several smaller ones. The idols are shaped like a man's bust. The big idol is in the middle, the others being placed on either side of it. On the left the second place is held by the god Sirmúrí, who is the god of Sirmúr, but who is not independent, being always found in the company of bigger god, and has no temple of his own. There is also an image of Déví Shimlásan. The idols on the immediate right of the big one only go to Hardwár and other places, while the rest are stationary. They go out because they are kept clean for that purpose. The others are in a dirty state. All these idols, except those of Sirmúrí and Shimlásan, represent Mahásu. The middle one is the most important, and there is no difference in the others. Milk and goats are offered in the temple, which is only opened every Sunday and Wednesday and on a Sankránt. Worship is held at 11 A.M. and at sunset in the same way as in Shirigul's temple, but there is one peculiarity, in that the devotees of Mahásu who own buffaloes generally offer milk on the day of worship. If there is a death or birth in the family of the Déwá, the temple must be closed for 20 days because neither a *játri* nor a Déwá can enter the temple within 20 days of a domestic occurrence. The Déwá must not indulge in sexual intercourse on the day of worship or two previous days, and hence only two days in the week are fixed for worship. The morning worship is called *dhúp déná* and the evening *sandhiá*. Legend says that one morning the god Mahásu appeared in a dream and told the ancestor of the present Déwá to seek in the Girí and build him a temple in the village. Accordingly the Déwá went to the Girí and found on its banks the big idol, which is also called *jalásan* (*i. e.* set up in water). Mahásu is not so widely believed in as Shirigul or Paras Rám. The present Déwá says he is 12th in descent from the man who found the idol.

The Jagra of Mahásu.—This festival, which is peculiar to Kángra in Tahsíl Rainka, is celebrated on the 4th and 5th day of the dark half of Bhádon. On the third of the same half the *deotá's* flag is erected on the bank of a stream, and on the 4th people arrive, who are served with free dinners. On the night between the 4th and 5th the people do not sleep the whole night. On the 5th, at about 3 P.M., the *deotá* is taken out of the temple. But if it is displeased, it becomes so heavy that even four or five men cannot remove it. The music is played and prayers offered. At this time some men dance and say an oracle has descended on them. They show their superior powers in curious ways. Some play with fire; others put earth on their heads. They answer questions put by those who are in want of the *deotá's* help. Some one among these dancing men explains the cause of the displeasure of the *deotá*, and then pilgrims and *pujáris* make vows, whereupon the *deotá* gets pleased and makes itself light and moveable. Now a procession is made, headed by the *deotá's* flag, which when brought to the stream, is sprinkled with water, after which the procession returns to the temple, where dancing is kept going till morning. A good dinner with wine is given to the people in the temple yard.

The Cult of Mahásu in the Simla Hills.[1]

Mahásu, who has given his name to the well-known hill near Simla, is a deity whose cult is making such progress that he is bound soon to take a foremost place in the hillman's pantheon. His history as told by the manager of his temple at Anel, the head-quarters of his worship, is as follows :—When vast portions of the world were ruled by demons, between the Tons and Pabar rivers dwelt a race of evil spirits whose chief, Kirmat *dánu*, loved to wallow in human blood. Twice a year he claimed a victim from each hamlet in his jurisdiction. In Madrat, a village above the Tons where the demons held their sports, lived two pious Brahmans to whom the gods had granted seven sons. Six of them had already been slain on the demon's altars and he had cast his eye on the seventh. His aged parents waited in dread for the half-yearly sacrifice, the more so in that he was the only son they had left to liberate their spirits at the funeral pile. But several months before the sacrifice the wife became possessed. A trembling fell upon her and in a piercing voice she kept on shrieking—" Mahásu—Mahásu—Mahásu of Kashmír will save our child." Her husband, Una Bháṭ, could not interpret the portent for he had never heard Mahásu's name, so he asked her what her raving meant. Still in her trance of inspiration she replied that in Kashmír there reigned Mahásu a mighty god who would save their son from the demon's clutches if he himself would but plead before his shrine. But Kashmír was far away and Una Bháṭ very old, so he laughed in sorrow at her fancy. " How can I," he asked, " who am stricken in years and weak of body make a pilgrimage to such a distant land ? The boy is already dead if his life depends on such a journey." But his wife did not heed his weakness and at length her possession grew so violent that the Brahman set out on his lonely journey, more to soothe her than from any hope of succour. He did not even know the road until a neighbour told him that at the famous shrine of Deví in Hátkoṭi there was a Brahman who had seen the holy places of Kashmír. Thither then he turned and begged information from the priest. But Paṇḍit Nág, the Brahman, scoffed at the idea of such an enterprise. " Your eyes are dim ", he said in scorn, " your legs tottering and your body worn and wasted ; you will surely die on the way. I, who am strong and in the prime of life, took full twelve years to do the pilgrimage." But Una Bháṭ having once left his home was eager to do his utmost to save his only remaining son ; and at last the Paṇḍit set him on his road with a blessing.

As the old man toiled up the hill path, his limbs were suddenly filled with youthful vigour and his body lifted into the air. Next he found himself by a tank beneath whose waters the great Mahásu dwelt,

[1] By H. W. Emerson, Esq., C. S.

though he knew it not. And as he stood in wonder on its margin one of the god's *wazírs*, Chekurya by name, appeared before him and asked him what he wanted. Una Bhát in eager words told him how a race of cruel demons vexed his country, how their chief had slaughtered six of his sons upon their altars and purposed to take the seventh, and how his wife had trembled and called upon Mahásu's name. When Chekurya had heard all this he bade the Brahman retire to a field behind the tank and there wait in silence for the coming of Mahásu who would help him in his need He had been gone but a short time when suddenly from the ground beside him arose a golden image which he guessed to be Mahásu. He clutched it tightly to his breast, pouring out a pitiful appeal. "I will not let you go", he cried, "until you pledge your word to rescue my only son. Either take my life or come with me" Mahásu comforted him with a promise of succour. "I have heard your prayer", he said, "and will surely save your child from the demon. Return now to your home and there make a plough of solid silver with a share of pure gold, and having put in it a pair of bullocks whose necks have never borne the yoke loosen well each day a portion of your land. On the seventh Sunday hence I, with my brothers, ministers and army will come and rid your people of those noisome spirits. But on that day be careful that you do no ploughing." These words were scarcely uttered when the image slipped from the Brahman's grasp and in the twinkling of an eye he found himself once more within his village. There having told of the wonders that had happened on his way, he made, in obedience to the god, a plough of solid silver with a share of burnished gold. Therein he yoked a pair of bullocks which had never drawn plough before and each day ploughed deep a portion of his lands On the sixth Sunday after his return he did his daily task but had only turned five furrows when out of each sprang the image of a deity. From the first came Bhotu, from the next Pabasi, out of the third rose Báshik and Chaldu from the fourth. All these are brothers called by the common affix of Mahásu. From the fifth furrow appeared their heavenly mother, and all about the field the god's officers and a countless army sprang like mushrooms through the loosened earth. Chekurya,[1] the minister, was there with his three colleagues, Kapla, Kailu and Kailat, as well as Chaharya who holds a minor office. When the Brahman first saw them he fell senseless on the ground, but the god's attendants soon revived his courage and bade him show them where the demons dwelt Then he took them to a deep dark pool where Kirmat *dánu* held his revels and there they found the demon king attended by his hosts of evil spirits. Forthwith Mahásu challenged him to mortal conflict and a sanguinary battle followed which ranged along the river bank and up the neighbouring hills. But the evil spirits had not the strength to stand before the gods so they were routed with much carnage and in a short time only their leader Kirmat *dánu* still lived. Alone he fled across the mountains until he reached the Pabar hard pressed by his relentless foes. They caught him at Niwára in the Dhádi State and hacked him up to pieces upon a rock, which to this day bears marks of many sword cuts.

In such wise was the land rid of the demons, but the lowlanders say the hillmen still have the manners of their former rulers. Their habits

[1] There is a Kailu in Chamba also.

are unclean, their customs filthy, they neither wash nor change their clothes nor understand the rites of true religion. However this may be, the army came back in triumph to Madrat, where the four brothers parcelled out the land between them dividing it to suit the physical infirmities of each. For a misadventure had marred to some extent the glory of their enterprise. Mahásu, it will be remembered, had pledged his word to Una Bháṭ that he would come and succour him upon the seventh Sunday but either in impatience or through a miscalculation of the date, the god arrived a week before his time. Thus the mother and her sons were waiting buried underneath the earth for Una Bháṭ to break its sun-baked crust and as he drove his plough three members of the family were injured by its blade. Bhoṭu was damaged in the knee so that thenceforth he was lame; Pabasi had a small piece cut out of his ear; whilst Báshik's vision was obscured by the thrusting of the ploughshare into his eye. The fault of course was not the Brahman's, for if the very gods select the sixth of any period to embark on a venture, they must expect the ill-fortune which attends the choice of even numbers to find them out. So Bhoṭu henceforth preferred to rest his injured leg within his temple at Anel and thence he exercises sway around its precincts. A portion of the Gaṛhwál State fell to Pabasi's lot and there he spends a year in turn at each of his six country seats. To him was allotted part of the tract now comprised in British Gaṛhwál and though defective eyesight prevents his making lengthy tours he journeys in successive years to the four main centres of his worship. Chaldu, it was justly felt, being sound in every limb could well fend for himself, so to him was granted no specific territory; so long as he observed his brother's rights, he was free to exercise dominion wherever he could find a following. Experience justified this estimate of Chaldu's powers, for his worship now extends over a wide expanse of country. It is he who is venerated in the Simla States, where his devotees are growing more numerous each year. Twelve years on end he spends in wandering amongst his subjects, and every house must then give Rs. 1-8 to his ministers. The priests and temple managers take the rupee for their own use, or current charges, but store the annas in the god's treasury. Besides this the peasants have to provide instruments of music and ornaments of silver in honour of their deity and also grain and other offerings to feed his following. They must therefore feel relieved when the long touring season is completed and the god can spend an equal period at ease within his shrine, which was built in a village close to where his brother Bhoṭu lives.

Chaldu Mahásu is the member of the family revered or dreaded as the case may be by many villages in Bashahr, but the people of that State tell a different story of his advent to those parts. The dynasty, they say, ruled in Kashmír where the first-born held his court attended by his brothers, ministers and hosts of minor deities. The only blot upon the brightness of his glory was the presence of a rival god, by name Chasrálu, with whom he long had carried on a bitter feud, but one day Mahásu lured his foe within his reach and drawing his sword smote him, below the belt. With a gaping wound Chasrálu fled in terror taking his life with him, whilst Mahásu with his whole army of retainers rose in pursuit. But the chase was long, for the fugitive was fleet of foot and had gone some distance before his enemies had grasped the situation. Over ranges of snow-clad peaks, down winding valleys and through dense forests for many days the hue and cry chased close behind the fleeing god, gaining slowly but surely on him until at length he was all but in their grasp. Chasrálu spent and worn was just about to yield his life when he espied a cavern with a narrow opening, going deep into the rocky mountain side and into this he darted as his nearest foe was in act to cut him down. There he lay concealed, gathering new strength and courage, whilst his ancient enemy held counsel with his ministers. 'Who of all my many servants', asked Mahásu, 'is bold enough to drive Chasrálu from his lurking place'? But no one had the courage to assault the god thus entrenched in his stronghold; only a minor deity whose name was Jakh proposed a plan. 'Let the accursed dog', he said, "stay in his gloomy cavern doomed to eternal darkness. I with four other of your gods will stand as sentinels upon the five approaches to his burrow, so that he cannot take flight either by the mountain passes or by the valleys or by the river. We will be surety for his safe keeping, if in return you grant us sole jurisdiction over our respective charges and pledge your word to leave us undisturbed." Mahásu would have liked to see his ancient enemy withered up before his eyes, but in default of any other way to wreak his vengeance he at last approved Jakh's plan, renouncing all control over the actions of his former servants. Then departing with his brothers and the rest of his court he found a heaven after many wanderings in the village of Anal which has ever since remained the centre of his worship. The five wardens of the marches on their part remained behind to keep unceasing watch and ward upon all exits from the cave. Jakh, who dwells in Janglik, watches the mountain passes to the north; Bheri Nág of Tangnu keeps guard upon the Pábar river and a valley to the west; whilst if the prisoner should escape his vigilance and hasten to the south he must pass the watchful eyes of Chillam and Naráin who have their temples in Dudi and Ghoswári. The last custodian is Nág of Peka or Pekian who stays as sentinel upon the road.

Though Chasrálu, cribbed, cabined and confined on every side had thus to stay within his dungeon yet as the years passed by he won his share of glory and renown. For up to recent times his cave contained a famous oracle where wondrous portents were vouchsafed upon the special festivals held in his honour at recurring intervals. On such occasions a skilled diviner went inside the cavern and as he prayed with tight shut eyes, held out the skirts of his long coat to catch the gifts which tumbled from the roof. Sometimes a calf would fall, a most propitious omen, for then the seed would yield abundant increase, the herds and flocks would multiply, and the peasantry be free from pestilence or famine. Sometimes again a pigeon came fluttering down, proving to be a harbinger of sickness and disease, whilst if a snake fell wriggling in the coat the luckless villagers were doomed to never-ceasing trouble until the year was over. Occasionally it happened that as the sorcerer muttered his prayers and incantations apparitions of the living passed before his eyes and though their human counterparts were well and healthy at the time they surely died within the year. The oracle was also efficacious in pointing out spots where hidden hoards lay buried. The would-be finder first sacrificed a goat and laid before the entrance of the cave its severed head, through which the god conveyed his message to the learned diviner who alone could comprehend its meaning. The people say the clues thus given led sometimes to the finding of hereditary treasure and then the lucky heir made dedicatory offerings of a field or house or other article of value to his god.

But Chasrálu's days of glorious miracle have vanished for Mahásu has declared that the god no longer lives within the cave. Some 20 years ago one of his priests, a man feared for his knowledge in the magic art, came to the group of villages where the five guardians were worshipped, and intimated that his master's ancient enemy had been dissipated into space. He did not blame the warders since the prisoner had not escaped through any lack of vigilance nor indeed escaped at all; he had melted into nothingness and merely ceased to be. But he argued, with unerring logic, that since there was now no prisoner to guard, it did not need five deities to hold him fast. Therefore his master, so he said, would deign to come amongst them and resume his former rule. The villagers were very angry at this wanton breach of faith and coming out with sticks and staves swore they would not allow Mahásu in their hamlets. Also they handled roughly the god's ambassador, threatening him with divers pains and penalties if he ventured in their midst again with such a proposition, so that he had to flee in haste, vowing vengeance as he ran. And from that day misfortune and calamity commenced and never ceased until the people gave their grudging homage to the forsworn god, through fear of whose displeasure they shrink from asking at Chasrálu's oracle. Jakh of Janglik has suffered in particular from the advent of his former lord, for previous to his intrusion there was an offshoot of Jakh's worship in the isolated sub-division of Dodra Kawár. There the local deity is also Jakh and till a few years ago a regular exchange of visits took place between the namesakes and their bands of worshippers. Now the people of Kawár deny that there has ever been affinity between the two but when hard pressed admit the bonds were broken when Mahásu entered into Janglik. They fear the Kashmír deity too much to run the risk of his invasion into their lonely valley, so they will neither take their god to any place within his sphere of influence nor allow the Janglik deity to come to them. The terrible Mahásu, they opine, might fix himself to one or other of the deities and it is easier to keep him out than drive him off when once he comes.

The superstitious terrors inspired by Mahásu and the methods he pursues may be illustrated by the following instance:—At one place the mere mention of Mahásu is anathema, for the village is the cardinal seat of Shálu's worship, a deity with whom the Gaṛhwál god is waging bitter war, the cause of which will be explained anon. In the adjoining hamlet also stands a temple to the glory of the local Shálu, and the brazen vessels, horns and rags hanging to its walls give testimony of the veneration extended to the god by former generations. But a sanctuary to Mahásu is near completion, so that in the near future the devotions and offerings of the peasants will be divided between the rival claimants, although the family deity is likely for some time to come to get the major share. The manner in which the interloper has gained a following and a shrine is typical. For some years the curse of barrenness had fallen on the women, crops and herds. Few children had been born within the village whilst those the wives had given to their husbands before the curse descended had sickened suddenly and died. The seed sown on the terraced fields had failed to yield its increase, or if by chance the crops were good some heaven-sent calamity destroyed them ere they were garnered in the granaries. The sheep had ceased to lamb and the goats to bring forth young, nay even the stock the peasants owned was decimated by a strange disease. At night-fall they would shut their beasts safe in the lower storeys of their houses, but in the morning when they went to tend them some half dozen would be either dead or dying despite the fact that on the previous evening they had all seemed well and healthy. At last a skilled diviner, to whom the lengthy story of misfortune was unfolded, was summoned to expound the meaning of these long continued omens of a demon's wrath With head thrown back, fists tightly clenched and muscles rigid he kept on muttering the incantations of his art, until successive tremors passing through his frame showed that some god or demon had become incarnate in his person. Then in a loud voice he told his anxious listeners, that unknown to them some object sacred to Mahásu had come within the village boundaries and with it too had come the god, for Mahásu never quits possession of any article, however trifling, once dedicated to his service. The oppression he had wrought upon the hamlet was but a means of signifying his arrival and until a fitting dwelling place was ready for his spirit, the inhabitants would fail to prosper in their ventures. Hence the half-built shrine above the village site Strangely enough the diviner in this instance, as in many others, was not connected with Mahásu's cult in any way and as the oracle was therefore free from interested motives it would seem that the general terror of Mahásu's name has obsessed the soothsayers as strongly as it has the people.

In the adjacent village distant but a mile or so, a former generation had raised a temple to Mahásu. It stood close to the road and facing it upon a narrow strip of land, once cultivated but long since given over to the service of the god. Within the courtyard were planted several images each consisting of a thin block of wood, with the upper portion cut into the uncouth likeness of a face. These were supposed to represent the five divine *wazírs* and a large pile of ashes heaped before the lowest proclaimed him as the fifth attendant, for ashes from the altars of his master or superiors are the only perquisites which come his way; from which it would appear that, like their human counterparts, the under-waiters of the gods received but little. Mahásu had remained contented with his shrine for many years, following a course of righteous living as became a well-conducted deity, but of late he had grown restive, developing a tendency to vex his worshippers. Crops had been indifferent on the lands for several seasons especially in the early harvest, a fact for which their northern aspect would afford sufficient explanation to any but the superstitious natives of the hills They, of course, assigned the failure of the harvests to a supernatural cause and to their cost called in the inevitable diviner. Mahásu, it then transpired, had nothing much to say against the fashion of his temple, it was soundly built, fairly commodious and comfortable enough inside; indeed it was all a god could reasonably desire: if the site had only been selected with a little more consideration. *That* was objectionable, for situated just above the public road it exposed his sanctuary to the prying eyes of the passing stranger, a fatal drawback which any self-respecting deity would resent. Now a little higher up there was a nicely levelled piece of land promising an ideal situation for a sacred shrine. Yes, he meant the headman's field, the one close to the village site, richly manured twice yearly so as to yield two bounteous harvests. If this were given to his service and a convenient sanctuary built thereon his present dwelling place would come in handy for his chief *wazír*, less sensitive, as became a servant, to the public gaze. Indeed in this connection it was hardly suited to the dignity of a mighty god, that his first minister should be exposed to piercing cold in winter and burning heat in summer without some covering for his head; and that was why the headman had lately dedicated to the god one of his most fertile fields within whose limits for the future no man would ever turn a furrow or scatter seed. The villagers too were only waiting for the necessary timber to erect a new and better sanctuary, a further act of homage which they were vain enough to hope would keep Mahásu quiet for some time. They apparently had overlooked the other four *wazírs* for whose comfort fresh demands were certain to arise and as Mahásu never asks but of the best one could only hope that he would cast his envious glance upon a field belonging to an owner rich enough to bear the loss. Shil is one of the earliest seats of worship of Mahásu in Bashahr in which State he gained a footing through the misplaced credit of a miracle in which he played no part. Several hundred years ago it happened that the ruler of Gaṛhwál set out upon a pilgrimage to the temple of Hátkoṭi, a very ancient shrine situated on the right bank of the Pabar. He was as yet without an heir, whilst Deví, the presiding goddess, was and still is famous for bestowing progeny on those who seek her aid. The Rájá had given timely notice of his royal pleasure to the local ruler who had issued orders to the *saildár* of the district and headmen of four adjacent villages to make all necessary preparations for the comfort of so powerful a prince. Either through carelessness or contumacy they shirked their duties and the Rájá with his suite suffered no little inconvenience in obtaining the requisite supplies,—a fact which ought perhaps only to have added to the merit of the pilgrimage. The chief however did not take this pious view and though he had no jurisdiction in the territory, this mattered little in the good old times when might was right, so after he had begged his boon and paid his vows, he seized the *saildár* and headmen, carrying them with him to his capital. There he threw them into a gloomy dungeon, whose inky darkness knew no count of day or night, to meditate in sadness on the ways of half-starved princes. Now in the dungeon there were other prisoners of State, natives of Gaṛhwál who owned Mahásu as their god, and from their lips the foreign captives heard many stories of his mighty deeds. As the months passed by without a sign of succour from their own ancestral god or ruler the *saildár* and his friends began to ponder on the wisdom of turning to a nearer quarter for deliverance. Accordingly, at last, they swore a solemn oath that if Mahásu would but free them from their bonds, they would forsake their ancient gods and cleave to him alone. By chance a few days later Deví vouchsafed an answer to the intercessions made by the prince before her altars, for to his favourite Ráni an heir was born whose advent was received with feelings of delight throughout the State. A day was set aside for general rejoicing and on it by a common act of royal clemency all prisoners were released, the *saildár* and his friends amongst the rest. Mindful of their oath, they ascribed their freedom to the mercy of Mahásu, not to the power of the goddess Deví to whom the merit actually belonged, and when they journeyed to their homes they carried with them one of his many images. This they duly placed in a temple built to his honour at Sanadur, and in addition each introduced the ritual of Mahásu's worship into his own particular hamlet. The *saildár* on returning to his home at Shil also told the people how a powerful deity had freed them from imprisonment and persuaded them to adopt his worship as an adjunct to the veneration paid to Shálu, their ancestral god. But neither he nor they accepted Mahásu as other than a secondary deity and when a shrine was raised to him, it was placed outside the village site, upon a plot of land below the public road. For some years sacrifices were duly offered to the stranger god and his *wazírs*, but as the memory of his timely aid began to fade, the peasants showed a falling off in their devotions, offerings were but few and far between, his yearly festival was discontinued and his very dwelling place fell into disrepair. This culpable neglect remained unpunished for some time until once a cultivator's wife fell ill, manifesting every sign of demoniacal possession. In the middle of a sentence she lost all power of speech, her lips moved but no sound came forth and as she struggled inarticulate a trembling seized upon her limbs. Then suddenly she fell prostrate in a swoon upon the ground, but almost at once leapt up again, her body still quivering and shaking as she gave utterance to fearsome shrieks which pierced the ears of all who heard. Then as suddenly she regained her sanity, showing no symptom of her temporary madness. For several days she went about her duties in the house and fields as usual, but all at once the same wild frenzy came upon her, and moreover as she shrieked her cries were echoed by a woman in another quarter of the village who too became as one possessed. As before the mania of both was followed by a brief period of complete recovery, but on the next outburst the two were joined by yet a third and so the madness spread until at length some half a dozen women made the hills and valleys re-echo with their hideous cries. Then it was deemed advisable to summon to their aid a wise diviner who might read the riddle of the seeming madness. Standing bareheaded in their midst, his frame racked by the paroxyams of divine possession, he told the people that Mahásu the terrible was angry, that his altars had remained so long neglected and his temple left to fall in ruins. If now they wished to check the mad contagion they must purchase expiation by raising a finer edifice, added to the sacrifice of many goats, both to the god and his *wazírs*. The price was promptly paid, so now womenfolk are free from evil spirits whilst a fairly modern sanctuary stands on the ruins of the ancient shrine.

But Maháśu still remains dissatisfied and the reason of his discontent is this :—Shálu, the hereditary god, dwells in a lofty temple, built in the centre of the village by a former generation which had never even heard the name of the great Maháśu. But the latter would evict the local deity and take possession of the shrine, founding his claim on the oath the erstwhile *saildár* swore that if the god but freed him from the darkness of the dungeon he would forsake his other gods and follow him alone. Shálu however is himself no weak-kneed godling to truckle to the self-assertion of any interloper from another land. He too commands a numerous following of pious devotees whose zeal is strengthened by a firm belief in the miraculous story of how he first revealed his godhead to their fathers. When in early summer the iron hand of winter has relaxed its rigors and the snows have melted on the lower passes it is the practice of the shepherds to drive their flocks up to the Alpine pastures. The owners of a group of hamlets collect their sheep and goats together in a central village, where they celebrate the massing of the flocks, before they speed the herdsmen on their journey to the dangerous heights, where the dread Káli loves to dwell. It was after such a gathering held in dim ages long past the memory of living man that the nomad shepherds of Pandarásan *pargana* set out upon their wanderings. Marching by easy stages in the early morning and late afternoon, they gave their footsore beasts a welcome rest during the midday heat, whilst at night their massive sheep-dogs crouching at the corners of the huddled square gave ready warning of the approach of man or leopard. Proceeding thus, they reached a level plateau, forming the truncated summit of a lofty mountain and tempted by the richness of the pasturage they resolved to make a halt until the luxuriant herbage should be exhausted. The sheep and goats were left to browse at will amongst the pastures whilst the men built for themselves rough shelters of piled-up stones for protection from the cold at night. That evening the dogs were sent as usual to ring the straggling beasts, but a continued sound of barking soon warned the shepherds that something was amiss. Fearing lest a panther had pounced down upon a straggler from the flocks they hastened to the spot, where on the edge of the plateau they saw a full-grown ram stretched calmly on the ground, indifferent to the onsets of the dogs which were rushing round him snarling and snapping in their vain attempts to move him. The men added their shouts and blows to the efforts of the dogs but all in vain, the ram still lay as though transfixed. At length angered by the obstinacy of the beast one of the men drew his axe and slew it as it lay. Another bent down to lift the carcass from the ground, but as he raised it, there lay revealed two dazzling images of an unknown god, whilst from a stone close by a supernatural voice was heard. Ere they could grasp the smaller image it started moving of its own accord, slowly at first but gathering speed as it went, until it reached the edge of the plateau down which it tumbled into a mountain torrent that bore it swiftly out of sight. The larger and finer idol still remained and this they carried to their halting place, first offering to the rock from which the mystic sound had rung the slaughtered ram, through whose inspired obstinacy the god had chosen to reveal his presence. At dawn the following morning they set out towards their starting place, for not one among them was skilled in the lore of heaven-sent signs to read the secret of the omen. On arrival there the wondrous news spread quickly through the countryside and a gathering of peasants larger even than that which had sped them on their way, assembled to hear from the shepherds' lips the oft-repeated tale and to see with their own eyes the precious image. A sooth-sayer too was summoned from a neighbouring village and he told them that the portent was propitious, for the god, who had revealed his presence to the lowly shepherds, would deign to live amongst them guarding them and theirs from harm if only they would forthwith build a spacious and lofty temple in honour of his coming. Willing hands soon raised the sacred edifice and on a happy day with the full ritual prescribed for installation of an idol the Brahmans placed the image in the upper storey of the temple. At the same time they gave the name of Shálu to the god, for in the language of the hills *shál* is the term used for the grand assemblage before the sheep and goats are driven to the Alpine pastures. This first temple to the glory of this god was built in the centre of the confederacy of villages, and though many local sanctuaries have been erected, as at Shil, this still remains the main seat of his worship. It is hither that the flocks converge each year, and as in the olden days, so now, a general gathering of the countryside precedes the exodus to the upper mountains. From here too the shepherds take with them in their journey the hallowed emblem of their god, lent them each year from the temple treasury. This is a drum-shaped vessel, sealed at either end, containing sacred relics of the deity whilst round the outer surface a goodly number of rupees are nailed. Only the leader of the herdsmen is privileged to carry it, slung by chains across his shoulders, but when the camp is reached it is unslung and placed with reverence in the midst of folds and shepherds and then both man and beast can sleep in perfect safety secure from all chance of harm. At nightfall the shepherds worship the sacred symbol, and at certain stages in their wanderings they sacrifice a goat or ram of which by ancient right their headman takes a shoulder as his private portion. Moreover when the grazing ground is reached where stands the stone, the former dwelling of the god, a customary offering of one rupee is added to the accumulated tributes of past years. The recognition of Shálu as a pastoral deity is shown in yet another way, for when he goes on progress every other year amongst his subjects it is his privilege to claim a ram each day, and though his journeyings continue for full three months he never asks in vain. With such old time memories cementing in a common bond the interests of god and peasant it is not surprising that the villagers even of a secondary seat of Shálu's worship are loath to oust their deity from his ancestral shrine in favour of a stranger. And in the meantime Mahásu carries on a relentless warfare which has been raging now for some ten years, during which time the owners of the houses which immediately adjoin the disputed sanctuary have experienced to their sorrow the power of his vengeance. Several families have vanished root and branch, others have been oppressed with sickness, whilst most have sunk into the direst poverty. A signal warning of the demon's wrath occurred some six or seven years ago. Almost next door to the shrine, perched on the edge of a precipitous slope, stood a building occupied by several humble cultivators, adherents, like the other villagers, of Shálu their ancestral god. One night, only a few days after the annual festival in honour of Mahásu had been duly celebrated, the master of the house was ladling barley from his store-bin. His wife stood by his side holding open the bag of goat-skin into which the grain was being poured. A second man, a near relation, had just crossed the threshold of the outer door. Suddenly without a moment's warning the building started to slide slowly down the steep hill-side and before the inmates could make good their exit the roof collapsed pinning them beneath the beams and rafters. For a hundred yards or so they travelled with the *débris*, until a clump of pine trees arrested further motion. So noiselessly had the incident occurred that their neighbours did not know until the morning what had taken place: then, descending to the mass of ruins they bewailed the loss of friends or relatives. But as they wept a voice came from the heaped-up pile of wood and stone, proclaiming the glad intelligence that one at least of the victims still survived. Quickly the stones and beams were thrown aside and from beneath them issued the men and women a little bruised but otherwise unhurt. Mahásu however as though to demonstrate his powers over life and death had killed the household goats which were tethered in the lower storey of the building.

The present *saildár*, a lineal descendant of the perjurer who brought such catastrophes upon the hamlet, recounted this story of Mahásu's 'playing', as he termed it and at the end in answer to a question maintained his firm allegiance to the cause of Shálu. But, as an afterthought, he added with a chuckle, that as his house was in a lower portion of the village, the 'playing' of the jealous god had so far affected neither him nor his. A survivor of the landslide was also present at the time and was asked whether he too would like the home of Shálu delivered over to his rival, so that henceforth the people of the quarter might live without the apprehension of impending evil. With a bold and sturdy spirit he answered that Shálu was the ancestral deity not to be renounced without good cause: if the god himself consented to deliver up his ancient sanctuary, then well and good, but otherwise he would remain faithful to the family god. Believing firmly as he did that Mahásu had toppled down his house, brought desolation or extinction to many of his neighbours, and that the tyranny would not cease until the sacred dwelling-place was handed over, this simple rustic with his devotion to his ancient faith displayed a heroism worthy of a better cause.

The latest incident in this battle of the gods had been the building of a smaller shrine a year ago to house Mahásu's chief *wazir*, the people blindly hoping that this fresh concession would appease the anger of the mighty spirit for some little time. The quarrel can however have but one issue. Mahásu's victory is assured and in all likelihood it only needs an unforeseen calamity to fall upon the *saildár* or his family to accelerate an unconditional surrender.

The justice of this forecast is indicated by the history of a village a little further on. Here too one of the liberated headmen incurred guilt or earned merit by the introduction of Mahásu's cult, its entrance in the village being followed by a bitter feud with the native deity. This was

Nágeshar, lord of serpents, who at the outset warned his worshippers that they would find it difficult to serve two masters with equal loyalty to both, bidding them beware lest the new divinity should prove a greater tyrant than the old. And so the sequel proved for the villagers, less stiffnecked than their neighbours, the followers of Shálu, had not the courage to hold out against a series of misfortunes succeeding one upon another in all of which Mahásu's hand was clearly visible. So since several generations Nágeshar had been termed the family god only by courtesy, whilst the real worship of the village has centred round the shrine of the invader. The ancient temple stood dilapidated and forlorn, the single offering of a metal pot nailed on its roof and long since blackened by exposure to the rains of many summers, only adding to its desolation. The buildings raised to the glory of Mahásu, on the other hand, filled up a portion of the village green and the neat group of arbours, granaries and smaller shrines which clustered round the main pagoda testified alike to the number of his votaries and the frequent calls on their devotion. Even the walls and gables of the newest shrine—erected for a minor minister some dozen years ago to check a cholera epidemic—were covered with the horns of sacrificial victims and other votive offerings. Thus if Mahásu had so far refrained from seizing on the temple of his rival the only reason was because he would not deign to grace a dwelling fallen to such low estate. Indeed the people said that the two were now the best of friends and this perhaps was so, for Mahásu could afford to be magnanimous towards a foe completely crushed and beaten. They denied also that the goddess Deví had played any part in rescuing their ancestors. Though the Rájá of Garhwál, they said, had come to seek an heir, it was not at the shrine of Deví that he sought him, but from the hands of the ruler of Bashahr For his only son had led some months before an army into Bashahr to join the local forces against the common foe from Kulu. The youth had perished honourably in battle, but his father in his frantic grief would not listen to the truth and insisted that the people of Bashahr were concealing him for their own ends. And so he took away the *saildár* and his comrades to hold as hostages and cast them into prison, binding them first with iron fetters. But Mahásu in answer to their prayers broke their chains asunder and burst aside the dungeon doors so that they escaped again to their own country. However this may be, the peasants of this hamlet were eloquent in praise of their imported god, protesting that he was the mildest mannered of all divinities, provided always that his modest demands were promptly met, for he was slow to brook delay and ever ready to accept the challenge of an opposition were it human or divine. Nor, in truth, is he without the grace of saving virtues for he cannot tolerate a thief nor yet a tale-bearer, and sets his face against the prayers and offerings of those of evil livelihood.

In the month of Bhádon each year the fourth day of the light half of the moon is set aside in honour of the god. Early in the morning the temple priests carry the images and vessels hallowed in his service to a neighbouring stream or fountain where they bathe them reverently according to their ancient rites. Wrapped in folds of cloth the images are carried on the shoulders of the Brahmans and so secured against contamination from the vulgar gaze. The company of worshippers watch the proceedings from a distance, for if they ventured near a curse would fall upon them. The rites completed, the images and vessels are conveyed in similar fashion to the temple and are placed in *parda*; except one small image which is set upon the car and left all day within the courtyard where the subsequent ceremonies occur. At night time it too is put inside the shrine safe from the hands of sacrilegious revellers. A high straight pole, cut usually from the blue pine tree, is planted firmly in the ground and bears a flag in honour of the deity. Another pole, shorter and thicker, cut off at the junction of many branches is also driven in the earth. The forking branches are lopped at a distance of several feet from the parent stem whilst in between them rough slabs of slate are placed so that the whole forms an effective brazier. At the approach of nightfall a ram and goat provided by the general community are sacrificed, the first beside the brazier, whilst the latter is led inside the shrine, for a goat is deemed a nobler offering than a ram. But the victim is not actually despatched before the altar, for the family of Mahásu has a strong aversion to the sight of blood, so after the god has signified acceptance of the offering through the trembling of the beast it is led outside again and slaughtered in the courtyard. When darkness falls the worshippers of either sex, with lighted torches in their hands, dance for some little time around the brazier on which they later fling the blazing faggots. All through the night the fire is fed by branches of the pine tree which flash the flaming message of Mahásu's fame throughout the chain of villages which own his sway across the valleys and along the hills, whilst the men and women spend the night in merrymaking, joining together in their rustic dances and time-honoured songs. At intervals, as the unceasing rhythmic dance circles around the fire, a villager drops from the group and manifests the well-known signs of supernatural possession. Then he must make an offering of a sweetened cake of wheaten flour, with a little butter to the god's *wazir* or, if well-to-do, must sacrifice a goat or ram. Sometimes a votary, snatching a burning torch from the fire, clasps it tightly to his breast, but if his hands are injured in the process, he is proved a low impostor and the slighted god exacts a fine of several annas and a kid. Also if many villagers become inspired there is a murmur that divine possession is growing cheap, implying that the would-be incarnations of the deity are simulating ecstatic frenzy. The general riot is heightened by a plentiful supply of home-brewed spirits, but the women do not drink nor is debauchery looked upon with favour. No one who tastes intoxicating liquor is allowed within the temple, and the priests who abstain themselves keep watch upon the portal. But when the revelry is at its zenith it sometimes happens that, despite their care, the drunken worshippers cluster around the porch and some fall helplessly across the threshold. Then the god inflicts upon the culprits the penalties imposed on mere pretenders to divine afflatus. At the break of dawn such of the merrymakers as are well enough to eat, enjoy a common feast for which each house provides a pound of wheaten flour and half a pound of oil. This ends the ceremonies and Mahásu is left in quiet for another year to prosecute his silent schemes by which he hopes to forge a few more links in the ever-lengthening chain that binds his worshippers in bonds of superstitious dread.

Síndhu Bír.—Síndhu Bír is the whistling god,[1] whose cult is found in Jammu, in the Kángra hills, and in the Jaswán Dún of Hoshiárpur, and whose whistling sound announces his approach. Síndhu is apparently an incarnation of Shiva conceived of as the storm-wind in the hills, and there may be some connection between this cult and the Jogi's whistle which is worn as denoting an attribute of the god. Síndhu is generally regarded as a malignant deity, causing madness and burning houses, stealing crops and otherwise immoral. But he is only supposed to burn down the houses of those with whom he is displeased, and the corn, milk, *ghí* etc. stolen by him is said to be given to his special worshippers. He can, however, be mastered by charms repeated at suitable places for 21 days. On the 21st he will appear after whistling to announce his approach, and sometimes with a whistling noise through his limbs, and ask why he was called. He should then be told to come when sent for and do whatever he is bidden. On the 22nd day a ram should be taken to the place of his manifestation and presented to him as his steed.

In places where the houses are liable to sudden conflagrations the people who come to beg in Síndhú's name are much dreaded and if they say they belong to his shrine they are handsomely rewarded. He is popularly believed to assume the form of a Gaddi, with a long beard, whence he is called Dáriála, and carrying a long basket (*kiro*) on his back, whence he is Kiromála. But he has several other titles: such as Lohe or Lohán Pál, 'Lord of metals' Sanghín Pál or 'Lord of Chains' and Bhúmi Pál or 'Lord of the Earth.'[2] In the form of invocation recorded in Kángra we find him addressed as grandson of Ngar Hír, Chatarpál, Lohpál, Agripál, Sangalpál, Thikarpal ('He of the potsherds'), daughter's son of Bhúínpál, son of Mother Kunthardi and brother of Punia. And the invocation ends with the words: 'Let the voice of Mahádeo work'.

Síndhú's principal shrine is at Basoli in Jammu territory, but he has smaller ones at Dhár and Bhangúri in Gurdáspur and at Gungtha in Kángra. Most Hindu cultivators in these parts have a lively faith in the Bír, and offer him a *karáhi* of *halwa* as sweetmeat at each harvest. Not only can he be invoked for aid, but he can also be directed by any one who has mastered his charms to cohabit with any woman, she thinking she is in a dream. Whenever a woman or a house or a man is declared by a *jogi,* locally called *chela,* to be possessed by the Bír, offerings of *karáhi,* a ram or he-goat should be made to him to avert illness. Those who have mastered his charms can also use him to oppress an enemy at will.

A very interesting feature of Síndhú's mythology is his association with the pairs of goddesses, Raṛi and Braṛi, said to be worshipped in Chamba, Andlá and Sandlá, two hill goddesses, the exact locality of whose cult is unknown, and Cháhṛi and Chhatráhṛi, also said to be worshipped in Chamba. The duality of these three pairs of god-

[1]In the Kángra District *sinḍh* or *sinḍhi* = a whistle, *cf.* Hindi *síti*: Kángra *Gazetteer*, Vol. I, pp. 77-8.

[2]See the *Song of Síndhu Bír, Ind. Ant.*, 1909, p. 295. *Loh*, pl. *lohan*, is said to = metal, not iron. Síndhu is said to have a chain (*sangal*) always with him, and so his votaries also keep one at home.

desses recalls that of the two Bíbís, wives of the Míán, whose cult is prevalent in the Hoshiárpur District. Bharmáni, a goddess of Barmaur in Chamba, is also said to dance with Síndhu.[1]

Bhairon or Bhairava, the terrible one, is a deity whose personality it is a little difficult to grasp. He is in the orthodox mythology the same as Shiva; Bhairon or Bhairav being one of the many names of that deity. But he appears also as the attendant of Kálí, and as such is said to be specially worshipped by Sikh watermen. At Benáres his staff is reverenced as an anti-type of that earthly deity, the Kotwál. More commonly he is represented as an inferior deity, a stout black figure, with a bottle of wine in his hand, whose shrine is to be found in almost every big town. He is an evil spirit, and his followers drink wine and eat meat. One sect of *faqírs*, akin to the Jogís, is specially addicted to his service; they besmear themselves with red powder and oil and go about the bazars, begging and singing the praises of Bhairon, with bells or gongs hung about their loins and striking themselves with whips. They are found mainly in large towns, and are not celibates. Their chief place of pilgrimage is Girnár-parbat in Kaṭhiawár, and the books which teach the worship of Bhairon are the *Bhairavashtak* and the *Bhairava-stottar*. That very old temple—the Bhairon-ká-sthán—near Icchra, in the suburbs of Lahore, is so named from a quaint legend regarding Bhairon, connected with its foundation. In the old days the Dhínwar girls of the Riwáṛí tahsíl used to be married to the god at Baododa, but they always died soon afterwards and the custom has been dropped. As a village deity Bhairon appears in several forms, Kál Bhairon, who frightens death, Bhút Bhairon, who drives away evil spirits, Bhatak Bhairon, or the Child Bhairon, Láṭh Bhairon, or Bhairon with the club, and Nand Bhairon. Outside a temple of Shiv at Thánesar is a picture of Kál Bhairon.[2] He is black and holds a decapitated head in one hand.[3] In the eastern Punjab he appears as Khetrpál, the protector of fields, under which name he is worshipped with sweets, milk etc. When a man has built a house and begins to occupy it, he should worship Khetrpál, who is considered to be the owner of the soil, the ground landlord in fact, and who drives away the evil spirits that are in it. He is also worshipped at weddings. Sometimes the Khetrpál is said to be an inhabitant of the *pípal* tree and to him women do worship when their babies are ill. Sometimes again he is considered to be the same as Shesh Nág, the serpent king. In Ferozepur he is known as Khetrpál, but his cult is probably more widely spread than the small numbers of his worshippers returned would appear to indicate, for in Gurdáspur the Hindu Kátil Rájpúts are said to consult Brahmans as to the auspicious time for reaping, and before the work is begun 5

[1] This goddess is said to have a temple in Bhat or Bhúṭán also. Síndhú is described as well-known and worshipped in Lahul and to affect mountainous regions generally.

[2] This picture is faced by one of Hanúmán whose shrine is sometimes connected with one of Bhairon. Sometimes too a shrine of Gúga will be found with a shrine to Goraknáth on one side and connected shrines to Hanúmán and Bhairon on the other.

[3] East of the Jumna Kál Bhairon is worshipped to a considerable extent, offerings of intoxicating liquor being made at his shrine by his votaries who consume it themselves. Vaishnavas, some of whom also offer to him, do not however offer him liquor but moles and milk.

or 7 loaves of bread, a pitcher of water, and a small quantity of the crop are set aside in Khetrpál's name. In Chamba too Khetrpál is the god of the soil, and before ploughing he is propitiated to secure a bountiful harvest, especially when new ground or tract which has lain fallow is broken up. A sheep or goat may be offered or incense is burnt. In the centre and west Bhairon is almost invariably known as Bhairon Jatí, or Bhairon the chaste, and is represented as the messenger of Sakhi Sarwar.

The Cult of Deví.

Maclagan, § 40.

Closely connected with the worship of Shiv, and far more widely spread, is that of his consort, Deví This goddess goes by many names, --Durgá, Kálí, Gaurí, Asurí, Párbatí, Kálká, Mahesrí, Bhiwání, Asht-bhojí, and numberless others. According to the Hindu *Shástras*, there are nine crores of Durgás, each with her separate name. The humbler divinities, Sítala, the goddess of small-pox, Masáni and other goddesses of disease, are but manifestations of the same goddess. She is called Mahádeví, the great goddess, Mahárání, the great queen, and Deví Mái or Deví Mátá, the goddess-mother She is known, from the places of her temples, as Jawálají, Mansá Deví, Chintpurní, Náina Deví, and the like.[1] In Kángra alone there are numerous local Devís, and 360 of them assembled together at the founding of the Kángra temple.

Deví is a popular object of veneration all over the Province, but her worship is most in vogue and most diversified in Ambála, Hoshiárpur and Kángra. The celebrated shrines of Deví are for the most part in those districts. At Mansá Deví, near Manimájra, in the Ambála district, a huge fair is held twice a year, in spring and autumn, in her honour.

Mansa Deví, sister of Shesh Nág, counteracts the venom of snakes. She is also called Jagadgauri, the world's beauty[2], Nitya and Padamavati. Her shrine is at Mani Májra west of Kálka. With Sayyid Bhúra, whose shrine is at Bári in Kaithal, she shares the honour of being the patron of thieves in the eastern Punjab, but it is at his shrine alone that a share of the booty appears to be offered.[3]

At Budhera in Gurgaon at the temple of Mansa Deví[4] a fair is held twice a year, on Chet *sudi* 7th or Asauj *sudi* 7th. This temple is about 125 years old. It is two yards square and the roof is domed. From the dome projects an iron bar from which hangs a *dhaja* or small flag. Of the 4 images of the goddess, two are of brass and two of marble, each about $\frac{3}{16}$ths of a yard high. They stand in a niche facing the entrance.

[1] Or rather, her cult names are used as place names.

[2] One of Deví's ten incarnations, assumed to receive the thanks of gods and men for the deliverance she had wrought.

[3] *S.C.R.* VIII, pp. 268, 277 and 266. Bhura is a title of Shiva.

[4] *Mansa* in Hindi means the desire or object of the heart.

At Chintpurní, in Hoshiárpur, there are three fairs in the year, and the *pujáris* make large profits at the shrine A large fair is held in Chet at Dharmpur in Hoshiárpur, and Nainá Deví, in Biláspur State, on the borders of the same district, is also a favourite place of pilgrimage. At Kángra is the renowned shrine of Bejisarí Deví, which Mahmúd of Ghazní and Fíroz Tughlak plundered in days gone by, and which is still one of the most famous in India. And at Jawálamukhi, in Kángra, is another and equally famous temple, where jets of gas proceeding from the ground are kept ever burning, and the crowds of pilgrims provide a livelihood for 'a profligate miscellany of attendant Gosáíns and Bhojkís.'

Jawálamukhi.—This Deví is the chief object of worship to the Telrája or Telirája *faqirs* who appear to be found chiefly in the United Provinces. The sect was founded by Mán Chandra, Rájá of Kángra. He was attacked by leprosy, so the Deví bade him turn ascetic and beg from Hindu women whose sons and husbands were living a little oil to rub on his clothes and body. By so doing he expiated the sins of a former existence, and was cured in 12 years. He retired to Kángra and founded the order, Srí Chandra, a Brahman, being his first disciple. Initiation consists in paying a fee of Rs. 5, or a multiple of that sum, and feeding the brethren. The novice then sips some *sherbet* upon which the *guru* has breathed. Some of Telrájas are Sikhs, others Hindus, but Deví Jawálamukhi is their principal deity. They beg oil from Hindu women who have only one son and put the oil on their clothes. When dead they are cremated. Some marry, others do not, and the only outward sign of the sect is that their clothes and bodies are smeared with oil.[1]

'Deví is worshipped under various other names in Kángra, *e.g.* as Janiári[2] in Samlohi, Bilásá[3] in Biláspur, Bharári[4] in Siál, Jalpá[5] in Jawáli, Bála Sundari[6] in Harsar, Baglá Mukhi at Nakhandi,[7] and Koṭla[8] and Chamda at Koṭla and elsewhere. It is impossible to reduce to rule anything connected with these temples. The priest is usually

[1] W. Crooke, N. I. N. Q., V., § 247. The Kankarián (literally gravel or pebbles) fair is held in Máler Koṭla on Asauj *sudi* 9th. When pilgrims set for Jawálamukhi to make the promised offerings, people accompany them on foot without shoes, so that pebbles may be trodden by their naked feet.

[2] From Jantára village or 'from certain bushes which grew near by.' This temple was founded by Rájá Tej Chand some 400 years ago. It is managed by a Bhojki.

[3] Founded by Rájá Dalip Singh in S. 1726.

[4] Founded by Fauja Wazír 200 years ago. Deví directed him to enshrine in it 'any stone on which people sharpened axes.'

[5] Founded by a Rání of Rájá Shamsher Singh of Goler in S. 1458.

[6] The story is that Rájá Hari Chand of Goler once when out hunting near Harsar, fell into a well. The goddess directed him to build her a temple on the spot, but he refused to do so as it was in foreign territory. This enraged the Deví and she prepared to punish him, caused him to fall into the well. In it again he remained 18 days worshipping the Deví and making vows to her. By chance some merchants passed by and one of them being thirsty went to the well and finding the Rájá pulled him out. He then built a temple here to Deví Bála Sundari. It is said that the merchants also settled here. The Deví is only worshipped by the chiefs of Goler

[7] Founded by Rájá Hari Chand of Goler in 1684 S. With this are connected the shrines of Shiva and Chatarbhuj.

[8] Founded by a Khatri of Amritsar in 1942 S.

a Brahman[1] but may be a Jogi or a Saniási. They may contain a single image or a number of images, varying in size and material. The ritual is equally diversified. For instance Deví Bharári is only worshiped on the Baisákhi, and on that day only is *bhog* offered and the lamp lit. As a rule the lamp is lit morning and evening or at least once a day. *Bhog* may be offered only once a day, but is generally offered twice. It is very varied. For instance Bála Sundari gets flowers in the morning and sweets &c. in the evening, but to Jalpá are offered rice and *dál* at morn and fruit at eve, and to Baglá Mukhi the morning *bhog* is offered after the images have been washed and in the evening *patáshas* and gram after the *árti*.

Deví is usually regarded as an activity of a god, but at Lagpata is a temple to Kaniya Deví the virgin goddess, whose fair is held on 9th Háṛ. Her Brahman *pujári* is a Bhojki and *bhog* is only offered and a lamp lit in the evening.

Other temples to Deví in Kángṛa are :—

1	2	3	4
Place.	*Pujári.*	Dates of fairs.	Ritual offerings &c.
Hári Deví in Bagroli, Núrpur Tahsíl. Rájá Nág Dev of Garh Gusnávi had 4 sons and a daughter. Rájá Bhúm Asar asked him for his daughter's hand which he refused, thinking it was not safe to marry a girl to a demon. So he abandoned his country and came here with his children. His daughter asked him to build her a temple so this one was built by one of her brothers and she turned herself into stone. It was founded by Rájá Gaḍi Ráj in the Duwápur Yuga some 5000 years ago.	Gosáín, *got* Attari	In Chet during the *naurátra.*	The temple contains a carving of an 8-sided figure on stone. Connected with it are temples of the Thakúrs and a tomb at which worship is performed simultaneously. These shrines contain stone *pinḍis* called Nársingh.

[1] Some of the Brahman *gots* mentioned in the accounts received do not appear in any list of Brahman *gots* in the notes furnished on that caste. *E.g.* Biláia Deví's *pújári* is described as a Brahman of the Chhapal Bálmík *got*.

1	2	3	4
Place.	*Pujári.*	Dates of fairs.	Ritual, offerings &c.
Deví Thal (fr. *atál*, 'eternal').	Brahman, *got* Mitte, *gotar* Koshal. The 11 groups of *pujári* take it in turn to manage the affairs of the temple	Baisákh 8th ...	*Parshád* or *púri* in the morning and *bhát* (boiled rice) in the evening.
The *mandir* of Bhagwati Kirpá Sundri in Bír is said to have been founded by a Rájá of Bangáhal.	An Osti Chandiál Brahman.	The 8 days after the Holi in Phágan.	No *bhog*.
The *mandir* of Chamundri Deví in Jadragal.	A Bhojki Brahman, caste Balútú and *got* Gautam.	On the Shivrátri the people gain a sight of the goddess who is said to have killed the demons Chand and Mund.	The temple contains an image of the Deví engraved on a slab, 6 spans long and 3 broad. On it are also engraved images of Manthasúr and Rakat Bij. The Chandiál and Gokhar Brahmans revere the goddess as their family deity and perform the *janeo* ceremony here. Five sweet *babru* (cakes) in the morning and fried grain in the evening form the *bhog*. *Sandhúr* (vermillion) is also offered monthly.
The *mandir* of Mata Deví Bajar Shúri at Kángra. Once Brahma with other gods went to do homage to this goddess. Their example was followed by other gods but they could not gain access to the Deví. So they resorted to Brahma who founded this temple where the goddess was enshrined. Many additions were made to it by rich votaries and Rání Chand Kaur, widow of Kharak Singh, gilded the dome etc.	Bhojki Brahmans, whose castes and *gots* are:— *Caste.* — Got. Chilián. — Markanda. Postu. — Bhárdawáj. Patiárach — Kásab. Masingan — Bhárdawáj. HadúKasú — Kásab. Kárbhárkhte. — Biás. Jagian — Kásab. Hatúrsú. — Kásab.	A great fair during the *naurátrás* in Chet and Asauj.	Worship is performed twice a day, morning and evening. Milk, fruits, sweetmeats, rice &c. form the *bhog* which is offered five times a day.

The following *mandirs* are connected with this :—

Laukṛa, Ganesh, Dharm-Rájá, Bhairon, Sher, Yogni, Lachmi, Gurú Sikh, Sat Náráin, Sítlá, Dhana Bhagat Shiva, Jateshar, Káli, Sarwasti, Bhadhar Káli, Singh Háthi, Suraj, Tarpar Súndrí, Chandka, Gauri Shankar, Káli, Hawan Kúnḍ, An Púrna, Káli Bhairon, Kangáli, Chetar Pál, Tara Yogni, Barái, Sundar San Chakar, Yag Yúp, Charan Padka and a *dharmsála*.

1	2	3	4
Place.	*Pujári.*	Dates of fairs.	Ritual, offerings &c.
The *mandir* of Jatanti Deví at Nandrol stands on a high ridge south of the Kángṛa fort. The meaning of the name is that the Deví killed all the *rákshasas* which used to vex the gods, so in return they worshipped her.	A Braman, Bhojki, *got* Bhárdwáj.	None, but people come to see the image on the Shivrátri.	The Brahmans and Rájpúts in the neighbourhood adore the Deví as their family deity. Worship is performed morning and evening. *Bhog* of *laḍḍú* or *peṛa* is offered.
The *mandir* of Ambká Deví in the Kángṛa fort dates from the times of the Pánḍavas. This Deví is the family deity of the Kaṭoch family.	Brahman, caste Sariál, *got* Sánḍal.	None ...	The usages of *bhog* and lighting a lamp have ceased.
Anjani Deví's temple at Ghiána Kalán. This Deví was a daughter of Gautam who, for unknown reasons, caused her to bear a son during her virginity, whereupon she abandoned her home and came here for devotion in seclusion. The temple was founded by Jamadár Khushhál Singh of Lahore in S. 1899.	Udási ...	Jeṭh 20th ...	The temple contains a stone slab on which are engraved images of Anjani and the hoof marks of the cows which gave her milk. Behind it are 3 *baolís* or springs formed by her miraculous power. Worship is performed morning and evening. Milk in the morning, rice at noon, and fried gram in the evening form the *bhog*. A sacred lamp is lit daily.
Mandir Sitlá Mahádev in Ṭíka Basdi.	A Giri Gosáín, *got* Atlas.	None ...	It contains a *pinḍi* of Shiva, one span high.
The *mandir* of Sítla Deví in Pálampur.	Bhojki ...	Each Tuesday in Jeṭh and Háṛ.	The temple contains a stone *pinḍi* of the goddess. No *bhog* is offered.

1	2	3	4
Place.	*Pujári.*	Dates of fairs.	Ritual, offerings &c.
Mandir of Deví Násna Sárwa.	Brahman caste Gaddítre, *got* Basisht.	Chet 12th. Formerly it used to last from 24th Bhádon to 1st Asauj and towards its close people used to throw stones at one another, to prevent cholera breaking out.	The temple contains a huge black stone 4 cubits high and 20 in circumference, having a figure of Deví carved on it and a trident painted with *sandhúr*. Bread is offered as *bhog* in the evening.
The *mandir* of Bhaddar Káli or Kálka Deví at Samírpur. Its foundation is ascribed to Panami Gurkha.	A Gir Gosáín. He is not celibate, but succession is governed by spiritual relationship though a son is also entitled to a fixed share in the offerings.	Hár 9th ...	The *pujári* lives on alms, and performs worship morning and evening. Rice in the morning and bread in the evening form the *bhog*.
Dholi Deví in Dabana in Núrpur. 500 years ago Dholi, a Rájpút girl, was being compelled to marry but she declined. When pressed she disappeared under ground on this spot.	Atari Gosáín ...	...	*Bhog* is offered in the morning, *árti* is performed and a lamp lighted every evening. The carving of the Deví, placed against a wall in the temple, is 2 ft. high. An image of Shiva 4 ft. high stands near it.

The shrines of Deví in other districts have seldom more than a very local reputation; the most famous, perhaps are the Bhaddar Káli temple at Niázbeg near Lahore, the Jogmáya temple in Multán, where offerings are made and lamps lit on the 1st and 8th of every month, and the old Jogmáya temple at the Mahrauli where the Hindus of Delhi hold their yearly festival of fans, the ' Pankha *mela* '.

There are, however, temples to various Devís scattered over the eastern districts and other parts of the province. Often associated with other cults the most important of these Devís are Saraswati at Pehowa, Bhiwáni at Thánesar, Mansa Deví in Gurgáon, Jhandka in Dera Ismaíl Khán and others :—

The most important old temples in Pehowa are those of Deví Saraswati, Swámi-Kárttika and Prithivishwara Maháděva :—

1. The two fairs at Saraswati's temple are held on Chet 1st, *chaturdashi Krishnapaksha*, Kártika *shuklapaksha* and *púranmási*. It is named after the daughter of Brahma and the stream on which it stands. When the Swámi Vishvámitra in his jealousy of Swámi Vasishtha invited Oghawati Saraswati to bring his rival to him the goddess carried the land on which Vasishtha sat to his abode, but divining his intention she bore the sage back again. Thereupon Vishvámitra cursed the stream, that her water should be turned into blood

and be no longer worthy of life. But Vasishtha invited all the gods and drew into the stream water from the Aruna *nadi*. When the gods assembled the *sthápan* of the goddess was first set up and the temple founded on the 14th of Chaitra. The junction with the Aruna was effected on the same date, and since then the water of the Saraswati became *amrit*, and the blood, which was food for evil spirits, was purged away. The confluence of the two streams removes all sins and a *pinḍadána* at the Kunḍ purifies even the *pisháoha* form. Hence the *chaturdashi* in Chaitra is also called Pishácha-Mochani. And a *pinḍodakakarma* on that date at the temple and stream according to Hindu belief releases the souls of *pitras* from Pretayoni and gives them *moksh* or emancipation. The fair has been held on that date every year in commemoration of the event. The second fair lasts 5 days in Kárttik from the *ekádshi* to the *púranmási*. It is held in the Krittiká *nakshatra púranmási* and to bathe in the Saraswati in that period gives health, wealth, prosperity and birth of children. It is impossible to guess the temple's age. The building is a small one and only contains an image of Saraswati riding on a swan and made of Makrana stone. The officiating Brahmans are Gaurs of the Kanaujia *got*.

2. The temple of Kárttikeya is visited on the *púranmási* in Kárttik. It contains his image but is dedicated to Kárta Skanda, the god of war, and was founded when the Mahábhárata was about to begin. The image of Kárttikeya has 6 faces as that god was named after his 6 nurses who form the stars of the Krittika asterism, the Pleiades, and is mounted on a peacock.[1] Vermilion and oil are invariably offered as acceptable to the god. Two lamps are kept burning continually.

3. No fair is held at the temple of Prithiwíshwara Mahádeva who is also called Prithúdakeshwara, 'lord of Prithudaka' or Pehowa. Prithiwíshwara means 'lord of the earth'. The temple was founded by the Mahraṭṭas during their ascendancy, and it is also said to have been repaired by one Kripálupuri Swámi about 100 years ago. Over the building is a large dome and its interior is 6 yards square. It contains a stone image of Mahádeva about 2 feet high. A *sádhu pujári*, who is a Sanyási, is appointed and kept by the *panchâyat* of Brahmans and is removable at their will. The Brahmans also do *pújа*.

At the Bhawáni Dwára at Thánesar the Deví's image is seated in a small building in the precincts of the main temple. It is 8 fingers high. Small images of Káli and Bhairon (Bhairav) also serve to decorate the temple.

At Pari Deví's temple in Banpuri in Gurgáon a fair is held on the 6th *sudi* of Chet and Asauj. The offerings are estimated at Rs. 400 a year. Nearly 90 years ago one Jawála of Fatehábád built the temple but the precise date of the year is not known. A *chirágh* fed with *ghí* is lit twice a day during Chet and on each *ashṭami* a virgin girl is fed with *karáh* or confection prepared for the occasion. When a goat is offered to the *mandir*, the *pujári* paints its forehead with *sandhúr* and turns it loose. It is generally taken by the sweepers

[1] The story goes that Kárttikeya on being deprived of the leadership of the *deotas* tore all the flesh from his body leaving only the bones. But the image does not appear to depict this. There are said to be really two images, one of stone, the other of wood.

of the village. The idols are of marble, one being 27 inches long and the other 18. The former is mounted on a lion. The administration vests in a Gaur Brahman who offers *bhog* and lights a lamp twice a day, morning and evening.

In Kohát Deví has her abode on more than one peak. Thus Hukman Deví occupies a peak in Shakkardarra which is visited by Hindus at the Baisákhi.[1] Chuka Mái is the highest peak on Shíngbar, and Hindus from afar visit it on the *naurátas* and *ashtami*. Khumari Deví is found in the village of that name and Asa Deví in Nar. Muhammadans also visit this village and call it *ziárat* Okhla.

The classical myths of Deví are very numerous and divergent. As Saraswati she is the goddess of learning, wife of Brahma in the later mythology, and personified in the river Saraswati in Karnál which was to the early Hindus what the Ganges is to their descendants.[2] As a destructress she is Káli,[3] as genetrix she is symbolised by the *yoni*, as a type of beauty she is Uma, and as a malignant being Durga. But she is also Sati, 'the faithful' spouse, Ambiká, Gauri, Bhawáni and Tára. As the wife of Shiva she is Párvati, 'she of the hills', her home is with him in Kailásha the mountain and she is the mother of Ganesha and Kárttikeya.[4] In orthodox Hindu worship the Earth is worshipped in the beginning as an 'Athar Shakti' or supporting force, and in several other forms of worship Earth is taken as a personification of some goddess or other. But the worship of an Earth or mother goddess is not very prevalent in this province except as part of some other worship.

But Káli or Durga must not be regarded as merely as a personification of lust for blood. Deví obtained her name of Durga by slaying the giant of that name. He had obtained Brahma's blessing by his austerities, but grew so mighty that he alarmed the gods.[5] The legend may recall in a dim way the extirpation of some tyrannical form of priest craft. But Deví's achievement did not end with the slaying of Durga. According to the *Márkandeya Purána*, the goddess assumed ten incarnations, including Káli the terrible and Chhinnamastaká, the headless.[6] In the latter guise she gained her famous victory over the *rákshasa* Nisumbha. Even the Káli incarnation was assumed in order to overthrow Raktavija, the champion of another *rákshasa*, Sumbha, just as that of Tára, the saviour, was assumed to destroy Sumbha himself. Deví also overcame a Tunda *rákshasa*, but his death is ascribed to Nahusha, the progenitor of the Lunar race, and his son Vitunda was killed by Deví as Durga, the 'inaccessible.'[7]

1 Similarly Chashma Bába Nának in Hangu is frequented by Hindus on the Baisákhí.

2 E. D. Martin, *The Gods of India*, p 90. For an account of her temple see *infra*.

3 In the Simla Hills besides the Greater (Bari) Káli we find a Lesser (Chhoti) whose functions are not at all clear. The Bari Káli hunts the hills. She is worshipped with sacrifices of goats, flowers, fruit, wheaten bread, and lamps. The difference between the Bari and the Chhoti Káli is this that the former has 10 hands and the latter only 4. Similarly in these hills we find a Younger Lonkra and a *chhoti* Diwáli festival. All attempts to obtain explanations of these reflected in duplicate gods and festivals have failed.

4 *Ib.*, p. 179 *f.*

5 *Ib.*, p. 183.

6 Chhinnamastaka is the modern Chamunda or Chaunda.

7 *S. C. R.*, VIII, p 276.

But in Kulu the legend regarding Tunḍi Bhút is that he was a *dait* or demon at Manáli (in Kulu) who having conquered the *dotas* demanded a sister of theirs in marriage. Básu Nag on this proposed to deceive him by giving him a mason or Tháwi's daughter named Timbar Shachka, who appears in other tales as a *rákshani*, and Manu the *Rishi* consented to make Tunḍi accept her. He overcame the *dait* at Khoksar, north of the Rohtang pass in Láhul, but in memory of his victory a temple was built to him at Manáli, south of that pass. He compelled Tunḍi to marry the girl. Tunḍi is in legend a demon who devoured men, until Manu put logs into his mouth and killed him. In front of this temple stands a pile of huge spruce logs, on an altar. These are said to be replaced three at a time every three years. At the annual fair called Phágali—held in Phágan—a *khepra* or mask (lit. evil form) of Tunḍi *rákshasa* is carried about.[1]

Káli as Chámunda, carrying her head in her hands, is worshipped at the Hoi, eight days before the Diwáli. At the beginning of the Kuljug death, pestilence and famine desolated the world although Brahmans prayed and fasted on the 7th of the dark half of each month. They would indeed have lost heart and given up that practice but for a Jhíwarni, who came and sitting in their midst encouraged them to persevere. After a while Kálka appeared and declared that as the ills prevailing were due to mankind's loose morals, it could only be saved by a fast on the 7th of the dark half of Kátik till moonrise or on the 8th till starlight. During this fast the Jhíwarni is exalted to a place of honour. She is petted by the ladies of the house who act as her tire-woman. After the house has been plastered with cow-dung, figures of a palanquin and its bearers are made in colours on the walls and worshipped in the usual way, offerings of radishes, sweet potatoes and other roots in season being made. This is the account given in the *Akártik Máhimála* where Pirthivi Ráj asks Nárada to account for the Hoi, and the sage tells him the above story. But another account is that Hui or Hoi was a Brahman maid of seven whom the Moslims tried to convert by force. She took refuge in a Jhíwarni's hut and when her pursuers overtook her disappeared into the earth. Since then the water-carriers have looked upon her as a goddess, other Hindus following their example.[2]

This goddess' name appears to have been transferred to Bába Chúda Bhanḍári whose shrine at Batála is affected by the Bhanḍári section of the Khatris[3] and the ear-piercing rite is performed there by its members. At some fight in its neighbourhood he lost his head, but his headless trunk went on fighting, sword in hand, into the town. In the streets it fell and there its shrine was built.[4]

Legends of headless men are also common in other connections. Thus when Parjápat, the Kumhár (potter), began to build Pánípat its walls and buildings fell down by night as fast as he built them by day

[1] N. I. N. Q., IV, § 35. The late Prof G. Oppert explained the story as a legendary account of the suppression of Káli worship, with its human sacrifices, by a purer faith, but it looks rather like an account of the extermination of an old Tibetan demon-worship by a cult of Káli herself.

[2] P. N. Q., II, § 799.

[3] *Cf. Vol.* II, p. 518, *infra.*

[4] *S. C. R.*, VIII, p. 266.

and so the Brahmans and astrologers bade him place the head of a Sayyid (Shahíd) in its foundations. By chance a Sayyid boy came straight from Mecca and him the people slew and put his head under the foundations. This drew down on them the vengeance of his kin, but the boy's headless corpse fought against them on the side of his murderers.[1] *Cf.* also the legend of Brahm Dat, *infra.*

But Deví has yet another attribute, that of self-sacrifice. The classical story is that Umá's spouse Shiva was not bidden to a great sacrifice offered by Daksha, her father. From the crest of Kailása she saw the crowds flocking to her father's court and thither she betook herself, but on learning of her husband's exclusion she refused to retain the body which he had bestowed upon her and gave up her life in a trance. Vishnu cut her body into pieces to calm the outraged deity by concealing it from his view or, as other versions go, Shiva himself picked up her corpse in his trident and carried it off. Portions of it fell at many places, such as Hingula (Hingláj) in Balochistán where the crown fell.

The Punjab can however not boast many of the sites at which fragments of the Deví fell. The top of her neck fell at Kasmíra, her tongue at Jawálamukhi, her right breast at Jálandhara, and her right ankle at Kurukshetra.[2]

The days most holy to Deví are the first nine days of the waxing moon in the months of the Chetr (March-April) and Asauj (September-October). Some persons will fast in the name of Deví on the eighth lunar day (*ashṭam*) of every month, and perform special ceremonies on that day. Sometimes they will light lamps (*jot*) of flour, and when a Brahman has read the *Deví-páṭh*, will prostrate themselves before the lamps. Sometimes it is customary to distribute rice and sweetmeats on this day to unmarried girls; and goldsmiths will often close their shops in honour of the day. The greatest *ashṭamis* of all are however those in the months above-mentioned; and of the two great yearly festivals, that of Asauj, the *naurátra* properly so called, is the greatest, following as it does immediately after the completion of the annual *shráddh* or commemoration of the dead. It is the custom in some parts of the country for worshippers of Deví on the first day of their festival to sow barley and water it and keep a lamp burning by it, and on the eighth day to cut it and light a sacrificial fire (*hom*), breaking their fast next day. Maclagan, § 49.

Deví is personified in a girl under ten years of age twice a year and offerings are made to her as if to the goddess on these occasions[3] On the 3rd of Chet *sudi*, there is, in Hissár, a special rite, unmarried girls making an image of Gangor of clay or *gobar*, which is loaded with ornaments and then, after its marriage ceremony has been performed, cast into a well. It is characteristic of the close connection between the peoples of the eastern hills and Rájpútána that this rite should be found in Kángra, under the name of Rali worship. Images of Siva and Párbatí are made by girls who perform their marriage and then throw them into a pool or river. The ceremonies commence in Chet and end on the *sankránt* of Baisákh and are traditionally supposed to commemorate the

[1] *S. C. R.*, VIII, p. 268.

[2] *Aín-i-Akbari*, II, p. 313-14. See also *S. C. R.* II, 419 *f.*

[3] Special feasts are given to little girls twice a year and they are given fees, as if they were Brahmans, P. N. Q., III, § 416.

suicide of a woman married to a boy much younger than herself, but a different explanation[1] has been suggested. The deities Siva and Párbatí

[1] Kángra Gazetteer, 1902. Golden Bough, II, p. 109. The legend goes that once upon a time a Brahman gave his full grown daughter in marriage to a child. When the ceremonies were over and the bride was sent to her husband's house, she saw how things really stood. So in her despair she stopped her *ḍolí* bearers on the road by a river, and called out to her brother Bastu: "It has been my fate to be married to a child, and I live no more. But in future in memory of my wretched fate, let girls make three toy images of earth, one of me, one of my husband, and one of you, my brother Bastu, and let them worship these images for the whole month of Chaitr (March-April) every year until they be married. Then let them marry these images, as I was married, on the 1st Baisákh, and on the 2nd or 3rd day thereafter let them take the images in a *ḍolí* to the banks of a river, and there let them drown them in it. And let this be done in honour of me, Rali the bride, Shankar, my husband, and you, Bastu, my brother. The blessing that shall spring forth from this rite shall be that she who performs it shall never marry an unsuitable husband." Saying this she sprang into the river, and was drowned, and in their grief at this, her husband and brother drowned themselves also. Ever since the worship of Rali, Shankar and Bastu, has been universal throughout the district of Kángra. The three chief fairs in honour of Rali are held at Baij Náth, at Dáda, half way between Pálampur and Dharmsala, and at Chari, three miles west of Dharmsála. Many songs are sung by children in honour of Rali, and the images are adorned with wild flowers. The children bathe every day during the month of Chaitr, and fast on the 1st, 2nd and 4th Mondays of that month. The images are dressed up according to the means of the parents, and are finally thrown into a river with songs and ceremonies.

This legend raises an interesting question. 'Did a custom ever exist of taking to wife an adult woman destined to be the bride of a grandson or grandnephew'? As to this problem see Dr. W. H. R. Rivers' *Kinship and Social Organisation*, 1914, pp. 33, 34, 37 and 56, and of the Simla Hills proverb:—

Chía chunḍíe ghugti básham, báno chunḍíe totá;
Kalí jugo rá póhrá lágá, dádí lái-guwá potá.

"A dove is warbling on the top of a pine, and a parrot on the top of an oak;
'Tis said of this iron age, that a grandson has taken away a grandmother."

Cf. the following note from the Indian Antiquary, Volume XI, p. 297:—The *Rali* is a small earthen painted image of Siva or Párvati. The Rali ka melá or Rali fair is a long business, and occupies most of Chet (March-April) up to the Sankránt of Baisákh (April). Its celebration is entirely confined to young girls, and is in vogue all over the district. It is celebrated thus:—All the little girls of the place turn out of their houses one morning in March and take small baskets of *dub* grass and flowers to a certain fixed spot, where they throw them all into a heap. Round this heap they stand in a circle and sing. This goes on every day for ten days, until the heap of grass and flowers reaches a respectable size. They then cut in the jungles two branches having three prongs at one end and place them, prongs downwards, over the flower heap so as to make two tripods or pyramids. On the single uppermost points of these branches they get a *chitera* or painted image-maker to construct two clay images, one to represent Siva and the other Párvati. All the girls join in collecting the clay for these, and all help as much as they can in the construction of the images themselves, this being a "good work." The girls then divide themselves into two parties, one for Siva and one for Párvati, and set to work to marry the images in the usual way, leaving out no part of the ceremonies, not even the *barát* or procession. After the marriage they have a feast, which is paid for jointly by contributions solicited from their parents. After this at the next Sankránt (Baisákh) they all go together to the riverside, and throw the *ralis* into it at any point where there happens to be a deep pool and weep over the place, as though they were performing funeral obsequies. The boys of the neighbourhood frequently worry them by diving for the *ralis* and rescuing them and waving them about, while the girls are crying over them. The object of this fair is to secure a good husband. These fairs are held on a small scale in all the principal places in Kángra, but the chief ones are at Kángra itself, where the Bangangа is the river used for the disposal of the *rali*, and at Chari, a village 10 miles from Kángra and 6 from Dharmsála, on the river Gajj. The largest fair is held there.

This recalls a rite practised by Hindus in Attock with a not dissimilar object, *viz.* to obtain rain in time of drought. In it boys and girls collect together: two dolls are dressed up as a man and a woman, they all say: *guḍḍí guḍḍa margia;* and then they burn them with small sticks and lament their death saying:—

Guḍḍí guḍḍa sáṛiá
Wae míṇ kália;
Guḍḍí guḍḍa piṭṭia,
Wae míṇ chiṭṭia;
Kále patthar chiṭṭe roṛ,
Baddal pia giránwáṇ kol.

"Dolls we burnt to ashes down,
Black cloud! soon come down;
Dolls well we bewailed,
Do, white rain! set in;
Stones black and pebbles white,
Cloud (rain) fell near village site."

are conceived as spirits of vegetation, because their images are placed in branches over a heap of flowers and grass, but this theory leaves many points unexplained.

The worship of young girls as Devís is always cropping up. Some years ago some enterprising people of the Kapúrthala State got two or three young unmarried girls and gave out that they had the power of Devís. The ignorant accepted this belief and worshipped them as goddesses. They visited various parts of the Jullundur District and were looked up to with great reverence everywhere, but as good results did not follow, the worship died out.

Maclagan, § 49

Those who are particularly the followers of Deví are called in an especial sense Bhagats, and the Bhagtas of our census returns are probably worshippers of this goddess. The sacred books of the sect are the *Deví Purán*, a part of the *Márkanda Purán*, the *Chandí Path* and the *Purán Sahasranám*.

In the west of the Province at any rate the Deví-upásak are chiefly Sunárs, Khatrís, Jogís, Saniásís etc. who follow the books specified above. Their places of pilgrimage are Jwálamukhi, Vaishno Deví in Kashmír and further afield the Vindhya hills, and Káli Deví near Calcutta. They are divided into two sects, the Vaishno Deví who abstain from flesh and wine and Káli worshippers who do not. They worship the image of Deví in temples, revere Gaur Brahmans, and pay special attention to sacrifices by fire (*hom*), fast every fortnight, and on Mondays break their fast by eating food cooked on the Sunday night and 'lighting a flame worship Deví.'

Maclagan, § 50.

THE BÁM-MÁRGIS.[1]—The most notorious division of the Shaktiks, as the followers of Deví are called, is that of the Bám-márgís or Váma-chárís, the 'left-handed' worshippers of Kálí. They are found in many districts, but they are said to be mostly prevalent in Kángra or Kashmír, and they are chiefly recruited from the Sainiásís and Jogis. The sect is said to have been founded by the Jogí Kanípa; their rites are as a rule kept very secret, but it is generally understood that their chief features are indulgence in meat and spirits and promiscuous debauchery. The Kundá-marg or Kundá-panthí preserve no distinctions of caste in eating, and they worship the fire. The Konla-marg appears to be called Kola-panth, Kola-marg or Kola-dharma, in the Punjab, and to be identical with the Kolá-chári who are worshippers of Saktí according to the left-hand ritual.[2] They preserve caste distinctions, in so far as they eat from separate vessels, and they worship Deví under ten separate names, to wit, Matangí, Bhawaneshri or Bhavaneshari, Baglamukhí, Dhumawálí,[3] Bhairaví, Tára, Chensara, Bhagwatí, Shâma and Bála Sundari.[4] Each man has one of them as his *isht* or peculiar patron goddess, and the Jogís and Saniásis are said to affect more especially Bála Sundarí. The book of the sect is called the *Kohanara*, and their creed claims to be founded on the *Shiva-Tantra*.

[1] The word "Márgí" means nothing more than one who follows a "path" or "sect." It may in some cases be a euphemism for Bám-márgí, but the greater part of the Márgís of our returns are from the Multán district, where the term is said to be applied generally to a class of followers of the Jain religion.

[2] P. N. Q., II, §§ 648-650. An account, full but very inaccurate, of the Kolá-chárís by Sirdáru Balhari, of Kángra.

[3] Or Dhumáwatí or Lalta-Dhumáwatí.

[4] (Lalta ?) Kálí, Kamala and Vidiya are given as variants of these four names or titles.

There are further and still more disreputable sections of the Bám-márgís, the nature of whose orgies is indicated by their names, such as the Cholí-márg and the Birajpání, whose peculiarities had better be left undescribed.

Orthodox Hindus will not sleep with their feet to the north, out of respect for the Deví who dwells in the Himalayas just as they will not sleep with them to the east out of respect for the Ganges.[1]

The Baurias sacrifice to Deví in a manner which is very common in the hills and is doubtless the normal rite everywhere. They immolate a goat, of either sex, at harvest time.[2] It must be healthy. They make it stand on a platform of earth plastered with cow-dung. They then secure its hind legs with a rope to a peg and taking a little water in the palm of the hand pour it on its nose. If it shivers after the manner of its kind, it is a token that the goddess accepts it and its head is at once struck off by a sudden blow, *jhatká*, of a sword. A few drops of its blood are offered to the goddess and its carcass is distributed to the by-standers. If the goat does not shiver, it is rejected and another is tried.

A circle is the sign of Deví, and a mark of it is made by women on a pilgrimage at every few yards, upon a stone, or some object near the road, with a mixture of rice-flour and water. These marks are called *likhna*.[3]

Akás Deví, 'the goddess of Heaven,' also called Gyásí Deví, is worshipped in the villages round Ambála. Her cult is said to be based on a passage in the *Deví Bhágavatí Purána*. Her temples contain no image. She is worshipped with the usual objects of procuring sons, effecting cures, and so on. Her temple stood originally at Jatwár village, but in a dream she bade the headman of Bibiál transport five bricks from the Jatwár temple to Bibiál so that she might find a resting-place there. He did so, and built round them a mud shrine, giving the offerings of corn etc. to a sweeper whom he appointed to look after the shrine. He also used to present coin to Brahmans. The fairs are held on the 8th and 14th *sudi* of Chet and on the same dates in Asauj *sudi* are called Gyásion ká mela.[4]

Behmátá is the goddess who records an infant's future at its birth. It is a deadly sin to refuse her fire when she demands it, and a *faqír* who did so was turned into a glow-worm and obliged to carry fire behind him for ever in his tail. Behmátá is Bidhimátá or Bidhná, and the glow-worm is called *honwála kíṛa* (? from *hom* or *havan*).

Kanyá Deví, who is worshipped in the Kángṛa valley, was the daughter of Brahmá Rájá, who was so enamoured of her beauty that he would not give her away in marriage. When pursued by him, she

[1] I. N. Q., IV, § 192.

[2] P. N. Q., III, § 721.

[3] Shib's mark is a circle with a line through it; a Siddh has a pair of foot-prints, *cf.* Oldham, in *Contemporary Review*, 1885, reprinted in P. N. Q., III, § 162.

[4] P. N. Q., II, § 445. *Cf.* Akás Ganga, the Heavenly Ganges, *ibid.*, § 523.

fled to a small hill, wherein was a huge rock which split as under and gave her a refuge. At her curse the Rájá was turned into a stone. Her shrine stands to this day on the hill near Nagroṭa and close by it lies the stone which, disintegrated by the noon-day heat in summer, becomes whole again in the rains. The Rájá's city too was overwhelmed by the mountains, and the tract on which it stands is a rocky and barren one to this day. It is called Munjeta or Pápnagara. Kaniyá Deví is worshipped like any other Deví.[1]

A shrine very similar to that of Bhúmia (but clearly one erected to a manifestation of Deví) is called Paththarwálí in Gurgaon. When a man who has in sickness put on the cord of Deví recovers he has to perform a pilgrimage to Nagarkoṭ or Jawálamukhi in Kángra, taking with him a *bhagat* or devotee of the goddess. While he is absent, the women of his family worship Paththarwálí.

Deví cults in Chamba.

The worship of Deví assumes the most diverse forms in the hills. It is not by any means always ancient, and though often of great antiquity appears to be quite distinct from that of the Nágs. Thus in Chamba the Devís are female deities, and are believed to have power to inflict and remove disease in man and beast. They are not associated with springs like the Nágs. It is common to find a Nág and a Deví temple side by side, and similar attributes are ascribed to both. Some of them, like the Nágs, have the power to grant rain. The worship is similar to that at Nág temples, and the offerings are disposed of in the same manner. The image is usually of stone in human form, but snake figures are not as a rule present. The temple furnishings are similar to those of Nág temples. In front of the Deví temples may usually be seen the figure of a tiger in stone: this is the *váhana* or vehicle of the goddess. The most famous Deví temples are those of Lakhshana Deví at Brahmaur, Shaktí Deví at Chhatrari, Chamunda Deví at Chamba and Deví Koṭhi, Mindhal Deví in Pángi, and Mirkula Deví in Láhul. Sen Deví at Shah in Sámrá has a temple ascribed to Músha Varma. Its fair is held on Baisákh 3rd, and her *chelas* are Ráthis.[2]

The following is a list of the principal Devís worshipped in Brahmaur and the southern part of the Sadr *wizárat* of Chamba :—

Name.	Village.	*Pargana.*	Date of fair.	*Pujáras* and *chelas.*	Founded in the reign of
Bál Bhairon and Ban-khandi.	Bhairon-gháti.	Brahmaur...	...	Charpat-Jogis Agásani Gaddis.	Sáhil Varma.

[1] P. N. Q., II, § 668.

[2] For some further details see Vol. II, pp. 218, 214, 269 and 271. On pp. 214 and 271 Chaund is undoubtedly to be Chámúnda Deví.

Name.	Village.	*Pargana.*	Date of fair.	*Pujáras* and *chelas.*	Founded in the reign of
Bharári ...	Tohogá ...	Trehtá ...	...	Shipyánu Brahmans.	Músh Varma.
Bharári ...	Chanhotá Lámun.	Chanotá ...	...	Ráthis ...	Músh Varma.
Bharári ...	Gáglá ...	Kalundrá ...	Katak, 6th-7th	Ráthis ...	Músh Varma
Brahmáni ...	Brahmáni ...	Brahmaur ...	...	Malkán Gaddi	Sajan Varma.
Chámundá ...	Sirná ...	Mahlá ...	*Jágrá* on Chet 30th.	...	Músh Varma.
Chámundá ...	Gawári ...	Sámrá ...	Asárh 7th or 8th.	Ránás ...	New.
Chámundá ...	Sher ...	Brahmaur ...	Bhádon 3rd ...	Khapri Brahmans.	...
...	...	...	...	Uren Gaddís ...	Uggar Singh.
Chámundá ...	Sanáhan ...	Sámrá ...	Asárh 1st or 2nd & Asauj 2nd or 3rd.	Sársut Brahmans, Ráthís.	Músh Varma.
Chhatrárhi or Adahakti.	Chhatrárhi	Píura ...	*Jágrá* on the 8th *shukal pakh* of Bhádon and 9th, 10th and 11th.	Sársut Bhárdwáj Rátan Totrán Gaur Bháradwáj Kalán and Ulyán Brahmans.	Meru Varma.
Hirimbá ...	Mahlá ...	Mahlá ...	...	Thitán Brahmans, Ghukán Gaddis.	Prithvi Singh.
Jakhná ...	Grimá ...	Brahmaur ...	...	Mogu Gaddís	Yugákar Varma.
Jálpá ...	Kareri ...	Mahlá ...	*Jágrá* on Sáwan 1st.	Pehnán Gaddís	Músh Varma.
Jálpá ...	Mahlá ...	Mahlá ...	*Jágrá* on Sáwan 1st.	Ghukán Gaddís, Ghukáran Gaddís.	Músh Varma.
Jálpá ...	Mahlá ...	Mahlá ...	Hár 5th-9th ...	Ghukárán Gaddís and Thulyán Brahmans.	Prithvi Singh.

Name.	Village.	*Pargana.*	Date of fair.	*Pujáras* and *chelas.*	Founded in the reign of
Jálpá ...	Bhatyárk ...	Lil ...	Baisákh 9th ...	Dumar Brahmans.	Músh Varma.
Jálpá or Khandrásan	Khandrásan	Lil ...	Hay 10th-12th	...	...
Jálpá ...	Girrer Mheusa.	Lil ...	Baisákh ...	Latnán Gaddís	Músh Varma.
Kabrá ...	Baloth ...	Lil ...	...	Báthís ...	Músh Varma.
Kalohálí ...	Kulethá ...	Trehtá ...	...	Hilak Brahmans.	Músh Varma.
Mahá Káli...	Kalhotá ...	Lil ...	...	Gadiálas Gaddís.	Músh Varma.
Mahá Káli...	Graundi ...	Lil ...	...	Báthís ...	Músh Varma.
Mahá Káli...	Launá ...	Mahlá ...	*Jágrá* on Sáwan 4th.	Aurel Gaddís	Músh Varma.
Mahá Káli...	Auráh ...	Brahmaur...	Sáwan 6th ...	Kurete Gaddís.	Bijai Varma
...	Leundi ...	Brahmaur...	...	Liundiál Gaddís.	Kirti Varma.
...	Tundáh ...	Brahmaur...	*Jágrá* on *puranmáshi* in Bhadon or Asauj.	Chhataryán Brahmans.	Suvarna Varma.
Káli Deví ...	Thalá ...	Brahmaur...	...	Dáhrán Gaddís.	Sáhil Varma.
Káli Deví ...	Mándhá ...	Brahmaur...	Asauj 1st ...	Brahmanetu Brahmans.	Suvarn Varma.
Káli Deví ...	Thouklá ...	Kothi Banhu	Bhádon 4th ...	Boti Brahmans	Músh Varma.
Káli Deví ...	Auráh ...	Brahmaur...	Sáwan 4th ...	Bhugahán Brahmans.	Bijai Varma.
Lakhná Deví (Bhadar Káli).	Brahmaur...	Brahmaur...	Asauj 10th and Bhádon 11th.	Sársut Ránetu Brahmans of the Bhumpál *gót.*	Meru Varma.
Maráli Deví	Chobhiá ...	Brahmaur...	...	Kawál Gaddís	Músh Varma.
Mehlá Deví	Gadhu ...	Trehtá ...	...	Daraklu Brahman.	Músh Varma.
Shakti Deví	Brahmaur Badgráin.	Brahmaur...	...	Harete Gaddís	Vidagdhá Varma.

Name.	Village.	*Pargana.*	Date of fair.	*Pujáras* and *chelas.*	Founded in the reign of
Shakti Devi	Jandrot Chhátrárhi.	Piurá ...	*Daljátras* in Bhádon or Asauj.	Kalán Brahmans.	Músh Varma.
Shiv Shakti Deví.	Bakán ...	Bakán ...	*Jágrá* on Hár 18th.	Ráthís ...	...
Tungásan Deví.	Gosan ...	Brahmaur... ...	Bhádon 1st ...	Ranon Gaddís	Yugákar Varma.

Brahmani Deví's history is this. A Brahmani had a son, who had a pet *chakor* (partridge), which was killed by a peasant. The boy died of grief, and his mother became *sati*, burning herself with her son and the partridge, and began to afflict the people, so they built her a temple.

In Pángi only four Devís are noted—Singhásan Deví at Surát in *pargana* Darwás, Shil at Sákhi, and Chaund at Re, Manghásan at Purthi, all three in Lách.

Deví Chámunda of Gawári revealed herself in a dream to Rájá Sri Singh, and ordered him to remove her from Prithvijor to this place. The temple at Sri was built by Rájá Uggar Singh who vowed to make it, if it ceased raining, it having rained incessantly when he had gone to bathe at Mani Mahesh.

Deví Chhatráhari or Ádshakti, "original power," has a curious legend. A land-owner suspected his cowherd of milking his cow in the forest, so he kept watch and found that the cow gave her milk at a spot under a tree. The goddess then appeared to him in a dream, and begged him to bring her to light. Searching at the spot the man found a stone *pindi* or image, which he was taking to his home, when it stopped at a certain spot, and there its temple was built.[1] Rájá Bala Bhadra (A. D. 1589—1641) granted it 36 *lahris* of land whence the Deví was called Chhatráhari.

The legend associated with Mindhal Deví is as follows:—The spot where the temple stands was originally occupied by a house, consisting of an upper and a lower storey, as is usual in Pángi, belonging to a widow with seven sons. One day in early autumn while she was cooking in the upper storey a black stone appeared in the *chula* causing her much annoyance. She tried to beat it down but in vain. At last she was seized with a trembling, and thus knew that the stone was a Deví. Rushing outside she called to her sons, who were ploughing in a field with two oxen to a plough, that a Deví had appeared in the house. They made light of the matter and asked tauntingly if the Deví would enable them to plough with one ox, or give them a *sásan*. Immediately the widow and her sons were turned to stone, she in the

[1] This temple was erected in the reign of Rájá Meru Varma (A. D. 680—700).

house and they in the field. From that time only one ox to a plough has been used in ploughing at Mindhal and the place has been a *sásan* grant for many centuries.[1]

Deví cults in Sirmúr.

There is a temple of Deví Jawálamukhi ('goddess of the flaming mouth') at Láná Rawána, concerning which the following legend is told:—Mahant Twár Náth and the Deví met at Hardwár, where they had gone to bathe, and, when leaving, the *mahant* asked the Deví when he should meet her again. The goddess promised to meet him after two years at Rawána, and duly manifested herself in his mouth, but the *mahant* being unaware of her advent struck his mouth and thus caused the goddess to flee from him. Simultaneously the whole surrounding forest caught fire, and the people, thinking the *mahant* must be an evil spirit who had enraged the goddess, called in Brahmans who found out the truth. It is said that the stones are still black from the fire which consumed the forest. The place having been purified, a temple was built and a Brahman *pujári* appointed. The *pujári* offers incense and *bhog* every Sunday morning and on the first day of the month (*sankránt*). The fair is held on the Durgá Ashṭmi day in Asauj.

Nagarkoṭi Deví. Nagarkoṭi Deví has her home at Sháyá Pajotha and Sharauli, and the legend states that the Páṇḍavás on their way from Kailás to Kurukshetra stopped at Sháyá, and built a temple here for the goddess, or, as some say, brought the goddess here. The temple faces south, and on the eighth day of the bright half of the month offerings are made to the goddess. Sapára is also associated with Nagarkoṭi Deví, but the place is one of peculiar sanctity whether the goddess be present or absent from it. There is also a Nagarkoṭi Deví at Daláhán, known also as Daláhán Deví.

Bis Nána is the home of Bhártí Deví, who is said to have been brought from Kidár Náth Badri Naráin in Dehra Dún. She is also called Kúshki Deví.

Lai Deví. There is a temple of Deví on the hill of Lai, built by Bhera Rangar,[2] the famous robber. Worship is performed here on the *sankránts* and every Sunday and *naurátra* in Asauj and Chet.

Bhangain Deví. Deví Bhangain has a *ling* temple in Dhár village, a mile north of Bhung. The legend runs that certain cowherds used to graze cattle in a forest, and their children, seeing a pointed stone, broke it in pieces, but next day the pieces had joined together and all traces of injury had disappeared. This occurred several times, and so the cultivators of Dasákna, convinced of the *ling's* miraculous power, erected a temple there. The Shiv Ling, four inches high and as many in girth, is known as Deví Bhangain, and is never clothed or ornamented. There is no special *pujári*, and pilgrims bring their own Brahmans. The offerings consist of milk, *ghí* and he-goats. The flesh of the latter is eaten by the pilgrims, the head being given to the Brahman *pujári*. The fair

[1] The people believe that if two oxen are used one of them will die.

[2] The term Rangaṛ or Raughaṛ used to be much more wide-spread than it is now. It was used, for example, of the people of Morinda Banganwála in Ambála and of those of Sathiála and Batála in Gurdáspur: Khazán Singh, *Philosophic History of the Sikh Religion*, Pt. I, pp. 211, 216.

is held on different dates in Asáṛh, and is attended by the goddesses Bijai and Ghatriáli. Only the people of Bhojes Ṭhakari and Dasákna attend.

Naina Deví.

The arrangements for the worship of Naina Deví at Baila are of interest. The *pujáris* belong to eight families of Deva Bháṭs, each family taking the duties for a month in turn and receiving a share of the produce at each harvest from the neighbouring villages. If the *pujáris* perform their service inefficiently and fail to exhibit in a convincing manner the virtues of the goddess, they receive no dues. The Deví has no temple, but her images are kept in the house of a Bháṭ. The original image, when brought from Keonthal, was first placed in that house, for which reason the people do not venture to place it elsewhere. The images are 15 or 16 in number, the oldest being fixed (*asthápan*). It is about a foot in height, with four hands, but only the bust is carved. It has a canopy of silver, and wears a necklace of rupees, silver ornament (*sis-phul*) on its head and a silver necklet (*gal-siri*) and has also a silver palanquin. The fair is held on the Ránwi Dhár above the village on the first three days of Sáwan, and is attended by the men of Karáli and the neighbouring *bhojes*, who sing and dance. On each evening of the fair the image of the goddess visits Thauntha, Mashwa and Tatiána villages, but in the day-time it remains at the fair. It is believed that if cholera or any other epidemic breaks out in a village it can be stopped by taking the image there.

Lá Deví.

The fair of the goddess Lá is held in the jungle near Naglá Toka on the *sankránt* of each month. The temple is small and of great antiquity, containing a stone image of the goddess. She is worshipped by Hindus and Muhammadan Gújars.

The new goddess.

About sixty years ago the people of *bhoj* Bajga proclaimed the appearance of the goddess of Tilokpur at Shakúr, so they built a temple to her as the new goddess. At her fairs on the *sankránt* of each month the goddess possesses a Kanet who dances in the temple, and then coming outside shows himself to the assembled multitude who hail him with shouts of *jai-jai*, and bow before him. In his ecstasy he prescribes remedies for afflicted men and beasts.

The goddess at Kawág on the *dhár* of that name is worshipped by Bháṭs alone, and only Bháṭs dance in her honour. Her ritual is the same as that of the new goddess. The temple is old, and now roofless.

The goddess at Belgí is known under that name, but is also worshipped as Simlásan.

Deví Kudín has her temple at Dúdam in Tahsíl Pachhád. The legend is that she was a daughter of Sur Purkásh, Rájá of Sirmúr, who was blind, and lived in Néri Jágilá. When the Rájá refused to pay tribute to the Mughal Emperor the latter sent a host against him through Dehra Dún, which was met by the Rájá's army under the princess herself. The Sirmúr forces were annihilated in the battle, and the *parohit* of the princess brought her head to Dúdam where he erected a temple and began to worship the princess. Another version says that the princess fell in an attack on Delhi, and after her death revealed to the *parohit* that he would find her at a certain spot, at which after a search the *parohit* found the image now in the temple. The fair is held on the *ikádshi* before the Diwáli, on which day the image is placed on a *singhásan* or throne. This is also done on each Sunday in Háṛ.

At Náog, now in Patiála territory, lived Lagásan Deví, the sister of Kudin. Her temple is at Khargáon. Her fair is held on the *ikádshi* before the Dewali. It is said that she appeared at the source of the river Giri, but others say she appeared from that river at Khargáon.

At Tilokpur is the temple of Deví Bála Sundri. There is held a large fair in her honour in the month of Chet when the Rájá attends and a buffalo and several he-goats are sacrificed. She is as commonly worshipped by hillmen as by people of the plains.

Devi Kat

The goddess Katásan has a temple at Barában, seven miles south of Náhan on the road to Paunta. In a battle between the Rájpúts and Ghulám Qádir, Rohilla, a woman appeared fighting for the former, when their defeat seemed imminent, and the Muhammadans were routed. The temple was built to commemorate the Rájpút victory. On the sixth day of the *naurátras* in Asauj and Chet *hawan* is performed in the temple, and the Rájá occasionally visits the temple in person or deputes a member of the royal family to be present.

Deví in the Simla Hills.

Deví Adshakti or Durga Mátá.—A Brahman of the Sakteru Pujára family relates that more than 100 generations ago his ancestors came from Káshi (Benáres) and settled at Hát Koṭi; and that one of them came to Kacheṛi village with Adshakti Bhagwati. This goddess, with her sister and Koṭ Ishwar, were shut up in the *túmbṛi* as has been told in the account of Koṭ Ishwar. Adshakti flew to the top of Tikkar hill above Ghámaná, a village in Kumhársain and settled there in the form of a *ling*. Her presence was revealed to a *mawanna* of Tikkar in a dream, and the *ling* was found and placed in a temple. The other *pujáris* of Kacheṛi say that Adshakti, commonly called Bhagwati Mátá, no doubt came from Hát Koṭi, but that she was never imprisoned in a *túmbi*, and that when the *pánda* of Hát Koṭi had shut up Koṭ Ishwar in the *túmbi* the two Durga sisters accompanied him, one walking ahead and the other behind him, looking for an opportunity to release him. When the *pánda* fell and Koṭ Ishwar escaped the two sisters also flew away. First they went to Rachtaṛi village and thence to Hátu, Durga Mátá settled at Tikkar in which neighbourhood Bhuṛia, once a powerful *mawanna*, had fallen into difficulties. He consulted Brahmans and then sent for a number of virgins and, having made them sit in a row, cried aloud that the spirit that distressed the *mawanna*, whether he were a god or a devil, should appear and reveal through one of the girls why he had harassed the *mawanna*. One of the girls began to dance in an ecstacy and said that Bhagwatī Mátá was lying on Tikkar hill in the form of a *ling* and that of the two sisters one lived on Kanḍa, the top, and the other at Munḍa, the foot of the hill. The *mawanna* and his

Brahmans excused themselves saying that they had not known of their presence, and they promised to build a temple for the Mátá. The girl in a trance walked up the Tikkar hill, the other virgins, the Brahmans and the *mawanna* following her. The girl pointed out the spot where the *ling* lay, and on that spot was built the temple called Mátri Deoṛi, which still exists. At that time Polas, a Brahmán from the Sindhu Des, came to Lathi village and began to worship Durga Mátá. He came to look after Koṭ Ishwar who would not appear before him, but at last after 12 years he revealed himself and then the Brahman began to worship him. Koṭ Ishwar gave the *pujáris* of Batáṛa village to Bhagwati Mátá for worship. These *pujáris* are said to have come from Koru Desh. The Mateog Brahmans were settled in Batáṛa and they worship Koṭ Ishwar daily, but at the four Sankránts in Baisákh, Sáwan, and Mágh and at the Diwáli the Sherkoṭu Brahmans officiate. Kirti Singh, the first Ráná of the Kumhársain family, acknowledged Durga Bhagwati as sister of Koṭ Ishwar and built her a new temple at Kacheṛi. Every third year a Púja *mela* is held and the State pays the expenses.

According to the custom of the Kumhársain family the *jadola* ceremony (cutting the hair of a son or wearing nose or ear-rings by the girl) is performed at Mátri Deoṛa. The Ráná and his Ránís go in person to this temple with their children for the ceremony. Similarly on ascending the *gaddi* the new Ráná with his family attends at the Mátri Deoṛa a ceremony called the Jawála Játra. Bhagwati Mátá holds a petty *jágir* from the State and also has a small *kelon* (*deodár*) forest. Goats are sacrificed to her, and every third year or when desired buffaloes are also killed before her at Mátri Deoṛa. Some people believe that though Mátá has temples at Mátri Deoṛi and Kacheṛi she is always sitting at her brother Koṭ Ishwar's side at Madholi. Benu and Bhuri are two *bhors* or servants of the Mátá. Benu was a Chot from Bena in Kulu and Bhuri came from Jo Bag at Halta. The latter is a female attendant and was originally a ghost. Both attend at the gate of the temple.

With the shrine of Deví at Hát Koṭi many wonders are associated. One of these may be cited. On one side of the portal of the goddess stands a large bronze vessel battered and soiled with age upon a metal plinth. Formerly its fellow stood on the other side, but one night in Bhádon when the river below was in spate, the pair of vessels moved from their pedestals of their own accord. Rocking jointly from side to side they took their way through the narrow gate of the courtyard until they reached the river bank and plunged with shrill whistles into the torrent. The priests pursued them, but were only just in time to rescue one and the second disappeared. The one thus saved is now securely chained to an image of Ganesh sitting in the temple, but sometimes still in the stormy nights of Sáwan and Bhádon it rocks upon its pedestals straining at its chains, and whistling and moaning as though pleading to be allowed to join his lost companion. At other times the peasant when planting out rice in the fields adjacent to the shrine sees the operation of a brazen vessel, mirrored in the water, which eludes his grasp as he tries to seize it.

Deví Kasumba at Khekhsu—Khekhsu is on the north bank of Sutlej in Kulu. Koṭ Ishwar's other sister, Kasumba Deví, settled here when he escaped from Pro. One of the Chhabishi Brahmans of Goan, a village in Kulu Saráj, saw in a dream a *pinḍi* or *ling*. The goddess then told him of her presence, and desired to have a temple built for her at Khekhsu. The people say that the artisan who made the image of Hát Koṭi Durga was called in to make her image. When he had finished that image the *mawanna* of Hát Koṭi had cut his right hand so that he might not make any more like it, but with his left hand he made a similar image at Khekhsu. Ráná Kirti Singh acknowledged this Deví as Koṭ Ishwar's sister and gave her a *jágír* worth Rs. 42-2-9. The original intention was that 9 *bharao* of *kiar* land at Khekhar and goats should be given by the State on both the *ashṭamis*, in Chet and Baisákh. This Deví also holds a *jágír* from Koṭgarh and Kulu. When Koṭ Ishwar has any *jag* she comes to Madholi and joins in it. A Deváli *mela* is held at Khekhsu. There used to be a *bhunda* every 12 years at Khekhsu, but Government has forbidden it owing to the risk of human life.

Bragu Deo is the *bhor* or servant of Kasumba. He was brought from Jundla in Kumhársain and was originally a devil.

In the Simla Hills was a goddess, who first settled in the Túná forest (a part of Chambi Kúpar) without any one being aware of her advent. But in the time of Ráná Naráin Singh of Koṭ Khái she came in a woman's shape, but dressed in old and ragged clothing, to Halái (a village near Kiári) where the Ráná had some fields. When he went to see his fields, he took her for one of his labourers, and abused her for her idleness, whereupon the Káli transformed herself into a kite and flew away saying— Káli Túná of Rakh Chambi Kúpar.

Túne ri Kálka Kiári dekhan ái.
Naráin Singh Ṭhákure rope rúm de lai.

'Káli of Túná came to see Kiári.
But Naráin Singh Ṭhákur employed her to transplant rice plants in his *kiár* (irrigated fields).'

From that time Káli has been worshipped in the forest and is considered the most powerful of all the Kális.

Deví Gayáshín's idol was brought to Shamánú village in Mahlog State by Surjá Brahman of Bhagrí in the Kuthár State. All the members of his family had been killed by Badohí Kanets, who were at that period troublesome dacoits, so he left his village for ever and settled at Shamánú where he built a temple for the Deví image. Her fair is held on the first Tuesday in Chet.

Deví cults in Saráj.

Durga Deví, sister of Lachhmi Naráin, is also called Deví Dhár. Once a girl appeared at a spring near Daogi, and declared herself to be the goddess and Lachhmi Naráin to be her brother.

Deví Gárá Durga's legend illustrates the disgrace which attaches to a girl's marriage with an inferior. Once a Ṭhákur was having a house built and the mason asked him to promise him whatsoever he might demand on its completion. When it was finished the mason demanded the hand of the Ṭhákur's beauteous daughter in marriage; and bound by his pledge, the Ṭhákur bestowed her upon him. The pair took their road to the mason's house, but on the way the mason bade his bride fetch him water from a stream. Unable to bear this disgrace she threw herself into the water, and when he went to look for her he found nothing but an image lying on the bank. This he brought home and worshipped.

Deví Baṛí has a temple in Koṭhi Ḍhaul. She first manifested herself at Charakh near Baṛí by taking the milk of a Ráná's cow. Convinced of the truth of his herdsman's story of this miracle the Ráná went to the spot and then had a black stone image made and placed in a temple. This idol is 2 feet high, and there are also masks of brass and silver in the temple. The *pujári* is always a Kanet and the Deví has a *gur*.

Daṛá Deví has a temple at Daṛá. A Ṭhákur's grain was all carried off by ants to the Deví's *pinḍi*, and so a temple was built in her honour.

Deví Kohla or the Deví of Kowel has a curious origin. The cows of the villagers used to graze near Nirmanḍ, and one of them was found to be giving milk to a cat. So the people began to worship the cat and an image of her was made. It is of black stone, 2 cubits in height. The *pujári* of the temple is always a *pánda*.

Pachlá Deví of Srígaṛh has also a curious tradition. Pichú Chand, Ṭhákur of Deohari, saw in a vision a black stone image which bade him go to see it lying at Kashṭa. He did so and brought it to Kashṭa and thence to Deohari, where he worshipped. Ṭhákur Jog Chand, his rival, in jealousy at his devotion, quarrelled with him and Pichú Chand made a vow on the goddess to kill him. He succeeded and built a temple to the goddess who was named Pichlá after him. This Deví has four temples: at Deohari, Kashtá, Chalâma, and Rúní. One fair at Deohari is held at the Diwáli in Maghar and another fair on the *ashṭami* in Asauj at Kashta. At Deohari a *shánd* is celebrated annually.

Kasumbha Deví has two temples on the Súi Dhár or range, one at Khaksu, the other at Buhṛa. A Rájá of Bashahr used to live at Khaksu, and in order to get a son he used to recite the *páṭh* of Káli. She manifested herself to him in the form of a black stone image and bade him worship it, so he founded the temple at Khaksu and named it after himself. It contains a black stone image, 1 cubit high, and a female figure, 3 cubits high, in metal. The *pujári* is always a Sársut Brahman. The goddess selects her own *gur*.

Deví Chebṛí's temple was founded by Deví Káli who killed a number of demons who used to devour the children of the neighbourhood. The idol is of black stone, 2 cubits high, and represents the goddess. There are other images also in the temple, but they are only one or two spans high.

Dhanah Deví has a similar legend. Káli defeated the *asurs* or demons and in her honour the people of Dhanáh built her a temple.

Deví Pujárli's temple is ascribed to a Brahman who, when ploughing his field, turned up a metal mask which he placed in a niche in his house. Soon after he fell ill and went to his former Deví, Ambiká, but she told him that her daughter had manifested herself to him and that he should make a vow to her for his recovery. The temple contains an image of black stone, 2 feet high. Ambiká's own temple at Nirmand is well known and Chandi Deví is said to have slain two *rákhshas*, Chand and Mund. Her temple dates from the same year as that at Nirmand.

Naina Deví owes her temple in Koṭhi Banogi to the discovery of an idol with beautiful eyes by a girl who was herding cattle near a stream. Its eyes became the object of the people's veneration. It is of black stone, 3 feet high. Its *pujári* is a Nola Kanet.

Deví Bári owes her temple at Bári to Brásanú, a Brahman who lived in Bári *phati*. He was childless, and in order to get a son, used to recite *paṭhs* to Káli, on the bank of a stream. One night, it was revealed to him that beneath the earth lay a black stone image of a goddess. She also bade him worship her, and he was blessed with a son. The Brahman then in fulfilment of a vow erected this temple in her honour, and it was named after him. Soon after this, the Rájá of Suket became a votary of Káli and built a temple in her honour at Chhikianá.

Three fairs are held annually at as many places, one on the 9th of Baisákh at Bári called the Tarslún fair. The Diwáli is held at Suket, when the Janamashṭmí festival is also observed. The Shánd is observed every 12 years.

The cult of Deví Bálá Durga is associated with that of Márkanḍa Deota. The temple at Márkanḍa was founded by a Sádhu from Triloknáth.

At Bargali is the *mandir* of Deví Durga called *mandir* Baggán Deoṛa. A fair is held from 1st to 3rd Phágan annually and is followed by the *naurátas* in Chet and Asauj during which girls are fed. On the Rikh Puniya a *jag* is celebrated. This temple has existed for a long time, but the date of its foundation is not known. It contains a stone idol of the goddess. A *kárdár* by caste a Kanet manages its temple affairs. The *pujári* is a Sársut Brahman. The *chela* or *gur* is a Kanet. Their offices are hereditary.

In Kulu proper the cult of Deví is even more popular than it is in Saráj. Her cult names are numerous. She is called Bhaga Sidh, Bhanthali, Bharari, Chamunda, Dasmi Barda, Garanpuri, Harnam Jagan Náthi, Jaishari or Mahi Kashar, Jawálamukhi, Káli Auṛi,[1] Káli Mahi Khasuri or Phungni, Khandásan, Kodanta, Kowanah Mahá Máyá, Mahá Mái Jagni, Nainan, Phungáni and Phangani Bari Shakh, Sri Ráni Neoli, Sanohia, Sarwari, Singhásan, Tripura Sundari and Rupashna.

[1] In Kulu there is at Harchandi village in *pháti* Nathán (Koṭhi Nagar) a temple to Káli, the idol consisting of a stone or image. *Auṛi* means a picture, monument etc. and is commonly applied to the stone put on end by a man on first visiting one of the numerous passes in Kulu, *e.g.* *Auṛi* Dhar means the "Ridge of the monuments." Such stones are very numerous on all passes in Kulu, and are set up on the occasion described, and a sheep or goat is killed and given to the companions, or some food is distributed. It is said to have once been customary to write the name on the stone, and the shapes certainly suggest the idea that once they were carved roughly in human shape.

The Deví Káli is said to have put the stone as her image at Archhanḍi.

The following is a list of the Deví temples in Kulu, their seats and the dates of their fairs and festivals. It is interesting to find a Siddh Deví :—

Name of Deví.	Site of temple	Dates of fairs.
Bhága Siddh[1] ..	Named after the goddess	12th and 13th Baisákh and for 8 days from 31st Sáwan.
Bhága Siddh ...	Ḍera ...	7th Jeṭh.
Bhága Siddh ...	Ḍera Dughi Lag ...	1st of Chet, 3rd of the light halves of Phágan and Chet, 1st of Baisákh, Jeṭh, Bhádon and Asauj, and on the full moon day of Maghar.
The goddess Hirmá ..	Dhungri Ḍera ...	Dhungri *játra* on the 1st Jeṭh for three days, on the Phágali, on the 4th Mágh, 1st of Sáwan and Baisákh.
Deví Harman ...	...	7th and 15th Mágh, 1st Baisákh and 1st Asauj.
Deví Káli Auṛi ...	Deví in Kothi Mángaṛh	1st Baisákh, 1st Bhádon and 3rd Jeṭh.
Káli Auṛi ...	Amhhandi Ḍera ...	1st and 2nd of Chet, 1st to 3rd of Baisákh, 1st of Bhádon and 1st of Asauj.
Káli Mahi Khasuri, Káli Auṛi or Phungni.	Ḍera Deví in Koṭhi Raisan	1st of Baisákh and Bhádon.
Deví Phungni ...	Ḍera Phungáni in K. Mandalgaṛh.	5th and 7th of the lunar months of Baisakh and Phágan and on Wednesday and Thursday in the light halves of Sáwan and Maghar.
Deví Phungáni ...	Ḍera Deví Phungáni in Biasar.	1st of Chet, 3rd and 5th of the light halves of Baisákh and Bhádon.
Deví Phangáni[2] ...	Tiun Ḍera in Koṭhi Mángaṛh.	In addition to fairs in Sáwan, Asauj, Maghar and Phágan, a fair is held on the 3rd, 5th and 7th in the dark half of Baisákh.
Deví Bhotanti[3] ...	Parai Ḍera in Koṭhi Chung.	1st to 3rd Asauj.

[1] The temples of the goddess Chámunda, of Narain, Doli Nág, the goddess Indarol and Dharat Pál are connected with this.

[2] South of the temple is a *bhanḍár* (storehouse) of the goddess and to the west are two rooms for cooking food. At 100 paces in the latter direction is a *marah* where a fair is held in her honour.

[3] Two temples are connected with this, those at Bháti Ḍera and Garan Ḍera. The goddess visits these temples on the occasion of the fair.

Name of Deví.	Site of temple.	Dates of fairs.
The goddess Bhanthali ...	Banthali Ḍera ...	7th of Jeṭh and 1st of Asauj.
Deví Bharári ...	Mel ...	3rd Asauj.
Deví Chámunda[1] ...	Dabogi Ḍera at Nashála	On the *dwádshi* (12th) in the light half of Phágan, 1st Chet, new year's day, 1st to 4th Baisákh, 1st Jeṭh, 1st Bhádon and 1st Asauj.
Deví Chámunda[2] ...	Nalar Ḍera ...	1st Sáwan.
Shri Deví Dasmi Barda	Kalar Ḍera ...	1st to 3rd Chet, 31st Chet to 3rd Baisákh, 6th to 3rd Háṛ, 31st Sáwan to 5th Bhádon and a *yag* every 12 years.
The goddess Ducha and Mucha.	Gajjan and Karjan Ḍeras.	The *gajjan* on the 4th Jeṭh and the *chachopali* on the full moon day of Chet, lasting four days
Deví Garan Puri ...	Naraini Garan Ḍera, Upar Rela Ḍera and Ringu Ḍera.	1st Phágan, 1st Baisákh, 8th Baisákh, Ganesh *chaudas* in Sáwan, in Háṛ, 1st of Poh and 21st Baisákh.
The goddess Jaggannáthi	Jaggannáthi Ḍera ...	8th to 11th of the light half of Baisákh, 7th to 10th of the light half of Háṛ, and 7th to 10th of the light half of Asauj.
Deví Jaggannáthi Ji ...	...	Baisákh *shudi ashṭami* 3 days, Háṛ *shudi ashṭami* 3 days, Asauj *shudi ashṭami* 3 days, besides 15th Phágan, 1st Chet, 1st of new year, 1st Baisákh.
Jaishari or Mahi Kashur[3]	Hat, in Bajaura Koṭhi	9th of Baisákh and 8th of Bhádon.
Jawálamukhi ...	Ḍera Pall Sari in Koṭhi Hurang.	1st of Baisákh, Jeṭh and Háṛ, and on the 2nd of the light half of Sáwan. A grand *yag* is performed every 12 years.
Jawálamukhi ...	Shamshi Ḍera in Koṭhi Khokhan.	1st of Baisákh, Sáwan and Asauj, and on the full moon day of Maghar. Each lasts one day.

[1] Another temple called Ḍera Nishála is connected with this. It contains an image said to be that of the goddess Bhága Sidh and it is worshipped in the same room as the other goddess.

[2] The temples at Dhara Ḍera and Sungal Ḍera are connected with this. The god's chariot is taken to these at a festival.

[3] The temple also contains an image of Bhole Náth. It is of stone, one cubit high. It is worshipped along with the goddess.

Name of Deví.	Site of temple.	Dates of fairs.
Deví Khandáman ...	Naumi Dera ...	The Japari *játra* in the beginning of the new year in the light half of the month of Chet for four days, and Sáwan *játra* on the 21st of Sáwan for four days.
Deví Kodaula[1] ...	Gohi Dera ...	2nd, 12th, 13th and 14th Baisákh, and 2nd Asauj.
Kowanal ...	Dera Soil ...	The *shivrátri* on the 4th of the dark half of Phágan, Phágli on the *ikádshi* of Phágan, *chacho-pali* on the full moon day, on the *bir shiv* on the 1st of Baisákh, the *bago* on the 1st of Jeṭh, the *sheono* on the 1st of Sáwan and the *sari* on the 1st of Asauj.
Deví Mahá Máya ...	Mahá Máya ...	Tuesday of the light half of Phágan.
Mahá Mai Jagni ...	Choppar.	
Nainan ...	Bhulang Dera in Koṭhi Khokhan.	1st of Baisákh, Sáwan and Bhádon, each lasting one day.
Phungni Bari Shahl ...	Dera Phungáni ...	3rd, 5th and 7th of the light half of Baisákh.
Phungni ...	Dera Phungni Gauuani in Hauani.	1st of Chet and 7th of the light half of Asauj.
Sri Ráni Neoli ...	Ráni.	
Deví Sandhia ...	Dera Deví Sandhia ...	4th to 7th of the dark half of the month.
Sarwari ...	Shuru Dera ...	*Naumí* (9th) of Baisákh.
Deota Singhasan ...	Singhásan Deví Dera ...	1st of Baisákh and illuminations on the *tij* (3rd) of Poh.
Tripura Sundari ..	Nagar ...	5th to 10th Jeṭh, 1st of Asauj, Durga *ashṭamí* in Asauj, 3rd of the light half of Poh, one day in the light half of Chet, 2nd and 3rd Baisákh.
Devi Rupashna ...	Sharani Beṛh in Koṭhi Harkanḍi.	1st Baisákh and *yag* every 3rd year on 2nd Bhádon.

[1] No temple is connected with this, but fairs are held on the 21st Maghar and 21st Sáwan when the gods and goddesses visit the fair and return in the evening.

Bhotánti Deví's original temple is at Jari in the Párbati valley. She and Parei Deví both have temples at Parei.

There is also a goddess of fire (or else the goddess is typified by fire) for when high-caste Hindu ladies hear a fire hissing they will say *bhakh nindia karanwá'í nún*, 'consume the back-biter', because the hissing expresses the wrath of the goddess at the evil habit of back-biting.[1]

In Outer Saráj Nirmand in the Núrpur Valley on the Sutlej Deví Ambka is worshipped, the great triennial fair being held in her honour. Every 12th year this fair is celebrated on a very large scale and is called the Bhunda. The following is an account of it :—

In the era of the Rishís, there were three kinds of sacrifice : the *narmedi*, *gaumedi*, and *asvamedi*, or sacrifices of men, kine and horses. These great sacrifices were performed by any one who had subdued the whole world, *e.g.* the Pándavas performed the horse-sacrifice. All the Rishís of renown used to assemble and sacrifice, and at the end of it they used to slaughter the man or animal, calling on the *deotá's* name and burning the flesh. Then the bones were collected, and their prayers had such efficacy that the man or animal was restored to life But after their era, goats and sheep began to be sacrificed, and, instead of killing a man, he was lowered on a rope, leaving it to chance whether he was killed or not. The Bhunda *melá* is the old *narmedi jag*, and the customs and rites are the same. This great fair is held at Nirmand, because Jamdaggan Rikhi being angry for some cause with his wife Ambiká, mother of Paras Rám, ordered the latter to beat her, and he did so. In expiation Paras Rám gave lands to the Brahmans of Nirmand who in return agreed to spend one-tenth of the produce on this Bhunda fair. As the Beḍa caste was appointed as before to ride down the rope, the fair was called Bhunda, though some say Bhunda is a corruption of *bhanḍár* or temple treasure-house. It is only held at fixed periods at Nirmand : elsewhere it is held when enough money &c. has been saved. The Nirmand fair is held in the same year as the Kumbh fair on the Ganges, *i.e.* once in 12 years. Three years after each Bhunda is held the Bharoji *jag* ; three years after that the Bhatpur *jag* occurs ; and again three years later, the Shánd *jag*. These though attended by several *deotas* are of much less importance than the Bhunda. They have no connection with Paras Rám and a Beḍa is not lowered on a rope.

Before the recent[2] Bhunda at Nirmand there had been Bhundas at Nithar (Buddha Mahádev), at Shamsar (Mahádev) in Naráingarh, at Baihna (Mahádev) in Sirigarh, and in December, 1892, at Gorah in Rámpur State, at which latter a Beḍa had been lowered on a rope.

The rope for the sacrifice is made of grass, cut at a propitious time, with music, two-and-a-half months before the fair, and the Beḍa himself makes it, performing constant ablutions while working at it. When

[1] P. N. Q., II, § 984. This is another instance of fire being a witness.

[2] This account was written in 1893.

it is made the right length it is placed in the temple, and if any one steps across it he is fined a goat, which is sacrificed, and the rope must be re-made. No one may approach it with shoes on or with anything likely to defile it It is reverenced as a *deota*. On the day of the fair it is lifted with great respect on the heads of men and taken to the cliff, where it is securely fastened. At every stage a goat or sheep is sacrificed to it, and when fixed the Beḍa is placed on it No other caste can make or ride it and the Beḍas regard this as a privilege and deem it disgraceful to refuse the descent It is a profitable venture, as the Beḍa is fed by the people for a year, besides obtaining Rs. 84 in cash, jewellery and clothes with other presents for his wife also. Sacrifices are begun in temples where means are available for a Bhunda 2½ years beforehand. Four Brahmans pray and sacrifice daily by burning rice, fruit, *ghi* and goat's flesh, the fire being placed in an earthern vessel sunk some four feet in the ground, an image of Káli being set up opposite to it, and small brass images of that goddess being placed near it. This vessel is called *nábhe kunḍ*, and it is only opened for the Bhunda, a large stone being placed over it on which the sacrifices at the Bhundas &c. are performed. Before the fair the *deotás* are summoned, and the ceremony cannot take place until they come. The *mohra* or image of a *deotá* does not attend, the *kals* or silver vessel full of water alone being brought. The *deotás* who must attend are those of Khán, Mahel (in Suket), Nirt Nagar (in Rámpur) and Nirmand (in Kulu). These are said to be five brothers. In addition thereof Lalsah, Dádsah, Sanír and Sanglah (in Rámpur) (called the *tadi deotás*) should also attend. Others may do so.

On a fixed day, called *chhilbichhli*, a picture of a pine tree is made of *sindúr* (vermillion) on a clean place in front of the temple, and the *deotá* who is to commence the fair is worshipped by the Brahmans. At this place also a fight takes place, and then all the *kalsás* of the *deotás* are collected and prayers recited. All the *deotás* then go into the *koṭhi* of the temple (where the treasure-house &c. are) on to the upper storey, and a *rath* of Shibji of white thread and a similar tree-picture to that outside are also made on the ground. On top of this is put a plate of *kansá* filled with rice, and a cocoanut wrapped in silk clothes is placed on top of the rice. In places on the picture are put cakes, rice and *másh* cakes with lamps at each corner. The *kalsás* are brought in and placed in order round the *ḍol* or *rath*, and if any *mohras* of the *deotás* have come they are placed on a clean spot near the wall. Grain is then given to the people from the temple store-house. This is called *chham-chani* or invitation. Next day the *deotá's gur* (*gurú*) comes with the *deota* and the people cook cakes and worship round the village (*astkpher*) in which the temple is Goats, sheep, and *sungar* (a kind of small pig) are killed, and again a mock struggle occurs, any one who likes taking an animal. When the circuit of the village is complete a number of sheep and goats are cruelly lain in the *koṭhi* of the temple. On the third day the rope is worshipped, and goats &c. sacrificed to it. The rope is then fastened on a cliff as described before, one end high up and the other lower down. The Beḍa bathes and is taken to the *kunḍ* (of sacrifice). The Brahman worships him, and he is considered a god, the same worship being paid him as is paid to a *deotá*. Five valuable things (*panchratn*) are placed in his mouth, as is done at the death of a Hindu. Then he is clothed in a *pagri* and *kurta*, and being placed on a goal is taken outside the temple. The Beda gives presents to the people, and is next made to ride on the *kárdár's* (manager of a temple) back, and music is played as at a funeral. His wife and children, unclothed, sit beneath the rope and lament. At the top of the rope four *kumbhs* or vessels are placed, over which a board is put. The rope is fixed in the earth, passing over the board. A wooden saddle, like those used on *jhúlas* or rope bridges, is placed on the rope, and on this the Beda sits, being firmly tied on to the rope. Skins of earth of equal weight are placed on each thigh and a white handkerchief is placed in his hand. He is lowered at first with ropes to test the balance, and then some barley is tied to his waist. These ropes are then cut and the Beda slides down. He is taken off at the bottom, and he and his family beg of the people, taking whatever they touch. He and his wife are taken to the temple, Rs. 84 and jewellery &c. being given them. They are danced two-and-a-half times round in a circle and dismissed. On the fourth day, after the temple gives presents to the *deotás* and people, the fair ends. This is called the Beái *jag*.

In 1893 a goat was lowered in place of a man, with the usual accompaniments. The rope is called *borto* and one account is that the *muáfidárs* of the temples usually make the rope The Bedas are a low caste of dancers. These fairs are held at Nirmand (Deví Ambká), Nithar, Dalásh, Dhamsa in Bashahr, and certain other places—all on the slopes running down to the Sutlej. Bhundas do not take place in Kulu itself, but very similar ceremonies (Ganer), in which grass ropes play a conspicuous part, are common, and there is a tradition that men used to be lowered over the cliffs on the Beás on ropes of their own making. Their names are recorded in the temple records and are remembered with honour. Further at *kíns* (Sk. kháyá ?) festivals the *panchrats* or five precious things are placed in a man's mouth.[1] The man who was sacrificed was called *jiáli*.

There is an account of a "Bhoonda" in Traill's *Statistical Account of Kumáon*, p. 69. (Reprinted from *Asiatic Researches*, Vol. XLI, in Batten's *Official Reports on Kumáon*, 1851.) Captain Harcourt also gave a short account in his *Himalayan Districts of Kooloo, Lahoul and Spiti*, 1874.

The goddess Hirma, who is said to be a sister of Jamlu,[2] is worshipped or at any rate invoked at the Káli-ri-diáli which is celebrated in Poh[3], late in December, not in November like the Diwáli in the plains It is, however, essentially a feast of lamps, for, according to one account it is inaugurated on the previous evening by a gathering of the men on the village greens where they sing indecent songs till a late hour, ending with a chorus in favour of Hirma. The dance is circular, each performer dragging his neighbour towards the inside or outside till one gets exhausted and lets go, sending

[1] N. I. N. Q., IV. 1893, § 144.

[2] See Vol. III, p. 267, *infra*.

[3] The Diáli in Kulu proper takes place generally in Poh on the Amáwas or last day before the new moon. But in Rúpi *wazíri* it occurs from Magh 7th—14th and is called the *sadiálá*, a corruption of *sai diálá*. *Diáli* is said to mean house of mercy.

all the rest sprawling. On the evening of the festival lighted torches are shown at every house, the signal being given from the castle at Nagar and caught up and down the valley.[1] Three days later comes the Ganeṛ. The Ganeṛ (from *gún*, a knot?) is perfomed on the *tíj* or third day of the new moon, *i.e.* three days after the Diáli. In former times, it is said, huge grass ropes used to be made and great feasts held, the people jumping over the ropes in sport. The Míáns of Kulu used to have ropes stretched between two posts and jump their horses over them, the people holding the posts, shaking them as they did so, so that sometimes the rider was killed at the jump, his horse catching in the rope.

But at one festival the people of Baṛágrán, a village on the west bank of the Beás (where it is also customary to hold it), got drunk, and the rope they had left lying about turned into a snake and went on to Nagar—across the river. As the snake went along, a dumb boy caught hold of its tail, and it coiled itself round him, but the Deotá Jiv Naráyan was on his way to Nagar, and one of his disciples seized the snake by the head, and it straightway became a rope again by the Deotá's power. Then the Nagar people insisted that the ceremony should be held henceforth at Nagar and not at the Rájá's race-course, and so the practice of stretching it on posts and jumping horses over it was discontinued. It then became, or still continued, customary to drag the rope down to the cliff overhanging the Beás, four men of Jána village and four of Nagar racing with it to the cliff. If the Jána men won, they had to pay the Nagar people a goat and two loads (*bhára*) of rice; but if the Nagar people won, the Jána people had to pay them Rs. 500. It is said that this racing was discontinued many years ago. The people of Nagar and Jána now simply run three times with the rope a few hundred yards towards the Beás, bringing the rope back each time. It is then broken, the Jána people taking one part (the head of the snake) and the Nagar people the other (its tail).

At this ceremony a ram's horns are placed on the head of a Chamár (currier) of a particular family of Nagar. This man is called the *jaṭhiáli* and has a sort of headship over the other men of his caste, who are called his *sewak* or disciples. He gets an extra share of the clothing given to the Dágís from the body of a Hindu at his burning. He is chosen every year, and the same man is often re-elected. When the horns are placed on his head, the *negi*, or headman of the *koṭhi* says—

He su mangal, kesu háth.
He su mangal, Rájá háth.
He su mangal, ri'aiyat háth.
He su mangal, sáwá háth.
He su mangal, dhariri háth.
He su mangal, Hirma háth.
He su mangal, kesu háth.

"Oh god (and) blessed one, aid the fruits of the earth, the Rájá, the people, the princes, the land, the goddess Hirma, the fruits of the earth."[2]

[1] Kángra *Gazetteer*, Pt. II, Kulu, p. 45.

[2] N. I. N Q., IV., § I.

The *negi* then places a rupee in his mouth as is done to a dead man. (This is also a feature of a similar ceremony).

After this every one sings and dances, and a feast is held. No offence is taken at anything said. The Dágans, or wives of the out-caste Dágís, abuse the better caste officials of the village, blowing pieces of grass at them out of their hands, and getting some money as a present. This part of the festival is called *kalagi*, lit. "tuft of the *munál* (pheasant) feathers" worn in the head-dress. It is said that in former times the high caste men used to sit and eat with men of any caste at the Diwáli when Shakti (Bhagwati) was worshipped, but this is not the case now. There is a story about the ram whose horns are used. When the Pál kings from Jagatsukh attacked the Ránás of Nagar, a ram fought for the latter, who were conquered, and the Páls captured him; but as he had fought so bravely, they honoured him by taking him to the Jagatipat or sacred stone (brought to Nagar by *deotás* in the form of bees), and putting a rupee in his mouth they killed him. His horns are now kept in a little temple close to Nagar. At this same fight certain *wazírs* who fought for the Ránás were also captured. The Pál king pardoned them and made them dance before him as a sign of subjection to him. Their descendants still dance at the Ganer, and are presented with a rupee each. The family is called Andrâo, *i.e.* 'inner counsellers.' At the *kalagi* ceremony an indecent song is still sung.

Appended is a portion of one of the songs sung at the *kalagi*:—

Jai Deví, Hirma Mái.

Victory Mother-goddess Hirma.

Terí khel khelní lái.

We begin to play thy game.

Posha máh, Poh parálí.

The month of Poh, Poh is the month of rice straw ricks.

Ihori bhosi, bahu jali.

Mágha máh, churní lomí.

In Mágh the icicles are long.

Deruá yár, khari komí.

Phágun máh, ila pila.

In Phágan, all is mud.

Khanju láuḍ, thoku kela.

Chetr máh, gáh garí ká.

In Chetr the place is dug.

Moslu jehá, leṭh paṭíká.

As big as the flail, or pole for husking rice—*membrum virile erectum est.*

Baisákhu máh, báthe kápu.

In Baisákh the cuckoo calls.

Pahle, pahle máushe laurá chápu.

Jeṭhá máh, gagri siḍá.
Jihun kúchá, tihun piḍá.
Shárá máh, bhar roní.
In Háṛ, the rice-beds are full.
Bhale mánshá begai nahín lení

and so on. The lines not translated are hardly fit for translation.

It is clear that the whole festival is older than the myth, which is equally clearly in part historical and in part an attempt to account for the rites.

Deví as the small-pox goddess.

Ibbetson, § 21C.

Sítala,[1] the small-pox goddess, also known as Máta, or Deví, is the eldest of a band of seven sisters by whom the pustular group of diseases is supposed to be caused, and who are the most dreaded of all the minor powers. The other six are Masáni, Basanti, Máhá Máí, Polamde, Lamkariá, and Agwáni, whose small shrines generally cluster round the central one to Sítala. One of them is also called Pahárwáli, or she of the mountains. Each is supposed to cause a specific disease, and Sítala's speciality is small-pox. These deities are never worshipped by men, but only by women and children, enormous numbers of whom attend the shrines of renown on Sítala's *saptami*, the 7th of the light half of Sáwan, when only light food is eaten. Every village has its local shrine also, at which the offerings are all impure. Sítala rides upon a donkey, and gram is given to the donkey and to his master, the potter, at the shrine, after having been waved over the head of the child. Fowls, pigs, goats and cocoanuts are offered, black dogs are fed, and white cocks are waved and let loose. An adult, who has recovered from small-pox, should let a pig loose to Sítala, or he will again be attacked. During an attack no offerings are made; and if the epidemic has once seized upon a village all worship is discontinued till the disease has disappeared. But so long as she keeps her hands off it, nothing is too good for the goddess, for she is the one great dread of Indian mothers. She is, however, easily frightened and deceived; and if a mother has lost one son by small-pox, she will call the next Kurria, he of the dunghill, or Báharu, the outcaste, or Máru, the worthless one, or Molar, bought, or Mangtú, borrowed, or Bhagwána, given by the Great God; or will send him round the village in a dust-pan to show that she sets no store by him. So too, many mothers dress their children in old rags begged of their neighbours till they have passed the dangerous age.

In Rohtak, where Sítala is also called Ganwali, her great days of worship are the Tuesdays in Chet,[2] though in some villages Mondays appear to be preferred. At Rabra again the Wednesdays in Háṛ are

[1] Sítala means 'cool,' from *sít*, and so small-pox is also known as Thanḍí, 'cold.' Cold water and cold food are offered at her shrines, either to propitiate her or as suitable food: P. N. Q., I., § 2. According to Sleeman, burning the bodies of children, who die of small-pox, aggravates the disease. Rambles, I, pp. 218 *et seqq.*

[2] In Máler Koṭla the Máta Ráni fair is held on the fourth Tuesday of Chet. Máta, the goddess of small-pox, is then worshipped and sweet bread and rice offered to her.

auspicious and at Anwali there is a great day in Asauj. At her shrine in Rohtak the concourse in Chet is a large one, and food is distributed to Brahmans, but the offerings are taken by sweepers. Sick or well the worship is carried on, and the rupee often seen on a boy's neck is frequently put on when he is supposed to be attacked by Sítala. It is particularly favourable to have a shrine at a crossways, and the goddess is then called Chauganwa, 'she of the four villages', or Chaurasta, 'she of the four ways', Mátá. At Ukhalchana and Kosli in Rohtak Lakaria,[1] her sister goddess, is also represented at her temple, but *her* shrine faces west. This title may, however, be only another name for Sítala, for she is said to live in the *kîkar* (*acacia arabica*) and its roots are consequently watered night and morning by Hindus. Her vehicle, the donkey, is for the same reason fed with *wet* gram and fried eatables, the idea of cooling thus coming into play.[2]

The shrines of Sítala, which are to be found near almost every town and village, are about 2 feet high and are generally built by Bánias *after* a patient has recovered, as a thank-offering. All through the small-pox season, which is generally in the cold weather, and especially during an outbreak of the disease, women may be observed going about carefully watering each shrine in a group to *cool* the goddess and so, vicariously, any patient they may be interested in, or to gain her favour.[3] Her shrines are called Sítala-ghar or in Guṛgaon Síyar, and the lamps burnt at them are of the *ekmukha* type, a pan with one light, and are lit on Mondays and Tuesdays. In the South West Punjab a mass of clinker, strongly reminiscent of a countenance deeply pitted with small-pox, may sometimes be noticed covered with *ghí*, flowers and grain. These are offerings to Sítala, the clinker being used as a shrine or rather altar possibly because in a country where Islam is dominant shrines could not be built.

At the temple of Sítala at Danathá in Guṛgaon fairs are held on the Wednesdays in Chet. 150 years ago a fair used to be held at Kharbala, but one Udáh, a Jáṭ[4], who used to worship the goodess, saw her in a vision and she bade him to remove her temple to Danathá, using some of the bricks of the old one. The temple is administered by the headmen of the village and they take all the offerings. Their *got* is Sháli. The story is that a Jáṭ used to beg in *faqír's* clothes and so his descendants came to be called *sháli*, and have been professioned beggars ever since. Every Wednesday a lamp is lit in the *mandir*. A sacred lamp is kept burning during Chet and it is also said that a lamp is lit 'after midnight.'

[1] Lamkaria appears to be another term for this goddess,—*vide* p. 350 *supra*.

[2] I. N. Q., IV, § 150.

[3] P. N. Q., II, § 646. When a child has small-pox, Hindus will also feed an ass as Sítala's chosen vehicle. In Kasúr this ceremony is said to be called *jandipuja*: III, § 686, IV, 150, *Ibid.* III, § 686.

[4] In Gurgaon Jáṭs take offerings to Sítala. There is an obscure tradition in that part of the Province that the Jáṭs are descended from 'Bhaddar, brother of Bhíl' but no connection with Bhaddar Káli is suggested.

Quite distinct from Sítala is Kandi Máta, so-called from the ring of spots which forms round the neck when the particular pustular eruption due to her takes place. Her shrine is usually smaller than Sítala's, but they are commonly many, not one. At Beri in Rohtak an avenue of them leads up to Deví's temple, as these shrines are usually built on recovery in fulfilment of a vow. The second Sunday after recovery is especially suitable for worship and Re. 1-4-0 are usually spent on distributing sweets. Regarding worship during health, customs vary in different villages, it being held every Sunday in some and in others only on those which fall in the light half of the month, while others only hold it on these days during an attack of sickness. In Bahádurgarh the 5th of Sáwan is a great day for the Bánia women to worship this goddess at *kair* bushes, on the road to the station, by sticking gram on the thorns and giving *chapatis* etc. to Brahmans. It is becoming usual, especially with Bánias, for the bride, bridegroom and bridal party to do *pújá* at this goddess' shrine. Her shrines at Chirána are of peculiar interest. The Jáṭs and Dhánaks have separate rows of them and the Jáṭs have one regular temple of the Kandi in which is an image of the goddess, without a head. As a rule her shrines contain no images. They are often to the north of the village, because the disease is supposed to have come from the hills.[1] Occasionally worship is offered by sprinkling gram before them in times of plague. But the plague goddess is one Phúlan Deví, whose half-completed shrine at Jasaur attests her ill-will or inability to stay the disease. Jagta is a shrine similar to that of Kandi, and it too appears to be erected to a goddess. It is worshipped at weddings with a prayer for offspring, and also when a disease, which seems to be eczema or itch, appears.

Masáni's shrines are hardly distinguishable from Sítala's. Most villages in Rohtak possess one. *Masán* is a disease that causes emaciation or atrophy in children, and she is propitiated to avert it. It occurs in Sirmúr where one of the two cures[2] in vogue consists in burning mustard and other oils in a lamp called *gaina*, with 32 wicks and a hollow in the centre. In this hollow pistachio nuts, flowers and perfumes are placed. Seven marks are made with vermillion on the lamp and one on the child's forehead. All the 32 wicks are then lit and after it has been waved round the heads of both mother and child it is carried out beyond the village boundary and placed in the forest. This may be in reality a rite in the worship of the goddess.

So also in Gurgaon, the chief fair held in the district is that of the goddess of small pox, Masáni, whose temple is at Gurgaon. A small *mela* takes place there every Tuesday, except in Sáwan, but the largest fairs are those held in Chet. The temple is held in great repute throughout this part of the country and is visited every year by pilgrims from the Punjab and United Provinces to the number of 50,000 or 60,000. The offerings which often amount to Rs. 20,000 were formerly appropriated by Begam Samru, but are now a perquisite of the land-owners of Gurgaon. Pilgrims visit the shrine on Mondays throughout the year but the biggest gatherings, amounting sometimes

[1] *Cf.* Paháṛwáli, above, as a title of one of Sítala's sister *devís*.

[2] For the other see Sirmúr *Gazetteer*, p. 25.

to 20,000 souls in one day, occur on the four Mondays in Chet. Tradition thus describes its origin :—

There was a shrine sacred to the goddess Deví, locally known as Masáni, at the village of Keshopur in Delhi. Some 250 years ago the goddess appeared in a dream to Singha a Jáṭ, of some influence at Gurgaon, and saying that she wished to leave Keshopur directed him to build a shrine for her in his own village. At the same time she authorised the fortunate Singha to appropriate all the offerings at her shrine, so her orders were promptly carried out. The shrine flourished until its fame reached Benáres. A visit to it is an antidote to small-pox, and women from great distances flock to it with their children to obtain this benefit all the year round. Singha and his heirs enjoyed the offerings for 200 years. The Begum Samru, when the *pargana* was under her rule, took the proceeds for a month in each year, but now they are again the perquisite of the village headmen. The temple is called the *mand* or temple of Masáni, *mand* generally meaning the domed roof of a temple. The origin of the name Masáni is not known, but probably it is connected with the disease of *masán*, to which children are very liable. Another story of its foundation is that the wife of the great saint Dronacharya, the *gurú* of the Pándus and Kurus, knew of a specific for the cure of small-pox, and so after her death this temple was raised to her memory. It has no pretensions to architectural beauty, being almost on a level with the ground. It comprises a main room some 8 ft. square with a small room at the back about 5 to 6 ft. sq. which is used for storing valuables.

There are 5 *dharmsálas* near it, all built by charitable persons and all far superior in beauty to the temple itself. They accommodate about 1000 pilgrims. The image of the goddess is of mixed metal bronzed over and about 9 inches high. It is not always kept in the temple but remains in the custody of a Brahman who takes it home and only puts it in the temple on fair days. In the centre of the temple is a small platform of ordinary brick about a foot high and on this the image after being clothed is placed in an ordinary wooden *singhásan*. A Brahman is employed to wash the image but his office is not hereditary. No special ritual is prescribed. Offerings consist of fruits, sweet, cash, flowers, live animals cowries etc., and no distinction is made between the rituals of different castes. A lamp is lit on fair days and only kept burning as long as the fair lasts. The fact is that the administration is carried on purely business lines. The annual contract for the offerings is put up to auction every year and the money realized is distributed amongst the landholders of Gurgaon in proportion to their shares in the village lands.

A Masáni fair is also held at the temple of Sítla or Budho in Mubárikpur. As at Gurgaon the largest gatherings take place in Chet and Baisákh, but people come to worship the *deví* at all times of the year except in Sáwan and Asauj. The fair is held on every Tuesday in Chet and continues till 10 A.M. on Wednesday.[1] The

[1] Whence the name Budho. But a more rationalistic explanation is that Mubárikpur lies about 12 miles from Gurgaon, so pilgrims to the Masáni at Gurgaon from the Delhi and Rohtak side usually visit the Mubárikpur shrine after they have worshipped the Masáni at Gurgaon. Generally they can only do this on a Wednesday, and so the *máta* has come to be called Budhomátá. But now of course Wednesday is deemed sacred to the goddess.

image is worshipped at night. Flowers, Mansúri *ṭakkas, laḍḍús* and cocoanuts form the chief offerings. It is said that seven sisters became goddesses: one is at Mubárikpur, another at Basant, the third at Gurgaon, the fourth at Kálka in Delhi while the whereabouts of the rest are unknown. The temple is 6 yards square. It has a dome and two doors and is surrounded on all sides by a platform two yards wide, the whole being enclosed by a wall. It is said that 200 years ago a *faqír* came here and asked the Jáṭ villagers to build a temple at the place where the platform stood of old. He said that there was a goddess there, who would be of great use to them, that her fair will be held every Wednesday and that she would be called Budho. In the western wall of the temple facing the door is a small platform ⅓the yard wide and ¼ long. On this stands an arch containing a painting in several colours. This is worshipped, there being no other image. Once it was proposed to set up an image but the goddess appeared to Basti Rám Jáṭ, who enlarged the temple, in a dream and forbade him to do so. The management is carried on by the *pujári* who sweeps the temple every morning and washes the painting. He is a Jáṭ, by *got* Sahrawat, and takes the offerings but bears all expenses. The small *mandhis* outside the temple are also worshipped by the pilgrims.

A local account from Ambála says that there are 10 Mahábidias or Adshaktis, 'chief goddesses', one of whom is Mátangi Shakti, the small-pox goddess. She has eight names, Ranká, Ghranká, Meḷá, Mandlá, Sítala, Siḍala, Durgá and Shankara Deví. By Masáni is meant Mátangi Deví and *she* is the protectress of children suffering from small-pox. Her ears are as large as a winnowing fan, her teeth projecting, her face hideous, eyes huge and mouth wide open; she rides an ass, carries a broom in one hand and a pitcher and ewer in the other and has a winnowing fan on her head. The offerings made to her are taken by Jogís as well as scavengers, but many people content themselves with plastering a small space with cow-dung and putting on them such flowers and eatables as they can afford. Her shrines are about 6 feet high, and consist merely of upright masonry slabs with triangular tops and a projection in front on which to place the offerings. There is always a niche for the *chirágh* or lamp.[1]

Rose, § 27. Deví is in Hissár essentially the small-pox goddess, and the rites to cure the diseases are all based on this belief. If a child be suffering from a mild attack, the disease is called Shukar (Venus), and *gur* is placed under a *gharwanji*, or stand on which pitchers are kept, and songs are sung. This is termed *nám-rakhá*, or 'naming' the disease. In the case of a severe attack it is termed *dúsri Shukar*, and on a Sunday a Brahman woman makes the child wear a *rakh*, or amulet with a gold bead, *kapúr* (mercury), and *marjan* (a precious stone), fastened with red thread. *Bhát* or coarse wheat-flour is given in alms in the afternoon, and that night the mother and child sleep on the ground. The former keeps the Monday as a fast and *bhát* and rice are cooked in the evening. On the Tuesday the child's forehead

[1] P. N. Q., II, § 647.

is marked with cow's urine and young girls are fed with the *bhát*, with rice and milk, and pice or *kauris* given them. On the Sunday and following days the mother pours *lassi*, or milk mixed with water, on a *jand* tree, sprinkling some also on the ground on her way to and from the tree. Girls are again fed on the Wednesday and on Thursday morning, and the mother again pours *lassi* on the *jand* tree, asking its forgiveness for her act. She should also sprinkle *lassi* on this day on every tree on her road, and round a kiln as well. On the Monday night following *bhát* is given in alms and finally women go in procession to Deví's temple, carrying an umbrella of paper, and accompanied by musicians. *Chhand* or hymns are sung daily to Deví, but the name of Rám may not be uttered, so he is addressed as Jaidewa. One of the lines sung is:—'O Deví, thou ridest a tiger under the shade of a canopy and a snake is thy whip.'

As long as the disease lasts *dhúp* grass and the dung of an elephant or sheep is burnt, and the child should wear a piece of tiger's flesh tied in a rag round its neck. *Ghí* may not be eaten in the house after the last visit to the *jand* tree, and the mother must avoid *ghí* for forty days, and fast every Monday. Visits of condolence, or receiving *bhájji* or food distributed at marriages are forbidden, and if any one comes to enquire as to the child's welfare he asks '*mahá mái khush hai*' 'is the goddess pleased?' and the reply is '*mahá mái mihr hai*,' 'she is kind.' The child is called '*mahá mái ká gola*' or slave of the goddess.

Here again we find girls feasted as incarnations of the goddess, and the attempt to transfer the disease to the *jand* tree, with due apology, is an orthodox treatment in cases of sickness. The other rites are less easily explained. Clearly there is some connection between the tiger's flesh worn as a charm and the conception of Deví as riding a tiger, but the exact train of ideas is obscure.

The worship of Deví Máta, who is propitiated by the lower classes of Muhammadans as well as by Hindus, is thus described in the *Yádgár-i-Chishti*.[1] When the child falls ill no one is allowed to enter the house, especially if he has bathed, washed or combed his hair, and any one who does come in is made to burn *harmal*[2] at the door. Should thunder come on before the pox has fully come out the sound is not allowed to enter the sick child's ears, copper plates etc. being violently beaten to drown the claps.[3] For six or seven days, when the disease is at its height, the child is fed with raisins covered with silver leaf. When the pox has fully developed Deví Máta is believed to have come, and, when the disease has abated and the sores become dry, a little water is thrown over the child's body This is called giving it the *phoa* or 'drop.' Kettle-drummers and Mirásís are then called in to make a procession to Deví's shrine and they march in front followed by the men, women and children related to the child who is carried in it, dressed in saffron clothes. A man who goes in advance sprinkles milk and water mixed

[1] N. I. N. Q., II, § 11.

[2] *Peganum Harmala*, a plant whose seeds are burnt to avert the evil eye or evil spirits: *Punjabi Dicty.*, p. 433.

[3] Mothers will also on such occasions ply their hand-mills to drown the noise of the thunder. P. N. Q., III, § 179.

with a bunch of green grass. In this way they visit some fig or other shrine of the Devi, and tie red ribbons to it, besmear it with red paint and sprinkle it with curds.

In Máṛwáṛ and Bíkáner inoculation for small-pox is not only practised but organised in a remarkable way Many years ago a Huda, a tribe of Jáṭs also found in Rohtak, received from Mahádevi (*sic*) the *kardan* or gift of suppressing small-pox and the tribe has been ever since the licensed inoculators of a great tract including Máṛwáṛ and Bíkáner, its members residing in scattered villages. When small-pox threatens, one of these practitioners is sent for and he on his arrival begins with rites and offerings to Deví. Children are then operated on by scores, the operation being performed on the wrist. The inoculator (*tonchara*) is paid in coppers and grain at three half-pence a head for boys. Girls are done at half-price. These inoculators have a high reputation for efficiency.[1]

Marí Mái is the cholera goddess, and failure to worship her, equally with personal uncleanliness, produces cholera. But it can be expelled by taking a young male buffalo, painting it with *sindhúr* or red lead, and driving it on to the next village. This is said to please the goddess. And she sometimes appears in human form. Thus in Sháhpur during the epidemic of 1893 two women were seen crossing the river in the ferry boats of whom one of them was asked where she had been and whither she was going: she replied that she had been staying for a time in Sháhpur, but was on her way north. She and her companion then disappeared. It was believed that this was the spirit of cholera going away, but unfortunately it broke out in the south of the district immediately afterwards.[2]

Marí Mái is in Káṅgṛa propitiated by the *panch-balá* and *sat-balá* rites. The former consists in offering four male animals, *viz.* a he-buffalo, ram, cock and he-goat with a pumpkin (*peṭha*) to the goddess at some chosen spot. The animals must be decapitated at a single blow, otherwise the ceremony fails and she is not appeased. The *sat-balá* is now out of date, as it consisted in the immolation of a pair of human beings, a woman as well as a man, to make up the mystic seven.[3]

Síta, as the goddess of cold or who can control cold, conferred a boon on the Dhobi caste for washing her clothes *gratis* and so they never feel cold from standing in the water washing.

[1] I. N. Q. IV, § 152. Among the Slavs also small-pox is conceived of as a supernatural female, indeed the Servians candidly call her the goddess, while the Greeks placate her by epithets such as the gracious or pitiful one, and the Macedonians style her 'lady small-pox.' All this is as like popular Hinduism as it could well be, and one is not surprised to learn that Russians look upon vaccination as a sin, equivalent to impressing on children "the seal of anti-Christ." Plague again is a gaunt old hag, on a par with the Indian notion which regards all diseases as manifestations of the goddess. Even scarlet fever is personified as the red woman or Rouse, just as the Persians typify that disorder as a blushing maid with looks of flame and cheeks all rosy red :—*V. G. F.* Abbott's *Macedonian Folk-Lore*, pp. 40-42.

[2] N. I. N. Q., III, § 226.

[3] Sir R. C. Temple, in P. N. Q., I, § 4. He suggests that *bála* = sacrifice, *cf. bal jáná*, to sacrifice onself. *Cf. Narain Bal.*

Traces of Deví-worship are to be found as far afield as Gilgit. In the Astor District Shri Bai, a goddess, lived on a rock, called by her name, a Nangan. This rock was always kept covered with juniper boughs and an attendant called Boh Bin looked after it. Before it barren women used to sacrifice goats and pray for offspring. After harvest too women dressed in their best clothes visited the Deví, singing on the way, and offered a goat to the Boh Bin who then threw up twigs of juniper into the air and the women tried to catch them as they fell, in the hope of bearing as many children as they caught twigs. Descendants of the Boh Bin survive, but the rites are no longer observed. A similar stone exists at Barmas near Gilgit where it is called Mulkum.[1]

In Gilgit the belief in giants (*yáth*, fem. *yáthini*) still subsists. At first the earth was enveloped in water, which was at some places frozen, and there some *yáths* took up their abode under Yamlo Hal Sgl, their ruler. He said he knew of a cunning wolf who lived at a place called Milgamok (old ice) who could spread earth over the water, and so they sent Nogi ('Fortune') to fetch him, but he refused to come. Then they sent 'Trust' to fetch him and he came, but bade them send for Garai Patan, a bird who dwelt in the snows of the Coscus mountain. Finally, Bojara Shah, the wolf, sent for a mouse which made a hole in the ice and spread earth over Garai Patan's wings and so over all the ice.[2] The *yáths* are here represented as benevolent, but the *yáthinis* were not so always. Thus one *yáthini* was a sister of the man-eating Shri Badat, king of Gilgit, and she devoured half the people who passed by her cliff at the junction of two streams near Gilgit. But a wizard (*Daniál*) named Soglio contrived to pinion her to a rock with nails and then turned her into a stone by prayers. He also begged the people to bury him when he died close to the *yáthini*, lest she should return to life and repeat her ravages, but they argued that she might return before his death and so they decided to kill him at once. This was done and he was buried close to the *yáthini*, who is represented by a figure of Buddha sculptured on rock.[3]

Deví Tárá of Tárab.

The Deví is the family deity of the Rájá of Keonthal, and her arrival dates from the advent of the Rájá's family in this part of the hills. Her legend is as follows:—Tárá Náth, a *jogi*, who had renounced the world and was possessed of miraculous power, came to Tárab to practise austerities. He kindled his fire, *dhúná*, in the jungle. When rain came not a drop fell on his sitting place (*ásan*), and it remained dry. Hearing of the supernatural deeds of the *faqír*, the Rájá went to visit him. The *jogi* told the Rájá to erect a temple to his goddess, Tárá Mái, on the hill, and to place her idol in it, predicting that this act would bring him much good, and that it was only with

[1] Ghulám Muhammad. *On the Festivals and Folklore of Gilgit*, Monographs, Asiatic Society of Bengal, I, pp. 108-09.

[2] Ghulám Muhammad, *ib.* p. 107.

[3] *Ib.*, pp. 105-09. How the Buddhist Shri Badat became a man-eater and how his daughter, Migo Khái Soni secretly married Shamsher and induced her father to disclose to her the secret that his sect could not stand intense heat as it was composed of *ghi* is told on pp 114-13. Shri Badat still lives under a big glacier and his return is so dreaded that the Talioo—at which singing and dancing round fires is kept up all night—and the Nisalo are held to prevent it: *ibid*, p. 118-10.

this object that he had taken up his abode on the hill. In compliance with these directions, the Rájá ordered a temple to be built, in which the *jogi* Tárá Náth placed the Deví's idol according to the rules set forth in the Hindu *Shástras* for *asthápan*, or establishing an idol. The Pato Bráhmans, who attended the *jogi*, were appointed *pujárís* of the temple. This Deví has eighteen hands, in each of which she holds a weapon, such as a sword, spear &c. and she is mounted on a tiger. The hill on which the *jogi* resided had, before his arrival, another name, but it was re-named Tárab after him As the Deví is the family deity of the Rájá, she is revered by all his subjects, and it is well known that whosoever worships the Deví will prosper in this world in all respects. It is also believed that she protects people against epidemics, such as cholera and small-pox. It is likewise believed that if the Deví be angry with anybody, she causes his cattle to be devoured by hyenas. The *zamíndárs* of *parganas* Kalánj and Khushálá have the sincerest belief in the Deví. Whenever sickness breaks out, the people celebrate *jags* in her honour, and it is believed that pestilence is thus stayed Some nine or ten years ago, when cholera appeared in the Simla District, some members of the Jungá Darbar fell victims to the disease, but the Rájá made a vow to the Deví, and all the people also prayed for health, whereupon the cholera disappeared. The people ascribe the death of those who died of it to the Deví's displeasure. Some four years ago, and again last year, small-pox visited *pargana* Kalánj, but there was no loss of life. Some two or three years ago hyenas killed numbers of goats and sheep grazing in the jungles round Tárab, and the Deví revealed the cause of her displeasure to the people, who promised to celebrate a *jag* in her honour. Since then no loss has occurred.

Close to the temple of Deví is another, dedicated to Siva, which was erected at the instance of the *jogi* Tárá Náth The first temple of the Deví was at Ganparí village in *pargana* Khushálá. This still exists, and the usual worship is performed in it. The Deví's original seat is considered to be at Tárab. Her oldest image is a small one

There is a legend that Rájá Balbír Sain placed in the temple at Tárab an idol made by a blacksmith named Gosáún, under the following circumstances :—One Bhawáni Dat, a *paṇḍit*, told Rájá Balbír Sain that as Tárab was a sacred place he ought to present an idol to it, which he (the *paṇḍit*) would place in the temple according to the Hindu ritual, and he added that the idol would display miracles. Accordingly the Rájá ordered Gosáún to make the idol required. The blacksmith made an earthen image of the shape suggested to him by the *paṇḍit*, who told the Rájá that while the idol was being moulded, he must offer five sacrifices. This the Rájá did not do, and moreover he had a brazen image prepared. Immediately after the blacksmith had completed his idol, he was attacked by a band of dacoits, who killed him with two of his companions, as well as a dog and a cat. Thus the five necessary sacrifices were fulfilled. The Rájá was then convinced of the veracity of the *paṇḍit's* statement and acted thenceforward according to his directions. He performed all the requisite charities and sacrifices, and, having seated the idol, took it to Tárab. He performed several *hawans* in the temple and placed (*asthápan*) the idol in it. This Deví is the one who is mentioned in the *Chandíki-Pothí* by Márkandá Rishi, who killed Mahí Kaháshor.[1]

The fair of Deví Tárá is held at Tárab in October on the Durgá *ashṭamí*, and lasts for a day. On the first *naurátra*, the Brahmans worship Durgá in the temple, and a he-goat is sacrificed daily, the Rájá bearing all expenses. On the morning of the *ashṭamí*, the Rájá, with his Ráṇí, and all his family, sets out from his court so as to reach the plain below the temple at ten in the morning, and there takes a meal, after which the whole Court goes in procession, preceded by a band of musicians, to the temple, which the Rájá, with the Rání, enters at about one in the afternoon. The Rájá first offers a gold *mohar* and sacrifices a he-goat, and each member of his family does the same. Everyone presents from one to eight annas to the *bhojkí* and the *pujárí*. After the ruling family has made its offerings, other people may make theirs, and money, fruits, flowers, *ghí* and grain are given by everyone according to his means. The *bhojkí* and the *pujárí* divide the heads of slaughtered goats, returning the rest of the flesh to the persons who offered them This worship lasts till four, and then the sacrifice of bull-buffaloes begins. These are presented by the Rájá as *sankalp* or alms, and taken to a place not far from the temple, where a crowd of people surround them with sticks and hatchets in their hands. The *pujárí* first worships the animals, making a *tilak* with rice and saffron on their foreheads.

Boiling water is then poured on them to make them shiver, and if that fails, cinders are placed on their backs. This is done to each animal in turn, and unless each one trembles from head to foot it is not sacrificed. The people stand round entreating the Deví with clasped hands to accept the offerings, and when a buffalo shivers it is believed that the Deví has accepted his sacrifice. The people then shout *Deví-jí-kí-jai, jai,*' 'victory to the Deví.' When all the buffaloes have been accepted by the Deví, the first is taken to the shambles and a man there wounds him with a sword. Then all the low-caste people, such as the Chamárs, Kolís, Bharos, and Ahírs, pursue the animal striking him with their clubs and hatchets and making a great outcry. Each is brutally and cruelly killed in this way, and it is considered a meritorious act to kill them as mercilessly as possible, and if the head of any buffalo is severed at the first stroke of the sword, it is regarded as an omen that some evil is impending and that both the person who inflicts the blow and the one who makes the sacrifice will come to harm in the course of the ensuing year, the belief being that as the buffaloes are the children of the Deví's enemies it is fitting to kill them in this way[2] After this sacrifice, food is offered to the Deví, and *ártí* is performed at six in the evening.

[1] (This reference is clearly meant to be classical, and for Mahi Kaháshor read Mahisásura.—Sir R. C. Temple).

[2] Mahí Khashwa, Mahisásura, who tormented the Deví, was a bull-buffalo, and, when he was killed, his descendants were metamorphosed into bull-buffaloes.

The fair is the occasion of much merriment and even debauchery. Women of all classes attend, unless they are secluded (*parda nashín*), and those of loose character openly exact sweetmeats and money for the expenses of the fair, from their paramours, and put them publicly to shame if they do not pay. The plain is a Sanctuary, and no one can be arrested on it for any offence, even by the Rájá, but offenders may be arrested as soon as they quit its boundaries and fined, the fines being credited to the temple funds. Offences are, however, mostly connived at. There is much drinking and a good deal of immorality, with a great many petty thefts. The Rájá, with his family, spends the night on the site of the fair. The *bhojki* and the *pujári*, who, with the *bhanḍári*, receive the offerings received at the fair, are Sarsút Brahmans of the Rai-Bháṭ group, while the *bhanḍári* is a Kanet. Brahmans girls are also brought to this temple, where they worship and are fed, and also receive money and *dachhna* (*dakhna*).[1]

On the third day of the Dasehra, the goddess is worshipped at 2 *p. m.*, in the *darbár*, all the weapons being first taken out of the arsenal and worshipped, and then all the musical instruments. The essential worship is that of the sword and flag. After this the Rájá holds a *darbár* with full ceremonial and then visits the temple of Ṭhákurji Lachhmi Naráyan, whence the image is brought in a palanquin, while the Rájá walks just behind it, attended by all his officials, in order of precedence, to the plain set apart for this festival. On this plain a heap of fuel[2] is piled at a short distance from a green tree, which is adorned with small flags and round which is tied a wreath containing a rupee. The Rájá with unsheathed sword goes round the heap, followed by the rest of the people, and the heap is then worshipped and set fire to. It is essential that the *wazír* of the State should be present at this ceremony, and if he is unavoidably absent a representative, who wears an iron *sanjuá*, is appointed, and the heap is then fired. The man who cuts the wreath on the tree in the midst of the burning fire and takes the rupee is considered a hero, and his prosperity during the ensuing year is assured. Before the heap is fired, a pitcher of water with a mark on it is placed close by, and whoever hits the mark is deemed lucky, besides receiving a prize from the Rájá. If no one is able to hit it, the man who represents Hanúmán, and who accompanied the idol, smashes the pitcher with his mace. The image is then carried back to its temple with the same pomp as before, and a turban is given to the Rájá on behalf of the Ṭhákurdwára, while his attendants are given *bhog* and *charnamrit*.[3] Wreaths of flowers are then distributed. The festival is believed to commemorate the conquest of Ceylon by Rám Chandar, the ancestor of the Rájpúts, which was accomplished after worshipping Deví.

A somewhat similar festival is the Saer fair held at Khad Ashni:—On the morning of the first of Asauj, a barber, having lighted a lamp in a *thál* (plate) and made an idol of Ganesh in cow dung, comes to the Rájá and his officials and makes them worship the idol.

[1] A fee for spiritual service.

[2] The stack is called *lauka*.

[3] The water with which the feet of the idol have been washed.

The Rájá and officials then give him presents according to their means. In the afternoon, the Rájá gives alms, and, accompanied by a procession with a band and his Ránís, sets out for Khaḍ Ashní. The inhabitants of the neighbouring villages assemble there in thousands to enjoy the sight. Some fighting bull-buffaloes, which have been reared for the purpose, are brought to the fair the day before and fed up with *ghí* &c. The Rájá himself rears six or eight buffaloes for this fair, and they are similarly prepared for the fight. The fair begins at one in the afternoon, when the he-buffaloes are set to fight in pairs; and the person whose buffalo wins is given a rupee as a reward by the Rájá. So long as the fight lasts, music is played.

The people at the fair distribute sweetmeats &c. among their friends and relatives. Swings too are set up and the people revel in drink. They can commit disturbances with impunity, as no offenders are arrested on this occasion Many people from Simla bring haberdashery for sale, and the articles are largely purchased by women. At five the people begin to disperse, and the Rájá returns to his *darbár*. About 6000 or 7000 persons assemble at this fair, and the Rájá distributes rewards among his servants on its termination. Its introduction is due to the Rájá, and it is not held in honour of any particular god. The place where the fighting takes place is dedicated to the god Badmún Formerly rams were also made to fight, but now only bull-buffaloes are used Before the commencement of the fight, a *roṭ* is given to the god This *roṭ* is made of 5¼ *sers* of flour, 5¼ of *gur*, 5¼ of *ghí*. The flour is first kneaded in *sharbat* of *gur* and then made into a thick loaf, which is then fried in *ghí*. When it is cooked, it is taken with *dhúp*, *tilak*, flowers and rice to the place of the god, and after worship has been performed, it is divided in two, one piece being left at the temple and the other distributed among the people.

According to one legend, this fair was instituted by the forefathers of the Rájá, who originally came from Gaur in Bengal and were an offshoot of the Sain dynasty. This festival is also observed in that country. It is said that the Rájás of the Sain dynasty were the devotees (*upásak*) of the Deví, who rejoices in fighting and the sacrifice of bull-buffaloes. Although this fiction is not generally accepted, the story is told by men of advanced age, and the late Rájá Maler Sain also ascribed the fair to this origin. It is said that Birju Deota is the *wazír* of the Deví, and therefore the fair is held at the place where there is a temple of the Deví or Biru It is also said that the day of the fair is the anniversary of that on which Rájá Rám Chandar constructed the bridge to Ceylon, and that the fair is held in commemoration of that event. In the everyday speech of the hill people Biru Deota is called Badmún Deota.

The Goddess Aṭh-Bhoja of Dharech.

Legend.—A Rájá of Kotlehr in the Kángra District, named Jaspál, had two sons. The elder succeeded to the throne, and the younger, in consequence of some dispute, quit the dominions of his brother, went to the hills, and took the name of Gajindar Pál. On leaving Koṭlehr, he brought with him an eight-handed image from the fort of Kángra, and came to Bhajji, where he begot four sons, Chírú, Chánd, Lógú, and Bhógú. On his death, these four partitioned his dominions thus: Chírú took the *iláqa* of Bhajjí, and Chánd that of Koṭí, while Lógú, and Bhógú received *pargana* Phágú in *jágír* The descendants of Chírú and Chánd are to this day the Ránás of Bhajji and Koṭí respectively. Bhógh married, and three families of his descendants, Marchítak, Phatík, and Halítak still exist in *pargana* Phágú. Lógú did not marry, but became a dacoit. In those days the country round Phágú was under the Ráná of Ratesh. Harassed by Lógú's raids, the people complained to the Ráná, but Lógú was strong and brave and the Ráná could not capture him. At last he commissioned a Chanál[1] to kill Lógú, promising him a reward if he succeeded, but though the Chanál pursued Lógú for some time, he failed to seize him. Lógú had a *liaison* with a Brahman girl, and one day she was sitting with him under a tree, when the Chanál chanced to pass by, and, taking Lógú off his guard, smote off his head and carried it to the Ráná, leaving his body at Hohán village, but the corpse of its own accord went to Dhar, a village surrounded by a rampart and with only one entrance, which was closed at that time. The headless body pushed open the gate, and entered the village. When the people saw it all besmeared with blood, they were terrified and gathered together, but the body disappeared, and though they searched for it, they could not find it. At last they discovered a stone *pinḍli* (an idol having no special shape). On consulting the astrologers, they were told that Lógú had been transformed into a *deota* and that they should place (*asthápan*) the *pinḍli* in a temple and worship it as a god Then Bhógú and other *zamíndárs* established the eight-handed Deví, which Lógú's father had brought from Koṭlehr, at Kiliya in Dhíraj village and placed Lógú's *pinḍlí* in the jungle of Dawán. The Brahmans who had come with the Rájá of Koṭlehr's sons were appointed *pujárís* of both deities, and it was then decided that Deví was the superior and that Lógú was her subordinate. Shortly afterwards several brazen images of Lógú were made and a handsome temple built to him in a Bakhóg village, where he is daily worshipped. In Dawán hamlet he is worshipped once every three years.

A fair is held at Deví's temple on the Durgá *ashṭami* day and at that of Lógú on the Salónó, *i.e.* the *púranmáshi* of Sáwan *sudi*, and at the Dewáli in the month of Kátak.

I.—The Zat Fair at Garen in Pargana Ratesh.

This fair is held on the 29th of Jeṭh. The images of the Deví Ratesh and Kalwa *deota* are brought in procession from the temple, where they are kept, to Garen, 400 or 500 persons accompanying them, and of these some 50 remain at Garen for the night, the rest returning home. By mid-day next day a great crowd of people collects, the men coming in bodies from opposite directions, each man armed with a bow and arrow and flourishing a *dángrá* (axe), with a band of musicians preceding them. A man in one of these bodies

[1] Chanál is a low caste in the hills.

shouts:—*Thadairi rá bhúkhá, awau jí jhamak lagí, thi,*[1] *hó hó*, I hunger for a shooting match: come, the fair has started, *hó, hó*. The others call out *hó, hó* in reply. The tune called a *thadairi* is then sung and matches are arranged between pairs of players One champion advances with his arrow on the string of his bow, while the other places himself in front of him, keeping his legs moving, so as to avoid being hit. The archer's object is to hit his opponent below the knee, and if he succeeds in doing so he takes a *dángrá* in his hand and dances, declaring that a lion's whelp was born in the house of his father at his home. The man who has been hit is allowed to sit down for a time to recover from the pain of the wound and then he in turn takes a bow, and placing his hand on his opponent's shoulder says 'bravo, now it is my turn, beware of my arrow.' If he hit his opponent he, too, dances in the same way, but if he fail his victor dances again crying, 'how could the arrow of such a jackal hit a tiger's cub?' This goes on until one or the other is beaten. The matches are usually arranged between men who are at enmity with one another. The play lasts for two days. Sometimes disturbances break out. These used to be serious, even resulting in men being killed on either side, but now-a-days a stop is put to the play, if a disturbance it feared, by pulling down the *deota's* flag, when the players desist of their own accord.

On the third day a goat and two buffaloes are sacrificed to Deví. The latter are killed in the same way as those at the Tárab Fair, but the shambles are at a distance from the temple, and two picked men take their stand, one on the road to Fágú, the other on that to Ratesh, to prevent the wounded animals going toward their respective villages, as it is believed that it is unlucky for one of them to reach either village, and bloodshed often results from the attempts of the different parties to keep the animals away from their village. Efforts have been made to induce the people to allow the buffaloes to be killed by a single blow, but the *pujáris* will not allow this, as being the offerings of Deví's enemies, they must be slaughtered with as much cruelty as possible. After this rite the people make offerings to Deví, the money going to the temple fund, while the other things, such as grain, goats &c. are divided among the *pujáris*. The *chela* of the Deví then begins to nod his head (*khelná*, lit., to play), and taking some grains of rice in his hand distributes them among the people, saying, 'you have celebrated my fair without disturbances, and I will protect you against all misfortunes throughout the year.' If, however, any disturbance has occurred during the fair, the offenders are made to pay a fine on the spot to obtain the Deví's pardon, otherwise it is believed that some dire catastrophe will befall them, necessitating the payment of a still heavier fine. The Deví passes the night at the fair, returning to her temple on the morning of the fourth day.

II.—The Ját fair, Bhaláwag.

This fair is held at Bhaláwag on the first Sunday in Hár. There is a legend that a *sádhú* once lived on the Chahal hill. He was famous

[1] Lit., 'you hunger after archery, come on, since you itch for it.' *Thadairi*, for *thoda*, an arrow, means archery, and one of the tunes or modes of the hill music is so called because it is played at archery meetings.

for his miraculous feats, and was said to be a *sidh*. He built a small temple to Mahádéo on the hill, and established a fair which was held continuously for some years. The offerings made at the temple were utilized to meet the expenses of the institution. After the Gurkha conquest this tract was ceded to the Mahárája of Patiála in the time of Rájá Raghúnáth Sain. Once Ráná Sansár Sain visited the fair, but a dispute arose, and the Patiála officials having used unbecoming words against the Ráná, he removed the *ling* of Mahádéo to his own territory and established it at Bhaláwag, and since then the fair has been held there. It only lasts one day. The Rájá with his Ránís &c. sets out with great pomp to the scene of the fair, the procession being headed by a band, and reaches the place about mid-day. People pour in from all parts, and by two in the afternoon the fair is in full swing. The Rájá takes his seat on the side of a tank, into which people dive and swim. A wild *leo* is also thrown into it as a scapegoat (*bhet*) and some people throw money into it as an offering. In the temple of Mahádeo, *ghí*, grain, and money are offered by the people according to their means. The *pujáris* of the temple, who are Brahmans, divide the offering among themselves. Worship is performed there daily, and on the *sankránt* days Brahmans of other villages come there to worship. On the fair day worship is performed all day long. People also give the offerings they have vowed. There is a legend about this tank which is as follows :—

Once a Brahman committed suicide in a Rájá's *darbár*. In consequence of this *hatiyá* (a profane act, especially the killing of a Brahman), the Rájá became accursed. He tried by all the means in his power to remove the curse, but in vain, for if he had a child born to him, it soon died, and though he performed worship and tried many charms and amulets, it was all of no avail. An astrologer then told him that as a *Brahman-hatiyá* had been committed in his *darbár*, he would never be blessed with a son, unless he sank eighty-four tanks at different places in his realm for watering of kine. The Rájá accordingly constructed eighty-four tanks at different places in the hills from Tajaur to Mattiána. Of these tanks some were very fine, and one of them is the tank in question. After making all the tanks, the Rájá sent for the builder, and, being much pleased with his work, gave him as a reward all that he asked for. But people then became envious of the kindness shown to him by the Rájá, fearing that he would be elevated to the rank of *musáhib* (courtier), and so they told the Rájá that if the builder did the same kind of work anywhere else, the Rájá's memory would not be perpetuated and that steps should be taken to prevent this. The Rájá said that this was good advice, and that, of course, he had already thought of it, so the builder was sent for, and although he tried to satisfy the Rájá that he would never make the same kind of tank at any other place, the Rájá paid no heed to his entreaties and had his right hand amputated. Thus disabled, the man remained helpless for some time, but having recovered, it struck him that with his skill he could do some work with his left hand, and he, accordingly, built two temples, one at Játhíá Deví and the other at Sadu, both now places in Patiála territory. When the Rájá heard of this, he at once went to see the temples, and was so delighted with their work that he gave a reward to the builder, but at the same time had his other hand cut off, and the man died a few days after.[1] It is said that after the making of the tanks, the Rájá celebrated a *jag* on a very large scale, and four years after was blessed with a *ṭíká* (son).

[1] This may be a variant of the superstition that the new structure must be guarded by a spirit as its custodian. Once granted that necessity, what spirit could be more suitable than that of the architect himself?

THE VAISHNAVAS.

Maclagan, § 53.

VISHNU.—We may turn now to the forms of worship which represent the Hindu spirit more truly than the strange practices of the Jogí and Saníasí sects. The Hindu, generally speaking, is not a Shaiva, but a Vaishnava, that is to say, he does not eat flesh, onions or garlic, and does not drink spirits. The main features of the Hindu pantheon are revealed to him in Vishnu or the incarnations of Vishnu. He worships the stone image of Vishnu in human shape. He reveres the Brahman and the cow. He wears the sacred thread (*janeo*) and the scalp-lock (*bodí*). He marries by walking round the sacred fire. He burns his dead, throwing the ashes into a river and taking a small portion of them to be thrown into the Ganges. He will often mark his forehead with one or more upright streaks of the calcareous clay known as *gopichandan*. His place of worship is called a *ṭhákurdwára;* and his places of pilgrimage are Hardwár, Gaya, Benáres, Jagganáth, Dwárka, Ajudhiá, Badrínáráin, Pushkar, Bindrában, Mathra, Pryág, Rámeshar, and the like. His sacred books are the four *Vedas*, the *Rámáyan*, the *Mahábhárat*, the *Bhágavat Gita*, and the *Vishnu-purán*. He is, in fact, the orthodox Hindu, and in our returns the word Vaishnav means, as a rule, little more than this. The Bania of the south-east, for instance, will often call himself a Vaishnav, when he means little more than that he is Hindu, and not a Jain. A Hindu, when asked his sect, is generally safe in replying that he is a Vaishnav: and the term covers a multitude of other sects regarding whom special separate information is also forthcoming. The numbers returned at a census as Vaishnavas exceed greatly the numbers returned under any other sect. The term is less distinctive, and the difference between the Vaishnav and the Shaiv is less marked in the Punjab than it is in the United Provinces and Rájpútána, where the mutual jealousy of the two sects is often very acute; and the Vaishnavs of our Census tables are mainly returned from the districts of the south-east border.

The Vaishnavs also include those who more particularly worship the god Vishnu under terms such as Bishnpuj, Bishní, and Mahábishn, or their adoration of the god as Ṭhákur, Ṭhákurjí or Srí Maháráj. He is also reverenced as Nirbhav, the fearless one, especially in Multán and Muzaffargarh. He is known also as Náráin, and is worshipped as Badrínárain at the shrine of that name in the Himalayas.[1] Another name for him which is common apparently in Hissár and Kángra is Visvakarma, Biskarma or Biskam, the Maker of all things, the Great Architect, and under this name is revered by the Tarkhán or carpenter caste, who, on the night of the Diwálí festival, will put away their tools and will not make use of them again until they have made to them due offerings of flowers and *gur* in the name of the god.

Of the minor *avitárs* of this deity, the only noticeable ones are those of Nársingh, the man lion, who tore into pieces the tyrant Harnákas (Hiranyakasipa) to save the pious Prahlád; and Parasrám the axe-hero, who fell with such fury on the Khatri caste. The most

[1] The Sat Náráins of Ráwalpindi are merley orthodox Hindus who observe the fast of Sat Náráin on the 18th day of the moon (*puranmáshí*).

popular incarnations are, however, of course those of Rámchandar and Krishna.

According to Sir R. G. Bhandarkar,[1] the various religious systems which prevailed in India in the 4th century B. C. included such sects as the Ajívakas and many others and those devoted to Vásudeva, Baladeva, Nágas, Yakkhas, Suriya, Inda, Brahmá, Deva, Disá and several others. The worship of Vásudeva, placed by a Buddhist on the same plane as that of the elephant, the horse, the crow and other animals, was destined to become the predominant religion of a large part of India even to the supersession of that of fire, sun, moon and Brahmá, as well as of animal-worship. Worshippers of Vásudeva were called Bhágavatas and their creed predominated in north-west India and was adopted even by Greeks.[1] The etymological sense of Vásudeva is given as 'one who covers the whole world and is the resting place, *adhivása*, of all beings. But the word may mean 'the son of Vásudeva' and it would appear that in the *Mahábhárata* two accounts are interwoven. In the earlier one the Supreme God is Hari and his worship has not completely emancipated itself from the religion of sacrifices. The later account connects a reform in this direction with Vásudeva and his brother, son and grandson and the new religion is represented to have been identical with that taught in the *Bhagavadgítá* and to have been promulgated by Náráyana himself. Possibly a religion of devotion had arisen yet earlier but only took definite shape when Vásudeva revealed the *Gítá* to Arjuna. Vásudeva's brother etc. were associated with him as his forms, *vyúhas*, who presided over certain psychological categories and the reformed sect became conterminous with the race of the Sátvatas', another name for the Vrishnis.[3] Sir R. G. Bhandarkar's conclusion is that the worship of Vásudeva owed its origin to the same stream of thought which in the east culminated in Buddhism and Jainism.

But Vásudeva soon came to be identified with Krishna and other names.[4] The process by which this identification was made is obscure. Krishna was a *rishi*, one of the composers of the Vedas, and Vásudeva seems to have been identified with him and given a genealogy in the Vrishni race through Súra and Vásudeva, although Krishna's patronym was Angirasa and he appears to have founded the Kárshnáyana *gotra*, or 'collection of Krishnas'.[5] The only possible explanation is that

[1] Sir R. G. Bhandarkar does not suggest any connection with the king Vásudeva of a later period. That king was a Kshatriya, whereas Vásudeva, the worshipful, belonged to the Vrishni race: *ibid.*, p. 4. It would be interesting to know if the Básdeo Brahmans, who are still officiants at weddings among the Muhammadan Nárus in Jullundur, are in any way connected with Vásudeva.

[2] The Ajívikas were a sect of Brahman ascetics devoted to Náráyana, as a form of Vishnu, according to Vincent Smith, *Asoka*, p. 145.

Other sects were the Jatilas or long-haired and the Nighanthas: *Grundriss, der Indo-Arischen Philologie etc. Vaishnavism, Shaivism etc.*, p. 3.

[3] Bhandarkar, *op. cit*, pp. 5-9, where the story of Nárada's visit to the 'white island' Svetadvípa. is given. But why should *dvípa* be translated 'island'? In Sangaladvíp it means at best a 'land between two rivers.'

[4] Janárdana and Keshava are the two others.

[5] A Brahmana *gotra* could be assumed for a sacrificial purpose by a Kshatriya. As the only *rishi* ancestors of the Kshatriya were Mánava, Aila and Pauravasa (which rather seem to be patronyms derived from the names of *rishis*) and as these names did not distinguish one Kshatriya family from another, the priest's *gotra* and ancestors were assumed: *ibid.*, p. 12.

Vásudeva assumed the title a Kárshnáyana and as such was called Krishna though it was a Brahmana-Páráshara *gotra*.

Just as Hari is older than Vásudeva so also is Náráyana or the 'place to which Náḍa or a collection of Náḍas go.' He is connected by tradition with the waters and the waters were called Náras or sons of Nara, and, since they were the resting place of Brahma and Hari, the two were called Náráyanas. Another form of the tradition is that Brahmadeva sprang from the lotus in the navel of Náráyana or Vishnu. But whatever form it may take the tradition reproduces the *Rig-Veda* X, 83, 5 & 6, which runs :—'Prior to the sky, earth and living gods, what is that embryo which the waters held first and in which all the gods existed? The waters held that same embryo in which all the gods exist or find themselves; on the navel of the unborn stood something in which all beings stood.' Here the embryo corresponds to the Brahma of the later tradition and the unborn to Náráyana.[1] The heaven of this Náráyana was the Svetadvípa or 'white land' which Nárada visited to learn the monotheistic religion of Vásudeva. The sage Markandaya tells Yudhishṭhira that Janárdana, or Vásudeva, is Náráyana and this concludes the question of his identity. Like Vásudeva, Náráyana in his four forms Nara, Náráyana, Hari and Kṛishna, is the son of Dharma and his wife Ahinsa, a metaphorical way of saying that righteousness and the doctrine that life was sacred begat a protest against the old sacrificial rites and the killing of animals connected with them.

It remains to trace Vásudeva's identification with the Vedic deity, Vishnu. In the *Rig-Veda* he measured the universe in three steps, the first two discernible by men, the third beyond their ken. Reverence for this third step raised Vishnu to a high position during the epic and Puranic period until three streams of religious thought, that flowing from the Vedic god Vishnu, that from the cosmic and philosophic god Náráyana and the third from the historical Vásudeva formed the later Vaishnavism.

Still later came the identification of Vásudeva Krishna with Gopála Krishna, the cow-herd god. No chapter in the history of Vaishnavism is more obscure than the process by which this was effected. The story of Krishna's boyhood in the Gokula or cow-settlement was unknown to literature till about the beginning of the Christian era. The cow-herds lived in a *ghosa* or encampment, as when they left Vraja and encamped in Vrindávan (Bindrában). *Ghosa* is defined as Abhíraphaili or the 'Ahírs' enclosure' and the cow-herds thus seem to have been men of that race who occupied the country from Madhuvana near Mathura to the region about Dwárka. Mentioned in the *Máhábarata* as having attacked Arjuna when he was taking the Vṛishni women, whose males had been exterminated, from Dwárka to Kurukshetra, they are described as Mlechha robbers living near Panchanada, the Punjab. They must have immigrated into the country in the 1st century, bringing with them the worship of the boy-god and the story of his humble birth, his reputed father's knowledge that he was not his son, and the massacre of the innocents. The stories of the Krishna's boyhood, such as that of

[1] 5. Bhandarkar, *op. cit.*, p. 31.

the slaying of the wild-ass demon, Dhenuka, were imported by the Ahirs, and it is just possible that they brought with them the name of Christ also, and this probably led to the identification of the boy-god with Vásudeva Krishna. Krishna dissuades his foster-father Nanda from celebrating a festival to Indra and induces him to worship the mount Govardhana instead.[1] His dalliance with the *gopis* or cow-herdesses was an aftergrowth.

Krishna's cult name of Govind may have had one of two origins. In the form of Govind it was an epithet of Indra in the sense of 'finder of cows', and Govid may be a later form of that name. But it does not appear to have been bestowed on Krishna because of his having had to do with cows, for Govinda is said to have been so called because in the form of a boar he found the earth (*go*) in the waters.[2] It would be quite in accordance with the laws of mythological evolution if Krishna took over Indra's title of Govid when he supplanted him and if the legend of the Gokula and the *gopis* were then all developed to explain the name Govind or Govid by a pastoral people as the Ahírs were. The theory of a Christian origin for the name of Krishna and the massacre of the innocents overlooks the fact that in primitive folk-lore the father who is ignorant of his son's existence and who takes steps to remove all children likely to be dangerous to himself is a stock character. We have another form of it in the legend that when the tyranny of the demon Kansa over the earth became intolerable she, in the form of a cow, complained to Indra who sought redress from Vishnu. The latter god plucked two hairs from his head, one white impersonated as Balaráma, the other black, as Krishna Soon after when Kansa was driving the *rishis* Vásudeva and his wife Deoki in a chariot a voice thundered from the sky that the eighth child of the woman whom he was driving would take away his life. So Kansa slew all Deoki's seven children, but Krishna, the eighth, was changed for the child of Nanda, the cow-herd, and he and his wife fled with the infant to Gokula, leaving their own child to be dashed against a stone by Kansa.[3] And to this day the eighth child is unlucky to its father.

THE INCARNATIONS OF VISHNU.—The incarnations avatáras) of Nárayana or Vishnu are variously given. The original six appear to be the boar (Varáha), man lion (Nrisinha), dwarf (Vámana) Ráma of the Bhrigu race and that assumed for the destruction of Kansa (Vásudeva-Krishna). Then to these were added Hamsa (the swan), Kurma (tortoise), Matsya (fish) and Kalkin, or future *avatáras*. The incarnations given however sometimes number as many as 23, and include sages like Nárada, Kapila, Datthátreya Risabha, undoubtedly the Jain Tirthankara, Dhanvantari, the teacher of medicine, and the Budha Finally ten incarnations seem to have been recognised as the orthodox number, and they were Matsya, Kúrma, Varáha, Nrisinha, Vámana, Parasuráma, Rám Chandr, Krishna, Buddha and Kalki These *avatáras* or descents are the distinctive feature of Vishnu who, whenever any great calamity overtook

[1] A mound in the characteristic shape of this mount may sometimes be noticed near a village by the side of a road in the Punjab.
[2] Bhandarkar, *op. cit*, pp. 35-38.
[3] E. Osborn Martin, *The Gods of India*, London, 1914, pages 133-34.

the sons of man or their progress was opposed by the *asuras*, came to earth in some form to rescue them and, his task fulfilled, returned to the skies. "Some of these are of an entirely cosmical character; others, however, are probably based on historical events ....." The course of evolution is also through the lower forms of life to the lowest form of manhood and thence to semi-divine man.[1]

Maclagan, § 59.

RAMCHANDAR AND KRISHNA.—The adoration of Rám is almost co-extensive with Hinduism. Every Hindu knows the main points in his history as told in the *Rámáyan*. Every Hindu sees his triumph in the yearly festival of the Dusehra; and the repetition of his name is the common method of salutation between Hindus all over India. Rám (or Rámchand, or Rámavtár, or Raghu Rám, or Raghnáth, as he is variously called) of Ajudhia or Oudh was the husband of Sítá, the son-in-law of Janak, the brother of Lachman; and these names are not uncommonly mentioned along with his Sítá especially is often worshipped in conjunction with Rám as Rádhá is with Krishn. Lachman, or Lachman Jatí, the chaste, is supposed to have gained superhuman power by his austerities, and his worship is especially popular in the central portions of the Punjab. His shrines are often attended by Musalman ministrants.[2]

Krishn, as a hero of romance, is as well known as Rám, and though the actual worship of this incarnation is probably not as extensive as that of the other there are particular bodies of men who venerate Krishn with an exclusive devotion such as is not found in the worship of Rám.

The scripture most intimately connected with the worship of Krishn is the *Bhágavat Gíta*, in which he is the principal speaker. The country round Mathra and Bindrában and the holy shrines at Dwárka are the chief places of pilgrimage affected by his followers. Srí Krishnají himself goes by many names. He is called Devkinandan after his mother, Nand Lál after his foster-father, and Vásdev after his real father. He is known also as Kesho or Smaljí or Murlídhar, as Gwáljí or Gopál, the great herdsman, and as Ranchor, the coward, from his Horatian discretion in the battle with Jarásindha. He is worshipped also in connection with his brother Baldeo and his wife Rádhá[3]; and one of the famous shrines of Rádhá and Krishn is probably that at Hodal in Gurgaon. Krishn is more particularly the patron of the Ahírs or cowherds; but his worship is also especially popular among the Bánias of the south-east and the Khatrís of the Central Punjab.

Sir Denzil Ibbetson did not classify the Hindu cults into Vaishnava and Shaiva. This was done by Sir Edward Maclagan and the

[1] Martin, *op. cit*, pp. 99-100, citing Kennedy, *Hindu Mythology*, p. 244.

[2] He is said also to be known as Pápúji and to be worshipped as such in Mewár by the Thorí and other castes. His followers in the Punjab are all returned from the Fázilka and Muktsar tahsíls of Ferozepur. There is another Lachman, a Mallí Jat, whose shrines are known as *máris* and who has a considerable reputation in Siálkot, more especially at a place called Badiána.

[3] The Rádhá-Swámís of our Census tables are a sect of recent origin, started by Rái Sálig Rám of the Postal Department in the United Provinces; details regarding their tenets will be found in *Punjab Census Reps*, 1902, pp. 130-1, and 1912, p. 141.

classification greatly aids us to understand the bewildering mass of details which a study of Hinduism in the modern Punjab reveals.

Vishnu, the sole survivor of the great Vedic gods in the modern Hindu pantheon, is essentially a personal god. Without dogmatising or laying undue emphasis on certain points of difference we may say that he is in marked contrast to Shiva because the latter is rather to be regarded as a deification of the material universe than as a personal god independent of that universe. Many qualifications must be understood and many points of resemblance admitted in thus distinguishing the conception of Vishnu from that of Shiva, but fundamentally it will be seen that the distinction is the key-note to much that is elusive in the two creeds. Vishnu as a personal god is the creator, loving and compassionate. Shiva is the destroyer, as well as the creator.

In speaking of the Vaishnava cults it must be borne in mind that there are two Krishnas—one of Dwárká, who was a great nature-god of immemorial antiquity, worshipped in the Kábul mountains and the Indus valley; the other the child Krishna. And in the Krishna of Dwárká again three Krishnas can be traced: (*i*) there is the chief of Dwárká, whom the bards of the *Mahábhárata* compliment with the rank of a Yádava, though he is clearly a dark-skinned indigenous hero of the lower Indus at a time when the Indus valley was a land of degraded Aryas, Shúdras and Abhíras, and the Kshatriyas were far inferior to those whom Parasuráma had destroyed.

(*ii*) As a god the dark Krishna is associated with his elder brother the white Balaráma, but in spite of his immemorial antiquity as a great god on the North-West Frontier he appears in what looks like a description of a historical siege of the city of the Daitya king Shálwa.

(*iii*) The original Krishna of the Indus valley underwent a gradual fusion, at first with Indra and then with the Vedic Vishnu. Though called Upendra, or the lesser Indra, and Govinda, or the herdsman of the rain-clouds, his final development came from the purely Aryan Vishnu, but was not completed till 400 A. D. He is identified with almost complete certainty as the Indian Dionysos who was worshipped in the hills and the Indus valley as well as in the regions north and north-west of the Indus, *i.e.* in Ariane, and possibly in Bactria also.

The child Krishna of Mathura first makes his appearance at the end of the 5th or early in the 6th century A. D.

The modern Hindu doctrine of works merits notice.[1] As it is assumed as the basis of the doctrine of *bhakti* that faith, and faith alone, can save a man, the question naturally arises as to what relation his good or evil works bear to his salvation. This question is mixed up with the puzzle of predestination, which has given birth to two schools, the 'cat'-school which teaches that Bhágavat saves the soul as a cat takes up its kitten, without free-will on the latter's part, and the 'monkey'-school which declares that in order to be saved the soul must

[1] Sir George Grierson, *The Modern Hindu Doctrine of Works*, in J. R. A. S., 1908, p. 337 *et seqq.*

reach out and embrace Bhágavat, as a young monkey clings to its mother. Nearly all the *bhakti* sects of Northern India are followers of the latter school and naturally investigate the problem of works. Their answer to it is that good works which are disinterested produce *bhakti*; and that it is *bhakti*, not the works themselves, which wins release from the weary round of endless births and re-births.

The Bhágavatas have taken the old Brahmanical system of ten *avatáras* and largely developed it. Usually translated 'incarnation', *avatára* has a much wider significance from their point of view and may be translated "descent."[1] The Supreme, as *Avatárin* or Descender, descends in one of four characters as (1) a Vyúha, or phase of conditioned spirit, (2) a *Vibhu* or *Vibhava Avatára*, (3) an *Antaryámin* or (4) *Arohá Avatára*. Of these the *Vibhu Avatáras* interest us more for the present purpose which is to show how the *bhakti* sects reconcile their tenets with the older Hinduism. These *Avatáras* may be *Púrna*, 'Complete,' as were Ráma-Chandra, Krishna, the Man-lion and, according to some, the Dwarf; or they may be *Ansa*, 'partial,' as were the Fish, the Boar, the Tortoise, *the Dwarf*, Hari, Hayagriva, Dhruva's Boon-giver, Nara-Náráyana, and perhaps Kapila, or they may be *Kalá* 'fractional,' as were the Swan, Datta, *Kapila*, Sanaka and his brethren, with perhaps Kalki, and Dhanvantari. All these are *Mukhya* or principal *Avatáras*.

Another class of *Avatáras* is called *Gauna* or subordinate. It includes Shakti, 'Power' or Kárya, 'purpose'; and Avesha, 'taking possession' *Avatáras*. Such are Parasu-Ráma, the Buddha, *Kalki*, Manvantara, the Vyása, Prithu, Yajna, Risábha, Dhanvantari, Mohini, Lakshmi-nivasa, and others. As the Bhágavata faith was originally propounded by Kshatriyas its followers naturally relegate Parasu-Ráma, the exterminator of the Kshatriya 'race', to a very subordinate place in the series of Avatáras.[2]

The *Vibhúti Avatáras* or Governance Descents include *Brahma, Nárada*, Shiva, Manu, Sváyambhuva, Rámánanda, and others.

Descent as an image or *Archa Avatára* is based on the theory that an idol, *múrti*, is merely stone or metal until it is consecrated. It then becomes a descent of the Supreme for worship.[3]

Thus the *Bhágavata Vibhu* descents alone number 24, as against the 10 *avatáras* of the Brahmanical system, which they place first. Space precludes fuller description of them, but they include the Hansa or Swan from whom three of the four great modern Bhakti-apostles trace their spiritual descent. The Swan taught Sanaka and his brethren[4] who taught Nárada (whom some identify with the Swan), who taught Nimbárka, the founder of the oldest, the Nimáwat, church of modern Bhágatvatism. The Swan also taught Brahmá who taught Subuddha, who taught Nara-

[1] J. R. A. S., 1909, p. 623.

[2] *Ib.*, p. 625.

[3] *Ib.*, p. 627.

[4] Sanakádi is the collective term for Sanaka, Sananda, Sanatana and Sanat-kumára, the four mind born sons of Brahmá. They enjoyed perpetual youth and innocence, and hence this incarnation is known as the Kumára Avatára, from Kumára, a youth. They are sometimes called the four "Sanas": *ib.*, p. 624.

bhari, who taught Madhva, founder of the Madhváchári church. Shiva who is the object of great veneration amongst all Bhágavatas, taught Nárada, who taught the Vyása of the Veda, who taught Shuka, who taught Vishnusvámin, who taught Paramánáda. Forty-eighth in spiritual descent from him Vishnuvámin was born again and then became the real founder of the Rudra *sampradáya* or Rudra church.[1]

Shiva is regarded as himself the first or primeval *bhakta* or 'faithful' devotee by the Bhágavatas.[2]

Bhágavatas also admit that Shiva became incarnate as Sankaracharya, the great teacher of the Advaita system of philosophy. As this doctrine is radically opposed to the central tenets of the Bhágavata cult, Shiva's connexion is got over by explaining that when the world was filled with Buddhism and other forms of false religion, the Adorable appeared to Shiva, directing him to become incarnate and to preach a doctrine invented by himself (Shiva), so as to turn people from the Adorable and to manifest His glory by the consequent destruction of unbelievers.

The commentators on the *Bhakta-mála* tell two stories which they say are not generally known, but which illustrate Shiva's *bhakti* towards the Adorable. Herewith is given a free translation of Priya-dása's version of these, filling up *lacunæ* from the commentary of Bhagawan Prasada and from the *Bhakti-premákara* of Kirti Simha. The latter tells the legends at greater length and in full detail.[3]

Satí, the wife of Sankara (Shiva), once, under the influence of delusion, asked why, if Ráma (an incarnation of the Adorable[4]) were really the Supreme Deity, he was wandering about in the desert distraught at the loss of Síta. Shiva warned her against such irreverent thoughts, but without success, and she went forth to test Ráma's divine knowledge. As she departed Shiva cautioned her to be careful as to what she did. In spite of this Satí took Sítá's own form, and, so far as she could imagine, made herself Sítá's exact image. She approached Ráma as he was wandering in the forest, but he at once saw that she was not his beloved and would not speak to her. Satí returned to heaven and told this to Shiva, who became greatly distressed, and reproached her with having ventured to take the form of the special object of his loving worship, Sítá, the divine spouse of the incarnate Adorable. Thereafter he refused to treat Satí as his wife or to be reconciled to her so long as she remained in her then birth. Satí accordingly destroyed herself by becoming 'suttee' at Daksha's sacrifice,[5] and being born again as Párvati was in due course wedded to Shiva. Priyá-dása adds to this story that it is very dear to him and that he sings it with especial delight.

The other legend is that one day Shiva and Párvati went out riding on the bull Nandi to visit the earth. On the way as they passed two

[1] J. R. A. S., 1909, p. 639.
[2] *Ib.*, p. 639.
[3] *Ib.*, p. 640.
[4] A parallel to 'He saved others, himself he cannot save
[5] Most Vaishnava sects worship Sítá as an incarnation of the Adorable, as well as Ráma. According to the usual account Satí killed herself because Daksha abused Shiva, her husband, whom he had not invited to the sacrifice.

mounds where there had once been villages, long since fallen to ruin, Shiva dismounted, and bowed himself to each. Párvati asked him to whom he paid reverence as there was no one in sight. He replied:—"Dearest, on one of these mounds there dwelt 10,000 years ago one who loved Ráma and Sítá, and who was supremely faithful (*bhakta*), and on the other, 10,000 years hence, will there be another king of *bhaktas*. For this reason both these places are to be highly reverenced by me." Párvati heard these words and kept them in her heart. Therefrom her affection for *bhaktas* increased beyond limit, so that now it cannot even be described. Yea, the white garment of her heart is dyed deep with love for them.

With the *Vibhúti Avatára*[1] Rámánanda we enter the domain of history. He founded the Rámávat sect of Rámánuja's Sri Sampradáya and to him Northern India really owes its conversion to modern Bhágavatism.

The following is a list of some of the principal Vaishnava shrines in Kángra:—

The *mandir* of Thákur Brij Rai in Núrpur was founded by Rájá Jagat Singh of Núrpur some 450 years ago. He conquered Chatorgarh and thence brought the Thákur's image.[2]	Brahman, *got* Káshab.	Three fairs are annually held in Jeth, Hár and Bhádon on Nársingh *chaudas*, *nirjala akádshi* and *janam ashtmi*.	The temple contains a black stone image of the Thákur, 5 ft. high, and one of Lachmi, 3 ft. high. *Bhog* is offered 4 times a day and consists of fruit, sugar, rice or bread. A sacred lamp, in which *ghi* is burnt, is lit daily in the evening. No distinction is made in the offerings of Hindus.
The *mandir* of Thákur Madan Mohan at Núrpur was founded by Rájá Madan Mohan nearly 1000 years ago. Shankar Swámi used to pay his devotions here.	A Saniási, *got* Dáchhni who is celibate.	None ...	Rice in the morning and fried things in the evening form the sacramental food. A sacred lamp is lit in the evening. The temple which is in bad repair contains a black marble image of the Thákur and a brass image of Bil Bhaddar both 2½ feet high.

[1] J. R. A. S., 1909, p. 642.

[2] Connected with this are the shrines of Rám Chandji, Lachmi Náráin, Ambká and Chaunda. The first contains images of Rám Chand and Sítá, Lachhman and Hanúmán, all of marble, set on a stone 5 feet high. The second Lachmi and Náráin—of black stone each a foot high. The third 3 images, between 1½ and 2½ feet high and the fourth a carving 2½ feet high. Four *pujáris* are in charge of these temples—caste Brahman, *got* Sársút.

Kidár Náth at Shurah. This temple is said to have been founded by Jaswant Singh's ancestor, a Gautam Rájpút.	A Jogi Náth, *got* Chauhán.	People gather on 25th Jeth and make offerings of wheat at every harvest.	The temple contains a black stone *pindi* of Shivji ½ span high and one in circumference. Worship is performed twice a day, rice or bread being offered as *bhog* morning and evening.
Kidár Náth's *mandir* at Sahúra.	A Giri Gosáín, *got* Bihingan.	The *panchmi tith* following the *amáwas* of Phágan.	It contains a black stone image one foot high and ½ foot in circumference. *Bhog* of fruit or sugar is offered in the morning and bread or rice is used as such in the evening.
In Bihlu Chiri Lachhmi Náráin.	Brahman, *got* Parásar.	On the day after the Diwáli a *jag* called *ankút*.	Bread fried in *ghí* in the morning and fried gram in the evening as *bhog*.
Lachmi Náráin at Gharoh	A Dhíchat Brahman, by *gotar* a Bashist.	None ...	The temple contains images of Náráin and Lachmi, engraved on a stone slab which is one cubit square. A *shivdiwála* containing a *pindi* of Shiva is connected with it, in which occasional worship is performed. Bread in the morning and soaked gram in the evening are offered as *bhog*.
The *mandir* of Lachhmi Náráin in Sangam on the Ban Ganga.	A Brahman, caste Dédal, *got* Koshal.	During the *naurátra* people come to bathe at the temple and a small fair is held.	The old image of Lachhmi Náráin has been replaced by one of Gauri Shankar engraved on a black stone slab, 1½ cubits long by 1 broad. Worship is performed only in the morning, when gram or fruit is offered as *bhog*.
Mandir or Thákardáwara Balkará at Ujain.	A Brahman caste, Lakhútra, *got* *Sandal*.	None ...	It contains marble images of Rádha and Krishna which are 1 foot high The temple is 15 cubits high. Worship is performed morning and evening. *Púri* in the morning and fried gram in the evening form the *bhog*.
Mandir Ganesh jí in Daulatpur. The building which is in a dilapidated condition stands on a platform called *tidlá*.	Brahman, caste Kamláyá, *got* Kodiná.	None ...	Worship is only performed in the morning when milk, *pera* or fruit is offered as *bhog*.

In the Kángra District about two-thirds of the women, and some of the men believe in Nársingh. It is said that he gives sons and assists in all difficulties His worshippers keep a *nárjil* (cocoanut) and *chandan* (sandal-wood, paste Every Sunday or on the first Sunday of each Hindu month they worship him by putting the *nárjil* on a brass plate (*tháli*), first washing it with fresh water Then they put a *tilak* of the *chandan* on it, just as Brahmans mark their foreheads, and then an *achhat* of as much washed rice as will stay on three fingers of the right hand *i.e.* on the thumb, first and second or middle finger. When this is done they adorn the *nárjil* with flowers, and then burn some *dhúp* (*dolomicea macrocephala*), besprinkled with powdered camphor, sandalwood, almonds and spices. It is made into pastilles, and when burnt emits a pleasant odour. The *nárjil* is then worshipped as Nársing and the sweetmeats offered to it are subsequently distributed to the children and other members of the household and to the neighbours. Nársingh's worshippers also wear a *bahuṭa* (amulet), containing a picture of him in the form of a man. This *bahuṭa* is of silver, and is worshipped like the *nárjil*. A ring, generally made of silver with a projection towards the nail, is also worn on the little finger in his honour and it too is worshipped. A special costume is also worn during this worship. When a mother or mother-in-law worships Nársing, her daughter or daughter-in-law must also do so. Barren women consulting a *chela* or a *jogi* are usually advised to worship Nársingh for offspring. He is believed to cohabit with women in their dreams in the form of a Brahman and aged from 12 to 20 years, and clothed in white When a woman is sick a *chela* is sent for to charm away her illness. If he says that Nársingh's anger has caused it he orders a *baiṭhak*. If she do not happen to have a *bahuṭa*, or the proper rings or clothes or a *nárjil*, the *chela* orders any of them that may be lacking to be procured before performing the *baiṭhak*. The *baiṭhak* ceremony is as follows :—On a Sunday, or any other fixed day, the *chela* comes with a *baitri* or singer of sacred songs, who plays on a *dopatra*, an instrument made of two *tumbas* (ascetic's bowls) connected by a bamboo rod. A wire runs along this rod fastened to its extremities so as to give out a sound when twanged. The *baitri* sings his song and the *chela* repeats his magic words, and then Nársingh comes and shakes the woman's body or of the *chelas*. The tremors last two hours or more, during which time the man or woman into whom the spirit has entered tells the fortunes of those attending the *baiṭhak*. They are usually told to worship some deity who will cure the sick woman. While the patient or the *chela* keeps shivering with the force of the spirit in him, the *baitri* sings an incantation, accompanying himself on the *dopatra*. The following is its translation :—

1. O friend born at the fort of Mathura, that wast incarnate in Gokal.

Refrain.

O my Nársingh, O great Naranjan !
O thou that hast captivated me (*bis*) :
O thou that hast captivated the whole world ;
O my Nársingh, O my Lord Naranjan.

2. O friend, son of Vásudeva, child of Yasodha.

3. Where the maids and virgins are, there is thy home.

4. Thy home is in the mangoes, in young mangoes, in wells and in tanks.

5. Thy home is in the *pípals*, in young *pípals* and the jasmines.

6. Red as red can be is thy turban flowered and crested, fine the robes on thy body.[1]

In Kulu Nársingh is regarded as one of the most potent demons of those spirit-haunted hills. He dwells in abandoned houses and in flower gardens, as well as in large temples, and is said to affect women and children more at night and noon-tide than at any other time. To cure one so affected a goat is sacrificed to him and sweet bread and a garland of flowers are offered. He is also made the patient's brother in this wise: a Brahman is given a turban and called Nársingh; and he treats the afflicted woman as his own sister. Thenceforth he and Nársingh are both regarded as her brothers. When Nársingh cohabits with women in dreams he is said to wear white garments, but his usual dress is a white *dhoti* and a turban, and he carries a cocoanut *huqqa*. This cult is special, if not restricted, to the twice-born castes.

At Nagar in Suket Nársingh is worshipped under the name of Pákhán, whose idol resembles those of Sálig Rám to be found in Punjab temples and is kept in a locked coffer in which there is a narrow hole through which Pákhán may be seen, but permission to look upon him has to be obtained from the State and even the *pujári* who bathes and feeds him has to keep him eyes closed and his face averted from him. It is dangerous to gaze upon him and a *sádhu* who was once allowed to do so died and thieves who stole from his temple were struck blind.[2] In Mandi Nársingh is found in temples to Gúga with many other deities.[3]

Other spirits classed with Nársingh are Kalia Bír, Dakni, Shamshán *bhút* and Banshera All these seem to have the power of assuming any shape or costume. They cause madness and disease, and to get rid of them spells are obtained from sorcerers and *sádhús* as well as from Brahmans and the *deotás* themselves

Kalia Bír seems to be the same as Kala Bíru, Kala-báhan or Kala Bhairon. He will possess any one with whom he is wrath but as a rule he will not affect a man until he is irritated by his *sadhak* (?) against him and then he will sometimes kill him. He can be propitiated by sacrificing a sheep etc. When he is a-hunting it is dangerous to see him as a sight of him causes possession by an evil spirit.

Nársingh photár, at the petrifying spring and cascade in the Katha gorge in the Salt Range, is a place of pilgrimage.

[1] "Anár Singh is the Nrisinha *avatára* of Vishnu, but the above song is to Krishna, some verses of which are commonly sung all over the Punjab at the Rás Líla, which commemorates the dance of Krishna with the Gopís. This mixing up of the Nrisinha and Krishna *avatáras* of Vishnu is very curious."—P. N. Q. I., §§ 585, 757. But this note confuses Nársingh with Narsingh who is the Man-Lion incarnation of Vishnu. In Chamba Nársingh is regarded as the *wazír* of Gugga Chauhán and the idea that he is identical with Nársingh is ridiculed.

[2] Suket *Gazetteer*, p. 22.

[3] Mandi *Gazetteer*, p. 39.

1	2	3	4
Place.	*Pujári.*	Date of fair.	Ritual offerings &c.
Amajgrán ...	Brahman, Rasontri by *got* and Gurg by *gotra*.	*Badi ashṭami* in Bhádon.	As *bhog*, any food prepared by the *pujári*, twice a day.
Sháhpur ...	Bairagi-Achhút ..	*Janam ashṭami* ...	Food cooked by the *pujári* as *bhog*.
Tirṭi founded in the time of Rájá Umed Singh of Chamba, 150 years ago.	Brahman-Koshal ..	None, but at the *janam ashṭami* people collect and the idol is placed in a *ḍol* (cradle) and worshipped.	Boiled rice in the morning, and bread in evening as *bhog*.
Tirṭi ...	Brahman—a Kashmíri by *got* and by *gotar* a Koshal	No fair, but same rite is observed.	Same, fruit being offered as *bhog* during a fast.
Rihlu, founded by a Brahman over 100 years ago when Rihlu was a part of Chamba.	A Kashmíri Brahman, Káship *got* (*sic*).	Same rite. This temple also contains a relief of Lachhmi.	Bread or rice in the morning and soaked gram in the evening.
Ghanhára, built 7 generations ago in time of Rána Partáp Singh Ghaniárach.	Brahman, *got* Chhatárani and *gotar* Batas.	Some 20 years ago Nársingh's image was thrown into a stream and replaced by one of Lachhmi Náráin, carved in relief on a slab with Sheshnág on one side and two boys on the other.	
The temple of Thákur Nársingh in Fatehpur was founded by Mahant Mohan Dás, a man endowed with power to work miracles. He brought a stone *pinḍi* from the Deccan which he enshrined in this temple 500 years ago.	Bairági, *got* Achchat.	*Janam ashṭami* in Bhádon, Holí in Phágan and *Rámnaumí* in Chet.	It contains images of Rám Chand, Rádha and Krishna, a *pinḍi* and a crane, made of marble and in height from one to two feet. Eleven lamps in which *ghí* is burnt are lit every evening. Muhammadans, Chamárs and other low castes are not allowed to make offerings.

VAISHNAVA CULTS IN THE HIMALAYAS.[1]

In the Sirmúr State, Punjab, the Hindus have two chief cults, one Vaishnava, the other Saiva. The former of these two is represented by the cult of Paras Rám and his derivative deities, which centres in Rainká-jío,[2] in the Ráinka *tahsíl* of the State at a great lake. Paras Rám's brothers are usually supposed to have become water, but, according to one local variant, Jámdaggan called his brothers cowards and turned them into women, so that now they are *devís* or goddesses, to wit: Lá Deví, Dormaí, Bhadwachhrí or Bhadarkálí, and Kamlí, all of whom have temples in the State. The local cult and ritual of Paras Rám are described in the *Gazetteer* of Sirmúr, 1904, and to that description may be added the following *mantra* or prayer, and the *kabits* or couplets which are given below :—

TRANSLATION.

The story of Sri Ragunáth of the thousand names, by whose grace we sing the praises of Hari.

Om! Om! Om! The stainless light of the letter Om![3] From the light the navel, from the navel the lotus, from the lotus was born Brahmá. He took his staff and bowl[4] and went to bathe. Shankásúr, the Dánav, was born.

[1] Compare *Indian Antiquary*, XXXII, p. 376, "Hinduism in the Himalayas."

[2] *Jío* is apparently an old form of *jí*, and the localised form of the legend runs that Jámdaggan Rishí used to practise austerities at a peak called Jambu-kí-Dhar, near Jambu, where a *márí* or temple still exists at the spot where the *rishí* had his *dhúní* or fire. The *pujárí* of Jambu still visits this *márí* every Sunday and *sankránt* day to worship there. Jámdaggan's wife, Rainka Jí, had a sister Bainka who was married to Rájá Sahansárbáhu ('of the thousand arms'), and once when *rishí* celebrated a *jag*, Bainka asked Rainka to invite her to it. Rainka begged the *rishí* to do so, but at first he refused, because he could not afford to entertain a *rájá* and his queen. He yielded, however, to Rainká's reiterated request and asked the God Indra to grant him Kámdhan, the cow of plenty, Kapl-brikhsh, the tree of paradise which yielded all manner of gifts, and Kuber, *bhandárí*, the celestial steward who could supply all kinds of luxuries. When the *rájá* arrived with all his court the *rishí* was thus enabled to entertain him sumptuously, and the *rájá* was so mystified as to the source of the *rishí's* wealth, that he deputed his barber to find out whence it came. Learning that Kámdhan was the main source of supply, the *rájá* asked for the cow as a gift, which the *rishí* refused, and so the *rájá* determined to take her by force, but the *rishí* sent her into the sky to Indra. Thereupon the *rájá* shot an arrow at the cow and wounded her in the foot, so the cow returned and attacked him. The *rájá* attributing this to the *rishí's* sorcery, put him to death and returned home, Rainka, taking the *rishí's* body in her lap, was bewailing his death, when she was divinely told that Kuber, *bhandárí*, had the *amrit* or elixir of life, and that a drop of it placed in the dead *rishí's* mouth would bring him back to life. So the *rishí* was restored to life and ordered his younger sons to kill Rainka, thinking that she had instigated his murder with intention of marrying Sahansárbáhu, but they refused. Then the *rishí* summoned Paras Rám, his eldest son, who was then practising austerities in the Konkan, and who appeared in an instant. Paras Rám killed his mother, and then, in consequence of the divine curse which fell upon him, went to the plains (*des*), and swore to kill all the Chhatrís and to swim in their blood, deeming Sahansárbáhu the cause of all his misery. Waging his war of extermination against the Chhatrís he had reached Kurukshetr, where Indra learnt what bloodshed he was causing in fulfilment of his oath and sent rain until the water rose to the height of man, and caused the upper currents to turn red. Meanwhile Jámdaggan had been searching for his son and, meeting him with his axe on his shoulders, was so pleased with his performances that he asked if he had any desire. Paras Rám in reply begged his father to restore his mother and brothers to life, and performed his mother's funeral rites. The *rishí* replied that his wife and sons had become *jal sarúp* or water, and that the former was in the larger and the latter in the smaller of the tanks at Rainka.

[3] *i. e.* first came the stainless light.

[4] *i. e.* the *dand* and *karmandal* carried by *faqírs*.

Brahmá then taught the Védas, and for that purpose Brahmá went to Siva's abode. (Said he): "Shivjí, thou art the slayer, thou art the Creator, thou knowest the meaning of the Four Védas."

Said Mahádév (Siva): "I meditate on the virtues (of God), I ask alms, I repeat (the name) of Harí (Vishnu). He is the slayer! He is the Creator! He knows the meaning of the Four Védas.

"For this he first assumed the Machh (Fish) incarnation. The mother of the Fish was Shankháwati, the father Purav Rishí, the teacher Mándhátá the birth-place Mánsarowar (Lake). He slew Shankhásúr, the Dánav.

"Secondly, Náráin (Vishnu) assumed the Kurm (Tortoise) Incarnation. The mother of the Tortoise was Karnáwati, the father Bilochan Rishí, the teacher Dhagisat Báwá Rishí, the birth-place Dhangarpurí. He slew Mádho Kítav, the Dánav.

"Thirdly, he assumed the Baráhrúp (Boar) Incarnation. The mother of the Boar was Líláwatí, the father Kaul Rishí, the teacher Sahaj Rishí, the birth-place Kanakpur. He slew Hirnákáshap, the Dánav.

"Fourthly, Naráin (Vishnu) assumed the Nársingh (Man-lion) Incarnation. The mother of the Man-lion was Chandrawatí, the father Harí-brahm Rishí, the teacher Káshi Rishí, the birth-place Multánpurí. He slew Hirnakhásh, the Dánav.

"Fifth, Náráin (Vishnu) assumed the Báwan incarnation. The mother of the Báwan was Langáwatí, the father Bilchan Rishí, the teacher Káshap Rishí, the birth-place Benáres. He deceived Balrájá and slew him.

"Sixth, Náráin (Vishnu) assumed the Paras Rámjí Incarnation. The mother of Paras Rámjí was Rainkájí, the father Jámdagganjí, the teacher Agast Munijí, the birth-place Kopalpurí. He slew Sahansár-báhu, the Dánav.

"Seventh, he assumed the Srí Rámchandarjí Incarnation. The mother of Rám Chandarjí was Kaushalyá, the father Dasrath, the teacher Bashisht Muní, the birth-place Ajudhiápurí. He slew Dshásur Ráwan.

"Eighth, Srí Náráin (Vishnu) assumed the Krishn Incarnation. The mother of Krishn was Dewkí, the father Básdev, the teacher Durbháshá Rishí, the birth-place Muthorápúri. He slew Kansásur.

"Ninthly, Náráin (Vishnu) assumed the Budh-rúp (Buddha) Incarnation. The mother of Budh was Padmáwatí, the father Bilochan Rishí, the teacher Dhagesat Bánú Rishí, the birth-place Parsotampurí. He slew Gayásur, the Dánav.

"Tenthly, Náráin (Vishnu) will assume the tenth Incarnation. When will he assume it? Now[1] he will assume it in the month of *Mágh*, in the light half, in the Réwatí Nakshatra, on Saturday, the

[1] At the following conjunction of the stars.

eighth of the month He will be a man thirty-two yards in (height), his sword will be eighteen yards (long), his swish will be nine yards (long). It will rain heavily. White his horse, white his saddle, heavy clouds about him, an umbrella over his head. Salt water will become sweet. The elephant will give milk. Sour milk will become sweet. The mother of Nishkalank[1] is Matangí, the father Dhanuk Rishí, the teacher Sahaj-rúp Rishí, the birth-place Sambhélángrí He slays Nishkalank (?), the Dánav.

The following are some of the couplets or *kabits* addressed to Paras Rám at Rainká-joi :—

THE *KABITS*.

1

Parbat chír tal band nír ghará jahán bhar mand hai,
Bádsháh gharíb dhiáwen kaláh jahán par chand hai.
The hill was broken, and the lake made full of deep water,
Kings and the poor worship (there), and the miracle is known far and wide.

2

Ashnán kíé páp ját, dhián kíé táp ját,
Darshan kíé saráp ját, máyá jahán aisí akhand hai.
By bathing sins fly away, by devoutly meditating trouble flees,
By looking at (it) curses depart, where such prosperity is ?

3

Chanan samán káshat jahán,
Kanchan samán pákhán jahán,
Shír samán nír jahán, aisá adhbat mand hai.
Wood is like sandal,
Stone like gold,
and water like milk at this wondrous place.

4

Rainká samán tírath nahíṇ, lók tarí lók bhawan meṇ,
Gupat jagah bás kíto chárón taraf jahán ban khand hai.
There is no place so sacred as Rainká,
The place that is holy and densely wooded all round.

5

Kitní hí tírath básí aisá rakhte hain agyán,
Jinko ashnán karná phánsí ke barábar ḍand hai.
Some pilgrims are so foolish,
That to bathe is to them as great a penalty as hanging.

[1] The name of the Tenth incarnation.

6

Man meṇ dhiáweṇ aur kám mukh se bóleṇ jai Paras Rám,

Din rát pare karén árám, jinkó darshan karná sehr hai.

They are thinking of other things, while with their lips they say 'Jai Pars Rám.'

They take their ease night and day, but to visit a temple is poison to them

7

Kahe Déwá Hírá Lál, men pápi ká chhor khiál,

Hoi Paras Rám diál, Jin par unki mihr hai.

Says Déwá Lál, 'Take no thought of your sin,

Paras Rám favours those to whom he is gracious.

The following list shows how numerous and important the Vishnu temples are in Kulu[1] and the variations in the dates on which the fairs and festivals are held :—

Deota Náráin	Garauge Dera ...	Either on Sunday, Monday, Wednesday or Saturday in the light halves of Phágan and Sáwan. A large fair is held every 12th year.
Ditto ..	Dera Náráin ...	On the 3rd, 5th or 7th of the light half of Sáwan and Phágan.
Ditto (a) ...	Dera ...	1st, 3rd and 8th Baisákh, and 1st to 7th Mágh.
Ditto ...	Dera Bishkola in Bishkola.	
Ditto (b) ..	No special name. In Dumchin.	Full moon day of Maghar, 9th, 15th and 16th of Bhádon and 2nd, 15th and 16th of Phágan.
Deota Lachhmi Náráin	Náráin Sari ...	1st Phágan, in Chet, 1st to 11th and 21st Baisákh, 1st Jeṭh, 7th Har, in Sáwan, during the Anant Chandas, 1st Asauj, in Har, 1st Maghar, and 1st Poh.
Ditto (c) ...	Dera Náráin Nahi in Bhallan. Also called Dera Bhallan.	1st, 9th and 11th Phágan, 1st to 5th Baisákh, 6th and 14th Baisákh, 18th Baisákh, 1st to 6th Sáwan, 7th, 9th or 11th Bhádon, in Bhádon, 1st Asauj, 1st Maghar, and 1st Poh.
Ṭhákur Lachhmi Náráin (d).	Lachhmi Náráin.	
Ṭhákur Lachhmi Náráin	Mandir Shailru ...	Third of the lunar month of Poh.

[1] For some further notes on Náráin etc. in Kulu see under Hinduism in the Himalayas—*infra*.

(a) Three small temples are connected with this.

(b) Another temple of this god in Dumchin is connected with this temple.

(c) The temple of Sheah Nág is connected with this. It is called Sara Aga.

(d) These two temples are connected with that of Rám Chander.

Thákur Lachhmi Náráin	Lakhshmi Náráin and Nársingh Jí temples in Chogan.	Rám Naumi, Janam Ashtami, Dasehra, Jal Buhar, Ban Beehar, Diwáli, Ankut, Nársingh, Chandas Phág, Panj Bhikhami and Utran.
Ditto	No particular name ...	No fairs.
Deota Lachhmi Náráin	Kharasui and Batadhi...	9th Baisákh and 6th Bhádon.
Bhaltu Náráin ...	Dera Bhalta ...	On Sundays, Mondays, Wednesdays and Thursdays in Phágan, Sáwan and Asauj.
Deota Chagard Náráin...	Chagari dera ...	1st of Chet and full moon day of Chet.
Thákur Chhamaini Náráin	Dera Chhamaini Náráin	31st Chet, 1st Baisákh and 32nd Hár to 2nd Sáwan.
Harangu Náráin ...	Dera Gadyára ...	Sundays, Mondays, Wednesdays and Thursdays in the light halves of Phágan and Sáwan, on the 2nd of Baisákh, the 3rd and 4th of Hár (Asárh), the 3rd of Asauj and on the full moon day of Maghar.
Deota Hebab Náráin ...	Naraindi Dera ...	Ikádshi of the light half of Phágan for 6 days, 1st and 2nd Baisákh, 1st of Jeth, 2nd and 3rd Bhádon, 1st Asauj, Uchhab Atrain Sankránt for one day, first Thursday in Poh, and a *yag* after 12 years.
Deota Karohali Náráin (*e*)	Kalun Dera ...	On the 3rd, 5th, 7th, 8th and 10th of the dark halves of Sáwan, Maghar, Phágan and Baisákh.
Karosi Náráin (*f*) ...	Naraindi Dera in K. Tarapur.	Yearly from Sunday to Thursday in the dark half of Phágan and on the same days in Sáwan. But in Baisákh the fairs are only held on the Wednesday and Thursday. Another is held for one day in Maghar. Every third year a large gathering takes place during five days in Sáwan.
Deota Kasoli Náráin ...	Kasoli Náráin in K. Kanáwar.	1st of Chet and Shivrátri.
Deota Kesho Náráin ...	Dhara ...	1st Baisákh, 1st Chet and 1st Asauj.
Deota Khalari Náráin ...	Dera Khalari Náráin ...	No fairs, but two festivals during light halves of Phágan and Sáwan.
Phalaini Náráin ...	Dera Phallan ...	Sundays, Mondays, Wednesdays and Thursdays in the light halves of Sáwan and Phágan.
Deota Sammon Náráin...	Dhedai ...	1st Phágan.

(*e*) Two temples and a *bhandár* are connected with this. The *bhandár* and one temple are in Garaling village and the other temple in Rajang.

(*f*) The temples of the goddesses Nanti Hothi Maháijani and Phungani are connected with this. The expenses of their worship are borne by the god himself.

Deota Sapurra Náráin or Sapat Rikhi (*g*).	Dera ...	5th Baisákh and 30th Chet.
Deota Sarachti Náráin ..	Basti Katon ...	First Sunday in Phágan, at the beginning of the new year and on the Dhougari.
Siam Náráin ...	Dera Siam Náráin ...	On the *dwádshi* of the dark half of Phágan. Another on the 1st half of Asauj lasts for three days.
Deota Sikho Náráin (*h*)	Nagi Dera ...	1st of Baisákh, 7th of Sáwan.
Thákur Tarjogi Náráin (*i*).	Tarjogi Náráin ...	18th Hár, Rám Naumi in Baisákh, Janam Ashtami in Bhádon, Holi in Phágan, Ankut and Dewáli in Kátak: also a *yag* every 3rd year on 18th Hár
Deota Náráin Lapas ...	Deota Náráin ...	9th and 10th Sáwan.
Deota Náráin Maha ..	Ditto ..	Phágan.
Deota Náráin Pulga ...	Dera ...	1st of Jeth.
Thákur Chatar Bhoj in Kothi Dugi Lag.	Thákur Dawála Dugi Lag.	On the full moon days of Phágan and Chet.
Thákur Gopál ...	Thákur Dawála Sarsai ..	Japari fair for half a day 3rd light half of the month of Chet, Uchhab Rám Naumi one day in the month of Chet, Uchhab Janam Ashtami one day in the month of Bhádon, Ankut Díp Mála for two days on the Amáwas of the light half of Kátak, Uchhab Phág one day in Phagan.
Sri Gopál Jí ...	Kastar Dera ...	One festival in the month of Chet.
Deota Hari Náráin (*j*) .	Dera Náráin ...	Full moon day of Maghar, on the 9th, 10th and 16th of Bhádon and on the 9th, 15th and 16th of Phágan.
Thákur Jagan Náth	Jagar Náth ra Dawála	Naumi of Chet, on the Janam Ashtami.
Thákur Mádho Rai (*k*)	Thákur Dawála Haripur	Dasehra for 6 days, Basant Panchami for 1 day, birthday of Ráma 1 day. Dev Saini on *ikádshi*, Janam Ashtami for two days, Holi for 8 days, Díp Mála of *ikádshi*, Ankut for 1 day.

(*g*) Besides this there is another temple belonging to this god in Barogi Náráin. The ceremonies performed at these places are the same.

(*h*) A temple of the god Manun Rikhí is connected with this and is situate in Bhati village. Manun Rishí came to Manáli in the guise of a *faqír*. He saw a woman named Gauri Mani and the *rishí* asked her for milk. She replied 'my cow has gone to graze in the jungle I cannot get you milk at present.' The Rishí bade her: "Milk these calves,' she did so and from them drew milk which the Rishí drank. He displayed another miracle by killing a demon who lived in the village. Seeing this the people began to believe in him and built him a temple. The *pujári* is a Kanet of the Káshab *got*.

(*i*) Close to the big temple there is a smaller one.

(*j*) Another temple of this god in Kokari village is connected with this.

(*k*) A temple of the goddess Bhalamásan is connected with this.

Thákur Murlídhar and Chatar Chug. (*l*)	Two temples which bear the names of the deities to whom they are dedicated	Ninth of Asauj and lasts till full moonlight half of Mágh for one day, one day in the light half of Phágan, and one in Jeṭh.
Thákur Murlídhar Jí ...	Name of the god.	
Thákur Murlídhar attached to Rám Chandr Jí.	Murlídhar ...	Dasehra.
Thákur Murlídhar ...	Thákur Dowára ...	No fair.
Thákur Har Sinhk Jí (*m*)	Thákur Dawála Lohal in K. Khokhan.	Ninth of the light half of Chet. On the Janam Ashṭami, *i.e.* the 8th of the dark half of Bhádon and on the day of the full moon of Phágan.
Thákur Nársingh Jí ...	Thákurdowára Nársingh Jí.	
Ditto ...	Dawála Karjan ...	In Mágh, Sáwan and Phágan.
Ditto ...	Harma Náinán Jí ...	Rám Naumi in Chet, on the Janam Ashṭami in Bhádon, on the Ankut in Kátak, on the Holi in Phágan and on the Dewáli in Kátak.
Ditto ...	Thákur Dawála Washal	Rám Naumi which may fall either in Baisákh or in the light half of Chet and Janam Ashṭami in the light half of Bhádon for one day.
Deota Naro Mani (*n*) ..	Dera in K. Kothi Kandhi	1st Baisákh, 1st Jeṭh, 15th Har, 3rd Bhádon and any day in Bhádon.
Thákur Nársingh Jí ...	In Jhatin known by the name of the place.	One day in the month of Bhádon, 1 day in Kátak, 3 days during the dark half of Kátak, 1 in the light half of Phágan, one in the light half of Baisákh, and one in the light half of Sáwan.
Srí Thákur Raghu Náth Jí.	Called after the god in K. Shari.	10th to 16th of light half Asauj, 5th of light half of Mágh, full moon day in Phágan, 12th of light half of Baisákh, and *ikádshi* of light half of Jeṭh.
Thákur Rám Chandar Jí	Thákurdawára Rám Chandar Jí in Dorab.	
Deota Rám Chandar ...	Known by the name of the god.	Full moon day of Asauj or Kaṭák.

(*l*) The temple Chatar Bhuj is connected with this. Its worship is performed in the same way as that of Thákur Murlídhar.

(*m*) Inside the temple are images of Thákur Murlídhar and Síta Jí. They resemble a human being in appearance. Each of them is of stone and 1½ cubits high. It is said that in the time of Rájá Kans who troubled Parichhat and oppressed the people, Sri Bhagwán appeared as an incarnation of Krishan and killed Kans. In the time of the hill chiefs these images were in Bir Koṭgarh whence they were removed by the *kárdár* of Ad Brahmá and made over to a Bairági for worship when this territory passed into the hands of the Sikhs. When the Bairági died they were brought to this temple. No muáfi is attached to these temples and the god Brahmma gives them some money as *dharam arth* to meet the expenses of worship.

(*n*) Including the big temple there are six temples in all and at each fairs are held and ceremonies performed.

Ṭhakur Rám Chander Jí (*o*), Raghu Náth Ji, Chatar Bhuj and Nársingh Jí.	Ṭhákurdawára ...	Dasehra on Dasmi.
Ṭhákur Rám Chander Jí	Rám Chandar Jí ...	Rám Naumi in Baisákh, Janam Ashṭami in Bhádon, Holi in Phágan Ankut and Diwáli in Kátak.
Ditto	Ṭhákurdawára ...	No fair.
Ṭhákur Sáligrám Jí .	Ṭhákur Sáligrám Jí.	
Ṭhákur Síta Rám ...	Síta Rám Jí ...	Ninth of the light half of each month.
Ditto ...	Síta Rám Jí, Koṭhi Mahárája.	Rám Naumi in Chet, on the Janam Ashṭami of Bhádon, on the Ankut and Holi in Phágan and on the Díp Malka (Diwáli) in Kátak.
Ditto ...	...	Díp Mála, Rám Janam, Baisákh Ichhia Tirpana, Bin Behar, Jal Bihar, Nársingh Chaudas, Janam Ashṭami, Dasami, Basant, Ankut.
Ditto ...	Gujar Dawála ...	Asauj, Ankut, Phág, Rám Naumi, Dev Sati *ikádshi*, Jal Bahar, Panj Bheesham, Díp Mála.
Deota Bishnu ...	Ḍera Bishnúwála.	
Ṭhákur Bishnu Bhagwán (*p*.)	Called after the name of the god.	Rám Naumi and on the Janam Ashṭami.
Deota Bishnu (*q*) ...	Ḍera Sajla in K. Barsai	The Jeṭh Bir Shiv on 1st of Chet, the Chachopali for 5 days on the full moon day of Chet, the Kanhiya Bir Shiv on 1st Baisákh, the Devkhel for three days on 6th Baisákh. Also the Kapu fair on 1st Jeṭh, the Sharhnu on 1st Har, the Deori Parabh on the 1st of Bhádon, the Janam Ashṭami in the dark half of Bhádon, the Sutari on 1st Asauj.

Lachhmi Náráin has at least four temples in Saráj. Regarding one the usual story, as usual, is that in the *duápar yug*, people used to graze cattle on this spot and once a boy noticed that a cow used to yield her milk to a black stone image every day. At last he told his parents of it and his father with other good men of the village came to verify his tale. When they reached the place they saw a *faqír* seated by the image, and he told them that it represented Náráin, promising prosperity to all who worshipped it. With these words he disappeared under the ground. The people then built a temple there and installed the image in it. It is believed to have been founded in the *duápar yug*, and is built of stone and wood. It contains a black stone image, 3

(*o*) The temples connected with this are those of Raghú Náth, Chár Bhuj, Nársingh, Murlídhar and Lachhmi Náráin.

(*p*) No other temple is connected with this except a *dharmsála* where *faqírs* put up.

(*q*) No temple save that that of Nág Dhumal is connected with this. It contains an image of stone about a foot high. Its worship is performed by the *pujári* of Bishnu *deota*.

feet high and 2 broad. Its administration is carried on by a *kárdár*, by caste a Kanet and by *got* a Káshab. He is married. The *pujári* is a Sársut Brahman by caste and by *got* a Gautam. These posts are hereditary. Thus in no respect does the temple differ from those to a Nág or any other *devta* in Saráj. The ritual has no distinctive features. A *bhog* of rice, *dál* or milk is offered once a day, and a sacred lamp lit every evening. No distinction is made in the offerings of different castes. The annual fair is held on 1st Baisákh. Connected with this are the shrines of Thách Deora and Dáogi. The fair at the former is held on the 1st Baisákh and at the latter from 1st to 3rd Phágan. The expenses incurred on these are borne by the respective gods.

Lachhmi Náráin's temple at Chíni was founded by a *thákur* who bestowed a plot of land on a *faqír* who declared himself to be Lachhmi Náráin. It differs in no essentials from the one first described. Two fairs are held, one on the 3rd Baisákh and the other on the *púranmáshi* in Bhádon.

Regarding the temple at Deori it is said that a *sádhu* came to a Brahman's house there and sitting at the door began to dig up the ground. In it he found a *pindi* to which a cow daily yielded her milk. This was noticed by a girl who was grazing cows near by. She told her father all about it. The *sádhu* told him that the *pindi* was the image of Náráin, and then disappeared under ground. The temple was founded in the *duápar yug*. It contains a stone *pindi* a foot high. Its administration is carried on by a Sársut Brahman *kárdár* and the *pujári* is also a Brahman. The god has two places for his worship, at each of which a fair lasting from 1st to 3rd Bhádon is held. Other fairs are held on 7th Baisákh and 7th Asauj every year.

The fourth temple at Chiṛ or Chiṛa Kelún, the deodár grove, owes its origin to a very similar accident. As a *thákur* was ploughing his field he saw a *pindi* appear above the ground. It told him that its name was Lachmi Náráin who desired to meditate on that spot, so he brought it to Chiṛa Kelún where a temple was built in its honour in the *duápar yug*. It contains the stone *pindi* and its administration is carried on by a *kárdár*. The *pujári* is always a Brahman. The disciple is called *gur* and special reverence is paid to him as he answers all questions put to the god in his trances. The fair begins on 1st and ends on 3rd Phágan. The Shivrátri festival is also observed. Another fair follows on 1st Chet. The 9th and 10th Baisakh are however the great festival days. The *jag* is annually celebrated on the *rikh puniya*.

Rámji has a temple at Rámgaṛh. In old times a devotee and a snake used to live on its present site from which the villagers used to cut grass and fuel. One day they observed a *pindi* at the spot where the devotee Rámjí had disappeared underground, so a temple was built and named after him. It has been in existence since the *tritiya yug*, and contains a stone *pindi*, a foot high. Its administration is carried on by a *kárdár* a Kanet who is by *got* a Káshab. There is also a *pujári*. *Bhog* is offered only once a month, on the *sankránt*, and a sacred lamp is only lit during Bhádon and in the evening. She-goats only are sacrificed at the temple. No distinction is made in the offerings of different Hindu castes. No other shrine is connected with this one.

The temple of Ṭhákur Murlídhar in Chíni owes its origin to the Rájás of Manḍi, the Ṭhákur's image having been brought there from Mathra by Rájá Mangal Sain of that State. The date of its foundation is not known.

The temple is of stone and wood, and contains a blackstone image of the god which is 2½ feet high. On either sides of it are seated the *pinḍis* of Shiva and Kidár Náth, each ½ foot high. Its affairs are managed by a *kárdár* and *pujári*, both Brahmans of the Dharmián *got*. The fairs are held on the *púranmáshi* in Phágan, *rámnaumi* in Chet, *janam ashṭami* in Bhádon and on the *dasmi* in Asauj every year.

The cult of Mádho Rai, who is Krishna in his *avátár* of Murlídhar or the flute-player, is important in Manḍi. He has a temple in the capital of that State which was dedicated to him by its Rájá Súraj Sain after the loss of his 18 sons,[1] and the god is still the head of the State. All the village deities visit this god at Manḍi during the Shibrátri *játra*.

Maclagan, § 66.

The Hindu revival in the South-West.—In Montgomery, Multán and Muzaffargarh considerable reverence is paid to the shrine of Ganjamáli in the Multán city. The founder of the sect was a Brahman who is said to have lived some 4 centuries ago, and to have obtained the title from his wearing a necklace (*mála*) of *gánja* seeds. He was a Gosáín, a resident of Multán and a worshipper of Krishn; he is now looked on by many of the Aroṛas as their *gúru*, and his cult is closely connected with that about to be described.

The most celebrated of all the Bairágí movements in the Punjab and by far the most predominant in the south-west corner of the province is that connected with the names of the Gosáíns Shámjí and Láljí. These two men were the leaders of a great revivalist movement among the Kiráṛs or Hindu traders of the south-west some three or four hundred year ago.

Shámjí, or Shám Dás, was a Khatrí, a resident of Dipálpur, who went to Bindrában when he was twelve years old and became a disciple in the temple of Sri Chetan Mahá Prabhú. The Gosáín in charge, Dwárká Dás, gave him his blessing, and he became endowed with miraculous powers. In the Sambat year 1600 (A.D. 1543) the god Krishn presented him with two idols and said: "The Hindus of the western country of the Sindh are ignorant of their religion. They have no *gurú* to guide them between good and bad. Go to the west and teach the Hindus the ceremonies of their religion and make them your disciples (*sewak*). Your words will have speedy effect." Shámjí thereupon set out, and on reaching the Indus commenced his mission by making two and a half disciples, namely, two Khatrís and half a Chándia Baloch! He settled down at Mauza Bapilwár

[1] Mandi *Gazetteer*, pp. 39 and 9. Súraj Sain had an image of the god made of silver. The number 18 seems to be conventional.

Fatteh Khán, and founded in the town of Ḍera Gházi Khán a temple in honour of Krishn as Nannit-praya, the lover of butter. This temple is one of the oldest in those parts and its present head is Gosáín Dharmí Dhar. There are other temples erected by or in honour of Shámjí at Dera Ismáíl Khán, Kot Sultán, Kot Addu and Multán.

Shámjí had three sons, Kahnjí, Dwárkánáthjí and Jugal Kishorjí; and his followers are derived from three sources—those belonging to the Gandia Jáṭs are called Rang Rangita, the Chándia Baloch are called Chhabala, and the Khatrís CHHABIHWALE.

Lálji was in a way the successor of Shámjí. He was a Brahman, a resident of Siwán in Sind, and was born in Sambat 1608 (A.D. 1541). He also went when quite a boy to Mathra and Bindrában, and while there in Sambat 1641 received from the god Krishn a divine errand similar to that of Shámjí. At first the young man refused, but the god told him to start for the Indus at once, adding that the divine image would follow him and that he would hear the tinkling of its anklets behind him. Whereupon Lálji set forth and on reaching the country west of Dera Ghází Khán he stopped and looked round. The idol then said: "You have stopped; and I too am going no further." So Lálji built a temple on the spot to Krishn under the name of Gopínáthji, and this temple still bears a considerable reputation in Dera Ghází Khán and its neighbourhood. Two other shrines were also established, one at Dera Ismáíl Khán, called Nágarjí and one at Baháwalpur, called Sri Girdhárí Jí. The miracles performed by Lálji were a very convincing proof of his mission, and his descendants still hold the temple of Gopínáthjí which he raised.

The influence of these men in favour of the Hindu religion has been enormous and they have in all probability reclaimed the whole of the trading community of the south-west from a virtual conversion to Sikhism or Mahomedanism. To be a Hindu by religion is in those parts almost synonymous with being a follower of these Gosáíns. The Khatrís and Aroras of the south-west are divided into Sikhs and Sewaks—the followers of Nának and the disciples of the Gosáíns; and it is due to the exertions of Shámjí and Lálji that the latter are as numerous as they are. The only object of reverence, which can be said in any way to rival Krishn and his apostles, is the River, and the people have gone so far as to confuse the two, and at times it is the Indus, at times Lálji, who is addressed and worshipped as Amar Lál, the immortal one.

The Gosáíns or priests of Shámjí and Lálji live largely at Leiah and Bhakkar and are Khatrís. The number of those who have succeeded the original pair is legion, and the sect itself is also known by various names such as Krishn Lálji, Mahán Prabhú, Sewak, Lílá Dhar, Bánsí Dhar and the like. These however may be separate sects or off-shoots of the parent sect, like the CHABEL DASIS.

The Chenáb is famous for its saints,[1] and these are by no means entirely Musalmáns. The Hindu saints of the Jhang district deserve Maclagan, § 68.

[1] The saying is: Satlaj Kírí Rávi amírí, Chenáb faqírí, Jhelam shaírí, wa Sind dilíri.

special metion, and the names of four of them, Rám Piára, Múla Sant, Bábá Shahána and Jinda Kaliána, may be noted. Of Rám Piára nothing can be ascertained except that he was *bhagat*, who generally resided in Jhang and Dera Ismáíl Khán and professed Vaishnava tenets.

There have been religious men of the name of Múla Sant both in Lahore and at Talagang in Jhelam, but the most celebrated Múla Sant was a famous Gauṛ Brahman of Wazírábád, who lived in the beginning of the 16th century. This man quarrelled with his caste-fellows in Wazírábád, and emigrated to a place called Sulimán in the Chiniot tahsíl of Jhang where he gave himself out as an Aroṛa. He was advised by Sayyid Jamal Sháh and Bábá Jinda Sáhib (of whom more hereafter) to visit the shrine of Badrínáráin; and at Badrínáráin he was ordered by the oracle to marry an Aroṛa woman. He complied, but of course a considerable stigma attached to the offspring of this irregular union, one Harídás by name, and it was only in consequence of Harídás's wonderful miracles that the matter was condoned. The tenets of Múla Sant were Vaishnava, and he is said to have spent 12 years worshipping in a hole which he had dug. His son Gosáín Harídás succeeded to his position at Sulimán, and his tomb there is still an object of great reverence among the Aroṛas who attend in large numbers to shave their chidren's heads (*jhanḍ utánṛá*) in honour of the saint. Fairs are held here in April and September. The Múlasanties or followers of Múla Sant are mainly found in Jhang, Sháhpur, and Gujránwála; they abstain from meat and wine, reverence Rám and worship no idols but merely the *sáligrám*. They are chiefly Aroṛas and make pilgrimages to his tomb at Sulimán.[1]

Like Múla Sant, Bábá Shábána was not originally a native of the Jhang district. He was a Gaurí Khatrí of Satghara in Montgomery who lived some 300 years ago. His original name was Mihra and his original occupation was boiling gram. One of his customers was a Musalmán *faqír*, who made him his *chela* and bestowed on him the name of Mihr Sháh. Mihr Sháh then emigrated to Leiah, in Miánwáli, where he converted two goldsmiths. From thence he moved to Kachian, a Khatrí village on the Chenáb, in Jhang tahsíl, which is now deserted; but his assumption of the Musalmán title Sháh offended the susceptibilities of the Khatrís and led to a good deal of cursing on the part of the saint, who shifted his quarters once more to Khíva, a village of the Mahni Siáls. The saint appeared in bad spirits, and the inhabitants to prevent more cursing gave him a house, a well and a plot of ground, which are still in the possession of the Bábá Sháhána *faqírs*. This restless devotee had however another and more celebrated residence at Gilmála, 12 miles from Jhang. He had shot an arrow into the air, and it fell at Gilmála, where now there is a large building inhabited by members of his order. A fair is held here on the first Friday in Phágan every year. The followers of Bábá Sháhána do not respect the *shástras* as they should; they call themselves " Sháh, " and they use the name of " Sat Sháh " in their prayers.

[1] Shahpur *Gazetteer*, 1897, p. 84.

Another Jhang sect, and one that worships one god only, is that of the followers of Jinda and Kaliána, two saints who are said to have lived in the early part of the 16th century. Jinda was a Ganidhar Brahman of Pírkot Sadhana, in Jhang tahsíl, who in early life was an Aghorí *faqír*, and his chief residence was Masan, in the Vichand, a few miles from Jhang. Kaliána was a Sáhar Brahman of Takht Hazára, in the Sháhpur district, who left his home for Siálkot and passed some time there in devotion on the bank of the Chenáb. From Siálkot he went to the Kiréna hill to compare his attainments with those of the Kiréna *pírs*. At Kiréna his miraculous powers became well established, but the Pírs suggested his moving on to Massan, and when he reached Massan, he met Jinda. As the two saints met they exclaimed simultaneously: *Jinda so Kaliána, Kaliána so Jinda.* 'As is Jinda, so is Kaliána'; the two are one and the same; and they are now known by the joint name of Jinda-Kaliána. There remained, however, the difficulty that Jinda was still an Aghori, while Kaliána was a Vaishnav; and it was not until Jinda has ascertained at the shrine of Jagannáth that he could drink a ser and a quarter of molten lead and pass it out in the ordinary way and had exhibited his ability to do this in the presence of ten *faqírs*, that he was able to renounce the old sect and enter the new. Jinda was a celibate and his *chelas* are the regular successors to the *gaddí* at Massan. Kaliána, on the other hand, married, at Jinda's instigation, a Brahman girl of Alipur, in Jhang tahsíl, and his offspring, still known as Gosáíns, are found in many villages of Jhang, are looked on with reverence by the people and are entertained with particular care by the *gadínashíns* of the Massan shrine. The buildings at Masan are striking in appearance, and an annual fair is held there. The two *samádhs* of Jinda and Kaliána are there, and the *mahant* of the place honours them by blowing his shell (*shankh*) morning and evening. Their followers are chiefly Brahmans, Khatrís, Aroras, Sunárs and Bhátias. They worship no god but Brahm, and they greet each other with the words "Sat Jinda Kaliána." Some accounts assert that Jinda and Kaliána were contemporaries of Gurú Gobind Singh,[1] and others would class them with the Nánakpanthís but the above is the received version, and though possibly influenced by Nának they do not appear to have been in any way his followers. The Jinda-Kaliána ke sewak make a pilgrimage to their tombs at Massan at the Dasehra.

To give further details:—

Jinda or Zinda, 'the living one,' was a Bunjáhi Brahman of the Genhdar[2] *got*, while Kaliána also a Bunjahi was of the Sahr *got*. Kaliána's natural descendants are now however Gosáíns by caste: but as Zinda was celibate his spiritual descendants are *faqírs* of Zinda-Kaliána.

The Mahant or Gurú is one of the *faqírs*. They wear a cap of silk (*daryái*, or *gulbadan*), round which they bind a black strip of woollen cloth (*seli*), shaving the head, but keeping the *choti* or tuft of hair,

[1] If not honoured by him as stated in the Shahpur *Gaz.*, 1897, page 83.

[2] The Genhdar are the Brahmans of the Muhammadan Siáls of the Jhang Bár.

like Hindus, and the beard and moustaches. They also wear shoes, a *majhla*, or waist-cloth, a *lingoti*, a *kurta* or shirt and a *chadar* or shawl. They also carry a *mála* or rosary and a necklace of *tulsi* beads. The Máhant, however, may not wear a shirt or shoes, though when walking he is allowed sandals. He must always sleep on the ground, or on a *manuha*, a square bed of grass made on the earth between four posts. The *chelas* or disciples may sleep on beds. Further, the Mahant must eat on a separate *ásan*, or mat, though the *faqírs* may eat on the same *ásan* and in the same *chauka*, with one another or with Brahmans: they may also eat in the same *chauka*, but on separate *ásans*, with Khatrís and Aroṛas. The Mahant may also take food from Brahmans, Khatrís or Aroṛas, but he can only drink water drawn with a *dur*, or rope, in a *lota*, but his *chelas* may use water drawn in earthenware. He also has a separate *huqqa*, but the *faqírs* may smoke with Brahmans, provided the latter are willing to allow them to do so.

The *faqírs* employ Brahmans for religious and ceremonial purposes but not so the Gosáíns, who, like other Hindu castes, call upon the daughter's son, the son-in-law, the sister's son and husband to take the place of the Brahman, who is only employed when no such relative is available. The *faqírs* receive the *bhenṭ* or offerings made to the *samádhs*: the Gosáíns receive *ardás* (alms) or *dán*. The former however now visit their followers to collect offerings. Near the *takia*, or residence of the Mahant, stand the *samádhs* or the tombs of Zinda, Kaliána, Amadiáli, and Darya Sáhib, a *chela* of Zinda, while close by is a house in which a sacred fire (*dhuán*) has been kept burning for four centuries. This house also contains a long red flag, which is worshipped, and conch shells and bells which are used when the *dubh* grass is reverenced. *Bhang* is offered daily and is also taken regularly by the Mahant. The *faqírs*, after preparing their own food, offer *bhog* (or sacramental food) to the *samádhs*. The *faqírs* and the public worship the *samádhs*, the *dhuán* or sacred fire, and a *tulsi* plant growing near by. The Gosáíns or secular priests intermarry with all the Panjábi Brahmans: and of course avoid widow re-marriage.

Maclagan, § 67.

SOME MINOR HINDU SECTS.—We have seen above that though the teaching of Rámánand was in the beginning an inroad on the caste principles of orthodox Hinduism, the influence of the Bairagí devotees, who look to him as their founder, has been almost entirely in favour of pure Hinduism, and the sect is in the Punjab as orthodox as any other. It would therefore be well if, before we go on to record the more liberal results of the teaching of Rámánand, we should glance at the names of various petty leaders of orthodox opinion in various parts of the Province. Even among these we shall find some whose doctrines are not in accordance with ordinary Hindu opinion, but this is the most convenient place to notice them.

The Bírbal-panthís are from the Marwat tahsíl of the Bannu district, and it would be interesting to know whether they really venerate the memory of Akbar's minister, or whether the object of their reverence is some other Bírbal. In Pesháwar and Kohát a few people return the name of Míran Bai, a famous poetess and devotee of

Krishn, who is said to have lived in the time of Akbar. Her shrine is at Udaipur in Rájpútána, and there are many legends about her, but that best known in the Punjab is connected with the supposed fact that the God Krishn partook of her *kacchi khichri*.

Lála Jasrae was a Khatri, whose shrine is in Dipálpur in Montgomery. A large number of Khatrís put their faith in him and take their children to his shrine to have their heads shaved. He is reverenced also at Lahore, Amritsar, Jálandhar and Jagráon. Kesar Sháh was a *faqír* in Gujránwála. Bábá Súraj of Chúhá Bhagtai, in the Kahúta tahsíl of Rawalpindí, was a Brahman, who some 200 years ago served a Jogí, and from him learnt a *mantra* by which he became a distinguished *faqír*. He is commonly known as Chúhewála and his followers as Bhagtís. Bál Gurú is a Kashmírí saint.

Mehr Dás was a *faqír* who resided at Ketás in the Pind Dádan Khán tahsíl, and Jodha Rám was a pious Brahman who lived at Hazro in Ráwalpindi. Regarding the Jairámís little seems to be known, except that the founder of their sect was also known as Bábá Kúrewála, or Bhangewála which would point to a low origin.

The Telírájás have been noticed above and the Martanís in Vol. III, p. 79.

Another and even smaller Vaishnava sect is the Diál-Bháwan-panth, founded by one Diál Bháwan, a cloth-seller of Girot, who was attracted to religion by an exhibition of second sight (*ilhám*) in a Pathán woman with whom he was staying. Its followers are initiated at the Ramsar tank at Girot where they are taught special prayers and have their heads shaved. Some wear the *janeo*, others not. The great fair on the Baisákhi at Girot is an auspicious day for a Hindu boy to have his head shaved and don the sacred thread.[1]

The Bairágís also claim to have won tolerance from Jahángír. When that emperor visited Káhnúwán in Gurdáspur the celebrated Bairági *faqír* Bhagwánji avoided his attempt to make his acquaintance by burrowing through the ground to Pindori, 10 miles to the north, and thence to Dhamtal across the Chakki in Kángra. The holes in the ground are still shown at Káhnúwán and Pindori. Jahángír subsequently found Naráin, Bhagwánji's disciple, at Pindori, but failed to make him speak as he was then undergoing a penance of silence, so Jahángír took him to Lahore and gave him 7 cups of poison each sufficient to kill an elephant, but he resisted its effects. Bhagwánji's explanation however not only satisfied the emperor but induced him to build a temple, domed like a Muhammadan tomb, which still exists at Pindori. The daughter shrine at Dhamtal was founded by Bábá Harí Rámji and possesses an inscribed magic crystal which dates from his time. At Pindori are 13 *samádhs* representing the 13 *gaddís* or successions of *gurús* of the shrine. Close to that of Bábá Mahesh Dásji, another disciple of Bhagwánji, is the *samádh* of his dog who is also said to have resisted a dose of 1¼ *mans* of opium administered to him by the *gurú* in proof of his powers. This shrine has 50 or 60 branches scattered all over India. Lahl near Dháríwál is an important branch and barren women

[1] *Shahpur Gazetteer*, 1897, pp. 82 and 83.

resort to it to obtain issue which the *mahant* is said to bring about by the use of *jantras.*[1]

The Láljís are described as 'a sort of Bairágis, followers of Lálji', of Dhiánpur on the Rávi in Gurdáspur. Their tenets are much the same as the Vaishnava Bairágís. They appear to be Rámánandís and Lálji who lived in the time of Shah Jahán had frequent discussions with that emperor's son, Dára Shikoh on the subject of monotheism. Pictures of these debates still exist on the walls of the main building at Dhiánpur.[2] The Shahpur *Gazetteer* states that Dára Shikoh was also a friend of Dádúji, himself a disciple of Rámánand, but Dádú's date is open to much doubt: see Vol. II, p. 215, note[3]. It also adds that the sacred tract of the Dádúpanthís is called *Dádú Bilás* which may be distinct from the *Dádú Bani* alluded to on p. 216 of that volume.

A sect called Ápá-panthi is described very briefly in Vol. II, p. 13, but the Ápá-panthi of Multán appear to be distinct from it. In September 1908 one Hem Ráj, son of Pokhar Dás, of Multán, who had turned *faqir* some 10 years before and had inaugurated a religion which he termed Ápá-panthi, died. His relatives and followers some 3,000 in number dressed his body in silk clothes, placed some *tiki* on his forehead, a garland round his neck and a *tiladár* (gold-laced) cap on his head. They then placed his body in sitting position in a coffin and after carrying it round the city, had it photographed. They then took it to the river arriving about 11 P. M., put it in the water, proceeded to cook and eat some *halwá* and finally returned with the grave clothes and coffin. Besides these proceedings, which were against the principles of Hinduism, they omitted to perform that portion of the funeral ceremony called the *kirya karm*. The Hindus were disgusted at these obsequies and with the relatives and followers for trangressing all the regular Hindu funeral rites.

Gurgáon. The fair at Baldeo Chhat lasts from Bhádon *sudi* 6th to 8th. The temple contains an image of Baldevji. It is about 200 years old. The image stands in the centre of a square in the west of the temple on a platform. It is of marble, 4 feet high and is dressed in clothes suited to the season. The *pujári* is a Gaur Brahman. He only looks after the temple and the image, bathing and worshipping it. *Jhánkís* are made in Sáwan. Another fair is held at Bahim in tahsíl Núh, but no temple exists there. It is held on Bhádon *sudi* 7th and lasts 2 days.

The Bisáh fair at Kásan is held once a year on Bhádon *sudi* 13th, when the pilgrims arrive, but the *zát* or worship takes place on the 14th. There is no image in the temple, only a niche. *Mansúri* pice form the chief offering. The temple is ancient. The legend goes that when Púran Mal a Rájá's son was engaged in austerities here, a Banjára passed with loads of sugar in bags. On being asked what

[1] Gurdáspur *Gazetteer* 1914, pp. 16, 27 and 31.

[2] *Ib.*, pp. 30-31.

[3] Shahpur *Gazetteer* 1897, p. 83.

they contained he replied 'salt'. Púran Mal said that it would be salt, and when the Banjára opened them he found salt instead of sugar. He sought forgiveness for his falsehood and the Rájá told him that he would sell the salt at the price which sugar would fetch. He did so and impressed by this the trader built a temple vowing to finish it in a single night. But some women began to grind corn at midnight, and the Banjára thinking it was morning went away and so the temple was not completed. It is 3 yards square and has a *chhatri* over it. It has four doors and the roof is domed. From it projects an iron bar to which is attached a *dhajá*. The management vests in the Gaur Brahman *parohits* of the villagers, but ⅛th of the offerings go to Marnáth Jogi and the rest to the Brahmans.

The Tijon fair is held at Gurgáon and Sohna on Sáwan *sudi tij* (3rd) for about 2 hours in the afternoon. Men and women, mostly young people, assemble in the fields and the girls swing on a rope thrown over the branch of a tree.

No account of what we may call the 'personal religion' of the Hindus would be complete without reference to the curious worship of the 'Name of God'. God (*Rám*), they say, is great, but the name of God (*Nám Rám Nám* or *Rám ká Nám*) is greater. There is abundant evidence of this in the songs. We have one often heard in songs in the Kángra valley :—

'Repeat always the Name of God,

To whom Thou hast to go.'

The original of which runs :—

'*Tun bhaj láe Rám ká Nám,*

Jithe tain jáná hai.'

These words admit of no double translation and are plain and clear. In a song given later, a hermit or saint (*jogi*) reads a homily to a young girl who comes to see him, and in it the 'Name of God' occurs three times as the object of worship. Thus she is bidden : *Simro nit Bhagwán ká Nám*, 'Call always on the Name of God' and again *Japá karo Bhagwán ká Nám*, 'Keep on repeating the Name of God'. She herself says once : *kaho, to lún Bhagwán ká Nám*, 'Say, and I will take the Name of God'. One of the *tuks* current in the valley may be translated thus :—

'He who repeats the one True Name

Holds a fruitful charm and Great.'

The original words are :—

Satt Nám ik mantar hai,

Jape soí phal pái.'

Here we have *Nám*, the 'Name', by itself, with the epithe *satt* 'true.' It is the Name, the True Name, the Name of God, that is the charm that will reward him who repeats it. Lastly, a song, which belongs properly, however, to formal religion, treated of later on, shows clearly the relative position of *Nám* and Rám in the popular estimation. In some parts of India, Kángra for instance, the 1st of Chet (March-April) instead of the 1st of Baisákh (April-May) is New Year's Day, when it is the custom for *ḍúms* (musicians) to go from house to house singing songs in its honour. It is very unlucky for any one to mention the day until the *ḍúm* has mentioned it. It is also a custom to dedicate the first spring flower seen on a tree to *Nám* and the second to Rám. Both these customs are exhibited in the *ḍúm's* New Year's song :—

The first of flowers for thee, O Name !
The second, Rám for thee.
The first of Chet brings luck to him
That hears it first from me.
O Krishna of the turban gay
With jewels fair to see,
Do thou live on a thousand years
With thy posterity !

The more important words in the original are :—

Pahilá phulji tún Náen ká !
Dújá nám Náráyaná.

which, translated literally, mean—

'The first flower thine, O Name !
The second name Náráyan.'

Observe the canonization *phulji*, of the first spring flower and the personification of 'The Name !' Sir Richard Temple was not prepared to explain the origin of this cult, which, however, is nothing new. It may have its origin in the fact that Rám, with whom *Nám* is now specially associated, was an incarnation of Vishnu, to repeat whose thousand names (Sahasra-náma) was an act of virtue from all time. That Vishnu himself was long ago connected with 'The Name' is shown by his Sanskrit epithets of Námi and Náma-námika.[1]

The custom is whenever a birth occurs in a house for *ḍúms* and musicians, such as Hijras,[2] and other harpies who scent a fee on these occasions, to collect there and sing congratulatory songs. It is wonderful how these people scent out a birth, so much so, that I have thought of employing them as registration agents. About the commonest and best known song, which is also rather inappropriately sung at weddings, is that here given. It is spirited and curious, and bears a resemblance in more ways than one to our own Christmas hymns. It describes the birth of Ráma Chandra, the great hero and incarnation of god (Vishnu), the god, in fact, of many parts of India, and god *par excellence* in the Sikh theology. His earthly father was the celebrated king Dasaratha,

[1] Some Hindu Songs and Catches from the Villages in Northern India, by R. C. Temple : *S. C. R.*, VII, pp. 421-2.

[2] Eunuchs who go about the Punjab and United Provinces dressed up as women, generally not less than three together, with a drum, and earn a living by attending weddings, births &c. Their fee is usually a rupee. They appear to be dying out ; at least, all I have seen are old people.

now known popularly as Jasrat Rái, and his mother was Kausalya. The song describes the birth as according to the usual modern customs. The child Rám Chandra is born; Jasrat Rái and Kausalya are delighted; the nurse takes and washes him; the barber comes (as is proper) to plant fresh *dub* glass for luck, while his wife summons the neighbours. The child's old grand-aunt brings him his first clothes, as is also proper and right, since it brings luck; his aunt is the first to hold him in her arms, and last, but not least, his father distributes presents to the poor, while the family priest comes prowling round for his dues. The name of the aunt, however, is Subhadra. Now Subhadra was never the aunt of Ráma Chandra, but the sister of Krishna, the great god of so many of the Hindus, and also an incarnation of Vishnu. Here, then, we have another instance of what is so common and puzzling in modern Hindu folklore, the mixture of classical legends. I have previously given two songs which also mix up the stories of Ráma and Krishna. The confusion may have arisen thus: both are 'God' and both favourite subjects of song: and besides there were three Ráms, all supposed to be incarnations of God. They lived evidently in different ages, and probably in the following order:—Parasu Ráma, axe Rám, root-and-branch Rám, the champion of the priests (Brahmans) against the warriors (Kshatriyas); Ráma Chandra, gentle Rám; and Bála Ráma, strong Ráma, brother and companion of Krishna. Bála Ráma and Ráma Chandra have probably been mixed up in popular songs, and there is nothing unlikely in this. It is a simple mess compared with some the bards have got into.

One of the prettiest and most widely-spread customs in North India is the swinging in Sáwan (July-August), when the rains are usually at their height, in honour of Krishna and Rádha. It is done for luck apparently, much as our Christmas pies are eaten, and seems to have no ulterior object. Everyone who wishes to be lucky during the coming year must swing at least once during Sáwan. Like most customs of this sort, it is confined almost entirely to women and children, whose swings may be seen hanging from the branches of trees in every garden and along the roadside, by villages, bazaars, and dwellings. Connected with this is the Doll fair (*Gurion ká mela*) carried on during the whole of Sáwan, and with the same object of procuring good luck in the future. Customs differ in various parts as to the manner of conducting the fair, but in Kángra every man, woman and child goes at least once to the riverside during the month, wearing a doll at the breast. The visit to the riverside must be on a Sunday, Tuesday or Thursday, and must have been previously fixed on by a kind of private promise or vow. Arrived at the river the doll is thrown in, and the superstition is, that, as the doll is cooled by the water, so the mind will be cooled (eased) by the action during the coming year. There is a song sung on these occasions by the children having allusion to the advent of the wagtails as a sign of the time for the Doll Fair having arrived. It is also sung in the Sáwan swings:—

Fly, fly the wagtails so;

Mother, 'tis the rainy month;

Mother, 'tis the rainy month,
Yes, my darling, mother O
Fly, fly the wagtails so;
Mother, we must go and swing,
Yes, my darling, mother O.[1]

THE PATRON SAINTS OF THE TRADER AND ARTIZAN CASTES.

The system of saintly patronage, exemplified in Mediæval Europe, was in force in Hindu society from an early period. Thus Visvakarma is the patron deity of the workers in wood and indeed of all craftsmen.

But the system found a fuller development in mediæval Islám. Thus "Adam was the first builder and sower; Seth the first manufacturer of buttons and wool-carder; Enoch the first tailor and clerk; Noah the first carpenter and joiner (in the later tradition of the Moslems Joseph was venerated as a carpenter and Jacob as a joiner); Hud the first merchant; Sáleh the first camel-driver; Abraham the first milkman and later, when he received from God the command to build the Ka'aba, the first builder; Ismaíl the first hunter; and Isaac the first herdsman; Jacob the first who led a life of contemplation; Joseph (the Egyptian) the first watch-maker, because he busied himself with this invention while in prison, in order to decide the time of the morning and evening prayers; Job, as the patient one, was the patron of all unfortunates; Jethro of the blind; Moses was a shepherd, as well as pastor of men; and his brother Aaron a *wazír*, *i.e.* minister and representative; Sil-kefel was the first baker; Lot the first chronographer, Esdras the first donkey-herd; Daniel the first interpreter; David the inventor of coats of mail; and Solomon gained his daily bread by basket-making; Zachariah was the first hermit; John a *shaikh*; Jeremiah a surgeon; Samuel a sand-diviner; Lokmán a learned man; John a fisherman; Jesus a traveller; and Muhammad a merchant.[2]

Hence the patron saint of the Hindu weavers being Kabír they call themselves Kabírbansi, just as the tailors are called Námdeví from Námdeo and are offended by being called Juláhá or Darzí. So too Hindu barbers sometimes resent being called Náí and call themselves Sainbhagtí.[3] Sain Bhagat was a Rájá's barber and deeply religious. Once sunk in meditation he forgot to wait on the Rájá but the deity did his work for him. When Sain Bhagat learnt of this he devoted the rest of his life to religion.[4] In the Punjab plains the Hindu weavers are also called Rámdásiás or followers of Gurú Rám Dás, but this term appears to be restricted to the Chamárs who live by weaving.[5]

[1] S. C. R., VII, pp. 426-7.

[2] Von Hammer: *Constantinopolis und der Bosphorus*, II, pp. 395-6. I am indebted for this reference to Dr. J. Horovitz.

[3] N. I. N. Q., I., § 72.

[4] *Ib.*, § 153.

[5] *Ib.*, § 648.

The spiritual ancestor, as he may be called, is held in such respect that a false oath is never taken on his name. Indeed there is much reluctance to swear by it at all.

The Muhammadan weavers are great observers of the 'Id-ul-fitr which is described as the festival of the Juláhás, just as the 'Id-uz-zuhá is said to be held in special esteem by the Qassábs, the Shab-i-barát by the comb-makers (*kanghíghar*) and the Muharram by the Sayyids.[1]

Sádhua *bhagat* is the patron saint of butchers. He was once going to kill a goat, but the animal threatened vengeance on him in the next life, so he joined the sect of 'Sádhs,' whence his name. Another story is that he was a Muhammadan, but this is inconsistent with his name, which appears in many folk-songs.[2]

Some other patron saints are: Omes Karím, Pír of the comb-makers; Sháh Madár, Pír of the jugglers; and Prem Tot, *gurú* of the Udásís. But the last-named appears unknown to the Udásís themselves and nothing can be ascertained regarding him.

[1] N. I. N. Q., I, § 643.

[2] *Ib.*, § 6.

Hinduism in the Himalayas.

In the preceding sections a good many facts relating to Hinduism in the hills have been given in their appropriate places, but many have been omitted. These are now given in a special sub-section in which the arrangement will be much the same as that in Hinduism itself. Distinctive as Hinduism in the Himalayas is, many or most of its facts could have been with at least equal propriety given a place in orthodox Hinduism, and very little doubt may be felt that a place in it could be found for every cult and temple, rite and observance, yet to be noted. But while Himalayan Hinduism does not really differ in kind from the Hinduism of the plains, it is highly distinctive in degree, retaining much that is older than Buddhism and more still that is older than latter-day Hinduism. Nág-worship for example must have existed long before Buddhism arose. It must have been absorbed by that creed after the first fervour of the early Buddhists had cooled down and left them more tolerant of popular and primitive cults, and then when Buddhism perished it must have survived in almost its original forms, unaffected by the religion which the State had adopted, but not imposed on the people.

Regarding the legend of Tikkar Nág, given at p. 159 *supra*, Mr. J. D. Anderson, C. S., writes:—

"The Nág never came down to Súni itself but stayed up round Tikkar, where the three States of Kumhársain, Madhán and Bhajji join (? is there always a Nág at a trijunction). The Koṭi people say that it ought to be a Ganesh, but this is, I think, a perversion. The Bhajji god who kept the Nág out from the Basantpur-Súni valley is called Dánu or Sarsahan, *i.e.* the god with the strength of 1000 arms. He is a god of the low ravines: whenever there is a considerable volume of water between Arki and Súni this god is worshipped. This is interesting, as Emerson has a certain amount of information to show that Nág is a river god. Here however the Nág is definitely the god of a high place, and his rival, who is anthropomorphic in the strictest sense, holds the river valleys — which incidentally swarm with snakes. He has however one point in common with the Nág: no one in his *iláqa* dares sleep on a bed, if they do the god at once tips him off. He is also a sanitary god: if any person washes clothes or his person in the *baolís* under his protection, he is stricken with leprosy."

In Kulu the rainbow is called Budhi Nágan the 'old she-snake': Diack, *Kulúhi Dialect*, page 54. This points to the Nág being regarded as a rain or water-god, as he usually is in the Simla Hills. But in Chamba the Nág is described as a whitish-coloured snake that frequents house-walls and is said to drink milk: its presence is regarded as a good omen and *púja* and incense are offered to it. The *sotar* is another snake, uniform in thickness and believed to have a mouth at each end, whence it is called *domúnha*, and it is believed that any one bitten by it will be bitten again every year.[1]

Ibbetson, § 237. *Hinduism in the Hills*—The Hinduism of the Himalayan areas differs considerably from that of the plains. It would seem that in all

[1] Chamba *Gazetteer*, p. 39.

mountainous countries, the grandeur of their natural features and the magnitude of the physical forces displayed lead the inhabitants to defy the natural objects by which they are surrounded, or rather to assign to each its presiding genius, and to attribute to those demons more or less malevolent character.[1] The greater gods, indeed, are not unrepresented in the Punjab Himalayas. There are the usual *thákurdwáras* sacred to Vishnu in some one of his forms, and *shiválas* dedicated to Shiva; but though Náths, with their ears bored in honour of the latter god, are to be found in unusual numbers, these deities are little regarded by the people, or at any rate by those of the villages. The malignant and terrible Káli Deví, on the other hand, is worshipped throughout the Kángra mountains; and to her, as well as to the *lha* presently to be mentioned, human sacrifices were offered up to the period of our rule. An old cedar tree was cut down only a few years ago to which a girl used formerly to be offered annually, the families of the village taking it in turn to supply the victim; and when the Viceroy opened the Sirhind Canal in November 1882, the people of the lower hills believed that 200 of the prisoners who had been employed on the works were released on condition of their furnishing a similar number of girls to be sacrificed at the inaugural ceremony, and lit fires and beat drums and sat up for several nights in order to keep off any who might be prowling about in search of female children for this purpose. But the every-day worship of the villager is confined to the *lhas* or genii of the trees, rocks, and caves of Láhul, and the local spirits or demons of Kulu, variously known as *deotás* or godlings, *Devís* who are apparently the corresponding female divinities, Rikhís and Munís or local saints, Sidhs or genii of the hill-tops and high places, Jognís or wood fairies, Págs or snake gods, and by many other names, though for practical purposes little distinction is apparently drawn between the various classes.[2] A favourite situation for a shrine is

[1] I shall not attempt to distinguish the various grades of belief which obtain in the different Himalayan ranges; but it may be said generally that the deeper you penetrate into the mountains, the more elementary is the worship and the more malevolent are the deities.

[2] "There is one curious difference between the gods of the hills and those of the plains and that is, that many of the former are purely territorial, each little state or group of villages having its own deity, and the boundaries between their jurisdictions being very clearly defined. The god Sípur, in whose honour the well-known Sípi fair is held near Simla, lost his nose in an attempt to steal a deodár tree from the territory of a neighbouring rival; for the latter woke up and started in pursuit, on which Sípur not only fell down in his alarm and broke his nose, but he dropped the tree, which is, I am told, still growing upside down to attest the truth of the story. The only territorial god of the plains that I can remember is Bhúmia, the god of the village. Perhaps the difference may be due to the striking manner in which Nature has marked off the Himalayan territory into small valleys separated by grand and difficult mountain ranges." So Sir Denzil Ibbetson wrote. But the feudalism of the hills is not wholly territorial. In this connection Mr. H. W. Emerson observes:—"In olden days the personal bond was so strong that it often continued to exist for generations after the hereditary ruler had ceased to exercise sovereign power over the lands of his former subjects. For example, the petty principality of Sairi was conquered by Bashahr many years ago and absorbed within the boundaries of the latter State. The peasantry, however, though compelled by force to pay regular imposts, steadily denied all obligation to contribute their monthly quota to the *corvée*, nor was it imposed upon them until two or three years ago. Also they still call the representative of the Sairi family by his ancient title, contributing towards his marriage and other expenses as though he was in fact their natural ruler. The nature of the link binding together the sovereign and the land-owning classes was the more appreciated by the latter because

a forest, a mountain peak, a lake, a cave, or a waterfall; but almost every village has its own temple, and the priests are generally drawn from among the people themselves, Brahmans and other similar priestly classes seldom officiating. Idols are almost unknown or, where found, consist of a rude unhewn stone; but almost every deity has a metal mask which is at stated periods tied on to the top of a pole dressed up to represent the human form, placed in a sedan chair, and taken round to make visits to the neighbouring divinities or to be feasted at a private house in fulfilment of a vow. Each temple has its own feasts also, at which neighbouring deities will attend, and on all such occasions sheep or goats are sacrificed and eaten, much hill-beer is drunk, and the people amuse themselves with dances in which the man-borne deity is often pleased to join. There are also other domestic powers, such as Kála Bír, Nár Singh, the *paris* or fairies, and the like who have no shrines or visible signs, but are feared and propitiated in various ways. Thus for the ceremonial worship of Kála Bír and Nár Singh, a black and white goat respectively are kept in the house. Sacrifice of animals is a universal religious rite, and is made at weddings, funerals, festivals, harvest time, on beginning ploughing, and on all sorts of occasions for purposes of purification, propitiation, or thanksgiving. The water-courses, the sprouting seeds, the ripening ears are all in charge of separate genii who must be duly propitiated.

"Till the festival of the ripening grain has been celebrated, no one is allowed to cut grass or any green thing with a sickle made of ir n, as in such case the field-god would become angry, and send frost to destroy or injure the harvest. If therefore a Láhulá wants grass before the harvest sacrifice, he must cut it with a sickle made of the horn of an ox or sheep, or tear it off with the hand. The iron sickle is used as soon as the harvest has been declared to be commenced by the performance of the sacrifice. Infractions of this rule were formerly severely punished; at present a fine of one or two rupees suffices."

Ibbetson, § 238.

All misfortune or sickness is attributed to the malice of some local deity or saint, and the priest is consulted as is the *bhagat* in the plains. Indeed the hill priests serve as a sort of oracle, and are asked for advice on every conceivable subject; when "by whisking round, by flogging themselves with chains, and so on, they get into the properly exhausted and inspired state, and gasp out brief oracular answers". Magic and witchcraft and the existence of witches and sorcerers are firmly believed in. In the Hill States, if epidemic attack or other misfortune befall a village, the soothsayer, there called *chela* or 'disciple', is consulted, and he fixes under inspiration upon some woman as the witch in fault. If the woman confess, she is purified by

they themselves relied, and in fact still rely, on a similar relation in dealing with their ancestral servants."

Mr. H. Fyson, C. S., notes a somewhat similar case of an ecclesiastical jurisdiction having no relation to any political one:-

"The Lagál *iláqa*, which comprises the four *kothis* of Tárapur, Chaparsa and Mángarh in *wazíri* Lag Mahárája, and Dughi Lag in *wazíri* Lag-Sari, has a separate system of *deotás* and *devís*. At its head is Deví Phungni and below her are the Naráins of the *kothis*, the *phâti devís* and village godlings. Of these Deo Gauhari alone seems to be not wholly of this *iláqa* as he has a temple also at Dhálpur on the plain near Sultánpur. Deví Phungni was called up by the Rái of Rúpi the other day and reproached with not having sent rain. She was given a date for it to fall — and it came! The Khaika ceremony is common and is probably a relic of human sacrifice as the man chosen (to represent the victim) is pelted with stones, shams dead and is carried round the village before he comes to again. But Lagál does not seem to have had a secular origin, for the people say that they never had a *thákur* of their own, but were always under the Rájás of Kulu".

the *chela*, the sacrifice of a he-goat forming the principal feature in the ceremony. But if she deny the accusation, she will be tried by one of several kinds of ordeal very similar to those once practised in Europe, those by water and by hot iron being among them. Tree worship still flourishes. Mr. Alexander Anderson wrote :—

"In matters of every-day importance, such as cattle-disease, health, good crops &c., in short in worldly affairs generally, the people of Kulu go to the old deodár trees in the middle of the forest where there is often no temple at all, and present a piece of iron to propitiate the deity. Such trees are common in Kulu, and the number of iron nails driven into them shows that this form of worship is not dying out [1]".

Both men and women of all classes eat meat, with the exception of widows; spirits and fermented liquids are commonly drunk, and Brahmans will eat when seated alongside of the lower castes, though not, of course, at their hands. The local saints and divinities are, unlike their rivals in the plains, all Hindu, with the doubtful exceptions of Gúga Pír, and of Jamlu, a demon of Malána in Kulu, who possessed great virtue before our rule, his village being a city of refuge for criminals, and whose hereditary attendants form an exceedingly peculiar body of men who are looked upon collectively as the incarnation of the divinity, are apparently of a race distinct from that of the hill-men, intermarry only among themselves, speak a dialect which is unintelligible to the people of the country, and use their reputation for uncanniness and the dread of their god as the means of wholesale extortion from their superstitious neighbours.[2] Jamlu is said to be a Musalmán because animals offered to him have their throats cut. But neither he nor his worship bears any other trace of Islám, and his attendants are Hindus. His incarnation, too, is known as *RA DEO*, while his sister is called Prini Deví.[3] The other *deotás* indeed refuse to visit him, and pretend to treat him as an outcast; but he revenges himself by assuming a superiority to them all which in old days sometimes took the practical form of a successful demand for a part of their property. In the lower hills the Muhammadan saints re-appear as Bába Fatu, Bába Bhopat, and their friends, and the majority of their worshippers are again Hindus.

In Suket the temple of the Sun, known as the Súraj Kunḍ, was built by the Rájá Garúr Chand (or Sain) and his consort. In front of it is a tank or *kunḍ* which gives it its name and adds to its beauty. The idol, of brass, is flanked by two horses, a *bálisht* in height, thus giving it the appearance of a chariot.[4]

Memorial tablets are also found at Rámpur in Bashahr. Occasionally they contain figures of male servants who died with their chief —

[1] The name *deodár* (*Deva-daru*) means 'the divine tree'. It is applied to the Himalayan cypress (*Cupressus torulosa*) in Kulu, and in Láhul to the *Juniperus excelsa*. The Himalayan cedar (*Cedrus deodara*) is called by the people *dear* or *kelo*, not *deodár*.—D. I.

[2] There is a tradition that they were deported to their present homes by one of the Emperors as a punishment for some offence. [D. I.]

[3] Mr. Fyson observes that the Prini people deny this relationship. Sir Alexander Diack says that Gyephan, the god of Láhul, is Jamlu's brother and Hirma, the goddess to whom is attributed the peopling of Kulu, his sister: *Kuluhi Dialect of Hindi*, p. 89.

[4] Suket *Gazetteer*, pp. 26-7, where a full account of its administration is given. Apparently it was not the erection of this temple under the Ráni's influence which led to the excommunication of the *sáchuban* Brahmans, but the Deví's warnings against the *parohits* and her infliction of epilepsy on his son.

a survival of the primitive idea that the Rájá must enjoy the same state in the next world as in this. Mr. H. W. Emerson has come across a curious *sati* superstition in Manḍi. He noticed that just before crossing a stream a villager picked up a stone and when he passed a certain spot threw it on a large pile of similar stones. He was told that a widow had been burnt there, that her spirit still haunted the place and that every passer-by must placate it with an offering.

Another interesting case of memorial stones is that of the rude slabs erected before a few village temples in Manḍi with figures of deceased diviners carved on them. The idea here is that their spirits should serve the god.

The Legend of Mahású Deota.

Mahású, doubtless a corruption of Mahá-Siva, is the god who gives his name to the Mahású hills. In the legend that follows he appears in quadruple form as four brothers, just as Ráná Sur had four sons.[1]

When Krishna disappeared at the end of Dwápar Yug, the Pánḍavas followed him. On their road to Badrí-káshram they crossed the Tons, and Rájá Yudhishthir, struck with the beauty of the place, ordered Viswákarmá to build a temple there. Here the Pánḍavas, with Draupadí, halted 9 days. They named the place Hanol, and thence journeyed by the Gangotrí and Jamnotrí ravines, through Kedár, to Badrí Náth, where they disappeared, and the Kalí Yug began.

At its commencement demons wandered over the Uttará Khanḍa, devouring the people and plundering towns and villages. The greatest of demons was Kirmar, who had Beshí, Sengí, and a host of minor demons under him at Maindárath, on the Tons, whence they ravaged towns and villages, until the people sought refuge in cliffs, caves and ravines. The demons devoured every one who came in their way. Once the seven sons of Húná Brahman, who practised penance in the Deoban forest, went to bathe in the Tons river and encountered Kirmar, who devoured them all.

As they did not return for some time, their mother set out in search for them, but when she reached the river without getting any clue to her sons, she sat down on its bank and began to weep bitterly. Meanwhile Kirmar, passing by, was struck with her beauty and asked why she wept. Kirtaká turned to him and said her seven sons had gone to bathe in the river and had not returned home. Hearing this, Kirmar said:—" I am fascinated by thy beauty. If thou wilt accede to my heart's desire, I will extinguish the fire of my heart and will be grateful to thee and try to help thee in this difficulty. I am a brave man, descended from Háwan. I have won the kingdom of these hills through the strength of my own arm ".

The chaste wife was terrified at these words and they increased her grief. In her distress she began to pray, saying, 'O Lord, the giver of all boons, everything rests with thee'.

[1] Temple's *Legends of the Panjab*, III, pp. 364 *et seqq.*

Dohá (*couplet*).

Puttar dukh dukhiá bhaí.
Par-bal abalá áj,
Satti ko sat ját hai.
Rákho, Ishwar, láj.

" I was distressed at the loss of my sons.

To-day I am a woman in another's power.

A chaste woman whose chastity is like to be lost.

O God, keep my chastity ! "

After this she took her way home, and by the power of God the demon's sight was affected, so that Kirtaká became invisible to him as she passed. She then told the story to her husband, saying with clasped hands that Durgá Deví would be pleased with her devotion and destroy the demons, for she alone was endowed with the power of averting such evil. The demons had corrupted religion, outraged chastity and taken men's lives.

On hearing this, her husband said they would go and worship Hát-koṭí Ishwarí Mátá. So Húna went to the goddess with his wife. He first offered her flowers, and then prayed to Háteshwarí Durga with the eight hands. While he prayed he unsheathed a dagger and was about to cut off his own head with it, when the goddess revealed her spirit to him, caught his hand, and said :—" I am greatly pleased with thy devotion. Go to the mountains of Kashmír, pray to God, and all thy desires will be fulfilled. Shiv-jí will be pleased and will fulfil thy desires. Go there cheerfully and there will be no obstacle in thy way ".

Obeying the order of the goddess, Húna went at once, and in a few days reached his destination. After his departure, he gave up eating grain and lived on vegetables. He also gave up clothes, using the bark of trees for his dress. He spent most of his time in worship, sometimes standing on one toe. When Shiv-jí was pleased with him, the spirit of the four-armed image addressed him, saying, 'I am greatly pleased with thee : ask me any boon which thou desirest '.

On hearing these words from the god Siva, Húna clasped his hands and said :—" O Siva, thou hast power to kill the demons. Thou hast power to repel all enemies and to remove all difficulties. I pray and worship the Ganges, the saviour of the creatures of the three worlds, which looks most beautiful as it rests on thy head. There are no words to describe thy glory. The beauty of thy face, which is so brilliant with the serpents hanging round thy neck, beggars all description. I am highly indebted to the goddess of Hát-koṭí, at whose feet I bow my head, and by whose favour I and my wife are so fortunate as to see thee in Kálí Yug ".

Uttar Khánḍ meṇ rákhas base, manukhoṇ ká karte áhár.
Kul mulk barbád kiyá, ábádí hogái ujár.

Tum hí Rudar, tum hí Bishnú Nand Gopál.

Dukh húá sur sádhúon ko, máro rákshas tat-kál.

Sát puttar mujh dás ke nahán gae jab parbhát,

Jab ghát gaye nadí Tons ke jinko Kirmar kháyo ek sáth.

"The demons who dwelt in the Northern region are preying upon the people.

They have laid waste the country and the people have fled.

Thou only art Ruddar (Siva), thou alone art Bishnú Nand Gopál.[1]

The sages and devotees are in distress, kill the demons at once.

Early in the morning the seven sons of me, thy slave, went to bathe,

When they reached the banks of the river Tons, Kirmar ate them at once".

The god Siva was pleased at these words and said :—" O Rikhi, the people of the Kálí Yug being devoid of religion have lost all strength. I admire thy sincere love and true faith, especially as thou didst not lose heart in worshipping me. Hence all thy desires shall be fulfilled, and I have granted thee the boon asked for. Be not anxious, for all the devils will be killed in a few days".

Dohá (*couplet*).

Bidá kiyo jab Bipra ko, díyé akshat, phúl, chirág.

Sakti rúp pahle pargat gai Maindárath ke bág.

Ghar jáo Bipra apne, rakho mujh par tek.

Sakti rúp ke ang se, ho-gaye deb anek.

Pargate ang se debte, rom rom se bír.

Istrí sahit bidá kiyó, 'rakho man men dhír'.

"When (the god) bade the Brahman farewell, he gave him rice, flowers and a lamp.

A Sakti (goddess) first appeared in the garden at Maindárath.

Go home, Brahman, and place reliance on me.

Countless divinities arose from the body of the Sakti.

Gods appeared from her body, and heroes from her every hair.

She dismissed him with his wife, saying 'keep patience in thy heart' ".

When the god gave Húna Rikhí leave to go, he gave him rice, a vessel containing flower and a lamp, and said, " O Rishi, go home and keep thy confidence in me. A Saktí (goddess) will first appear in the

[1] Explained to mean 'the son of Nand, *i.e.* Krishna'.

garden at Maindárath. Numerous demons will come out of her thimble, and every hair of her body will send forth a hero. Do not lose courage but go home with thy wife. Keep the garland of flowers, the rice, and the lamp which I have given thee concealed beneath the *pípal* tree which stands in the garden behind thy house, and perform the customary daily worship of all these. Light this lamp and offer me flowers and incense on the *amáwas* of Bhádon and thereafter worship me with a sincere heart. Also perform a *jágaran*[1] on that date for one day and night. By so doing thou wilt, on the third day, observe a Sakti emerge from the ground with a fountain. Flames will then be visible all around. From her forehead and other limbs will spring gods, who will be named after the member from which they were born. The four gods, called the Nág Chauth or Mahású, will appear on the fourth of the light half of Bhádon. Those who appear on the following day, *i.e.* the 5th, will be called Kiyálu and Banár. Moreover, many distinguished above the rest by their courage will spring from the Sakti's hair. They will kill the demons and give great happiness to the people. They will fix their capital at Hanol, which was founded by the Pándavas".

When this boon was granted to Húna Rikhí, he walked round the god and paid him obeisance. After this he went his way homewards and the god disappeared.

After many days the Rikhí reached home with his wife, and acting on the god's directions carefully placed the lamp, flowers and rice on the prescribed spot. On the *amáwas* of Bhádon he worshipped and lighted the lamp. On the third day a fountain sprung up, wherein the Sakti appeared.

Chaupái.

Bhúmí se upní Mátá Deo Lárí.
Thán Deo Mátá ko Kongo re Bárí.

"Mother Deo Lárí appeared from the earth.
The temple of Deo Mátá (was named) the Bárí of Kongo".[2]

Tú hí yog, yugtí, tú hí yog máí.
De, Mátá, bachan de painde men láí.

"Thou only art devotion and the law, thou art the mother of the age
O Mother, give us thy promise to lead us on the (right) path".

Máthe bale Máí re agní re gethe.
Bothá rájí Mahású hoi súraj re bhekhe.

"On the Mother's head burnt a fire of faggots.
Mahású was born with lustre like the rays of the sun".

[1] *Jágaran* (from Sanskrit *Jágarana*) means keeping awake the whole night in devotion.

[2] By Mahású, because it was close to his own temple.

Chháti se márte Chakkar chál,
Janamá Chálḍa, Mátá re lál.

"Placing her hand round her breast,
The Mother brought forth her son, Chálḍa".

Mátá Deo Lári ne háth kie khare
Báshak Pabási dono háth đó jhare.

"Mother Deo Lári raised her hands.
Báshak[1] and Pabási both sprang from her two hands".

Chauth men upne Mahású chár.
Panchmí huí tithí dí Deo Kiyálú Banár.

"The four Mahásús were born on the fourth.[2]
On the fifth were created the gods Kiyálú and Banár"[3].

Sher Káliá Kiyálú hoe Boṭhe re wazír.
Romo hoe romo de nau lákh bír.

"Shér Káliá and Kiyálú became the ministers of Boṭha.[4]
Nine *lákhs* of heroes sprang from every hair".

Háth joṛe Húna gayá paire pe jái:
'Sab manukh líe, Malká, rákshasá khái'.

"Húna fell at her feet with clasped hands:
'All mankind has been devoured by the demons, O Mistress'".

Háth bande pair shir láyá jánú:
'Maindárath Tálo dá Kirmar dáno'".

"With clasped hands and feet he placed his head on her knees:
'Kirmar, the demon (dwells) in the Maindárath Lake'".

Kaṭhṭhí hoí sainá Maindárath ke bág.
Chár bhái Mahású kardí re ág.

"The armies were arrayed in the garden of Maindárath.
The four Mahású brothers were like the fire"[5].

[1] Báshak is also called Chálḍa, *i.e.* the 'goer', the serpent.

[2] Of the light half of Bhádon.

[3] That is to say, two of the four Mahású were created on the 5th of the light half of Bhádon.

[4] Mahású.

[5] Of a cow-dung cake.

Húne jaise rikhie ati bintí lái :
Isí ke káran chár Mahású ái.

"Húna, the Rishí, made a great prayer :
'The four Mahásús for this purpose have come'".

Sabhí jabí debte ne bintí lái :
'Kyá dewe ágyá Deo Lárí Mái'?

"All the gods made a prayer (saying) :
'What are the orders of the goddess Deo Lárí Máí'"?

Jab dí ágyá Srí Deví Mái :
'Kirmar Keshi rákshas ko tum do ghái'.

"Then Srí Deví Máí gave orders :
'You must kill the demons Kirmar and Késhí'".

Chambola.

Rájá Rikh-choliyá láyo tero náw.
Rájan ko ráj náw tero náw.

"Thy name is king of Rikh-choliyá.
Thy name is king of kings".

Kungú, kastúri, Rájá, guglá ko dhúp,
Chár Bhái Mahású Naráin ko rúp.
Rájan ko ráj náw tero náw.

"With saffron, musk, and fragrant resin and incense, Rájá,
The four Mahású brothers are Naráin incarnate.[1]
Thy name is king of kings".

Háth shankh, chakkar, gal sámp ke hár,
Chár bhái Mahású Buddar avatár ;
Bhekh-dhári rájan ko ráj, náw tero náw.

"With conch and quoit in their hands, and serpents round their necks,
The four brothers Mahású are Buddar incarnate,
In spite of all disguise, thy name is king of kings".

Háth shankh, chakkar gajjá, tirshúl,
Nách láyo parí ro, barkhá hoe phúl,
Bhekh-dhári rájá láyo tero náw.
Rájan ko ráj, náw tero náw.

[1] *i.e.*, Siva.

"Conch, quoit, mace and trident in hand,
Dance of fairies and rain of flowers,
In spite of all disguise kingly is thy name,
Thy name is king of kings".

Uliyá ko nátí Rájá Bhimlá ko jáyo.
Kashmíre chhorí Rájá Maindárath áyo.
Rájan ko ráj, náw tero náw.

"Uliyá's grandson and Rájá Bhimlá's son has been born,
The Rájá left Kashmír and came to Maindárath,
Thy name is king of kings".

Dohá (*couplet*).

Tháro ant koí nahín jáne, lílá param apár.
Bhagat hit kárne tum kaí bidh sete ho avtár.

"None knoweth thy infinity, thy glory is infinite,
Thou dost take many shapes in order to do good".

Binti sun rikhí kí, parsan hue atyant.
Hukam diye sainápatíon ko 'máro asur turant'.

"Hearing the prayer, great was the joy of the saints,
They gave the order to the leaders to slay the demons forthwith".

Agyá páí, Mahású kí mungar liyo háth,
Mahán rath par Chálḍa baiṭhe nau lákh sainá sáth.

"Receiving the orders, the Mahásús took bludgeons in their hands.
Chálḍa sat in his great war chariot at the head of nine *lákhs* of men".

Pirtham yudh húá Maindárath men, sainá márí apár,
Aise Shib Shankar bhae jo santan prán adhár.

"Battle was first joined at Maindárath and armies were slain.
It was Shiv Shankar who thus came to save his disciples".

When the whole army of the *rákhshasas* had been killed, Kirmar beat a retreat and came to Majhog, the abode of Singí, the demon. There they collected their scattered forces, intending to give battle afresh.

Dohá (*couplet*).

Jab Majhog men devat pahúnche án,
Singí máro jab dait, húá yudh ghamsán.

"When the *deotás* reached Majhog,
They killed Singí, the demon, and a desperate battle was fought".

On hearing of the slaying of Singí Rákhshas by Sher Kulí, and that most of his men were slain, Kirmar fled to Kinárí Khandái, a village on the river bank, but was pursued by the *deotás*. When he was about to hide in a ravine of Mount Khandá, he was overtaken by Chálda Mahású, who rode on a throne of flowers borne by two soldiers.

Dohá (*couplet in Pahárí*).

Khandán jáne khe páwá thá tháo,

Bír bháne[1] *the Rájle khánde ré láo.*

" He took refuge under a rock in the village of Khandái,

Intending to smite with his sword his opponent ".

When Srí Chálda[2] killed the demon, a large force of other gods reached him.

Dohá (*couplet in Pahárí*).

Sáth larau deote kharie[3] *khánde,*

Ghái huwe[4] *rákshas lái lái bánde.*

" All the gods attacked with their swords

And cut the demons to pieces ".

After killing the demon Kirmar, all the gods threw flowers over Srí Chálda and paid homage to him.

Dohá (*couplet*).

Ádi Kalí Yug men Kirmar kíyó ráj,

Sant mahátmá ko dukh díyo dait samáj.

" Kirmar ruled the world in the beginning of the Kálí Yug.

The demon brotherhood caused great trouble to the saints and the men of God ".

Sab devan ke deb hai Mahású kartár,

Kirmar ádi márke, dúr kiyo mahi-bhár.

" The lord Mahású is the god of all gods,

Killing the great Kirmar, he has lightened the burden of the World ".

Yah charitr Mahádev ká chit de sune jo koí,

Sadá rahe sukh sampadá aur muktí phal hoí.

" He who listens to this story of Mahádev with a sincere heart,

Will always remain happy and attain the fruit of salvation ".

[1] From *bháda-na*, to break, in Pahárí.
[2] Lit., 'raising high'.
[3] *I. e.*, Mahású.
[4] *Ghái huwe*, 'are killing'.

After killing Kirmar, all the gods encamped in a field near Khanḍái and the place came to be called Dev-ká-kháṭal. It still forms the *jágír* of Dev Banár. The place in Khanḍái, where Kirmar met his death, still retains the marks of his sword on a rock. Travellers and passers-by worship this stone by offering flowers, and also express gratitude to Mahású.

Next morning at daybreak Húna Rikhí came to Mahású with clasped hands and expressed joy at Kirmar's death. He further begged that the demon, Keshí, who had made Hanol his abode and was destroying its people should be killed, adding that the place was a delightful one, as it had a fine temple, that the rippling waves of the river by which it lay added beauty to its scenery, that it was a place of sanctity and would be better under his rule than under the demons, and that it was therefore right that the demon should be killed.

Hearing this the god marched his army in that direction, and on the march they passed Salná Patti, a village in Ráwíngaṛh, near which lived another demon in a tank, receiving its water from the Pabar. When the flower-throne of Mahású reached this spot he saw a demon dancing in the tank and making a noise. Sri Naṭárí Jí said to Mahású :—' This is a fearsome sight'. When Mahású heard Umá Shankwrí's words he knew by the might of his knowledge that this was the demon spoken of by the *rikhí*. He stopped his throne and destroyed the demon on the spot by muttering some charms, which had such power that even to this day the river does not make any sound as it flows. Hence the place is called Nashudi.

Dohá.

Bájá jari-bharthá deote re bájá,

Boṭha Bájá Mahású Hanola khe birájá.

" *Jari-bharth*, the music of the gods, was played,

When Boṭha, Rájá and Mahású left for Hanol ".

Maháráj Mahású Chálḍa Pabási,

Hanol dekhíro bahute mano dé hásé.

" Maháráj Mahású, Chálḍa and Pabási,

The gods laughed greatly in their hearts on seeing Hanol".

Chhoté chhoté bahuté deo,

Srí Boṭha Mahású deote rá deo.

" There are many minor gods,

But Srí Boṭha Mahású is the god of gods."

When Srí Mahású reached Hanol with his army, he asked Húná Rikhí if it was the resort of Keshí the demon. The latter humbly replied that it was, but he added that the demon sometimes haunted the Masmor mountains, and had perhaps gone in that direction and that preparations for his destruction should be made at once. Upon this all the gods held a council and sent Srí Chálda with Sher Kaliá, Kolú and others to the mountains of Masmor to kill the other warrior-gods. They set out in search of the demon. This song of praise was sung :—

Terí Hanole, Rájaá, phúloṇ kí bárí,
Chár bhái Máhasú Mátá Deo Lárí.
Rájan ko ráj, náw tero náw.
Bhesh-dhári Rájá-jí
Ráni, Rájá náwe, parjá náwe.'

" Rájá thou hast a garden of flowers in thy Hanol,
The abode of the four Mahásús and their mother.
Thy name is king of kings.
In spite of all disguise thou art Lord,
The queen, the king and his subjects bow down to thee ".

Potgi.

Khanḍáil dákú námí chor,
Le chalo pálgí merí ubhí Masmor.
Rájan ko ráj, náw tero náw.
Kashmírí Rájá dewá kathí ? Bhimlá kí or.

" Thieves and robbers of Khanḍáí,
Bear ye my palanquin up to Masmor.
Thy name is king of kings.
Whither is the king of Kashmír gone ? He is gone towards Bhimla ",
Kailás Kashmír chhóro rájasthán Maindárath áyá.
Rájan ko ráj, náw tero náw.

" Thou hast left Kailás and Kashmír and came to Maindárath.
Thy name is king of kings "!

When Srí Chálḍa's throne reached the hill with his bandsmen playing music, the demon Keshí witnessed his arrival, and thought him to be the same who had killed his lord Kirmar, and had come there for the same purpose. So he made ready for battle and said, ' It is not right to fly'. Thinking thus, he took a huge mace and spear to attack the god. When about to shatter the god in pieces with his mace, the god's glory was manifested and the demon's hand hung motionless. Srí Chálḍá ordered Sher Kaliyá to kill the demon at once. This order was instantly obeyed. The people of the place were exceedingly glad at this good news, and there was much throwing of flowers over Mahású.

Verse.

Khushí howe ádamí paháro re sáre :
'Káre ṭek khaumpaní kúto re méro.'

" All the hill people rejoiced :
'Accept as thy revenue the offerings made out of our (share of the) produce' ".

'Kár deo khaumpaní páre Hanole láe'.
Sadá bárwí de barshe deo Bharánsí le bulác'.

" We will work and send tribute in our turn to Hanol,
And will bring the god for worship to Bharánsí every twelve years".

'Sadá kahen, Mahásúwá, mulak tihárá,
Sál deo samato rá kúto rá kárá'.

" O Mahású, we say this land is thine for ever.
And we will give thee each year every kind of grain in due season".

'Bhút, kar, rákshas, paret, chhal,
Kár deo khaumpaní sadá rahai parjá tumhárí.
Achhiddar do aur karo rakkshá hamárí'.

" Protect us from the evil-spirits, spirits, demons, ogres and goblins,
And we will give thee tribute and ever remain thy subjects.
Give us prosperity and grant us protection".

After killing the demon, Srí Cháldа Mahású seated himself on his throne and came with his forces to Hanol in great state. He brought with him all the offerings in gold and silver, as well as a gold *kaḍḍú*. taken from the demons.

On reaching the place he recounted the death of Keshí to Boṭha Mahású, saying :—" All the demons have been killed by thy favour, and all the troubles removed. Accept these offerings which I have brought and send them to thy treasury".

Hearing this, Boṭha Mahású said : -" O Srí Cháldа, go with all these heroes to the places which I name and divide the country among them, so that they may rule there, and guard the people against all calamities. The people of these lands will worship thee as thy subjects and be dependent on thee. Every person will offer thee silver, gold, brass or copper on the attainment of his desires. Wherever thou mayest go, the inhabitants will worship thee, performing a *jágrá* on the Nág-chauth and Nág-panchami days, which fall each year in Bhádon. They will be amply rewarded for these annual fairs". And he added : - " Thou shalt be worshipped like myself, and be highly esteemed throughout my kingdom, but thou wilt have to pay the *málikáná* dues for each place to the other gods. When a grand *jágrá* is performed, thou wilt be invited to present offerings to me".

Báje tál mardang shankh báje ghánte

Sabhí Srí Mahású jí ne debton kó ráj díno bánte.

"The cymbal, the *mardang* and the conch were sounded and bells were rung

When Sri Mahású divided his kingdom among his minor gods".

Ráj sabé deoton kó is tarah bántá,

Rájdhání Pabásé dená Deban rá ḍanḍá.

"He divided his State to the gods thus,

Giving the territory of Mount Deban to Pabásí".

Báshuk ko Báwar díno poru Bilo bolí Sáthe,

Pabásí Bel díno punwáso jo Bel Páshe.

"To Báshuk he gave the whole of the Báwar territory with the part of Bilo on this side of Sáthi.

To Pabásí he also gave the country of Sháthi which is on the bank of the Patwál".[1]

Kálú Koṭlá hú díno Kyálúe Banár.

Boṭhé Chálḍé Mahású ro ráj howá sarab pahár.

"To Kiálú and Banár he gave Káló and Kotlá also.

And Boṭha and Chálḍa Mahású became rulers of the whole of the hill tract".

Bothá Chálḍa Mahású sab deban re deo.

Pújané rá Mahású re jánade ná asau.

"Boṭha and Chálḍa Mahású are the gods of all the gods.

The people do not know how to worship Mahású".

Sab richá dení Húná Rikhí khe Vedo rí batán.

'*Isí bidhi kár mere debte rí pújan karái*'.

"The hymns of the *Vedas*[2] were dictated to Húná Rikhí:

'Perform my worship according to them'".

Sab gwe debte apne sathάno khe jái.

Vedo rí richá dení pújane lái.

[1] This is the meaning as explained by the descendant of Káverú, *lit.* the translation appears to be — to Pabásí he gave Bel on the day of the full moon, and so it is (now) called Bel Páshé.

[2] That is, in regard to the worship of this god.

"All the gods went to their own capitals.

The Vedic hymns should be used in worship".

Srí Mahású ke sáth sab debte gae ái,

Is Khanḍ Uttar men dete mántá karái.

"All the gods who had come with Mahású,

Are worshipped in this Northern Region".

Notáre Pokho chhoṛá jo maréshwar Mahádeo.

Hanol meṇ Boṭhá Mahású jo sab deban ke deo.

"Noṭáre[1] and Pokhú remain, Mahádev the god of the burning places.

Boṭhá Mahású is the god of gods in Hanol".

Chúrí meṇ Chúṛeshwar wahí Mahású hai deo.

Desh chhore deshore Ḍúm ádi Bhindrá deo.

"That same Mahású as Chúṛíshwar is the god of the Chúr Peak.

Ḍúm, Bhindrá and others are in charge of the other parts of the plain country".

Naráin, Ruddar, Dhaulú, Ghorḍú debte gayé Bashahro rí nálí.

Hát-koṭí meṇ Mátá Háṭéshwarí aur pahár pahár men Kálí.

"The gods Naráin, Ruddar, Dhaulú and Ghorḍú were sent towards the valley of Bashahr.

Mother Háṭéshwari was in Hát-koṭi and on every hill was Kálí".

Sabhún kí pújan Bhái huí 'jai jai' kár.

Kirmar ádi már ke ánand bhayo sansár.

"All worship the Brothers and give them (the cry of) 'victory.'

The world became very happy at the death of Kirmar and the other demons".

Désh huwá muluk, Srí Chálḍea, tumhárá.

Hanolo khe bhejná kúto rá kárá.

"Srí Chálḍa, all this country is thine.

Thy servants give thee tribute in Hanol".

"Thus was a separate tract assigned to each, and they were sent each to his own territory. Húna Rikhí was loaded with blessings in money. After this, Mahású disappeared and an image of him with four arms appeared of its own accord. It is worshipped to this day".

Sab gaye debte apne apne asthán,

Jab Boṭhá húe Shrí Mahású-jí antar-dhyán.

"All the gods went to their own places,

And then Boṭha Srí Mahású disappeared".

[1] In Gaṛhwál.

Kiyálú Banár diná uṛáo,
Kúí rí serí dá pákṛá tháo.

"Kiyálu and Banár flew away,
And took possession of the fields of Kúí".[1]

The following story is connected with these two places:—The capital of the two gods is Pujárli, a village at the foot of the Burgá Hill, beyond the Pabar stream.

When all the gods had gone to their own places, all the land was regarded as the kingdom of Mahású, and his capital was Hanol. It is now believed that if any irregularity occurs in this territory, the gods in charge of it and the people are called upon to explain the reason. The people of this country believe Mahású to have such power that if a person who has lost anything worships the god with sincere heart, he will undoubtedly achieve his desire.

Dohá (*couplet*).

Lílá iskí barnan sakke koí kaun?
Adi deban ke dev hai, Mahású kaháwe jaun.

"Who can praise him?
He is the chief god of all gods, and is called Mahású".

Jo jan dín-ho-kar unko dhyáwe.
Woh ant samay man-bánchhit phal páwe.

"He who remembers him with humble mind,
Shall at last have all his desires fulfilled".

Aise bhae yih Ruddar avatár,
Jin tárá sakal sansár.

"So (great) is the incarnation of Ruddar,[2]
That all the world is delivered from transmigration".

Wohí Shib Shankar avatár,
Jinkí máyá ne bándhá sansár.

"He is Shiv Shankar incarnate,
And the whole world is enthralled by his illusion".

Aisé hain woh Shib Shankar ánandá,
Jin ke simran se káte har phandá.

"Such is Shiv Shankar ever pleased,
Who remembers him passes safely through the whole maze".[3]

Jis ne is men shanká uṭháe,
Woh narak hí men hai Shambhú ne páí.

"He who has doubts as to these things,
Is doomed to hell by Shambhu".

[1] Kúí is a place in Rawaingaṛh, near the Burga Mountains.

[2] Shivá.

[3] Or we may read *Har phandá* and translate: 'By remembrance of him (mankind) may be delivered from the maze of Har (Shiv)'.

Woh Shib Shankar antarjámí,

Jin ko dhyáwat sur nar gyání.

"He is Shiv Shankar, the heart-searcher,

On whom meditate the heroes and the sages".

Yih Shambhu Jagat sukh dái,

Jin ká pár koú nahíṇ pái.

"He is Shambhu and gives blessings to the world,

And no one can fathom his doings".

Bháva, Sharva, Rudra, Pashu-pati, Girisha, Mahesha, mahán,

Jin ke gunánu vád ko gáwi Veda Purán.

"He is Bháva, Sharva, Rudra, Pashu-pati, Girisha, Mahesha, the great one,

Whose virtue is sung in the *Vedás* and *Puráns*".

Aise bhae woh Mahású sukh-dáyí,

Jal thal meṇ jo rahe samáyí.

"Mahású comforts every man,

And his glory pervades both sea and land".

Koú barnan ná sake unkí prabhutái;

Brahmá, Vishnu, Sáradá ant nahíṇ pái.

"We lack words to tell his greatness;

Brahmá, Vishnu, and even Sáradá could not know his reality".

Tín lok ke náth haiṇ ant nahíṇ kachhu pái:

Brahmá, Vishnu, Sáradá, hár gaye man mehí.

"He is the king of the three worlds and is infinite:

Even the gods Brahmá, Vishnú and Sáradá could not stand before him".

Háth joṛké Brahmá, Vishnu, khaṛí Sáradá mái:

'*Tín lok meṇ játe bháe pár láne nahíṇ pái*'.

"Brahmá, Vishnú and Mother Sáradá stood with clasped hands before him:

'We have been round the three worlds, but could find no end (to his glory)'".

Hár mán kar thakat bhae pár nahíṇ jab pái,

Háth joṛkar ṭháḍḍé bhae náth-pad sís nái.

"When they could find no end to his glory,

They came before him with clasped hands and bowed heads".

Sís nawáí ke náth pad ke kíní bahut pukár :

'Tum deban ke deb hó lílá param apár.'

"They bowed their heads to the god and praised him aloud :

'Thou art the god of all gods and wondrous is thy glory' ".

'Hai Chandra-chúra madanáksh-shúl páni kar jaisá :

Tín lok ke kartá kartá deban deb Maheshá.'

"Thy light is like that of the moon and thou art full of water like the ocean :

Thou art Mahású, the creator and destroyer of the three worlds".

Jahán tahán bhae Mahású antar-dhyán,

Tab se unkí astuti karat Hanóla Sthán.

"From the time that Mahású disappeared,

He began to be praised in the Hanol temple".

Woh sthán hai Uttar Khand máhí :

Nadí kináré Tons ke mandir baná táhín.

"His place is in the Northern Region :

His temple is built on the bank of the river Tons".

When all the gods went to their own places, the other gods agreed to pay tribute to Hanol according to the directions of Mahású. They also agreed to pay *mál.káná* dues on the birthday of Mahándátá to the inhabitants.

In Kulu Mahású is known as Kashu-báhana and when disputants take an oath they drink water in his name. The party telling an untruth suffers from the draught thus drunk.

Shiv worship is very common in Mandi, both in the town and in the *iláqa* — much more so than in Bashahr where Káli worship is far more important. The veneration of Shiva however is not universal. In several *iláqas* adjacent to Kulu the *shivrátri* receives very casual notice whereas Deví worship is general there. Mr. H. W. Emerson does not think it safe to say that the cults of Shiva are imported or that they are merely the cults of the educated classes. In the hills, as a rule, the low aboriginal castes are the greatest worshippers of Shiva, but the Kanets also — though the custom varies considerably — are very zealous observers of the *shivrátri*. There is also a close association between Shaivism and Nág worship — the Nágs are his (or Káli's) favourite servants. *Lingams* are common and in more or less orthodox temples are found with the *yoni*. Near the entrance to the *haram sarái* there is a very horrible image of Durga with a realistic *lingam* in front round which a cobra is coiled with the canopy over the top of the *lingam*. The *shivrátri* is the great official festival of Manḍi, corresponding to the Dasehra of Kulu. The gods are all brought in and do obeisance first to Mádhu Rái, the real ruler of the State, and then to the Rájá his vice-regent. The latter always goes behind Mádhu Rái in the procession.

In Manḍi the cults of Shiva are chiefly affected by Brahmans, Rájpúts, Khatrís and Bohras which may point to their imported origin, or merely indicate that they are the cults of the educated classes as opposed to the cultivator masses. In Manḍi town a temple is dedicated to Shiva Ardhnareshwara or Shiva as half himself and half his consort Gaura or Párbati, the first creator of all things, older than sex itself. On the left bank of the Biás is a temple to the Pancha-baktra or 'five-faced' Shiva and on the right bank one to Triloknáth, 'lord of the three worlds', with three faces. It would be interesting to know if these temples are complementary to each other like those of Ḍera Dín Panáh in Muzaffargaṛh. Another and a very old temple to Shiva is that of Bhát Náth in Manḍi town, regarding whose idol a legend of the usual type is told. A cow was seen to yield her milk to a stone, and beneath it Rájá Ajbar Sain (c. 1500 A. D.) discovered the idol and founded the temple in consequence of a dream.[1] Bálaknáth, son of Shiva, has a temple on the bank of the Beás. He is not to be confounded with Bálak Rúpi. Bhairoṇ is a disciple of Shiva[2] and a Siddh, and Ganpati or Ganesh is his most dutiful son, as elsewhere. In Suket Rájá Madan Sain founded a temple to Astan (? Sthamba) Náth, apparently a form of Shiva.

Although out of 49 fanes in Manḍi town no less than 24 are dedicated to Shiva, the Gosáíns, his votaries, have declined in importance.[3]

In Kulu the tradition is that the *deotas* represent the *rishis* and other great men who were in existence at the time of the Mahábhárat. After that war the *deotás* and *rishis* of that epoch came and settled in the Kulu valley and the autochthones built temples and raised memorials to them. The reason advanced for this tradition is that all the temples and *deotás* bear the names of those *rishis* and heroes. But the temples at Maníkaran (Rámchandar's), Sultánpur (to Raghúnáth), Mahárája and Jagat Sukh are ascribed to the time of Mahárája Jagat Singh while the Sikh temple at Harípur was erected by Rájá Hari Singh.

In Manḍi Tomasha *rishi* is still worshipped by Brahmans at Rawálsar lake, as well as by Buddhists under the name of Padmasambhar.[4]

[1] Women visit this temple every Monday and sing hymns with lamps in their hands. For a beautiful illustration of a temple to Bhút Nátha in Madras see *Arch. Survey Rep.*, 1913-14, Pt. I—Pl. VIII.

[2] In the Hills Ganesh is known as Binúyák or Sidhi-Binúyak and in Kángra his picture, called *jag-jáp*, is carved in stone or wood and set up in the house-door when ready: J. A. S B., 1911, pp. 183, 235, 175. Havell's explanation of Ganesh's elephant head is worth citing. He describes him as the god of worldly wisdom and as the 'protector of households', representing the wisdom which brings to mankind a great store of this world's goods; the sagacity of an elephant which keeps the mind tied to earth, not the spiritual power of Shiva, which can take wings and lift the soul to heaven: wherefor he is the patron deity of scribes and publishers. But how much of this explanation is due to Mr. Havell's own ingenuity and how much to orthodox or current belief? *The Ideals of Indian Art*, pp. 51, 82.

[3] Manḍi *Gazetteer*, pp. 38-39.

[4] Francke's *Antiquities of Indian Tibet*, p. 123.

The following is a list of the temples in Kulu dedicated to various *rishis* :—

Name of *rishi*.	Site of temple.	Date of fair.
Kártak Swámi ...	Ḍera at Sheonsar ...	5th of Baisákh.
Do. ...	Ḍera or Ḍeri ...	6th of the light half of Baisákh, 1st of Chet, commencement of the new year in Chet, and 1st of Bhádon.
Do. ...	Ḍera at Shaushar ...	5th of lunar part of Baisákh, 20th Bhádon and 20th Mágh.
Kapal Muni ...	Ḍera at Kalath ...	On the Rám Naumi, the 16th of Chet, and the *janam ashtami*, the 21st of Bhádon.
Do. ...	Ḍera at Bashona ...	25th Baisákh and a *yag* every year on 1st and 2nd Sáwan.
Bashist Rikhi ...	Bashist Ḍera ...	1st of Baisákh and 12th of Kátak.
Gautam Rishi[1] ...	Ḍera Gautam Rishi ...	12th of Phágan and 1st Baisákh.
Gautam Rikhi or Ghumal Rikhi[2]	Ḍera in K. Kot Khandi...	1st Phágan.
Gamal Rikhi[3] ...	Loni Ḍera	*Ikádshi* of the light half of Phágan.
Parásar Rishi ji[4] ...	Kamandu Haru ...	In Mágh, Chet, Baisákh and Sáwan.
Chiman Rikhi or Chirmal.[5]	Ḍera	7th Phágan, 11th Baisákh, and 5th Jeṭh.
Do. ...	Chiman Rikhi ...	1st of Phágan.
Sándal Rikhi ...	Dera Kahim in K. Manali	8th of Phágan, 2nd of Baisákh, and the *janam ashtami*, the 26th of Sáwan.
Márkanda[6] ...	Mukrah temple ...	1st Phágan, 1st Baisákh, and 20th Sáwan.

[1] The temple of Beás Rikhi is connected with this, the *Puráns* say that the place where he practised penance was the source of the river Biás. Any one visiting Beás Kunḍ is fed here. The *pujáris* are Gaurs, Kanets and Bairágís.

[2] At another temple the chariot of the god is kept. It is decorated with fine clothes, as well as ornaments of silver and gold, and the images of gods are arranged in it. The chariot is also worshipped at the fair.

[3] A temple called Guran Ḍera is connected with this. When the chariot is elsewhere the god is kept in the temple.

[4] This *rishi* also has a temple in Sanor in Manḍi (*Gazetteer*, p. 40).

[5] Two other temples are connected with this.

[6] Márkanḍa fair is held annually on the 1st Baisákh in Kángra. Márkanḍa was an ascetic, but his name is now applied to any water which flows eastward. On the Saukránt of each month people bathe in this water and give alms. In Kulu proper Márkanḍa's image seems to have been placed on bridges and as guardian of bridges he would appear to have been known as Mangleshar—unless that was the name of his spouse. The god Mangleshar Deo is alluded to in the triplet :

Mangli Ráni, Mangleshar Deo
Dhauns phúṭi, Saund seo,
Markanḍa Makrál seo.

"When Mangli was queen Mangleshar's drum was burst; the bridge of Saund carried the god Márkanḍa to Makrál".

And the legend goes that when queen Mangli ruled at Jía, at the junction of the Beás and Párbati rivers, the latter used to be spanned by a bridge at Saund, just above the confluence. When the drum used in the worship of Mangleshar burst the bridge fell, but the idol of Márkanḍa, which was on the bridge when it fell, was carried on the timbers of the fallen structure down the river to Makrál where Márkanḍa's temple now stands : Diack, *Kuluhi Dialect*, p. 39.

In Saráj there are several minor cults of interest. Besides that of Jamlu who is identifiable with Jamdaggan *rishi*, Márkanda and Shringa[1] *rishis* are the objects of worship. The former has three temples. That at Manglaur, which derives its name from one name of the temple, is also called Kanderi. From 1st to 5th Phágan a fair is held here every third year, and on the *shivrátri* in Chet a *brambhoj* (free distribution of food) is celebrated and girls are feasted. On 1st Baisákh a *jag* is held at which the god is taken to the nearest river to bathe. Small fairs are also held during the first week of Baisákh. During Bhádon the god is invited by all the neighbouring villages, and for many nights an illumination is made before him. Throughout Poh and Mágh the god is shut up in the temple which is re-opened in Phágan. Once upon a time, the story goes, a Ráná in Manglaur asked a Brahman to recite the *Chandi* to him and while he was doing so a *sádhú* appeared. It was declared that Márkanda *rishi* had thus manifested himself, and many people became his followers. His fame soon reached the ears of Rájá Mangal Sain of Mandi who gave land in *muáfi* for the maintenance of his shrine. After the Rájá's death a *ṭhákurdwára* was built at Manglaur in his memory, but the exact date of its foundation is not known. It contains a stone *pindi*, 2 feet high, as well as a stone image. Its affairs are managed by a *kárdár* by caste a Gaur Brahman. A Sarsút *pujári* is employed for worship. The *gur* is also a Brahman. These persons are not celibate and their offices are hereditary. A *bhog* of sweetmeat, *ghí*, rice etc. is offered daily and a sacred lamp is lit every evening. No other shrine is connected with this one.

The story about Márkanda's other temples is that he is in the habit of manifesting himself through his *gur*, who goes into a trance on 2nd Phágan every year. While in this state he declares that there are seven Shivas in Triloknáth in Láhul, who begot seven devotees named Márkanda: that one of them stayed at his birthplace, while the other six came to Rothí Koṭ. One of them settled in Makláhr, while the rest set out for Kanglaur. There one of them carved out a principality and the other four made their way to Balágád, Fatehpur, Mandi and Núr. Núr was governed by a *ṭhákur* whom the devotee killed and took possession of his territory. After this Márkanda disappeared below the earth, whereupon a *pindi* of stone appeared. Two temples were built at this place. The date of their foundation is not known. One of them contains a stone *pindi*, 3 feet high, and the other a chariot of the god. Their administration is carried on jointly by a *kárdár* and the villagers. The *pujári* is Bhardawáj Brahman. He is not celibate and the succession is governed by natural relationship. Special reverence is paid only to the *gur*. No special rites are performed by the *pujári*. The usage of *bhog* is not known. No sacred lamp is lit, nor is fire maintained. Connected with this are the shrines in Núr and Nolu. The annual fair is held on 19th and 20th Baisákh. A *jag* is celebrated after every 12 years, at which a few he-goats are sacrificed. It generally falls in Maghar or Kátak.

Márkanda and Deví Bala Durga have a temple at Márkanda where a fair is held on 5th Phágan, and at the Holí it lasts from the end of

[1] Popularly called Singa *rishi*.

Chet to the 10th of Baisákh. Other fairs are also held on 12th and 15th Baisákh. During the *naurátra* festivals also virgins are fed and worship performed. The story is that once a *sádhú* came from Triloknáth and declared that the places should be consecrated to the worship of the Deví and Márkanḍa. Accordingly they were installed here. The temple was founded in the Dwápar Yug. It contains a stone *pinḍi*. Its affairs are managed by a *kárdár*. For worship a Brahman is employed. The *kárdár* is a Gauṛ Brahman and the *pujári* a Sársut. All the questions put to the god are answered through a *gur*.

Deota Shringá Rikhi in Chaihni has two temples: one in Sikarn and the other in Bijepur. The fair at the former is held annually on the last day of Baisákh, and at the latter on any auspicious date in Phágan. Besides these, a fair is held at Banjár on 2nd Jeṭh. The story is that Shertángan, a Kanet of Rihlu, was once ploughing his field on the Tirthan Khaḍ when he heard a voice saying: 'I will come'. This was repeated on three successive days, and on the morning of the last day of Baisákh a *pinḍi* in the image of a man emerged from the Khaḍ and approached the man. It directed him to carry it to the place where during the Dwápar Yug it had performed asceticism. On the way it stopped at two places, Bijepur and Sikaru, where the temples were afterwards built. Here a *chela*, during the night, learnt in a vision that the god's name was Surangá Rikhi. The temples were founded in the Dwápar Yug. It contains a black stone *pinḍi*, 2¼ feet long. Its administration is carried on by a Kanet *kárdár*. A Brahman *pujári* is employed to perform all the rites. His caste is Sársut and *got* Dharmíán. A *bhog* of rice, *dál*, milk, *ghí* or sugar is offered twice a day, and a sacred lamp is lit every evening. Low castes are not allowed to offer any edible thing as *bhog*, but no distinction is made in their offerings of other things. Connected with this are the shrines in Chaihni and Bági.

In Saráj Jamlu and Devi Jalpá have a temple at Galun Deora, where a fair is held every year from 21st to 28th Phágan, and another from 21st to 26th Sáwan. The *navrátras* in Chet and Asauj are also observed as fairs. Virgins are worshipped and a *páth* is recited. The story goes that a *sádhú* was found in Galun sitting absorbed in meditation. A *thákur* asked him who he was and whence he came. He replied that people called him Jamdaggan Rishi and added that he desired a temple to be built in his name. The *thákur* built a temple, but it did not satisfy the *sádhú* who, taking an image of the *deví* from his hair, said that a temple should be built for her residence also. This demand was not acceded to; so eventually both were installed in the same temple. It is said to have been built in the Dwápar Yug, and contains stone *pinḍís* of the god and goddess. A silver club and a silver horse are also kept in it. Its administration is carried on by a *kárdár*, by caste a Kanet. A Brahman *pujári* is employed for service in the temple, while the *gur* is the disciple of the god. These three incumbents are not celibate and the succession follows natural relationship. The *pujári's* position is good, but special reverence is paid to the *gur* who answers all questions put to the god. A *bhog* of sweetmeat, milk, rice etc. is offered daily, and the sacred lamp lighted every evening. Connected with this is the shrine in Sinoh.

The principal fair in Saráj tahsíl is that of Sing or more correctly Shringá Rikhi. It takes place at Banjár, the head-quarters of the tahsíl on the second of Jeṭh and lasts from 10 P. M. to 4 A. M. Men and women dance in crowds, a dance which is called *nati*. All offerings below two annas, including sweetmeats, grain and fruit, go to the *pujáris*, those of that amount and above it are credited in the god's treasury. Some 2000 or 3000 people attend the fair. Sweetmeats, fruit and clothes are given to relatives, especially to women. Men and women swing on *handolás*, sing the songs called *jhanjhotis* and make other forms of merriment. A considerable amount of trade also takes place.

THE CULT OF JAMLU (JAMDAGGAN).

The cult of Jamdaggan Rishi is widespread in the Kángra hills, the temple at Baijnáth being dedicated to him. In Kulu he is especially worshipped at Malána, the remote valley whose people are called RADEO.

The following is a list of his temples in Kulu proper:—

Name of god.	Site of temple.	Date of fair.
Deota Jamlu ...	Kharon Mandir in Koṭhi Malána.	10th of Maghar, full moon day of Maghar, one day in the dark half of Poh, one Thursday in Mágh, one day in the light half of Mágh, one in the light half of Phágan, 8 days in Phágan, 2 in Chet, 10 in the light half of Chet, 1st and 2nd of Baisákh, one in the light half of Baisákh, 1st of Jeṭh, 1st of Har, 3 days in the light half of Sáwan, 31st of Sáwan to 5th of Bhádon, Sheori Shankránt for 2 days, 5 in the light half of Asauj, and 1st of Kátak.
Deota Jamlu ...	Dera Jamlu Saman in Saman.	*Ikdam* of Phágan *sudi* lasting 4 days, 1st of Chet, 1st of Bhádon, lasting 4 days, and full moon of Maghar for 2 days.
	Dera Jamdaggan Rishi in Sati.	One lasting 4 days from the *ikádshi* of the light half of the month, another on 1st of Chet, a third lasting 4 days in Bhádon, and a fourth 2 days on the full moon day of Maghar.
	Dera Daifri in Daifri ...	4 days in the light half of Phágan, 2 from 1st Chet and Baisákh, 4 days from 1st Bhádon, in Sáwan, and 2 days on the full moon day of Maghar.
	Dera Shangchar in Shangchar.	7 days on the *ikádshi* of the light half of Phágan, 2 days beginning on 1st of Chet, 1st of Baisákh, and 1st of Bhádon, lasting 4 days.

Name of god.	Site of temple.	Date of fair.
Deota Jamlu	Dera. Shegli Jamlu in Shaigli.	4 days on the *ikádshi* of the light half of Phágan, 2 days on the 1st of Chet and Baisákh, 4 days on 1st Bhádon, and in Sáwan.
		Phágli from 7th to 10th Phágan, Khauni *Phágli* on 1st of Chet, and Sáwan *játra* on 1st Bhádon.
	Dera Sakho Sah in Parain	Baisákh and Phágan
	Dera Jamdaggan Rishi ...	1st of Bhádon, full moon day of Maghar, 9th of the light half of Phágan, and 1st of Chet.
	Dhari Narol in Jagat Sukh	Phágan and Chet, a Sáwan *játra* in Sáwan and Bhádon, and a fair on the full moon day of Maghar.
	Dera in *mauza* Shiah ...	1st Baisákh and 24th Sáwan.
	Dera in Jamdaggan Rikhi Ursu village.	7th Baisákh.
	Páshi Dera or Khalangoha Dera in Páshi.	7th Phágan and 1st to 7th Baisákh also Rakhri Punián.
	Jamdaggan Rishi's temple in Neri.	On the *ikádshi* and *dwádshi* of Phágan, 1st of Chet and Bhádon, and on the full moon day of Maghar.
	Dera in village Sisa ...	12th Bhádon, 3rd Phágan, and 1st and 3rd Baisákh.
Deota Jamlu Badagaran	Dera Deota Jamlu ..	8 days from the *ikádshi* of the light half of Phágan, 1st of Chet for 2 days, 1st of Baisákh for 2 days, 1st of Bhádon for 5 days, in Sáwan, and on the full moon day of Maghar for 2 days.
Deota Jamlu Baharka	Naroli re Deri ...	5 days in the light half of Phágan, 2 in the light part of Chet, 3 days on the 1st of Bhádon, and *sokhab bir pája* for one day.
Deota Jamlu Gajjan Wala.	Gajjan Dera ...	1st of Chet.
Deota Jamlu Karjan Wála.	Dera Karjan ...	*Phágli* in Mágh on the *ikádshi* of the lunar month for 2 days, *phágli* on the full moon day of Chet, Sáwan, *játra* from 1st to 4th of Bhádon, and in Maghar on the full moon day.
Deota Jamlu Kasheri	Dera Jamlu Kasheri ...	On the *ikádshi* of the light half of Phágan for 3 days, 1st of Baisákh for 2 days, 1st of Chet for 2 days, 1st of Bhádon for 4 days, and 1st of Asauj for 2 days.

Name of god.	Site of temple.	Date of fair.
Deota Jamlu Kulang	Dera Jamlu ...	7th of Phágan till 10th and Sáwan *játra* on 1st Bhádon.
Deota Jamlu Majachh	Do. ..	*Phágli kanni, phágli* and Sáwan *játra* on 7th Phágan, 1st Chet, and 1st Bhádon, respectively.
Shakohri Jamlu ..	Mehr Bari ...	On the Holi in Sáwan and on the *naumi* of Maghar. A large gathering also takes place every third year in Sáwan.
Deota Jamlu Soil Wála	Dheri Narol ...	5 days in Bhádon, *phágli* in Phágan and Chet, *dhara pujani* in Asauj and *pons* for 2 days in Maghar.
Deota Jamlu Tapri ...	Dera Jamlu ...	*Ikádshi* and *dwádshi* of the light half of Chet, 1st Friday of Bhádon, and 1st of Bhádon.
Deota Jamlu Tos ...	Deota Jamlu ...	Tuesday of the light half of Bhádon.

In Maṇḍi the tradition is much the same In that State most of the *deotás* are *rishis* or saints of Hindu mythology, but others are named after the hills on which their temples stand. Devís, especially, control rain, like Phugni Deví in Chohár and so do Naráin and Pusakoṭ. The two latter also dislike smoking. Tandi, Laogli and Tungasi are well-known deities in Maṇḍi Saráj. Barárta Deo, whose fair is held on Sáwan 2nd on Lindi Dhár or ridge, is effective in curing barrenness in she-buffaloes.[1]

But the Deví-cults in Maṇḍi are of a higher type than those of a mere rain-god. Srívidya or Rájeshwari is not only popular but ancient as the old Rájás used to worship her. Bagla-mukhi or the heron-faced Deví is affected by the *parohits* of the ruling family. She wears yellow and holds a club in one hand, in the other a demon's tongue. Like Srívidya, Bála and Tára have four arms, but their attributes are different. Kálí assumes many forms. Dichhat Brahmans are her chief devotees, and her shrine is on the large tank at Maṇḍi. Less orthodox *devís* are Shikári or the huntress in Nachan, who dwells on a lofty hill and is fond of the blood of goats, Tunga in Sanor who is angered by evil deeds and when offended kills people by lightning, and Nawahi in whose honour a great fair is held on Baisákh 5th at Anantapur, where her temple is surrounded by many smaller ones of some antiquity.[2] The ruling family of Suket has been long under the protection of Deví. Rájá Madan Sain removed his capital from Pángna on her warning him in a dream that it was her ancient *asthán* and by her Garúr Sain was admonished against his disloyal, though apparently hereditary, *parohits* who were ex-communicated by his successor and were not re-instated for some time.

[1] Maṇḍi *Gazetteer*, pp. 40-1.
[2] *Ib.*, pp. 39 and 41.

In this State Hindu women observe the *chirya-barat* on the 3rd of the bright half of Bhádon. This fast is kept by eating no food prepared on a hearth and no plantains, but only milk and other fruits. Sparrows, 5 of silver and 20 or 25 of mud, are prepared, the former being clothed and adorned with silver ornaments and a gold nose-ring put in the beak of each, and then given to Brahmans, while the mud images are given to children. Párbati by observing this rite obtained Shiva as her spouse, and women still observe it to ensure long life to their husbands.[1]

The following are some temples in Kángṛa which cannot be classified with any certainty :—

Name of god.	Site of temple.	Date of fair.	Images, etc.
Mandir Báwa Bhúpa in Pargor. The story is that the Báwa before his death desired his heirs to burn his remains at this place This was done and his tomb erected where the present *mandir* stands. There is also a *dharmsála* in its precincts.	Rájpút ...	Jeṭh 1st ...	It contains images of the Báwa carved on a stone. Worship is performed morning and evening, *halwa* being offered as *bhog* every morning.
Mandir Báwa Daya Gir Swámi. The Swámi used to live in the building; so when he died his tomb was built here. He possessed a good knowledge of Sanskrit. The temple was rebuilt of brick in S. 1914 by a disciple.	Brahman ...	The fair on 3rd Jeṭh has been held for 20 years. It is patronized mostly by the villagers.	It contains a tomb on which is seated a brown stone *pinḍi* of Gauri-shankar, 2 spans high.
Goriya Sidh's *mandir* at Sidhbári. A Rájpút sept lived at this spot, and owing to the attacks of Bháṭs of Chamba they resorted to a Goriya Gosáín who lived at their gate. He bade them cast themselves into a well, and he himself followed their example, after he had covered it with a stone slab. Shortly after the curse or *khot* of the dead men tormented the villagers who began to propitiate and worship them as their family deities or *kúlja*. Another story is that beneath the Sidh's image is a deep hole meant for receiving the water of a libation.	Abdhút Gosáín...	Jeṭh 11th ...	The stone image of the Sidh is a span high. Bread or rice in the morning, milk or gram in the evening form the *bhog*.

[1] Suket *Gazetteer*, pp. 8, 12 and 22.

Name of god.	Site of temple.	Date of fair.	Images, etc.
Thákur Guptushar's *mandir* in Khaḍ Manúni in Sanhára. Owes its origin to the same Gosáín.	...	...	The stone image lies under a large slab of stone and is 4 fingers high
Tirti to Rai Singh of Chamba who fell in battle against R. Parkásh Chand of Goler and Sansár Chand Katoch in S. 1850.	Brahman, *got* Ipat, *cotar* Bashist.	Háṛ 6th. The temple contains an idol of Mahádev Rámeshar.	Rice in the morning and bread in the evening is offered as *bhog*; soaked gram or fruit is also used in worship. It is said while the Rájá was dying, he smeared his hand with his own blood and marked it on a stone, over which a smaller temple was raised. Here lamps are lit on the fair day.
Mandir Báwa Janti Dás in Matúr. Founded in Sikh times.	Khatri ...	Háṛ 1st ...	Worship is performed morning and evening, but a *bhog* of *halwa* is offered only once a year, at the festival. Connected with this is the same Báwa's shrine at Nandpur at which a fair is held simultaneously.
Mandir Apsara Kunḍ.[1] Hindu women mostly frequent this temple and offer fresh grain during Phágan, Chet, Baisákh, Jeṭh and Háṛ. It is also frequented by people of the neighbouring towns, who often bathe in the *kunḍ* or spring, which is fed by the Gupt Ganga with water from the Ban Ganga.	Brahman, caste Húlar, *got* Kodina.	...	The temple contains a stone image of Apsra, the fairy, 1½ cubits high. By its side is a *pinḍí*.

At the *mandir* of Ajia Pál in Teri no fair is held. Ajia Pál was a Rájá of Ajmer, who was adored by the people of this place. In his lifetime he enshrined a small image which was eventually worshipped as the Rájá himself. Tho temple has existed for 400 years, but the old building was replaced by one of masonry under Sikhu Brahman some 60 years ago. It contains a conical stone 2 spans high called Ajia Pál.

In conclusion, attention may be called to the side lights often cast on history by the legends and occasionally by the records of these temples. Thus the story of Udah Deví's temple at Bhagwára is that

[1] The *mandir* of Sháh Madár is connected with it and all offerings made by Muhammadan women bathing in the *kunḍ* are taken by the Muhammadan *faqírs* who are the guardians of the shrine.

once it was revealed in a vision to Rájá Tej Chand that he should go to Básan, where she would appear, and worship her there if he desired to regain territory lost to the Rájá of Mandi. Before long he achieved a complete success. When the news of his defeat reached the Rájá of Mandi, he carried away by stealth the Deví's image in a *pálki*, but when it reached the Kángra boundary the bearers, to take a rest, placed it on the ground, and when they tried to lift it up again they could not do so. So they left it there and took their way homewards. In the morning the Kángra men came and tried to carry it back, but equally in vain. So Rájá Tej Chand erected this temple at the spot and there the fair has been held ever since. The date of foundation is not known. The temple stands on a raised *chabútra*. It contains a stone *pindi* of the goddess, the height of which is only equal to the breadth of 2 fingers.

List of unclassed deotás *in Kulu.*

Name of god.	Site of temple.	Date of fair.
Baradhi Bír ...	Nandi Dera ...	1st Baisákh, in Bhádon, 1st Asauj, during *naurátras*, 1st Poh, 1st Phágan, and in Phágan.
Berruthan ...	Berraithan in K. Mahárája.	From end of Phágan to 1st of Baisákh, from end of Chet to beginning of Baisákh, from end of Sáwan to beginning of Bhádon.
Panj Bír ...	Dera	In Sáwan and Baisákh.
Bír Náth ...	Dera Bír Náth Mandrol in K. Pashan.	Full moon in Maghar and on the *janam-ashtami*
Gauhri ...	Dera Deota Gauhri ...	1st Chet, 1st Baisákh, 1st and 2nd Asauj, and festivals during light half of Sáwan and on 15th Phágan.
Bír Náth ...	Dera Bír Náth Dachani in Dorah.	12th of Baisákh and full moon of Maghar.
Gushri ...	Lakri Shiva ...	1st of Baisákh, Chet and Asauj.
Bír Náth or Gahri ...	Dera Deota Gcahri in Bissar.	1st of Jeth.
Deota Bír Náth ...	Dera Bír Náth.	
Gauhri ...	Dera Gauhri in Karain.	
Gauhri ...	Dera ...	5th Phágan and 3rd Baisákh.
Gauhri ...	Dheri Bhosh Jeth Bír Shiv in Bhosh.	2nd of Chet and one day at the new year.
Bír Náth or Gauhri...	Gauhri Dera in K. Mahárája.	1st of Chet and Baisákh, and on the 16th of Baisákh.

Name of god.	Site of temple.	Date of fair.
Bír Náth ...	Dera Sargnti Padhár in Paugan.	1st of Chet, 1st of Jeṭh, light half of Sáwan, 1st of Asauj. 5th of light half of Asauj, 10th (Dasehra) of the light halfof Asauj. light half of Maghar, 12th of Phágan, and light half of Jeṭh.
Gauhri or Bír Náth...	...	4th of Bhádon, 1st of Baisákh, Bhádon and Asauj, and on the day of the full moon of Maghar.
Gauhri or Bír Náth ..	Hatai Ḍera ...	1st of Asauj and 3rd, 5th and 7th of dark half of Phágan.
Basheshar Náth ...	Hatai Ḍera ...	No fair.
Ajmal	Ajmal Naraindi ...	1st to 7th Phágan, 31st Baisákh and 1st Jeṭh. Every 12 years a *yag* from 1st to 3rd Bhádon.
Amal	Naraindi Ḍera ...	Seven days in the light part of Phágan, 3rd of Baisákh, 1st of Haṛ, and in Bhádon.
Arjan Gophar ...	Arjan Gopha ...	...
Bania Masho ...	Lain Ḍera	From Sunday to Thursday in the dark half of Sáwan and Phágan and on 1st of Mágh.
Chánga Shin ...	Chkráhan Ḍera ...	1st to 3rd Jeṭh.
Damohal ...	Maror	1st Asauj.
Dhonbal ...	Ḍera Deota Dhonbal in K. Hawang.	Friday to Monday in Phágan.
Dhonbal ...	Ḍera Dhonbal in K. Badagara.	11th to 20th of Phágan and on Tuesday.
Durbha Sharshi ...	Pagli Ḍera, Dhara Ḍera, Gahra Ḍera, Bawara Ḍera and Mohani Ḍera.	1st Baisákh, 11th Baisákh, 26th Baisákh, 9th Jeṭh, on *deo saini thádashi* in Asauj or Bhádon, 5th Poh
Donkhru ...	Mewa	*Amáwas* in Bhádon.
Gauhri Mahu Khat ...	Gahri Mahu Khat ...	*Shivrátri.*
Jagitam	Naráin-di Ḍera in K. Badagar.	For three days from 1st of Baisákh.
Jagti pat ...	...	...
Jagmátá ...	Dhara Ḍera	*Amáwas* in Bhádon.
Kamardan ...	...	In Phágan, on the 1st of Asauj and on the full moon of Maghar.
Mandasan ...	Ḍera	29th Chet, 8th Baisákh, 25th Baisákh and 5th Asauj.

Name of god.	Site of temple.	Date of fair.
Nawani	Kasanti Dera ...	3rd, 5th, 7th and 8th of the dark half of Baisákh, Phágan and Maghar.
Píth	Shakai	7th Baisákh and 1st Asauj.
Raimal	Dera Narol in K. Bhalat, Naráin Nabi.	*Bhog* on 11th Baisákh, 9th or 11th Maghar, *beth* on 9th or 11th Baisákh, *nágni panchmi* in Bhádon, and *parchain* on 1st Phágan.
Raupal	Lohal Dera in K. Khokhan	1st of Chet and Baisákh, on the 23rd and 24th of Baisákh, and on the 1st of Sáwan and Bhádon.
Resha	Talarah Dera or Rurah Dera, Dhemol Deota, Gausari Dera, Chantala Dera, Pabhiari Koṭ, Pabhiari Koṭ, Pabhiari Parol, Ghat Koṭ, Kaniargi Dera, Kaniargi Mara, Kaniargi Koṭ, and Rupiali Dera in Bhai Roṭ.	9th and 10th Baisákh, 9th and 10th Bhádon, 11th Baisákh, 11th Bhádon, *dwádshi* of Sáwan, 1st Phágan, 3rd to 5th Phágan, 1st of Chet, and first Sunday of Sáwan.
Gurg Resha ...	Dhara in K. Dera. ...	12th Baisákh and 9th Hár.
Reshi Chashbui ..	Gara Dera	*Rakhri punián*, birthday, *sháwan-játra*, after 6th and 11th days of the birthday, *janam-ashṭami* in Bhádon, *Kosheri játra* on 1st Asauj, *mahta játra* on *Panu Bhikha ashṭami*, *purchhani játra* on 1st Phágan, and *bir shiw játra* on 1st Baisákh.
Resha	Mahashui Dera ...	7th Jeṭh.
Surajpál	Dera	1st of Hár.
Thán	Bahuthi Dera in K. Tárápur.	1st of Chet, Baisákh, Sáwan, Bhádon, and Asauj.
Thán	Thán	1st of Chet, 7th of Baisákh, and 1st of Asauj.
Thán Balurga ...	Dera Deota Thán ...	1st of Phágan, 7th Mágh, and 1st Bhádon.
Thir Mal ...	Narian-di Dera ...	1st to 9th Phágan and 1st to 5th Bhádon.
Shargan ...	Dera Deota Shargan ...	1st and 2nd or 3rd of Chet.
Shubh	Naráin-di Dera ...	9th of Phágan, 1st of Hár, and 1st of Baisákh.
Rawal	Dera in Garahan ...	2nd and 3rd Bhádon.
Do.	Rawal in Uch ...	9th and 10th Baisákh.

Nauni is a *jogni*, a malignant demon, who is worshipped at Khopri in Tárapur *koṭhi* and at Kashánṭi, a village above Karaun. No other *deota* is worshipped there. She has no image.

Gramang *deota* at Rujag in Chuparsa has two temples (*dehru*), the smaller up the hill-side, the larger lower down. In the light halves of Sáwan and Maghar he visits the village for a day, and pays it a longer visit of three days in the light half of Phágan, spending an hour or two in the upper temple and the rest of the time in the lower. He is one of the lesser Naráins and though regarded as Parmeshar he is not asked for rain, as that is demanded of Phungni *deví* — in Tiun and Mángaṛh. Gramang Naráin came from Dariáni in Mángaṛh *koṭhi*, where he has a *dehru*. In Gramang, a village in Balh *pháti*, Naráin has two *dehrus* and a *bhanḍár* in which a *chhatchi* or umbrella is kept, but no *pinḍi* or image. No oaths are taken on him, and his *pujári* etc. are all Kanets. The villagers go to Rujag for the fair in Phágan and the *utsabs*, held in Sáwan and Maghar, which are lesser fêtes. Related to this Naráin are Kadrusi Naráin in Tárapur, Phalani in Dughi Lag and Hurangu Naráin in Tandari. Hurangu Naráin came from Hurang near Sil Badwáni in Manḍi, but the Kulu gods have now no relations in Manḍi, though, it is noted, the Kulu people intermarry with those of Manḍi. From this part of the valley hail fell when the *deotas* all went to the Dasehra at Sultánpur, so now only Hurangu of Tandari, Gilhṛu Thán[1] of Bhuthi in Tárapur and Bhága Sidh of Dughi Lag go to it.

Kudrási Naráin has a temple at Bhuthi in *pháti* Bhaliáni on a *soh* called Dochig where the road bends to descend to a bridge. He has a *jach*, e.g. in Baisákh *obti* or light half, at the same times and places as Gilhṛu Thán, though he is a great *deota*, ranking above Gramang Naráin. Ropri may however be regarded as his head village and he has three places there, a *dehru*, a *marh*[2] and a *bhanḍár*. He also has a temple at Chathání, a hamlet in *pháti* Bhaliáni — and one in *pháti* Bhamtir, where he is worshipped with Shela Deo. In other villages too he is worshipped but not alone, Gauhri Deo and Gramang Naráin being also worshipped. Deo Gahri ranks below him and his *pujári* etc. are all Kanets. He has a temple at Sultánpur and another, with a *bhanḍár* at Brahman village, which contains a *chhatar* or canopy and a white stone but no *múrat*.

In Kulu Deo Amal has nine small temples in all, the chief being at Jugogi hamlet.

Another godling Dani, also called Rachhpál, is worshipped for increase of the flocks and for prosperity in general, a sheep or goat being

[1] *Gilhṛu* means goitre and *thán* a place where the earth split and a *pinḍi* emerged. Gilhṛu *Thán* as a *deota* has however no apparent connection with goitre, though the water of the Sarwari is supposed to cause that disease. Though his temple is at Bhuthi his *bhanḍár* is at Nanadi and there his *pujári* and *guṛ* live, while his *kárdár* is at Kasheṛh. He has no big fair but *utsabs* on 1st Baisákh, Chet and Sáwan, with dancing, as well as one at the new moon in Chet when the new Sambat year begins. No villages but Bhuthi, Narádhi, Kasheṛh and Ghaliána worship Gilhṛu Thán. A *thán* can be made by placing a stone under a *bhekal* bush, and then sacrifices are made at it for good harvests.

[2] The *maṛh* is a place where lights are placed and food cooked on one day in the year.

offered to him. But he is not avoided (?) in any way. A *pujári* worships him on the sacrificer's behalf.

In Kulu Gash *deota* takes the place of Kashgi in the Simla Hills. His cult is peculiar to Brahmans and the twice-born castes, and if one of them wishes to injure an enemy, he wears an image of Gash round his neck and gets him to eat some of his leavings (*júṭha*). If he can manage this, Gash will surely injure his enemy in some way. But Gash is also worshipped at weddings.

A number of deities exercise similar functions. Such are:— Shanghari, Tharu-bateri, Thumbardeví, Suthankal, Karani, Nanhda, Tharapere of Shamshi, Montha-Makan, who will at the earnest request of clients kill or injure their enemies.

An aggrieved person will go to a temple, pull out his hair and pray that evil may befall his enemies. Such prayers are sometimes heard and the life or property of an enemy thereby lost or injured. This is called *nihása* or *gál*.

To avert such a curse, the transgressor must placate the man he has injured by the *chhidra* rite, which is thus performed:—

A piece of *kusha* grass or *sarkhara* is held by the transgressor at one end and by the injured person or one of his relations (or in their absence by an idol of flour or earth made to represent him) at the other. Then a Nar or a *chela* of the local *deota* asks them to take oath that if so-and-so have injured such a one, 'it is his *chhidra*,' and he hereby begs his pardon: after this the Nar or *chela* cuts the grass in the middle, a goat or sheep is sacrificed, and the villagers and relations are entertained. Sometimes some barley corns are also thrown over the grass before it is cut.

Precedence.—The principal temple of a *Thakur* is that of Raghúnáth, near the Rái's palace at Sultánpur. All the other *ṭhákurs* are dependent on him and have to make him certain offerings. Originally their *jágírs* and *muáfís* were a part of his *muáfí* and he allotted them as grants in return for presents.

All the gods have to wait on Raghúnáth at Dhálpur at the Dasehra. They have also to visit their place of origin (*phágli*) in Phágan. At the latter ceremony goats are sacrificed and a feast held.

The minor gods in the villages are subordinate to the god who is commonly regarded by one or more *koṭhís* in which the villages lie as their chief god. At festivals and fairs such godlings make certain offerings to their superior and he in return supplies them with all their necessaries.

Subordinate gods.—The following are the subordinates of each god in Kulu, namely, Kokal, Chungru, Thomber, Dohangnu, Makal, Mahti, Sarmkaul. They are called his *báhan*. At each festival or feast these are given a sheep and a *pinḍ*.

A superior has the following subordinate *deotas*:—

(1) Jagru, (2) Dani, (3) Dohagnu, (4) Phangi etc.

These appear to be called, collectively, *bathu*, minor godlings or second class *deotas*.[1]

[1] Diack, *Kulahi Dialect*, p. 50.

At the festivals held in the temples and at a wedding or a *jag* these servient *deotás* are given a *bheḍu* or *bakra* (a sheep or goat).

The *ṭhákurs* and Shivji do not visit any fair or *tirath*.

Forms of temples and their appurtenances.—The forms of the temples vary greatly. Sometimes the building, which may have one to five storeys, is called a *bhandár* or *koṭhi*. These are picturesque structures in no way differing from ordinary dwelling-houses except that the *deotás'* houses have larger and stronger timbers to support the floors, because there may be one or more above the lowest storey. The images are kept in the inner room, and in the verandahs the staff and musicians are accommodated. There are also many *ṭhákurdwáras* and *shiválás*. Stone structures, called *shail*, for the most part, they generally have only one storey. In the *shail* is kept the image of the *ṭhákur*, Shiv or Deví, as the case may be. Attached to the *shail* are houses for servants and menials.

Other houses or rooms attached to a temple are the *dehri*, *dehra*, and *maṛh* : but the god only comes to live in them at fairs and festivals.[1]

No place for bathing the god exists outside a temple, but a compound is attached to it for the people to stay in at the fairs or when they have to offer prayer or make enquiries at it. This is called the *deota's* seat and contains a platform for the *chela* to play on.

In Himri *koṭhi* the house in which the image is kept is generally one-storeyed,[2] while the buildings attached to it have from 2 to 4 storeys.[2]

In Chambá little 'chapels of ease' exist. They are called *páduke* or foot-print pillars and consist of a pile of stones covered by a flat slab, on which is carved a trident (*trisúl*), with a foot-print on each side of it. They are seen by the roadside often at a considerable distance from the temple with which they are connected, their object being to enable passers-by to do obeisance and present offerings, usually flowers, to the deity without having to go all the way to the actual shrine. They are also found in front of temples.[3] No trace of such *pádukas* seems to exist in Kulu.

Position of images.—An image of Sri Rámchandar or Raghúnáth should be placed on the right hand, and that of Jánki or Síta on the left of Krishna's. An image of Rádhka is also kept in such temples. The rule as to placing images to the right or left is based on seniority, *i.e.* a superior god must be placed to the right and a servient one to his left hand according to their spiritual positions.

In a *ṭhákurdwára* it is necessary to have an image of Garúṛa placed near that of the latter : in a *shivala* the presence of a bull is necessary as Shiv's vehicle : where there is an image of Rámchandar there must be one of Hanúmán : and in a *deví-dwála* the presence of a lion is essential, because they are considered to be the attendants of that god or of the goddess.

[1] Other houses attached to every temple are the Chhoṭi Deví,-Maṛh Chughandi and Koṭhi Mandlar.

[2] In the temples of Saráj, where the number of storeys and rooms varies from 1 to 7, the image is by preference kept in the north-eastern room.

§ Chamba *Gazetteer*, pp. 48-9.

The *pujáris* are generally Brahmans, but may be Kanets, Kumhárs or goldsmiths by caste. All the offerings are placed in the god's store-house; the *pujáris* do not get any share in them, as a rule. But Brahman or Bhojki *pujáris* often get a share out of the offerings, besides holding the revenue-free lands assigned in *muáfi* to the temple. At marriages one rupee is offered to the local god, but there are no other fixed times for making offerings. None of the temple officials are hereditary. They hold office only as long as they do their work well, and they are liable to dismissal for misconduct. All the secular affairs of a temple are controlled by its *kárdár* (manager). The *bhog* presented to the image is taken by the *pujáris*, tenants and other office-holders. All offerings are voluntary. The *kárdár* is respected and the tenants readily obey his orders. All classes serve the local god according to their callings, but tenants have to render special services, in return for which they are allowed the drum and other temple instruments free at weddings etc.

The god is usually worshipped twice a day, except when his idol is shut up in the store-house, in which case worship is only held twice a month, on the 1st and 20th.[1]

The *Tala*.—For this rite the villagers open a subscription list and on the day fixed by the *deota* at their request the ceremony begins with the ordinary *Ganesh púja*. A jar full of water is placed in the *deota's* compound and a *mandap* (a place for him to sit) is prepared, and the *naugrahs* (nine *deotás*) worshipped. A stick of the *rakhál* tree 1½ *háths* long is set up by the *deota's thán* (resting place). This is followed by *shánti-hawan* and the sacrifice of a sheep to the *naugrahs*. A large fire (*jagra*) is lit and the *chela* on a sheep's back goes thrice round the fire and then the sheep is thrown across the fire and killed. A large rope of straw and a woollen thread are wrapped round the stick, stuck near the *thán* (place), and it is then taken out by the people who accompanied the *deota's rath*. The sorcerer, drummers etc. go round the village pitching, setting up a stick in each of the eight directions, sacrificing a fish on each. On reaching the spot whence they started, a *shánti-hawan* is performed and the *parohit* is given *dakhshna* amounting to annas 8 or Re. 1. This part of the ceremony is called *shánd* or *sutarbandh*.

Early next morning a Dági (called the *jathiáli*), with an empty *kilta* (basket) on his back and a fowl in his hand, followed by the *deotá's* sorcerers and other people dancing and singing, visits each house in the village: every household offers a piece of cloth to the sorcerer and *satnája* (7 kinds of grain), wool and nails are put in the *kilta* which the *jathiáli* carries. After going through the village the party proceeds to the nearest river or stream, and there a pig, a fowl, a fish and

[1] This may account for the auspiciousness of the number 20. Sometimes a *jantar* is made so that the figures in each line, whether added perpendicularly or lengthways, make 20. This is called the *bisa jantar* and as the proverb goes:—

Jis ke ghar ko jantar bísa,
Us ke ghar men pání bharen jal dísa;

but few know this *jantar* and it is very difficult to make it complete (*sidh karna*). It is worshipped for the first time during an eclipse or on some other auspicious day with *mantras*, and when *sidh* or complete it is carefully preserved in the house and worshipped at every festival.

a crab, brought with them, are killed and the *jathiáli* throws the *kilṭa* into the water: this finishes the ceremony and the party returns to the *deotá's soh*, where the *parohit* is given annas 8 or 4 at least as *dakhshna*. The villagers entertain each other, *sur* or *lugri* being drunk.

As in the Simla Hills, the *gharásni*, which consists in killing a goat and worshipping the family priest at home, is observed in Outer Saraj. But in Kulu the *gharásni*[1] *jag* is unknown and another ceremony, the *sutarbandh*, takes its place: the *parohit* and local god's *chela* are invited, the former performs the *shánti-hawan* and the latter arranges for the *bali* sacrifices: a stick or peg (of *rakhál*, 'yew') is stuck at each corner of the house and a rope made of rice-straw tied to them: a sheep and a goat are sacrificed. The *parohit* gets from annas 4 to 8 as *dakhshna* and when the ceremonies are finished a feast is given, and all the people (even the twice-born) drink *sur* and *lugri*.

Four branches of a *kelu* tree are pitched in the form of a square tied at their tops with a piece of cloth, this is called *káhika*.[2] Beneath it the *parohit* performs the *shánti-hawan*, and a man selected from the Nar caste performs the *chhidra*[3] *shánti* ceremony with a wooden drum. The Nar together with his wife and an unmarried girl of that caste and the *deota's* sorcerers dance before the *deota*: a turban and some cash by way of *dakshhna* are given to the Nar and a *dopatta* to the Nar girl. The fair lasts all day, people offering pice, fruit and flowers to the *deota* and joining with the Nar in the performance of the *chhidra*. In the evening the *deotá's chela* shoots the Nar with an arrow in the breast, making him insensible and a rupee is put in his mouth. He is taken into the *káhika* with two yards of cloth on his body as a shroud, and the *chelas* by reading *mantars* and burning *dhúp* (incense) restore him to his senses. This *jag* is celebrated during the *shukla paksh* (full moon days) of Jeṭh at Shirrah in Koṭhi Raisan, every second year in memory of Káli Nág *deota*. The other *deotás* can only afford to perform this *jag* at considerable intervals.

When rain is wanted a feast is given either by the *zamíndárs* themselves or by the local *deota*. In the latter case the cost is met from the *deota's* treasury, in the former from subscriptions raised by the *zamíndárs* themselves. The feast is called *paret pújan*, *phungni* or *jogni*. A lamb is sacrificed on a hill, *jogni deota* is worshipped, and a flat stone adorned with flour, *pinḍs* of dung, and the heart of the lamb being offered to the *jogni*. Formerly the Rájás used to pay for such feasts, but now local deities or the *zamíndárs* do so.

The *phungni* is also called *tikar-jag*, which is thus described:—The villagers go up a hill, taking with them a lamb, goat or sheep: there they worship the *jogni* and painting a large flat stone with different colours spread over it the liver of the animal brought with them, as an offering to the *jogni*.

To preserve a heap of grain a large sickle and a *pinḍ* (ball) of flour are placed on top of it. When a new animal is brought home branches

[1] Fr. *ghar wasná*.
[2] In Kulu called *kai* I think, or *khai*, Sansk. *khaya*, expiation.
[3] We shall come across the *chhidra* later.

of the *bhekhal* after being touched by the animal are buried beneath a large stone. Great precautions are taken in bringing grain home during the *bhadra nakshatra*. If the crops are very good the grain heap is worshipped, a goat killed preferably on the threshold and a feast held. In Inner Saráj the land is also worshipped on the *Somwári amáwas* in Bhádon, in addition to the goat sacrifice and a *hawan* performed. If in a piece of land the seed does not germinate, while round it it does, a goat is killed on the spot and its head buried there so as to get rid of the evil which prevented the seed from coming up.

The ceremony of *jagru jag* is performed when on account of illness offerings have to be made to the *deota*. On the evening preceding it men, women, children go to the temple, pass the night in dancing and singing. Early next morning the necessary offerings are made, a goat is sacrificed and Brahmans are fed.

Release from an oath can be secured by observance of the *chhidra* or *chhua kholná* rite. This is practically similar in all parts of Kulu. In Inner Saráj the consent of the local god being first obtained, a feast is held at which the parties at enmity with each other are made to eat together. This feast is called *Brahm bhoj*. Or both parties contribute one goat each and some flour to the local god's temple, loaves are prepared and given to those present. This is called *chhua kholná* or 'reconciliation'.

In Himri *kothi* both parties go to the temple of the village god and worship the earth there : the god is offered Rs. 18 and a goat, which is afterwards killed, and a feast is given : thus the two parties are reconciled.

The abandonment of property.—When the owner of a house has no son, or if he or his family are constantly ill, or his cattle do not prosper, or if a *chela* declare that some demon or *jogan* lives there, he abandons it as inauspicious. He will also show some earth from inside it to the *deota's* sorcerer, and if he too confirms his doubts he will promise to offer land, a house or cash to the god, provided the latter helps him to surmount the trouble. If the calamity is got rid of, the promise must be fulfilled by gifting the land etc. to the god.

If the *gur* or sorcerer of a *deota* declares a thing to be needed by any demon or god, it is abandoned in his name or stored in the local god's *bhanḍár* (treasury).

First fruits.—The usages regarding first-fruits are variously described. Speaking generally, food is given to Brahmans, *sádhus* and the local god before fresh grain is used by cultivators. In Inner Saráj high caste people offer some of the new grain before they use it, and when it is brought home incense is burnt and a lamp lit before it is stored. In Kulu proper some of the new grain is thus offered and the Brahmans etc. are also fed. Then the neighbours and relations invited for the occasion are fed, and the guests say *ago bhí do*, 'give in future too'; and the spirit in reply says *ago bhí kháo*, 'eat in future too'. On this occasion sometimes goats are also killed, while Kanets and other Sudras drink *lugri* and *sur*.

The *chela* of a *deota* is also invited after the Rabi and some ears of barley are offered to the god through him; a goat or sheep is killed and a general feast (*salhor*)[1] is held in Jeṭh. Again at the Kharíf a subscription list is opened for the purchase of a goat, which is sacrificed over the god and a feast is held just as after the Rabi. This is called *giári*.

Equally various are the beliefs regarding cracks in the soil and other omens. The *bejindri* is called *waliyati*, and an *ol* or *khol* is called *khāman* in Kulu. Both are inauspicious, and to avert the evil a sheep or a goat is killed on the spot and in the case of a crack its head and legs are buried in it.

But in Inner Saráj, where a crack is called *baindri*, only one which occurs at the sowing of the Rabi crop is considered inauspicious, one in the Kharíf not being so regarded. In the former case a Brahman is fed or a goat is killed and its head buried in the crack. In Himri *kothi* (Outer Saráj) a crack which suddenly appears in a field is called *kalai*.

But an abnormally good crop is sometimes considered inauspicious, and a goat is sacrificed to avert its evil effects—such as death or other injury.[3] If one stalk brings forth two ears it is a good omen[4] as is also a bird building its nest in a field out of ears taken from it. But if it build its nest elsewhere than in the field from which it took the ears the omen is unfavourable.

In Kulu if a snake (*siánlu*) cross in front of the ploughshare or both oxen lie down when ploughing, or if blood comes at the milking of a cow, it is considered an unfavourable omen, and the owner's death or some other evil is feared. *Jap* and *páth* are used to avert it.

Tuesday and Friday are auspicious days for commencing ploughing in either harvest. Indeed Tuesday is considered best for beginning any agricultural work, but the rule is not strictly observed. Cattle are not sold on a Wednesday, Thursday and Sunday.

When going on a journey, paying a visit to superiors or to court, it is well to meet a jar full of water, any loaded man or animal, any one with fruit or game, or a dead body. On the other hand an empty jar, basket, or basin and sneezing are bad omens.

At the *mandir* of Chambhú-*deotá* in Randal two fairs are annually held on the 7th Baisákh and on a date fixed by the people in Maghar. At these all visitors are fed free. The story is that all the Ránás, save one of Somibadgani, were killed by this god, who then took up his abode in the dense forest at Randal. Here he manifested himself

[1] Salhar: ? on 1st (Sṅjá) of Jeṭh, Diack, p. 87. The offerings to the *deota* are essential, feeding Brahmans being optional. At the harvest-home in Kulu no ceremony is performed.

[2] Or *bejendri batái*, which strictly speaking means a gap between two furrows into which no seed happens to have dropped.

[3] The idea seems to be that harm will only result if a he-goat is not sacrificed, as in default death or other harm is to be apprehended.

[4] But it is also said:—

Two cobs sprouting out of one ear, the falling of a heap of grain on the *khirmángáh* or of a pile of loaves, is considered inauspicious and some sacrifice is made to avert the evil.

in the usual way—a Brahman's cow used to yield her milk to a black *pinḍi* in the forest. One day the Brahman saw this and inferred that the *pinḍí* was possessed of miraculous powers, so he told his Ráná, who with his wife and family went to the spot and paid their devotions to it. The date of the temple's foundation is not known. It contains the black *pinḍí*, a foot high and 4 in circumference, as well as carvings of many deities. Silver and brass masks are kept in the temple. Its administration is carried on by a Brahman *kárdár*, by *got* a Gautam. The *pujárí* is also a Brahman, by *got* a Gautam also. Neither is celibate and succession is governed by natural relationship. The *gur* receives special reverence, but the rites are performed by the *pujárí*. *Bhog* of rice, milk, *ghí* etc. is offered daily, and the sacred lamp is lit morning and evening at the times of worship. At the fairs he-goats are sacrificed. No distinction is made in the offerings of different Hindu castes, but low castes are not permitted to offer any edibles. No other shrine is connected with this.

At the other *mandir* of Chambhú at Kasholí two fairs are held, one on 1st Jeṭh and the other on the *chaudas* in Maghar. To both other gods are invited and fed free. The story is that Chambú had three brothers, all bearing the same name. One night the Ráná of the tract saw a light at a distant place which he visited next morning, and here found a stone as white as snow which he brought home. After a time he fell ill and went as usual to Ambiká Deví to pray for his recovery. The goddess directed him to propitiate her son, the white stone, which he did. He enshrined it in a temple built on a site where 7 Brahmans had once dwelt and where 7 *jáman* trees also stood. The date of its foundation is not known. It contains a black stone image, 3 feet high. Two silver masks are kept on the god's chariot. Its administration is carried on by a Kanet *kárdár*, by *got* a Bhárgú. The *pujárí* is a Brahman, *got* Bhárdawáj. He is not celibate, and the succession is governed by natural relationship. Special reverence is paid only to the god's disciple because he nods his head and answers all questions put to the god. The use of *charas* is not known. A *bhog* of *ghí*, rice, milk and sugar is offered daily. The sacred lamp is lit in the morning and evening at the time of worship. No distinction is made in the offerings of Hindu castes, but the low castes are not allowed to offer *bhog*. No other shrine is connected with this.

At the *mandir* of Dakhnashúri in Nirmanḍ[1] an annual fair is held on the *satmí* in Bhádon. This god is said to have come from the Deccan and settled here after he had killed a demon which was a terror to the people. After his death the temple in which he was enshrined was built. The date of its foundation is not known. It is of stone and wood, and contains a stone image 3 feet high. Its affairs are managed by a Brahman *kárdár* who is generally appointed by a committee of the god's votaries. He is by caste a Bháṭ, *got* Káshab. The *pujárí* is a Brahman. Succession is governed by natural relationship. No *bhog* is offered to the god, and the sacred lamp is lit only in the evening. No distinction is made in the offerings of different Hindu castes. No other shrine is connected with this.

[1] For the inscriptions at Nirmand see *Corpus Inscriptionum Indicarum*.

At the *mandir* of the Chaurásí Sidh at Pekhri[1] fairs are held on 3rd Phágan and 3rd Baisákh every year. Once a shepherd grazed as *ṭhákur's* sheep near a tank. As he felt thirsty he went to drink at it and saw an image emerge from the water. In the evening he took this image home and gave it to his master, the *ṭhákur*, who kept it for some days in a niche in his house-wall until one day it occurred to him that a temple ought to be built in its honour. So he founded this temple and called it Chaurási after the village. The date of its foundation is not known. It is built of stone and wood and contains images of gold silver and brass. The stone image taken out of the tank is also installed in it. Its affairs are managed by a *kárdár*, by caste a Kanet, *got* Káshab. The *pujári* is also a Kanet. They are married and are always of this caste. *Bhog* of *ghí* &c. is offered in the morning only, but a sacred lamp is kept burning all night. The low castes are not allowed to offer edible things. Seven shrines are connected with this one.

Deota Jalándí's annual fairs are held on 1st Sáwan and at the Diwáli in Maghar. The tradition is that once a *ṭhákur*, named Pairam, daily went tobathe in a pool called Mansarowar. One day the god manifested himself and the *ṭhákur* begged him to accompany him to his house. To this he agreed and there the god was seated at a place in a grove of oak (*kharshú* trees). Temples were eventually built at these places and called after the names of the trees &c. The date of their foundation is not known. There are 4 images of the god. The stone *pinḍí* is ½ foot high; the bust is made of brass; the third is of stone and 2½ feet high; and the fourth is the chariot of the god. The temple administration is carried on jointly by the villagers and a *kárdár* who is also its *pujári*. By caste he is a Nolu Kanet. He is not celibate. A *bhog* of flowers, scent &c. is offered in the morning at the time of worship. No lamp is lit nor is sacred fire maintained. No distinction is made in the offerings of different Hindu castes. Connected with this are the shrines of Kanḍu Shailtor, Barámgaṛh, Bag Deora and Saráhan.

Mandir Khuḍíjal in Deohri.—The tradition is that in former times a *ṭhákur*, named Thúlá, had a cow called Kailṛi who used to yield her milk to a black stone *pinḍí* in Khuḍi village. Her master, enraged at his loss, determined to break the *pinḍi*, but the cow told him that the *pinḍí* should not be broken as Jamdaggan *rishi* had manifested himself to it, but he ignored her warning and struck the *pinḍi*. No sooner had he done so than he died on the spot, owing to the *rishí's* miraculous power. So the people took to worshipping it and eventually a temple was built on this spot. The date of its foundation is not known. It contains a black stone *pinḍi*, 2 feet high. Its administration is carried on by a Kanet *kárdár*. The *pujári* is a Brahman, by *got* a Bhardhwáj. He is not celibate. A sacred lamp is kept burning all through the night. No distinction is made in the offerings of different Hindu castes, but a low caste man is not permitted to offer edible things. No other shrine is connected with this one. For 11 days ending with the *púranmási* in Sáwan or Bhádon the fair is in full swing. The place is also enlivened by visitors at the Diwálí. Small fairs such as *shánd* or *thiarshú* are held on 1st and 16th Phágan, 9th Baisákh and 20th Háṛ.

[1] In Uchandi *koṭhí*.

Deota Chambhú has a temple in Deogi. The story goes that on the site of the present temple a cow used to yield her milk to a small black stone set in the ground. One day this was noticed by a herdsman who followed the cow. He returned home and told the people of his town all about it They went to the spot and found his tale was true, so they founded a temple in which the image was enshrined. The exact date of its foundation is not known, but tradition says that it was built in the Tretiya Yug. It contains a smooth, black stone image, 2¼ feet high. The temple walls are decorated with various pictures and busts of brass and silver are also kept in it. A Kanet *kárdár* manages its affairs. He is married. The *pujári* is always recruited from the Brahmans. He is not celibate either. The *gur* is held in greater respect than either the *kárdár* or *pujári*. The use of *charas* is not known. *Bhog* is offered daily to the god. A sacred lamp is lit daily morning and evening when worship is held in the temple. No distinction is made in the offerings of different Hindu castes, but low castes are not allowed to offer edible things. No other shrine is connected with this one. The annual fairs are held on 11th Baisákh, 12th Bhádon, and on 2nd, and 3rd Asauj. Illustrations are also displayed on the Diwáli in Maghar.

Pubhári, the god on the Jalori Pass, has 5 temples called after the names of the villages in which they are situate. At these annual fairs are held: at Kotarshu on 12th Baisákh, 12th Sáwan, on the Diwáli in Maghar, and on the 1st of Phágan; at Dim on 20th Sáwan; at Jalauri on 15th Sáwan and 3rd Kátak; at Kanár on 3rd Phágan; and on 18th Baisákh at Sariwalsar. The story is that a man of Kota Thirshu chanced to find a metal mask which bade him enshrine it in a suitable place. So a temple was built and the mask placed in it. The dates of the fairs were fixed by a committee of the villages in which shrines were erected. The stone image is 1¼ cubits high. The date of foundation is not known. Its affairs are managed by a Kanet *kárdár*. Under him are a *bhandári* (store-keeper), a *gur* and *pujári*, all Karaunks. They are all married. Special reverence is paid to the *gur*. A *bhog* of rice, meat &c. is offered daily, and a sacred lamp lit in the evening. No distinction is made in the offerings of different Hindu castes. Connected with this are the shrines in Koṭ, Dim and Jaun.

Konerí *deota* has a temple in Kuinri. His main fair is held annually at the Diwáli in Maghar, and it is followed by small fairs called *shánd* and *thirshu*, on 1st and 16th Phágan, 9th and 20th Hár. The story is that Karm Deo, a Brahman of the village, used to bathe daily in a spring. One day he found a black stone or *pinḍi* in the water which said it was Biás *rishi* and had come from Kuinri. He worshipped it and his example was followed by others. Eventually a temple was built, but the date of its foundation is not known. It contains a black stone *pinḍi*, 2¼ feet high. Its administration is carried on by a Kanet *kárdár*. The *pujári* is always recruited from the Brahmans. His *got* is Bhárdhwáj. He is not celibate. A sacred lamp is lighted in the evening at the time of worship and kept burning the whole night. No distinction is made in the offerings of different Hindu castes. No other shrine is connected with this.

No particular fair is connected with the *mandir* of *deota* Pauj. Bír, but a he-goat is sacrificed at the *shankránt* of Asauj and Phágan.

The story is that on the site of the present temple a Brahman used to meditate, recounting the names of God on his rosary. One day perchance it fell from his hand and struck against a stone which burst into many pieces and from it sprang 5 images each of which told the Brahman that they were 5 *bîrs* (or heroes) and brothers, adding that people should adore them. At this spot a temple was erected in their honour. The date of its foundation is not known. It contains 5 brass carvings of Bhairon, each ½ foot high. Its administration is carried on by a Kanet *kárdár*, by *got* a Káshab. The *pujári* is a Brahman, by caste a Gaur and by *got* Sársut. He is not celibate. Special reverence is paid to the *gur*. *Bhog* is offered on the first of every month and particularly on the *shankránts* of Phágan and Asauj, on which occasions a he-goat is sacrificed. A sacred lamp is lit every evening for half an hour only.

Deota Shang Chul has a temple in Koṭhi Shángaṛh. Three fairs are held annually, one on the 3rd Háṛ at Damardwará, another on the 1st Asauj at Nagari, and the 3rd on 8th Phágan at Batáhr. The story goes that a cow used to yield her milk to a stone *pinḍi* hidden under ground. A Brahman observed this and dug up the place. The *pinḍi* was found and from the hole came out a snake which declared that he must be worshipped. The date of foundation is not known. All the four temples are of wood and stone. One contains a stone *pinḍi*, a foot high. *Mohrás* of gold and silver are also kept in the temple. Its administration is carried on by a *kárdár* who is also *pújári* and *gur*. His caste is Gaur and *got* Sársut. He is not celibate. *Bhog* is only offered at festivals. The sacred lamp is lit only in the evening. No distinction is made in the offerings of Hindu castes. A low caste is not allowed to offer edible things. Connected with this are the shrines in Batáhr, Jiladhura, Dharadeora, Nagari and Lapa.

Deota Sandeo has 3 temples at which annual fairs are held on the last day of Sáwan, and on the 2nd and 8th of Phágan. On these occasions a *hawan* or sacrificial fire is lighted, and the rite is repeated on the 2nd Baisákh every year. It is said that three gods sprang from a hailstone. Two of them carved out principalities in Nohanda, while the third took up his abode in Shríkoṭ which had already been occupied by the god Márkanda, so the latter left the place and went to Manglaur. After that the people began to worship Sandhu. The date of the temples' foundation is not known. None of them contains any image, but gold, silver and brass *mohras* (masks) are used in adorning the god's chariot. The administration is carried on by a Kanet *kárdár*. The *gur* and *pujári* are also Kanets. They are not celibate. Special reverence is paid only to the *gur*. A *bhog* of rice, *ghí*, milk &c. is only offered at festivals. A sacred lamp is lit morning and evening at the times of worship. No distinction is made in the offerings of different Hindu castes, but a low caste is not permitted to offer edible things. Connected with this are the shrines of Naráin, Kandi and Guda Deora.

The Cults of the Simla Hills.

The Simla Hill States form a network of feudal States with dependent feudatories subordinate to them, and the jurisdictions of the local godlings afford a striking reflection of the political conditions, forming a complex network of cults, some superior, some subordinate.

To complete the political analogy, the godlings often have their *wazírs* or chief ministers and other officials. Perhaps the best illustration of this *quasi*-political organization of the hill cults is afforded by the following account of the 22 Ṭíkás of Junga. At its head stands Junga's new cult. Junga, it should be observed, is not the family god of the Rájá of Keonthal. That function is fulfilled by the Devi Tára.[1]

THE CULT OF JUNGA.[2]

Legend.—The Rájá of Koṭlehr had two sons, who dwelt in Nádaun. On the accession of the elder to the throne, they quarrelled, and the younger was expelled the State. With a few companions he set out for the hills and soon reached Jakho, near Simla. Thence they sought a suitable site for a residence, and found a level place at Thagwa in the Koṭí State. Next morning the Mián, or 'prince', set out in a palanquin, but when they reached Sanjauli, his companions found he had disappeared, and conjecturing that he had become a *deota,* returned to Thagwa, where they sought him in vain. They then took service with the people of that part. One night a man went out to watch his crop, and resting beneath a *kemú* tree, heard a terrible voice from it say, 'lest I fall down!' Panic-stricken he fled home, but another man volunteered to investigate the business and next night placed a piece of silk on the platform under the tree and took up his position in a corner. When he heard the voice, he rejoined 'come down', whereupon the tree split in half and out of it a beautiful image fell on to the silk cloth. This the man took to his home and placed it in the upper storey, but it always came down to the lower one, so he sent for the astrologers, who told him the image was that of a *deota* who required a temple to live in. Then the people began to worship the image and appointed a *chela* through whom the god said he would select a place for his temple. So he was taken round the country, and when the news reached the companions of the Nádaun prince they joined the party. The god ordered temples to be built at Nain, Bojári, Thond, and Kóṭi in succession, and indeed in every village he visited, until he reached Nádaun, where the Rájá, his brother, refused to allow any temple to be built, as he already had a family god of his own named Jípúr. Junga, the new god, said he would settle matters with Jípúr, and while the discussion was going on, he destroyed Jípúr's temple and all its images by lightning, whereupon the Rájá made Junga his own deity and placed him in a house in his *darbár.*

Jípúr is not now worshipped in Keonthal, all his own temples being used as temples of Junga who is worshipped in them. Nothing is known of Jípúr, except that he came in with the ruling family of Keonthal. He appears to have been only a *jathera* or ancestor. Junga has another temple at Pajarli near Junga, to which he is taken

[1] An account of this goddess will be found on p. 357 *supra.*

[2] (The family likeness of the legends connected with these hill deities of the extreme North of India to those connected with the 'devils' of the Tuluvas on the West Coast, very far to the South, is worthy of comparison by the student. See Devil Worship of the Tuluvas, *Ind. Ant.*, XXIII—XXVI, 1894—1897.)

when a *jag* is to be celebrated, or when an heir-apparent, '*ṭika*', is born to the Rájá, on which occasion a *jágra* is performed. On other occasions the images made subsequently are alone worshipped in this temple. The ritual is that observed in a *shwála*, and no sacrifice is offered. There are 22 *tikás* or "sons" of Junga. None of these can celebrate a *jag* or observe a festival without permission from the Junga temple, and such permission is not given unless all the dues of Junga's temple are paid. Thus Junga is regarded as the real god and the others his children.

THE TWENTY-TWO ṬÍKÁS OF JUNGA (KEONTHAL), NEAR SIMLA.

The State of Keonthal is one of the Simla Hill States in the Punjab, and its capital, Junga, so called after the god of that name, lies only a few miles from Simla itself. Besides the main territory of the State, Keonthal is overlord of five feudatory States, *viz.* Koṭi, Theog, Madhán, Gúnd and Ratesh. Excluding these States, it comprises six detached tracts, which are divided into eighteen *parganas*, thus :—

I.—Southern tract, comprising ten *parganas* :—(1) Fágu, (2) Kháláshi, (3) Tir Mahásu, (4) Dharech in Fágu tahsíl, (5) Ratesh, (6) Karoli, (7) Jái, (8) Paráli, (9) Jhajot, (10) Kalánj in Junga tahsíl.

II.—Northern tract, which includes four *parganas* :—(11) Shilí, (12) Matiána, (13) Rajána, (14) Matiána, in Fágu *tahsíl*.

III.—Pargana Ráwin, and

IV.—Pargana Púnnar, together forming Ráwin tahsíl.

V.—Pargana Rámpur, and

VI.—Pargana Wákna, both in Junga tahsíl.

The three *tahsíls* are modern Revenue divisions, but the 22 *parganas* are ancient and correspond in number to the 22 *ṭíkas*, which are described below. It does not appear, however, that each *pargana* has its *ṭíka*, and the number may be a mere coincidence. The fondness for the Nos. 12, 22, 32, 42, 52 etc. in the Punjab, and indeed, throughout India, is well known, and goes back at least to Buddhist times.

The following are the 22 Ṭíkás of Jungá :—

(1) Kalaur.
(2) Manúni.
(3) Kaneti.
(4) Deo Chand.
(5) Shaneti.
(6) Mahánpha.
(7) Tíru.
(8) Khateshwar.
(9) Chadei.
(10) Shanei and Jáu.
(11) Dhúru.
(12) Kulthi.
(13) Dhánún.
(14) Ḍúm.
(15) Ráíta.
(16) Chánana.
(17) Gaun.
(18) Bíju.
(19) Kúsheli Deo.
(20) Bál Deo.
(21) Rawál Deo.
(22) Kawáli Deo.

(1) *The Cult of Kalaur.*

Legend.—A Brahman once fled from Kulu and settled in Dawan, a village in *pargana* Ratesh. There he incurred the enmity of a Kanet woman, who put poison in his food. The Brahman detected the poison, but went to a spot called Bangápáni, where there is water, in Doran Jangal, and there ate the food, arguing that if the woman meant to kill him she would do it sooner or later, and so died, invoking curses on the murderess. His body disappeared. In the Garhál-ki-Dhár plain was a *bakhal* plant. One day a Brahman of Garáwag observed that all the cows used to go to the plant and water it with their milk, so he got a spade and dug up the bush. He found under it a beautiful image (which still bears the mark of his spade) and took it home. When he told the people what had happened, they built a temple for the idol, and made the Brahman its *pujári*. But the image, which bore a strong resemblance to the Brahman, who had died of the poisoned food, began to inflict disease upon the Kanets of the place, so that several families perished. Thereupon, the people determined to bring in a stronger god or goddess to protect them from the image. Two Kanets of the *pargana*, Dhelí and Chandí, were famed for their courage and strength, and so they were sent to Láwi and Pálwi, two villages in Sirmúr State, disguised as *faqírs*, and thence they stole an *áth-bhojáwáli*, 'eight-handed', image of Deví, which they brought to Dhawar in Ratesh. The people met them with music and made offerings to the stolen image, which they took to Walán and there built a temple for it, ceasing to worship Kalaur. The plague also ceased. The people of one village Charej, however, still affect Kalaur.

(2) *The Cult of Manúni.*

Manúni is Mahádeo, and is so called because his first temple was on the hill of Manún.

Legend.—A Brahman of Paráli, in the Jamrot *pargana* of the Patiála hill territory, a *pujári* of Deví Dhár, and others, went to buy salt in Mandi, and on their way back halted for the night in Máhún Nág's temple at Máhún in the Suket State. The Brahman and the *pujári* with some of the company, who were of good caste, slept in the temple, the rest sleeping outside. The *pujári* was a *chela* of the god Dharto, at that time a famous *deota*, revered throughout the northern part of the Keonthal State. On starting in the morning, a swarm of bees settled on the baggage of the Brahman and the *pujári*, and could not be driven off. When the party reached Munda, where the temple of Hanúmán now stands, the swarm left the baggage and settled on *bán* tree. Here, too, the *pujári* fainted and was with difficulty taken home. The astrologers of the *pargana* decided that a god had come from Suket and wished to settle in that part, and that unless he were accommodated with a residence the *pujári* would not recover. Meanwhile the *pujári* became possessed by the god and began to nod his head and declare that those present must revere him (the god), or he would cause trouble. They replied that if he could overcome the god Dharto, they would not hesitate to abandon that god, though they had revered him for generations. Upon this 'a bolt from the blue' fell upon Dharto's temple and destroyed it, breaking all the idols, except one which was cast into a tank in a cave. The *pujári* then led the people to Munda, where the bees had settled and directed them to build a temple at the place where they found ants. Ants were duly found in a square place on Manún hill, and a temple built in due course, but when only the roof remained to be built, a plank flew off and settled in Parálí. Upon this the *pujári* said the temple must be built there, as the god had come with a Brahman of that place, and so a second temple was built and the image placed in it. That at Manún was also subsequently completed, and a third was erected at Koṭi Dhár. The cult also spread to Nala, in Patiála territory, and to Bhajji State, and temples were erected there. The Brahmans of Parálí were appointed Bhojkís and the *pujárís* of Koṭi Dhár *pujárís* of the god. Meanwhile the image of Dharto remained in the tank into which it had fallen. It is said that a man used to cook a *rot* (a large loaf) and threw it into the water as an offering, requesting the god to lend him utensils which he needed to entertain his guests. This Dharto used to do, on the condition that the utensils were restored to the pool when done with. But one day the man borrowed 40 and only returned 35 plates, and since then the god has ceased to lend his crockery. Beside the god's image is another, that of a *bír* or spirit, called Tonda. Tonda used to live at Paráli in a cave which was a water-mill, and if any one visited the mill alone at night he used to become possessed by the *bír*, and, unless promptly attended to, lose his life. But once the *pujári* of Manúni went to the mill, and by the help of his god resisted the attempts of the *bír* to possess him. In fact he captured the *bír*, and having laid him flat on the grind-stone sat on him. Upon this the *bír* promised to obey him in all matters if he spared his life, and so the *pujári* asked him to come to the temple, promising to worship him there if he ceased to molest people. The *bír* agreed and has now a separate place in the temple of Manúni, whose *wazír* he has become.

(3) *The Cult of Kaneti.*

Legend.—After the war of the Mahábhárta, when the Pánḍavas had retired to the Badri Náth hills to worship, they erected several temples and placed images in them. Amongst others they established Kaneti in a temple at Kwára on the borders of Gaṛhwál and Bashahr, and there are around this temple five villages, which are still known after the Pánḍavas. Dodra and Kwára are two of these. The people of the former wanted to have a temple of their own, but those of Kwára objected and so enmity arose between them. The Dodra people then stole an image from the Kwára temple, but it disappeared and was found again in a pool in a cave. It then spoke by the mouth of its *chela*, and declared that it would not live at Dodra, and that the people must quit that place and accompany it elsewhere. So a body of men, Kanets, Kolís and Túrís, left Dodra and reached Dagon, in Keonthal State, where was the temple of Jípúr, the god of the Rájá's family. This temple the new god destroyed by lightning, and took possession of his residence. The men who had accompanied the god settled in this region and the cult of Kanetí prospered. Áicha, Brahman, was then *wazír* of Keonthal, and he made a vow that if his progeny increased, he would cease to worship Jípúr and affect Kaneti. His descendants soon numbered 1500 houses. Similarly, the Bhaler tribe made a vow to Kanetí, that if their repute for courage increased, they would desert Jípúr.

(4) *The Cult of Deo Chand.*

Legend.—Deo Chand, the ancestor of the Khanogo sect of the Kanets, was *wazír* of Keonthal and once wished to celebrate a *jag*, so he fixed on an auspicious day and asked for the loan of Junga's image. This the *pujáris* refused him, although they accepted his first invitation, and asked him to fix another day. Deo Chand could not do this or induce the *pujáris* to lend him the image, so he got a blacksmith to make a new one, and celebrated the *jag*, placing the image, which he named Deo Chand after himself, in a new temple. He proclaimed Deo Chand subordinate to Junga, but in all other respects the temple is under a separate management.

(5) *The Cult of Shaneti.*

There are two groups of Kanets, the Painoi or Painúi and the Shainti. Owing to some dispute with the *pujáris*, the Shaintís made a separate god for themselves and called him Shaneti.

(6) *The Cult of Mahánpha.*

The Chibhar Kanets of Jatil *pargana* borrowed an image of Junga and established a separate temple.

(7) *The Cult of Tíru.*

Legend.—Tíru is the god of the Játik people, who are a sept of the Brahmans. A Tírú Brahman went to petition the Rájá and was harshly treated, so he cut off his own head, whereupon his headless body danced for a time. The Brahmans then made an image of Tíru, and he is now worshipped as the *jathera* of the Játiks.

(8) *The Cult of Khateshwar.*

The Brahmans of Bhakar borrowed an image of Junga and built a separate temple for it at a place called Koṭi, whence the god's name.

(9) *The Cult of Chadei.*

The Nawáwan sept of the Kanets brought this god from *pargana* Ratesh, and built his temple at Charol, whence the god's name.

(10) *The Cult of Shanei and Jáu.*

Junga on his birth made a tour through the Keonthal territory, and having visited Shaint and Jáu villages, ordered temples to be built in each of them. Shanei is subordinate to Junga, and Jáu to Shanei. Both these temples are in the village of Koṭi.

(11) *The Cult of Dhúru.*

A very ancient god of the Jai *pargana* of Keonthal. All the *zamíndárs* who affected Dhúru died childless. The temple is financed by the Rájás and the god is subordinate to Junga.

(12) *The Cult of Kúlthí.*

The Chibhar sept of the Kanets affect this god. His temple is at a place called Kawálath.

(13) *The Cult of Dhanún.*

Legend.—The image of this god came, borne on the wind, from Nádaun, after Junga's arrival in the country. It first alighted on Jhako and thence flew to Neog, where it hid under a rice plant in a paddy-field. When the people cut the crop they spared this plant, and then turned their cattle into the fields. But all the cattle collected round the plant, from under which a serpent emerged and sucked all their milk. When the people found their cows had run dry, they suspected the cowherdess of having milked them, and set a man to watch her. He saw what occurred, and the woman then got enraged with the plant, and endeavoured to dig it up, but found two beautiful images (they both still bear the marks of her sickle). The larger of these two is considered the Rájá and is called Dhánún (from *dhánd*, rice), and the smaller is deemed the *wazír* and is called *wano* (meaning 'tyrant' in the Pahāṛí dialect).

This was the image which assumed a serpent's shape and drained the cows. Two temples were erected to these images, but they began to oppress the people and compelled them to sacrifice a man every day, so the people of the *pargana* arranged for each family to supply its victim in turn. At last weary of this tyranny, they called in a learned Brahman of the Bharobo sept, who induced the god to content himself with a human sacrifice once a month, then twice and then once a year, then with a he-goat sacrificed monthly, and finally once every six months, on the *ikádshís* of Háṛ and Khátik *sudí*. The Brahman's descendants are still *pujáris* of the temple and *parohits* of the village, and they held Bhiyár free of revenue until Rájá Chandar Sain resumed the grant They now hold Sigar in lieu of service to the god.

(14) *The Cult of Ḍúm.*

Ḍúm has a temple in Katián, a village of Phágu *tahsil*, and goes on tour every five or ten years though Keonthal, Kothár, Mahlog, Bashahr, Koṭ Khái, Jubbal, Khanár, Bághal, Koṭi and other States. In Sambat 1150 he visited Delhi, then under the rule of the Tunwars, many of whom after their defeat by the Chauháns fled to these hills, where they still affect the cult of Ḍúm. He is believed to possess miraculous powers and owns much gold and silver. He became subordinate to Junga, as the god of the State.

(15) *Ráltá.*

This god has a temple in *pargana* Parálí.

(16) *Chanana.*

He is the deity of the Doli Brahmans.

(17) *Gaun.*

The image is that of Junga, who was established by the Rawal people.

(18) *Bíju.*

Bíju was originally subordinate to the god Bijat, but as he was in the Keonthal State, he became subordinate to Junga. His real name is Bijleshwar Mahádeo, or Mahádeo, the lightning god, and his temple stands below Jori Chandni in the Jubbal State.

(Regarding Nos. (19) *Kúsheli Deo*, (20) *Bál Deo*, (21) *Rawál Deo* and (22) *Kawáli Deo*, no particulars are available.)

The *deotás* of the Punjab Himalayas include a number of divine families each ruling over its own territory, just as the ruling families of the Hill States rule each its own State or fief. In the Simla Hills for example we find a family of Nágs, another of Ḍúms and a third called Marechh, besides the more orthodox families of Koṭ Ishwar and the Devís.

The Cult of the Ḍums.

One of the most remarkable cults of the Simla Hills is that of Ḍúm, who appears also as one of the twenty-two *ṭikas* of Keonthal. In that State he is a subordinate deity, but elsewhere he is a godling of the first rank. His cult extends to several other states, *e.g.* to Bashahr and Kumhársain. *Zamíndárs* offer him *ghí* every time they clarify butter, otherwise he would prevent their cows yielding milk. Every three years the accumulated *ghí* is spent on the god's entertainment. He is closely allied with *páp* or *newá*, and one account thus describes his origin :—Khalnidh, an aged Kanet, went to worship Hátkoṭi *deví*, and pleased with his devotion the goddess gave him some rice and told him that two sons would be born to him. When they grew up they used to graze a Brahman's cattle, and the goddess conferred on them the power of doing anything they wished. On their death their *páp* or *khót* began to vex the people of this *iláqá*, so they were propitiated by worship ; and one of them stayed in the State while the other took up his abode at Kuthán in Keonthal.

The *deota* Ḍúm or Nagarkoṭia, as he is also called, of Katián (properly Gathán), a village in the Shilli *pargana* of the Phágu tahsíl of Keonthal, is the brother of Ḍúm *deota* of Sharmala,[1] which is his capital, lying in the Kumhársain State. The latter's history is as follows :—

An old Kanet, named Shura, living in Hemri village (now in *pargana* Chagáon in Kumhársain), had no son. His wife, Párgi, was also old and she asked her husband to marry a second wife in order to get a son, but Shura refused on account of his advanced age. His wife induced him to go to the goddess Hátkoṭi Durga and implore her aid, threatening to fast even unto death unless she promised him a son. Shura reached Hátkoṭi in seven days (though it was only a two days' journey) and for seven days sat before Durga Deví fasting. The goddess was so pleased at his devotion that she appeared before him with all her attributes (the *sankh*, *chakkar*, *gadda*, *padam* and other weapons in her right hands) and riding on a tiger. She granted his request and bade him return home. Overjoyed at this *bar* or 'boon', he went home and told his wife the good news, and three months later she gave birth to twin sons, but both parents dying seven days later, they were nursed by a sister named Kapri. While quite young the orphans showed signs of superhuman power. Their sister too soon died

[1] Sharmala lies in *pargana* Shil of Kumhársain and Dúm is worshipped by all the people of *pargana* Ubedesh and by some of *pargana* Shil.

and the boys were employed as cowherds by the people, but they were careless of their cattle and devoted themselves to their favourite game of archery. So the people dismissed first one and then the other. Both of them then took service with the Ṭhákur of Darkoṭi, but were again discharged for idleness. They then roamed the country seeking service, but no one would help them, and so they went down to the plains and reached Dehli, where they enlisted in the king's army. To test the skill of his archers the king set up a *tawa* (pole ?) from which hung a horse hair with a small grain in the centre. No one in all his army could split the grain with an arrow, except these two recruits, and the king was greatly pleased with them, but as his Ráni told him that they were not common soldiers but possessed of magical power and should be dismissed to their native hills with a suitable reward, he gave them a huge vessel (*cheru*) full of coins which they could not lift, and they were about to depart when two *deotás*, Mahású and Shrígul, who were prisoners at Delhi,[1] appeared and calling upon the brothers for help, as they belonged to the same hill country as themselves, promised that if they petitioned the king for their release they would be set free.

The Ḍúm brothers implored the king for the *deotás'* release, and their request was granted. The *deotás* were so pleased that they bade the youths ask of them any boon they liked, and they asked their help in carrying the vessel home. The *deotás* told the brothers to mount their aërial steeds, look towards the Kailás hill, touch the vessel and whip up their horses. So they did, and their steeds carried their riders high up into the sky, flying northwards over the hills and halting at Binu, a place near Gathán village. The gods went to their dominions and the vessel full of coin was buried at Binu, where it turned into water, which was made into the *baoli* now on the boundary of Kumhársain and Keonthal. The aërial steeds disappeared on Mount Kailás after leaving the young Ḍúms at Binu. Binu then belonged to the Ṭhákurs of Rajána, and the Ḍúm brothers made themselves very troublesome, breaking with their arrows the *gharás* full of water which the women were carrying home on their heads[2] or setting their bundles of grass on fire. The people became so alarmed that at last the whole countryside with the Ṭhákur at its head brought the brothers to bay in a battle in which the elder, who was called Ḍúm, was killed. Kon,[3] the younger, also died and both were cremated on the spot where they had fallen, but they emerged from the ashes in the form of idols. These miraculous images punished the Ṭhákur in many ways, haunting him in his sleep and overturning his bed. To appease the images, who were thus become *páp*, the Ṭhákur conveyed them to Nagarkot in Kulu, but when presented there before the goddess they vanished. The people were distressed at their loss and fasted before Durga until she made them re-appear. So she gave them back the images; but some say that she gave them other images in lieu of the originals. Thereafter Ḍúm

[1] The *deotás* Mahású and Shrígul were captives kept at Delhi for being devil oppressors in the hills.

[2] See the note in the account of Gúga.

[3] The descendants of Kon settled in Keonthal State and are called Kathán.

deota was also called Nagarkoṭia *deota* of Sharmalla. One image was brought to Sharmalla, where Ḍúm was established, while the image of Kon was taken to Gathán village. Temples were built for the residence of each at those places. But some say both images were first established at Sharmalla. People used to invite the *deotás* to their houses, but the Sharmalla people refused to send them to Gathán, and so the people of the latter place stole one of the *deotás* and established him there. Ḍúm of Sharmalla is worshipped daily by Brahmans, but his *gur* (the man into whom the spirit comes and through whom it speaks) is always a Kanet. The *deota* has his *kárdárs*, the chief among them being the *bhanḍári* in charge of the stores. The Sharmalla women call him by the pet name of Nánu, but other people call him Ḍúm. His annual *mela* is held on the Bishu day in Baisakh, but his *játra* is held every 7th or 8th year. When a new Ráná ascends the *gaddi* a *rajáoli mela* is held and the *deota* tours in the villages of his devotees. The Shánt *mela* is held every 50 years. The *deotá's* followers are found mostly in Ubdesh *pargana*, but he is also worshipped in several other scattered villages in Bashahr, Khaneti, Theog and Shill. He used to have a *mela* at Shamokhar. Some say that the *deotás* Magneshwar, Koṭ Ishwar and Ḍúm sat in their respective places and the *mela* began, but the trio quarrelled and the *mela* was forbidden to be held in the future by Government. The Dagroṭ people in consequence pay a *chershi*[1] of Rs. 30 to Manún or Magneshwar every third year. The *deota* helped Kumhársain to gain its victory over Keonthal, and when besought by a Ráná of Jubbal blessed him with a son for which the Ráná presented him with a gold image. Ḍúm's original image is of brass, but a few smaller images have been added as its companions. The Ṭhákur of Rajána was also blessed with a son at an advanced age, and he presented Ḍúm with a silver chain worth Rs. 140. The *deota* is rich, having silver instruments (*narsinga* and *karnál*) of music, while a necklace of gold *mohars* and gold ornaments always adorn him. He is not *dhudadhári*, but goats are sacrificed before him. He is believed by his devotees to be a very powerful god, blessing the people but distressing those who do not obey him. He had a large dominion of his own, but Ḍúm of Gathán has a much larger one. The Ḍúm of Sharmalla had seven *khúnḍs*[2] (descendants of *máwis* or *mawannas*) who recognised his authority. These are—Baghalu and Charogu in Khaneti, Aṭnet and Relu in Bashahr, Dogre and Rachla in Kumhársain and Dharongu in Balsan. The Charogu, Relu and Dharogu valleys were seized by Ḍúm of Gathán and added to his dominions.

The following is another account of this strange quarrel:—The worshippers of Mauni *deota*, whose real name is Magneshar Mahádev and whose temple is in Mauni, a village in Shil, are

[1] *Chershi* is a fine levied thus:—The god every third year visits the villages from which the fine is due. This fine comprises a goat, Re. 1-4-0, and as much grain as will suffice for the worshippers who accompany the god.

[2] *Khúnḍ* also appears to mean a tract of country. The Khúnḍ Kanets are in Bashahr distinguished from the Ghára Kanets. They are sometimes called Neru or Niru, and certain religious ceremonies, such as the *bhesda* and *shánt* are only performed in villages where there are Khúnḍ Kanets.—Simla Hill States *Gazetteer*, Bashahr, p. 21.

confined to that *pargana*. Nearly 70 years ago the worshippers of both the gods, Mauni and Ḍúm, used to assemble with their gods at a fair held at Shamokhar, an open space on the borders of the Ubedesh and Shil *parganas*. About 65 years ago, in the time of Ráná Prítam Singh, of Kumhársain, the worshippers of Ḍúm objected to the admission of Mauni *deota* and his worshippers into Shamokhar. This led to a feud between the two parties, and the case came before the Ráná, who in Sambat 1907 decided that if Mauni *deota* was not allowed to be brought into Shamokhar, the inhabitants of Dakún, Rabog and Jadún (the worshippers of Ḍúm) should pay a fine called *chershi* to Mauni *deota*.

Koṭeshar *deota* (also called the *deota* Koṭi), the State god who has a temple in Madholi village, was offended by the above decision, so he prohibited both the gods from coming to Shamokhar. As he was the State god, the Ráná was bound to obey his orders, so both the *deotás* were prevented from coming. When the worshippers of Mauni found that the decision went against them, they solicited the aid of a favourite *khawás* of the Ráná who was a daughter of Utenun, a Kanet of the Moroshla family and a worshipper of Mauni. Through her persuasion the Ráná gave permission to Mauni to come to Shamokhar. This partial judgment caused a quarrel between the rival factions, so both the gods were prevented from coming to Shamokhar in the future, but the *chershi* continued to be paid as usual to Mauni *deota*. During the chief's minority payment of the *chershi* to Mauni *deota* was not enforced, and his worshippers asked either that they might be allowed to hold their fair at Shamokhar, or that the *chershi* should be paid to them; but no decision was given, and the dispute was not settled. Subsequently the *chershi* was paid to Mauni, but later on the authorities thinking that the god's visits to the village were likely to cause disputes, stopped its payment and arranged for the payment of Rs. 30 in cash every third year as *chershi* to Mauni.

The *deota* Ḍúm of Hemri has the same history as the Ḍúm of Sharmalla. Shura and Párgi lived at Hemri, and it is said that when the Ḍúm brothers were killed their images were brought to Hemri and thence taken to Sharmalla and Gathán. Some say that the Ḍúm brothers were killed by *máwis* even before the Ṭhákurs of Rajána ruled the country. There is an image of Ḍúm at Hemri temple where the people of Hemri, Kathrol and Guma worship him. This *deota*, when necessary, goes to Kángra on a pilgrimage (*játrá*). A *mela* is held at Hemri on the Sharono (Salono) day in Bhádon. The Balti *mela* is held every third year. A Brahman is his *pujári*, but he is generally worshipped by the Kolís and Lohárs of Hemri.

Ḍúm of Kaṛel is worshipped at a temple in that village. He too is also an offshoot of the Ḍúm brothers. People say that Ḍúm first went from Hemri to Gathán, whence an image of him was brought to Kaṛel, although Hemri and Kaṛel are close together. The Kaṛel people worship Ḍúm in Gathán, but as a mark of respect they keep an idol of him in a temple in their own village. A Balti fair is held every third year and a Bhúṇḍa *mela* whenever the people wish, generally after 10 or 15 years. Every house gives some goats to be killed, people inviting their kinsmen, especially their *dhi-dhiáns* and sons-in-law and their children. The Bharech Brahman does *púja* in the morning only.

Bháṭ *deota* also resides with Ḍúm in the Kaṛel temple. Originally a Sársut Brahman living at Mateog, a village just above Kumhársain itself. Bháṭ was prosecuted by a Báná of Kumhársain and ordered to be arrested, but he fled to the Kulu side pursued by the Kaṛel sepoy who had been sent to seize him. He was caught on the bank of the Sutlej, but asked the sepoy to allow him to bathe in the river before being taken back to Kumhársain, and then drowned himself. He became a demon and haunted the sepoy in his sleep until the latter made an image in his name and began to worship him at Kaṛel. The other people of Kaṛel out of respect for the image placed it in the temple besides that of Ḍúm.

The people of Jhangroli in Chagaon *pargana* also brought an image of Ḍúm from Gathán and made him a temple. He is worshipped with *dhúp díp* every 5th day, but has no daily *púja*. The people hold Gathán Ḍúm to be their family *deota*, but the temple is maintained in the village as a mark of respect.

Though the Ḍúm *deotás* have their chief temples at Gathán and Sharmalla, there are a number of Ḍúms with temples in Saráj, as already noted. Ḍúm also came in Shadhoch and there are four temples to Ḍúm in the following villages of *pargana* Chebishi :—

(1) *Ḍúm of Pharal.*—It is not known when this Ḍúm was brought from Sharmalla. A man of this *pargana* lived in Saráj, whence he brought an image and placed it in a temple at Pharaj with the express permission of Malendu *deota*, who is the family *deota* of the Chebishi people. This Ḍúm has no *rath* and his function is to protect cattle. If a cow does not give milk, he is asked to make her yield it in plenty and the *ghí* produced from the first few days' milk is given to him as *dhúp*. No *khin* is performed for him, but Kanets give him *dhúp díp* daily. He has no *bhor*.

(2) *Ḍúm of Koṭla.*—Koṭla has always been held in *jágír* by the Kanwars or Miáns of Kumhársain, and the Ḍúm temple there was founded by one of them.

(3) *Ḍúm of Kupṛi.*—The people of Kupṛi village say that more than 700 years ago they came from Rewag, a village in Ubdesh *pargana* in Saráj and settled at Kupṛi in the Chebishi *pargana* of Shadoch. Their ancestors brought with them Ḍúm, their family *deota's* image, and placed it in a temple. A field at Kupṛi was named Rewag after their original village. The people of this village do not regard Malendu as their family god. There are at present nine images of Ḍúm in the Kupṛi temple and a small *píṛí* (bed) where it is believed a Bhagwati lives with him The Kanets are his *pujárís* and also his *gurs*. A Khin. *mela* is held every three or four years at night and goats are sacrificed.

(4) *Ḍúm of Parojusha.*—Nearly 200 years ago, Káji, a Shadhoch man who had lived in Saráj, returned to his village and brought with him an image of Ḍúm, which he presented to his fellow-villagers at Beshera, and made them also swear to worship him. This they did, presumably with Malendu's permission. More than 100 years ago one of the villagers killed a *sádhu* whose spirit would not allow the people to live at ease in their village, so they all left it and settled in Parojusha. A Bhagwati is believed to live with him in the temple. The Kanets worship him but their family god is Malendu. He has no *bhor*.

THE FAMILY OF MARECHH.

The Marechh family is represented by seven members.[1] The *deota* called Dithu or Marechh has his temple at Dholaser, close to Kumhársain itself. The story goes that he came from the Mansarowar lake nearly 4000 years ago.[2] On his way down he met Bhambu Rái at a place now called Bhambu Ráiká Ṭibba, a peak between Bághi and Kadrála, where the ruins of his palace are said to still exist. Bhambu Ráo, who was a Rájpút[3] Rájá like Kans, is looked upon as a *maleksh* or *daint* (devil). His favourite meal was a woman's breast and he ate one every day. He used to go to bathe in the Sutlej, thence go to Hátkoṭi for worship, and return to dine at his palace every day, a daily round of about 100 miles which he accomplished in six hours The people were grievously oppressed by him, and at last the *deota* of Shuli (in *pargana* Kanchin of Bashahr) killed him. But after his death his evil spirit (*páp*) began to torment the Shuli *deota*, and in order to appease him Shanti built for it a resting place at Shuli in a separate temple. Every twelfth year Bhambu Ráo comes out seated in his *rath*, by night, never by day, and carried by the people rides and dances in it. Women and children shut themselves up in their houses while he is out at night. He was very powerful when Dithu *deota* was coming down from the Mansarowar lake, and near Kadrála refused to let him pass, so a great fight was fought in which Bhambu Ráo was worsted. Dithu then halted on his way at Márni in a ravine near Madháwani in the valley north of Nárkanḍa in Kumhársain, hid himself in a cave and ate human flesh. He used also to accept human sacrifice. A long time after, when the *deota* Koṭ Ishwar held his *mela* at Chhachhori, Dithu hearing the notes of the *karnál* and *narsinga* came out of his cave and joined in the fair. Both the *deotas* made friends, and Kot Ishwar invited Dithu to his temple at Koṭi. When Koṭ Ishwar and Bhura *deota* entered the temple two goats were, as usual, offered for sacrifice, but Koṭ Ishwar declined to accept them saying that he had with him a third *deota* as his guest, and that a third goat should be offered for him. So the people brought a third goat, but Dithu refused to accept it saying that he preferred human flesh, and that a virgin girl

[1] Of whom three are found in Kumhársain, two in Shángri, one in Koṭgarh and one in Kulu, thus :—(1) Dithu at Dholaser, (2) Marechh of Malendu at Malendi, (3) at Bareog in Kumhársain, (4) at Shawan in Shángri, (5) at Banar in Shángri, (6) at Kirti in Koṭgarh and (7) at Baina in Kulu.

[2] In the year 1000 of Yudhisthir's era, or 4000 years ago.

[3] He is said to have come from the Bángar Des, apparently meaning the Kurukshetra. He was called Ráo or Rái.

should be sacrificed. Koṭ Ishwar was displeased at this and ordered Dithu's arrest, and he was not released until he had sworn never to taste human flesh again. This pleased Koṭ Ishwar and he made Dithu his *wazír*. He was given a place called Dholaser, where his temple still exists. Koṭ Ishwar also assigned him his favourite Kotálu, the *mawanna*, as his *kárdár*, and to this family was given Bai, a village close to Dholaser. Dithu brought with him from Márni a *mohru* tree, which, with some *kelo* trees, still stands near his temple. Ráná Kirti Singh, founder of the Kumhársain State, affected this *deota*.

Dithu comes out of his temple when Koṭ Ishwar rides on his *rath* at a *mela*. A Balti *mela* is held every third year.

The Marechh of Malendi is also called Malendu, or 'he of Malendi'.

The people of Chebishi *pargana*, who are his devotees, say that the seven Marechh brothers came from the Mansarowar lake and fought with Bhambu Ráo when he barred their way. After his overthrow they came to Háṭu, whence they scattered. Malendu went to Chhichhar forest and after a time flew to the top of the Dertu hill above Chebishi *pargana*. A Káli or Kálka called Bhágwati, who lived on this peak, received him kindly, but after a while she desired him to acquire a territory where he could be worshipped, and recommended to him the Chebishi *pargana*, as it was subsequently named. So this *deota* Marechh left the Kálka and came to Lanki forest. Thence he descended to the Nálá and reached Janjhat, a place where he found a brass *báoli* with brass steps leading down to the water. But some say either that he did not reach the brass *báoli* or that from the *báoli* he went to Dheongli and sat under a *bes* tree. The story goes that this Marechh being anxious to make himself known to the people transformed himself into a serpent, and sucked milk from the cows that grazed near by. A cow-girl saw him and informed a Deongli Brahman. When he came the serpent resumed his original form—an *ashtdhátu* image—and sat in his lap. The Brahman gave him *dhúp díp*. At that time the *mawannas* of Bashera and Pharal were powerful, so the Brahman carried the image to Bashera and the Bashera *mawanua* in consultation with him of Pharal informed *deota* Koṭ Ishwar of the new arrival. Koṭ Ishwar treated Marechh kindly and gave him the present Chebishi *pargana*, but only on condition that he would not oppress the people, and that he should only be allowed goats and rams, *kháḍu* but not *bher*, to eat. He was given a *jágír* in four villages, as well as fields in several others. It was also agreed that Malendu should not go out for a ride on a *rath* unless Koṭ Ishwar gave him leave and his *rath* is never decorated until Koṭ Ishwar sends him a piece of *masru* cloth in token of his permission. Like Dithu he only comes out of his temple when Koṭ Ishwar does so. Malendu was further ordered to observe the following *teohárs* or festivals (at each of which Koṭ Ishwar sends him a goat), *viz.* the Bishu, Rehálí, Dewálí, Mágh and Sharuno. Lastly, the god was asked to select a place for his temple, and he chose Malendi, and there it was built by the Bashera and Pharal *mawannas*. It is believed that this *deota* is absent from his temple on the Mághi Shankránt for seven days, during which period the temple is closed and all work stopped till his return. The popular belief is that the *deota* goes to fight with the *rákshasas* and *daints* at Bhonda Bil, somewhere in Bashahr, and returns after bathing at Kidárnáth. On his return the temple is re-opened and his *gur* or *dewa* dances in a trance (*chirna*) and through him the *deota* relates all his strife with the *rákshasa*. Strange to say, if the *rákshasas* have won, it is believed that a bumper harvest will result; but if the *deotás* win, there is danger of famine. Yet, though there be good harvest, if the *rákshasas* win, there is a danger that pestilence may afflict men or cattle, and if the *deotás* win, though there may be famine, they will avert pestilence. A *deota* never speaks of himself but only of the other *deotás* who fought with him. If he says that a certain *deota* left his bell on the field, it is believed that his *gur* will soon die; if he says a musical instrument was left, that the *deotá's* Turi (musician) will die; or if a key was left, that the *deotá's bhanḍári* or a *kárdár* will die. If Koṭ Ishwar throw dust towards a *rákshasa* and retire from the field, there may be famine or some part of Kumhársain will be encroached upon or given to another State. There is a pond at Bhonda Bil and a Brahman of Bashahr puts up two hedges—one on the side believed to be the *deotás'* side and another on that believed to be the *rákshasas'* side. If the hedge on the *deotás'* side falls down, they are believed to have suffered defeat, but if the *rákshasas'* hedge falls, they are worsted. No one but Maon Nág of Suket plunges into the pond, and by the flash of his plunge the other *deotás* bathe in the water sprayed on its banks. If defeated, the *deota* says he is *chut chipat* ('impure') and then a Balti *púja* is held on an auspicious day. On the Shankránt days Brahmans do *púja*, reciting *mantras* and offering *dhúp díp*. These *mantras* are not found in any Veda, but are eulogies of those concerned in the Mahábhárata war. They are called *karasni*.[1] The bell is rung and *dhúp díp* is given in a *dhurna* or *karach*.

Certain Brahmans are believed to know Sabar-bidia or magic[2] lore. Their books are written in a character something like Ṭánkri, but the language is different and very quaint. Sabar-bidia is only known to a few Brahmans, and they do not readily disclose its secrets.

Malendu has no connection with any other *deota* save Koṭ Ishwar, and it is believed that at the time of pestilence or famine he comes out at night in the form of a torch or light and tours through his dominions. The image of this *deota* is of *ashṭ-dhát* (eight metals), and is seated on a *pujri* or small four-sided bed, but it has no *singhásan*. The *deota* has a *jágír*, and one of his *kárdárs*, called *mashána*, is appointed by the State. A *mashána* is changed when necessary by the State. His *gur* is also called a *ghanitta* and his *kárdárs* are commonly called *mahtas*.

Malendu has two *bhors*, Jhatak and Lata. Jhatak is of an *uch* or superior, while Lata is of a *nich* or low caste. Jhatak lived at Urshu, a place also called Jhaila; so he is also called Jhaila

[1] The Mahábhárata praises a song called 'Karasani.'

[2] (1) Tantar; (2) Mante; (3) Jadu.

at Urshu.[1]

Some say that Koṭ Ishwar gave Jhatak as *wazír* to Malendu. On one occasion Lata left Malendu and fled to Koṭ Ishwar, but on Malendu's complaint Koṭ Ishwar restored him to his master who took him back to Malendi.

Banka is another *bhor* who lives at Shelag. Kolís generally worship him, and he drives away ghosts etc. He was originally a devil in a forest, but was subdued by Malendu.

The Marechh *deota* of Bhareog is the family god of the Sheon *pargana* people, and a small *jágír* is held by him of the State.

Paochi, a Brahman village, in *pargana* Chebishi, has a temple to Shawan Marechh. His image was brought from Shawan, a village in Shángri, and set up here.

Concerning Marechh of Kirti two traditions are current. One is that his image was brought by the villagers of Kirti from a place known as Marni, situated on the borders of the Kumhársain and Kanehti States, and that it was called Marich after the name of that village. The other is that originally the worship of this *deota* consisted in burning the hair of the dead in *ghí*, whence he was called Malichh or 'dirty', and that name has been corrupted into Marichh.

The Cult of Mul Padoi.

But beside these families there are several independent *deotás*. Examples of these are Mul Padoi, who has temples at several villages in the States of Bhajji, Shángri and Kumhársain. He is one of the biggest *deotás* in the Simla Hills, and appeared from a cave called Chunjar Malána near Muthiána 1500 years ago. About that time a prince named Dewa Singh[2] had come from Sirmúr, as he had quarrelled with his brothers, and accompanied by a few of his *kárdárs* or officials took refuge in that cave. He also had with him his family god, now called Narolia. While he was dwelling in the cave, Padoi, who was also called Mul, used to play musical instruments and then cry out, *chutun, parun*, 'I shall fall, I shall fall'. One day the prince replied that if the god wished to fall, he could do so, and lo! the image called Mul fell down before him. Mul

[1] He became Malendu's *wazír* soon after he came to Malendi and his dwelling is a *thanb*, a long log of wood which stands before the temple. The *wazír's* function is to drive away evil spirits (*bhút, pret* and *churel*), if they possess anything or man. He also protects people under Malendu's orders from visitations of any *chai chidar*, plague, famine etc. Lata was originally a Koli by caste who lived at Kalmu village. He died under the influence of some evil spirit and became a ghost. As he troubled the Kolís of Kalmu and Shelag, they complained to the *deota*, who accompanied by Jhatak visited the place and caught him. At first Lata would not come to terms, but *deota* Malendu promised him his protection, and that he should be worshipped by the Kolís and a *roṭ* (loaf) be given him on the four *shankránts* (Bishu, Rehálí, Dewáli and Mágh), and that he should be presented regularly with *dhúp dip* after he had himself received it, and that Kolís should sacrifice ewes (*bheṛí*) to him. Lata accepted these terms and swore to trouble the people no more, but he explained that he could not sit still, and so Malendu erected the wooden log in front of his temple, and in it Lata is doubtless ever moving.

[2] Dewa Singh was also the name of one of his descendants who held Koṭi State in Kandru.

wished him to accept a kingdom, but he said that he was a vagrant prince who had no country to rule over. Thereupon a Bári (mason) from Koṭi in Kandru *pargana* came and told the prince that he had led him to that cave, and he sought him to follow him to a State which had no chief. The prince replied that he could not accept its chiefship until the rest of its people came and acknowledged him as their Rájá. So the mason returned to Kandru and brought back with him the leading men of that tract and they led the prince to Koṭi. There he built a temple for the *deota* and a palace for himself. Tradition says that the palace had 18 gates and occupied more than 4 acres of land. Its remains are still to be seen near the temple. Some say that the Rájá placed the *deota* Narolia along with Mul Padoi in the temple, which stood in the middle of the palace. The *deota* Narolia never comes out in public except to appear before theRáná of Kumhársain, if he visits him, or before the descendants of the mason who led the prince to that country. The *deota* never comes out beyond the Koṭi *bása* (dwelling-house) to accept his dues (*kharen*), which consist of a small quantity of grain. A few generations later it befell that a Ṭhákur of Koṭi[1] had four sons who quarrelled about the partition of the State. One son established himself first in Kulu and then at Kangal (now in Shángri); the second went to Tháru in Bhajji State: and the third settled at Malag, now in Bhajji, while the Ṭikka or eldest, as was his right, lived at Koṭi.

It is said that Rájá Mán Singh of Kulu took Kangal fort and also overran Koṭi, but others say that Kumhársain took it. Koṭi appears, however, to have been reconstituted as a State soon after the disruption of Rajána, and the latter State is only remembered in connection with Mul *deota's* story and the songs (*bars*) sung in his honour in Bhajji.

On the other hand, some people say that in the Chunjar Malána cave four images fell, while others think that there are four Muls in as many temples. Their names are Mul, Shir, Sadrel and Thathlu and their temples are at Koti, Padoi and Kangal in the Simla Hills and at Saran in Suket. But doubtless the devotees of Mul *deota* multiplied the Mul, carrying his images with them and building temples to him wherever they went. Wherever there is a temple to Mul he is now generally called Padoi. His principal temple is at Padoa in Bhajji, on the east bank of the Sutlej, but Koṭi is his Jethu-Sthán or Senior Place. Shanglu and Rirku are his *bhoṛs* or ministers.

Rirku was a *deota* at Padoa who in the spirit came flying to Mul at Koṭi. He ate a loaf given him by Mul and accepted him as his master. He now drives away *bhút-pret* when commanded by Mul. The same tale is told of Shanglu.

Thathlu *deota* is the *wazír* to the Mul of Koṭi, and when a rupee is presented to him 4 annas are given to Thathlu. Thathlu's temple is at Thatha in Kumhársain and in it his image is kept, but people

[1] The parent State appears to have been known as Rajána. Its capital was at Koṭi, and it split up into four States, Koṭi, Kangal, Tháru and Malag. The *zamíndárs* of Thathlua village claim to be descendants from the Sirmúr prince, though they have now sunk to Kanet status. The Miáns of Gheti and Karioṭ in *pargana* Chebishi are descendants of the *ex*-Ṭhákur of Kangal.

believe that Thathlu is always with Mul, his elder spirit, and only comes back to his own temple when invoked or to take *dhúp díp*. Thathlu calls Mul his *dádu* (elder). Mul goes to Suni every year at the Dasahra, and his spirit also goes to Shuli to bathe. Padoa and Dharogra in Bhajji have large temples to Mul, and there is a big temple at Parol in Shángri also. Mul Padoi is very useful if his help is asked in hunting and shooting.

There are also two temples to Padoi in Chebishi *pargana* at Shaila and Gheti.

When the Ṭhákur of Kangal fled or died his fort was burned by the Rájá of Kulu, and his descendants came to Kumhársain. This happened in the time of Rání Rám Singh, who gave them Gheti village in *jágír*. The Koli fort was taken by them and they held it for about 20 generations. They had brought with them to Gheti silver and copper images of Mul, and these are kept in the Gheti temple to this day. Other descendants of the Ṭhákur settled in village Karioṭ. The Gheti people too were carrying their family god to Karioṭ, but on the road they came to Shaila. Nág *deota* used to be the god of the Shaila people, but a leper in that village laid himself on the path and begged Padoi to cure him. Padoi said that if he cured him, he must disown the Nág *deota* who was living in the village. The leper promised to do so and was cured. The people thus convinced of Padoi's superiority over the Nág sent the latter off to Dhali village where the people still worship him, but his temple at Shaila was taken over by Padoi and he lives there to this day.

Only a couple of years ago a devotee of Padoi went to Theog and there built him a temple. It is said that with the prince from Sirmúr came a Brahman, a Kanet named Gosaon and a Turi (musician) whose descendants are to be found in Kumhársain, Bhajji and Shángri.

Some minor cults of the Simla Hills.

The cult of the deota *Magneshwar Mauni of Mánun.*

At a village called Jalandhar in Kulu lived a Brahman whose wife gave birth to a girl when she was 12 years old. She, though a virgin, gave birth to twin[1] serpents, but kept it secret and concealed her serpent sons in an earthen pot, and fed them on milk. One day when she went out for a stroll she asked her mother not to touch her dolls which were in the house, but unfortunately her mother desiring to see her child's beloved dolls uncovered the pot and to her dismay the two serpents raised their hoods. Thinking the girl must be a witch she threw burning ashes on them and killed one of them, but the other escaped to a *ghara* or pot full of milk and though burnt turned into an image. Meanwhile the virgin mother returned and finding her loving sons so cruelly done by, she cut her throat and died on the spot. Her father came in to churn the milk and in doing so broke the *ghara* in which, to his surprise, he found the image which the living serpent had become. Distressed at his daughter's suicide he left his home taking the image, found in the milk, in his turban and roamed from land to land. At last he

[1] Another version says three.

reached Sirmúr whose Rájá had no son. He treated the Brahman kindly and on his asking the Rájá to give him his first-born son, if by the power of his image he had children,[1] he accepted the condition, and by the grace of the image was blessed with two sons, the elder of whom was made over to the Brahman together with a *jágír* which consisted of the *parganás* of Rajána, Mathiána, Shilli, Sheol and Chadara now in Phágu tahsíl in Keonthal. It was called Rajána and its old Ṭhákurs have a history of their own. The family ruled for several generations. Hither the Brahman brought the Rájá's elder son and settled him at Rajána village, commonly called Mul Rajána, in Shilli *pargana*. The Brahman settled at Mánun, a village to the north-west of Rajána where another *deota* was oppressing the people, until the Brahman revealed his miraculous image and people began to worship Magneshwar as a greater *deota*. He killed the oppressor and the people burned all his property, certain Máwis who resisted being cruelly put to death by the devotees of the new *deota*. Deori Dhár village was set on fire and the people burnt alive in it. Later on when the Giáru family of the Kumhársain chiefs had established themselves in the country the *deota* helped the Ṭhákur of Kumhársain to gain a victory over the Sirmúr Rájá. The Kumhársain State gave a *jágír* now worth Rs. 166 to the Magneshwar *deota* of Mánun. He has a large temple and the chief among his *kárdárs* is the *bhanḍárí* who keeps the *jágír* accounts. *Sadá barat* (alms) are given to *sádhús, faqírs* and Brahmans. He is worshipped daily morning and evening by his *pujárís*. A *mela* is held annually at Mánun on the 17th or 18th Baisákh and another at the Diwáli by night. Every third year another *mela* called the Shiláru Púja is held. A big *púja mela* is performed every 7th or 8th year and a still bigger one called Shánt every 30 years. When a new Rána ascends the *gaddi* the *deota* tours the country belonging to him. This is called *rajaoli játra*. The Nagarkoṭia or Ḍum *deota* of Sharmalla was on friendly terms with this *deota*, but they quarrelled while dancing at Shamokhar as related above on page 451.

The cult of the deota *Melan or Chatur Mukh in Koṭgarh.*

This *deota* is believed to be one of the most powerful gods in these hills. He is the family god of the Koṭ Khai and Kanehti chiefs and of the Ṭhákur of Karangla. More than 3000 years ago when there were no Rájás or Ránás in the country (excepting perhaps Banasur in Bashahr) the people obeyed the *deotás* as spiritual lords of the land, while *mawannas* held parts of the country. *Deota* Kána was supreme in Koṭgarh and the Kanehṭi Shadhoch country. As he had only one eye he was called *kána*. He delighted in human sacrifice and every month on the *shankránt* day a man or woman was sacrificed to him as a *bali*. Each family supplied a victim in turn. Legend says that there was a woman who had five daughters, four of whom had in turn been

[1] Another account says: The Brahman gave him three grains of rice and told him that by the *deota* a son should be born to him. The Rájá divided the rice among his three Ránás, and on his return after a year the Brahman found that three sons had been born to them. He demanded the eldest from the Rájá as his reward, and brought the boy with him to Mauni.

devoured by Kána Deo and the turn of the fifth was fixed for the *shankránt.* A contemporary god called Khachli Nág dwelt in a forest called Jarol near a pond in Kanehti below Sidhpur (on the Hindustán-Tibet road to Kotgarh). The mother went to him complaining that Kána *deota* had devoured hundreds of human beings and that her four daughters had already been eaten and the fate of the fifth was sealed. She implored the Nág to save her daughter and he having compassion on her said that when Kána Deo's men came to take the girl for the *bali* she should look towards the Nág and think of him. The woman returned home and when Kána Deo's men came for the girl she did as she had been told. At that instant a black cloud appeared over the Jarol forest, and spread over Melan village and Kána Deo's temple with lightning and thunder. There was heavy rain, the wind howled and a storm of iron hail destroyed both temple and village, but their remains are still to be seen on the spot. Large stones joined with iron nails are said to be found where the temple stood, and images of various shapes are also found in the Nála. There now remained no other *deota* in this part of the country and people were wondering how they would live without the help of any god. They could hold no fair without a god riding in his *rath,* so they took counsel together and decided that Nág *deota* of Khachli should be the only god of the country. They chose his abode in the forest and begged him to accept them as his subjects, promising that they would carry him to Melan and build him a new temple : that on *mela* days he should ride in a *rath,* be carried from place to place and worshipped as he pleased. But as Nág *deota* was a pious spirit his ascetic habits forbade pomp and pageantry so he declined to be chosen god of the country, but said that he was a hermit who loved solitude, and that if the people were in earnest in wishing for a god they should seek one at Kharán (a village in *pargana* Baghi-Mastgarh, now in Bashahr) where three brother *deotas* had a single temple. He advised them to beg these *deotas* to agree to be their lords and promised that he would help them with his influence.

The Kharán *deotas* came in their *raths* for a *mela* at Dudhbali (in *pargana* Jao, now in Kumhársain) and the Shadhoch people proceeded to obtain a *deota* as king over their country. While the three Kharán brothers were dancing in their *raths* they prayed in their hearts that whichever chose to be their god might turn his *rath* as lightly as a flower, while the other *raths* should become too heavy to move. They vowed that the one who accepted their offer should be treated like a king, that of silk should be his garments, of silver his musical instruments, that no sheep or she-goats should be given him but only he-goats, and that his domain should spread far and wide from Bhaira near the Sutlej to Kupar above Jubbal. The custom is still that no sheep or she-goat is sacrificed before Chatur Mukh *deota* and no cotton cloth is used. Their prayer was accepted by the second brother who was called Chatur Mukh (four-faced). The name of the eldest brother is Jeshar and of the youngest Ishar. When Chatur Mukh caused his *rath* to be as light as a lotus flower, eighteen men volunteered to carry it away from the *mela* and dancing bore it home on their shoulders. The Kharán and Jao people finding that Chatur

Mukh was stolen from them by the Shadhoch people pursued them, shooting arrows and brandishing *dangras*. The brave eighteen halted on a plain behind Jao village where there was a fight, in which Kachli Nág mysteriously helped them and Chatur Mukh by his miraculous power turned the pursuers' arrows against their own breasts and their *dangras* flew to their own heads until hundreds of headless trunks lay on the plain while not one of the Shadhochas was killed. The Shadhoch people then carried the *rath* in triumph first to Shathla village (in Kotgarh) choosing a place in the centre of the country so that the god might not be forcibly carried off by the Kharán and Jao people. Thence the *deota* was taken to Sakundi village, in Kotgarh, but the *deota* did not choose to live there either and bade the people to build him a temple at Melan nearly a furlong from the ruined temple of Kána Deo towards Kotgarh. This was gladly done by the people and Chatur Mukh began to reside there.

The people say that nearly 150 years ago Chatur Mukh went to Kidár Náth on a *játra* (pilgrimage) and when returning home he visited Mahású *deota* at Nol, a village in Kiran (once in Sirmúr), as his guest. But one of Mahású's attendant *deotás* troubled Chatur Mukh in the temple at Nol and frightened his men so that they could not sleep all night. This displeased Chatur Mukh and he left the temple at daybreak much annoyed at his treatment. He had scarcely gone a few steps when he saw a man ploughing in a field and by a miracle made him turn towards the temple and ascend it with his plough and bullocks. Mahású *deota* asked Chatur Mukh why he manifested such a miracle and Chatur Mukh answered that it was a return for his last night's treatment; that he, as a guest, had halted at the temple to sleep, but he and his force (*lashkar*) had not been able to close their eyes the whole night. Chatur Mukh threatened that by his power the man, plough and bullocks should stick for ever to the walls of the temple. Mahású was dismayed and fell on his knees to beg for pardon. Chatur Mukh demanded the surrender of Mahású's devil attendant and he was compelled to hand him over. This devil's name is Shirpál.[1] He was brought as a captive by Chatur Mukh to Melan and after a time, when he had assured his master that he would behave well, he was forgiven and made Chatur Mukh's *wazír*, as he still is, at Melan. Shirpál ministers in the temple and all religious disputes are decided by him, *e. g.* if anyone is outcasted or any other case of *chua* arises, his decision is accepted and men are re-admitted into caste as he decrees. Some other minor *deotás* are also subordinate to Chatur Mukh, the chief among them being :—(1) Benu, (2) Janeru, (3) Khoru, (4) Merelu and (5) Basara.

These Deos are commonly called his *bhors* (servants). The people cannot tell anything about their origin, but they are generally believed to be *rákshasas* who oppressed the people in this country until Chatur Mukh subdued them and made them his servants. These *bhor* Deos are his attendants and work as watchmen (*chaukidárs*) at the temple gate. Benu is said to have come from Bena in Kulu. He was at

[1] *Shir* means stairs and *pál* means watch: hence *shirpál* means a servant at the gate.

first a devil. When it is believed that a ghost has appeared in any house or taken possession of anything or any one Deo Benu turns him out. Janeru came from Paljara in Bashahr. He too is said to have been a devil but Chatur Mukh reformed him. His function is to protect women in pregnancy and child-birth, also cows etc. For this service he is given a loaf after a birth. Khoru appeared from Khoru Kiár in Kumhársain. He too was originally a devil and when Rájá Máhí Prakásh of Sirmúr held his court at Khoru and all the hill chiefs attended it this devil oppressed the people, until Chatur Mukh made him captive and appointed him his *chaukídár* at Melan temple. Merelu came out of a *marghát* (crematorium). He too is looked upon as a *jamdút* or *rákshasa.* He had frightened the people at Sainja in Kotgarh, but was captured and made a *chaukídár* at Melan. Basara Deo is said to have come from Bashahr State, and some say that he was a subordinate Deo of Basaru *deota* at Gaoró and troubled his master, so Basaru handed him over to Chatur Mukh, but others say that Powari, *wasír* of Bashahr, invoked Chatur Mukh's aid as he was distressed by the devil Basara, and Shirpál, Chatur Mukh's *wasír,* shut Basara up in a *tokni.*[1] Thus shut up he was carried to Melan and there released and appointed a *chaukídár.* This Deo helps Benu Deo in turning out ghosts (*bhút, pret,* or *churel*). To Basaru Deo were given Mangshu and Shawat villages where only Kolís worship him. The people of Kirti village in Kotgarh worship Marechh Deota. Less than 100 years ago Deota Chatur Mukh came to dance in a *kirtijubar* and Marechh *deota* opposed him, but Chatur Mukh prevailed and was about to kill him when Tiru, a Brahman of Kirti village, cut off his own arm and sprinkled the blood upon Chatur Mukh who retired to avoid the sin of *brahm-hatia* (murder of a Brahman). Chatur Mukh feeling himself polluted by a Brahman's blood gave Marechh *deota* the villages of Bhanana, Kirti and Shawat and then went to bathe at Kidár Náth to get purified. Every 12th year Chatur Mukh tours in his dominions and every descendant of the 18 men who brought him from Dudhbali accompanies him. They are called the 9 Kuin and 9 Kashi. Kuin means originally people of respectable families and Kashi means 'those who swore' as the 9 Kuin had taken with them 9 men who swore to help them to carry Chatur Mukh from Dudhbali. When the *deota* returns from his tour these 18 families are each given a *pagri* as a *viddigi* or parting gift and all the people respect them. An annual *mela* is held at Dudhbali to which Chatur Mukh goes to meet his two Kharán brothers. A big Díwáli *mela* is also held at Melan every 3rd year. Every year Chatur Mukh goes to the Dhadu *mela* in Kotgarh, and he goes to tour in the Shadhoch *pargana* of Kanehti in Sáwan. The old *pujáris* of Kána *deota* were killed by lightning or drowned with him and when Chatur Mukh settled at Melan, the Kharán *pujáris* also settled there and they worship him daily, morning and evening. His favourite *játra* is to Kidár Náth and this he performs every 50 or 60 years. He does not approve of the *bhunda* sacrifice, though every 12th year his brothers in Kharán hold one, at which a man is sent down a long rope off which he some-

[1] This utensil is still kept at Melan.

times falls and is killed. Chatur Mukh however goes to see the *bhunda* at Kharán though he does not allow one at Melan. There is a Balti fair at Melan every 3rd year. The *deota's* image is of brass and silver. When he returns from Kidár Náth a *diápan jag mela* is held. People believe that Chatur Mukh is away from his temple in Mágh every year for 15 days, and that he goes to bathe at Kidár Náth with his attendants They say that the spirits fly to Kidár Náth and all work is stopped in those days. His *bhanḍár* (store-house) is also closed and his *dewa* or *gur* (through whom he speaks) does not appear in public or perform *hingárna*. The people believe that Chatur Mukh returns on the 15th of Mágh and then his temple is opened amid rejoicings. Some say that there is a place in Bashahr called Bhandi Bil where the hill *rákshasas* and devils assemble every year early in Mágh, and Chatur Mukh with other hill *deotás* goes to fight with them and returns after 15 days. People also say that Chatur Mukh has 18 treasures hidden in caves in forests, but only three of them are known. The treasures were removed from the temple when the Gurkhas invaded the country. One contains utensils, another musical instruments and the third gold and silver images. The remaining 15 are said to be in caves underground. One was once robbed of some images. The *deota* holds a large *jágír* from the Bashahr, Kumhársain, Koṭ Khśi and Kanehti chiefs,[1] as well as one from Government worth Rs 80. Kumhársain has given him a *jágır* of Rs. 11 and Kanehti one of Rs. 22. The three Kharán brothers once held certain *parganas* in *jágír*, *pargana* Raik belonging to Jeshar, *pargana* Jao to Chatur Mukh, and *pargana* Samat to Ishwar, but they have been resumed. Nearly 150 years ago Melan temple was accidentally burnt down and when a Sirmúr Ráni of Bashahr, who was touring in her *jágír*, came to Melan the *deota* asked her to build him a new temple. She besought him to vouchsafe her a miracle, and it is said that his *rath* moved itself to her tent without human aid, so she then built the present temple at Melan, some 30 years before the Gurkha invasion. The devotees of other *deotás* jest at Chatur Mukh's powers. Till some 7 generations ago the Ránás of Koṭ Khśi lived there and then transferred their residence to Koṭgarh. When at Koṭgarh the Ṭíka of one of the Ránás fell seriously ill and the people prayed Chatur Mukh to restore him. Chatur Mukh declared he would do so, but, even as the *gur* was saying that the Ṭíka would soon recover, news of his death was received. Thereupon one Jhingri killed the *gur* with his *dangra*, but the Ráná was displeased with him and the family of the murderer is still refused admission to the palace. Some say that the blow of the *dangra* was not fatal and that the *gur* was carried by a Koli of Batari to Kanehti where he recovered. Chatur Mukh has given the Kanehti men the privilege of carrying him in front when riding in his *rath* while the Koṭgarh men hold it behind. Another mark of honour is that when Chatur Mukh sits his face is always kept towards Kanehti. He is placed in the same position at his temple. Chatur Mukh does not like ghosts to enter his dominion and when any complaint is made of such an entry he himself with his

[1] His chief *kárdárs* are the *gur*, *bhanḍári*, *khazanchi* and *dárogha* of accounts: four of them being from Koṭgarh and two from Kanehti. All business is transacted by a *panchâyat*.

bhors visits the place and captures the ghost. If the ghost enters any articles such as an utensil, etc. it is confiscated and brought to his temple. Chatur Mukh is a disciple of Khachli Nág who has the dignity of being his *guru* or spiritual master. Deota Kepu at Kepu in Kotgarh is Mahádeo and Chatur Mukh considers him as his second *gurú*. Ḍúm *deota* at Pamlai in Koṭgarh, a derivative of Ḍúm of Gathán in Keonthál, is considered subordinate to Chatur Mukh and has a separate temple at a distance. Marechh *deota* of Kirti and Mahádeo of Kepu can accept a cloth spread over the dead, but Chatur Mukh and Ḍum cannot do so. What became of Kána *deota* after the deluge at Melan cannot be ascertained, but a story believed by some is that he took shelter in a small cistern in Sawári Khaḍ. A woman long after the deluge tried to measure the depth of the cistern with a stick and Kána Deo's image stuck to it, so she carried it to her house and when his presence was known Chatur Mukh shut him up in a house at Batari village. Some say that the woman kept the image of Kána in a box and when she opened she was surprised by snakes and wasps that came out of it. The box is buried for ever.

According to another account there are two traditions as to this name. According to one, Chatur Mukh means four *or five* mouths, the original idol having had, according to this story, four faces; this idol is kept in the temple treasury, and nobody is allowed to see it, a one-faced image, which can be seen and worshipped by the people being placed in the temple instead. The other tradition is that the *deota* is called Chhatar Mukh as being the mouth of the Rájá of Koṭ Khái (*chhatar* meaning Rájá, *i.e.* one who has a *chhatar* (umbrella) over his head), and the name would thus signify that whatever is ordered by this *deota* is regarded as the Rájá's own command.

The cult of Jít Dánon (Mahlog State).

Jít Rám, a Kanet of Sherla village, was as a child carried off by his brother's wife to Dún, a low-lying village which is surrounded by hills. When he grew bigger he was employed in grazing cattle, and was so simple that he believed his own village to be the whole world. Once some of his cattle went to Jatáon village while grazing, and on his following them he saw, to his great surprise, a new world. On his return he told his brother's wife and she scornfully replied: 'You are merely a grazier of Dún, and so foolish as not to know yet that the world is not limited to the two villages you have seen. On hearing this he left Dún for Jatáon, telling her that she would have no butter, milk etc. until she worshipped him. He remained at Jatáon and worshipped God all his life. After his death he was worshipped by the people as a *deota* or *dánon* and since then he has been called Jít Dánon. Every man in the State offers him a goat and 1½ *sers* (*khám*) of *ghí* when his cattle calve, and it is believed that any one who does not make this offering will get little milk from his cattle.

The cult of Deo Ghurka (Mahlog State).

Ghurka, who fought bravely in the Mahábhárata war, was the

son of Bhím (one of the Pándos) by a Rákhshani, named Harimbhá. On his death a temple was built to him in Gharshi, a village on the Ghurka Dhár (hill). Another *dhár* opposite Ghurka *dhár* is called Harimbha, after the name of Ghurka's mother and a village of the same name.

Baindra of Devri.

A man named Baindra came to this place from Náhan in Sirmúr, and at first he dwelt at a place in the Kalála Forest, called Chortha. One day a woman of the Kerh tribe while grazing her cattle passed by the spot where Baindra was sleeping and awakened him by striking him with a stick. Baindra woke in a rage and cursed her, saying: 'Be a *deodár* tree': whereupon she was at once transformed into a *deodár*, and this tree, which stands near the temple of Baindra at Chortha, is still worshipped. After Baindra's death he was worshipped as a *deota* and temples built to him at Chortha and Devri.

Chambi of Bareon.

A man (whose name is not known) was born at a place called Chambi in the Balsan State. He displayed miracles, and in the last stage of his life moved from Chambi to Bareon. After his death an image of him was made, and it has been worshipped ever since. A temple was also constructed at Chambí, his birth place.

Nandhrari of Pujarli.

The present site of Nandhrárí village was in old times a piece of waste land, called Nandhrárí, where a fish lived in a fountain. This fish vomited up an image of a goddess, which was named Nandhrári after the place, and was brought to Pujárlí where a temple was built for it. Another temple was erected at the fountain in Nandhrárí.

The deota *Baneshwar of Pujárli.*

Pujárli is a village in the Ubdesh *pargana* of Kumhársain and its *deota* is said to be very ancient. Some say that in the early times of the *mawannas* three *máwis* lived to the south of Bagli, at Kero, Gahleo and Nali. The Kero *máwi's* fort lay in the modern Kanehti and the Gahleo *máwis'* in Kot Khái, while the Nali *máwis* had theirs at Mal, now in Kumhársain, below Háthu and close to Bagli.[1] The *máwis* of Gahleo brought this *deota* from Bala Hat in Garhwál and built him a temple at Chela, a village in Kot Khái, as he was the family *deota* of all three *máwis*.[2] But they were nearly all killed by Sirmúr and their houses burnt, so the surviving Gahleo *máwis* concealed the *deota* in a cave in the cliffs above Chela. Thence his voice would be heard, with the sound

[1] The *máwis* were so wealthy that one used to spread his barley to dry on a carpet, another could cover a carpet with coin, and the third had a gold chain hung from his house to the temple. Two of the *máwis* appear to have been named Nalo and Gahlo.

[2] His family was called Molta, but only one house of it survives. The present Brahmans of Pujárli hail from Tikargarh in Bashahr. The *pujáras* of Pujárli appear to be called Kacheri (by *got* or family) and they founded Kacheri, a village near Kumhársain.

of bells and the scent of *dhúp*, so a Brahman of Pujárli went to the cave and brought the *deota* to a temple at Pujárli. He is regarded as their family *deota* by the people of Pujárli, Nagan, Karáli and Banal. As he is *dúdhadhari* goats are not sacrificed to him. When the spirit of the *deota* enters (*chirna*) his *gua* the *deota* says through him :—*Nálwa, Gahlwa ! na áp chhare, na an chhara,* 'Nahlo, Gahlo ! You spared neither yourselves nor me'!—because the *máwis* had involved him in their own ruin.

The following are the principal *deotas* of the Koṭi State. It will be noticed that though all are described as Deo, yet they are of very diverse origins :—

(1) *Klainú Deo.*—The name Klainú is from 'Kulú-fa-ánú' meaning 'brought from Kulu.' In Kulu the god is called Jamnú from the Sanskrit Jamadagni. Apparently the deity was a saint called Dúdádhári, Sanskr., Dudáhhári, 'vegetarian.' Being a saint he never accepts animal sacrifice. His temple is near Kiár on a ridge called Deodhár.

(2) *Sip Deo* (probably from Shiva) came with the ancestors of the present Ráná of Koṭi from Sidhapur in Kángra. His temple is on a small ridge near Mul Koṭi. He is worshipped by the people of Shuhawli and Dharthí *parganas* in Koṭi, but they believe that he is Nrisingha Vishnu or Nársingh.

(3) Sharáli Deo is also called the Deo Junga because he was brought from Junga. He too is Dudhádhárí. His temple in the Sharál village in Koṭi territory.

(4) *Gambhír Deo,* the legend of whose origin goes thus :—Dhír Chand and Gambhír Chand were two sons of Ṭhákar Jajhár Chand of Koṭi, the former by his Kumhársain and the latter by his Kotgarh Rání. They were born on one day, the former in the morning and the latter in the evening. Though by different mothers, they were very fond of each other. Gambhír Chand was anxious to get Chanari village just opposite Koṭi, as his *jágír*, but as it was already held by Brahmans in return for service as State cooks and gate-keepers his wish could not be gratified. In his disappointment Gambhír Chand resolved to commit suicide, and so he rode his pony to a place about a furlong from the palace and there holding up his pigtail with his left hand, and taking a sharp sword in his right, he cut off his head with one blow. His head fell to the ground and rolled down the slope about 60 yards from the body. It is said that the suicide's spirit began to vex his elder brother Dhír Chand, and was only propitiated by the erection of a large temple at Chanári to which local Brahmans were appointed *pujárís* and *díwáns*. Two small temples were also built, one at the spot where the body fell, the other where the head fell, and every year during the Dasehra a sheep is sacrificed at each

(5) *Dhándi Deo,* whose legend is thus described :—Dhándi and Gándhi were two brothers, Kanets by caste, living in Pagog, a village in Koṭi. Dándhi devoted much time to the worship of Klainú, so much so that he used to bring milk every day from Pagog to Deodhár, a distance of about 6 miles. Klainú Deo was so pleased with him that

he accepted him as a deity on his death. So Dhándi became a deity, and his temples are at Pagog and Kamháli in Koti. The potters of these villages became his *pujáris* and *díwáns*, and are now looked upon as respected Kanets.

(6) *Bhát Deo.*—The legend goes thus:—There was a Brahman living with his wife in Badaih village in Koti State. He earnestly besought a boon from villagers, but was refused. Thereupon both he and his wife committed suicide and, as ghosts, began to terrify the villagers who at last accepted the man as a deity. Thus Bhat, meaning a Brahman, has become the deity of Badaih village.

(7) *Korgan Deo.*—The temple of this deity is at Chhabalri village in Koṭi State. The history is as follows:—There was a Rájpút in Sirmúr State, who fell in love with a woman. The *samíndárs* forbade him to visit her, but he paid no heed. At last he was killed together with his groom, a man called Mashadi, and his spirit began to trouble the villagers. He was only propitiated when the villagers took him as their deity. It so happened that the Ṭika of Koṭi went on a trip to Sirmúr, and the deity was much pleased with him, and told him that he would accompany him to Koṭi. Thus he was brought to Koṭi and a temple was erected for him in the Chhabálri village.

(8) *Nnál Deo.*—This deity was brought by Kogi *pargana* people who are immigrants from Suket State. His temple is at Kogi village under Náldera, and there is also a small temple at Náldera, which means 'the temple of Nnál'. It is said that this deity is not on good terms with Síp deity, so it never goes anywhere beyond the Kogi *pargana.*

(9) *Dhánu Deo* is a deity of the Keonthal State, and was brought with them by the people of Chhabrog *pargana,* originally natives of Keonthaḷ. His temple is at Chhabrog village in Koṭi State as well as in Keonthal.

(10) *Shyáni Deo.*—His temple is at Kyáli village in Kalálthi *pargana* of Koṭi State. He is supposed to be a cook residing with all of the aforesaid nine deities.[1]

Bághal State boasts three Deos, two of whom are Shiva, while a third is the spirit of a sonless man. They are:—

(1) *Bára Deo,* who has a temple on the Bari *dhár,* a ridge running in a north-westerly direction from Bahádurpur fort in Biláspur to the junction of the Gambhar and Jol streams. The temple is on the highest point of the ridge, 5,789 feet above the sea level. A fair is held on the 1st Asáṛh. The god is properly Shiva, but as is usual he is generally called by the name of his place of worship.

(2) *Har Sang Deo,* whose home is at the highest point of the Har Sang *dhár,* which runs northwards to the Sutlej on the boundary of Bághal and Bhajji States. This god's fair takes place on the 1st Sáwan. He too is Shiva.

[1] Simla Hill States *Gazetteer,* Koṭi, pp. 8-9.

(8) *Madhor Deo.*—His temple is at the village of Mangu, where a fair is held on 1st Baisákh. This deity was originally a sonless man, a class of person whose spirit the hillman often considers it advisable to conciliate by worship after death. Such a spirit sometimes, as in the present case, rises to the position of a god in course of time.[1]

In the Lower Simla Hills Deo Súr is a greater than Nársingh Bír—there the women's god as he is in Kángra. Indeed Nársingh Bír is said to be his servant. He is universally accepted as the deity of the women of the lower hills. A large fair is held in his honour in the month of Jeṭh at Sairai in Patiála on the Simla-Subáthu road, to which women gather from far and wide. The ritual performed consists of the women sitting in rows while a drum is beaten. During the drumming they sway their heads about from side to side, and when it stops they sit still. This is evidently a representation of the tremors caused by the entering in of the spirit of the god, such as takes place at the *baithak* of Nársingh (see *Kángra Gazetteer*). A similar fair on a larger scale, which lasts eight or nine days, is held at Joharji, also in Patiála, in November. It is supposed that any woman who has become a devotee of Súr and fails to attend one of these fairs will be visited with misfortune. Like Dewaṭ Siddh, Súr is worshipped on the first Sunday of the month[2]

Another Biju, not to be confounded with Biju or Bijat, the lightning god, is a *deota* in Kutiár and its neighbourhood. Ajái Pát, a Rájá of Koṭguru, had a son named Bijái Pát who showed preternatural wisdom in infancy and power to interpret oracles. He succeeded to his father's kingdom but turned *faqír*, and one day reached Deothal on the Gambhar river, 4 miles from Subáthu. There he vanquished Shrí Gul and took possession of his temple. Several smaller temples in his honour have been built of stones from Deothal at various villages.[3]

As instance of *deotas* migrating is furnished by the following legend:—The Rájá 24th in descent from Rám Pál of Kothiár in Kángṛa had five sons and a daughter. His eldest son succeeded him then, but the other four and his daughter crossed the Sutlej into Mal Bhajji in the Nauti valley below Mahásu. Chiru and Chand founded the dynasties of Bhajjí and Koṭi, but the third son, Shogu, became a *deota* at Fagu,[4] while the daughter became the goddess, of Dharch in Keonthal.

But besides these local godlings, there are certain deities of the first rank which merit a fuller description than it has been found possible to obtain. These are the Lesser Káli and the Younger Lonkṛa.

The difference between the Baṛí and the Chhoṭí Kálí is this that the former has 10 hands and the latter only 4.

The Baṛí Kálí haunts the hills. She is worshipped with sacrifices of goats, flowers, fruit, wheaten bread, and lamps.

[1] Simla Hill States *Gazetteer*, Bághal, p. 6.

[2] *Ib*, Biláspur, p. 10, and Baghát, p. 7.

[3] Kuthár, p. 5; Bhagnát, p. 7.

[4] The fourth, Bhoga, married a Kanet girl and begat the Fagiána Kanets, *ib.*, Koṭí, p. 6.

Yáma, the god of death, is supposed to live in rivers. He is propitiated by making an image of gold according to one's means. This is worshipped and then given to a Brahman.

Besides the gods, spirits of various kinds are believed in and propitiated.

Such are the *bhúts* or ghosts, *parís*, especially the *jal-parís*, or water-sprites, also called *jal-mátris*, the *chhidras* and *banshira*.

The *bhút* is the ghost of the cremating ground.

Pret is the term applied to the ghost for one year after the death of the deceased: *rishet*[1] is its name from the end of that year to the fourth.

Jal-parís are conceived of as female forms, some benevolent, others malevolent. To propitiate the former a sacrifice is required.

The *chhidra* is conceived of as a terrifying spirit which must be propitiated by incense of mustard seed.

The *banshira* haunts old buildings, valleys and peaks. It is propitiated by sacrifices of goats, or, in some places, by offerings of dust or gravel.

In lieu of sacrifice a *púja*, called *kunjhain*, is offered to Káli and to *parís* or *mátris*. A tract of hill or forest is set apart as the place of their worship, and even if the rest of the forest is cut down the part consecrated to the goddess or spirit is preserved for her worship, none of the trees in it being cut, or their boughs or even leaves removed.

Dágs are the demons specially associated with fields. If the crop yields less than the estimated amount of produce it is believed that the difference has been taken by the *dág*.

Dúdadhári or *mánashári* haunts burning *gháts*, and is averted by wearing a silver picture round one's neck. If possessed by the former one should abstain from meat.

Ghaṭiálu or *Gaṭerir* is a demon known in Dhámi. He is said to possess people, and is propitiated by the sacrifice of a *khádhu* (ram). He is embodied in a stone which is kept in the house and worshipped to protect the cattle from harm. He is said to have come from Bhajji State.

Newa is a spirit also, closely resembling the *Páp*. When a man dies sonless and his brethren inherit they are frequently haunted by his ghost and so a Brahman must be consulted. He directs an image of silver, copper or stone to be made and worshipped after the *amávas*. Then one of the heirs hangs the image, if of metal, round his neck, and, if of stone, places it in a water-trough.[2] This image is called *newa och*, *dia* or in Kanaar *gurokách*. In some places a plot of land

[1] Fr. *rishi*, a sage.

[2] Like brooks and springs, *báolis* or cisterns are supposed to be haunted by *jal-parís* (water-sprites) and *mátris*: Simla District Gazetteer, p. 42. The object probably is to confer fertility on the *newa* in the next life.

called *sog* is set apart in its name and never cultivated. A hut is also erected on the land and on it a wooden image placed and worshipped at each *amávas*. Sometimes a *newa*, like a *páp*, attains to the position of a *deota* in course of time.[1]

Páp in the Simla Hills is the ghost when body has not been accorded due funeral rites. In order to prevent its haunting the family home and tormenting its survivors a shrine of four low walls and a small roof is built in the midst of a field and dedicated to it. This shrine is called *dareoti* and flowers are often offered at it by the family which believes that the spirit has been safely lodged in it.[2] Otherwise the *páp* will cause disease, barrenness or other calamities, and a Brahman must be called in to divine the cause. In the Pandra Sau tract of Bashahr this belief is common, and the shrine is styled the *páp ká chauntrá*.[3]

The principal Hindu festivals of Northern India are observed in the Simla Hills, with the usual rites. Chet is the first month of the year and Turís go from village to village to entertain the people with songs and music throughout the month. Chet 1st is New Year's day.

The nine days from the 1st of the bright half of Asauj are called the *navarátras*, or 9 nights on which a fast is kept and the goddess worshipped. *Batri*, from Sanskrit *vrata*, = a fast. In the upper hills they call the fast or the 9 days of it *karáli* also.

Sája in Kulu is the 1st of any month (Diack, *Kulúhi Dialect*, p. 87). In the Simla Hills, *Sáer sáji* is the 1st of Asauj, *sáji* being the actual passage of the sun from one zodiacal sign to another: Ṭika Rám Joshi in J. A. S B., 1911, p. 228. In Kulu the 1st of Chet is called *lingti*.

The *Chár* or spring festival in Chamba celebrates the defeat of winter. The latter, personified as an evil demon (*kulinsa*) by a man wearing a mask, is pelted by the villagers with snowballs until he drops his mask and takes to flight, after which he joins in the dance with the *gámi* and *mesmi* or masks which represent a man and a woman, respectively, at Triloknáth.[4]

Narathe, *navarátri*, are also defined to be the 9 days of Chet and Asauj in which Devi is worshipped.

These and other festivals some of which are peculiar to the Hills are given below in chronological order :—

Lingti.[5]	Mrig Satái.
Narathe.	Ledaṛ.
Chitráli.	Dasúni.
Naumi.	Gīl.
Salhor.	Rakharpunia.

[1] Simla Hill States *Gazetteer*, Bashahr, p. 33.

[2] Simla District *Gazetteer*, p. 42.

[3] Simla Hill States *Gazetteer*, Bashahr, p. 33.

[4] Chamba *Gazetteer*, p. 45.

[5] J. A. S. B., 19, pp. 133, 217, 218 and 226.

Chár.	Parrewi.
Sgoh.	Bháidúj.
Párthivapúja.	Karma chauth.
Nág Ashtmi	Deothan.
Janm Ashtmi.	Pandru.
Badranjo.	Magar.
Dagiali.	Tarain Saja.
Málpunya.	Khrain.
Saer Suji.	Bhartu.

The Chitráli in Kulu are the nights in Chet when the women assemble and dance on the village green. The men look on but take no part in the dancing. The women dance to their own singing, each song or air having a dance peculiar to itself. The song of Runjke is sung by the women when formed in two lines, facing each other, one representing the lover, the other his mistress. As one line advances the other retreats and the sitting and rising alluded to in the song are acted by the singers.[1] Each woman in the line crosses her arms behind her back and then clasps the hands of the woman next to her.

Naumi, the 9ths of Chet and Asauj, on which Devi is generally worshipped. They are regarded as fast days.

On Jeth 1st an offering (*sálhor*) of flowers is made to *deotás*, and on 1st Baisákh the god's history is recited (*bártha*) at most temples: Diack, *op. cit.*, pp. 87 and 47. On the 1st Baisákh also *sain*, an offering of flowers or grain, is hung up on the house-wall (*ib.*, p. 88). This may be an oblation to the household god whose ark (*kalká*) holds (or constitutes) him and is kept in the verandah or sometimes indoors (p. 70).

Mrig-satái, the fortnight from 22nd Jeth to 8th Hár, during which sunshine is wanted for crops.

Ledar, a feast held on 1st Har.

Dasúni, Dsúni, a festival observed on the 11th of the bright half of Hár.

Gíl, the 16 days, including the last week in Hár and the first in Sáwan, believed to be auspicious for planting trees.

Rkhrunya, from *rakhri*, a thread, and *punya*, full moon, is a festival held on the full moon in Sáwan when the twice-born castes don a new sacred thread consecrated by Vedic hymns and a thread (*rakshá*, *rákhi* or *rakhri*) is tied by a Brahman round one's wrist to protect one for a year. Gifts are made to Brahmans and friends feasted.

Sgoh, the 16 days, including the last week of Sáwan and the first in Bhádon, during which sunshine is undesirable.

Janmashtmi, or 8th of dark half of Bhádon.

The Badranjo in Kulu is a festival held in Bhádon in honour of the plough-cattle which are decked with flowers and not worked on that

[1] Diack, *Kulúhi Dialect*, p. 12: Runjke may be the Ránjha of the South-West Punjab

day.[1] After it the rope strung with leaves which has been tied round their necks is hung between two trees.

Nágpanchami is a festival observed throughout India. Women keep fast and worship Shib. It takes place on the 5th of the bright half of Bhádon, whence it is also called Bhadronji.

The Chrewal or 1st Bhádon, at which gods (Shivs) are made of clay and worshipped, light being shown to the god (Shivling) every evening throughout the month. This is called Párthivapúja.

Dagiáli, the *chaudas* and *amáwas* of the dark half of Bhádon, on which date the *ḍags* assemble.

Every year on the night of the 16th Bhádon all the *deotás* congregate at Dhár Kambogir in the Manḍi State. The four *jognís* from the east, west, south and north also come and a battle rages between them and *deotás*, until one party defeats the other. If the *deotás* win, the land yields a good harvest that year, but the victory of the *jognís* is calculated to bring famine.

The following facts are given in proof of the above story:—

(1) Buffaloes and other cattle graze day and night on the *dhár*. On the night mentioned the owners of cattle bring their she-buffaloes down from the Dhar Kambogir lest the *jognís* kill them.

(2) On the night of the 16th Bhádon Hindus of the Hill States in the neighbourhood of Manḍi distribute rapeseed in order to avert the influence of the *jognís*.

Málpunya, a festival held on the full moon in September, at which cows are worshipped and fed. At Koṭi it is followed by the Bláj.

Sáer-sáji, 1st Asauj.

Bhái-dúj, a festival held on the 2nd of the bright half of Kátak, when a sister is visited, and food taken from her hands in return for a present.

The Karuwa Chauth is a Hindu festival that takes place on the 4th of the dark half of Kátak.

Deoṭhan, a festival held on the 11th of the bright half of Kátak.

Pandru, a festival observed on the 15th Poh in Jubbal, Koṭgarh and Kot Khái, Simla Hills.

At Rámpur in Bashahr the Rájá's *shikári* throws a garland of musk-pods on his neck. In the upper hills the people observe it as a day for rejoicing, rich cakes being prepared and distributed among friends and relatives.

Magar, the fortnight including the last week in Poh and the first in Mágh, supposed to be a time of heavy snowfall.

[1] Diack, *Kaláhi Dialect*, pp. 48 and 70 (*s. v. Kandu*).

[2] For festival days in the Simla Hills see Tika Rám Joshi, *Dicty. of Pahári*, in J. A. S. B., 1911, pp. 211, 200, 207, 149, 155, 167, 226, 231, 176, 147, 228, 203, 155, 217, 202 and 195; also pp. 188, 217, 218 and 226.

Mágh 1st is the Tarain *sája* (*Kulúhi Dialect*, p. 94).

Khrain, a festival observed in Mágh by Kanets. It resembles a *jágra*, but instead of remaining for the night in his host's house the *deota* returns the same day to the temple.

The following are held on varying dates or occasions :—

Bláj, fr. S. Valirája, the king Vali, is a night fair.

Bishu, S. Vishuva : (1) the moment of the sun's reaching Aries, and (2) a song sung by low-caste people in April. Twine, to which rhododendron flowers are attached, is hung on every house at the Baisákhi *sankránt*, called *bishu*.

Pánjag, the *nakshatras* Dhanistha, Shatbikha, Púrvábhádrapadá, Uttarábhádrapada and Revati, S. *panchaka*.

Parewi, the first of the bright or dark half of a month.

Rhyáli, a fair held in the monsoon at which archery is practised in the Madhán, Theog, Balsan and Jubbal States, Simla Hills.

Perhaps the most characteristic festival of the Hills is the Sheri or Saer, held on Asauj 1st, when barbers show well-to-do people their faces in a mirror, and every family makes an image of clay, puts flowers on it and places it before his house. Rich food is also prepared. In the evening lights are lit all round the image, and it is worshipped.

Jágra, from Sanskrit *jágarana*, vigil, is a rite offered to any village deity. Either he is invited to one's home or it is performed at his temple. The day of its performance is first fixed and then all the people of the *pargana* go to the temple or the house as the case may be. A great feast is given to all present, and if the chief is also invited he is paid Rs. 80 in cash.

Mr. G. C. L. Howell, C. S , has recorded two stories which illustrate the beliefs current in the ruling family of Kulu :—In Rájá Jagat Singh's time (A. D. 1637-72) a large grant of rice land was conferred on his Ráj-gurú—or spiritual preceptor—as a reward for a spell which he had woven for the Rájá and contrary to custom the land was settled on the Ráj-gurú's sons and grandsons. What the spell was intended for we are not told, but it may have been for the destruction of some of his opponents. Of Jagat Singh it is related in the chronicles that a Brahman had a pot of pearls which the Rájá wanted to possess and which the owner refused to give up. After repeated refusals the Brahman told the Rájá that he would give up the pearls on the latter's return from Manikarn whither he was going. On his return, however, the Brahman set fire to his own house, consuming to ashes himself and his family, as well as the pearls which had excited the Rájá's avarice. On re-entering his palace at Makaráha Jagat Singh ordered dinner, but when it was placed before him the rice all turned to worms To have been indirectly the cause of a Brahman's death was a heinous sin, almost beyond the possibility of atonement. It was however at last atoned for by the Rájá having the image of Raghunáth brought from Ajodhia to whom he assigned his kingdom and ruled only as the god's vicegerent. The assignment to Raghunáth under the name of Mádho Rái in Mandi took place about the same time. It may have been in connection with this incident that the spell was sought by Jagat Singh.

The following paper by Mr. H. W. Emerson, C. S., records a chapter in the history of Bashahr and various beliefs, one of which at least opens up a new field of inquiry :

Tikrál now forms part of the Bashahr State having been annexed some three centuries ago. Previous to annexation it was under the jurisdiction of a local Rájpút *thákur* whose descendants give their place of origin as Garhwál. While their invasion and conquest must be placed at a comparatively early date, it is doubtful whether the inhabitants of the remote portions of their *thákurái* were reduced to more than a nominal allegiance. At any rate, the people of the district now in question appear to have retained their own internal form of government, in which the confederacy of the five gods played a leading part. A survival of their theocratic rule exists in the appointment of a divine representative known as the *jana*. The qualifications essential for the office considerably restrict the field of selection. The incumbent must be a male child of not less than two years of age and not more than ten years and must belong to one of certain families of Pekha village that alone enjoy the privilege of providing candidates. Both his parents must be living and the ceremony of cutting the hair and of naming must not have taken place. The appointment is made direct by the council of the five gods who on the day fixed for election assemble in their palanquins at the temple of Nág of Pekha, a member of the *panchâyat*. With them there come a crowd of worshippers; but no person of low caste is allowed to be present nor yet a stranger, even though he be a Kuran, who is not subject to the jurisdiction of the gods. Such intruders, in the olden days, paid for their indiscretion with their lives and even now are looted of all that they have with them at daybreak, the heads of families possessed of eligible vows are placed in a line a few paces apart, inside the temple courtyard. The gods are then carried down the line by their appointed bearers who oscillate the palanquins as a sign that the divine spirit has animated the image Jakh of Junglik, the chairman of the council leads the way, followed by the others in strict order of precedence. When Jakh reaches the father of the future *jana* he bows his head in token of acceptance and the other four do likewise as they pass. The test is then repeated until the choice has fallen three times in succession on the same family. If it contains more than one male child eligible for election these are then produced, the same method of selection being employed. The boy chosen is bathed in the five products of the cow, dressed in a suit of new clothes and seated with honour on a consecrated square. The gods next endow him with divine strength, each diviner laying the standard of his deity, usually a sword or dagger, on the head, hands and other parts of his body.

This completes the main part of the consecration ceremony and the rest of the day is spent in feasting at the expense of the parents of the boy. But the latter is taken to his house and, with exceptions to be mentioned presently, remains there in strict seclusion until the period of his office ends. His parents alone can tend him; but they must bathe him every few days, offer incense before him and burn lights in his honour. His chief food is rice and sweetened milk: fish, and liquor are forbidden. He must not see a crow, a Koli or a stranger, nor must they see him, and hence before his mother takes him into the verandah of the house she must look carefully to see that none of these are about. Worshippers of the five gods can look at him but only from a distance unless they be persons specially privileged to approach him. In any case they must join the palms of their hands and put them to their foreheads in token of adoration. They make offerings in his name and this they often do. Should any woman give birth to a child, or a cow calve inside the house he must be carried to a temple a few miles away and remain there until the period of impurity had passed. The journey must be done at night so that he be safely hidden before a crow caws or a low caste fellow or a stranger comes along. Should these taboos be broken the gods dethrone him, and in any case his period of office ends with the death of either parent. The gods do not approve a representative who has reached years of discretion, as soon as the *jana* begins to reason for himself he is dismissed. This is the ordinary cause of removal for his parents take good care that he is not contaminated in any way, since both he and they are fed and clothed (for the full term of office) at the expense of the community, which under favourable circumstances may last for seven or eight years. Moreover, apart from its perquisities, the post is regarded as one of great honour.

As soon as the gods declare the office vacant the late incumbent returns to his ordinary mode of life. His hair, which has remained unshorn, is then cut and he is given a name in the usual way. His former clients no longer contribute to his maintenance nor does he appear to benefit in any way from his existence as a god.

Owing to the dissensions of the gods an interregnum sometimes occurs, but this is rare, for while the incumbency is associated with good fortune a vacancy is supposed to bring calamity. Moreover, certain mystic rites connected with the worship of Chasrálu cannot be celebrated without the presence of a *jana*. These take place at intervals of 3 or 5 years at Chasrálu's cavern, a period of retirement in the wilderness preceding their observance. The *jana* is accompanied by the heads of the families who are alone permitted to share in the ceremonies. They leave the village at night, one of them going in front of the party, blowing a conch-shell to give warning to travellers or Kolís that the *jana* is abroad and must not be seen by them. They spend the first night on the road and the next two in a lonely cave where the main rites are performed, but of their nature one can learn little as the greatest reticence is observed, the celebrants being pledged to secrecy. A kid is sacrificed which must be roasted over a fire and not boiled in a cauldron, nor must it be eaten with salt. For the rest the singing of the song of Kali appears to be the most important duty. This song was sung by her when in human guise. She surprised a band of hunters, who had taken refuge for the night in the same cave. It can be sung only by the senior male of each branch of their descendants and a father who has learnt the words must teach them only to his eldest son, when the two are alone together grazing their flocks on the hillside. It can be sung only in the cave, and should a person sing it elsewhere or at other than appointed time the goddess drives him mad. The *jana* learns the words when he takes part in these secret ceremonies, and this fact appears to give a clue to his title, which may be derived from *gáná* to sing. If this is so, the *jana* is, therefore, one privileged to sing the song of Káli. Having performed the remaining rites, whatever they may be, the party journeys to a hamlet, where two nights are spent. The sixth night is passed on the road to Chasrálu's cave where the general body of worshippers awaits their coming. The *jana's* face is then screened from afar from the vulgar gaze, but the privileged persons may approach him. Chasrálu's diviner can alone enter the cave; the *jana* with his escort remains at some little distance while the remainder of the assembly look on from afar. The *jana* himself does not appear to take any part in the ceremonies nor are sacrifices offered him. But it is clear that the period of retirement is connected with his divine office since the people believe that for the next few days he is endowed with supernatural powers to an extraordinary degree, and his sayings are, therefore, regarded as peculiarly inspired.

Such then are the main facts relating to this curious institution as it now exists; and when I was first told them I regarded the *jana* merely as an embodiment of divinity, who, like an idol or other sacred emblem, has to be protected from pollution. But this first impression was materially changed when I was told later that the *jana* was formerly the *Rájá* of the tract, that he used to settle all disputes, and that his worshippers still refer to him to some extent, his decision being binding. Now one could understand a boy of 8 or 10 years of age giving a more or less intelligible answer to a question addressed to him, but how a child hardly able to talk could satisfy disputants passed my comprehension. The explanation given was a typical one. In such cases they said, the five gods having been brought into the presence of the child, charged and recharged him, as it were, with divine inspiration until he said something from which a meaning could be deduced, or at other times the parties each made a ball of earth in which a blade of grass was hidden These were placed before the infant judge without his knowing which was which and the owner of the one on which he placed his hand was deemed to be the party in the right. That one of these procedures was actually adopted is the more probable because it is entirely in keeping with the characteristics of the hillman: his firm belief in divine possession and his intense distrust of human agents. For instance, I have known a man, who wished to call up the spirit of a deceased relative, identity and sex unknown, that had visited him under the painful guise of boils, insist on the officiating Brahman to employ as his medium a boy and girl, both of tender years, who would not dupe him.

Similarly the condition that the *jana* should always be a child of little understanding was obviously imposed as a safeguard against fraud. As regards his jurisdiction in mundane matters it must be remembered that many Himalayan gods annually distribute the grazing grounds among their worshippers, decide the rotation of irrigation and are even consulted by prospective bridegrooms before they choose their brides, There is thus nothing improbable in the theory that the *jana* was the theoratic ruler of a group of Kanets, appointed directly by the gods whose vice-regent he was, that his sayings were regarded as inspired and therefore binding, that he exercised temporal as well as spiritual authority, and that the confederacy of villages under his jurisdiction at one time acknowledged no other ruler. In support of a wide application of the same principle it may be observed that the jurisdiction of local gods corresponds closely to natural divisions, that they are known as *kul ke devata*, gods of the family, and that the worship of a common deity is still of very strong bond of unity among his worshippers

Again, the association of the *jana* with prosperity and good fortune connects him with the magical aspect of early kingship This point is brought out more clearly in the neighbouring territory of Narain of Jabal, where the institution exists in a modified form. There a *jana* is appointed only when certain ceremonies are celebrated at intervals of 3 or 5 years. These last for about three weeks and when completed the tenure of office ends. The qualifications and the nature of the taboos are identical in many respects with those already described, but this *jana* is removed from the custody of his parents and his wants attended to by certain privileged persons. He is not kept in one house, but tours throughout his jurisdiction according to a fixed programme being lodged in each village in a building specially reserved for his use. Provided the taboos are not violated he is supposed to bring good fortune to every place he visits, and his tour is associated with the pronouncement of prophecies concerning the harvest of the coming year. If he cries in a village the omen is bad, but only for that particular place ; hence no means are spared to keep him happy, and within lawful limits he is given whatever he may ask. In former times there is little doubt that human sacrifice was offered to him, and he now takes part in a ceremony in which a scapegoat, the acknowledged substitute for a man, is slaughtered before him. He is worshipped as a deity and the people are inclined to think the deity is Káli, but they are vague on this point. At any rate the celebrations are in her honour and the boy is dressed in girl's clothes and decked with female ornaments. The explanation given of this disguise is as follows :—The *jana*, they say, was originally a girl, but on one occasion many generations ago when she was being carried round the tour she died from cold and exposure on the road, the month being December when snow was laying on the ground. Her escort were in a state of consternation, for the festival could not be celebrated in the absence of a *jana*, and its abandonment would bring the anger of the gods upon their heads. At length the happy idea was conceived of stealing a boy from the nearest village, dressing him in the girl's clothes and passing him off as the genuine *jana*. This was done, and the deception proved so successful that it has been continued ever since. As tradition is usually reliable in the hills this version may perhaps be true. On the other hand, the custom of dressing boys in girl's clothes in order to avoid the evil eye is a common device, and taking the attendant circumstances into consideration it appears probable that in this instance the disguise is only one of many expedients employed with the object of conserving unimpaired the beneficial powers of the disguised.

As far as Bashahr is concerned the institution exists only in the two cases mentioned, and there is good reason to believe that the two are closely connected, the one being merely a modification of the first. As such it may be a connecting link between the permanent appointment of a divine ruler and the casual worship of small girls as incarnations of the goddess Deví. The latter custom is not found in Bashahr, and my information with regard to it is incomplete. But I believe that it is widely practised in Kángra, more particularly during the Dasahra when the worship of maidens as representatives of Bhagwati is considered essential. There appear to be no taboos observed as with the *jana*, but there is the same condition that the girls should not have reached years of understanding. At times other than the Dasahra, a favourite method of acquiring merit or removing trouble, is the worship of one or more girls; and if there are more than a certain number a boy is joined with them and regarded as Launkra, the *bír* or minister of Káli. The worship should be performed in the early morning before its objects have tasted food; but apparently this is the only restriction. The sayings of the girls are, or were, regarded as inspired, and there is one well-authenticated case in which a *faqír* cut off a portion of his tongue at the bidding of one of these incarnations of Bhagwati. In some respects, therefore, the same attributes are ascribed to these youthful goddesses as to the *jana*; but there is not a direct appointment by the god, no regular system of taboo and no continuous tenure of office. Any girl of suitable caste can apparently be taken as Deví's deputy for the time being; but when the ritual is finished she at once resumes her normal position. Nevertheless, the points of resemblance do suggest the remote possiblity that the custom of girl worship is a survival from a very early state of society in which the recognised form of government was a theocracy, exercised through a human agent, preferably a child. Why a girl should have been chosen in some cases and a boy in others is not obvious. The choice may have depended on the sex of the local deity, a boy being selected as the representative of a god and a girl as that of a goddess. Or the practice of dressing the boy in girl's clothes as a protection against the evil eye may have ultimately led to the substitution of females when the origin of the disguise had been forgotten. But these explanations are at best conjectural and would not be advanced if the existence of the *jana* in Bashahr did not appear to open up a new field of inquiry. It seems to be far more improbable that the institutions I have described are local curiosities, than that they are survivals of what was once a popular method of government.

So much for the general discussion of the subject. As regards the nature of several of the taboos a few words may be said, as they are of world-wide currency. There is, for instance, the respect shown for that bird of ill-omen, the crow. I have found this particular form of superstition in connection with other mystic rites in the hills, and especially in such as relate to the promotion of the fertility of the soil by burying in it an image or sacred clod of earth. This rite must be performed before sunrise, in secret and by the head of the family who must complete his task before he hears a crow caw. If he does not, he must start all over again on a more auspicious day. As to the reputation of the crow family in general one cannot do better than quote from a zoological study that appeared recently in the *Times*:—"In all times and countries," the author writes, "man has regarded crows with superstitious awe, knowing them for birds of ill-omen, the familiars of witches and evil spirits, and the confidants of deities whom they never failed to betray. Odin took them for his heralds and councillors, but could not trust them, and they blabbed the secrets of Valhalla. They were the scandal-mongers of Olympus, and to their evil tongues poor Coronis owed her death. Indra, in wrath at their tale bearing, hurled them, we are told, down through all the hundred stages of his heaven. No bird surely had nobler opportunities, none has been so highly honoured; and everywhere it proved itself unworthy of its trust."

All of which considered the Kuráns are well advised to screen their *jana* from the sight of such an evil bird. Again, it is a far cry from Tikrál to ancient Rome; but one condition imposed on the *jana* associates him with an incident of the Roman priesthood. The Flamen Dialis was bound to vacate his office on the death of his wife; and as the reason for this rule is obscure it has been the subject of a controversy, the main points of which are given in Sir John Frazer's volume of the *Golden Bough* which deals with the worship of Attis, Adonis and Osiris. Dr. L. R. Farnell explains the provision on the supposition that death brought in its train the taint of ceremonial pollution, and so compelled the resignation of the priest. In support of his theory he cites instances of Greek ritual, which requires that certain sacred offices should be discharged only by a boy both of whose parents were alive. Sir John Frazer, on the other hand, contends that the priest had to resign because his wife was essential to the worship of the pair of divinities they served; and in the course of his argument he makes a theory point of the fact that if Dr. Farnell's theory is correct then every orphan is ceremonially unclean for life, and therefore incapable of performing sacred duties. As this restriction is obviously too far-reaching for the affairs of practical life he rejects the pollution theory, and with the view of discovering a more reasonable explanation proceeds to examine all the cases known to him in which the children of living parents could alone take part in ritual.

The list is a long one, but naturally enough it does not contain the case of the *jana*. And at first sight the *jana* provides an excellent argument in support of the disqualification arising from the impurity of death. It will be remembered that not only have his parents to be alive at the time of appointment, but that the death of either of them *ipso facto* brings about his dethronement. Moreover, the birth either of a cow or a calf in his house entails his hasty removal to another dwelling place; and in this case there is no doubt that fear of ceremonial contamination is the reason for his flight. It would therefore be natural to suppose that the inevitability of uncleanness in the case of death was the factor that terminated his office. But his clients were emphatic that this was not so. At the same time the only explanation they could give was that the five gods did not approve an orphan and by way of justification asked indignantly who would. Thus the analogy of the *jana* supports Sir John Frazer's objection to the pollution of death theory, and it is interesting to consider whether his general conclusions apply to this case also. After reviewing the evidence he sums up as follows:—"The notion that a child of living parents is endowed with a higher degree of vitality than an orphan, probably explains all the cases of the employment of such a child in ritual, whether the particular rite is designed to ensure the fertility of the ground or remove the curse of barrenness or to avert the danger of death and other calamities. Yet it would probably be a mistake to suppose that this notion is always clearly apprehended by the persons who practise the customs. In their minds the definite conception of super-abundant overflowing vitality may easily dissolve into a vague idea that the child of living parents is luckier than other folk."

When regard is had to the beneficent functions ascribed to the *jana* it must be confessed that the vitality theory does supply a satisfactory motive for the condition of living parents. But the same cannot be said of the case already cited in which the soul of a departed relative spent its leisure moments in tormenting a man with emerods. For there also the boy and girl employed as mediums were the children of living parents, and in this and similar cases the more vitality a child enjoys the less reality would he yield to the influence of an invading spirit. The employment of the children of living parents in such cases of Himalayan ritual as are known to me seems to be based not so much on their merits as on the demerits of orphans. This distinction is brought out very clearly in marriage ceremonies. In many parts of Bashahr it is considered essential that the parents of the *vakil* sent to arrange a betrothal should both be alive; and in all parts it is regarded as desirable. But should an orphan be sent the outraged party does not ask why a person who would bring good luck was not employed; they abuse the culprits charging them with having sent a wretch who has already eaten his father or his mother as the case may be. Similarly a posthumous son is an object of general derision on the ground that he killed his father without even seeing him. An unfortunate orphan is thus regarded not as the passive victim of adverse circumstances, but as an active agent who has contributed to his own misfortune. He is possessed by an evil genius that brings about his own undoing as well as that of those connected with him. This conception may be peculiar to the Himalayas; but it is obviously a very primitive one, and is in strict conformity with animistic beliefs which underlie so many religious and temporal observances. That a person possessed of a spirit with homicidal tendencies would be a dangerous person to employ in sacred or profane rites is self-evident; and this attribute of orphans will probably explain the employment of children blooming on both sides in all known cases. Finally, it will be remembered that the *jana* must be a boy who has not received a name and whose hair has therefore not been cut, since both ceremonies are performed at one and the same time. The non-cutting of the hair is here the important element, not the absence of a name; so that we are again brought into touch with a series of superstitions so well known as to make commentary almost superfluous.

Firstly, there is the belief that a man's strength resides in or is at least dependent on his hair. Secondly the hair is often worn long as a mark of dedication, and this is certainly the explanation of the veto on cutting often imposed by a hill god on his diviner during the interval between two *jags*, which may be as long as twelve years. It may also explain the fact that carpenters, smiths and other labourers employed on the erection or repair of a temple are allowed to cut neither their hair nor beards until the work is completed. But more probably the prohibition in this case is founded on the widespread belief that if a magician obtain possession of a man's hair or of the parings of his nails, he can work what will he likes. This is of course the reason why in Bashahr the hair of the tonsure ceremony of a boy is either taken to the top of a pass where it is hidden in a cairn and dedicated to Káli; or thrown secretly into a stream or else placed in a sacred tree, the holy emanation from which is supposed to counteract baneful influences. The fear of magic is also the most reasonable explanation of the taboo placed on the *jana.* One more illustration of this superstition must suffice, and as it is appropriate that at least one reference should be made to historical records we will quote some of the duties (of a chamberlain of the palace under the Chand Rájás of Kumáon) (as given in Atkinson's *Himalayan Gazetteer*):—They were these :—He should see that the cook did his duties conscientiously and well. He should taste everything used for the Rájá's food, and never allow the cook to be out of his sight. He should constantly move about and threaten the servants, whether there was cause or not, so that no one might become careless. He should never speak of poison, opium and *bhang*, nor ever touch them. And finally he should never speak of spells, as they were only used for evil purposes; nor cut his nails nor shave within the limits of the palace. It was not sufficient that the chamberlain should be a man of proved integrity; there was always the danger that sorcerers would pervert his morals. The prohibition of shaving and nail cutting only within the precincts of the palace is curious, and can only be explained on the supposition that the Kumáon Rájás believed the spirit of the place, as well as of their chamberlain, essential for the efficacy of magic spells. We can only hope that their confidence was not misplaced.

Traditions in Kamru.

Many centuries ago, so runs the first legend, the Baspa valley was invaded by an army from Tibet, before which the local ruler and his followers fled for refuge to the Kamru fort. The enemy pitched their camp upon the hill slopes which overlook the fortress, and from there sent emissaries in all directions to bribe the neighbouring chieftains to fight against their overlord. One of these envoys found his way to Chíni, then the capital of a semi-independent *thákur*, whom the Rájá of Bashahr had lately reduced to vassalage. Uncertain of his loyalty, the latter sent his warning that if he helped his country's enemies it would be a *darohi*[1] and he would have to pay the penalty. The warning was a solemn one, for *darohi* was a form of oath the Rájá could impose upon his subjects, by which he lay a prohibition on any purposed course of action. In its origin it was perhaps a kind of royal *tabu*, invested with semi-divine attributes of the personage from whom it issued; in its development it proved a source of power in the days when kings were glad for their own safety to fence themselves around with supernatural

[1]This word reappears in South India. *Rájá-droha* was the offence of 'injuring the interests of the king', and *grámi-drohia*, one who injured the interests of the village: Mathai, *Village Government in British India*, London, 1915, p. 85, citing *Madras Epigraphy*, Ann. Rep., 1910-11, p 75.

safeguards. The oath is still employed both for official and private purposes. In its public aspect it is a useful method of insuring obedience to executive orders with a minimum of friction or delay, and as such is used by certain village officers invested with authority to impose it. To give a simple example. A headman of a village is called upon to supply a number of coolies, one of whom prefers to stay at home rather than carry loads. 'If you do not go', the headman warns him, 'it will be *darohi*, a sin, against your ruler'. In the vast majority of cases, the cooly goes; but should he prove recalcitrant, a headman can bring him before a magistrate who imposes a trifling fine upon the culprit. But superstitious qualms rather than fear of civil punishment supply the sanctions by which the system works. Again, resort is often made to this expedient in private disputes. Two neighbours had a quarrel about a piece of land, and one of them, anxious to plead possession, starts to plough the area in dispute. The other finds him with his plough and oxen on the land. 'If you turn the soil before the case is settled by the cours', he threatens, 'it will be *darohi*'. As a rule the intruder stops his ploughing.

But on the occasion now in question, it so happened that the Ṭhákur of Chíni chose to ignore the warning and joined his forces to the Tibetan hordes. Another of the Rájá's subjects, a low-bred tailor, living in a village close to the fort, also played the traitor and sold the enemy secret information relating to the structure of the citadel. He told them of the central bean which if dislodged would bring the fort down with it in a mass of ruins, and for the remainder of the siege the Tibetans directed all their efforts towards its downfall. But each time the goddess Káli turned aside their missiles, so that at length disheartened by the supernatural forces ranged against them, or fearful of the coming winter, they raised the siege and left the Rájá free to wreak his vengeance on his treacherous subjects. He again reduced the Chíni *ṭhákur* to vassalage, and as a general warning to traitors ordered that a man of Chíni should henceforth present himself at Kamru on every triennial celebration held there in honour of the goddess Káli. This festival is still observed, its national character being apparent both from the grants made from the State treasury and from the presence of Brahmans of the ruling family who bring with them small images of Bhíma Káli from Saráhan. Sacrifices are offered on a liberal scale, the sacred fire is burnt for several days and the peasants from the neighbouring villages assemble with their gods. Moreover, a representative from Chíni, called the Chínchang, attends the festival, being accompanied by a man from an adjacent village, who by ancient right acts as his escort. During the eight days of the celebration, the Chínchang is freely plied with liquor, so that on the final day he is in a state of almost complete insensibility. Rusty armour is put upon his body and a helmet on his head, and thus attired he is made to dance first round the building and then inside the courtyard of the fort, a laughing stock to the assembly of villagers and village gods. Further he is accompanied in his dancing by a descendant of the tailor who sold the information to his country's enemies many centuries ago. Formerly, before the dance began, a priest poured holy water on their heads—a ceremony which left no doubt as to the nature of the punishment inflicted on their ancestors. For the sprinkling of water on a creature's head is the means employed to produce the shaking by which a deity accepts the dedication of a sacrificial victim. Sometimes the victim's head is severed from the body first and water poured on immediately while the nerves are still sensitive to shock; but the general rule is for the sprinkling to precede the slaughter. A similar device was practised by the Greeks so that it is perhaps worth noting that in the Himalayas the tremor implies far more than the mere formal acceptance of the victims. The quivering, in the popular imagination, denotes the actual entry of the god into the body of the animal, and it is the divine spirit—and not the water as one might suppose—which is responsible for the animation. The significance of the ritual is unique; and so, even if local tradition did not support the obvious interpretation, there could be little doubt that the triennial festivals at Kamru were formerly associated with human sacrifice. Even to this day there is little competition among the Chíni villagers for the privilege of attending at the celebration A superstitious belief prevails that the actor in the drama will die within the year, a belief, however, which has weakened since change was made in the ceremonial some 50 years ago. Up to that time, although the actual sacrifice had been abolished for several generations, the water was still poured on the Chínchang's head. The Chíni villagers, from whom the representative is chosen by lots, objected to this dedication at the shrine of Káli, formal though it were, and so their fears were partially allayed by a promise that for the future the water should be poured upon the hands and not upon the head. But even now, during the Chínchang's absence at Kamru, his family continue in a state of mourning, consoled only by the hope that the lamps they keep burning day and night inside the house will win the mercy of Naráin, the village god.

The second story associated with Kamru is likewise concerned with human sacrifice and, here again, Káli in her form of Párvati, the mountain goddess, plays a leading part. The only road to Kamru from the Sutlej valley lies along the Baspa river which for some 10 miles above its junction with the Sutlej rushes down a narrow gorge shut in on either side by precipices which block the view in front. The path then winds above the river, emerging on the shoulder of a ridge from which the so-called Kailás peaks are first visible in all their grandeur. To the Western traveller they convey mainly a sense of beauty and isolation, but to the hill-man they are invested with the supernatural dangers inseparable from the goddess of destruction. To him the topmost pinnacles of the line of jagged peaks are the favourite thrones of Káli, from which she radiates her vital or destroying energy. And hence her worship predominant through the State reaches its zenith in the Baspa valley, where no means are left untried to win her favour or placate her wrath. The superstitious terrors inspired by the nearness of her presence were shared alike by prince and peasant, and so it happened that the visits of a Rájá to his capital were attended by ceremonies of some significance.

During the first stages of his progress, continues Mr. Emerson's account, the Rájá was borne in a palanquin, preceded by musicians and State officials, and escorted by his subjects. But on the last day when the procession drew near the ridge whence Káli's home burst on the vision, a halt was called. While still sheltered from her eyes and those of her sentinels the Rájá descended from his palanquin, doffing robes, ornaments and head-dress, in which a Matas of Sapni, a village near by, attired himself, while the Rájá donned inconspicuous garments of grey. A priest waved a vessel of holy water round his head and then poured its contents over the Matas' head. Then the latter was borne in the royal palanquin, and treated like the Rájá, who himself walked in the crowd until the procession entered the fort. He then resumed his dignities, but the robes and ornaments worn by the Matas became his perquisite. Probably he himself was sacrificed in bygone days within the fort, and they fell to his heirs. He was called the *Rája-ki-bali* or king's sacrifice, and as in the case of the Chínchang the first sacrifice was a punishment for treachery.

On the last occasion—30 years ago—when the heir-apparent visited Kamru the old rites were all observed, but the water was poured on the Mahtas' hands, instead of on his head; and the man who then took the part declares that he is the first of his family to survive the ordeal by a year. The people see in him a decoy on which Káli's envy may fall before it reaches the Rájá. But Mr. Emerson points out that if the fact of sacrifice be one admitted to have occurred it is difficult to accept that theory.

As late as the middle of the last century no act of State was performed without the approval of Bhima Káli, who was regarded as the ruler of the land, she having granted the regency to the Rájá's ancestor six score generations ago, just as she had conferred the hereditary priesthood to the senior branch of his family. In much the same way the sovereignty of Kumhársain vests in Koṭ Ishwar Mahádev, and it is he who instals each Rána on its throne. Jagat Singh, Rájá of Kángṛa, carried the fiction further when he placed Ṭhákur Raghúnath's image on the throne, and proclaimed himself to be only chief ministrant of his temple. From that time the Rájá was, in constitutional theory, only the god's chief priest, the god himself being ruler of Kángṛa.

Makaráha.

There has been much confusion regarding the site of this place which Mr. A. H. Francke was able to clear up. The Chronicle of Tinán in Láhul speaks of Bahádur Singh residing at 'Makarsang'—and this is the Bunán locative of Makarsa—and means 'at Makarsa'. The name Makarsa in the Bunán dialect of Láhul means 'the place of Makar'. All tradition in Kulu supports the statement of the Chronicle of Tinán and the statement of Hardiál Singh that Bahádur Singh of Kulu rebuilt the ruined town of Makaráha. This lies on the plain on the left bank of the Beás near the débouchement of the Hurla Khaḍ, south of Nagar and easily accessible from Bajaura. As regards Moorcroft's identification of Nagar with Makarsa, he only casually looked at the place from the other side of the river, and might quite easily have failed to catch what was said to him or he was misinformed. Rájá Bahádur Singh and his descendants used to like to live at Makaráha, and imagine that they were descended from the great kings who built this town. Most unfortunately some British officials with unpardonable iconoclasm used most of the beautiful stone carvings of Makaráha to build the bridge over the Beás at Dilásni which was washed away, as well as some other bridges. But enough remains to show that the place was founded by some civilized dynasty which had attained to a very high order of art, for the stone work is really very beautiful. The founders were many degrees removed from the semi-savage Badánís, who never produced anything better than the crude wood carvings at Dhungri temple and whose attempts at imitating the stone work of ancient days were pitiable. It seems probable that one highly advanced civilization was responsible for the beautiful carvings of Makaráha, of those in its immediate neighbourhood near Bajaura, and of Nast near Jagat Sukh at the head of the valley. At any rate the connection between these different carvings is well worthy of the attention of archæologists. The sites would probably repay excavation. As for Bahádur Singh, Makaráha was doubtless a convenient place of residence for him during the time that his generals were campaigning in Saráj. He never took the field himself apparently, and as long as the right bank of the Sáinj Nála was occupied by his troops he would be quite safe at Makaráha[1] and in touch at once with Nagar and the army in the field.

This valuable account of Makarása, which seems to mean the land of alligators (*magar*) or that of sea-monsters (*makar*[2]), is from the pen of

[1] The Makaráha referred to is nearly opposite Bajaura on the left bank of the Beás. It was an ancient place founded before the Christian era: but was soon abandoned and remained a ruin till the time of Bahádur Singh, 1532-59, who rebuilt it and virtually made it his capital. From his time Kulu was called Makarsa or Magarsa from the name of this town, the proper spelling of which is Makarása—'the region of Makar', who was the founder of a primitive dynasty of Rájás in Kulu, before the Pál dynasty. *S* is pronounced as *h* in many parts of the hills to this day, and in ancient times this pronunciation was universal. You will find it Makaráhar in some places, but the final *r* must be redundant. Harcourt has the correct spelling in his book. It seems probable that Nagar also was called Makarsa as late as the time of Moorcroft who calls it by this name. We have documents in Chamba in which Kulu is called *Makarsa* as late as A. D. 1809. The Kulu Rájás continued to reside at Makaráha till the reign of Rájá Jagit Singh, A. D. 1637-72, who conquered the neighbouring state of Lag on the right bank of the Beás and then transferred the capital to Sultánpur and lived there. After this Makaráha was again deserted and fell into ruins.

[2] Platts, *Hindustani Dicty.*, p. 1058.

Mr. G. C. L. Howell, I. C. S., as is that which follows. By a coincidence Dionysius Periergetes gives the name Megarsus to the Sutlej.[1] This may give a clue to the origin of the name and to the extent of Makarása. It possibly originated as a description of the alligator-infested Sutlej, was transferred to a kingdom on that river and finally was applied to another hill kingdom in the upper reaches of the Beás. This is of course pure speculation. No evidence exists so far to connect the Makarása on the upper Beás with Megarsus, the Sutlej or some section of that river. The Mrichh[2] in Kulu do not appear to have been inhabitants of Makarása as one is tempted to suggest. Philologically the derivation is untenable.

A Note on Ancient Trade Routes in Kulu.

Geography makes history all the world over, and nowhere is this more palpably true than in the Himalayas. Kulu history is based on evidences which are meagre, and, more especially in the case of the so-called chronicle of the old Rájás of Kulu, often unreliable. But from the legends of an untutored mountain race and the ineradicable record inscribed on the face of the slowly decaying ranges, it is sometimes possible to reconstruct something of a picture of what life was like before the advent of the British.

The position of the valley, it has always seemed to me, is peculiar. Here is no backwater like the neighbouring State of Chamba, in which an ancient Rájpút line has been sheltered and able to maintain an unbroken rule from a period preceding the dawn of civilization in Europe. Kulu and Láhul lie full in a channel, through which have ebbed and flowed for ages the tides of racial and religious antagonisms. The people have acknowledged many masters—Aryan and Mongolian; but through it all Indian markets have always demanded salt and wool and borax—to say nothing of the more precious merchandise of Central Asia—and while armies marched and fought, the hungry Tibetans would still risk much to get the wheat of the plains and the incomparable barley of Láhul. The trade therefore went on. It was quite by chance that I discovered the ancient trade route. One must remember that the Beás was nowhere bridged, and everywhere an impassable torrent; that there were no made roads; that every height was crowned with a fort, held by a garrison of marauders; that the Kulu farmer then as now regarded travelling sheep as 'fair game'; that there was a custom house below Ralla at the cañon, still known as the 'customs-house' (Jagát-khána), where no doubt a foreigner's life was made a burden to him, and that there would be endless bickering and bargaining at every halt before a caravan of laden sheep could get any grazing. All this is plain to any one who can imagine the Kulu people set free from the restraints which the British Ráj imposes.

So the trade avoided the Hamta Pass and the Rohtang and the comparatively broad paths which led to destruction in the valley.

[1] *Arch. S. R.*, II, p. 12. Cunningham suggested some connection between the Megarsus and the Megh tribe, but the seat of the Meghs is not on the Sutlej. It lies along the Jammu border, west of the Rávi for the most part: see Vol. III, p. 77, *infra.*

[2] Vol. III, p. 180, *infra.*

Arrived at the summit of the Baralacha Pass the Tibetans turned sharp to their left and followed down the left bank of the Chandra. Here was pasturage and to spare of the finest fattening grass in the world wherever they chose to halt. There were no torrents which were not easily fordable in the morning: and there was not the least fear of molestation in an uninhabited and to the Indian mind most undesirable region. Past the beautiful Chandra Lake the trade sheep marched to and grazed on the plain near Phati Rúni (split rock) still known as the 'plain of the Kanauris'. There the middlemen from Kanaur in Bashahr and probably from Koṭhi Kanaur at the head of the Párbati valley met them. The big 50-lb packs of salt and other merchandise were unpacked, the big Tibetan sheep were shorn and for a week or so the trading went on, and finally the little Bashahri sheep marched off, not laden so heavily as the Tibetan *liangis* or trade sheep, while the latter returned with their packs to Rudok and Leh.

But the Kanaurís had no thought of moving through Kulu. They went up the valley, which is now blocked by the Shigri glacier; across the head of the Párbati valley: along the old mountain sheep route, which is still known, though seldom used; always through uninhabited safety to the Sutlej valley at Rámpur. There they met, and let us hope were a match for, the wily trader of the plains.

In 1836, tradition says, the Shigri glacier bursting some obstruction on the hill top overwhelmed the Chandra valley, dammed the Chandra river till it rose within measurable distance of the Kunzam Pass into Spiti, and finally destroyed the old trade route. The Spiti people had pickets out at the summit of the pass to warn them in case the river headed up high enough to flood the pass and flow down to Losar. There are however some landmarks on the old road, which I suspect was abandoned much more gradually than tradition states.

The Kanaurís, who speak a Tibeto-Burmese language closely allied to those of Láhul and Malána, have left their name on the 'Kanaurís' Plain' near the modern camping ground of Phati Rúni and the whole of the upper Párbati valley is known to this day as Koṭhi Kanauri, while its inhabitants, though they have forgotten their language and are rapidly becoming assimilated to the Kulu people, are still regarded as foreigners and often show markedly Mongolian features. Probably they are the descendants of Kanaurís who gave up trade for farming generations before the road was abandoned. But they still know the road from Phulga to Rámpur.

Section 5—Islam.

Notes on the religious History of Islám.

The history of Islám in the Punjab begins with the conquest of
Multán by Muhammad ibn Qásim in 712 A.D.,[1] and the extreme south- 93 H.
west of the Province shared the fortunes of the Caliphs, Ommayad and
257 H. Abbásid, until 871, when Sindh became virtually independent of the
Khiláfat. Soon after, in or before 879, the kingdom of Multán was 265 H.
established, but Islám had made little or no progress in the rest of the
Province.

287 H. In 900 Amír Ismáíl the Sámáni subdued 'some part of Hind', doubtless in the Indus Valley. Fifteen years later Mas'udi visited that country, and in his *Meadows of Gold* describes the state of Islám therein. The Amír of Multán was an Arab of the noble tribe of the Quraish, and the kingdom had been hereditary in his family for a long period nearly—'from the beginning of Islám'. The *khutba* was, however, read in the name of the Caliph. The Amír's dominions extended to the frontier of Khurásán, and the temple of the Sun at Multán, which was still an object of pilgrimage to the Hindus, yielded the greater part of his
revenues. Sixty years later, in 976, Ibn Haukal found the Sun temple 366 H.
still flourishing. The Amír indeed resided outside the city which he held as a hostage, a threat to destroy the idol in the temple being always sufficient to avert any threat of a Hindu insurrection. Thus the Arab tenure of Multán, virtually independent as it was of the Caliphs, was weak in the extreme and Islám had found few converts among the Indians.

375 H. But in or about 985 events occurred which eventually changed the whole aspect of affairs. The Qarmatian heretics, recently expelled from Egypt and Iráq, sought and found a refuge in the remote provinces of the Indus valley. By them the idol of the Sun was broken in pieces and the attendant priests massacred.[2] Nevertheless the Qarmatians made or found many adherents in Multán.

Mahmúd of Ghazni was far from finding in Multán a *point d'appui* for his inroads into the Punjab. Its ruler, Abú-'l Fath, the Lawi, indeed, actually allied himself with Anandpál, and necessitated
Mahmúd's third expedition into India in 1006. 396 H.

That the Qarmatian heresy had taken deep root in Sindh is proved
by the fact that the Sumras had been won over to it before 1032, in 423 H.
which year an epistle, preserved in the sacred books of the Druses, was sent by Muktana Bahá-ud-Dín, the chief apostle of Hamza and the principal compiler of the Druse scriptures, to 'the Unitarians of Multán and Hindustán in general, and to Shaikh Ibn Súmar Rájá Bal in particular'.[3]

The assassination of Muhammad of Ghor in 1206 is ascribed to the 602 H.
Khokhars by some and to the Maláhidah by earlier and better authorities. The Imám Fakhr-ud-Dín Rázi was accused of having brought it

[1] Muhálib's invasion of 664 A. D. may be mentioned. He came as far as Multán; his object was to explore the intermediate country. Al-Biláduri indeed says that he advanced as far as Bannu and Lahore: E. H. I., I., p. 116.

[2] E. H. I., I., p. 470.

[3] *Ib.*, p. 491.

about on account of his friendship with Sultán Muhammad, the Khwárazm Sháh.[1]

571 H. In 1175 Muhammad of Ghor led his forces to Multán and delivered that place from the hands of the Qarmatians.

At this period Uch, now in the Baháwalpur State territory, was
the great centre of Moslem learning and propaganda in the south-west
Punjab. It possessed the Fírúzi College to which in 1227 Minháj-i- 624 H.
Saráj, the historian, was appointed, and he also held the Qáziship of the
forces of Alá-ud-Dín Bahrám Sháh, son of Násir-ud-Dín Qubácha.

626 H. In 1229 Altamsh received a diploma of investiture from the Abbási
Khalífa of Baghdád, confirming him in the sovereignty of Hindustan.[2]
743 H. Again in 1343 Muhammad ibn Tughlaq, holding that no king or prince
could exercise regal power without confirmation by the Khalífa of the
race of Abbás, made diligent enquiries from many travellers about the
Khalífas of that time, and learned that its representatives were the
Khalífas of Egypt. Accordingly he sent despatches to Egypt, had his
own name and title removed from his coins and those of the Khalífa
substituted. In 1343 Háji Sa'íd Sarsari came to Delhi from Egypt
bringing the Sultán honours and a robe from the Khalífa. He was
received with great ceremony, the Sultán walking barefoot before him,
and two years later a diploma was obtained from Egypt constituting the
Sultán a deputy of the Khalífa.[3] The historian Zia-ud-Dín Barani
indeed writes as if some previous Sultáns had received such confirmation
757 H. but not all.[4] In 1356 however Sultán Fíroz III followed this precedent
and was invested by the Khalífa with the title of Sayyid-us-Salátín,
robes being also sent at the same time to him and to his heir and principal minister.[5]

Meanwhile Delhi had replaced Uch as the centre of Moslem learn-
630 H. ing. In 1232 Altamsh made Minháj-i-Saráj, the historian, Qázi, Khatíb
and Imám of Gwálior, and five years later he was made chief of the
Násiriah College at Delhi, and Qázi of the empire in 1242, but in the 639 H.
following year he resigned those appointments. In 1246 he was re- 643 H.
appointed to the college, and obtained the lectureship of the Jámi'
Masjid with the Qáziship of Gwálior. In 1251 he again became Qázi 649 H.
of the empire and the capital, but was deprived of the post in 1253. 651 H

He was however appointed Qázi for a third time in 1256 and 653 H.
probably retained the office till his death.[6] His name does not however appear in the list of the Qázís of the court of Altamsh, but that

[1] T. N., p. 485.

[2] E. H. I., II., p. 293, *cf.* p. 575.

[3] Farishta, Persian text, Pt. I, p. 66; Thomas, *Chronicles*, p. 47; Lane Poole, *Muhammadan Dynasties*, p. 296.

[4] He had probably solicited it in 1340: Duff. pp. 219, 220, E. H. I., III, pp. 249 and 250. But the date is not certain: *cf.* p. 568, note 1. For Delhi as Dár-ul-Khiláfat under Qutb-ud-Dín Ibak, *cf.* T. N., p. 525: Farishta, Persian text, Pt. I, p. 140.

[5] E. H. I., III, pp. 387 and 342-3. Farishta, p. 146; Táríkh-i-Firoz Sháh by Ziai Badni, p. 598.

[6] T. N., pp. xxv-xxxi. Raverty adds some interesting information regarding Minháj. He was a Súfi, a scholar and one of those who would become filled with religious ecstasies, on hearing the singing at *zikrs* and *taskírs*, and when he became Qázi of Hindustán that office assumed integrity and rectitude: *ib.*, p. xxx.

office may have been separate from those he held. We read of three such Qázís and a fourth was styled 'Qázi of the army'.

In the beginning of Sultán Raziyyat's reign one Núr, a Turk, incited an outbreak among the Qirámita and Mulâhida heretics. They collected at Delhi from Sind, the Jumna valley and many other parts, as well as from the immediate neighbourhood of the capital and pledging fidelity to one another in secret they conspired against Islám, the mob listening openly to the harangues of Núr. He used to denounce the Ulamá as Násibi (setters-up) and Murjís (procrastinators),[1] especially those of the Hanafi and Shi'a sects. In 1237 these sectaries made a desperate attack on the Muhammadans in the Muizzi College, which they had mistaken for the Jámi' Masjid, but they were suppressed not without much bloodshed.[2] 634 H.

Khwája Qutb-ud-Dín Bakhtyár Káki of Ush near Baghdád came to Multán, in the time of Násir-ud-Dín Qabácha, and subsequently to Delhi, where Altamsh offered him the office of Shaikh-ul-Islám which he refused. To his memory Altamsh erected the great Qutb Minár at Old Delhi. He died in 1235.

He was, it is said, the disciple of Qázi Muhammad Hamíd-ud-Dín Nágauri, and the following table of spiritual descent may be drawn up according to the Chishti tradition :—

Hamíd-ud-Dín of Nágaur.
Qutb-ud-Dín Bakhtyár.[3]
Faríd-ud-Dín Shakarganj.
Khwája Nizám-ud-Dín Aulia.
Nasír-ud-Dín Chírágh-i-Delhi.

. . . .

Fakhr-ud-Dín.
Sháh Niáz Ahmad.
Núr Muhammad of Mahárán.
Khwája Sháh Sulaimán of Taunsa Sharíf.

At Kot Karor was born in 1170 Shaikh Bahá-ud-Dín Zakaria, who subsequently became a pupil of Shaikh Shiháb-ud-Dín Suharwardi of Baghdád. Thence he returned to Multán and became the intimate friend of Shaikh Faríd-ud-Dín Shakarganj.[4] The latter, perhaps the most famous Muhammadan saint of the Punjab, flourished in the 12th century.[5]

Nizám-ud-Dín Aulia taught at Delhi during the latter half of the 13th century and the early part of the 14th.[6] One of his pupils was the poet Amír Khusrau.

[1] Who consider good works unnecessary and believe that faith alone suffices for a Moslem's salvation, hell, being reserved for infidels : Sale, *Koran*, pp. 122, and 130-1.

[2] T. N., pp. 646-7.

[3] Sleeman says that Qutb-ud-Dín was a disciple of Moín-ud-Dín of Ajmer, the greatest of all their saints : *Rambles and Recollections*, II., p. 165.

[4] Beale, *Oriental Dicty.*, p. 97.

[5] Born in 1173, he died in 1265 at the advanced age of 95, *ib.*, p. 129. 569 H.-664 H.

[6] He was born at Budáon in 1233 and died in Delhi in 1325, age 89. 634 H.-72.

The Shaikh Jamál-ud-Dín, Bustámi, was the first to hold the office of Shaikh-ul-Islám at Delhi and on his death, according to Raverty, Altamsh wished the Khwája Qutb-ud-Dín Káki to accept the office. This is, however, very doubtful for the latter saint died in
633 H. 1235 and the former in 1239. However this may be, the Shaikh-ul-
657 H. Islám took part in politics at a very early period, for it was on secret instructions received from Shaikh Jamál-ud-Dín, the Sayyid Qutb-ud-Dín and the Qázi Shams-ud-Dín Bharaichi that the rebels under Ulugh
655 H. Khán attacked Delhi in 1257.[1] Jamál Dín then must have lived till after 1257 and on his death two years later could not have been succeeded by the Khwája.

Jalál-ud-Dín Firoz Sháh II was remarkable for his clemency, but his only act of capital punishment led in popular belief to the down-
C. 1295. fall of his dynasty. In his reign one Sídí Maula, a *darwesh* from the upper country,[2] who had come to Delhi in Balban's time, acquired a position of extraordinary influence in that city. He offered prayers, but never in mosques. He received no offerings, yet he distributed vast doles to travellers, and others. Upon a magnificent *khánqáh* he expended thousands. He visited Shaikh Faríd at Ajodhan, but disregarded that saint's advice to abstain from meddling with politics and made a disciple of the Sultán's eldest son who called himself the Sídí's son. Other Muhammadans of position eventually conspired with him to waylay the emperor on his way to the mosque on the Sabbath and assassinate him, which done the Sídi was to be proclaimed *khalifa* and marry a daughter of Sultán Násir-ud-Dín. Information of this conspiracy was, however, soon brought to the Sultán, but the conspirators strenuously denied their[3] guilt and no evidence could be obtained against them. Nevertheless Sídi Maula, despite the failure of the legal process against him, was destined to suffer death. The Sultán bade the *darweshes* avenge him of the *maula* and one of them attacked him with a razor and an elephant was made to trample him to death. Forthwith, says the chronicler, a black storm arose which made the world dark and trouble arose in the State. Famine prevailed throughout Siwálik in that same year. This event must have occurred about 1295.[4] Yet
when a thousand *thags* were captured he refused to execute any one of 694 H.
them and sent them in boats towards Lakhnauti where they were set free.[5]

695 H. The year 1296 was marked by a remarkable assassination. The saint Nizám-ud-Dín Aulia,[6] whose shrine is at Delhi, had roused the jealousy

[1] T. N., pp. 718, 622 and 707. According to D. B. Macdonald (*Muslim Theology*, p. 118) the dignity of Shaikh-ul-Islám was not created in Turkey till 1453.

[2] *Wiláyat-i-mulk-i-bálá.*

[3] It was not, says the *Táríkh-i-Firoz Sháhi*, the custom in those days to extort confession by beating. A large fire was, however, kindled and orders given to place the accused in it, but the lawyers urged that the ordeal by fire was against the law, and the evidence of one man insufficient to convict of treason. So the ordeal was countermanded and the leader of the conspiracy Qázi Jalál Kasháni actually sent as Qázi to Budáun, the remainder being banished.

[4] E. H. I., III, pp. 144-6.

[5] *Ib.*, 141.

[6] Born in 1236, he died in 1325 on 18th Rabi I, 705 H.: Beale, *Oriental Dicty.*, p. 302.

of the emperor Jalál-ud-Dín Fíroz Sháh Khilji by his influence and display,[1] and he had threatened to humble the proud priest on his return to Delhi from the Deccan. The saint's friends urged him to quit the city and seek safety elsewhere, but his invariable reply to their entreaties was *Hanoz Delhi dúr ast*,[2] 'Delhi is yet afar', a saying which has passed into a proverb. His courage or confidence was justified by the event, for Fíroz Sháh was treacherously murdered at Karrá on the Ganges by his nephew and son-in-law Alá-ud-Dín and never reached the capital.[3] With reference to this event Sleeman writes as follows:—"One is tempted to ask why Nizám-ud-Dín Aulia countenanced Fíroz Sháh II's murder if he was a *thag* of great note, seeing that the Sultán had been, as we have seen, extremely, not to say absurdly, lenient towards that fraternity"[4], and Mr. Muhammad Hamíd adds:—"The phrase 'Delhi is far off yet' is said to have been uttered by Sháh Nizám-ud-Dín, Mahbúb-i-Iláhí, of Delhi—wrongly supposed by some European scholars to be the *pír* of thieves and robbers—when he was pressed under threats of death to repay several lacs of rupees which he had received as alms from Násir-ud-Dín Khusrau Khán. Though Tughlaq Sháh had already reached Kílokherí, about two miles from Delhi, the saint persisted in repeating the phrase and it is said that that very day the king died a sudden death—the roof of the wooden palace falling in upon him". Sleeman clearly did not believe the tradition that Nizam-ud-Dín was the patron saint of thieves. The origin of the tradition will be discussed later.

699 H. Alá-ud-Dín's reign was also marked by an outbreak of religious fanaticism at Delhi itself. In 1300 one Háji, a *maula*, *i. e.* a slave or rather client of a *kotwál*, seized his opportunity while the Sultán Alá-ud-Dín was besieging Rentambhor to raise a revolt in the city. He placed on the throne a descendant of Ali, who was also a grandson of Altamsh on his mother's side. The revolt was however suppressed with little difficulty, and great severity.

702 H. In 1303 occurred one of the then frequent Mughal raids into the Punjab. Their army under Turgai invested Delhi, where Alá-ud-Dín unable to meet them in the open field entrenched his camp. Their retreat after a two months' siege was attributed to the power of the famous saint Nizám-ud-Dín Aulia.

The saints were revered and feared even by the governing bodies who are represented as always befriending them. Their anger was apt to bring the most unexpected disasters on the offending party, as, for example, the *Sairu-l-'Árifín* and the *Tazkírah-i-Auliyá-i-Sindh* mention the sudden death of Ghiyás-ud-Dín Tughlaq Sháh in 1325 owing to a 725 H.
curse uttered by the great Sháh Rukn-i-'Alam of Multán, who felt insulted at some remarks made by that sovereign.

[1] He was believed to possess the *dast-i-ghaib* or invisible hand because his expenditure was even more lavish than the emperor's own, though he had no ostensible source of income.

[2] Equivalent to 'there's many a slip 'twixt the cup and the lip'.

[3] E. H. I., III, pp. 175-8.

[4] Sleeman says 'it is very likely that he did strike this army with a panic by getting some of their leaders assassinated in one night'. There appears to be no historical evidence whatsoever to support this conjecture.

Fíroz Sháh III owed his elevation to the throne of Delhi in 1351 in large measure to the support of the *shaikhs*.[1] 752 H.

Fíroz Sháh built a large number of cities, forts, *bands*, mosques and tombs. His cities were Hisár Fírozah, Fatehábád, Fírozábád, Fírozábád Harni Khírá, Tughlaqpur Kosna, Tughlaqpur Malúk-i-Makút and Jaunpur, and everywhere he erected strong places for halts in travelling. His palaces were also numerous and he erected several *bands*, including the Band-i-Fath-Khán, Band-i-Malja (to which he supplied Ab-i-Zamzam[2]), Band-i-Máhpálpur, Band-i-Shakr Khán, Band-i-Sálúra, Band-i-Sáhpanáh, and Band-i-Wazírábád. He also built monasteries and inns for travellers. It is recorded that he erected 120 monasteries in Delhi and Fírozábád so that travellers from all parts might be received as guests in each of them for three days, and so might remain for 360 days in all. Superintendents of the Sunni faith were appointed to them and funds for their up-keep provided from the treasury. Malik Ghází Shahna was their chief architect, and held the gold staff of office while Abdul Haq (Jáhir Sundhár) had a golden axe. A capable *shahna* (superintendent) was appointed over each class of artisans. Fíroz Sháh repaired the tombs of former kings and restored the lands and villages formerly assigned to them. He also repaired the graves of saints and learned men of the faith. In the tombs of kings and saints he placed *takhts* (sofas or beds) of sandal wood.[3] At the close of his life Fíroz Sháh took special pains to repair mosques, and appointed to each of them a *muazzin* and an *imám*. He also provided for light and carpets.[4]

Fíroz Sháh showed much respect for saints and whenever he rode abroad he visited all those of Delhi. Towards the end of his reign he himself became *makluq*, by having his head shaved like a *qalandar*.[5]

Fíroz Sháh suppressed all practices forbidden by religious law, such as the painting of portraits, directing that garden scenes should be painted instead. He forbade the making of images and abjured the use of silver and gold vessels. He also abolished imposts which were against the law such as the *dángána*, an impost levied at one *danga* per *tanka*; *mushtaghal* or ground rent, also called *kirá-zamín*; *jazari*, an impost on butchers at 12 *jitals*[6] for every ox killed; *duri* or *rozi*, one levied on traders who brought grain, salt etc. into Delhi on bullocks. Once they had to carry the bricks from the old cities of Delhi to Fírozábád[7] on bullocks. Fíroz Sháh levied *jazya* from the Brahmans who had been exempt in former reigns. They protested but finally agreed to pay it at the lowest rate, *i.e.* 10 *tankas* and 50 *jitals* per head.[8]

Fíroz Sháh visited the tombs of the saints of Bhakkar, and renewed the former grants of the people of that place. Thence he

1 E. H. I., III, pp. 275-6.

2 Zamzam is the well at Mecca held sacred by Muhammadans.

3 *Táríkh-i Fíroz Sháhí* by Shams Siráj Afif, Persian text, pp. 329-33. *Takht* here is explained to mean the Hindi *chhaparkhat*—a bed with a canopy. What the king actually presented were canopies supported on a sandal-wood frame and pillars.

4 *Ib.*, p. 511.

5 *Ib.*, pp. 271-2.

6 A *jítal* = ⅓rd of an anna.

7 *Táríkh-i-Fíroz Sháhí*, pp. 378-79.

8 *Ib.*, pp. 382-4.

went to Uch where he rebuilt the monastery of Shaikh Jamál-ud-Dín
of Uch, and restored villages and gardens to his sons and bestowed
fresh pensions and presents on them and other people of Uch.[1] He
also repaired the monastery of Shaikh Faríd-ud-Dín[2] at Ajudhan, and H 282.
granted robes of honor to his descendants and confirmed them in
possession of their villages and lands.[3]

Sultán Fíroz has left an interesting account[4] of the heretical movements of his reign—and of his methods of dealing with them. He suppressed the Rawáfiz, a Shi'a sect, by burning their writings and punishing them in various ways, but apparently without bloodshed. Another sect of heretical sectarians, *mulhid abáhtián*, used to meet by night to drink wine and indulge, he writes, in promiscuous intercourse. He beheaded its leaders and banished or imprisoned other members of it. Another sect he describes as atheistical and at the same time as worshippers of one Ahmad Bahárí who was regarded as God. Its members were imprisoned and banished. Another self-styled prophet, Rukn-ud-Dín, asserted himself to be the Imám Mahdi, claimed omniscience and a special knowledge of the science of letters which he said had been revealed to him. He was torn to pieces by the people of Delhi. Sultán Fíroz based his fiscal system on the letter of the law at a considerable sacrifice of revenue,[5] and in return for the tax of toleration (*zar-i-zimmiya*) exacted the abolition of new idol temples and put down proselytising innovations with great severity.[6] But he appears to have respected existing Hindu institutions. The reign of Sultán Fíroz, however, was chiefly remarkable for his educational policy and his re-organization of existing institutions. To enable us to realise what he achieved an excursus on Moslem education in the Middle Ages and subsequent times down to the close of the Mughal period will now be useful.

Moslem education in Mediæval and later times.

The Muhammadans established several educational institutions in the Punjab. Of these the earliest was probably the Muizzi college at Delhi, doubtless founded by Muhammad of Ghor or one of his successors in the Muizzia dynasty which he founded and which was called after his name of Muizz-ud-Dín.[7] Next in point of time came the Fírúzi College at Uch[8] (c. 1227). Jálandhar probably possessed another ancient college,[9] but the origin of the famous Saints of Jálandhar dates

[1] *Táríkh-i-Fíroz Sháhí* by Zia-i-Barni, Persian text, pp. 538-9.

[2] This Sultán's orthodoxy is highly commended by his historian. He showed great respect to the Shaikh-ul-Islám Ala-ud-Dín and his successor Faríd-ud-Dín ot Ajudhan. Towards the close of his reign he himself took the tonsure and became a *mahlúk*. A less pleasing feature of his reign was the levy of the *jizya* from Brahmans: E. H. I., III, pp 362-3 and 366.

[3] *Ib.*, p. 543.

[4] In his *Fatúhát*: E. H. I., III, pp. 378-9.

[5] *Ib.*, p. 364.

[6] *Ib.*, p. 380.

[7] It is only alluded to in T. N., p. 646. It was not among the buildings repaired by Sultán Fíroz: E. H. I., III, p. 383 *f*.

[8] Raverty's *Tabaqát-i-Násiri*, London, 1881, p. 541: it was probably founded by the Malik Fírúz-ud-Dín, Altamash, the Sálár, prince of Khwárazm, *ib.*, p. 625, a noble of the Sultán Altamsh.

[9] *Ib.*, p. 679.

from a much later period, probably not earlier than the close of the 13th century. These saints were of Afghán or kindred origin and among the earliest was the Imám Násir-ud-Dín Shíráni. Another was an ancestor of the saint, influential in the Afghán hills, known as the Pír Roshan, the founder of the Roshanía schism.[1] But Delhi was the principal centre of religious instruction. The Násíriah college was founded there, probably by Altamash[2] who appointed the Persian historian Minháj-ud-Dín, formerly principal of the college at Uch, to this foundation in 1237 A. D.

The later and more orthodox Muhammadans generally had their educational institutions or *madrasas* attached to mosques or tombs. It is believed by them to be a religious act, conferring the blessing of God on the soul of the deceased buried in the tomb or on that of the founder of the mosque. Sometimes, however, they were founded independently, but such cases were not very many. This system is to be met with practically in the whole Muhammadan world, and still prevails.

Delhi.

(*i*) After the Muizzi and Násíriah colleges at Delhi comes Alá-ud-Dín's college, which was attached to his tomb near the Qutb Minár, within its enclosure. It was repaired by Fíroz Sháh.[3] The building is totally ruined but has recently been cleared from débris.

(*ii*) Fíroz Sháh, who was very fond of buildings and erected as well as repaired a large number of them, constructed two *madrasas.* One of them was built at the Aläi tank and known by the name of *Madrasa-i-Fíroz Sháhi.* Ziá-i-Barni, a contemporary historian, has lavished much praise on this building and says that Mauláná Jalál-ud-Dín Rúmí, a scholar of great repute, was appointed to teach *tafsír* (commentaries on the Qurán), *hadis* (tradition), *fiqh* (Muhammadan Law) in the *madrasa.*[4]

(*iii*) The second *madrasa* built by Fíroz Sháh was at Siri. It also has been greatly praised by Ziá-i-Barni who records that Najm-ud-Dín of Samarqand, a great scholar of the time, gave religious instruction in that *madrasa.*[5]

(*iv*) There was also a third *madrasa* built by Fíroz Sháh in connection with his son Fateh Khán's tomb known as Qadam Sharíf.[6]

(*v*) In the year 1561 Maham Angah, the wet nurse of Akbar, built a *madrasa* attached to the mosque known as Khair-ul-Manázil[7] near the old Fort.

(*vi*) There was a college or *madrasa* on the roof of the tomb of Humáyún. It was at one time an institution of some importance and men of learning such as Mauláná Núr-ud-Dín Tarkhán were appointed to the charge of the place.[8]

[1] Temple, *Legends*, III, p. 150 *f.*

[2] One of his titles was Násir-i-Amír-ul-Múminín. It can hardly have been founded by Násir-ud-Dín Kabája, since Sultán Fíroz relates how he rebuilt the college (*madrasa*) of Altamsh which had been destroyed: E. H. I., III, p. 383.

[3] *Asáru-s-Sanádíd* (ed. Cawnpur, 1904), ch. III, pp. 27-8.

[4] *Táríkh-i-Fíroz Sháhi* by Ziá-i-Barni, p. 562-5.

[5] *Ib.*, pp. 565-6.

[6] *Asáru-s-Sanádíd*, ch. III, pp. 37-8.

[7] *Ib.*, ch. III, p. 54.

[8] Carr Stephen, Delhi, p. 207.

(*vii*) Ghási-ud-Dín Khán built a *madrasa* in connection with his mausoleum, which he erected in his own lifetime.[1] It is still used as such, being occupied by the Anglo-Arabic High School.

(*viii*) The *madrasa* of Raushan-ud-Daula associated with a mosque in Daríba Bazar, Sháhjahánábád, Delhi, was built by Nawáb Sharf-ud-Daula in 1135 Ḥ. (1722-3 A. D.) during the reign of Muhammad Sháh.[2] The *madrasa* no longer exists, but it is referred to in the inscription on the central arch of the mosque.

(*ix*) The tomb of Safdar Jang is locally known as *madrasa* but no reference to it is to be found in any book. It is possible that the rooms in the enclosure may have been used for the purpose which has given it the name of *madrasa.*

Lahore.

In Lahore, Dái Láḍo, wet nurse of Jahángír, founded a school which continued to flourish till the collapse of the Mughal power.[3]

Batála.

During the reign of Bahlol Khán Lodi in 1472 A. D. Batála in Gurdáspur was founded by Rai Rám Deo, a Bhaṭṭi, to whom the tract between the Sutlej and Chenáb had been farmed by Tátár Khán, viceroy of Lahore. Rám Deo was converted by Shaikh Muhammad Qádiri of Lahore. In later times Batála enjoyed a great reputation for learning and the saints Shaháb-ud-Dín Bukhári, Sháh Ismáíl Sháh Niámatulla and Shaikh Alláh Dád lived there. The tomb of the first-named still exists in the quarter occupied by his descendants, the Bukhári Sayyids, and that of his still more distinguished kinsman Mauj Darya stands at Khán Fateh, five miles to the west of the town. But the last-named may be really buried at Lahore.

Agha Badí-ud-dín Shahíd, 11th in descent from Sayyid Abdul Qádir Jíláni, migrated to India in the time of Humáyún, and 6th in descent from him was Khán Bahádur Qázi Ináyatulla[4] whose eldest son Sayyid Muhammad Akram was *qázi* in Montgomery. Another son, Muhammad Fazl Dín, settled in Batála about 300 years ago. He founded its Madrasa Qádiria in Aurangzeb's reign, and in that of Farrukhsiár about 100 villages were granted him in *jágír*. On his death S. Ghulám Qádir Sháh, whose books on *tasawwaf* were well-known in the Punjab, became *sajjáda-nashín* and obtained villages worth Rs. 12,000 a year from Ahmad Sháh Abdáli. His *gaddi* is still held by his descendants, one of whom, S. Ahmad Sháh, assisted Lt. W. M. Murray in his historical works.

Muhammad Fazl's college attracted many students, but it was destroyed by Banda and the town soon lost its title of Sharíf.[5] Banda indeed set fire to the whole town and pillaged it, beginning with the Qázís' *mahalla*, then its wealthiest quarter.[6]

Siálkot.

Mulláh Abdul Hákim and Sádulláh 'Allami, afterwards the grand *wazír* of Sháh Jahán, were class-fellows and studied together in the

[1] Carr Stephen, Delhi, pp. 263 *et. seq.*
[2] *Asáru-s-Sanádíd*, ch. III, p. 81.
[3] *Hist. of Lahore*, p. 286.
[4] *Qázi* at Siálkot, in Montgomery, Kashmír and Kábul from time to time, and founder of Chak Qázi in Gurdáspur, where he died.
[5] Gurdáspur *Gazetteer*, 1914, p. 28.
[6] Khazán Singh, *Philosophic Hist. of the Sikh Religion*, I., p. 216.

maktab at the Kashmíri mosque near the Imám Sáhib's mausoleum. Both were poor and Mulláh Abdul Hákim's parents were weavers. The most famous of his teachers was Mulláh Kámal Akhúnd of Kashmír. Abdul Hákim distinguished himself in logic and philosophy, but his renown did not spread abroad until his introduction to the court of Sháh Jahán which occurred in this way: Sádullah 'Allami, when he rose to the dignity of *wazír*, remembered his class-fellow as they had been great friends in early days. He mentioned the name of Abdul Hákim to the emperor and praised him so much that the emperor ordered him to be sent for. He came to Delhi where some time after his arrival a discussion on the existence of God took place. Mulláh Abdul Hákim was required by the emperor to join in the discussion and he brought forward so many convincing arguments that all admitted his intellectual superiority. The emperor himself was greatly pleased and requested the *mulláh* to arrange those arguments in the form of a pamphlet which is still extant. In its introduction the author relates the above story and says that he wrote at the express desire of the emperor. The *mulláh* lived for a long time at court, but finally came back to Siálkot and buried himself in imparting knowledge to all. He opened a *madrasa* in a mosque in Rangpura where men from all parts of the world came to hear his discourses, even from Basra, Egypt, Baghdád, Pengál, Kashmír, Turkistán and Persia. He used to dictate explanatory notes on difficult books of logic and his pupils used to take them down in class. His elucidations of difficult works of old philosophy are still printed and in recent years a book published in Egypt under the name of 'The Reflections of the Siálkoti' is still used and appreciated by students of philosophy. It is a text-book in the Colleges there. Besides this his 'elucidations' or *Háshiah* of books on philosophy are still printed in Arabia and Egypt which shows that they have not lost their hold on the public mind and have not become stale with the lapse of time and the introduction of new theories about philosophical doctrines has not impaired them.

Sháh Jahán was so pleased with the *mulláh* that when he came back from Delhi to Siálkot he granted him land and had a tank dug for his ablution. This tank still exists near the American Mission School. The emperor also had a canal dug for his special use, the traces of which are still found at some places near the tank. The reason for the digging of the canal was that Mulláh Abdul Hakím professed the Shafái doctrine of Islám, according to which ablutions are only lawful if performed in running water.

He had an extensive library in which valuable books were collected. After his death his descendants did not inherit his intellectual powers and in the last years of the 19th century, one of them Mián Ghausa disposed of all his valuable manuscripts out of sheer poverty. Mián Ghausa died recently and now nothing remains of the old philosopher but a confused heap of stones to mark the last resting place of one who once ruled the intellectual world of India. He is buried at Siálkot near the tank and his mausoleum was once imposing, but owing to the vandalism of the Sikhs, who used it as a magazine, they say, it is now in ruins.

To resume the notes on the religious history of Islám :—

Religious history of the Mughal period.

Akbar's policy was one of toleration and in fact he incurred the charge of heterodoxy by his attempts to bring all religions into one comprehensive fold. His historian Abul Fazl's account of his measures must be read with caution as that writer's own father had been accused of Shi'á tendencies and sympathy with heresy.[1] He was a Súfi, but disapproved the ecstacies of music and dance affected by that sect; and also eschewed silk, though he changed his views in this respect.[2]

Akbar's measures were far-reaching. He abolished the poll-tax on infidels in the 9th year of his reign and also the tax called *karmi* levied apparently on Hindu pilgrims to sacred shrines.[3] This led to a rebellion, the emperor's innovations being objected to in so far as they led to the withdrawal of grants of rent-free land. But Akbar does not appear to have acted in this matter without some justification. The department of the Sadr-i-Jahán had been very great before the time of the Mughals and even during Akbar's reign he ranked as the fourth officer of the empire. His edict legalised the *jalús* or accession of a new king.[4] But the department had become most corrupt and especially so in the administration of the *sayúrghál* or grants Akbar's Sadrs were :—

1. Shaikh Gadáí, until 968 H.[5]
2. Khwája Muhammad Sálih, until 971 H.[6]
3. Shaikh Abdunnabi, until 986 H.[7]

[1] See the guarded account in the *Aín-i-Akbari*, Blochmann's Trans., III, p. 420 *f*.

[2] Blochmann, *op cit.*, p. 440.

[3] E. H. I., VI, pp. 29-30, and *Aín*, I, 189.

[4] *Aín*, I, p. 270.

[5] To the vitriolic pen of Al-Badauni we owe many details regarding these Sadrs Akbar's efforts to revise the lists of religious grants seem to have given grave offence to Al-Badauni. Possibly his own pocket had been affected.

Shaikh Gadái, Kamboh, was the son of Jamál, Kamboh, a poet of Delhi, who after the second defeat during the 'exile at Gujrát' had come to the Khán Khánán. Through his influence he was appointed Sadr in 995 H. The Khán Khánán and even the emperor himself attended singing parties at his house, which Al-Badauni describes in severe terms. Shaikh Gadái drew the pen of obliteration through the grants and pensions of old servants of the Crown, but to any one who disgraced himself by attending his levées he gave a *sayúrghál*. He died in 976 H. : *Muntakhab-ut-Tawárikh*, translation W.H. Lowe, II, pp. 22 and 124 ; *Maasir-ul-Umara*, II, pp. 540-41.

[6] In 969 H. Khwájgí Muhammad Sálih of Hirát, grandson of Khwája Abdulla Marwáríd, a well-known *wazír*, was appointed Sadr, but without fully absolute powers of granting *aukáf*, and subsistence (*ma'adí m'ash*), as they were subject to administrative control : *Mun'akhab-ut-Tawáríkh*, Lowe, II, pp. 48-9.

[7] In 972 or 971 H. Akbar sent for Shaikh Abd-un-Nabi, the traditionalist, grandson of Shaikh Abd-ul-Quddús of Gangoh, one of the greatest Shaikhs of Hind, and made him chief Sadr, so that acting with Muzaffar Khán, he might pay the pensions. He soon acquired absolute power over the grants of allowances, lands and pensions, but by degrees matters reverted to their old position. About 983 H. when Shaikh Abd-un-Nabi was rising to power, the emperor used to go to his house to hear lectures on the traditions of the Prophet, and make Jahángír attend his school to learn the 40 *ahadis* of the renowned master, Mauláná Abdur Rahmán Jami. Once or twice the emperor placed the Shaikh's slippers before his feet. In this year Akbar gave orders that no *a'imae* in the empire should be recognised by the *karori* (revenue officer) of a *pargana*, unless the *farmán* by which the

4. Sultan Khwája, until his death in 993 H.[1]

5. Amír Fathullah Shírázi, till 997.[2]

grant had been made was produced before the Sadr for verification. This brought numbers of worthy people from the east of India and so far west as Bhakkar to Court. If any of them had a patron in one of the Amírs, or a friend of His Majesty, he could get his affairs settled, but such as lacked recommendations had to bribe Sayyid Abdur Rasúl, the Shaikh's headman, or his chamberlains, door-keepers and sweepers. Many of the *a'imadárs* died without effecting their object from the heat caused by the crowds. The Shaikh would for example allow a teacher of the *Hidáya* and other books 100 *bighas* more or less; and though such a man might have held long possession of a greater area, the Shaikh would take it away. But to men of no repute, even to Hindus, he would grant lands. Thus learning and learned men fell daily in estimation. Even in the hall of audience the Shaikh used to insult great Amírs and even courtiers, who endured it in order to help poor suppliants. Never by any emperor had such absolute power been given to any Sadr. Once Shaikh Abd-un-Nabi told Akbar that a certain *mujtahid* had nine wives, but on another occasion when the emperor asked him how many wives a man could marry, he gave a different answer and so annoyed the emperor that he never forgot it. In 987 H. Shaikh Abd-un-Nabi and the Makhdúm-ul-Mulk tempted mankind by suggesting that the *Qurán* was a forgery, by casting doubts on the authority of the prophets and Imáms and denying the existence of demons, angels, all mysteries, signs and miracles. At length owing to the enmity of the Makhdúm-ul-Mulk and others, he lost the emperor's favour. But perhaps the chief reason of his fall was the execution of a Brahman.
1578-9 A.D. In 986 H. Shaikh Abd-un-Nabi and his enemy the Makhdúm-ul-Mulk were banished
to Mecca, the post of Sadr being conferred on Sultán Khwája. In 990 H. they
returned to Gujrát, where the Makhdúm-ul-Mulk died at Ahmadábád. Shaikh Abd-un-Nabi 1582 A.D.
went to Fathpur, and tried to regain his former position but he used such rude language that the emperor struck him in the face. He had apparently been given Rs 7000 before he went to Mecca and seems to have been unable to account for it on his return, so he was handed over to Rája Todar Mal and imprisoned like a defaulting tax-gatherer and the historian adds that one night a mob strangled him. This took place in 991 H.: *op cit.*,
Lowe, II, p 70, Persian text, II, pp. 204, Lowe, pp. 207-8, 211, 231, Pers. Text, II, pp. 1583 A.D.
276, 311 and 83.

[1] In 984 H. Sultán Khwája (Abdul Azím, son of Khwája Kháwand Mahmúd) was appointed Mír Háji and given six *lákhs* of rupees to distribute among the deserving poor of Mecca and Medina and build a *khánah* in the sacred precincts. He returned in 986 H., bringing back Arab horses, Abyssinian slaves, and other presents for the emperor, who made him Sadr of all Hindustán with the rank of 1000. A disciple of the emperor, he died in 992 H. and was buried in Fathpur fort. Akbar bestowed his daughter in marriage on his son the prince Dániyál: *Muntakhab-ut-Tawáríkh*, Lowe, II, pp. 243 and 275; and *Maasir'ul-Umara*, II, pp. 379-81.

[2] In 990 H. Mír Fathullah of Shíráz who in theology, mathematics, physics and all sciences, both logical and traditional, and in *talismas*, incantations and discovering treasure was unrivalled in that age, in obedience to a *farmán*, left Adil Khán in the Deccan and came to Fathpur. The Khán Khánán and Hákim Abdul Fath by imperial command met him, and brought him to the presence. He was made Sadr, but his only duty was to confiscate the lands of the poor. When the emperor learnt that he had been a pupil of Mír Ghiyás-ud-Dín Mansúr of Shíráz, who was none too strict in religion, he fancied that he would gladly accept his schemes, but Fathullah was so staunch Shi'a that even in the hall of State he said the Shi'a prayers with perfect composure, a thing no one else would have dared to do. His Majesty therefore classed him as a bigot, but connived at his practices, and married him to a daughter of Muzaffar Khán, associating him in the wazírship with Rája Todar Mal. Mír Fathullah also taught the Amír's children. He also accompanied the emperor in the chase. In 993 H. Akbar gave Sháh (afterwards Mír) Fathullah the title of Azud-ul-daulat and a present of Rs. 5000, appointing him Sadr-in-chief of Hindustán, but posted him to the Deccan. His deputy Kamali Shírázi remained at the capital 'to bring to court the lackland *a'imadárs*, some of whom were still left, scattered here and there'. Under him the sadarate reached its zenith, but by degrees things came to such a pass that Sháh Fathullah, for all his pomp, could not grant 5 *bighas* of land. Nay, after the withdrawal of the grants the very soil became the haunt of wild beasts instead of *a'imadárs* and husbandmen. In 993 H. Akbar sent Azud-ud-Daulat from the Court to Málwa, in 995 H. he was sent to govern Berár and in 996 H. he received Basáwar in *jágír*, with all its charity lands. In 997 he died of fever in Kashmír and was buried on the Takht-i-Sulaimán, a hill near a city of that province: *Muntakhab-ut-Tawáríkh*, Lowe, II, pp. 325-6, 354, 372, 379, and 381.

6. Sadr Jahán, whose name coincided with his title.[1] He had been *Mufti-i-mamálik-i-mahrusa* and continued to serve under Jahángir.[2]

Another Sadr was Mauláná Abdul Báqi, of unkonwn date. Shaikh Gadái began the resumption of the endowments, but Abdunnabi was invested with wide discretionary powers and made grants lavishly though, if his detractors are to be believed, capriciously until his downfall. Under Sultán Khwája who had adopted the 'Divine Faith' of Akbar, matters took a very different course, the lands were steadily withdrawn and as the emperor inquired personally into all of them the power of the Sadr was completely broken and many Muhammadan families were utterly ruined.[3]

In 989 H. Akbar again entrusted the Punjab to Saíd Khán, Rájá Bhagwán Dás, and Mán Singh. To investigate the management of grants in the province, he appointed a Sadr to each Doáb, *viz.* Mulláhs Illahdád of Amroha, Sheri the poet, Illahdád Nabawi of Sultánpur, and Sháh Muhammad of Sháhábád. The first two were remarkable for their goodness and the last two for their badness. He also appointed Shaikh Faizi Sadr of a Doáb (probably that between the Sutlej and Beás). But Hakím Humam and Hakím Abdul Fath, the Sadrs of the capital, he sent beyond the Ganges.[4]

Akbar presumably conducted ecclesiastical business in much the same way as his successors, for instance Sháh Jahán, of whom it is recorded that after the emperor had disposed of purely administrative business the chief Sadr reported to him any important point in the despatches received from the provincial Sadrs. He also brought to his notice cases of needy scholars, Sayyids, Shaikhs and holy men and obtained grants of money for them.[5]

Nevertheless Akbar's toleration of other creeds and his measures against the holders of religious grants did not alienate all Muhammadan sympathy from him. On the contrary several of the highest ecclesiastical officials in the empire in 987 H. signed a document declaring the superiority of the Imám-i-ádil or just leader over the *mujtahid*.[6]

[1] Besides these there were provincial Sadr-i-juz in each Súbah under the (direct ?) orders of the Sadr-i-Jahán, Sadr-i-Kul or Sadr-us-Sudúr as he was also called. The Sadr-i-Jahán often wielded great powers, *e.g.* Abdunnabi had two men put to death for heresy: *ib.*, III, 271.

[2] Sadr Jahán, *mufti* of the imperial dominions, who had been appointed to a commandership of 1000, joined the Divine Faith, as did also his two foolish sons in 1004 H: *Muntakhab-ut-Tawárikh*, Lowe, II, p. 418.

[3] *Ib.*, III, pp. 278-4 and 270. These grants were designated *a'ima*, and the holders *a'imadár*. The former word is still found as a place-name in the Punjab, *e.g.* in Hoshiárpur.

[4] *Ib.*, II, p. 304, Persian text, II, pp. 295-6.

[5] Sarkar, *Anecdotes of Aurangzeb*, p. 169. Abid Khán was Sadr of Aurangzeb's reign: *ib.*, p. 90.

[6] *Muntakhab-ut-Tawárikh*, Lowe, I., pp. 185-6. This document was signed, not without much debate and many mental reservations, by Qázi Jalál-ud-Din of Multán, Qázi-u-quzzát, Abdunnabi, Sadr Jahán as *mufti* of the empire and others.

This document made Akbar supreme head of the faith and was soon followed by the attempt of Háji Ibrahím of Sirhind, who is said to have translated the *Atharva Veda*,[1] to adduce proofs that the emperor was the Sáhib-i-Zamán, or 'Man of the Age', a title frequently given to the Imám Mahdi, who was to reconcile the 72 sects of Islám, and in 988 H. this movement received some support from the learned.[2] Among Moslem doctors who are mentioned as having influenced Akbar's conduct is Shaikh Táj-ud-Dín of Delhi, son of Shaikh Zakaría of Ajodhan and a disciple of Shaikh Zamán of Pánipat. Táj-ud-Dín was styled Táj-ul-Arifín, or crown of the Súfis, and the emperor listened whole nights to his 'Súfic trifles' according to Al-Budauni.[3]

Muhammad Akram was appointed Qázi of the imperial court in 1698 and died in 1705.[4]

But tolerant as Akbar was of religious convictions he persecuted doubtless in self-defence and in the interests of toleration itself, many learned men and lawyers. The *ulamá* as a class appear to have come in for very severe treatment and many Shaikhs and *faqirs* were sent to Qandahár and elsewhere to be exchanged for horses. The sect of the Iláhís met with similar treatment.[5]

The story of Dárá Shikoh may now be read in J. N. Sarkar's *History of Aurangzeb*[6] and his place in literature in Pandit Sheo Narain's paper.[7] In the *Safinat-ul-Aulia* he calls himself a Hanafi and his poetical name was Qádiri, but it is not certain that he belonged to that or any other particular sect or order. His views were exceedingly broad and liberal and though he seems to have been initiated into the Qádiria order by Muhammad Sháh Tisán-ullah in 1049 H., he may have been influenced by political motives to adopt a vague Súfiism which would win him support from the Hindus without alienating the more moderate Muhammadans. However this may be, many folktales recall his Hindu leanings, and his dialogues with Bába Lál show that

[1] *Muntakhab-ut-Tawárikh*, pp. 189 and 105.

[2] *Ib.*, p. 190. The *Muntakhab-ut-Tawárikh*, Lowe, II, p. 295 (Persian text, pp. 286-7) ascribes this incident to 990 H. and adds that Khwája Maulána of Shiráz, 'the heretic of Jafrdan', brought a pamphlet by some of the *sharifs* of Mecca, which quoted a tradition that the earth would exist for 7000 years, and as that period was now over the promised Mahdi would soon appear. 'Many others also produced such pamphlets and all this made the emperor the more inclined to claim the dignity of a prophet, perhaps I should say, the dignity of something else (of God)'.

[3] *Ib.*, p. 181. Shaikh Zamán was in Súfiism and pantheism second only to Shaikh-ibn-Arabi. He was the author of one commentary on the *Lawáih* and of another comprehensive one on the *Nuzhat-ul-arwáh*.

[4] Sarkar, *op. cit.*, p. 142. The kind of question that was referred to the *muftis* is illustrated by an incident of Aurangzeb's reign. Some Hindus were taken prisoner at the siege of Satara and the emperor directed the Court Qázi Muhammad Akram to investigate the question with the help of the *muftis*. He reported that under the canon law they could be released if they accepted Islám—but that the Muslims taken should be imprisoned for 3 years: *ib.*, p. 141. But he soon reviewed his decision in the light of the *Fatáwa-i-Alamgiri* and the prisoners were impartially executed. The function of *mufti* was to expound the law and assist the Qázi by supplying him with *fatáwas* or decisions: p. 142.

[5] *Muntakhab-ut-Tawárikh*, pp. 278 & 191.

[6] Two vols., Calcutta, 1912.

[7] Punjab Historical Society's *Journal*, 1912, p. 21.

they are founded on fact. Though specially fond of Lahore his influence was felt further afield, and the shrine of Jati Abdál or the chaste Abdál at Rámpur in Kabírwálá tahsíl, Multán, was founded by one of his servants. No woman is admitted into this shrine.[1]

The austere orthodoxy of Aurangzeb found no nobler field for its activity than the reformation of abuses within the fold of Islám itself. He showed much self-restraint in the exercise of his despotic powers, but his firmness in carrying out the measures, which he considered necessary, was beyond all praise He endowed learned men and professors but was apparently enabled to prevent the abuses rife under Akbar. While he observed the Sháfian tenets[2] he recognised in legal matters the authority of the Hanáfi School and caused a digest of the conflicting rulings of the *qázís* and *muftís*, which had been delivered without any authority, to be drawn up by a commission under Shaikh Nizám. As its members were well paid this commission cost about two *lakhs* of rupees.[3] The *Fatáwa-i-Alamgiri*, which is known at Mecca as a *Fatwa-i-Hind*, was composed of extracts in Arabic from several collections of *fatáwas* of older date and also from other legal treatises of a more abstract character by writers of the Hanífia School. It was commenced in the 11th year of Aurangzeb's reign (1670 A.D.) and was completed before his death.[4] Sarkár describes it as a mere compilation though it cost nearly two *lákhs* of rupees.[5]

That writer adds that in the same year the four degrees of devotion to His Majesty were defined. They consisted in readiness to sacrifice to the emperor property, life, honour and religion. Whosoever sacrificed one of these four won a degree. The courtiers put down their names as faithful disciples of the throne.[6]

Aurangzeb changed the title of the imperial slaves from *ghulám* to *chela* because he considered it an act of impious presumption for one man to call another *ghulám*, men being slaves of God alone.[7]

In 1680 the emperor re-imposed the *jizya*, a measure which led to a commotion at Delhi. The *Muntakhab-ul-Lubáb* implies that it was imposed to curb the infidels, *viz.* the Satnámis, who had broken out just before. But the *Ma'ásir* places that outbreak five years before the re-imposition.[8]

It was again abolished in the brief reign of Abul Barakát (1719).[9]

[1] Multán *Gazetteer*, p. 22.

[2] E. H. I., VII, p. 158.

[3] *Ib.*, pp. 159-60

[4] Two books of this digest are translated in a condensed form in Baillie's *Moohummudan Law of Sale* (London, 1850), and it was largely used by the same author in his *Digest of Moohummudan Law* (London, 1875). But no translation of the work as a whole exists in English.

[5] *Op. cit.*, p. 142.

[6] *Muntakhab-ut-Tawáríkh*, Lowe, II, p. 299, Persian text, II, p. 291.

[7] Sarkar, *op. cit.*, p. 101 Does this account for the existence of a Chela sept among the Siáls, Vol. III, p. 419, *infra*? Possibly the Chelas were originally Ghuláms, as on the frontier.

[8] E. H. I., VII, p. 296.

[9] *Ib.*, p. 479.

No trace seems to exist in the Punjab of the *hisba* jurisdiction, though Sarkár cites an order of Aurangzeb reproving the Prince Muhammad Azam Sháh for taking upon himself the functions of the *muhtasib* or 'censor of morals'.[1] The *muhtasib* exercised *quasi*-judicial functions of a very delicate and important kind.

Sirhind. Sirhind was a considerable centre of Muhammadan learning during the Mughal period. It must have possessed a college, for Shaikh Abdulla, surnamed Mián, taught there, one of his pupils being Shaikh Muhammad Baká, author of the *Mirát-i-Alam* and a disciple of Shaikh Muhammad of Sirhind.[2]

Sirhind was a wealthy town, learned and religious men in great numbers residing there when it was sacked by the Sikhs under Banda in 1708.[3]

Siálkot. Siálkot also held some position in the learned world, for Chulpi Abdulla, son of the celebrated Mauláná Abdul Hakím of Siálkot, was employed to translate the *Fatáwa-i-Alamgiri* into Persian.[4]

Lahore. 1709-10. Notwithstanding the recent sack of Sirhind by the Sikhs Lahore was in 1121 H. the scene of a riot caused by an imperial order that the word 'heir' should be inserted among the attributes of Ali in the *khutba*. Against this innovation Ján Muhammad and Háji Yár Muhammad, two of the most eminent scholars in the city, protested and after other and more violent protests had been ignored the *khatib* of the mosque was stabbed by a Túráni Mughal and finished off by the mob in the forecourt of the mosque[5] Apparently the imperial order implied a claim by the emperor to be styled or regarded as the Khalífa. Háji Yár Muhammad stoutly opposed the innovation in an audience at Delhi also and though the form used in the reign of Aurangzeb was eventually restored the Háji and two other learned men were sent to a fortress.[6]

Islamic Theology.[7]

In order to understand the present position of Islám in the Punjab, the condition of its institutions, and its aspirations, a sketch however brief of its theological history is indispensable. The constitutional history of Islám has been that of a conflict between two principles, the authority of the *Qurán* and the various influences which sought to modify it. The contribution made by the Prophet to Islám was legislation pure and simple. Since his death there has been no legislation, properly so-called, but only interpretation of the *Qurán*. This is the more momentous in that the sphere of law is much wider in Islám than it has ever been with western nations. Passing over the various sources,

[1] Sarkár, *op. cit.*, p. 70 Under Aurangzeb, at any rate, beside the *qázís* or judges of canon law, *ádils* or judges of common law were also appointed, but the emperor himself was the fountain of justice and the highest court of appeal. He took the law from the *ulmá* or canon-lawyers: Sarkár, *op. cit.*, p. 175, *cf.* p. 178.

[2] E. H. I., VII, p. 153.

[3] *Ib.*, VII, p. 415.

[4] *Ib.*, p. 160.

[5] *Ib.*, VII, p. 421.

[6] *Ib.*, pp. 427-8. Prince Azím-us-shán secretly countenanced this opposition.

[7] Throughout this sub-section D. B. Macdonald's *Development of Muslim Theology, Jurisprudence and Constitutional Theory* (London, 1903) has been drawn upon freely.

such as the *hadís* or tradition, which were drawn up to interpret, amplify and modify the *Qurán* we find four great legal schools developing in succession. Of these the first was that of Abu Haníla, the first teacher to leave behind him a systematic body of teaching and a missionary school of pupils. A Persian by race he does not seem to have held office as a judge or to have practised law, but to have been a philosophical jurist. Finding that the law of the desert not only failed to apply to town and agricultural life but was even directly mischievous, he reduced to a definite principle the consideration of local conditions under the formula of *istihsán* or 'holding for better'.[1] Although his system was never reduced to a code and was vehemently attacked by his opponents it was perfected by his pupils and their successors and has withstood all attacks. It is the leading one of the four existing schools and prevails over all northern India. Abu Haníla died in 782 A. D., 176 H.
and 29 years later died Málik ibn-Anas who had given form to the historical school of Madína. While Málik relied more upon tradition and took refuge less frequently in opinion, he accepted the principle of *istisláh* or 'public advantage' with clearness. The result was that it is not easy to make much practical distinction between his school and that of Abu Haníla, and it had little influence in the east.

We next pass from simple development to development through conflict. Hitherto dissension had only covered points of detail. Now it touched a vital question of principle. The traditionists said that law should be based solely on the *Qurán* and tradition. The modernists contended that it was better to work out a legal system by logic and the necessities of the case. Between these extremists Ash-Shafi'i (died
204 H. 819 A. D.) struck out a middle course. An absolutely authentic tradition he regarded as of equally divine authority with the *Qurán*, but he recognised also as inevitable the maintenance of usages which had grown up in individual life, in the constitution of the State, and in the rules and decisions of the courts. To prevent the overthrow of this established order of things Ash-Sháfi'i erected the theory of *ijmá* or agreement, already adumbrated by Málik, into a principle, and taught that whatever the community of Islám has agreed upon is of God. But he also accepted *qiyás* (analogy) as a guide and thus gave elasticity to his system. Ash-Sháfi'i is one of the greatest figures in the history of law and with him closes the great development of Muhammadan jurisprudence But he has had little influence over the development of law in the Punjab. His doctrines are only professed by a few depressed tribes like the KEHALS as an excuse for eating the flesh of unclean animals.

Against Ash-Shafi'i's teaching the principal revolt was headed by his own pupil Dáúd-az-Záhiri, 'David the literalist', and he founded a school which lasted for centuries and had important historical and theological consequences, though it was never acknowledged as a regular school of Moslem law. The dignity of the fourth school was reserved for that of Ahmad ibn Hanbal, a theologian of the first rank but not a lawyer, who minimised agreement, rejected analogy and favoured literal interpretation. His school was not progressive and has had little influence, if any, on the Punjab, unless we except the Ahl-i-hadís of

[1] *Lit.* 'approving, praising', . . or 'considering as a favour': Catafago.

modern times.[1] Ahmad bin Hanbal died in 855 A. D. 341 H.

The present position then throughout the Moslem world is that besides the codices of canon or theoretical law there is an accepted and authoritative body of statutes (*qánúns*) promulgated by secular authority. How far this system ever applied to India it is difficult to say.

The above account omits any mention of Shi'ite and Ibádite laws. The latter has had no influence on the Punjab as far as can be seen. The Shi'a legal system is based on the authority of the Hidden Imám. They utterly reject the idea of co-ordinate schools of law, and to the doctrine of *ikhtiláf* or 'variability' under local conditions they oppose his authority. They still have *mujtahids,* divines and legists, who have a right to form opinions of their own, can expound the original sources at first hand and claim the unquestioning assent of their disciples. But in these provinces, even among so strictly Shi'a a tribe as the Túrís, the office of *mujtahid* is either in abeyance or not disclosed.

So far we have dealt with law as a branch of theology, a perfectly legitimate method in an account of Moslem religious development. Its purely theological history can only be dealt with here cursorily. The two earliest schools of theological thought were the Murji'ites and Qadarites. The former 'postponed' judgment until it is pronounced by God on the Day of Judgment. Their principal contribution to theology is the doctrine that faith and faith alone saved, and as a party their doctrine that the good of the Moslem community required obedience to the ruler of the time, even though his personal unworthiness were plain, must have had important consequences throughout Islám. The sect with which we are more nearly concerned is that of the Qadarites. Deriving its name from the tenet that a man possessed *qadr* or 'power' over his actions, it disappeared as a sect much earlier, it would seem, than the Murji'ites, but its teaching was destined to have far-reaching results. The story of its founding connects with the outstanding figure of Al-Hasan-al-Basri, though he was not its originator, and its principal exponents were a disciple of his called Wásil ibn-i-'Ata[2] and his disciple in the second generation Abu-Husail Muhammad-ul-Allaf. These founded the sect of the Mu'tazila or Secessionists, from an expression used by Al-Hasan-al-Basri himself. Wásil accepted the doctrines of *qadr* and of faith as sufficient for salvation, but he taught that if a believer (*mo'min*) died unrepentant of great sin he went to hell but after a time would be permitted to enter heaven. Abu Husail further developed the doctrine of *qadr*. Holding that in this world man was endowed with free-will, he taught that in the next all changes were predestined. Further he rejected the evidence of tradition for things connected with *alghaib,* the unseen world,[3] and taught that it

[1] Macdonald, *op. cit.,* p. 115, says: 'Practically only the Wahhabites in Central Arabia are Hanbalites', but as literalists the Ahl-i-Hadís wherever they may be found must accept or be influenced by Hanbalite doctrine.

[2] Died 131 H. Others say that Amr-bin-Ubaid was the pupil of Al-Basri who seceded from his teaching. He died in 144 H. For a sketch of Hasan Basri's life and teachings see Claud Field, *Mystics and Saints of Islám,* p. 22*ff*.

[3] The place given to dreams in Moslem works on and means of spiritual re-union with God has puzzled some writers; *e.g.* Major J. Stephenson in his translation of the *Hadiqat*.

was not to be accepted unless among the witnesses to them there were one at least of the People of Paradise or Friends of God, some of whom, he taught, were always in the world. These are the *auliá* whose existence in the Punjab is still an important article of faith and who will be described later.

This period and the one which followed it was one of extremely acute theological speculation. How far it was due to contact with Greek thought it is impossible to gauge, but the times were the golden age of Muslim science and of broad-minded toleration. But the Mutazilite ascendancy if great was destined to be short-lived. Its chief opponent was the jurist Ahmad ibn Hanbal, who staunchly maintained the authority of tradition (*naql*) in theology as against reason (*'aql*) as he had done in law. Its decline was followed by a period of scholasticism which in turn declined, even in the writings of the devout and versatile Al-Fárábi into encyclopædism.

We now come to what Macdonald[1] calls the great mystery of Muslim history, the Fatimid movement, which certainly appears to have been one which favoured progress and enlightenment. From the earliest times the family of the Prophet had unquestionably fostered science. Obscure though the historical material may be it is amply sufficient to prove that the movement appealed largely to the educated and enlightened elements in Islám. Closely allied with the movement and with Al-Fárábi was the semi-secret society of the Ikhwán-as-safá which flourished for a brief period at Basra in the middle of the 4th century of the Hijra. Its methods resembled closely those of the Ismailians or Assassins. Its leaders raised difficulties and suggested serious questionings, and it is possible that its elevated eclecticism was the real doctrine of the Fatimids, the Ismailians, the Qarmatians and the Druses. Another eclective sect, but based on very different principles, was that of the Qarramites,[2] of which Mahmúd of Ghazni was an adherent. Murjiites in that they held faith to be only acknowledgment with the tongue, the Qarramites took the *Qurán*

ul-Hdqiqat of Hakím Abú'l Majd Majdúd Saná'i of Ghazna says: "A portion of the book (pp. 51-6) is, curiously, devoted to the interpretation of dreams; after which the author treats of the incompatibility of the two worlds, again of the abandonment of earth and self, and of the attainment of the utmost degree of self-annihilation (pp. 56-8)"—see p. xxix of the Introduction. Saná'i's chain of thought is perfectly logical as dreams are revelations or communications from the 'invisible world'. Ibn Khaldún writes on the 'Science of the interpretation of dreams' after his description of Sufiism (De Slane, *Les Prolégomènes d'Ibn Khaldoun*, III, pp. 114 *ff.*, Paris, 1868). Both writers treat the interpretation of visions as a science complete in itself. 'A cook means great riches, just as a butcher means that one's affairs are ruined. A physician is pain and sickness, especially to one who is wretched and needy. The tailor is the man in virtue of whom troubles and affliction are all changed to good fortune'; and so on with every thing and person that may be dreamt of. The unseen world has its *pír* and the *dast-i-ghaib* is a feature in countless legends of saints.

[1] *Op. cit.*, p. 165. On p. 166 he points out that Al-Ma'mun had combined the establishment of a great university at Baghdád with a favouring of the Alids and the Fatimids in Cairo used all their influence for the advancement of learning. The obscurity and paucity of the historical data are doubtless due to the fact that most of it perished with the downfall of the Fatimids and their kindred dynasties.

[2] Founded by Abu Abdullah ibn Karram, an ascetic of Seistán, who died in 256 H. 679 A.D.

in its most literal sense.[1]

By this time the doctrine of *kashf*, 'revelation', the unveiling of the mysteries which supplemented tradition and reason—*naql* and *'aql*—had been greatly expanded and developed on two sides, an ascetic and a speculative. As regards the Punjab the former was destined to be the more important. Although 'there is no monkery in Islám' it was influenced from the earliest times by the *hanífs* or recluses of pre-Muhammadan Arabia and the *sá'ihs* or 'wanderers' and *ráhibs* or monks of Christianity and other creeds. Their Muslim imitators were called Súfis, *záhids* (ascetics), *ábids* (devotees) and *walís* or saints, but these terms had also special significance as will be seen later. With
the accession of the Abbassides in 750 A.D. came a development of 132 H.
asceticism. The old believers found an outlet in the contemplative life, withdrew from the world and would have nothing to do with its rulers.[2] This spirit has unfortunately survived to the present day and leads some of the finest characters in Islám to stand rigidly aloof from civil life. The mystics of Islám are numerous and only a few of their names can be barely mentioned here. One of the earliest was Ibráhím ibn Adham, a wanderer of royal blood who drifted from Balkh to Basra and Mecca.[3] Another, Al Fudail ibn Iyaz, was a native of Khorásán.[4] These earlier ascetics were contemplative quietists. But ecstatic mysticism soon displaced quietism. The famous Ma'ruf al Karkhi[5] adopted similes from human love and earthly wine and his greater disciple Sari-as-Saqati[6] followed him. The latter is also credited with the first use of the term *tauhíd* to denote union of the soul with God.

But perhaps the greatest name in early Sufiism is that of Al-Junaid,[7] on whom no shadow of heresy ever fell. Ash-Shibli[8] was one of his disciples and in his verses the vocabulary of amorous intercourse with God is fully developed. The last of this group was Abu Talib al-Makki.[9] The earlier Súfis had fled into the wilderness from the wrath to come, and wandering singly or in companies was the special sign of the true Súfi. But they soon began to gather in little circles of disciples round a venerated Shaikh or prior, and fraternities began to form under masters like al-Junaid or as-Saqati. Monasteries were formed later, but as early as 200 H. traces of such an institution are found in
A. D. 816 Khorásán. The organization of these institutions followed later.

[1] Macdonald (*op. cit.*, p. 171) speaks of the Karramite movement as 'a frank recoil to the crudest anthropomorphism', but it must not be forgotten that under the Ghaznivides Ghazni was a brilliant centre of learning and culture.

[2] Macdonald, pp. 174-5.

[3] Died in 161 H. A long poem current in the Jumna valley describes Adham *faqir*
A. D. 777. and his marriage with a king's daughter. It doubtless preserves a tradition of this mystic For a sketch of his teaching see Field, *op. cit.*, pp. 36 *ff*. His story realls the renunciation of Buddha, and he may have been influenced by Gnostic doctrines: Nicholson, *The Mystics of Islam*, pp. 14 and 16.

803 A. D. [4] Died in 187 H.. For a sketch of his teaching see Field, *op. cit.*, pp. 46 *ff*.

816 A. D. [5] Died in 200 H.. Karkh is a suburb of Baghdád.

871 A. D. [6] Died in 257 H.

909 A. D. [7] Died in 297 H.

946 A. D. [8] Died in 334 H.. Nicholson gives many details concerning him: *op. cit.*, pp. 34-5, 48, 52, 55, 62 and 116.

996 A. D. [9] Died in 386 H.

The Súfis provoked orthodox criticism less by their theological speculations, of which Islám has generally been remarkably tolerant, than by their mode of life. Their introspective practices seem to have evoked little condemnation.[1] But their prayer-meetings or *zikrs* were fiercely attacked by the orthodox as opposed to recognised public worship. The Súfi principle of *tawakkal* or dependence upon God was also reprobated, and even the more sober Súfis approved the principle of *kasb* or industry, citing the example of the husbandman who first casts his seed into the ground and then trusts in God.

Meanwhile the speculative, theological side of Súfiism had also made
headway and when it gained the upper hand *záhid* (ascetic) and Súfi
were no longer convertible terms. This movement roused more bitter
hostility than the other in cases where its exponent was suspected of
political leanings towards the house of Ali. Abu Yazíd al-Bistámi[2]
in spite of his pantheistic leanings died unpersecuted in 261 H., but A. D. 875
al-Halláj,[3] the cotton-carder, a disciple of al-Junaid, was put to death
with great cruelty in 309 H.. What his real views and aims were
931 A. D. it is impossible to say. In spite of his assertion: 'I am the Truth'
he was defended by the great doctor al-Ghazzáli[4] who upheld his
orthodoxy, while lamenting some incautious phrases used by him.
To the Súfis he is a patron saint and martyr who represents the spirit
of revolt against formalism and dogmatic scholasticism.

The Islámic hierarchy.

The office of Qázi-ul-quzát or head of the Qázís (judges), also known as Sadr-i-Jahán, appears to have been one of considerable antiquity. It was an estalished office under the latter style at Ghazni, and at Fíruzkoh under the Ghorian Sultáns.[5] Known also at Dehli, as the

[1] There is a striking resemblance between the Súfis, seeking by patient introspection to see the actual light of God's presence in their hearts, and the Greek monks in Athos, sitting solitary in their cells and seeking the divine.

[2] For Abu Yazíd al Bistámi (Bayazíd Bustámi) see *infra*, p. 540. See also Nicholson, *op. cit.*, pp. 17 and *passim*.

[3] For a sketch of (Husain ibn) Mansúr Halláj see Field, *op. cit.*, pp. 68*ff*. His teaching was from the Moslem standpoint a heresy of the worst kind, for he preached a doctrine of personal deification, saying, *ana'l-Haqq*, 'I am God'. He held that as the humanity (*násút*) of God comprised the whole bodily and spiritual nature of man, God's *láhút*, 'divinity' could not unite with that nature except by means of an incarnation or an infusion (*hulúl*) of the divine spirit. The Hulúlis, who believe in incarnation, are repudiated by the Súfis in general quite as vehemently as by orthodox Moslems: Nicholson, *op. cit.*, pp. 150-1. The *nafs* of Halláj was seen running behind him in the shape of a dog (*ib.*, p. 40), but such an idea was not peculiar to him. His apologists have denied that his words have the meanings attributed to him.

[4] For a sketch of al-Ghazzáli see Field, *op. cit.*, pp. 106*ff*. He was a great exponent of *zikr* and anticipated Jalál-ud-dín Rúmi's teaching that this is the best of all possible worlds; evil being a part of the divine order and harmony: Nicholson, *op. cit.*, pp. 14, 46 and 96.

[5] T. N., p. 3, § 9. At Cairo the dignity of grandmaster of the lodge, *dai-'l-duát* was, frequently combined with that of *qázi-ul-quzát* or chief justiciar. Von Hammer gives the following classification of the degrees of the Assassins:—

Shaikh, grand-master.

Dai-ul-kabír, grand prior, or the *dai-ul-kirbal*, three in number who ruled the three provinces of the Assassins

Dai, master or prior, and fully initiated.

Rafík, fellows, in process of initiation who were clothed in white with red insignia.

Fidwi, *fidái*, agent or devoted one, or the young men employed to carry out secret murders who were intoxicated with *hashísh*.

Lasik, lay brother or aspirant: *History of the Assassins*, pp. 79 and 80. But *dai* appears to have been synonymous with *khalífa* and *hudshet* (*hujjat*): p. 108.

Sadr-ul-Islám, it was the principal court of justice and lawyers and learned men, whether inhabitants of the country or foreigners, were under its inspection. The Shaikh-ul-Islám, corresponding to the western Shaikh-ush-Shuyúkh, had similar jurisdiction over all *faqírs*, native or foreign.[1]

The name of the earliest holder of the office of chief Qázi is not known.

At the time of the accession of Altamsh it was held by Wajíh-ud-Dín Kásáni who, with the lawyers, first took the oath of allegiance to him.[2] A later holder of the office was the chief Qázi of Hind and Sind, Kamál-ud-Dín Muhammad, son of Burhán-ud-Dín, of Ghazni, who occupied it under Muhammad Tughlaq.[3]

In Peshávar, if anywhere, one would expect to find the Muhammad priesthood organised on regular lines. Bearing in mind that the people of this district are nearly all Sunnís and the Afgháns generally of the Hanafi sect[4] it is not surprising to find the clergy fairly well organised. The *mulláhs* or priests, as distinguished from the *astánadárs* or holders of a place (*astán*) who may or may not be devoted to religion, are the active clergy and are divided into four classes, *viz.* the *imám*, the *mulláh* proper, the *shaikh* and the *tálib-ul-ilm*. The *imám* is merely the leader of the congregation (*jamá'at*) of a mosque in prayer, but he can hardly be described as the head official attached to it.[5] Several *mulláhs* are generally attached to each mosque and one of them generally succeeds to the office of *imám*. They also act as his deputy when absent and call the *azán*, but they are mostly occupied in teaching the village children. The Shaikh is one who having renounced worldly pleasures has become the disciple (*muríd*) of a *buzurg* or saint, while the *tálib-ul-ilm* is in theory a seeker after knowledge.

Alongside the regular clergy and independent of their organization is the hierarchy whose members are collectively styled *astánadár*, a term which implies that its holder had an ancestor who acquired the title of *zburg* or *buzurg* by holiness or miracles in life and at death left a shrine, mosque or sacred spot as a memorial or at least a reputation for sanctity. His shrine is an *astán* or *ziárat*. Any Mussalmán may

The *dai* was also called *naqíb*, but while the *dai* corresponded to time the *hujjat* corresponded to space : *Encyclopædia of Islam*, p. 895.

The people ranked below these degrees or formed the lowest of them.
Another series of Ismailian grades was:—
The Imam.
The *hujjat* or proof, designated by the Imám and also called *iade*, or seat. He corresponded to the grandmaster.
The *sumassa*, corresponding to the grand prior.
The *dai*, missioners.
The *masumi* or friends, corresponding to the *rafík*.
The *mukallabi*, or doglike, corresponding to the lay-brethren
The *mumini*, believers, or pupils : *ibid*, p. 58.

[1] E. H.I., III, pp. 578-79. According to Macdonald, *op. cit.*, p. 118, the dignity of Shaikh-ul-Islám was first created by Sultán Muhammad II in 1453. His court stands at the head of the judges of the canon law, who have jurisdiction over marriage, divorce, inheritance, and all private and family affairs. Other courts administer the custom, *urf* or *ádat*, of the country, and the will of the ruler of the country, often expressed in statutes *qánúns*.

[2] *Ib.*, p. 591.

[3] *Ib.*, pp. 590, 594.

[4] Peshávar *Gazetteer*, 1897-8, p. 110.

[5] *Ib.*, p. 112.

become the founder of such a family of *astánadárs*, but the Afgháns recognise four classes among them whose precedence is based on descent. First come the Sayyids, always addressed as 'Sháh' and claiming sacred descent. Next come the *pírs*, descendants of Afgháns, addressed as *bádsháh* and endowed with many privileges including the *entrée* to the women's apartments. Third come the *miáns* whose ancestors were not Afgháns but *hamsáyas*, enjoying similar privileges except the right of *entrée* specified. Last come the *sáhibzádas*, of a somewhat lower sanctity and less numerous though more wealthy than the *pírs* and *miáns*. Practically synonymous with *sáhibzáda* is the term *akhúndzáda*. These terms do not denote the sect of the holder. For instance, the *pír* Abdul Waháb was an *ahl-i-hadís* by sect and was called the Manki *mulláh* from his residence at Manki in Naushahra tahsíl.[1]

The famous *akhúnd* of Swát Abdul Ghafúr was a Gujar who earned that title by his learning and his descendants are styled *Akhúndzáda* or collectively *Akhúnd Khel*. The latter term is applied to many Awáns and Gujars who have little claim to the title, but who very often pretend to be Sayyids. They cannot be correctly classed as *mulláhs* as they perform no priestly functions but cultivate land or graze cattle like Paṭháns. In Hazára, however, any one who has studied the religious books of Islám appears to be styled *mulláh* or among the Afghán tribes *akhúndzáda*.[2]

Less than half a century after the Hijra the first Moslem anchorite appeared in southern Arabia. This was Awís or Ovais bin Umr, called al-Karani, from Karn his birthplace in Yemen. By command of the archangel Gabriel whom he saw is a dream Ovais abandoned the world and led in the desert a life of contemplation and penitence— 639-59 H. His followers became the Awísia or Ovaïssi order, and in memory of the two teeth lost by the Prophet at the battle of Ohod Ovais had all his removed and imposed on them the same sacrifice.[3] In the pedigrees of the Paṭháns the name of a Sultán Wais or Uvais appears and this may signify their spiritual descent from this hermit.

But the mystic teachers of Islám form two great schools, according to the two-fold system of purification which they inculcate. The interiorists or Bátinia, themselves sub-divided into two classes, form one school and the Záhiria or 'exteriorists' the other. The first sub-class of the former starts with the consciousness of man that he is constantly seen and observed by God. In consequence the ascetic watches his heart lest it be invaded by worldly thoughts. Thus the divine majesty displays itself to him in all its splendour and the ecstacy which its sight produces leads the mystic to the very sight of his *shaikh*. For the more advanced a shorter method is indicated, but it does not differ from the former in principle or results. In the second sub-class the contemplative method is more physiological and less abstract, but the object in view is the same, *viz.* absorption in God. To attain it the aspirant must engrave on his mind the image of his *shaikh* and regard it as his right shoulder. Thence he must trace a line to his heart, destined to give passage to his *shaikh's* spirit, so that he may come and take possession

[1] Peshâwar *Gazetteer*, pp. 144-5.
[2] Hazára *Gazetteer*, 1883-4, p. 59.
[3] Petit, *Les Confréries Musulmanes*, Paris, 1902, p. 6.

of that organ. By repetition the religious chief invoked absorbs the aspirant in the fullness of his being. The Zábiríás instead of aiming at absorption in the Divine by quietism aspire to attain it by voiced prayers designed to drown the spirit in the ocean of the divine being. The most efficacious of their formulas is of course the *Lá-iláha-ill-Alláh*. To obtain the desired result by its recital the eyes must be closed, the lips shut, the tongue folded back against the palate and the hands held against the thighs—in the ordinary attitude of prayer. The formula is repeated while the breath is held and the head turned alternately to the left and right. All the Islámic orders have adopted one or the other of these two methods, so that all are in some degree either interiorists or exteriorists; but the Naqshbandís allow both of them simultaneously.[1]

Rose, § 48. *The Shi'a tenets.*—The *usúl* or fundamental tenets of the Shi'ás or 'followers' of Ali are five:—(1) the unity of God, (2) his justness, (3) the divine mission of all the prophets, of whom Muhammad is the chief, (4) to consider Ali the Khalífa and his descendants from Hasan to 'Al-Mahdi,' the 12 Imáms, and (5) the resurrection. Of these the fourth has led to the greatest dissensions in Islám. It is based on the doctrine of appointment (*alqá'ilú ı bilanas*) held by the *ahl-i-Imámia* as adherents of Ali and the holy children of Fátima as contrasted with the *ashâb ul-ikhtiar*) or doctrine of election held by the *khawárij* Murjia, some of the Mutazala, and a section of the Zaidia.[2] The Shi'a doctrines thus rest generally speaking on the absolute sanctity of the descendants of Ali to whom in consequence almost divine honours are paid: the Sunnís, while respecting the house of Ali, accord them no authority, and thus the tenets of the two great sects are irreconcilable. Yet so deeply rooted is this belief in inherited sanctity that the Sunnis hold in theory that the Khalífa must be of the Quraish tribe, though in practice the rule has never been observed. This doctrine of inherited sanctity is dependent on, or at least closely connected with, the belief in the metempsychosis, and has rendered it possible for the Shi'a sect to admit of many developments, so that from the cardinal tenet of the unity of God was eventually evolved a system of pantheism. This was due, probably, to the introduction of the Súfi doctrines, which occurred in the second century of the Hijra, and had been preceded even then by an earlier mysticism. The initial inspiration (*ilhám*) is gained by repeating in absolute seclusion the name of Allah, until the utterance becomes mechanical, and then divine enlightenment ensues, as in the *yoga*. The esoteric teaching of the Súfis compares sensuality to ecstasy, and in this too has analogies in the Sháktak practices. As an organization Sufiism recognizes two grades, persons of admitted piety and acknowledged sanctity, being divided into two classes, *viz.* :—(1) the *mujas*, or those who are authorized to establish *bai'at*,[3] or spiritual discipleship, and (2) the *ghair-mujas* or those not

[1] Petit, *op. cit.*, pp. 85-87.

[2] For a sketch of the philosophy of the Muta'zalas see Amír Ali, *op. cit.*, p. 335*ff*. The term Qadaria was applied by their opponents to the extreme Mutazilas who held the doctrine of *tafwis* or absolute liberty (free-will).

[3] For a note on *bai'at* or self-surrender see end of this section. Latter-day Shi'aism is essentially quietist and the Ním or Khafif Shi'as are hardly to be distinguished from the Sunnís: Multán *Gazetteer*, p. 119.

so authorized, who are engaged only in the amelioration of *nafs* or self. The *Qurán* is valued as a divine revelation, but in practice the voice of the *pír* or spiritual director is substituted for it, and the *muríd* or disciple has no further responsibility. Here again we find a resemblance to the *Gurú-sikhi* system of spiritual relationship in Sikhism.

The Shi'a sects.—The doctrine of the Imamate contained within it the germs of schism. The Imamate being a light (*núr*) which passes (by natural descent) from one to the other, the Imáms are prophets and divine, and this heritage is inalienable. Thus the second Imám, Hasan, the eldest son of Ali, could resign his title of Khalífa, but not his Imámat which had descended to him and on his death passed by his inheritance to Husain. Its subsequent devolution followed the natural line of descent, thus :— Rose, § 44.

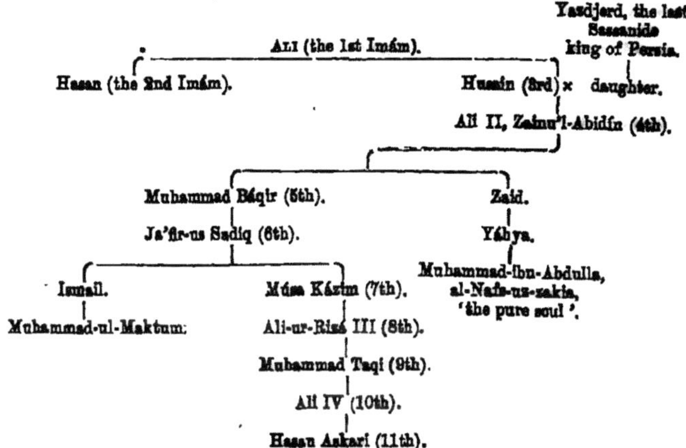

In the time of Ali II, the fourth Imám, the Imamites, as we may term the Shi'as, formed themselves into a secret order, with a series of seven degrees, into each of which its votaries were formally initiated. This movement transformed the Shi'a sect or faction into a secret society, or group of societies, and had far-reaching results, though at first it appears to have been merely a measure of self-defence against the oppression of the Sunni sect. It was soon followed by the great Shi'a schism, which arose out of a dispute as to the succession to the Imamate. Jáfir, the sixth Imám, nominated Ismail, his eldest son, but on the latter's premature death he declared that Músa was his heir, to the exclusion of Ismaíl's children. The succession to the Imamate was thus governed by the usual rules of inheritance, the uncertainty of which has so often led to fratricide and civil war in eastern empires. The claims of Ismaíl were supported by one party among the Shi'as, despite the declaration of Jáfir, and thus was founded the Ismailía sect. The other party, the Imamites, supported the claims of Músa, and this sect of the Shi'as believes that the twelfth Imám, Muhammad, is still alive, that he wanders over the earth, and is destined to re-appear. The Ismailians on the other hand hold that the last visible Imám was Ismaíl, after whom commenced the succession of the concealed Imáms. And to go back for a moment the Nosairians held that Ali was the last, as well as the first, Imám, and it thus appears that the Shi'a sects originated, historically, in divergent views as to the personal claims of the Prophet's natural descendants to succeed to the Imamate.

Rose, § 45. *The Ismailians.*—The history of the Ismailians is of great interest not only in itself but also in that the tenets of the sect are still a living force in the Muhammadanism of this part of India. The sect was also called Sabiún because it acknowledged seven Imáms, ending with Ja'far-us-Sádiq and Ismaíl; and yet it held that the Imamate descended to Ismaíl's son, etc.. History does not tell us what became of the children of Ismaíl, but their sacred character lent itself to the foundation of one of the most remarkable and important organizations known to history. The Ismailians were first organised by Abdullah, a native of the Persian province of Khuzistán, who retained or revived the organization of the sect into orders which had been introduced in the time of the fourth Imám. His successors however gave an entirely new character to the sect. The descendant—probably a spiritual not a natural descendant—of Abdullah the Ismailian proclaimed himself the legitimate descendant of Ali and Fátima, and assuming the title of Al-Mahdi, usually given to the last Imám, founded the Fatimite dynasty in Egypt. His descendant Muhammad-ibn-Ismaíl indeed went a step further and accepted the doctrine that the Khalífa was an incarnation of the invisible Imám and as such a god on earth, abandoning apparently the pretence of actual descent from Ali. To this teaching the sect of the Druses owes, in some obscure way, its origin, and the idea that the Mahdi need not necessarily be re-incarnated in a descendant of Ali was fruitful in its results, for to it may be traced the claims of various Imáms to that title. In India Shaikh Alai of Agra claimed to be Al-Mahdi and as among his disciples was Shaikh Mubárik, the father of Abdul Faiz, the *wazír* of Akbar, it is probable that that emperor was greatly influenced by Mahdavi ideas. To the same teaching may be ascribed the origin of the Bábi sect in modern Persia, whose doctrines appear not to have penetrated to India, and various other movements in the Muhammadan world.

When the fortunes of the Western or Egyptian Ismailians were on the wane, the sect was revived, in Syria, by Hasan Ibn Sabáh,[1] who was like Umr Khayyám a companion and protégé of Nizám-ul-Mulk, *wazír* of Alp Arslan, Seljuk. Hasan reorganized the order, which he divided into four[2] grades, the *fidwi*, or 'consecrated,' *rafík*, *dai*, and

[1] His full name was Alá-ud-Dín, Hasan, son of Ali, son of Muhammad, son of Jáfar son of Husain, son of Muhammad, who claimed descent from us-Sabbáh-ul-Hamairi: Raverty, *Tabaqát-i-Násiri*, II, p. 1187.

[2] Other authorities say seven but Amír Ali says that the Eastern Ismailians (Alamútias or Muláhides of Kohistán) had four degrees. He ascribes the foundation of the Eastern Ismailians to Abdulla Ibn Maimún, a Magian according to his enemies, a descendant of Ali according to his followers. Amír Ali traces his sect to the Manichaeans through the Paulicians. It branched off into sub-sects:—(i) The Egyptian Fatimites held that Ismaíl was not the last Imám, the Imám having re-appeared in Obaidulláh-al-Mahdi, Abu Muhammad Abdulláh, the son of Muhammad-al-Habíb, the last revealed Imám: (ii) The Qaramitas (Qarmatians), founded by Hamadán: pp. 308-7.

a fourth, and which became popularly known as the Hashishi, or hemp-eaters, a term soon corrupted into Assassin in the European languages. Of this order Hasan was the first Shaikh, or chief, a title somewhat unfortunately translated Grand Master, seeing that the Shaikh claimed to be—at least in the person of Muhammad Kiah, the third Shaikh—an incarnation of the concealed Imám, wielding supernatural powers, and not merely the head of a militant religious order.

From their stronghold at Alamút in the Elburz[1] the Shaikhs dominated Muhammadan Asia, by a perfectly organized system of assassination during a century and a half, until, towards the close of the thirteenth century, the last Shaikh was overthrown by Húláku Khán, the descendant of Zenghiz Khán. The sect however was not exterminated, and, though it had lost its power, continued to exist, but rather as a sub-sect of the Ismailians than as an independent organization, in Irak and the anti-Libanus. Its present head, a lineal descendant of the fourth[2] Shaikh, is His Highness the Agha Khán of Bombay, who has a considerable following in the Punjab and the regions of the Hindu Kush.

SHI'A DISSENT.

The Shi'as have however themselves suffered from dissents and dissenters from their dissent are called *rawáfiz*[3] who are also styled Zaidias. The Imamate passed, according to one branch of the Zaidias,[4] from Ibrahím to Idris, the founder of the Idriside dynasty of Mauritania.

Other dissenting Shi'as are the *ghair-mukallad* or Rafi-ud-dín, and the *mukalladin*. The former make movements[5] while praying etc., and after praise of God repeat the *amin* aloud. These two sects do not pray together and indeed the *ghair-mukallad*, whose head-quarters are at Delhi under Názir Husain, have a separate mosque at Bhiwáni.

Lastly the Jibriyas[6] had a preceptor at Hánsi in Saráj-ul-Haq—a descendant of the four Qutbs. He was against both Shi'as and Sunnís, and his followers reason away the *Qurán* and the *hadís* and believe that they will go to Heaven however sinful they may have been.

[1] Elburz, the Sanskrit Haraithi, would seem to have been famous for its hemp (*Soma*) in Vedic times: Oldenberg, *Religion der Veda*, p. 178. Elburz means 'eagle's nest,' in Turki. Amír Ali describes it as 'near Kaswin in Upper Persia'.

[2] The fourth Grand Master was the Ala-Zakrihi-us-Salám, 'Zikr-us-Salám', and from him the Agha Khán is descended: Sir Amír Ali, *The Spirit of Islam*, p. 313. Some authorities say he was descended from the fifth Imám.

[3] See under Ráfizi, Vol. III, p. 268, *infra*.

[4] Further the Zaidias split into four sub-sects:—

(*i*) Járudias, who deny the succession of Isa, maintaining the claims of Muhammad Nafs-uz-zakiya.

(*ii*) Sulaimánias, who preach a secular Imámate.

(*iii*) Tabarias, } who accept as rightful the *khiláfat* of Abu Bakr and Umr,
(*iv*) Sálehias, } but not that of Osmán: *Spirit of Islam*, pp. 294-5.

[5] At one time they stretch their hands outwards, at another they fold them down, keeping the fingers straight in the direction of the Kaaba.

[6] The Jabarias are a very ancient sect in Islám. They were rigid adherents of the doctrine of predestination: Amír Ali, *op. cit.*, pp. 331-2. They had three sects, and at least two off-shoots, the Sifátias, 'attributists', and the Mushabbahas.

A priest, one Isá Qázi, a follower of this sect in Toshám, was dismissed from his post as being unorthodox.

THE SECTS AND ORDERS IN ISLÁM.

'IT is a fairly safe rule', writes Lukach, 'to measure the unorthodoxy of a Moslem sect by the extent to which it exalts Ali', but in Moslem dissent there are many varieties of belief. The Shi'as who prefer the term Imám to that of Khalífa include many sects of which the Imámía may be regarded as orthodox Shi'as. They believe in a succession of 12 Imáms of whom Ali, his sons Hasan and Husain were the first and the last named's direct descendant Muhammad Abu'l-Qásim the last. But he is believed to be not dead and is destined to reappear in the last days to rule the world, for seven years with the title of Imám-ul-Mahdi or the Imám or 'Director'.[1]

The Shi'as proper are Asna-a'asharias, 'duo-decemians' as they believe in the twelve Imáms, but they are now called Shia's or Imámías *par excellence*. At an early period they were divided into two main sects or schools, the *usúli* guided by principles, and the *akhbári* or traditionists.[2] Other Shi'a sects were the Kaisánías and Hashimías (now extinct), the Ghállías or Ghullát—extravagantists, really descendants of the Gnostics—and the Nusairís who believed in the divinity of Ali while the Ishákías, Numánías and Khitábías were anthropomorphists, believers in incarnations and the metempsychosis.[3]

According to von Noer Mukhtár-ibn-Abaid's heretical hordes followed a decorated chair said to be Ali's, and so too Umer Roshanía had Báyazíd's bones placed in an ark and borne before him in battle etc.: II, p. 169. Amír Ali says the Roshanías were the exact counterpart of the Illuminati of Christendom and that Báyazíd, an Afghán of Arab extraction, acquired a taint of Manichæism from the Ismailías who still flourished in the hills of Khorásán. His later teaching was that all existing objects are but forms of the Deity, that the *pír* represented Him and that the ordinances of the law have a mystical meaning: perfection being once attained through the *pír's* instructions and religious exercises, its exterior ordinances cease to be binding: numbers of Ismailians are to be found in Gilgit and Hunza: *op. cit.*, pages 314-15.

It is often said that Islám has 72 sects, but each sect asserts that all of them have gone astray and that the only true order is itself the 73rd, the *firqat-i-naját* or party of salvation. This accords with Muhammad's prophecy that his followers would separate into 73 sects and that of these all but one, the Nájía or 'Saved Ones', would go to hell.[4]

[1] Lukach, *Fringe of the East*, pp. 209, 211.

[2] Amír Ali, *op. cit.*, p. 313.

[3] *Ib.*, p. 314. Some popular Shi'a beliefs seem to be based on their theological doctrines, *e.g.*—

A Shi'a if offered bread divided into four parts will not eat it, possibly because he suspects the giver of wishing to make a Sunni of him, as Sunnis believe in four Khalífas while Shi'as only acknowledge one: P. N. Q., I, § 538.

Shi'as do not eat the hare because it was originally born of a woman and they say that by washing its flesh all runs away in the water, leaving only the bones: *Ib.*, II, § 990—see I, § 108.

[4] *Fringe of the East*, p. 151.

SUFIISM.

In the belief of the orthodox Sunni sect itself the instruction imparted by the Prophet was of two kinds:—

1. *Ilm-i-záhir* or knowledge of the rules and regulations of religion by books. Those learned in this knowledge are called *mulláhs* and *maulavís*.
2. *Ilm-i-bátin* or the concentration of the mind on God by worship. Those who apply their minds in this concentration call themselves Súfi.

The best Súfís of one class can impart instruction according to the methods of another class also, but ordinary people should adopt the tenets of one class only.

Another definition is that:—"Those Muhammadans who follow *tasawwuf*, the theology of the Súfís or contemplation, are called Súfís"

They have four *pirs* as follow:—

1. Imám Hasan.
2. Imám Husain.
3. Imám Hasan Basri.
4. Qumail, son of Zyád.

The principal obstacles to a clear description of the Súfi doctrines are the fact that the term is applied generically to a number of orders and sects which differ widely in their practices and tenets, and the failure of writers on Sufiism to distinguish between those bodies when describing them.

The term Súfi is derived from *súf*, 'wool'[1], but this is not inconsistent with a theory that it was originally an adaptation of the Greek *sophos*. The term appears to have been first applied to wandering monks who wore woollen garments in imitation of the Christian *ráhibs* or the Arabian *hanífs*, a theory open to the obvious objection that wool is not proved to have been worn by either of those classes in climates where it would be a penance to wear it, and where its use cannot have been very common.

With a vague tradition that the original order was the Sabátia, the ancient Sabians, the Súfís were early divided into two orders, or schools, the Hulúlia or inspired which held that the divine spirit enters into all who are devout, and the Ittiháadia, or unionists who hold that the soul by union with God becomes God.[2]

From these two schools sprang five sub-orders, *viz.*—

The Wáslia, 'joined' to God.
'Ashaqia, 'lovers' of God.
Talqínia, 'instructed'.
Zakia, 'penetrated'.
Wáhidia, 'solitary'.

[1] Macdonald, *Muslim Theology*, p. 130. E. B. Havell has called attention to the fact that the word *urna*, which in Buddhist (and other) images symbolised the divine eye, literally meant 'wool'. But his explanation that the Divine Light was conceived as converging towards the centre of Buddha's forehead and so suggested a tuft of wool seems far-fetched: *The Ideals of Indian Art*, pp. 50-1.

[2] God is joined with every sentient being. He is as flame and the soul as charcoal. Brown (*The Dervishes*, p. 58) gives all these seven orders, but calls the Wáslia 'Wasúlia', the Zakia 'Zarkia' and the Wáhidia 'Wahdattia'.

The term Bátinia, 'esoteric', is applied to several Súfi sects[1], and, according to Wilberforce Clarke, to the order of the Assassins. No general doctrine corresponds to this name, each sect having tenets of its own, but some of the ideas belonging to it recall the system of Avicenna. 'All that proceeds from truth will be united in the universal soul, and all that partakes of the nature of evil will return to Satan, *i.e.* to nothingness. This is what sectarians call the Resurrection'.

The Súfís acknowledge four stages, material or outward observance—*pardakht jismáni* :—

tariqat, the path,
m'arifat, divine knowledge or intuition,
haqiqat, truth, and
wasl, union.

The organization of religious institutions in Islám dates from a very early period. Although in Islám is no monachism,[2] in the 2nd year of the Hijra (=623 A. D.) 45 men of Mecca and as many of Medína joined themselves together, took an oath of fidelity to the doctrines of the Prophet, and formed a fraternity to establish community of property and to perform daily penances. They are said to have taken the name of *súfi*, but it is also said that that term was first employed by Abú Háshim, a Syrian *záhid* who died in 780 A. D. However this may be, during Muhammad's lifetime Abu Bakr, afterwards the first Khalífa, and Ali had established *jamá'at*, 'assemblies', wherein vows were made and exercises practised; and in 657 A. D. Uvais-i-Karáni had established the first religious order of the greatest austerity. Abu Háshim appears to have built the first *takia*, 'convent'.

The institution of the *khánqáh*, a term also translated convent, is of unknown origin but its constitution is recorded. The men of it form two parties, the travellers and the dwellers. After a stay of three days the former must seek service in the *khánqáh*, unless their time be spent in devotion. The dwellers are again divided into three groups, the *ahl-i-khidmat* or servitors, the *ahl-i-suhbat* or associates and the *ahl-i-khilwat* or recluses. The first-named are novices who do service in order to become acceptable to the men 'of deeds and of stages', *i.e.* to those who are engaged in practices and have advanced some stages on the path or way. By service they acquire fitness for 'kinship', *i.e.* admission to the next degree in the order, and thus become a slipper out of the garment of alienation and of farness, *i.e.* put off the garment of separation from the Divine. Abu Yakúb, Súsi, commends retreat (*khilwat*) to the old and *suhbat* to the young. Some convents at any rate insisted on fitness for service by outward resemblance and inward and pure desire—whereby the candidate acquired kinship with *súfis*. Exclusion was inflicted as a punishment, but the seeker of the pardon

[1] It was also applied to sects outside Islám, such as the Mazdakites, a Manichæan sect. In Iráq the Bátinites were called Qarmatians and Mazdakites, in Khorásán Ta'limites and Malhids: *Encyclopædia of Islam*, p. 679.

[2] Wilberforce Clarke, II, p. 952. *The Awárif'ul-Ma'árif*, p. 1.

could be re-admitted on payment of a fine (*gharámat*) which took the form of victuals.

Khánqáhs were sometimes endowed, and sometimes not. If endowed and it was the testator's wish that the income of the convent should be spent on the purposes of the lords of desire, *i.e.* those who have mastered their passions, and on travellers by the path (*tariqat*) it was unlawful to expend it on the habituated, *i.e.* on professional beggars, or the crowd that from bodily sins or attachment to the world had not attained to the stages of the heart, advanced, that is, along the path of spirituality. These provisions were clearly intended to secure the proper administration of *waqf* or trust properties and guard against abuses like those which fostered the sturdy mendicancy of the Middle Ages in Europe.

Khánqáhs without an endowment were ruled by the head or if the brotherhood had no head (*shaikh*) it had a discretion, like a head who could direct the brethren to abandon *kasb*[1] and, putting them on *tawakkul*, bid them rely on alms for their subsistence. To brotherhoods, not under a *shaikh's* headship, whose members were 'of the crowd of strong and of travellers', who formed, that is to say, a body of able-bodied wandering *faqírs*, the latter course is commended, but weaker brotherhoods could choose either *kasb* or mendicancy.

It is curious to observe the transformation in meaning which the term *khánqáh* has undergone. It now means ordinarily a tomb, especially that of a *pír* or *faqír*, a saint or holy man, not necessarily one of the regular clergy. Such *khánqáhs* become surrounded by trees as no one dare cut one down or even remove fallen wood from a *faqír's* grave. They also tend to become sanctuaries for property as no one will venture to steal in the vicinity of a *faqír's* tomb. The tomb may be merely a grave of earth, but is more often a pile of stones or bricks, with a wall to enclose the grave. As it is usual to make vows (*mannat*) to such tombs, branches of the trees above them are often full of rags (*barak*) tied to the twigs ; or if a specific prayer has been answered appropriate offerings are hung up, such as a cradle for a child bestowed, a halter for a stolen bullock recovered and so on. A *khánqáh* too may itself cure disease. Thus one at Ishar in Sháhpur is famous for the cure of toothache and ague. The sufferer throws cowries down at the grave and his pain does not recur for as many years as he presents cowries.

But a shrine is not necessarily a tomb and must be distinguished from it. Thus above Kathwái in the Salt Range is a shrine to Gorra, ancestor of all the local Awáns. As he passes it an Awán vows to put up a stone there if successful in his journey and so the trees around are full of such stones.[2]

The adoption of the *khirqa* or *darvesh's* mantle is not prescribed by the *sunnat* but only by the *hadís* or tradition of Umm-i-Khálid. The *khirqa* is of two kinds, that of desire and that of blessing. When

[1] W. Clarke translates *kasb* by 'acquisition', but it clearly means 'industry' in this context: see Catafago's *Arabic Dicty.*, p. 805. Industry was permissible just as it was and is to certain religious orders in Christendom. Macdonald translates *kasb* by 'gaining of daily bread by labour': *op. cit.*, p. 179.

[2] Shahpur *Gaz.*, 1897, p. 86.

the *shaikh* is convinced of the *muríd's* desire for God he indues him with the former.* The latter is bestowed upon him who with the *shaikhs* hath a good repute. To these two some add a third, the *khirqa* of holiness, which is bestowed when the *shaikh* wishes to appoint a *muríd* his own *khalífa*. Thus the *khirqa* is a mark of initiation into an order and may also be given to designate the right of its recipient to succeed the *shaikh* in his office.

The rules as to the colours of the *khirqa* are elastic. The form and colour of the *muríd's* garment depend on the *shaikh's* intuition. If he sees him inclined to fine raiment he makes him don the coarse *khirqa* of grass, but if he finds him disposed to hypocrisy and ostentation he clothes him in soft silk. He forbids him any fashion or colour which he would affect. The white garment prescribed by the *sunnat* is only for *shaikhs* that have gained freedom from *nafs*, the lusts of the flesh. The coloured garment is chosen for others as less time is required for its cleansing than would be taken up by white raiment, and blue is the choice of the Súfís, though black is better against defilement, because that colour is fit only for him who is sunk in the darkness of lust. In the flame of the candle one part is pure light and the other pure darkness. The place of their union appeareth blue and that colour is suitable to the *hál* or 'mystic state' of the Súfi.

Each order has moreover its distinctive *khirqa*. Thus in Egypt the Rafa'i wore a black turban with a red edging at one end.[1] The patched *khirqa* or *muraqqa'at* is the outward sign that the mystic has emerged from discipline of the 'Path' and is advancing with uncertain steps towards the Light, as when a toil-worn traveller having gained the summit of a deep gorge, suddenly catches a glimpse of the sun and covers his eyes.[2] But the traditional and more probable explanation of the patched garment ascribes it to the Prophet's *mihráj* on ascension, when the angel Gabriel showed him a coffer full of garments of many colours. The Prophet took these robes and divided them among his companions who transmitted them to their heirs, thus giving rise to the Islamic practice of bestowing garments or patches of them to consecrate the bonds which unite the master to his disciples.[3] The rending of the *khirqa* also has a mystical significance.

Zikr is the repeating of the name of the God, the profession of His unity etc. in chorus, accompanied by certain motions of the head, hands, or whole body. It is performed near a saint's tomb, in a sepulchral *masjid* or in a private chamber, and generally on the occasion of a nativity (*maulúd*).

Most of the orders distinguish between the daily *zikr* or *zikr-ul-auqát* and the 'solemn' *zikr-ul-jallála*. The former is recited silently, after each of the five daily prayers. The latter is used at ceremonies of the cult, especially at those observed on Friday. The Khálidia, a Turkish branch of the Naqshbandís, has adopted almost exclusively the *zikr-ul-kháfi* or mental and silent *zikr*.[4] But the Naqshbandís

[1] Petit, *op. cit.*, p. 44.
[2] Nicholson, *The Mystics of Islam*, p. 49.
[3] Petit, *op. cit.*, p. 44.
[4] Petit, *op. cit.*, pp. 48-51.

generally belong to the Záhiriá school and so they especially affect a deep-toned *zikr*.[1]

The *zákirs* sit cross-legged, in a circle, within which are four candles. At one end of it are the *murshids* (verse-reciters) and the player on the flute (*nai*). The *shaikh* of the *zákirs* exclaims *al Fátiha* and all recite that, the opening chapter of the *Qurán*. Then begins the *zikr* proper. 'There is no God but God' is chanted to different measures, first sitting then standing. Before the end of the *majlis*, as the whole performance is called, the *zákirs* ejaculate the words rapidly, turning their heads violently, shaking the whole body, and leaping.

The recitation of the whole of the *Qurán* is called *khatm* and is performed by *faqihs*. When performed after a death its merit is transferred to the soul of the deceased.

Peregrination (*safr*) is commended as spirtually beneficial and the Sufís are in sympathy with Isá (Christ) because throughout His life he was in *safr*. Twelve rules are laid down for the guidance of pilgrims.

The men of this path, the path of the Súfi, are of three grades, the *mubtadiyán* or beginners, whose will is surrendered to the *shaikh* and to whom no raiment, goods or aught else is lawful save by his desire : the *mutawassitán* or middle ones, who have surrendered their will to God and who submit, as occasion demands : and the *muntahiyán* or perfected who, by God's will, are absolute, what they choose being His will.

Observing retreat (*khilwat*) in the way of the Súfís is another innovation on the *sunnat*, although Muhammad himself used to practise it in the caves of Hara, passing nights there in *zikr* and devotion. Retreat for 40 days lifts every day a veil which keeps one separated from the hidden world. It should be observed once a year and consists in a collection of practices hostile to *nafs* and in austerities (*riázat*) such as eating and speaking little, shunning companionship, perseverance in *zikr*, denying thoughts and steadfast awed contemplation. But in the opinion of the Súfis *khilwat* is not restricted to 40 days. The practice of *khilwat* translates into action, so to speak the renunciation of the world (*ázalat án un-nás*), the vigil, *as-sahr*, and abstenance, *as-siám*. Naturally it has endless variations among the different orders.[2]

To a beginner it is prescribed that he should confine himself to divine precepts, the *sunnat* of prayer and, at other times, *zikr*. For a middle one assiduity in reciting the *Qurán* after the performance of divine precepts is best.

The *zunnár* in Súfi parlance means something whereby they may attain oneness. Háfiz alludes to it in the story of Shaikh Saná'n, a Qalandar who in the paths of wandering or apostacy held mention of the rosary of the King, in the girdle of the *zunnár*. Being in love with a Christian damsel he left Islám and took to music, wine and swine-herding but he put on the religious cord,[3] strove to be even

[1] Petit, *op. cit.*, p. 52.

[2] Petit, *op. cit.*, pp. 48-9.

[3] The passage in the *Divan* (I, p. 170) is obscure. Apparently the religious girdle of a Christian order is alluded to. Shaikh Saná'n however never abandoned the Muslim rosary of 99 beads (p. 169). Elsewhere Háfiz calls the patched garment the *zunnár* of the 'way' (*tariqat*) : II, p. 807.

as the beloved (Christian) and within the religious cord mentioned his love (of God ?). He had been influenced by the evil prayer of Ghaus-ul-'azam, but was brought to Islám by an invisible hand and with his beloved made a pilgrimage to Mecca.

The institution known as *pír murídi* in the Punjab is typical of Sufiism though it cannot be said with certainty to be confined to it. The *pír* is also known as *murshid* and corresponds to the *shaikh* of the Súfi. Next in order to a prophet ranks the *shaikh*, a term which signifies being a *khalífa*, a deputy or vicar whose duty it is to call men by the path of Muhammad to God. His condition is called *shuyukhiyat* and 15 admirable rules are laid down for his guidance in relation to his *muríd*. He must show no greed for his property or services.

The *murshid* is also called, mystically, the *sáqi* or cup-bearer, the *mutrib* or minstrel.

The perfect *murshid* is termed the vintner, *khammár*.

The *murshid* of love who calleth the disciples to the path of God is called the *malláh*, sailor.

Jibrá'il, Muhammad's *murshid*, has his mansion in Sidra, the tree of Paradise which is sometimes identified with the Túha or lotus tree (*Zizyphus Lotus*), but more generally with the tree of Paradise. Sámiri, a sorcerer of Sámra, cast dust from Jibrá'il's path into a calf of silver and gold, whereby it became alive and spoke: I, p. 311: *cf.* Exodus VI, 1-6.

Thus in Muzaffargarh every Muhammadan has a *pír*, but he need not be learned or even of known piety—indeed many are notoriously immoral. But he should have a reputation for being able to secure the objects of his *muríd's* vows. The *pír* is commonly chosen by lot. The *muríd* secures his *pír's* intercession by an annual offering called *buhal* which is collected by the *pír* himself or his deputies in the most shameless way, even force being resorted to.[1]

Súfi Literature.

There are hundreds of books on Sufiism, in Arabic, Persian and Urdu. The most important and generally recognized are :—the *Fasús-ul-Hikam*, *Tafsír-ul-Qurán* and *Futúhát-i-Makki*, in Arabic, by Shaikh Muhy-ud-dín, ibn-'Arabi: the *Díwán*, *Lawáiha* and *Rubá'iyát* (in Persian) by Abdur Rahmán Jámí: the *Kashf-ul-Mahjúb* by Shaikh 'Alí Hajwírí: the *Mathnawí* (in Persian) by Maulavi Rúmí: the *'Awárif-ul-Ma'árif* (in Persian) by Khawája Shaháb-ud-Dín, Suhrwardí: the *Tazkirát-ul-Auliyá*, *Iláhi Náma*, *Baisar Náma*, *Jauhar-uz-zát*, *Montaq-ut-tair* and others (in Persian) by Shaikh Faríd-ud-Dín Attár: the *Ihyá-ul-'ulúm* (in Arabic) by Imám Muhammad Ghazáli: the *Fath-ur-Rabbáni* and *Futúh-ul-ghaib* (in Arabic) by Shaikh 'Abdul Qádir Jíláni. The *Hadiqate* of Hakim Samáli is also worth mentioning.

[1] Muzaffargarh *Gazetteer*, 1883-4, p. 62: *cf.* p. 66 also. Wilberforce Clarke mentions an extreme development of the institution. An order of the Súfís called the Murtaza Sháhi make an image in clay of the *murshid*. This the *muríd* keeps to prevent him from wandering and to bring him into identity with the *murshid*: *op. cit.*, p. 10.

Some of those by authors who lived or live in the Punjab are given below, but it should be understood that the list is not at all exhaustive:—

The *Khazinat-ul-Asfiyá* by M. Ghulám Sarwar of Lahore, the *Qánún-i-'Ishq*, the commentary on the *káfis* of Hazrat Bulla Sháh of Kasúr, the *Majmú'ah-i-Qánún-i-tauhid*, the *Qánún-i-sulúk*, the *Qánún-i-m'arifat*, and a lecture on Muhammadan Súfi Philosophy by H. Anwar Alí of Rohtak, the *Tuhfat-úl-'Ashiqin*, the *Gulzár-i-faridi* and the *Kashaf-ul-mahjúb*.

A monthly journal issued at Lahore is devoted specially to the subject of Sufiism. Its name is the *Anwar-us-Súfiyah* and an association called the Anjuman Khuddam-uṣ-Sufiyah, whose president is Sayyid Háji Jamá'at Alí Sháh of Alípur Sayyidán in Pasrúr Tahsíl, Siálkot, also exists.

The older Súfi historical books are *Safinat-ul-Auliyá*, *Rauzat-ul-Asfiyá*, *Khazinat-ul-Asfiyá*, *Sair-ul-Aqtáb*, *Silsalat-ut-tahsib*, *Ganjina-i-Sarwari*, *Ihyá-ul-Ulúm* and *Kimiya-i-Sa'ádat* by Imám Muhammad Ghazáli.

A modern historical work is the *Sair-ul-Árifín* by Maulavi Ghulám Ahmad of Sambhal.

The special books of the Qádiri teaching are:—the *Guldasta-i-Karámát* of Hazrat Sháh-i-Jílán Ghauth-i-'Azam Mírán Muhy-ud-Dín (Pír Sáhib Baghdádí): the *Manáqibat* of Hazrat Mahbúb-i-Subhání the Pír Dastgír who has about 99 names: the *Manáqib-i-Hazrat Sháh Kangal* which is greatly revered in Kashmír, Káshghar and other places. Hazára.

As to the Chishtís, the only book known in Hazára is the *Ma'fúzát-i-Chisht*.

Muhammadans in general and especially the Súfís hold that the whole world is divided into circles (*wiláyat*) each in charge of a living *wali* or saint, called *sáhib-i-wiláyat*, who controls all temporal affairs therein. For instance this belief is expressly stated to prevail in the Ambála District.

The doctrine of the *aulia* appears to owe its origin to Abu Huzail Muhammad al-Allaf[1] who taught that there were at all times in the world these 'Friends of God' who were protected against all greater sins and could not lie. Their words are the basis of belief and the tradition is merely a statement of what they said. The Súfís recognised *walias* or women *walís*,[2] but none appear to be known in the modern Punjab. The last of the Muwahids or his disciples extended the doctrine and held the *wali* to be higher than the prophet, *nabi* or *rasúl*.[3] Later Islám regarded all members of a religious order as *darwesh*, but only those gifted by God with miraculous powers as *walís*.[4] But Ash-Sha'ráni[5]

[1] He died *circa* 266 H. and was a disciple in the second generation from Wásil: Macdonald, *Muslim Theology*, p. 139.

[2] *Ib.*, p. 173.

[3] *Ib.*, p. 263.

[4] *Ib.*, p. 208.

[5] *Ib.*, pp. 279 and 281-5. He was a Cairene and died in 973 H.

developed the doctrine at length, teaching that the *walís* possess a certain illumination (*ilhám*) which differs however from the inspiration of the prophets, so that they never reach their grade but must always walk according to the law of a prophet. They are all guided by God, whatever their rule or *tariqa* may be, but that of al-Junaid is the best. Their *karámát* are true miracles and are a reward of their devout toil, but the order of nature will not be broken for any one who has not achieved more than is usual in religious knowledge and exercises. All *walís* stand under a regular hierarchy headed by the Qutb, yet above him in holiness stand the Companions of the Prophet. This teaching marks a re-action from that of many Súfís who had held that the *walís* stood higher than even the prophets themselves. The Wahábís rejected the intercession of the *walís* with God, but for the body of the people lives of the *walís* abounding in tales of their miraculous achievements still command credence.

The doctrine of the *walís* was however extended by various Súfi writers on lines already familiar to us from the accounts above given of the spiritual degrees among the Ismailians. Hujweri, the great exponent of this teaching, tells us that the saints form an invisible hierarchy at whose head is the Qutb (axis), the most eminent Súfi of his age. He presides at their spiritual and miraculously convened parliaments. Below him stand the following grades in ascending order :—

Lowest of all are the 300 *akhyár* or 'good' and the 40 *abdál* (substitutes) and then come the seven *abrár* 'pious'; then four *autád* (supports) and the three *naqabá* or overseers. The members of this celestial hierarchy can only act by mutual consent, but it is the special task of the *autád* to go round the whole world every night and if on any place their eyes do not fall, some flaw appears in it next day and they must then inform the Qutb so that by his blessing the defect may be repaired.

This is Nicholson's account,[1] but other authors give variants of it. Thus Petit describes the belief that there are always a fixed number of saints on earth, 4000 according to some, only 356 according to others. Divided into seven classes, corresponding to their degrees of holiness, these privileged beings have, after this life, access to heaven and formed by their union Ghaus-ul-Alam[2] or 'refuge of the world'. At the head of the hierarchy is the Ghaus-ul-Azam or 'great refuge', the saviour whose merits can atone for the sins of others without compromising his own salvation. No one knows him, nor does he know himself. Next to him comes his *wazir*, the Qutb, the most influential saint of his generation, the pole round which humanity revolves unceasingly. More precisely he is called the Qutb-ul-Waqt, or 'Pole of the Age', or Qutb-ul-Aqtáb, 'the Pole of Poles'. Below him come the *autád* or 'pickets', one for each of the cardinal points, with Mecca for centre. Contrasted with the *autád* are the *khiár* or 'elect', only seven in number but ever on their proselytizing journeys to spread the light of Islám. Petit

[1] *The Mystics of Islam*, in the Quest Series, pp. 123-4.

[2] Ghaus is a title of Moslem saints whose limbs in the ardour of their devotion fall asunder. Its literal meaning is said to be 'redress'. Ghaus-ul-'azam was a title of Abdul Qádir Jiláni.

translates *abdál* by 'changing,' because their cadre is always fixed, and as soon as one dies another takes his place. But authorities differ as to their number, some fixing it at 70, others at 40, and some at only 7. While they live chiefly in Syria the *najab* or 'excellent', 70 in number, prefer Egypt, while the 300 *naqáb* or heads of groups protect the rest of Africa *Wali* is a title only borne by dead saints, so that it results from a kind of popular canonization.[1]

Somewhat analagous to but not apparently connected with this system of *walis* is the belief in the Pir Gháib, regarding whom Mr. Muhammad Hamíd writes:—"The Pír Gháib or Gháib Pír appears to be a name given to a class of saints whose names are not known or whose miracle it was to hide themselves from the people at some particular period of their life, or it might be that the body of the saint disappeared after his death. With the concealed Imám (Imám Mahdi), however, the Gháib Pírs do not seem to have any connection. I know of a shrine of a Gháib Pír at Jaláli (Alígarh District), whose name is not otherwise known and it is this ignorance of his name that has probably given him the epithet of Gháib Pír. Pír Gháib is the name of a place at Jullundur regarding which a remarkable legend is current. Imám Násir-ud-Dín was a native of Nákshab.[2] He lived from
252—334 H. 866-945 A. D. and came to Jullundur where he miraculously restored to a widow her son who had been buried alive beneath the walls of Jullundur as the sole means of keeping what had been built during the day from falling down at night. He afterwards converted the Jogi who had been guilty of this nefarious sacrifice. It is most meritorious to work the well near this saint's tomb during his fair and there is much rivalry among the owners of bullocks for the privilege of doing so.

The significance of this legend seems obvious. The Imám converted a people, it says, who believed in sacrificing human beings in order to supply guardian spirits to the walls of a town, saving youths from such a fate, and supplying a more efficient guardian in the Pír Ghaib. The Imám Násir-ud-Dín appears in the *Saints of Jálandhar* as Násir-ud-Dín Shírázi. To make room for the mosque erected in his memory the shrine of the Jogi Jálandhar Náth is said to have been pulled down—a highly probable tradition, though it is difficult to think that he was not earlier than Násir-ud-Dín Awadhi, the preceptor of Nizám-ud-Dín Aulia, as Temple has suggested.[3]

Súfi Orders.

The Súfís are divided into 14 orders—9 of which are Qádiria and 5 Chishtia. In the former are included the Suharwardi. These three, with the Naqshbandi and Naushábia orders or sects, are spread all over India. This classification differs somewhat from that given in Volume III, p. 431, and many differences of opinion exist as to the history of the various orders, as will be noted below. But the following pedigree

[1] *Les Confréries Musulmanes*, by the Revd. Père Louis Petit, Paris, 1902.

[2] 'A place said to be in Persia, but perhaps the same as Kárshi in Bokhára': Purser Jullundur *S. R.*, § 17, p. 58. But Nákshab is the place where the veiled prophet of Khorásán performed his miracle of making moonshine.

[3] *Legends of the Panjab*, III, pp. 158, 199.

able which traces the foundation of all the orders to natural or spiritual descendants of Ali or Abú Bakr is of some interest :—

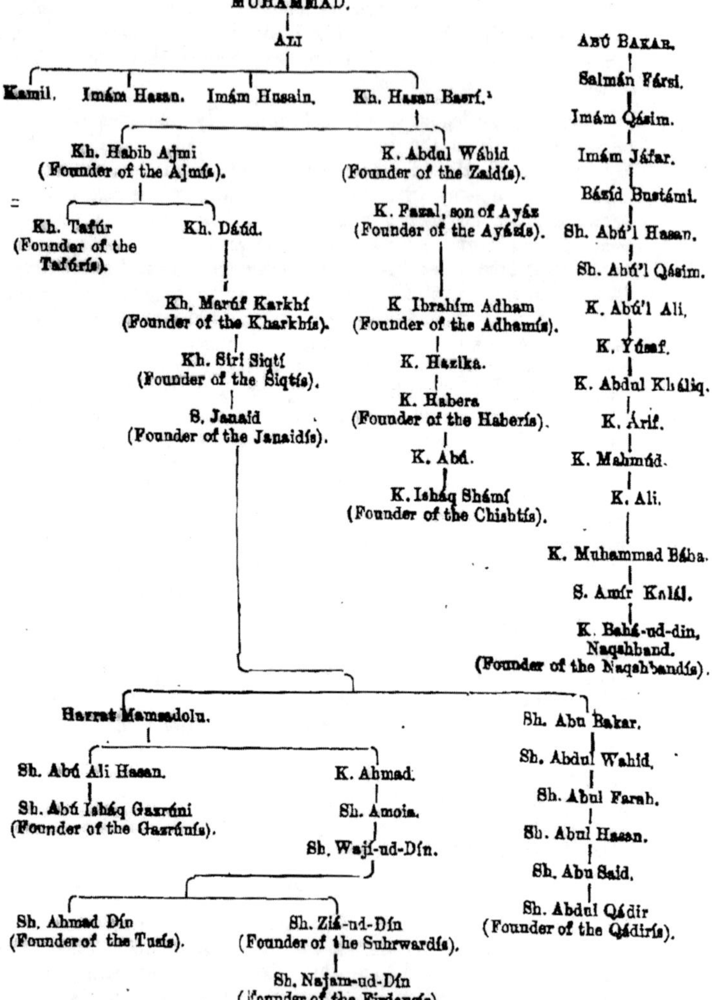

Of the four principal spiritual orders, descended from the Prophet, the Naqshbandi descends through the Caliph Abú Bakr, the Suharwardi through the Caliph Omar, and the Chishti and Qádari through the Caliph Ali. Below is given the genealogical table of the Sabiri sub-division of the Chishtís. The names are given as spiritually descended, and are not the only ones. For example Caliph Ali had many disciples besides the Imám Hasan Basri, but they have their own lines of descent and that is the case with other notables also.

[1] *N. B.*—That this table is not confined to *natural* descent but includes *spiritual* affiliation.

THE PROPHET, from whom was spiritually descended :—

Hazrat Ali (son-in-law of Prophet).

Imám Hasan Basri (of Basra).

Khwája Abdul Wáhid.

Khwája Fuzail bin Ayáz.

Sultán Ibráhím bin Adham of Balkh (the king, who abdicated his throne).

Khwája Hazifa-al-Marashi.

Kháwja Hubera-al-Basri (of Basra).

Khwája Aluv Mamshad.

Khwája Bu-al-Isháq Shámi (of Syria).

Khwája Abu Ahmad Abdál, the first Chishti (of Chisht).

Khwája Muhammad Záhid Maqbúl Chishti (of Chisht).

Khwája Yúsúf Násir-ud-Dín Chishti (of Chisht).

Khwája Qutb-ud-Dín Maudúd Chishti (of Chisht).

Khwája Háj Sharif Zindni.

Khwája Usmán Harvani,

Khwája Múin-ud-Dín Chishti (of Chisht), the saint of Ajmer.

Khwája Qutb-ud-din of Delhi, the Qutb Sáhib.

Shaikh Faríd-ud-Dín, Shakarganj, the famous Bába Faríd of Pákpattan.

Hazrat Makhdúm Alá-ud-Dín Ali Ahmad *Sábir* of Pírán Kaler (near Rurki). His spiritual descendants are called *Sábiris*.

Hazrat Nizám-ud-Dín of Delhi, whose spiritual descendants are called Nizamís.

Sh. Shams-ud-Dín Turk of Pánípat.

Sháh-i-Waláyat Sh. Jalál-ud-Dín of Pánípat.

Sh. Abdúl Haq of Radauli (U. P.).

Sh. Arif Sáhib.

Sh. Muhammad Sáhib.

Sh. Abdul Qadús Sáhib Qutb of Gangoh (U. P.).

Sh. Jalál-ud-Dín of Thánesar.

Sh. Nizám-ud-Dín of Balkh.

Sh. Abú S'aíd of Gangoh.

Sh. Muhammad Sádiq of Gangoh.

Sh. Dáúd Sáhib of Gangoh.

Sháh Abul Maíali.

Hazrat Miran Syed Sháh Bhík, the famous Mírán Sáhib, whose tomb is at Ghurám, in Patiála State: and so on.

and so on.

In the mystic language of the Súfis these four sects, the Naqshbandi, Qádiria, Suharwardi and Chishti, are called *khanwadas* (houses) and are sub-divided into minor sects known after the leading members of the parent sects.

In the Punjab disciples of the Chishti, Qádiria, Suharwardia and Naqshbandia orders are found but adherents of the others are very few in number. They profess Islám and are religious orders, not castes though they tend to become tribes. A Muhammadan of any caste or tribe can adopt the teaching of any Súfi order and retain his caste. Celibacy is not strictly observed by these orders, but it is preferred by their leaders. These orders differ in their practices and religious doctrines.

The Chishtia Order.

In contradiction to the generally accepted account[1] the foundation of the Chishtia order is by some ascribed to Khwája Ahmad Abdál[2] of Chisht, where he was enshrined in 355 H. He was the disciple of Abú Isháq Shámi who was buried at Akka in Shám (Syria) and not in Chisht, as often stated. The order claims to originate from Ali the fourth Caliph himself through Hasan Basri and thus appears to be the youngest though it is the most popular of the four great Súfi sects.

Chistia methods and practices.

At initiation a disciple first recites two *raka'ts* of *namáz* or prayer and is then given certain instructions, which he is directed to observe without demur, such as the precepts :—(1) that a *faqír* takes food in the name of God, (2) that he spends his life in remembrance of God (*yád-i-Iláhi*), (3) that he sleeps with death, and (4) arises with the *kalima*. He is exhorted in these words :—" O disciple thou hast become a *faqír* and shouldst follow these precepts : and as the word *faqír* contains 4 letters *fe, qáf, ye* and *re*, the *fe* which expresses *faqah* or fasting, the *qáf*, *qanaat* or contentment, the *ye, yád-i-Iláhi* or remembrance of God and the *re, riyásat* or penance, so shouldst thou possess these four qualities " : *vide* the *Bágh-o-Bahár* of Mír Umman.

After this he is bidden to concentrate attention on his *murshid* or spiritual leader in a certain way every day, then some *ism* or sacred name is disclosed to him and he is directed to go to a shrine, to fast there for 40 days called *chila kashi* and to keep on repeating the sacred name. Lastly the spiritual pedigree of the order is declared to him. By degrees he makes spiritual progress and sees visions of all things and places up to *'arsh* or heaven. In this state when the two stars, Nasíra and Mahmúda,

[1] See Vol. II, p. 172, and *cf.* the *Khazínat-ul-Asfia*, Vol. I, pp. 239-40.

[2] See art. on Abdal in Vol. II, p 1. The Abdáls, known in Turkey as Turkalu, are there described as wearing no clothing. They lived entirely on herbs and held women in horror, yet achieved such an evil reputation that early in the 19th century they were almost exterminated. Yet even of recent years they were frequently seen on high-roads and in provincial towns and held in respect and even awe by the populace, who term them Abdals: W. S. Monroe, *Turkey and the Turks*, London, 1908, pp. 280-1. The Abdáls are undoubtedly supposed to be living representatives of the 70 *abdáls* who succeed to the 40 *rijal-ul-ghaib* : Brown, *The Dervishes*, pp. 82-3. See also *supra*, p. 524.

become one he attains the condition of *sehawa* or spiritual waking consciousness, and thus he reaches the *loh-i-mahfúz* or protected plank. Past, present and future things manifest themselves to his sight, that is to say he gets a vision of all the worlds and thus when he repeats his meditation from his very heart, a condition of *taqwím* or deep trance supervenes and he learns or perceives the all-pervading spirit and meets the mystery of *nás* and *nayás*; *nás* orders but *nayás* is silent, and the great mystery of *ism i-zát* or 'name of self' reveals itself to him.

The five Chishtia sub-orders.

1. Zaidi, from Khawája Abdul Ahad,[1] son of Zaid, whose shrine is at Basra.

2. Ayázi, from Khwája Fuzail, son of 'Ayáz, whose shrine is at Kufa.[2]

3. Adhami, from Khwája Sultán Ibráhím, son of Adham, whose shrine is at Baghdád.[3]

4. Chishti, from Khwája Abu Isháq Shámi Chishti, whose shrine is at Chisht, a town near Herát in Afghánistán.

5. Hubairi, from Khwája Hubairat-al-Basri.[4]

The Zaidi, 'Ayázi, Adhami and Hubairi sub-orders have long since ceased to be recognized as distinct and the only descriptions of them in almost all the Súfi books are to be found under the Chishti order.

Formerly the Chishtia order was one, but now it is split into two sub-orders: (1) Nizámia from Nizám-ud-dín of Delhi, (2) Sábiria from Khwája Ala-ud-dín Ahmad Sábir, nephew and son-in-law of Bába Faríd-ud-Dín Shakarganj.

The Sábir Chishtís have an important shrine at Thaska Míránji in Karnál. It is called Rozái Sháh Bhík and a fair is held there on the 10th Shábán. It was founded by Nawáb Roshan-ud-Daula, minister of Muhammad Sháh, at a cost of some ten *lákhs* of rupees in the time of Muhammad Fázil, successor of Sháh Bhík from whom it takes its name and was begun in 1131 H. It is administered by Mián Imám Sháh 7th in succession to Sháh Bhík who is celibate like most of his predecessors and the *faqírs* of the sect, the succession being governed by spiritual relationship.

Drugs such as *bhang*, *charas*, tobacco and liquors are strictly forbidden to be brought or used in the shrine or its precincts.

[1] In the account of the Zaidi in Vol. III, p. 510, Abdul Ahad is incorrect, it should be Abdul Wáhid. A sect called Zaidi is dominant in Central Yemen, where it was established by the Imám-ul-Hadi Yahya in 901 A. D. and through him the present Imám of Yemen claims descent from Ali and Fátima. Unlike other Shí'as the Zaidi regard Ali as the first rightful Khalífa by personal fitness and not by selection. They pilgrimage to Mecca and regard one made to Karbala as a work of supererogation: G. Wyman Bury, *Arabia Infelix*, pp. 38, 82-4. A Sayyid *family* in Multán is sometimes called Zaidi as descended from Zaid Shahíd, grandson of the Imám Husain: Multán *Gazetteer*, 1901-2, p. 154.

[2] The shrine of Khwája Fuzel is not in Kúfa. It is in Mecca: *vide Khazínat-ul-Asfia*, Vol. I, p. 230.

[3] The name of Khwája Ibrahím Adham is wrongly given as Ibrahím Adhím Khán (*ibid*, p. 236). His shrine is not in Baghdád. It is in Shám.

[4] The shrine of Habera Basri is not in Marash but in Basra (*vide Mahbúb-ul-Arfan*).

BBB

Tombs of Sháh Bhík's disciples form the seven or eight minor shrines subordinate to this. They are at Talakam in Jagádhri tahsíl, at Handi Khera in Naraingarh tahsíl, at Gangheri and Thaska Ali in Thánesar tahsíl, at Ramba in Karnál tahsíl and at Kuhrám in Patiála. Although the saint died on the 5th Ramzán his *urs* is not kept on that date as it falls in a month of fasts and his disciples decided to hold it a little earlier; so the *urs* is held on the 10th of Shábán and lasts till the 13th. It is the occasion of a big fair.

The name Sábir is thus explained :—One day Bába Faríd Sháh Ali Ahmad's spiritual director and maternal uncle bade him give food and alms on his behalf to the poor. This he did and though stationed at the *langarkhána* (refectory) night and day he did not quit it to take his food at his own house. As he got weaker day by day, his mother asked the reason and he replied that he had taken no food for several days as his leader's orders were to distribute it to others but did not authorise him to take any for himself and also that as he was required to be present at the poor house, he could not leave it. For this he received the name of Sábir the 'patient' or 'contented'.[1]

The following is a list of some of the best known Chishti shrines :—

Name.	Place.	Hijri year of death.
The shrine of Qutb Sáhib at Mihrauli near Delhi. This saint forbade a building to be erected over his tomb.	Delhi	14th Rabi-ul-awal 633.
That of Khwája Nizám-ud-dín Aulia, Sultán-ul-Mashaikh, commonly called Sultánji Chishti, at Arab Sarái near Delhi.	Do.	
The shrine of Bu Ali Qalandar Chishti known as the Qalandar Sáhib, at Budha Khera in Karnál.	Karnál	724
Khwája Shams-ud-dín Chishti Sábiri called Sháh Wiláyat, at Pánípat. He was a spiritual descendant of Ali Ahmad Sábir.	Panipat	
S. Jalál-ud-dín Kabír-ul-Aulia Sábiri called the Makhdúm Sáhib, at Pánípat. He was a Turk, and descended from the foregoing.	Ditto	
Sháh Lakhi	Ambála.	
Sháh Bhik Míránjí or Mírán Sáhib ...	Thaska.	
Míránjí	Thánesar tahsíl.	
Sh. Faríd-ud-Dín	Pákpattan	644 or 669
Sh. Sharf-ud-Dín	Pánípat	724

[1] Ali Ahmad's shrine is at Pírán-Kaliar near Roorkee. His life is given in the *Gulzár-Sábiri*. The Prophet gave him the name of Ala-ud-Dín before his birth and his parents that of Ali Ahmad.

Name.		Place.	Hijri year of death.
Kh. Amír Khusro	...	Near Delhi	725
Sháh Nasír-ud-Dín, Roshan Chiragh Dihlwí.		Delhi	757
Sháh Kaku ...	...	Lahore (Delhi Gate)	880
Sh. Jalál-ud-Dín	...	Thánesar	979
Sh. Ján Ulláh	...	Lahore	1029
Sh. Háji Abdul Karím	...	Kot Nahli in Lahore	1045
Sh. Abdul Khalik	...	Lahore	1059
Sh. Muhammad Arif	...	Do.	1071
Sh. Muhammad Siddiq	...	Do.	1084
Sh. Abdul Muali	...	Do.	1116
Sh. Abdul Rashid	...	Jullundur	1121
Sh. Atiq Ullah	...	Do.	1131
Sh. Muhammad Salim	...	Lahore	1151
Sh. Bahlol ...	...	Jullundur	1170
Sháh Latíf Ullah	...	Do.	1180
Mauláná Fakhar-ud-Dín	...	Delhi	1126
Syad Alim Ullah	...	Jullundur	1202
Sh. Nur Muhammad	...	Tajasarwar near Muhar, a town in Baháwalpur.	1205
Sayad Ali Shah	...	Jullundur	1213
Sh. Muhammad Said	...	Sharaqpur, Lahore	1214
Sh. Mahmud Said	...	Jullundur	1220
Sh. Khair-ud-Dín	...	Lahore	1228
Hafiz Mui ...	...	Manakpur	1245
Kh. Muhammad Sulaimán	...	Taunsa in Sanghar tahsíl.	1267
Maulvi Amánat Ali	...	Amroha	1280
Hájí Ramzán...	...	Lahore	1282
Sh. Faiz Bakhsh	...	Do.	1286[1]

Some Chishti saints.

The full name of Bu Ali Qalandar was Shaikh Sharf-ud-Dín Bu Ali Qalandar. Born at Pánípat, it is not certain as to whose disciple he was, some holding that he was the *khalífa* of Khwája Kutb-ud-Dín, others that he was a disciple of Nizám-ud-Dín Auliya. He wrote many works on Sufiism and in one of them, the *Hikmat-Náma*, he gives a short autobiography Among his numerous disciples were Sultán Ala-ud-Dín Khalji and Jalál-ud-Dín Khalji. In the *Hikmat-náma* he says that at the age of 40 he left Pánípat for Delhi where he was entrusted with the office of *mufti* and teaching Islamic law for 20 years. When his abstraction increased he gave up teaching and his office and spent the rest of his life as a Qalandar. He accepted no presents from disciples. He performed many miracles and died on the 13th Ramzán 724 H. (11th January 1324 A.D.). His tombs are at Pánípat and Karnál.[2]

At the *siáratgáh* of Bu Ali Sháh Qalandar the *urs* is held from 9th to 12th Ramzán, during which days the place is illuminated and

[1] Many important saints are omitted from this list, to wit Mauláná Fakhr-ud-dín of Delhi, Sháh Kalímullah Jahánábádi etc.; while minor saints like Sulaimán of Taunsa etc. are mentioned.

[2] *Khazínat-ul-Asfiya*, pp. 326-8; *Asrár-i-Abrár*, pp. 100-1; *Miftáh-ut-Tawáríkh* Persian text, by Beale, p. 79.

Qawáls (singers) sing *ghazals* or hymns etc. Another fair, called the Badakharah, is held on every Thursday in Jeṭh and Háṛ. Once it is said the Sháh was sitting on a wall of the building when a *faqír* riding on a lion drew near. The Sháh ordered the wall to pay its respects to him, whereupon it moved up and down in token of respect. So the people founded the fair in honour of the Sháh. The shrine has been in existence for 600 years. It contains the Sháh's tomb, made of marble, on which flowers are carved. The administration is carried on by a Shaikh *majáwar*.

Ibbetson, § 224. Another saint of great celebrity is Boáli Qalandara, contemporary of Bába Faríd. He used to ride about on a wall, but eventually settled at Pánípat. The Jumna then flowed under the town: and he prayed so continuously that he found it convenient to stand in the river and wash his hands without moving. After seven years of this he got stiff, and the fishes ate his legs; so he asked the river to step back seven paces and let him dry. In her hurry to oblige the saint she retreated seven miles; and there she is now. He gave the people of Pánípat a charm which drove away all flies from the city. But they grumbled, and said they rather liked flies, so he brought them back a thousandfold. The people have since repented. There was a good deal of trouble about his funeral. He died near Karnál, and there they buried him. But the Pánípat people claimed his body and came and opened his grave, on which he sat up and looked at them till they felt ashamed. They then took some bricks from his grave with which to found a shrine; but when they got to Pánípat and opened the box they found his body in it, so now he lies buried both at Pánípat and at Karnál. His history is given in the *Aín-i-Akbari*. He died in 724 Hij. (1324 A. D.).

The following Chishti saints have shrines in Jínd:—

Sayyid Jamál-ud-Dín or Sháh Waláyat has his shrine at Jínd town. He belonged to the Chishti order and accompanied Shaháb-ud-Dín of Ghor in his campaign against Rái Pithora. He was killed in battle at Jínd, where his shrine was built. A fair and *urs* are held here in Muharram every year. His sister's son also has a tomb there and so has Shaikh Wali Muhammad. Both belonged to the Chishti order.

Sháh Sondha's shrine is at Safídon town. He belonged to the Chishti and Qádiria orders.

Hidáyatullah or Mubáriz Khán has his shrine at Kaliána in the Dádri tahsíl. Mubáriz Khán was made commander-in-chief by Alaf Khán, son of Tughlaq, King of Delhi, and was deputed in 730 H. to fight against Rája Kalián, ruler of Kaliána and the country thereabouts. He was killed and his shrine was built. A full account is given in the Jínd State *Gazetteer*.[1]

Shaikh Mahmúd has his shrine at Dádri town. He belonged to the Chishti order.

Dáta Ganj Bakhsh, 'the saint, the bestower of treasure', was really named Ali Makhdúm Hujweri[2] and a son of Usmán, son of Ali

[1] Phulkián States *Gazetteer*, Jind, pp. 262 and 335.

[2] Hujwer was a suburb of Ghazni: *History of Lahore*, p. 179.

Jaláli of Ghazni. He was a disciple of Shaikh Abul Fazl, son of Hassan Khutbi. He followed the armies of Mas'úd, son of Mahmúd, to Lahore where he settled in 1039 A. D. The authorship of the *Kashf-ul-Mahjúb* or 'Revelation of the Unseen' is ascribed to him. He was a precursor of the Chishtís, for Khwája Muín-ud-Dín of Ajmer is said to have spent 40 days at his tomb.

Chishti shrines are not numerous at Lahore but that of Sháh Rahmatullah Sháh (d. 1708 A. D.), who was the spiritual guide of Abdus-Samad, viceroy at Lahore, merits notice. The saint is now known as Pír Sámponwálá or 'saint having command of snakes' owing to an incident which occurred near his tomb in Ranjít Singh's reign.[1]

In Baháwalpur the Chishtís are important though only one shrine, that at Chishtiána, is held by them. Shaikh Táj-ud-Dín, a grandson of Báwa Faríd-ud-dín, converted various Rájpút tribes in Bíkáner and this brought him into collision with the unconverted clans. They attacked him and the women of his household were swallowed up by the earth. A tower which marks the spot is visited by women who make vows there. Various stories associate Khwája Nur Muhammad Mahárvi and Bába Nának with the shrine of this saint, at which the Lakhweras and other Joiya septs make vows for sons, while Muhammadans in general after the *istisqá* or prayer for rain sacrifice goats &c. and Hindus offer a chintz cover to the tomb for restoration to health and distribute sugar and boiled grain as a thank-offering for rain.[2]

Khwája Núr Muhammad was a Kharral Panwár Rájpút. Born
1142 H. in 1746 in the Shahr Faríd *iláqa* of Baháwalpur, he obtained the *khiláfat* from Mauláns Fakhr-ud-Dín Muhíb-un-Nabi at Delhi and the name of Núr Muhammad from his disciples as he was the perfect 'light' (of God). Better known as the Qibla-i-Alam, he performed countless miracles and could send his invisible body (*wajúd-i-silli*) where he liked. He appeared after death to read the *janása* at the funeral of a *muríd*. He had 4 *khalífas*, Núr Muhammad II of Hájípur, Qázi Muhammad Aqil of Mithankot, Háfiz Muhammad Jamál of Multán, and Khwája Muhammad Sulaimán Khán of Sanghar. Their deputies in turn founded *gaddís* in Baháwalpur, Sindh and the Punjab, among them those of Muhammad Akbar at Ránia in Hissár, Makhdúm Sayyid Mahmúd of Sítpur and Muhibb-i-Jahánián at Shahr Sultán, and others. This saint, who must be classed as a Chishti, has thus exercised a profound influence over the whole of the south-western Punjab.[3]

The shrine of Hujra Sháh Mohkam in Montgomery is the subject of the *Tazkirát-i-Mohkami*, compiled in 1747. The descent of its founder is thus given:—Ghaus Muhi-ud-Dín Chishti, Abd-ur-Razáq, Sayyid Ali, S. Muhammad Mushtáq, S. Momani, Shams-ud-Dín (I and II), Zahúr-ud-Dín, S. Sadr-ud-Dín, Fateh Ulláh, Zain-ul-Abidín, Ala-ud-Dín Surakh-posh, Táj Muhammad Budáúni and Bahá-ul-Haqq, Budáúni Hujrái. On the death of the last named, its founder, in 1565

[1] *History of Lahore*, p. 187.

[2] Baháwalpur *Gazetteer*, pp. 174-5.

[3] *Ib.*, pp. 176-8.

his younger son Sháh Mohkam was elected to succeed him. Bahá-ul-Haqq or Baháwal Sher left Budáún and settled on the bank of the Sutlej in a small village inhabited by Dhid Jáṭs.[1] By the miraculous use of his staff the saint caused the river, then divided into several streams, to flow in a single channel. Once he rode to Pákpaṭṭan and tore off the tapestries from the tomb of Shaikh Faríd Badr-ud-Dín Shakarganj, by which apparent sacrilege he enabled that saint to attain the highest heaven, into which his entry had hitherto been impeded. Apparently this saint supported the cause of Humáyún against the house of Sher Sháh Sur, for in his restoration he entertained the emperor at a banquet for which a valuable horse presented to the saint by Akbar had been slaughtered. As late as the reign of Ranjít Singh, however, the partizans of the shrine seem to have carried on a religious war with those of Shaikh Faríd.[2] This legend may give a clue to the significance of the shrines which have no roofs. In the *Punjab Historical Society's Journal*, 1914, pp 144-5, the present writer gave instances of hypæthral shrines in the Punjab. To that list may be added the shrine of Khwája Báqi-billáh Naqshbandi at Delhi, and the Chishti Qutb's at Mihrauli: the roofless tomb of Pír Aulia Ghori near Bahádurpur in Multán[3] and that left incomplete in honour of Gujari, a *sati* in Nábha[4]: and doubtless many other examples could be cited. These shrines are all Muhammadan—with the possible exception of the *sati's* in Gurgáon—but they do not appear to be confined to any particular sect. Muhammad Latif says that *hujra* in Persian means 'building, mosque or mausoleum without roof,'[5] but all roofless shrines are not styled *hujra* in the Punjab.

Jawáya Sháh whose *takia* is at Basti Kamboánwáli in Ferozepur was a Máchhi and a *faqír* of the Chishti school. Born in Ferozepur city, he went to live in the Basti when it was founded, and was buried there. No fair is held.

West of the town of Hánsi are the tombs of the four Qutbs, Qutb Jamál-ud-dín and his three descendants. Tradition makes 'Sultán' Jamál-ud-Dín a scion of the Ghaznivides who accompanied Mahmúd or else Muhammad of Ghor in his invasions. The tomb of Ali Tajjár, 'a disciple of Qutb-ud-Dín', stands in the enclosure. Ali Tajjár was his chief purveyor.[6] The 2nd Qutb was his son Burhán-ud-Dín, the 3rd Manawwar-ud-Dín, and the 4th Núr-ud-Dín, Núr-i-Jahán. In another enclosure are the graves of the four Díwáns or successors of the Qutbs whose descendants are still *sajjáda-nashíns* and known as the Díwán Sáhibs. Shaky as the traditions are as to chronology the 1st Qutb is described as a disciple of Bába Faríd Shakarganj and the second as also a companion of H. Nizám-ud-Dín of Delhi. Hence the institution must be classed as a Chishti one, though it is possibly older in origin than the time of Báwa Faríd.

[1] A tribe otherwise unknown.

[2] P. N. Q., III, §§ 593, 643 and 732.

[3] Multán *Gazetteer*, 1901-02, p. 123.

[4] Vol. II, p. 312, *infra*.

[5] *Hist. of Lahore*, p. 165.

[6] So the Hissar *Gazetteer*, 1904, p. 319.

Another tomb at Hánsi is that of Sayyid Niámat Ullah Shahíd killed in Muhammad-ibn-Sám's attack on the place, in 588 H. probably.[1] Tradition adds that he was present at the battle of Thánesar and killed Khande Ráo, brother of Prithi Ráj. However this may be, the fair held in Chet at his tomb is called the *mela-i-neza* or fête of lances. His comrades who fell were buried at the Ganj Shahídán 3 *kos* from Hánsi.

An interesting Chishti shrine at Gula in Hissár is that of Míran Nau Bahár—the name signifies eternal prosperity—a disciple of Bába Faríd of Shakarganj. On his return to Gula he was given some bricks, blessed by the curses of evil spirits, which he put into a *mári*. Whosoever is affected by evil spirits or hysterical fits has only to put his head in the *mári* to be rid of them. The date of the erection of the *mári* is that of the annual fair.

It is generally believed that the *khánqáh* was built about 750 years ago. Its administration is carried on by Mirán's descendants who are Tirmizi Sayyids, while the keeping of it clean rests with an old family of *khádims*.

The fair begins on the *púranmáshi* of Jeṭh *sudi* and lasts 2 days longer. People affected as above are cured thus :—They are made to eat *ním* leaves wetted in the oil of a burning lamp and then made to put their head into the *mári*. The evil spirit appears, talks, says why he troubled the man, prescribes a remedy and then departs.

The *khánqáh* of Sháh Kaiím ud-Dín is attached to this shrine. It is about 500 yards from it. He was some relation of Míran Nau Bahár's father.

The shrine of Dáta Sher Bahlol.—This saint's shrine lies a mile east of Hissár. His name was Abdul Razzáq, Data Sher Bahlol being his *laqb*. In 1340 (757 H.) he lived where his shrine now stands in a wilderness which was the hunting ground of Fíroz Sháh Tughlaq, son of Sálár Rajjab, a cousin of Sultán Muhammad Tughlaq. In 1340 when Fíroz Tughlaq came here to hunt he was astonished to see Sher Bahlol living without water etc. and had a wall built round what is now the town of Hissár and a canal brought from the Jumna to it. A *mela* is held on the 6th of Muharram. On Thursdays and Sunday the Muhammadans and Hindus of Hissár gather there for *ziárat*.

The shrine of Sháh Junaid.—This shrine stands 300 yards south of the Nagauri gate of the town. It comprises a small *gumbad*, a mosque, a well in the compound and some other tombs of the saint's relatives. Junaid, son of Chandan and grandson of Mahmúd, was a native of Ajadhan (now Pákpaṭṭan) and a descendant of Bába Faríd Shakarganj. An inscription in Arabic on the shrine runs—'Built on the first of Rabi-ul-Awal 927 H. (1510 A. D.): here lies Junaid bin Chandan'. Every year a *mela* is held on 27th Ramzán.

The shrine of Ismail Sháh.—This shrine stands close to the western side of the town. Ismail Sháh settled here in 1800 A.D., and by his high character achieved such popularity that many became his

[1] *Epigraphia Indo-Moslemica*, p. 12.

disciples, many villages in Bíkáner were assigned to him and other states also gave him a yearly income.

The shrine of the Chihl Háfiz.—This shrine is called that of the forty reciters of the *Qurán* who were 40 wandering *darwesh* of Baghdád. Arriving here in 1340 A. D. in the reign of Fíroz Sháh Tughlaq they settled at the place where the shrine now stands to enjoy the society of Dáta Sher Bahlol. All 40, it is said, were buried in one and the same tomb after they had been put to the sword by the Ḍogars of Agroha.

Two shrines exist in Sirsa—one called Abu Shakúr Silmi and the other Shaikh Allah Dád Sáhib. The former, a native of Salam in Arabia, came here in the time of Sultán Mahmúd Ghaznawi. A very learned *darwesh*, he belonged to the Ibráhím sect founded by Ibráhím of Balkh who abandoned his kingdom and used to live in solitude in the hills. He wrote a work, called the *Tamhíd*, on purity of mind. The 14th Shabán is the date for the *mela* at the shrine The four cupolas one on each side of the shrine are called the four *chilás* :—of Bába Faríd Shakarganj, Baha-ul Haqq-wá-l-Dín Zakaría Multáni, Sayyid Jalál and Bába Nának—since these four came here at different times and spent some time in meditation on Abu Shakúr Silmi.

A yearly fair is held at Palla in tahsíl Nuh, in the *khánqáh* of Khwája Músá Chishti on the 27th and 28th of Jamádi-ul-awwal. The *khánqáh* was built by Khwája Abdul Samad, a descendant of Kh. Músa in 1142 H.; and the buildings attached to it by Nawáb Shams-ud-Dín Khan of Ferozepur-Jhirka. The grave is of white marble enclosed on all sides by a marble palisade, but open on the top. Surrounding the *mazár* are some houses in which people can put up. There are two gates, one to the east, the other to the south. The management vests in the Quraishi Shaikhs of Palla, the descendants of Shaikh Músa. In the fair each person offers a pice to the *mazár* and also *reori* or *batáshas* with one pice The following offerings are also made :—

Cloth from 5 to 100 yards to cover the grave, a *jhárú* (broom) which is deemed to possess the virtue of removing pimples from the skin, *malída* (bread mixed with *ghí* and sugar) and milk and curd. No other shrine is connected with this.

At the tomb of Sháh Chokha[1] or Sayyid Akbar Ali a fair is held every *chánd-rát* of the Muhammadan month of Jamádi-ul-awal, ending on the 8th of that month, in this wise :—When the new moon is seen a drum is beaten and the tomb is lit up. Every subsequent evening and morning a gathering for *fatihá-khwáni* takes place and sometimes

[1] The saint of the Meos, see Vol. III, p. 84, *infra*. A still more curious Chishti shrine is described below :—

The *khánqáh* of Dáda Tím Sháh at Lakhháji in Ferozepur has a fair on the 4th Hár every year. The story is that Dáda Yatím Shah was a Chishti juggler. He came from Ajmer and settled in Marapah in Muktsar some 120 years ago. Thence he was brought to Lakhaháji by Kalu and Lakha, Ḍogars. He had a disciple named Sayyid Lakhan Sháh Bukhári. On the day of the foundation of Lakhaháji, Dáda Yatím Sháh breathed his last. The fair is attended by some 200 men and *qawáls* or singers are invited to it. Some of the visitors go into a trance by waving their heads violently. *Faqírs* are fed free with bread, rice and meat. *Faqír* Bahádur Sháh, Qureshi, is its *majáwar*. Succession is governed by natural relationship, but in the absence of a son, the inheritance would pass to a *chela*. Lamps are lit every Thursday night, when people offer cash, or sweets. The *khánqáh* of Lakhan Sháh is connected with this.

verses are also sung. The drum is beaten five times each day. *Faqírs* and shopkeepers encamp on plots of ground from 1st to 3rd of Jamadi-ul-awal, and shops are opened on the 4th. The *fátiha-khwáni* is finished on the 5th, and the fair ends on the 8th. Forty or even fifty thousand people of every sect visit this fair.

Sayyid Akbar Ali was a Charkalot Meo. Chokha means 'good', and probably the saint was so called on account of his miracles. The tomb is said to have been built in the reign of Akbar, but its *khádims* state that the Persian phrase *sanni-zuhák* expresses the year of its foundation which would thus be 939 H., but the words are meaningless. The tomb is enclosed by walls on all four sides, the outer walls being about 100 yards long, and 5 or 6 yards high, with two gates, one in the northern, the other in the southern wall. The *naubat* or drums are kept at these gates. In both these walls are smaller doors for the convenience of the public. Inside all the four walls are *hujrás* and *dáláns* in which visitors to the fair put up. Between the outer and inner walls are many small tombs in which shop-keepers set up booths during the fair. In the north-western corner is a small mosque without a dome. The inner circuit has two gates, one in the southern, the other in the western wall. Inside it are two *dáláns*, known as the *bára-dari*. Under one is a *tah-khána* and there are five or six small graves in the courtyard. At the north-eastern corner is a small roofless mosque in the form of an *ídgáh*. North of the tomb stands a large mosque in which the *Qurán* is read. Behind this mosque is a three-doored room built of red sand-stone, which seems to be new for the middle door has an inscription in Hindi.[1] In the inner circuit is a large stone tomb. Above it is a large egg-shaped dome surmounted by a golden *kalas*. This tomb has two doors, one to the south, the other to the east. Inside this building is the grave of Sháh Chokha covered with a green cloth kept in position by a few stones (*mírfarsh*). Inside the building on the northern wall hang a stick, a wooden bow, a stone *kantha*, two wooden swords (one of them a *khánda*), 5 small glass beads, and an iron bead known as 'the *simurgh's* egg'. By the grave are two *Qur áns*, two iron candelabra and an iron *fatilsoz*.

The administration of the temple vests in the villagers who style themselves descendants of Sháh Chokha. All the *khádims* are Chishtís. Every Thursday at the *fátiha-khwáni lobán* or incense is burnt. The tomb of the *pír* or religious teacher of Sháh Chokha is said to be at Nárnaul in Patiála.

All that can be ascertained of Sháh Ahmad Chishti is that he was the son of Shah Ismaíl. His father came to reside at Sajwári from Dasna in the Balandshahar District. After his death Sháh Ahmad Chishti took his *gaddi*. His fame rests upon a tradition that once a Banjára bringing valuable goods from abroad met him. Sháh Ahmad asked him what they were. The Banjára named some inferior goods. Sháh Ahmad said 'Yes. It must be what you say'. When the Banjára reached his destination and opened the goods he found that they had been transformed into what he had misrepresented them to be to the Shaikh. He came back to him and begged for Gurgáon.

[1] Kewal Rám, son of Sálig Rám, Kalál of Mathra, S. 1840.

pardon, which was granted and the goods were restored to their original condition. So the Banjára had this shrine raised to the Shaikh's memory. It is much worshipped by people of the surrounding villages some of whom have assigned lands to it. Nawáb Murtaza Khan assigned 4 or 5 hundred *bighas*. The pepole of Mahalla Qánúngoyán in Palwal generally have their children shaved at this place. The annual festival takes place on 12th Rabi-ul-awwal.

The influence of the Chishtís has penetrated into parts of the hills. Thus at the *khánqáh* of Bara Bhái is the shrine of Abd-us-Salám, a Chishti, founded by a Rájá of Nasrota. Its fair is held on a Thursday in the light half of Jeth.

The Qádiria Order.[1]

Abdul Qádir Jiláni was born at Gilán or Jilán in Persia in 1078 A. D. His titles were Pírán-i-Pír, Ghaus-ul-Azim, Ghaus-us-Samdáni, Mahbúb-i-Subháni, Mírán Muhay-ud-Dín, Sayyid Abdul Qádir Jíláni, Hasan-ul-Hussaini.[2] Abdul Qádir Jíláni's nephew (*bhánja*) was Sayyid Ahmad Kabír (not Qabír) Rafái,[3] the founder of the Rafái or Gurzmár *faqirs*.

Abdul Qádir is said to have left his tooth-brush at Ludhiána. It has grown into a *ním* tree at his shrine which stands in an open space near the fort. His fair is called Roshani and begins on the 11th of Rabi-us-sáni. Hindu as well as Muhammadan villages light lamps at his shrine and women desirous of offerings make offerings at it. Jáṭs also bring cattle to it and make them jump for luck. The fair lasts 3 or 4 days and songs of all sorts are sung by the ever-moving crowds both night and day. Prostitutes frequent it.

But the following local account of the fair makes no mention of Abdul Qádir or of the *ním* tree and assigns a very different origin to the shrine :—

The Roshani Fair is the most famous in Ludhiána. It is held in that town at the *khánqah* of the 'Pír Sáhib' and people of all classes, mostly Muhammadans with some Hindús, attend it. Beginning on the 10th of Rabi II it should end on the 12th but it generally goes on for a week, more people visiting it at night than by day. Visitors present cash, sweetmeats, goats, milk, cowries &c., as they think fit. Every Thursday too there is a small gathering at the *khánqáh*, especially of Muhammadans. This Pír was Sayyid Muhammad, progenitor of the Súfi Sayyids of Ludhiána. At the site of the *khánqáh* he practised

[1] See Vol. III, p. 431.

[2] Herklot's *Qanoon-e-Islam*, p. 155.

[3] *Ib*, pp. 157 and 193. Abdul Qádir Gíláni was the son of Abi Sálih and a disciple of Shaikh Abu Sa'íd. Born on the 1st Ramzán 470 H., at the age of 18 he left Gilán for Baghdád where he began his studies, and in 521 H. he began to preach. More than 70,000 people are said to have attended his lectures. He could talk with the Invisible (Rijal-i-ghaib), as well as with Khizr, and performed many unique miracles. Many saints who had lived before him had prophesied concerning him. He died on 9th Rabi II, 561 H., at the age of 90 and was buried at Baghdád: *Khazínat-ul-Asfia*, I, pp. 94-9; *Safínat-ul-Aulia*, pp. 43-53. For a hymn to Abd'ul-Qádir Jiláni see Temple's *Legends of the Punjab*, II, p. 153. The tale of the miraculous rescue of the drowning bridegroom by the saint may be purely allegorical. The saint's chief *fête* is celebrated on the *yárhi*—11th (*gyárwín*) of Rabi. II: *ib*. p. 153, citing Herklot's *Qanoon-e-Islám*, p. 155 *ff*.

12th February 1166 A.D.

chila for 40 days shut up in a hut. At its close his disciples came to revere him and thus the Roshani fair was instituted. Sayyid Muhammad was a *khalífa* of Hazrat Hujat-ul-Aulia Shaikh Dáúd Gangú. From the *Hadiqá Dáúdi* it appears that he was contemporary with Alamgír and probably the *khánqáh* was founded in his reign. Its mangement vests in the descendants of Sayyid Muhammad, and for its service one or two *mujáwars* or *faqírs* are employed.

In imitation of this fair, another Roshani fair is held at Ráipur in Ludhiána tahsíl on the same date, but it only lasts a day and a night. It is held at Pír Daulat Sháh's *khánqáh*, and his disciples (*muríds*) gather there.

Brown gives various details regarding the Qádirís. According to him Abdul Qádir's title was Sultán-ul-Aulia or sovereign of the *walís* (saints).[1] The insigne of the Qádirís is the rose, because once the Shaikh-ul-Sa'íd Abdul Qádir Gílání[2] was directed by Khizr to go to Baghdád and on his arrival the Shaikh (apparently the chief of the town) sent him a cup full of water to signify that as the town was already full of holy men it had no room for him. But the saint put a rose in the cup, although it was the winter season, to signify that Baghdád could find a place for him. He was then admitted to the city. Abdúl-Qádir represents the *atwár-i-sab'a* or seven paths.[3] The initiatory rites *mubáya'at* of a *muríd* include the *bai'at* or giving of the right hand clasped in the Shaikh's right hand with the two thumbs raised up against each other.[4]

The Qádirís have three grades of *dirwesh*, the *muríd*, *khalífa* and *shaikh*. The *khalífa* is the *shaikh's* vicar, *e. g.* Shaikh Ismail or Rúmi, originally a Khalwatti, became the *khalífa* of Abdul Qádir. Sir Richard Burton was initiated into this order, first as a *shaikh*, then as a *murshid*, or one allowed to admit *muríds* or apprentices.[5]

The Qádiria methods and practices.

In the Qádiria method of contemplation the disciple is instructed to attain union with God or reach to Him by the practices of *yak-zarbi*, *dú-zarbí*, *seh-zarbi* and *chahár-zarbi*, four methods of repeating the name of Alláh, and he must recite His name in a voice so pitched as not to arouse sleeping people. In *yak-zarbí* he repeats the word Alláh with a certain pitch and length of voice from the heart and throat with emphasis once and then stops until his breathing is regulated and *Zikr.*

[1] Brown, *The Dervishes*, p. 80.

[2] *Ib.*, p. 89, apparently Abdul-ul-Qádir himself or one of his successors.

[3] There are 7 names of Alláh, used in *zikr*, each having its peculiar light, prayer and number of times which it must be repeated :—

1. Lá-Illahi-ill-Ullah, blue, 100,000 times.
2. Alláh the *'ismi jalíl* or beauteous name, yellow, 78,536 times.
3. Ismi Hú, red, 44,630.
4. Ismi Hai, white, 20,092.
5. Wáhid, green, 93,420.
6. Azíz, black, 74,644.
7. Wadúd, no light, 30,202.

These numbers total 447,574, but their mystical significance is not stated. It used to be necessary to recite the names the above number of times in order to qualify for the degree of Shaikh.

[4] *Ib.*, p. 95.

[5] *Al-Madina*, I, p. 14.

then he recites the word Alláh and so on. In *zikr dú-zarbí* he sits in the posture of *namáz* (prayer) and recites the name of Alláh once turning his head to the right and again in the heart. In *zikr seh-zarbí* he sits cross-legged and recites 'Alláh' first to the right, next to the left and thirdly in the heart with a loud voice. In *zikr chahár-zarbí* he sits cross-legged and recites Alláh first on the right side, then on the left, thirdly in the heart and fourthly in front with a loud voice. They are also taught to pronounce the words *la-Iláh a-Illilla* in a certain way sitting with eyes closed.

The nine Qádiria orders are the :—

1. Habíbi, from Khwája Habíb of Ajmi.
2. Tafúri, from Khwája Bayazíd of Bustám.[1]
3. Siqti, from Khwája Imám Sirri, and Siqti.[2]
4. Karkhi, from Khwája Marúf Karkhi.
5. Junaidi, from Khwája Junaid of Baghdád.
6. Gazrúni, from Khwája Najm-ud-Dín Kubru.
7. Túsi, from Khwája Abú'l-Faráh Tartúsi.
8. Firdúsi, from Khwája Abú S'aid Khizri.
9. Suharwardi from Khwája Abú Najíb Suharwardi.

Like the Chishtia the Qádiria order is divided into two sub-orders, the Razáqia from Shahzáda Abdul Razáq and the Wahábia from Shahzáda Abdul Waháb.

The following is a list of Qádiria shrines :—

Name.		*Place.*		*Hijri year of birth.*
Mauláná Ghaus Ali Sáhib	...	Pánípat in Karnál.		
Sháh Qumais or Qumes	...	Sádhaura in Ambála.		
Sayyid Muhammad Ghaus	...	Uch in Jhang	...	923
Mír Sayyid Sháh Fíroz	...	Lahore (Dandi Gardan)	...	933

[1] This and the Junaidi are not always given as Súfi orders. But as given in the *Taríkh-al-Aulia* and the *Anwár al-Arifín* the 14 Súfi orders are :—

1. Zaidi,	8. Karkhi,
2. Ayázi,	9. Siqti,
3. Adhami,	10. Junaidi,
4. Hobari,	11. Gazrúni,
5. Chishti,	12. Túsi,
6. Habíbi,	13 Sahrwardi, and
7. Tafúri,	14. Firdúsi.

Bustám is a village near Wad, a city in Persia. Bayazíd, founder of the Tifúri, Tafúri or Taifúri order, was an interesting personality. His full name was Taifúr bin Isa or Abu Yazíd and his Sufism made him a true pantheist. Whatever attains to God, he held, becomes God and his sanctity was such that he wrought miracles and wounds inflicted on his person when in a state of ecstasy appeared on the bodies of those who inflicted them. His townsmen feared his supernatural power and cast him out of their city seven times, only to receive him back again. A tenet he inculcated was that loving-kindness should be shown not only to men but to animals and the story goes that once he and his friend Qásim carried an ant away from its home unnoticed in their belongings. At Qásim's request Bayazíd set out to restore it to its home whereupon a halo encircled his hand and the inhabitants of Shahrud and Bustám fought for possession of his person. Qásim was killed in the fray and when Bayazíd on his return learnt of his death he rebuked his townsmen so vehemently, that they stoned him to death. Both he and Qásim are buried at Bostám: William Jackson, *From Constantinople to the Home of Omar Khayyam*, pp. 200-1. For a sketch of Bayazíd Bustami's life and teaching see Claud Field, *Mystics and Saints of Islam*, pp. 52 *ff*: and for Habíb Ajami, pp. 79 *ff*.

[2] The Siqti and Karkhi orders have long ceased to be so called, and their followers find a place under the Qádiri order in all books on Súfi history written in Persian or Urdu.

Name.	*Place.*	*Hijri year of birth.*
Sayyid Abdul Qádir II ...	Uch in Jhang ...	940
Sayyid Muhammad Hazúri[1] ...	Near Mián Mír road	942
Mírán Sayyid Mubárik ...	Uch in Jhang ...	956
Sháh Latíf Barri ...	Nurpur in Ráwal-pindi ...	950
Sayyid Baha-ud-dín ...	Hujra ...	973
Sayyid Hamid Ganj Bakhsh...	Uch in Jhang ...	978
Sh. Daud ...	Shergarh ...	982
Sh. Bahlol ...	Chiniot ...	983
Sh. Abu Isháq ...	Mozang (Lahore)	985
Sayyid Muhammad Núr ...	Chúnián in Lahore	988
Sayyid Músa ...	Multán ...	1001
Sh. Hussain (Lál Hussáin) ...	Lahore ...	1008
Sháh Shams-ud-Dín ...	Do. ...	1021
Sháh Khair-ud-Dín ...	Do. ...	1024
Sh. Muhammad Táhir[2] ...	Do. ...	1040
Sh. Muhammad Mír (Mián Mír)	Do. ...	1045
Sayyid Shah Biláwal ...	Outside Lahore ...	1046
Sh. Madhuri ...	Near Lahore ...	1156
Khwája Bihári ...	Near Mián Mír's shrine ...	1060
Sháh Sulaimán ...	Bhilowál ...	1065
Sayyid Ján Muhammad ...	Near Garhi town	1065
Sayyid Abdul Razzáq ...	Lahore ...	1068
Sh. Sháh Muhammad (Mulla Sháh) ...	Outside Mián Mír's tomb ...	1069
Sh. Háji Muhammad ...	Chhani Sahanpál in Gujránwála...	1103
Sayyid Hasan ...	Pesháwar ...	1015
Sháh Raza ...	Lahore ...	1118
Inait Sháh ...	Do. ...	1141
Sh. Muhammad Fazal ...	Batála ...	1151
Sháh Pir Muhammad ...	Naushahra in Guj-rát ...	1152
Sháh Muhammad Gaus ...	Lahore ..	1152
Sh. Abdul Rahmán ...	Birhi in Gujrán-wála ...	1158
Sayyid Bahli Sháh ...	Kasúr ...	1171
Sh. Abdulla Sháh ...	Mozang in Lahore	1212
Sh. Ghulám Hussain ...	Wayánwáli in Guj-ránwála ...	1260
Sh. Qaisar Sháh ...	Ditto ...	1283
Sh. Lahe Sháh ...	Lahore ...	1253

[1] The Hazúri family of Lahore is so called because its disciples are, it is believed, quickly admitted into the presence of the Prophet. Originally of Ghor it settled at Uch but migrated to Lahore under Sháh Jahán. Their tomb has two domes and in it are buried Muhammad Hazúri and his son Sháh Núr-ud-Dín, and Ján Muhammad and his son Sarwar Dín : Ján Muhammad, who died in 1708, was a man of profound learning : *Hist. of Lahore*, p. 171.

[2] Shaikh Táhir Bandagi, who is buried at Lahore, his native place, was a disciple of this Shaikh Ahmad.

Some Qádiria saints.

The pedigree of the saint Sháh Qumes makes him a descendant of Abdur-Qádir Jiláni through a son of his named Abd-ur-Razzáq who is otherwise not known. Sháh Qumes most probably flourished in the 16th century as tradition connects him with Akbar and with Humáyún's wars against Sikandar Sháh Sur, though even so his birth cannot be carried back to 1425 as in the genealogy.[1] His cult is said to be connected with Bihár and three large fairs are held, one in that Province, one at Ludhiána and a third at Sádhaura itself.

Sháh Biláwal, son of S'aid Usmán, son of S'aid Isa, who came from Herát to India with Humáyún when he reconquered India with Persian aid, was a disciple of Sh. Shams-ud-Dín Qádiri and a tutor of Maulavi A'bul Fateh. He died in 1636 A. D. and was first buried beneath a high dome on the banks of the Rávi, but on account of that river's encroachments Faqír Azíz-ud-Dín 200 years later exhumed his body and re-buried it a *kos* east of Lahore. The coffin was found suspended to the roof by an iron hook and the body in perfect preservation. The fort of Shaikhúpura with its environs was held in *jágír* by this Sayyid.[2]

Sháh Shams-ud-Dín who predicted Sháh Jahán's accession was also a Qádiri and offerings are made to his shrine in fulfilment of vows (*mannat*). He died in 1618 A. D. and Sháh Jahán constructed his tomb.[3]

The tomb of Sháh Raza, described as belonging to the Shattaria Qádiria family,[4] is on a platform in an open courtyard. Súfís assemble at the annual fair held at this *khánqáh*, to sing hymns when in the ecstatic state. Sháh Raza died in 1706 A. D. and disciple Sháh Ináyatulla had as his disciple the famous poet Bhulla Sháh.

Sháh Jamál described as a Qádiri Sahrwardi who died in 1650 A.D. has a tomb at Ichhra near Lahore. It is on a mound, in the form of a battery and so is called the Damdama Sháh Jamál. His brother Sháh Kamál is buried in the adjoining village of Vona. When Jamál used to sit on this *damdama* the ladies of the royal household could be seen bathing in Jahángír's tank close by, so they objected, but the *faqír* in a curse predicted that neither palaces nor tank should remain. Nevertheless in a fit of *wajd* or ecstasy he danced so hard that 5 storeys of the building sank below the ground, and so reduced the height of the *damdama* that people could not see the ladies bathing from it and only the present two storeys of his shrine remained.[5]

The Pír Dastgír.

Sháh Muhammad Ghaus, whose shrine is at Lahore, is held is great esteem from Delhi to Peshāwar. He died in 1739. His father, Said

[1] Given in Temple's *Legends*, III, pp. 92-3, where a full account of the saint's miracles and history will be found.

[2] *Hist. of Lahore*, p. 159. He was noted for his charities and established an alms-house : p. 59.

[3] *Ib.*, pp. 201-2.

[4] *Ib.*, pp. 200-1.

[5] *Ib.*, pp. 200-1.

Hasan, whose tomb at Peshâwar is also much respected, was a lineal descendant of the Pír Dastgír.[1]

The descendants of the Pír Dastgír include some patron saints of industrial castes or at least of local guilds. Thus at Lahore Fíroz Sháh Giláni, a disciple of Sháh Alam, became the saint of the Dandigars or *kherádis* (turners). He died in 1527 A. D. and was succeeded by Shaikh Abdulla. Similar saints are known in other parts of the Moslem world. Thus Abu Zulaima is the patron saint of the seas about the Gulf of Suez. He watches over the safety of mariners, sipping coffee, brought raw from Mecca by green birds and prepared by angels: Burton, *Al-Madina*, I, p. 199.

But other patron saints do not appear to be so regarded. Thus Hassu Teli, a saint contemporary with Lál Husain, is essentially the saint of the oilmen and his tomb is the scene of an annual fair. His shop too, at which he sold corn, is still respected and a lamp is lit daily at his residence. He was a disciple of Sháh Jamal Qádiri whose tomb is at Ichhra, and he died in 1593 A. D.[2] Shaikh Músa was an *áhangar* or ironsmith and his tomb is revered by people of that occupation. Once it is said, a Hindu woman brought him a spindle to straighten. Smitten by her beauty he forgot it and when she taunted him he replied that in looking at her he was only contemplating the maker's skill and taking the spindle he passed it over his eyes which remained unhurt while it turned into pure gold. The woman embraced Islám and her tomb is close to his. He died in 1519 A. D.[3]

The dyers of Lahore similarly affect the tomb of Ali Rangrez which is also that of his brothers Wali and Bahu.[4]

Pír Hádi, the 'shewer of the way', is much reverenced by the Khojas of Lahore.[5] His pedigree is :—

S. Shams-ud-Dín Tabriz

|

S. Abdul Qádir

|

Pír Hádi Ráhnuma. Mohsin Sháh. Abdulla Sháh.

Sháh Chirágh (Abdul Razzák), a descendant of the Pír Dastgír, has a lofty tomb at Lahore, erected by Aurangzeb. It is the scene of an annual fair.[6]

The Qalandars.

The Qalandars,[7] according to Brown, are not an order. One of the *darvesh* of the Qadirís was named Sháhbáz-i-Qalandari and another

[1] *Hist. of Lahore*, pp. 168-69.

[2] *Ib.*, pp. 202-03.

[3] *Ib.*, pp. 204-05.

[4] *Ib.*, p. 209.

[5] *Ib.*, p. 208.

[6] *Ib.*, p. 193.

[7] Described in Vol. III, p. 257 *infra*. The Sháh Báz settled on the Peshâwar border may be this Sháhbáz, the Qádiri. The shrine of Sháh Chokha, as already stated, is held by Chishti *khádims*.

of the Maulavís was called Shams-ud-Dín Tabrízi Qalandari.[1] But the Qalandars also appear to be connected with the Bektáshis some of whom wear the cap called Sháhbáz-i-Qalandari which is said to have been assumed by the Sháh, Adham, of Balkh and which is therefore called Adhami.[2]

THE SUHARWARDI ORDER.

The account given of the foundation of this order in Vol III, p. 432, is almost certainly incorrect. It was founded either by Shaikh Shiháb-ud-Dín Suharwardi who died in 632 H. and is entombed at Baghdád (and not in the fort of Multán, as erroneously stated in that art.) or by Shaikh Ziá-ud-Dín).[3] Shaikh Shiháb-ud-Dín's disciple Bahá-ud-Dín Zakaría is buried in the fort at Multán and hence is sometimes called Bahá-ud-Dín Zakaría Multáni.[4] Suharwardi comes from Suharward, a village in the Oxus valley.

At initiation into the Suharwardi order the *murshid* or spiritual guide first bids the disciple repent his sins, great and small. He is then directed to recite 5 *kalimas* and to attain to full conviction of the true faith, to recite the *namáz* regularly and to observe the fasts (*roza*). This is called *muríd hona*, 'to become disciple.' Jalál-ud-Dín, Mauláua Rúm, author of the *Masnawi*, belonged to this order. He was born at Balkh about 1207 A. D.[5] His parents claimed descent from Abú Baki,

[1] *The Dervishes*, p. 84: Brown however also gives the tradition that the Qalandars were founded in Spain and says the title means 'pure gold': p. 241.

[2] *Ib.*, p. 150.

[3] *Nafhat*. p. 873. Sh. Shiháb-ud-Dín did not come to India. It was Sh. Baháwal Dín who came to Multán: *vide Khazinat-ul-Asfia*, Vol. II, p. 19. The nightingale of Shíraz Sádi was the disciple of S. Shaháb: *vide Nafhat*, p. 441. Shaikh Ziá-ud-Dín was a son of Najib Suharwardi, uncle of Shaikh Shaháb-ud-Dín Suharwardi. Shaháb-ud-Dín's tomb is in Baghdád. Ghází-ud-Dín Khán Fíroz Jang Bahádar, father of the first Nizám of Haidarábád, was a grandson of Alam Shaikh, a saint and scholar of Samarqand who claimed descent from Sh. Shaháb-ud-Dín: Sarkar, *op. cit.*, p. 92.

[4] The learned Shaikh Baha-ud-Dín Zikaría Multáni, son of Wajíh-ud-Dín, was one of the greatest saints of his time. A disciple of Shaikh Shiháb-ud-Dín Umar Suharwardi of Baghdád, he received the garment of succession from him. The mildness of his nature earned him the title of Baha-ud-Dín, the 'angel'. His miracles were numerous and Bába Faríd Shakarganj addressed him as the Shaikh-ul-Islám. When Sultán Shams-ud-Dín Altamsh became king, Sultán Násir-ud-Dín Qabácha, governor of Multán, Uch and Sind planned a rebellion against him. Learning this Baha-ud-Dín Zikaría and Qázi Sharf-ud-Dín wrote to inform Altamsh of his intentions but their letters were intercepted by Qabácha. In revenge he sent for the writers and placing the letters before them asked if they were theirs. Qázi Sharf-ud-Dín admitted their authorship and was straightway beheaded, but Baha-ud-Dín declared that he had written them by a divine command, and they contained nothing but the truth. Overawed by his words Qabácha begged his forgiveness and let him go. He died on Thursday the 7th Saffar 666 H: *Saffinatal Aulia*, pp. 114-5; *Askar-i-Ahrar*, pp. 55-6; Farishta, Persian text, pp. 404-9; *Khasinatul Asfia*, II, pp. 19-26, and Beale, *Miftah-ut-Tawáríkh*, Persian text, p. 62.

[5] Described as 'the greatest pantheistic writer of all ages,' Jalál-ud-Dín died in 1272 A.D., 7 years after Dante's birth, and did not live to finish the *Masnawi*. His teaching is summed up in his last charge to his disciples:—'I bid you fear God openly and in secret; guard against excess in eating, drinking and speech; keep aloof from evil companionship; be diligent in fasts and self-renunciation and bear wrongs patiently. The best man is he who helps his fellow-men, and the best speech is a brief one which leads to knowledge. Praise be to God alone!' He bade man choose a *pír* to represent for him the Unseen God. His praise of the reed flute has made it one of the principal instruments in the melancholy music which accompanies the dancing of the Maulavi *darvesh*. 'It is a picture of the Súfi or enlightened man, whose life is, or ought to be, one long lament over his separation from the Godhead, for which he yearns till his purified spirit is re-absorbed into the Supreme Unity. We are here reminded of the words of Novalis, 'Philosophy is, probably speaking home sickness; the wish to be everywhere at home'. Field, *op. cit.*, pp. 148 *ff*.

father-in-law and successor of Muhammad. He had a mysterious friend in Shams-ud-Dín of Tabríz. Jalál characterised Shams-ud-Dín as a great alchemist and as a scholar in every science known to man, who had renounced them all to devote himself to the study and contemplation of the mysteries of Divine love. It would seem that under his influence Jalál instituted religious dancing or *hál khelná* amongst his disciples and on this account they earned the name of dancing *darvishes*. Shams met his death, it is said, during such a religious entertainment.

According to Petit the Suharwardi cover themselves with many pieces of different stuffs to remind them that 'man is ever naked and observed by God'.[1] But he also observes that their many-coloured costume represents the infinite variety of the creatures placed by God at man's service.

Shaikh Shams-ud-Dín Tabrízi, whose real name was Muhammad, was the son of Ali, son of Malik Dáda. Some say he was the disciple of Shaikh Abúbakr Silla-Báf Tabrízi; others that Kamál Khujandi or Shaikh Rukn-ud-Dín Sanjási was his father. Born to saintship he fasted for 40 days without a break even when a mere boy. Mauláná Jalál-ud-Dín Rúmi had great faith in him. Once, it is said, Shaikh Shams-ud-Dín reached Baqunia and found Jalál-ud-Dín sitting by a tank with some books busy teaching. After exchanging a few words with the Mauláná the Shaikh threw the books into the tank. The Mauláná was grieved to lose the books and said that some of them were rare and had belonged to his father, so the Shaikh put his hand into the water and took out all the books which were quite dry. The Mauláná thus became his disciple. One night the Shaikh was talking to the Mauláná in a private room, when a man came to the door and called him out. The Shaikh at once stood up and bidding farewell to the Mauláná said that men had come to kill him. As soon as the Shaikh went out seven men attacked him with daggers, but when he uttered a cry they all fell unconscious on the ground. On recovering they saw nothing but a few drops of blood, but no trace of the Shaikh could be found. It is not known where he was buried as his tomb is stated to be at two or three different places. His death occurred in 645 H. 1247 A.D.

The *wazír* of Qonia had built a college and himself took part in the dancing at the opening ceremony, but he discourteously collided with Shams-ud-Dín during the performance. Confusion resulting the police of the Sultán were called in and they led Shams-ud-Dín away and put him to death without further inquiry. Jalál-ud-Dín wrote this strange sentence on the door of Shams-ud-Dín's lodging—'This is the abode of the loved one of Elias, on whom be peace.' Jalál-ud-Dín's disciples followed their leader's example and practised dancing as a spiritual exercise but equally naturally strong objection was raised against it as being only worthy of mad men, the objectors going so far as to take legal advice which declared dancing, music and singing unlawful. Some of his chief disciples aver that his reason for instituting musical services in his order was that God had a great regard for the Roman people. Many objections were raised against dancing and religious ecstacies but

[1] *Les Confréries Musulmanes*, pp. 44 (citing Senoussi in Rinn, p. 210) and 45.

the Chishtia order now declares that *hál khelna* is lawful, though the other orders declare these practices unlawful.

Shaikh Shams-ud-Dín Tabrízi, whose tomb is at Multán, is a different saint. He was a Musavi Sayyid and his descendants who profess Shi'a tenets are known as Shamsi Sayyids: *Khazinat-ul-Asfiya*, II, pp. 268-70; *Safinat-ul-Auliya*, p. 179.

This order is closely connected with Multán. It is the home of an important Shi'a family who call themselves descendants of a saint of Multán named Shams Tabríz to whom in 1787 A.D. a large tomb was built. The name Shams, 'Sun', is peculiarly appropriate to the saint of a place like Multán, one of the hottest in India, and the story goes that the sun broiled a fish for him there when he was denied food by the citizens. Moreover the legend of the celebrated Shams-ud-Dín Tabrízi, who was killed at Qonia in 1247 A.D., was flayed alive and wandered about for four days afterwards with his skin in his hand, is also told of this Shams-ud-Dín of Multán, though his principal attribute is that he brought the sun nearer to the world at that place than any where else on earth.[1] The Shi'a guardians of the shrine indeed declare that the name Shams Tabrez is an error and that his real name is Shams-taprez or 'heat-giving'.[2]

The following is a list of shrines of the Suharwardia order:—

Name.	*Place.*	*Died in Hijra.*
Sh. Baha-ud-Dín	Multán	666
Sh. Sadr-ud-Dín	Do.	684
Sayyid Jalál-ud-Dín	Uch in Jhang	690
Sh. Ahmad	Multán	723
Sh. Rukn-ud-Dín	Do.	735
Sh. Hamíd-ud-Dín	Mau, a town in Multán	735
Sayad Jalál-ud-Dín	Uch in Jhang	785
Sh. Sadr-ud-Dín	Do.	827
Sayad Nasir-ud-Dín	Do.	847
Sh. Abdul Jalíl[3]	Lahore (Old Qila)	910
Sayyid Usmán	Lahore	912
Shaikh Músa	Lahore (Gumbaz Sabz)	925

[1] Temple: *Legends of the Punjab*, III, p. 87.

[2] Multán *Gazetteer*, Lahore, 1902, p. 350, citing Sir Alex. Cunningham, *Archæological Survey Reports*, Calcutta, 1875, V, pp. 135 and 184.

Possibly a similar origin may be ascribed to the Shamsi Táláb or Sun Tank at Mihrauli near Delhi. On its bank stands the Jaház Mahal, a curious building which bears no resemblance to a ship, as its name would imply, though it is popularly ascribed to such a likeness or to its proximity to water. This Táláb is famous in Muhammadan folk-lore: Annual Progress Report of Superintendent, Muhammadan and British Monuments, Northern Circle (Allahabad), 1914, p. 41. It was known to Timúr as the Hauz i-Shamsi or Cistern of Shams-ud-Dín Altamsh, the first Turk emperor of Delhi.

[3] Shaikh Abdul Jalíl or Shaikh Chuhar married a daughter of Sikandar Lodi and died in 1534 leaving a son, Abdul Fateh. His miracles are recorded in the *Tazkara Qutbia* and his descendants who live in Batta Pírán, in Siálkot, are still much respected: *Hist. of Lahore*, p. 205.

Name.	*Place.*	*Died in Hijra.*
Sh. Sayad Haji Abdul Wahâb	Delhi ...	932
Sayad Jamál-ud-Dín ...	Do. ...	948
Sayad Jhulan Sháh ...	Lahore ...	1003
Sh. Hasan Ganjdagar ...	Do. ...	1012
Mírán Muhammad Shah ...	Do. ...	1014
Sháh Jamál	Near Ichchra in Lahore	1049
Sháh Daulah Daryái ...	Gujrát ...	1075
Shaikh Ján Muhammad ...	Lahore ...	1082
Sh. Muhd. Ismaíl ...	Do. ...	1085
Sh. Ján Muhd. II ...	Do. ...	1120
Kh. Ayúb	Do. ...	1055

Shaikh Hamíd ud-Dín Abulgais, entitled Shaikh Hákim, 16th in descent from Záid-ud-Din Háras Muhammad Asghar and 17th from 705 H.
Ali himself, was a governor of Kich Mekrán in 1208. The warning of a female slave whom he had caused to be flogged induced him to renounce the world. He came to his mother's father Sayyid Ahmad Tokhta at Lahore and also received instruction from Shaikh Shahâb-ud-Dín himself, Baha-ud-Dín Zakaría, and Shaikh Rukn-ud-Dín Abul Fath, who appointed him his *khalifa* with a mission to preach Islám between Neh and Sakkar. At Mau a Jogi was converted by him and took the name of Zain-ud-Dín. His descendants are the present *mujáwars*. Shaikh Hákim corrected the faulty orientation of the great mosque built by Altamsh at Delhi, but his request for the hand of that ruler's daughter led to his imprisonment. But eventually his miracles compelled the king to bestow on him the hand of his daughter the *patráni* Aisha, and a great *jágír* between Multán and Bhakhar. That lady's tomb is at Lahore close to that of S. Ahmad Tokhta, but Shaikh 770 H.
Hákim's body was buried at Mau Mubárik. He died in 1368 at the age of 222, an age not attained by any other Suharwardi saint. Vows are made and vigils kept at his shrine.[1] An interesting feature of his career was his emancipation of his Hindu slaves who in gratitude embraced Islám. The *maliks* among their descendants were originally his door-keepers and their real tribe was Pargár or Palhár.[2]

Sháh Dujan has a shrine at Jínd town, and a full account of it is given in the Jínd *Gazetteer*.[3] Sháh Dujan was a disciple of Shaikh Sadar-ud-Dín Máleri and was appointed by him as Sháh or spiritual governor of Jínd. He died in 964 A. H. There were two tombs, one of the Sháh himself and the other of his wife.

The Naqshbandi Order.[4]

Khwája Baha-ud-Dín of Turkestán, founder of this order, who died in 792 H. and was buried near Bukhára, must not be confounded with Baha-ud-Dín Multáni. Khwája Ahmad Naqshband, who died in 1034 H.

[1] Baháwalpur *Gazetteer*, pp. 167-8.
[2] Clearly Pratihára or 'chamberlain'; *cf.*, the Scotch Durward.
[3] In Phulkián States *Gazetteer*, 1904, Jínd, p. 261.
[4] Vol. III, p. 157.

and is buried at Sirhind in Patiála, was the disciple of Khwája Baqí' whose shrine is at Delhi where he too was buried in 1012 H.

Khwája Baha-ud-Dín Naqshband had four important disciples, one of whom Khwája Yaqúb Charkhi is buried at Malafko in Hissár.

The method of *tasawwuf* in the Naqshbandia order is as follows:—

The disciple is first directed to put aside all external and internal anxieties and to sit in solitude, having no thought of enmity or anger, to be moderate in eating and to bring death before his mind, and to ask pardon of his sins from God. Then he must close his eyes and lips and draw breath into his heart or stomach or in other words stop breathing. This is called *habs-i-dám*. After this he must utter the word *lá* from his heart and prolong it from his *náf*, navel, to his right side up to his shoulder and then repeat the word 'Alláh' and then the words 'illa-Alláh'.

According to Punjab traditions the following is the line of the Naqshbandi *Pírs*:—

No.	Name.
1	The Prophet.
2	Abu Bakr as Saddiq the 2nd Caliph.
3	Silmán Fársi.
4	Imám Qásim bin Muhammad, son of Abu Bakr.
5	Imám Jáfar Sádiq.
6	Bayazíd Bustámi.
7	Khwája Abul Hasan Khargáni.
8	" Abul Qásim Gargáni or Kerkiápi.
9	" Abu Ali Farmadi or Farmandi.
10	" Abu Yúsuf Hamdani.
11	" Abdul Khálíq Ghajdawani.
12	" Muhammad Árif Reogari or Riokari.
13	" Mahmud Abkhair Faghnawi.
14	" (Azizan) Ali Ramitani or Rametni.
15	" Muhammad Baba Sammasi.
16	" Sayd Amír Kalál or Gulan.
17	" " Bahá-ud-Dín Naqshband.
18	" Ala-ud-Dín Attár.
19	" Yáqúb Charkhi.
20	" Nasir-ud-Dín Ubaidullah Ahrár.
21	" Muhammad Záhid.
22	Mauláne Darvesh Muhammad.
23	" Khwajgi Amkinki.
24	Khwája Muhammad Baqi Billa Berang.
25	Imám Rabbáni Mujadid Alif-sáni Sh. Ahmad Farúki Sirhindi.[1]
26	Khwája Muhammad Másúm.
27	Sh Saifuddín.
28	M. Háfiz Muhammad Muhsin Dihlawi.
29	Sayyid Núr Muhammad Badauni.
30	Shams-ud-Dín Habíbulláh Mazhar Shahíd Mirza Janjanan.
31	Mujaddid Mistusáliswal Ashar Sayyid Abdulla (Sháh Ghulám Ali Ahmadi).
32	Sháh Abu Said Ahmadi.
33	Sháh Ahmad Said Ahmadi.
34	Háji Dost Muhammad Qandhári.
35	" Muhammad Usmán (shrine at Kuláchi in Dera Ismaíl Khan).

[1] He is considered the reformer of the second thousand years after the Prophet.

This agrees fairly well with Brown's account.[1] He, however, traces the spiritual pedigree of the order from Ali, through the Imáms Husain Zain-al-Abidain, Muhammad Báqir and Já'fir Sádiq, to Sh. Báyazíd Bustámi and adds :—'Báyazíd Bustámi was born after the decease of the Imám Já'far Sádiq, but by the force of the will of the latter received spiritual instruction from him. Imám Já'far also spiritualised Qásim, grandson of Abu Bakr'. From Báyazíd he brings the line down with one or two additions to Alai-ud-Dín Attár, but after him he gives a different succession of the Naqshbandi *pírs*.[2] The Punjab line appears to begin with the Khwája Baqi-billa who is buried at Delhi.

The members of the order are styled Khwájagán or teachers, and the *khalífas* and disciples of Obaidulla were *walís* whose shrines are scattered over the countries of Sind, Bukhára, Persia and their confines.[3] Various members of it enunciated different opinions, one declaring that the soul returns to earth in a new body. Others taught the necessity of *khalwat* or meditation so profound and continued as to completely absorb the mind, so that even in a crowd the meditator can hear no sound. Every word spoken by others will then appear to him *zikr*, and so will his own words also when spoken on other topics. The practice of *zikr* is highly elaborated, according to Brown, and by it, by *khalwat, tawajjuh, murákaba, tasarraf* and *tawassuf* the fervent *darwesh* attains peculiar spiritual powers called *quvvat-i-ruhi bátini* or inward spiritual power and in a *shaikh* or *pír* the exercise of these powers is called *quvvat irádat* or will-power. It extends to the ability to cause death even at a distance.

Petit[4] regards the Naqshbandís as one of the convulsionary orders, to a certain extent. Armed with long sticks and with hair streaming in the wind they utter loud cries, and trample on sharp stones until they fall insensible from pain. These exercises are chiefly practised in Persia. Petit also speaks of their ideal which is to be absorbed in God by developing the *quvvat-ul-irádat* or strength of will. Familiarised thereby with the various phenomena of mental suggestion they are regarded by the people as having a discretionary power over nature. Their lesser attributes consist in foretelling the future, settling events in advance, healing at a distance, and smiting their enemies from afar. When in their contemplations ecstacy is slow to supervene, they are said to use opium and its preparations.

According to the *Rashihát* the Khoja Ahmad Tasawwi aided Sultán Abu Sa'íd against Bábar and saved Samarkand when he attacked that place. That saint claimed to be able to affect the minds of sovereigns by *taskhír* or the subduing faculty.[5] Brown's account of the *tarks* varies. He describes the Naqshbandís as wearing caps of 18 *tarks*[6]

[1] The *Rashihát 'Ain-al-Hayát* or 'Drops from the Fountain of Life' ascribes the order to Obaidulla, and makes Baha-ud-Dín merely a learned exponent of its principles : Brown, *The Dervishes*, p. 127.

[2] *Ib.*, pp. 125-6.

[3] All this appears to be based on the *Rashihát*.

[4] *Op. cit.*, pp 15 *f*. The parallels between these practices and the Hindu *yoga* are self-evident.

[5] Brown, *op. cit.*, p. 137.

[6] *Ib.*, p. 53.

or only 4.[1] The cap, generally white, is always embroidered and used to contain a verse of the Qurán. The order performs *ikhlás* or prayers seated, each member reciting one *ikhlás* until 1001 have been said. The number is checked by the use of pebbles as tallies.

The Nurbakhshis[2] are evidently an offshoot of the Naqshbandis, but Brown, who gives their spiritual descent,[3] says nothing about their practices.

Naqshbandi shrines are found as below—

Name.	*Place.*
Khwája Baqi-billa Naqshbandi ...	Delhi.
No building over his grave exists.	
Sáín Tawakkal Sháh Naqshbandi ...	Ambála.
Qutb Sáhib	Tháneaar.
Mujaddid Sáhib Shaikh Ahmad	Sirhind
Sh. Ahmad Said Sh. Mohámmad Masum Sh. Saif-ud-Dín	Sirhind
Kh. Khawand Mahmúd	Lahore
Sh. Sadi	Mozang, Lahore.
Sayad Núr Muhammad Sh. Abdul Ahd Sh. Muhammad Abid	Sirhind
Sháh Abdullah	Delhi
Sháh Abu Saíd	Tonk
Hazrat Ghulám Mohiy-ud-Dín ...	Kasúr
Sayad Imám Alí Sháh	Ratr Chhatr in Gurdáspur.[4]
Sh. Mahmúd Sháh Sh. Hájí Muhammad Sa'íd Ján Muhammad ...	Lahore

THE NAUSHAHI[5] AND QAISARSHAHI ORDERS.

These are two recent offshoots or sub-orders of the Qádria. The founder of the Naushábi is also said to have been named Shaikh Háji Muhammad whose tomb is at Chhani Sahnpal, on the Chenab

[1] Brown, *The Dervishes*, p. 57.

[2] Alluded to in Vol. III, p. 174, *infra*.

[3] Brown, *op. cit.*, p. 126.

[4] Near Dera Nának. Like Masánian near Batála this is a seat of Sayyid *pírs*. Both possess Muhammadan buildings of some interest: Gurdáspur *Gazetteer*, 1914, p. 31.

[5] Vol. III, p. 166.

opposite Rámnagar in the Wazírábád tahsíl. The Qaisarsháhi derive their name from Qaisar Sháh, whose shrine is at Wayánwáli in the same tahsíl. Many followers of these two sub-orders are to be found in the Gujránwála District.

Like the Chishtís the Naushális are deeply attached to spiritual and moral hymns and in ecstasy forget themselves and everything under the sun. Other Súfi orders do not bind themselves to any such observances and lay great stress on the simplicity observed in the time of the Prophet and his four companions.

The rites observed by each Súfi order after prayers differ slightly, but the spirit of them all is the same and leads to a common goal, *viz.* the annihilation and absorption of self and everything else in the unity of God.

A Naushálhi shrine at Lahore is that of Fazl Sháh, a native of Sai'dpur in Zafarwál tahsíl, Siálkot. First the *mulláh* of a mosque, then a maker of spectacles, he became a disciple of Rahmán Sháh Naushálhi and a *mast faqír* who squandered the money given him by his follower Rájá Dína Náth and in his fits used to abuse and pelt him with stones. He died in 1854 and was buried in the tomb which the Rájá had made for him in his life-time.[1] He appears to have given its name to the Masti gate of the city.

Pír Sháh, whose *takia* stands at the Zíra gate of Ferozepur city, belonged to the Naushális. One of his followers is in charge of the tomb. A fair is held here in Bhádon when alms are distributed.

At a small gathering held at Cháwa in Bhera tahsíl during the Muharram Naushálhi *faqírs* have hymns sung which cast some of the hearers into ecstasy. The patient becomes unconscious or raving and is then suspended by his heels from a tree till he recovers. But such practices are reprobated by the learned.[2]

THE MADÁRI ORDER.

To the account given in Vol. III, pp. 43-4, some additions may be made. According to the legends current in Patiála, the Madári owe their origin to Badí'-ud-Dín, Madár, a son of Abu Isháq, the Shámi, and their *mír ḍera* or chief shrine in Patiála is the *takia* of Murád Ali Sháh at Banúr. They have other *ḍeras* in that tahsíl, but the most interesting feature in their cult is their connection with the shrine of Háji Ratan near Bhaṭinḍa which is held by Madári *mujáwars* descended from a Madári with the Hindu name of Sháh Chand who came from Makanpur in Oudh. Tradition makes Háji Ratan himself a Hindu, by name Ratan Pál, who assumed the title of Háji Ratan on conversion.

Ratan Pál or Chan Kaur—the latter name could hardly be borne by a man—was *díwán* to a Hindu Rája[3] of Bhaṭinḍa but he betrayed that fortress to the Moslems.

[1] *Hist. of Lahore*, p. 182.

[2] Sháhpur *Gazetteer*, p. 88.

[3] Bina Pál or Vena Pál.

Born a Chauhán Rájpút, like Gugga, his knowledge of astrology told him that a prophet called Muhammad would be born in Arabia who would spread the religion of Islám. In order to be able to see the Prophet he practised restraining his breath, and after the prophet had performed the miracle of splitting the moon into two he set out to Mecca in order to meet him. There he embraced Islám and lived with him 30 years, so that he was numbered among the *asháb* or companions of the Prophet. After that period he returned to India by order of the Prophet and stayed at the place where his shrine is now and where he continued the practice of restraining his breath. When Shaháb-ud-Dín Ghori proceeded to Bhaṭinḍa to fight Pirthi Ráj he went to pay a visit to the Háji who miraculously supplied his whole army with water from a single jug. The invader asked him to pray for the conquest of the fort of Bhaṭinḍa, whereupon the saint replied that it would be conquered by the help of two Sayyids of his army. The sign by which he could recognise them would be that while a storm would blow down all the other tents of the camp their tent would not be hurt and they would be found in it reading the *Qurán*. When the king had found out the two Sayyids, they declared themselves ready to undertake the task in which however they foretold they would lose their lives. The fort was conquered, the two Sayyids fell as martyrs and their tombs are now to the north of the shrine of Bába Ratan. The Bába himself died shortly after the conquest of the fort at the age of 200 years.

This is the legend as told at Bhaṭinḍa But Bába Ratn was destined to find a much wider field of fame. Several Muhammadan writers of the 7th and 8th centuries of the Hijra mention having seen Ratan and one of them, Daúd Ibn As'ad of Assisiút in Egypt, calls him Ratan the son of Medan, the son of Mandi, the Indian money-changer. The story which he heard from him was to the effect that after having gone to Syria where he found Christianity to be the ruling religion he turned Christian, but later on in Medina he became a convert to Islám. According to Daúd the Háji's death took place in 608 H. (1277 A. D.). Another account gives some particulars of his appearance. His teeth were small like those of a snake, his beard was like thorns, his hair white, his eyebrows had grown so long that they reached down to his cheeks and had always to be turned up with the help of hooks. He was known in Mesopotamia. A Ratan Sháh is known to Kashmir legends and in the 11th century a traveller informs us that Bába Ratan was considered by the gardeners of Constantinople to be their patron saint. This post however he owes probably to some of the Sufic orders which we know exercised in all Muhammadan countries a great influence on the guilds of the various trades and their organisation. Among the patrons of the various guilds we very rarely find saints that were not exceptionally long-lived and it is probably chiefly as a *mu'ammar* or long-lived person that Bába Ratan has attained this rank.[1]

The Jaláli Order.

This order described in Vol. II, p. 350, as one of the regular Muhammadan orders is perhaps an off-shoot of the Suharwardia and in Patiála its *faqírs* are said to be distinguished by their glass bracelets which

[1] See also *Journal, Punjab Hist. Society*, II, p. 97 *f.*

recalls the sect which wears women's clothes in Sind. When epidemic disease breaks out among goats people offer them goats to stop the evil. They repeat the words 'Panjtan' and 'Dam Maula'. They have a *dera* at Ghanaur in Patiála.[1] Brown[2] ascribes the foundation of the order to Sayyid-i-Jalál who gives his name to a cap worn by the Bektásh which has seven *tarks*.[3]

The *sáin* in charge of the Musallis' *takia* in Ferozepur also belongs to the Jalális. His predecessor became its incumbent in the time of Rání Lachhman Kaur. The well, *takia* and mosque belonged to the Musallís and they settled him (Ináyat Sháh) here.

Hasan Ali was a Bukhári Sayyid of Bahra who belonged to the Jaláli order. His tomb lies in the *takia*, known as that of Guláb Sháh or Ghore Sháh on the road from the Ferozepur Municipal Board School to the Sadr. Prayers are said and alms distributed here in Muharram at the Chihlam or 40th day.

The Bektáshi order is ascribed to Háji Bektásh Wali, but the accounts of him are quite legendary. They say he belonged to Níshápur, was a pupil of Ahmad Yesewi and died in 1337, but the figure 738 H. is merely arrived at by calculating the letters in the word 'Bektáshia'. The tradition that Bektásh blessed the Janissaries under Orkhán appears to be based on their later connection with the order. Its existence under this name can only be proved for the 16th century, but the movement organised by it in western Turkey is older and moreover after the order was founded that movement spread far beyond its limits. In Albania the Bektáshís are a sect rather than an order. The Qizil-básh and Ali-iláhís agree in the main Bektáshi doctrines. In those doctrines Súfi ideas about the equality of all religious and the worthlessness of external ceremonies play an important part. Professing to the Sunnís for the most part they are extreme Shi'as, recognizing the twelve Imáms, and especially Ja'far-us-Sádiq, with the fourteen Ma'súm-i-pák or 'pure children', who are mostly Alid martyrs. Prayers offered at the graves of saints may take the place of ritual worship, and Bektáshís have often settled at old and famous places of pilgrimage and so made them their own. They have the doctrine of the Trinity, Ali taking the place of Jesus (Alláh, Muhammad and Ali), and celebrate a communion of wine, bread and cheese at meetings in the *maidán oḍasy*, or hall of assembly in the monastery (*takia*).[4] They deny that they have *zikr*. They also confess to their *bábás* and receive absolution. Wine is not forbidden, owing to the importance of the vine in their cult, nor do their women wear veils. One section still lives in celibacy—which was

[1] Phulkián States *Gazetteer*, Patiála, p. 80.

[2] Brown, *The Dervishes*, p. 150.

[3] For a song about Jaláli the blacksmith's daughter see Temple, *Legends*, II, p. 168. This tale seems purely mythical. Jaláli was carried off by a local king and rescued by Bode Sháh, the shaven *sádh* or priest, also called Jaláli. Legend says he came from Mecca and connects him with Abdul-Qádir Jíláni. He has a shrine vaguely described as near Lahore on the Amritsar road. His great feat was making the *dúb* grass of India green and sweet for ever, so he is clearly a survival of nature-worship merged in the Jaláli tenets.

[4] Similarly, the Qizzilbásh in Eastern Anatolia who must be regarded as a branch of the Shi'as, 'combine the identities of Ali and Our Lord, of Ali's sons Hasan and Husain and SS. Peter and Paul, of the twelve Imáms and the twelve Apostles': Lukach, *City of Dancing Dervishes*, p. 187.

UUU

probably the original rule for the whole order. They have adopted the mystic doctrine of numbers, particularly that of four, and also believe in the metempsychosis. The head of a monastery is called *bábá*, and all celibates have since the middle of the 16th century had a head of their own, the *mujarrad babasy*. The ordinary *darvesh* is called a *muríd* and a layman attached to a *takia*, *muntasib*. The dress of the order is a white cloak and cap (*sikke*) made of 12 (usually) or several triangular bits of cloth, corresponding to the twelve Imáms. Round the cap the *bábás* wear the green turban. An amulet of stone (*taslím tásh*) is generally worn round the neck.[1] The double axe and long staff complete the full dress, celibates also wear earrings as a distinguishing mark. The Bektáshís were chaplains to the Janissaries and overwhelmed in their ruin in 1826, but they have recovered much ground.

Members of the order are affiliated with French masonic lodges. Its headquarters are at Rumili Hissár.[2] But the mother-monastery (*pír ewi*) is at Háji Bektásh between Kirshahr and Kaisariye, and there its Grand Master or Chalabi resides.[3]

The cult of the vine was a feature of the old pre-Zoroastrian cult of Armenia.[4] The double axe is peculiarly interesting in view of its associations with an early Greek or Mycenæan divinity.[5]

The 'howling' *darvesh* also carry an axe, but it is not double.[6]

Brown's account of the Bektásh is full and worth quoting at some length, not only as an instructive example of a Muslim order and its developments but also because it casts much light on the kindred orders, the Qalandars and Naqshbandís. According to one of his informants Háji Bektásh,[7] Ján Núsh, Sháhbáz-i-Qalandari, Jalál-i-Bukhári and Luqmán Qalandari were all disciples of Ahmad-al-Yassavi and originally Naqshbandís. But each founded a separate order and the tombs of Jalál and Sháhbáz are at Simna near Kurdistán while that of Ján Núsh

[1] Or 'stone of submission' regarding which various interpretations are current. One is that it is worn to commemorate the Prophet's gift of Fátima to Ali: Brown, *The Darvishes*, p. 151. Another is that it is the *darvesh-darveshán* or miraculous stone with 12 holes worn by Moses: *ib.*, p. 149.

[2] W. S. Monroe, *Turkey and the Turks*, p. 281.

[3] All the foregoing is taken from the *Dicty. of Islám*, pp. 691-2. For the Bektáshís in Albania, see p. 452.

Lukach records that the Chelebi Effendi derives his title from Ar. *salib*, 'crucifix': *The City of Dancing Dervishes*, p. 22.

[4] *Encyclopædia of Religion and Ethics*, I, p. 794.

[5] A. J. Evans, *The Mycenæan Tree and Pillar Cult*, 1901, pp. 8 *ff*.

[6] See illustration at p. 284 in *Turkey and the Turks*. This or some other modern work illustrates a Turkish *darvesh* with a dagger thrust through both cheeks. As showing how religious symbolism and practices tend to reproduce themselves Bishop Whitehead, *The Village Gods of South India*, p. 79, may be cited. The devotee of Durga pins his cheeks together with a long safety-pin to ensure concentration of mind when drawing nigh her shrine. In both cases the origin of the practice may be similar.

[7] But Brown also predicates two Bektáshes, one Bektásh 'Kúli' the 'servant' of God, author of the *Bostán-i-Khiál* or Garden of Reflection; the other Háji Bektásh who lived in Asia Minor under Sultán Murád I and blessed the Janissaries. Brown reproduces a curious note on the origin of the Bektáshís which says that the *musáfirs* of Rúm are divided into four classes, the *gházís* or heroes, *akhián* or brothers, *abdáls* or ascetics, and the *hem-bajis* or sisters. 'Háji Bektásh chose the Bájián-i-Rúm among the Bulaurs (whoever they may be) and made over his principles of spiritual power to the Khátun Anádur (a lady of the latter name) and then died': *op. cit.*, p. 142.

is in Khorásán. All except Jalál wore the costume of the order of Háji Bektásh, but while Ján Núsh had 12 *tarks* in his cap, Sháhbáz had only 7 and Luqmán 4, while the dissentient Jalál had only one. The spiritual descent of Háji Bektásh is traced up to Ali through the same or almost the same steps as that of the Naqshbandís.[1] But the Bektásh have a characteristic legend regarding the preaching of their spiritual doctrines. As the angel Gabriel had invested (with a cloak and so on) Adam, Abraham and the Prophet, so the last named invested Ali, he Salmán-i-Fársi and Umr Ummia Bilál Habshi, and these did the same for 12 others, including Zu-n-Nún Misri who was sent to Egypt, Suhaili who went to Rúm, Dáúd Yamani to the Yemen and Salmán to Baghdád.[2]

The rites of the Bektásh are numerous and elaborate and with them religious symbolism has reached a high development. At initiation the *muríd* is deprived of nearly all clothing[3], his breast being bared, and anything metallic or mineral on his person is taken from him, to symbolise that he sacrifices the world and all its wealth. His initiation is preceded by the sacrifice of a sheep, as among the Rafáis, and with a rope made of its wool he is led into the hall of the *takia* by two *turjumáns* or interpreters. This hall is square and in its octagonal centre is one stone called the *maidán tásh* on which stands a lighted candle, while around it are 12 seats of white sheepskin, *post* or *postaki*. At an initiation the candle on the *maidán tásh* is replaced by one placed in front of each post. The *murshid* or *shaikh* is seated on one *post* and 11 members of the order on the others. The *muríd* is led to the central stone on which he stands with crossed arms, his hands resting on his shoulders, his whole body leaning towards the *shaikh* in a prescribed attitude. The litany of initiation is simple, but it is accompanied or ratified by the *muríds'* kneeling before the *shaikh*, their knees touching, while each holds the other's right hand, the two thumbs raised in the form of the letter *alif*. Every incident in the ritual has its meaning. The *maidán tásh* represents the altar on which Abraham was about to offer up his son, or the stone of contentment which is also worn in the girdle of this order. The 12 Imáms are represented by the 12 members seated on the *posts*. The Bektáshis are credited, as usual in the case of such orders, with secret panthëistical or even atheistical doctrines and it is said that the *muríd* is required to admit that there is no God, meaning that all nature is God, but this is not proved. The *shaikh* is said to represent Ali, but the *muríd* makes his vows to the *pír* or founder of the order, not to the *shaikh*. Before his initiation he is tested for a full year during which he is styled a *mahaqq* or catechumen, being entrusted with false secrets to test his powers of guarding the real mysteries of the order. He is guided to the *takia* by two *rahpars* who remain outside it armed with the *tabbar*, a halberd of

[1] Abu Bakr as-Sadiq, 1st Caliph, and Ali both taught Salmán Fársi and *he* taught Muhammad Sádiq (son of Abu Bakr) who passed on the tradition to his son Ja'far, he to Abu Yazíd (*sic*) Bustámi, he to Abul Hasan Harrakiani, he to Abu'l-Qásim Karkáni, he to Ali Ali-al Farmadi, he to Yusuf Hamadáni and he to Ahmad Yassavi.

[2] Salmán's name seems to occur in two capacities. Zu-n-Nún, the Egyptian Sufi, is said to have been the first to formulate the doctrine of ecstatic states (*hál*, and *maqámát*). His orthodoxy was not above suspicion. He died in 245 H.: Macdonald, *op. cit*, p. 176.

[3] He is only stripped if he intends to take the vow of celibacy (*mujarrad iqrár*).

peculiar shape. But as these *rahpars* are two in number and do not enter the *takia* it can hardly be said that the *rahpar* represents Muhammad and the idea that the Prophet is thus placed lower than the Caliph appears to be unfounded. The *iqrár* or vow is comprehensive and concludes with the *muríd's* acceptance of Muhammad as his *rahpar* and Ali as his *murshid*. The dress of the Bektáshi consists of a sleeveless vest (*haidri*) with a streak supposed to be the word Ali, and 12 lines symbolizing the Imáms: a *khirqa* with a similar streak: a girdle of white wool: a cord (*kambaria*[1]) of goat's hair to which is attached a crystal called *najf*[2]: earrings[3] (*mangosh*) like those of the Rifá'is; and a cap. This cap is called *táj* and in the case of a *shaikh* has 12 *tarks* which are of 4 doors, but in the case of a lower degree it is simply made of white felt in four parts, signifying *shari'at*, *tariqat*, *haqiqat* and *ma'rifat*. The *táj* is however the subject of much mystic symbolism and as already noted the number of the *tarks* is not fixed. Passing over the significance of such ritual paraphernalia as the *dolak* or legging, the *lavank* or long robe and the *muliffah* or wide dress (the two latter garments were worn by the Prophet when he declared his light and Ali's to be one), the *kashgúl* or beggar's bowl, the *figni* or pilgrim's staff, the *chillik* or rod,[4] used in punishment, and the *luffar* or horn, this account of the order may be closed with references to two points of general interest. The Bektáshís appear to lay peculiar stress on the docrine of the *misál* or spiritual counterpart of the body which is its spiritual *pír*. It dies 40 days before the temporal self and so forewarns the body to which it belongs of impending events. God, it is held, does not make saints of the ignorant. He has them first taught by the *misál* and then makes them *aulia*. It is regrettable that our knowledge of this doctrine is not fuller. Another doctrine of the Bektáshis finds a curious parallel in the eastern Punjab. As the *shaikh* in the assembled *takia* represents Ali, so the next *post* is that of the cook, or Said Ali Balkhi, a *khalífa* of the order: the 3rd that of the breadmaker, Bahím Sultán: the 4th that of the *nakíb* or deputy *shaikh* after Gai Gasus: the 5th, that of the *maidán* is occupied by the Superintendent of the *takia*, representing Sári Ismáil: the 6th that of its steward, called after Kúli Achik Hájim Sultán: the 7th of the coffee-maker, after Shazali Sultán: the 8th, of the bag-bearer, after Kara Daulat Ján Baba: the 9th, of the sacrificer, after Ibrahím Khalíl-ullah (Abraham): the 10th, of the ordinary attendant of the services, after Abdul Musa: the 11th, of the groom, after Kamber, Ali's groom; and the 12th, of the *mihmándar* or entertainer of guests, after Khizr.[5]

[1] Ali's horse, Duldul, had a groom Kambaria who used to tie its rope round its waist. It had 3 knots, *ul-bághi* (hand-tie), *dil-bághi* (tongue-tie) and *bel-bághi* (rein-tie). The *kambaria* thus reminds its wearer that he must not steal, lie or commit fornication.

[2] Apparently the same as the stone of contentment.

[3] The *mangosh táshi* is shaped like a new moon and commemorates the horse-shoe of Ali.

[4] Brown describes this as kept 'in the *takia*' (p. 153) and as, like the *fiqui* and *tabr* carried when on a long journey (p. 159). The *jamjama* is a skin thrown over the shoulder when travelling.

[5] Brown, *op. cit.*, p. 153. Khizr seems to be specially affected by the Bektáshis. With 15 other prophets he wore their girdle which was first worn by Adam. He is called the chief of all the *auliar*: *ib.*, p. 145.

A curious parallel to this list is afforded by the Sayyids of Karnál.

Mr. J. R. Drummond, C. S., first called attention to the fact that the Sayyids of certain villages in Karnál, who are of the Bára-Sa'ádát, had a curious system of clan names, and subsequently the following account of them was obtained by Sayyid Iltáf Hussain, Honorary Magistrate at Karnál:—

The Bára-Sa'ádát have a curious system by which the inhabitants of each hamlet or *basti* are known by certain nick-names These Sayyids are descended from Sayyid Abdul-Farash Wásiti, son of Sayyid Dáúd or Sayyid Hussain. A list of the *bastis* and nicknames is appended :—

Name of Basti.		*Nickname.*
Sanbalhera	..	Kafandozi, or sewer of shrouds.
Mojhara	...	Confectioner.
Míránpur	...	Sheep-butcher.
Kethora	...	Butcher.
Tandhera	...	Bhútni, she-ghost.
Khojera	...	Ghost.
Kakroli	...	Dog.
Behra	...	Chamár, scavenger or leather-worker.
Morna	...	Camel.
Jatwára	...	Pig.
Nagla	...	Barber.
Jansatha	...	Chirimár, bird-catcher.
Chitora	..	Mimic.
Kawal	...	Jariya, one who sets glass or stone in ornaments.
Jauli	...	Teli, or oilman.
Tasang	...	Dúm.
Salarpur	...	Chútiya, fool.
Ghalibpur	...	He-ass.
Sedipur	...	She-ass.
Kelaudah	...	Kunjra, green-grocer.
Bahari	...	Goldsmith.
Baháđurpur	...	Kungar, rustic.
Biláspur	...	Khumra, a cutter of mill stones.
Palri	...	Kamángar, a bowman or bow-maker.

Name of Basti.		*Nickname.*
Saudhawali	...	Dár-ul-Himaqat, house of foolishness.
Pimbora		
Sarái	...	Bhatiára, baker.
Churiyala	...	Manihár, bangle-maker.
Tassar	...	Sweeper.
Sakrera	...	Owl.
Muzaffarnagar	...	Eunuch.

At first sight some of these names look like totems, and one is tempted to see in them traces of Arabian totem-clans, which would be in accord with the claim to be descended from the tribe of Quresh. This, however, does not appear to be the true explanation of the names, which, it should be noted, are called *palwal*, or 'countersigns' by the Sayyids themselves. Moreover, the Bára-Sa'adát are all Shi'as, except those who live in Latheri village, and even they intermarry with the Shi'as.[1]

The nicknames given above appear to be in reality relics of a system of initiation into the degrees of a secret order, and are paralleled in Turkey in the order of the Maulavís, in which the novice is called the scullion, and so on. The Shi'as have always tended to become organized into orders, or secret societies, and the Assassins of the Elburz formed in the Middle Ages the most powerful and famous of these associations. They also had a system of degrees into which their adherents were successively initiated. The Turís of the Kurram Valley, who are or claim to be Shi'as, also have signs by which they ascertain if a man is straight, *i.e.* a Shi'a, or crooked, *i.e.* a non-Shi'a.

The Rafá'i.

The Rafá'i, briefly described in the article on Gurzmár in Vol. II, p. 321, is one of the most interesting of the Islámic orders. Macdonald ascribes its foundation to Ahmad ar-Rifa'a in 576 H. and is of opinion that the Auládd Ilwan or sons of Shaikh Ilwan who is said to have founded the first monastic order as early as 49 H. are a sect of the Rifa'ites.[2] But Brown says its founder's name was Ahmad Sa'íd Rafá'i whose claim 'to have his foot over the necks of all the saints of Allah' is admitted by his followers. The Rafá'is are chiefly distinguished by their *ridáli khirqa*, which must have a green edging,[3]

[1] The Bára Sa'adát were also settled in the Punjab, *e.g.* at Sirhind: see Temple, *Legends, III*, p. 327. The tale is that Sayyid Asmún, son of Sayyid Akbar Shah, governor of Sirhind, was killed at Sháh Jahán's court. Probably it is historically incorrect, but recalls some events of religious importance. Bára or Bárha Báwín near Sirhind may still exist.

It is characteristic of the Qádiriás in Arabia, also that the celebrated saint Shaikh Hámid, founder of a long line of holy men at Madína, bore the title of *al-sammán*, 'the seller of clarified butter': Burton, *Al-Madinah*, p. 162.

[2] *The Dervishes*, pp. 267-8. The *khánqáh* of Mían Shakúr in Ferozepur with which no fair is connected has the following history: Shakúr was a *faqír* possessing miraculous powers and the *khánqáh*, which contains his tomb, was in existence before the village was founded in 1869. It contains a grave enclosed by a wall. Its management is in the hands of Mían Núr Sháh *faqír*, a Gurzmár. He sweeps the floor daily, beats a drum every Thursday; and keeps a green cover over the tomb. Worshippers may offer new green covers to the tomb. The *mujáwar* himself keeps charge of the fire (for *hukkahs*) and lives on alms collected from the villages.

[3] *Op. cit.*, p. 113, where the origin of this is explained by a legend.

and their *táj* or cap. The *táj* is white and has 8 or 12 *tarks* each signifying a cardinal sin abandoned. The turban is black and the *shaikhs* generally wear black or green garments with a black shawl. They practise *ri'a* or abandonment, which is the principal of four forms of that practice, and their *shaikh* wears a *táj* of 12 *tarks*, signifying the 12 Imáms, and of these 4 are called 'doors' to represent the forms of *ri'a*.[1] At initiation the *murid* provides a sheep or lamb for a sacrifice which is offered at the threshold of the *takia*, the flesh being eaten by all its members and the wool made into a *taiband* or belt for the *murid*.. The initiated also wear earrings, being called Hasani is only one ear if drilled and Husaini if both. At initiation the shape of the cap is also changed, apparently to represent progress in grace and the abandonment of sins. The Turkish Rafá'is do not seem to have much in common with the Gurzmárs though they wear a *kan'at táshi* of one to four stones in the girdle to appease hunger, in the belief that before it is necessary to compress the stomach by four stones Providence will have supplied food. The Rafá'is of Egypt are however very like the Indian Gurzmárs and surpass them in self-torture.[2] Its founder is there styled Sa'id Ahmad Rifa'a-al-Kabír and is regarded as one of the four Qutbs.

[1] Brown, *op. cit.*, p. 113.

[2] *Ib.*, pp. 245, 249, 262, 264, citing Lane's *Modern Egyptians*.

Moslem cosmogony and belief in spirits.

According to the *Qurán* (ii, 20 and lxxviii, 6) the earth was spread out as a bed or as a carpet, and the belief is that there are 7 heavens one above the other and seven earths one beneath the other. An angel supports the earth on his shoulders, and beneath his feet is a rock of ruby with 9000 perforations, from each of which pours a sea. The rock stands on the bull, Kuyúta, with 4000 eyes and other features, and below the bull Batamút (Behemoth), the giant fish which rests in water and that in darkness. A general belief is that below the darkness lies hell with its seven stages.[1]

In Moslem cosmogony each of the seven planets has had its age of 7000 years and we are now in the last, the *daur-i-qamar* or age of the moon, the end of time.

The first planet, Utárid (Mercury), is the *qázi* and *dabír* of the sky. His mansion is in Jauza (Gemini), and with Jauza he keeps his quiver. The hair of Jauza's face is called arrows. From Utárid come the world's disasters. Heaven hath 9 or 7 steps or degrees:—(1) the welkin, the circles of the (2) sun, (3) moon and (4—8) five planets; and (9) the empyrean, which is God's abode. From Zuhra in the third heaven come song and singing. From Muríkh (Mars) in the fifth comes tyranny. The conjunctions of Venus with Jupiter and with moon, and of the moon with Jupiter, are exceedingly auspicious.

When the Shaitáns attempt to overhear words from the lowest heaven they are struck down by shooting stars, some being consumed while others fall into the waters and become crocodiles. Others alighting on land become *ghúl* which is properly female, the male being *qutrub*. The *ghúl* appears to men in the desert in various forms and lures them to sin. These beings and the *ghudar* or *gharar* are the offspring of Iblís and a wife created for him out of the fire of the Simúm. The *ghúl* takes any form, human or animal, and also haunts burial-grounds.

The account of the Creation in the *Qurán* (xli 8 ff) was supplemented by the traditions which declared that "the angels were created from a bright gem and the *jinn* from fire without smoke, and Adam from clay."[2]

The *jinn* consist of five orders:—

(1) The *jánn* or metamorphosed *jinn*—just as an ape or swine may be a transformed man—created from smokeless fire—the fire of the Simúm:

(2) the *pari* or *dev*, renowned for beauty, but

(3) the *shaitán*, any evil *jinni*, created from fire just as the angels were created from light and Adam of earth.

(4) Ifrít, a powerful *jinn*, and

(5) Marίd, a most powerful *jinn*.

Aljánn also signifies Iblís (= Shaitán), a serpent, a *jinn* and the father of all the *jinn*.

[1] E. R. E., Vol. 4, p. 174.

[2] *Ib.*, p. 174.

Among the Ját and Baloch tribes of Dera Ismáíl Khán and Míánwáli it is very difficult to get people to talk about *jinns*. The more intelligent profess a disbelief which they do not really feel : while the poorer and more ignorant will not say much, either from fear of ridicule or to avoid being questioned. The latter consider the *jinns* helpful people who should be propitiated : but the former consider them harmful. The favourite haunts of the *jinns* are ruined wells, old *khánqáhs* and graveyards as well as the many lonely tracts in these districts. The dust pillar is a *jinn*. There is a very strong belief in the *jinns* who inhabit desolate tracts and in a woman's voice call men back by name. Two men have told me that this has happened to them. Safety lies in going on without turning round. I heard a curious story—much like that of the death of Pan and other European variants of the same idea :—A man was riding after nightfall near the village of Tibbi. A *jinn* called to him and bade him ride to the ravine near the village and cry 'The mother of Bardo is dead'. He did so. He could see nothing in the ravine, but the bushes stirred and there was the sound of many women wailing. The *jinn* takes an active and mischievous interest in agricultural operations. Every heap of grain has the *bismilláh* written by the village *mulláh* stuck on it in a cleft stick. The *dátri* or sickle and wooden fork are also left sticking in the heap, points upwards, to keep off the *jinns*, who would otherwise fetch away the grain. Cattle sickness is usually caused by *jinns*. Either the cattle are driven at evening into the village under a *Qurán* held aloft by two men or the *jinns* are driven away by guns fired into the air. The Akhúndzáda *faqír* at Paroa in Dera Ismáíl Khán writes a verse of the *Qurán* on paper, washes off the ink into water and sprinkles the cattle with it. In the notorious village of Murisli, close to Dera Ismáíl Khán town, lives a *maulavi's* daughter who charms a stick by reading certain passages of the *Qurán* over it. This too is efficacious when passed over the cattle. To cure *muṅh khúri* a lamp made from the hoof of a dead horse is used. Sickness disappears from the area illuminated by its light. *Jinns.*

Cases of women and men who are supposed to be possessed by evil spirits are common. Only the lineal descendants of Lál Isán and Pír Mohammad Rájan (whose two shrines are both in Míánwáli) can exorcise them. These spirits are known by name. They are Atá Muhammad, Núr Muhammad, Fateh Muhammad and Zulf Jamál. They have a sister known as Mái or Bíbi Kundái. Those possessed will say which spirit troubles them. A man possessed by Bíbi Kundái assumes *parda* and always covers his face. The sick are taken on camels to the fairs of Kot Isán and Pír Rájan. Usually the patient dismounts on seeing the shrine and runs madly towards it. Exorcism usually consists, I believe, in anointing with oil, reading particular verses of the *Qurán*, reciting the mighty names *isnam* and attributes of God and, I have heard, of whipping on the back. Offerings are usually given yearly to prevent a return of the spirit. There are also two Hindu *jinns* of this class, named Rám Diwáyá and Rám Rikkí. They do not attack Muhammadans. The *murids* of Taunsa Sharíf are supposed to be immune. The same belief and customs prevail in Multán. Demoniacal possession.

Ibbetson, § 219.

Khwája Khizr, or *the god of water*, writes Ibbetson, 'is an extraordinary instance of a Musalmán name being given to a Hindu deity. Khwája Khizr is properly that one of the great Muhammadan saints to whom the care of travellers is confided. But throughout the Eastern Punjab at any rate, he is the Hindu god of water, and is worshipped by burning lamps and feeding Brahmans at the well, and by setting afloat on the village pond a little raft of sacred grass with a lighted lamp upon it'. His original name is said to have been Ablia, the son of Mulkan, 6th in descent from Noah. He wears a long white beard and one of his thumbs has no bone in it. As he is always dressed in green he is called Khizr and it is believed that wherever he sits or prays the soil becomes green with verdure.

According to the *Sikandarnáma* Khwája Khizr presided over the well of immortality and directed Alexander the Great, though in vain, as to where he should find it.[1] As giver of the waters of immortality he too is called the Jinda or Zinda Pír, a title which is however more commonly used of Gugga.[2] The Khwája in this tradition appears as the brother of Mihtar Iliás, who is Lord of Land as the Khwája is Lord of Water, and both are attendants of Alexander. When the latter set forth to discover the waters of life they accompanied him, but when they came to where two roads met, the king with a few attendants took one and the two brothers the other. At a wayside fountain they all roasted fish and flung a bone into the water in which it came to life again as a fish. Both then drank of it and returned to tell the king of their discovery. He went back with them and finding the birds at the fountain featherless asked them the cause. They replied that as they had drunk of the living water, they would not die till the Judgment Day, but having eaten and drunk all that they were destined to consume they were doomed to live on in that condition. Alexander abstained from drinking of the fountain lest the same fate should befall him. But the two brothers who had drunk of its water prayed for such dignities as would enable them to live in comfort till the last day. In response God bestowed upon the Khwája the control over water and upon Iliás power over the daily changes in the market rates for grain and the guidance of lost travellers.[3]

The Moslims usually confound Khizr with Phineas, Elias and St. George, saying that by metempsychosis his soul passed through all three. Others say he was Balya ibn Maikán, a contemporary of Farídún, B. C. 800, and that he lived in the time of Músa. Others again that he was a general of Alexander and a nephew of Abraham, who guided Moses and Israel in their passage of the Red Sea, and led Alexander to the Water of Life in the Zulmát or Darkness.[4] Khizr is believed to be

[1] P. N. Q., II, § 8.

[2] A Zinda Pír is also one who is recognised as a saint even in his lifetime. Thus the Shaikh, Sadr-ud-Dín, the founder of the Máler Kotla family, was so accounted.

[3] Crooke gives a version of this legend current in Sahāranpur and points out its resemblance to the tale of the cunning of the devil and of secret judgments of God in the *Gesta Romanorum*, lxxx, the origin of Parnell's *Hermit*: N. I. N. Q., IV., § 389.

[4] For the ten meanings of the phrase *khasra-i-daman* or 'green of vegetation', see Wilberforce Clarke, *Díwán-i-Háfiz*, I, p. 149. They include the world, alchemy, a beautiful woman of unworthy origin, one possessed of unusual power of miracles, unlawful wealth &c. *Cf.* also pp. 198-9 and 211.

concealed like Muhammad Báqir who is still alive and a wanderer over the earth. A section of the Syrian Ismailites is called Khizrawi, owing to its extraordinary veneration for the prophet Eliás.

In Jalálpur Jaṭṭan in Gujrát a script called Khizri is well known. The writers say that Khwája Khizr taught their forefathers the art of writing.

The Khizri gate of Lahore city is so named because it was the river-gate when the Rávi flowed under the fort.

Khwája Khizr surpassed even Moses in learning. Once when the latter went to see him the Khwája took a plank out of a boat and disabled it. Then he killed a handsome boy and a third time he, with Moses' assistance, repaired a ruined house-wall without being asked by any one to do so. He accounted to Moses for his deeds by pointing out that the boat belonged to an orphan and was about to be seized by an oppressive governor, that the boy whom he had killed was of bad character, and that under the ruined wall lay a buried treasure which belonged to some poor boys, and that its fall would have obliterated the marks which indicated its place of concealment.

Another story about his patronage of learning says that Hazrat Imám Ghazáli was devoted to learning but being very poor could not devote his whole time to it. Once Khwája Khizr appeared in a dream and bade him open his mouth so that the Khwája might put salvation in it and so enable him to imbibe all the sciences at once. But Imám Ghazáli said that knowledge so won would be useless because it would have cost him nothing and so he would not appreciate it. Khwája Khizr then gave him some casks of oil to enable him to prosecute his studies.

Khwája Khizr[1] has various names, such as Khwája Khása Durminda, Dumindo, Jinda Pír,[2] and, in Chamba, Bir Batál.

As Dumindo he appears to be confused, or identical, with Shaikh Dúndu, an effigy of cloth stuffed with straw which is used as a charm against rain.[3]

Khwája Khizr is often identified with Mihtar Ilyás (Elias), but the latter is the patriarch who presides over jungles to guide travellers who lose their way, while the Khwája is the tutelary saint of sailors and boatmen.[4]

In popular lithographs Khwája Khizr appears as an old man standing on a fish, and he is named indifferently Khwája Sáhib, Pír or Gurú. He is reverenced by all classes, both Hindu and Muhammadan, but more especially by the Jhínwars, Malláhs and all whose occupation is connected with water in any form.[5] Persons travelling by river

[1] The *Mutawakkil-i-áb* of the Persians.

[2] P. N. Q., I, § 836.

[3] *Ib.*, I, § 953.

[4] *Ib.*, III, § 7.

[5] Even apparently dyers and *dhobis*, as in the United Provinces.

or sea, and those descending into a well will propitiate him. Parched gram is distributed and lights placed in wells in his honour. On Thursdays the low castes place *ekmukha* lamps on his shrines.

Not only is Khizr worshipped when a boat is about to sail, but he is propitiated when a river is low or threatens to wash away land. Thus in Montgomery vows (*assa*) and sacrifices are made to rivers, but in his name by Muhammadans who offer wheat porridge mixed with *gur*, while Hindus offer *chúrma*, part of which is thrown into the river. They eat what remains themselves, but Muhammadans give what remains of their offering to the poor.[1] When a village is in danger from a river the headman offers it a rupee and cocoanut. He stands in the water and if it rise higher enough to take the water out of his hand it is believed the river will recede. Sometimes 7 handfuls of boiled wheat and sugar are thrown into the stream or a male buffalo, ram or horse (with its saddle) is cast in with its right ear bored.[2]

Ladhar Bábá is said to be or have been a *sádhu* in Jhang whose followers affect Khwája Khizr.

In order to procure sons Hindus will place lamps made of dough on the platform of a well and light them every night. They also clean the platform in the early morning. This is all done to please the Khwája, who is a lord of fertility.[3]

Khwája's relish being the fish, Hindus regard a pair of fish, male and female, painted, facing each other, over a doorway as a good omen.[4]

Khwája Khizr is invoked, with Sháh Madár, in a charm for headache.[5]

Lastly he haunts bazars early in the morning and fixes the prices for the day. In his matutinal wanderings he also blesses white articles of food and obviates the effects of the evil-eye, to which they are peculiarly subject. This, however, is a purely Muhammadan view as Hindus think that such articles, when so affected, cannot be digested.[6]

One of the *tinds* on a Persian-wheel is called Khwája Khizr's *ghora* (Khijr Khwája-da-ghora) and when a new *mahl*[7] is put on, it is fed with grass. It follows the *rer*, or thick cross-piece which keeps the two wheels apart. The *tind* and *ghora* are tied on the next *reri* by the string. This is done by both Hindus and Muhammadans. The belief is that so long as the Khwája's steed is with the rope it will move, just as a carriage is drawn by a horse. When a person is standing at or near a well he is sometimes adjured thus :—*Hun tusi Khijr Khwája de utte khalote ho, hun sach bolna.* "Now you are standing on Khwája Khizr, now speak the truth".

Khwája Khizr is also said by Muhammadans to have found and drunk of the fountain of eternal life.

[1] Montgomery *S. R.*, p. 65.

[2] N. I. N. Q., I., § 20.

[3] I. N. Q., IV., § 277.

[4] Shi'a Muhammadans often have a similar design painted over the doorway, but it does not appear to refer to Khwája Khizr: I. N. Q., IV, § 276.

[5] I. N. Q., IV, § 113.

[6] *Ib.*, §§ 25 and 26.

[7] The *mahl* is the rim, joined by cross-pieces (*rer*, diminutive *reri*) to the second rim between which the wheel works.

By Hindus the Khwája is no doubt reverenced, or perhaps it would be more correct to say that he is equated to Varuna. As such he is specially affected in Asauj and Kátak (September-October) by Hindu ladies who light lamps on tanks, wells and streams every morning and evening.

Hindu water-carriers sacrifice a goat or sheep to Khizr every 2nd or 3rd year in the rainy season, and cook its flesh at home, roasting the liver, and, wrapping up its four feet and head in the skin, go to the river with some kinsmen beating drums. Having made a small boat of reed or straw, they put in it a lamp of wheat flour with four wicks, a roll of betel leaf and a wreath of jasmine. Those present then bow down, drop pice one by one in the boat, and let it float away, but not before they have taken out all the pice save two. Then they make for home, after flinging the feet, head and skin of the goat into the river. When the boat has floated away, they feast their relatives, *faqirs* and the conjurers called Malangs, and distribute sweetmeats bought with the pice taken out of the boat. This is called a goat sacrifice to Khizr.[1]

When Hindu water-carriers sink a well, they also sacrifice a goat to Khizr, and give a feast of its cooked meat to relatives and *faqirs* with genuflexions to the mound of the well.

Water-carriers, both Hindu and Musalmán, at every harvest, cook 5½ *sers* of porridge and go to a well, throw small portions of it thrice into the water and distribute the rest among children, Hindus on a Sunday and Musalmáns on a Thursday.

The first day that a farmer uses his well, he also gives 5¼ *sers* of porridge, but now-a-days most Musalmáns do not do this, and those who do, cast some of it into the well in three lots, giving the rest to small children—like the water-carriers. Most Musalmáns on the first Thursday of the new moon cook 5¼ *sers* of porridge and distribute it as described above.

When a boat is caught in a storm its passengers vow to offer porridge to Khwája Khizr, if they reach the shore.

Among Musalmáns who do not observe the *pardah* system, when a child is one month and ten days old, its mother bathes, puts on new clothes and putting on her head a couple of pots filled with boiled wheat or maize goes to a well and performs the ceremony mentioned above. She then fills the pots with water and returns home.

If a water-carrier gets praise he offers porridge to Khizr. Oarsmen also sacrifice a goat, or offer cooked porridge to him, and Hindu water-carriers regard him as a living prophet.

When a Persian wheel at work utters a shriek (*kúk*) unusually loud it is considered an evil omen and to avert disaster the owner will sacrifice a sheep or goat and smear the blood on the pivots of the gear.

[1] This rite is said to be observed in Dera Ghási Khán, especially on Thursday evenings Bhádon. The feast of boats is held in honour of Khizr.

The cult of Sakhi Sarwar Sultán.

Sir Edward Maclagan, whose description of the Sultánís or followers of Sakhi Sarwar, has been reproduced in Vol. III, pp 435-7, appears to have accepted the theory that Sakhi Sarwar was a historical personage, and the cult of Sakhi Sarwar is thus described by him :—

Maclagan, § 71.

First and foremost is the following of the great saint Sultán Sakhi Sarwar. No one knows exactly when Sultán lived. Sir Denzil Ibbetson places him in the 12th century and Major Temple in the 13th; while there are accounts in the Sákhís of the Sikhs which represent him as a contemporary of Gurú Nának, and as having presented a watermelon to him. Whatever the exact time of his birth and death, Sultán was practically one of the class of Musalmán saints, such as Bahá-ud-Dín and Shams Tabríz who settled down and practised austerities in the country round Multán. Sakhi Sarwar Sultán, also known as Lakhdáta or the Giver of Lákhs, Lálánwála, or He of the Rubies, and Rohiánwála or He of the Hills,[1] was the son of one Záinulábidín, and his real name was Sayyid Ahmad. Of his life there is little to tell but a mass of legends.

"Hazrat Zainulábdín", it is said, "had two sons,—one was Saidi Ahmad, afterwards known as Sakhí Sarwar, the other was Khán-Dodá,[2] who died at Baghdád, and was not famous. There is a shrine to him between Dera Ghází Khán and Sakhi Sarwar, at a place called Vador. Saidi Ahmad studied at Lahore, and from there went to Dhaunkal, near Wazírábád, in Gujránwála. Whilst at Dhaunkal he saw a mare, the property of a carpenter, and asked the carpenter for it. The carpenter denied having a mare, whereupon Saidi Ahmad called to the mare, and it came up to him of its own accord clearing the Sulaimáns by leaping through the range. Saidi Ahmad then told the carpenter to sink a well, which he did, and the descendants of the carpenter are the guardians of the well, at which a fair is held every year in June to Sakhi Sarwar's honour.[3] After this Saidi Ahmad, by his father's order, went to reside at the foot of the Sulaimán range, and settled at the place now called after him Shortly after retiring into the desert, Saidi Ahmad performed another miracle. A camel belonging to a caravan, which was going from Khorasán to Delhi, broke its leg. The leader of the caravan applied to Saidi Ahmad, who told him to return to where he had left the camel, and he would find it sound. The merchant did as he was directed and was rewarded by finding his camel recovered. On arriving at Delhi, the merchant published the miracle, and the emperor heard of it. The emperor, anxious to enquire into the miracle, sent for the camel and had it killed.

[1] The Sultánís return themselves at the Census under such terms as the following : - Sarwaria : Sultánia Sultán wa Deví : Sewak Sultáni : Sanáthan Dharm Sarwaria : Sakhi Sewak : Hindu Sultáni : Sarwaria Sultánia : Nigáhia : Sultán-pírías : Sarwar Sakhi : Sewak Sakhi Sarwar : Sarwar Ságar : Lakh Dátá : Sultáni Rámráe : Sarwar-panthi : Sakhi Sultáni : Chela Sultán : Rámdásia Sultánia : Gurú Sultánia : Nigáha Pír : Dhaunkal Sewak : Khwája Sarwar ; Lálánwála, and so on.

[2] Dhond or Dhoda. *Calcutta Review*, LXXIII, 1881, p. 271, or S. C. R., VII, p. 808.

[3] The local legend at Dhaunkal is that the well is due to Sakhi Sarwar having struck his staff on the ground when thirsty. Its waters are said to be good for leprosy, and the village is much haunted by lepers. The offerings at the Dhaunkal shrine are shared by the owners of the twenty-one wells, and the transfer of a well carries with it a transfer of a share in the offerings. Sakhi Sarwar ordered a bull to be milked at Sodhra in Gujránwála.

The leg was examined and found to have been mended with rivets. The emperor convinced of the miracle sent four mule-loads of money to Saidi Ahmad, and told him to build himself a house. Sakhi Sarwar's shrine was built with this money. One Gannu, of Multán, now gave his daughter in marriage to Saidi Ahmad, who had miraculously caused two sons to be born to him. Ganuu endowed his daughter with all his property and it was for the generosity in distributing this property to the poor that Saidi Ahmad obtained the name of Sakhi Sarwar, or the bountiful lord or chief. Sakhi Sarwar now visited Baghdád. On his return he was accompanied by three disciples, whose tombs are shown on a low hill near Sakhi Sarwar".[1]

A local account says that the shrine was built by the king of Delhi and the footsteps by Díwáns Lakhpat Rái and Jaspat Rái of Lahore. Temple identifies the former with the Díwán killed by the famous Sikh leader Jassa Singh Ahlúwália in 1743: *Calcutta Review*, lxxiii, 1881, p. 254. Another account of the saint, supplied to Major Temple by a *munshi* from Lahore, runs as follows:—

"The father of Sayyid Ahmad, surnamed Sakhi Sarwar, was one Sayyid Zainulábidín who migrated to India from Baghdád in 520 A. H., or 1126 A. D., and settled at Shahkot, in the Jhang District, where he married 'Aesha, the daughter of a village headman, named Pirá, a Khokhar. By 'Aesha he had a son, Sayyid Ahmad, afterwards the great saint known as Sakhi Sarwar. Sayyid Ahmad was much ill-treated by his own people in his youth, and on the death of his father left India in 535 A. H. or 1140 A. D., and went to Baghdád, where he obtained the gift of prophecy (*khiláfat*) from the saints Ghaunsu'l 'Azam, Shaikh Shaháb-ud-Dín Suharwardi and Khwája Maudúd Chishti. (Ghaunsul 'Azam is Abdul Qadir Jiláni, who flourished at Baghdád in 1078-1166 A. D. Shaikh Shahab-du-Dín Suharwardi flourished at Baghdád in 1145-1234 A.D. Kawája Maudúd Chishti died in 1150 A. D. This tradition is therefore fairly correct as to chronology.) After dwelling at Baghdád for some time, Sakhi Sarwar returned to his native land and dwelt at Dhauokal, in the Gujránwála District, for a time. He then went to Multán, the governor of which gave him his daughter Bái in marriage. Here he also married another woman, the daughter of one Sayyid Abdur Razzáq. He next visited Lahore, where he obtained proficiency in secular knowledge under Sayyid Isháq (this is an anachronism, as Mauláns Sayyid Isháq was born at Uch, in the Baháwalpur State, and studied under his uncle Sayyid Sadru'ddin Rajú Kattál at Sahárampur, where he died in 1460 A. D.), and finally returned to Sháhkot, where he settled. Here he became famous as a worker of miracles, and obtained many followers, which excited the envy of his relatives, who determined to put him to death. But the saint, having heard of their intention, fled into the desert and settled at Nigáha, in the Dera Ghází Khán District, in company with Sayyid 'Abdul Ghani, his brother, Bái, his wife, and Sayyid Surájud Dín, his son. His family, however, followed him, and falling upon him in large numbers, slew him and his companions at Nigáha in 570 A. H. or 1174 A. D. The saint was buried on the spot, and there his shrine stands to this day."[2]

[1] Dera Ghází Khán *Gazetteer*, p. 89.

[2] *Panjab Notes and Queries*, III, § 154. The remarks in brackets are by Major (now Colonel Sir) Richard Temple.

Maclagan, § 72.

The shrine of Sakhi Sarwar.—The above may be taken as representing roughly the outlines of a legendary life round which numberless additional tales have gradually collected. Those who would know, for instance, how he raised a boy from the dead for Dáni Jaṭṭi, how he used Bhairon as his messenger, how Isa Bánia in the time of Aurangzeb built him a temple, and so on, will find all they want in the interesting *Legends of the Punjab* published by Major Temple. There is little enough of history in all this, and the main fact we can determine is that for some reason or other the saint fixed on Nigáha, in the Dera Ghází Khán District, at the edge of the Sulaimán mountains, as his residence, 'the last place', it has been said, 'that any one with the least regard for his personal comfort would choose as an abode'. The present shrine at Nigáha is built on the high banks of a hill stream, and a handsome flight of steps made at the expense of two merchants from Lahore leads up from the bed of the stream to the shrine. The buildings of the shrine consist of Sakhi Sarwar's tomb on the west and a shrine to Bábá Nának on the north-west. On the east is an apartment containing the stool and spinning wheel of Máí 'Aeshán, Sakhi Sarwar's mother. Near this is a *ṭhákurdwára*, and in another apartment is an image of Bhairon who appears in the legends as the saint's messenger. There is clearly some close connection between the worship of Bhairon and this cult, even Bhái Pheru (whose wife was Deví), the *numen* in the small whirl-winds so common in the Punjab, is represented as a disciple of Sultán Sarwar. The shrine is approached by a defile, at whose entrance is a cliff some 80 feet high, called the robber's leap (*chor-i-ṭap*), because a thief when pursued threw himself over it, vowing if he survived to sacrifice a sable heifer to the saint. He escaped unscathed.[1] To the west of the out-houses and within the shrine enclosure are two dead trees (a *jál* and a *kauda*) said to have sprung from the pegs which were used for the head and heel ropes of Kakki, the saint's mare. Behind the shrine are the dwellings of his son Ráu'ddín[2] and his brother Dhodha. To the west near the shrine, but away from it, are the tombs of Núr and Isháq, two of his companions; and similarly to the east are two more tombs to his comrades, Ali and Usmán. The tomb presents a peculiar mixture of Muhammadan and Hindu architecture. In 1883 it was destroyed by fire, and two rubies presented by Nádir Shah and some valuable jewels presented by Sultán Zamán Shah were consumed or lost. Since then the shrine has been rebuilt.[3]

"The present guardians of the Sakhi Sarwar shrine," according to the *Gazetteer*, "are the descendants of the three servants of Gannu who attached themselves to Sakhi Sarwar. They were Kúlang, Káhin and Shekh. Sakhi Sarwar limited the number of the descendants of

[1] Here we have a legend which reminds us of the Bhairava Jhamp, the cliff at Kidárnáth in Kumáun whence pilgrims used to precipitate themselves as an offering to Siva, and of the somewhat similar Bihunda rites on the Sutlej at which men of the low Beda or 'sheep' caste are lowered on ropes down a precipice in honour of Mahádev.

[2] But he was also called Rána and the sacred grove of plum-trees (*beri*) near a spring in the neighbourhood of Nigáha is said to have been planted by him: *Calc. Rev.*, 1881, p. 271, or S. C. R., VII, p. 308.

[3] See Dera Ghází Khán *Gazetteer*, p. 40; and *Punjab Notes and Queries*, I, § 999, III, § 83.

these three men to 1650[1] which number has been strictly observed ever since. The number is thus distributed :—

Descendants of Kúlang	... ...	750
Descendants of Káhin	... ...	600
Descendants of Shaikh	... ...	200

"All the offerings made at the shrine are divided into 1650 shares and it is said to be a fact that there are never more nor less than 1650 *mujáwars* or descendants of the three original keepers of the shrine. This number includes women and children. It is not however a fact that there are not more nor less than 1650 *mujáwars* as was ascertained when the village pedigree title deed was prepared. The *mujáwars* are all equal, and an infant gets the same share of the proceeds of the shrine as an adult. The *mujáwars*, after the annual fair which is held in April, almost all disperse over the Punjab as pilgrim hunters. It is only at the great annual fair that the treasure box of the shrine is opened and its contents distributed. Throughout the year the shrine is the resort of mendicants and devotees, but the mendicants usually receive nothing more substantial from the shrine than an order upon some worshipper of the saint given under the seal of the shrine. This order, when presented, is paid or not according to the respect in which the shrine is held by the presentee. When Mr. Bull, the Assistant Secretary to the Lahore Municipality, was attacked by a fanatic, an order from the Sakhi Sarwar *mujáwars* was found upon his assailant. This at first gave rise to a suspicion that the guardians of the shrine were in some way implicated in the murder. The order had however been granted merely in the ordinary course".

Pilgrimages to Sakhi Sarwar—The pilgrimages to the shrine from the centre of the province are a special feature of the cult of Sultán, which are worth mentioning, and in the early months of the year there are continual streams of pilgrims of all creeds—Hindu, Sikh and Musalmán—pouring towards Nigáha. I cannot do better than quote Mr. Purser's account of the pilgrimages made from the *Jullundur* District :—

"The company of pilgrims", he writes, "is called *sang* and their encampment *chauki*. The main route is through the following villages :—Hánsron, Mukandpur, Kuleta or Barapind, Bopárae (Phillaur), Rurka Kalán, Bandala, Jandiála, Bopárae (Nakodar), Khánpur, and thence to Sultánpur. Along this route the *sang*, which is originally formed by pilgrims from Garhshankar, in the Hoshiárpur District, is joined by detachments from the districts to the south of the Sutlej and from the lower half of the Jullundur District. It is known by the special name of Kálikamlí, because so many of the pilgrims have black blankets[2] to

[1] Ano her account says that after the burial of Sakhi Sarwar three persons, Gobra, a leper, Hibrat Nigáhi, a blind man, and Ahmad Khán, Afghán, an impotent man, came to the shrine and were cured of their respective infirmities. From these are descended the present *mujáwars*, who are divided into three classes,—Kúlang, Mauhan and Shaikh. The number of descendants is said to be 1350 and by a miracle of the saint never to alter; but this is not true, as all the *mujáwars* claim an equal share in the annual profits and their number can be ascertained at any time. See *Punjab Notes and Queries*, III, § 156.

[2] Black is the colour of Shiv : H. A. R.

protect them from the cold. Another route is by Adampur, Jullundur, Kapúrthala and Wairowál, which is taken by pilgrims from the north of the Doáb. Those from about Kartárpur assemble there and proceed to Kapúrthala. On the road these people sleep on the ground, and do not wash their heads or clothes till the pilgrimage is accomplished, and the more devout remain unwashed till their return home. The pilgrims are personally conducted by the Bharáís, and call each other *pír bhái* or *pír bhain* (brother in the saint or sister in the saint). Ibbetson says it is probably from this latter circumstance the Bharáís derive their name (Pír Bhra or 'Saint Brothers'). People who cannot undertake the pilgrimage usually go to one of the *chaukís*, or, if they cannot manage that, to any other village, for a night. If they cannot go anywhere, they sleep at home at least one night on the ground, as a substitute for the complete pilgrimage. A pilgrimage to Nigáha is commonly made with the object of obtaining some desired blessing from the saint, or in fulfilment of a vow. The pilgrims have a local self-government of their own on the road. Leaders from Chakchela and Kangchela (Kang Kalán) in the Nakodar tahsíl attach themselves to the southern band, and hold an assembly called *díwán* every evening in which they administer justice, and are assisted by assessors from Bilga, Jandiála, Barápind, and other villages. There is much rivalry between the Kangchela, and Chakchela leaders, but the latter hold the supremacy".

There are other shrines of this saint, and in fact almost every village in the Central Punjab contains one. But the most celebrated are those connected with the annual fair at Dhaunkal in Gujránwála, the Jhanda *mela* at Peshávar, and the Kadmon-ká-mela" in Anárkali at Lahore. At Dhonkal, Sultán had taken up his abode and procured a miraculous stream of water. His house was in the time of Shah Jahán turned into a mosque and the well was much improved and beautified. The fair here, which lasts for a month in June and July, is attended by some 200,000 people, who drink the sacred water and take away fans and sprigs of *mehndi* as mementos of their visit. The Jhanda *mela* in Peshávar is of less importance; it takes place in the first or second Monday in Maggar, and the festival is put off if there is rain. The *mela* is in commemoration of the death of Sakhi Sarwar, and has its name from the flags exhibited there by the *faqírs*. The Kadmon-ká-mela, in Anárkali, is held at the shrine of Sakhi Sarwar near the Police *thána*, on the first Monday after the new moon in February. Offerings are made on the tomb, and a certain class of musicians, called *dholís*, take young children who are presented at the tomb and dance about with them.[1]

A typical shrine of Sakhi Sarwar is that at Moga. It is called Nagáha Pír, and was founded in 1869 S. by a Patiála man. It contains no image but has a *chabútra* or platform. The *pujári* is a Khatri and succession follows natural relationship. Fairs are held on the 8 Thursdays

[1] At Máler Kotla the Nigáha *fair* is held on the first Thursday of Poh. It is a copy of that held at Multán. The Dhúni fair is held on the first two Tuesdays of Poh. The Bharáís light a *díwa* at a place to which both Hindus and Muhammadans go and offer bread and grain. Next day they start for Mári where the shrine of Gugá Pír is situated.

of Chet and Asauj, when offerings of cash and *chúri* are made to the shrine. Another shrine of Sakhi Sarwar is at Nagáh, where a fair is held on the light Thursday of Phágan. It contains a place which is worshipped. It was founded some 200 years ago by the Sirdár of Mansa. When subjected to severe trials they were bidden in a vision to go to Moga and there build a temple. So they constructed this shrine and all Hindus and Muhammadans in this part are its votaries, offering it grain at each harvest. It also has a *chhabíl* where the poor travellers drink water. At the fair visitors are fed free. A Brahman is employed as *pujári*.

The Bhádla fair in Ludhiána is held at the *khánqáh* of Sakhi Sarwar at that village on the 1st Thursday of the light half of Jeṭh. Inside it is a cenotaph of Sakhi Sarwar. People attending the fair cook a huge *roṭ*, which, after presentation to the *khánqáh*, they divide with the poor. The management of the *khánqáh* vests in the Ghumman Jáṭs and Bharáís of the place and they divide the offerings in equal shares.

The cult of Lakhdáta or 'the Bountiful' is found in Chamba, in which state it is recognised as the same as that of Sakhi Sarwar Sultán. His shrines in the hills are resorted to by both Hindus and Muhammadans. In most cases the incumbents of his temples, *astháns* or *mandárs*, are Muhammadans (*mujáwars*), but at Bari in *pargana* Chanju the *pujára* is a Billu Brahman, and at Phurla in Himgari the *pujára* or *mujáwar* is a Ráthi and the *chela* a Muhammadan. These offices appear to be always hereditary. Wrestling matches—called *chhinj* and associated with the Lakhdáta cult—are held yearly in every *pargana* of Churáh and in some *parganas* of the Sadr *wizárat*, as well as in the Bhattiyát. No satisfactory explanation of this association is forthcoming.

There is a *khánqáh* to Sakhi Sarwar at Náhan, and his cult is spread beyond the Punjab. In Saháranpur he is worshipped by a sect of Jogís called Far Yai[1] (*sic*), who are initiated by their clansmen at the age of 10 or 12. The ceremony of initiation is said to be simple, for the parents of the boy merely place some sweets before the Jogi who is their religious guide, and the latter offers them to the saint, after which they are eaten by the Jogís present. The boy then learns the song which describes the attempt to convert a bride to Sikhism and its consequences, for Sakhi Sarwar commanded Bhairon to punish the evil-doers, who at once became lepers and blind, but they were cured again at the bride's intercession. Yet there is no real hostility at present between Sikhism and this sect, and a case has been known of a gift of land being made by a Sikh Jáṭ[2] to the shrine at Nigáha.

In the east of the Punjab, at least, the cult of Sakhi Sarwar is peculiarly favoured by women, which is consistent with its connection with Bhairava, the earth being the emblem of fertility, and this again

[1] *North Indian Notes and Queries*, IV, § 90.

[2] The orthodoxy of his Sikhism may be debateable: Temple, *Calc. Review*, 1881, p. 255, or S. C. R., VII, p. 292, speaks of Dáni as a Sikh, but she is merely called a Jaṭṭi, *not* a Sikh in the poem of *Sakhi Sarwar and Dáni Jaṭṭi Legends*, I, p. 66 *ff*. Possibly the Handáli sect of the Sikhs was more in sympathy with the Sultánís and Temple identifies the 'city of the *gurú*' in the poem with Jandiála the head-quarters of that sect, but by city of the *gurú* 'Nigáha itself may conceivably be meant'.

is in accord with the somewhat Paphian rites observed at the shrine itself. Further the theory that the worship is really one of the earth-god would account for its being essentially the cult of the Ját peasantry. In the legend of Dáni the Jaṭṭi the saint bestows a son on her after 12 years of childless marriage in response to a vow. She breaks her vow but the boy is restored to life by the saint.[1] At Multán his followers eat all the kids of the flock, but he takes the bones and skins, puts them in a heap and restores them to life by prayer.[2] He makes the wild oak (*pilú*) fruit in the midst of winter at the request of *Kakki*, his mare, for the support of the followers in the jungle.[3]

The cauldrons of Sakhi Sarwar recall those mentioned in the account of Sikhism below and in the legends of Ḍúm above.

One is called *man*, the other *langar*. The former holds 8 *mans* of *gur* (mollases), 5 of *ghí*, 20 of *dalia* (boiled wheat) and one of fruit etc.. *Langar* holds 3 *mans* of molasses, 2 of *ghí*, 8 of boiled wheat and 20 *sers* of fruit etc. Once a year, in May or June, both are filled and the cooked food distributed to the public.

Qásim Sháh, father of Naurang Sháh, whose shrine is in Dera Ghází Khán, came there from Sindh. Naurang Sháh remained a devotee of Sakhi Sarwar for 12 years and became famous for his miracles. His descendants connect his pedigree with Hazrat 'Ali.

The Five Pírs.—In some parts of the country the Hindus are fond of representing themselves as followers of the Panj-Pír or Five Saints. Who these five saints are is a matter which each worshipper decides according to his taste. Sometimes they are the five Páṇḍavas; sometimes they are the five holy personages of Shi'aism, *viz.* Muhammad, Fátima, Ali, Hasan and Husain; sometimes they are a selection of Musalmán saints, as Khwája Qutb-ud-Dín, Khwája Mu'ain-ud-Dín Chishti, Shaikh Nizám-ud-Dín Aulia, Nasír-ud-Dín Abu'l Khair, and Sultán Nasír-ud-Dín Mahmúd or as Khwája Khizr, Said Jalál, Zakaria, Lál Sháhbáz and Faríd Shakarganj. The Bhaṭṭís of the Gujránwála District will tell you that the five saints are Shaikh Samail, Sháh Daulat, Shaikh Fateh Ali, Pír Fateh Khán and Sháh Murád, all patrons of the Bhaṭṭí race; and each tribe will have its own selection. In the centre and west of the province, however, we meet with queer admixtures of Hindu and Musalmán objects of worship. The same list will contain Sultán, Deví, the Gurú, Khwája and Gúga Pír; or (as in Ludhiána) Khwája Khizr, Durga Deví, Vishnu, Sakhi Sarwar and Gurú Gobind Singh; or (as in Simla) Gúga Pír, Bálaknáth, Ṭhákur, Sakhi Sarwar and Shiv. The five saints are in fact any five personages the worshipper likes to mention; and the fact that a man describes himself as a Panjpíria implies generally that he is indifferent as to the saints whom he worships and is probably a man of the lower orders. Panjpírias are found all over the province from Muzaffargarh to Delhi, and there is a place in the Sháhpur District, 10 miles south of Sáhíwál, where a large fair is held every year in honour of the Panjpír. Some persons, wishing to be more specific, declare themselves to be followers of the Chahár Pír or Four Saints; by

[1] *Calc. Review*, 1881, p. 254, or S. C. R., VII, p. 291.

[2] *Ib.*, p. 273, or S. C. R., VII, p. 310.

[3] *Ib.*, pp. 268, 272, or S. C. R., VII pp. 305, 309.

this is generally implied the four friends of the Prophet, whose admirers are found both among Musalmáns and Hindus.

The *khánqáh* of the Panj Pír at Abohar is not covered with a roof. The fair is held annually on the 15th Hár. Few people attend it, mostly Madári, Naushábi etc. Tradition says that nearly 900 years ago. Abohar was ruled by Rájá Aya Chand who had an only daughter. On his death-bed he expressed deep regret that he had no son, to go to the Panj Píran at Uch in Bahāwalpur and mount the horses there. His daughter courageously assured him that she would go and fetch the horses from Uch. So accompanied by a small band she went there and carried off the horses of the Panj Pír. They came after her and begged her to return them, but she refused and so they had to wait in patience for their return. The Pír's wives being tired of waiting followed their husbands to Abohar where with their beloved spouses they breathed their last, cursing the lady and the place. Before long their prophecy was fulfilled and the place became a desert. The five Pírs were interred at a place in the village and near them the remains of their wives. The shrine contains the tombs of the 5 Pírs and those of their 5 wives, which are surrounded by a brick wall, but have no roof. The administration of the *khánqáh* is carried on by two Musalmán *faqírs*, caste Lád. They keep it clean and light a lamp in the evening.

[1] See Temple's *Legends of the Panjab*, II, p. 372. See also an exhaustive account of the Panj Pír of the United Provinces in *North Indian Notes and Queries*, II, § 10, and subsequent numbers.

Religion of the dominant tribes of Kurram, *e.g.* the Turi, Zaimusht and Bangash.

The Turís are all Shi'as. The Bangash of Lower Kurram are all Sunnís, but those of Upper Kurram, with the exception of the Bushera and Dandar Bangash, are also Shi'as. Taking the numbers of the Bangash of Lower and Upper Kurram into consideration the proportion of Shi'as to Sunnís among the Bangash may be put at 3 to 1. The menial classes of course accept the religion of their patrons. Even some of the Jajís, who cross the border and become *hamsáyas* of the Turís, adopt Shi'aism. The Zaimusht however are all Sunnís.

Imáms are regarded as without sin, and it is believed that those who follow them will be saved in the world to come. The Imáms, it is believed, will, on the day of resurrection, intercede for those who believed in them and have followed their directions. The Imám Jáfar Sadíq is supposed to be the most learned of the Imáms, and his teaching in religious matters is commonly observed. The Sunni Bangash and Zaimusht are all followers of Imám Numan who is called Abu Hanífa.[1] There is no difference in belief between the Turi and Shi'a Bangash, but one point is worth noticing. The Bakar Khel branch of the Shalozán Bangash do not believe in *pírs* as they do not regard the Sayyids and Qázís of Kurram as competent to impart religious instruction. This is presumably because they are in the habit of constantly going to Karbala, and have to pass through Persia where they meet educated people ; doubtless other people from Kurram also go to Karbala, but they are in most cases altogether illiterate, and hence cannot easily grasp what they hear from educated people. The majority of the Shalozán Bangash can read and write, and hence they do not believe in *pírs* and do not follow them like the other Turís.

Almost every village in Kurram has a *mulláh*. The children of the village go to him, and he gives them some religious teaching. The first duty of the *mulláh* is to teach them the *Qurán* in the orthodox way, with all the prayers that are recited in *namáz*. If any one wishes to go further with his spiritual education he reads other religious books in which the praises of Hazrat Ali, Hasan, Hussain and other Imáms are recorded.

The Sunni Bangash and Zaimusht keep *mulláhs* in their mosques. Their duty is to teach children the prayers that are used in the *namáz*. Children whose parents place a higher value on education are taught the *Qurán* as well, and after finishing it some Persian and Arabic books also. Among the Sunnís, *i.e.* the Zaimusht and Bangash, the *mulláhs* preach to the people when they get an opportunity, particularly on Fridays. They get no fixed remuneration, but each gets something at harvest from every one in the village. Among the Shi'as there is no preaching, but some of the Sayyids and other educated persons read books containing *marsiás* and other eulogies of Ali, Hasan and Hussain to the people. A number of Turís go to Tehrán for religious instruction.

Amongst the Sunnís the subject of these teachings is usually the praise of God and his Prophet Muhammad. Sometimes books containing eulogies of saints, or on the laws and morals of Islám, are also read.

[1] Also called the Imám-i-Azam.

These preachings often take place in mosques and when a man dies the *mulláh* of the village, if he be educated, reads to the people.

Amongst the Turís and other Shí'as in Kurram there is nothing so important as the *mátam* or 'mourning' for the sons of Ali. To it the month of Muharram is devoted as a whole, but the first 10 days of Muharram, called Ashúra by the Turís, are observed as days of special mourning. Almost all the Turís fast during these days, the more orthodox extending the period to 40 days. *Mahfils* or meetings are also held for the sake of lamentation, and they are attended both by men and women. At them Persian *marsiás* or dirges are recited in a plaintive tone, while the bare-headed audience shed tears of sorrow. Breast-beating is not uncommon and sometimes the people go so far as to flagellate themselves with iron chains in a most cruel manner. Clothes are not changed during these 10 days and no rejoicings of any kind take place. Even laughing is prohibited. Clothes dyed almost black in indigo are worn for 10 days at least. *Sherbat* made of sugar or *gur* is distributed among the poor and alms given in the name of Hussain. Volleys of curses are hurled at Yazíd, his counsellors and companions, and their faults and shortcomings are painted as black as possible. The 10th of Muharram is the climax as on that day Hussain is said to have been decapitated by Yazíd. This is called the Shahádat Waroz or yaum-i-Shahádat (day of martyrdom), and on it a *rausa* (something like an effigy) made of coloured paper is taken to the cemetery, followed by a mourning crowd composed of men, women and children who beat their breasts and faces. A pit is then dug in the cemetery and the *rausa* formally interred in it with all the ceremonies attending a funeral.

On certain days of the other months, the Sayyids and other educated people among the Shí'as read books containing *marsias* and eulogies of the Imáms and the *Charsdah Masum*. These books are usually read in the *mátamkhánás* and sometimes in the mosques.

According to the teaching of the Sunnís, *i.e.* the Zaimusht and some of the Bangash, there are four *farz* for every one, whether male or female, to observe, *viz.* *namáz*, fasting, *haj* and *zakát*. *Namáz* is offered five times in the 24 hours of the night and day. Moreover, on certain days of the months some other prayers called *nafal* are offered. There are four kinds of these prayers or *namáz*, viz. *farz*, *sunnat*, *wajib* and *mustahab*. *Farz* and *wajib* are supposed to have been prescribed by God and the *sunnat* by the Prophet. The *mustahab* were not prescribed, but are prayers offered without regard to time. The *mustahab* are also called *nafal*.

The month of Ramzán is generally observed as a fast, but the Drewandís observe it with great strictness, while the Miánmurid observe the Ashúra (in Muharram) as a fast more rigidly. Besides this, fasts are kept in other months but they are not *farz*. *Haj* means to go to Mecca in the month of *Zul-haj*. *Zakát* means the paying of a $\frac{1}{10}$th or $\frac{1}{40}$th[1] of one's property to poor people not possessed of property worth more than Rs. 51.

[1] In fact there are different rules for different articles—cattle, grain, money, ornaments &c. &c.. *Zakát* is not paid to Sayyids.

The above four *farz* are all observed by the Shi'as, and in addition to this they have to give a ⅕th of their income to poor Sayyids exclusively. This is called *khamas* (a fifth). The Shi'as, moreover, consider a pilgrimage to Karbala an important thing. They do not regard it as *farz*, but consider it to be a very urgent duty.

Sunnís offer prayers in a mosque, usually with an Imám if they can manage to do so easily, whereas Shi'as offer their prayers alone. They say the presence of a learned man is highly desirable for prayers with an Imám, but as they cannot find one they offer their prayers alone. Almost every Shi'a keeps a piece of *khák-i-Karba'a* upon which they place their foreheads when they offer their prayers.

Festivals or mourning celebration.

Amongst the Sunnís there are only two festivals, *viz.* the *'Id-ul-Fitr* and the *'Id-ud-Duha*. The 'Id-ul-Fitr is held in commemoration of the pleasure enjoyed after the month of Ramzán and the 'Id-ud-Duha in commemoration of the reconstruction of the building at Mecca for which Ibráhím sacrificed his son Ismáil.

The following are the days on which the Sunnís observe mourning:—the Muharram, the Bára-wafát and the Shab-i-Qadr. In the Muharram they do not weep like the Shi'as, but abstain from pleasure and enjoyments. It is useless to relate here how the *mátam* in the month of Muharram came to be observed. There was a dispute and afterwards a battle between Hussain, son of Ali, and Yazíd, son of Muawiah, about the leadership of the Muslims at the time, and in that battle Hussain, with his relatives, was killed.

The Bára-wafát is observed by Shi'as on account of the Prophet's illness. It is held on the 27th of the month of Safar. The Sunnís hold that on the 23rd Ramzán (Shab-i-Qadr) the *Qurán* descended to earth. The Shi'as observe the Shab-i-Qadr as the day on which Ibráhím was thrown into the furnace by the idolatrous king Nimrod for refusing to worship his idols, and was saved by God.

All these festivals and mournings are observed by the Shi'as, but besides this they observe other festivals and mournings too. The 'Id-ul-Ghadir is held on the 18th of Zul-haj in commemoration of Hazrat Ali's election to the leadership of the Muslims. There is another 'Id called the 'Id-ul-Umr, which is held on the 3rd day before the Bára-wafát in Safar. The 'Id-ul-Umar is observed in commemoration of the killing of Umar, son of Kattáb, by Abu Lolo. Umar was the enemy of Ali. Hence it is a day of rejoicing to the Shi'as and of mourning to the Sunnís.

The 20th of Safar is supposed to be the 40th day after Hussain's death, and hence it is regarded as a day of mourning. The 23rd of Ramzán is regarded as the day on which Ali died and hence is also considered a day of mourning

Shrines.

The Turís of Kurram, as Shi'as, are great admirers of Ali and his descendants, and have a large number of Sayyid shrines (*ziárats*)[1] which

[1] The shrines roughly described as *ziárats* are really of three kinds—

(*i*) a *ziárat* proper, where the saint lies buried or is reported to lie buried.

(*ii*) a *maqám*, where a saint rested in his lifetime or where his body was temporarily interred before removal to Karbala.

(*iii*) a *khwáb*, where visions of the Imáms and Saints have appeared to holy persons.

The ceremony of *ziyárat* or visitation at the Prophet's tomb at Medina is fully described by Burton. *Za'irs* or visitors are conducted by *mazawwir*. The *haj* is quite distinct, the observances differing in every respect: Burton, *Al-Madina*, I, pp. 305-6, 307, 309, are held in profound veneration and periodically visited. Boys are shaved at these *siárats* for the first time and vows are made. The principal are the following :—

At Peiwar—

(1) Ali Mangula[1] *siárat*, visited by the Peiwarís on the two 'Ids.

(2) Sayyid Mahmúd *siárat*, visited by the Turís of Peiwar on the 10th of Muharram.

(3) Sháh Mardán : where a vision of Ali appeared—see note 2 on page 579 *infra*.

(4) Sika Rám *siárat* on the summit of Sika Rám, the peak of the Sufed Koh or 'White Mountain' about 15,000 feet above sea level. It is held in high repute both by Hindus and Muhammadans, and is believed to be the resting place of a Sayyid recluse, by name Sáíd Karam, who is said to have lived there for a long time and tended his flocks on the summit, which came to be known after him as the Sáíd Karam (corrupted into Sika Rám) peak.

Sáíd Karam had two brothers, Mander and Khush Karam, who lived and prayed on two other peaks called after them the Mander and Khush Kurram peaks, respectively. The Mander peak is on the Afghán side of the border opposite Burki village and its shrine is visited by Jogís. The Khush Kurram (corruption of Khush Karam) peak being on the British side of the border in the south of the Kurram Valley above the Mukbil encampment of Ghozgarhi is visited by the Turís of Kurram. Both these peaks are studded with lofty *deodár* trees and ever-green shrubs which the people ascribe to the numerous virtues of the holy men.[2]

At Shalozán—

(1) Imám *siárat*.
(2) Sayyid Hasan.
(3) Mír Ibráhím or Mír Bím *siárat* : see below.
(4) Sháh Mír Sayyid Ahmad *siárat*.
(5) Bábá Sháh Gul *siárat*.

[1] *Mangula* = hand-mark (of Ali on a stone).

[2] But another Muhammadan legend makes the name Sika Rám a corruption of Khwája Wasi Karam who is said to have been a saint in the days of the Muhammadan kings of the valley. He is said to have gone to the top of the mountain to avoid the notice of the people. It is said that Bíbi Badina was his sister and a woman of pure morals. Khwája Khuram (*sic*) is said to be the brother of Khwája Wasi Karam. He was also a saint. The Hindu version, however, is that an Indian hermit of the name of Saki Rám or Sika Rám used to frequent the peak and pray in solitude to his *deotas*, and that the place was called Sika Rám after him.

According to the Hindu legends Sika Rám went to the top of the Sufed Koh, and by a stamp of his foot produced a tank called the Sika Rám Sar which they say exists. The Badina Sar is similarily named after Bíbi Badina and the Khush Kharam Sar after Khwája Khuram. It has been suggested that Sika Rám is a corruption of Síta Rám, a Hindu Rájá whose coins are found everywhere in the hills of Afghánistán. They are called Síta Rámi. Both Turís and Bangash admit that Sika Rám was a Hindu, and had nothing to do with the Musalmáns, though some of the latter lay claim to him.

As far as can be ascertained no manuscript histories of any of these shrines exist. The legends are said to have been handed down orally to the present day.

At Malána—

Sháh Talab *ziárat.*

At Zerán—

(1) Sháh Sayyid Rúmi *ziárat.*

(2) Mír Kásim or Mast Mír Kásim *ziárat* is annually resorted to by the Malli Khel, Hamza Khel and Mustu Khel *kuchi* (nomad) Turís, in the month of Safar and a regular fair is held.[1] Sheep and goats are also slaughtered as offerings to the shrine. All the people visiting the *ziárat* are fed by the Zerán Sayyids, who are said to have been ordered by the saint to do so.

At Karmán—

(1) Sháh Sayyid Fakhr-i-Alam *ziárat:* see below

(2) Mír Karím *ziárat.*

At Sadara—

Abbás *ziárat,* visited by Turi women.

Children are shaved here and vows are made for sons.

At Kharláchi—

(1) Burqa-posh *ziárat:* see below.

(2) Lála Gul *ziárat.*

At Nasti Kot—

Dwalas (twelve) Imáms' *ziárat,* said to be the resting-place of the 12 Imáms of the Shi'as.

At Ahmadzai—

(1) The *ziárat* of Mirak Sháh, a descendant of the 7th Imám Músa Kazim. Mirak Sháh was the grandfather of the present Sayad Haníf Ján of Ahmedzai.

(2) Arab Shah *ziárat.*

At Samir (Hassan Ali Qilla)—

Hazrat Abbás *ziárat,* visited by the Ghundi Khel on both the 'Ids and at the Muharram. Hazrat Abbás is buried at Karbala.

At Alizai—

Sháh Isháq *ziárat,* visited by Alizaís, Bagazaís, Hamza Khel and Mastu Khel of Chárdíwár.

At Balyamín—

Mír Humza *ziárat,* visited by Mastu Khel and Hamza Khel *kuchi* Turís and the Ghilzaís of Afghánistán on their way to India.

[1] It is said in connection with this fair, which is held annually in the end of May or beginning of June, that the parents of Mír Kásim suggested that he should marry. He replied that rather than marry he would prefer to excavate a water-course from a spring above Zerán and lead it to the *ziárat.* Accordingly the chief feature of this fair is the periodical excavation of this water-course when men and women mix freely just as they do at Chintpurni near Bharwain, in Hoshiárpur.

At Shakardarra—

The *ziárat* of Mián Mír Akbar who died in 1912.

In the Darwázgai Pass—

The Diwána Malang[1] or Laila Majnún *ziárat*, in the Darwázgai Pass, is annually visited by the Malli Khel, Hamza Khel, Mastu Khel and Duperzai *kuchi* Turís. A fowl is killed as an offering for every male member of the family. An iron nail is then driven into the trunk of a tree close to the shrine. There is a legend that if a man can climb up the tree at one bound he is sure to get a horse after a year. A huge black stone lying near the shrine is said to have been split in two in obedience to Laila's command.

At Tongai—

Hazár Pír *ziárat*, visited and venerated both by Shi'as and Sunnís.[2]

At Bagzai—

Sháh Ibráhím *ziárat*, visited by the Turís of Bagzai and Chárdíwár. A visit to it is said to be a specific for smallpox.

At Shabak—

The Zarauna Buzurg *ziárat*, near Shabak, is also visited by the Turís. The Turi belief is that a gun will not go off at this shrine.

Of all the shrines of the Kurram Valley, the following five are the most important. They all belong to Sayyids and are called the 5 *khanwadas* (families). The Sayyids of the Kurram Valley are descended from these five *khanwadas*.[3] An account of each is given below :—

I. *Sháh Sayyid Rúmi*, grandson of Imám Ali, the 4th Imám whose shrine is at Zerán, is the patron saint of Zerán. His descendants, who are called Rúmí Khel, Mashadi or Imam Razái Sayyids, are

[1] The Mián Muríd state that when the Malangs hear the praises of Hasan, Hussain and Ali with music they lose their senses and become altogether distraught. Their flesh and blood become solid like iron, and they can then jump into fire without being burnt. They can even put fire into their mouths and devour it or catch a fowl or chicken and eat it without killing it in the proper way. This they call *jabka*. They believe that their salvation is absolutely dependent on their Imám's intercession for them on the day of the resurrection.

[2] Hazár Pír is in fact not a shrine. It is only said that the Amír-ul Mominín, *i.e.* Ali, was seen by somebody in a vision there.

The same story is told with regard to the shrines of Abbás Ali at Hasan Ali, and Sháh Mardán at Zerán. The exact dates of these visions are not known.

Mír Jamál is reported to be a descendant of Sayyid Asháq, grandfather of the Mahur Sayyids.

[3] Charms of different kinds, given by the five Sayyid families or *khanwadas*, are considered potent enough to cure various sorts of ailments. *Dam* or cure by blowing is also practised by the *mulláhs* and Sayyids. The blind, it is said, are cured by going to the Hazár Pír, Abbás Ali, Sháh Mardán, Fakhr-i-'Alam and Lála Gul, or to Sayyid Mír Ibráhím, Mír Jamál and Sayyid Asháq. Various other miracles are ascribed to these saints.

confined to Zerán and Shal Khána, and are much revered by the Turís. The charms of the Rúmi Khel Sayyids are considered potent for the cure of many ailments. Many legends are told about this miracle-working saint :—(1) On one occasion he is said to have presented the building at Mecca to certain Sayyids of the Fakhr-i-Alam Kaol. A stone bearing the names of Allah, the Prophet, Ali and his family is preserved at Zerán as a testimony to this miracle. (2) He is said to have once flung a club from Zerán to Shanai, a distance of about 6 miles, and as a reward he was given the land between those two places by the Bangash, and his descendants still enjoy it. (3) A woman who is said to have taken refuge with him from her enemies was miraculously transformed into a stone. The outline of her ornaments and features are still seen on the stone.

Numerous other miracles are said to have been wrought by this saint, whose ancestral home is traced to Rúm or Turkey.

II. *Mír Ibráhím* or *Mír Bim,* a descendant of the 7th Imám Músa Kázim, whose shrine is at Shalozán, highly revered by the Turís of Kurram. He is the patron saint of Shalozán and his descendants, who are called Ibráhím Khel or Imám Musa Kazimi Sayyids, are found in Shalozán, Nurkai, Ahmadzai and Nasti Koṭ and are much respected. The shrine is visited both by Sunnís and Shi'as. Children are shaved, animals and sweetmeats offered, flags hung and vows made for success against enemies. Two miracles are ascribed to this saint :—

(*a*) At the request of the Shalozánís he is said to have increased the water of spring which had hardly been sufficient for their requirements.

(*b*) A dry olive tree is said to have become green when touched by him.

Mír Ibráhím, great-grandfather of the Ahmadzai and Nurki Sayyids, is said to have come from Surkháb in the Amír's territory, and with the Turís. He occupied the spot where the present village of Shalozán lies. At that time Zable was Khán of the Shalozán Bangash. One day Mír Ibráhím's camels were grazing in the Khan's fields and a villager reported to him that a stranger's camels were grazing on his crops, so he ordered the trespasser to be brought to him, and asked him why he had grazed his camels on his crops. The Mír replied that his camels had done no damage. This the Khán could not believe so he went to see for himself, and on arriving at the spot found that the camels were not touching his crops. The Khán thought that the Mír must be a saint, and asked him how much land he would accept. The Mír replied that he would throw his staff, and that as far as it flew the land should be his. To this the Khán agreed, and Mír Ibráhím then cast his staff as far as Ahmadzai. But the Khán was unwilling to give him all that land, though assured he was a saint. Some lands at Ahmadzai and Shalozán were then given him and his descendants hold them to this day.

III. *Sayyid Fakhr Alam*, whose shrine is at Karmán, is held in high repute not only by his disciples there, but also by those of Shalozán and other places. His descendants are known as Husaini Sayyids, and are found at Karmán, Shalozán, Darawi, Ali Sheri and even in Tiráh. Regular fairs are held annually at this shrine at both the 'Ids and on the Muharram days. People from distant villages attend them. Almost all the visitors are Shi'as, Sunnís being very seldom seen. Sheep and goats are slaughtered and distributed among the guardians (*mujáwars*) of the shrine, and the people attending the fairs. Prayers are offered to the soul of the saint. The story of a miracle wrought by this saint is as follows :—

It is said that Hujaj, a tyrannical king, was a great persecutor of the Sayyids, whom he could recognise by a peculiar fragrance which came from their mouths. The Sayyids thereupon rallied round Fakhri Alam and begged him to request the Prophet to remove the fragrance which was so dangerous to them. Fakhri Alam accordingly went to Medína, bowed before the mausoleum of the Prophet and made the request. He then went to sleep, and in a dream saw the Prophet who told him that his request had been granted. Fakhri Alam then came back to Kurram. While passing through the outskirts of Karmán, he prayed that the stones and pebbles, which had proved so gentle to his bare feet, might be changed into fine white sand. The prayer was heard and the sand is still seen in its vicinity. He also blessed the fields of Karmán, which have since begun to yield abundant harvests.

The following is another version of this legend which is current among the saint's descendants :—

Hujaj Abn-i-Yúsaf, ruler of Turkey, was hostile to the Sayyids. He had put numbers of them to death and was hunting out the rest when one night in a vision he was directed to give his daughter's hand to a Sayyid of pure descent. On rising next morning he ordered his *wazírs* and *amírs* to have search made for a Sayyid of pure blood, and so they sent messages all over the kingdom to spread the news of the king's clemency. This proclamation produced the desired effect. Within a week over a thousand Sayyids were present in the king's *darbár*, every one declaring himself to be of the purest descent. The king then told the story of his vision to his officials who advised that all Sayyids who claimed to be of noble birth should be sent under escort to the Prophet's tomb at Medina there to prove themselves pure Sayyids by the following test :—

"Each should walk by himself round the Prophet's tomb and ask the Prophet to call him. If the Prophet replied to him the Sayyid would be deemed of pure blood and could receive the hand of the King's daughter on his return. When this proposal was disclosed to the Sayyids they all, with the exception of Sháh Abul Hasan and Sayyid Jalál (the great-grandfather of Pahlewán Sháh of Mahura), left the King's *darbár* and disappeared. These two, however, went to Medína and walked round the Prophet's tomb. Sayyid Jalál, they say, failed to produce the desired reply from the tomb, but when Sayyid Sháh Abul Hasan asked the Prophet whether he was his descendant of pure blood or not, the Prophet replied 'Yes' and said 'henceforth you must be called Fakhr-i-Alam'. He was then ordered by the Prophet to go to a place named Kirmán. Sayyid Fakhr-i-Alam, they say, married the

King's daughter, and the Qabat Shah Khel of Zerán regard themselves as her descendants. The Sayyids of Grám and other places are descendants of Sayyid Fakhr-i-Alam by his first wife who was a Sayyidáni. Fakhr-i-Alam, they say, went in search of Kirmán and eventually reached the place he sought, and there he stopped.[1] This happened prior to the occupation of the Kurram valley by the Bangash."

This version of the story is, however, not accepted by the descendants of Sayyid Jalál who point to the great honour done to the tomb of Sayyid Jalál at Uch in Baháwalpur and Bilot in Dera Ismail Khán as proof that he was the person who had his pedigree verified in the manner above quoted.

IV. *Lála Gul,* another descendant of the 7th Imám whose shrine is at Shakh, is much resorted to both by the Malli Khel and Duperzai Turís and the Muqbils of Kurram. His descendants, who go by the name of Lála Gul Kawal Sayyids, are found in Kharláchi, Shal Khána, Sultán and Shakh. Lála Gul is also known as the Yakh-posh, 'endurer of cold', saint, for having passed a night in a pool of frozen water at Istia. According to another legend, he sat on a burning pile of wood without being injured, and in return for this miracle he was given by his disciples a piece of land near Shakh, which his descendants still enjoy. Lála Gul's father Burqa-posh is also much revered by the people. He is said to have requested the Amír-ul-Mominín Ali to show him his face and on receiving no answer, he put on a *kafan* (winding sheet) and went to the cave of a big serpent known to be the guardian of a hidden treasure at Pír Ghar, about 2 miles from Kharláchi. As soon as the Burqa-posh (wearer of the veil) went near the serpent, it lowered its head as a tribute to his virtues. The Burqa-posh then took up his abode in the serpent's cave and it became as harmless and tame as a domestic animal. After a few days three Muqbils of Istia, thinking that the serpent was dead and that Burqa-posh was in possession of the treasure, determined to kill him and steal it. But when they neared the cave, the serpent gave a furious hiss and all three were burnt to death. Three black stones are still preserved as evidence of the incident. Burqa-posh then lived peacefully for some time in the cave with the serpent which provided him with sustenance. One night he had a dream in which Ali appeared to him and told him to pay a visit to the Shapola hill, close to Pír Ghar. Next morning he went to the Shapola hill, and was much astonished to see a wall miraculously rise around him and some sheep descend for him from heaven. Almost immediately after this he saw the face of Ali which was like a full moon. Burqa-posh then bowed before the Amír-ul-Mominín (commander of the faithful) and received from him, as tokens of his love, a gold ring and a golden flag. Thenceforth Burqa-posh always kept his face under a veil and never showed it to the people, signifying that nobody was worthy to catch sight of him. That is why he was known as Burqa-posh. His shrine is at Shakh close to Lála Gul's shrine.

This saint recalls the Veiled Prophet of Khorásán, Al-Muqanna' 'the

[1] Lumsden's statement that the shrine of Fakhr-i-Alam, the father of Nádir Shah, which is considered very sacred by the Turi tribes, is in the Karmán Valley, is totally incorrect.

concealed' whose name was Hakím Bin Háshim and who wore a golden mask. He was also called the Sázindah-i-Máh or the moon-maker, because he produced a miraculous illumination by night from a well at Nákhshab which caused the place to appear moon-lit. Mokanna' taught that God has assumed the human form since he had bidden the angels to adore the first man, and that since then the divine nature had passed, from prophet to prophet, to Abu Muslim who had founded the Abbassides, and had finally descended to himself. He founded in Transoxiana the sect of the Sufedjímagán or white-clothed. The Burqái, a sect found, like the Ráwandi, in Transoxiana, were so called because Muqanna' had veiled his face. They would appear to be identical with the Sufedjámagán.[1]

Three centuries later the Assassins adopted white garments and were called Muhayasa or white, as well as Muhammara or 'red' because they also adopted red turbans, boots or girdles.

The Ráwandís also acknowledged Abu Muslim as their head and he seems to have been the first to import the doctrine of transmigration (*tanásukh*) into Islám. To this doctrine Moqanna' added that of the incarnation of the divine and human nature.

Mr. Muhammad Hamid on this suggestion writes as follows:—'Al-Muqanna'[2] originally belonged to Merv in Khorásán, and served for some time as a secretary to Abu Muslim, governor of that province under Al-Mahdi, the third of the Abbaside Khalífas (A. D. 775-785). Afterwards he turned soldier, passed from Khorásán into Transoxiana and proclaimed himself a prophet. By Arab writers he is generally called Al-Muqanna' or sometime Al-Burqa'i (the veiled) because he always appeared in public with his face covered with a veil or gilded mask. The real cause of his always appearing in a *burqa'* was that he did not like to show his defects to the people. He was short in size, blind of one eye which he had lost in one of the wars—deformed in body, stammering in speech and otherwise of a despicable appearance. His followers, however, alleged that he hid it lest the splendour of his countenance should dazzle the eyes of beholders. Not content with being reputed a prophet he arrogated to himself divine honors, pretending that the supreme Deity resided in him. He alleged, as proof of his claim, that the first man was worshipped by angels and the rest of creation. From Adam, he asserted, the Deity had passed to Noah and so on to the prophets and philosophers until it resided in the person of Abu Muslim and after his death had passed on to him. He gained a large number of followers, deluding them by many so-called miracles, the chief of them being a moon which he caused to appear from a well for several nights together at a fairly long distance from his residence. Hence it is that he is also called Sázindah-i-Máh or Sáni'-i-Máh (the Moon-maker). His disciples increasing in number occupied several fortified places in Transoxiana and the Khalífa

[1] Amír Ali assigns the Ráwandís' foundation to 141 H. (758 A. D.), *op cit.*, p. 481. He terms Muqanna' the 'infamous' founder of the Sufedjámagán, pp. 481-2. But he writes as if the Indo-Magian sect of the Ráwandís, who taught the metempsychosis, were distinct from the Sufedjámagán.

[2] Ibn Khallaqán makes him a washerman of Merv. His real name, he mentions, was Aṭa but that of his father is not known. He is sometimes called Hakím.

was at length obliged to devote his energies to repressing the formidable rebellion headed by him. At the approach of the royal forces, Al-Muqanna' retired into one of his strongest fortresses (Sanám ?) in the city of Kash, which he had well provided against a siege and sent some of his chosen followers abroad to convert people to his heresy alleging that he raised the dead to life and knew future events. But being hard pressed by the besiegers, when he found that escape was impossible, he gave poison to his family and followers and when they were dead, burnt their bodies together with their clothes and all the property and cattle in the fort and then to prevent his own body being found jumped into the flames. Another tradition says that he threw himself into a tub of a poisonous preparation which consumed every part of him except his hair. The besiegers entered the fort but could find nothing but one of his concubines, who, suspecting his designs, had concealed herself, and disclosed the whole matter.[1]

Ibn Khallaqán gives another and somewhat different account of his death. He says that he administered poison in drink to his family (but not to his followers) a portion of which he drank himself, thus dying at his own hands. The besiegers, he says, forced the entrance of the fort and killed all the followers of Muqanna' found in the stronghold.[2] The remainder of his followers still adhered to his teachings as he had promised them that his soul should transmigrate into a grey-bearded man riding a greyish beast, and that after many years he would return to them. This expectation kept the sect alive for many generations after his death which occurred in 163 H. = 778-9 A. D.

A careful examination of the accounts of Al-Muqanna' and the Burqaposh of Kurram shows that there is no direct connection between them. The former died in 779 A. D. The latter seems to be much later but he is probably a true saint, never pretending to be a diety or even a prophet.

The Burqa'i sect of Transoxiana where Muqanna' first spread his heresy may be descended from some of the surviving disciples of the impostor. Muqanna' is called 'the veiled prophet of Khorásán' simply because he originally belonged to Merv in that province; but in fact his heresy spread over Transoxiana and he was besieged and defeated in the latter province. Again if the sect of the Sufedjámagán was founded by Muqanna', it is more than probable that they are identical with the Burqa'is.

Sayyid Lála Gul's descendants are the Sayyids of Kharláchi. It is said that Lála Gul migrated from Kashmír. When he came to Kurram the valley was full of the Karmán Sayyids, and when the eldest of them heard that a new Sayyid had come to the valley he sent him a glass of milk as a hint that the valley was full of Sayyids. Lála Gul then put a flower in the milk and sent it back to the Karmán Sayyid, thereby signifying that though the valley was full of Sayyids he would trouble no one. From Kurram he went towards Lohgar and after a while came again towards Kurram. Passing through the Chakmanni country he was recognized by the people as a saint. It is stated that a headman of the village of Dhunda asked him to remove the *jhil* which had made his lands a swamp. This Lála Gul did by throwing his staff into

[1] *The Sword of Islam*, pp. 489 and 138.
[2] Ibn Khallaqán, *Fihrist*, Part I, p. 319.

it. The village, however, still retains its old name. The land where Kharláchi lies was in possession of the Bangash. They gave some land to the Sayyid, but after a while were themselves driven from the place.

V. *Sayyid Isháq,* grandson of the Sayyid Jalál just mentioned, whose tomb is in Alizai, was the ancestor of the last of the five recognised *khanwadas* of the Sayyids. His descendants are called Bukhári Sayyids and are found at Paiwar Mahura, Agra, Tutak, Makhezai and Nasti Kot. His shrine is visited by the Hamza Khel and Mastu Khel of Alizai, Bagzai and Chárdíwár. Offerings are made, and the *mujáwars* and poor people are fed. Flags are also hung here. Many miracles are ascribed to this saint. By the most important of them all he perforated, by means of his club, a hill which obstructed the water of the Alizai Canal. That tunnel still exists, and through it flows the water of the canal. As a reward for this miracle he was given a piece of land called Bargherai which is still in possession of his descendants.

Sayyid Isháq was the great-grandfather of the Mahera Sayyids and came to the Kurram valley from Pesháwar, where the Karímpura Bázár is named after Sayyid Karím Shah, his grandfather. Sayyid Isháq's father, Muhammad Sháh Tájdár, died on his return from a pilgrimage to Meshed and was buried at Grinch, a place between Herát and Kandahár. Sayyid Isháq, returning to Peshávar *viá* the Kurram, stayed in the Kurram and died there. He is buried at Alizai. According to another account, however, he was not buried in Kurram, but there is a place in Alizai where he is said to have stayed.

In addition to these shrines, the Turís make long and perilous journeys to the famous shrines of Karbala and Mashad in Persia. In former days when there were no facilities of communication they had to travel the whole way on foot, but now the greater part of the journey is made by rail and steamer. Sometimes a whole family migrates to these shrines and takes up its permanent abode there. This is called *hijarat* by the Turís. Well-to-do people often send the bones of dead relations to the Karbala cemetery to be buried there.

The origin of the Mián Muríd and Drewandi factions among the Sayyids.

It appears that the Kurram Valley already possessed four classes of Sayyids, as stated above, when one of the Tíráh Sayyids came to the valley to try his fortune. Some of the people owing to a political disagreement with the Kurram Sayyids flocked to him and became his *muríds*. He used to stay a while with them and then return to Tíráh where he spent the greater part of his time. It is stated that one Amír Shah Sayyid of Kharláchi preached that the Tíráh Sayyads were superior in every way to the other Sayyids in Kurram, which so irritated the other Sayyids of the valley that they took up arms to kill him. The Tíráh Sayyids' *muríds* defended him, but owing to the smallness of their numbers could not protect him, and so Amír Sháh was killed. This was the beginning of the Mián Muríd and Drewandi factions. The Mián Muríds though few in number nevertheless managed to oppose the Drewandi faction with some success. The Mián Muríds were at one time called Ting or 'rage' Gund and the Drewandis, the Sust or 'slack' Gund.

Their disputes lasted for a considerable time, until the British Government put a stop to them, but the two factions still exist.

The Mián Muríds generally believe that the assistance of their *pír* is required for entering Paradise. The other Sayyids are only *pírs* in name, and their *muríds* do not put much faith in them. The main cause of the differences between the Drewandi and Mián Muríd factions is said to be that the former object to the Malangi institutions fostered by the Mián Muríds. A Malang is the religious devotee of a Sayyid and the Mián Muríds declare that his devotion (to a Sayyid of their persuasion) will be rewarded by Paradise.

These sectarian differences are further cross-divided by the Spín[1] and Tor *gunds* or factions. None of the Turís or Bangash can say when these *gunds* arose. A Ghalzai version is that a long time ago there was in Afghánistán a Khán who had two sons. The eldest was called Spín Khán and the younger Tor Khán. After their father's death they quarrelled about the supremacy and this led to a fight between them. As both were wealthy they subsidized the neighbouring tribes who took part in their fights which lasted for a considerable time. The tribes who joined Spín Khán's faction were called Spíngundi and those which joined Tor Khán's Turgundi. The Turi and Bangash do know of this tradition, but they can give no other explanation of the origin of the two *gunds*.[2] This feud breaks out occasionally but it is chiefly observed in matters which have no connection whatever with any religious question. In fact it may be said to have become extinct as such but the factions live, and influence the tribes in their dealings with each other. All the Torgundi are Sunnís, whilst the Spín *gund* comprises some Shi'a and some Sunni tribes.

The Sayyids of Tíráh, Gram and Ahmadzai are the most honoured families in Kurram. The Sayyids of Mahura and Kharláchi come next to them.

I.—Shrines of the Kurram Wazírs.

1.—*The ziárats of Pír Sábiq and Pír Rámdín.*

These two shrines lie close to each other at the junction of the Thal and Biland Khel boundary, about four miles from the latter village, and are held in high veneration by the Biland Khels, Thalwáls, Khattaks and Kábul Khel Wazírs, who pay annual visits to them and make vows for the increase of their cattle, wealth, and sons. In former days, cows and sheep were slaughtered as offerings here, but no sacrifices are now made. Hindus also resort to them, but Shi'as never visit them, although the saints were Hussaini Sayyids. The descendants of Pír Sábiq and Pír Rámdín are known as the *pírs*, or religious guides, of the Biland Khels and comprise no less than fifty families. They own one-fifth of the Biland Khel possessions, and are a powerful community.

[1] Vol. III, p. 428.

[2] A characteristically cynical folk-tale says that the origin of the Tor and Spín *gunds* is due to a discussion about a bird called *gobaka* or *kajkas*. Some people said that the bird had more white feathers than black, others that its black feathers were more numerous than its white. This led to two political parties, the Tor and Spín *gunds*, being formed.

The Kábul Khel and other Wazírs, when proceeding to the Shawál and other places in summer, leave their grain, hay and household property within the precincts of these shrines and find them intact on their return in winter. The shrines are covered over with domes shaped like canopies, and are consequently called the *duá-gumbat ziárat,* or shrines with two domes.

The story about the miraculous power of the saints is as follows :—The Biland Khels, being in want of water for the irrigation of their lands, begged Pír Sábiq and Pír Rámdín to dig them a canal from the Kurram river, and this the saints undertook to do. Though they had no money, they commenced excavation, and when in the evening the labourers came to them for wages, they directed them to go to a certain rock, where they were paid. Nobody could tell how they came by the money. One day, while excavating, the labourers found their way blocked by a huge stone, which they could neither remove nor blow up. The saints thereupon ordered them to leave it alone and retired. In the morning when the labourers returned to work they found that the rock, which had to them appeared an insurmountable obstacle, had been driven asunder by the saints, who had made a passage for the water to flow through. Two years after the completion of this canal the saints died. The Biland Khels, who are their chief disciples, attribute their prosperity to their patronage and the proximity of the two shrines. To cut trees in the vicinity is looked upon as sacrilege.

2.—*Rámdín Ziárat.*

This shrine lies midway between Biland Khel village and the shrines of Pírs Sábiq and Rámdín. This Rámdín was a descendant of Pír Sábiq, and should not be confounded with the Pír Rámdín who was Pír Sábiq's contemporary. He was a great Arabic and Persian scholar, and endowed with saintly powers before he came of age. When a child of four, as he was seated one day on a low wall, repeating verses from the *Qurán* and meditating on their import, he happened in his abstraction to kick the wall with his heels, which began to move, and had gone seven or eight paces before the saint became aware of what had happened and stopped it. The wall can be seen even to this day.

One day he went to a hill, sat down under a *pleman* tree and began to repeat verses from the sacred book. The shade of the tree pleased him so much that he determined to plant one like it near his own house. Having finished his reading, he walked home and was surprised to find the tree following him. He turned round and ordered it to stop. The tree is now known as the *rawán pleman* or 'walking *pleman*' and is held in high esteem by the surrounding tribes. Its twigs, when worn round the neck, are said to cure jaundice. A stone enclosure about fifty yards in diameter surrounds it, and to this day the Kábul Khel Wazírs bring diseased cattle there. The moment they taste the earth of the enclosure they are cured.

3.—*Sar Prekarai Faqír—The Shrine of the Beheaded Saint.*

This shrine lies about four miles from Biland Khel village. The saint is said to have been a cowherd, and one day, while grazing his herds on a hill-top, he was attacked by a gang of Malli Khel Turís, who killed him and carried off his cattle. Tradition says that the severed head of the saint pursued the raiders for nearly a mile, and that when they turned and saw it they fled in dismay, leaving the cattle behind. The cattle were thus recovered. There are now two shrines, one at the place where the saint's body fell, and the other where his head was found. As he was a great lover of cattle, all those desirous of increasing their herds visit his shrine, fix small pegs in the ground and tie bits of rope to them, as a hint that they want as many cattle as there are pegs; and the belief is that their efforts are not in vain. The saint's descendants, who go by the name of Manduri Sayyids, are found in Kurram and the Bannu District. They are supposed to possess the power of curing people bitten by mad dogs. Their curse is much dreaded by the people, and nobody ventures to injure their property. In the tribal *jirgas*, whenever one party wishes to bring the opposite side to a permanent settlement or termination of a feud, it invariably secures the attendance of a Mandúrí Sayyid at the *jirga*, as no one will venture to violate or contravene an agreement drawn up in his presence. People whose property is insecure in their houses take it to the precincts of this shrine in order to secure its safety, and no thief will venture to touch it. A jackal is said to have once entered the compound of the shrine with intent to steal, but it was miraculously caught in a trap and killed. The head of the *faqír* is buried in the Miámi country and his body in Malikshâhi.

4.—*Ziárat Sarwardín.*

This shrine is situated about hundred yards from the shrine of Rámdín (No. 2). This saint also was a Sayyid. His descendants, who live in the surrounding villages, are said to have been much oppressed by the high-handedness of the Thalwáls (inhabitants of Thal), who maltreated them and forcibly diverted their water. One day descendants of Sarwardín, exasperated by the excesses of the Thalwáls, went to their ancestor's shrine and prayed against them, and it so happened that one of the men, who was actually engaged at the time in injuring them, died within twenty-four hours. Another man, who had stolen some grass from the field of a descendant of this saint, saw in a dream that he was stabbed by a horseman and when he awoke he went mad, ran about like a wild animal and died soon after. The descendants of this saint are also respected and dreaded by the people, though not to the same extent as those of the Sar Prekaṛai saint.

5.—*Násimu'lláh Ziárat.*

This shrine is about three hundred paces from Biland Khel village. The saint belonged to the Qáz Khel family and lived a life of great austerity. He very seldom spoke, always remained bareheaded, and passed his days and nights, both summer and winter, in water. He left to his posterity a green mantle and a green cloak. The popular belief is that these clothes, when drenched in water, have the power of bringing down rain from the sky. His descendants look upon them as a sacred and valuable legacy and would not part with them for anything.

6.—*Khalifa Nika Ziárat.*

This shrine lies about a mile from the village of Biland Khel. The saint, who goes by the name of Khalífa, was a beloved disciple of Háji Bahádur Sáhib, whose shrine is at Kohát, and he is said to have been allowed by his spiritual guide to lift kettles of boiling water on his bare head. There is a belief that if a man receive a piece of cloth from this saint's descendants and dip his head along with it in boiling water, it will come out unscathed. This shrine is visited both by men and women and vows made for the birth of sons and increase of wealth. The Kábul Khel and Khojal Khel Wazírs make frequent visits to it. A stone taken from the *ziárat* and passed over the body is looked upon as a potent charm against evil spirits.

7.—*Khand Ziárat.*

This shrine is close to the village of the Karmandi Khel Wazírs and is highly venerated by them and by the Máyamis. Khand was a Mandúri Sayyid, and the popular belief among the Karmandi Khels is that the vicinity of the saint is a strong safeguard against the prevalence of cholera, fever, and small-pox. The Karmandi Khels, on proceeding to their summer settlements in the Shawál hills, leave their household property in the precincts of this shrine and find it untouched on their return in the following winter.

8.—*Saif Ali Ziárat.*

This shrine stands six miles from Spínwám. The saint was a Kábul Khel Wazír. His descendants, who are known as Isa Khel Kábul Khels, are much respected by the people. A man, who stole a bundle of hay from the precincts of this shrine, became blind and his house was burnt down the same night. The saint's descendants are held in repute by the Wazírs of the Karmandi Khel section, and when the rains hold off they are fed by the people by way of offering, the belief being that a downpour will immediately follow. They are also empowered to give charms to the people, which they say have a wonderful effect in curing various diseases.

9.—*Ghundakai Ziárut.*

This shrine stands on high ground and is known as the shrine of the Asháb, or Companions of the Prophet. In its precincts the people stock their crops, after they are cut, and they are then safe from the hands of an incendiary.

II.—Shrines of the Madda Khel and other Wazírs of the Tochi Valley and of the Ahmadzai Wazírs and others of Wana.

1.—*Máman Ziárat.*

This shrine lies in a village, called after it the Ziárat Qil'a, which stands within a bugle sound of Sheranna. The saint is a descendant of the famous Dangar Pír, whose shrine is in the Gyán country in Khost, Afghánistán. Almost all the tribes of the Tochi Valley, *viz.* the Madda Khels, Khizzar Khels, Dangar Khels, Tannís, and Daurís, visit it, and to its presence they ascribe their prosperity, security, and very existence. The tribes living close to the shrine visit it almost every Friday. Those living farther away resort to it at the 'Id and Muharram. It is guarded by Wazír *mujáwars* (guardians) who are entitled to one *osha*[1] of grain per house from each crop. They also receive a share of the alms of pilgrims, who make offerings and slaughter sheep, goats, and cows at the shrine. Vows are made here for an increase in wealth and the birth of sons. The Sperkais, Wali Khels, Tori Khels, and Madda Khels when going to Shawál, and the Kábul Khels when returning to Margha, on their way to Kurram, deposit in the precincts of this shrine all such property as is not required for immediate use. The belief is that it is immediately transformed into a snake if touched by a strange hand. A murderer wishing to make peace with his enemies resorts to the shrine for seven consecutive Fridays and thereby succeeds in his object. During his lifetime the saint is said to have asked one of his *shaikhs* (disciples), called Dále, to cook a *kok*[2] two maunds in weight, and the story goes that the *shaikh* succeeded in so preparing it, that when it was weighed it was found correct. The saint is said to have blessed Dále for his deftness, and the following proverb is associated with his name : '*Dále dang dáikoke dang dai*' 'Dále is tall and his *kok* is also tall.' The large boulders seen near Dagar Qil'a are said to have been detached from the hill by the miraculous power of this saint. On one occasion he sent his *shaikh* to Páolai, a gardener, to fetch fruit, but the latter refused to give him anything. On this the *shaikh* called out 'fall, fall,' and the fruit began to fall one after another. The gardener was frightened and gave him as many as he could carry. Lunatics, who cannot otherwise be cured, are tied up by the side of this shrine and recover in a week. It is said that unholy persons cannot pass a quiet night within the precincts of the *ziárat*. The descendants of Máman are known by the name of *piran*. The shrine is also called Miánji Sáhib. Dangar Pír was a follower of Háji Bahádur Sáhib of Kohát. In addition to the Tochi tribes mentioned Zadráns, Khostwáls and Bannúchís visit the shrine in large numbers. Another account says : 'Isperka and Tori Khels do *not* go to Shawál and the Wali Khel enter Shawál by a different route and do not deposit their property in the *ziárat*. Madda Khels leave property there on their way to Mazdak, and it is believed that any one touching property left at the shrine is either struck mad or blind.'

2.—*Bába Ziárat.*

This shrine stands near Dande village and is visited by Madda Khels, Tori Khels, Daurís and other tribes of the valley, who make offerings of live animals. The flesh is distributed among the poor and needy Wazírs, who hang about the place at such times. The descendants of this saint are called *faqíran* and are looked upon with respect by the people. Offerings are now usually made in cash.

3.—*Mara Panga Shahíd* (*Martyr*).

This shrine is situated on the slopes of the Char Khel Range and is held in esteem by the Machás, Ismáíl Khels, Nazar Khels, Khizzar

[1] About 20 *sers*.

[2] A *kok* is a Wazír loaf, round like a ball, and cooked on the embers by placing a hot stone in the centre.

Khels, Tannís, Janbey Khéls,[1] and Bakhshi Khels, who visit it in the hot weather *en route* to their summer quarters. A goat or sheep is slaughtered for every flock that passes by this *ziárat*. All those visiting it go on a Friday morning, and after throwing some wood-chips round about the tomb, fall asleep and in their dream see their desires fulfilled. On waking they pray to the soul of the saint, slaughter a sheep or goat, and distribute its flesh among the poor. All who have once slaughtered a sheep or goat at this shrine become the saint's disciples, and it becomes incumbent upon them to slaughter a sheep every year by way of offering to the shrine. *Ghí*, querns, beams and mats are deposited within the precincts of this shrine by the nomad tribes. Flags are also hung here, and a bit of stuff taken from them and tied about the neck is looked upon as a safeguard against all diseases.

4.—*Chang Mangal Ziárat.*

This is situated close to Achar, a village about twelve miles west of Datta Khel. The saint was a Mangal and passed a pious life in this vicinity. He has no descendants here. The shrine is visited both by Madda Khels and Achars. A thread, equal to the length of this tomb, worn round the neck, is said to be a specific for fever and jaundice.

5.—*Dangar Pír Ziárat.*

This is a most important shrine, situated in Gyán and periodically visited by almost all the tribes of the Tochi, Khost, Zadrán, and Urgún. The saint was a Sayyad and an ancestor of Máman. His descendants are called Dangar Khels and are found at Ghazlámi and other villages of the Tochi Valley. They are called *pírs* by the Tochi tribes and are highly venerated by them. Their displeasure is much dreaded, especially by those who become *muríds*, or disciples of Dangar Pír. The name Dangar, which means 'lean', was given to the saint on account of his physical condition. His home is traced to Egypt, of which country he is said to have been king. He is afterwards said to have laid down his sceptre for a saintly staff and to have travelled to this country. In his travels he was accompanied by Miso or Musa (now known as Musa Nikka) and Máman (now called Máman Pír). People take special care never to offend the descendants of Saint Dangar, for it is said that whenever anybody does so, the saint in his rage miraculously flings blades of iron at him, and destroys him and his family. These iron blades are called *saghbírs* by the people.

6.—*Máman Pír Ziárat.*

This shrine is about two hundred yards from Dangar's shrine. In the autumn a joint fair is held by the Gyáns at the shrines of Máman Pír and Dangar Pír, at which a sheep is slaughtered by every family attending it. Máman Pír belonged to the Abbaside dynasty, and the following saying shows how much, according to popular belief, he was loved by God :—

مامن عباسي ـــ خداي درسی په يين داڵی غو په تندي حسي

"God is as enamoured of Máman the Abbaside, as a cow is of her new-born calf."

[1] A sub-section of the Madda Khels.

7.—*Musa Nikka Ziárat.*

This shrine stands on the right bank of the Shakin Algad in Birma on the Wána Urgún border. Musa Nikka claims to be the ancestor of all the Wazírs, whether in Wána, Birmal or the Tochi. The Ahmadzái Wazírs and others on their way to Birmal in summer leave their superfluous property in the precincts of this shrine and on their return in autumn find it intact. The belief is that any one stealing property thus deposited is immediately struck blind.

The Musa *ziárat* is visited by the Ahmadzáís and Mahsúds of Wána, the Saifalís and Paipalís of Birmal and the Madda Khels and others of the Tochi. Many stories are told of the miraculous powers of this saint, as, for instance :—One day the saint's brother Isa was grazing his flock in the hills. There was no water in the neighbourhood. Isa and his flock both became parched with thirst. Just then Musa came to his brother's help and with his stick made a small hole in the ground, covered it with his mantle, and began to pray. After a while he told his brother Isa to remove the mantle. The tradition says that a spring of clear water began to ooze from the hole, at which Isa and his flock quenched their thirst. Musa then closed the hole and the spring dried up. The site of this spring is in the Warmána Nála, close to which are seen two large heaps of stone called the *chillas* of Musa and Isa. Within the walls of this shrine are three trees, which are believed to be endowed with different miraculous qualities. To embrace the first will give a man a wife ; to climb the second will give him a horse ; and to swing from the third will give him a son. Close to the Musa Nikka *ziárat* are two others, known respectively as Shin Starga *ziárat* and Baghar *ziárat*. All three shrines are visited on one and the same day and joint sacrifices made.

8.—*Michan Bába Ziárat.*

This shrine stands about eight miles east of Wána. The descendants of this saint are not found in Wána, but it is probable that the scattered families of Michan Khels, found in the Bannu District and elsewhere, are his descendants. The shrine is visited by the Zalli Khels and Madsúds and vows made for the birth of sons.

III.—Minor shrines occasionally visited by the Ahmadzai Wazírs and others.

1.—*Umar Aga.*

A Daftani saint, who has a shrine at Dhana, about twelve miles north-west of Wána.

2.—*Khojaki Ziárat.*

This is situated at Maura. The saint was a Sayyid and the shrine is visited by the nomad Wazírs.

3.—*Madár Bába Ziárat.*

This is about fifteen miles west of Wána and has a well close to it, where Wazírs encamp every year.

4.—*Mámin Ziárat or Patán Ziárat.*

This is situated on a hill near Madár Ziárat.

TAHSÍL HARÍPUR.

1. The Bhorewáli shrine, on the bank of the Johi *nála*, Mohri-Malya, 9 miles from Harípur, is known as the *ibádat-gáh* (place of prayer) of one Sháh Maqbúl, who came from Baghdád and spent 24 years there in prayer. His *bhora* or cell still exists, though in ruins. His grave is at Peshâwar in the *Mohalla Dabgari*, but this shrine is also greatly revered by the people of Hazára in the belief that a visit to it will cure certain diseases. The descendants of this *faqír* are still to be found at Bhedián in Attock and at Kokaliya in Hazára.

2. The shrine of Sháh Maqsúd, 6 miles east of Harípur and on the bank of the Dor *nála*, in Maqsúd. The grave is of one Sháh Muhammad Gházi, who came from Sukkur and was buried there by a spring of clear water. This shrine is of great repute.

3. The *ziárat* of Bibi Puránïwáli, a virgin recluse, in Dehdar alongside the main road leading to Hassan Abdál, is ascribed to the Muhammadan period. Every Sunday women assemble there to get relief from *parchhâwan*[1] (the shadow of a demon or apparition). It has a pond in which sick people bathe. The villagers have allowed an acre of land as *seri* to its *mujáwar*.

4. The Dári *ziárat*, 6 miles north of Harípur, in Dari, is the shrine of Sháh Sher Muhammad Gházi, who is said to have come from Sayyid Kisrán in Káwalpindi. People generally visit it to get cured of sore eyes. It is also the scene of a fair at each 'Id. Sick persons resort to it every Thursday. *Túti* is also played.

5. The *ziárat* of Chhajka in a glen of Sowábi Mira in tahsíl Harípur is visited by the people of that tract to cure colic. Every Thursday nearly 150 souls assemble there.

6. The *ziárat* of Sakhi Habíb, 2 miles east of Harípur in Mának Rái, is the shrine of a *Pír* held in high esteem by the people, who generally resort to it of a Thursday to obtain their desires. They give what is called *gaddí podi* to the *mujáwar*.

7. The *ziárat* of Jatti Pind, 4 miles north of Harípur, lies in a dry plain in that village. It is said that a hermit came here from Gujrát in Muhammadan times. Every Thursday people suffering from neuralgia make a pilgrimage to the shrine to get cured.

8. The Qázián *ziárat*, 2 miles north of Harípur, in Qázián, is the shrine of Miyán Abdul Wahâb Gházi, who migrated from the Awánkári *iláqa*. His descendants still live in this and the two adjoining villages of Malakyár and Padhána. Every Thursday it is the scene of a large gathering of people suffering from coughs.

9. The *ziárat* of Mián Mardán Sáhib lies in Darwesh near Harípur. People believe that a bath in its tank on a Thursday will cure scabies.

10. The shrine at Paháru is known as that of Haqáni Sháh, whose native place was Saiyad Kisrán in Káwalpindi. This is a well-known *ziárat* where people assemble every Thursday in large numbers in order to obtain their desires.

[1] The local pronunciation is *pachâwan*.

11. The *ziárat* at Kharkoṭ is the shrine of Bába Sajalif of the Awán Qutb-Sháhi tribe whose native place was in the Awán-Kári, whence he went to Pakhli, but not finding it to his liking he flung his horse's reins which fell at Kharkoṭ and then took up his abode there and was buried there on his death. People assemble there every Thursday in order to secure male issue.

Tahsíl Mánsehra.

1. Díwán Rájá Bábá was a well-known saint in the Pakhli tract near Baffa in the Mánsehra tahsíl and it is the common belief of nearly all the people in that district that the notoriously oppressive Turk Rájá was expelled from his kingdom and dethroned because he incurred the displeasure of this saint. Soon after the Rájá was warned to mend his ways, the Swátís came over and defeated him. The only thing is that they can only say and do what they see will be done by the Almighty and be contented to do whatsoever He will. The shrine in Guli Bágh near Baffa is visited by almost every one in Hazára and is generally called the *gumtánwali ziárat.* At this shrine is a spring in which the sick bathe. At the 'Id on one day only women and next day only men assemble. Among the men the principal game is the *túti*, a kind of prisoners' base. The people of the Pakhli plain, of the Swát glens and of Feudal Tanáwal are the principal visitors at the gatherings which are in the main festive, though the shrine is held in high repute.[1]

2. The shrine of Mián Kháki Sáhib in the Agror valley is famous.

3. The shrine of Sultán Mughal Sáhib in Mián Kháki-da-Bágh in Tanáwal is also famous and it is believed that he was blessed by Hazrat Mián Sáhib at Mangal.

Another shrine in Leúng, a village in Mánsehra tahsíl, is also much respected.

5. The other shrines are in Independent Territory in the trans-Agror valley, *i. e.* Paimál Sharíf, or in Muzaffarabad in Kashmír.

6. The *ziárat* of Hayát-ud-Mír, 24 miles north-east of Mánsehra at Bálákot on the bank of the Kunhar *nála,* is in Muhammadan belief the sitting place of Sakhi Hayát-ul-Mír who is said to have been endowed with life everlasting, while according to Hindus it is the sitting place of Bhái Bála. At the 'Id one day men and the next day women assemble there. It has a spring, known as *sharbat,* which has medicinal properties, being believed to cure leprosy and other diseases and 20 or 30 sufferers are generally to be found there.[2]

7. The *ziárat* at Nankoṭ in the Pakhli plain is the tomb of Saiyad Ali Hamdán Bábá. He had also some *nishastgáhs,* or sitting places, in Kashmír which are held in high esteem. Every Sunday, especially the first in every bright half of the lunar month, there is a large gathering of women with their children afflicted with *parchhawán.* The sufferers are passed under the olive tree at the shrine.

[1] *Hazára Gazetteer,* 1883-4, p. 59.

[2] *Ib.,* p. 60.

8. The *ziárat* of Sayyid Jalál Bába at Bhogarmang commemorates a leader under whom the Swátís of what is now Mánsehra tahsíl wrested their present seats from the Turks.[1]

9. The ancient *ziárat* known as that of Sufaidáhwála Bába lies at Khatai in the Agror *iláqa*. This *faqír*, who lived quite naked, was a Sayyid by caste.

10. At the shrine at Dogái (the 'junction' of the Sarori and Unár streams) in the Agror *iláqa* people assemble every Thursday and Sunday. The name of the *faqír* entombed there is not known, but he was a Sayyid of Ogh.

11. The Takiáwáli shrine at Torawára in Agror is the tomb of Akhúnd Sa'ad-ud-Dín who with the aid of Suba Khán, leader of the Tanáwalís in Hazára, conquered Agror. Swátís and other tribes visit this shrine.

12. The *ziárat* at Gházikoṭ or Tútni-ki-ziárat lies by the road leading to Abbottabad. People suffering from stomachache visit it every Thursday and Friday.

13. The shrine of Sháh Sharíf Qalandar lies at Sufaidáh near Mánsehra. The saint entombed therein was a Sayyid. The inhabitants of the Pakhli *iláqa* and Garhián in Tanáwal assemble there for prayer in times of drought. The water of its tank is possessed of medicinal properties in some ailments.

14. The *ziárat* Takiya Mahándri in Jaríd by the road leading to Kágán is the tomb of Pír Gházi Sháh. He is believed to have struck a stone with his *'asá* or 'stick' and from it gushed a spring which still exists.

15. The *ziárat* Síri Panjaulwáli is the shrine of Khitáb Sháh whom the Swátís brought here from Yághistán and entombed after his death. He was by birth a saint. The villagers visit his shrine at both 'Ids.

16. The Báwájiwáli *ziárat* is the shrine of Sháh Waláyat Sháh, who went to a distant land, but his body was brought back and buried near Icharián. He was deemed an able man of enlightened mind. At the 'Ids people go to his shrine to *salám*.

Tahsíl Abbottabad.

1. *Ziárat* Báwáji Sáhib is a shrine at Máíngojri in Tanáwal. The Báwáji came here from Chandaur, in Tanáwal, Tahsíl Haripur. He is also known as the '*buzurg* of Chhatti Mohri', an estate or tract still held by his survivors. According to the popular faith a visit to the shrine will cure every disease.

2. The *ziárat* of Miyán Sultán Gházi lies at Kháni Tathára in Tanáwal and midway between Johrípur and *thána* Sharwán. It is a resting place for travellers as it has a spring of sweet water and shady trees. Several diseases are cured by paying it a visit.

3. Chila Sháh Barri Latíf is a place for the worship of Sháh

[1] Hazára *Gazetteer*, 1883—4, p. 60.

Barri Latíf, whose shrine is at Núrpur Shéhán in tahsíl Ráwalpindi. This *ibádatgah* lies one or one-and-a-half miles from Dakhan Pesor in the Nára *ilága* on *nála* called the Haru Dhundán. It has a grove of shady trees and is much revered by the people who to the number of nearly 20 assemble there every Thursday.

4. The Khandwála Pír Sáhib shrine at Sajkot, in the Nára *iláqa*, is so called because, according to the people, a rain of *khanḍ* (sugar) fell at his death. Hence the offerings to it consist mainly of sugar. Some 4 or 5 persons visit the shrine daily. One's desires can be fulfilled by paying it a visit.

5. The Numána Sháhwáli *ziárat* in Chanáli near Nagri Totial is the tomb of a *faqír* whose native place is said to be Kashmír. After praying here for some years he was buried on this spot at his death. According to the people a visit to it is an antidote for fever

6. The *ziárat* at Mángal or Miyán Kangál Sáhib is the shrine of Gul Muhammad, lying 8 miles north of Abbottabad in Jalápura, the former site of Mangal. His *pír* was Shaikh Abdus Sabúr Qádiri of Kashmír who was also called Bastal, c. 1145 H. (1732 A. D.). A large gathering of men and women is held every Thursday.

7. The *takiya* at Tarchh, near Majohán, is the very old shrine of Pír Sattár Sháh Ghézi and is situate on the bank of the Jhelum.

8. Other shrines are that of Jamál Ghási at Dhamtaur where there is a fine grove of some size and to which Muhammadans make offerings: that of Sáín Malpat in Abbottabad tahsíl: and in Mánsehra tahsíl, that of Shaikh Bála and Mehr Ali Bába at Bajna near Shinkiári: that of Qalandar Sayyid at Bálákot: that of Naubat Sháh Sayyid at Lachimang in Konsh: that of Tortom Bába Sayyid at Shamdhara: and that of Haidar Bába at Ghanián, both in Agror. The last-named lies at the foot of Black Mountain and is the tomb of Miyán Haider Bába, grandfather of the Sayyids of Atir. It is the scene of a fair at the 'Id.

SHRINES ON THE FRONTIER.

Pesháwar. Jogian Sar is a *ziárat* on the summit of the Tortaba spur of the Ilam mountain which is visited in spring by both Muhammadans and Hindus, in separate parties. The latter term this festival Rántakht. It lasts three days and is described as a mixture of religious devotion and debauchery. Pír Bába is a *ziárat* in Buner which is a sober place of pilgrimage without a fair owing to the unsettled state of the country.[1]

Kohát. The *ziárat* of Shaikh Yúsaf in Chillibágh at Sherkot village, Kohát tahsíl, *tappa* Samílzai, consists of a masonry tomb in an adobe building surrounded by *shísham* trees and beds of narcissus. People from the neighbouring country assemble on Thursdays between Chet and Bhádon, the gatherings lasting from one to four days, and, on the first Thursdays of Hár and Maghar especially, visitors bring bread and *khichri* which is all collected and after being blessed is distributed to those present. This gathering is called *laghra*. Visitors ask for happy marriages, sons, wealth, recovery from disease and forgiveness of sins. Goats and sheep

[1] *Pesháwar Gazetteer*, p. 113.

are sacrificed and the heads and legs offered to the *siárat* to be eaten by the man in charge. Coverlets, oil, *gur*, rice etc. are also offered. Gatherings are held both in the light and dark half of the month, in which both Hindus and Muhammadans join.

The *siárat* of Mír Habíb Shah, near the spring of Khwája Ashraf in village Jangal Mír Asghar Mela, is a thickly wooded place in a picturesque situation where the saint is said to have prayed. Gatherings take place at the end of Sáwan when the grapes are ripe.

The *siárat* of Sháh Ismáíl Sáhib, between Samari Bála and Páyán, Kohát tahsíl, *tappa* Baizai, consists of tombs surrounded by a grove of trees. Gatherings from villages near and far take place every Friday in Chet and Baisákh, both in the dark and light half of the month, and last for one or two days. Visitors kill goats and sheep, offer a part to the priest in charge and ask for all sorts of blessings. This shrine is held in great reverence by the Khattaks, Bangash and Tíráhwáls. Tradition says that the saint was a Sayyid of Bukhára who, with some companions, visited Mír Khweli and thence cast a stone which fell near the shrine. So he dwelt here. But a serpent bit his finger and he died. There are now three graves, one of the saint, another of the bitten finger and a third of the snake!

The *siárat* of Háji Bahádur Sáhib consists of a masonry mausoleum, with a mosque and tank attached to it, in Kohát town. It is the most frequented shrine in the district. The saint was a Mír Ahmad Khel, Bangash, and his original name was Mián Abdulla. From boyhood he was fond of religious studies and became a disciple of Shaikh Adam Banúri who with his disciple set out on a pilgrimage to Mecca. During the voyage, the ship was brought to a stand-still by a storm. At his preceptor's instance, tradition says, Mián Abdulla lifted the ship on his head and set it agoing, but the exertion bruised his scalp and caused baldness so since then all his descendants are born bald. At Mecca the preceptor's son died but was restored to life by Mián Abdulla's prayers. In recognition of this miracle he was styled Háji Bahádur by his preceptor. On his return to Kohát Háji Bahádur assumed the title of *khuda-i-bín* or 'seer of God'. This offended Aurangzeb and the Háji was summoned to Lahore by the emperor and challenged to display his supernatural powers or undergo punishment for his heresies. Tradition says that he accepted the ordeal and asked the emperor to look at some water which he was dropping through the holes of a *pípal*. The emperor became insensible at the sight and fell from the throne. When he was himself again he testified to the Háji's supernatural powers and granted him the village of Mián Khel. It is also claimed as a proof of existing sanctity, that in seasons of drought, stones placed on the tomb, if dipped in the tank, are sure to bring down rain. Four well-known verses commemorate the date of the Háji's death. It is even said that he married Aurangzeb's daughter.[1] This shrine is respected by the Bangash, Khattak, Afrídi, Orakzai, Wazír and Kostwál Pathâns.

The *siárat* of Tor Kamál near Kamál Khel is that of a saint who came from Turak with Sultán Mahmúd of Ghazni and was killed here.

[1] See paragraph 4, App. I to Tucker's Kohát *Settlement Report*.

The Khulai *siárat* in Marchungi is resorted to every Thursday by people suffering from rheumatism. This saint was killed in a religious war, but he took up his severed head and walked away. People noticed this and began to talk about it, whereupon the head fell off near the site of the *siárat.*

At the *siárat* of Pír Futeh Sháh Sáhib in Kohát town gatherings take place on the 'Id-ul-Fitar, 'Id-ul-Zuha, the 8th day after the 'Id-ul-Zuha, and the Nauroz. Visitors eat a little salt placed on the grave and also touch the stones with their eyes.

The *siárat* of Sháh Sa'id Halim Bukhári on the left bank of the Kohát Toi close to the Railway Station was believed to be respected by the Toi, but now it has been washed away. Men given to intoxicating drugs often resort to its shady grove.

The *siárat* of Sháh Abulla Namázi near Sir Sháhzáda Sultán Ján's cemetery owes its origin to Gauhar, a *kárigar,* who had a dream about it and so the *siárat* was made.

The *siárat* of Shaikh Alladád in Kahi Circle, Kohát tahsíl, is that of a saint, a Khaṭṭak Paṭhán who used to pray in the Mandúri hills and then settled here. The Jawakki Afrídís and others visit it in large numbers on the first Thursday of the light half of the month. It is a fine masonry building consisting of two mausoleums, one of the saint, the other of his son.

The *siárat* of Sandali or Fateh Gul Bábá in Torastáni marks where that saint prayed on the Sandali hill.

The *siárat* of Faqír Sáhib in the village Nariáb, Hangu tahsíl, is visited by people of this district as well as of Tíráh on Thursdays and lamps are lit at it.

The Nawan Faqír *siárat* in Darsamandi on the road to Torwári is visited by rheumatic people on Thursdays.

The *siárat* of Sháh Almás, on a high hill north of Hangu, is believed to be the tomb of the ancestor of the present Sayyid in Hangu. People assemble on both 'Ids and a lamp is lit every Thursday.

The *siárat* of Miánji Sáhib, Shakardarra Circle, Kohát tahsíl, on the Makhaḍ road is visited by people with toothache who put one stone above another to invoke its blessing.

The *siárat* of Háji Kamál Sáhib, near Miánji Khel in Teri tahsíl, is said to be the tomb of the ancestor of the Miáns of Miánji Khel. It is very popular among the Khaṭṭaks and Wazírs.

The *siárat* of Miánji Sáhib in Shiwáki is the tomb of the ancest of the Sayyids of Shiwáki.

The *siárat* of Saráj Khel is a well-known shrine. The saint was the ancestor of the Sayyids of this village. People visit it every Thursday in Chet.

Shrines in Dera Gházi Khán and Muzaffargarh.

The shrine of Pír Adil or 'the just saint' lies 9 miles north of Dera Gházi Khán town. The saint, Sayyid Sultán by name, came from Baghdád in 439 H., but the shrine was only built in 814 H. by Nawáb Gházi Khán. Sayyid Sultán's son Sayyid Ali one day killed a goat-herd whose mother complained to the saint. He handed over his son to her to wreak her vengeance on him and she killed him He thus earned the title of Pír Ádil and survived his son 26 years. The annual fair is held in Chet. But another version is that the saint only came from Mashhad in the 9th century of the Hijra and it adds that after the tomb was finished Ghází Khán came to see it and asked the *pír* to manifest himself. This he did by thrusting his arm through the masonry of the tomb and a circular hole still remains in it to testify to the truth of this story.[1]

Tahsíl Rájanpur.

The shrine of Muhammad Aqil Sáhib at Koṭ Miṭhan was in the old town of Koṭ Miṭhan, but when in S. 1919 both town and shrine were washed away by the Indus, the coffin containing the body of Muhammad Aqil Sáhib was disinterred and brought to the present shrine. Muhammad Aqil Sáhib traced his descent from Abbás Alí who came from Khorásán to dwell in Sindh and Muhammad Sharíf Sáhib came here in 1090 H. The pedigree is :—

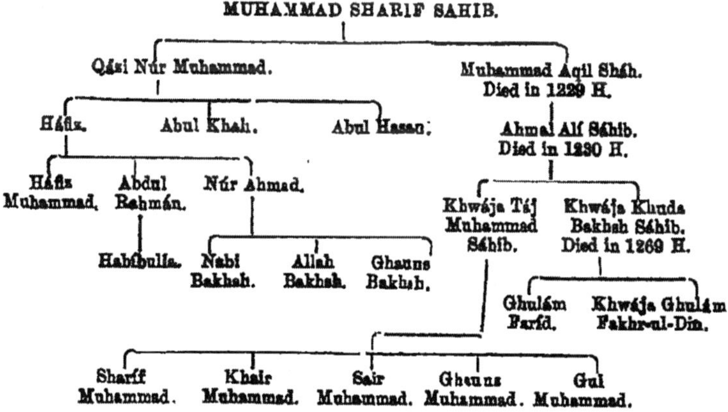

A legend about the miracles of Muhammad Sharíf Sáhib says that once he had to cross the Indus but there was no boat, so he put all the water of the river into a jug and went across, but on reaching the western bank he emptied the water out of the jug and so became

[1] Dera Ghází Khán *Gazetteer*, 1898, p. 55.

known as Karbacha. The shrine is a handsome dome and the *urs* is very largely attended.[1]

Another shrine at Rájanpur is known by the name of Khalífa Mián Muhammad Sáhib. It has existed for 40 years only. One *urs* is held in Safar.

The shrine called Aṭháran[2] Imám and Sayyid Bukhári has existed for 150 years. Its *khalífa* is Ghulám Muhammad, *mujáwar*, and its *gaddínashín* Sayyid Gul Sháh, *saildár* of Murghái. Every year in Chet a fair is held there lasting over 7 days. People of all creeds attend it, and they bring their own bread. The offerings go to the *khalífa*. A story about Tagia Sháh, a descendant of Ṭháran Imám Sháh, is that once a potter moulded an earthen horse and Tagia Sháh mounted it and it ran hither and thither. Tagia Sháh said that Ṭháran Imám Sháh had given him the horse and from that day the shrine has been greatly revered. The descendants of Ṭháran Imám Shah, Gedi Sháh and Dalan Sháh live at Murghái and those of Bande Sháh at Bhágsar.

Tahsíl Jámpur.

The shrine of Mossan Sháh of Jámpur is the scene of a fair from the 14th to 20th of Rabi-ul-awal. It is managed by descendants of the saint's daughter's son in default of male issue. His tomb is of adobe with a four-walled enclosure.[3]

Lál Parwána or 'the red moth' also has a shrine at this town, but the wall round the tomb is of brick. The saint left no sons but a *faqír* sits at his tomb and his *urs* is held on the 13th of the same month.

In the Kaha Pass at a distance of 5 miles from Harrand is the shrine of Khalíd, son of Walíd, known as Isháq Asháb, as he is said to have been a companion of the Prophet. * A pilgrimage to his shrine is regarded as equal to one to Mecca and it is visited on the 'Id-uz-Zuha.

A tomb, held in great respect, though no shrine has been erected, is that of Shaikh Raís Sáhib of Gadi in Sangaṛh tahsíl at which visitors pray for what they want, presenting offerings expressive of their wishes. The tomb is in consequence hidden under a heap of toy cradles, bullocks, camels, yokes, strings of cowries with which camels are ornamented, and the like.

The shrine of Khwája Núr Muhammad Sáhib Norúwála at Hájipur.—Born in 1134 H. this saint went to Multán to learn Persian, Arabic and Philosophy in 1148 H. and completed his studies in 1160. At the age of 30 he became a disciple of Mián Sáhib Núr Muhammad Mohaṭwali and went to Hájípur with the *Burra*, men of his caste. He dwelt on the Norúwála well at Sikhaníwála whence he was known as Norúwála; his own caste was Pirhár. He spent a large part of his life in devotion, not sleeping by night and fasting by day. People regard

[1] Dera Ghází Khán *Gazetteer*, 1898, p. 55.

[2] *Ib.*, p. 56.

[3] Recalling the 'eighteen Naráins' of Kulu, the eighteen Imáms must be a purely conventional number, but though 18 is a very common number in Hinduism, no other instance of it is known in Islám.

him as an *aulia* and he worked miracles. He died in 1204 H. at the age of 70. The present shrine was built in 1206 H. by Islám Khán Dáúdpotra, an uncle of the then Nawáb of Baháwalpur, with 3 doors on the north, south and east. People say that once Maulavi Azíz Ullah, a disciple of the Khwája Sáhib, was in a difficulty and one night he went inside the shrine and prayed for his *pír's* help when suddenly Muhammad entered it from the southern door and his difficulty was solved. This door is now named the door of Heaven and is kept closed all the year, being only opened for two days on the 6th and 7th of Muharram, and those who visit the shrine always enter it by this door.

Two arms of the Indus are held in special veneration. One in Rájanpur tahsíl is called Taran Imám or the 'Imám's Ferry' and though long silted up is still held in honour. To say: *Taran Imám ká dur, Malik Osmán* (or any name chosen) *ká kur*, is to attribute falsehoods as numerous as the dust of the *taran* to Malik Osmán (or the other person selected). The couplet doubtless originated in a Shí'a curse on the Caliph Othmán. The other arm is called Dhand Lálgír after a saint of that name who diverted the waters of the Indus by his prayers.[1]

Bábá Lálgír, a saint who gives his name to an arm of the Indus in Dera Ghází Khán tahsíl, diverted by his prayers the water of the Indus, but it found its way into the creek again, though the fine *banian* tree which forms a place of pilgrimage is, or was till 1898, still standing.

At a distance of 8 *kos* from the Shori pass is the shrine of the Zinda Pír, Lakha Lahri, a son of Sháhbáz Aulia. He is, as his name implies, an immortal and invisible saint.[2] His father only looked at a woman and she conceived Lakha Lahri who is said to be still alive concealed in a large cave. In the Shori hill torrent are hot springs in which people suffering from boils, syphilis and leprosy wash and recover their health. Once a housewife was cooking something in a pot or *deg* to give away in charity but it was slow to boil, so Zinda Pír broke the *deg* with a kick in anger and the housewife was buried with it beneath the earth—whence the hot spring.

An ancient shrine in Rájanpur is that of Shahíd Mard at Sikhánívála. The tomb has existed for some 500 or 600 years, but a few years ago one Ditta, a Gopáng Baloch, built a shrine (of which he is now *gaddí-nashín* or incumbent). He takes the offerings and feeds the people who collect at the annual *urs* on 12th Muharram.

It is possible for a *gaddí-nashín* to be a pluralist. Thus at the modern shrine of Maulavi Muhammad Hasan, a great *faqír*, the *khalífa* is Ghulám Muhammad Awán, and at the annual *urs* in Safar people of all creeds attend and are fed by the *sajjáda-nashín*. But the *gaddí-nashín*, Maulavi Ghulám Faríd, is also incumbent of another great *faqír*

[1] D. G. Khán *Gazetteer*, 1898, p. 55.

[2] The shrine consists of a house built for his residence and furnished with beds etc. and a copy of the *Qurán*. It is much visited—especially in March: D. G. Khán *Gazetteer*, 1898, p. 55.

Maulavi Aqil Muhammad Sáhib's shrine. Each of these shrines contains three tombs and otherwise resembles the other.

At Rájanpur the shrine of Sayyid Nur Sháh Sáhib has existed for about two centuries. It has no *urs* but people of all creeds frequent it daily and the offerings go to the *khalífa.*

A very old shrine is that of Hamza Sultán at Soman 6 miles west to Dajal. This saint was an *aulia* and as he left no male issue the offerings are received by the *mujáwars.*

The shrine of Maulavi Núr Muhammad Sáhib at Muhammadpur.—A son of Maulavi Aqal Muhammad Burra of Burra, a village in Dajal, this saint was made a *khalífa* by Khwája Núr Muhammad Sáhib of Hájípur, and went to reside at Muhammadpur. He was recognised as a *wali* and had many disciples. As he left no sons his sister's son succeeded him. The annual fair is held on the 16th of Ramzán.

The shrine of Sháh Lál Kamál in Dera Gházi Khán.—Some 300 years ago this saint came here from Chotar Lahri. He was famed for his miracles and died in 1069 H. His *urs* is held annually.

The shrine of Sayyid Nabi Sháh at Kot Chutta, 14 miles south of Dera Gházi Khán.—He left no issue so his collaterals succeeded him. He died in 1200 H. and his *urs* is held in Asauj. He is regarded as a *wali.*

The shrine of Sháh Sadar-ud-Dín, 15 miles north of Dera Gházi Khán.—He is said to have been a disciple of Baháwal-haq of Multán and descended from the same family as Pír Adil. He left no issue, so four *faqírs* look after his shrine and a fair is held annually on the first Monday in Chet when people collect and offer presents. They also get their sons shaved there.

The shrine of Khwája Muhammad Sulaimán Khán at Taunsa.—Khwája Muhammad Sulaimán was the son of Zakría Khán, a Jáfir Afghán, a native of Khorásán. His ancestors came to live at Drug, in the hills west of Taunsa, and Muhammad Sulaimán Khán was born at Gargoji hill in 1179 H. He was named Mana, and educated at Taunsa and Shekho Langáh as a boy; after that he acquired knowledge at Miṭhankot, and at the age of 16 became a disciple of Khwája Núr Muhammad Pír Mokorwála who named him Muhammad Sulaimán Khán. In 1199 H. he went on a *pír's* pilgrimage to Delhi and Ajmer and returning to Gargoji lived there for a while, but eventually made his abode at Taunsa where he spent his time in devotion and gave whatever he received in charity. He bore a simple character and had no pleasures except devotion to God and charity. His reputation as *nek-bakht* or fortunate grew and people from far and near became his disciples, among them a Nawáb of Baháwalpur. He was also known as a worker of miracles. His son Gul Muhammad had predeceased him when he died in 1267 H. and so he was succeeded by Mián Allah Bakhsh, his grandson, commonlly called the Hazrat Sáhib. The present shrine was erected in 1272 H. by the Nawáb of

Baháwalpur at a considerable cost. Ghulám Mustafá Khán, Khákwáni of Multán, also had a *majlas khána* built and Ahmad Khán, Afghán, had a well sunk and masonry buildings have been built out of the income from offerings. An *urs* is held twice a year in Safar and Rabí-us-sáni. The shrine is frequented by Muhammdans of every sect.[1]

The shrine of Mián Ahmad Sáhib at Taunsa has also existed for about 60 years. It is largely visited by hill tribes such as the Baloch. No special fair etc. is held.

At Siál Sharíf, south of Sáhíwál in Sháhpur, is the shrine of Khwája Shams-ud-Dín, a branch of that at Taunsa Sharíf.[2]

At the shrine of Sháh Shams, ancestor of the Sayyids of Sháhpur, a large fair is held on Chet 23rd to 25th. Tent-pegging and other amusements are provided. According to Maclagan another fair is held every year in honour of Sháh Shams at Shaikhpur, near Bhera in the Sháhpur District, where the sick and ailing from all parts of the province present themselves at the appointed time to be bled by the barbers of Bhera. These worthies are said to do their work with great efficiency, and the whole neighbourhood is soon reeking with horrid rivulets of human blood. But according to the Shahpur *Gazetteer*[3] this fair is held in honour of Sultán Ibrahím on four Sundays—the two last in Chet and the two first in Bisákh in spring and the operation performed on these auspicious days protects the patients from all diseases.

Dín Panáh was a Bukhári Sayyid who settled in the north-west corner of Muzaffargarh about 330 years ago, in the house of Suhágan, wife of a Makwál Jáṭ called Akku. When her daughter was married Dín Panáh gave himself as part of her dowry. He died in 1012 H. on the west bank of the Indus, whence the Makwál of the east bank tried to steal his coffin. This led to a feud in the tribe which was eventually settled by the saint who in a dream bade Akku's brothers make him a coffin for the east bank in which his body would also be found. He has now a shrine on each bank and the Makwál are still *khádims* of his tombs. Daira Dín Panáh in Muzaffargarh is a favourite shrine for the observance of the *jhanḍ* among Hindus as well as Muhammadans. The *daira* is the centre of a set of beggars, called Sháh dá faqír, who are self-elected, any idle or discontented rascal who wraps a brown *pagri* round his head being entitled to beg within 14 *kos* of the *daira* under a traditional saying of the saint. These beggars require no authority to beg from the keeper of the shrine and they compel the people to give alms by abuse and curses.[4]

The shrine of Hazrat Dín Panáh Sáhib in Daira Dín Panáh in Dera Gházi Khán has existed from the time of Akbar. Hindus

[1] For a description of the buildings, see Dera Gházi Khán *Gazetteer*, 1898, p. 54.

[2] Sháhpur *Gazetteer*, 1897, p. 87.

[3] *Ib.*, p. 88.

[4] Muzaffargarh *Gazetteer*, pp. 62-3. It would not be difficult to point to several elements of nature-(river-) worship and a fertility cult here.

and Muhammadans alike go there to pay respects. In the month of Chet 4 fairs are held on Fridays, called the Jumásháh fair. The tradition about it is that the Hazrat caused boats to run on land and as these boats are still to be found in Beohra village the people gather there also for worship.

The shrine of Karm Sháh Sáhib at Bughláni has existed for about 400 years. The Bughláni and Mongláni Baloch of Sokar revere it and a small fair is held there on a Friday in Hár.

Other small shrines at different places are those of Ghaghu Sultán Sáhib, Sakhi Sathan Sáhib, Lajmír Sáhib, Sultán Naurang Sáhib, Shaikh Sultán Sáhib, Shaikh Ibrahím Sáhib &c.

Alam Pír (Shaikh Alam-ud-Dín), a Bukhárí Sayyid, descended from the Makhdúms of Uch, has a shrine at Shahr Sultán, which is remarkable for the frenzy which attacks the persons, especially women, who resort to it. It even attacks women at home as the fair time, in Chet, draws near, and is believed to be due to possession by *jinn*, the woman being said *jinn khedan*, lit. 'to play the devil.' In the houses of the *makhdúm* and other Sayyids of his family women of the upper class have the *jinn* cast out to a drum accompaniment played by a *mirásan*. For ordinary people four sites are chosen, over each of which a *khalífa* of the *makhdúm* presides. The women possessed pay him a pice or fowl, take their seats and begin to sway their bodies to and fro, with gradually increasing violence. The excitement is increased by a drum. The *khalífa* goes round and lashes the women with a whip and pours scented oil on them. As each woman gets weary the *khalífa* pronounces some words and sprinkles a little water over her. The *jinn* is cast out and the woman is dragged away in an exhausted condition by her friends.[1]

Bagga Sher is a shrine 6 miles north of Muzaffargarh which is so called because a 'white tiger' there defended the saint's cows from thieves. During an epidemic it is good for cattle to visit this shrine. The saint's name was Shaikh Muhammad Tahir.

Mián Hayát has a shrine 7 miles south of Muzaffargarh, with a stone image of the camel he used to ride and a grove of date-palms the branches of which are like cobras. A branch kept in one's house will drive those snakes away. The saint was a nephew of Ghaus-ul-Azam, and his fair is held in Ramzán.

Dedha Lál has a fine domed shrine at Harballo in Muzaffargarh. Cattle visit it as they do Bagga Sher. Originally named Shaháb-ud-Dín, the saint got his other name on conversion by Makhdúm Jahánián who turned milk into blood and made Dhedha drink of it.

Shaikh Ladhí's shrine is similarly visited.

[1] Muzaffargarh *Gazetteer*, p. 64. The *karmal*.

Músán Shah, where wrestling matches are held at the fair on 5th Asauj :

Muhíb Jahánián, where wrestling and occasionally horse-races are held.

Núr Sháh

Shaikh Pallia

Háji Isháq

Pír Ali and Pír Kamál are *naugasas.*

Shaikh Alláh Dád Quraishi who came from Arabia had acquired sanctity in the service of Makhdúm Jahánián Jahán-gasht and settled in Rámpur in Muzaffargarh. His shrine is known as that of Dáúd Jahániah, Dhudhu Jahániah or simply Dhudhu, and is celebrated for its cures of leprosy. The patient bathes in baths of hot and cold sand prepared by the attendants of the shrine and on recovery presents models of the diseased limb in silver or gold. The repute of the shrine extends to Kashmír. The Shaikh's descendants are now Metlá Jats, because, they say, so many Metlás live in the neighbourhood. Hindus also frequent the shrine, where a fair is held every Thursday, especially in Chet and Sáwan. A vow common at this shrine is the *atta ghatta.*[1]

Saints and shrines in Multán and Baháwalpur.

Some of these have already been noticed under the various Súfi orders, but many more might be described here if space permitted. Reference may be made to the Multán *Gazetteer*, 1901-02, *passim*, especially to pp. 121-3, and 339-43. The most renowned in the district are the shrine at Sher Sháh and that of Sultán Ahmad Qattál at Jalálpur Pírwála. The former was built in honour of Sháh Ali Muhammad
Husain who came from Mashhad in 1499. The latter came to Jalálpur 905 H.
990 H. in 1582. Many of the shrines in Multán offer features of great
interest in their cults or traditions, but in this respect they are excelled by those in Baháwalpur. In that State Uch Sharíf is unrivalled in India for the number of its shrines. The most celebrated of its Bukhári saints was the Makhdúm Sher Sháh, Jalál-ud-Dín, Surkh-posh,
Bukhári, the Second Adam. Born in 1199[2] he is credited with the 959 H.
conversion of Chingiz Khán, as well as of many tribes indigenous to Baháwalpur. His grandson Sayyid Ahmad Kabír, the Makhdúm Jahánián Jahángasht, and his descendants are numerous and widely scattered. Later in date came the Giláni Sayyids, descendants of Bandagi Muhammad Ghaus, 7th in descent from Abdul Qádir Giláni,
887 H. who reached Uch in 1482. The other saints are variously descended
and at their shrines many varieties of ritual and miracles are performed.[3]

THE SAINTS OF FEROZEPUR.

Núr Sháh Wali, the saint of Ferozepur City.

In the time of Rání Lachhmankaur, there was a fort at the site where this tomb is now situate. The Rání had a stable here, but what-

[1] Muzaffargarh *Gazetteer*, 1883-4, p. 63.

[2] The date is doubtful. Temple gives 1188-1283 as the dates of his birth and death *Legends*, III, p. 184.

[3] Baháwalpur *Gazetteer*, 1904, pp. 159-182, and Chap. IV.

ever horses were tied there, one used to be found daily dead or injured. The Ráni was perplexed at this and made enquiries about its cause. The third night she had a dream in which the saint told her that the cause of the trouble was the disrespect shewn to him by allowing horses to stand at the place where he was buried. He also told Ráni his name. She thereupon ordered the stable to be removed, and on this being done, a pucca grave was found to exist there. One Sayyid Naqi Sháh, who was the ancestor of the present occupants of the shrine (*khánqáh*), was employed in the cavalry (*risála*) of the Ráni. She ordered him to take charge of the *khánqáh* as she said he was a Sayyid and the *khánqáh* was also a Sayyid's. All the land appertaining to the fort was assigned to him. The Ráni used to support Naqi Sháh as he had to give up his service in the cavalry. Naqi Sháh was succeeded by Najaf Ali Sháh and the latter by Hussain Ali Sháh who was succeeded by Rahmat Ali Sháh the present incumbent. When British rule commenced the then Deputy Commissioner Captain (Sir Henry) Lawrence ordered the fort to be demolished, so it was pulled down and the ground sold. The tomb was the only thing left untouched, but no one listened to the attendants of the shrine until Captain Lawrence had a dream in which he saw the saint and had some sort of compulsion laid upon him.[1] In the morning he ordered that the tomb should not be disturbed and moreover he had it repaired, gave Rs 500 as a present to Naqi Sháh and promised to grant a *muáfi* to the *khánqáh*. That very day he received a telegram to say he was transferred. The tomb with the ground surrounding it was left in Naqi Sháh's charge.

Pír Baláwal Sháh's khánqáh in Ferozepur tahsil.

When Mírán Sháh Núr was living at Khái, Akbar sent Pír Baláwal, whose real name was Diláwar Khán (or rather Baláwal Beg), Súbah of Delhi, with troops to bring the saint to the capital. When he arrived he found the Sháh had gone to bathe at a tank, whither he went and delivered the emperor's message. The Sháh forthwith dived into the water and reached Delhi where the emperor and his wife were at supper. The Begam observing a third hand on the table told the emperor who replied: 'If you see it again let me know.' When the hand again appeared, reaching towards the dishes, she pointed it out to Akbar who seized it and enquired what the matter was. The Sháh said: 'You summoned me and I am here.' Akbar was delighted. When the saint took his leave he asked for a token to show the Súbah at Khái. Taking a handful of rice, a handkerchief and an order under the imperial seal the Sháh immediately re-appeared at the tank. All this only took as long as a man would spend in a single dive. The Sháh showed the thing to the Súbah and said: 'Do you mean to take me to Delhi?' Diláwar Khán said: 'If I get a token from the emperor, what more is needed?' The Sháh made over the things aforesaid to the Súbah which so completely upset him that he took off his uniform and turned *faqír* on the spot, saying he would serve

[1] This is a very common incident in hagiolatrical legends: *cf.* Temple in *Indian Art*, *XI*, p. 42, for account of this shrine and in *Folklore Record*, *V*, p. 158, for an account of Khajúria Pír. The same writer records a similar experience attributed to himself in *Selections from the Calcutta Review*, Second Series, VIII, page 278.

the True King and not an emperor of this world. So he remained with the Sháh, attaining perfection and dying in the lifetime of the Sháh. He is indeed popularly said not to have died a natural death but to have become a Shahíd or martyr in this wise:—Certain thieves came to offer him a share of the plunder, but when they arrived he was asleep, so they placed a part of the booty at his pillow, and went away. Meanwhile the owner came and found the Pír still asleep, with the property by him. Thinking him to be a thief he killed him. Míran Sháh Núr ordered him to be buried in his blood-stained clothes, as he lay, without being washed. His brother came from Delhi, buried him and built his tomb. He also purchased the four wells on each side of it and made them over to the Sháh's son Míran Sháh Jamál. Subsequently Míran Shah Núr's grandson Imám Sháh came from Kasúr and tried to take possession of the shrine, but Qutb Alí Sháh, another grandson who was in possession of it, gave his daughter in marriage to the son of Imám Sháh. The disciple of Imám Sháh, Maula Madat Ali Sháh, settled the dispute, so Imám Sháh took possession of the shrine, *jagír* etc. of Pír Baláwal Sháh and settled there. There used to be four fairs, but two are now held—one on the 2nd Asauj, which is the *urs sharíf* or wedding (death) of the Pír, at which beggars are fed—and the second and greater on the 10th Muharram, when the *tásias* of Ferozepur city are all buried there. Prayers on both dates are made for the Pír's soul. Hindus frequent the fairs but do not join in these prayers.

Lál Muian (Mohsin) Sáhib Láhori.

His tomb, which is coloured green and lies in the Mandí Kalálán or spirit-sellers' market, was founded 141 years ago. This saint was a Sayyid, a son of Sultán Arab, who was of the royal family. He was a saint from birth and having finished his course of worldly education in his 11th year went with his father to Multán and there became a disciple of Shaikh Bahá-ud-Dín Zakaría Multáni and a perfect saint the same day. Those on whom he cast his sight used to become senseless and for this reason very few used to visit him. Whoever made him an offering of one *dínár* begat a son. He was married to Bíbi Milkhi, a pious daughter of Shaikh Zakaría, who was a Sirdár of Matila, a village between Thatta and Multán. She also was a saint from birth. The saint had four sons: Shaikhs Yáqub, Isháq, Ismáil, and Ahmad. He went to Gujrát and stayed in the house of Mahmúd, a blacksmith. The king asked leave to see him, but was not allowed. A Hindu woman came to the blacksmith to have her spindle straightened and the Shaikh seeing her said, 'she savours of Islám' and looked at her. The woman finding the Shaikh gazing at her, asked the blacksmith, 'what sort of *faqír* is this who is gazing at me?' The Shaikh said: 'if I looked at you with bad intent, I will touch my eyes with the spindle, and may God deprive me of my sight.' Saying this he touched his eyes with the spindle which was on fire, but it did not injure them in the least, nay it became gold. Seeing this miracle the woman became a Muhammadan, but her parents hearing of it tortured her and she died. While the Hindus were taking her body away the Shaikh, hearing of her death, reanimated her and caused her to recite the *kalima*. This made him widely known and the people used to visit him to such an extent that he was obliged to remove to Lahore, where he died on Thursday the 18th Safar 962 H.

Pír Karam Sháh's fair is held on every Akhiri Chahár Shamba (a Muhammadan holiday), and alms are distributed to beggars and blessings invoked.

Mái Amírán Sáhiba's fair is held on the Bárawafát day, alms being distributed to *faqírs* and blessings are invoked. She was a great *majhab* and a perfect saint. She came from down-country.

Roḍe Sháh's *takia*, on the road from Ferozepur to Malwal or Moga, belongs to the Qádiri sect. No fair is held. The saint was a disciple of Iqrár Husain whose tomb is near that of Mái Amírán Sáhiba. Iqrár Hussain was a disciple of Jáfar Husain whose tomb is at Kishenpura in tahsíl Zíra.

The shrine of Mírán Sháh Núr at Mírán Sháh Núr in tahsíl Ferozepur.

Some 500 years ago, in the time of Akbar, Mírán Sháh Núr was born at Chúnián in Lahore, and Shaikh Alamdí (Ilam Dín), a dyer of that place, and his wife, Mái Chhinko, having no children, adopted the boy at the age of 5 or 6. When he was aged 14, Shaikh Alamdí bade his wife test his conduct, so she took him to the jungle and invited his advances. But he seized her breasts and began to suck therefrom. She told her husband of this as proving that he was untainted by the world. Shaikh Alamdí had his dyeing vat on the fire that day and into it he threw the Sháhzáda (Mírán Sháh Núr) and shut down the lid. After 24 hours his wife, searching for the boy, asked him where he was, but he did not reply. Lifting up the lid she saw the Sháhzáda sitting cross-legged inside and when she had taken him out the Shaikh said :—'Had he remained another day and night his children one and all would have been the friends of God. Now however only one of them will always be so'. And to the Sháhzáda he said :—'I have given you all I had. As I am a dyer and you are a Sayyid you must choose a perfect master and placing your hands in his' do homage (*ba'át*)'. Then he told the boy the name of Sayyid Sultán Lal Músán (Mohsin) Núrí Láhorí as one who was to be his master. Accordingly Mírán Sháh Núr went to Lahore and served him and was made his disciple. He too was also a Sayyid and the boy remained with him for a year. He gave the boy a tiger's skin, a handkerchief, a staff, bedding etc. and said :—'Wherever by the power of God this skin falls, there make your house and deem it your tomb also'. So the boy left his master and came to the bank of the Sutlej, but found the ferrymen had started with the boat. He asked them to take him across also, but they said the boat was full and had left the shore, so they would return and fetch him; whereupon the youth stepped into the river, calling on God and his master, and straightway the water fell until it became fordable, so that he crossed before the boatmen could return. Then he returned after his wanderings to Chúnián and married into a Sayyid family of Dholanwál, settling in Gulnaki village where he sunk several wells. After 23 years, leaving his three sons and daughter there, he came alone as a traveller to Ferozepur, where an old fort stood long before the Sikh rule arose. There he abode with a miller named Núr for 7 years in the fort, engaged in the worship of God. Eventually the place in Sikh times became known as Núr Sháhwáli. In Rání Lachhmankaur's time some one had tethered horses in this sacred place, but the Rání was told by Mírán Sháh Núr in a dream that this should be forbidden, and he told her his name, condition, and caste. So the place was deemed blessed, and a great shrine built there by degrees. Thence Mírán Sháh Núr went to Khéí where Ghází Khán was in power and the country all round was dense forest, and the river and rains had filled the tanks so that the land was desolate, only a small space being clear. There Mírán Sháh Núr built his house. After the ablutions of prayer, they say, he buried his tooth-brush which by the power of God became green and grew into a *pílú* tree which is still visible in front of the shrine. He summoned his family from Gulnaki and from his preaching and piety gained wide recognition.

One day six Hindu women came and prayed for issue, Mírán Sháh also prayed and told Shaikh Ratu Sáhib, his chief disciple, to give each of them a loaf and some of the meat which he was himself eating. Shaikh Ratu did so and five of the six women ate each her loaf and meat without aversion. The sixth however did not do so, but threw the food under a bush as she went away. In due course the five had each a son, but the sixth had none. All six came to Mírán Sháh Núr, the sixth complaining and asking what sin she had committed that no son was born to her. He replied :—'Your child is lying under the bush' and when she went to look at the spot where she had thrown the loaf and meat she saw an embryo in the very form of a child and became ashamed. Many other miracles and mercies of this kind occurred. Shaikh Ratu, Pír Baláwal, and other elders as well as his four sons became his *khalífas* (successors). His tomb, they say, was built in his life-time, though Akbar's agent made it under his orders and at his expense. A great miracle occurred in its building. A *lohár*, blind from birth, begged the Sayyid to restore his sight, and agreed to place eight iron bricks in the tomb if this were vouchsafed. By the power of God he forthwith gained his sight and made the bricks of iron which are still within the shrine. The great fair of this shrine is held on the 4th Asauj when *faqírs* are fed.

The *khánqáh* of Sayyid Miráj-ul Dín was built some 80 years ago by a descendant of the founder of Zíra. Poor travellers can put up in this shrine. The tomb is surrounded by a brick wall, near which are interred all the dead of the saint's family. Its administration is carried on by the Sháh's descendants who also hold the *gaddi*, and at present a lady manages it. At a fair held in Asauj or Kátak only *faqírs* assemble. They are fed and make free use of *charas*.

The *khánqáhs* of Ahmad Sháh, Qutab Sháh and Rode Sháh are managed by the Muhammadans of Zíra. They are all nearly 100 years old. A brick mosque and well are attached to the *khánqáh*.

The *khánqáh* at Jalálábád.

A *khánqáh* of Hazrat Sayyid Kabír lies to the east of Jalálábád. In its enclosure are interred the dead of his family, and in the midst lies the tomb of the Sayyid. A great fair is held on the second Thursday of Chet, when people from distant parts come to pay homage to the shrine to which they offer a gift in cash or kind according to their means. The Sayyid recipients are responsible for repairs to the tombs etc. Eatables offered are distributed there and then. Both Hindus and Muhammadans attend the fair. It is said that the tomb is 200 years old.

The shrine or *siáratgáh* of Pír Gúrah is situate at Sultánpur village. Its building was completed in S. 1907. Pír Gúrah was a good *faqír* and after his death his disciples built his *siáratgáh*. A fair held on the 1st of Háṛ is attended by some 2000 persons and prayer is offered. Every Thursday a drum is beaten at the shrine. Its administration vests in the owners who keep it clean. *Paṭáshas* are offered and their value is estimated at Rs. 15 a year which is spent on the up-keep of the shrine.

The Pír Mál *khánqáh* in Khwája Kharak is also called Pír Kál Mál. No fair is held in connection with it.

The village of Khwája Kharak has existed for 70 years, but the *khánqáh* was already known by the name of Pír Mál when it was founded. The villagers have the right to appoint any one as *mujáwar* for sweeping the *khánqáh* etc.

Shrines in Ferozepur tahsíl.

The *khánqáh* of Rori in Atánwáli, founded some 70 years ago, has no fair connected with it. When the village was founded, some bricks were found lying near it and Ṭhákar Daya Singh built a *koṭha* (hut) of them, but it fell down twice or thrice so a *faqír* Nathe Khán built a brick tomb. A well and mosque were also built. A *faqír* used to live in the *khánqáh*, but it has been quite neglected since his death, and no *mujáwar* is employed in it. The offerings of milk, *paṭásha* and *chúrma* when made are distributed among those present at the *khánqáh*.

At the Karím Sháh *khánqáh* in Sidhúán a movable fair is held in Háṛ or Sáwan every year, on a date fixed by the *mujáwar*. Maulavi Karím Sháh Qázi of Mislam is said to have got a *ghumdo* of land from the people of Sidhúán, and built his grave at this spot some 18 years ago. As he was a devotee and his prayers were heard people worshipped him. The *mujáwar* is a Bhaṭṭi Musalmán. He sweeps out the *khánqáh* twice a day. Celibacy is not obligatory, but succession is governed by spiritual relationship. The *mujáwar* receives special respect and is provided with grain etc. by the villagers, while *chúrma* or milk is offered as *bhog* to the *khánqáh*.

The *khánqáh* of Sháh Sikandar in Arafke has no fair. It is said that when a house was built on the tomb of this saint its owner was directed in a vision to abandon it. He obeyed and rebuilt the saint's tomb 80 years ago. The *faqír* is a Ḍogar. He sweeps the tomb twice a day and lights a lamp every Thursday. At every marriage four annas are offered to it.

The *khánqáh* of Janḍla in Arafke also has no fair Janḍla was said to be possessed with power to work miracles and to fulfil the desires of all who resorted to him. After his death the people built his tomb and began to worship it 40 years ago. Its administration vests in a Malang who sweeps it out twice a day and lights a lamp every Thursday.

At the *khánqáh* of Makhi Sháh a fair is held every year on the 9th Asanj. Makhi Sháh was possessed of miraculous powers and after his death his remains were kept in a box in a house, and are still preserved in the *khánqáh*. It is believed that the encroachments of the river on his *khánqáh* are barred by his power. It was built 60 years ago. Its manager is a Bukhári Sayyid who sweeps it out and lights a lamp every Thursday. On marriages a rupee is offered to the *khánqáh* and food given to the manager.

The shrine or Ḍera of Usmán Sháh has no fair connected with it. Formerly this *khánqáh* contained the grave of Jiwan Sháh but his remains were removed to Rangoon, so those of Usmán Sháh were interred in it. It was built 50 years ago. The manager is a Manar Ḍogar who lights a lamp on the tomb. Succession is governed by spiritual relationship. The priest is held in special respect and a rupee is paid him on a marriage. *Charas* is not used. *Chúrma* is offered. The *khánqáh* of Dátá Núr Sháh at Aṭári has no fair. It was built 60 years ago. The *mujáwar* is the manager and he is an Usmán *faqír*, by *got* Gurzmár. He sweeps out the *khánqáh* daily and lights a lamp in it. Succession follows natural relationship.

At the *khánqáh* of Baji Sháh a fair is held on the 20th Sáwan. Baji Sháh only died on November 18th, 1892. Succession follows spiritual relationship.

At the *khánqáh* of Ináyat Sháh, who died in Bhádon S. 1933, succession follows spiritual relationship. The *mujáwar* feeds poor *faqírs* but himself lives on alms. The use of *charas*, opium, and *bhang* is common. A lamp is lit on every Thursday.

At the *khánqáh* of Bír Sháh a fair is held on 22nd Háṛ; Bír Sháh died in Sambat 1924. Succession follows spiritual relationship. The *faqír* who dwells at the shrine lives by begging. The use of *charas* or *bhang* is common. The *khánqáhs* of Sáiṇs Majnu, Fi Sháh and Malli Sháh are connected with this.

At the *khánqáh* of Núr Sháh Bal a fair is held every Thursday, Succession is governed by spiritual relationship.

At the *khánqáh* of Nau-Gaza a fair is held every Thursday.

The *khánqáh* of Bohar Sháh has no fair. This saint died in S. 1932. Succession follows spiritual relationship. The keeper of the shrine is a *faqír* who lives on alms. Lamps are lit every Thursday.

At the *takia* of Roḍa Sháh a fair is held on the 20th Bhádon. Roḍa Sháh died on 8th April 1902.

The *takia* of Mai Mírán has an annual fair held on 12th Háṛ. It was founded on 12th Chet S. 1946. The *mujáwar* is a *faqír* who lives on alms.

The *khánqáh* of Wali Sháh has a fair on 15th Jeṭh.

The *khánqáh* of Makhu Sháh has a fair on 22nd Sáwan.

The *khánqáh* of Rafi Sháh has no fair. It dates from 1929 S.

The *khánqáh* of Husain Sháh has no fair. It is called after Husain Sháh. The *khánqáh* was founded in S. 1929. People of all castes make offerings to the shrine.

At the *takia* of Ghoṛe Sháh a fair is held 40 days after the Moharram. This shrine was first occupied by Husain Ali, a *faqír* possessed of power to work miracles, but he had a disciple named Ghoṛe Sháh after whom it is known.

The *khánqáh* of Bhakhar Sháh in Machíwára has no fair.

The *khánqáh* of Sháh Baka in Malwal has no fair.

At the *khánqáh* of Wahàb Sháh in Lodhra a fair is held annually on 15th Háṛ. Wahàb Sháh was a juggler. It has been in existence for 200 years. At the fair many jugglers visit the shrine and Qawáls are invited to sing at it. Many visitors go into a trance and then their limbs are bound up and they are hung on trees. The visitors are fed at night by the holder of the *gaddi*, and lamps are lighted at the shrine. Succession is governed by natural relationship. People make offerings of *chúri* to the *khánqáh*.

The *khánqáh* of Khwája Roshan Dín—in Pir Khán Shaikh—has a fair every year on the first Thursday in Háṛ. It was built some 150 years ago. Its administration is carried on by a descendant of the Khwája. He is not celibate, but succession is always governed by spiritual relationship.

It is said that when Khwája Roshan Dín chanced to pass through Mohanke he spent the night in the house of a Ḍogar Sardár whose descendants always keep a lamp burning in their house in commemoration of the Khwája's visit. Of the 400 people who visit the fair many go into a trance.

The *khánqáh* of Ramzán Sháh Qureshi in Kurma is named after a Háshami saint whose *urs* is held annually in the last week of Háṛ. He used to live in Malikpur but went to Lahore whence Varyám knowing him to be a devotee brought him to lay the foundations of Kurma. Ramzán had a son named Khudá Bakhsh, also a devotee, and so great reverence was paid them by the Nawábs. Both their tombs and that of the grandson, Ghulám Sháh, lie in the *khánqáh*. At the *urs* only verses from the *Qurán* are recited. People make offerings to the shrine at marriages etc.

The *khánqáh* of Sáíṇ Sher Sháh has no fair. One Jíwan, a weaver of Kurma, used to go into a trance, and so he learnt of the existence of the tomb of Sher Sháh, no trace of which then remained, and he pointed out the spot, which was enclosed some 60 years ago. Women of the village light lamps here on Thursday nights.

The tomb of Sáíṇ Tokal Sháh in Kurma lies near the house of Allah Ditta, a butcher, and lamps are lit at it on every Thursday night.

The *khánqáh* of Pír Pake Sháh is in Jamad. Once Mala headman built a cattle-pen here, but in a vision he saw that the place contained a *faqír's* tomb, so he abandoned it and rebuilt the tomb. Another story is that the clay horses offered at the tomb fight at night and are found broken in the morning. This has been witnessed by one Jaimal, son of Himmat, a Ḍogar of Algu

The *khánqáh* of Sayyid Nazar Sháh in Jhok Ṭehl Singh.—This Sayyid was a grandson of Mírán Sháh, Nawáb. He had a Gujar disciple named Dág Sháh. Founded 140 years ago, the tomb contains the Sayyid's *guḍri* or wallet and the story is that the Sikh owners of the village once determined to eject Dág Sháh and destroy the shrine, but they resisted so they set fire to the *khánqáh*. So Dág Sháh covered himself with his *guḍri* and lay in a corner of the shrine, which was reduced to ashes but he was unhurt. The fame of this incident spread far and wide. The offerings are taken by Dág Sháh or Míran Sháh.

The *khánqáh* of Sayyid Mahmúd Sháh was founded 120 years ago. The Sayyid left a disciple Bani Sháh who kept up the fair for some years but it ceased on his death. Offerings of *chúrms, paṭáshaks* and other sweets are eaten by those present.

At the *khánqáh* of Máma Sultán in Máma a fair is held on 12th Asauj. This saint was a Husaini Jáṭ who lived in Pákpaṭṭan. While grazing his cattle on the river bank he chanced to come to the site of the present village and built a hut there. His example was followed by others and so the village grew up. It was named Máma after him. His two brothers were Sháh Jíwan and Núr Muhammad, and his disciple Pír Ser. The fair is attended by 100 *faqírs*. The shrine is run by Máma's descendants whose caste is Jara and *got* Husaini. Milk, *khír* and *paṭáshaks* are offered.

At the *khánqáh* of Sayyid Chirágh Sháh in Máma a fair is held on 12th Asauj. This saint, a descendant of Hazrat Mírán Sháh Núr Muhammad, died on 5th Asauj S. 1949 and his disciple built his tomb of brick and enclosed it by a wall. Soon after one Muhammad Nai began to take bricks for his own use out of it, but his house fell down and in order to avert a recurrence of this he offered a *deg* of rice to the tomb and then rebuilt his house without difficulty. This incident contributed to the fame of the fair at which *faqírs* are fed on rice and meat Founded in S. 1949, its administration is carried on by one Shaikh Dín Dár who is not celibate as *mujáwar*. The Jáṭs of the village mostly make offerings. The *khánqáh* of Mírán Sháh Núr Sáhib is connected with it.

The *khánqáh* of Sayyid Bahádur Sháh in Khai has been in existence 100 years. It contains two tombs, one of Bahádur Sháh and another.

At the *khánqáh* of Mírán Sháh in Núr a fair is held on the 15th Asauj at which *faqírs* are fed on sweet rice, bread and *dál* or pulse. Many go into a trance (*hál*) by shaking their heads, in which state they are hung on trees with their legs tied together. Mírán Sháh died on 27th Muharram, 1035 H., but the *khánqáh* was founded in Akbar Sháh's time. The *khánqáh* has 3 storeys and is built of brick. It contains 4 rooms with as many tombs—of Mírán Sáhib, Mírán Sháh Jamál and Jamál Khán.

The *khánqáh* of Núr Sháh in Jhok Ṭehl Singh and many tombs of this family in Wazír Khán's mosque at Lahore are connected with this shrine.

At the Rauza of Pír Baldwála in Khilji a fair is held on 10th Muharram every year. The Pír was one of Akbar's high officials. When Mírán Sháh was working miracles the Pír came to him and was so impressed with his powers that he became a *faqír* and entered his service. Mírán Sháh asked him to live in Khilji. Six thieves robbed a rich man's house and vowed to give the Pír an eighth of the booty. So they went to him, but finding him asleep laid his share by his bedside. Meanwhile the owners in pursuit of the thieves came to the Pír's residence and found their goods there and thinking the Pír had robbed them, they murdered him out of hand. People then built his tomb on the spot. At the fair all the *tázias* used in the Muharram are buried here. The shrine was laid some 350 years ago. It contains three tombs :—of Pír Bald, Sayyid Amám Sháh and Mard Ali.

At the *khánqáh* of Sháh Sikandar in Mamdot an *urs* is annually held on the 10th of Muharram. The two brothers Sayyid Kabír and Sháh Sikandar came from Bukhára and settled in Mamdot and Fatehpur respectively. When Sháh Sikandar died his tomb was built in H. 905. The *khánqáh* contains the tombs of the dead of his family. Gujars mostly affect this Pír's cult. Kabír's *khánqáh* in Fatehpur is connected with this.

The *khánqáh* of Sáíṇ Khwáj Bakhsh in Mamdot.—The Sáín came from Montgomery and died here. At the fair held on the 1st Sáwan *faqírs* shake their heads and go into a trance. Kálu Sháh, a disciple of the Sháh, used to feed visitors with rice, bread and meat.

The *khánqáh* of Sultán Mahmúd, *murshid* of Sáíṇ Khwája Bakhsh, at Abarbara in Montgomery, is connected with this shrine.

The Rauza of Sáíṇ, son of Mash Sháh, in Keluwála.—This saint was a Qureshi Chisti who lived in Ferozepur. The tomb of Muhammad Akal the Sáíṇ's *murshid* is at Mitthankot in Baháwalpur.

The *khánqáh* of Sayyid Sher Sháh in Azim Sháh has a fair in Háṛ. This saint was headman of this village, and died only few years ago, when the *khánqáh* was built. His brother Haidar Sháh granted and for its maintenance. The *faqírs* attending the fair are fed free.

The *khánqáh* of Sáíṇ Roshan Sháh in Jhok Hari Har existed long before the foundation of the village.

The *khánqáh* of Mírán Sáhib in Bazídpur.—The Sáiṇ came from Bukhára in Ranjít Singh's time. He died and his grandson constructed his *khánqáh*. People light lamps on Thursday night and offer a rupee at marriages.

The *khánqáh* of Sháh Kumál, who is said to have lived in Sikh times, lies in the middle of the village

The *khánqáh* of Sayyid Lál Sháh in Khánpur has a fair on the 25th Haṛ every year. This Sayyid was a Bukhári *faqi* in Sikh times.

A *faqír* named Kumál Sháh has been living here for 22 years and he laid the foundation of the fair. *Faqírs* practise *hál* and are fed free.

The *khánqáh* of Pír Kále Sháh at Norang Siál has an *urs* on 15th Chet.

The saint Mián Mír, whose real name was Sh. Muhammad Mír, was a man of learning and sanctity. He visited Jahángír at Agra,[1] and was visited by Sháh Jahán. But his principal *rôle* was that of spiritual adviser to Dárá Shikoh[2], though his disciple Mulla Sháh or Sháh Muhammad is also said to have filled that office.[3] However this may be Dára Shikoh built Mulla Sháh's tomb at Lahore apparently before his death in 1661.[4] Dára Shikoh also commenced the building of a mausoleum to Mián Mír who died in 1635 at the age of 88.

Dára Shikoh gives a pedigree of Mián Mír which makes him one of the sons of a Qázi Sáínditta. He was born in Seistán but lived almost all his life at Lahore. He appears to have affected the Pír Dastgír and at any rate had such respect for his memory that he never mentioned his name without ablution.[5] His long life was attributed to the practice of *habs dam* or slow breathing. His disciple Mulla Sháh followed him in this and also in remaining unmarried and never lighting a lamp in his house[6]

Mián Mír's disciples included the scholar Mulla Sháh of Badakhshán who died in 1614[7] : Khwája Bahári, who was credited with many miracles[8] : Shaikh Abu'l Ma'ali,[9] a native of Bhera : his *khalífa*

[1] *Hist. of Lahore*, p. 47.

[2] *Ib.*, p. 59.

[3] *Ib.*, pp. 175 and 64.

[4] *Ib.*, p. 178 Dára Shikoh was hardly in a position to do so after 1659 in which year Aurangzeb reached Lahore : p. 65.

[5] *Ib.*, p. 175.

[6] *Ib.*, pp. 59, 175-6 and 178.

[7] *Ib.*, p. 59. Mulláh Sháh was a great mystic. Born in 1584, he died in 1661 at Lahore and was buried there in a shrine of red stone erected by the princess Fátama, sister of Dára Shikoh. The orthodox taxed him with imitating Mansúr Halláj and he was sentenced to death by Shah Jahán, but saved by Dára Shikoh's intercession. His disciples included Mír Baqi and Akhúnd Mulláh Muhammad Syud (? Sa'id). Mián Mír taught him Súfi exercises according to the Qádiria rule : Field, *op. cit.*, pp. 194-189.

[8] *Ib.*, pp. 60 and 178-9.

[9] *Ib.*, p. 68. Abul Ma'ali (Sháh Khair-ud-Dín) was a saint in the reigns of Akbar and Jahángír who built a great part of his tomb in his lifetime. On his death in 1616 A.D. it was completed by his son. A large fair is held there on his *urs* : p. 208.

Abdul Ghani[1], whose *maqbara* was built by Dárá Shikoh : and Abdul Haq who cursed the kiln of Buddhu because he was refused its warmth on a rainy day.[2] Another disciple was Mír Ináyatulla, surnamed by his *pír* Miskín Sháh on account of his secluded life. When asked how his disciple supported life his *pír* replied that he was *miskín amrí*, a poor man supported by God's *amar* or will, and so in no need of help. Dára Shikoh also built his shrine.[3]

Maulavi Muhammad Ismaíl, generally known as Mián Wadda, has a spacious tomb Lahore at where he built a *madrassa* in Akbar's reign Born in 1586 he became a disciple of Makhdúm Abdul Karím of Langar Makhdúm on the Chenab and died in 1683. He desired that no dome should be erected over his grave, but the present *sajjáda-nishín* has built a grave in which he sits daily, reading the Qurán[4] His disciple was Ján Muhammad, the first *imám* of the mosque built in 1649, the year in which Sháh Jahán sent Aurangzeb to recover Kandahár.

Maulavi Nizám Dín, whose tomb is at Lahore, is known as Pír Mohka, meaning one who cures warts. Sufferers are said to be cured by making a vow to this saint to offer a broom and a garland. He died in 1705 A. D. and his *maqbara* or mausoleum is a fine one.[5]

Addul Razzák Makái of Sabzwár settled in Lahore in Humáyún's time and when he died was buried in the closet in which he used to pray. His tomb long remained without a dome, and a lion was believed to sweep it out every Thursday with its tail until the guardian of the shrine saw in a vision Mauj Daryá Bukhári who bade him construct a large dome over the saint's remains.[6]

Mádho Lál Hussain is the name of a famous pair of tombs at Lahore. The actual tombs are in an underground chamber, signs of them being reproduced on a lofty platform. Mádho was a Brahman boy of whom Lál Hussain became enamoured and who became a Moslem under the name of Shaikh Mádho.[7] Lál Hussain was a historical saint who lived in Akbar's reign and is mentioned by Dára Shikoh and other writers. Two great fairs, the Basant and Chirághán, are held annually at this shrine. The former was celebrated with great display under Ranjít Singh.

[1] *Hist. of Lahore*, p. 144.

[2] *Ib.*, pp. 151, 167.

[3] He died in 1647 A. D.

[4] *Hist. of Lahore*, pp. 156, 212 and 166.

[5] *Hist. of Lahore*, p. 164.

[6] *Hist. of Lahore*, pp. 145, 192-3. Shaikh Mádho is a name which could not possibly be borne by a Muhammadan, not even by a convert. The clue to the meaning of the cult is probably to be found in works like the *Baharsa* or *Haqiqat-ul-Fuqrá*.

[7] *Ib.*, p. 158.

Ghoṛe Sháh whose real name was Bahá-ud-Dín, a Bukhári Sayyid, a grandson of Sa'id Usmán of Uch, was affected with palsy and so was known as the Jhúlan Sháh or 'Sháh who shakes like a swing'. He was credited with having been born a *wali* and before the age of 5 displayed such horsemanship that he is called Ghoṛe Sháh, and any disciple who presented him with a horse got what he desired. Even the present of a toy horse had the same effect. But his display of saintly power at such an early age brought down upon him his father's curse and under it he died at the age of 5 in 1594. A fair is held at his tomb to which toy horses in thousands are presented.[1]

Pír Zaki, who gives his name to the Yakki Gate of Lahore, was a warrior of the same type. According to the *Tuḥfat-ul-Wásilín* he was killed fighting against the infidel Mughals, and his head is buried in the gateway, while his body rests at a spot close by where it fell.[2]

At Ambála town is the shrine of one Lakkhe Sháh Darvesh. One legend is that he lost his head in a great war in Multán, but fought his way to Ambála. A well then stood at the site of his shrine and from the women who were drawing water from it he begged a draught, but they ran away and so he fell down there and died, but not before he had uttered the curse : *Ambála shahr diṭṭha, andar khárá, báhir miṭṭhá,* 'Ambála town have I seen, sweet without and bitter within'. So to this day that well has been dry and any well sunk within the town always yields brackish water.[3] Another legend is that after the English had taken possession of Ambála, the magistrate, Mr. Murray, wished to make a road from the town in the fort (since dismantled), and destroyed the Sháh's tomb. A man in black came by night and overturned the magistrate's bed but he was not dismayed. Next night however he threw him off his bed and this frightened him so that he sat outside his house all night. After that he changed the line of the road and rebuilt the tomb with its four gateways.

[1] *Hist. of Lahore*, p. 158.

[2] *Ib.*, pp. 86 and 280.

[3] *S. C. R.*, VIII, p. 272.

THE SHRINES OF THE IMÁMS AT PÁNÍPAT.

The shrine of Imám Badr-ud-Dín—Sayyid Badr-ud-Dín is said to have suffered martyrdom in one of the first Muhammadan inroads. The story goes that Rájá Anang Pál of Pánípat resolved to build a castle. He consulted all the Brahman astrologers and told them to fix the most auspicious moment for laying its foundation. They advised him to get hold of a Muhammadan and secure its good fortune by laying its foundations on his head. As a Muhammadan was a rarity in those days in Hindustán the Rájá disregarded their advice, but soon after two Muhammadans by chance fell into his hands and he caused one, a Sayyid, to be killed under the northern wall of the fort; the rest of his body being similarly placed under other parts of it. Accordingly there are two shrines, that of the head on the summit of the fort and the other of the body below it. The Rájá reaped the fruit of his inhuman conduct, for having sacrificed the Sayyid he escorted his wife or sister with all care to the frontier. There she related the episode and Badr-ud-Dín and Akbar Ali with other Sayyids girt up their loins to wage war and by spiritual insight obtained the Prophet's sanction. Sayyid Badr-ud-Dín with his relations and friends, numbering not more than 300 in all, gathered all the information they needed from the lady and set out disguised as dealers in Arab horses. On arrival at Pánípat they took up their abode near the Rájá's palace. When apprised of this arrival the Rájá inquired their purpose in visiting his capital and bade them leave it at once. After much negotiation fighting ensued and the sons of Háshim displayed such valour that despite the limited force at their disposal the Musalmáns killed many of their opponents. Whenever a Sayyid fell in the action, drinking the cup of martyrdom, his place was mysteriously taken by one of the enemy: while from the souls of the dead there sprang a number of Sayyids, with heads and hands cut off, who were seen to slay many who possessed heads and hands. Seeing such miracles many of the Hindus embraced Islám and fought against their countrymen; and one Baram Jít, a Hindu commander, thus became a Muhammadan and was killed fighting against his former co-religionists. The tombs of these converts are still to be seen in the open ground near that of Sayyid Badr-ud-Dín, the martyr. None of his offspring survived him. The date of the Sayyid's tomb is not known, but the present dome was built some 50 years ago by Khwája Muhammad Khán Baraich.

The shrine of Khizar Khán and Shádi Khán.—The author of the *Zubdat-ul-Táríkh* says that Khizar Khán and Shádi Khán were two brothers, akin to Ala-ud-Dín Khilji, and men of great influence. According to the *Sharf-ul-Manáqib* the Sultán stood much in awe of the greatness of Hazrat Sharaf-ud-Dín, and frequently consulted him in difficulties relating to his empire, seeking his help and guidance. One day the Hazrat asked the Sultán to build his tomb, telling him that his death was at hand and that there should be no delay in its construction. The Sultán lost no time in obeying his orders and appointed his son to supervise the work. The tomb was built in 717 H.

The shrine of saint Sháh Sharaf-ud-Dín.—This saint, before the arrival of Khwája Shams-ud-Dín, used to live in Pánípat. But after the

Khwája's arrival he left it and went to settle in the village of Budha Katra. Here he spent most of his time, but often visited the town as it was his birth-place and the place where his parents were buried. He was greatly attached to Mubárak Khán and Shaikh Jalál-ud-Dín. The former died in 715 H. and his tomb was built in Pánípat. Knowing that death was near the saint asked Sultán Ala-ud-Din Khilji to build his tomb near that of his follower Mubárak Khán. He died on Ramzán 29th in 724 H. in Budha Khera. The residents of Karnál and Pánípat spent the day in deep regret, and next day his remains were brought to Karnál. But one of his followers named Mauláne Siráj-ud-Dín had been told in a vision that his body should be interred in the grave which had been built for him, and as the saint had also told him that he had been released from bodily imprisonment, the Mauláne set out next morning with the saint's nephew and others for Karnál to fetch the body which was brought to Pánípat and interred there. He was a great teacher and reputed to possess power to work miracles. He adopted the creed of the Súfís, because according to their belief the souls of prophets and saints obtain eternal bliss on leaving the material body. It is said that in his lifetime one Malik Ali, Ansári, of Herát, became his follower, and that Amar Singh, a Rájpút, whose descendants are still found in Pánípat, also embraced Islám. The so-called tomb of Sháh Sharaf-ud-Dín at Karnál should probably be regarded as a *mazár* or nominal shrine.

The shrine of Shaikh Jalál-ud-Dín.—This Shaikh, one of the chief saints in Pánípat, traced his descent from Khwája Abdul Rahmán Usmáni who flourished in the time of Mahmúd Ghaznavi. Noted for his generosity he had been brought up by Khwája Shams-ud-Dín, Turk, and like his father he used to distribute food daily to 1,000 persons. He often besought Sháh Sharf-ud-Dín for the gift of saintship, but was assured by him that it could only be had from Khwája Shams-ud-Dín. Eventually the latter appeared in Pánípat and bestowed it on him. At the same time the Khwája directed him to marry. From the union he had five sons and two daughters whose descendants, still found in Pánípat, are generally known as the *Makhdúms*. Dying in 800 H. at the age of 170 his tomb was built in 904 H. by Muhammad Lutaf Alláh Khán in the reign of Sikandar Sháh Lodi. But the *Sair-ul-Iqtibas* places his death in 765 H.

The shrine of Sharaf-ud-Dín Bu Ali Qalandar.—Sharf-ud-Dín, son of Sálár Fakhr-ud-Dín, was a descendant of Imám Azam Abu Hanifa of Kúfa who claim descent from Nausherwán. Born at Pánípat, in the early years he became well versed in all kinds of religious knowledge, and according to the tradition in the *Iqtibas-ul-Anwár,* he taught the people in the great *minár* in the Quwat-ul-Islám mosque at Delhi for 30 years. Eventually he attained absorption in divine meditation, and so spent the rest of his life. Although his system resembled that of Shaháb-ud-Dín, the lover of God, yet he received the spiritual power entitling him to rank as a saint from Ali Murtaza[1] without undergoing the required training and ranked foremost among the saints. His fame spread far and wide. His sayings recorded by the *mutádis* of Delhi in the

[1] Whence his title of Bu Ali or 'the spirit of Ali'. He is said to have taught the *tariqa-i-mujáhida* or duty of defending religion.

book called the *Takmil-ul-Imám* are still current. Born in 604 H. he died in 724 and the latter is the probable year of the erection of his tomb.

The shrine of Sálár Qamar-ud-Dín of Iráq, father of Sháh Sharaf.—According to Muhammad Bin Ahmad a descendant of Nizám Iráqi and author of the *Sarf-ul-Munáqib,* Sálár Qamar-ud-Dín and Bíbi Háfiz Jamál, the parents of Sharaf-ud-Dín, came to Pánípat in search of Nizám-ud-Dín their eldest son who had come to India for trade, but the beauty of the place induced them to settle in it. Sálár Qamar-ud-Dín had two sons and three daughters. One son Nizám-ud-Dín was born in Iráq, the other Sharaf-ud-Dín in Pánípat. The tombs of Sálár Qamar-ud-Dín, Nizám-ud-Dín his son, Bíbi Háfiz Jamál, his mother and of two of the daughters are all under one dome, but the date of their erection is not known.

The shrine of Sayyid Mahmúd.—This Sayyid was one of the ancient martyrs—a fact attested by Hazrat Sharaf-ud-Dín and Khwája Shams-ud-Dín. It is said that the Prophet in a vision directed Jalál-ud-dín to visit the tomb of the Sayyid daily and offer prayers.

The tomb of Sálárganj was founded in Hijri 1132.

The shrine of Sayyid Sháh Shamas-ud-Dín, Turk.—This Sayyid, a native of Turkistán, had a son Sayyid Ahmad, to whom the present family traces its descent. The *Sair-ul-Khitáb* says that one of the family held the rank of a Panjhazári under Sháh Jahán, but tired of worldly pleasures he chose the life of a devotee, and still in need of a spiritual guide he left home in search of one and travelled afar. When he arrived in India he chanced on Makhdúm Ala-ud-Dín Ali Ahmad, the Patient, a successor of the saint Ganjshakar of Kuler.[1] He became his follower and attained saintship. On his death-bed his guide thus addressed him :—"Shams-ud-Dín, my death is at hand, when I am buried, stay a while at my tomb and then go to Pánípat to give guidance to its people. The gift of saintship was handed down to me by Jalál-ud-Dín[2] and the same I now give you". The disciple gladly undertook the duty of cleaning the tomb daily, but this offer the dying saint declined, so when he was dead Shams-ud-Dín, after spending three days at the tomb, set out for Pánípat. On his arrival there, he sat at the foot of a wall. His fame spread through the town and reached the ears of Jalál-ud-Dín, who had also been directed in a vision, by Makhdúm Ali, to do him homage in return for spiritual blessings. So Jalál-ud-Dín served him faithfully for some time, and on his death in 716 H. succeeded him.[3]

A story of Khwája Shams-ud-Dín, given in the *Sair-ul-Khitáb*, is that, after acquiring spiritual perfection, he, with his teacher's permission, entered the service of Sultán Ghiás-ud-Dín Balban, but kept his spiritual perfection a secret. By chance, however, his holy spirit manifested itself in a miraculous and supernatural way, and the Sultán who had

[1] Or Kalár.

[2] The Jalál-ud-Dín Pánípati already mentioned. Another account says that Shams-ud-Dín reached Pánípat in the guise of a *qalandrana* or 'keeper of bears', and that Jalál-ud-Dín handed on to him the *ni'amat báini* or 'inward delights' delivered to him by Ala-ud-Dín in trust for Shams-ud-Dín. He was learned in both sciences, *naql* and *'aql*.

[3] This is the date given in the *Sair-ul-Iqtibas*.

made vain efforts to conquer a fortress, came to know of it, and said that it was a pity that he had not been benefited by the saint's powers. At first the saint tried to conceal his spirituality, but he gradually yielded to the king's importunity and offered up prayer for his success and the fortress fell.

The shrine of Imám Qásim.—Sayyids Abul Qásim and Abul Isháq, it is said, were members of Sayyid Badr-ud-Dín's party and leaders of his vanguard. They suffered martyrdom and when Sayyid Badr-ud-Dín reached Pánípat and learnt of their deaths he was greatly enraged and began to fight. The descendants of Sayyid Abul Qásim say that formerly he was interred near Badr-ud-Dín's tomb and so the place came to be called Shahídpura or habitation of martyrs. Descendants of these martyrs, called 'the children of Mír Abdur Rahmán', are still found in Pánípat. The present dome of Imám Qásim was built 80 years ago by Khwája Ain-ud-Dín, an Ansári *maulavi*. The founder of the old shrine is not known. After these Sayyids had fallen Mahmúd of Ghaznavi reached India, and according to the author of the *Mirat-ul-Asrár*, that Sultán having conquered the country up to Kanauj returned home in 407 H. In 416 H. he again plundered it as far as Somnáth. From that year the propagation of Islám in India began and many Muhammadans settled in different places. One of them, Khwája Abdur Rahmán, in many ways the precursor of Shaikh Jalál-ul-Dín, settled in Pánípat and for a time ruled it absolutely, levying tribute and acquiring wealth. After this great numbers of Muhammadans continued to visit Indian cities, and the Rájpúts, who in reality were the chiefs of India, after many struggles were entirely put to the sword by the royal forces, so much so that none of them escaped but a pregnant woman, and she after undergoing various hardships succeeded in reaching the house of her parents. She gave birth to a son, and his descendants increased in the village of her parents. One known as Amar Singh was one of them. The shrine has been in existence for 900 years.

Champions as saints.

Mírán Sáhib is worshipped in the Nardak. With his sister's son Sayyid Kabír he has a joint shrine at Sonepat. Another shrine at a spot midway between Bhaṭinda and Háji Ratan in Patiála is known as the shrine of Máma-Bhánja or the 'Uncle and his Sister's Son'. The latter pair are described as leaders of Shaháb-ud-Dín Ghori's army who were killed in the capture of Bhaṭinda.[1] But the story in the Nardak differs. According to it a Brahman appealed to Mírán Sáhib for help against Rájá Tharu of Habri. The fight extended over the whole country to Delhi and the so-called Sayyid shrines are the graves of the Moslems who fell. Mírán Sáhib had his head struck off in the battle but he went on fighting until a woman exclaimed: 'Who is this fighting without his head?' Then he fell down and died, but not before he had cursed all Tharu's villages which

[1] Phulkián States *Gazetteer*, 1904 (Patiála), p. 81. The names of the pair are not given. Sayyid Mírán *Sháh* has a tomb at Bhaṭinda. In the Kabírwála tahsíl, of Multán, Mámán Sher has a shrine at the large mound outside Tulamba. This saint was martyred with Dáta Ganj Bakhsh at Lahore, but rode back without his head to the place where he is now buried: Multán *Gazetteer*, p. 122.

were turned upside down, all their inhabitants save the Brahman's daughter being killed. Mírán Sáhib was buried at Habri. Who this Mírán Sáhib was is not very clear.

To get rid of *karwa*, a fly which injures *bájra* in bloom, take your sister's son on your shoulder and feed him with rice-milk while he says: 'The sister's son has got on to his uncle's shoulder: go, *karwa*, to another's field',—just as he has climbed on to a stranger's shoulder.[1]

Sirkap Sháh or the headless saint has a tomb at Ladwa in Ambála. Long ago by prayer and fasting this *faqír* obtained the power of granting sons to the barren, and many women visited him, but his refusal to allow more than one woman at a time into his hut caused scandal so the people tried to poison him, but he frustrated their attempts and bade the women visit him no more. But they disobeyed him and in revenge their men-folk attacked the saint and beheaded him His headless trunk however slew them all within four hours, leaving so many widows that the place was called Randwa Shahr or the 'widows' town' in consequence.[2]

A *naugaza* is a deceased saint whose tomb is supposed to be 9 feet or as many yards long and whose remains are believed to be of proportionate length. They perform miracles, grant sons, and so on. At Guptsar (in Sirsa apparently) where Gurú Govind Singh is said to have encamped, he found a *faqír* who had built himself a masonry tomb 9 yards long, leaving on one side of it an opening large enough for him to be put in when he died.[3] Cunningham says that every such tomb is described as that of a Ghási and Shahíd, 'champion and martyr', who fell fighting for the faith and that their length varies from 10 to upwards of 50 feet. But he also records that the two tombs ascribed to the Prophets Seth and Job (Sis and Ayub) at Ajudhia and to Lamech in Lamghán are the extreme limits of their occurrence, so they are dedicated to prophets also. At Multán there are 15 of them, including that of Pír Gor Sultán near which lies a *manka* or gigantic stone ring, said to have been worn by the saint as a necklet or thumb-ring. At Harappa near the tomb of Núr Sháh *naugaza* there were three undulated stone-rings called the *nál*, *manka* and *nag* (gem) of the giant. This tomb seems to have grown from 18 feet to 46 in length since Burnes saw it.

The *naugaza* shrines are common all over the Punjab and a Buddhist origin has been suggested for them.[4]

[1] Sirsa *Sett. Rep.*, p. 256.

[2] *Selections C.R.*, VIII, p. 274.

[3] Sirdár Sir Atar Singh, *Sákhis*, p. 77, quoted in P. N. Q., I., § 486. The *faqír* is said to have been of the Wahmi order, an order not mentioned elsewhere apparently. The term *wahmiyat* signifies the faculty by means of which one grasps the qualities of objects, and forms one's opinions (*wahm*. *Wahm* seems to connote acquiescence in a proposition, but the assent to it is not ordinarily free from doubt (Slane's *Ibn Khaldoun*, I, p. 199). Hence it also denotes illusion (*ib.*, III, p. 97). Hence the *wahmi* would seem to be a philosophic doubter.

[4] A. S. R., V., pp. 130, 131 and 106. The 15 at Multán include the tombs of a king Mírán Samar (?), Lál Husain Bairági, a converted Hindu, Sabz Ghási, Qázi Qutb Kāshāni, Pír Adham, Pír Díndár, Pir Ramzán Ghási, Pir Gor Sultán, Shádna Shahíd and 5 of unknown saints. Shádna Shahíd should be invoked to get a thing done quickly: Multán *Gazetteer*, pp. 346-7. Major C. H. Buck describes Núr Sháh as a giant who came from Arabia and laid waste the country: *Faiths, Fairs, and Festivals of India*, p. 210.

The tomb of a Naugaza Sáhib, whose real name was Hazrat Imám Ja'far Sádiq, one of the companions of the Prophet, is found at Ferozepur. It is said that once when the Prophet fought with the infidels the Naugaza Sáhib had his head cut off in the fight, but the rest of his body remained fighting and by his miraculous power reached this place where it stopped as soon as a party of women saw it. No fair is held but offerings are made every Thursday.[1] Temple records another nameless *naugaza* at Baṭṭala in Amritsar (? Gurdáspur) regarding which the stock legend of a man stealing the saint's bed and being overturned when he slept on it is told.[2] The nebulous character of the saint and his identification with the Imám Ja'far suggests some connection with the concealed Imám, but the origin of the term is as obscure as that of the shrines themselves.

Sháh Rahma is the whirlwind saint in Sháhpur, where once, when his shrine was neglected, he cursed the district that whirlwinds should blow for nine days in succession. This ruined the wheat harvest and so now his fair is regularly attended.[3]

Jamme Sháh is a giant who is confined in a well at Kastewál in Amritsar. He is only allowed to leave it on one night, on 18th Jeṭh, in the year, and on his return all the lamps in the village are extinguished. The rattling of his chains is heard and an evil smell pervades the place on this occasion.[4]

Khajúria Pír had an old tomb in the Paget Park, Ambála Cantonment. Growing out of it is a date-palm—whence his name. His dealings with English Officers are described in *Folklore Record*, V., p. 158.[5] He visits Alláh Bakhsh, a saint who occupies a room in the Cantonment Magistrate's cutcherry at Ambála, where he is regularly worshipped by suitors and accused persons. He had in life a favourite station under a *bahera* tree near the race-course and still visits it torch in hand at night. Palsy is attributed to him and to cure it a white cock in full plumage and a plateful of sugar and cardamums should be offered to him.[6]

The *khánqáh* of Mián Mohkam-ud-Dín, a Rájpút of Ambála, was built at Jagráon in 1915 S. and the annual fair is held on 14th Phágan. It now lasts for 3 days and nights, and many lamps are lit round it at night during that period. The Mián had a disciple in Bhái Basant Singh whose *samádh* at Kakra in Moga tahsíl is the scene of a fair on Sáwan 1st as well as of a fair every Thursday. It is in charge of a *dárvesh* named Híra Singh, who is celibate. At Jagráon too succession goes by spiritual descent.

At Jangpur in Jagráon is held a fair in honour of Mián Búre Sháh on the night between Asauj and Kártik. This *khánqáh* was founded

[1] J. R. A. S., XIII, N. S, p. 183.

[2] S. C. R., VIII, pp. 273-4.
N. I. N. Q., I., § 396.

[4] *Ib.*, § 18.

[5] S. C. R., VIII, p. 273.

[6] P. N. Q., II, § 1066.

in 1841 S., the year of the Mián's death. He was a saint of such high character and of spiritual powers that people irrespective of caste or creed loved him and held him in high esteem, and on the anniversary of his demise gathered to worship his tomb, and pray for fulfilment of their wishes. He was a native of Uch and belonged to the Husain-sháhi sect, to which its incumbents still belong. By degrees this fair grew so popular that now about 10,000 people assemble at the *khánqáh* by night. Some also bring cattle with them. and having remained there for a night go away. Lamps also are lighted on all sides of the tomb, as well as inside it. It contains another tomb besides the saint's, that of Bíbi Khusrálo, a Brahman girl, who was disciple of the Mián and who died 40 years after him.

The story about the shrines of Wiláyat Sháh and Hásham Sháh of Ghairatpur Bás in the Meo country in Gurgáon is that two *faqírs* so named died in that village and so their shrines were built there. There is no *urs* or annual celebration at Hásham Sháh's tomb, but at Wiláyat Sháh's his disciple Chaitan Sháh collects about 20 *faqírs* each year on 11th Zikád and feasts them. Wiláyat Sháh died in 1825.[1]

Another 'Sháh Wiláyat' has is tomb at Palwal.[2] His name was Sayyid Baha-ud-Dín and a *khalífa* of Ali Ahmad Sábiri of Gangoh.

The fair called Nishán is held every Wednesday in the middle of Mágh. The visitors are mostly Meos. When Sálár Ma'súd Gházi conquered this part 400 or 500 years ago he made many converts to Islám and they are called Meos. His standard or *nishán* is set up every year and the fair held around it, but no temple or other building exists. Three hereditary *faqírs* manage the fair and they sing songs in honour of Sálár when the flag is put up. It is carried from village to village while songs are sung and offerings of grain collected. Rice and *chúrma* are cooked and distributed as *darúd*.

Sháh Badr Díwán, whose mausoleum is at Masánián in Batála tahsíl, Gurdáspur, has a *chilla* at Lahore. At Masánián his *khánqáh* is called 'Husaini' or 'Gíláni'. Its annual festival is held on 12th Rabi-ul-Awal and the monthly fête or *nau-chandi* on a Thursday at the appearance of the new moon. Sháh Badr-ud-Dín was born in Baghdád in 861 H. He left his home in 904 H. and came to Masánián where he died in 978 H. and this *khánqáh* was built. It contains the tombs of Bíbi Murassa, his wife, Sayyid Ali Sábar, his eldest son, and Sháh Abdul Shakúr, Sayyids Ahmad Sháh and Khwája Ján, his grandsons. The tombs bear some modern inscriptions.[3]

At Kástiwál, a fair is held annually on the *púranmáshi* or full moon of Jeṭh for 4 or 5 days. The shrine, which is named after the village in

[1] These two shrines may be those of twin gods. The latter's ministers once allowed his shrine to fall into disrepair, whereupon he afflicted them with sickness until they restored it. Wiláyat Sháh protects travellers and once when a villager's cart wheel gave way he vowed 5 balls of *gur* to his saint if he got his cart to his village. His cart duly reached the village boundary, but got no further: Gurgáon *Gazetteer*, 1910, pp. 6 and 9.

[2] *Epigraphia Indo-Moslemica*, p. 1. Palwal also boasts a Sayyid Chirágh and the tombs of Fattan and Umr Shahíds, as well as that of the well-known martyr Ghází Shiháb-ud-Dín, concerning whom the usual story is told that after his head was cut off, he rode his horse to the spot where his grave now lies.

[3] *Hist. of Lahore*, pp. 189.

which it stands, owes its origin to one Bába Godar Sháh who is said to have come from Sirsa. A disciple of Alláh Dád Khán, he built him a hut to live in, but a body of demons living in the forest threatened to burn him alive in it, if he did not leave it. The Bába however blew some verses of charm on to water which he sprinkled on the demons, and so caused them to stand on one place like statues. Next morning the Bába found them all unable to move, and when they saw him they implored him to set them free. He threw some water on them, and revived them. They then left the place, but one of them Júme Sháh begged to be made his disciple. He soon acquired miraculous powers. Once he placed a big beam on the shrine which 20 persons could not lift. When on the point of death Júme Sháh asked the Bábá's leave to go to his fellow demons and live with them, but he asked the Bába to grant him a room in the shrine and the latter gave him one in a *burj* or dome, which is still called after him. At that time the forest was uncultivated and the village of Kástiwál stood on a mound, but the Bába built a wall round the shrine and also a mosque with ten *hujrás* or chambers.

The fair is held on the anniversary of the Bába's death, prayers being offered for the benefit of his soul.

Founded in 1062 H. or 3 years before his decease its present manager is a Ját whose duties are to meditate on the name of God, to feed needy travellers, and look after the *khánqáh*. The holder of this office is celibate, and succession is governed by spiritual relationship, the disciples being always selected for the *gaddi*.

At the Jogiánwála well near the *khánqáh* Bhumar Náth Jogi used to live. Once an old woman was about to offer milk to the Jogi, but when near the *khánqáh*, the Bába bade her offer it to the shrine. She did so and next morning found that her cow yielded much more milk than before. This miracle impressed the people of the neighbourhood, and the Jogi in jealousy at the Bába's fame summoned him through one of his disciples. The disciple told the Bába that the Jogi, his Gurú, wanted him, but he bade him sit by him for a moment and then he would accompany him. Before long the Jogi despatched another disciple with the same request, and the same thing happened. At last the Jogi himself came and challenged the Bába. The latter asked him to show him a miracle. On this, the Jogi put off his sandals and flew towards the sky. The Bába then ordered his sandals to chase the Jogi and bring him back to him. The Jogi was accordingly pursued by the sandals, which overtook him and brought him back to the Bába. The Jogi thus defeated implored the Bába to give him shelter. The latter sent him to the village of Jhakhar in Pathánkoṭ. The Jogi on his departure asked the Bába whether he could do him any service. The latter replied that as he was going to a place where wood and bamboo were abundant, he might send him a wooden plate (*prát*) and a bamboo basket. The custom of supplying these articles is in use ever since.

The *khánqáh* of Bhíkha Sháh in Kángra is the scene of a large fair, which lasts from 5th to 7th Jeṭh every year. The story goes that Bhíkha Sháh was a Brahman who lived in Jaisingpur, and became a disciple of Masat Ali. He miraculously restored a corpse to life.

Thereby he incurred the displeasure of his *gurú* who ran after him to chastize him, but the *chela* disappeared underground and took up his abode at the place where the shrine now stands. The fair was first celebrated in 1907 S.

At the *khánqáh* of Pír Salohi at Kaluah in Núrpur tahsíl annual fairs are held on Mágh 7th, on both Thursdays in the second half of Jeṭh; and on the first two in Háṛ. The story is that Pír Salohi asked some shepherds here for water to wash his hands and face before he offered his prayers. The shepherds said that none was to be had near by, whereupon the saint struck the ground with his *khúnḍi* (an iron rod) and a spring gushed out. Then the saint went to the house of Jaimal, a *samíndár*, and asked if he was at home. His mother gave the saint a cup of milk, and he then returned to the place whence he had started. Here he disappeared underground. During the night it was revealed to Sháh Fakír in a vision that a lamp should be kept burning on the spot where the saint had said his prayers. The shrine was founded in 1794 S., a date verified from its records. Three sacred lamps are always kept burning at the shrine, a number increased to 7 on Thursdays. Sacred fire is also kept alight. Both Hindus and Muhammadans pay their devotions and no distinction is made in their offerings.

In the Attock Hills Ghází-Walípuri is the popular name for a huge boulder at Háji Sháh, which is covered with irregular cup-marks. No tradition regarding it seems to exist.[1]

A shrine of which little is known is that of the Pír Abd-ur-Rahím, Abd-ur-Karím or Abd-ur-Razák, at Thánesar, where it forms 'one of the most striking of picturesque monuments in North India',[2] with its pear-shaped dome and flowered lattice of white marble. Ascribed to the time of Dára Shikoh, all that is recorded of the Pír is that he wrote a book called '*Lives of the Walís*', and is known as Shaikh Tilli or Chilli. In the Punjab Shaikh Chilli seems to have no great vogue, but a Shaikh Chilli holds in the United Provinces the same position as Nasr-ud-Dín, 'the Khoja of Aqshahir', does in Turkey. 'His character is a curious blend of cunning and naïveté, of buffoonery and shrewdness'.[3]

Chirágh Sháh, Chirágh Chand Sháh or Sháh Chirágh has a tomb at Ráwalpindi which is famous throughout the Sindh Ságar Doáb. He was a Sayyid, born in 1360 A. D.

The death of Sher Sháh Sur is attributed in folk-tales to a headless man. Dharm Dat, a Bánia, had two fair daughters whom the emperor demanded and on the Bánia's refusal he was beheaded, but his headless trunk seized the sword and slew the emperor as he had threatened to do before he was executed.[4]

[1] P. N. Q., II, § 1023. Regular cup-marks occur at another place, half a mile from Háji Sháh, with out-line engravings of deer-hunting. Close by is an ancient Buddhist well—with an inscription. Cup-marks also occur at Koṭ Bithaur in these hills: *ib.*, III, §§ 56-7 and 180.

[2] Cunningham, A. S. R., II, p. 223. The Imperial *Gazetteer* does not mention this tomb.

[3] Lukach, *The City of Dancing Dervishes*, p. 34 *ff*. *Cf.*, N. I. N. Q., *passim*.

[4] S. C. R. VIII, p. 275. Sher Sháh was killed at the siege of Kalinjar in 1545.

Ghaibi Pír or the hidden saint has a square shrine on the top of the Bahrámpur hill in Rohtak. It is in the form of a tomb but with no cenotaph and is open to all four winds. The tale told of it recalls that of Púran Bhagat and other legends. When a wayfarer passed by the *faqír* with a load of sugar and was asked what he had, he said 'salt.' 'Salt be it', said the *faqír*, and salt it was; but he repented and it became sugar again, so in gratitude he built the shrine. But no one knows the saint's name or where he lies. Popular rationalism says the sinner mistook the *faqír* for a customs line officer. Crowds visit the shrine on Sundays. A Pír Ghaib has a small shrine at Halalwaja in the Shujábád tahsíl, Multan.[1]

An invisible tomb is found in Baháwalpur tahsíl. There the 7 tombs of Ali Asháb include one which is not seen. The other 6 are ascribed to Ali Asháb, Gul Ahmad, Pír Zakaría, Mubárik and Tangre Sáhib, all companions of the Prophet who fell in battle. Five of the tombs are 9 yards long, and apparently *naugasas*, the sixth being only 3 yards in length. They are frequented by people sick of fever or headache, by those desirous of a wife or offspring, or in distress. Even thieves make vows at them in order to escape punishment. Seven fairs are held on Fridays in Jeṭh and Háṛ, and Hindus who are in debt or childless offer the flour and goat sacrifice. A Hindu making an offering must fast, as must his wife also. He must then cook a kid's liver, and get the *mujáwar* to recite a *khatam* over it and give a piece of it to the wife to break her fast. Cattle are also taken to the shrine to cure farcy etc. The *mujáwars* are Ansárís or Thalims and their offices are hereditary.[2]

Barat Sháh, a saint of Kasúr, has a shrine there and near it is a pond in which children are bathed to cure them of boils (*pániwáte*).[3]

Sháh Abdul Azíz of Delhi was a noted interpreter of dreams and he once advised a disciple to go to Tonk. He entered the Nawáb's service and under his directions the Nawáb sided with the British.[4]

Mián Ahmad Khán, a *darvesh*, has a shrine at Kasúr in which the attendants place white pebbles. These stones are known as Ahmad Khán's lions and are bought by his devotees to tie round the necks of children whose sleep is troubled.[5]

Mián Miṭṭhu, a saint extensively worshipped in the western part of Gurdáspur, has a shrine at the village which bears his name. He was a Nawáb at the imperial court and was sent to suppress a revolt, but on the march his favourite horse died and he was so impressed by the sorrow which death could cause that he threw up his command, turned *faqír* and withdrew from the world. Once a Hindu *faqír* appropriated the milk which the villagers used to supply to him, justifying the act on the ground of his own superior sanctity. The

[1] Multán *Gazetteer*, p. 128.

[2] Baháwalpur *Gazetteer*, p. 159.

[3] P. N. Q., III, § 181.

[4] N. I. N. Q. I., § 980.

[5] P. N. Q., III, § 376.

Mián challenged him to a practical test of their spiritual powers. The Hindu flew up into the air, but the Mián brought him down with a shot-gun and was voted the holier man. The Hindu turned Muhammadan and became his disciple. The Mián is greatly reverenced, however, by Hindus and they make offerings to him. They also eschew the use of burnt brick because his shrine is built of them, and so strict is this prohibition that several large villages in the neighbourhood are entirely built of adobe bricks.[1]

Sayyid Miṭhha may be connected with the foregoing. His name was Muín-ud-dín and his father Sayyid Jamál-ud-dín was a native of Khwárazm. The invasion of Changiz Khán drove him to take refuge with Jalál-ud-dín of Ghazni and with him he fled to India when Ghazni also fell to the Tartars. The fame of his son surpassed his own and he made many disciples at Lahore where he died in 1262. 661 H.
His tomb is held in great respect.[2]

Pír Ghaṛe Bhan is 'the saint of the broken pitchers'. His shrine at Kasúr is a platform where pitchers are broken in pursuance of vows to do so if desires are fulfilled.[3]

Pír Chíthri is one of a group of *pírs* whose insignia are of the humblest. Chíthri is a *pír* whose cairns of brushwood are common in the Bár between Lahore and Multán, and if a traveller throw a stick upon one of them intimation is at once conveyed by the Pír to his home that he is safe. Pír Thigri is a similar saint. If a man's wishes are fulfilled he places branches of trees (*gohá*) and shreds of cotton at a certain place in accordance with his vow, and the place is called Pír Thigri.[4]

Pír Tingri is also represented by shreds of cotton, but in his case they are tied to a tree,[5] and Pír Roṛe by one brickbat placed on another. They are both worshipped by thieves who offer them sweetmeats if successful.[6]

Bába Wali Qandahári, who has 126 other names, is the saint of Hasan Abdál. One Hasan, a Gujar, owned a cattlepen on the site of the modern town and used to water his cattle in the Haroh river. The Bába arrived, performed a *chihla* and asked for water for his ablutions. Hasan went to the Haroh for it, but the saint in his impatience struck his tongs into the limestone and water gushed out. The Bába's shrine is on the hill-top, and the town derives the second part of its name from one of his titles, Sháh Wáli Abdáli. As he is still, it is said, alive

[1] P. N. Q., II, § 377. The *tabu* or *pakka* brick is also found among certain tribes, *e. g.* the Mián Miṭhú is quite distinct from Mihr Miṭhá as to whom see Vol. II, p. 286. Mián Miṭhú is also a sobriquet for the parrot and to call oneself Mián Miṭhú (*apne mún áp Mián Miṭhú banná*), means to sound one's own praises: *ibid.* III, § 317, IV, § 472. It is also styled Ganga Rám.

[2] *Hist. of Lahore*, p. 229.

[3] P. N. Q., III, § 759.

[4] For a Thikar Náth see *Legends of the Punjab*, II, p. 441.

[5] In Baháwalpur when a young tree is peculiarly vigorous it is dedicated to a *pír* and even called after his name. Offerings are made to it and villagers often visit it in groups. By degrees the tree is anthropomorphised into the saint himself, the *pír* most implicitly believed in by the villagers, and distinguished by a flag which is fastened to it.

[6] P. N. Q., III, § 487.

he is also called Haiátu'l Mír. A modern accretion to the legend avers that Bába Nának visited the place and sent two of his disciples to demand water from Bába Wali. The latter retorted that if Nának were a saint he could procure water where the wished. He also sent a stone rolling down the hill after the disciples, but Bába Nának stayed it with his outstretched hand and left its impress on the stone, from beneath which a spring of water has flowed ever since.[1]

Among Muhammadans in Attock various methods of causing rain are in vogue. One consists in collecting grain from each house, boiling it and then taking it to the *masjid* or *khánqáh* when after prayers it is divided among those present, confectionery being added in Attock tahsíl. Another consists in simply collecting together, repairing the mosque and cleaning it, and praying there. Women join in these gatherings. In a third a boy's face is blackened and a stick put into his hand. He then collects all the other children and they go round begging from house to house calling out :—

Aulia ! Maulia ! Míṇh barsá,
Sádi koṭhí dáne pá,
Chiriye de múṇh páni pá.
'Aulia ! Send rain,
Put grain in our house,
And water in the beaks of the birds.' !

Whatever grain is collected is boiled and divided. Lastly there is the *zári* rite in which *mulláhs* and others go to the mosque, calling the *báng* seven times at each corner as well as in the village. Crowds of villagers assemble and pray, religious books are read and presents made to priests and shrines, a common offering being a ploughshare's weight in grain.[2]

The Muhammadan rosaries are as various as those of other creeds and comprise the Sunnis' *aqiqul'-bahar* of dark stone : the *káṭh kí tasbíh* of variegated wooden beads ; the *tasbíh* of *kánch* or variegated glass : the *sang-i-maqsúd* of yellow stones : the *kahrubá* of amber, used by *maulavís* ; and the *sulamáni* of various stones also used by them. The four last named are also used by all *faqírs* Shi'as use the *khák-i-shifá* or ' dust of healing', made of particoloured earth from Karbalá[3]

[1] P. N. Q. II, § 980. Lalla Rukh lies buried at the town of Hassan Abdál.

[2] Attock *Gazetteer*, pp. 108-9.

[3] I. N. Q., IV, § 146.

The Chúhás, or Rat-children of the Punjab, and Sháh Daula.

(i) *The Chúhás.*

The Chúhás or Rat-children are an institution in the Punjab. They are microcephalous beings, devoid of all power of speech, idiots, and unable to protect themselves from danger, of filthy habits, but entirely without sexual instincts.[1] They are given names, but are usually known by the names of their attendants, whose voices they recognise and whose signs they understand. They have to be taught to eat and drink, but cannot be allowed to go about unguarded. Their natural instinct is to suck only, and, when they have been taught to eat and drink and can walk, they are made over to a *faqír* of the Sháh Daula sect, who wanders about begging with his 'Sháh Daula's Rats'.

The popular idea is that these unfortunate beings have been blessed by the saint, Sháh Daula Daryáí of Gujrát in the Punjab, and that, though they are repulsive objects, no contempt of them must be shown, or the saint will make a Chúhá of the next child born to one who despises one of his *protégés.* It is this fear which has brought about the prosperity of Sháh Daula's shrine at Gujrát.

The common superstition as to the origin of the Chúhás is this: Sháh Daula, like other saints, could procure the birth of a child for a couple desiring one, but the first child born in response to his intercession would be a Chúhá—brainless, small-headed, long-eared and rat-faced. The custom used to be to leave the child, as soon as it was weaned, at Sháh Daula's *khánqáh*, as an offering to him. After the saint's death the miracle continued, but in a modified form. Persons desiring children would go to the saint's shrine to pray for a child, and would make a vow either to present the child when born or to make an offering to the shrine. In some cases, when the child was duly born in response to the prayer, the parents neglected to make the promised gift. Upon this the spirit of the offended saint so worked on the parents that the next child born was a Chúhá, and all subsequent children as well, until the original vow was fulfilled.

The tomb and shrine of Sháh Daula lie on the eastern side of Gujrát town, about 100 yards from the Sháh Daula Gate. His descendants dwell near and round the shrine, and their houses form a suburb known as Gaṛhí Sháh Daula. The shrine itself was built in the latter part of the seventeenth century by a 'saint' named Bháwan Sháh and was rebuilt on a raised plinth in 1867. In 1898 it was put into thorough repair by the followers of Sháh Daula.

The cult of Sháh Daula offers few unusual features. No lands are attached to the shrine and its *pírs* are wholly dependent on the alms and offerings of the faithful. Three annual fairs are held at the shrine, one at each *'Id* and a third at the *urs* on the 10th of Muharram. A weekly fair used to be held on Fridays, attended by dancing girls; but this has fallen into abeyance. There are no regular rules of succession

[1] For medical opinion on the Chúhás, see an article in the *Indian Medical Gazette*, for May 1st, 1866, by E. J. Wilson Johnston, M. D., M. R. C. S. E. This article is reprinted in *Panjab Notes and Queries*, 1885, III, §§ 117-118; see also II, §§ 69 and 172.

to the shrine, and each member of the saint's family has a share in it. Three of them, however, have a special influence and one of these three is generally known as the *sijjáda-nashín*, or successor of the saint. The general income of the sect is divided into three main shares, each of which is divided into minor shares—a division *per stripes* and *per capita*. The shareholders also each take in turn a week's income of the shrine.

The principal *muríds*, or devotees of the sect, are found in Jammu, Púnch and the Frontier Districts, and in Swát, Malákand and Káfiristán. Sháh Daula's *faqírs* visit each *muríd* annually and exact an offering (*nazar*), usually a rupee, in return for which they profess to impart spiritual and occult knowledge. Some of these *faqírs* are strongly suspected of being concerned in the traffic in women that exists between the Punjab and Púnch and Jammu, and it is from these districts that the Chúhás are chiefly recruited.

There is a notable off-shoot of the Sháh Daula *faqírs* in an order of *faqírs*, who properly own allegiance to the Akhúnd of Swát. A disciple of the Akhúnd, named Gházi Sultán Muhammad, a native of Awán, a village in Gujrát District on the Jammu border, has established a considerable following. He lives now at Sháh Daula's shrine, but has built himself a large stone house at Awán.

(*ii*) *The Legend of Sháh Daula, by Major A. C. Elliott.*

Sháh Daula was born in A. D. 1581 during the reign of Akbar. His father was Abdu'r Rahím Khán Lodi, a descendant of Sultán Ibrahím Lodí, grandson of Bahlol Sháh Lodi who died in A. H. 894 (A. D. 1488). This would make him a Paṭhán by descent, but he is nevertheless claimed by the Gújars of Gújrát as belonging to their tribe. His mother was Niámat Khátun, great-granddaughter of Sultán Sárang Ghakhar.

In the reign of Sultán Salím, son of Sultán Sher Sháh (A. H. 952-960 or A. D. 1545-1553) a large force was sent to subdue Khawás Khán,[1] who had rebelled in support of Adil Khán, Salím Sháh's elder brother. Khawás Khán met with a crushing defeat and sought refuge with the Gakhars, who supported him, and a battle was fought near Rohtás in the Jhelum District, in which Sultán Sárang Ghakhar was killed, and all his family were afterwards made captives. A daughter of Gházi Khán, son of Sultán Sárang, was among the captured, and she had at the time an infant daughter at the breast. This was Niámat Khátun, who was taken with her brother to Delhi and in the first year of Akbar's reign (A. H. 963 or A. D. 1556), shortly after Humáyún's death, she was married to Abdu'r Rahím Lodi, then an officer of the imperial household. But Sháh Daula was not born of this marrige till the 25th year of Akbar's reign (A. H. 989 or A. D. 1581) which was also the year of his father's death.[2]

Where Sháh Daula was born is not known, but his widowed mother returned to her native country, Pathás, now represented by the Jhelum

[1] For a *Legend of Khán Khwás and Sher Sháh Chaughatta* see *Indian Antiquary* 1909.

[2] [This story reads like the familiar fictitious connection of local heroes in India with the great ones of the land.—Ed., *Indian Antiquary*.]

and Ráwalpindi Districts. On her arrival, however, she found that, though she was the great-granddaughter of Sultán Sárang, she was as much a stranger there as in Hindustán and that no one had any regard for herself or her fallen family. For five years she had to earn her living by grinding corn in the village of Sabhála in the *pargana* of Phirhálat, whence she removed to Kaláh, where she died in A. H. 998 or A. D. 1590 after four more years of toil.

Sháh Daula, now left an orphan and friendless, determined to go a-begging. In the course of his wanderings he reached Sakhi Siálkot, where he met one Mahta Kíman, a slave of the Qánúngos of that place, and a rich and generous, but childless man. Moved by pity and favourably improved by his looks, he adopted Sháh Daula and brought him up in luxury. Sháh Daula's intelligence attracted the notice of the Qánúngos, who gave him charge of their *tosha-khána* or treasury, but so generous was Sháh Daula by nature that he could never turn a deaf ear to a beggar. The result was that not only all his own money, but also all the valuables, cash and furniture of the *tosha-khána* disappeared! The Qánúngos refused to believe his story that he had given everything to mendicants and had him imprisoned and tortured.

In his extremity under torture Sháh Daula declared that he had buried the money and would dig it up again if released from prison. He was led to the *tosha-khána* where he at once seized a dagger from a niche and plunged it into his belly. This act put the fear of the authorities into the Qánúngos, and they sent for a skilful physician, who bound up the wound, from which Sháh Daula recovered in three months.

The Qánúngos then set him free and he went to Sangrohi, a village near Siálkot, where he became a disciple of the saint, Sháh Saidán Sarmast. Sháh Daula now ingratiated himself with one Mangu or Mokhu, the saint's favourite disciple, and spent his time as a mendicant The scraps he secured as the proceeds of his begging were placed before the saint, who ate all he wanted and passed the remainder on to Mangu. After Mangu was satisfied, the small portion that remained was given to Sháh Daula, whose hunger was rarely appeased. But such poor earnings in kind failed to satisfy the saint, who set Sháh Daula to work and earn money with which cooked food might be bought, as a substitute for the stale scraps received as alms.

At that time a new fort was being built at Siálkot out of bricks from the foundation of some old buildings, and Sháh Daula was sent to dig as an ordinary labourer at a *taka* or two pice a square yard of brick-work dug up. So hard was the material that most powerful men could not excavate more than two or three square yards in a day, but Sháh Daula worked with such amazing energy that he dug up seventy square yards on the first day and separated the bricks. The officials, recognising superhuman aid, offered him seventy *takás*, or full payment for his work, without demur, but he would only accept four.

With the four *takás* thus acquired, he bought a savoury dish of *khichrí*, which he presented to the saint, before whom he was inclined to boast of his powers. But the saint showed him his own hands, all blistered with the invisible aid he had been rendering to Sháh Daula. As a mark of favour, however, the saint gave him some of the *khichrí*, which produced such excruciating pain in the second finger of his right-hand on his commencing to eat it that for days he could neither sleep nor rest, and at last asked the saint to relieve him. Mangu also interceded and at last the saint told Sháh Daula to go to the Butchers' Street and thrust his hand into the bowels of a freshly slaughtered cow. As soon as he had done this there was immediate relief and he fell into a deep sleep for twenty-four hours; but on awakening he found that the finger had dropped off! He returned, however, to the saint and thanked him for his kindness, whereon the saint said :—'Man, thus much of self-love hadst thou, but it has gone from thee now and love for others only remains. Be of good cheer. Thou art proven worthy of my favour, and of the knowledge of God'.

For twelve years Sháh Daula remained in the service of the saint, Sháh Saidán Sarmast, who was a *faqír* of the Suharwardi sect. At the end of the twelfth year the saint saw that his own end was approaching and asked who was near him. The reply was, 'Daula', but the saint told him to go and fetch Mohku, *i.e.* his favorite Mangu. But Mangu refused to come as it was night. Thrice Daula went and thrice Mangu refused. The saint then remained silent for a while, but towards morning he roused himself and said :—'God gives to whomsoever He will'. He then made over his *dalg* (*faqír's* coat) to Daula, and when the latter said that he knew Mangu would not let him keep it, the saint said :—'Let him keep it who can lift it'. And so he gave the *dalg* into Sháh Daula's keeping, gave him his blessing also, and died.

When the day broke it became known that the saint was dead and Mokhu and all the other disciples took their parts in the funeral ceremonies. They then attempted to seize the holy *dalg*, which fell to the ground. Each in turn tried to lift it and then they tried all together, but it would not move until Daula grasped it with one hand, shook it and put it on, thus proving his right to the name and title, by which he has always been known, of Sháh Daula.

Making his way out of Siálkot, and leaving the jealous disciples, he hid himself for a while outside the town. For ten years after the death of Sháh Saidán Sarmast he remained in the neighbourhood, growing yearly in reputation and power. He built many buildings, mosques, tanks, bridges and wells, the most notable of which was the bridge over the Aik. After this Sháh Daula moved to Gújrát and settled there permanently in obedience to divine instructions.

Faqírs believe that each city has its guardian saint, and Sháh Daula is looked on as the guardian of Gújrát. During his life he devoted himself to works of public utility and the construction of religious buildings. His principal works were the bridge in front of the eastern gate of the town of Gújrát over the Sháh Daula Nálá, and the bridge over the Dík in the Gújránwálá District. It is said that he never asked for money and that he paid his labourers promptly. He was also most successful in finding the sites of old ruins, whence he dug up all the materials he required for his buildings. He was liberal to the poor, irrespective of creed, and had a peculiar attraction for wild animals, keeping a large menagerie of all sorts of beasts and birds. His tolerance made him beloved of all classes and there were both Hindus and Musalmáns among his disciples. He became very famous for his miracles and received large gifts. The attraction towards him felt by wild animals largely contributed to the general belief in him.

The emperor Akbar died whilst Sháh Daula was still at Siálkot, and it was in the seventh year of Jahángír that he went to Gújrát, in A. H. 1022 or A.D. 1612. No meeting between Sháh Daula and Akbar is recorded, but the following account is given of an encounter between him and the emperor Jahángír :—

Sháh Daula used to put helmets, with *raurís* sewn over them, on the heads of his favourite animals. One day a deer thus arrayed strayed near the place where the king, *i.e.* Jahángír, was hunting at Sháhdara near Lahore. The king saw the helmeted deer and enquired about it, and was told about Sháh Daula and his miracles. The deer was caught and two men were sent to fetch Sháh Daula who at that time was seated at his *khánqáh*. During the day he had remarked to his disciples :—'What a strange thing has our deer, Darbakhta, done! It has appeared before His Majesty and caused men to be sent to call me before him. They will come to-day. Cook a delicious *pilão* and all manner of food for them'. The astonished servants prepared the meal and towards evening the messengers arrived with His Majesty's order.

Placing the order on his head, Sháh Daula wished to start at once, but the hungry messengers had smelt the supper and so they stayed the night at the *khánqáh*, and did not take the Sháh to Sháhdara till the next day. When he arrived, he called for ingredients and made a large cake which he wrapped in a handkerchief and offered to the king when summoned. The king was seated on his throne with Núr Jahán Begam near by, and they were both much struck by his holy appearance. The king asked Sháh Daula where he had found the philosopher's stone, but he denied all knowledge of any such stone and said he lived on alms.

The king however saw in him a wealthy and influential person, capable of raising a revolt, and Núr Jahán suggested that he should be made away with. At the king's order the imperial chamberlain produced a poisoned green robe, which Sháh Daula put on without receiving any harm. A robe smeared with a still more deadly poison was then put on him and again no injury resulted. Upon this the king ordered a cup of poisoned *sharbat* to be mixed, but his throne began to quake, the palace rocked violently, and faces of *faqírs* were seen everywhere. The king in his fear recognised the saintship of Sháh Daula and dismissed him with honour and two bags of *ashrafís*. Giving the king his blessing, Sháh Daula departed after distributing the *ashrafís* to the royal servants. Hearing of this the king summoned him again and asked him if he would accept a grant of 5000 *bighás* of land. Sháh Daula replied that he did not want any land, but would avail himself of the offer later on, if necessary. Upon this the king allowed him to depart after showing him much reverence.

The building of the bridge over the Dík came about in this way: During one of the journeys of the emperor Sháh Jahán into Kashmír, the private belongings of Dára Shikoh and Hari Begam and many pack animals were lost in the Dík, which was in flood. The Faujdár of the District, Mirza Badi Usmán, was accordingly ordered to have a large and permanent bridge ready by the time the royal party returned. The Faujdár set to work, but could get nothing but mud bricks and so he imprisoned all the brick-burners. The result was that when the emperor returned the bridge was not even commenced. On being severely reprimanded, the Faujdár remarked that only Sháh Daula could build the bridge. The emperor at once ordered him to fetch Sháh Daula. By a stratagem he was induced to enter a palanquin and was carried off, but he remarked :—'There is no need to force me to obey the emperor's orders. I know them and will carry them out'.

Arrived at the Dík, Sháh Daula procured the release of the brick-burners and set about building the bridge. A wicked *gurú*, who inhabited the spot, destroyed the work as fast as it was done, but after a controversy in which he was overcome the *gurú* was lured into a lime-pit and buried up to his neck in lime and mortar by Sháh Daula.

Sháh Daula met with many other obstacles. Among them was one raised by Búta, the land-owner of the neighbourhood, who made money out of the ford at that spot. Búta cut the dam in order to drown the *faqírs* encamped underneath it, but Sháh Daula cleverly frustrated him by making a second dam below it. A *faqír* was sent to report on Búta's behaviour to Sháh Jahán, who ordered him to be sent to Lahore bound hand and foot, there to be beheaded and his head to be hung on a *ním* tree. But Sháh Daula interceded for him and obtained his release. Búta after this rendered every possible assistance, the bridge was duly built and Sháh Daula returned to Gújrát.

About this time a *faqír*, named Saidán, came to Gújrát and claimed the guardianship of the town by divine appointment in order to discredit Sháh Daula. By spiritual means Sháh Daula convinced the impostor that he was wrong, and the *faqír* disappeared and was never heard of again.

At that time female infanticide was rife in Rájaur, now a part of the Jammu State. Rájá Chattur Singh of Rájaur was a devoted follower of Sháh Daula, but he always killed his female children at birth. However, on the birth of one girl, Sháh Daula told him to let the child live, as she would be very fortunate and become the mother of kings. The child was therefore allowed to live and grew up a fair and lovely maiden, and when Sháh Jahán was passing through Rájaur on one of his journeys to Kashmír, the Rájá presented her to him as a *nazar*. The girl was accepted and bestowed on Prince Aurangzeb, who married her.

Later on, the prince, being anxious to know whether he or one of his brothers, Dára Shikoh and Murád, would succeed to the throne, went to see Sháh Daula and presented him with a *sar-murgh* (golden pheasant), a foreign cat and wooden stick. If the saint accepted all but the stick it was to be an omen that the prince would succeed. But Sháh Daula, as soon as he saw the prince, arose, saluted him as 'Your

Majesty', and giving him a cake, returned the stick and said :— 'God has sent you this cake, and this stick is granted you as the sceptre of your authority. Be of good cheer'. Aurangzeb told the tale to the Begam Baí, who confirmed him in his belief in it by relating Sháh Daula's prophecy that she herself would be the mother of kings. Her sons were Mu'azzim and Mahmúd, of whom the former became the emperor Bahádur Sháh.

At a later period, after he had become emperor, Aurangzeb again sent for Sháh Daula, who appeared before him in a miraculous manner. The emperor was dining by himself, but he saw that a hand was eating with him. Calling his attendants he told them of this, and said that the hand was the hand of an old man with the second finger missing. One of the attendants, named Bakhtáwar, said that the hand was probably Sháh Daula's. The emperor thereupon summoned the Saint to appear, when Sháh Daula at once stood revealed, and was dismissed, loaded with presents by the amazed sovereign.

Many other tales of his miracles are told of Sháh Daula, but that which is chiefly associated with his name is the miracle of the Chúhás or Rat-children, said to be born through his agency with minute heads, large ears, rat-like faces, and without understanding or the power of speech.

Sháh Daula lived to a great age, commonly stated to have been 150 years, and was contemporary with Akbar, Jahángír, Sháh Jahán, and Aurangzeb. He was born in the 25th year of Akbar, A.H. 989 or A.D. 1581 and died, according to the anagram of his death, *Khudadost*, in A.H. 1087 or A.D. 1676. He was therefore really 95 years old at his death.

His usual title is Sháh Daula Daryáí, because of the numerous bridges that he built. To the end of his life, princes and nobles, rich and poor alike, sought his blessing. At last, when he saw his end approaching he sent for his disciple, Bháwan Sháh, duly invested him with the *dalq*, and installed him as *sijáda-nashín* and successor.

The existing members of the sect of Sháh Daula claim that Bháwan Sháh is the son of the saint, but whether he was a real or an adopted son or *bálká*, the present *pírs* are the descendants of Bháwan Sháh.

Notes by the Editor, Indian Antiquary.

There are some points worth noting in the stories of Sháh Daula's Rats and of Sháh Daula himself.

In the first place it seems pretty clear from what has been above recorded that the ascription of the Chúhás to the agency of the well-known saint of Gújrát is posthumous. One suspects that Bháwan Sháh of the Sháh Daula Shrine created the cult, much in the fashion that Ghází Sultán Muhammad is creating one now out of the shrine which he has set up round the tomb of the great local saint. All the circumstances point to such a situation. These are the extreme modernness of the cult, the fact that a band or order of *faqírs* make a living out of a certain class of local microcephalous idiots, and the convenient existence of an important shrine Then the absence of landed property in possession of the band, or of any recognized right to succession to the leadership, and the entire dependence on earnings, in turn dependent themselves on the gullibility of the 'faithful', all make it almost certain that Bháwan Sháh took the opportunity of the then recent decease of a well-known ancient and holy man to find a sacred origin for the unholy traffic of his followers. The division of the income thus earned is just such as one might expect of a body that had no other source of cohesion originally than profit out of a common means of livelihood.

As regards the legend of Sháh Daula himself, we have the usual ascription of a direct connection by birth of a local holy man with the great ones of the earth in his day, with the usual clear openings for doubt in the account thereof, and we have also the ascription of miraculous powers common to Panjábí saints. There is nothing in the story that could not have been picked up by the tellers out of the tales of other saints commonly current in the country. No doubt there did live, during the seventeenth century, a holy man in Gújrát town, who died there at an advanced age and had a tomb erected to him, which became venerated. It is quite probable that he was instrumental in forwarding works of public utility in his neighbourhood, and was notorious for his charity to the poor and needy, led an excellent life, and was venerated by the nobility around him. Considering the situation of the town of Gújrát, it is quite possible also that he attracted the attention of the emperor Sháh Jahán and his suite, during their many journeys to and fro between Kashmír and their Indian court. But all this affords no ground for supposing that he had anything to do personally with the poor idiots now exploited by the sect, band, or order of *faqírs* that have fastened themselves on to his name.

As regards the Chúhás themselves, it is quite possible that there is a tendency to produce such idiots among the population of given districts, such as Púnch and Jammu, but one cannot help suspecting that, owing to the necessity for a continuous supply being forthcoming for the well-being of those who live on them, some of these unfortunates are artificially produced after their birth as ordinary infants. It would be so easy to accomplish this on the part of the unscrupulous.

The Cult of Mián-Bíbí ; or the Prince and His two Wives.

I.

The Legends of Mian-Bibi.

1. There are various stories as to who these saints were and when they first appeared. According to one account, Khwája Kasmi had five sons, Sháh Madár, Bholan Sháh, Shaikh Madu, Pír Sultán Sháh and Pír Jholan Sháh, and five daughters, Jal Pari, Mal Pari, Asman

Pari, Hur Pari and Sabz Pari. Of these, the tomb of Bholan Sháh exists at Jhonawál in tahsíl Garhshankar in Hoshiárpur. The other brothers and sisters are said to have become famous in other countries and died there. Another story is that Sháh Madár, who is referred to throughout the songs sung by the followers of Míán-Bíbí, was a Shaikh of Rúm by name Badr-ud-Dín. Being an adventurous man he migrated to India and took lodgings in the house of a person whose profession it was to amuse the king of that time with tricks. After his arrival in the house the host gained increasing favour from the king, which he thought was due to Sháh Madár's spiritual influence. Sháh Madár was called *Míán* by the daughter of his host, and they were called by him in return *Bíbí*. The girls became more and more attached to the Míán, and their belief in his supernatural powers grew stronger day by day. One day, it is said, the king, instigated by a minister who was jealous of the favour shown to the jester, ordered the latter to fight with a tiger. The jester, not being able to do this, asked the Míán's aid, and he by a miracle caused a tiger to go into the king's *darbár*, kill the jealous minister, and desist from doing further mischief at the bidding of the Míán's host. This astonished the king and the people, who sought out the author of the miracle, but the Míán was not pleased with the exposure of his powers and desired to leave the capital. The girls insisted that the Míán should not leave them, but he could not be persuaded to remain. At last seeing that the girls were determined to live or die with him, the Míán and his virgin-companions disappeared underground. It is not known where and when this happened, but the general belief as to the origin of Míán-Bíbí is as above described.

2. Another, and perhaps the most plausible story, is that Míán was a Shaikh by name Saddú of Delhi. He was well versed in medicine and pretended to have influence over evil spirits. He had a number of followers and maid-servants, the principal among whom were Míán Bholan Sháh, Míán Chanan, Míán Sháh Madár, Míán Maleri, Sháh Pari, Húr Pari, Mehr Pari, Núr Pari, Usmán Pari, and Gungan Pari. These are not Indian names, but the addition of the distinctive word *pari* signifies the exquisite beauty of these female companions of the Míán. These *paris* were more commonly called Bíbí, and the Shaikh was on account of his attachment to the women called Míán-Bíbí. The party travelled through many lands and preached the wondrous powers of their head, the Míán, and the women, being credulous, believed in the spiritual powers of the Míán, held him in great respect, and kept his memory green after his death by playing Míán-Bíbí in the manner explained later on. The Míán was extremely fond of women; he was shrewd enough to know that his pretensions would be readily believed by the weaker sex and worked exclusively among them, curing their diseases by his medical skill and attributing the success to his spiritual powers. It is said that the Míán was in possession of a lamp like the one Alauddín of the Arabian Nights had, and that with the aid of this wand he could get any woman he liked. It is said that the king's daughter fell in love with the Míán, and this being brought to the notice of the king, the Míán was killed and the lamp destroyed. His companions, fearing a similar fate, fled in different

directions, Bholan Sháh finding his last place of rest in Jhonawál, tahsíl Gaṛhshankar, and Mián Maleri at Malér Kotlá. Shah Madár escaped to the Deccan and Mián Chanan to Afghánístán, where their tombs are still found. It is said that this happened after Akbar's time.

The worshippers of Mián-Bíbí.

3. As above stated, the Mián and his wives were all Muhammadans, and their influence was at first confined to people of that creed. Gradually, as the time went on and communion between Hindus and Muhammadans became more general, the former followed the practices of the latter and *vice versâ.* The principal followers are Báhtís, Sainís and Mírásís, but Rájpúts and other classes of Hindus and Muhammadans are also found among them. In no case, however, does a male member propitiate the Mián-Bíbí *which is a deity of the female sex alone.* It is also remarkable that in most cases it is the young women who worship Mián-Bíbí, and as they become old they neglect it, although their regard for the deity is not diminished.

The method of Worship.

4. No fixed fair is held, nor is there any fixed time for the worship. Generally when the new harvest is gathered, and the people are at their best in point of wealth, a young woman who is a believer of the Mián-Bíbí prepares herself for the worship. None but a woman in want of a child, or of a bride for her child, or for relief from some distress, follows this practice, her object being to invoke the assistance of Mián-Bíbí in getting her wishes fulfilled. Mírásí women (professional songstresses) are called in with their instruments. The woman puts on a new dress, adorns herself as on her wedding day and sits in front of the *mirásans.* The latter sing songs in praise of the Mián, his manly beauty, and his devotion to the Bíbís and their mutual love and attachment. While singing, the *mirásans* also play on their instruments which consist of small drums. The worshipping woman moves her hands wildly, nods her head, and as chorus grows, she becomes excited and almost frenzied. At this stage it is believed that she forgets all about herself and that her spirit mingles with the thoughts of the Mián, whom she personifies so long as the fit caused by the excitement lasts. Other women who have belief in the spiritual powers of the devotee come and offer grain and sweets, which the *mirásans* appropriate. After making their offerings they put questions as to coming events in their families. Such questions generally relate to family distress and wants, and the devotee, knowing full well the wants of her neighbours, answers them in ambiguous terms, on which the women putting the questionf place the best possible construction and prove the spiritual power of mind-reading displayed by the devotee. It is believed that the Mián answers the questions through the devotee and fulfils the desires of those believing in him. The women practising the Mián-Bíbí devotional exercises in the above manner are distinguished by a silver tablet or piece hanging round their necks on which the Mián's picture is engraved and an amulet with the Bíbí's picture on it. [LALA DINA NATH.]

II.

Songs sung when Mián-Bíbí sways his head in an emotional trance.

A.—The káfís.

1. A *káfí* of Mián Sháh Madár.

Khele zinda Sháh Madár
Main tán tán jíwán,
Terá núr bhará dídár,
Terá maulá nál qarár
Khele zinda etc.

If the living (ever-living) Sháh Madár sways his head in an emotional trance or a hysterical woman falls into a trance, I shall live.

Thy (Sháh Madár's) countenance is beaming with the (heavenly) light and thou converseth with God.[1]

2. A *káfí* of Bullán Sháh.

Mián Bullán Sháh jawání mane,
Karm kare tán mainún jáne,
Terián ditián lakh karorán,
Tere wich darbár jo áwe,
Apnián man dián murádán páwe.
Terián ditián etc.

May'st thou, O Bullán Sháh, live long. If thou lookest kindly on my condition, thou wilt come and know of me. Thou hast blessed me with a myriad favours. He who appears before thee (*lit.*, in thy *darbár*) attains his heart's desires.

3. A *káfí* of Pír Bana Banoi.

Pír Banna jí main arz karán tere age,
Sab dulián nún pák jo
Kardá rati der na láge
Jinnán bhútán nún dúr tún kardá
Jot terí oh sahne láge
Pír banná.

To thee, O Pír Bannají, I present my appeal. Thou purifiest all who have lost heart and this thou does without the least delay. Thou drivest away (all) *jinns* and evil-spirits who flee in fear of thy glory.[2]

4. (a) A *káfí* of Mián Ala Bakhsh Gangohí.

Mere peshwá Ala Bakhsh Peshwá—
Mahbúb-i-Khudá Mámún Ala Bakhsh Peshwá
Mere Sáhib-i-Auliá Ala Bakhsh Peshwá
Doli pák karo mere Ala Bakhsh Peshwá.

On thou my Leader! Thou Ala Bakhsh, Peshwá! Thou art beloved of God and art protected by his peace.[3] Thou art protected by and beloved of God! Thou Ala Bakhsh, Peshwá! who art the best of saints! May'st thou purify my *doli*.

[1] The original is *Terá maulá nál qarár*, which may be translated, 'thou reposeth in peace in God'. *Qarár* means 'repose in peace.' But it is also explained to mean '*Terí báten khudá se hotí hain*', 'thou holdest conversation with God'.

[2] The original is *Jot terí oh sahne láge*, which is thus explained, *woh tere jalwá ko bardásht karne lag játe hain*, meaning 'they gradually bear thy glory.' But it is also explained to mean, *Tere jalwe se khauf khákar daur játe hain*, which is the translation given above.

[3] Mámún is explained as *Khuda ke amán se mahfúz*, or 'protected by the peace of God'.

4 (*b*). ANOTHER *káfí* OF THE SAME.

Mámún Ala Bakhsh pán ká birá
láwán tere pás.
Je tún kapron ká jorá mángen,
darsí buláwán tere pás
Je Mámún Ala Bakhsh dúdh pere
mujh se mánge,
Halwáí ko buláwán jhaṭ tere pás.
Je Mámún Ala Bakhsh pán birá
mánge,
Main panwárí ko buláwán fauran
tere pás.

O Mámún Ala Bakhsh! May I bring to thee *pán birá*. If thou needest clothes, I will call the tailor to thee. If thou wishest to have milk and *perá*, I will forthwith call the confectioner to thee. If thou desirest *pán*, I will at once call the *panwári* to thee.

5 (*a*). ANOTHER *káfí* OF BULLÁṆ SHÁH (to whose tomb it is addressed).

Tán main áwán tere pírá,
Deh murádán tún man dián pírá.
Terí chahár díwárí sariánwálí,
Terí qabar te jale charág pírá.
Tán main etc.
Khúhí terí thanḍí pírá,
Tere bágín bolan mor pírá.
Terí chahár diwárí khulí pírá
Tere hath wich sádí pírá.
Tán main etc.

To thee, O Pír! I will come if thou givest me my heart's desire. The four walls of thy house are studded with pearls, and lamps are lit on thy tomb. The water of the well of thy house is exceedingly cool and peacocks sing in thy garden, and thy enclosure walls are very wide. Thou art owner (protector) of good and bad actions.

5 (*b*). ANOTHER *káfí* OF BULLÁṆ SHÁH.

Bullán Sháh jawání máne.
Hun báhuren tán jánán.
Terián lakh karoran ditián.
Mián fazal karen tán jánán

May'st thou, Bulláṇ Sháh, advance in years. If thou art kind to me and fulfillest my desire, I shall know that thou art a true saint. Thy favours and boons are given in myriads. I will have faith in thee if thou dost kindness unto me.

6. A *káfí* OF GHAUS AZAM, PÍRÁN PÍR OF BAGHDÁD.

Mansá karat sukh charan tiháre
Merí murádán parsan piáre.
Jo sukh áwe so phal páwe
Ghauns Nabí ke láge piáre.
Mansá karat etc.

O thou, who fulfillest my desire I pray to thee on my knees. He who cometh to thee with a desire secures it and is beloved by Ghauṇs Nabí (a saint).

7 (*a*). ANOTHER *káfí* OF SHÁH MADÁR.

Sháh Madár main díwání dekho,
Sháh Madár main díwání.
Pírá tere áwan de qurbán, tún tán
roshan dohín jahánín
Kálá bakrá sawá man áṭá deo shá-
hán mihmání.
Sháh Madár main díwání, dekho
Sháh Madár main díwání.

See, O Shah Madár! I am mad with love for thee, O saint! If thou comest (to me), I will sacrifice myself to thee. Thy name is a light in this and the next world. If thou comest, I will offer a black goat and 1¼ maunds of flour for a feast to the saint. See, O Sháh Madár! I am mad with love of thee.

7 (*b*). Another *káfi* of the same.

Gund liyái málan phúlon ká sihrá.
Áj Míán tere sir ko mubárak.
Áp Míán jí ne kanganá bandháyá,
Núr ká batná ang lagáyá
Táj kuláh sir chhatar jhuláyá
Áj banrá tere sir ko mubárak.
Áj Míán etc.

The flower-girl has brought garlands of flowers. I congratulate thy head, O Míán! to-day. The Míán has his (left) wrist encircled with a bracelet and his body[1] besmeared with *batná*. I congratulate thy head, O bridegroom! thou who hast a crown and a cap on thy head and an umbrella over it.

B.—The thoughts of the Míán.

1. Khialat[2] Míán: *rág Kalián Áiman.*

Zinda Sháh Madár,
Allah kine áundá dekhiá?
Madár ní Madár,
Níle ghore wálá,
Sabz doshále wálá,
Bánkián faujáṇ wálá,
Kine áundá dekhiá.
Zinda Sháh Madár.

Has anybody seen the living (ever-living) Sháh Madár coming? Sháh Madár has a blue horse to ride and a green shawl to wear. His retainers are very handsome. Has anybody seen him?

2. Another song: same *rág.*

Berá banne láde jí merá berá banne lámná
Tárián denáṇ aukhí melá jí main
Sarwar semiáṇ mushkil karde ásán.
Tárián denáṇ etc.
Puttáṇ de kárau Dúlo seman máiyáṇ,
Man dián murádáṇ mere pír ne pujáiyáṇ.
Mushkil kar de ásán.
Tárián dená.

Oh Míán! let the ship of my life sail to the end, *i.e.*, let all my difficulties be removed. I have invoked thee in the time of my distress. Mayst thou remove my difficulties! O generous one, women worship thee for sons. I have attained my heart's desire by the grace of my Pír.

3. Another song: *rág Bihág tár tín.*

Kar nazar mehar dí jí
Míráṇ, jí Míráṇ
Main tain par bári-sadqe kítí qurbán Míráṇ
Kar nazar mehar dí jí Míráṇ.

Be kind unto me, O Míráṇjí (another name of the Pír). I sacrifice myself to thee. Be thou kind unto me.

4. Khial II., *Bihág tár tín.*

Mainuṇ hál Míráṇ dá dasiṇ?
Mainúṇ hál Míráṇ dá, etc.
Chár díwárí jhurmat wálí wich Míráṇ dí chaukhandí be.
Mainúṇ hál Míráṇ dá dasiṇ etc.

Tell me in what state is Míráṇjí? The four walls of Míráṇjí's house are shaded with rows of trees and he has a seat in the house (This refrain is repeated.)

[1] Meaning thereby that the Míán has besmeared his body with the light of God. This song is sung at wedding when the flower-girl brings garlands of flowers.

[2] A *khiál* is sung by *faqírs* with regard to the time of the day or night. A *khiál* must be sung at its proper time.

5. A *káfí* of Sháh Madár : *Rág Manji.*

(1) *Mírán áe ré Sháh jí áe ré,*
Sháh Madár áe re.
Albelá banrá Mírán áe re.
Mírán kí majlus khúb baní hai, pánch phúngal páe re.
Mírán áe re etc.

(1) Míránjí has come! Sháhjí has come! Sháh Madár has come! (These three names are identical.) The giver of desires, the bridegroom, the one devoid of care has come. His assembly is brilliant and a garland of flowers has been placed round his neck.

(2) *Nainán dá chálá sánún de gayá, main wári ho Mírán*
Nainán etc.
Laṭ paṭ chírá re,
Kesariá bándhí ré, ghúnghaṭ main kuch kah gayá.
Main wárí haún Mírán
Nainán dá chálá sánún de gaya etc.

(2) Míránjí has made me restless by the winking of his eyes. I sacrifice myself on thee, O Míránjí! His head-dress is dishevelled and it is of saffron colour. He has playfully whispered something to me in a language half concealed. I devote myself for thee, Oh! Míránjí! there is meaning in his playful glance.

(3) *Zindá Sháh Madár*
Merá Mírán áundá dekhá, hai Madár, hai.
Madár ní uddhár,
Merá Mírán áundá dekhá.

(3) Oh living (ever-living) Sháh Madár! I have seen my Mírán coming. He is Madár; He is Madár! (my) deliverer.

(4) *Sháh Madár, teríán Chaunkíán bhardí*
Núr bhariá dídár, Mera Mírán áundá dekhá.

(4) Oh Sháh Madár! I am waiting for thee.[1] Thy countenance is beaming with the light of God. Has anybody seen my Míránjí coming? (Here follows the refrain.)

6. Khial Kanhra : *rág Bíbí.*

(1) *Ala albelarían—Ala albelarían*
Merí Sháh Parí
Bhig gaíyán súhián chúnarían.
Main chalí piá bágh tamáshe,
Bhig gaiyán súhián chúnarían.
Ala albelarían etc.

(1) Oh my God! The *Bíbíán* (*i.e.*, Shah Parí and others), are free from care and all control. Oh my Shah Parí! Thy red-coloured *dopaṭṭa* (body-sheet) is wet. I am going to witness amusement in the garden of my beloved.

(2) *Sháh Madár ke darbár men khele Sháh Parí, ohdíán kasumbarián cholarián re, báhín chúre hare re, merí Sháh Parí.*
Sháh Madár etc.

(2) Shah Parí, who is attired in a *cholí* (petticoat) dyed with *kasumbha* and who wears green glass bangles (*chúrís*) round her wrist, is swaying her head to and fro in a frenzy in the Darbár of Sháh Madár.

[1] *Chaukí bharná.* When women have made vows to saints and their vows are fulfilled, they repair to the saint's residence and sit there for a day and a night. This is called *chaukí bharná.* The Bharáis or priests of Sakhi Sarwar derive their name from this rite.

III.

The most remarkable fact about this cult of Míán-Bíbí is that it has been so completely Muhammadanized; and it is suggested (I., 2 above) that this cult was introduced into India after Akbar's time, *i.e.* after that ruler had attempted to found a new religion amalgamating all the creeds of his empire. On the other hand, it is clearly connected with the famous shrine of Shaikh Máler, the founder of the Máler Koṭla State in the Punjab. There a similar cult exists, an account of which is given in the *Gazetteer* of that State. It might be imagined that the cult is a mere adaptation of a Hindu myth, but this is by no means certain, and it is quite possible that it is an importation of pure Muhammadan mysticism :—

Shaikh Sadr-ud-Dín.—Shaikh Sadr-ud-Dín, the founder of the Máler Koṭla ruling family, flourished during the reign of Sultán Bahlol Lodhi, who gave him his daughter in marriage in 1454.[1] Commonly styled Hazrat Shaikh, Sadr-ud-Dín or Sadr Jahán left Darában, his birth-place in Afghánistán, and settled at Máler on an old branch of the Sutlej. An aged Musalmán woman, named Máli, became his first follower and from her Máler takes its name. From the princess are descended the keepers of the shrine while the Nawábs of Máler Koṭla are descended from a Rájpútni whom the Shaikh also married. His shrine, surrounded by four walls believed to have been built by genii in one night, lies in Máler. His fair, held on the first Thursday of every lunar month, is largely attended by Hindus and Muhammadans from the State as well as from distant places. Various offerings are made, such as horses, donkeys, cows, buffaloes, goats, fowls, clothes, money, grain of all kinds, food (especially sweet bread and that cooked in a frying pan) etc. Of these offerings the *khalífa*, a descendant of the Shaikh, takes elephants, horses, donkeys, complete suits of clothes and rupees, while all other offerings are taken as of right by the *majáwars*. People of all castes have great faith in Hazrat Shaikh. No marriage is considered blessed unless the bridegroom attend the shrine and *salám* to it immediately after donning the wedding wreath and before leaving for his bride's home. Women believe that all worldly desires are fulfilled by the Shaikh. To gain any wish they vow to make a specified offering to the shrine in case it is realised. They often perform the ceremony called '*Hazrat Shaikh ki chauki*'. Sometimes they keep awake the whole night and employ a *mirásan* who sings songs, especially eulogies of the Shaikh, and sometimes play the *chauki* in the day time. The woman who is to do this, bathes, puts on the best new clothes she can get and sits on the bare ground with other women round her. The *mirásan* beats her drum and sings the Shaikh's praises. At first the woman sits silent with her head lowered and then begins to roll her head with hair dishevelled. Then the *mirásan* sings more vigorously, generally repeating over and over again the part of the song at which the woman showed the first signs of having fallen under the Shaikh's influence. In a few moments the Shaikh expresses through the woman what he wants of her and what she must do for him and where. After this all the women round her question her and receive her responses. She then attends the

[1] Just as tradition says Adham Faqír married the King's daughter.

shrine and offers something according to her promise. In Jeṭh and about the time of the Namáni fair, on the Jeṭh *sudi*, the attendance at the fair of Hazrat Shaikh is very large, people of all creeds and ages and of both sexes being attracted to it from long distances.

A curious parallel to the cult of Míáṇ-Bíbí is afforded by that of Síndhu Bír who, like the Míáṇ, has three pairs of attendant goddesses, *viz.* Ráṛi and Bráṛi, Cháhṛi and Chhatrahṛi, all worshipped in Chamba, and Andla and Sandla who are worshipped in the hills. The goddess Bharmáni of Barmaur, in Chamba, is also associated with Síndhu. The cult of Míáṇ-Bíbí is probably of phathic origin, though such a theory cannot be definitely proved. The parallel afforded by Síndhu's pairs of wives is, however, too striking to be accidental. Síndhu is certainly a god of fertility adored by all the seven 'Banáspati Mothers', who are goddesses of vegetation. But he is also 'lord of metals', Lohán Pál, of the earth, Bhúmi Pál, and of chains, as Sanglíṇ Pál. As the last-named he has with him always a chain and his votaries also keep one at their homes. Síndhu Bír affects mountainous regions generally and is even said to be widely worshipped in Láhul. He becomes enamoured of fair maidens and they dance with him. But he has small ears or none at all, and often carries a broom on his back. He wears a cotton girdle though the rest of his costume is like that of Gaddi or shepherd and when not whistling he makes the sound *chhuá chhú* which shepherds use when grazing their sheep, resting or fatigued. Indeed he is also called Laknu Gadetu or 'Lukhna the Gaddi youth', with whom Gaddi maidens fall in love.[1]

A NOTE ON *BAIAT*.

Baiat, bai, or 'sale' of self, denoting 'one should give up one's own desires and submit wholly to the will of him to whom one sells oneself.' To make *baiat* implies faithful obedience as set forth in the Holy *Qurán* and the doctrines inculcated by the Prophet as well as by the acts of his Caliphs.

The *baiat* made at the hands of Prophets and the appointed ones of God is made solely with a view to attain to piety. God said to His Prophet Muhammad—

"Those who pledge their faith to thee pledge it to God, the hand of God is over their hands—hence whoever shall break his oath will suffer for it and whoever shall perform what he covenanted with God to him He will give a great reward."

In the Chapter called *mumtahina* (Examination or Trial) God addresses His Prophet thus:—

"O Prophet when believing women come unto thee and make *baiat* that they shall not confuse anyone with God, nor steal, nor commit fornication, nor kill their children, nor come with a calumny which they (the women) have forged in front of their hands and feet, nor be disobedient to thee in doing good things; take their pledge and pray to God to forgive their sins—God is prepared to forgive and is merciful."[2]

[1] For a song to Síndhu Bír see *Indian Antiquary*, 1909.

[2] Verse 10—Chapter Fatah (Victory) of the *Qurán*.

It is mentioned in the *Sáhih Bokhári* in the conditions on which the Imám should accept a pledge that Ismaíl, son of Abu Obais, said that he had been told by Imám Málik, who was told by Yahya, son of Said Ansári, who was told by Ibada, son of Walid, who was told by his father, who in his turn was told by his father Saint Abada that:—"We pledged our faith to the Prophet to bey his orders in prosperity and in suffering, to acknowledge the supremacy of him who should be fit for it and not to dispute with him—that we should adhere to what is right wherever we lived—that we should tell the truth and that in God's path we should not fear the reproach of any persecutor. We were told by Abdulla, son of Yúsaf, who was told by Imám Málik, who was told by Abdulla, son of Dínár, who was told by Abdulla, son of Umar, that when we pledged our faith to the Prophet that we would obey his orders he said: 'Say so far as may be possible.'"

Baiat should be made thus:—If the one who makes it is a man he who accepts his pledge should take his hands in his own and recite the words pertaining to *baiat* and the other who makes the *baiat* should repeat them; after the repetition of the *baiat* the Imám, *i.e.*, the receiver of the pledge, and those present should pray for the stability of the faith of the pledger. If the plighter of faith be a woman an oral pledge is taken from her—but her hand is not touched—as is described in the *Sáhih Bokhári* regarding Hazrat (holy) Aisha that the Prophet received oral pledges from women in accordance with the *mumtahina*. The Prophet's hand touched no woman save his own wives. But now-a-days some receive the pledge from a woman by holding a cloth which is also held by her.

LEGEND OF DÚLLÁ BHAṬṬÍ.

Argument.

Dullá or Dúllá, son of Faríd Khán, is a Bhaṭṭi Rájpút of the Sandal Bár or Sandalwál. He goes to Naina Bás village to enjoy the *phág* festival in the Holi and during his absence Jalál-ud-Dín, his uncle, goes to Akbar, the Mughal emperor, to inform him that Dúllá is a highwayman. The emperor deputes Mirzas Alá-ud-Dín and Ziá-ud-Dín to seize Dúllá. Alá-ud-Dín goes to the Sandalwál with 12,000 men. Núramde, Dúllá's wife, dreams that her golden bedstead is broken and interprets this omen to mean that Dúllá's misdeeds will end in disaster. But her mother-in-law boasts of Dúllá's strength. A Ḍogar woman announces that during Dúllá's absence the imperial troops are advancing to the attack. She borrows the five garments of Dúllá's wife and goes among the soldiery hawking curds. Alá-ud-Dín wants to buy some and puts his finger into the jar to taste the curds, whereupon the Ḍogari grips his arm with such strength that he cannot make her let go. The Mirza, in admiration of her physique, offers to make her his chief wife—he has 360 already—and mounts her on his horse. On the road she borrows his sword, on the pretence that she will chase deer, and plunges it into his heart. She carries off his five garments to Dúllá's mother. Ziá-ud-Dín, the murdered Mirza's brother, hearing of his death lays waste the Sandalwál. Núrá, Dúllá's son, rejecting his teacher's advice to flee, demands his father's sword from his grandmother. Ignoring his mother's entreaty that he will save himself he takes the sword and kills 25 of his opponents, but his sword breaking he is captured, and all his relatives with him. His younger sister begs Jalál-ud-Dín to effect her release, but he basely refuses. Dúllá's wife now sends a *mirási* with a letter to Dúllá imploring aid. Dúllá immediately attacks the Imperial troops and rescues his son, with the others. He is about to put Ziá-ud-Dín to death when his mother intercedes, saying he will dishonour her by the murder, but, disregarding her prayers, Dúllá smites the Mirza on the mouth and knocks out his teeth.

The following songs and ballads are inserted here for the sake of the light which they cast on Punjab ways of thought and the relations which exist between the various creeds and castes. The Tale of Mirza and Sáhibán is peculiarly rich in omens :—

Qissa Dúllá Bhaṭṭí Rájpút sákin mausa Sandalwál, ya Sandal Bár Jangal, mutallaqa Zilla Montgomery.

Akbar Sháh bádsháh ke samána meṇ Dúllá Bhaṭṭí Rájpút thá.
Líjie nám Rabb ká, kardega berá pár.

QISSA.

1. *Chandá kí bairí bádlí, machhlí ká bairí jál :*
Bandá kí bairan maut hai, nahí ke din char.
2. *Mardáṇ núṇ badíáṇ likhdí, loháṇ núṇ kíte ṭá'ú :*
Mirgáṇ núṇ dhúpán likhdí, súráṇ ko kíte ghá'ú.
3. *Sukh se soyí sej par supná ágyá rát,*
Sowarn palang marhiá, ṭúṭe chároṇ sál.[1]
4. *Máthe kí bindí bhúṇ parí, merí nau bal khága'í náth,*
Churá phúṭá háthí dánt ká, phíká pará suhág.
5. *Ghore áweṇ ṭhumakde, karde máro már,*
Kiá Dúllá terá qaid meṇ, luṭjá Sandalwál :
6. *'Sás! Yih badíyáṇ haiṇ burí!'*

JAWAB LADDHBI WALIDA DULLA AE BAHU :—

7. *Bolí Laddhí : "Kya kahe? sunle bahúr bát :*
Gidrí ne jáye pánch sát, maiṇ shíhní ne jáyá ek ;
8. *Jad mera Sher dharúktá kartá máro már!*
Faujáṇ bádsháhí bhágjáṇ, murke ná letí sáṇs."

BAHU SAS SE KAHTI HAI :—

9. *Bole Núramde : "Kya kahe? sunle sású, bát :*
Kiá choráṇ ke mámla, kiá jhúṭe ká 'aitbár?
10. *Jaisá Dúllá túṇ janá, aisa jane ná ko :*
Rát nachdwe kanchaní, din meṇ khele shikár.

[1] *Lit.* the horizontal pieces, *shál*, not the legs. The breaking of a bed is always regarded as a disastrous omen, and the overturning of a bed under a sleeping man is a favourite way of manifesting divine or saintly displeasure against him.

11. *Bhíṛ purí meṇ bhágjá, hamko ná lejá sáth.*
Ai sás rí. Tu barjle pút ko, badíyáṇ haiṇ búri".

Kalam Ḍogari az walida Dulla :—

12. *Bole Masto Ḍogarí: "Sunle, Laddhí bát!*
Páṇcho lá de kapre, solá láde singár".
13. *Páṇcho pahne kapre, bharla'e solá singár.*
Sir dhar maṭkí dúdh kí, áwe lashkar darmiyán.
14. *Dahí dahí púkártí lashkar ke darmiyán:*
Dahí mángí Mirza 'Alá-ud-dín: "Maináṇ thora dahí de chakhá'e!"
15. *Bharke únglí chakh dá pahúnchá pakṛá já'e,*
"Gud budh, gud budh kyá kare? Sidhí bolí bol!
16. *"Márúngí lapeṛá khenchke, tere battís jhar jáeṇge dánt:*
Dekhá nahíṇ Dúllá Rájpút ká? Terá lashkar dúṇ luṭwá'e,
17. *Bhalá cháhe, ḍerá úṭhá le, nahíṇ lashkar dún luṭwá'e".*
Bole Mirza: "Kyá kahe? Sunle, Masto, bát!
18. *Us Dúllá ke kyá kare? sang hamáre chal,*
Begamát tín sau sáṭh, sab kí karúṇ sirdár.
19. *Sone meṇ kardúṇ chamakdí, sang hamáre chal.*
Maṭkí chaṭki phorde, charhle ghoṛe par."
20. *Pakaṛ báṇh bíṭhálaí, pare Dehlí ke ráh.*
Dekh súrat ko ro parí, Mirza kare jawáb.
21. *Je kaṭárá mere háth de, mirgáṇ ko márún já.*
Súṭke kaṭárá Ḍogarí ne báhdíá Mirza ke kalje máṇh.
22. *Páncho̤ṇ líye kapre, páncho̤ṇ líye hathyár:*
Ghoṛá joṛá lelíá, áwe Sandalwál.

23. *Ghoṛá ládía thán se, Laddhí se karí salám:—*
'Ibárat. Mirza 'Alá-ud-dín jab márágyá, to bhái Mirza Ziá-ud-dín ne suná, to woh Sandalwál ko lúṭne lagá.
24. *Dúm aur Bháṭ lúṭíye dete kabit suná'e.*
Khási kanchaní lúṭíye, luṭgyá mál hawál.
25. *Dúlle ká chácha lúṭíye, luṭgyá mál hawál,*
Maulá kaláli lúṭíye, dende phúl sharáb.
26. *Bole Miáṇjí: "Kya kahe? Sunle Núre bát!*
Já beṭe, bhágjá, nahín parjá bádshdh kí qaid."
27. *Je, Qázi, maiṇ bhágjáún, kul ko áwe láj.*
Chalke Núrá dándá áwe mahlán ke mán:
28. *Háth bándh karúṇ bentí, dádí, sabko merá sát salám,*
Maináṇ mián ká khaṇḍá ánde pahunchúṇ faujon darmiyán".
29. *Bole Laddhí: "Kyá kahe? Sunle, beṭe, bát!*
Já, beṭe mere, bhágjá, nahíṇ parjá bádsháh kí qaid".
30. *"Jo, dádí, maiṇ bhágjáúṅ, mere kul ko áwe láj"*
Miáṇ se súte misrí, áwe dehorí kí bár.

31. *Pachchhís jawánán ko káṭdá káṭe Mughal Paṭhán,*
Amar se khanḍá túṭgyá, lohe ne dedí hár.
32. *Sir se chíra tárke da'í mushkán bándh,*
Núrá paṛgyá qaid men, paṛgya bádsháh kí qaid.
33. *Núramde Phulamde bánd hogaí, pargayí bádsháh kí qaid:*
Mátá Laddhí bandhgayí, paṛgayí bádsháh kí qaid:
34. *Phúpphí Shamash bandhgayí, paṛgayí bádsháh kí qaid:*
Beṭí Salemo bandhgayí, mián kahtí já'e?
35. *Bole Salemo: "Kya kahe? Sunle, dádá Jalál Dín, bát!*
Bándí karke chhúṛá, húngí dáman gír."
36. *"Bádsháh kí qaid men tum parí, potí, mere ghí ke bali chirágh"*
"Dádá, tukhm Rájpút ká nahín hai, kisí bándí ká jám."
37. *"Jo jítí muṛke ágayí, dángí khál kaḍhá'e!"*
(Líjiye nám Rab ká, kardegá beṛá pár!)
38. *Bole Núramde: "Kyá kahe? Sunle, mirásí, bát!*
Le parwána pahúnchiye, jáye Nainá bás."
39. *"Chaṛhná ho, tum chaṛh chalo, luṭgayí Sandalwál."*
Le parwána mirásí ne já día Dúllá ke háth.
40. *Bole Dúllá: "Kyá kahe? Sunlo, jawánon, bát!*
Jhaṭá jhaṭ káṭhí parga'í, bandhgaí sone ke zín."
41. *De dobáglí pasne áwen lashkar darmiyán.*
Lashkar báje misrí karte máro már.
42. *Fauján Sháh kí bhágján, bháge Mughal Paṭhán.*
Bole Núra: Kya kahe? Sunle, mián, merí bát!
43. *Zara mushkán kholde, dekhle Núre ke háth.*
Jhaṭá jhaṭ múshkán khulgayí, ghoṛí ká kíá sowár.
44. *Lashkar báje misrí, karte máro már.*
Chalke Ziyá-ud-dín awtá áwe Laddhí ke pás:
45. *Beṭá karke bachále, main húngá dámangír!*
Itne men Dúllá pahunchgyá, áwe mátá ke pás:
46. *"Ran ká chor baládde, Mátá, sach batá"!*
"Beṭá ran ká chor bhággyá: pahúncha Delhí darmiyán"
47. *Bole Mirza: "Kya kahe? Sunle, mátá, bát!*
Beṭá karke bachále terá húngá dámangír."
48. *Bole Laddhí: "Sun, beṭá Dúllá, bát!*
Jo tú usko márta, merí battís dhár hardm."
49. *Márá leperá khenchke Mirza ke battís jhaṛgaye dánt.*

Misri Talwar.

Dullá Rájpút beṭá Faríd Khán rahnewála Sandalwál ká thá. Mauza Nainá Bás men Holí ká phág khelne giáhuá thá. B'ád uske jáne ke uske chháchá Jalál Dín Akbar bádsháh Delhí ke pás gíá and jákar faryád kari ki Dullá musáfaron ko lúṭ letá hai. Bádsháh ne Mirza 'Alá-ud-Dín wa Ziá-ud-dín ko bhejá ke Dullá ko pakaṛ láo

Mirza bárá hazár fauj lekar Sandalwál men ayá. Ek roz rát ko Núramde Dullá ki istrí ne supná dekha, ki sowarn palang ṭúṭ gaya, bas apní sás se yeh kahá ki yeh hái burí hotí hai, tera beṭa musáfron ko lúṭta hai: sás ne kaha ki mene apna beṭa aisa jana hai ki mánind Shair ke hai. Ḍogrí guwálan Dullá kí mán ke pás áí, us se Dullá kí mán ne kaha ki merá beṭa yahán maujúd nahín hai. Badsháhí fauj larne ko áyí hai kiya karún. Ḍogri guwálan ne kahá ki apni lahú ke páncho kapre mujhe dede men lashkar ki khabar láún. Woh kapre pahankar dahí kí hánḍi sir par rakh kar fauj Bádshahí men dahí bechne ko áyí aur lashkar ke darmiyán án kar kahá ki aisa koí hai ki jo merí dahí mol le. Mirza 'Alá-ud-dín ne dahí mángí jab woh lekar gayí Mirza ne unglí dahí men bhar kar zubán se lagání cháhí thí ki Ḍogrí ne Mirza ká háth pakar liya aur woh is qadr táqat rakhtí thí Mirza ne harchand cháha ki háth chhuráláún magar nahín chhura saka. Mirza ne apne dil men kahá ki agar isko men apne ghar lejáún aur is se bálbache paida honge to niháyat zoráwar honge. Mirza ne us se kahá tú mere sáth chal, merí tín sau sáṭh begamát hain, unpar sirdár tujh ko karúnga. Woh uske sáth holí, rástah men mirg ghás chug rahe the. Mirza ki súrat ko dekh kar roparí. Mirza ne púchha kis wáste rotí hai, usne kahá ki mere pás hathiár hota to unko martí: main aksar shikár khela kartí hún. Mirza ne apna khanḍa usko dedíya, us ne qábú pakar Mirza ke khanḍa márá woh margaya aur Mirza ke pánchon kapre lekar Dullá kí mán ke pás áyi.

Ziyá-ud-dín Mirza 'Alá-ud-dín ke bhái ne yih hál suna, usne bázár men lúṭ lagádí. Miánjí ke yahán Dullá ká beṭá Nurá nám parhtá thá. Miánjí ne us se kahá ki bhágjá, usne kahá ki merá kám bhágne ka nahín hai, merí kul ko láj áwe. Miyánjí ke pás se apne mahlon men áyá, apni dádí se háth jorkar kahá ki merá sat salám hai, miyán ká khanḍa dedo. Mán ne kahá ki beṭa tú bhágja nahín to bádsháh kí qaid men parjáwega, usne kahá ki jo main bhág jáúnga to kul ko láj lagegí aur talwár lekar pacchís jawán máre. Amar se khanḍa ṭúṭgaya, tab Ziyá-ud-dín ne giraftár karlíya aur uskí mushkán bándhín aur uskí dono mán ko giraftár karlíyá aur uskí phúphí ko giraftár karlíyá aur us kí bhain ko giraftár kar líyá. Woh larkí Jaláldín se kahne lagí ki dáda mujko qaid se chhuráo, usne kahá ki main nahín chhuráúnga. Dúllá kí zojah ne parwána likh kar Mirásí ko diya ki yeh Dullá ke pas lejáo. Woh parwána lekar gaya aur Dullá jhaṭ paṭ agaya aur bádsháhí fauj ko márne laga aur apní beṭe kí mushkán kholdí aur Mirza Ziyá-ud-dín ke márne ko chala. Ziá-ud-dín Dullá kí mau ke pás ayá aur us se panáh mángí, us ne apne beṭe se kaha, jo tu isko márega merá dudh tere par harám hai, usne ek tamáncha aisa Mirza ke márá ki Mirza ke battí dánt ṭúṭ gaye.

TRANSLATION.

The story of Dúllá, the Bhaṭṭí Rájpút, who dwelt in Sandalwál village or in the Sandal Bár, a steppe adjoining the Montgomery District.

In the time of the emperor Akbar there lived one Dúllá, a Bhaṭṭí Rájpút. Take the name of the Lord, He will grant victory.[1]

[1] Literally, will bear the boat across.

Story.

1. The cloud is the enemy of the moon, and the net of the fish:
   Man's enemy is death, and his days of doing good but a few (*lit.* four).
2. Trouble is the lot of Man, and often is the iron plunged into the fire:
   The sun is the lot of the deer, and wounds are a hero's lot.

Song.

Dúllá's wife:—

3. "I was asleep on my bed at ease, when last night I had a dream,
   My golden bed creaked and its four legs broke.
4. My frontlet fell to the ground and my nose-ring twisted badly,[1]
   My ivory wristlets broke, and my wedded happiness turned to sadness.
5. The horse came galloping rapidly;
   Dúllá has been captured, and the Sandal Bár been raided![2]
   (She moralises on her dream:—)
6. Oh mother-in-law! These deeds (of Dúllá) are indeed evil."
   Reply of Dullá's mother, Laddhí, to her daughter-in-law:—
7. "Said Laddhí: what sayest thou, listen, daughter-in-law!
   The jackal had a litter of five or seven, I, the lioness, brought forth one only."
8. When my lion roars, he shouts: 'Kill! kill!'
   The king's forces flee and do not turn to take breath.
   The daughter-in-law says to her mother-in-law:—
9. Said Núramde: "What sayest thou, listen, mother-in-law,
   Why dost thou boast of a robber's and a liar's deeds?
10. May no one bear a son like Dúllá:
    By night he holds a dance of courtezans, by day he hunts (*i.e.*, he robs).
11. In trouble he flees away and takes not us with him.
    O good mother, admonish thy son, his deeds are indeed evil."[3]
    The Ḍogar's wife speaks:—
12. Said Masto Ḍogarí: "listen, Laddhí, to me,
    Bring the five robes and sixteen ornaments."

[1] Literally, nine times.

[2] This is part of the dream.

[3] *Cf.* verse 5 above.

13. She put on the five robes and bedecked herself with the sixteen ornaments.
Putting a pot of milk on her head she went in among the troops.

14. She hawked her curds among the troops.
Mirza Alá-ud-Dín asked for a curd, he said "give me a little to taste!"

15. Taking it up with his fingers he tasted it. She grasped his arm and said:
Why dost thou talk nonsense? Talk plain sense.

16. I will buffet you, and all your thirty-two teeth will fall out:
Hast thou not seen Dúllá Rájpút,

17. If you wish for your own good, strike your camp, else I will have it plundered.
Said the Mirza, What sayest thou? Hearken Masto!

18. What wilt thou do with thy Dúllá? Come with me.
I have three hundred and sixty ladies, of all will I make thee queen (mistress).

19. I will make thee glitter with gold. Come with me.
Break the jar, and mount my steed.

20. Grasping her arm he placed her in the saddle, and took the Delhi road.
Looking in his face she felt a-weeping and the Mirza inquired the cause.

(The Ḍogrí replied)—

21. "If thou wilt give me your dagger, I will go and kill deer."
Drawing the dagger she, the Ḍogrí, thrust it into the Mirza's heart.

22. She took the five robes and the five weapons.
Taking his horse and his garments she came to Sandalwál.

23. She tethered the horse in the stable and greeted Laddhí.
When Mirza Alá-ud-Dín had been killed his brother Mirza Ziá-ud-Dín heard of it. He began to ravage the Sandal Bár:—

Verses.

24. He plundered the Ḍúm and the Bhâṭ; they chanted verses.
He plundered the chief prostitutes, goods and chattels.

25. He plundered Dúllá's uncle of his goods and chattels:
He plundered Maulú the vintner who sold the wine.

26. The Míáṇ said to Núrá[1]: listen to me.
"Fly hence or the King will cast you into the prison."

[1] Dúllá's son.

27. O Qází, if I flee dishonour will fall on my family.
Núrá went to his palace.

28. "With joined hands, grandmother, I beseech thee sevenfold greeting to all.
Give me my Lord's sword: I will go among the forces."

29. Laddhí said:—"What sayest thou? Hearken, my son!
Flee or the royal prison awaits thee."

30. Grandmother, if I fly, disgrace will befall my kin.
He drew the sword from its scabbard, and came out of the porch.

31. He slew outright twenty-five of the Mughal Paṭhán youth.
By fate's decree his sword broke and the steel betrayed him.

32. Taking the turban from his head they bound his hands behind him.
Thus was Núrá taken, taken and cast into the imperial prison.

33. Núramade and Phulamde [1] were taken captive and cast into the imperial prison.
The mother Laddhí was taken, and cast into the prison.

34. Shamash, the aunt of Dúllá, was taken, and cast into the prison.
Salemo, his daughter, was taken, calling on her father.

35. Said Salemo:—"Listen grandfather Jalál-ud-Dín
Release me as a slave girl, or I will seize thy skirt!" [2]

36. "Thou hast fallen into the imperial prison. I will fill my lamp with *ghí*." [3]
"Grandfather, thou art of no Rájpút stock, but the son of a slave-girl."

37. "If I return alive, I will have thee flayed."
Repeat the Lord's name [4] for He will take the boat across.

38. Said Núramde:—Listen *mirási*,
Take this letter to Nainabás.

39. If thou desirest to attack, then attack quickly, Sandalwál has been plundered.
The *mirási* took his letter and gave it into Dúllá's hand.

[1] Wives of Dúllá.

[2] In the next world. A better translation appears to be —Thou hast got me imprisoned at last, but at the Day of Judgment I will seize thy skirt, *i. e.* 'accuse thee of this wrong.' Salemo knows Jalál-ud-Dín to be the cause of her distress, but will not stop to implore his mercy.

[3] In sign of rejoicing.

[4] Spoken by the poet.

40. Dúllá said 'Listen, comrades!'
And in a moment the saddles were on, with the gold laced saddle cloths.

41. On both sides they attacked and came into action.
Swords rang in the field, and (Dúllá's men) slew right and left.

42. The King's forces fled, fled the Mughal and Paṭhán.
Said Núra :—"Listen father, to my words !

43. Loose my bonds a little and see Núra's deeds."
Speedily his bonds were loosened, and he mounted a mare.

44. Swords rang in the field and (Dúllá and his men) slew right and left.
Ziá-ud-Dín came on foot to Laddhí :—

45. "Save me as if I were thy son I will cling to thy skirt (hereafter)."
Meanwhile Dúllá came up and drew near his mother : —

46. "Point out to me the thief[1] of the field ; mother tell me truly.
My son the chief of the field has fled and reached Delhi."

47. Said the Mirza : "Mother hear me !
Save me as thy son or I will seize thy skirt."

48. Said Laddhí—Listen Dúllá, my son
If you slay him you will defile my thirty-two streams of milk.

49. He gave the Mirza a buffet which knocked out his thirty-two teeth.

THE STORY OF DAYÁ RÁM THE GUJAR, BY KALA JOGI, OF KHAUḌA IN THE AMBÁLA DISTRICT.

Jag meṇ rahe Gújar jaisí nanhí dúb,
Aur ghás sab jal jáengí, rahegí dúb kí dúb.
Gújar kí Gujráṭi bóle : —" Sun Dayá, merí bát,
Soná chándí bohtá pahná, motí pahne ná'e,
Liáde mujhe sánche mótí.
Motí kí larián láde, pahnáṇgí sánche motí,
Motí par shauq merá, motí bigar[2] maiṇ na jítí."
Jíse Dayá Rám dádhárí, sohní súrat par wárí.
" Gujarí ne tere bolí márí bhar ke márá tír
Yá láde mujhe sánche motí yá hojá faqír.
Chádar Gujrát kí láde, lahṇghá Multán ká láde
Sálú Sángáner ká láde, kanghí Karnál kí láde,
Missí Dihlí kí láde, mehndí Nárnaul kí láde,

[1] Runaway.
[2] *Bigar*, for *baghair*.

*Chá*ṛ*á Pánípat ká láde, surma Panjáb ká láde.*
Jútá Péshâwar ká láde."
Jíwe Dayá Rám dúdhárí, sohní súrat par wárí.
*Ba*ṛ*í Gujarí motí mánge, chho*ṭ*í ho dilgír,*
Rotí Gujarí sás pá áwe, nainán ḍ*haltá nír :—*
" Saukan merí motí mánge, Dayá kahín márájágá
Gánwarí súnni hójá'égí,
*La*ṛ*ke máre ro marenge,*
Motí kis par pahnégí "
Jíwe Dayá Rám dúdhárí, sohní súrat par wárí.
" Ná mátá merí sár sár ro'e, na jhúre man mén,
Ab ke phere yún karjánye, Dayá janmán ná'ie,
Moi'e ká to sóg[1] *na kaííye, ranwás*[2] *kí sewá karíye,*
*Ran men be*ṭ*e ko páe, Gúmri ká ráj karíye."*
Jíwe Dayá Rám etc.
" Lá Gujarí, mere pánchon kapre, lá mere pánchon hathiár,
*Thán se lá merí Lailí gho*ṛ*í, main ho chalún sawár,*
Ḍ*olán ko jáke gherún lá dún tujhe sánche motí,*
Gujarí tujhe án pahnádún."
" Saián mere jítá rahye !
Amí[3] *jal pítá rahye*
*U*ṛ*já'e terá bhawar nimáná,*
Dunyá se kyá le jáná ?
Nekí tere sang chalegí,
Badí badsháh ke já'ége."
Jíwe Dayá Rám etc.
*Chhinkte Dayá ne gho*ṛ*í perí cha*ṛ*h ton* ṭ*ú*ṭ*á tang,*
Yá Gújar kahín márájá'egá, yá machégá jang.
Jíwe Dayá Rám etc.
Orá barje,[4] *Dhore barje, barje sab parwár,*
*Ujalapúr kí ran*ḍ*í barje, ' mat já tú merí yár,'*
*Sandal terí be*ṭ*í barje, ran men térá be*ṭ*á barje,*
Bábal[5] *biná na jíwenge ka*ṭ*árí khá'e marenge.*
Jíwe Dayá Rám etc.
Ankh Dayá, terí madh ke pidle,
Bhau'án baní kamán
Achhá sohná gabrú Dayá rúp diá Kartár,
Mánchhán terí bal khá rahín.
Jíwe Dayá Rám etc.
*Pán sau ghorí chhe*ṛ *Dayá ne rasta gherájá'e,*
Shahr Dehlí ḍ*ola chale, Mírápur ko já'e.*
Dayá ne rasta gherá.

[1] *Sog*—sorrow, mourning.
[2] *Ranwás*—one who dies on the field of battle.
[3] *Amí*, S.—water of life, nectar.
[4] *Barjná* — restrain.
[5] Babal, husband.

Jíwe Dayá Rám etc.
Naubat Khán jab Súba [1] *kahtá :—"Suno, jawáno, bát,*
Tum main Dayá kaunsá mujko do batá'e
Uske main sisko kátún jíte ko kabhí na chhórún"
Já Dayá Rám paṭṭhe ne jhuk ke karí salám.
Naubat Khán ne bhálá márá,
Dayá gyá bachá'e.
Dayá Allah ne rakkhá.
Jíwe Dayá Rám etc.
Ḍola meṇ ek begam bole :—"Suno, Dayá, merí bát, yih ḍola tere yár ke kahíṇ hone de parle pár.
Terá insáf karwá'úṇ gámrí jágír diwá'úṇ."
Jíwe Dayá Rám etc.
Ná lúṭún terá mál khazána, ná lúṭúṇ bandúq.
Woh chízáṇ batládo, begam, jaháṇ hai sandúq.
Kahiye jis meṇ sánche motí
Motí ka maiṇ bhúká áyá,
Gujarí ne motí mánge
Jíwe Dayá Rám etc.
Nán bá'í ke nán lúṭe pán wále ka pán
Ek tambolaṇ aisí lúṭí lákh ṭaká qurbán.
Zúlfáṇ wain bal khárahí
Jíwe Dayá Rám etc.
Motí kí tíṇ laṛiáṇ lúṭí,
Chádar Gujrát kí lúṭí,
Lahngá Multán ká lúṭá,
Sálú Sángáner ká lúṭá
Kanghí Karnál kí lúṭí,
Chúṛá Pánipat ká lúṭá
Jíwe Dayá Rám etc.
Sáchche motí lúṭ Daya ghar ko pahúṇchá já'e,
Yih motí kí laṛián, Gújarí, pahno man chit lá'e,
Gújarí singár bandwe :—
"Saián merí jítá rahye,
Amí jal pítá rahye
Uṛjá'e terá bhaur nimáná,
Dunyá se kyá lejáná ?
Nekí tere sang chalegí,
Badíán bádsháh ke já'engí.
Jíwe Dayá Rám etc.

TRANSLATION.

The Gújars are like *dúb* grass,
Other grasses get burnt up, but the *dúb* is ever green
The Gújar's wife said :—"Listen, Dayá Rám,
I have had gold and silver to wear in plenty, but never a pearl,
Bring me real pearls !

[1] Suba = Governor.

Bring me strings of pearls, I would wear real pearls.
On pearls have I set my heart, without pearls I cannot live."
Long live Dayá Rám,
Let me immolate myself for the beauty of thy face!
"Thus the Gújarí mocked at thee, and the arrow hit the mark!
Either bring me real pearls, or turn beggar,
Bring me a shawl from Gujrát and a gown from Multán,
Bring me *sálú* from Sángáner, and a comb from Karnál.
Bring me toothpowder from Delhi, and henna from Nárnaul.
Ivory bangles from Pánípat, antimony from the Punjab,
And shoes from Pesháwar."
Long live Dayá Rám etc.
The Gújar's elder wife demanded pearls and his second wife was vexed.
In tears she went to her mother-in-law, her eyes shed tears.
"My co-wife is demanding pearls, and Dayá will be ruined.
The village will be ruined.
Our sons will perish.
On whom wilt thou put pearls?"
Long live Dayá Rám etc.
"Do not weep, mother, do not repent and consider.
That Dayá was never born.
Mourn not my death, but worship me as I die on the field of battle.
Send me to the battlefield, and rule my little village."
Long live Dayá Rám etc.
"Bring Gújarí, my five garments, and my five weapons.
From her stable bring Lailí, my mare, I will mount her and away.
I will lay in wait for a palanquin, and bring real pearls,
My Gújarí, for thee to wear."
"May Heaven prolong my husband's life!
Long may he drink the water of life.
The soul is to quit this body.
What can be taken away from this world?
Good deeds will go along with thee,
With the king will go ill deeds."
Long live Dayá Rám etc.
He saddled the mare while sneezing, and the girth broke as soon as he mounted.
Either the Gújar will perish somewhere or a battle will begin.
Long live Dayá Rám etc.

HHHH

Aura, Dhaura and the whole family restrained him.

The courtesan of Ujálapur dissuaded him, saying, 'don't go, my beloved.'

Sandal, thy daughter, dissuaded thee, and to the battlefield thy son would not have thee go

Without my father we will not live, we will die by the dagger.

Long live Dayá Rám etc.

His eyes are cups of wine,

His eyebrows are like a bow,

A fine and handsome lad is Dayá, to whom the Creator gave beauty.

Thy moustachios are twisted.

Long live Dayá Rám etc.

Urging on 500 horse Dayá stopped the highway,

From Delhi city went the palanquin, on its way to Míránpur,

Dayá stopped the way.

Long live Dayá Rám etc.

When Naubat Khán, Governor, said :—" Listen, my men,

Where is Dayá, tell me,

I will cut off his head, and never let him go alive."

Dayá Rám went and bowed.

Naubat Khán hurled a spear,

But Dayá Rám dodged it.

Dayá was preserved by God.

Long live Dayá Rám etc.

In the palanquin a lady spake :—" Listen, Dayá this palanquin belongs to a friend of thine, let it pass.

I will see that justice is done thee, and have a village bestowed on thee."

Long live Dayá Rám etc.

I will not rob thy treasure, or thy fire-arms,

Tell me, lady, what things are in your coffers,

Tell me, where are the real pearls ?

For pearls I came in search,

My Gújarí yearns for pearls.

Long live Dayá Rám etc.

The baker's loaves were looted and the betel leaf-seller's betel leaves,

A *tamolan* (female betel leaf-seller) was looted who was so beautiful that one would not care to part with a hundred and thousand *takas* for her sake.

Her locks were curled.

Long live Dayá Ram. etc.

He plundered three strings of pearls,

A shawl of Gujrát,

A gown of Multán,
Sálú from Sángáner,
A comb from Karnál,
Bangles from Pánípat.
Long live Dayá Rám etc.

He stole real pearls and brought them home, and asked Gújari to wear the pearls with pleasure.

And his Gújarí adorned herself :—
" Long may my consort live,
Long may he drink the water of life,
Thy soul is to fly away,
What can be taken from this world ?
Good deeds will go along with thee,
With the king deeds evil."
Long live Daya Ram, etc.

KISSA MIRZA AUR SÁHIBÁN KÁ.

Pírán dá Pír Mohi-ud dín, ghausán dá Qutb Faríd !
Ziárat chalná pír dí, ráhín ghat wohír !
Bolan khumre khumríán, japan faqír Faríd,
Nangián dendá kapre, bhukhe bhojan khír !
Ás kar áwan mangte, Dillí chhad Kashmír,
Ás pújánwdá jumal dí, merá Shaikh Baháwal pír.
Charhde Mirse Khán nú mán mattí de kharí :—
' Jis ghar hoe dostí, us ná jáyo gali.
Tapan kardhe tel de sir wich lát lalí.
Supne andar máryo, teri súrat khák ralí.'
Charh de Mirse Khan nú, Wanjal [1] *dendá mat :—*
' Sun farsandá meriá lajj di bannhín pag !
Rannán Bhattán dí dostí, khúri jinhán dí mat !
Ape láwan yáryán, ápe dendíyán das !
Pare bigání baiṭhke, mandí ná karye kat !
Lathí hath náh ánwdí dánishmandán dí pat.'
Bhain ne wágán pharlayán Ghat Allah dí kár :—
' Suní, wírá Mirsá merá ! Bah ke káj sawár !
Ek jánjí, ek mánjí, ek tere wekhan hár !
Hathí sardi batkhán, tásí jhúlen darbár !
Káj wahúna main phirán : mainú ki káján nál ?
Ka'i mahín ka'i ghorián, únṭhán dí ditti katár !
Aj dá wár ṭalá já, wág pichhán bhuwá.

Jawáb Mirza kí phupphí :—

' Suttí supná wáchá, supná burí baláe !
Búrá jhoṭá kheldá, Muglán kúthá de!
Kálí jehí ḍúmní lagí, birhon ay !

[1] Wanjal, Mirsa's fat her,

Siroṇ mándra ḍhai payá, mahal giá karkáye !
Aj ká wár ṭalá já, wág pichháṇ bhawá !
Beṭe Hazrat Alí de, Hasan Hussain bhirá !'
Larde nál Yahúdíáṇ, karde bahut jangáye.
Honí ná miṭe paighambaráṇ, tún bhí mann rasáye.

Yih gal karke Mirza chalagayá, rástá meṇ ek nái se milá, us se púchhá: Tere pás kí hai? Usne kahá:—' Mere pás piṭári suhág sutráh dí hai.' Mirza ne piṭári kholí, apní bakki nú chabúk máriá, tad Bakkí ne jawáb dittá:—

Jawáb Bakkí ká.

' Mainúṇ márá koṛá, jadd nú láyo láj ;
Maiṇ háráṇ dí bhain Padmani, utrí taínúṇ dáj ;
Merí qadar na páyo dekha, haisen jat nibhág.'

Bakkí se Mirza ne háth joṛkar kahá ke maiṇ bhúl gayá. Phir Bakkí dauṛ chalí, aur janj núṇ ja milí. Phir Mirze ne sáre janj wáloṇ kí pagrí utárli, aur apní mású Bíbo ke ghar chalágyá. Jab logoṇ ne janj ko bagair pagrí ke dekhá to janj ne jawáb día ki:—' Tumháre dohte ne sádí pagṛí utárlí.' Unhoṇ ne kahá: ' Sánúṇ khabar nahíṇ Mirza kiththe hai.' Ih gal sunke Mirze ne Bíbo ko ákhiyá: ' Mású hun Sáhibán núṇ láweṇ, to main bachdá háṇ.' Bíbo ne apne bhirá ko kahá: ' mainh suí hai, kaṭṭá nahíṇ jhaldá. Log kahdeṇ haiṇ ke je gáné baddí bakliyán chárs táṇ kaṭṭa jhalle.' Uske bhirá Khíwá ne apní gáne baddí dhí núṇ uhde nál kardittá. Mirze kol legayé. Dono ápas meṇ mile. Milkar Sáhibán apne makán ko haṭṭí.

Changí bhalí ghalíoṇ, aíoṇ moḍhe lagg !
Kise ghási gaj máriá gáyá kaléja chat ?
Sáhibán ghalli tel núṇ gayí pasárí dí haṭ.
Púrá kise ná toliá, jin toliá tin ghaṭ.
Mirze killián ṭhokíáṇ, mahlíṇ charhá jáye.
Hathoṇ golá deke, Sáhibán laddijáye.
' Je tú bhúkha dudh dá deváṇ, dudh piyá.'
' Maiṇ bhukhá nahíṇ dudh ká, dudhoṇ bhukh ná já.
Bhukhá tere 'ishk dá, khol tani gal lá !
Chalíye Dánáwádá núṇ: jehṛí kare Khudá !

Kalám Sáhibán.

' Kalí bárí ránglí, thalloṇ áuwdí toṛ.
Je nahíṇ si ghar báp de, mang líáwaṇ hor.
Ghore wír Shamír[1] *de sabhe rátab khor,*
Kháṇḍe khanḍ nihárydṇ, turde summ ṭakor !
Bhaniyán ján na denge, ádalliyáṇ de chor !'

Jawáb Mirza.

' Bakkí wekh na ḍublí, jhúre chit ná pá !
Uḍḍe nál pakherúáṇ, tási kaun baláye.
Bakkí nán rowan farishte, mainú roye Khudá !

[1] Brother of Sáhibán

Charh merí bel te, Kábá sís niwáye!
Le chalán Dánáwád ná, tainú tattí ná lage wá!'

Log kahte hain.

''Ashak ratte ashkán, kolhú ratte tel!
Janj wagútri rahgayí, búhe baithá mel!
Thálí batná rahgayá, kuppí tel phulel!
Jhánjar sane pitárián, gahne sane hamail[1]*!*
Sáhibán Mirza legayá, ghat Bakkí dí bail!'

Musannif kahtá hai.

'Jand, karír, wán, beryán, bárí jhall ghane,
Sáwín sanj de nikle, sárí rát bhane.
Tángu malle maut de, khallán wáng dhawen,
Hánj bigání márke báre kiyon sawén?'

Jawáb Samma Máhí.

'Sammán máhí kúkiyá, jhang siyálán dí bár,
Kahende bari hai ná, tain ná mutyár.
Ujar mallo piyádo, dandí mallo aswár!
Sáwán Mirza márná, karke kaul karár.'

Jawáb Mirza.

Panje sáni bálde, panje thaddi de jund
Gol kiye goliyán, wekh mah gayín de and.
Daih daih márgaye súrmán, bárí pahan chorang
Main wadhiyá nak jinhá dá, langaya panj nad
Merá mathá Danáwád nún dittí, siyálán nú kand.

Jawáb Kalda Jogní.

'Bhukhí Kalle púkárdi, je Sumer wejí,
Jándi war de main ditthí, ek Bakki, do jí!
Kanní bunde sir midhiyán, kise bhalí dí dhí,
Uhde munh ton pallúlah gayá, ná láj na líh!
Jamná te marjáwana, mauton darná kí?'

Jawáb Sáhibán.

'Uth Mirza suttiyá! Kai áye aswár'
Jaiththán neze rángle, karde 'máro már.'
Nahín dhúndaú ápne, nahín mír shikár,
Uth! Bakkí te charh bahye! Warye Dánáwád.'

Jawáb Mirza.

Unche disde jhaunrre rukhán báhj girán,
Bháyíyán báhj ná joryán, puttán báhj ná nán!
Wekh jandore ki chhatri, thandí is dí chhán
Palk dhaunká leliyá, jag wich rahúgá nán.

[1] *Hamail*, a pocket *Qurán*, worn in token of pilgrimage, in a gold embroidered crimson velvet or red morocco case slung by red silk cords over the left shoulder: Burton's *Al-Madina*, I, pp. 142, 289.

Jawáb Sáhibán.

Kutte mír Shamír de, chhapri án wape!
Lamb jawán mukhrá (bhan!) hatti ran charhe!
Gal wich paṭke maut de (wahyán) án phaṛe!
Jáṭ núṇ sángán áthíhián, pakkhi pain gaṛe!
Kharí ne háni láṭá líya, látyá khub raṛe!

Jawáb Mirza.

Mandá kítá, Sáhibán! Tarkash tangio jand!
Sau sath kání khán dí diyan siyálmwand!
Pahle Khán Shamír núṇ, duje kulle de tang!
Tíje máráṇ us nú, jidhí pahlí tú mang!
Chauthí wich asmán de jhar, jhar payen patang!
Talwárán jhurmaṭ ghaṭṭayá, tíráṇ páyí ḍanḍ!
Siroṇ múdasá lehgayá, nangí ho gayí jhanḍ
Kallá Mirzá máriá, múḍh ná bháyí band!
Je bháyí honde ápne laye Siyáláṇ nu wanḍ!

TRANSLATION.

Saint of all saints is Muhí-ud-Dín and the axis of all devotees is Faríd!

On a pilgrimage to this saint would I go! O guide put me on the way!

The doves male and female coo the name of Faqír Faríd

Who giveth clothes to the naked and feedeth on rice and milk the hungry!

Full of hope come the needy, from Delhí and Kashmír,

And the desires of all are fulfilled by my Shaikh, Baháwal Pír.

By Mirza Khán as he was mounting to set forth, his mother stood and advised him :—

'Enter not the street wherein dwells your sweetheart,

I saw cauldrons of heated oil whence arose fiery flames.

I dreamt Thou hadst been slain and thy body mingled with dust.'

To Mirza Khán as he was mounting to set forth Wanjal gave counsel :—

'Heark O my son! Bind fast the turban of honour!

Vain is the friendship of women and dancers, for they are rotten!

They themselves make friendships, which they themselves betray.

Sitting in a stranger's company, speak ill of no man!

Even the wise when they have lost honour cannot regain it.'

His sister too seized his reins and bade him trust in God :—

'Hearken, Mirza, my brother! stay and set thy affairs a-right!

On the one hand are the wedding party and its attendants, on the other the lookers-on!

The elephant moves in Winter, but only the racer is found at Court !

Listlessly I wander about, for what have I do with them ?

So many milch-buffaloes, so many mares and strings of camels !

Let but this day go by ! Turn Thy steed again !

The reply of Mirza's father's sister :—

'Whilst I slept I dreamed a dream—a fearful dream !

That while a buffalo-calf was lowing the Mughals came and slaughtered it !

A dark-browed songstress stood beside the porch !

The lofty towers fell down, and the palace crushed in ruin !

Let but this day go by ! Turn thy steed again !

Sons of Hazrat Alí were the brothers Hasan and Husain,

Fighting with the Jews they fought many battles

Even the Prophets escaped not what was doomed to pass, do thou also yield to Fate !'

Thus speaking Mirza went his way and meeting a barber on the road asked him what he had. He said :—he had a small basket of toilet requisites'[1] This Mirza opened. Then he struck Bakkí his mare with his whip and she replied :—

'By whipping me thou hast brought dishonour on thy ancestry ;

I am sister to the virgins of Paradise, as Padmaní come to thee in dower ;

My worth thou hast not prized, my lover, being but a luckless *hoor*.

Clasping his hands together Mirza spoke to Bakkí : –I forgot. Then Bakkí galloped on and overtook the wedding processions and Mirza took off all the *pagrís* of its members and went to his mother's sister Bíbo's house. When people saw the procession without a *pagri* in it its members retorted that it was her daughter's son who had removed them. The people said *they* did not know where Mirza was. Hearing this Mirza said to Bíbo:—'Aunt ! I can only be saved if thou bringest Sáhibán.' Bíbo said to her brother : 'Our she-buffalo has calved, but she will not suckle her calf. People say that if a newly wed girl feed her on boiled grain she will suckle her calf.' Thereupon her brother Khiwá sent his newly wed daughter along with her. She took her to Mirza. They met, and after meeting Sáhibán went off home again.

I had sent them hence hale and hearty, but thou comest leaning on another's shoulder !

Has some *ghási* pierced they liver through with his goad ?

Sábibán was sent to fetch oil and went to the grocer's shop.

[1] Lit containing henna, a comb, red thread etc.

Yet no one gave her full weight, whosoever weighed gave short weight.

Mirza drove in pegs and by them climbed into her mansion.

After searching (the text is obscure and not translatable here).

Sáhibán says :—

'If thou art athirst for milk I can give thee milk to drink.'

Mirza says :—

'I am not thirsty for milk. Milk would not appease my thirst.'

I hunger for thy love' ! Now loose thy girdle and embrace me !

Let us then go to Danáwád, and may God do what He wills !

Sáhibán's reply :—

'Thy light brown mare hath come afar from the steppes.

If thy father's house had not another, thou should'st have borrowed one.

The steeds of Shamír, my brother, all are stall-fed on sweetened food,

Fed on sugar and flour mixed together they stamp their hoofs !

So fast are they that they will not let seducer escape or runaways like us take flight ! '

Mirza's reply :—

Think not that Bakkí is lean, nor let despair afflict them !

She can outpace the birds in their flight and no racer can match her.

For Bakkí the angels weep as weeps God for me !

Mount my steed, bowing thy head to the Ka'aba !

I will carry thee to Dánábád, not even the sirocco shall catch thee !'

People all say :—

'Lovers are with lovers, as is an oil-press with oil !

The wedding procession was left in the lurch, and the visitors sitting at the door !

In the dish pomade remained, and in the goatskin some scented oil !

In the box ankle-rings yet left and ornaments of all kinds, even the *hamail*.

Mirza put Sáhibán on the back of his mare and carried her off !

Saith the poet :—

Thro' the dense jungle studded with *janḍ, karír* and wild shrubs,

Setting out at dawn they spent the whole night travelling.

Death watched his opportunity, the pair panting like bellows.

Stealing another man's property why do you sleep in the forest ?

Sammáṇ's reply :—

' Sammáṇ Máhi called aloud,

The brown milch buffalo in the dense forest is missing and the belle is not among the spinsters spinning.

Follow the untrodden path ye who are a-foot and follow the beaten path ye who are mounted.

Pledge your honour and kill Mirza alone.'

Mirza's reply :—

My face towards Dánáwád, and my back towards Siál.

Kal's reply :—

' Kalla empty stomached called out—live, O Sammír live !

I saw Bakkí with two riders entering the jungle !

With rings in her ears, wearing her hair braided,—the daughter of a man,

Goes unveiled without shame or sorrow !

Man is mortal, wherefore then fear death ?'

Sáhibán's address :—

' Rise sleeping Mirza ! Many horsemen have arrived,

With coloured lances in their hands, crying 'kill him,' 'kill him.'

They are not looking for themselves, nor are they a hunting party.

Get up and mounting Bakkí let us reach Dánábád.'

Mirza's reply : —

The cottages in a village look high when no trees surround it,

No pair can be without a brother and no name without a son !

Look at the shady *janḍ* tree and its refreshing shade,

Let me snatch a short rest and leave my name in the world.

Sáhibán's reply :—

Lo ; Shamír's dogs have come and entered the pond !

A tall youth with muffled face has come !

The angels of death put round our necks the rings of death !

As a Jáṭ struck with hail on his side,

Mirza was openly plundered, losing his all !

Mirza's answer :—

Sáhibán thou did still to hang thy quiver on the *janḍ* tree !

My 160 arrows would have the Siáls !

My first arrow would have hit Khán Shamír and my second struck the flank of his steed !

With the third I should have aimed at him to whom thou wast betrothed !

My fourth would have flown to the sky and brought down moths !

Now are they encompassed by swordsmen urged on by bowmen !

The turban fell from his head, and his hair was uncovered !

Mirza fell alone, unaided by brother or kinsman !

If his brothers had been there, each would have coped with band of the Siáls.

GÍT MÍRÁN SAYYID HUSSAIN WÁLÍ.

THE SONG OF MÍRAN SAYYID HUSSAIN, THE SAINT

Shaikh musáhib buzurg the dáná,
Míráṇ Sayyid Hussain nál já parhá dogáná.

Shaikh Shaháb se le le masláh,
Khásí poshák mangá'í.

Chírá hará, hará thá jámá,
Paṭká hará kamar se bhárí.

Harí dáp talwár nál jí,
So kamar bich laṭká'í.

Gainde kí ḍhál par hará phúl ji,
Roghan kí chamke siyáhí.

Khásah kaṭár pah zálim dhár jí
Gúthí maine kí harí laga'í.

Tukke hare bhare the tarkash,
Tín san chátar chatrá'í.

Nesá hará, harí thí bairakh,[1]
Harí bhaundi si nál jhan ná'í.

Khanká ghorá sás sab zín hará jí,
Aur sar kalghí harí súhá'í.

Hará posh aur bakhtar posh jí,
Aur Míráṇ ke sang chalte súr sipáhí.

Míráṇ bhaye aswár khing ke úpar,
Sang harí fauj báná'í.

Káfar bahut, Turk the thore,
Míráṇ Sayyid Hussain sídhe kíye ghore.

Míráṇ ne sídhe kíye ghore,
Báje tabal aur ṭakore.

Alí Alí karke jore,
Ran meṇ larte nárá súre.

Míráṇ kí chalí hál aswárí.

Faujáṇ gaḍ baḍ bahín hál,
Líyá teghe ko nikál,

Larte ápá meṇ hasmál,
Ran meṇ phailá hai gulál.

Ran kí suno bis taiyárí.

Ran meṇ hone lágí karolí,
Beṭe Rájpútáṇ máreṇ golí.

Aisí machí jaisí holí,
Bhígí rakton meṇ cholí.

Chhúṭ rakt bharí pichkárí.

[1] *Bairaq,* P. Bairak or-kh, H. — a flag.

Úṭhí ándhí to gambhír,
Úrtí rotá jo 'abír.

Chhúṭe bálochhí aurá tír,
Dúbá lohú meṇ sharír.

Waháṇ paṛá judh ek bhárí.

Ran meṇ kúdá ek Shaikh,
Maulá rakhtá úskí ṭek!

Tárá sarmukh áyá dekh,
Usne balochhí márí phek.

Tárá ne simat sáng jab mare.

Zakhm Shaikh Ábu ne kháyá,
Aur unko Maulá ne bacháyá.

Sote tege ko lagáyá,
Káṭ Tárá ko giráyá.

Rájá ke lagá zakhm tan kárí.

Gayí káfar kí ján,
Aur jaltá dozakh ke darmiyán.

Laṛá Míráṇ ká jawán,
Húá Maulá miharwán.

Rájá kí bhág gayí fauj sárí.

Khabardár khabreṇ daiṇ:
Rájá yeh hí 'arz hai merí:

Khet rahá Míráṇ jí ke háth,
Dhan dhan Sayyid aur saiddd!

Laṛte guzrí sárí rát,
Kahí halkáre ne bát.

Rájá kí ghúnghat fauj khá gayí sárí.

Jab Tárá márá gayá,
Míráṇ fateh karí Kartár,

Khabar bhayí Pirthí Ráo ko,
Sun ulṭí kháí pachhár.

Ulṭí kháyí pachhár jí nainoṇ nír áwe bhará.
Ko'í láwe loth úṭhá ke yúṇ hukm áp Rájá kará.

Rájá farmáwe bhá'í ko búláwe,
Are á'í re bahiyá máno bát hamárí!

Tárá márá jáwe ná tujhe láj áwe?
Are á'í re bahiyá ṭúṭí báṇh tihárí!

Nahíṇ autár lenge isí jagat miyáni,
Bár bár janmoṇ nahíṇ mathárí.

Is zindgí se hai marná khásá,
Are de re bahiyá karo hál taiyárí!

Rájá sun líjiye mujhe hukm díjye
Gír'un jáe ran meṇ karún már bhárí.

Rája farmáyá ḍanká dilwáyá,
Á'í sunkar fauj simat kar sárí.

Áye Rájpút wa kitne rájá,
Hainge fíl aswár baṛe baṛe chhatar dhárí.

Pánchoṇ hathyár Rájá áp sájá,
Tarkash, tír, talwár aur adhál kárí,

Diá ṭop, sar par liá pahan bakhtar
Rá'o kamar ke bích meṇ khoshá katárí.

Rájá áp terá lá'o háthí merá
Jis par jhúl kanchan kí hai jhál kárí.

Kishná chaṛhá píṭh háṭhí kí,
Aur kar kúdá Megal aswárí.

Kishná háthí pah chaṛhá,
Yádá Sambhú ko kará.

Thá wuh ghusse meṇ bhará
Holá áge ko baṛhá.

Rájá liye kaṭak fauj dal bhárí.

Man meṇ yád Shambhú ko kare
Jab Kishná háthí par chaṛhe.

Bhá'í ká badlá líjo já'eke
Yúṇ hukm áp Rájá kare.

Pirthí bát kare bhá'í se
Tum já'e Turk ko máro,

Usko máro, uskí laskhar luṭo,
Yúṇ Rájá jawáb thakáro.

Kishná bát kahí bhá'í se:—
Jo bidhná likhá leláro,

Qismat ke likhe honge sohí,
Jo rachá áp Kartáro.

Rájá be yaqín nahíṇ samjhe dín re
Woh Rájá baṛá ganwáro!

Uske sahs háthí chaleṇ kor meṇ
Sang beshumár aswáro.

Baṛí baṛí topeṇ Rájá jutwáwe,
Liye kainchín bán sab niyáro.

Rájá pahúnchá já'e kaṭak dal andar
Jaháṇ lothoṇ kí paṛe kardro.

Chíl aur gidh, mar raí rahe re
Aur le Shambhú ká nám sáng jáe gáro.

Rájá pahúnchá án jahán thá maidán jí
Aur háthí par se Kishná khaṛa lalkáro

Ae Musalmán Míráṇ Sultán lo kahá mán!
Kiún ná laṛo án jí?

Jín ne máro bír hamáro.

Khabardár khabreṇ dayí
Khaṛeṇ kaheṇ Míráṇ se hál

Ran meṇ marúṇ tabal phir se bajáe
Suno Zaid Alí ke lál.

Khabardár jásús ne khabreṇ díṇ
Ají aje merá áyá chhár rájo.

Chaṛhe hál lalkár ke áp Míráṇ
Hegá khing chaṛhne ká dín ájo!

Míráṇ ne farmáyá khing ko mangáya
Jis par zín kanchan kí yeh shakal sájo.

Chaṛheṇ Shaikh Shaháb aur asp Bokhárí
Chaṛheṇ Rúmí, Halbi aur Irán sárí.

Chaṛheṇ hál lalkár ke dín kájú.

Míráṇ pahúnche án jahán thá maidán jí
Gaye bhág káyar jab himmat hárí.

Jaháṇ ran kambhá gáṛá Sayyid wahín tháṛá
Bhiṛe súr se súr sunke káyar bháge.

Rájá pahúnchá án jahán thá maidán jí,
Aur háthí par se khaṛá Kishná lalkáre.

Míráṇ khaṛe sarmukh dete jawáb,
Sher sarmukh á'úte kyá rahí gídaṛ mén táb.

Míráṇ ko dekh Rájá kahne lagá,
Abhí hai bálí umr nádán.

Makke ko phir jáyio tú kahá hamárá mán

Lo kahá mán merá Sultán jí,
Yaháṇ náhaqq ján gawáyo.

Maiṇ máráṇ tumheṇ láj áwe mujko,
Yúṇ Rájá jawáb sunáno.

Míráṇ kalmoṇ mukh jharéṇ phúljí,
Míráṇ sunke bát muskáyáno.

Rájá tujhko máráṇ tére gaṛh ko lúṭúṇ.
Ae nahíṇ dín nabí ká máno.

Itná sukhan suná Rájá ne,
Wuh ghussah joṛ dil kháno.

Rájá ne apní fauj ko líá bulake,
Rájpút Ráo kiyá Ráno.

Main púrí Chauhán Búndelá,
Rahe ranke bích lay cháno.

Míráṇ ko chároṇ taraf se líá ghér ke,
Jaise badlí meṇ chánd chhipáno.

Main kaháṇ tak siffat karúṇ Sayyidoṇ kí,
Jinke sháken jagat bakháno ?

Jis waqt Míráṇ pakre shamsher ko,
Rájá kí sátoṇ súrat gahlaháno.

80 *Pakar shamsher lai dast meṇ,*
So rann ke bích Míráṇ kharo.

Aré Rá'o Kishná sun-líjo
So hál kalmah mukh se bharo.

Are Rá'o Kishná lená mán kahá !
Parho hál kalmáh Míráṇ farmáyá re.

Rájah sun páwe ghussá jí meṇ kháwe,
Unne apní faujoṇ ko bulwáyán re.

Rájá hukm kíná topeṇ dágh díná,
Dhúáṇ dhár ghubár woh sarsáyínyá re.

85 *'Ashaq falak topeṇ chhuteṇ dana nan,*
Dhan dhan jinnán karke golá ayiyáṇ re.

Ká qá kahqá karke hawáí topáṇ chhútti,
Jaise khuk aur súr machávyán re.

Tan man káfar chogor waháṇ to golí barse,
Jaise Indar barsát jhar láyán re,

Mírán Sayyid Hussain liye kamán dastoṇ,
Ghussah karkar karke karkayiyán re.

Mírán ke tír chhúṭe áke ran meṇ ṭúṭe
Sáná ná nán karke woh phan náiyán re.

90 *Lágá teghá chalne sunke káyar bháge,*
Túṭe tír talwáro jhan nayiyán re.

Nesá khod bakhtar waháṇ to giren kaṭ kaṭ,
Lágá tan meṇ zakhm woh bhal káyiyaṇ re.

Súr bír lare ranke darmiyán jí,
Aur chhátí se chhátí bhir jáyán re.

Jogan lálkáre Shimbhú sáng gáre,
Woh kaṭár úpar naubat ayiyán re.

TRANSLATION.

1. Shaikh Musáhib was a sage,

And he used to say the morning and evening prayers with Mírán Sayyid Hussain.

On the advice of Shaikh Shaháb,

He sent for fine raiment.

Geren was his turban, green his coat,
Green his waistband round his waist.
Green was the shield, with the sword
Hung round his waist.

5. On the shield of rhinoceros hide was worked a green flower,
And it was lacquered with black varnish.
A good dagger with cruel edge
In a sheath of green chintz.
Green were his arrows,
All three were perfect.
And green the quiver deftly wrought,
Green was his spear, and green his standard.
And over it was a green knob which whirled round and round.
His horse carried a green saddle and trappings,
And on his head he wore a green helmet.

10. Dressed all in green, and harnessed in green,
Míráṇ was attended by gallant men-at-arms.
Míráṇ mounted his steed,
And led his troops all clad in a green uniform.
Countless were the unbelievers, and but few the Turks,
Míráṇ Sayyid Hussain rode his steed upright.
When Míráṇ rode his steed upright,
The drums were beaten.
Side by Side, calling upon Ali,
The gallant warriors fought in the battle.

Thus rode the Míráṇ's chivalry.

15. The troops fell into an ambuscade,
All drew their swords,
And fighting on the defensive,
Besprinkled the field of battle with red.[1]

Learn the twenty ways of waging war.

Loud rose the din of battle,
As the sons of warriors fired their pieces.
The battle was in full swing, like the Holí festival,
And garments were drenched in blood,

As if squirts full of blood were being discharged.

A heavy dust-storm arose,
Sand scattered like powdered talo.

[1] *Lit.* red powder, *gulál*, which is used at the Holí.

20. Spears and arrows were thrown,
Bodies became wet with blood.
A terrible combat raged.
In the midst of the battle uprose a Shaikh,
Whose honour was safe with God!
Tárá seeing him advanced, came before him
And the Shaikh cast his lance at him,
But Tárá drew back and threw his spear.
And the Shaikh and his companions received wounds,
But God saved their lives.
Drawing his sword
He attacked him, and cut down Tárá,
The Rájá receiving a mortal wound.
25. The infidel lost his life,
And burns in the midst of Hell.
Míráṇ's brave youths fought on,
And God was kind.
All the Rájá's army fled.
The scouts brought in words,
(Saying) "Rájá! This is our report:
The field remains in Míráṇ's hands,
Honour to the Sayyid and his race!
The whole night passed in fighting."
Thus spake the messengers.
The Rájá's army fled in shameful rout.
30. Tárá was slain,
And God gave the victory to Míráṇ,
When Pirthí Ráo learnt the news,
Hearing it, he fell prone.
He fell prone, and his eyes were filled with tears.
He himself gave the order that his body should be brought in.
And he bade them call his brother,
"O my brother! Hearken to my words!
Art thou not ashamed that Tárá has been killed?
Oh my brother! One of our arms hath been broken!
35. We shall never be re-born in this world,
Our mother will never again give us birth.
'Twere better to die than to cling to this life,
Oh my brother! Forthwith make ready"!
"Oh Rájá! Hear me, and give me thy commands!

Though I perish on the field I will deal our enemies a heavy blow."
By beat of drum the Rájá proclaimed his orders,
Hearing it, all his forces assembled.
Rájpúts came, and many a Rájá,
Mounted on elephants, with umbrellas over their heads.

40. The Rájá put on the five arms,
The quiver, the arrow, the sword, and the strong shield,
He put on also his helmet and his armour,
And stuck his dirk into his girdle.
The Rájá himself bade them bring his elephant,
On which was a saddle-cloth embroidered with gold.
Krishná rode on the elephant's back,
And Megal also rode forth.
Mounted on his elephant, Krishná called to mind the god Shambhú.
45. Full of wrath he
With a mighty force advanced.
Remembering the god Shambhú in his heart,
When Krishná mounted his elephant,
"Go and take vengeance for thy brother."
Thus the Rájá bade him.
And again addressing his brother,
(He said) :—"Go and smite the Turk
Smite him, and plunder his camp"
Such were the Rájá's orders.

50. Krishna spake to his brother :—
"Whatsoever be written in the book of fate,
Whatsoever is written, that shall come to pass,
As predestined by God."
The Rájá was a sceptic, and did not comprehend the faith of Islám :
Such a clown was he !
Twenty-two elephants moved with him in line,
Countless horsemen rode with him.
The Rájá had his heavy guns yoked,
Taking cross-bows and various weapons
55. The Rájá won his way to the midst of the dense throng
Where the dead lay in heaps.
Over them hovered kites and vultures,

Invoking Shambhú's name he couched his lance.
The Rájá reached the scene of battle,
Standing on his elephant Krishna shouted aloud,
"Thou Musulmán! Míráṇ Sultán! Grant me this boon!
Why dost thou not come forward to meet me in fight?"
Scouts brought in the news,
And told Míráṇ this news:—
"O son of Zaid Alí! In the battle beat the drum!"
Careful spies brought in word
That the Rájá has come forward.
Then Míráṇ himself mounted his horse, and shouted aloud:—
"This is the day to mount our steeds!"
Míráṇ bade them bring his horse,
On which was a golden saddle.
And Shaikh Shaháb rode on Bokhára steed,
And the men of Turkey, Aleppo and Irán all mounted.
All rode impetuously in the cause of the faith, shouting aloud.
Míráṇ reached the field of battle,
And the coward fled when his courage failed him.
Where the battle raged most fiercely, there stood the Sayyid steadfast.
With the brave fought the brave, but the faint-hearted fled.
The Rájá reached the field of battle,
And from his elephant's back Krishná shouted,
Standing faced him and thus answered his challenge.
Míráṇ seeing the Rájá, called to him:—
"When the lion comes forward, what strength remains to the jackal?"
Seeing Míráṇ the Rájá spake:—
Thou art but young in years and ignorant,
Get thee gone to Mecca, and listen to my words.
"Hearken, O Sultán, to my words,
Here thou wilt but vainly lose thy life.
If I slay thee, I shall be put to shame,"
Thus the Rájá answered.
From Míráṇ's mouth came words like flowers
Hearing these words Míráṇ smiled.
"Rájá! I shall slay thee and plunder thy stronghold
Unless thou wilt embrace the Prophet's faith."
Hearing this the Rájá was enraged at heart,
The Rájá summoned all his forces,

All his Rájpúts, Rá'os and Ránás.
"I am a Chauhán of Bundela,
I will that the combat begin now."
Míráṇ was surrounded on all sides,
As the moon is hidden by the clouds.
How shall I sing the praises of the Sayyid,
Whose exploits are known throughout the world?
When Míráṇ grasped his sword,
The Rájá's seven senses were lost.
80. In his hand he grasped his sword,
As he stood among the horsemen.
Hail! Rá'o Krishná! Hear me,
Repeat the *kalma* with thy lips.
Hail! Rá'o Krishná! accept my counsel!
"Repeat the *kalma*!" Thus commanded Míráṇ.
As the Rájá listened he grew enraged at heart,
And called upon his soldiers.
He bade the cannon open fire,
And they belched forth smoke.
85. The cannons opened fire
And the balls fell in showers.
The round iron discs flew into the air and made a noise like the grunting of wild boars.
In his hands Míráṇ Sayyid Hussain took his bow and Míráṇ's arrows flew, just as Indra sends down rain in torrents.
90. When the swords began to play, the cowards fled,
Arrows, swords and spears were broken into pieces.
Lances and armour were splintered into fragments,
Bodies were wounded and cries of pain arose.
Brave men fought in the midst of the battle
Breast to breast
Jogan Lál saith: Shimbhú threw away the spear,
Now came the time for the dagger.

Section 6—Sikhism and the story of Banda Bairágí.

1469. **Life of Nának.**—Nának, the founder of the Sikh faith, was the son of Kálú Chand,[1] a Khatri of the Bedi section, and was born at Talwandi,[2] a village on the Rávi not far from Lahore, on the full moon day in Kátak Sambat 1526, or 14 years earlier than Luther. His father was a simple peasant, employed by Rái Boe, a Muhammadan Rájpút of the Bhatti tribe, the owner of the village, as an appraiser of produce. His mother's name was Tripta.

When only 5 years old the sister of Nának's mother, Bibi Lakho, came to see her sister and observing the boy's indifference to wordly things said to her: 'Thy son is soft headed.' Nának rejoined: Thine will be four times as soft headed; thus predicting the birth of the famous saint Bába Rám Thamman whose shrine is at the place of that name near Kasúr.[3]

Of Nának's life few authentic details have come down to us, and these are contained in a *janmsákhí* or biography, assigned by Trumpp to the later years of Gurú Arjan or his immediate successors. This work refers to hymns in the *Granth Sáhib* and must therefore have been compiled after it. Mohsan-i-Fáni appears to refer to separate stories which even in his time were not collected in one work. This biography contains few of the miracles and other incidents found in the later *janmsákhís*, and as it is an early record of Nának's life and teaching it may be regarded as authentic in all material points.

[1] One account avers that Kálú or Kallu had no sons until one day a *faqír* visited his hut and was there fed, whereupon he sent some fragments of his meal to Kallu's wife promising her a famous son. She went as is customary for her confinement to Mári near Kot Kachwá (or Kána Kachha, 15 miles south of Lahore) where her parents lived. Here her son was born and he received the somewhat disparaging name of Nának, because he was born in the house of his *náná* or *maternal* grandfather. See McGregor's *History of the Sikhs*, I, p. 32, and Cunningbam's ditto, p. 40, and note. This account is rejected by the better-informed who say that Hardiál, the family priest, drew up the boy's horoscope and divined for him the name of Nának to which his parents objected as it was common to both Hindus and Muhammadans. The priest rejoined that his calculations disclosed that the boy was destined to be revered by both creeds: *Philosophic Hist. of the Sikh Religion*, by Khazán Singh, Lahore, 1914, p. 55. B. Gurbakhsh Singh however writes:—"Gurú Nának's sister was older than himself and she was named Nánakí. The brother was given her name, as very often happens. This is a simpler and more natural explanation than the other two given. Perhaps the girl was born in her maternal grandfather's house and so named Nánakí."

[2] Talwandi Rai-Bulár or "of wit and wealth" is now called Ráipur: McGregor, I, 32. The date of Nának's birth is also given as the 3rd of light half of Baisákh.

At Talwandi now stands the famous Nankána Sáhib on the site of the house, in which Nának was born; the Kiára Sáhib, the sacred field into which Nának when absorbed in contemplation let his father's cattle stray but in which no sign of damage done to the crop could be found; a temple on the site where a snake shaded his face with its hood while he lay sunk in contemplation and another where the shade of the tree stood still: Khazán Singh, *op. cit.*, p. 60.

[3] Khazán Singh, *op. cit.*, p. 56. Rám Thamman was a Bairági, and a cousin of Nának: see vol. II, p. 87 *infra*. *Thamman*=*dhamman*, the *Grewia oppositifolia* or *elastica*, or *dhámar*, a grass *Pennisetum cenchroides*, *Panjabi Dicty.*, pp. 1123, 295, 294. But possibly *thamman* is derived from *thamm*, a post or pillar, Sanskr. *Sthamba* and may thus be connected with Stamb Náth, a form of Shiva.

As a child Nának was devoted to meditation on God, and at the age of 7 he was sent to the Hindu village school, where he composed the 35 verses[1] of the *Patti* in the Rág Asá of the *Granth*. Here Nának received all his secular instruction, for he was early employed by his father as a buffalo-herd.

In due course he married and two sons were born to him, but this did not prevent his leading a life remote from thoughts of this world and his superhuman character was revealed to Rái Bulár, the son of Rái Bhoe, who found him one day sleeping beneath a tree whose shadow had stood still to shelter him, while those of the other trees had moved, with the waning noon.[2]

Nának showed no bent for any worldly vocation, but delighted in the society of saints and even wandering *faqírs*, and at last his father in despair sent him to Sultánpur, a town now in the Kapúrthala State, where his brother-in-law Jairám, husband of his sister, Nánaki, was employed as a factor to Nawáb Daulat Khán the Lodi, who after his long governorship of the Punjab called in Bábar to aid him against his master's injustice.

At Sultánpur Nának devoted himself to his duties, but his wife and children were left or remained at Talwandi, sometimes regarded as an indication that his domestic life was not happy. His wife however rejoined him after his travels and lived with him till his death. There too he was joined by an old acquaintance, Mardána the Dúm, an itinerant musician, who accompanied his improvised hymns on his *rabáb* or harp.[3]

At Sultánpur too Nának was destined to receive that definite call to the office of religious leader to which he owes his title of Gurú. While bathing one day in the canal he was taken up by angels and transported into the presence of God who gave him a goblet of nectar with the command to spread the fame of God (Hari) through the world. Meanwhile his servant had carried home the news of his disappearance in the water, and the Khán had actually set fishermen to drag the canal for his body, when he re-appeared.

After this event Gurú Nának took the decisive step of distributing all that he had among the poor and accompanied by Mardána he left his house and began to preach. In popular phrase he turned *faqír*. His first pronouncement 'There is no Hindu and no Mussalmán' led to his being cited, at the Qází's instance, to appear before the Nawáb, who

[1] 35, not 34 as usually stated. Each verse began with a letter of the alphabet. The letters are exactly the same 35, as are now found in the Gurmukhi alphabet, even including the letter (ṛ) which is peculiar to Gurmukhi, thus proving that the Gurmukhi alphabet existed before his time and was not invented by the second Gurú, Angad, though the name Gurmukhi may have replaced its original name, which was possibly Tánkre. See the pamphlet: *The Origin of the Gurmukhi Characters*, Coronation Printing Works, Hall Bazar, Amritsar. Sir George Grierson holds that the alphabet is derived from the Sárada through the Tákri of the Hills and the *landa* script of the plains: J. R. A. S., 1916, p. 677.

[2] Subsequently the legend ran that a huge black snake had raised its hood over Nának's head to shield him from the sun's rays while he slept.

[3] Mardána was the founder of the Rabábi group of the Dom-Mirási. Cunningham calls him the harper, or rather a chanter, and player upon a stringed instrument like a guitar: *Hist. of the Sikhs*, p. 42.

invited him to accompany him to the mosque. Nának did so—and while the Qází led the prayers, he laughed. To the Qází's remonstrances he replied that the latter had left a foal in his own courtyard and had throughout the prayers been anxious lest it should fall into the well. Amazed at Nának's power of reading his thoughts the Qází fell at his feet and acknowledged his power.

After this incident Nának set out on what are often called his five pilgrimages, thus beginning his mission to call the people to the right path. The first lay eastward,[1] to the shrine of Shaikh Sajan who had built a temple for Hindus and a mosque for Muhammadans—a proof of the religious toleration in fashion at this period of Indian history. But the Shaikh was given to murdering those who put up with him in his shop and stealing their property, until the Gurú saw through him and made him become a repentant follower of his teaching. Tradition also takes Nának to Delhi, where he restored a dead elephant to life and interviewed the Mughal emperor. Besides Shaikh Sajan he encountered many other *thags*, whom he converted. At the sack of Sayyidpur he was captured by Bábar's troops and carried off, but coming under Bábar's own notice he was honourably used and set at liberty.[2]

But he soon set out on his second or southward pilgrimage. That he ever reached Ceylon or formed there a *sangat* (congregation) of his disciples is hardly probable, and if he did so few authentic details of this journey have been preserved.

At Siálkot he heard that Hamza Ghaus was undergoing a 40 days' fast in order to acquire power to destroy the town, so he sat under a plum (*ber*) tree and called thrice to the *faqír*. Receiving no reply he stood up and gazed at the lofty tower in a vault of which the *faqír* had shut himself, and burst open its walls so that the sun fell on the face of the recluse. This saint had promised sons to a Khatri of the town in return for a promise that the first-born should become his disciple and as the vow was broken had condemned all the inhabitants to annihilation. The Gurú impressed on him the injustice of punishing all for the faults of a few.[3] The Ber Bába Nának still commemorates this incident.

On his 3rd tour the Gurú who was returning from Russia and Turkistán reached Hassan Abdál in 1520. On the top of the hill was a spring of water. Its summit was occupied by Wali Qandhári, a Muhammadan saint, who grew jealous of the Gurú and refused to let

[1] Khazán Singh locates Sajan at Tulamba and places the incident in the second tour. The Shaikh inveigled Mardána into his house and maltreated him, hoping to secure the Gurú's accumulated offerings in his possession. Tulamba had been in Taimúr's time a considerable centre of religious learning for his biographies speak of its Saiyids, *ulamás* and *shaikhs*: E. H. I., III, pp. 418, 484, cited in the Multán *Gazetteer*, 1901-02, p. 373*f*. No mention of Sajan is traceable. But at Chawali Masháikh in Mailsi tahsíl is a Darbár Sáhib of Bába Nának: *ib.*, p. 128. So too at Nigáha there is a shrine to Bába Nának north-west of the shrine of Sakhi Sarwar: Dera Ghází Khán *Gazetteer*, 1898, p. 53.

[2] This must have occurred in 1524, and though Nának does not mention the occurrence in the *Granth*, it may well have happened. In this pilgrimage to the East Nának supplemented his imperfect schooling by constant dialectics with Muhammadan Shaikhs and other *faqírs*. He then returned to Talwandi.

[3] Khazán Singh, p. 75.

Mardána draw water from it, so the spring dried up and re-appeared at the spot where the Gurú had halted. The Wali cast a huge rock down from the hill upon it, but the Gurú stopped the rock with his hand, leaving an impression of it on the hill-side.[1] Thence he continued his tour through Siálkot and witnessed the sack of Saídpur, near Eminábád, which he had foretold.[2]

Again Nának returned to Talwandi, but only to make thence his third pilgrimage northwards into Kashmír, where he climbed Mount Sumera and had a lengthy discussion with the chiefs of the Jogís and according to some accounts with Shiva himself.

His fourth pilgrimage was to the West to Mecca, where he lay down and by chance turned his feet towards the Ka'aba. When reproached for this by the Qázi, Rukn-ud-Dín, he challenged him to lay his feet in any direction where God's house did not lie, and wherever the Qází turned Nának's feet, there appeared the Ka'aba.[3]

Gurú Nanak's fifth and last pilgrimage may be regarded as purely allegorical. He went to Gorakh-hatri where he discoursed with the 84 Siddhs, or disciples of Gorakh Náth. A temple exists at Nánakmáta in the Kumáon or Naini Tál Tarai, about 10 miles from Khatima, a station on the Rohilkhand-Kumáon Railway. Not far from this place are still to be found several *maths* of *yogís*, from one of which sweet soap-nuts (*mitha retha*) are obtained by the *mahant* at Nánakmáta. Two such trees are known in the Almora district; one at the place called the *Gulia ritha* by the hillmen, the other on the road from Lahughát to Dhunnaghát. It appears that where new shoots spring from old decayed trunks, the fruit they bear loses its bitterness. Gorakh-hatri may be the name of some *math* of *yogís* in these hills. 'It was also,' observes S. Gurbakhsh Bakhsh, 'the name of a well-known *math* at the Indian end of the Khaibar Pass, about two stages from Peshávar. Bábar, who went twice to visit the place, gives an account of it and describes it as a well-frequented place to which Hindus came from distant places, and went through the ceremony of shaving themselves clean. Several low underground cells, entry to which was obtained by crawling along on all fours, and immense heaps of hair marked the place.' This seems to be the well-known Gor-Khatri at Peshávar. Other authorities say that this the Gurú's last pilgrimage was to the East and that it took him to Gorakhmátá or Nánakmata.

Other accounts give more detailed and less ambitious accounts of the pilgrimages. On his first the Gurú visited Eminábád where he meditated on a bed of pebbles (*ror*) where the Rori Sáhib now stands.[4] Here he composed a hymn in which he reproached the Khatrís for subsisting on alms wrung from the people and expounded the merits of earning a livelihood by honest labour.

[1] Khazán Singh, p. 101.

[2] *Ib.*, p. 102.

[3] The *chola* or cloak said to have been presented to him at Mecca is preserved at Dera Bába Nának. It is inscribed with thousands of words and figures: Gurdáspur *Gazetteer*, 1914, p. 30.

[4] Khazán Singh, p. 70.

Nának went to several other places also. At Haridwár he pointed out to the Hindus the hollowness of sending water to their forefathers. At Kurukshetr he proved the uselessness of such vain beliefs as not eating meat at an eclipse. At Jagannáth he pointed out the right way to worship God and said that it did not consist in lighting lamps and so on. Among the other countries that he visited were Kábul, Baghdád etc. But this pilgrimage is rejected altogether by the reforming Sikhs.

Nának died at Kartárpur on the banks of the Rávi in the Jullundur District in the house of his family, with whom he appears to have been reconciled. Before his death he transmitted his Gurúship to Lahna, surnamed Angad, the second Gurú, by a strikingly simple ceremony. Nának laid five pice before Angad[1] and fell at his feet. This event occurred in 1537 A. D.

1594 S. The successive Gurús transmitted their office by this rite, but later on a cocoanut[2] was also laid before the successor thus appointed. Gurú Nának also went four times round his successor and then said that his own spirit had gone into his body so that he was from that moment to be regarded as Nának himself. It is now a common Sikh belief that each Gurú inherited the spiritual light of Nának and the doctrine is as old as Mohsin-ul-Fáni.

Bhái Budha, a Ját, affixed the *tilak* or coronation mark on Angad's forehead and survived to witness the installation of no less than four of Angad's successors. Tradition says that while very young he came to Nának and referring to the devastation of the unripe crops wrought by Bábar's troops said that he was afraid of being untimely carried away by the angel of death. Nának replied: 'Thou art old (Budha) not young.' So he was named Bhái Budha and lived till 1627. The significance of the *tilak* is well known. It is often if not generally affixed by a dominant or autochthonous agricultural class and in this instance the choice of Bhái Budha represented the Ját recognition of the Gurú's chiefship. To his sons' protests against their father's choice of Angad, Gurú Nának replied that not even the Gurú's dogs suffered want, and that they should have clothes and food enough. In accord, probably, with this tradition, we find the Nának-putra or descendants of Nának employed towards the close of the Sikh period in *banda-bhara*, a practice whereby traders entrusted goods to a Nánakputra who engaged to convey them for a stipulated sum from Jagádhri to Amritsar, then the emporium of the Sikh states, paying all duties. The Nánakputras, from the sanctity which attaches to their persons, engaged enjoyed certain exemptions and were less subject to molestation from custom-officers' importunity than others.

[1] Angad is said to mean 'own body' (fr. *ang*, Sanskr. 'body'), because Lahna obeyed Gurú Nának's order to eat of a corpse which vanished when he began to do so: McGregor's *Hist. of the Sikhs*, I, p. 49, and Malcolm's *Sketch*, p. 208. But a more probable account is that he was blessed by the Gurú and proclaimed as flesh of his flesh and blood of his blood; as the Gurú's self, in fact.

[2] *Als eine Art Reichsapfel* (Trumpp, *Die Religion der Sikhs*, p. 11)—*cf.* Murray's *History of the Punjab*, I, p. 169. But Khasán Singh says that the cocoanut was used at Gurú Angad's nomination.

Nának's attitude to Islám is illustrated by several incidents in the above sketch of his life. To these the latter *janamsákhís* make many additions, which at least record the traditional attitude of the earlier Sikhism to Islám. Thus immediately after Nának's election for a spiritual life he is said to have been visited by Khwája Khizr, the Muhammadan saint, who taught him all earthly knowledge.

The traditional account of Gurú Nának's funeral also records his attitude towards the two religions. When the Hindus and the Muhammadans both claimed his body he bade them lay flowers on either side of it, for Hindus on the right and for Muhammadans on the left, bidding them see whose flowers remained fresh till the following day. But next morning both lots of flowers were found fresh, while the body had vanished, signifying that it belonged to neither, yet equally to both the creeds. Nának expressed his religious thought in verses, composed in Panjábi, which form no insignificant part of the *Granth*. Nának was absorbed, to use the Sikh phrase, on the 10th of October 1538 (the 10th of the light half of Assuj, Sambat 1596).

His successor, Gurú Angad, was a Khatri of the Tríhun section, who had fulfilled the Gurú's ideal of unquestioning obedience to his will. Though perhaps illiterate, the invention of the Gurmukhi alphabet in
1590 S. 1533 is ascribed to Gúru Angad[1] and he also had much of what he had learnt about Nának from Bálá, the Sindhu Ját, a disciple of that Gurú, reduced to writing.

He himself however composed a few verses which are preserved in the *Granth*. He earned his living by twisting the coarse twine made of *munj*, thus following Nának's teaching about alms. His death
1609 S. occurred in 1552 or 1553 at Khadúr near Govindwál on the Biás, where he dwelt in seclusion since his accession to the Gurúship. He had appointed his follower Amar Dás, a Khatri of the Bhalla section, to succeed him, passing over his own sons as unworthy.

Gurú Amar Dás resided at Govindwál whence he sent out 22 of his numerous disciples to various parts of the country to preach, dividing it into as many *manjas* or dioceses.[2] He also built Kajárawál. But his most important act was the separation of the passive recluses of the Udási order from the active lay Sikhs, thus giving the latter body something of a social character in addition to the religious ties which held it together. He organised and maintained a public refectory (*langar*) at which all the four castes ate together and no question was raised as to whether the food had been cooked by a Brahman or a low caste Sikh.[3] Before his accession he had been a Vaishnava, and after it he built at Govindwál the grand *baoli* or oblong well with its 84 steps

[1] B. Gurbakhsh however writes :—" The tradition that the second Gurú invented the Gurmukhi alphabet is based on a misreading of the spurious book called the *Janamsákhi of Bhái Bálá*. Gurú Angad only secured the *Janampatri* or horoscope of Gurú Nának from his uncle Lalu: see the introductory portion of this *sákhi* given in Dr. Trumpp's *Translation of the Granth*. The peculiar script of Gurú Gobind Singh's letters is an earlier stage of Gurmukhi.

[2] The *Panth-Prakásh* calls them *gaddis*. *Manja* means a large couch so that 'see' would be a good translation of the term. *Cf.* Akbar's 22 provinces: G. C. Narang, *Transformation of Sikhism*, p. 23.

[3] Khasán Singh, p. 113.

and landing places. It is a general belief among the Sikhs that whoever bathes on these steps one by one on the same day repeating the *japji* with sincerity to the last step shall be saved from the 8,400,000 transmigratory forms and go direct to heaven. Gurú Amar Dás also pronounced against the Brahmanical rite of *sati*, reformed the ceremonies in vogue at marriage and death, forbade pilgrimages and the like, and added largely to the poetical literature of the Sikhs. His verses in the *Granth* are distinguished for simplicity and clearness. Gurú Amar Dás left two sons Mohan and Mohari, but bestowed the *barkat* or apostolic virtue upon Rám Dás, his son-in-law, as a reward for his daughter's filial love and obedience as well as the worth of Rám Dás himself.

Rám Dás succeeded as Gurú in 1574. He was also a Khatri of the 1631 S.
Sodhi section, which has played so pre-eminent a part in Sikhism. Gurú Amar Dás is said to have found an attentive listener in Akbar, but Rám Dás entered into still closer relations with that tolerant emperor, and is said to have received from him the grant of a piece of land whereon he founded Rámdáspur, subsequently known as Amritsar, or the 'pool of salvation' from the ancient tank which lay in it, and which he repaired and enlarged. According to some authorities he also built in its midst the Harimandar, or temple of God (Hari), in which no idols were set up.

Gurú Rám Dás' poetical contributions to the *Granth* are clear and easy to understand, reproducing the traditional circle of Sikh thought as enunciated by the earlier Gurús.

This, the fourth Gurú, was succeeded by Arjan, his youngest son,[1] and henceforth the office becomes hereditary in the Sodhi section. Moreover with the accession of Arjan on the 3rd Bhádon *sudi* 1580, accord- 1638 S.
ing to the oldest known record, the Sikh community enters on a new phase. He laid aside the rosary and garb of a *faqir* and dressed in costly raiment. Though not, it is sometimes said, a Sanskrit scholar, Gurú Arjan was a man of considerable literary attainments and nearly half the *Adi Granth* was composed by him.

He also collected the hymns of his predecessors and adding to them selections from the writings of the earlier reformers, Kabír, Námdeo, Rávi Dás, and others, compiled the *Granth* or 'Book' of the Sikh commonwealth. A decalogue of ten commandments ascribed to this, the fifth Gurú, has recently been discovered in Eastern Bengal. It is naturally very like the Mosaic, but one of the manuscripts indicates that the Sikhs were being boycotted and found it difficult to marry.[2]

But Arjan's activity was not confined to spiritual affairs. Hitherto the Gurús had lived on their own earnings like Angad, or on the voluntary offerings of their followers though these seem to have been in the main ear-marked to charitable purposes by Amar Dás, but Gurú Arjan established the beginnings of a fiscal system, appointing collectors, called *masands*, to each of whom was assigned a definite district.

[1] Not his eldest son. Arjan's elder brother Pirthi Chand had founded a rival sect, the Mínás. The eldest son was more than once set aside as personally unfit or not available.

[2] *Dacca Review*, 1916, p. 378.

Their deputies were called *meorás*,[1] a term borrowed from Akbar's system. These appointments indicated an attempt at regular administration. Some writers hint that the 22 secs or *manjas* of Gurú Amar Dás became the 22 fiscal units of Gurú Arjan. If this was so the change is significant of the gradual transformation of Sikhism even at that early stage. But disciples were also sent to Kábul,[2] Kandahár, Sindh and even Turkistán not only to spread the Sikh faith but also for purposes of trade. He also permitted himself to be addressed as *sacha pádsháh* or 'true king,' 'Sodhi Sultán,' the Sodhi Sultán.[3] Apparently he obtained this title in consequence of the dignities bestowed on him for his services against Nálagarh. He continued Nának's policy of toleration for and good relations with the Muhammadans, for the famous saint Mián Mír was a great friend of his and the happening to visit the Gurú at this time he was asked to lay foundation stone
1646 S. of the Harímandar in 1589. But it was not well and truly laid and though the mason righted it the Gurú prophesied that the temple would fall down and have to be rebuilt.[4] In 1590 he founded Tarn Táran.

Gurú Arjan's chief opponent was Chandu Lál, a *díwán* or finance minister of Akbar, whose daughter the Gurú refused to accept for his son Har Govind. This led to an enmity which had dire results. Chandu Lál denounced the Gurú to the emperor as an enemy of Islám and though Akbar himself was not induced to persecute the Gurú—on the contrary he honoured him in various ways and an account of Akbar's visiting Gurú Arjan at his home and remitting the land revenue on a famine-stricken area at his request is given in the *Seirul mutakharin*—Chandu Lál's hostility predisposed his successor Jahángír against him It was he who informed that emperor of the Gurú's loan of Rs. 5000 to Prince Khusru. Indeed the *Dabistán*,[5] which contains the most probable account of Gurú Arjan's death, says he was accused, like

[1] Khazán Singh. p. 118. Akbar had employed Meoras or Mewátis, of the Mewát, as dák-runners, spies and on other delicate duties: *Aín-i-Akbari*, I, p. 252. The definition of *meora* as 'a Gurú's priest' cited in Vol. III, p. 86 *infra*, is misleading.

[2] Narang, p. 35. He suggests that *masand* is a corruption of *masnad-i-álá* or 'Excellency,' a title of the Mughal governors, and that though there are now no Sikh *masands* the system still continues in the sect founded by Banda, and the *masands* exist under the style of Bhái (in that sect). But a writer in the *Dacca Review* for January 1916 (p. 317) speaks of the term as equivalent to *sangatia*. And he writes:—'the original number' (of the *masands*) got very much multiplied (under the successors of that third Gurú. With the gradual transformation of Sikhism, this system also underwent a change and the bishops did not remain purely spiritual guides, but became collectors of tithes etc. (p. 316) This confirms the view expressed in the text. Followers of *masands*, who were in charge of *sangats*, were called *sangtias* or *masandias*, not *masands* themselves. Trumpp says Gurú Arjan introduced a regular system of taxation, compelling all Sikhs to contribute 'according to their means or other gains.' But this Gurú appears to have established the tithe, *dasaundh*, *daswandh*, 'a regular tenth contributed to the Gurús': *vide Panjabi Dicty*, *s. vv.* In the Western Punjab, at any rate, this title was called *sikhi* or was replaced by a new tax called by that term.

[3] According to Khazán Singh (p. 130) these titles were assumed first by Gurú Hargovind.

[4] Khazán Singh, p. 119. Gurú Arjan's *baoli* in the Dabbi Bazar at Lahore was also made by the Muhammadan governor, Hosain Khán: p. 121.

[5] II p. 272 *et seq.*

many other Punjab notables, of actual participation in Prince Khusru's rebellion. It is certain that he was condemned by Jahángír to a heavy fine.[1] Unable or unwilling to pay the sum demanded he was exposed of the sun's rays and perished of exhaustion in 1606. 1663 S.

Arjan's son Har Govind succeeded to the Gurúship. He wore two swords typifying *amíri* or secular and *faqíri* or spiritual authority, and he was the first Gurú to take up arms against the Muhammadans to whom he certainly ascribed his father's death, whatever the precise circumstances may have been. He built the stronghold of Hargovindpur on the upper reaches of the Beás, and thence harried the plains. To his standard flocked many whom want and misgovernment had driven from their homes. But at last Gurú Har Govind fell into the hands of the imperial troops, and Jahángír kept him a prisoner at Gwálior for 12 years, until in 1628, on that emperor's death, he obtained his freedom by sacrificing his treasures.[2] Returning to Kíratpur the Gurú renewed his attacks on the Muhammadan land-owners and imperial officials of the plains. One of his last exploits was an expedition to Nánakmaṭa, in the Tarai near Naini Tál, whose *faqír* Almast, the Udási, complained that he had been expelled from his shrine by the Jogís, who had also burnt the *pípal* tree under which Gurú Nának had held debate with the followers of Gorakh Náth. This or another Almast had been deputed by this, the sixth Gurú, to Shujátpur near Dacca and had there founded *sangat*. This *sangat* at Shujátpur was called after Natha Sáhib, third in succession to this Almast.[3] In
1693 S. 1636, the Gurú restored him to his shrine and returned to Kíratpur

[1] According to the *Túzuk* of Jahángír he waited upon Khusr when the latter halted at his residence, and placed the saffron finger-mark or *ṭíka* upon his forehead: J. A. S. B., 1907, p. 608. The meeting took place at Tarn Táran according to Khazán Singh, p. 125.

[2] The Sikh accounts aver that Chandu Lál continued his intrigues against Gurú Har Govind and prevailed on Jahángír to demand payment by him of the fine imposed on the father, but the Gurú forbade the Sikhs to raise the money. Mían Mír however interceded with Jahángír at Delhi and not only obtained his release but reconciled him to this emperor whom he accompanied on his tour in Rájpútána and who even employed him to subdue the rebellious chief of Nálagarh: Khazán Singh, p. 129. This account is easily reconcilable with that of the *Dábistán* (II, p. 274) which represents Gurú Har Govind as entering Jahángír's service and continuing to serve Sháh Jahán: yet the latter emperor sent troops against him and they drove him out of Rámdáspur (Amritsar) and plundered his lands there. The Gurú was victorious in his struggle with Painda Khán, who resisted the fortification of Hargovindpur, but imperial troops intervened and drove him to seek refuge amongst the Hill States: *ib*, p. 277. The testimony of Mohsin-i-Fáni is in some ways all the more valuable in that he was a Muhammadan.

Malcolm's *Sketch* (p. 82) reproduces a tradition which is not based on any written or authentic proof.

Other authorities say that the Gurú was invited by the emperor to Delhi and thence accompanied him to Agra. There misled by an astrologer the emperor requested the Gurú to fast and pray for him for a period of forty days in the solitary hill fort of Gwálior. This was a plot on the part of Chandu and other enemies of the Gurú to get him out of the way. But the emperor soon realized his mistake, sent for the Gurú and at his request liberated many of the hill Rájás imprisoned in Gwálior.

[3] *Dacca Review*, 1916, p. 228, *Sikh Relics in Eastern Bengal*. The Nánakmaṭa near Naini Tál seems to have been called the 'Nánakmaṭa of Almastráj.' B. Gurbakhsh Singh writes regarding the *sangat* at Shujátpur: 'The inscription on a stone in the well of this *sangat* commemorates the name of the original founder and his "Mother Lodge" of Nánakmaṭa. This new *sangat* was not named Nánakmaṭa, but it was under the Lodge at Nánakmaṭa in Naini Tál, and its priests were appointed or removed by the head at that place.

through Alígaṛh, Dehli and Karnál. This life of active military enterprise, lightened at intervals by sport,[1] absorbed all Har Govind's energies and he contributed nothing to the *Granth*.

But interesting stories are recorded of his aversion to the ostentatious or undue exercise of spiritual power. Bábá Gurditta, his eldest son, had restored to life a cow accidentally killed by a Sikh. The Gurú rebuked him for this uncontrolled exhibition of spiritual force and the Bábá went to the tomb of Budhan Sháh, a Muhammdan *faqír*, where he lay down and gave up his soul. Similarly, Aṭal Rái, his fourth son, as a boy of 9 restored to life a playmate who had died of snake-bite and he too when reproached by the Gurú for vying with the giver and taker of life by exercising miraculous power over death covered himself with a sheet and breathed his last. His tomb is close to the Kaulsar at Amritsar and is the highest building in that town.[2]

Gurú Har Govind was known also as the Chhatwán Bádsháh or 6th king among the Sikhs and so offerings of *kaṛáh parshád* are made at the Darbár Sáhib at Lahore on the 6th of every month and the building is illuminated.[3]

On his death at Kíratpur in 1645[4] his grandson Har Rái succeeded 1701 S.
him.[5] Of this Gurú we have an account by the author of the *Dábistán*, who knew him personally. Less warlike than his grandfather, Gurú Har Rái still maintained the pomp and circumstances of a semi-independent military chieftain. His body-guard consisted of 300 cavalry with 60 musqueteers, and 300 horses were stalled in his stables. His alliance was successfully sought by another rebellious scion of the Mughal house, Dárá Shikoh, who soon perished. Thereupon the Gurú retreated to Kíratpur whence he sent his son Rám Rái to Delhi to negotiate pardon. Aurangzeb received the young envoy graciously, but detained him as a hostage for his father's loyalty. Har Rái contributed not a
single verse to the Sikh scriptures. Dying in 1661 at Kíratpur he 1718 S.
left his office to his second son Har Kishan, the 8th Gurú, and as yet a minor.[6] Rám Rái, still a hostage, appealed to Aurangzeb, who seized

[1] His prowess as an archer is still remembered for he would shoot an arrow from Srígovindpur to the shrine of Damdama, a distance of about half a mile: Gurdaspur *Gazetteer*, 1914, p. 17.

[2] Khazán Singh, pp. 140-1.

[3] Muhammad Latíf: *Lahore, its History* etc., p. 197.

[4] Macauliffe places this event in Sbt. 1701 (= 1644 A.D.), but this appears to be an error. The *Dábistán* gives the year as 1645 and its correctness has now been proved, by a manuscript recently found in Eastern Bengal. Its author had seen this Gurú at Kíratpur in 1643 A. D. Macauliffe rightly rejected the Hindusing version of the Gurú's death, according to which he caused himself to be shut up in Patálpuri and bade Gurú Har Rái not to open the door till the 7th day, when he was found dead: *Dacca Review*, 1916, p. 378.

[5] Gurditta, his father and Har Govind's eldest son, had become an Udási, and this disqualified him for the office of Gurú, now a quasi-secular chiefship. From a tent-peg driven in by him sprang the Tahli Sáhib, a large *shisham* at Ghakhar Koṭli, a village in the south-west of Shakargaṛh tahsíl: Gurdaspur *Gazetteer*, 1914, p. 17.

[6] We do not know why Rám Rái was passed over. As a hostage he may have been held ineligible. A somewhat similar incident occurs in Baháwalpur history. According to the Sikh accounts he had misquoted a verse of Gurú Nának: Khazán Singh, p. 145. An early tradition recorded by the Court Historian of Mahárája Ranjít Singh makes Rám Rái, the brother of Har Rái, son of Bábá Gurditta, on being superseded appeal to the emperor, who would not or could not help him, and upheld the election. Bábá Gurditta had married a second wife much against the wishes of his father, and Rám Rái was his son by that wife: see the *Umdat-ul-Tawáríkh* by Lála Sohan Lál, Súri. Vakíl, Lahore Darbar.

the pretext for interference in the Gurú's domestic affairs and summoned
1712 S. Har Kishan to Delhi. There he died of small-pox, after declaring that the Sikhs would find the next Gurú in Bakála, a village on the Beás. Disputes regarding the succession inevitably arose and some of the Sodhís set up a Gurú of their own,[1] while Rám Rái urged his claims in reliance on imperial support. This, however, only alienated his own followers, and despairing of success he retreated to Dehra Dún, where he founded a sect of his own.

1721 S. At length in 1664 Teg Bahádur[2] obtained recognition as the 9th Gurú. Teg Bahádur was a great figure among the Sikhs. From his birth he was destined to be a scourge to his enemies, and foreseeing this his father named him Teg Bahádur. His personal likeness to Bábá Nának was also striking. Nevertheless his recognition was keenly contested by Dhir Mal, the elder son of Gurditta, the Udási,[3] and Teg Bahádur was driven to seek refuge on a piece of land which he purchased from the Kahlúr Rájá. Here in 1665 he founded Anandpur. Still harassed by his opponents the Gurú set out on a progress through the Málwa country—a tract still dotted with shrines, tanks and *dharmsálas* which commemorate his visits. Then he wandered through the Kurúkshetra, and thence into Lower India, where the Sikh faith had many scattered adherents. The Sikh accounts of this progress are perhaps inaccurate in detail, but it is certain that Teg Bahádur's itinerary was designed both to foster the Sikh faith where already established and to preach the Sikh doctrine throughout Lower India. Incidentally the existing records show that the net-work of Sikh organisation had been spread as far east as Patna and even Dacca, where a *masand* was posted.[4] Dacca indeed became a *hazúr sangat* or provincial *sangat*, at first under the

[1] Sikh authorities say that 22 Sodhís of Bakála each claimed to be the rightful Gurú, but they all failed to stand the test of divining what sum one Makhan Sháh, a Labána, had vowed to offer the Gurú when he escaped shipwreck.

[2] Teg Bahádur was the 5th son of Gurú Har Govind and his wife Nánaki, and was born at Amritsar on Baisákh *badí* 5, 1678 Sambat (1621 A.D.).

[3] Trumpp is almost certainly wrong in making Dhir Mal a son of Gurú Rám Dás: *Ádi Granth*, p. cxvi. He is cited by Maclagan, §§ 101 and 104. The genealogy given in the latter paragraph should be as follows:—

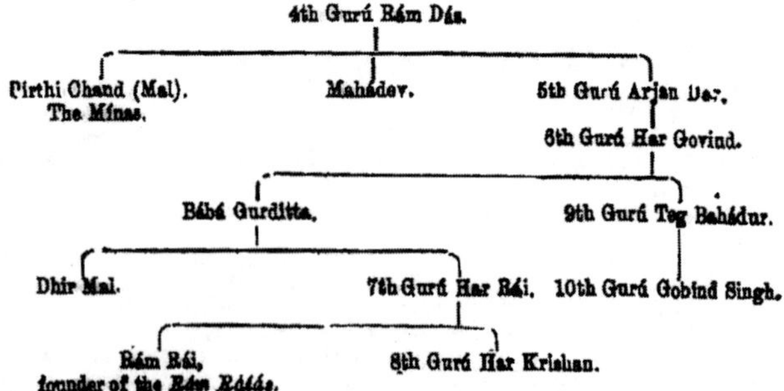

Khazán Singh does not say whose son Dhir Mal was, but he states that he had possession of the *Granth* and supported Rám Rái's pretensions: pp. 150-51.

[4] We also find the Gurú assigning the offerings of Hánsi and Hissár to Galara, a *masand* who lived at Chúhka.

pontifical throne at Anandpur and later under the *takht* or archbishopric at Patna.[1] The *sangats* thus established were not merely places of worship but also wayside refectories which gave food and shelter to indigent wayfarers and each was under a *masand*, a term equivalent to viceroy. When in 1666 Teg Bahádur visited Dacca he found prosperous *sangats* at Sylhet, Chittagong, Sondip, Lashkar and elsewhere and by the time of Gurú Govind Singh Dacca had earned the title of the home of Sikhism.[2] At Paṭna in 1666 was born the future Gurú Gobind Singh. Not long afterwards the Gurú returned to the Punjab, but Govind Singh remained in his native land until the Gurú sent for him and he went to Anandpur.

Recent research has thrown considerable light on the life and propaganda of Gurú Teg Bahádur. At that period the Aroras went north to Kábul and Kandahár, Balkh, Bukhára and even Russia, while the Khatrís monopolised the markets of Eastern and Southern India. Hence when Teg Bahádur was persecuted by his Sodhi brethren and when even the *mutsaddis* of the temple at Amritsar shut its doors against him he found adherents in the Khatri communities dotted all over Hindustan, the Deccan and Eastern Bengal.[3] These colonies probably preserved the secular Kshatriya tradition of the independence of thought and freedom from Brahmanical control.

The enterprise of the Sikh missioners and the distances to which they travelled may be gauged by the recently discovered itinerary of a pilgrim to the Sikh temples in Southern India and Ceylon. The author
1732 S. must have lived long before 1675, but he must have taken boat at Negapattan on the Coromandel coast and returned through Malayalam, in which country he found stray colonies of Bhaṭra Sikhs and met Mayadaman, grandson of Shivanáth,[4] at Sattur. Inquiries recently made by B. Gurbakhsh Singh have thrown much light on the history of Sikhism in Southern India.

The author of the itinerary mentions a viceroy at Tanjore—Airapati Naik. This and other indications would fix his date soon after the battle of Talikoṭe in Akbar's time. Other details as regards topography are also substantially correct. This account places Shiv Náth at Jaffna, in the extreme north of Ceylon. Sikh temples still exist at Rámeshwar, Salur, Bhaker and Shivkanji in Madras and Colombo in Ceylon. Old temples also exist at Burhanpur, Súrat,

[1] There were four of these *takhts* or 'thrones' at Anandpur, Amritsar, Patna, and Nander (Haiderábád, Deccan).

[2] *Dacca Review*, 1915, p. 225 *f*.

[3] *Ib*., 1916, p. 377 *f*.

[4] *Ib*., 1916, p. 376. Trumpp discredited this story, but its substantial truth must now be regarded as established in spite of the pilgrim's exaggerations in his account of the victuals consumed at the daily *yagya* in the principal temple in Ceylon. The name given in the Sikh books is Shivnábh and not *Shivnáth*. *Náth* in Buddhist literature means an evil spirit and *nábh* has sacred associations as in *Padam-nábh* etc. It is quite possible that the name was changed on purpose and the Sikh books give it correctly as known at Jaffna. Another explanation is that Shivnáth in Persian character was misread as *Shivnábh* by early chroniclers. Even in Gurmukhi Shivnábh is apt to be misread as Shivnáth, the letters *b* and *th* being so alike. For a similar reason Banda would be obliged to call himself a Kshatriya instead of a Khatri in the Deccan, where the term Khatri is used for Dheḍ weavers.

Bombay (and Mahalakshmi, Grant Road), Amráoti, Nirmal (District Adilábád—in the Nizám's Dominions). Manuscript copies of the *Granth Sáhib* are to be found at Burhánpur and Súrat, and another old copy with one Bolaji Tripathi at Lonovala (Poona).

The *sangat* at Colombo is in Colombo fort and a Brahmin Misra Jawála Parshád is now in charge. A Sindhi firm—Ṭopan Singh, Moṭhúwál—claim to have been established in Ceylon from before Gurú Nának's time. Their head office is at Karachi and their *munib* or agent in Colombo, Gopál Dás by name, is still known to be a good Sikh. Certain Egyptian mummies in the Colombo Museum are curiously enough identified by the local Sikhs as Shivnáth, his wife and son! Large numbers of Khatrís have been established in Burhánpur from very remote times, and are found as far south as Madras, where a Khatri, Rája Tuljarám, lived not many years ago in Tirmalkheri (Madras town).

At Salur where Gurú Nának is supposed to have held discussions with *yogís* many *maths* or *yogi* temples are found.

Meanwhile Aurangzeb's policy was bearing fruit. In his attempt to Muhammadanize India he had excited grave opposition and Gurú Teg Bahádur recognised that if Gurú Nának's acquiescence in the Moslem sovereignty was to be revoked his own life must be the price of the revocation.[1] Accordingly he sent the Kashmíri *paṇḍits* who had appealed to him in their distress to make a petition to the emperor in these words :—'We live on the offerings of the Kshatrís. Gurú Teg Bahádur, the foremost among them, is now seated on the throne of Gurú Nának and is Gurú of all the Hindus. If thou canst first make him a Mussalmán, then all the Sikhs and Brahmans who follow him, will of their own accord adopt thy faith.' The emperor accordingly summoned the Gurú to Delhi and he replied that he would come after the rains. That season he passed at Saifábád[2] with Saif-ud-Dín whom he converted and then dismissing all his followers save five, among whom was his *díwán*, Mati Dás Chhibra, he set out for Delhi. At Samána a Paṭhán offered him a refuge, but the Gurú went on to Delhi. There he was seized and resisting every inducement to forsake his faith was eventually put to death. To his son Govind Rái he sent a dying message to abide fearlessly in Anandpur. Govind Rái, then a boy of 9, received this behest at Lakhnaur, whence he and his mother retired to Anandpur.

There he received his father's head, which was cremated at that place. Govind Rái was then acknowledged as the 10th Gurú in 1675.

The Sikhs' relations with the Hill States.

The first of the Hill Rájás to accept the teaching of the Gurús was the Rájá of Haripur, in Kángra. He was permitted to see the Gurú

[1] Gurú Nának, it was said, had promised Bábar the empire for 7 generations. Six emperors of his line had reigned, and Teg Bahádur would offer his own life in lieu of the 7th.

[2] Saifábád lies 4 or 5 miles from Patiála.

Govind Rái was here visited by Bhikham Sháh, owner of Kuhrám and Siána, 4 miles from Lakhnaur, and of Thaska which the emperor had bestowed on him. Govind Rái guaranteed his possession of Thaska during the future Sikh domination. Govind Rái's close connection with leading Muhammadans is remarkable.

Amar Dás after eating from his kitchen at which food was prepared and eaten by all castes without distinction.[1] This occurred before 1574.

In 1618 Gurú Har Govind had subdued Tárá Chand, Rájá of Nálagaṛh, who had been in revolt against Jahángír. He was brought before the emperor and the Gurú for his services obtained the honorary command of 1,000 men and 7 guns, with high judicial functions and other honours.

1684 S. In 1627 Gurú Har Govind was invited by some of the Hill Rájás to visit their territory, but he sent Bábá Gurditta, his eldest son, to the (Jaswán) Dún and Hindúr (Nálagaṛh) and he founded Kíratpur in that year.[2]

1692 S. In 1635 however we find Gurú Har Govind himself visiting Rájá Tárá Chand's territory.[3]

1696 S. In 1642 he joined forces with this State and helped the Rájá to defeat the Nawáb of Rúpar.[4]

1713 S. About 1656 we find the Sikhs reducing the Rájá of Kahlúr (Biláspur) to submission.[5]

1739 S. In 1682 Rájá Bhím Chand of Biláspur, in whose territory the Gurú Govind Singh was then residing, demanded gifts which included an elephant called Parsádi (or loans which he did not intend to return) from his guest. He deputed his *wazír*, Parmánand, to obtain these exactions, but the Gurú declined to lend the offerings of the Sikhs. The Rájá's personal threat of explusion was equally ineffectual and so he attacked the Gurú but was routed, losing many men.[6]

1741 S. In 1684 Gurú Govind Singh visited the Sirmúr territory at the Rájá's invitation and founded Páonta on the banks of the Jamna.[7]

Bhím Chand's defeat, however, had rankled and he leagued himself with the Rájás of Goler, Kaṭoch, Jaswál, Káthgaṛh and Nálagaṛh against him.

1742 S. In 1685 they attacked him at Páonta and won over 500 Paṭháns who had been discharged from the imperial service and whom he had

[1] Khazán Singh, p. 118.

[2] *Ib.*, p. 133.

[3] *Ib.*, p. 136.

[4] *Ib.*, p. 139.

[5] *Ib.*, p. 143.

[6] *Ib.*, p. 164. The Sirmúr *Gazetteer*, p. 15, gives a slightly different account. It says that the Gurú declined to surrender an elephant to Rájá Bhím Chand and Hari Chand, both of Biláspur, so they compelled him to leave Anandpur, then in that state, and he came to Toka whence he was brought to Náhan by the Rájá of Sirmúr. Thence he proceeded to Páonta. Meanwhile the Biláspur Rájá had returned the presents made by the Gurú to Rájá Fatah Sháh of Gaṛhwál whose daughter was marrying a Biláspur prince. This insult determined the Gurú to prepare for war and at Bhargani, 8 miles from Páonta, he defeated both Hari Chand and Fatah Sháh. The Gurú resided at Páonta from 1686 to 1689: *Ib.*, p. 112. 1743-6 S.

[7] *Ib.*, p. 166.

employed on the advice of his friend Budhu Sháh of Sádhaura. An equal number of Udásis also deserted him though they had long been fed on his bounty, and if Budhu Sháh had not joined him with 2000 disciples the day would have gone against him. The Gurú then left Páonta for Anandpur and founded Anandgarh, Lohgarh, Kesgarh and Fatehgarh to keep the hill states in check.[1]

The attempt of the Delhi government to collect revenue from the hill Rájás however led some at least of them to change sides, for we soon find the Gurú aiding them with troops to repel a force sent against them. Bhím Chand too had certainly concluded peace with the Gurú, and the Biláspur chronicles even say that in alliance with him he defied the imperial authorities at Kángra and defeated the governor Alif Khan at Nádaun,[2] but many hill Rájás joined Ghulám Husain Khán in his expedition from Lahore.[3] Before he reached Anandpur however he was opposed by one of the hill Rájás who aided by forces sent by the Gurú completely defeated him.

1757 S. But in 1700 disputes arose about fuel and grass and Rájás Bhím Chand and Alam Chand with the help of the Rájás of Biláspur and Nálagarh attacked the Sikhs in the forest, only to be completely routed. Bhím Chand[4] then convened a council of the Rájás of Sirmúr, Kángra, Daraul, Parauli, Dadwál, Srínagar (Garhwál) and other states, besides those mentioned above and they attacked Anandpur with 20,000 men, but failed to take it by siege and were dispersed. But obtaining promise of a reinforcement of 2000 men from the Mughal governor of Sirhind they treacherously attacked him again, only to meet with a second reverse, and yet they were able to compel Ajít Singh to evacuate Kíratpur. The history of this episode is obscure. The Gurú was apparently on friendly terms with the Ráj of Basauli and in 1701 he concluded peace with Bhím Chand once more, though he had been the leader of the confederacy against him. Soon after the Gurú visited Rawálsar in Mandi.

Gurú Govind Singh is said to have come up into the hills from Bilás-pur at the end of the 17th century and went as far as Sultánpur in Kulú There the Rájá asked him to perform a miracle whereupon the Gurú

[1] Khazán Singh, pp. 167-9.

[2] Simla Hill States *Gazetteer*, Biláspur, p. 6. The year of this victory is not stated but it appears to have been won late in Bhím Chand's reign. 1665-92 A D. B. Gurbakhsh Singh points out that it must have occurred before S. 1755 at any rate, as in that year Gurú Gobind Singh wrote an account of all these engagements. The elephant came from Dacca. Unfortunately neither this letter nor the one that followed a few months later is dated, but they were certainly sent after 1748 S. which is the date of the first letter, written while peace still prevailed, though war material was being collected. So the hostilities must have commenced between 1748 and 1755 S., more probably nearer the former date, say about 1749 S. or 1692 A. D. Gurú Gobind Singh's letter to the ancestors of the Phúlkián chiefs, now preserved at Patiála, is dated 1753 S. It invites them to aid him with their horsemen. This appears to have been the last engagement of Gurú Gobind Singh with the hill Rájás, and an account of it is given in the introduction to his *Bachitra Nátak*, completed in 1755 S. The dates of these engagements therefore fall between 1748 and 1755 S.

[3] Khazán Singh, p. 169.

[4] Khazán Singh says Rájá Bhím Chand of Biláspur, but a few lines before he writes as if another Bhím Chand were meant and in this he is correct for Bhím Chand of Biláspur had abdicated in 1692 ; Simla Hill States *Gazetteer*, Biláspur, p 6.

took hold of his own beard and drew it out to a great length, but the Rájá in his turn breathed out a flame which consumed the Gurú's beard and also had him imprisoned in an iron cage.[1] The Gurú then caused himself to be carried through the air, cage and all to Manḍi, where the reigning chief—Rájá Sidh Sain, A.D. 1684-1727—received him with honour and treated him hospitably.[2] Govind Singh's journey into the hills seems to have been with the object of seeking assistance from the hill chiefs against the Muhammadans. He remained some time at Manḍi and the Rájá became his disciple. On his departure he told the Rájá to ask anything he might desire and it would be granted. The Rájá expressed a wish that his capital might never fall into the hands of an enemy, and this promise was given in the following cryptic couplet still current in Manḍi:—

Manḍi ko jab lúṭenge,
Ásmáni gole chhúṭenge.[3]
"When Manḍi is plundered
Heavenly shots will be fired."

Vigne who visited Manḍi in 1839 says that down to that time the Sikhs had never entered the capital though the State had long been tributary to them—indeed from 1809—and for some superstitious notions connected with the above prophecy no servant of Mahárája Ranjít Singh had ever been sent to Manḍi.[4] The receiver of the revenue on behalf of the Sikhs was quartered outside the town and the Mahárája's officer in attendance on Vigne did not enter it.

By some the promise is said to have been made by Banda, the follower of Gurú Govind, but there is no evidence to prove that he ever visited Manḍi.

Manḍi continued to enjoy immunity from Sikh intrusion till 1840 when a force under General Ventura was sent into the hills under the orders of Nao Nihál Singh, grandson of Ranjít Singh. Manḍi was occupied and the Rájá taken by treachery and sent as a prisoner to Amritsar, where he was confined for some time in the fort of Govindgaṛh. In the following spring, soon after the accession of Mahárája Sher Singh in January 1841, the Rájá was released and allowed to return to his capital.[5] General Ventura when returning to Lahore at the close of his expedition took with him the trophies of 200 hill forts—chiefly in Manḍi and Kulu—including those of Kamlágaṛh, the famous Manḍi stronghold which till then was a virgin fortress.[6]

The Sirmúr Gazetteer (p. 15) which is silent regarding the events
1811-27 S. of 1700-01 says that Kírat Parkásh, Rájá of that State from 1754-70, turned his arms against the Sikhs, taking Naráingaṛh, Morni,

[1] Vigne's *Travels*, Vol. I, pp. 99-100.
[2] *The Rájás of the Punjab*, pp. 580-86.
[3] Manḍi *Gazetteer*, p. 9.
[4] Vigne's *Travels*, p. 100.
[5] Manḍi *Gazetteer*, p. 11.
[6] Khan 'n Singh, pp. 175-8.

Pinjaur and other tracts (from them apparently). He then entered into an alliance with Rájá Amar Singh of Patiála.

According to the Biláspur chronicles Mahán Chand, Rájá of that State, 1778-1824 A. D., waged war with the Rájás of Nálagaṛh and Kángṛa and the Sodhís of Anandpur, but they do not state expressly that the Sodhís were in alliance with those states.[1]

An account of the latter Sikh incursions into the hills will be found in Barnes' Kángṛa *Settlement Report*, §§ 56-82, and one of their rule in Kulu in Sir James Lyall's Kángṛa *Settlement Report*, §§ 82-5. No attempt was apparently made to proselytise the hill people and to this day a Rájpút is very rarely a Sikh. Nevertheless there were a few Sikh shrines in the hills at Páonta, in Sirmúr, and at Harípur in Mahlog is a *gurdwára*, the see (*gaddi*) of a sect of *gurús* widely reverenced by Sikhs and Hindus in the lower hills and adjacent plains. This see was founded by Jawáhir Singh,[2] who appears to have been the great-grandson of Ganga, founder of the GANGUSHÁHÍS (Volume II, p. 278).

Elsewhere in the hills hardly a trace of Sikhism exists. In Kángṛa Nának's teachings resulted in the foundation of a shrine near Ráníwál, but it differs little if at all from any other shrine in Kángṛa. It is called Báwá Fathu's shrine.

Three hundred years ago a Brahman of the Bhari *iláqa* in Ráwalpindi asked Bedi Báwa Parjapati for a charm, as his children had all died and vowed to give his first-born to him. The Brahman had five sons, but failed to keep his word, so two of them died. Thereupon he brought one of his sons, Fathu, to the Bedi, who kept him with him. So Báwá Fathu became a *sádhu* and people began to pay him visits. The Brahmans of the shrine are descendants of Báwá Parjapati, a *bhagat* of Gurú Nának. The fair is held on 1st Baisákh.

In Chamba Sikhism never obtained a footing.

The first mention of the Sikhs in connection with Chamba is in the reign of Ráj Singh (A.D. 1764-94), when that Rájá obtained the help of the Rámgaṛhia Sardárs against Jammu and Basohli in 1774-5. In the following year the state became tributary to Jai Singh Kanhiya and paid Rs. 4001 of tribute.[3] This probably continued to be the case till 1785-6 when Jai Singh having been defeated in the plains was compelled to retire from the hills—the suzerainty of the hill states of the Kángṛa group passing into the hands of Sansár Chand of Kángṛa.[4] Chamba came under Ranjít Singh's control in 1809, but was only once visited by a Sikh army in 1844.[5]

Basohli was under the Sikhs in 1783 when Forster passed through it. They had probably been called in in the previous year on account of the invasion of Ráj Singh of Chamba in 1782, referred to by Forster.

[1] Simla Hill States *Gazetteer*, Biláspur, p. 7.

[2] *Ib.*, Mahlog, p. 6: *cf.* Biláspur, p. 12.

[3] Chamba *Gazetteer*, p. 99.

[4] *Ib.*, pp. 100-101.

[5] *Ib.*, p. 108.

In the inner mountains of Bhadrawáh and Kashtwár Sikhism seems never to have obtained any real footing. Kashtwár was under Muhammadan rulers—who were nominally at least subject to the Durránís in Kashmír and later to Ranjít Deo of Jammu, and finally to the Rájás of Chamba, to whom the suzerainty of these states was transferred by Jammu towards the end of the 18th century.

In the outer hills from the Sutlej to the Jhelum Sikh influence began to be felt soon after the middle of the 18th century. In their conflicts with one another the hill chieftains often called in to their help one or another of the Sikh leaders, and the latter took advantage of the opportunity thus given them to establish their power in the hills. The first of these to acquire supremacy in the hills to the east of the Rávi was Jassa Singh of the Rámgarhia *misl* who had probably in the first instance been called upon for help in the way described.[1] He assisted Ráj Singh of Chamba in expelling the Basohli army in 1775 and the latter state received help from another *misl*, probably that of Jai Singh Kanhíya in 1782-8.[2] In a similar manner, when a feud took place between Ranjít Deo of Jammu and his son Brijráj Deo in A.D. 1774, the former received help from the Bhangi *misl* and the latter from the Sukarchakia *misl*, the Sikhs being only mercenaries and ready to sell their swords to the highest bidder. When they came they generally came to stay, and by the beginning of the 19th century all the states of the outer hills, except Kashtwár, had become tributary.

That the tenets of the Sikh faith took root to any extent in the hills is highly improbable, though some of the Rájás may have given a nominal adherence. Between Ranjít Singh and the hill chiefs no love was lost. They despised him as an upstart of lower status socially than themselves: and possessing no claim to their homage and allegiance To Ranjít Singh the Rájpút chiefs "were an object of special aversion, for they represented the ancient aristocracy of the country, and declined to countenance an organization in which high caste counted for nothing."[3]

Among the common people however a certain amount of veneration was developed for the personality of Nának and his descendants called Bedís. For a long time probably the Sikhs in Chamba and possibly in other parts of the hills have been in the habit of transmitting a yearly offering in cash to one of the Sikh shrines in the plains and about 80 years ago this usage spread almost all over the state, but more especially in the Churáh *wizárat* and assumed the character of a voluntary cess on the Hindu community. This cess is farmed out by some Bábás or descendants of Nának, residing in Chamba, at the rate of 4 *chaklís* (nearly an anna) in cash and one *máni* of grain (4 *kachcha sers*) for each household, the cash being paid to the Bábás and the grain going to the collector of the cess as his remuneration.

[1] Chamba *Gazetteer*, p. 99.

[2] Forster's *Travels*.

Ranjít Singh—*Rulers of India*.

Nának as a saint is believed to control one of the infectious fevers, probably typhus, and the offering is meant as a propitiation to ensure protection from the disease. This belief is probably prevalent in other parts of the hills also.

In the Simla Hills an Udási ascetic has become a Hindu god under the name of the Dughli *deota,* whose temple is on a peak of the Darla *dhár*, a smaller range running from south-east to north-west through the centre of the State, parallel with the Bári *dhár*. A fair is held on the 1st Asauj. Dughli is the name of the place. The temple was erected over the tomb of an Udási *faqir* of noted piety. It is a resort of Udásís, and the local people have converted the original saint into a god.[1]

Gurú Govind Singh.—We now come to that great historic figure, the 10th and last Gurú of the Sikhs. Surrounded during his childhood by Hindu influences, Govind Rái succeeded to his office under every temptation to remain within the pale of orthodox Hinduism, and indeed one tradition asserts that his first act was to ascend to the temple of Nainá Deví which stands on a precipitous hill overlooking the Sutlej. Here the Brahmans called on him to sacrifice one of his four sons to the goddess, but their mothers refused to surrender them for this object, and finally five Sikhs offered their heads. One of them was duly offered to the goddess, who promised a world-wide fame for the Gurú's creed. Mythical as the story undoubtedly is, it does not do more than show that Govind Rái was in no way hostile to Hinduism at his accession. But it is not accepted as even metaphorically true by more advanced Sikh opinion. The cult of Deví is no doubt often alluded to in the Sikh writings and histories. Thus Gurú Angad's father had been a devotee of Jawálamukhi, but the Gurú himself was not. His successor Amar Dás had been a Vaishnava, but he was a firm adherent of Nának's teaching. Nevertheless we hear of no explicit condemnation of the cult of Deví until the time of Gurú Govind Singh whose ideas were opposed by the priests. They proposed the performance of a great *homa* rite for the propitiation of Durga, so that she might appear and bless the new Khálsa sect, and they also preached the power of the goddess, persuading the Sikhs to make offerings and sacrifices to her in order to obtain invincibility. The Gurú assented to the proposal in order to prove the hollowness of this cult of Deví and a peak close to Nainá Deví was chosen for the rite. The recitation of hymns began in
1753 S. 1697 and was kept up for a whole year, the chief *pandit* constantly prophesying her advent and finally declaring that she would require the sacrifice of some holy person, hinting at the Gurú's eldest son. But the Gurú suggested that the *pandit's* superior sanctity qualified him as the victim. This suggestion led the *pandit* to depart, never to return, and his companions followed suit. The Gurú cast all the accumulated *ghi* &c. into the great fire pit and declared that the sword he held in his hand was the Deví's symbol. She did not appear. Then the Gurú feasted Brahmans, but expounded to them the brotherhood of man.

[1] Simla Hill States *Gazetteer*, Bághal, p. 6. The place-name Dughli is clearly derived from the *deota* whose own name would seem to mean thin or 'emaciated.'

Soon after the Gurú however began to lead a life of seclusion and the masses believed that his mind had suffered by the appearance of the Deví or some such cause.[1]

The account current in the hills of this event is characteristically different and illustrates the conflict between the teaching of the Sikh Gurús and the orthodox cult of Deví. The story goes that Gurú Govind before embarking on his campaign against the Turks sought the aid of Nainá Deví. He brought with him a Brahman of Benáres and for months kept up the *homa*. At last the Deví appeared and the Gurú, awe-stricken, presented his sword which she touched and disappeared. The Brahman, however, declared that the stigma or defect in the rite caused by the Gurú's display of fear could only be removed by the sacrifice of one of his sons. To this he agreed, but the mothers of his four sons objected. So one of his followers was sacrificed, the goddess re-appeared and promised prosperity to his sect.[2]

Gurú Govind Singh was, however, bitterly opposed to Islám. The execution of his father called for retribution, and the Gurú early instituted the *pahul* or rite of initiation whereby a chosen few[3] were admitted into a sacred brotherhood, called the Khálsa or 'pure' commonwealth of the Sikh votaries. To emphasize the change thereby effected in the initiates' being the Gurú altered his cognomen, whatever it might formerly have been, into Singh,[4] he himself assuming the style of Govind Singh instead of Govind Rái.[5]

As the outward and visible sign of this initiation the Sikh was enjoined to wear the 5 K's—

the *kes* or long hair ;

the *kachh* or short drawers ending above the knee ;

the *kara* or iron bangle ;

the *kripán* or small knife with an iron handle round which the *kes* is rolled and fastened to the head[6] : (some authorities give instead the *khanda* or steel knife)[7] ;

and the *kanghá* or comb.

1 Khazán Singh, pp. 170-78.

2 Simla Hill States *Gazetteer*, Biláspur, pp. 13-14.

3 According to some writers the Gurú initiated five Sikhs only by the *pahul*. Each was styled Bhái, to denote that he was spiritually a brother of his fellows. These appear to be the five alluded to below. Their names were Sáhib Singh, Dáya Singh, Himmat Singh, Dharm Singh and Mohkam Singh.

4 Lit. 'lion.' Singh had long been an affix of names among the military classes of India, though not, I think, confined to Kshatriyas (Temple, *Proper Names of Panjabis*, p. 14).

5 A precisely similar change of suffix is usual (*i*) among *faqirs*—on entering a religious order, and (*ii*) among heirs to the crown—on ascending the throne.

6 Macauliffe in *Calc. Rev.*, 1881, p. 162.

7 The error is due apparently to the fact that the *pahul* of Gurú Govind Singh was called the *khanda pahul* or initiation of the dagger, whereas Banda initiated by the *charan pahul*, whereat the initiate drinks water in which the Gurú's foot (*charan*) has been washed : Khazán Singh, p. 219. The Sikh was always to go armed. Malcolm says an initiate was presented with 5 weapons, a sword, fire-lock, bow and arrow, and a pike ; *Sketch*, in *Asiatic Researches*, XI, p. 285. Cunningham, p. 79.

In accord with, and in amplification of, these signs the Sikh initiate was enjoined, as one under a vow, not to cut his hair or beard,[1] or indeed to shave any part of his person.[2]

[1] In Sikhism the number 5 has always had a mystical significance Gurú Govind Singh deputed 5 chosen Sikhs to Banda's army, and bestowed on him 5 arrows to protect him in extremity: *ib.*, p. 157.

[2] Macauliffe, in *Calc. Rev.*, 1881, p. 162.

But the *pahul* was the essential rite. It is difficult to say why it has ever been described as a form of baptism. The initiate, after bathing and donning clean clothes, sits in the midst of an assembly generally summoned for the purpose, some sugar is mixed with water in an iron basin and five Sikhs in turn stir it with a double-edged dagger chanting certain verses of the *Granth*. After this some of the solution is sprinked over the hair and body of the initiate and some of it is given him to drink. The *raht* or rules of Sikh conduct are also explained to him. The solution is called *amrit*, and *amrit chhakná*, 'drinking nectar,' is thus another name for Sikh 'baptism.' The *amrit* is supposed to confer immortality on this new son of Govind Singh, to make him a Singh (lion) and a true Kshatriya. Finally *karáh prashád* (*halwá*, sweetmeats) is distributed among those present: Narang, p. 81, *cf.* p 78. At initiation the Sikh also becomes a son of Mátá Sáhib Deví, the childless wife of Gurú Govind Singh, who asked for issue and was told she would become the mother of the whole Khálsa: Khazán Singh, p. 163. Women are also initiated by the *khandá pahul* and Khazán Singh says that Mughal and Sayyid women were so initiated in 1750. They were taken in marriage by the Singhs: p. 249. On the other hand Macauliffe says that Gurú Govind Singh appears to have left no instructions regarding the forms of prayer for women or their initiation in the new religion. Nevertheless they offered him homage in his wanderings, ministered to his necessities and received salvation from him as the reward of their attentions. Childless women who visited him miraculously received the gift of children. Mothers, he indicated, could expiate the dread crime of (female) infanticide by simply bathing in full costume in a sacred tank. Women are said to have fought in his battles and to have been wounded on behalf of the Khálsa; and it is recorded that the saintly and childless Máí Bhágo, attired in the Sikh *kachh* and a *pagha* or turban, and armed with a ponderous javelin, commanded a body of the ten faithful Sikhs with whom she watched over the Gurú in his nightly slumbers: *Calc. Rev.*, 1881, p. 75.

Pandit Sheo Naráin, R.B., gives an interesting history of the rite of initiation in his paper on *Pahul* (*Sikh* baptism) in *Journal of the Punjab Historical Society*, IV, pp. 62-7. Deriving the term from *paw*, 'foot' and *hal*, 'shaken' or 'stirred,' he ascribes its origin to Gurú Nának. In its inception the rite consisted of washing a toe of the Gurú in a basin of water which was then drunk by the initiate who had had to spend some time as a novice in the service of the Gurú of his order and attain a certain degree of self-abnegation. Bhái Káhan Singh states that the initiate also drank water touched by the foot of other devout Sikhs, whatever their original castes, so that all pride of caste was destroyed. In the time of Gurú Arjan the water was not touched by the Gurú's toe, but simply placed under the *manja* or *masnad* of the Gurú. But Gurú Govind Singh greatly elaborated the rite and changed its significance.

At the *khanda pahul*, instituted by him, an *iron* vessel is filled with water and sugar, wafers are mixed in it. Instead of being placed below the *masnad* it is set in front of it. The presence of the *Granth Sáhib* is indispensable, together with a reader (*granthí*) and five initiated Sikhs, of pure and unblemished character, called *piárás*. (The *Granth* now-a-days represents the Gurú and the five *piáras* the original five companions.) The novice constantly mutters the *Wáh Gurú*, standing throughout the rite. The *granthi* and the five ministers then announce to the congregation that a candidate desires to enter the fold of Sikhism and on its tacitly assenting the *granthí* exclaims: *Sat Gurú de-ágaya*, 'the true Gurú has assented.' Then prayers are offered, the Gurú's spiritual presence invoked and the novice blessed by the ministers who assume the *birásán* or soldierly pose. One of them holds the vessel with both hands, another fills it with water, a third puts in sugar, a fourth draws a sword and sits opposite the holder of the vessel, and the fifth, the leading minister, thrusts a two-edged dagger into the water and stirs the sugar unceasingly, while he recites the *Japji*, *Jap Sáhib*, *Chaupái* and *Swayyás* from the *Granth*. He then passes the dagger to his colleagues who repeat the rite. On its return to him he also repeats the rite, but recites the *Anand*. Then all five stand up and offer a prayer. The initiation begins with an invocation by the leading minister, after which the *granthi* again asks the congregation to assent and repeats the phrase *Sat Guru de-ágayá*. Then the five ministers approach the candidate who repeats the *mál-mantra* (root text), the first stanza of the *Japji*, five times. Instructed in the

He also wore blue clothes, a colour abhorrent to the Hindu,[1] though anciently worn by Balráma[2] himself. He also avoided the use of tobacco.

Lastly, the Gurú enjoined ablution of the head, arms and thighs (*panjnanish, or pani ishnáná, i.e.*, washing of 5).

The first initiates of the Gurú were 5 men of various different castes and hailing from distant parts of India. They were a barber of Southern India, a Khatri of the Punjab, a Kahár of Jagnanáth, a Ját of Hastínapur (Delhi), a Chhípa of Dwárka in Guzerát, just, one may say, the very classes among which Sikhism has had its fewest converts.[3]

The Gurú also denounced 5 bodies of men, *viz.* (*i*) the Mína-Dhirmallia sectaries, (*ii*) the Rám Ráiás, (*iii*) the *masandias*,[4] (*iv*) the *kuṛímárs*, or those who destroyed girl infants,[5] and (*v*) the *bhaddanis*, who shaved their children's heads. The Gurú also denounced certain practices, *viz.* the use of the *janeo*, the *karma* or belief in metempsy-

essentials of the Sikh creed he bows before the *Granth* and sits in a soldierly posture. Five handfuls of *amrit* are placed in his hands and he repeats the *Wáh Gurú ka khálsa* etc. over each. He then sanctifies his sight by gazing at the principal minister who sprinkles the mixture five times over his face. Then the rest of it is given him to drink, and if more than one novice be initiated at the same time the cup is passed from mouth to mouth to obliterate all caste scruples.

The addition of sugar to the water is accounted for by the following episode:— Gurú Govind Singh intended to use pure water in the rite, but Máta Sáhib Dewán brought *patáshas* and mixed them with it. The Gurú remarked that he had meant to use water stirred by a sword, but the Wáh Gurú intended otherwise. The sweetness added signified that although a Sikh should be a soldier yet he should enjoy peace at home, with God, his *Gurú* and the world and that he is only to fight defensively. Tradition adds that once the Gurú spilt some of the *amrit* and the birds drank it and began to quarrel. The Máta Sáhib to avert this omen persuaded the Gurú to mix *patáshas* in the water. Women also receive the *pahul*, but in their case a single-edged dagger is used, though it is said that efforts are being made to review the ancient practice which used a two-edged one in their initiation also.

The whole history of the rite, its origin and development, show how fundamentally it differs from the ritual significance of baptism. A similar custom will be noticed among the Baloch.

[1] But Muhammadans often prefer blue to any other colour for clothes. No Sikh will or should wear clothes dyed *kasumbha*, or saffron, the favourite colour of Hindu devotees. Govind Singh escaped disguised in blue clothing when he escaped from the battle of Chamkaur, personating a priest of Uch.

[2] Cunningham (p. 79) following Bhái Gurdás Bhalla says 'Krishna' but Balrám is alluded to.

[3] The list was clearly an appeal to the non-existent sentiment of nationality.

[4] The causes of Gurú Govind Singh's hostility to the *masandias* are quite obscure. Malcolm says he put to death many of this *tribe* (*sic*), and described them as 'a sect who call themselves Gurús, or priests, and endeavour to introduce heterodox doctrines': *Sketch* in *As. Res.*, XI, p. 286. They opposed him in his propaganda of the sword, rebelled, established their own sects, and were the *sangatias* referred to in his letters.

Other Gurús retained their *masands* and at Ghuráni in the Sáhibgaṛh tahsíl of Patiála the Marwáha Sarín Khatrís are still *masands* of Gurú Rám Rái in Dehra Dún. They are descendants of Bhái Bálú of Gondwál in Amritsar who was appointed by Gurú Amr Dás and whose shrine is at Dádan in Ludhiána. They now serve the *gurdwárá* in Dehra Dún and also the *darbárs* of Máta Rájkaur at Mani Májra and Bábá Gurditta at Kíratpur: Phulkian States *Gazetteer*, 1904, p. 95.

[5] Cunningham, pp. 78-9. For *bhaddanis* P. Sheo Naráin says 'huqa-smokers' (*nari-már*) is now substituted in the *pahul* rite, but aloofness from either class is now regarded as impracticable.

MMMM

chosis, the distinction of castes (*kelnas*), and division of classes. Their watchwords must be *Kritnásh, kulnásh, dharmnásh, karmnásh*, 'Forsake occupation and family, ritual and ceremonies.'[1]

The transition from theocracy to monarchy.—Gurú Govind Singh perished or disappeared in 1708, a year after Aurangzeb had died in 1707. He was succeeded as military leader, but not as Gurú, of the Sikhs by Banda, the 'Slave' of the departed Gurú once a Bairági devotee but converted to the Sikh faith by the Gurú's supernatural powers. But Banda was nothing more than a devoted, almost fanatical, military commander and under his leadership the political development of the Sikhs ceased. Banda's religious doctrines indeed showed Hinduizing tendencies.[2] His rule was, however, too short to be an enduring influence in Sikhism, for in 1716 he was captured by Abdul Samad Khán, governor of Kashmír and the Punjab, and put to death at Delhi.

The Bandái Sikhs.—The régime founded by Govind Singh was however destined, even before its birth, to be profoundly affected by separatism and even schism. The principal exponent of a more violent policy than the Gurú's was the famous Banda. The death of Aurang-
1118 H. zeb in 1707 was followed by dissensions among his sons. Govind Singh found a protector or at least a sympathiser in the emperor Bahádur Sháh, but he was not able or willing to restrain the activities of Banda. This man had a curious history. By birth a Rájpút[3] of Rajauri in Kashmír he had changed his name of Lachhman Bála to Naráin Dás at the shrine of Rám Thamman near Kasúr and became a Bairágí in 1686. But in 1691 he became a Jogí and an adept in occult science[4] with the name of Mádho Dás. Meeting the Gurú, probably at Nader,[5] he was given the title of Bahádur, with that of Banda which he had earned by his submission to the Gurú, together with five arrows and other weapons. But he was not initiated with the *pahul*[6] and while imparting to him his spiritual power the Gurú enjoined on him five rules according to which he was to remain strictly celibate and truthful, not to start a new sect or use a cushion in a Sikh temple, or allow himself to be styled Gurú, but live in peace with the Singhs.

Banda proceeded to wage open and relentless war on all Muhamdans and he was joined by the Singhs. He exacted vengeance for

[1] According to Cunningham, p. 74.

[2] *Ib.*, pp. 94-5.

[3] Another account makes Banda also a Punjab Khatri of the Siálkot District—perhaps of the Kapúr section. The verses quoted at the end of this section also make him a Khatri of the Sodhi clan. He was married in a Mehra or Marwáha family. The former would make him a Kapúr or a Khanna and the latter a Sodhi according to the endogamous laws prevailing in the Punjab. See note on p. 722.

[4] He possessed a volume called the *Sidh Asúnia*, compiled by a disciple of Gorakhnáth: Macauliffe, *The Sikh Religion under Banda* in *Calc. Rev.*, 1881, p. 155.

[5] This is very uncertain, as indeed is the whole question of Banda's relations with Govind Singh: see Khazán Singh, pp. 198-200. There seems some reason to believe that he had been active before the death of Govind Singh and possibly it was that Gurú's death which caused the leaderless Sikhs to flock to his standard.

[6] Other authorities say he *was* so initiated.

the execution of Gurú Teg Bahádur and for the treachery of the Paṭháns of Damla. Moreover he reduced Sádhaura in spite of its adherence to the Gurú,[1] and some four months before his death he destroyed Sirhind with merciless slaughter. To its province he appointed a governor and a *díwán*, organised its administration and the collection of its revenue.

This victory made many join the Khálsa, but it was not followed up at least by Banda himself. One of his first acts was to chastise the Rám Ráiás of Páel,[2] and then after exacting contributions from Máler Koṭla and Ráikoṭ he retreated to Mukhlasgaṛh in the hills, renamed it Lohgaṛh[3] and provided it with immense stores, but he himself retired into the Joharsar hills for religious meditation. Meanwhile the Sikhs met with defeats at Tirauri and Kharar,[4] but were joined by Banda at Burail and a victory there enabled them to regain Sirhind, which they had lost. But he failed to take Jalálábád by siege and after defeats at Ladwá and Sháhábád in 1709, Sirhind was re-occupied by the Muhammadans and the Sikhs retired to the hills. Banda had apparently again retired to Lohgaṛh whence he emerged for another advance on Sirhind and regained all the country lost by the Sikhs.[5] But again his triumph was short lived for he met with a crushing reverse at Sahárantpur-Buria at the hands of prince Rafi-us-shán and was driven back to Lohgaṛh. Thence he escaped in disguise, fleeing into the hills[6] and getting possession of Sirhind again, but only for a short time as in 1711 the emperor's appearance in person made him seek refuge in the hills once more. At Paṭhánkoṭ he had a successful encounter with the Mughals, killing Shams Khán, a *faujdár*, and Bázíd Khán. The emperor issued an edict that all Hindus should shave off their beards and that all Singhs should be indiscriminately massacred, a step which led to the slaughter of thousands of Hindus on suspicion.[7]

1763 S. Bahádur Sháh's death in 1712 led to the usual strife amongst his sons for sovereignty and Banda took full advantage of it to occupy Sirhind again and compel the Rájás of Sirmúr, Nálágaṛh and Biláspur to submit formally to his allegiance. He reduced the Muhammadan *jágirdárs* of Rúpaṛ, Bassi, Kiri and Bahlolpur to a similar position, and in 1714 was strong enough to hold a regal *darbár* at Amritsar, at which he appeared in royal dress with an aigrette on his head.[8] His

[1] Khazán Singh, *op. cit.*, p. 208.

[2] *Ib*, p. 210. Páel is now in Patiála; Phulkián States *Gazetteer*, 1904, p. 200.

[3] Lohgaṛh, the Sikh name for Mukhlispur, stood on a steep hill a few miles from Sádhaura. Irádat Khán calls it Daber. Its site is now only marked by a mound on a hill encompassed by two mountain streams: G. C. Narang, p. 110. It must not be confounded with the fort in Gurdáspur, also styled by some Lohgaṛh, *ib.*, p. 114. But the precise site of this latter Lohgaṛh is also in dispute. It is identified with Gurdáspur itself and with a village still called Lohgaṛh near Dínanagar, but its site is probably a mound in Bathwála, a village one mile north of Gurdáspur: Gurdáspur *Gazetteer*, 1914, p. 18.

[4] Khazán Singh says Tiravṛi, Sirhind and Kharaṛ, and then observes that the third battle took place at Buṛail. He probably means Tirauri in the province of Sirhind.

[5] *Ib.*, pp. 211-13.

[6] The Rájá of Sirmúr was charged with having allowed him to pass through his territory and was sent a State prisoner to Delhi: *ib.*, p. 214.

[7] *Ib.*, p. 215.

[8] *Ib.*, p. 216.

next step was to take Gurdáspur, Paṭhánkoṭ and Baṭála, which last named town he gave up to indiscriminate pillage and massacre, beginning with its wealthiest quarter, the *muhalla* of the Qázís. These events were followed by the reluctant submission of the Kángṛa chiefs.

In 1713 Farrukhsiár's reign began and he promptly attacked the Sikhs on two sides, calling in a large army from Kashmír and sending picked forces from the east against them at the same time. The Sikhs rallied at Sirhind, but were compelled to fall back on Lohgaṛh which was besieged, until Banda sallied forth from his hill fastnesses and drove back the imperialists, thus bringing the country between Lahore and the Jumna under Sikh control. Farrukhsiar next tried to use the influence of Gurú Govind Singh's widow against Banda, who was excommunicated on eight counts in that he had married, started a new creed, substituted a *charan pahul* for the Sikh *khanda pahul*, invented the war-cry of *fateh daras* (victory of faith), in lieu of the Sikh war-cry, attired himself in royal robes, styled himself the 11th Gurú and claimed to rule the Sikhs, his followers being called Bandái instead of the Singhs of the Gurú.[1] Banda's answer to these charges was significant. He said he was merely a Bairágí *faqír* and not the follower of Govind Singh : yet that he was merely carrying out his orders for the campaign of vengeance and the protection of the Khálsa.

This edict led to the disruption of the Sikhs, the true or Tat Khálsa holding Amritsar, while Banda went to Gurdáspur. His power lay chiefly along the Jammu border as far as Attock, but he had adherents also in Ambála whose *faujdár* they defeated. But all his efforts at a reconciliation with the Tat Khálsa failed and in 1711 he was captured at the siege of Gurdáspur. He is generally said to have been put to death with great cruelty at Dehli, but another tradition is that by a mental process he survived his tortures and resuscitated himself. Refusing the offer of some Singhs to place themselves under his leadership he retired to Bhabbar on the Chenab in the Riásí *pargana* of Jammu where he died in 1741, leaving a son whose descendants still hold charge of his shrine.[2]

Banda's relations to the Tat Khálsa are not very clear.[3] It certainly fought against him at his siege of Lahore, but generally refused to do so. It had made terms with the Mughal governors, but was certainly reluctant to join them in repressing Banda. The Imperialist attitude to the Sikhs indeed changed as soon as Banda had been captured, and the
1782 S. Singhs retaliated. In 1725 they proclaimed their intention of holding the Díwáli fair at Amritsar, but the Bandái Sikhs, still more numerous than the Singhs, disputed the claim. It was settled by lot and most of the

[1] According to Macauliffe (*Calc. Rev.*, 1881, p. 159) he prescribed garments dyed with safflower and red turbans in lieu of the blue clothes of the Sikhs.

[2] The followers of Banda Bairágí are said to still form a sect in the south-west of the Punjab under the name of the Banda-panthi : Maclagan, § 107. Cunningham also mentions them : *Hist.*, p. 378.

[3] According to Macauliffe Banda's hostility to the Sikhs became acute in his later years and he openly proclaimed his purpose to establish himself as Gurú and offer hecatombs of Sikh opponents to Kálí. 'Such sacrifices, initiated and sanctioned by Govind, Banda declared necessary for the success of a new religion ; and his would succeed, when he had filled with human blood the *khapaṛ* or sacred cup of the malevolent deity': *Calc. Rev.*, 1881, p. 159. *Khapaṛ*=skull.

Bandái Sikhs went over to the Tat Khálsa, being initiated by the *khanda pahul*. Confused, desultory fighting ensued with the Imperialists, but in 1731 a Sikh force surprised their main body at Bhilowál, 20 miles from Lahore, and then Farrukhsiár weakly offered them a *jágir* of Rs. 100,000, with the title of Nawáb to cease their depredations. This latter offer the Sikh leaders one and all rejected, but Kapúr Singh of Faizullapur, then working a hand-*pankha*, was decked in the imperial robe, and proclaimed Nawáb. Whatever the truth of this story may be, Kapúr Singh became a notable figure among the Sikhs. He had succeeded his father as leader of the Singhs who subsequently formed the Faizullapuria *misl* in 1915, and in various battles received no less than 48 wounds. It was considered a great honour to be initiated by him and among many others Ala Singh, Rájá of Patiála, and many of his relations received the *pahul* at his hands.[1] He paved the way for the Khálsa's rise to power and its transformation into a monarchy.[2] He appears to have designated Jassa Singh Ahlúwália as his successor in the leadership of the Khálsa.

The Singhs or their leaders however certainly accepted the Dipálpur, Kanganwál and Jhabal *parganas* in *jágir* and abandoning plunder contrived to subsist on its income. But as their numbers increased
1791 S. they divided in 1734 into two *dals* or armies, one called the Budhá or veteran, the other the Ṭaru or young.[3] The latter had five *jatthas*, companies or groups, *viz.* the Shahíds, Amritsarias (headed by Khatrís of Amritsar), the Dallewálias (headed by Khatrís of Dallewála), that of Bábá Kahn Singh,[4] and the Rámdásiás (headed by Rámdásís or Mazhabi Singhs) These *dals* fought in unison, especially in the submontane tracts along the Jammu border, and the division had no religious significance.

The events of the next few years can only be very briefly touched upon. It is however necessary to hark back first for a moment to Banda's relations with the Rájpút chiefs of the Kángṛa hills and the adjoining tracts in the north-west corner of the Punjab plains. As already described the Kángṛa chiefs had reluctantly submitted to him in 1714, and he had undoubtedly found allies in the hills whence he descended in that year to fall upon the country round Baṭála and Kalánaur, and whither he fled when imperial troops were sent against him. In 1716 however he again emerged from his strongholds, falling upon the two towns just mentioned and sacking them with much slaughter of the Muhammadans, including the famous family of Shaikh-ul-Ahmad. But some of the hill Rájás sided with the Mughal governors, for Abdul Samad Daler-jang, governor of Lahore, set out in pursuit of him assisted not only by the *hákims* of Eminábád, Pasrúr, Paṭṭi and Kálánaur but also by Rájá Bhím Singh of Kaṭoch and Dhrúva Deva of Jasrota.[5]

1795-6 S. But Nádir Shah's invasion in 1738-9 appears to have led indirect-

1 Khazán Singh, p., 286. But *cf.* p. 277 f.

2 *Ib.*, pp. 277-8, where an account of Kapúr Singh is given which totally negatives the idea that he ever worked a pankha.

3 G. C. Narang calls it the Tarúna-ḍal, p. 126. Neither form is given in Maya Singh's *Punjabi Dicty.*

4 Its leaders were Dhillon Jáṭs and an Ahlúwália: *ib.*, p 287. The Dallewália of the Taru *ḍal* appear to be quite distinct from the Dallewália *misl.*

5 *Ib.*, p. 289.

ly to a general combination between the Mughal governors and the Hill Rájás to put down the Sikhs, although they had fiercely assailed the invader on his retreat. The Sikhs had seized the opportunity allowed them by the confusion created by the invasion to plunder Muhammadan villages and Nawáb Kapúr Singh had refused to join Nawáb Zakaría Khán, governor of Lahore, in resisting them. A demand for restitution of half the booty wrested from Nádir Sháh was rejected by the Sikhs and this exposed them to the enmity of Hindus as well as Muhammadans.
1805 S. After Ahmad Sháh's invasion of 1748 a proclamation issued for their extermination. Abut 15,000 Sikhs had collected in the dense jungle of Káhnúwán which Lakhpat Rái, Khatri, chief minister to the governor at Lahore, invested. His blockade lasted three months and when the Sikhs had exhausted their ammunition they tried to cut their way out towards the hills through Paṭhánkoṭ, only to find the passes all blocked by the Hill Rájás under orders from the governor of Lahore.[1] Finally they broke through towards the south and directed their course towards the Málwa. This fight was known as the Chhoṭa Ghallu-
1813 S. ghara. Again in 1756 when Adína Beg, governor of Lahore,[2] fled before Ahmad Sháh's invasion of that year he sought protection under the Hill Rájás.[3]

After Banda's execution the Sikhs waged implacable war against the Muhammadans, but made no attempt to establish an organised government. In 1748, Cunningham states, the *ḍal* of the Khálsa, 'the army of the elect,' was proclamied by Jassa Singh Kalál, one of their ablest leaders and head of the Ahlúwália *misl*,[4] and a few
A.D. 1757-8. years later he struck coins in the Mughal mint at Lahore with the legend: "Coined by the grace of the Khálsa in the country of Ahmad, conquered by Jassa the Kalál."[5] In 1761 when Ahmad Sháh retired from the Punjab after his great victory at Pánípat, Jassa Singh attacked him while he was crossing the Biás and released about 22,000 Hindu captives, male and female.[6] For this feat he was popularly known as Bandichhoṛ or 'the liberator.' He also occupied Lahore. But the Sikhs had to cope with internal dissensions, for about this time the *mahant*, who was Hindál's successor at his shrine in Janḍiála, turned against the Singhs and tampered with Nának's biography. He had destroyed hundreds of innocent Singhs and now called in the aid of the Abdáli whose forces in 1862 raised the siege of Janḍiála which the Sikhs abandoned, concentrating at

[1] Gokal Chand Narang, *Transformation of Sikhism*, p. 114, citing Muhammad Qásim's *Ibratnáma*, p. 51.

[2] *Ib.*, p. 244.

[3] *Ib.*, pp. 247-8

[4] *Hist.*, p. 101. It would appear that Jassa Singh only revived the *ḍal*, no longer divided, but whether he gave it a new significance cannot be affirmed with any certainty.

[5] Cunningham, p. 105 G. C. Narang gives the inscription:—

Sikka zad dar jahán bafazl-i-Akál,
Mulk-i-Ahmad girift Jassa Kalál,

Which would give rather a different meaning. He adds that the Sikhs used the old Mughal mint and that Jassa Singh was styled Pádsháh by his own followers, but the Sikhs never regarded him as such, nor did he claim any superiority over the Khálsa: p. 147. Lepel Griffin says that 'Akál,' not 'Khálsa' is the correct reading, but he points out that no such coins are extant and that the *qázis* and *mulláhs* very possibly struck a few to incite Ahmad Sháh's resentment against the Sikhs; *The Rájás of the Punjab*, p. 461.

[6] Khazán Singh, p. 253.

the siege of Sirhind which they would probably have taken in that year but for the advance of the Sháh's forces, allied to the Muhammadan chiefs of Máler Kotla, Baroch and other places.[1] Their great defeat at the hands of the Abdáli near Hathúr—the *vada ghallu ghara* or great defeat—followed in the same year.

Nevertheless in 1763 the Sikhs took Sirhind, sacked and destroyed it. This event virtually decided the fate of the Punjab proper as far as the Abdális were concerned, and the generally received account is that in 1762 Alá Singh of Patiála received the first title of Rájá ever bestowed on a Sikh chieftain,[2] and, though no coins of his appear to be extant he seems to have minted rupees in 1763 or two years before his death which occurred in 1765.[3] The Sikh policy was radically changed from that time. The Phúlkián chiefs became sovereigns in their own States. Tradition indeed describes how after their victory at Sirhind in 1763 "the Sikhs dispersed as soon as the battle was won, and how riding day and night, each horseman would throw his belt and scabbard, his articles of dress and accoutrement, until he was almost naked, into successive villages, to mark them as his." This description may well have been true of their earlier conquests, but the old Mughal province of Sirhind was partitioned in a much more systematic way.

In 1764 the Sikh chiefs assembled at Amritsar and proclaimed their supremacy and struck the Nánakshâhi or Govindshâhi rupee which bore the inscription :—

Deg wa Teg wa Fatih nusrat be drang,
Yáft az Nának Gurú Govind Singh.
"Gurú Govind Singh received from Nának,
The Sword, the Bowl and Victory unfailing.[4]

This inscription was adhered to in the main by later Sikh chiefs, including Ranjít Singh, though petty chiefs occasionally inserted the emperor's name.[5] It was also retained by Nábha, but never adopted by the other two Phulkián States.

From time to time attempts were made to restore the Sikh theocracy, under representatives of the sacred Khatri families. For instance in 1800 Sáhib Singh Bedi, a descendant of Bábá Nának, 'pretended to religious inspiration,' collected a large force, invested Ludhiána, took Máler Kotla and 'called on George Thomas to obey

Sahib Singh, Bedi.

[1] Khazán Singh, p. 255.

[2] Khazán Singh however gives a different account of the Abdális' 'lease' of Sirhind Province to the Patiála chief. According to him it was offered by Ahmad Sháh in 1765 to the Pathâns of Máler Kotla and the chiefs of Ráikot, but they refused it owing to their fear of the Sikhs. It was accordingly farmed to Alá Singh with the title of Rájá-i-Rájagán Mahindar Bahádur and he was at the same time permitted to strike coin in his own name. The Singh chiefs declined to accept *jágírs* offered to them through the Rájá. Khazán Singh adds that he was put under a religious ban for his submission to the Abdáli: p. 260.

[3] See Griffin's *Rájás of the Punjab*, pp. 26, 285-8. For the curious inscription on the coins of Patiála and Jínd see pp. 286-7.

[4] Khazán Singh, p. 264. The *deg*, lit. a big cooking vessel, typifies the earth which produces food for the world: *ib.*, p. 507. Teg Bahádur had disclaimed that designation, saying that he aspired to be called Deg Bahádur or 'the lord of bounty' not 'lord of the sword': *ib.* p. 150. *Cf.* Cunningham, p. 59, note.

[5] Cunningham, p. 111, note.

him as the true representative of the Sikh prophet.'[1] But the time had gone by for militant religious leaders and the Bedi soon retired north of the Sutlej.

THE SIKH RÉGIME.

The Sikh government was a curious mixture of theocracy, democracy and absolutism. At its head stood the Gurú, and in later times the Mahárája. Below them was the Gurúmaṭṭa or council of the Gurú which was in theory convened in any emergency. Of its precise constitution little is known, but it included the Sikh chiefs and was held at Amritsar. It was convened by the Akális (or according to other authorities by the *granthís*), and was, like them, established by the 10th or last Gurú Govind Singh,[2] its last meeting being held in 1805 when the British drove Holkar to seek an asylum in the Punjab. Its main function, or one of its chief functions, was to choose a leader of the Khálsa armies, but on occasion it acted as a judicial body, deciding a case of disputed succession. Its meetings were conducted with religious solemnity. When the members were seated the holy books were placed before them and to these they bowed with the customary exclamations: '*Wáh Gurúji ká Khálsa! Wáh Gurúji ki fateh.*' One account has it that cakes of wheat, butter and sugar were placed upon the volumes and covered with a cloth. After they had received the salutations of the assembly its members rose, the *granthís* or Akális prayed, and music was performed.[3]

When the prayers were finished the *granthís* bade the assembly be seated, and the cakes were uncovered, to be eaten by all, whether Hindu or Muhammadan, high or low, as a token of union in a common cause. The Akalís then proclaimed: 'Sirdárs! This is a Gurúmaṭṭa,' whereupon prayers were again said aloud. The chiefs then swore on the *Granth* to lay aside all feuds, and proceeded to the business of the assembly.[4] After this council ceased to meet the Akális lost much of their influence.

After the Gurúmaṭṭa had ceased to meet the army gradually came to be the representative assembly of the Sikhs, and it in turn was represented by a committee or assemblage of committees, termed *panch or panchá-*

[1] Cunningham, p. 181.

[2] Macauliffe, indeed, states that the *Gurúmaṭṭa* was established by Gurú Hargovind (*Calc. Rev.*, 1881, p. 63), while Cunningham says that perhaps the first regular Gurúmaṭṭa was held in 1762 when the army of the 'Khálsa' assembled at Amritsar (p. 108), but it is very doubtful whether the Sikhs were strong enough in that year to hold Amritsar in any force. This is, moreover, intrinsically improbable. The Gurúmaṭṭa, it is most likely, was founded by Gurú Govind Singh in pursuance of his general and well-defined policy, especially in view of the fact that with him the line of the Gurús would end. In 1762 the Sikhs had no known democratic leader and their whole policy was on the verge of a complete reversal, from democratic theocracy to monarchy.

Khazán Singh gives a very different meaning to the term *gurúmaṭṭa*. He applies the term to a resolution passed by any assembly of 5 orthodox Singhs, the Gurú (Govind Singh) having laid it down that wherever 5 such Singhs were gathered together the Gurú must be considered as present among them, and enjoined that all affairs of State or religion must be considered at such an assembly: p. 265. But he adds, 'all State affairs were carried out by *gurúmaṭṭas* (resolutions of a cabinet-council) and the resolutions passed were strictly adhered to.'

[3] Lepel Griffin: *Law of Inheritance to Sikh Chiefships*, p. 50.

[4] Murray's *History of the Punjab*, pp. 181-2.

yat, *i.e.* a jury or committee of five, composed of men selected from each battalion, or each company, in consideration of their general character as faithful Sikh soldiers, or from their particular influence in their native villages.[1] Under this system, rude as it was, the relation of the Sikh army to the State had wholly changed: it was no longer the willing instrument of the Government, but looked upon itself and was regarded by others as the Khálsa itself assembled by tribes or centuries to take its part in public affairs. Even in the crude form of representation thus achieved, the Sikh people were enabled to interfere with effect, and with some degree of consistency, in the nomination and removal of their rulers, but in this large assemblage military license was sometimes added to the popular tumult, and the corrupt spirit of mercenaries to the barbarous ignorance of ploughmen.

The head of the Khálsa exercised both spiritual and temporal authority, and this office devolved by appointment, not by natural descent, until the demise of the 10th and last Gurú. Thus Bábá Nának bequeathed his spiritual office to Lehna, a Trihún Khatri, who took the title and name of Gurú Angad. His two sons were not even initiated as Sikhs and his office descended to Amar Dás, a Bhalla Khatri, who had served him in the capacity of a water-carrier. Amar Dás left a daughter, on whose husband Rám Dás, a Sodhi Khatri, he bestowed the *barkat* or apostolic virtue, as a reward for her filial love and obedience. It is also said that Rám Dás' wife obtained from Gurú Amar Dás a promise that the sacred office should remain with her posterity. However this may be, the fatal principle that spiritual sanctity follows natural descent was now introduced and Arjan Dev, Rám Dás' eldest son, succeeded his father. Under him the customary offerings of the Sikh converts or adherents were reduced to a systematic tax, and the first attempts at regular administration were made. On his death his brother Pirthí Chand aspired to the succession, but his son Har Govind, although only a boy of eleven, was acknowledged as Gurú.[2] Har Govind was succeeded by his grandson, Har Rái, the younger son of his elder son, Gurditta.[3]

Har Rái also left two sons—Rám Rái, the offspring of a hand-maiden and Har Kishen. The latter was duly acknowledged, but died in childhood, and the succession passed to Teg Bahádur, the third son of Har Govind. From him it descended to his only son Govind, the tenth and last of the Gurús. But on his death in 1708 the line of the Gurús came to an end, for, in anticipation of his death, after he had been mortally wounded by one of Painda Khán's two sons, he appointed the *Granth Sáhib* as his successor, with the customary rites of a Gurú's installation, and entrusted his Khálsa to the bosom of the ever-lasting Divine, declaring that the appointed ten had accomplished their mission.[4]

Gurú Govind organised the Sikhs as a militant democracy. He

[1] Cunningham's *History of the Sikhs*, pp. 258-4.

[2] Pirthi Chand however retained a few followers, called Mínas according to Cunningham, *History of the Sikhs*, p. 57 n. His descendants hold Gurú Har Sahái in Ferozepore.

[3] This is Murray's account—in his *History of the Panjab*, I, 97. Cunningham, however, speaks of Dir Mal as Gurditta's younger son: p. 64 n.

[4] Khazán Singh, p. 203.

instituted the *pahul*,[1] a rite of initiation, on the one hand : on the other requiring his followers to break the Brahminical thread: and this rite was far from being merely religious.

The initiated Sikhs (*pahulias* or Singhs) formed the Khálsa,[2] the 'chosen' or 'elect,' the commonwealth or state of the Gurú and year by year the *sarwat Khálsa* or whole Sikh people met once at least at Amritsar during the Dasehra.[3]

This commonwealth was organised into a number of *misls* or confederacies.[4]

These confederacies were loosely organised and varied from time to time in power, and even in designation. They are usually recorded to twelve in number, but more correctly as eight, supplemented by four *dehras* or camps.

The following were the Sikh *misls*, and the castes from which they were, at least mainly, recruited :—

No.	Name.	Caste.	Capital.	Possessions allotted in 1759.
I	The Bhangís, so called because they were addicted to hemp (*bhang*).	Játs ...	Amritsar ...	Amritsar, Tarn Táran, Gujrát, Wazírábád, Siálkot and Chiniot.
II	Nishánias, or standard-bearers, from *nishán*, a standard.	Khatrís and Rangrethas[5] or converted sweepers.	Ambála ...	...
III	Rámgarhias, from Rámgarh, a village near Amritsar.	Tokhás or Bharáís (carpenters) and Játs.	Sri Hargovindpur.	Hargovindpur, Batála and Mukerián *parganas* on the Biás.
IV	Ahlúwálín, from Ahlú, a village near Lahore.	Kaláls ...	Kapúrthala	Núrmahal, Talwandi, Phagwára, Kana Dhillon, and Hariána
V	Kanhia or Ghania, from Ghani, a village near Lahore.	...	Sohíán ..	Ajnála, Sohíán, Nag, Gurdáspur, Dehra Bábá Nának, Kalánaur, Pathánkot and Sujánpur.
VI	Faizullapuria, or Singhpuria.	Játs ...	Jullundur	Jálandhar, Haibatpur, Patti etc.
VII	Sukr-Chakia ...	Játs .	Gujránwála	Gujránwála, Kunja etc.
VIII	Dallawália[6]	Játs ...	Ráhon	Nakodar, Talban, Badála, Ráhon, Phillaur etc.

[1] *Pahul* possibly means 'gate,' Gr. *pute*; if this is so, the idea underlying the rite has some striking analogies with the modern Pers. *báb*. But a better explanation is that it means 'whetting,' as a blacksmith hardens soft iron.

[2] *Khálsa* for *Khálisa*, Ar: lit. pure, special, free. In India its original meaning was apparently "crown province" or domain : *Tabaqát-i-Násiri*, Raverty's Translation, II, pp. 746, 767 *bis*, 768 n. Khálsa was originally used to denote the followers of Gurú Govind as opposed to the Khulása, *i. e.* those of Gurú Nának, but this latter term has now fallen almost entirely out of use.

[3] Cunningham, p. 112.

[4] *Misl* is also an Arabic word, meaning, literally, 'alike' or 'equal.' For the equality among the Sikh Sirdárs see Lawrence's *Adventures in the Punjab*, pp. 131, 132 (k).

[5] This word is of obscure origin, and various etymologies have been proposed, but it is suggested that it is a corruption of the English word 'recruit.' It occurs at least as early as 1849 in Cunningham's *History of the Sikhs* (pp. 75 n. and 379) but *lambar* (from number) appears to have been adopted quite as early by the Sikhs.

[6] Not to be confused with the Dallawália of the Taru Dal.

The four dehras.

No.	Name.	Caste.	Capital.	Possessions allotted in 1759.
I	Shahíds, or 'martyrs'[1] ...	Játs ..	Sháhzádpur	...
II	Nakkais,[2] from Nakka ...	Játs ...	Chúnián ...	Chúnián, Bahrwál, Khem Karn, Khudián etc.
III	Panjgarhias or Krora-Singhias, who were divided into (a) Shám-Singhan and (b) Kalsias, the latter being further subdivided into Laud-pindián and Barápindián or Birk and Jahálián.[3]	...	Bhúnga ...	The Karorís got Nawashahr, Burka, Bassián, Pindorián, Hoshiárpur, Bhanga and Kathgarh.
IV	Phúlkián ...	...	Patiála, Nábha &c.	...

Territorial divisions.—The Sikhs formed several territorial groups. The two principal divisions were, and still are, the Mánjhi and Málwáí. The former derived its name from the Mánjha or 'mid land' and originally included all the Sikhs north of the Sutlej, while the term Málwáí was applied to all south of that river, though the Málwá only includes the tract which lies between Sirhind and Sirsa. But besides these two divisions minor groups were distinguished. The Sikhs settled in the Sindh Ságar Doab were known as Dhanígheb Singh, and those in the Chinhat Doáb as Gujarát Singh. Those of the Rachna Doáb were designated Dharpí Singh, the term Mánjhi being sometimes confined to the Sikhs of the Mánjha proper. The Sikhs in the Jullundur Doáb were known as Doába Singhs, and those of the country south of the Sutlej as Málwá Singhs.[4]

Taxation.—From the tracts of country which the Sikhs subdued but could not hold, they exacted *rákhi* or the price of 'protection.' This tribute was regularly levied and varied in amount from a fifth to a half of the revenue or government share of the produce.[5]

The Sikh military resources.—The great mass of Sikhs were horsemen and speedily became famous for their effective use of the matchlock when mounted. Infantry was used almost solely to garrison forts, and cannon, among the early Sikhs, was unknown. Very varying estimates were formed of their numbers. In 1783 Forster estimated them at 200,000, but others put them at 300,000 men! Browne reckoned them at 73,000 horse and 25,000 foot. Twenty years later Franklin declared they mustered 248,000 cavalry, but, apparently on George Thomas'

[1] Khazán Singh justly describes this as a religious rather than a military body: p. 280. It was a militant order of Sikhism, but not to be confused with the Akális or Nihangs, as G. C. Narang appears to suggest: p. 180. Founded by Díp Singh, a Ját of Pohu in Amritsar, its most prominent member was Suchs Singh.

[2] Sometimes called, quite erroneously, the Nagarias.

[3] Wynyard's *Ambála Settlement Report*, pp. 19 *ff.*

[4] Murray, I, 31.

[5] Cunningham's *History of the Sikhs*, p. 118 n.

authority, subsequently reduced their effective strength to 64,000, within 1800, only 40 field guns.

In later times the Sikhs enlisted Muhammadans in their light cavalry and they were called *gurcharas*.

Sikh quoits.—According to Osborne the quoit is an arm peculiar to the Akális. It is a steel ring, 6″ to 9″ in diameter, and about 1″ in breadth, very thin and with its edges ground very sharp. The Akális are said to be able to lop off a limb at 60 or 80 yards distance, but Osborne had a poor opinion of their skill.

Rosaries.—The Sikh rosaries are :—

All Sikhs	...	*lohe kí mála*, of iron beads.
Nánakpanthís	...	*sphatik*, white crystal.
Kúkas	...	*un kí mála*, black (and white) beads of wool.

Sikhs also use a rosary of 27 beads and a head bead, black and made of iron.[1]

Sikhism in art.—In art Sikhism cannot claim an exalted place. The Sikhs had indeed begun to counteract some of the tendencies of the later Muhammadan style. The Sikh wood-carving was their most characteristic medium. It is distinguished by elaborately lined and twisted foliage, with small grotesque figures of men and animals, but it retained the late Mughal pillar, pilaster and *mihráb*, with flatness of relief, absence of under-cutting, a free use of geometric diapers, incised in line merely, in relief or in framed lattice-work.[2]

The following notes supplement the account of the Akális (Vol. II, p. 9) and that of the Nirmalas (III, p. 172):—

The Bibeki Akális.—The strictest of the Akális acquired the title of Bibeki (from a Sanskrit word 'meaning discrimination') or 'the conscientious' and engrafted on their own creed all the prejudices of Hinduism. With the Vaishnavas they would not eat meat or any article of food or drink not prepared with their own hands. To such an extreme was this rule pushed that they would not taste food cooked by their wives, eat fruit bought in the market or drink water which they themselves had not drawn from the well. They considered it a sin to eat bare-headed and would pay a fine to the temple if they did so inadvertently. They did not remove the hair from any part of their persons and in lieu of the Hindu *janeo* wore a sword. They were very strict in wearing the 5 *Ks.* and will not drink water without immersing in it a knife or dagger. They added the word *singh* as an affix to all substantives and sometimes the other parts of speech, and they transposed all feminine nouns into the masculine gender. Thus they would say: 'place the inkstand *singh* on the table *singh*,' and *kanghi* a comb became *kangha*.

Some Akális call themselves Nihangs, from *nihang* 'a crocodile.' Their high-peaked turbans are said to have earned them this title from

[1] I. N. Q., IV, § 146.

[2] Journal of Ind. Art, I, p. 29.

Gurú Govind Singh, but another version has it that during one of Zamán Sháh's marauding inroads they donned the high-peaked turbans of the Turki soldiers and so disguised attacked his force at night and destroyed it. Yet a third account is that the lofty turban or *dumbálá* ('high-tailed') was not adopted by them till Ranjít Singh's time when the example of Bholá Singh, a gigantic Akálí whose height was enhanced by his high-peaked turban, induced them to adopt a similar head-gear.[1]

Authorities differ as to the origin of the blue dress. It is said to have been adopted in imitation of Gurú Govind Singh who escaped by donning the blue garb of a Muhammadan pilgrim to Mecca and personating a priest of Uch when he was driven from Chamkaur and pursued into the wastes round Bhaṭinda.

According to Macauliffe[2] the Nirmalas do not deem the *pahul* or rite of initiation of vital importance though they are baptised Sikhs. Many do not wear long hair and for the *kachh* they substitute the loosely tied *langoṭa* or loin-cloth of the Hindu *faqír*. Above all they wear the ochre-coloured *bhagwa*, a colour forbidden to all true followers of Gurú Govind Singh.

Some account of the Sanwal-sháhís, an off-shoot of the Sikhs, will be found in Volume III, page 380 *infra*. The conjecture put forward in the Punjab *Census Report*, 1902 (page 135), that they are identical with the Cháwal-sháhís appears correct, since their founder Somán was an Aroṛa of the Cháwala section. The title of Sháh was bestowed on him by Gurú Arjan as a reward for his zeal in helping to construct the Hari-mandar tank at Amritsar. To its cost he devoted his income. His descendants continued to serve the Gurús, and when the tenth Gurú gave *amrit* to his disciples Mihar Sháh, a descendant of Somán Sháh, was allowed to take it also. Hence the Gurú added the title of Singh to that of Sháh and his descendants still bear the double title. The Gurú also conferred on him the right to levy *sikhí*[3] in Sindh etc. and made him Gurú of those parts of India. He also bestowed on him 5 gifts, *viz.* a writ of appointment, a copy of the *Granth* in his own hand-writing, a drum, a hammer and 5 *sers* of *khichrí*. He was enjoined: (1) to keep alive the memory of *kál* (death) and *Akál* (God), (2) to propagate religion and take peaceful measures for the public weal, (3) to rise in the last watch of the night in order to show humility by worshipping God, (4) to maintain the Gurú's *langar*, (5) to lead people to the right path; and (6) to cherish a sincere belief in the *bachans* (sayings) and *bánís* (hymns) composed by the Gurú. Many people of all castes, Brahmans, Acharajs, Bhāṭs, Khatrís and other Hindus became his disciples. His followers are to this day found in Kábul, Kandahár, Khost, Bangash and Dawar, as well as all over the Western Punjab. They pay an annual *nazráná* as well as dues at marriages and deaths.

[1] Macauliffe, *The Sikh Religion under Banda* in *Calc. Rev.*, 1881, p. 164 *f.*

[2] *The Sikh Religion under Banda* in *Calc. Rev.*, 1881, p. 168.

[3] *Sikhí* was equivalent to the *dasaundh* or else replaced that tithe, the right to collect which had been abused by the *masandias*.

Mihar Sháh Singh's son, Gharíb Sháh Singh, followed in his father's footsteps. Of his three sons, Himmat Sháh Singh, Samran Sháh Singh and Sanwal Sháh Singh, the eldest had a son Sundar Sháh Singh, whose descendants, found in Isa Khel, Lakhi and Bannu, are known as Sundar Sháhias. The descendants of the other two sons are found in Bhakkar and Dera Ismáíl Khán. Of them one family went to tahsíl Rangpur and one to Odo-Sultán in Jhang. The Sanwal-sháhís must not be confused with the Bhái Khel, who are not Cháwalas but Hojás. They collect *nazrána* in the Western Punjab and pay a fixed contribution to the Gurús of Gurú Koṭ and Har Sahái in Ferozepur but do not act as their agents, and if they cease to pay their quota they cease also to collect *nazrána*. All affect the title of Singh, whether they wear the *kes* or not. The Cháwala Sánwal-sháhís take brides from the Utrádha Aroṛas and give them to be Bhái Khel and others.

Some Sikh shrines.

The principal Sikh shrines are at Amritsar and in the Gurdáspur District. A description of them here would require too much space, but a few notes on the lesser shrines in Gurdáspur and elsewhere may be of interest.

In Gurdáspur the *mandir* at Dehra Bábá Nának is visited by Sikhs on the Baisákhi, on the *púranmáshi* in Kátik, the Diwáli, and from 21st to 23rd Phágan when the Chola Sáhib ceremony is observed. Built in 1744 S. the *mandir* contains the tomb of Gurú Nának. Its affairs are managed by an Udási *mahant* who is celibate and succession is governed by spiritual descent. A *bhog* of *kaṛáh parshád* is offered every morning and on fast days milk is offered as such.

At the Ṭahli Sáhib *mandir* no fair is held. Bábá Sri Chand is said to have cleaned his teeth here with a *dátan* (toothbrush) and to have planted it in the ground. From it sprang the *ṭahli* tree, after which the temple is named. Portraits of Gurú Nának and his son Bábá Sri Chand are painted on its walls. Its affairs are managed by an Udási *mahant* who is also celibate. Food cooked in the temple is offered to the *Granth*. Another Ṭahli Sáhib has a similar origin. It also is in charge of an Udási *mahant*.

At the *mandir* of Sri Chola Sáhib annual fairs are held on the *púranmáshi* in Kátak, Baisákhi, Diwáli and on 21st, 22nd and 23rd Phágan. It is called after the Chola Sáhib or 'gown' preserved in it. Founded in 1941 S. it contains a *Granth* and its affairs are managed by Báwás, but its *pujári* is a Bedi who is not celibate and succession is governed by natural relationship.

Connected with this are some smaller temples in the town—all managed by the *mahant*. Another Sri Chola *mandir* is visited on 21st, 22nd and 23rd Phágan. Founded in 1947 S. it contains nothing but the *chola*. Its *pujári* is a Bedi who is not celibate. A *bhog* of flowers is offered in the morning.

A shrine of peculiar interest is the mosque (*masjid*) of Gurú Har Gobind Sáhib. No fair is held here. An adversary of this Gurú in the service of Sháh Jahán complained to the emperor that the Gurú was biased against the Muhammadans, whereupon the emperor held an enquiry. The officers entrusted with it came to the Gurú and found him building this mosque, but the precise year of its foundation is not known. Its affairs are managed by one Sáín Pohu Sháh, a Qureshi. The Imám is held in respect both by the Hindús and Muhammadans.

At the *mandir* of Manji Mátá Sáhib no fair is held. It is said that the mother (*mátá*) of Gurú Bhág Singh, a descendant of Dhir Mal, performed her devotions on a bed where the present temple stands. The date of its foundation is not known. It contains the Manji Sáhib or bedstead. Its *pujári* is a Brahman, appointed by the Gurú of Kartárpur. It is connected with the chief *mandir* in Kartárpur.

At the Damdama Sáhib *mandir* a monthly fair is held every *púranmáshi*, and once a year on the Baisákhi.

Gurú Har Gobind used to walk along the bank of the Beás to practise archery. After his death it was revealed in a vision to Bhái Káhn Singh that the point of an arrow once shot had stuck in the *tharra* or platform which formed the Gurú's seat. He was also directed to build the *mandir*. Founded in 1855 S., it contains no image, but a *Granth* is kept in a *báradari*. Its affairs are managed by an Udási *sádhu*. A *bhog* of *karáh parshád* is offered to the *Granth*, a sacred lamp is kept lit and fire burning at all times.

The history of the Darbár Sáhib in Niohla Kalán in Batála tahsíl, a *gurdwára* at which 4 fairs are held, on the Baisákhi, during the *shrádhs*, on Mágh 1st and the *Amáwas* of each month, is obscure. An old man, it is said, had been given the power to work miracles by Gurú Nának. He lived in the village of Rám Dás. After his death, one Sáhib Rám Kaur, seventh in descent from him and blessed with the same gift, was installed on the *gaddi*. But of his four sons, Kishen Kaur, Mohar Singh, Anúp Singh and Jawáhir Singh, only Mohar Singh succeeded him. He was on bad terms with his brothers, and so once when Sáhib Rám Kaur and Anúp Singh went out shooting they found themselves shut out of the temple on their return. By the advice of the neighbouring villagers they took possession of land in Nicha Kalán where after Anúp Singh's death a *samádh* of brick was built—nearly 200 years ago.

At the *mandir* of the Darbár Sáhib in Dera Bábá Nának fairs are held on the *shankránt* or 1st of every Hindu month, and also on the *púranmáshi*. Gurú Nának's wedding was celebrated here in the light half of Bhádon in 1548 S. His father-in-law was Múla, a Khatri, and this *mandir* was erected in commemoration of the marriage. Mahárája Sher Singh began the masonry building but it was not complete till after his death, according to the *janamsákhi*. The *Granth Sáhib* reposes in its centre. On all four sides are rooms for *parkarmán* or circumambulation. On its walls are pictures of the ten Gurús. Its manager is an Arora of Batála, and his duties are to recite the *Granth* and look after the *mandir*. The *mantras* for worship are *shabds* or hymns from the *Sukhmani* and *Granth Sáhibs*.

Hindús and Sikhs offer cash, grain, clothes etc. At 9 A. M. *kacha bhojan* or *bhog* is offered. A *bhog* of *karáh* is offered on the *sankránt*, *amáwas* and *púranmáshi*, *i. e.* on the new and full moon days of each month. During the night lamps are lit. The masonry *thara* on which the wedding party of Gurú Nának rested is much respected by the people.

The Darbár Sáhib fair at Barbata village is held on the Baisákhi. Báwá Sri Chand, its founder, came here to meditate on God. The *Granth* reposes on a Manji Sáhib. The *pujári* is a Sársut Brahman and recites the *Granth* daily. He also feeds all travellers lodging in the *mandir*. A *bhog* of food prepared in the morning or *karáh parshád* offered by votaries is first laid before the *Granth Sáhib* and then distributed among those present.

A curious feature of the Paṭṭi Sáhib at Lahore, which includes a number of buildings in a walled enclosure, is the fact that a *samádh* of Nág *deota* is found in it side by side with one of Báwa Sri Chand, and another of Kubha Díwán, the hump-backed accountant of Ranjít Singh, to which no sanctity seems to attach.

The Gurú *Sar* or 'tank of the Gurú' at Khosa Kotla, in Zíra tahsíl, Ferozepur, lies near the village where the Manji Sáhib of the 6th Gurú, Har Gobind, is kept. It was founded nearly 100 years ago. An Udási *sádhu* is in charge and a fair is held on the Mághi festival. Visitors, both men and women, dig earth from the tank and make offerings of grain, *gur*, milk, cash etc., all of which the *sádhu* takes to the Manji Sáhib before which they bow. *Karáh parshád* or confection is distributed among them. Earth is also dug from a *chhappar* or pond of Bábá Andehr, but no fair is held at it.

The *sthán* or sanctuary of Gurú Har Gobind in Sahif village is also called Gurú Sar. A fair is held there at the Mághi and Baisákhi when the *Granth* is opened and read, Sikhs paying it special reverence and making offerings to it. The temple was founded nearly 150 years ago. Its *pujári* is a Soḍhi. The *Granth* is opened on the 1st of every Hindu month and verses recited. At the *gurdwára* situate at Takhtupura an annual fair is held on the 12th January. Most of the visitors are Sikhs who bathe and make offerings to the temple. The village was founded by one Takhtu. Bábá Nának is said to have honoured it with his presence, and so did Gurús Har Gobind and Gobind Singh. The tank near the temple was made by Ranjít Singh, and some small *gurdwáras* are attached to it. It is in charge of an Udási.

The *mandir* at Daroli in tahsíl Moga is called Mátá Damodari, and two annual fairs are held at it, one on the Lohri, the other on the Baisákhi. Mátá Damodari was a goddess and a disciple of Gurú Har Gobind, and her tomb lies near the *mandir*. This temple was built in S. 1710. No Brahman is employed as the *pujári* is always a *Sikh*. He keeps the *mandir* clean, washes the *chabútra* or platform in the morning and lights a sacred lamp in the evening. Lastly a drum is beaten. At a *maṭṭri* near the *mandir* a lamp is lit every evening. The *maṭṭri* is also washed in the morning. The temple at Sirái Mangha in tahsíl Muktsar is known as Gurú Nának *ji ká gurúdwára* and a fair is held there on the Baisákhi While touring through the country, Gurú Nának came to this place and while resting on a mound used a *dátan* or toothbrush which he thrust into the ground It grew into a tree which still thrives. Some 65 years ago one Bhái Bálá raised a wall round the *mandir*. The *mandir* contains no image, but only a stone with Gurú Nának's foot-print on it. Its administration is carried on by the Bhái's descendants and they employ an Udási, who keeps it clean, lights a lamp in the evening, and gives food and water to travellers from the *langar*. The servants of the *mandir* had always been *sádhus*, and succession had been governed by spiritual relationship until the death of Bhái Bilu whose natural descendants succeeded him as he left no disciple. At the fair the *Granth* is recited and *karáh parshád* offered as *bhog* to it. Visitors make offerings and receive *karáh parshád* which they deem sacred. A lamp is always kept burning and Hindus also make offerings to the *Granth*.

The *mat* or monastery of Gurú Angad is at his birthplace and people makes vows and offerings to it if their prayers are fulfilled. The *pujáris* take all the offerings. No lamp is kept burning.

The Gurdwára known as the Sri Darbár Sáhib is the scene of a fair held from the 1st to the 3rd of Mágh every year. It is so called because when Gurú Gobind Singh fled before the Mughal army he took shelter here and recited the *Granth* on May 17th, 1767. Ever since then the fair has been celebrated. In olden times the tank here was called Ishar or Khandrána, but after the battle in which his followers fell and received *mukt* or salvation it was named Mukatsar or the 'pool of salvation.'

The *mandir* was founded in 1718, and was built by Sardár Udhe Singh of Kaithal. The Darbár Sáhib contains a sword, disc etc. Its administration is carried on by a Bhandári Khatri, and by the 11 members of the Darbár Sáhib.

Two of them are attached to the *mandir* to supply water and prepare and distribute food. The manager is responsible for all the expenditure. The members meet at night in the temple after the *rah-i-rás* or evening prayer, and before the distribution of food, some 10 loaves with pulse are offered to the *Granth*, a conch being sounded to inform those present in the temple that the food is ready. It is then brought out and distributed among them and they receive the loaves which are believed to be sacred. All that remain are taken to the *langar*. Offerings are made by Hindus in general as well as by Sikhs.

Other temples connected with this are:—the Shahíd Ganj, Tibbi Sáhib, Mukh-manjan Sáhib and Tambu Sáhib. The Shahíd Ganj is where Gurú Gobind Singh's followers were slain and burnt. The Tibbi Sáhib is where he fought the enemy. This sanctuary lies a mile to the west of the Darbár Sahíb. From it the Gurú went to the waste lands, west of the Tibbi Sáhib, which are called the Mukh-manjan Sáhib, because the Gurú cleaned his teeth there. The Tambu Sáhib is so called because Gurú Gobind Singh pitched his tent there. It was founded by Mahárája Karm Singh, Chief of Patiála, in 1900.

The *mandir* in Gurú Har Sahái is called 'Pothi-Mála.' No fair is held here, but the Baisákhi is observed as a fair. It is so called because it contains a *pothi* or religious book and a *mála* or rosary said to have belonged to Gurú Nának, and its foundation dates from his time. They are kept by the Gurú's descendants, who hold charge of the temple, in the house believed to have been occupied by him. Ten years ago a new building was constructed and the *mála* and *pothi* brought from Chúnián and placed therein. The *gaddi* is always occupied by the eldest son of the family. When people come to do homage to these relics the *pujári* bathes and dons the *topi, chola* etc., which were worn by Gurú Nának. He then displays the *pothi* and *mála*, provided a *nazrána* of Rs. 101 is laid before them. *Karáh parshád* is offered daily as *bhog*.

When votaries in distant places, such as Bannu, Kohát, Peshávar, Hazára and Kábul, dedicate offerings to Gurú Nának at weddings etc. they are sent to this temple.

The temple at Chúnián in Lahore is connected with this *mandir*, and it is held by a member of the same family. An ordinary fair is held there on the Baisákhi.

At the *samádh* of Bhai Sarúp Dás at Bagahke, a fair is held on the Baisákhi. Some 50 years ago the corpse of Bhái Sarúp Dás was burnt at this spot, where his disciple Púran Dás built a *samádh* in 1921. The administration of the *mandir* vests in Bhái Sáhib Dás, a disciple of the late Púran Dás. But an Udási disciple, who is employed in the *mandir*, lives in a separate house near the well attached to the main temple which he keeps clean and in which he lights a lamp. Only the Bairági *sádhu* however officiates in the temple, and he receives all the offerings with a fee of Re. 1-4-0 at every wedding. On the Baisákhi *karáh parshád* is offered as *bhog* and then distributed among those present. A lamp is always kept burning in the temple. All Hindús make offerings according to their means.

At the temple called Gupt Sar a fair is held on the Baisákhi. When Gurú Gobind Singh during his war with the Muhammadans reached this place his soldiers demanded their pay and he found a hidden treasure in a tank most of which he distributed to them. The balance, it is said, disappeared at the same spot. Hence the tank came to be called the Gupt Sar or 'tank of the hidden store.' The temple possesses a *chakkar* (disc) and *jhanda* (banner). No Brahman is employed, but a lamp is kept burning and Hindus make offerings to it. Cash collected is spent on the up-keep of the *mandir*.

At the Gurudwára in Ropána no fair is held. The people gather there on the Baisákhi and offer *karáh parshád*. Gurú Gobind Singh threw away his used *dátan* or toothbrush here and it turned into a green tree, a miracle which caused people to worship the place. In the temple are deposited a *chakkar, nishán* (standard) and other weapons. Its administration is carried on by the present *pujári*, a Jái No Brahman is employed. It rests with the residents of the village to employ any person whom they deem fit. It is said that once a Sikh Gurú visited this place, and after his departure it was held sacred by the Hindús and Sikhs who bathe in the pond. The use of *charas* and *bhog* is not common. A lamp is lighted at the temple.

At the *mandir* called Faqír Sar in Muktsar tahsíl an annual fair is held.

At a pond in Bhondar village a fair is held annually at the Baisákhi. As Gurú Gobind Singh's horse drank water from it people bathe in it every year, but no building is attached to it. Formerly a *faqír* used to live at the pond but after his death some 12 years ago, people simply collect on the day of the fair to pay homage to the pond and play *saunchi*.

At the *mandir* of Gurú Gobind Singh at Harípur near Abohar, two fairs are held, one on the *púranmáshi* in Kátak, the other on the *Chetar chaudas* in Chet. About 800 persons, Bágri Jáṭs etc. attend them. Charn Dás took up his abode in Harípur in S. 1927, and founded the temple in Sáwan S. 1933. When the people of the Bágar began to worship the *mandir* he sank a well for drinking water. When he had got 1½ yards down, an iron box was found in which were an image of Nársingh, an iron disc, a footprint of Gurú Nának on a stone, an iron rod, a sword, a closed book etc. The image of Nársingh is carved on a stone slab. These things were sent to Mr. Wakefield, then Deputy Commissioner of Sirsa, but they were brought back and placed in the *mandir*. Since then Hindus frequent it to see the relics. The foot-print on the stone is regarded as that of Gurú Nának and a hand print on the other side is supposed to be that of one Kirpál Udási. The administration of the *mandir* is carried on by one Charn Dás. Its income from offerings is estimated at Rs. 125, excluding Rs. 7, the value of the grain offered, which is divided equally between Charn Dás and the Bishnoi *faqírs*. The former keeps the *mandir* clean and burns incense twice a day. *Karáh parshád* is distributed among those present. The fair is patronized by Jáṭs, Aroṛas, Sikhs, Bágris and Bishnois. It only lasts one day.

At the Gurú Sar in Bázídpur, tahsíl Ferozepur, a fair is held on the *Basant panchmi*. Gurú Gobind Singh rested here for a short time, so the place was held sacred. In the time of Ranjít Singh a *faqír* constructed a *gurudwára*. At the fair the Farídkoṭ State supplies 50 *mans* of grain and one of salt for the requirements of visitors who are all fed free. Báwá Sidha Dás *faqír*, a Chhímba, lives in the temple and recites the *Granth* in the morning. Disciple succeeds *gurú*. A kettle-drum is beaten at night. *Charas* is not used nor is there any rite of *bhog*. Lamps are lit in the evening. The *gurdwára* in Sayyidpur is connected with this.

In Ludhiána the Bhái Bálá fair is held on the 10th *sudi* of Mágh in the waste land of Dad. Bhái Bálá was a disciple of Gurú Nának and at his *samádh* here about 10,000 people from the neighbourhood visit the fair. Hindus offer grain, cash etc. which are taken by Masand Khatrís of Kudhani in Patiála. People also bring curds made the pre, vious night, and after being presented to the shrine they are distributed and eaten. There is also a pond here, and people attending the fair consider it a religious duty to dig out of it seven handfuls of earth with their hands.

A temple in Kángra is :—

Mandir Dera Bába Nának. Bába Nának is said to have stayed here for a while and wrought miracles. The temple contains a stone on which his foot-print is marked. Its length is a cubit and breadth a foot. It stands on a pedestal. A flag is also planted on one side of it. Near it is the tomb of Báwa Mehr Dás, one of the Biláspur chiefs.	Udási ...	None ...	Food cooked by the *pujári* is offered as *bhog*, but on the first day of every month *halwá* or confection is prepared and offered to the *Granth*. A sacred lamp is lit daily.

THE PHILOSOPHY OF SIKHISM.

A Sikh gentleman contributes the following instructive note on Sikh ideals :—

The Gurú observed :—'All men are suffering in one way or another; the source of all misery is attachment to material things. Desire generates attachment; desire precedes illusion. Illusion is removed by the knowledge of the spirit; the spirit lives in every particle of the universe; it lives within us, without us and everywhere. God is all 'Life,' 'Knowledge' and 'Bliss,' and to know God is to *be* God. Therefore happiness cannot be obtained in material enjoyment but in the knowledge of God. This is the essence of Sikhism. Until the soul has become free from desire of material objects, it has to suffer births and rebirths under the law of transmigration of souls.

The stages of practice.—The next question is how to become one with God and secure a stage of eternal happiness. The Gurú says there are three stages :—(1) Discipline, (2) Meditation, and (3) *Giána.*

(1) *Discipline.*—The beginner must begin by keeping the company of good people (*sádh-sangat*) and cultivate purity of character. Character (*achar*) supplies the soil for the sowing of the seed which is meditation on the name (*Nám*) and *giána* is the fruit (*sukhphal*). Discipline means total subjugation of the lower instinct (*ausri gunas*), of lust (*kám*), anger (*karodh*), blind attachment (*moh*), covetousness (*lobh*), vanity (*ahangkara*); and development of the higher virtues (*daivi gunas*), such as the proper use of the bodily essence (*sil*), contentment (*santokh*), kindness of all forms of life (*daya*), faith in Divine existence (*dharma*), purity of body and mind (*such*), charity and benevolence (*dan*), toleration (*dhiraj*), and thoughtfulness (*vichár*). To discipline his mind one must always keep (*sat sang*), the company of holy men and learn to live independently by earning an honest livelihood. True

discipline is cultivated not by living in seclusion but by leading a life useful in all respects. The Gurú's tenet is: 'Fulfil all the duties of domestic and social life, but let not your heart forget your spiritual nature.'

(2) *Meditation.*—When the character-building is complete the *adhkári* is initiated into the society of the pure (*khálsa*). He is baptised (given *amrita*) by the 5 chosen Khálsa (Pánch Gurú Khálsa) and taught the method of meditation on the true name (Satnám). The message communicated to him at the *amrita* runs: 'Henceforth you belong to the community of the Khálsa, your father is Sri Gurú Gobind Singh (protector of the universe), your mother Sáhib Devi (the supreme power), your abode Anandpur (the city of bliss), your caste Sodh-bans (the family of the Lord). You will be bound to wear the 5 national symbols (*rahit* of the five *ka's*): (*i*) The *keshas*, to preserve your brain in its normal condition. This is the sign of Yogi, implying abhorrence of all artificialities due to the desire to appear beautiful: (*ii*) *kach*, meant to teach you the habit of using the life-fluid properly: (*iii*) *kirpán*, to teach you the necessity of cultivating physical development and warn you against the danger of bodily deterioration: (*iv*) *kara* to bind you to obedience of the Gurú's law as given in the Holy *Granth*: (*v*) *kangha*, as the comb keeps the hair pure, even so twice a day you should try to purge away all filthy thoughts from your mind. You shall also recite five *bánís* every day:—

1. *Japp*—Comprising the main principles of Sikh spiritualism, ethics and divinity.
2. *Jap*—Giving the attributes of God, personal and impersonal.
3. *Swayas*—Inculcating the transitoriness of material enjoyments and emphasising the brevity of human life.
4. *Rahirás*—The prayer for peace.
5. *Sohála*—Praise of the Divine.

You shall believe in the Gurús as the 10 manifestations of one and the same Lord: and obey the commandments given in the Holy *Granth*.

You will have to meditate on the holy name with full concentration of mind every day in the early morning.

You must perform all ceremonies (*sanskaras*) according to the instructions of the Khálsa.

Methods of meditation.—In the first stage attention must be fixed on the personality of the Gurú by reading his life and by constantly thinking of the attributes to be cultivated. Afterwards, silent repetition of the name together with the understanding of the sense in the mind. By constant practice the name itself vanishes and the spirit makes itself manifest in the devotee's heart according to his conception.

(3) *The* giána *stage.*—Ultimately the individual soul enjoys perfect union with the supreme soul. In this stage the *bhagat* sees the one God

within, without and everywhere and realises that:—'In Him he lives, moves and has his being.'

Notable features of the Sikh ideals.—The Sikh believes that the supreme soul has fully manifested itself in the Gurú. He is therefore, the creator, the preserver; and it is he who is the destroyer of the universe. He thus concentrates all his love on the Gurú in a manner so earnest that he is ready never to flinch from the path laid down for him by the Gurú even at the risk of his life. History narrates that in the time of Furrukhsiar Rs 80 were offered as a prize for the head of a Sikh with his *keshas* (hair) yet never was Sikh known to betray his faith for worldly gain, however much he was tempted. Day and night the Sikh meditates on the self-radiant point ever effulgent in his breast through the grace of his Gurú, and moves in the world self-poised, self-satisfied, and self-contented. He has full control over his temper and it is his object to make the most of the chances given him by serving others in all possible ways.

He has realised that as no form can endure he must one day pass away. The hour of death being uncertain he must use all his energy, wisdom and wealth in philanthropic deeds. Free from all vanity, he has totally resigned his will to the Gurú. He is indifferent to pleasure and pain and is heedless of eulogy or abuse. Gold and dust are equal in his eyes. Thus ever singing his master's praises, he goes to the Home of Bliss after death, which he has really conquered in this life.

Growth of the Khálsa community.—Gurú Nának Deva spent his whole life travelling from place to place, sowing the seed of divine love wherever he met a true seeker of God. In the course of time millions in distant lands became his followers.[1]

[1] *Gurú Nának.*—Gurú Nának did not receive any secular education. The following verses show that he did not attend to lessons taught in school. One day he was asked to write out some Arithmetical tables. He replied:—

" Burn worldly love, grind its ashes and make them into ink, turn the superior intellect into paper.

Make divine love thy pen and thy heart the writer: ask thy Gurú and write his instructions,

Write God's name, write his praises, write that he hath neither end nor limit,

O Master! learn to write this account,

So that whenever it is called for a true mark may be found thereon.

There greatness is obtained, everlasting joys and everlasting delights,

They in whose hearts is the true name have the mark of it on their brows,

By God's mercy men obtain it and not by idle words;

One man cometh, another goeth, we give them great names,

Some men God created to beg and some to preside over great courts,

When they have departed they shall know that without the name they are of no account;

I greatly fear thine anger, O God! my body pineth and wasteth away;

They who had been called Kings and Lords are beheld as ashes,

Gurú Angad worked on his lines and devised a new Panjábi alphabet in which the lives, hymns, and sermons of the Gurús were written.

The efforts of Siri Gurú Amar Dás were mainly devoted to the abolition of caste distinctions. He taught 'that good actions are commendable to God and that all men are equal.' He introduced the system of performing all ceremonies with the help of the Gurú Bani and instructed the Sikhs to throw off the yoke of the Brahman priesthood.

The fourth Gurú Ram Dás began the Golden Temple at Amritsar as a centre for the Sikhs, to which they might come from all parts to unite themselves by the bond of brotherly love so essential to strengthen the national tie.

Gurú Arjan ordered every Sikh to set apart one-tenth of his income for religious and charitable purposes. He framed rules of devotion and collected all the hymns of his four predecessors into the holy scripture called the *Granth* to which he himself largely contributed. This new form of Sikhism raised up many enemies to the Gurú, and so he instructed his son Gurú Har Govind to devise means of safety for his disciples.

Gurú Har Govind introduced military exercises and horsemanship among his Sikhs. In course of time they became good soldiers, and whenever their foes became aggressive they gave proofs of their valour, courage and military skill.

Nának when men departeth all false affections are surrendered.

Upon this the School-master acknowledged Gurú Nának as a perfect saint and did the homage to him."

The incident called the *sacha sauda* may also be mentioned :—Kálu, father of Nának, desired his son to embrace a mercantile life, so he sent him to Chúharkána now in Gujránwála and buy articles for trade. Nának set out with a servant and on his way met some holy men. He spent all the money in their service, and on his return home when censured by his father he replied that he had done 'true trade.'

The Gurú's condemnation of the rite of investiture with the *janeo* (sacred thread) :—

Pandit Hardiál, family priest, was invited to perform this ceremony and when all the members of Kálu's brotherhood were present, Gurú Nának enquired its meaning. The priest explained that the *janeo* was the basis of the Hindu religion and without it a man would remain a Sudra. Hearing this the young Gurú uttered the following hymn in the *Asa De Wár* :—

1. Make mercy thy cotton, contentment thy thread, continence its knot, truth its twist,
2. That would make a soul; if thou have it, O Brahman! then put it on me;
3. It will not break, or become soiled, or be burned or lost;
4. Blest the man, O Nának! who goeth with such a thread on his neck.
5. Thou purchasest a *janeo* for four *damrís* and seated in a square puttest it on
6. Thou whisperest instruction that the Brahman is the Gurú of the Hindus
7. Man dieth, the *janeo* falleth off and the soul departeth without it.

The Pandit was angry at this and the Gurú then uttered the following :—

1. By adoring and praising the NAME honour and a true thread are obtained.
2. In this way a sacred thread shall be put on which will not break, and which will be fit for entrance into God's court.

The story about Naina Deví has been wrongly represented in the text The idea of the Gurú was to show the Pandits and the people the hollowness of the cult of Deví. The first Gurús had already refused to accept the worship of any deity except the one Almighty God. Gurú Gobind Singh was not bitterly opposed to Islám and the *pahul* or *amrit sanskár* was not for the purpose of retribution. The *pahul* in fact is a form of baptism, and the method of its administering proves it.

THE SIKH VIEW OF TRANSMIGRATION.

The following gives the Sikh conception of the manner in which souls emanated from God :—

As from one fire millions of sparks arise, though rising separately, they unite again in the fire,

As from one heap of dust several particles of dust fill the air, and on filling it again blend with the dust,

As in one stream millions of waves are produced, the waves being made of water all become water,

So from God's form non-sentient and sentient things are manifested.

Springing from Him shall all be united in Him.

THE CONCEPTION OF DIVINITY.

'God is without passion, without colour, without form, without outline,

He is without wordly love, without anger, without enmity, without jealousy,

He is without Karma, without error, without birth and without caste,

He hath no friend, no enemy, no father, no mother etc.'

THE DEFINITION OF KHÁLSA, THE PURE.

1. He who repeateth night and day the name of Him whose enduring light is unquenchable, who bestoweth not a thought on any one but the one God.

2. Who hath full love and confidence in God, who putteth no faith even by mistake in fasting or worshipping, cemeteries, places of cremation, or Jogis' places of sepulchre,

3. Who only recognizeth the one God and not pilgrimages, alms, the non-destruction of life, Hindu penances and austerities,

4. And in whose heart the light of the perfect one shineth, he is recognized as a pure member of the Khálsa.

THE BALLAD OF HARÍ SINGH NALWÁ OF AMRITSAR.

Lardí Sirdár Harí Singh Nalwá sakna Shahr Amritsar.

1. { *Sohná baniá Ambarsar, sohná baná darbár ;*
Sang marmar patthar lagiá chándí chárhe kewár.

2. { *Kai lakh ohná soná lagiá, motí lakh hazár;*
Koí koi hat-wányán basdá, basde sáhúkár.

3. { *Mahán Singh de ghar Ranjít Singh jamiá, jamiá bará autár;*
Kai hazár usne ghore rakkhe, faujáṇ lakh hazár.

4. { *Wich Khaibar de laggí larái, lishkí hai talwár,*
Othe ghaldio Harí Singh núṇ, faujáṇ dá Sirdár.

5. { *Tejá Singh dí fauj dá Sikho, mainúṇ naháṇ itibár,*
Pahlá ḍerá Rávi de kaṇḍe, dúja Ráwi de pár;

6. { *Tíjá ḍerá Púl Kanjrí de, chauthá Wazírábád;*
Chambe ghore núṇ dewe thápíáṇ 'tú rakh dhauliáṇ dí láj.'

7. { *Nikki jehí uṭṭhí badlí, míṇh barsá mohle dhár;*
Chhappariáṇ dá pání píke, Sikh hogaye khabardár.

8. { *Chalo bhiráo merio main rallíá tuhádé sáth.*
Otthe margayá Harí Singh, bíráṇ dá jamádár!

9. { *Otthe margayá Tejá Singh, faujáṇ dá Sirdár.*
Ek jo uṭṭhá ranyá gayá Harí Singh núṇ sár.

10. { *Dúroṇ Láhoroṇ chaliá Farangí karke mandá bháná;*
Majlíṇ majlíṇ ánke áthe maliá Ludhiáná.

11. { *Dar dar usdi chaunkí bahgayí, shahríṇ bahgayá tháná,*
Sikháṇ núṇ Angrezáṇ ne márliá hoyá Rab dá bháná.

12. { *Dúroṇ Láhoroṇ ayá Firangí, sir par rakhkar ṭopí;*
Baṛe rájáṇ se-sark puṭṭái, hath wich pakarke soṭí.

13. { *Srak terí sohí puṭṭange, jinháṇdí kismat khoṭí;*
Bháná Sikháṇ de utte bartiá, kaí na chaliá sáthí.

TRANSLATION.

1. Beautifully planned is the city of Ambarsar with a stately and imposing Darbár. In it white marble was used, and the doors are covered with silver.

2. Many lakhs worth of gold and a thousand lakhs of pearls were used. It is mainly inhabited by bankers, petty shop-keepers being few.

3. In the house of Mahán Singh was born Ranjít Singh, the great soul descended from Heaven. He had thousands of horses and maintained armies numbering a thousand lakhs.

4. In the Khaibar Pass war began, and swords flashed like lightning. Thither Hari Singh was sent in command of the forces.

5. 'O Sikhs, I trust not Tejá Singh's army. So my first camp will be on the hither side of the Rávi's bank, and my second beyond it.

My third halt will be at Púl Kanjrí and my fourth at Wazírábád.'

6. Patting his bay steed Ranjít Singh said: 'Save my honour for the sake of my grey hairs.'

PPPP

7. A small cloud arose and rain began to fall in torrents. The Sikhs drinking water from the ponds became anxious.

8. 'O my brothers, press on, for I am with you.' There has Hari Singh, commander of the forces, been killed.

9. Sirdár Tejá Singh has also been killed. One of the warriors went to burn Hari Singh Nalwa's body.

10. From Lahore set out the Firangí obeying the impulse of pride and marching stage by stage met the Sikhs at Ludhiána.

11. Posts were opened at every door, and a police station established in the midst of the city. The English defeated the Sikhs, for it was the will of God!

12. Straight from Lahore came the Firangí with hat on head and employed many masons in metalling the roads, holding a stick in his hand.

13. 'Thy roads will be metalled by those who are unfortunate.' Trouble seized the Sikhs at last and none sided with them!

THE TALE OF LACHHMAN DÁS, OTHERWISE BANDA SÁHIB, DISCIPLE OF THE GURÚ SÁHIB, THE SINGH.

Ahwál Lachhman Dás urf Banda Sáhib, Chela Gurú Singh Sáhib.

Dohá.

1 { *Abchalá nagar hai Srí Gangá ke pás,*
Sádhú Lachhman Dás hai bairágí, kare nivás.

2 { *Khatrí Sodhí-bans, sún, bhayo, bairágí á'e,*
Abchal nagrí Gangatat, sádhe tap ko já'e.

Chaupáí.

3 { *Sundar Rám bághíchá lágá,*
Sukh samlhú, dukh nirkhat bhágá.

4 { *Anek bhánt phal phúl suhá'e,*
Khag, mirg, gunjad, lahut sukh dá'e.

5 { *Wá ke madh baní ámrái,*
Sukh-su-vás sab bhánt suhá'í.

Dohá.

6 { *Amrái ke bích ek palang bichhá sukh-sár,*
Chár bír chau tarf rahen rakhwále, balkár.

Chaupái.

7 { *Aur koí baiṭhe taháṇ jáí,*
{ *Paṭak bhúm máreṇ so táiṇ.*

8 { *Jo palang ke neṛe jáwat,*
{ *Phir júwat páchhe naháṇ áwat.*

9 { *Pakṛ pachháreṇ Gangá táe,*
{ *Turt kareṇ Amrapur wáe.*

Dohá.

10 { *Srí Gurú ke panth meṇ sakal bhaye balwán,*
{ *Bádsháh daswáṇ bhae Gurú Gobind Singh án.*

Kabit.

11 { *Gurú Nának, Gur Angad, Gur Amardás, Gurú Rámdás, Gurú Arjan dháro,*
{ *Gurú Hargobind, Har Rái, Harí Krishn bicháro,*

12 { *Tegh Bahádar, bhayo, nám dhar ek man líno,*
{ *Sabd gurú updésh dán sangat ko díné.*

13 { *Kalá dhár Gurú Gobind Singh bhae, amar bhae Kalú meṇ sákhí,*
{ *Jhankár, bhayo, tirlak meṇ bírd, paj satgur ki rakhí.*

Dohá.

14 { *Srí Gurú Gobind Singhjí dháró dharm Autár,*
{ *Máléchhaṇ ke hat karne parbal, bhayo, balkár.*

Kabit.

15 { *Ashp ke aswár bhayo, Gurú Gobind Singhjí sail sadháyo,*
{ *Gang ashnán kiyo hit hit, sún bhayo, Lachhman Dás ke bágh meṇ áyo.*

16 { *Palang bichheṇ bano ati sundar baiṭhat wáhpah harkh, widháyo,*
{ *Bír rahe bal lá'ei ná lágat dhan, Gurújí ko tej sowáyo.*

Kabit.

17 { *Lachhman Dás Sádhú Gang ashnán kar pújá páṭh mantr jap amráí áyo haiṇ,*
{ *Áge sú Gobind Singh baiṭhat par pank máhín, dharm autár shubhr ajit soháyo haiṇ.*

18 { *Nirkh chakrit, bhayo, aiso baiṭh kaun áyo, tej wá partáp ján bismay suháyo haiṇ.*
{ *Bíráṇ ko ágiá kar palṛ ke pachháro nar, aiso ahankárí budh de kaun áyo hain?*

Chaupái.

19 { *Bíraṇ ánk bhánt bal láyo;*
{ *Palang naháṇ so úṭho uṭháyo.*

20 { *Guru Gobind Singh jo abtár,*
{ *Kiá'e kareṇ bíráṇ balkár?*

Dohá.

21 { *Púchhat Gurú Gobind Singh tum ho sádhú kaun?*
At-parchanḍ újjal tuje kiúṇ ḍhar baiṭhe maun?

22 { *Sáhib ke banda bhaye, ehhí hamáro nám,*
Nis din japde baiṭhke Parmeshwar Srí Rám.

Chaupái.

23 { *Tum banda sáhib ke piyáro,*
Te jas así tap karnewále.

24 { *Ab kar apne shashtar ḍháro,*
Dharm káj yeh bachan hamáro.

25 { *Malechhan, sun, judh racháo,*
Banda Sáhib nám kaháo.

26 { *Lachhman Dás jí sant ne lío teg kar ḍhár,*
Mughlaṇ ke hat kárne lage karan dangár.

27 { *Wáhe Gurú ki fatah, so wáhe Gurú ká ráj!*
Gurú Gobind Singh amar haiṇ, kíó ḍharm ká káj.

Chaupái.

28 { *Judh karat Turkáṇ sún bhárí,*
Mughláṇ kí buh sen sanghárí.

29 { *Jang Sarandh ánk bidh bhayo,*
Tiág deh Gur surpur gayo.

Dohá.

30 { *Ḍhúṭá Labáná, bhayo, sikh Gúrú ká ján,*
Ik shat mohar Gobind Singh déní thá mán.

Chaupái.

31 { *Dhuṭhe ko Gurú bachhan sunáyá,*
Sikh Gurú ká bahut suháyá.

32 { *Ab tum jáó apne gám,*
Kíjó já'e tiháṇ bisrám.

Kabit.

33 { *Gurú Gobind Singh kahe Dhúṭhe kó: gám tumháre áwenge,*
Do unglí tumrí kar apní pakar nishání láwenge.

34 { *Sikh apná bhej tujhí ko apne pás mangáwenge,*
Tab jáno tum Gurú hamárá ek sau moharáṇ páwenge.

Chaupái.

35 { *Chaṛh bibán Gur surg sadháe,*
Ḍhúṭá apne dwáre áye.

36 { *Bahut díwas sún phír kahe jáe,*
Gur ke charnoṇ láge áe.

37 { '*Kab Gur is des meṇ áweṇ,*
Do unglí muj kó pakṛáweṇ;

38 *Ek sau mohar mo se mángen?*
Dhan bhág more jab jágen.'

Kabit

39 *Chandr-Bhágá nadí kináre Bandah tap ko áyo hai,*
Mahán pawittar bhúmí ká dekhí baiṭh kahun sukh páyo hai.

40 *Desan ke bhúpál áeke, sab ne mátho náyo hai,*
Ḍhúṭhe got Labáne Gur ke áge sís lagáyo hai.

Chaupái.

41 *Ḍhúṭhá apne pás pás mangáyo;*
Bandah Sáhib bachan sunáyo.

42 *Do únglí tin ko pakr aí,*
Ek sau mohar nám sunáí.

43 *Ḍhúṭhe man men parm úchhdhá,*
Dhan dhan karat charn lipṭdhá.

44 *Bahor apne ghar ko áyá,*
Sakal kuṭúmb pás mangwáyo.

45 *Ek sau mohren thál bhardyá,*
Bhúkan bistar sang suháyá.

46 *Khán pán sakale pakwán,*
Sang lí'o parwár suján.

47 *Bájen ḍhól sang sukh-dáí,*
Náchen Ḍhúṭa bahor suháí.

48 *Náchat kúdat Gur pah jáwen,*
Mukh se gáwat sabd suháwén.

Kabit.

49 *"Gur ládho re, Gurú ládho re, Gur ládho, Gurú suháyo re,*
Jin Turkán ke sís útáre, so Gur milú hamáro re.

50 *Dhan Gurú Gobind Singh újjal dharyo dharm abtáro re,*
Dhan Gurú Gobind Singh sáhib jí áb Ḍhúṭe ko táro re.

Chaupái.

51 *Wáh Gurújí bhág hamáre,*
Aj Gurú jí mile piáre.

52 *Tégh úṭhái Mughal jin máre,*
Sakal Hind ko dharm sudháre.

53 *Jo Gur apne ko manáwen,*
Charn gahe muktí phal páwen.

54 *Gur ke charn rahún lipṭái,*
Ant kál Gúr hót saháí.

55 *Ḍhól bajen bahe, Ḍhúṭá náoh en,*
Prem bhará bah údham náchen.

56 *Náchat gáwat Gur pah áyo,*
Charn Gurán ke sis niwáyo.

Dohá.

57 *Bádsháh daswen, bhayo, Gurú Gobind Singh áy'e:*
Ikádas Banda Sáhib ji, táro sikh su há'e!

58 *Chandr-Bhágá Gangá ke nikaṭ niwás kíno parbal trikuṭh dhár sundar súhát haiṇ,*
Kanchan ke thamb chapáṭ bane, kanchan ke kanchan ko mandar jorṭ bahú bhánt haiṇ.

Anek hí parkáran ke bájat bajantr mahá gáwat sabd nek bhánt ke súhát haiṇ.
Chár khúnt chale át mátho já'eṇ ko nivrit dhan Gurú Bandah Sáhib dharo ghaṭ haiṇ.

Kabit.

60 *Des hi des chale buh áwat, kos hasároṇke sikh súháweṇ,*
Wáhe Gurú Bande Sáhib ko buh'nám japeṇ muktí phal páweṇ.

61 *Ḍhol mirdang pakháwaj sang bajáwat báje sabd jo gáweṇ,*
Utr des niwás kiyo; jo nám japeṇ muktí phal páweṇ.

62 *Srí Gur Bande Sáhib ko dharo parm síhá'e,*
Ujjal Hákim Rae ne sobhá kahí baná'e.

TRANSLATION.

1 Abchal[1] is a town close by holy Ganges,
And in it lived a saint, one Lachhman Ḍás Bairágí.

2 He was a Khatri of the Sodhí sect, but he became a Bairágí,
At Abchal town on the Ganges bank he performed penance.

3 In it lay a beautiful and pleasant garden,
In it (was found) every kind of pleasure, without pain.

4 In it were countless kinds of fruits and flowers,
Birds and deer added pleasure to its delights.

5 In it stood a summer house, just at its centre,
A pleasant dwelling which afforded joys of every kind.

6 In it was spread a luxurious couch,
Which was guarded on all four sides by four champions, powerful men.

7 If any one went to sit thereover,
They straightway threw him on the ground.

8 Whosoever even approached the couch,
Never came back alive

9 They cast him into the Ganges,
(And) forthwith he entered Heaven.

10 All the Gurú's followers became powerful,
Gurú Govind Singh was the 10th King.

[1] Possibly an allusion to the four *takhts* of the Sikh Gurus.

11 Know then the Gurús :—
Nának, Angad, Amar Dás, Rám Dás, Arjan, Hargobind, Har Rái, Hari Krishn.

12 Teg Bahádur, who believed in the unity of God
Gave the boon of the Gurú's teaching to his followers.

13 Gurú Govind Singh was glorious, and in the Kali Yuga immortal,
His story resounded through three worlds, and he kept up the glories of his Guru

14 Holy Govind Singh was an incarnation,
He showed his might in assaults on the Mlechhas,

15 Mounted on his horse Gurú Govind Singh went forth,
Bathed joyously in the Ganges and so came to Lachhman Dás' garden.

16 There he found the splendid couch and seated himself thereon with great delight,
In vain the *bírs* (champions) put forth all their strength:
Blessed be the glorious Gurú!

17 So Lachhman Dás the saint, after bathing and reciting his prayers, returned to the summer house,
Where he found Govind Singh seated on the couch, (him) who was an incarnation of God and most glorious!

18 Seeing him he was amazed (and said): 'Who is seated here,?'
Seeing his glory and his splendour he was astounded.
(And) he bade the guardians (saying): 'Cast out this fellow, who is seated so arrogantly here!'

19 The champions exerted all their strength,
But the couch did not move.

20 Gurú Govind Singh was an incarnation of God,
What could the mighty champions do?

21 Gurú Govind Singh asked: 'What saint art thou?
Thou who art so glorious, why art thou silent?'

22 'I am the Servant of God, *that* is my name!
Day and night I repeat God's *name*.'

23 Thou art the beloved Servant of God,
Glorious one! and a performer of penance.

24 Take warlike weapons in thy hand,
And listen to my preaching.

25 { Attack the Mlechhas courageously,
And earn the title of 'God's Slave.'

26 { Lachhman Dás, the holy one, took in his hand the sword,
And resolved to put the Mughals to death, in battle.

27 { (His war-cry was) 'Victory to the Gurú! Thus shall be the Gurú's reign!'
Gurú Govind Singh is immortal, he hath done works of piety.

28 { He made fierce war on the Turks,
Many Mughals were destroyed.

29 { He fought at Sarandh with all his might,
The Gurú gave up his life, and went to Heaven.

30 { Ḍhúthá Labána became a disciple of the Gurú,
And had a mind to offer him 100 gold *mohars.*

31 { The Gurú exhorted Ḍhúthá,
And he, the Gurú's disciple, was greatly pleased.

32 { The Gurú said: 'Now get thee to thy village,
And dwell there in peace.'

33 { Gurú Govind Singh said to Ḍhúthá: 'We will come to your village,
Grasping two of your fingers we will make a sign.

34 { I shall call you to me through one of my own disciples,
Then know that your Gurú will accept the 100 *mohars.*'

35 { Ascending his (celestial) chariot, the Gurú went to Heaven,
And Ḍhuthá returned home.

36 { Many days he waited there,
In expectation of his Gurú's coming.

37 { (Thinking) 'When will the Gúrú come to this country,
And give me his two fingers to hold?

38 { And ask me for the 100 *mohars*?
Blessed then will be my lot?'

39 { To the bank of the Chenab river came Banda to do penance,
Seeing the great purity of its soil there he rested.

40 { All the rulers of the land came to do him homage,
Ḍhúthá Labána bowed his head to the Gurú.

41 { He called Ḍhúthá to him,
Bandá, 'God's Slave' spake to him.

42 { He gave him his two fingers,
And mentioned the 100 *mohars.*

43 { Ḍhúthá was greatly delighted in his heart,
Saying again and again 'Blessed one!' he clung to his feet.

44 Then he returned home,
And sent for all his kinsmen.

45 He filled a platter with the 100 *mohars*,
And a quantity of jewels and clothes.

46 With food and drink and all kinds of sweetmeats;
Taking his whole family with him.

47 Drums were beaten for joy,
Ḍhuthá danced before them from love.

48 Dancing, leaping, he went to the Gurú,
With his lips he sang his praises.

49 I have found my Gurú, my Gurú, and he hath comforted me!
He who had cut off the Turks' heads, he is my Gurú.

50 Blessed be Gurú Govind Singh, who is an incarnation of God,
Blessed be Gurú Govind Singh, who has *saved Ḍhúthá!*

51 O! blessed Gurú, happy is my lot,
To-day have I met with my beloved Gurú.

52 Taking up the sword he has slain the Mughals,
Restored religion to all India.

53 Whoso believeth in his Gurú,
And embraceth his feet, will get the reward of salvation.

54 Let me remain clinging to the Gurú's feet,
In the end the Gurú will save me.

55 Many drums were beaten, and Ḍhúthá danced,
Filled with love he danced fervently.

56 With dance and song he went to the Gurú,
And bowed his head at the Gurú's feet.

57 Gurú Govind Singh appeared as the 10th King,
The 11th was Banda, 'God's slave.' Save thy disciples!

58 He made his abode by the Chenab's holy stream, where is the goddess, most powerful and ever glorious has golden pillars.

59 Numerous hymns are sung there with musical instruments which are pleasing to the ear,
People from all directions come and pay homage there. Blessed is the advent of Gurú Banda Sáhib in this world.

QQQQ

60 People from all countries and Sikhs from thousand *kos* come there and repeat the name of Wáhgurú Banda Sáhib and obtain salvation.

61 They sing the hymns there with different kinds of drums. Banda has taken up his abode in the northern country, he who will repeat name will obtain salvation.

62 All should deeply love Gurú Banda Sáhib and see how Hákim Rái praises the unique being—The Sublime.

CHAPTER II.

RIGHTS AND CEREMONIES.

SECTION I.—HINDU PREGNANCY OBSERVANCES.

The first menstruation after marriage.

The first menstruation after the marriage has been consummated is the occasion of a strict *tabu* in Manḍi. The wife must touch no one, and should not even see any one, to secure which she is shut up in a dark room. She must not use milk, oil or meat, and while she is still impure the following rite is performed:—On a day chosen as auspicious by a Brahman, all the wife's female relatives assemble, and kinswomen wash her head with *gondhana*. Then after she has bathed, five cakes of flour, walnuts and pomegranates are put in her lap, with a pretty child, in order that she too may bear such a child.[1] Looking into its face she gives it some money and cakes, and then the family priest makes her worship Ganpati. In return he receives a fee in money, with the things offered to the goddess. The women spend the ensuing night in singing.

The earlier observances in pregnancy.

If a woman's children all die, she procures, in the third month of her pregnancy, a piece of iron, taken out of a sunken boat, and from it has a *karí* or manacle made. This she wears on her right leg, and it is believed to prevent her future children's premature death. [Dera Gházi Khán District.]

In Fázilka an observance, now nearly extinct, is observed by Hindu Aroṛas in the third month of a first pregnancy. It is called the *ánkh salái*, because after it the wife ceases to apply antimony to her eyes. Her parents send her rice which is distributed among her kin.

In Siálkot the observance of the third month is called *thákni*.[2] Dried dates and pieces of cocoanut are given to the wife, and of these she eats a little, the rest being distributed among her kinsmen. In Hoshiárpur a similar rite is observed; loaves of wheat flour fried in *ghí* are distributed among the brotherhood, and both husband and wife put on new clothes and worship the family god.

In the extreme south-east hardly any observances during pregnancy are reported, though in Hissár the *kanjí* rite—described below—is in

[1] In Patiála if the woman eats real pearls in her menses she will also give birth to a male child.

[2] But in Gurdáspur the rite known as *thankni* (clearly=*thákni*) is said to be observed on the first day of the sixth month. The woman on this date washes her head with curd and puts on new clothes: saltish comestibles, such as *pápaṛs*, *pakauṛas* and *sewiáṅ*, or vermicelli, being distributed among the brotherhood. The *thankni* is followed by the great *rít*, held early in the eigth month, which is a religious ceremony. The woman's parents send her presents, and she washes her head etc. as in the *thankni*. But a *panḍit* is called in and performs certain religious rites. The women of the family also sing certain ritual hymns, and the occasion is one of great rejoicing. *Pun-savan*, defined by Platts (*Hindustani Dictionary*, p. 270) to mean "causing the birth of a male child—the first of the essential ceremonies of Hindu initiation—held on the mother's first perceiving signs of a living conception," is now obsolete in the Simla hills. So, too, is the *símant*, which used to be performed in the sixth month.

vogue in some parts. But elsewhere such observances are usual and somewhat elaborate. Thus in Jínd during a *first* pregnancy (*jeṭhá hamal*) we find the *miṭṭhá bohiá*,[1] a social ceremony, in which at the end of the third month a basket full of sweets is sent to the woman by her mother, with a suit and a half of clothes, and Rs. 5 in money. At the fifth month a second similar ceremony, the *sáḍh*,[2] is observed, the mother sending her daughter two and a half suits of clothes, one and a quarter maunds of sweetmeats, and Rs. 7.

Later observances.

During the seventh month occurs a rite of a religious character, called the *bíbián ká bhoján bharná*. This consists in the woman's offering four and a quarter *sers* of rice to the *bíbís* or spirits, in ten *thális* or plates, of which one is given to a Ḍúmni, another to a land-holder's wife, a third to the husband, a fourth being allotted to the woman herself, and the rest to other relatives.

The pregnancy rites, however, which are, strictly speaking, religious, are the *garbh sanskár*, and foreshadow the *janm*, *múṇḍan* and *janeo sanskárs*[3] or rites at birth, (first) tonsure and initiation, which will be described in due course.

The *garbh sanskár* includes two distinct rites, the *chhoṭí* or lesser, and the *baṛí rítáṇ* or greater rites, which are observed in the fifth and seventh months, respectively, of the pregnancy throughout the Central Panjab.[4] In the former the woman bathes, her hair is plaited and she is dressed in clothes presented by her parents. Her neighbours and kinswomen also assemble to sing songs and fill her lap with grain and cakes made of grain flour fried in *ghí*. Her mother-in-law is also congratulated, and similar eatables distributed among the husband's brotherhood.

At the commencement of the seventh month the husband's parents celebrate the *baṛí rítáṇ*; but first of all the wife's parents send her a new *tewar*,[5] a cocoanut, dried dates and money, together with a present of clothes to her husband's parents, who on their part present her with new clothes. On a lucky day chosen by the Brahman, the husband and wife, dressed in new clothes, sit side by side and revere images of the gods drawn by the Brahman on the floor. The husband's mother then places a cocoanut and dried dates in the wife's lap, and congratulations are exchanged. Huge loaves of flour fried in *ghí* are then distributed among the brotherhood.

In Ferozepur these rites are replaced by the *jár bharnekí* and *bhog bharnekí* observances. Of these the former simply consists in making *kachchí pinní*[6] or rolls, of which two are marked with saffron and given to the wife, who either eats them or divides them among young girls and the brotherhood. The second rite is however far more elaborate.

[1] *Miṭṭhá* 'sweet': *bohiá* a small basket, *Panj. Dicty*., p. 283.

[2] *Sáḍh*, s.f. lit. "a half."

[3] To these four *sanskárs* should apparently be added a fifth, the *nám karn* or naming which precedes the *múṇḍan*.

[4] *E.g.* by the Lahoria Khatrís, but the Bunjáhi Khatrís are said only to observe the *baṛí rítáṇ*.

[5] *Tewar*, or *teur*, three articles of clothing; a trousseau consisting of a gown, shawls and shift (*ghaghri*, *dopaṭṭa* and *kurta*). The *beur* consists of two articles only.

[6] The *pinnís* are made in the following proportions, rice flour 5¼ *sers*, sugar 2½, and *ghí* 1 *ser*.

The wife's parents send her a double *tewar*, with a shawl and turban for the husband, and other things. Then, on the day of the new moon, the wife visits each member of the brotherhood in her house, and gives him some rice as a summons to the rite. Before the kinswomen assemble a corner of the eastern wall of the house is plastered, and seven hand marks made on it with rice-flour mixed in water. A wooden plank is also set up before the wall and a lamp lighted. The kinswomen bring with them some of the grain and rice given them the previous day, and scatter the rice near the lamp, piling the grain in a heap close to it. The plates are then put in one place; twenty-two *sers kham* of rice are then boiled, with five of sugar and two and one-half of *ghi*, the mixture being divided in precisely equal portions on the plates among the kinswomen, who object if one gets more than another. The idea, doubtless, is to convey equal fertility to all.

The clothes presented by the wife's parents are next put on her, and her skirt tied to that of an unmarried kinsman. The pair then walk round the plates seven times, and are asked to bow to the lamp. It is believed that the boy will thus soon be himself married. Their skirts are then untied.

A vessel is now placed in the wife's hands and each kinswoman gives her a little rice from their plates, which she eats. Her husband's mother is then congratulated. The grain brought by the kinswoman is shared equally by the Maihra? (waterman), and her Brahman priest.

Mid-pregnancy.

It is clear that the *chhoṭi ritán* are observed at or about the time when half the period of gestation has elapsed, and indeed the rite is called the *adh gabh* in Amritsár,[1] Gujránwála, and in Baháwalpur. In Hoshiárpur it is not known by that name, but it is observed on the second evening of the lunar month in the fifth month of pregnancy,[2] and a second rite corresponding to it is held on the second day of the ninth lunar month. In Jhelum it is observed on an auspicious day in the fourth or fifth month. The wife bathes, and is dressed in new clothes, her hair is plaited and her hands stained with henna. Her kinswomen sing songs throughout the night. All this is supposed to prevent miscarriage. Her parents also send her some sweets which are put in her lap. In Siálkoṭ the *adh-gabh* is also said to be observed, but not by the Jaṭs, and is described as simply consisting in the distribution of *pápars, pakauras* etc. among the brotherhood.

In Siálkoṭ the mid-pregnancy rite is called the *páoṇ bhári* or the 'heavy feet.'

In Rájanpur tahsíl a rite called *chilwáṇ* from *chhil*, 'loin', is commonly observed among Hindús as well as Muhammadans. After six months in every conception the pregnant woman is required to bathe

[1] But Bániás, who come from the south-east, do not observe the *adh-gabh*. One account says it is observed in different ways, 'by all sects of Brahmans and Hindus'; another, that it is called *rít* and is observed, in different ways, by Brahmans, Mahájans, Khatrís, Sunárs and Jhíwars, but *not* by Jaṭs; while a third alleges that the *adh-gabh* is performed in different ways, but on the same principle, by all Hindus; whereas the *kanjí* is confined to Brahmans, Khatrís and Aroṛas. In Ajnála it is said not to be observed at all.

[2] In Hoshiárpur the wife's parents send her a piece of red *sálú* and some rice. She bathes and puts on the *sálu*. Rice is also distributed among the brotherhood.

under the direction of a *dái* (midwife) who ties beads round her loins, thereby implying the safe completion of the conception and easy labour.

The seventh month : kanjí.

Corresponding again to the *bari rítán*, described above, is the *kanjí*,[1] which is usually observed in the seventh month, though sometimes postponed to the ninth. It is very generally observed, except in the extreme south-east, but it varies in details and often bears no distinctive name.

In Hissar it is observed in the seventh or ninth month, and among the Bágrís the wife's parents send clothes for herself and her husband.

In Hoshiárpur this ceremony is called *rít*, and is observed on the first of the lunar month (seventh or eighth). The present wife's parents send her ten to twenty loaves fried in *ghí*, *pápars* and *pákauras*, clothes for herself, and her husband, one or two ornaments, and from one to seven rupees in cash. Food is also distributed to the brotherhood and menials, Brahmans being also fed in the name of ancestors. In some places the wife's parents feed Brahmans, giving them wheat-flour and *karí*.[2] Or again the wife's parents send her clothes and money, after which she bathes, and then both she and her husband pray that the child may be a boy.

In Amritsar the *kanjí* is observed in the seventh or ninth month, by all castes but not in all parts of the district. In Ajnála it is called *rítán*.

In Gujránwála the *kanjí* or *rít* is very similar. It is observed in the eighth month, and is sometimes held in the house of the wife's parents.[3]

In Gurdáspur a wife, when pregnant for the first time, is sent to her parents' house in the seventh month, and presented with a *ser* of jaggery, as an intimation to them of her condition. Her parents give her clothes for herself, her husband and his mother, and other presents, with which she returns to her husband's house. On the rising of the

[1] Apparently *kanjí* is a kind of sweetmeat: Hoshiárpur.

[2] Made of gram flour and curds fried in oil.

[3] But in Ramnágar, a town in the Gujránwála District, it is said that no rite is observed in the seventh or ninth month, only the *adh-gabh* being observed.

In Muzaffargarh no special rite is observed during pregnancy by Muhammadans, but Hindus usually observe the *malhwan* and *kanjí* during the 6th and 8th months when a woman is pregnant for the first time. This is an occasion for feasting and rejoicing. The parents of the pregnant woman send her clothes and other presents at the *kanjí*; she bathes, washes her hair, and puts on her new clothes and ornaments. This ceremony is intended *inter alia* to make the fact of the first pregnancy of a bride public, or at least well-known in the brotherhood. A particular custom among Muhammadans of good family is called *gudd dena*. It is performed at the end of the 8th month. The *dái* brings the pregnant lady a basket of fruits and having washed and dressed in red from head to foot the lady takes the fruit in her hands or handkerchief or other cloth. The *dái* then divines the sex of the child and generally informs the mother of it.

In Jínd tahsíl during the seventh month among Hindu Chhímbas the pregnant woman performs the rite of *bhog bharna* offering 10½ or 5¼ *sers* of rice to the Bíbís or spirits, while rice with *gur* is distributed among the brotherhood. Among Muhammadan Saqqás during the seventh month the woman's parents send her a suit of clothes which she puts on, and a feast is given to the brotherhood.

new moon in the seventh month, a Brahman is called in, and the husband and wife are seated side by side, with their near kinsmen. A jar (*kumbh*) is then filled with water, and a lamp filled with *ghí* put over it and lighted. The Brahman makes an idol of Ganésh out of flour, and worships their ancestors. The garments of the pair are then tied together (a rite called *gand chitráwa*), and their pedigrees to the third degree recited, their ancestors' names being also written on a sheet of paper which is hung up on the wall. Rice is next distributed among the brotherhood. A small gold ornament, presented by her parents, is also hung round the wife's neck, and this is eventually given to the child when born.

In Siálkot the rite is not very dissimilar. The wife's parents send her presents, and on the appearance of the new moon, *i.e.* on the second of the lunar month, she is bathed and dressed. Ancestors are worshipped. This rite called *rít* in Panjábi, *bahore*[1] in Lahore, *bhora* in Montgomery and *símanat* in Sanskrit, is known as *sawáni* in Jammu, in which tract the Dogras celebrate it by feasting kinsmen.

In Jhelum the rite is kept in the seventh or ninth month. The wife's parents send her sweets and fruits, and these are put in her lap. After this she must not leave her house. Both at the *kanjí* and *adhgabh* in this district the wife bathes, and then receives a gift of clothes from her husband's younger brother, or other young kinsman, in whose face she gazes before she puts them on.

In Talagang the *kanjí* or *rít* is observed on an auspicious day in the seventh month at the house of the wife's parents, and all males are excluded from it, and not even informed of it, though boiled rice is distributed to the brotherhood on this occasion. In Hazro this *rít* is observed at 4 P. M. on the day of the new moon in the seventh month, and the priest's wife conducts it. Some jaggery is cut up with a knife and a portion given to her, while the rest is distributed among the near kin.

The Dewá-dhámí.

Another ceremony, with which the husband's parents are closely associated, is the *dewá-dhámí*.[2]

In Montgomery this rite is observed in the seventh or eighth month. The family priestess lights a lamp fed with *ghí* in a corner of the house, making a hearth and seven cakes of earth, and covering the latter with vermilion. Before these things the husband and wife prostrate themselves, and big loaves of flour fried in *ghí* are then distributed among the brotherhood. Until these articles have all been removed, the women of the family do not spin or do any other work. The things are then collected and given to the parents, who in return present the wife with a *trewar*,[3] a rupee and a half *ser* of jaggery. This rite is observed three days *before* the *kanjí* ceremony. But in Gujránwála it is said to

[1] *Bhahore* in *Punjabi Dictionary*: s.v. *Kanjí*, p. 550.

[2] *Déwá* or *díwá*, a lamp; *dhámí*, not given in the dictionaries, is possibly to be derived from P. *dhám*, s.f. a feast.

[3] *Trewar* = *tewar*: see note [5] to p. 782 *supra*.

be held at the same time as the *rít,* and it must be held in the lower storey of the house, by night, the lamp being lighted in the southern corner.

In Hazro, the *dewá-dhámí* is also held on the same *rít,* by the kinswomen and the priest's wife—all males being excluded. The priestess begins by kindling a lamp and causing the wife to worship Ganesh. Sweetened rice or bread is then distributed Next morning rice is boiled or *halwa* made; and the wife is bathed and dressed in the clothes sent by her parents. Another woman is then seated by her to represent her husband, and on her knees are put all the clothes received for him. Seven vessels and covers of cowdung are then made, and cardamoms, rice, barley, *mung* (pulse), *piwa* and two copper coins are placed in each. These vessels are then put between the two women, and the wife removes the covers, which the other woman replaces. This is done thrice. Then both dip their fingers in milk and water and each tries to seize the other's fingers thrice. Both then chew cardamoms, which they spit over each other, and finally the rice or *halwa* is given to the priestess, who also gets five annas or Re. 1½. Next day she is called in again and lights the lamp, which she extinguishes with milk and water. This ends the *rít.*

In Bahãwalpur, on the other hand, the *dewá-dhámí* is preformed by the husband's father, who lights a lamp in a corner of the house, making an effigy of Ganesh and worshipping his ancestors, with his face turned to the north or towards the Ganges. While worshipping he must unloose the string of his *chola* or shirt, or the gods will not accept his devotions.

In Mandi the *ríts* of the fifth and seventh months are not observed at all, but in the beginning of the eighth month the *athwahán*[1] is celebrated by putting an idol of Ganpati on a red *chaukí;* and this the wife worships for a month, during which period she must not bathe, change her old clothes, or cross a river. In the beginning of the ninth month follows the *baránwín,* at which the wife's kinswomen assemble to bathe her, make her put on new clothes and look at a handsome boy to ensure her own child being a son. This boy is dismissed with a present of money. Then the wife is made to stand up, and a kerchief is tied round her waist, cakes, money, gold and silver, flowers, a cocoanut, a pomegranate, and a mixture of rice, sesame and sugar, sent by her parents, are put in her lap. Of the money, part goes to the priest, and the rest to the midwife. On this occasion her nearest relative also gives the wife money and ornaments for her own use. Then the wife revers Ganpati, and a vessel (*kalas*) of earth, brass or copper is put in an octagonal *jantar* (diagram), and in it is placed a cocoanut, with an image of Vishnu. The wife is then directed to worship the *kalas* and after that a *hawan* is performed, a he-goat[2] being sacrificed to appease the fire deity. Brahmans and near relatives are then fed, and the kinswomen sing songs and make merry all night. This rite is observed in every pregnancy.

[1] The Sanskr. *pun san.* In the parent State of Suket the *athwán* is observed in the eighth or ninth month. The woman's parents send her clothes for herself and the child. The clothes are perfumed. A rupee is also sent. They also send one or two garments for the husband's mother.

[2] Or vicariously a cocoanut, which is split into two pieces.

The eighth and ninth months.

If we exclude such of the foregoing observances as are postponed till the eighth or ninth month, there are few which are necessarily held in either of these two months. In Hissár the *kanji* is observed in the seventh or ninth month,[1] and in some places the *adh-garbh*[2] is actually said to be deferred till the ninth month. In parts of Hoshiárpur there is, however, a distinct rite in the ninth month, on the second day, thus corresponding to the rite in the seventh. A corner of the house is plastered, and the wife is seated there, with her face to the east, and made to worship Ganesh. A cocoanut and a rupee are also put in her lap by way of *shagún* or good augury, and boiled rice is set before. Sweets etc. sent by her parents are distributed among the brotherhood.[3] In the northern part of the same district it is said that the *rít* is held in the ninth month, and consists simply in the distribution of *kari* (gram flour cooked in whey) to the brotherhood in order to proclaim the pregnancy.[4]

Athwánsá.

At the commencement of the eighth month the Shaikháwat Rájpúts observe a rite called the *athwánsá*. The wife's parents send her clothes, ornaments, fruit, money, and on their receipt all her kinswomen assemble. Brahmans then worship the gods and the wife bathes, after which she puts on the new clothes. With this the following custom among the same people appears to be connected.

After birth a child of either sex is bathed in the blood of a he-goat and a necklet of its flesh is put round the child's neck. Then it is dressed in a blue *kurta* and cap, with a belt of blue silk round its waist. These clothes are worn for six or seven months, but the necklet is retained for two years and the belt worn till it reaches the age of five.

Máwali.

All Hindús who believe in the god Máwali perform the following rite in the seventh month: a mixture of rice, *múng* and barely is made and an earthen vessel sent for from the potter's house. This is marked seven times with three things, henna, black and red colouring. Then boiled rice and the dish described above are placed in her lap seven times, some cooked *múng* being also put in the middle of the vessel. Lastly, a red thread is put in it and taken out by the midwife, who deposits it under a *ber* tree. All the members of the family then eat the food.

1 In Fázilka the *kanji* is said to be held only in the ninth month. In Gujránwála it is observed in the seventh or eighth.

2 *Adh-garbh* = *adh-gabh*.

3 The Básdeo Brahmans observe this rite in the eighth month, and feast the whole brotherhood, males and females, on this occasion, great quantities of curd and sugar being given them.

4 It is also said that the *rít* in this part varies in different castes, and that it is repeated 'several times.' It is specifically described as being observed thrice, in the fifth month (when *kanji* and *pakauras* are distributed); in the seventh (when boiled rice and pulse are sent round), and in the ninth (when moist gram and jaggery are distributed among the brotherhood). It is not stated that all three rites are observed by the same caste.

The following rites are observed during pregnancy in Chamba :—The woman should not go near a dead body even of a near relative, nor cross a stream, especially in the evening, lest the water spirit exert an evil influence on her, nor should she visit a woman newly delivered. In all these cases the danger feared is abortion from the influence of evil spirits. If a snake appears and is trying to escape the people believe that the shadow of a pregnant woman falling on it will cause it to crawl slowly.[1]

Eclipses in pregnancy.

During pregnancy the parents are both peculiarly susceptible to the effects of an eclipse, and it is safest for the wife to keep her bed and not even see the eclipse, in Ambála, but the father is not under any such necessity. In Dera Gházi Khán, however, either parents must avoid applying antimony to the eyelids, or a *tilak* to the forehead, during an eclipse, lest the child be so marked. Both should also avoid locking or unlocking a lock, lest its fingers be bent and powerless. If they cut wood with an axe, the child will have a hare-lip ; or if they break anything, such as a piece of wood, its fingers will be marked. In short, anything such as stamping or printing done during an eclipse is liable to leave its impress on the child's body.[2]

Abortion.

If abortion has ever occurred, or is feared for the woman, *syánas* or wizards prevent it by giving her (*i*) a piece of wood from a scaffold on which a man has been hanged, or (*ii*) pice which have been thrown over the *biwán* or bearse of an old person, or (*iii*) a tiger's flesh or claw. The idea in each of these charms is to increase the vitality or prolong the life of the child.

Section 2.—Hindu birth observances.

I.—Observances before and at birth.

Lucky and unlucky births.—The auspiciousness—or the reverse—of a birth depends upon several factors, such as the season or time of its occurrence, its sequence relative to preceding birth in the family, [3] and the child's position at birth.

Premature birth.—Birth in the eighth month of pregnaoy is attributed to a cat having entered the mother's room in a former confinement. A child born in this month will, it is believed, die on the eighth day, in the eighth month, or eighth or eighteenth year, after birth.

[1] In Kángra in the eighth month of pregnancy the pregnant woman is seated inside a *chauuk* in which *bel-búte* 'leaves' are placed and in which a small lamp is lit. *Púja* is done to Ganesh. This is called *athwá*.

[2] During an eclipse of the sun or moon a pregnant woman should lie with her body straight, lest the child be born crooked. Every morning she should be careful to look first at her husband's face, so that the child may resemble him. If any one else is frequently seen it will take after him. If her husband is absent she should look at the faces of her other children or at her own face in a looking glass, or at her sister's face, but not at her brother's.

[3] For the significance of the sequence of births, see *Folk Lore*, vol. xiii, pp. 63—67, and pp. 279—280.

Hence the number eight is never mentioned in speaking of a child's age, *un-ginat* or 'uncounted' being used instead: thus, *an-ginat din* = eighth day,[1] *an-ginat barha* = eighth year.

The aṭhwáhá.—In the Ḍera tahsíl of Kángṛa a child born in the eighth month is called an *aṭhwáhá* (fr. *aṭh.*, 8), and is regarded as unlucky to both its parents, foreboding the father's death. As a remedy a spinning-wheel is passed thrice round the mother's head, and then given to the midwife.

In Kángṛa a child which dies at birth, or immediately after it, is inauspicious, and its nose is bored, for a gold ring to be inserted, in order to avert its evil influence.

Monday is an unlucky day for birth, and as a remedy the child's nose or ear is bored. In some parts, *e.g.* among orthodox Hindús in Baháwalpur, Ferozepur and Manḍi, the following remedies are used to counteract the evil influences of the various planels:—

Saturn: seven kinds of grain, or anything black, such as iron or a black buffalo, should be given away in charity.

Mars: articles such as copper, *gur*, cloth dyed red, oil etc.

The Sun: reddish things, such as *ghí*, gold, wheat, a red-coloured cow etc.

The Moon: white articles, such as silver, rice, a white cow, white cloth etc.

Mercury and Venus: green articles such as *múng* (a kind of pulse), green cloth or fruit, such as oranges etc

Jupiter: yellow things, such as yellow cloth, gram-pulse, yellow sweetmeats (*nukhti* and *laḍḍu*), gold etc.

To avert the evil effects of Ráh (or ascending node): coconuts, *ghí*, sugar (*khanḍ*) and *másh* (a kind of pulse); and that of Kret or typhon (the descending node): *samosa* (a kind of sweetmeat) and *bluish cloth* are given in charity.

This is termed *girah-púja* (or worship of the planets).

A birth which occurs during the *panchak* period will, it is believed, be followed by the birth of three children of the same sex.

The *gandes* are five days which fall in the dark half of the lunar month, and a child born on any of these dates bodes ill to its parents. Accordingly, the father must not see the child until, in the recurrence of the *nakshatra* in which it was born, he has worshipped the gods, or until five dolls have been made, put in a copper vessel and anxiously propitiated. Fruit is placed before them, as they are believed to eat; and Brahmans recite *mantras*. Lastly, an earthen jar is pierced with twenty-eight holes and filled with water and various drugs. It is then hung up some distance from the ground and the water allowed to trickle on to the parents' heads. After this the Brahmans are rewarded.

[1] But the same writer (S. Gurdiál Singh in *J. A. S. Bengal*, lii, Pt. I, p. 205), says that a child is never said to be so many days or months old, but so many *years*, *e.g.* *chár barhe* = four days or four months old, as well as four years.

As we have already seen, eclipses affect the parents during pregnancy. So too a child, of either sex, born during an eclipse brings ill luck, to avert which the following observances are in vogue, at least in Kángṛa :—

The image in gold of the deity connected with the asterism in which the eclipse occurred, and one of the sun (if it was eclipsed), or of the moon (in the case of its eclipse), together with an image of Ráhu, are reverenced. A *hawan* is also performed, *ak* wood being used if the sun was eclipsed, or, if the moon, *palas*. Like other unlucky children, a child born under an eclipse is weighed every month, on the *sankránt* day, against seven kinds of grain, all of which is given away.

A child (unlike a calf) born in Bhádon is lucky, while one born in Kátak is inauspicious, and the mother of such a child should be turned out of the house, though she may be given to a Brahman and then redeemed from him. Children born under certain asterism are peculiarly liable not only to misfortune themselves, but to cause evil to others, and various rites are performed to avert the consequences of their birth.

A child born in Kátak must either undergo symbolical birth from a cow (*goparsab*), or also both it and the parents must bathe on the first *sankránt* after the end of Kátak in water drawn from seven wells and mixed with turmeric, sandal, ginger and other drugs. These are termed *sarbokhadi*, and are placed in an unbaked earthen jar, with 1000 orifices and a lip, the appropriate *mantras* being duly recited. Water from seven wells or rivers is then similarly purified by *mantras*. The parents, with the child in its mother's lap, are then placed under a sieve, through which the water is poured. *Hawan* is then performed, and lastly a tray of *ghí* is given away by the parents in charity.

A child born when the moon is in the sixth or eighth zodiacal sign is ill-omened, and to avert its influence the following rite is observed: On the twenty-seventh day after the birth a basket made of bamboo is filled with sixteen *sers* (thirty-two lbs.) of rice, some camphor, a pearl, a piece of white cloth and some silver and given away in charity, together with a team of white calves yoked, and vessels of milk and *ghí*. Worship, in which white sandal-wood and white flowers figure, is also performed. This, however, is an orthodox rite, and in Kángṛa the popular idea is that a child born in the *ghāti-chandarmán*, *i. e.* when the moon is inauspicious, is not ill-omened.

The unlucky *tithi* or lunar days for birth are the *amáwas*, or last day of the dark half; and the *chatúrdashi* (vulg. *chaudas*) are fourteenth, the last day but one. Children born on the former day are unpropitious to the father, those born on the latter to the mother. To avert their evil influence an idol of Shiva is made of silver, and in an earthen jar are placed leaves from various trees, mango, *palas*, *pípal* etc. A cocoanut is then placed on the jar, which is covered with a red cloth; and on this is put the idol of Shiva, after it has been purified by *mantras*. *Hawan* is performed with sesame, pulse (*másh*) and white mustard. The idol is given to a Brahman.

The following thirteen *nakshatras* are unlucky :—

1. Asauni,
2. Rawati,
3. Maghán,
4. Shelkhán,
5. Múlan,
6. Jeshṭan,
7. Grahn (eclipse),
8. Atepát,
9. Shankránt,
10. Gand,
11. Chandas,
12. Amáwas,
13. Bhadra,

especially 1 to 6[1]—each *charan*[2] having special influence of its own. Thus in Shelkhán the second *charan* is fatal to wealth, the third to the mother, and the fourth to the father.[3] In the Jeshthá asterism, which is divided into ten *charans*, each of six *gharís*, we have the following scheme :—

Birth in second *charan* : father. Birth in first *charan* : mother.

Father. Mother, fourth *charan* ; brother,[4] third *charan*.

Elder brother, eighth *charan* child, to itself if born in fifth *charan* ; to the 'members of its family' if in sixth or seventh ; to its father-in-law in the ninth ; and to everything in the tenth.[5]

In the Múl asterism the first *charan* is unpropitious to the father, the second to the mother, and the third to wealth.[6]

[1] In Núrpur tahsíl of Kángra the evil influence of a birth in any unlucky *nakshatras* is averted by bathing the parents and child with water from a jar, containing 1000 holes, into which leaves from 108 male trees (mango, *pípal*, banian, are male ; while *nákh*, 'pear,' and *beri*, 'plum,' are feminine). Children born in the remaining seven of the thirteen *nakshatras* specified are not very unlucky, and the planets are merely worshipped by more rigid observers of Hindu precepts.

[2] Lit. 'foot.'

[3] To avert the evil influence five earthen jars, filled with water and leaves (*pípal* etc.) are covered with a red cloth, and the golden image of a serpent placed on them and worshipped. The person to whom the birth forebodes evil gives alms, and a *hawan* performed with *ghí* : Kángra. In Dera the five jars should contain gold images of Brahma, Vishnu, Mahesh, Indra and Varuna.

[4] Special attention may here be directed to the position of the mother's brother in astrology. The part played by him in weddings *may* conceivably have an astrological basis. He is curiously affected by his sister's child cutting its upper teeth first : see *Indian Antiquary*, vol. xxxi, 1902, p. 292.

[5] To avert the evil a piece of ground is plastered with cow-dung and a platform for a *hawan* made on it. On this platform *mantras* are written in flour. In five jars, full of water, are put the leaves of five trees (*pípal*, mango, *palákhar*, *palas*, and a fifth), with *panchamrit* and *panchgarbh*. In a sixth jar, unbaked, with 1000 orifices are placed 107 different drugs. The parents and child are then drenched through a sieve, and then they join in the *hawan*, which must be celebrated by sixteen Brahmans. Finally parents and child bathe in the water from the five jars. [Kángra.]

[6] The rites are the same as in the case of a Jéshṭa birth, except that the idol made is a gold one of a *rákkhasa* : Kángra.

Among Hindus in Ambála astrologers are consulted about the auspiciousness of the birth. If the child was born at an inauspicious time, called *gandmul*, 27 days after the birth the child and its mother are bathed in water containing drugs in solution. The water is poured on them from a pitcher with a hundred holes bored in it. In some parts if the child is a male the father gets certain incantations recited over food which is given to the poor so that his ancestors' souls may benefit thereby.

The Gands.—The fourth *charan* in the Shelkháṇ Jeshṭhá and Reoti asterisms, and the first in the Múl, Ashwini and Maghá are called *gands*, and a birth in these is unlucky: if it occur by day, to the father; if by night, to the mother; and if in the morning or evening, to the child itself.[1]

But all these refinements are hardly known to popular astrology, and the general practice is to regard births in Jeshṭhá, Múla, Ashlekhán and Maghán asterisms only as unlucky.[2]

In the Simla hills the evil influence of a birth in the Krishnpak *chaudas* is averted by propitiating the nine planets. A birth at the end of a month and in the Jamgandhjag, Kalijag etc. is unlucky to the parents etc.; and they should not see the child's face until alms have been offered. Triplets portend the speedy death of parents, and to avert the evil, *hawan* is performed, alms are given to the *parohit* and the *shánti mankal* is read.

The couvade.

Repeated inquiries had hitherto failed to elicit any trace of the *couvade* in these Provinces, but Mr. H. W. Emerson, C.S., has now found it in Manḍi where 'the man goes to bed when a son is born: either the mother or the father must be on his back for three months and as the mother does most of the work the father does most of the lying-in.'

The first-born.

Speaking generally, the birth of the first-born child, provided it is not a girl, is the occasion for special rejoicings—and in Káugṛa a pilgrimage is made to the family god (*kul-deota*), and a he-goat, called the *kudnu randá*, is let loose in his honour, another being also sacrificed at his shrine, and a feast given.[3]

In Saráj a few people of the village visit the parents' house and fire off guns. The father feasts them, and gives each guest a small turban and a rupee; the village *deota* and musician also receiving each a rupee. This money is called *wadhái ka rupiyá*, and it is all deposited with an honorary treasurer, and when enough has been collected a great feast is held.

In Hamírpur the *panjáb* rite, which consists in giving alms to the poor, is observed on the eleventh day after the birth. Brahmans and the kinsmen are also feasted, menials also receiving gifts. A good deal of money is thus spent.

[1] The rites resemble those in the Jeshṭha or Múl cases, but a cow is also given as alms in the child's name: Káugṛa.

[2] In the Ḍera tahsíl of Káugṛa the rites observed on such births, or in those which occur under an inauspicious (*ghatak*) moon, are simple. Images of Brahmá, Indar, Súraj (Sun) and the Moon (Chandarmá n) are placed in four jars, with the leaves of seven trees; the jars are then filled with water and covered with a red and white cloth. Mother and child are then sprinkled with the water.

[3] A great many Hindu women who have never had children, or been unable to bring up any, propitiate the Deity by vowing that their *first-born*, if preserved, shall, till he comes of age, or of a certain age, serve in the procession of the Tazia as a water-carrier, or in some other capacity; and such sons always wear the green uniform till they attain that age during the Muharram, and serve as their mothers have vowed, they shall serve, but return to Hindu rites and ceremonies as soon as the Muharram is over, without prejudice to their caste or reproach from their associates. MS. note in a copy of *Sleeman's Rambles and Recollections* (? by the late Mr. Carr Stephen).

The first-born has always held a peculiarly sacred position, especially if born to parents who have long been without offspring in answer to a vow, in which case sacrifice of the child was common in India.[1] The Mairs used to sacrifice a first-born son to Máta, the small-pox goddess,[2] while Muhammadans throughout Northern India believe that first-born children can stop excessive rain by certain rites.[3] On the other hand a first born son will in Telingana attract lightning.[4] A first-born child (Jesṭh) must not be married in Jesṭh: P. N. Q., III, § 10. Twins, as is well known, are peculiarly uncanny.[5]

But many remarkable ideas cluster round the third conception or round a child of one sex born after three children of the other sex. Thus in the South-West Punjab on the borders of Sindh the former superstition prevails and its results are thus described :—

Trikhal is the third conception after two births (without regard to the sexes of the former children). It is a Jaṭki word, meaning 'third' and implies contempt. This conception is considered unlucky among Hindus, especially in Jámpur tahsíl. Every effort is made to effect abortion, and in many cases it undoubtedly takes place. It is also suspected that the third child is killed at birth if the attempts to cause abortion have failed, but fear of the law prevents any attempt to kill it if it survives its birth.

The Trikhal.—This however appears to be a local variant as the other superstition is far more prevalent and its effects and the measures taken to avert them are thus described :—

A child of one sex born after three children of the other sex is called, in Punjabi, *trikhal*, as, for example, a boy born after three girls. Such a child is considered unlucky, and its birth portends—(1) the death of a parent; (2) loss of wealth by the parents; (3) the taking fire of the house in which it was born; or (4) some other calamity, such as lightning or snake-bite.

If this child grows up without its parents suffering any injury, and is taller than the parents, they are benefited instead of injured by the birth, their lives are prolonged, or if poor they become rich and are protected against all misfortunes. Many Hindús also believe that the children born *after* a *trikhal* cannot live long.

The following remedies are adopted at the birth of such a child to avert its evil effects :—

(1) The father pours a quantity of *ghi* down the gutter of the roof of the room in which the child was born

[1] Moore's *Hindu Infanticide*, pp. 198-9.

[2] Sherring: *Hindu Tribes and Castes*, III, p. 66.

[3] P. N. and Q., I, §§ 116 and 468.

[4] N. I. N. Q., I, § 378.

[5] But in Dahomey a boy born *after* twins has a special name (*dosu*), according to Burton: *Mission to Gelele King of Dahome*, I, p. 33, *Memorial Edition*.

(2) A brass tray is broken in the centre and the child passed through the hole.

(3) A horse-shoe is painted with *sandúr* (red oxide of mercury) and scented with *gugal* (a drug) and attached to the bed of the mother. The shoe is re-painted with *sandúr* and scented every Tuesday.

(4) If the third day after the birth be a Sunday, a ceremony known as *trikhal shánti* (or propitiation of the *trikhal*) is performed. Green leaves from seven trees are collected and put in an earthen pitcher with 101 holes in its bottom. Another pitcher is filled with water taken from seven wells. The mother, with her child, sits under the drain of the roof of the house in which the child was born. A *pandit* recites to her a *katha* from the *trikhal shánti shástra* while a kinswoman of the mother holds a sieve over her head. The pitcher containing the green leaves is placed on the sieve, and the father pours the water of the seven wells down the drain of the roof, so that the water passing through the pitcher and the sieve may trickle slowly over the mother's head.

(5) If the charm, whose figure is given below, be set in gold and tied to the neck of the mother all evil is avoided :—

Teri jan men ya na jan men mere kharne ko jagah de.

ya meri sunnat	ya meri sunnat	ya meri sunnat
ya meri sunnat	ya meri sunnat	ya meri sunnat
ya meri sunnat	ya meri sunnat	ya meri sunnat

This belief relates chiefly to the first *trikhal* born in the family : it applies to boys more than to girls (and indeed it is said in Kasúr [1] that a *girl* after three boys is not unlucky at all) and evil is to be feared by both parents but principally to the parent of corresponding sex. Moreover, a boy born after three girls is also apt to be himself unlucky.

The ceremonies used to avert the ill-effects are often those employed when a child is born under an evil *nakshatra* but for a *trikhal*—

Five earthern pitchers filled with water containing gold images of Brahma, Vishnu, Mahesh, Indar and Rudar are worshipped, whereas in the case of a birth under the asterisms of Jesta, Mula, Ashelkán and Magán the leaves of 7 trees [3] are used as described above and in the case

[1] P. N. Q., III, § 458.

[2] And in Amritsar a girl so born is called '*bakhai*' or lucky child : *ibid*, II, § 824, also § 186 (in Bombay)

[3] They should be male trees (*katha, anár, tút* etc.) according to an account from Jhelum.

of a child born in Kátak —

Four images of Brahma, Indar, Rudar and Súraj are placed in 4 pitchers covered with red and white cloth and a little of the water sprinkled over the mother and child.

Lastly for a child born during an eclipse —

Three gold images, one of the *nakshatra* of birth, another of Ráhu and a third of the sun or moon (as the eclipse may have been), are worshipped.

Another name for the *trikhal* is *tretar* (said to be derived from Skr. *tri*, 3 and *attar*, enemy), and in Hoshiárpur the performance of a fire sacrifice with the aid of a Brahman after the *sútak* period is usual. *Pala* wood is burnt and sugar etc. thrown on to it.

In Karnál and Rohtak a son born after three girls is usually called *telar* (or named Telu Rám) and in Rohtak various ways of averting the evil he may bring are described. In one the parents sit on a plough and bathe from an earthern vessel containing 108 or 101 holes with water from the Ganges and 27 wells, 108 medicines and milk. The water is passed through a sieve, but in some places a sieve is held to be unlucky. In another ceremony the parents bathe in water (passed through a sieve) drawn from 27 wells and in which stones from 27 places and leaves from 27 trees have been placed. This must be done 27 days after the birth. 27, 14 or 7 Brahmans are also feasted. After these ceremonies a pair of snakes are made of a precious metal and given with 7 kinds of grain to the Ḍakaut Brahman. In another right a horse-shoe, painted with vermilion figures, is burnt on the third or tenth day after the birth. It is lucky if this day falls on a Sunday.

The superstition appears then to take various forms and the rites practised are very diverse, those used to avoid other unlucky births being often resorted to, though it appears that strictly speaking special rites should be performed. It is said to be confined in Sirmúr State to immigrants from Hoshiárpur It is possibly connected with the astrological doctrine of trines but the powers of the first-born are not thereby explained. The belief and rites are said to be described in the *shástras*. In 1885 a Sanskrit book called *Trikhal-shánti* was published at Lahore giving an account of the belief. The sage Pushkar asks Bhargat how a *trikhal* can be propitiated. The reply is that it should be abandoned as it will cause the death of its parents and maternal uncle [1] within 7 months and also destroy itself.

The eighth child.[2]—The eighth child is very unlucky if a son as he is sure to cause his *father's* death.[3] But in Karnál the 8th child is regarded as peculiarly dangerous to the *mother*. The remedy is to pass a *charkha* or spinning wheel thrice round the mother and give it to the midwife. The *charkha* must be in perfect order.

[1] The part which the maternal uncle plays in marriage rites is well known. He is in grave peril if his sister's child cut its upper teeth first.

[2] Connected apparently with the eight names of Rudra, Muir's *Sanskrit Texts*, IV, pp. 388, et *seqq*.

[3] I. N. Q. I., V, § 94.

Dhái sira or '2½ heads.'—Mr. W. S. Talbot writes that in Jhelum *trikhal* is drilled with 2½ holes—a local expression meaning 2 holes in one ear and 1 in the other, or 1 in each ear and 1 in the nose. In Muzaffargarh a *dhái-sira, mula or sat-sira* is a child whose head has not been properly shaped.

There is no objection to twins. But in Kángra if a boy and a girl be born together it is sometimes regarded as unlucky.

In Karnál different classes have different ideas about twins. Among both Hindús and Muhammadans some consider them a good omen while other Hindús think they forebode ill-luck. Women do not consider their birth evil and they have a proverb that the woman who gives birth to twins goes straight to paradise on her death.

In Ambála twins being weaker than single children frequently die, and so they are considered ominous It is believed that if at intercourse air gets in it splits the seed in two and thus gives rise to twins. It is also said that if a pregnant woman eats a fruit which has grown in a pair, she will give birth to twins.

In Hoshiárpur a child which first teethes from its upper jaw is considered unlucky to its maternal uncle. To remove the evil effects its mother goes beyond the limits of her village on the path leading to her parents' house. From the opposite direction comes the maternal uncle of the child, bringing with him a white brass tray, 1½ *sers* of rice, 7 pice, a yard of cloth and 4 iron nails, all except the tray and nails, knotted in the cloth. The maternal uncle drives the 4 nails in the ground in a square, touches the child's teeth with the tray, and then puts the tray and the cloth with the other articles wrapped in it within the square between the nails and returns home. The uncle and his sister must not talk or see each other's faces. The sister sits with her child clinging to her shoulder, her veil drawn and her back towards her brother, and he returns in silence after the ceremony, which is called *dánton ka thakna* or 'the charm of the teeth.'

In Karnál when a child of either sex cuts the front teeth of its upper jaw first it is a bad omen to the maternal uncle. His sister, the mother of the child, sends him word of the event. On receiving the message the maternal uncle takes a bronze cup of medium size, a quarter of a *ser* of *kasár* or *ganjíri* (wheat flour baked in *ghí* and mixed with sugar) and half a cocoanut in a piece of red cloth (*khárwa*) and proceeds to his sister's house without informing her or any other person in the house of his arrival, which is kept strictly secret. He goes quickly on to the roof of the house in which his sister lives and puts the cup &c. on it, or if there is no staircase he throws them upon it. After this ceremony he retraces his steps silently without speaking to, or even seeing the face of, his sister and returns home. When it is known that the ceremony has been finished the things are taken from the roof and used without scruple.

It is performed differently in villages situate in the neighbourhood of Patiála. A time is fixed and a place appointed for the ceremony. The child's mother goes to the place, which is always fixed beyond the limits of the village on the road to her brother's house. He starts from his own village and halts a mile from the place till he gets news of his sister's arrival. He brings with him an old three-pie coin (*Mansúri paisa*) with an iron nail, but nothing else. When he is informed that everything is ready, he proceeds to the place. His sister takes her child up in her arms so that its face is towards the way her brother is coming, she herself standing facing the village whence she came. The brother comes silently and opens the mouth of the child, touches its teeth with the *paisa* and iron nail, without showing himself or seeing his sister's face and after burying these things on the spot returns to his village.

Place of confinement. –It is a very general, but by no means universal custom for the wife to return to her own parents' house for her first confinement.

A child born in the house of his *náná*, or mother's father, often receives the name of Nának.[1]

Care is taken not to let the fact that the pains of labour have begun be noised abroad, lest publicity increase their severity. And if the pains are severe a tray (*thálí*), on which a charm is written, is shown to the patient in order to remove them.

It appears to be the universal custom for delivery to be effected on the ground.[2] But after it is over the mother is usually seated on a mat or cassock. It appears to be almost the universal custom to tell her that she has given birth to a girl, [3] in the curious belief that if she were to learn that she had become the mother of a son, the after-birth would not come away.

As a rule the umbilical cord is cut with a sharp knife, but in Ludhiána it is tied with the *janeo* of an elderly man belonging to the family. This is also the usage in Hoshiárpur and Siálkot, but in these districts, if the child be a girl, the cord is tied with the thread of a spinning-wheel. Any other method is supposed to injure the child. In Gújránwála the cord is not cut till two or three hours after birth.

Disposal of the after-birth.—In Ferozepore the secundines are buried in a corner of the house.

In Mandi the after-birth is buried at the spot where the child was born, after the eldest matron of the family has made the mother worship it.

Death in child-bed.—If a woman die within thirteen days of her delivery it is believed that she will return in the guise of a malignant spirit to torment her husband and family. To avert this a *shánti* is performed at her funeral, a piece of red cloth and the grass image of her child being placed on the bier. Some people also drive nails through her head and eyes, while others also fasten nails on either side of the door of their house.

[1] *Cf.* Temple in *Proper Names of Panjábis*, p. 50.

[2] In Hoshiárpur delivery is said to be effected on a *chárpái*.

[3] And if she has given birth to a girl, she is told she has borne a stone.

In Hoshiárpur a woman whose child has died within forty days is called a *parchháwán*,[1] and she must not see a woman in confinement during the first forty days after birth.

II.—Observances subsequent to the birth.

The observances after birth are manifold, and their character complex, so that it is as difficult to distinguish between the religious and social observances, as it is to say what usages are based on magic and what on the first glimmerings of medical skill. Nevertheless, under much that is barbarous and puerile there are traces of more rational ideas regarding cleanliness, and even a kind of primitive anticipation of antiseptic treatment. One important point to note is that the observances are far less elaborate in the case of a girl child, and this idea, that the birth of a girl is a misfortune, re-acts injuriously on the mother, less care being bestowed upon her, and every observance being hurried over and many stinted, if the child is not a boy. Thus in Ráwalpindi the mother of a son is carefully tended for forty days, but if the child is a girl for only twenty-one

The period of impurity.—The period of impurity is most commonly called *sútak* but it is known as *chhút*, especially in the north-west of the Punjab.

Its duration is, in theory, ten days among Brahmans, twelve among Khatrís, fifteen among Vaisyas and thirty among Sudras, thus varying inversely with the purity of the caste. But in practice it is eleven days among Brahmans and thirteen among Khatrís; or only eleven or thirteen for all castes.[2]

Among the Jaṭs of Hoshiárpur, who may in this connection be regarded as typical of the Hindús of the Punjab proper, the following is the method of treatment after birth:—

The midwife washes the child in a vessel into which silver has been thrown, before she gives it to the mother. But the child is not suckled for one and a half days.

[1] *Cf.* Parchhaiṇ, shadow.—*Panjabi Dictionary*. p. 868.

[2] In Rohtak and Lohárn it would appear to be only ten, expiring with the *dasúthan*. In Gujránwála it is said to be thirteen days for Brahmans and sixteen for others.

In Patiála it is generally believed that death in child-bed is ominous for the other women of the family who may yet bear children, and more or less so for the husband also should he take a second wife, because the dead woman's evil spirit will vex her; the prophylactic measures, generally undertaken, with slight modification in different localities are:—Just after the death 4 iron nails are driven into the ground round the corpse, and when it is taken from the house-door to the burning-ground rape-seed is scattered all the way behind it, and a wizard follows it reciting incantations. Midway the bearers set the body on the ground and 4 more nails are driven into it. On reaching the burning-ground it is cremated without any ceremony, but on the 3rd or 4th day when the ashes have cooled the unburnt bones are picked up and the ashes collected into a conical heap on which the lower part of a hand flour-mill is placed while two iron nails are driven towards the head and two towards the feet of the body as it lay when placed on the pile, and the wizard reading some incantation completes the ceremony. After all this the husband still has to go to Pehowa where he undergoes purification under the guidance of the Brahmans of that place.

In Sangrúr the *Gayathri mantra* is recited by a Brahman when a woman dies in child-birth among the Naís, to prevent her becoming an evil spirit. The sweepers drive an iron nail in the ground for the same purpose, and the Jhínwars send for a Qázi to recite some words called *kilna*. No unusual treatment is practised among other low castes in this tahsíl.

The pap must be washed by the husband's sister before the child can be fed. For this she receives a fee.

As on all auspicious occasions, oil is thrown on the ground and under the mother's bed, beneath which green *dúb* grass is also placed, as it is a sign of prosperity; and as such some is also presented to the child's father by his friends :—

To prevent mischief to the mother or the child, a number of precautions are taken :—

(*i*) Fire must be kept in the room, as must also

(*ii*) Grain close to the bed, as an emblem of good luck.

(*iii*) Water must also be kept there, as it is a purifier; and

(*iv*) A weapon should be placed close by the mother.

(*v*) Under the bed should also be kept the handle of a plough.[1]

(*vi*) There should be a lock on the bed, or else it should have a chain round it. This is termed *bel maria.*[2]

(*vii*) On no account should a cat be allowed in the room, nor should the mother hear one call, or even mention the word 'cat.' It is most unlucky for her to dream of the animal, and if one is seen in the room, ashes should be thrown over it.

(*viii*) The house should not be swept with a broom—lest the luck be swept out of it.

(*ix*) No small drain into the room should be left open, lest ill-luck enter by an aperture which must be unclean.

(*x*) A lamp must be kept burning all night, and allowed to burn itself out in the morning. A son is called *ghar ká díwá,* so if the lamp were blown out, he too would be destroyed.

Neither mother nor child must come out of the room for thirteen days.

On the thirteenth day the mother gives her old clothes to the midwife, who sometimes shares them with the *nain*. The latter brings some cow's urine in a *ṭhikra* or jar, with green grass, a *supára*, and a *naherná*, or nail-parer She sprinkles the cow's urine over the mother with the grass, burns some incense, and pares her nails for the first time since her confinement. Then the mother must put on the *nai's* (the *nain's* husband's, not the *nain's*) slippers, and walk out of the room carrying the child The *nain* sprinkles oil on the ground outside the door,[3] and there the *jhíwari,* or some other menial, stands with a

[1] Probably because the plough turns the soil which produces grain, and so witches will not come near it.

[2] In Panjábí *belná* or *velná*—to press or roll; also to strike the bridegroom's hand at a wedding. *Bel márná* is not traceable in the *Panjabí Dictionary*.

[3] In Jínd the *nain* makes a *satya* (a mark said to be like a cross) on the wall near the door, and receives a rupee and some rice; and the mother eats some *khichṛi* (rice and some pulse, cooked) on this day.

pot of water and some green grass. Both she and the *nain* are paid for their services.

In the outer room Vidháta (vulg. Bidh) Máta is worshipped, no men, not even a Brahman, being present. The women make an idol of *gobhar*, covering it with a red cloth and offering to it the food cooked for the feast. Drums are then beaten, Brahmans and relatives fed, and the members of the household congratulated. The idol is kept for one and a quarter months and then deposited near the well.

The period of confinement lasts forty days, and the mother must not stain the palms of her hands with henna, nor wear clothes dyed with *kasumbha*, until the ancestors have been worshipped and kinsmen feasted. On this occasion the *dhiánís*,[1] or girls born in the tribe, must also be fed, fee'd and reverenced.

Third day.—On the third day the observance called *báhir* is current in Rohtak, and, as the name denotes, the mother on this day comes 'outside,' from the room in which she was confined, at an auspicious hour fixed by a Brahman. The women of the brotherhood assemble at her house, each bringing half a *páo* of grain. The *nain* makes a *chauk* on the ground, in which are depicted the planets. The eldest woman of the family then puts five *sers* of grain, some jaggery and oil on the *chauk*, and all the others follow suit. Then the mother comes out of her house and touches the grain, which is divided, with the jaggery and oil, between the *nain*, the Brahmani and the midwife. A *chhaṭák* of jaggery is then given to each female of the brotherhood present, and songs are sung. Menials also get their dues, and, when the mother comes out of the house, the *nái* waits at the door with a *naherná* with which he touches the boy, for which he gets a rupee. He also puts blades of *dabh* grass in the turbans of the child's forbears, in order that they may multiply like the grass. For this he receives a second rupee.

In Hoshiárpur the mother in some places is bathed on the third day, if she has given birth to a girl: a function postponed to the fifth day if her child is a boy. In Sirmúr, too, she bathes on the third or fifth day; and in Mandi a rite called the *tirphal ká gontar*[2] is observed

[1] Or *dhidhan* or *dhián*, a sister or daughter. The term is used by Brahmans, *mírásis* etc. in addressing the daughter or sister of a patron.

[2] This rite is thus described: The courtyard of the house is swept, and circles drawn on it with mud. These circles are called *mahol*. The threshold of the house is painted red. The person who sweeps the yard gets *puṛá tar* (rice, sugar, cash etc.). Then the mother is bathed in hot water and made to worship Ganpatí, whose idol is put on a yellow *chauk*, and offerings made to it. A Brahman now makes *panchgabh*, mixing it up in a jar with a blade of *dabh* grass. He gives three spoonfuls of this mixture to the mother and thus removes her impurity. He next receives his fee in money, and then places a ball of cow-dung, containing gold, silver, a pearl, and a bead of coral, near the idol. This ball is called *biyáhí*, and is worshipped like the goddess. After all this, the mother's breasts are washed and she suckles the child. Then balls of boiled rice are placed daily in the *chauk* for three days—until the impurity has been removed—and are then given to the midwife. The mother's brother then goes to the forest with a Brahman and a musician, and cuts four branches from a *thohar* (Euphorbia Royleana), and these he is made to worship by the Brahman, who receives a fee for this from the mother's brother. Of these four branches the Brahman places two, one on each side of the door of the house in which the birth took place, and sticks two in cow-dung near Ganpatí's *chauk*. They are then covered with a red cloth The mother's brother's forehead is then marked with the *tilak*, and the nearest kinsmen are fed. Songs are also sung. The eldest matron of the family also gives the mother rice mixed with salt, a dish called *pichhlagra*. (*Pichchh*=rice water.)

on the former day. In Ráwalpindi the mother bathes on the third, fifth or seventh day, and *chúri* (baked bread, sugar, and *ghí*) is then distributed among the females of the brotherhood. In the evening of the same day she puts the child in a winnowing basket and takes it outside the village gate—accompanied by the midwife.

Fourth day.—As a rule the mother bathes on the third day, or on one bearing an odd number after it, but in the Dasúya tahsíl of Hoshiárpur she is bathed on the fourth, seventh, thirteenth, twenty-first, thirtieth, and forty-eighth days.

Fifth day.—Excluding the bathing already mentioned, the rites of the fifth day are confined to Jhelum, in which district the *panjwáṇ* or fifth-day observance simply consists in a bath, and Hoshiárpur. In the latter district a foster-brother is made for the child out of cow-dung, and grain, sweets and bread placed beneath it. A red cloth is then thrown over it. All these things are the midwife's perquisite. The rite is performed both for a girl and a boy. The mother also bathes on this occasion, and her head is washed with milk and cow's urine. Elsewhere in this same district the mother is bathed on the fifth or seventh day, and the *nain* plaits her hair. Then she is brought out into the courtyard, wearing the *nain's dopaṭṭa* or shawl. The yard is previously plastered with cow-dung, and in it the mother is seated on a stool, and given cow's urine and Ganges water to drink. She then re-enters the room in the house, which has in the meanwhile been re-plastered with cow-dung. Inside she sits by a wall, close to which is placed some grain on which a lamp is lit. Each of the kinswomen then brings some grain and money and puts them by the lamp. Then rice, loaves and *másh* are distributed among the brotherhood, the grain and money brought being divided by the midwife and the *nain*.

Sixth day.—The ceremony called the *chhaṭi* was doubtless originally, as the name implies, observed on the sixth day, but it is now extinct (in Sirmúr), or else held on the sixth or any subsequent date.[1] Only in Manḍi must the rite called *chhaṭi gontar*[2] actually be held on the sixth day.

Elsewhere the *chhaṭi* is known as the *dhamán*, and is held only in cases when the child was a boy.

[1] In Gujránwála the *chhaṭi* is described as being observed on the fifth day, on which day the child is named.

[2] This resembles the *tirphalla*. The house is swept, as before, and Ganpati again worshipped. Then images of a cow, a calf, and a herdsman are made of brass. These are known as *dádá wachha*, and are placed near the goddess' idol. *Panchgabh* is given to the mother. The females of the brotherhood assemble and sing songs. They are regaled on moist grain, and red thread is then sent to the mother's parents, a custom called *ḍart dena*, or 'giving the thread.' In return they send money and sweetmeats. In Manḍi is also performed the third or last *gontar*. On the evening preceding the day fixed for this rite, the house is swept. All the near kinswomen are invited, and they spend the night in singing, while the priest makes the mother worship Ganpati. Alms are also given to avert evil planetary influences. On the following day the priest performs a *hawan* (*hom*), in much the usual way. The mother and all the members of her family are then purified, and finally a *biyáhí* of cow-dung is made, and the mother instructed to clean her teeth with twigs of a fragrant plant. These twigs are struck in the *biyáhí* and preserved as long as the child lives, being worshipped at its birthdays. The *biyáhí*, with the twigs struck in it, must, at this *gontar*, be set afloat on a river or stream.

When the mother goes to her parents' house for her confinement the *chhaṭi* is observed on her return to her husband's house, and in Ferozepur it is in this case postponed till the twenty-first day.

In Ludhiána the rite is simple. The mother is bathed (*chaṭṭí ka ashnán*), and boiled rice and sweets are distributed among the members of the brotherhood. The mother fasts all day until sunset, when she is given starch to eat and then she is brought out of the room by the midwife with a lamp burning in the winnowing basket. After the sixth day the mother is not so carefully looked after.

In Amritsar the *chhaṭí* is said not to be observed by Brahmans or Khatrís, but only by Aroṛas.

In Montgomery the *chhatí* is termed *sathi*,[1] and the Brahman suggests the boy's name—no such observance being required for a girl.[2]

In Rohtak and Lohára it is said to be the occasion on which the goddess of fortune will visit the house and partake of grain and water therein, so water is set forth, and pen, paper and ink placed ready for her to record a happy future for the child.

The kinswomen and the priest's wife sing songs all night, the idea being that the goddess will record a better fate for the child if they are awake and a lamp is kept burning. After this the mother is allowed to eat grain, and the child is dressed in a *kurta* and cap, and ornaments are put on it. If it is a boy, mango leaves are hung on the door of the house, and *thápás* or hand-prints made on either side of it in the corners, with henna.

Special care is taken that the sounds of mourning may not reach the mother's ears if a death occurs in the neighbouring houses.

Dhamán.—In the Hazro tahsíl of Attock the term *dhamán* is applied to the custom whereby the mother keeps her bedding on the ground.[3] On the first Sunday or Thursday after the birth, mother and child are bathed and dressed in new clothes. They are then placed on a *chárpái*. Sweet porridge is also distributed among the brotherhood on this day. If during the *dhamán* period thunder is heard, a pewter vessel is beaten, lest the sound of the thunder reach the mother's ears.

Seventh day.—The *satwán*, or seventh-day observance, is only known by that name in Jhelum and Ráwalpindi, in which districts it consists merely in a bath—as in Hoshiárpur—in lieu of or in addition to those previously taken.

Tenth day.—The tenth day is not generally marked by any special rites, in spite of the fact that it gives its name to the *dasúṭhan* (lit., bathing on the tenth day after childbirth).[4] In Sirmúr it is also called *sondhia*, and is observed at any time before the child is five years old.

Dhamán.—In Siálkot the *dhamán* rite is observed on the eleventh day by Brahmans, and by other castes on the thirteenth, *i.e.* after the *sútak* is over. Four copper coins are placed under the mother's feet,

[1] By corruption, apparently.

[2] In this district, the *dhamán* appears to be observed, as a distinct rite, on the first Sunday or Wednesday after the birth.

[3] According to the *Punjabi Dictionary*, *dhamán* or *dhamaṇh* in Potohárí means 'the period of child-birth.'

[4] Platts, *sub voce.*

and an idol made of cow-dung. After bathing and putting on new clothes the mother worships a lamp, placed before the idol on a pile of grain (which is the midwife's perquisite). Each woman of the brotherhood then gives her a cocoanut and five dates. She is then taken to the kitchen, where a Brahman administers the *panchgan*, receiving a fee of annas four or eight, and a meal. Lastly the idol is taken away outside the village and placed under a plum tree. On this same day the child is invested with the *taragga*,[1] a thread on which are strung a cowry, an iron ring, another of green glass, a tiger's claw, and a piece of the child's umbilical cord, cut off after its birth. The kinswomen are also feasted on this occasion. In the Ḍogar country this thread is made of silk.

Thirteenth day.—The thirteenth day is important, because the *sútak* period very commonly ends on that day, and it is therefore signalised by rites of purification. Very generally the mother is bathed, all the earthen vessels in the house are broken[2] or replaced, and those of metal cleaned. Clothes also are washed, and the house plastered. Brahmans are sometimes fed, and occasionally the child is named on this day or dressed for the first time.

Twenty-first day.—The twenty-first day is merely marked in Hoshiárpur by bathing the mother and purifying all the vessels used by her since the birth by fire.

Thirtieth day.—The thirtieth day is only the occasion for a bath, in Hoshiárpur.

Fortieth day.—On the fortieth day the mother bathes for the last time, and then ceases to be even ceremonially impure, and can take part again in the duties of the family kitchen. Strangers also can now take food from the house

The chụṛa karam.—In Manḍi an observance called the *chúra karam* or *jarolan* is held in the third or fifth year of the child's life in Mágh, Phágan, Baisákh, Jéṭh or Háṛ, which months are auspicious for it. Two children must undergo the rite together. All their relatives are summoned the previous day. On the day fixed a *chauk* is painted red, and over it is placed a platter, made of cow-dung, and containing four hollows, one of which is filled with cold water, another with hot, a third with milk, and a fourth with curds. In each a little Ganges water is also poured, and a bundle of *dubh* grass is placed on the platter. A little oil is then dropped on the children's heads, and their bodies are rubbed with *baṭná*.[3] They are next bathed, and the eldest matron of the family passes sweets round their heads to avert evil spirits from them. Then they are made to reverence Ganpati, and the priest parts their hair into three, tying each with red thread. A young girl is then told to apply all the contents of the platter, with the *dubh* grass, to their

[1] Like the *tagaḍhri*, in some parts of the Punjab, and probably, the *sútra* in Amritsar, the *taragga* appears to foreshadow the *janeo*, and to be a stop-gap for it during childhood, until the child is of an age to be invested with the sacred thread. For *taragga*, *cf.* *tarágai* or *tarági* (*tarr*—also), which means a string tied round the waist: a string or silver string worn round the waist of men or boys, especially Márwáris (*Punjabi Dictionary*, p. 1106).

[2] This is not done in Amritsar, in which district the room is simply cleansed.

[3] Hindi *ubṭan*, a paste made of meal, turmeric, oil and scent, used to clean and soften the skin.

hair.[1] Brahmans are then fed. Next day at dawn the priest makes the two children worship the nine planets, and then he receives his fee in money. Oil is then poured on their heads and the barber cuts their hair, which must fall into the mother's skirt. The barber is paid his due The mothers offer the hair at the temples of their family goddesses. Then the children are bathed and dressed in new clothes, their brothers' wives, or their sisters, painting their eyes with antimony. A goldsmith then bores their ears and puts gold ear-rings in them, receiving a he-goat and some cash as his fee. Copper coins are finally distributed among the poor, and a feast given to the Brahmans and near kinsmen.

Well worship.—In Rohtak, a month or so after the birth of a boy, a rite called *doghar púja* is observed. If the mother is very weak the other women of the house place a jar of water by her, and they themselves visit the nearest well, singing songs as they go. The well is worshipped, rice and *dubh* grass being offered to it. On their return copper coins are given to the menials. Or if the mother cannot perform this rite herself, it is observed at home. In Ferozepur the mother goes, on the twenty-first day, to a well, and there distributes boiled barley amongst children.

Suckling.—Suckling the child for the first time is the occasion for a curious rite. At sunset the midwife washes the mother's breasts with water, using some blades of *dubh* grass as a brush. They are again washed by the child's sister or some other female. The midwife gets annas two or four, the sister a rupee, for this. Next day the midwife brings some green *sarín* leaves and ties them with a *mauli* thread to the house door—a fee of annas two or four being paid her for this also. In Ferozepur the child is not suckled till the evening after its birth, and then the mother's breasts are washed by a young girl, who gets a rupee if the child is a boy, but only annas two or four if it is a girl. Jaggery is applied to the child's lips before it is given the breast. If the milk does not flow freely the child is given sheep's milk.

Fosterage.—Fosterage is not very common in the Punjab, and sometimes it is a mere concession to superstition, as when a Brahman declares that it is inauspicious for a mother to see her child it is put out to nurse, if the parent can afford it.

Head Compression.—For some notes on this practice in the Punjab reference may be made to *Man*, 1902, No. 2.

Chola.—The ceremony of clothing a child for the first time is usually called *chola*, and is held on various dates. In Ráwalpindi a Brahman fixes a day; in Amritsar also this is the usual custom, but often Aroras and Khatrís hold it on the thirteenth day.

In Ferozepur the *chola* ceremony is elaborate, and is thus described:—A part of the house is plastered and a figure of a cow made by the midwife — both with cow-dug. This image is covered with red cloth and designated the Bidh-máta, or 'goddess of fortune' Next the barber brings cow's urine in a cup, in which he also puts some blades of *dubh* grass. Then the mother puts on the barber's shoes, and, holding his skirt in her hand, she reverses the Bidh-máta, her children sitting on

[1]This rite is called *jaru senchna.*

her lap. Two copper coins, the barber's perquisite, are also placed beneath her feet. The barber now applies the cow's urine to the child's lips, with the *dubh* grass, and then gives it to the mother, who is thus purified, as is the child. If the latter is a boy the parents place a rupee in the cup, but if it is a girl annas two or four suffice. *Pinjiri* and lumps of parched wheat are distributed to the brotherhood, and the females belonging to it place grain before the image of bidh-máta. This grain is divided between the barber and the midwife. The mother is given strengthening food after this. The ceremony [1] appears to be usually observed on the thirteenth day, but this is not always the case.

In Montgomery the *chola* also takes place on the thirteenth day, but if the boy was born on one of the six unlucky asterisms, the observance is postponed till the twenty-seventh. In Gujránwála, however, the *chola* is held as early as the first day, *i.e.* immediately after birth, or on any day till the thirteenth. Speaking generally, the customs connected with the rite are social rather than religious, but in Hoshiárpur the family god's temple or some Muhammadan saint's shrine is usually visited.

Chhuchak.—In Rohtak the mother's parents send her clothes and ornaments for herself, the child, and her husband. This present is called *chhuchak*, and it is sent in response to the *badhái* (*vide supra*).

Festivals.—The Lohri following a birth is observed with special pomp, copper coins and cowries being given away to the poor.

So, too, the next Díwáli is celebrated by a grander illumination than usual, sweets being also distributed among the brotherhood.

Tonsure.—The first tonsure of a child is an important rite, but it is known by various names and celebrated in various ways by different castes, [2] and in different localities. In the south-west it is known as the *jhanḍ* [3] and elsewhere as the *múnḍan* or *bhaddan*.[4] If the mother has made a vow prior to the birth of her child to observe the rite at a certain shrine or temple, it is duly carried out there; otherwise it may be done at home.[5] An auspicious hour should be fixed by a Brahman, or the rite should be performed on the marriage of a near kinsman, or on the Baisákhi or Dasehra. In Hoshiárpur [6] a boy's ears are bored on this occasion, and some people smear his forehead with goat's blood.

In Ludhiána the rite is, like the birth observances, described as the *múnḍan sanskár*, and it is unlucky to shave a child's head until it has

[1] The accounts of the *chola* rite are very confused, because *chola* literally means a cloak, and the child is dressed in that garment on other occasions, *e.g.* on the fifth, seventh, or ninth day; when the mother is bathed the child is dressed in a yellow *chola*. And a boy, born after several successive female children, is dressed in one made of cloth, which must be given by a friend (Ferozepur). But in Ráwalpindi the cloth is got from a friend or the mother's relatives under any circumstances.

[2] The Hindu Bánias of Mahráj in Ferozepur have a special time for the rite *viz.*, the light halves of Asauj and Chet, and a lock of the hair is then left uncut.

[3] *Jhanḍ*, lit. *lanugo*, or down, is the hair on the head of a new-born child.

[4] *Munḍan* — *Munna*, to shave. *Bhaddan*, s.m — shaving.

[5] Some sections have fixed places for the observance of the rite, *e.g.* the Khanna Khatrís observe it at Dípálpur. In Ráwalpindi, most of the Khatrís observe it at home, but not so the Jaggi and Awal sections, and some families observe it at Katás in the Baisákhi, or at the Jogi shrine at Kot Sarang.

[6] But in this district a distinction appears to be drawn between the cutting off of the *jhanḍ*, which is removed at a tank or under a *janḍ* tree, before the child is three (though only a few families observe this rite), and the regular *bhaddan*, which is performed at a *ṭhákurdwára* or *gurdwára* between three and five years of age, and is often celebrated with considerable pomp.

been performed. The menials receive fees, and the brotherhood is regaled with sweets at the first tonsure, after which *bodí*[1] or tuft of hair is allowed to grow,[2] but it is more usual to let the *bodí* grow after the marriage of a near kinsman

As a rule the rite is performed between the ages of one and a quarter[3] and four years, or, in Ferozepur,[4] as soon as the child has cut its teeth. Sometimes the rite is repeated once or twice. In Gujránwála the observance is called *rít* and is held in the third or fifth year.

In short, the observance is essentially a domestic usage, varying in its details according to the ancestral custom of the caste, section, or even family. Sometimes women vow that a child's hair shall never be cut (Montgomery), and a girl's hair is never cut. Among Sikhs the rite is not very common, and, if practised, is observed when the child is only two or three months old. In a well-to-do family the rite is the occasion for a feast to Brahmans, otherwise Brahmans appear to have no part in it.

The janeo *or sacred thread.*—We are accustomed to talk of the *janeo* or 'sacred thread of caste,' as if it were invariably worn by the three higher or 'twice-born' castes, and not by the fourth or Sudra caste, and as if the 'sacred thread' were the same or only slightly different for all the three higher castes. But an examination of the facts as they stand not only shows the extraordinary variety of form which the *janeo* takes but also proves that it is inaccurate and misleading to call the *janeo* 'the thread of caste.' At the present day it is not always worn by the higher castes, while on the other hand the so-called Sudra castes not infrequently wear it.

As a general rule we may say that the form of the *janeo* varies in every caste or group or sect. It will thus be most convenient to deal with the form of *janeo* as worn by each caste.

The tagádhri.—It was formerly customary among Hindús for children to wear the *tagádhri* before they reached the ages at which the *janeo* could be worn, and in some parts of the Punjab the custom still survives. The *tagádhri* is worn round the waist, and is made of *munj* or, if the parents are wealthy, of silver.

Making the janeo.—Pure cotton is purchased in August, and on the 13th day after the new moon it is spun into thread by a Brahman girl (Jhelum), or by a married woman whose husband is alive (Gujrát), never by a widow. The cotton should be picked from a field free from filth.

A *janeo* may consist of one or two *agras*.

The making of on *agra* is thus described :—There are three lines on the fingers. The Brahmans should wind the single thread over the upper line 96 times, the Khatrís over the central line 86 times, and the Vaisyas over the lowest 76 times. The thread is then made into three folds and twisted on a *kath*, a special tool used in preparing the *janeo*. It is then

[1] *Buddi*, syn. *munna* or *rabbat*.

[2] In Ferozepur the *bodí* is allowed to grow on the Beisákhi or Dasehra, and in Ráwalpindi on the seventh day after the *jhand*.

[3] One account puts the minimum age at five months (Ferozepur).

[4] It is stated that in this district some people shave the child on an auspicious day *without informing the parents*. If this is so, comparison may be made with the idea that unlucky children should not see their parents.

folded in three folds a second time so that there are now 9 threads in the cord. To make an *agra* it is again folded thrice, making 27 threads in each *agra*. The number of *granthis* or knots in a *agra* depends on the number of *parvaras* or famous ancestors in each *gotra*. One *agra* is allowed to a Brahman in the Brahmchári or discipleship stage, the second being added when he reaches the second, the Grihasthashram or house-holder stage. The first thread should be twisted from right to left, the second from left to right, (and so on).

The second *agra* is made in the same way. When two *agras* are worn they are knotted together by three or five knots.

The most usual or orthodox rules appear to be that the material, length and age of initiation for each caste or *varna* should be :—

	Uarna.	*Material.*	*Length.*	*Ages.*	
For a	Brahman...	Cotton	96 *chappas*	8th year up to 16th	after conception.
	Chhatri ...	Hemp	95 „	11th „ „ „ 22nd	
	Vaisya ...	Wool	94 „	12th „ „ „ 24th	

A *chappa* is four fingers' breadth. The first year in each case specified above is called *mukhai kál*, *i. e.* the precise or proper time. After that *janeo* may be put on in the *gaun kál*, *i.e.* up to the last year specified, after which the man is *anadhiman* or disqualified.

There are, however, modifications. Thus if a Brahman wishes to become learned in the Vedas, he should assume the *janeo* in his 5th year, if a Kshatriya desire strength, in his 6th year, and if a Vaisya desire success in cultivation, in his 8th year : Manu *Smriti*, Chap. II, 36 and 37.

The Khatri's *janeo* should, according to one account, be of silk thread, and the Vaisya's of *pashmina*. In Benáres a *janeo* of silk lace is made into which certain *mantras* are interwoven. Sometimes in Sirmúr it is made of fibre from the bark of the *gudála* tree.

The rules as to material are not now observed at all strictly. As we shall see the *janeo* of wool is now characteristic of certain religious castes. But the rules as to length are still very generally observed.

E. g. the Gaddís of Kángra have four social groups :—

1. Brahmans with a *janeo* of ... 96 *chappas*
2. Rájpúts „ ... } 95 „
3. Khatrís „ ... }
4. Rathís „ ... 94 „

The ordinary *janeo* is of three kinds :—

Brahmgandh { (*i*) with 5 knots for the higher grades of Brahmans. (*ii*) with 3 knots for the lower grades of Brahmans.

Vishnugandh, with 1 knot, for all other castes.

Initiation.—The ceremony of initiation should take place at an auspicious time.

When the ceremony is performed the boy's head is shaved, only the *shikha, bodi* or *chota* (the lock of hair on the top of the head) being left. He then bathes

He is then seated on the skin of an animal (deer, sheep or goat according to his caste), and is given a stick or staff of a particular tree. Or according to another account he must don a deer-skin (*mrig charam*), take a *palas dand*, or staff of *dhák* wood, in his hand, and put on *padakas* or *khuraos* (wooden shoes). The rites in ancient times included various burnt offerings made in pits (*hawan-kund*), over which a wooden frame (*bedi*) was placed. The 9 planets were also worshipped.

Then the *gurú* seats the boy on his left side, and after making him promise to obey the orders he will receive, covers both their heads with a long cloth (*sáfa*), and amidst the beating of drums and sounding of conches (to prevent others hearing what he says to the boy), whispers in his right ear a *mantra* which is never revealed[1] to any one but himself.

Then the boy goes to his mother and first begs alms of her, subsequently begging of all the women of the assembled brotherhood. Alms, consisting of rice, money, both small silver and copper, silver rings, etc., are thrown by them into his *jholi* or pilgrim's wallet. These are offered to the *gurú*, who then puts the *janeo* on the boy.

The modes in which the janeo *is worn.*—The *janeo* is ordinarily worn over the left shoulder, across the back and chest, and under the right shoulder.

But in worshipping the gods there are three distinct ways in which the *janeo* should be worn :—

(*i*) *nitya-shabik:* in worshipping the gods the *janeo* is still worn on the left shoulder, but is held across the palm under the thumb of the left hand. The right hand is kept over it forward.

(*ii*) *ap-shabik:* in naming the *pitris* the *janeo* is worn on the *right* shoulder, and the libation of water made with the fingers of the right hand, the palm being kept above them so as to pour the water to the left. This is the worship of *pitris* or ancestral *manes*.

(*iii*) In worship of the *rishis* the *janeo* is placed round the neck and allowed to fall like a necklace. The libation is made with both hands so as to pour it inwards towards the chest.

The janeo *of the Jogís.*- All twelve *panths* or orders of the Jogís wear the *janeo*, which is made by certain special members of the sect and not by ordinary Jogís or by Brahmans. 16 strands, each 9 cubits long, are taken. These strands are divided into 8 parts, each of 2 strands, and each part is then wrapped round a stick and twisted to the right. All 8 parts are then twisted into one rope, which is again divided into 8 strands. These are finally knotted together by a Brahm knot, and to them is attached a *pawittri* (a ring of gold or rhinoceros horn), and to this again a *nad*, also of the latter material. This *janeo* should be of black wool, and is worn like a necklace).

The Kalli-sutar.—Besides the *janeo*, Achárj Brahmans, Vaishnav and Bairági *sádhús* wear a *kalli-sutar*, or thread round the loins, made of wool or *munj*.

[1] This Mantra is called *Gáyatri* and runs :—

Tat Savitur varenyam bhargo devasya Dhimahi dhi yo yo nah prachodayat, "Let us worship the supreme light of the Sun, the God of all things, who can so well guide our understanding, like an eye suspended in the vault of Heaven."

SECTION 3.—MUHAMMADAN PREGNANCY OBSERVANCES

Charms against miscarriage.

Among some tribes a woman who has previously miscarried wears a charm, such as a thread or amulet, on her navel; others wear a cowry on that part to avert the child's being born dead. The charms are blown upon before being put on, the fee paid depending on one's means.

Satwáhin.

In Ambála the observance in the seventh month, or *satwáhin*, is said to be confined to the towns. It simply consists in the parents sending sugar, rice etc. to their daughter on her first pregnancy; a woman related to the family also drops fruit into her lap.

In Sirmúr the woman's parents try to arrange for her to be sent to their house, but if this cannot be done they send her presents of rice, sweets, fruit etc., with clothes for hereself and the child. This is called *kioka.*[1]

In Kángra on the commencement of the seventh month the woman's parents bring her presents consisting of red clothes, dry fruit, henna, scented oil, and *missí*, with other perfumes and an ornament, preferably one for the arm. These gifts are brought in a procession, musicians and singers accompanying it. On arriving at the husband's house, they make their daughter sit on a stool, while the *nain* dresses her in the red suit and dyes her hands with the henna. She is also garlanded with flowers, and her lap filled with dry fruits, such as cocoa-nuts or dates. These are all eaten, apparently by her husbands' parents, she herself not being permitted to partake of them. Then the husband's parents make *karáhi* (of flour, *gur* and *ghi*), and this is eaten by people of the *gotar*, but by no others. Persons not belonging to the *gotar* are feasted separately. Prior to this observance a pregnant wife may not wear new clothes or ornaments. After it she must not go to her father's house until forty days have elapsed from her confinement.

In Kapúrthala the parents first send their daughter clothes etc. in the sixth or seventh month, and then she is taken to their house, the sweets sent by them being divided among her husband's kin. Similarly in Ludhiána it is thought that the first confinement ought to take place in the woman's own house. In Máler Koṭla the Muhammadans, especially the dominant Paṭhán families, observe two distinct customs on a first pregnancy. As a rule the first, the *satwáhau*, takes place at the husband's house. The woman's mother is formally notified of the fact that her daughter is in the seventh month of her pregnancy, and she comes to the house, bringing a suit of clothes, sweets and dried fruit. Towards the end of the seventh month the woman bathes and puts on new clothes brought by her mother, perfuming herself with scents. Fruit is then put in her lap, and she then sits on a floor which has been plastered while a *mirásan* sings the appointed eulogies, called *sohla*, of Shaikh Sadr Jahán, to a drum accompaniment.

[1] *Kioka*, not traceable in the dictionaries.

Throughout this performance the woman sits with her head bent down, and her hair unloosed, but combed and oiled. Occasionally she falls into an ecstasy under the influence of the Shaikh, who often makes her his mouth-piece. Sweets are then sent round to relations and neighbours, and the *mirásan* dismissed with her fee. In the evening the *darweshes* are fed at the mother's expense, and next day she takes her daughter home, if the husband's parents agree to this.

In Lahore the *rít* is observed in the beginning of the seventh month, as follows:—The kinswomen assemble and eat out of one tray, the matrons of the family giving the woman fresh fruits as an auspicious omen. The mothers of the couple are also congratulated. Then the kinswomen are feasted, and a Dúmni sings songs. After this the woman is dressed in coloured garments, and puts on ornaments of flowers. At night her hands are stained with henna and the girls of the family sing. This observance is only held by the lower classes of Muhammadans, such as the Kakezais (distillers), Qasábs (butchers), Aráíns (market gardeners), Dhobís (washermen) and *máshkís* or watermen. Among all classes the woman's mother brings her to her own house at the commencement of the ninth month, and on the day of her arrival sends for the almonds, dates, saffron etc. required on or after her delivery. *Patáshás* are distributed among the family, and also among the women of the quarter, a rite called *sauda* by the women.

It is a very general rule among all Muhammadan castes in the north of the Punjab that the woman should avoid eating fruit, wearing fine clothes, or any kind of adornment until the *rít* is performed on the commencement of the seventh month. This *rít* consists merely in feasting the brotherhood, but it is also not uncommon for the woman's parents to send her a present of a *trewar*, and to boil rice which is eaten at a feast in the name of their ancestors. The *trewar* is then given to the husband's sister or the daughter of his nearest kinsman. After the *rít* the woman may use scent. Wheat, too, is parched, mixed with jaggery, and made into balls, which are distributed among the brotherhood

In Ráwalpindi a pregnant woman avoids the use of antimony, or *dandása.*[1] She also avoids the shade of the *dharek* [2] and the shadow of a woman suffering from *athrá*,[3] *i.e.* one whose children die in infancy.

In Fatehjang *rít* is observed in the seventh month, *halwá* being distributed among the brotherhood. This is done either in her parents'

[1] *Dandásá* or walnut bark is used as a toothstick (the literal meaning of the word), or for chewing, in order to redden the lips.

[2] *Dhárek*, the Melia Azedarach.

[3] *Athrá* (? lit. a bead—the word does not appear in the *Panjabi Dictionary*). An *athráwálí* is a woman whose children are born prematurely and generally die. A bead, which changes its colour, is believed to counteract the effects of *athrá*. This bead is rare and is sold by gipsies at fancy prices. It is also tied to the leg of a new-born child as a talisman against *athra*: and *athri ka manka* means one of a changeable, volatile disposition (*manka* = bead in Panjábi).

house, or in her husband's, but in the former case the consent of the husband's parents is necessary.

The satwánsa.

Muhammadans in Hánsi observe the *satwánsa* in the seventh month of pregnancy. Seven or nine jars of water are brought from as many different wells, and the woman bathes in the water thus brought. Some Muhammadans take the woman to the nearest mosque with the jars on her head, and make her draw water from the well attached to the mosque. Her nearest kinswomen accompany her and the observance is often held at night. Others simply give the woman a hot bath.[1]

Friday, at the time of the Asar prayers, is an auspicious day for this ceremony, in connection with which alms are given in the names of ancestors and the Prophet.

Some castes send the woman a suit of green clothes, red bangles, a *naherna,* some *mehndi,* and a silver vessel. The clothes and bangles are worn by the woman, but the henna is used not only by her, but by her friends as well, if they are desirous of offspring, while the *naherna* and silver vessel are kept for the *chhaṭí*. After this one and a quarter *páos* of sugar are sent to each relative and friend. Some families boil rice with sugar, and with it feast the woman and seven others who are also married, some being also given to *faqírs*. After this the woman is given vegetables and sweets.

In Sirsa the rite is called *satwánsi* and simply consists in the parents sending their daughter a gift of clothes, henna and dried fruit in the seventh month of her pregnancy. In Rohtak the *satwánsí* is held at the beginning of the seventh month. The woman is dressed in red, and sugar also put in her lap. The Ḍúm woman, who sings on the occasion, gets a rupee or two.

In Rohtak among the more orthodox Muhammadans there are no regular rites during pregnancy, but the barber is sent to announce it to the mother's parents, and he takes them a rupee as *til cháwalí*.[2] In the seventh month one or two men, and several of the women, bring parched unhusked rice, *patáshás* and fruit, with some red cloth, to the woman, with cloth for her husband's parents and near kinsmen. The woman puts on the red cloth, and the rice etc. is thrown into her lap. The menials also get certain dues. This ceremony, however, is not universal.

The determination of sex.

If the milk in the woman's breasts before birth be thin the birth of a boy is anticipated, otherwise a girl is expected. Or sometimes some of the milk is put in a shell and fire applied to it; if it dries up completely, a girl is expected, otherwise a boy. Hissár.

[1] The Hammáls of Hánsi have a curious custom, which looks like a relic of the *couvade*. The woman's parents send her a present of Rs. 5, a suit of clothes, some scent and a comb. After bathing she puts on her husband's trousers, and a chaplet of flowers. Dúm women also sing songs on this occasion. Boiled rice is distributed among the brotherhood.

[2] *Til cháwalí* is simply rice and *til* mixed: it is used as a food.

In the city of Delhi, where Muhammadans of good birth are numerous, many elaborate customs connected with pregnancy survive. The craving for tart, savoury food has given rise to the polite phrase: *in ká khaṭṭe-miṭhe ko jí châhtá hai,* lit. 'her heart yearns for bitter-sweet things,' *i.e.* 'she is pregnant.' Other phrases are *páoṇ bhári honá* (to be heavy-footed), *do-jíya hona* (to have a second life), *din charhná* (to dawn), *umed hona* (to have hopes) etc.: and women friends say *mubárak salámat*! *i.e.* 'may you be blessed and the child be safe!' to the expectant mother.

The satwánsa in Delhi.

When the seventh month begins the woman's parents bring her *sadhár,*[1] a Hindu custom. This *sadhar* consists of kinds of vegetables, dried fruits, cakes etc., and at 4 P.M. the woman's lap is filled with these things; then she bathes and is dressed in coloured garments, with a red sheet over her head, and flower ornaments are put on her—to make her, as it were, *again a bride.* Her husband's sisters then fill her lap with the seven kinds of fruit etc. and receive presents of money in return. They get the vegetables, dried fruit, the head sheet, and the rupees of the *neg,*[2] all the rest being divided amongst the other members of the family. A cocoanut is then broken in half; and if the kernel be white the woman will have *ujlá phúl* or white fruit, *i.e.* a boy. This cocoanut is called *jhanḍúla,* or 'hairy,' just as a new-born child is so called.[3]

The naumása in Delhi.

At the beginning of the ninth month, the woman's parents send her various presents, including a red veil, seven kinds of fruit, *neg* for the husband's sisters, and rupees to buy the *panjírí,*[4] which must be made at the woman's house. Her lap is filled, as in the *satwánsa,* by the husband's near kinswomen. The midwife at this stage rubs the woman with oil, and receives a fee, to which all the women contribute. The fruit is the perquisite of the husband's sisters, together with the *neg* and the red veil, as before. The midwife gets the nail-parer, one of the presents given by the woman's parents, and the silver oil-cup used for the oil. The woman now goes to her parents' house—an observance called *páoṇ pherná,* or turning the feet, with some *panjírí,* and returns some six or seven days later, bringing with her fresh fruit and sweets. After the *naumása* is finished, the midwife goes to buy the *kioka*[5] or various drugs required for the confinement.

In Dera Gházi Khán some Muhammadans have the Hindu superstitions regarding the effects of an eclipse on the fœtus, if *either* parent undergo violent exertion.

[1] *Sadhar* is said to mean seven things in Hindi. In some families it is brought in the fifth month.

[2] *Neg* is any customary present at weddings etc. made to relatives or to servants, v. Shakespear's Hindustani Dictionary, s. v.

[3] In songs a new-born child is often so termed: *cf. solar.*

[4] *Panjírí* consists of five (whence the term) ingredients, *viz.*, dry dates, gum, water-lily seed, cocoanut and ginger—all mixed with *súji* or meal and fried in *ghí.*

[5] *Cf. supra,* p. 729: the word seems to have a different meaning in Sirmúr.

SECTION 4.—MUHAMMADAN BIRTH OBSERVANCES.

When the birth-pains commence, *Bíbí Mariam ka panja*,[1] a leaf whose shape resembles that of a hand, is put in a jar of water. As delivery approaches, the leaf opens out, and as it does so the birth takes place. This observance also, it is believed, facilitates the delivery.

Sayyids and *faqírs* also indite charms, which are tied round the patient's waist, or sometimes a Muhammad-Sháhí rupee, on which is inscribed the *kalima*, is put into water, which is then given her to drink. In Kángṛa the *báng*, or call to prayer, is pronounced in the room set apart for the confinement by one of the men of the family, the call being a prayer used in any time of trouble.

Birth ceremonies.—As among Hindús, delivery is usually effected on the ground,[2] the mother being made to lie on a quilt with her head to the north and her feet to the south. She thus faces Mecca, and if she dies in child-birth she expires in the posture in which Muhammadans are buried.

If the child is a girl, the parents give some grain in an old black *hánḍí* (an old used pot) to the midwife. But if the child is a boy they give her a rupee, and the relations also give her money, called the *wel*, according to their means.

Whether it be the hot or cold season, the mother remains in confinement for one week. If in good health she is bathed on the sixth day, provided that it is a Friday or Monday, the latter being the day on which the Prophet was born.

During the actual confinement only those women who are closely related to the patient are allowed to be present, but her mother is sure to be one of them. Some stand in the courtyard in the open, with outstretched arms, and, looking upwards, pray: *Iláhí! is kí mushkil ásán ho!* ('God! grant that her troubles may be lightened!'); others vow *dauna* (sweets put in cups made of folded leaves) to Mushkil-kusha.[3] Meanwhile the midwife tells the mother: *Jheli do, jheli*, i.e. 'bear down.'

A child born feet foremost is called a *pa'el*, and women believe that a few gentle kicks from one so born will relieve pains in the back.

As soon as the child is born the mother is told that she has given birth to a one-eyed girl in order that the heat engendered by this ill news may force out the after-birth quickly, and that the joy of having given birth to a male child may not retard it.

Immediately after the child has been born its umbilical cord is tied up with *kaláwa*, a bit of thread dyed red and yellow, and severed with a knife, the thread being thrown round the child's neck[4] until the rest of the cord falls off. The part actually cut off is buried in a pot inside the

[1] This leaf is said to be imported from Arabia. But one account speaks of it as a kind of grass or piece of wood shaped naturally like a hand, obtained from Arabia.

[2] But in some parts, *e.g.* in Jínd and Karnál, she is allowed to lie on a bed.

[3] Alí, the son-in-law of the Prophet, is so-called on account of his humane qualities.

[4] This is also done in Lahore.

house,[1] a charcoal fire being kept burning on top of it for six days until it is all burnt up. Into this pot the near kinswomen put annas two or four, as a present to the midwife. Some betel-leaf and silver are also placed in it, and when buried, turmeric and charcoal are thrown in to keep off evil spirits. The cord of a *pahlaunṭhí*,[2] or first-born child, is invariably so buried, but if a woman's children do not live she has it buried outside the house. The midwife now gets her *nál kaṭái* or fee, for cutting the cord, in money ; but among the wealthy the mother's parents and her husband add gold or silver bracelets, according to their position.

In Amritsar and Gujrát the parents' or mothers' formal permission to the severance of the cord must be obtained by the midwife. But in Ráwalpindi the eldest and most respected woman of the family takes up the child as soon as it is born in order to communicate her own virtues to it. She also buries the secundines on the spot where the birth has taken place, and cuts the cord, which is preserved with great care. The Ghebas do not use a knife to cut the cord, but a *narra* or *nalla* or 'spindle,' obtained by the midwife from a weaver's house. With this the midwife cuts the cord, after pressing it with her feet, and then buries it in the ground.[3]

After birth a child is bathed, its head being pressed to give it a round shape,[4] and tied up in a *qasába* or handkerchief folded in a triangle. The nose also is pressed to prevent its hardening on exposure into a bad shape.

The *mulla* is next sent for without delay. He repeats the *subah kí asán* [5] in the child's right ear, and the *takbír* in its left. *Batáshás* chewed, or something sweet, are also applied to its palate.

[1] People are believed to be deeply attached to the spot where their navel-string is buried, so that to say to a man : *Yahán tera nál to nahín gaṛa, jo tu jáne ka nám bí nahín leta?* 'Is your cord buried here that you do not even talk of going?' is equivalent to saying that nothing will induce him to budge.

[2] The first-born child is supposed to be peculiarly susceptible to the influence of genii, evil spirits, lightning and the evil-eye.

[3] The Khattars of Ráwalpindi have the uncut part of the cord, after it has dried up and fallen off, encased in silver and hung round the child's neck as a charm against stomachache.

Throughout the south-east Punjab the umbilical cord is carefully buried, often with the after-birth, in an earthern vessel (*ṭhíkri*) in a corner of the house. In Hissár, neither parent should touch the cord. In Kángra, the midwife cuts the cord on the coin which she gets as her fee. Besides this she receives presents from the kinswomen etc. and these are called *nár kaṭái*. Among the Kashmírís only the secundines are buried, the piece of the cord cut off being kept to cure the child if it gets sore eyes In Amritsar the uncut piece is preserved with the *jhanḍ*. In Dera Ghási Khán the cord is carefully preserved and buried on the right of the house-door. In Multán it is buried where the birth took place.

[4] This is also done in Hissár, but neither there nor in Delhi is any vessel used to force the head into a round shape.

[5] 'The morning call to prayer.' But usually the *asán* pure and simple is specified (for this see Hughes' *Dictionary of Islám*, s.v. *Asán*). The usual synonym for *asán* is the P. *báng*, lit. : a call, or cock-crow. In the south-east of the Punjab it is whispered, in Baháwalpur repeated in a loud voice, and elsewhere recited or repeated apparently in the ordinary voice.

The *mulla* receives a gift.[1] After bathing, the child is made to lick honey, and then the *ghuṭṭi* is administered.

After the *ghuṭṭi* has been given, *i.e.* on the third day, the child's father's sister[2] washes the mother's breasts with milk or with water squeezed out of kneaded flour,[3] and then her hair, in which some green blades of grass are woven. The following song is sung by her or on her behalf :—

Bírán, bháiya, main teri má kí jáí,
Holar sunkar, badháwa lekar áí,
Bírán, bháiya, main teri má kí jáí :
Chháti dhulái kaṭori lúngi, to lat dhulái rupaiyá,
Páun dhulan ko cherí lungi ; to khasm chaṛhan ko ghorá.

"Brother ! I am thy mother's own daughter, and hearing that a son has been born into the family, I have come to felicitate thee. For having washed the breasts, I expect a silver cup as a present, and money for washing her tresses. I will accept from thee a hand-maiden to wash my feet, and for my husband a horse to ride."

For this observance the father's sister receives a *neg*, varied according to her brother's position, but not less than Re. 1 as. 4.

From the time the child is born a knife, sword, or piece of iron is kept under the mother's head, to ward off evil spirits.

On the next or a subsequent day the husband's sisters make and distribute the *achhwáni*[4] amongst the kinsfolk and receive a present in return ; but amongst the poor the mother alone is given *achhwáni*.

For six days the mother is never left alone, partly lest she overlay her child, partly to keep off evil spirits. Amongst the well-to-do a lamp is kept burning continuously for forty days (but only for six among

[1] His fee varies, depending mainly on the child's sex. If it is a boy he gets a rupee or more, with some flour and sugar ; if a girl, only an anna—in Hissár. Sometimes he whispers the call to prayer through a *saṛa* or tube ; and, if the child is a girl, he sometimes whispers the *takbír* in both its ears, not the *báng*. If a *mulla* is not available, any man of reputed piety may perform the rite, receiving some sweet stuff only, not a fee. In Karnál a man of good repute is called in to perform on the third day, and he receives no fee, but sweets are distributed. Or the eldest male of the family may perform it in lieu of a *mulla*. In Kángra this duty devolves on the child's uncle, or any pious member of the family. In Máler Koṭla the rite is administered with considerable solemnity. A woman stands with her back towards Mecca, holding the child so that it may face the Qibla. As the *mulla* repeats the *azán* she turns its right ear towards him, and then its left as he recites the *taqbír*. Until the *azán* is thus repeated, the belief is that the child is convulsed with fear. In Jínd some juice of the date is poured into the child's mouth, if it is a boy, in token of welcome.

[2] She is called *dhiyáni*. But in Siálkot the breasts are washed by the *nain*

[3] Called *áṭe ka dudh* or milk of flour, and it is used because amongst Hindús it would be a sin to throw the milk after it had been used for washing, on the ground.

[4] *Achhwáni* (or *chha*—in Sirmúr) = candle, Platts, s v., where it appears to be traced back to *ajwain*. It may, however, be derived from *chhe*, six. It is giv..n to the mother for six days. A cup of it is sent to every house in the brotherhood on the day of the birth (Hissár), but not universally. The *chhawáni* (or-*a*) is also distributed among kinsmen and neighbours in Máler Koṭla, and in return they send money to the midwife, according to their means. It is also given to the mother, but only for three or four days. Its ingredients vary, and for delicate women *'unnáb* or jujube is substituted.

the poor), and a stove is kept alight, in hot weather or cold. Wild rue is also burnt for six days, to keep off the evil-eye and purify the air. Lest the mother sleep on, and her blood so stagnate and gets cold, women take it in turns to sing *jachágirián* or lullabies, of which the following are examples :—

1. *Mere bábal ko likhío sandes, jhanḍúlá aj húá :*
Bábal hamáre rájá ke chákar ; birán ṭále bhes :
Jhanḍúlá áj húá.

"Tell my father that his daughter has borne a son : my father is a servant of the Rájá, *i.e.* he is well-to-do ; and that my brother is yet a child : the young one was born this day."

2. *Áj janam liyá mere ráj duláre ne, pálná banáúngí, rí, pálná banáúngí !*

Ghí khichṛí bhejí, bábal,

Hubrang, sughar jachá ko maiṇ táre

dikháúngí, rí, pálná banáúngí !

"The beloved of my kingdom, my prince was born to-day. I will make a cradle for him to sleep in, dear women ! I will assuredly make a cradle for him ! My father, having heard this news, has sent *ghí* and *khichṛí* for me. Hubrang (the poet who wrote this song), says 'I will show the stars to this accomplished mother, *i.e.* I will perform the ceremony of the *chhaṭí*.'"

3. *Jachá, merí káhe ko rúṭhí, maiṇ terá itr, khilauná rí !*

Kaho to jachá rání, dáí ko bulá dúṇ—kaho kone palang bichhá dúṇ—kaho thaí thaí náchúṇ.

Chorus—Jachá merí &c., &c.

Soṇṭh maiṇ bhúl áyá, ab la dúngá, rí !—háth meṇ kúndí, bagal meṇ soṭá láyá, rí ! soṇṭh bhúl áyá, rí !

Chorus—Jachá merí &c., &c.

Tere holar ká naukar, ae begam, maiṇ terá naukar, terá chákar, rí, soṇṭh maiṇ bhúl áyá rí !

Chorus—Jachá, merí káhe ko rúṭhí, maiṇ terá itr, khiláuná, rí !

This is a comic *sachágirí*—as if it were made by, and sung for, the husband. The husband addresses the wife and says: "Beloved *sachá*, why are you sulky with me ? I am in truth your scented toy : if you require a midwife, I will send for her ; if you desire a bed, I will make one for you in the corner—should even this not please you I will dance (*thái thái*)[1] to amuse you. I confess that I forgot to bring dry ginger for the *sachá-khánâ*, but I can go for it immediately and bring it quickly—my hand was employed bringing the *kúnḍí* (stone mortar), and under my armpit I had the *soṇṭá* (a heavy wooden

[1] To beat time, as in music, and dance, clapping the hands.

club, used as a pestle), which were for your use—so you see, my dear, I could not help it: O my queen! I am your child's servant—your servant—your own servant. Why are you displeased? No doubt, I forgot to bring the *sonth* (dry ginger)."

4. *Albele ne mujhe darad díyá—sánwalyá ne mujhe darad díyá:*

Sánwalyá ne mujhe darad díyá, pátalya ne mujhe darad díyá:

Jáe kaho larke ke báwa se, únche naubat dharáo re!

Chorus—Albele ne &c.

Jáe kaho larke ke nána se, rang bharí khichrí láo re!

Chorus—Albele ne &c.

Jáe kaho larke ke mámú se, hansli, kare gharháo, re!

Chorus—Albele ne &c.

Jáe kaho, larke ki khálá se, kurte, topí láo, re!

Chorus—Albele ne &c.

Jáe kaho larke kí báwá se, bhand, bhagatie nacháo, re!

Chorus—Albele ne &c.

"The fine, beautiful, nut-brown, slender child, to show his beauty in the world, has given me the pains of childbirth: go, and tell its father that he should proclaim its advent by a *naubat* (music on the upper storey or roof); have *nafírí* played, so that I may be rewarded for my pains by its soothing melody: and tell the mother's father of the child to arrange to bring the *khichrí* with all due magnificence, for the *chhattí* (sixth day) is given by him: go, and tell the mother's brother of the child also to make ready the *hanslí* (necklet) and *kará* (wristlets), *i.e.* give orders to the goldsmith to prepare them: go also, and tell the mother's sister to have ready the *kurte* (shirts) and caps, for these are supplied by her: warn the farther also that on this joyous occasion he must give us a dance by the *bhánd* and *bhagatie*."

This last song, though it is in reality the pæan of joy sung by Deokíjí on the birth of her son Krishna, is still sung among the Muhammadans.

The clothes worn by the mother at her confinement are given on the day of birth to the midwife, and are replaced by new ones on her *chhattí* or *chila*.

It was formerly the custom that the lobe of that side of the ear by which the child was born was pierced, the object being that the child might live—women having a belief that the piercing of a vein in the ear is a preventative of mortal disease (presumably convulsions); further with the same object, the end of the nose was also pierced on the same day and a nose-ring inserted: but this custom is now rare among the lower castes.

From the day of birth, the *nakti* ('nose-cut,' or noseless one, *i.e.*

the cat) is not allowed in the mother's room, in the belief that she is possessed of genii, or more probably in order to protect the buried umbilical cord from any possibility of injury, and she is kept out till the *chhaṭṭí or chilla.*

It is also worthy of remark that a *hijrá* (eunuch) goes daily to each *mahallah* (street) and cries *Huá ṭeṭá? Kaun sá ghar jágá?* (*i.e.*, 'Has a son been born?' 'Which house has awakened?') Some child, or the sweepress of that quarter, informs him of the family in which a son or a daughter was born; going to that house he gets two pice for a daughter and four for a son, and informs all the *bhaṇḍs, bhaṇḍelas* etc. (players, actors, buffoons, etc.); from that time the *bhaṇḍele zanane, hijre, sháh ṭaiyam-taiyá, chúne-wáliyáṇ*, and *bháṇḍ, bhagatye* of the town, all those whose business it is to sing, dance, play, or amuse, begin to come, and after singing or acting for an hour or two demand their presents and go away, only to come back again on the *chhaṭṭí*.

Ṭhíkri.—All the females in the house at the time of the birth drop some coins, from one pice to two annas, into a *ṭhíkrí*, the lower part of an earthen jar, the first to do so being the patient's mother or mother-in-law. If any near kinswoman is negotiating a betrothal, she drops a rupee into the jar, and this renders the agreement irrevocable. This is called the *ṭhíkrí kí sagái.* The money dropped into the jar is the midwife's perquisite.

The aqíqa *or tonsure.*—The *aqíqa* is an orthodox Muhammadan rite, consisting in shaving the child's head for the first time, on the seventh, fourteenth, twenty-first, twenty-eighth, or thirty-fifth day after birth, and sacrificing two goats or sheep for a boy and one for a girl.[1] This simple rite has, however, been confused with, or influenced by the observances proper to, the *jhanḍ;* in places, it has never been adopted, or if adopted has become obsolete.[2] As a rule the *aqíqa* is celebrated within seven days of the birth.[3]

The child's head is shaved, and the weight of the hair in gold or silver given away as alms.[4]

[1] The meaning of the word *aqíqa* is disputed. It may mean (1) the hair on a new-born child's head, like *jhanḍ;* or (2) be a derivative of the root *aq* (to cut or sacrifice). Even amongst orthodox Muhammadans the observances vary, *cf.* the *Mishcát-ul-Masábih*, Mathews, II, pp. 315, 16.

[2] In Bhiwáni it is only observed by well-to-do people, never by the peasantry, *as nomine*, but on the *chaṭṭí* the child's head is shaved. Occasionally a vow is made that the child's head shall not be shaved unless and until it can be done at a specified place. Or part of the hair is left uncut, to be subsequently shaved off in fulfilment of the vow. In Siálkot the *aqíqa* is displacing the old *dhamán* rite.

[3] It is very commonly held on the *chaṭṭí*, or on the seventh, fourteenth, twenty-first, or twenty-eighth, in Hissár; on the seventh or tenth in Bhiwáni; on the seventh, fourteenth, or fortieth in Sirmúr; at any time within six months in Kángra, very commonly on the fifth, or in Núrpur, on the eighth; in Máler Koṭla on the sixth; on the seventh, eleventh, or twenty-first in Lahore; it is also very common in the central Punjab to perform it on the sixth, thirteenth etc. day, *e.g.* if the birth occurred on a Monday, it would be held on the following Sunday, and so on.

[4] In Delhi, and some other parts, this is the barber's perquisite.

The hair itself is carefully buried in the earth.[1] For a boy two he-goats are sacrificed and for a girl one.[2] The bones must not be broken, but carefully buried in the ground.[3] The flesh is distributed[4] among the brotherhood uncooked; or else they are feasted on it.

But the child's parents, and its parents' parents[5] must not eat of the flesh. Such are the main outlines of the rite.

Beri barhana.—A blue cotton thread, called *beri*, is tied to the left foot of a child[6] in the name of Muin-ud-Dín Chishti of Ajmer, and when it is three or four years old it is taken to the shrine of that saint, and the parents there make an offering of five and a quarter *sers* of *maledá*,[7] two pice and a trouser-string.

Bindú bandhna. —If a man's children die in infancy, he puts a bit of *bindú* or silver wire in the left ear of his next child.

Petá charhāná.—Women desirous of offspring often vow to offer *petá*[8] to the shrine of Dána Sher at Hissár, if their wish is granted. A little of the *petá* is given to the custodian of the shrine, and the rest is distributed among the brotherhood.

The chhaṭṭí *or sixth day.*—The religious observance of the *aqíqa* is closely associated with the *chhaṭṭí*, the *chúchak*, and the naming of the child, three observances which will now be described.

As among the Hindús, the *chhaṭṭí*, in spite of its name, is not necessarily held on the sixth day of the birth Thus in Delhi the mother and child are bathed on the Monday or Wednesday nearest the sixth day, the former being an auspicious day because the Prophet was born on that day, the latter because: *Budh is liye ki sab kám sudh hon, i.e.* 'Wednesday, in order that all things may be right,' and thus all subsequent children may be sons.

[1] But in Delhi it is made over to the washerwoman, to be thrown into the river: in Hissár it is carefully preserved; in Máler Koṭla it is kept wrapped up in bread; in Ráwalpindi the hair is caught by the sister, or father's sister of the child, lest it fall on the ground, and kept in the house with great care.

[2] In Kángra the goats must be young and free from blemish, and of a uniform colour for a girl; the latter is the only essential condition.

[3] Or as carefully preserved; while the head and feet are given to the barber, and the skin to the waterman or the *malláh* (Hánsi). In Kángra, the bones are buried within the house. In Amritsar, a portion of the flesh is given to the midwife, and the rest distributed among the brotherhood; both bones and blood are buried. In Sháhpur the flesh is given to the poor, and the bones are buried in the graveyard, after being placed in an earthen jar. In Dera Ghází Khán, both bones and blood are carefully preserved (? buried) *at separate places.*

[4] If the flesh is thus distributed it would appear that the bones need not be kept intact (Ludhiána).

[5] Only the grandparents, the great-grandparents apparently not being debarred.

[6] In Rohtak the thread is described as black, and as being tied on both feet. The child's hair is also allowed to grow until the period of the vow has expired, when it is cut at the shrine.

[7] *Maleda*, thick hand-made bread broken or pounded, and then mixed with sugar and *ghí*.

[8] *Petá* = intestine.

The mother sits on a stool while her husband's sisters pour milk, or water squeezed out of flour, over her head; green grass or a thin slice of betel-leaf are put into the water or milk. In return the sister-in-law receives presents (*neg*). Then the mother bathes, and taking the child in her arms, puts on her nose-ring and sits on the bed. The guests, mostly women—though among the higher classes near male relatives are also invited—come in. Outside the men are entertained by eunuchs, *bhánds, Shah-tiayam-taiya*, and dancing-girls; while inside the house Ḍomnís and *chúnewálian* give displays of dancing. The mother, with her head wrapped in gold lace, sits enthroned like a queen, the child's head being also enfolded in a kerchief. *Mubárak búdián* or congratulatory songs are sung, such as:—

Jami jam shádián, mubárak bádián;

Báwen farzand salámat, salámat-badián.

"May you be ever blessed with such happiness; nay, may you, with your son, ever enjoy peace."

Or—

Naurang chúre-wálián, meri jachá ránián:

Suhá jorá pahin suhágan motí bharí ránián:

Naurang chúre-wálián.

"Our Zacha queen, with bracelets of many colours and robe of red, a wife whose lord is alive, and the parting of whose hair is decked with pearls, yea, she is our bride."

In Hissár the *chhaṭṭí* is observed on the sixth day, the mother and child being bathed, the brotherhood feasted and the mother dressed in new clothes. Her father also sends the *cheochak*, or gift of clothes, and the *aqíqa* is observed on this day. If a man does not observe the *chhaṭṭí* it is said:—*Chaṭṭí na chhillá hogayá.*

Like the Hindús, Muhammadans imagine that on this the sixth night the child is peculiarly subject to demoniacal influences.[1]

In Lahore the mother and child are bathed on the first Thursday or Sunday: this is called *chhaṭṭí ká ghusal*, and food called *sudak ká khána*[2] is sent to all the women of the family.

The chhúchhak.—The *chhúchhak* is very commonly observed on the *chhaṭṭí*, but it may be postponed to the fortieth day, and indeed there appears to be no absolutely fixed day for its observance. In the central Punjab the first confinement ordinarily takes place at the house of the mother's parents, and in this case the mother, if the child is a boy, brings back with her some gold and silver ornaments for herself and the boy on her return to her husband's house. These gifts are called *chhúchhak*. In the south-east the first confinement is arranged for at

[1] Among the *zamíndárs* of Baháwalpur and Ahmadpur a ceremony called the *doyán* is observed on the sixth or eleventh day after birth; *chilire* or small loaves, also termed *wadián*, are cooked, dipped in syrup, and distributed among the brotherhood.

[2] *Sudan.*

her husband's house, but the mother visits her father's house some four or six months later and then brings back the *chhúchhak*.[1]

Generally speaking, the *chhúchhak* appears to be used for any present sent to the mother or child on the *chhatti*, *aqiqa* etc. by her parents or other relatives, or even by relatives of the child's father. In Rohtak, indeed, the term appears to be limited to the presents made by the father's sister of the child.

In Hissár mention is made of a gift called *jamawana*, made by the mother's parents to her. It consists of gum, *ghí* and sugar, with clothes and ornaments for the child, and would appear to be distinct from the *chhúchhak*.

Weham.—Closely analagous to the *chhúchhak* is the *weham* observance, which is widely spread throughout the submontane and south-western districts.

In Lahore the *weham* is, among well-to-do people, a link in a chain of elaborate observances. On the *chhila*, or fortieth day, the women of the family assemble and make presents to the mother and child, who are then taken to a shrine. *Chúri* is then distributed among the women, and the kinswomen of the mother's mother are also given food from her house. Her mother then sends her clothes and ornaments, for herself and the child. These gifts are called *weham*. The observance is only observed on the birth of a first-born child. Poor people also observe it, but on a smaller scale.[2] After it, the midwife is dismissed.

On the day after the mother goes to her parents' house and returns with her child and the *weham* presents, the women of the *mahalla* come to view them, and the child's grandmother distributes sweetmeats and *panjíri* to the brotherhood In return the women each give the child a rupee, or less.

In Amritsar the term *weham* is applied to the presents made by the mother to each of the kinswomen assembled on the fortieth day.

In Baháwalpur the parents give her on the eighth, twenty-first, or fortieth day, when she bathes, *pinnis*,[3] and a *trewar* for herself and her child: together with other clothes for it, according to its sex. If wealthy they also give a silver bracelet, or *hasli*, a silver necklet or a gold *mohar* for the child.[4]

[1] Platts, *sub voce*, says *chhúchhak* is the ceremony observed after childbirth (when the mother visits her father—generally forty days after childbirth—and returns with presents: so the presents made on this occasion. The derivation of the word is obscure. In Hissár it takes the form *chhochhák*.

[2] In Kapúrthala the observances are simple. On the third day the father sends a *man* of *khichri* to his wife's father, and he, on the eighth day, sends in return *pinjiri*, clothes and ornaments for the mother.

[3] *Pinnis* are rolls made of *ghí*, flour and *gur*, and weighing about half a *páo* each.

[4] In Siálkot the parents send their daughter *ghí* and sugar on the same day, with or without *pinnis*, to recruit her strength. They also send clothes for the midwife, as well as to the mother and child, and an ornament for the latter. Well-to-do people also permit the ornament to be given by the father's sister.

The treatment of the mother.

In theory the mother is bathed on the tenth, twentieth, thirtieth and fortieth days, as in Rohtak, Hissár, Karnál, Ambála[1] and Sirmúr; but to this rule there are numerous exceptions.[2]

The bath on the fortieth day is called *chhilla* (lit., fortieth), and that on the tenth *daswáṇ*, on the twentieth *biswáṇ*, and on the thirtieth *tiswáṇ*. But in the Karnál District these three earlier baths are called *chhoṭá chhillá*; and in Delhi, the *daswáṇ chhillá* (tenth), *biswáṇ chhilla* (twentieth), *choṭa chhilla* (thirtieth), and *baṛa chilla* (fortieth)—a curious instance of the confused use of precise terms in Indian observances.

Showing the stars to the mother.—On the night of the *chhaṭṭí*, mother and child are both dressed, their heads being enfolded in three-cornered embroidered bands (*qasába*), and the mother is seated on a low stool placed in the courtyard of the house. Two women, holding naked swords in their hands, bring her out; the midwife carrying a *chaumak*[3] to light the way. Standing on the stool with the child in her arms and the Qurán on her head, the mother looks towards the sky and counts seven stars, while her companions bring the points of the swords together over her head, forming a crescent so that *jinns* and *parís* may not pass over her, and from this day the danger that they may overshadow her ceases.

Meanwhile the father goes to the mother's bed, and standing thereon repeats the *bismillah* in full. He then shoots an arrow into the ceiling, at the *mirg*. Hence this observance is called the *mirg márna*, and the wife's mother gives her son-in-law a *neg* on the occasion.

Once, on the birth of a prince in the family of Bahádur Sháh, King of Delhi, the poet Sháh Nazir of Delhi, described this custom thus:—

Wuhíṇ phir sháh ne yih rasm kí wa'ṇ:
Chhaparkhaṭ par qadam rakh, ho ke shádáṇ,
Adá kar harf i 'Bismillah' sárá,
Kamán-o-tír lekar mirg márá;
Namúṇdár is tar'h tha saqf meṇ ṭír,
Falak par kahkasháṇ kí jaise tahrír.

[1] As well as on the sixth *chhaṭṭí*.

[2] *E.g.* in Sirsa she is said to be bathed (? only) on the sixth and fortieth days. Or on the fifth, seventh, or tenth (Karnál), every eighth day (Kapúrthala). In one account from Hissár it is said that the *chhilla* is only given on the fortieth day if it falls on a Friday. In Lahore the seventh, eleventh, twenty-first and thirty-first are said to be the days for the baths; or according to another account, on the first Friday (*chhaṭṭí ka ghusal*) and on the tenth (on both these days the midwife gets dues), on the twenty-first (when *panjírí* is distributed and a feast held in memory of the ancestors), and on the thirtieth and fortieth days. In Siálkoṭ the mother is bathed on the fifth, if the child be a girl, and on the eighth if it is a boy.

[3] Fr: *chaumakh*, *i.e.* 'with four mouths.' It is made of dough, in the shape of a four-cornered cup, to hold four wicks and is fed with *ghí*.

"Forthwith (while his consort was viewing the stars) the king observed the rite, standing on his wife's bed with a bow and arrow in his hand, and after repeating all the *bismillah*, his arrow shot by him into the roof looked like the Milky Way in the firmament."

After seeing the stars the mother returns and seats herself on her bed; a table-cloth is spread in front, the stool being used for a table, and on this is placed food, including seven kinds of vegetables and various dishes. The *sachá ráni* or 'queen mother', together with seven other women, whose husbands are living, takes a little from each dish, and the only words heard are *mubárak*! *salámat*! Songs are also sung:—

Jachá jab dekhne ko áí táre,	*Chhaṭṭí kí dhúm jo pahunchí falak tak,*
Sitáre charkh-i-gardúṇ ne utáre:	*Qamar aur mushtarí donoṇ pukáre,*
Huá farzand yih sab ko mubárak:	*Khudá ne kyá khushí donoṇ ko dí hai:*
Kaho, laṛke ká báwá, mirg máre:	*Damáme baj gae—gúṇje naqáre.*

"When the mother came out to see the stars, the revolving heavens were pleased, and showered stars upon her head (showered stars over her, like the money thrown at weddings etc. upon the chief character in the ceremony). As the child that was born will be a blessing to all, tell his father to perform the *mirg márná*, whereby his courage may be proved. When the sounds of rejoicing at the *chhaṭṭí* reached the skies, the Moon and Jupiter cried: 'What joy hath God bestowed on both (the parents), that the drums have thundered forth their happiness.'"

Some rupees are now thrown into the *chaumak* as a present to the midwife.

In the imperial family another custom, called *Bigír-bachchá*, also prevailed, and the other Mughals of Delhi also observe it with slight variations. A big, sweet loaf was made of 5½ *sers* of flour, baked in the ground, and the middle portion taken out, leaving only the rim; on top of this naked swords were placed, and on the right and left arrows stuck into it; seven *suhágans*, three in front of the loaf and four to the left of it, stood in line; one woman passed the child through the hole, saying, *Bigír-bachhá*, 'take the child'; the next one would say, *Alláh nigahbán, bachcha*, 'God is the protector of the child'; and, passing the child between her legs, would say to the third *Bigír bachchá*. In this way, each of the seven *suhágans* passed the child seven times through the loaf, and between her legs. This is the only Mughal custom foreign to India, all the others being similar to those prevailing in it.

This observance is very widespread, but there are several interesting local variations. Thus, in Ludhiána the Jáṭs, Gujars, Aráíns, Dogars etc. observe this rite on the third day, and the mother goes to the door of the house accompanied by a boy who has a *phálá* (ploughshare) over his shoulder and a *paraiṇ* or ox-goad in his hand. In Máler Koṭla the rite is called *chhaṭṭí ke táre dekhánâ*, 'to show the stars of the sixth.'

The mother comes out attended by the midwife and a woman carrying a lamp. A man of the family carries the *Qurán*, out of which he reads certain passages to the child. In her mouth the mother has some uncooked rice, and in her hand an iron weapon or implement, while in her lap is some uncooked *khichrí*. Thrice she spits rice out of her mouth to the right and thrice to the left. The reader of the *Qurán* gets a silver coin and some *gur*, and the midwife takes the *khichrí*. On this day, the sixth, the mother is bidden to eat her fill, otherwise the child will have an insatiable appetite all its life.

In Kángra the mother sees the stars on the seventh day, unless it fall on a Friday.[1] She bathes and observes the chief points described above in this ceremony, but the sword is held over her head by her husband, and a woman reads the *Qurán*. In Gujrát the Chibh Rájpúts have an observance of their own. On the third, fifth, or seventh day the mother leaves her room. A square is made with whitewash or rice-flour in a wall, and red lines drawn across it diagonally. At their intersection a picture of the new moon is made, and a sieve placed over it, at which one of the child's near kinsmen shoots seven arrows.

Sardán karne kí rasm.—Just after the *táre dikhánu* the families of the old Mughal dynasty performed another called the *sardán*[2] *karne kí rasm*; which is also observed by people of the city of Delhi, but not necessarily on that date, as any time before the child teethes will do. Women believe that if a child which has not teethed be lifted above the head, it will pass white motions, for which this observance is a preventative, or, if the disease has begun, a cure. It is performed thus:—The ropes used to tighten a native bed are loosened, and two women, who must be mother and daughter, are called in: one of them gets on the bed, with the child in her arms, while the other sits on the ground towards the foot of the bed. The former then passes the child through the opening in the loosened ropes down to the latter, and she passes it back again to the former. This is done seven times. The two women receive the same gifts as are given in the *bigír bachcha* ceremony. In Delhi city this observance is called *shírdán*, and is only practised if the child actually gets ill. The women add the question *shírdán gayá?* They reply *gayá* each time they pass the child through the ropes.

Menials' offerings.—Offerings made by menials to the child play an important part in the observances in Ráwalpindi and Gujrát. In the former district a boy is presented with a *totá*[3] by the tailor: with a chaplet of *dharek* and siris leaves by the flower-woman[4]—this is hung on the outer door as a safeguard against the influence of women who have miscarried; the washerman daubs the wall near the outer door with stuff from his washtub, as a charm against the evil eye: the *máchhí* makes a net and casts it over the child, as an augury that he may remain dutiful and obedient to parental control; the sweeper (*musalli*)

[1] Because if she bathe on a Friday she will be barren for twelve years! Tuesday and Sunday are the lucky days for the bathing.

[2] *Sardán*; possibly a contraction of *sar-gardan*, *i.e.* that which is passed over the head; *shírdán* clearly from *shír*, milk.

[3] A toy made of several pieces of cloth of all colours, strung on a thread like the tail of a kite. This is hung on to the roof of the house but without any express meaning. This is also done in Gujrát.

[4] This is done in Gujrát by the Aráín or flower-woman and she receives a rupee.

brings a small bow and arrow, placing them near the boy's head, so that he may be manly; the shoemaker presents a deerskin; and the *kamángar* or painter brings a paper horse. Each of these dependants receives his customary dues in return.

In the villages of Gujrát the family Brahman of a Muhammadan family makes an imitation *pípal* tree, before the fortieth day, and receives from rupee one to five, according to the family's position.

Dhamaṇ.—The *dhamaṇ* rite is observed among Muhammadans in Siálkot and Gujrát. In the latter district the mother bathes on the fifth or seventh day and puts on new clothes. Bread with *halwá* is distributed among the brotherhood. This is called *dhamaṇ karná.*[1] In Siálkot the observance merely consists in the kinswomen assembling a few days after the birth, and in distributing *halwá* and *chapátís* among the brotherhood.

Pichháwáṇ.—The belief in the evil effects of the shadow (*pichháwáṇ*) of a woman whose child has died young survives among the Muhammadans of Gujrát. Every precaution is taken to prevent her getting access to mother or child, and green *saríṇ* leaves are hung over the outer door to avert the *pichháwáṇ*. Certain tanks are believed to have the power of curing children who are affected by *pichháwáṇ* and so waste away, if bathed therein.

Kunisht.[2]—A curious custom, not very clearly described, is observed in Siálkot by certain tribes. During the first year, if the child be a boy, the wives of the family prostrate themselves before a heap of sugar, which is spread out on a blanket and divided into as many shares as there are proprietors in the village, invoking the elders' good-will. The daughters of the tribe are strictly forbidden to use this sugar, when it has been distributed among the brotherhood, presumably because they will on marriage cease to be members of the tribe or of the village community.

Fosterage.—In well-to-do families a wet nurse (*anná*) is chosen from some decent family, with a nurse (*máni*) to dress the children; a *dádá* to bring them up, and a girl (*chhochho*) to wash soiled clothes, and to play with the children, under the mother's supervision.

In the morning the *chhochho* plays with the children, humming the following verses:—

For boys—1. *Miáṇ áwe dúroṇ se,*
Ghoṛá bándhúṇ khajúroṇ se.
"My master has come from a far country;
I will tie his horse to a tall palm tree."

[1] Among the Gujars the Brahman actually comes in on this day and makes a *chauka* in which a lamp of flour is lit. Huge loaves of bread, each weighing a *topa*, are given to the menials and the Brahman himself gets a *topa* of flour. In well-to-do families a special kind of *halwá* is made and eaten by the members of the *got*, but no one else may partake of it. Even married daughters cannot eat this *halwá* because in marriage they cease to be members of their paternal *got*. On the other hand a share is sent to a son's wife if she is absent.

[2] *Kunisht* means apparently, 'hell,' 'younger,' 'of the lowest degree.' in Punjábi.

2. *Miáṇ áwe daur ke.*
Dushman ki chháti tor ke.
"My master comes dashing in, after smashing in the foe's breast."

"Master comes with a rush;
Giving the foe's breast a crush."

Or 3. *Jug, jug, jug, jug*[1], *jia karo,*
Dudh malida piyá karo.
"Long, long, may you live on;
Milk, crushed bread with butter, live on."

When the *dádá* washes the child's face she sings:—
Chhichi chhichi kawwá kháe;
Dúddá bháti nanna kháe.
"The dirt, the dirt, the crows may eat;
Milkie, ricie, tiny will eat."

At noon, the *anná* sings the following lullaby (*lori*):—
Á já, ri! nindiyá tú á kyuṇ na já?
Mere bále ki ankhoṇ meṇ, ghul mil já.
Áti húṇ, bíwí, áti húṇ:
Do, chár, bále khiláti húṇ.
"Come, Lady Sleep! why don't you come?
To the eyes of my baby, O come!
I am coming, Lady, coming!
Playing with a few children—I am coming!"

Or *Tú so, mere bále! tú so mere bhole! jab tak báli hai nínd:*
Phir jo paregá tú dunyá ke dhande, kaisá hai jhúlá! kaisí hai nínd!

Chorus.—Tú so, mere etc. etc.

Khel, tamáshe, kar le tú sáre; kahtí húṇ tujh se, ánkhoṇ ke táre!
Zindá hai máṇ bhí, báp bhí báre: kar le tú árám Sayyad piyáre.

Chorus.—Tú so, mere etc. etc.

Khel tum aise khelná, lalná! jin sena ho máṇ báp ká jalná:
Dunyá se ḍar, ḍar, sanbhal-kar chalná; sakri hai ghátí, rásta phisalná.

Chorus.—Tu so, mere etc. etc.

"Sleep, my babe! my innocent babe! while to the child there's sleep,
Caught up in the whirl of (life's) business; where is thy cradle, where thy sleep!

[1] Hindi for an age, epoch, period, long time, always.

Chorus.—Sleep, my babe! etc. etc.

All fun and frolic, go enjoy : I am telling you, my dearest boy!

Your parents are living yet; Sayyid, dear, take the rest you can get.

Chorus.– Sleep, my babe! etc.

Play such games, my dear boy, as your parents won't annoy :

Walk the world in fear, in careful mode; narrow its vale, slippery its road.

Chorus.—Sleep, my babe! etc.

At night, on seeing the moon, he is thus amused :—

Chandá mámúṇ, dúr ke.	*Piyálí gai túṭ,*
Bare pakáweṇ, búr ke;	*Chandá mámúṇ gae rúṭh,*
Áp kháweṇ tháli meṇ,	*Piyáli ái aur,*
Ham ko deweṇ piyálí meṇ;	*Chandá mámúṇ áe daur.*

"Uncle moon afar, fries fritters of saw-dust; he himself eats off plates and gives me (food) in small cups : the cup broke, and uncle moon was angry : another cup came, uncle moon came running."

Sometimes the nurse sits near the lamp, and, reaching out her hand to the flame and passing it close to her face and eyes, repeats :—

Akkho! makkho!	"Akkho! makkho!
Mere miyáṇ, Alláh! rakho.	God! preserve my master."

When the child is just able to articulate, she sits him on her knees, and swings him, resting on her back, and moving her knees up and down, while she sings :

Jhujjhú Jhoṭe, jhujjhú-jhú :
Jhujjhú kí ḍálí jhúm paṛí;
Miyáṇ ne chun, chun, god bharí.
Pakke, pakke, miyáṇ kháeṇ;
Kachche, kachche naukar kháeṇ.

Jhujjhú=jujube or *ber* tree. The purport is that her little master is supposed to be on a swing, hung on a tree, which are her legs, and that as the branches swing, the fruit drops down, the child fills his lap, eating the ripe ones himself, and the servants the unripe ones. Afterwards she puts up her legs as high as they will go, and says : —

Khabardár rahiyo, buṛhiyá! rájá ká koṭ girtá hai : Agá! rá! rá! dham!

"Look out, old woman! the king's fort is tumbling down : crash crash! down! thud!"

WWWW

If it is a girl, she amuses her thus :—

1. *Bíwí rí! tú báí, change din áí:*
   Jíweṇ tere báp aur bháí!

   "Miss, you are princess; you have come at a nice time:
   May your father and brother live long."

2. *Bíwí, beṭiyáṇ, chhaparkhaṭ meṇ leṭiyáṇ:*
   Máre magrúrí ke jawáb na detiyáṇ!

   "Miss daughter, you lie in a mosquito curtain:
   Through pride, you don't answer me!"

3. *Akkho! makkho! merí bíwí ko, Alláh! rakho.*

   "Akkho! Makkho! O, God! preserve my lady!"

If, while asleep, the child smiles, they say that *Biháí* is making it laugh. *Biháí*, or *Beh Mátá*, is a Hindu goddess, who, it is believed, makes the child smile at times, and at others weep, by whispering in its ear that its mother is dead or alive.

Rat-jagá or vigil.—The name *rat-jagá*, or vigil, is applied to any merry-making which is kept up all night by the women. A vigil is kept on the occasion of a *chaṭṭí dúdh-chuṭáí, sál-giráh, bismilláh*, or wedding. The frying-pan is kept on the fire all night, and fritters are made, *Allah miyáṇ ká rahm* [1] being also baked. This is done to ensure divine favour. At the same time, the *bíbí kí niás*, or offering to Fátima, daughter of Muhammad, is also made. Seven kinds of fruit and vegetables, in plain or sweetened [2] rice, are served in new earthen vessels. On this offering are also placed some *missí, phulel* (scented oil), *surma* (antimony), henna, *kaláwa* (coloured thread), sandal-wood and five annas as *chirághí* or lamp fee. Formerly it was also customary to put some sláked lime in a small plate, into which the *pák-dámanáṇ* or chaste wives, who partook of the food offered in the *niás*, dipped their fingers, and licked off the lime which adhered to them, in the belief that blood would thereby be caused to flow from the mouth of those who were unfaithful.

Circumcision.—Around so primitive a rite as circumcision, cluster, as might be anticipated, countless local and tribunal usages, accretions on the orthodox observance. This is simple. Though not even alluded to in the *Qurán*, the rite is held to be *sunnat, i.e.* founded on the customs of the Prophet,[3] but no religious observances appear to be prescribed in connection with it.

[1] A kind of biscuit, flat and round, made of a kind of *halwá* prepared from a rice and flour, kneaded in *ghí* and sugar, and in which are mixed dried fruits.

[2] The proportions being 5¼ *sers* of rice to 2¼ *sers* of sugar and 2¼ of curd.

[3] See article in Hughes' *Dictionary of Islám*. In the Punjab the rite is commonly called *khatná*, *cf.* A. *khatnah* or *khitán*; but the term *tahor*, i.q. *tahúr* (purification) is also used.

Circumcision should be performed between the ages of seven and twelve, but it is permissible on or after the seventh day after birth. It is very commonly done in the *chhaṭṭi*.

As a rule the operation is effected at home, but in places the boy is taken to the mosque, and it is done in front of the door.

The keynote to the observances connected with the operation lie in the fact that it is regarded as a wedding—indeed, in the south-west of Baháwalpur it is actually termed *shádi*. In accordance with this idea the boy is treated like a bridegroom, dressed in yellow clothes, and mounted on a horse. Before the operation the brotherhood is sometimes notified, sugar or dates being sent out to its members.

On the day itself the brotherhood is feasted, and entertained with dances. The women sing songs, and sometimes *ḍomnís* are employed to keep the singing up all night.

It is not unusual to half intoxicate the boy with *ma'jún*, so that he may not feel the pain.

As a rule the barber operates, but in Kángṛa the Abdál is sometimes employed, and in the west of the Punjab the Pirhain. In Baháwalpur the boy is told by the guests to slap the Pirhain, who gets as many rupees as he receives slaps. Naturally as the father has to pay, he urges the boy not to slap the operator.

In Kángṛa the boy is seated on a basket, in which is placed a cock, the barber's perquisite. In Lahore he is seated on a stool, to which his hand is tied by a piece of *mauli* thread, and unless a companion in suffering has been found for him, the top of an earthen vessel is simultaneously cut off.

The barber receives a substantial reward. He puts his *kaṭori*, or cup, on the stool in the midst of his assembled guests, and each of them puts a coin into it.

In Máler Koṭla the boy is ceremoniously bathed on a wooden stool, and then his mother's brother ties a *kangna* of thread, called *khamani*, on which are strung a betel nut, an iron ring and a piece of liquorice. After the operation the barber bids the uncle take the boy away, and he does so carrying him in his arms.

In Baháwalpur the boy's mother stands by with a *Qurán* on her head during the operation, her women friends standing round her while she dips the hem of her petticoat in a vessel full of water.

The foreskin, when removed, is generally buried, but sometimes it is thrown on the roof, or even attached to it with a piece of straw, in Hissár. In Baháwalpur it is called *khol*, and is carefully preserved, being sometimes buried in the floor, which, being near the water pitchers, always remains wet. In Delhi it is tied together with a peacock's feather to the boy's left foot, so that no one's shadow may affect him; but this custom is falling into disuse.

In Ráwalpindi the operation is often carried out on the same day as the *aqíqa*. The child's sisters and his father's sisters are presented with clothes, and they sing:—

Hariá ní maye Háriá,	*Ohio ghar bhágíbhariá,*
Hariá te bhágí bharia,	*Hariá ní máye Háriá,*
Jis ghar eh beṭrá jamiá,	*Hariá te bhági bhariá.*

"Oh, mother! How blessed and peaceful is that house in which such a son has been born! Mark well that daughters alone have been useful on the occasion."

Vows.

A vow (*H. omannat*, in Punjabi *manaut*) is not infrequently made by a barren woman that she will offer a cloth, light a lamp, and have her child's first tonsure performed at a specified shrine if offspring be vouchsafed to her. The period for such an observance is always specified in the vow, but it is usually limited to a time before the child attains the age of twelve years.

Badháwa.—Another type of vow is to place a silver necklet round the child's neck every year, or to make him wear a *hama'il*, and add one rupee or more to it every year until he attains the age of seven, ten or twelve, when the accumulated silver is sold and the proceeds given to the poor.[1] If the necklet is sold at the age of ten the observance is called *dasaundh.*[2] The necklet should be put on the child's neck on the last Wednesday in Safar, the second month of the Muhammadan year. In Amritsar this is called Badháwa Pír Sáhib.

In Siálkot the term *banháwa*[3] is applied to the custom of putting on the *hamá'il* and adding a rupee year by year. After the twelfth year it belongs to his wife, but the vow may stipulate that a certain share of the value shall go to a certain shrine, and the number of years may vary. In Ludhiána the sale-proceeds are often supplemented by further gifts, and go to feed the poor. The object is to invoke God's favour on the child.

Half-heads.—(In fulfilment of vows) in Ludhiána, some people shave only half the child's head at a time, every week. The right half is first shaved, from back to front; then the left. This is done for some years, and then a *niáz* is offered, and the whole head shaved.[4]

Imámon-ka-paik.—During the first ten days of the Muharram, some people get their children made messengers of the Imáms (*imámon-ka-paik*), thus: ten yards of muslin are cut into four equal parts, lengthways, and two are dyed green and two black. One of each colour is then taken and made into a sheet, giving two sheets, of which one is wrapped round the head and the other round the waist. Some ten or fifteen small bells are then strung on a cotton thread, which is also tied round the

[1] But in Siálkot and Baháwalpur the *hasli* or *hama'il* becomes the property of the boy's wife when he marries. In Hissár the sale-proceeds are sometimes spent in sweets, which are distributed among the brotherhood. In Kapúrthala the necklets are sometimes sent to the shrine to which the vow was made, and sometimes they are divided among the near kinsmen of the child's mother.

[2] *Dasaundh, lit.* a tithe, also a votive offering made at the age of ten: see *P. Dictionary, sub voce daswandh.* Sometimes a rupee is simply put by each year till the child is ten.

[3] *Badháwa*—lit. increase, growing. But in *P. Dictionary* it is said to mean the ornament put on a child's neck in fulfilment of a vow.

[4] In Siálkot this custom is modified: only children whose brothers and sisters have died, or whose parents are old, are treated thus—half the head being shaved, and the other half left, in order that the Angel of Death may pass them by as too ugly. This is equivalent to giving an opprobrious name to the child.

waist. The boy goes barefoot, but his *pagri* is adorned with feathers.[1] On the tenth day of Hasan's martyrdom, rice and milk are cooked and distributed among Muhammadan households.

Jhand.—In contrast to the religious rite of *aqiqa* is that called the *jhand*, which is done either in accordance with an express vow, or which may be regarded as the fulfilment of a tacit vow. In Hissár the rite is said to be extinct, but other accounts appear to contradict this.[2]

The *jhand* is commonly observed within the *chhila*, or forty days from the birth, but it may be deferred till a much later age. In Kapúrthala the *aqiqa* is called *jhand utárna*, but in Máler Kotla, if the *aqiqa* is not performed, the *jhand*. *i.e.*, a lock of hair is left on the head and cut off generally at shrine of Shaikh Sadr Jahán, a vow being made that it will be done if the child live a certain time, generally twelve years.

The *jhand* rite is not confined to boys, but is observed in the case of girls also—the only difference being that the barber's fee is diminished by half in the latter case.

In Kángra the hair is mixed with flour, baked into a loaf, and thrown over running water; but as a rule the hair is weighed and its weight in silver given to the barber. In Lahore, however, great importance is attached to the *jhand* or first tonsure. It is generally removed on the fortieth day after the *chila* observance is over, but some people do this on the *aqiqa* day. In either case the hair is scrupulously preserved, and sometimes placed in a silver amulet or always carried about with one. The hair is deemed sacred, and kept by one on commencing any new work. Women believe that no evil influence can prevail over one who has it near her. But some people tie the hair to the child's bed. The barber is paid from rupees one to five, and other menials get dues from the mother's mother. *Jhand*, too, is very often performed on the seventh, fourteenth, twenty-first or fortieth day, and silver equal to the weight of the hair is given away in charity, the hair being then buried in the ground. But if a vow has been made the rite is carried out in fulfilment of that vow, and the *jhand*, or a lock of the hair, removed at the specified shrine. There, too, a he-goat is sacrificed, and some people even sacrifice a he-goat every year until the child attains the age of twelve or twenty-one. Besides which bracelets are put on the child until he is twelve.

Among the Chibh Rájpúts of Gujrát the first tonsure must be performed within seven years at the shrine of the martyr Shádí, ancestor of the tribe, and until it is done the mother must abstain from meat. If the hair is cut a lock must be left. This lock is called Bábú Shahíd. At the shrine a goat is sacrificed, the mother eats the liver, and the rest is given away as alms.

In Sháhpur the *jhand* is observed on the seventh, eighth or ninth day, a *chúri* of bread, *ghi* and *gur* being distributed among relatives

[1] If the boy be a Shia his remaining garments will be black; if a Sunni, green.

[2] Vows appear to be made at the shrine of Dána Sher of Bhauna to cut the *jhand* there at a specified age but this seems to be regarded as part of the *aqiqa*.

or friends. But a lock of hair called *liṭ* is kept and removed some years later at a Pír's shrine; but the observance is not common.

In Ráwalpindi the *jhanḍ* is removed between the seventh and twelfth days; the sister or father's sister holds the child in her lap and catches the hair. The Ghebas keep three locks or tufts of hair—called *suchi bodi*—which remain until the child is circumcised.

In Ráwalpindi, when a child has been shaved on the seventh day, a lock of hair is left, to be removed at the shrine of a saint at the time fixed in the vow. Other people, in accordance with a vow, place a *hanslí* on the child's neck and sell it at the end of the seventh year, offering the money to the shrine. Other but similar vows are made, and in fulfilling them the parents put on new clothes, fast, and feed the poor with the food specified in their vows.

Marúnḍon kí rasm.—When the child is about five or six months old its mother's mother sends some *marúnḍe*,[1] and these are distributed in the family. The *marúnḍe* are balls made of wheat or parched rice mixed with sweets, or else of *moṭí chúr ke laḍḍu múng kí dál* mixed with syrup, together with poppy seed or boiled wheat. The balls are made by closing the fist (*muṭṭhí ke band karne se*), and are sent because at this age the child begins to open and close its fists.

Section 5.—Hindu betrothal observances.

Shastric ideas on betrothal.

A Hindu friend[2] has furnished me with following account of orthodox Shastric ideas on the subject of betrothal, and I prefix it to my notes on 'Hindu Bethrothal Observances in the Punjab,' as it contains many points of interest.

The relatives who can give a binding promise of betrothal are:—the father, paternal grandfather, brother, a *sakulya*,[3] and lastly the mother. But if any one of these disregard the *prikraṭi* or *kúlachar* (family custom) he loses his or her privilege and it devolves on the next in order. *E.g.* if the father is inclined to sell his daughter, the right to betroth devolves on the grandfather, and so on.

Betrothal being governed by various considerations, it is no hardship on a boy or girl to betroth them in infancy. The guardian of the girl should not only see the boy's body, but have regard to his conduct, family means, education and repute. He should choose one whose age is double that of the girl, but not treble her age or more. The boy should be sound in body and in mind, and his family should be free from hereditary disease. He should not live too far away, be constantly

[1] *Marunḍa* or *murunḍa*, a ball of parched sugar mixed with crude sugar, sometimes of a large size: *P. Dictionary*, pp. 731, 777, 779.

[2] Pandit Shib Rám Dás, a Brahman of the Ganghár section (Bashist *gotra*) of Bunjáhí status, whose family was originally settled in the Jhang District.

[3] The *sakulyá*, *i.e.* one of the same *kul* or family.

engaged in war, or an ascetic, and, apart from these general considerations, he should have the following particularized qualifications :—

> Broad or deep should be his chest, face and forehead, his navel, voice and *satya* (inherent power).
>
> Short his throat, back, male organ and legs.
>
> Fine (*sukhsham*) his hair, nails, teeth, flesh and the joints of his fingers.
>
> Long the distances between his eyebrows and his breasts, his arms, his nostrils and his chin.
>
> Red should be his palate and tongue, the soles of his feet and the palms of his hands, and both the corners of each eye.

Countless other points of palmistry have also to be considered. Thus, a boy with no lines, or too many, in his hand will be poor and short-lived. Lastly horoscopes have to be consulted, and it is important that neither party should have been born in the *mangal ras*, or house of Mars, because, if so, his or her mate is doomed to an early death.

On the other hand the girl should be *aspinda*, *i e.* not related to the boy within the following degrees, thus : —

> She should not be of the same *gotra* as the boy. (The *got* of the maternal grandfather is also sometimes avoided.)

She should be a virgin, beautiful, young and free from disease. She should also have a brother, for otherwise, according to the marriage contract, her first-born son would have to be given to her father, in order that he might become his maternal grandfather's heir. Various other qualifications are prescribed ; health, good repute, a swan-like gait, fine teeth and hair, delicate limbs and soft red-soled feet without prominent joints. Her fingers and toes should be separated, and the palm of her hand shaped like a lotus for luck. Her shape should be fish like, and on the soles of her feet there should be the marks of a goad and barley-corns. Her knees should be round, her legs free from hair, her forehead broad and prominent, the navel deep, with three deep wrinkles in the abdomen, the nipples round and hard, the throat like a lion's, the lips as red as a *trsuha* fruit, the voice soft like a cuckoo's, the nostrils evenly matched, and the eye like a lotus. Lastly, her little toes should not touch the ground lest she become a widow; the second toe should not project beyond the big toe lest her character be lost, and her legs should not be long and thin, for that, too, is an omen of widowhood. Hair on the legs presages misfortune, and a prominent abdomen lasting sickness and sterility Her eyes should not be a reddish brown, nor like those of a cat, for the latter denote easy virtue. Hair on the nipples will bring misfortune on her husband. Dry hair and everted lips show a quarrelsome temper, and so on.[1]

[1] Some of the Pashtu verses descriptive of good looks popular in Kurram run :—

Nis mein o li dalla chhi pasár thée guléna

Narai mollá sarinda zálf táróna

Nis mein o lidalla díng gárdán mirmána

Shastric law classifies women into four groups; Padmani, Chitarni, Sankhani and Hastni.

When all these points have been investigated and the betrothal decided on, an auspicious day is fixed for its celebration, which should not take place in the month of Poh, Kátik or Chet, when Venus and Jupiter are on the wane, during the *shrádhas*, annual or general, *dwitik* (intercalated month), or the *anatrá*, when Venus and Jupiter are in the same *rás*, and so on. Sundays, Tuesdays and Saturdays are also to be avoided.

Betrothal was generally observed during the following *Nakshatras* (asterisms):

Utrán and Parhán { Phalgani. / Khárán. / Bhadarpadán. }

Also in Rohni, Kritkán, Mrigshár, Maghhán, Hust, Swáti, Utradhán, Kután and Reota.

On the day appointed for the rite the boy's party go to the girl's house and both parties are there seated, while Brahmans recite the *mangha-charan* or benedictory prayers, and Shri Ganeshji is worshipped

Zi ghan jan kúm thha maula ká laghrúna
Chhoh wishtillai chhoh naraibu faryadúna
Khúdai thhi mihrban jorawi thha súratúna
Thha adrai gútti malúchho ní pastaithhi
Thha sarhai shhundi laalo pa shhawa sari thhi
Samandai júna ta naistargi sari thhi
Khúdai mihrbán thhi jorawi thha suratúna
Thha khhumari istargo si ajab thhithhan thhi
Thha ding gardan khoi seir mer ta mastigar thhi
Thha mayanon urko mukhh ki istir safar thhi
Bakhhtawar thhi chhi khhuri shhúndi sarúna
Nin main chhi púm okro ding gardan masalai hee
Ding serai poza pa mukhh ki tajalla kai
Kawum yank bakhtawar thha sanni pa khwali ki
Shirin alab thhi mer shá ta dir chu khúmáa
Mahomed Ali Khan dair gunahgár thhi hila adlári kádima
Peroopa iyar talo o lidalla nasimua
Bala tar singa thha showdo wawro na iepina
Maulah thha mukhi rashha chha pair armanddna.

The complexion should be fair, the face and brow broad, the chin round, the nose thin and aquiline, the eyes black, and (one regrets to say) lustful. The hair, eyebrows and eyelashes should all be long and black, the teeth white and the lips red: the charms of rosy cheeks are enhanced by a black or a green mole: the neck should be ong, the fingers tapering and the waist slim.

in a brass dish (*thál*); rice is thrown on Ganeshjí and the boy's party, and sometimes red-coloured water is also sprinkled over them. The girl's guardian then announces that the girl, daughter of so-and-so, is betrothed to the son of so-and-so. This is called the *wákdán*, *i.e.* 'the *dán* or gift by word of mouth,' and is the essence of the betrothal contract. It is now irrevocable, and there is a very strong feeling against breaking it.

When once the promise has passed the lips of the girl's father, it can only be withdrawn for grave causes. A Sanskrit adage says:—*Sakrit pradiyate kanya*, 'a girl is given but once.' Formerly, in respectable families, a betrothed girl whose *fiancé* had died could not be married, and if such a marriage occurred it brought social discredit on the family. A Mirotra Khatri family in Multán is still looked down upon because it once contracted a marriage of this kind.

Then a *janeo*, or sacred thread, fruit, flowers and some clothes are given to the boy by the girl's brother or Brahmans. The girl's Brahman applies the *tilak* to the boy and his kinsmen. The boy's parents and kinsmen make gifts to Brahmans and distribute money among them, an observance called *náwáṇ* (lit. name).

The boy is next taken to his father's house when a morsel of bread, butter, sugar and *khichri*[1] is given him. This rite is called *Gráhin dena* (or gift of a morsel of bread). The females also distribute *khichṛi* to the brotherhood, who, in return, give them presents. Till far into the night, songs are sung by the women.

Betrothal thus effected creates a kind of relationship, so that if one of the parties to it dies, the other is counted impure for three days.

In some families *gur* and a rupee, five pieces of turmeric, some *supári* (betel-nut), rice and fruit are thrown into the laps of the boy's party at the betrothal.

Taking money for a girl is strictly forbidden by the Shástrás, and one who takes it goes to hell.

A proverb says:—

Kanjar te Qasái, chút nál chút waṭái—meaning that low-caste men are divided into (*i*) Kanjars who prostitute their girls; (*ii*) butchers, who kill them; and (*iii*) those who exchange their persons.

Modern Hindu observances.

Amongst the Hindús betrothal is a contract, and is, as a rule, an indispensable preliminary to the marriage of a girl, though a woman once married cannot again be betrothed according to the ceremonies of a first betrothal.[2]

Betrothals are of three kinds:—

(*i*) *dharm*[3] or *pun*, in which the girl is given by her parents as a quasi-religious offering to her future husband.

[1] This is the custom in the Jhang District.

[2] *Punjab Customary Law*, ii, p. 118.

[3] *Dharm dí pachár* in parts of the South-West Punjab.

(*ii*) *waṭṭa saṭṭa* [1] (exchange), in which two or more families exchange brides.

(*iii*) *ṭakke* or *ṭakkián dí pachár*, in parts of the south-west Punjab, in which a bride-price is more or less openly paid.[2]

(*i*) The *dharm* or ritual form of betrothal is a religious rite. In it the initiative is almost invariably taken by the girl's parents.[3]

Thus in Gurgáon her father sends his family barber and priest to search for a suitable boy. When they have found one they return, and, if horoscopes are kept, compare those of the pair to see if they are in accord. If the girl's father approves of the match he sends the two delegates again to the boy's house with the signs of betrothal called *ṭiká* or *sikka*.[4] If the boy's father approves of the match,[5] he calls his kindred together and in their presence the delegates[6] place the tokens in the boy's lap, and some sweets into his mouth, simulaneously proclaiming the girl's name. The girl's barber or priest also makes a mark (*ṭika*) on the boy's forehead with his thumb.[7] During the ceremony the boy is seated on a wooden plank (*chauki* or *paṭri*) slightly raised off the ground, on which, after it has been swept and smeared with cow-dung, a square (*chauk*) has been traced with flour.

The signs of betrothal vary, but in the South-East Punjab there is almost always a rupee, often a cocoanut and sometimes clothes.

Elsewhere in the Province the cocoanut is replaced by dates, usually five in number, but often two or seven; thus in Gurdáspur the girl's father sends seven nuts (*chhowára*), one or more rupees and some clothes as a *shagún* or conventional gift to the boy. These are made over to him by the *lági* (a priest, a barber, or a bard) at his parents' house in

[1] *Waṭṭi dí pachár* in parts of the South-West.

[2] Such a betrothal (or the price paid for it) is said to be called *dambah* in Ludhiána. *Pun* betrothal is confined to the higher castes, and instances rarely occur among them of the initiative being taken by the boy's people. Indeed, the instances noted are all from the Western Punjab, where the Hindu element holds a subordinate place under the Muhammadan tribes. Thus in Shahpur, among most of the Khatrís and Aroras, the boy's father takes the first step, but among the Khokharain, or upper class Khatrís, the girl's father does so (xv, pp. 22-3). In Muzaffargaṛh and Dera Ghází Khán, on the Indus, the boy's father always appears to take the initiative (xx, pp. 14-15; xvi, pp. 2-3), but this is not the case in Pesháwar (xvii, p. 28).

[3] In Hindi a betrothal is called *sagái*, in Punjabi *mangewa* or *mangní*, from *mangná* 'to beg in marriage'. *Kurmái* is a term widely used, especially in the Punjab. In Muzaffargaṛh (South-West Punjab) *pachár* is the term used by Hindús. *Ropná* is also used in the Eastern Punjab for betrothal, but it literally means the present (of seven dried dates etc.) sent by the girl's father to the prospective bridegroom.

[4] Also called *ropna* (in Sirsa). The use of the term *ṭika* (*ṭikkà* in Punjabi) in this sense is unusual and apparently confined to the South-eastern Punjab. Thus in Hánsi the girl's father sends a barber with a rupee to the boy's house, and the barber gives this rupee (which is called *ṭiká*) to the boy. In Jhelum *ṭiká* is used as equivalent to *tilak*.

[5] No public inquiry is made about the girl, but the women find out among themselves.

[6] Called *sagí* as entitled to *sag* or *lâk*, *i.e.* dues, in the South-East Punjab. But a commoner term is *lági*, *i.e.* one entitled to *lág*, dues.

[7] This mark is more correctly and usually called *tilak*. It is usually made on the boy's forehead by the girl's Brahman with turmeric and rice. Occasionally her barber affixes it. In Jhelum it is affixed during the reception of the *shagún*.

the presence of his kinsmen, and in return he sends the girl a *shagún* of ornaments and clothes.[1]

In the Western Punjab the rite is quite as distinctively religious. Thus in Muzaffargarh, although the boy's father and kinsmen take the initiative and go empty-handed to the girl's house,[2] they are there met by her father or guardian with his kinsmen and presented with *gur*, fruits or clothes, and the Brahman, if present, performs the worship of Ganesh and recites the *gotrachár*. The *gur* and fruits are taken to the boy's house and there distributed.[3]

This rite is held on an auspicious day and must be solemnized at the girl's father's shop or pleasure-house, but not at the house where his women-kind live,[4] and after it the boy's father is called *putreta* and the girl's *dheta*, the relationship called *sain* or *senr* henceforth existing between them. This relationship prevents their visiting each other or even eating together, while the future son-in-law (*jawátra*) may not even speak to his father-in-law (*sohra*).

Thus betrothal in the South-West Punjab is a solemn rite and the tie it creates is irrevocable, so much so that it can only be annulled owing to impotence or incurable disease, and even when the boy or girl is thought to be dying the tie between the pair is solemnly cancelled by the following rite:—

In Muzaffargarh, where the rite is called *páni piláwan* (*i.e.* giving water to drink), the boy is called to the girl's death-bed and made to stand by her pillow and drink some water. The girl also drinks, and then the boy says, 'Thou art my sister.' This, of course, dissolves the betrothal, but it is understood that if the patient recover the tie will hold good. In the event of the boy's not arriving till she is dead the girl's body is not burnt until he has looked upon her face, or if the body has to be burnt before his arrival some cotton is smeared with blood from her forehead and thrown into his house. Every effort is however made to prevent the cotton being thus thrown into the house and a watch is kept over it, the belief being that, if the cotton is thrown in, it will bring ruin upon the dwelling. After four days the blood-stained cotton cannot be thrown in and the house is safe.

In the adjacent State of Baháwalpur a very similar ceremony called *mathe lagáwan* is performed to cancel the betrothal. Thus, if the girl be at the point of death the boy goes to her and standing by her death-bed gives her some sweets, saying, *hán káki miṭhái ghin*, 'dear sister, take this sweetmeat,' and she must reply *liá bhirawá*, 'brother, give it me.'

[1] *P.C.L.*, xii, p. 3.

[2] They say they have come to arrange for the *pachár* (betrothal) of so-and-so *chaudhrí's* (notable's) son. The reply is that the girl's father will consider the proposal (*wichár karná*), and it appears to be etiquette for him to promise a reply in a week or a fortnight's time, when the boy's people again approach him.

[3] *P.C.L.*, xx, p. 15.

[4] In Jhang there is a survival of this rite, a girl being shown her betrothed's bier, if the latter die before their wedding; or she breaks a clod of earth at his door or behind his bier, and, having washed her clothes, returns home.

This cancels the betrothal, but if the sick child recover and the parents of the couple agree to the renewal of the contract the betrothal ceremonies are again performed by the parties

The *mathe lagáwan* must be done at the house of the sick child, but his or her parents do their utmost to prevent it as it brings calamity upon their family. If they knowingly permit it no other Kirár will contract an alliance with them. Consequently guards are posted at the door of the sick child's house to keep out the intruder who makes every effort to get in. Both sides resort to violence, so much so that sticks are sometimes used and serious affrays ensue. Disguise is even sometimes resorted to in order to obtain access to the sick child; for instance, the garb of a sweeper etc., but if this too fail it is sufficient for the betrothed to strike his or her forehead against the wall of the sick child's house. This knocking the wall, which is termed *Sawan*, must be performed within four days from the sick child's death, after which it is of no avail. If a child fails to perform the *mathe lagáwan* or *sawan* he or she cannot secure a second betrothal, being regarded as ill-starred, but if the ceremony be duly performed he or she is considered purified, and can readily contract a second betrothal.[1]

(*ii*) Betrothal by change is further divisible into three or more varieties, *viz.*: (i) *amho samhaná* or simple exchange; (ii) *treabanj* or threefold barter [2]; (iii) *chobhanj* or fourfold, and so on, in Muzaffargarh.[3] In all these the parties concerned meet at one place by appointment, and enter into the contract of giving the girls, one to the other, after which each girl's guardian gives *gur* or fruits to the guardian of the boy to whom his girl is betrothed. Then the Brahman, if present, performs worship of Ganesh and recites the *gotrachár*. The *gur* or fruits are taken home and distributed.

In Jhang exchange betrothal is called *amo sámne*, a term which in Multán is applied to direct, as opposed to *tarain vatni* or indirect exchange. In Ludhiána betrothal by exchange is called *határh*.

In Ludhiána exchange marriage (*baṭṭe ká biyáh*) sometimes takes the form called *bádhe ká biyáh* in which a girl of, say, eighteen years of age is exchanged for one of five. In such a case, a kind of disparity fine (*bádhá*) has to be paid to the party giving the adult girl.

Among the Gaddís of Chamba, marriage by exchange is called *bola*, and the first of the rites observed resembles those described below in a *dharma-puna* betrothal. But when all the boy's people go to complete the alliance, a grindstone, pestle and *sil* (mortar) with three or five lumps of *gur*, *supári bihan*, and *rolián*, are placed before them, and the *parohit* taking the *supári* etc. in the fold of his garment puts them in the mortar, receiving a fee of four annas from the boy's father before grinding them. He then mentions the names of the betrothed pair, and pounds up the spices. Then the *supári* etc. is put in a dish with the *gur* broken into small pieces, and distributed among the guests, the boy's

[1] The *mathe lagáwan* is also observed in the villages of the Multán District.

[2] In which three betrothals are arranged in connection with one another.

[3] *P.C.L.*, xx, p. 15.

father first taking a piece. The elder members of the bride's family do not take any, as that would be contrary to etiquette. Then the boy's father puts one rupee four annas in the dish, and from this silver the girl's parents have an ornament made for her. She also presents herself before the boy's father, and he gives her a rupee. The rest of the ceremony resembles that observed in a *dharma-puna* betrothal, but the coins put in the vessel come out of the boy's father's pocket. The whole rite is repeated in the other family's house, but not necessarily on the same day. Tuesday, Friday or Saturday is an unlucky day for these observances.

(*iii*) In betrothal by purchase the essential difference is that the initative is taken by the boy's people, who go to the girl's house and there make the bargain. Then the girl's parents send their *lágis* (or more usually one man, the *sái*) to the boy's house where the ordinary rites are gone through.[1]

In the north-eastern (Himalayan) corner of the Punjab, the initiative is usually taken by the boy's people. After certain preliminary negotiations, they go to the girl's house with their priest (*parohit*) to perform the rites. In a *dharma-puna* betrothal the girl's father gives the *parohit* some *dubh* grass, with at least four copper coins, which are to be handed over to the boy's father in token that he accepts the alliance. All remain the night at the bride's house, and after a meal, her father gives eight copper coins to the boy's father These he puts in his dish as a perquisite for the man who cleans it.[2]

In Kulu, among the higher castes, the *parohit* fixes a day for the rite and is then sent with one or two men, with a present of clothes, ornaments, and money to the bride's house. There he makes the girl worship Ganesh, and she is then dressed in the clothes, and *gur* is distributed among the villagers or neighbours. In return her parents send a sacred thread and a betel-nut for the bridegroom, in whose village also *gur* is distributed on the *parohit*'s return.

Among the Kanets, the local god fixes the auspicious day for the rite, and on that day, the boy's father or brother with two companions, takes the clothes and ornaments to the bride's house. She puts them on and *gur* is then distributed without any worship of Ganesh. The lower classes have the same rites, but among them the boy also goes to his father-in-law's house at the betrothal.

When the initiative is not taken by the girl's father, it is fairly safe to assume that the parties are of low status or caste, and that the contract was not *pun*. Thus in Siálkot, among the Chúhrás, the boy's father goes to the girl's house with a female kinsman, and is then feasted, giving her father two rupees. Next the visitors are given an ordinary meal, and the girl's father gets another rupee. After this a blanket

[1] *P.C.L.*, v (Ludhiána), p. 43. But in Muzaffargarh Ganesh is not apparently worshipped in *takke* betrothals, xx, p. 16.

[2] The above are the customs in vogue among the Gaddís of Chamba, but in the Churáh sub-division of that State the custom is for the boy's father or brother to place eight copper coins or as much as a rupee in the dish from which he has eaten. This is called *júth*, and the act *júth dálná*. On the following day the betrothal contract is made.

is spread on the ground, and the girl's father, in the presence of his kin, brings a flat dish into which the boy's father puts the betrothal money, which varies in amount but is always considerable, sometimes amounting to fifty rupees.[1]

Briefly, the essentials of a valid contract of betrothal are the public acceptance of the match, feasting and the exchange of gifts, the religious rites, if any are observed, being of secondary importance, even indeed if these are necessary to the validity of the contract.

It may be said generally that a contract of betrothal is irrevocable, except for certain definite causes, or in cases when it has become impossible of fulfilment. Even when its literal fulfilment is impossible owing to the death of the boy, there is a widespread feeling that an implied contract subsists to marry the girl to another member of his family. Instances of this custom are found in the Gujars, Rors and Jats of Kaithal,[2] the tribes of Sirsa,[3] and in the Sháhpur District, where the general feeling is that the girl is a valuable piece of property, and that betrothal is a contract to transfer her ownership to the boy's family, when she reaches a marriageable age, but the boy's death cancels the contract.[4] It would appear that the castes or tribes which allow widow re-marriage have a strong feeling that the betrothal duly effected gives the boy's family a claim on the girl's hand, so that, in the event of her original fiancé's death, she may be married to another boy of the family. In Jhelum, on the other hand, the contract is revocable unless the formality observed be the *waq*, which is to all intents a marriage.[5]

Thus the advantages of the contract are all on the boy's side, in having secured a valuable chattel, little is thought of the girl's claim on the boy, only very exceptional circumstances would make the boy's family refuse to find another match for her in the event of his death. If the girl die the contract is void, her family having contracted to transfer a specific article, to wit a particular girl to the boy's family, and as that article no longer exists the bargain cannot be fulfilled, and her family has no claim to marry another of its girls to the boy.

The causes which justify a refusal to carry out a contract of betrothal are mainly physical (*e.g.*, leprosy, impotence, blindness, or mortal disease in either party). Immorality on the part of the girl is generally also a valid cause. As a rule immorality on the boy's part is not recognized as a cause for refusal to carry out the contract, and, speaking generally, the contract is considered much more binding on the girl's relatives than on those of the boy, so much so that among the Jaṭs of Lahore this principle is pushed to an extreme, and it is alleged that the boy can break off his betrothal at pleasure, whereas a girl cannot.[6]

A betrothal is also said to be revocable on other grounds, *e.g.* on the discovery that the parties are within the prohibited degrees of re-

[1] *P.C.L.*, xiv, p. 5.
[2] *P.C.L.*, *loc. cit.*
[3] *P.C.L.*, iv, pp. 89-94; *cf.*, ii (Gurgáon), pp. 116-119.
[4] *P.C.L.*, pp. 24-5.
[5] *P.C.L.*, xix, p. 18.
[6] *P.C.L.*, xiii, p. 4.

lationship,[1] or that they belong to different tribes,[2] and apostasy would also justify its revocation.[3]

As a rule, among Hindús, priority of betrothal gives the girl a social, though hardly a legal, claim to be married first, *i.e.* to be married before the fiancé takes another wife. The reason is that in a Hindu household the first married wife occupies a more or less privileged position.[4]

The ages of betrothal.

The age at which betrothal may be effected is not fixed, and it varies among different tribes and in different localities, so that it is impossible to generalize regarding it. Thus in Kaithal the Rájpúts assert that betrothal cannot take place before the age of ten, and girls are certainly betrothed at a much later age among Rájpúts than among other (and lower) tribes, so much so that it is common to defer a Rájpút girl's betrothal till she is fifteen or even twenty.[5] In Ambála, the Gújars of Rúpaṛ put the lowest age of betrothal at five weeks; many tribes putting the maximum age at forty years,[6] but it is not usual below five. Similarly in Gurdáspur,[7] Siálkot,[8] Shahpur, Jhelum, Dera Gházi Khán, and Muzaffargaṛh there is no restriction as to age, but the actual customs differ greatly according to circumstances. Thus there is a tendency to defer betrothal among the higher castes to a somewhat later age than is usual among the middle castes; *e.g.* in Lahore, Jáṭs betroth from four to six; and Rájpúts from twelve to fourteen,[9] in Shahpur, Hindús betroth from eight to twelve, and in Jhelum, before ten.[10] Generally speaking in the Western Punjab girls are betrothed at a very early age, much earlier than is customary among the Muhammadans, but boys are often not betrothed till puberty or later. The feeling that it is a disgrace to have a grown-up daughter unmarried is very strong among Hindús. Throughout the Punjab pre-natal betrothal is unusual, but not unknown.

Some observances subsequent to betrothal.

These are purely social and of little importance. In Hánsi the boy's father sends sweets etc. for the girl on festivals. These she returns with some money. Later the boy's father sends her ornaments—called *buba*. These, too, are returned with some cash, oil and clothes added, only three or four ordinary trinkets being retained.

[1] *P.C.L.*, x, p. 4.

[2] *P.C.L.*, viii, p. 3; x, p. 4.

[3] *P.C.L.*, x, p. 4; xii, p. 4; xiv, p. 6; xix, p. 18; xx, p. 16.

[4] Whereas among Muhammadans the four wives are, in the eye of the law at least, absolutely equal.

[5] *P.C.L.*, viii, p. 2.

[6] *P.C.L.*, x., p. 5.

[7] *P.C.L.*, xii. p. 3.

[8] *P.C.L.*, xiv, p. 3.

[9] *P.C.L.*, xiii, p. 3.

[10] *P.C.L.*, xv, p. 20; xix (?), p. 17.

In Multán and Muzaffargaṛh, there is a similar custom called *subha,* which consists in the exchanging presents of sweets at festivals. Clothes and toys are also sent. These presents, too, are sometimes returned by the girl's people. This custom is spreading, it is said, into Sirmúr.[1]

Muzaffargaṛh also appears to have some distinctive local customs in the *ság* or *wat walawan,* which consists in the girl's father sending the boy's a request for *ság* (vegetables).

The request is complied with and fruit of any kind in season sent. After this the fathers may have dealings with each other—a thing wholly forbidden to them before this observance. After it too comes the *watr sákh,* in which the girl's father sends the boy's fresh fruit or green stuff. In both cases the fruit etc. is distributed among relatives and neighbours.

In Multán the betrotheds' fathers do not even salute each other when they meet, after the betrothal has once been effected, until the *Rám sat* observance has been duly performed. For this a lucky day is chosen, and then the girl's father with some of his kinsmen takes some sweets and Re. 1-4-0, Rs. 3 or Rs. 5 in cash to the boy's home, where he finds the latter's kinsmen also assembled. He presents the boy's father with the sweets etc. and salutes him, saying 'Rám Rám' (the usual Hindu greeting). After this the two fathers may salute each other if they meet.

In Jhang some time after the betrothal an observance called *piridai* is in vogue. The boy's kinsmen with some of his kinswomen visit the girl's home where they receive sweetstuff or a rupee each, and the women of the boy's party are seated on a *píṛí.*[2]

[1] Very similar to the *subha* observance, yet distinct from the observance called *guṛ* in Multán. It consists in sending *guṛ* (jaggery), fruit and vegetables with two rupees (Baháwalpur coinage, which is cheaper) to the boy's father, 'some time after the betrothal has been completed.'

[2] Betrothal among Hindús in large towns is arranged by the womenfolk, the mother, grandmother or some other relative of the boy visiting the girl's mother till she gives her consent or refusal. Betrothal is formally announced by the girl's parents sending a lump of *guṛ* with a rupee to the boy's. In well-to-do families this ceremony, which is called *shagún,* 12 to 25 rupees with 100 *kúzás* (sugarcandy) are sent. In the case of a *májú* (a widower) of good social status and well-to-do the amount often rises to Rs. 500 or even Rs. 1000.

After the betrothal comes the *pair páná* (to put in one's feet) ceremony. At this the girl's people send as many as 51 trays of *laḍḍu, láchí* and other sweets to the boy's parents, followed on the same day by a formal visit paid by the women of the boy's family (neighbours and friends are also invited, but no males) to the girl's. These ladies are served with light refreshments and among well-to-do families the boy's kinswomen get a cup of milk with a rupee each. The boy's mother takes the girl in her lap and a *sarwárna* of Re. 1-4-0 is done. When the boy's party have left, the girl's in turn go to his house, where the girl's mother takes the boy in her lap and gives him a *mohar* or a half *mohar.* One rupee each is given to all the other relatives of the boy, but his father and grandfather get a whole or half a *mohar* according to the status of the family. The girl's party are not served with refreshments. The boy's parents then celebrate the *bháji.* In the case of a *májú* there is no *pair páná,* strictly speaking, nor is there in that of a *saukan* (second wife when the first is still alive). In the latter case as much secrecy as is possible is observed by the boy's people.

SECTION 6.—HINDU MARRIAGE OBSERVANCES.

Among Hindus marriage is of two kinds, regular and irregular. The former is a sacrament and in theory indissoluble, so that formal

A few days before the wedding on an auspicious day the *dhang* and *milni* ceremony is observed. On this occasion too the girl's people send 51 trays of *laḍḍu* &c. with a big *chāṭi* full of *dahi* (whey) to the boy's house. No females accompany these trays, only males doing so. They are met in an open space by the men of the boy's party, assembled there for the purpose. The *milni* (= to meet) is now performed, the girl's party standing on one side and the boy's on the other. To begin with the girl's people present money to the boy's through their *parohit* commencing with Rs. 3 and rising by odd numbers, 5, 7 &c. to Rs. 17. Then the girl's people present jewellery and this is followed by the *salámi*, which involves the gift of a rupee by the girl's relatives to each of the boy's. At the *milni* the kinsmen formally meet one another, and the boy his father-in-law to be. On the wedding night the girl's people send a mare to the boy's house to fetch him. After the necessary *púja* in his house, he dons a *mukaṭ* and then he and his *sarbála* (a boy under 10 years of age and closely related to the bridegroom) don clothes specially prescribed and march out of the house after the *tambol* has been taken. The boy carries a sword in his hand. The boy then mounts the mare with the *sarbála* behind him. The mare is fed on *dál*. The boy's sister then holds the reins of the mare and refuses to release these until she gets some money as *wag phaṛái* (= to catch the reins). She sings the following song :—

Kí kuchh dena vírá wág phaṛái
Kí kuchh vírá dál chardi.

'Brother dear ! how much would you give me for catching the reins ?
Dear brother, how much would you give me for feeding your mare on *dál* ?'

The boy and his *sarbála* then ride off to the girl's home accompanied by a couple of friends and a servant. On dismounting at it he is beaten with thin sticks (*tíli márna*) by little girls who sing :—

Sas puchhdí, jawái mera kehṛa,
Jide hath gáná sir sehra.
"The mother-in-law asks : 'who is my son-in-law ?'
One with a *gáná* round his wrist and a garland of flowers on his head."

This done the girl's relatives try to put a *lahnghá* (an old skirt) round the boy's neck, but he resists in every possible way, being helped in this by the friends who had accompanied him. If the girl's relatives succeed it is anticipated that the boy will always remain obedient to the girl, otherwise it will be the other way round. This over, the boy goes into the house marching under a sieve with a lamp in it which he knocks over with his sword. He is then accommodated in a room till the time for the *láwán* comes. In this room he is surrounded by girls and other females of the bride's family, who jest with him getting him to bow down before an old shoe of the girl wrapped in red cloth which is represented to him as a goddess but the boy does not always submit to this as he has been warned by his mother, sister &c. against such traps. When the time for the *láwán* draws nigh, he goes to the *bedi*, and is seated on a *khárá* turned upside down with the girl similarly seated alongside him. Here too a number of small girls behind him try to beat him with tiny wooden boxes called *ḍabbián márná* and annoy him with various tricks. He tries to snatch from them as many of the *ḍabbíá* as he can.

The wedding rite having been gone through the *khatpújná* is performed. In this the bride and bridegroom are seated on a bed with everything that forms a part of the dowry on it. The boy is asked by the bride's kinswomen to recite some *chhands* and for these he is paid a rupee each.

The *chhands* are :—
Chhand paráge di jái chhand práge kesar.
Sas meri Párbati, sauhra merá Parmeshar.

After this the girl is taken to the *ḍoli*, but before doing so the following song which moves every body to tears is sung :

Lai challe bábalá lai challe wai.

Mainán ḍoli pa kahár bábalá lai challe wai.

Rakh lai bábalá rakh lai wai.

Mainán rakh hun dihára chár

Hun ki bábal tera dáwa.

Was pardí kíra dáwa,

divorce is not recognized. The latter is a civil as opposed to a religious union and is often dissoluble in practice. Thus there are, as it were,

"Father dear! they are taking me away!
Father dear! the *kahárs* are taking me away in a *doli*!
Father dear, father dear! Keep me with you, do keep me with you.
Keep me a little longer!
Father dear! you can claim me no more!
I belong to some one else, your claim now is false."

When the bride has been seated in the *doli* often with a little girl beside her, she goes on crying. The *doli* is carried a few paces by her nearest relatives and then by the *kahárs*, the bridegroom going in front of it.

A few days before the marriage singing parties are invited to their houses by the parents of the pair. They consist of females only and sing at night when they are served with light refreshments. The songs sung at the girl's house are called *sohág* and those at the boy's *ghoriáṇ*.

Sohág.

Desáṇ da rájá báp chhaḍiá, mahláṇ rání máṇ,
Paṭṭi likhda vir chhaḍiá, chhaḍiá sab parwár.

"I am leaving now my father, king of many a kingdom, and my mother, queen of many a palace!

I am leaving my dear brother who writes on *paṭṭis*. I am leaving the whole family."

Ghoriáṇ.

Sir tere naurangia chírá, kalgí dí ajab bahár.
Pair tere makhmal dí juti turnáe pabbáṇ de bhár.

The Lohṛí festival.

A month or so before the Lohṛi small boys and girls go from house to house begging for wood and cowdung cakes which they collect till the Lohṛí night when a big bon-fire is lit and the girls sing:—

Soṭí soṭí wai lokaṛio soṭí sí,
Rab deve Mohan Lál tsinúṇ wauṭi sí.
Is wauṭí dí vel wadhai ṣí.
Ghar baihiáṇ wán sakkí bhábí di sí.
Pá mái pá kále kutte núṇ wí pá.
Kálá kuttá de duáṇ, teriáṇ jíwaṇ majhi gáiṇ.
Mohmdi de ke já dáhṛi phul pawá ke já.
Dáhṛi teri hari bhari, motiáṇ nál jaṛi bhari.
The boys sing—
Suṭ gohá, khá khoyá.
Suṭ lakaṛ, khá shakar.
Isa O! Isa khol bhái khisa.
Hilna O! hilna, ai ke hilna.
"If you cast cow-dung cake you will get *khoya* to eat.
If you throw wood you will get sugar to eat.
Brother dear! open your purse!
We won't move till we get something!"
Sádí waṭṭí dae ní mási lumaṛai.
Sáde chúhe kha ní mási lumaṛai.
"Give us our turn! aunt fox!
Eat up our rats! aunt fox?"

degrees of marriage, with something like corresponding degrees of legitimacy.

Of the eight ancient (so called) forms of Hindu marriage traces still survive. Thus in Gurdáspur it is said that the *Brahmana* form is still observed by Brahmans and Khatrís, while among Játs marriage generally takes place according to the *asura* form, in which a pecuniary is struck.[1] In Baháwalpur also the Brahm *biáh* in which the bride's father so far from receiving a price for her gives her as much as he can afford is in vogue among the higher classes, while among the lower the *asur biáh* is practised. In the latter the girl's father receives a consideration, no doubt, but neither in Gurdáspur nor in Baháwalpur does there appear to be any real difference in the ritual of these two kinds of marriage. Both are called *biáh* in Baháwalpur, and such differences as exist are matters of caste, *i.e.* social and not ritual.

In the hills the names of one or two of the old forms are said to be still in use Thus in Kulu marriage is said to be of three kinds: (*i*) *bedi biáh*, the ordinary Hindu forms; (*ii*) *ruti mandi*, 4 or 5 men go from the bridegroom to the bride's house, dress her up, put a cap on her head, and then bring her home to the bridegroom; (*iii*) *Ganesh púja*, the form used by Brahmans, Khatrís, Sunárs (goldsmiths), etc. in marrying a Kanet girl.[2] But another account distinguishes the three forms as *Brahm*, *gandharb* and *gharbiáh*, and a third classifies the usage in vogue thus:—

(*i*) Brahm
(*ii*) Arsh (*asura*) } By the twice born castes and Kanets.

(*iii*) Gandharb, by low castes.

Side by side with these are current four forms of customary marriage, *viz.*—

1. *Ghar-biáh*, performed at the house of either party.
2. *ruti mandi*, in which the bridegroom accompanied by 4 or 5 kinsmen goes to the bride's house and brings her home.
3. *madkhúia*, concubinage.
4. *randol*, widow-remarriage.

These four forms are more or less observed in all tribes. In Nos. (*iii*) 1 and 2 Ganesh worship is necessary; whereas in Nos. 3 and 4 a goat or sheep is sacrificed and kinsmen are feasted. The inconsistencies in these accounts show how fluid the customs in Kulu have become, and before describing any of the forms it will be convenient to glance at the classifications in vogue elsewhere in the hills.

[1] P. C. L., xii, p. 7.

[2] P. C. L., ii, p. 185.

In Chamba the Gaddís recognise only three forms, *bidh*, *i.e.* regular marriage, *jindphuka*,[1] and *jhanjarira* or widow-remarriage. But in the Churáh *wizárat* of that State regular marriage would seem to be either (1) *jandi* or (*ii*) *sir gaddi*[2]; corresponding to the *jindphuka* is the *man-marzi* or marriage made by a couple of their own free will; while widow-remarriage is called *bandha lána*.[3]

The term *Jhanjrára* is used for the remarriage of a widow in Kángra and Kulu as well as in Chamba. But in Sirmúr 'regular' marriage is termed *jhajra*, in contradistinction to *rít* or marriage with a woman purchased from her former husband—the *madkhúla* of Kulu; but the *jhajra* is not the orthodox Brahmanical marriage, which is all but unknown in the trans-Giri part of Sirmúr. *Jhajra* is in fact solemnised without the *phera* and is thus performed: After the betrothal the bridegroom's father or in his absence any near relative with two or three other persons goes to the bride's house, taking with him a *nath*, some dresses, and as many ornaments as he wishes to present to her. The *pandit* reads certain *mantras* at an auspicious moment and the women sing the wedding songs. Then the *pandit* puts the *nath* into the bride's nose; and after that *gur* or sugar is distributed among those present. When this is over the bride puts on a red dress and follows the visitors to her husband's house, one or two relatives accompanying her. At an auspicious hour fixed by the *pandit* she enters her husband's house in which a pitcher of water has been placed, with quaint figures painted on the walls and an (earthen) lamp put near them. The bride and bridegroom are made to sit in front of these and incense is burned. *Gur* or sugar is then given to the bridegroom and he puts it in bride's palm and she eats it. In the same manner the bride gives *gur* to the bridegroom and he too eats it. This completes the marriage and the custom is called *gharautni*. Two or three days after this the bride's father goes to the bridegroom's house, accompanied by his friends and relatives to the number of 300 to 400, and the party are entertained there, first with sweet food and then with meat. No entertainment, however, is given if the bride's father has taken compensation for bringing her up. The whole ceremony is called *jhajra*.

Apparently then *jhajra* means 'putting the *nath* or nose-ring in the bride's nose,' but to the west, *i.e.* in Kulu and Kángra the term has come to be applied to widow-remarriage.

[1] It appears to be also called *jar phuka* and is solemnised by burning a *karjora* or *kahmali* bush, *i.e.* by setting light to the bush and tying the end of the bride's sheet to the bridegroom's woollen girdle and going round the fire eight times. This form is only permissible in the case of an educated girl marrying her paramour, or when the bride's parents will not consent to the marriage though they gave their consent to the contract of betrothal. It is celebrated by the mutual concurrence of the bride and bridegroom, and no priest or relations are required to attend its celebration.

[2] At a *jandi* wedding 5 or 7 men accompany the bridegroom to his father-in-law's house and there give the members of the bride's party Rs. 3 and a he-goat: in a *sir guddi* double that amount is paid, but not always accepted, and the bridegroom is only accompanied by 3 men. In both forms a rupee is given to the bride for her *bandha*, an ornament.

Jandi appears to mean presents: in Kulu it means presents made to members of the *bardt* or wedding party

Sir guddi means 'plaiting the hair' and is an incident in formal marriage.

[3] *Bandha lána*, lit. to put on the *bandha*, the ornament which distinguishes a married woman.

Ritual marriage in the hills—In Kulu the *parohit* is sent for and given sweets and money. He then fixes an auspicious date for the wedding and prepares a *lakhnotari* or programme. This he takes to the bride's house and expounds to her family. The day once fixed cannot be changed even if a death occur in either family. In Chamba among the Gaddís after the *parohit* has fixed a day two men are sent to the girl's house with some *ghí* and if her people approve of it messengers from both sides go to the *parohit* and get him to prepare the *lakhnotari*.

2. *Naming the day.*—When both the parties are ready for the wedding an astrologer is asked to examine their horoscopes and fix a propitious time for the ceremony. The wedding is generally celebrated at night but in special cases it is performed during the day (*hathlewá*).

3. *Investiture with the sacred thread.*—In the twice-born castes (Brahman, Kshatria and Vaisya) the boy must be invested with the sacred thread before the wedding can take place.

4. *Pera.*—This is the first of the wedding ceremonies. *Pera* is made of *másh* or pulse, finely ground, called *piṭhi*. The bridegroom takes his seat on a wooden plate and the help of the principal deities is invoked, especially that of the goddess of wealth, who is represented by a current coin. This coin is used in every rite and is carefully preserved. After the marriage is over these deities are represented by images made of flour. *Piṭhi* is distributed among all the relative and friends, with a sweetmeat made out of it.

5. *Lagan.*—The bride's father sends to the other party clothes, jewels, cash, and cattle according to his circumstances. Among the Hill Rájpúts these presents are made by the bridegroom's father.

6. *Sáhá chiṭṭhi.*—A letter fixing the date for the wedding and settling the number of followers in the bridal party is despatched by the bride's father.[1]

7. *Macha.*—A barber is sent by the boy's father to measure the girl for her wedding garments.[2]

8. *Brahma bhoj*—Sweetmeats and cash are distributed among the Brahmans of the place. The distribution is three-fold, (1) per head; (2) per family; (3) per branch of that family.[3]

9. *Del.*—A distribution of money among Brahmans and barbers, each of whom receives so many *dels* or shares according to the number of relatives he may be connected with, in some instances one man getting as many as 60 *dels*. Barbers get half as much as Brahmans. In the trans-Sutlej districts the ceremony is called *thámа*, and the

[1] Among the Khatrís and Brahmans of Gurdáspur along with the '*sáhá chiṭṭhi*' are sent some cash, from Re. 1 to Rs. 250 in amount, ornaments and clothes for the *kurmani* (boy's mother): also a *katora* (cup) resembling a *tabalbáz*, some *misri* (refined sugar), a cocoanut and a rupee for the boy These articles are known as the *tikka*. The boy's parents give the bearer of the *chiṭṭhi* a bag containing bits of cocoanut, almonds, dried dates &c. weighing at most 20 *sers*. They also give the bearer a *bid* (gift) for the girl.

[2] Now-a-days in Gurdáspur the girl's boy's parents with the *sáhá chiṭṭhi* send the boy's parents a *mauli* as a *macha* or measure for the preparation of the girl's garments.

[3] These offerings are made not only at weddings, but on all auspicious occasions of a similar nature.

number of *dels* is fixed at 252 altogether.

The minimum rate per *del* is a quarter of an anna and the maximum one rupee among persons of ordinary means; and the bridegroom's father is put to ruinous expenditure on that ceremony which arises solely from a desire for ostentation. (This custom prevails generally among the Kaláls.)

10. *Hath bhrx, chonk ulanga.*—This ceremony is observed by the women only. The bridegroom's mother or in her absence his nearest kinswoman, after bathing, dons new clothes and passes over the place where her son has performed the rites mentioned above. She then effaces the flour images used in them and stamps her handprint over the house door. It is considered a disastrous omen if any one save the mother or nearest kinswoman pass over the place in question.

11. *Máián.*—The bridegroom after performing the usual religious rites is made to sit on a wooden stool. The near relatives rub perfumed oil and a fragrant substance called *baṭna* over his face, and he is supplied with a weapon to guard himself from sudden attack; he is girt with an auspicious thread called the *kangna*, and from this time he is never left alone till the wedding is over. On this day too four small earthen vessels are hung up by a string in the middle of the courtyard of the house, and in these some medicines &c. are placed to purify the air, and to protect the house from evil spirits or enchantments. In Gurdáspur the kinswomen assemble and 5 or 7 of them whose husbands are alive oil the bridegroom or bride, as the case may be. This ceremony is also called *tel charhána*, 'to apply oil.' *Waṭna* or *baṭna* is also rubbed on their bodies. On the same day *pakauṛás* (lumps of flour) sweetened and fried and rice are distributed among the kindred, and the *kangna* or *gána*, a coloured thread, is tied round the bridegroom's right wrist.

These ceremonies are performed by both the families concerned.

12. *Chakki chung, kothi áṭa &c.*—The special millstone which is to be used to prepare the marriage feast is tested by some women of the family, who join in grinding a little corn in it in order to ensure that it is not impregnated with any poisonous substance. They in like manner examine the place where the flour and corn to be used in the wedding are kept. These are precautionary measures for the safety of the guests invited on the occasion.

There are also some other minor ceremonies observed by the women.

In Gurdáspur 5¼ *sers* of wheat are ground on an auspicious day. The flour being put in an earthen vessel (*kothi*) which is also decked with a thread (*mauli*), and some of it is mixed with the flour meant for use of the wedding party. The hand-mill, in which the wheat was ground, is also decked with a *mauli*.

13. *Shánt.*—This ceremony is performed on the morning of the wedding day. The bridegroom takes *nalu*, and the help of certain deities is invoked, so that no misfortune may befall during the continuance of the marriage. He dons a gorgeous red dress with a crown (*mukaṭ*) and a garland of gold or lace on his head. All his kinsmen and friends pronounce blessings on him and money, called *bhur*, is distributed

among the Brahmans present. A boy relative of the bridegroom is made his *sarbálá*, and if the bridegroom die the bride is wedded to the *sarbálá*, as her marriage must never be postponed, under any circumstances whatsoever, when she has once gone through the ceremony of *jal charhánά*.

14. *Ghorí charhna, jandi káṭná.* – In the evening the bridegroom proceeds to the bride's house with his *sarbálá* riding on a horse, the whole wedding procession following him. On his way he cuts a branch of a *jand* tree with a sword. *Aphar* is made on this occasion.

In Gurdáspur after the boy has mounted the mare the women sing songs and some cash (as *siráwára*) is waved round his head and then distributed among the *lágís* etc.

The first day in the bride's house.

15. *Júṭhá ṭikka.*—While the *barát* is waiting outside the town this rite is performed. A line (*ṭikka*) is drawn in saffron on the bridegroom's forehead, the residue being sent for the use of the bride. The object is that she may always remain obedient to her husband. Then some respectable persons of the town proceed in token of respect towards the *barát* to conduct them to the place appointed for their residence. *Afshár* is now made.

16. *Bateri.*—On the first evening some uncooked food and sweetmeats are sent by the father of the bride for the bridal party's dinner. A small quantity of sweetmeat is sent back to the bride after the bridegroom has eaten of it.

17. *Milní.*—At twilight the wedding party goes to the bride's house, some of whose inmates appoach and receive it with due respect. First *sarnasár* is interchanged between the parties, and then an elderly kinsman of the girl presents *nazar* to the boy's father or other kinsman; sometimes a horse, cow or she-buffalo is given. This occasion is celebrated with fire-works and dancing, and the front of the house is illuminated. This done the bridegroom enters his future father-in-law's house, and the rest of the party return to their abode.

The real rite according to the *shástrás* is that the girl herself should come forward and present a *nazar* to her lord as a mark of obedience. But this custom is not now observed, as the marriage is celebrated in her childhood.

18. *Chánní jorna*—An examination of the bridegroom to see whether he is an expert marksman or not. A *chánní* with a lamp burning in it is hung in the middle of the doorway, and the boy takes it out with a sword.

19. *Ghorí.*—Before the bridegroom enters the house the bride is brought outside the door where she meets him, kneels and makes him an obeisance as a token of homage. Under the existing custom she is wrapped up in a blanket and taken under the bridegroom's horse.

20. *Jhilṛián.*—Some married women go and bring water from a neighbouring well, singing wedding songs. With some of this water they make the bride bathe, and the rest is put into small mud vessels with which they make the bridegroom undergo certain ceremonies, intended to test his physical dexterity and capacity. The boy is further made to

utter some rough verses called *chands*, for each of which he is given presents in cash by the kinswomen of the bride.

According to religious doctrines either the girl's brother or a learned Brahman should be present to examine the boy at the betrothal, and he should then address these words to him in presence of the assembly : " My father or *yajmán* (as the case may be) will bestow his daughter on you in marriage subject to the following conditions :— (1) that you bathe before the nuptial rites in order to prove that you are free from all dangerous diseases ; (2) that there is no defect in any of your organs : (3) that your manners are gentle and your life blameless ; and (4) that you are not impotent."

This custom, however, is now dropped.

21. *Suhág-paṭṭári, satsaroch.*—The bridegroom sends the following articles for the bride as a first gift :—

(1) A looking glass ; (2) a comb ; (3) perfumed oil ; (4) saffron ; (5) jewels ; (6) a shawl.

This is to signify that in future she will have to adorn herself only with what he may from time to time provide. Some sandalwood, medicines and spices are also sent with them, to express the hope that she may enjoy worldly pleasures with him in perfect health and happiness.

22. *The nuptial fire.*—In the courtyard of the house is erected a quadrangular structure of young trees framed in a square and prettily decorated with split and festooned leaves. This is called *bedi* and this rite is performed under it.

A priest, conversant with the Vedás, ignites the sacred fire and pours into it with due *mantars* a libation of clarified butter. Then the father of the bride welcomes the bridegroom in the prescribed form by offering water to wash his feet and by the well-known oblation called the *arghya*. He then gives his daughter's hand to the boy thrice, reciting a holy *mantar*. This time both the boy and girl are installed on two separate stools, and for the first time see each other's faces. The boy afterwards worships according to the ordinance the fire compound, and taking his wife's hand by general invocation prays to the principal deities that they both may pass their lives in comfort, faithful to each other, and that their union may be blessed with healthy children. Both then walk round the nuptial fire, the wife holding the hem of her husband's garments, to call to witness that effulgent light which pervades every quarter of the globe, that neither in thought, deed or word will either swerve from the path of duty. The husband then sprinkles holy water on his wife, and invokes that element that she may ever remain chaste and gentle and that her eyes, heart and mind may be his and his hers always.

A number of Vedic *mantars* are recited on this occasion, invoking the help of the Natural Power, personified in different gods, as well as beseeching the one Universal Spirit pervading all to bless the married pair. From these *mantars* it appears that marriage among the Aryans is not a civil contract,[1] but a spiritual union of two souls for

[1] As in Islám

their worldly happiness, the propagation of the race, the performance of the sacred sacrifices, the attainment of true knowledge of the secrets of nature, and the final absorption of the soul in the Absolute Soul, the source of all existence, conscientiousness and bliss, marriage for the mere satisfaction of lust being held abominable. It was for that reason that the Arya Shástrás prohibited remarriage of widows, for ties once consecrated by Vedic ceremonies were considered indissoluble for ever.

23. *Lassi pair.*—At the time when the nuptial rites are being performed, the mother of the bridegroom in her own house, in company with other relatives of the same sex, puts her feet in water mixed with milk. She then asks the old women to give her son and daughter-in-law their blessings that as the milk is mingled with the water so they may ever live in loving kindness one with another.

The second day in the bride's house.

24. *Mitha bhat.*—In the afternoon the marriage party is entertained with a feast worthy alike of the guests and the host. Various kinds of sweetmeats are laid out in an oval form over a white *chaddar.*[1] Before they commence eating a senior male relative from the girl's side presents a *nazar* and sweetmeats to the father or a near kinsman of the boy. (This custom is not practised among the Hill Rájpúts.) Each of them eats separately out of *pattals* made of leaves. At night supper is supplied.

The third day in the bride's house.

The bridal party is entertained in the same manner as before.

25. *Vará súi.*—In the evening costly costumes, beautiful gold and silver ornaments, prepared for the bride, are sent to her, as well as some *hennah,* almonds and cocoanuts. The pomp displayed on this occasion is proportioned to the wealth of the family. The parents of girl keep some of these articles for immediate use and the rest are sent back.

26. *Khat* (dowry).—Under the existing custom parents supply their daughter and son-in-law with all household furniture, such as clothes, kitchen utensils, cash, jewels, bedstead, razáis, carpets, cattle,—in short with every necessary article. These are kept outside for some time for the public view. The boy and girl are then made to sit on a bed, when with an eloquent and clear voice the fathers of both the parties pronounce blessing on the girl in these words :—'Be thou unto thy husband as Sita [2] unto Ráma, Rukmani [2] unto Krishn, Damodri [2] unto Ráwan, Sachi[2] unto Indr, &c.' [3]

[1] In Gurdáspur this usage is also called *kharki.* The rest of the sweets is given to the bridegroom's barber. Similarly on the second day the *barát* is entertained with sweets called *bina bhat*, the residue being given to the bride's barber. The sweets served on the third day are called *danda.*

[2] These heroines were famous for their chastity and attachment to their lords.

[3] At the *khat* in Gurdáspur the bridal pair are seated on the couch given to the bridegroom in dower, and Ganesh and the nine *garahas* are worshipped. Then the bride's father presents (as *sankalp*) the bridegroom with all the ornaments, clothes, untensils, sweets, etc., which he means to give his daughter in dower having regard to his means. Then the heads of the pair are made to touch each other (a usage called *sir jori*) and a rupee is waved round their heads and given to the barber. The *barát* or wedding party then departs.

27. *Dákhila.*—When the bridal party returns home, on their arrival in the town the procession moves slowly through the bazár with great splendour. The boy mounted on a horse proceeds first and the wife is borne after him in a *doli.*[1] Among the Hill Rájpúts the girl is carried first. *Apshar* is made at this time.

When the couple approach the house some women of the family receive them with due honour. The mother waves a cup of water seven times round her son and daughter-in-law, which she then drinks. This means that she, with pleasure and for her son's love, takes on herself every misfortune that may in future time befall either of them.

28. *Til khelna.*—The senior relatives of the boy in succession put a handful of sesamum into the hands of the girl, which she returns to them at once.

This ceremony signifies that they wish the bride to bear children as numerous as the sesamum seeds which fall to the ground. Then the women sing :—

Jitne dharti til giresi,

Utne bauhti put janesi.

'May the bride bear as many sons as sesamum seeds have fallen to the ground.'

29. *Bari háth dálná.*—A purse containing money is made over to the wife. She is at liberty to take any amount out of it to spend at her pleasure. The signification of this rite is that the husband entrusts to the care of his wife all his worldly goods. She then promises that she will spend nothing without his knowledge.

30. *God lená larke ká* (to adopt a son).—A little boy is made to sit in the lap of the newly married girl, as a sign that she may also be a mother of sons. She then presents *nazars* to the elder relatives of her husband, and in return gets presents and clothes from them.

31. *Got kúndla.*—To convert the new girl into her husband's *got* all the women of the family, including the girl, eat together rice and sweetmeat out of the same dish.

32. *Sat horá.*—The mud vessels that are hung in the middle of the house are now taken out.

33. *Kangna khelná.*—The sacred thread with which the waists of the husband and wife are encircled are now taken off and put into a large dish, when each of them tries to take possession of it and to achieve victory over the other. This is the last rite of marriage.

34. *Mukláwá.*—After a stay of few days the girl returns to her father's house. The husband with some servants after a period varying from one to three years from the date of marriage goes to take her back. His father-in-law on this occasion supplies him with some clothes and jewels.

[1] In Gurdáspur this observance is also called *wápasi* or returning and the rite of waving the cup round the boy's and girl's heads is known as *pání wárna.*

SECTION 7.—MUHAMMADAN BETROTHAL OBSERVANCES.

Terminology.

Among Muhammadans 'betrothal' is known as *mangewá*, *mangni*, *mangan* (and other forms of that word,[1] which literally means 'asking' or 'begging'). It is also called *sagái*, especially in the south-east, and *kurmái*.[2] Another term is *ropná*, which literally means the present or token consisting of seven dried dates and various other things sent by a (Hindu) girl's father to his prospective son-in-law at or before the betrothal. It corresponds to the *shagún*[3] among the higher castes, *e.g.* in Hoshiárpur. The Arabic word *nisbat* is also used, chiefly in the towns. Another common term is *nátta* or *nátá*, which has a somewhat derogatory meaning, so that *nátá dená* means to give girl in marriage, an admission of inferiority in status. The bridegroom is styled *mangedar* or *mangetar*,[4] a term also applied to a betrothed girl, while *bendhá* is used in the south-east. In the north-east he is called *dúlo*, or *dulhá*, or *naushâh*,[5] *nausho*, *naušá*, or *naudho* being variant forms of the latter word, and in Gujránwálá *lárá* is also used. In the Talagang tahsíl of Jhelum he is called *nadha* and his bride is *kuri*, literally a girl or a virgin. In the south-west *ghot* is in common use.

The bride is correspondingly *bendháni*, *dulhan*, or *kwár* in the south-west, and after she is married *nodh* or *bahú*.[6] The latter term means literally son's wife.

In the Pashto of Pesháwar betrothal is called *koyidán*. The bridegroom is called *changhál* and the bride *chunghalá*. During the days of marriage the *changhúl* and *chunghalá* are respectively called *khâwand* and *náwí*.

The boy's father is particularly, and the boy's kinsmen are generally, called *putreta*. Similarly the girl's father or party is *dheta*.

Preliminaries in betrothal.

In Arabia, it is said, marriage is usually adult, and it is not regarded as indecent that the bridegroom should see his future wife, but the seclusion of women in India renders this impossible, at least among the better classes. In consequence a *máshshâta* or go-between is often employed to spy on the girl and report on her looks etc. to the boy's people. These go-betweens assume various disguises, such as cloth-sellers, in order to obtain access to the girl's house, while, on the other hand, a girl is not infrequently substituted for the one seen and reported

[1] *E.g.* *mangarn* in the Rájanpur tahsíl of Dera Gházi Khán.

[2] Fr. *kuram*, 'a relation of marriage.'

[3] Or *shagan*, lit. 'an omen.'

[4] *Man ge ata*, from *man ge ati* is also used.

[5] This word appears to mean 'new king.'

[6] See Maya Singh's *Punjabi Dicty.*

on by the go-between. Unpleasantness not unnaturally frequently results from such a deception. In theory Muhammadan law attaches great importance to mutual consent in marriage, but in India the practice is very often opposed to allowing even grown-up girls to express any opinion on a proposed betrothal. In fact, among the Muhammadans of Delhi there is a custom of pre-natal betrothal which is called *ṭhikri kí máng*,[1] because, if a girl be born according to anticipation, the boy's mother drops a rupee into the girl baby's bath or mixes sugarcandy in the *ghuṭṭi* given to her, as an earnest of the betrothal contract thus ratified. In Rohtak a boy's mother or any near kinswoman may drop a rupee into the vessel used by a midwife, and by so doing apparently bespeaks the new-born girl for her son. The betrothal is there and then announced and congratulations are exchanged.

Contrary to the usual practice amongst Hindús, the proposal among Muhammadans comes almost invariably from the boy's side. The term *bátáná bat-jáná*, to propose, is used when negotiations are opened by the boy's people. When both sides are satisfied as to the suitability of the match a day is fixed 'for sweetening the mouth' (*múṇh miṭhá karne ká din*), and on that day a number of women, with a few men of the boy's family, go to the girl's house to perform the betrothal rites.[2] In the Sangrúr tahsíl of Jínd the request by the boy's father is called *dhuk* and he visits the girl's father in the evening. The *duá-i-khair* is then observed, the senior member of the boys's party commencing the prayer.

In Dera Ghází Khán the negotiations which precede a betrothal are called *sawál* or 'request,' and may take place a month or more before the betrothal is solemnised.

The negotiations are, however, not infrequently opened by the girl's people among the rural classes who are converts from Hinduism. Thus among the Meos of Guṛgáon the girl's party first visits the boy's father, and reaches his house on the evening of an auspicious day in the lunar month. If they find the boy to their liking they are feasted, after giving a rupee each to the boy, his father, brother, father's sister, and his *mírási* and barber. The party is also feasted on the 2nd and third days, after which it sets out for its home, giving the boy's parents Rs. 11 or 22 as a farewell gift. Of this sum a rupee is left in the vessel in which it was presented; the barber and *mírási* take one rupee and the balance is given to the poor. The girl's father in turn gives a rupee to the boy's father. This is called *miláp*. Among other Muhammadans the observances vary. A ring or two is often sent to the boy, with other presents, and the rings are put on by the boy amongst his assembled kinsmen.[3] A ring is often presented in sugar, and the kinsmen feasted with more or less ceremony.

[1] Fr. *ṭhikra*, an earthen vessel. *Máng*, asking.

[2] This paragraph applies to Delhi city.

[3] The barber is given rice, *ghí*, and sugar, but nothing containing salt should be offered him on this occasion.

When such a negotiation is initiated by the girl's father certain special observances may occur. Thus in Siálkot a *mírási*, barber, or even a Brahman, is sent to the *putreta* or boy's father, and when he reaches his house a little oil is dropped on the threshold before he enters it. This observance is called *tel dálná*. The *putreta's lágis* also assemble, and the *dhetá's lági* is given some sugar in a plate, from which he takes a little in his mouth. This observance is called *munh juthláwná* or *juthálná* or *juthalnna* = to defile: *P. D.*, p. 522. Then the *lági* is given *khichri*. He eats some of it and drops a rupee and some copper coins in the plate. These are distributed among the *putretá's lágis*. Next day the boy's kinsmen feast the *lági* on rice and sugar or mutton and bread. At the *zuhr* prayer carpets are spread in the boy's house and the whole brotherhood assemble. The boy is seated in front of the *lági*, who gives him from Re. 1 to Rs. 25 as well as a date or sugarcandy to eat. Then he exchanges congratulations with them and observes the *niyat khair*. After this all present congratulate the boy's father. The *dhetá's lági* presents a sum varying from Re. 1 to Rs. 11 for distribution among the boy's *kamíns*. The boy's people also distribute *tapásás* of sugar among the people on this occasion. Some well-to-do Jats and Rájpút families also send a camel, a horse, and ornaments such as bangles or *butkián*[1] for the boy's mother. This is called *tikká bhejná*. On this occasion drums &c. are beaten in the boy's father's house. The persons present on the occasion give a rupee each to the boy's father to be given to the *lági*. On the *lági's* departure the boy's father gives them as *wadáigi* from Rs. 4 to Rs. 8, which is divided into four shares, three being given to the *lágis* named above and the fourth to the *lági* of the maternal relatives. No mention is made on this occasion regarding the date of the wedding.

A very few wealthy families in Gujránwála also observe this custom of sending a *tikka*, but in a slightly different way. It consists in sending a barber, a *mírási*, a Brahman, and a tailor, with a horse, a camel, clothes for the boy and his parents, a gold finger-ring for the boy, Rs. 21 in cash, five lumps of candy, and some dried dates. On the arrival of the *lágis* named, the boy's father invites his kinsfolk to his house and displays the gifts mentioned. Congratulations are then exchanged and *tapásás* distributed among those present. Rs. 2 to 5 are given to each of the bride's *lágis*, and they are then sent back. Various intermediaries are employed in the preliminary negotiation. Thus in the Bhakkar tahsíl of Míánwáli, on the Indus, a Sayyid, *maulavi*, *faqír*, or any respectable elder, is sent to the girl's father by the boy's to make a request (*dhukná*) for her hand. If it is meant to accept it an ambiguous answer is given until the proposal has been repeated four or five times. Meanwhile the boy's kinswomen begin visiting the girl's family with presents, and finally the offer is accepted provided the parties be related or the boy's father promises compensation or a girl in exchange. In the Leiah tahsíl of this district among the leading families, almost all Syyids and dominant Baloch, the first step to take when a boy reaches a marrying age is to send a *dhuk* or embassy of picked members of the family to the girl's father. His refusal will be definite,

[1] *Budki*, a gold coin worth Rs. 5: *P.D.*, p. 168.

not to say abrupt, but his acceptance ostensibly reluctant and well-considered. The families now begin to associate, but the girl veils herself from all the males of her intended husband's family.

But in Hazára generally no intermediary is employed save the barber, and he is not called when the parties belong to the same brotherhood, for then the womenfolk arrange matters. In Peshâwar an elderly kinswoman of the boy acts as *dalála*, or go-between, and it is only when she has succeeded in securing a bride for him that a *jirga* of Sayyids and *ulamas* is sent to the girl's parents. If they are wealthy they put off the *jirga* twice or thrice before finally consenting.

Even after these preliminary negotiations the final betrothal does not always take place at once. Thus in Bhakkar and Leiah a few days after the negotiations have closed the boy's people go to the girl's house and formally present her father with a few gold or silver ornaments for her use, and after the *duá-i-khair* has been repeated distribute sweetstuff. This observance is called *nishâni*, or 'token.' In Bhakkar the boy's father is said to place a ring on her finger and a *bhochhan* or sheet on her head, and this is called *nishâni*. The betrothal follows a month or two later. But among the Utmánzais in Hazára the *nishâni* only precedes the betrothal by a couple of days, and is observed in rather a curious way: the boy's party takes present to the girl's village. After nightfall they are invited to her house, and the *mírási* brings a plate, into which the boy's father puts the ornaments. Of these the girl's father takes two or three by way of *nishâni*, and then the betrothal is announced, the *duá-i-khair* recited, and congratulations exchanged. The *mírási's* fee for this service varies from Rs. 4 to 8, twice that of the barber, so the part he plays must be regarded as important. The boy's teacher gets from Rs. 1 to 5. Among the Jadúns in this district the *nishâni* appears to be the betrothal itself, for when a match has been arranged the boy's father sends food—called *jirga ki roti*—to the girl's and then pays a visit (*jirga*), which must be made on a Monday or a Friday, and by night, to her house. The *jirga* or visitors are then fed, and a barber presents sugar in a plate to one of its members. He drops Rs. 30, 50, or whatever the girl's father demands, into it and the barber carries it into the house. The girl's father accepts part of the money and returns the rest. The *duá-i-khair* is then recited, and a rupee [1] given to the mosque. A barber then gives the boy's kinsmen in a cup (*katora*), into which they drop a rupee. In another cup *mehndi* is brought, and this is applied to each man by way of *nishâni*. Another rupee is dropped into this cup also. Within a week of the *jirga's* departure, some of the boy's kinsmen take a sweetmeat called *pakwán* to the girl's house, where they spend the night. The return visit is called *milni*. At the next 'Id the boy's parents send the girl clothes and uncooked food, with an ornament if well-to-do, and similar presents are sent on every 'Id and Shab Barát until the wedding.

In Peshâwar also the *nishâni* is the *nátá* or betrothal. When the last *jirga* has obtained a definite promise of the girl, a body of the

[1] Called *duá ká rupia.*

boy's kinsmen go to the girl's house, and take one to seven ornaments with them as *nishání*. When they arrive they are seated on a carpet, and the barber brings a *patnos* into which each puts some money. The ornaments, too, are put in, and then the *patnos* is sent inside to the girl's womenfolk. The amount of money agreed upon and the *nishání* are kept, and the *patnos* with the balance sent out again to the boy's kinsmen. The betrothal is completed by the father paying certain fees to the barber, the *imám* of the mosque, and the *mutrib*. On the third day after this the girl's parents send the boy a ring and a suit of clothes—a gift called *jorá*—and at each fair and festival his parents send her presents till the wedding.

In the Utmánnáma Tappa of Pesháwar the *nishání* observance appears in all essentials under the name of *thál*—the plate in which the ornaments for the girl are placed. The *thál* ceremony concludes with the return, it is said, of all the ornaments and cash offered. However this may be, at its close each person present drinks some *sharbat* and puts some *mehndi* on his hands—an observation called *ghúnt*, which is held to make the betrothal binding. The third day after the betrothal the girl's kinswomen go to the boy's house for two or three days, and when they depart his parents give his future mother-in-law and sister-in-law a rupee each 'by way of *parona*.' This observance is called *channa arta*. Again, two or three days later the bridegroom, with two or three friends and females, goes by night to his father-in-law's house taking with him sweetmeats and cash Rs. 2 to 10. The party are feasted and then the bridegroom puts the money into the plate and sends it with the sweetmeats to his mother-in-law as *salámána*. Shortly afterwards the bride's parents come, flinging jets at him, and sprinkle scented water over him. This is called *ubáachwal*. At each fair and festival after these ceremonies the bridegroom sends gold or silver ornaments for the bride.

In the Chakwál tahsíl of Jhelum a very similar custom exists. To ratify the understanding already arrived at, the boy's father goes one day to the girl's and presents her with sweetstuff and Rs. 21 in cash in the presence of her brotherhood. Her father accepts from Re. 1 to Rs. 5, rarely taking the whole, and coloured water is sprinkled over the whole of the boy's party. The *duá-i-khair* is recited at night, and they return next day. This is called *nishání rakhná*. The boy does not accompany the party on this occasion. On the first 'Id after it, the boy's father sends presents for the girl, and if he is well-to-do he sends clothes to her mother and sister as well—when the gift would be called *dhái tewar dená*, 'to gift 3 (literally 2½) sets of clothes'. The fathers may also exchange gifts of clothes, but if the bride's parents only receive garments for her they need only give sweetmeats in return. If this gift is brought by a barber the girl's father gives him a rupee, a turban, and a *kurta*—an observance called *kapre dená*. At the next 'Id clothes &c. are only sent to the girl. In Talagang tahsíl the *nishání* is merely a present of Rs. 5 in cash and as many *paos* of sugar made, it seems, at betrothal. So, too, in Haripur tahsíl, in Hazára, it is an ornament given to the girl at the *mangeva*. Finally, in Hoshiárpur, at least among the Paṭháns, we find the *nishání* following the solemn betrothal, at which a *maulavi* invokes the *niyat khair* twice and the girl's father gives dried dates and sugar to the boy's party by way of *shagún*. The contract having thus become irrevocable, some date of the lunar month is fixed for the *nishání*, which merely consists in the interchange of presents, feeing of *lágís*, and the payment by the girl's father of sufficient money to buy the boy a ring.

Betrothal as an usage and as a rite.

In the Western Punjab Muhammadans tend to assimilate the betrothal to the regular *nikáh*, or wedding. This is especially the case in Hazára. In that district some people celebrate the *mangewa* only at betrothal, others solemnise the *nikáh* simultaneously with it, but without fixing the amount of the dower. That appears to be fixed subsequently, and the *nikáh* is regarded as irrevocable when the amount of dower has been fixed. In Harípur tahsíl, after the *duá-i-khair*, the ritual of offer and acceptance is solemnised at the betrothal. In Attock tahsíl, too, a *mulláh* officiates at this ceremony.

In the Rájanpur tahsíl of Dera Ghází Khán the position is this: When persons of the same tribe make a betrothal by exchange, the *nikáh* is not performed at the betrothal, but the *mangní* is performed, and the *duá-i-khair* is recited in connection therewith. But if a betrothal is made in consideration of a cash payment the *nikáh* is solemnised simultaneously with the *mangní*. The amount paid varies from Rs. 100 to 300. But elsewhere it is rare to find betrothal regarded as a religious rite, though occasionally the *níyat khair*, or invocation of a blessing, is invoked by the Qází's reciting the *duá-i-fatih-khair*, as in Ferozepur. In that district this is the only ceremony at a betrothal, the boy's father visiting the bride's and receiving a red *khes*, or *mutáhá*, after the *níyat khair*, while the boy does not accompany his party. In Mandí the following times are considered inauspicious for a betrothal, and in fixing the date for it a Qází is consulted :—

(1) The first ten days of the month of Muharram.
(2) The month between the 'Id-ul-Fiter and the 'Id-ul-Zuhá.
(3) The month of Jamádi-us-Sání.
(4) The last day of every month.
(5) The 3rd, 8th, 13th, and 18th of every month.

Auspicious days for a betrothal are :—

(1) The 7th, 11th, 14th, 25th, and 27th of every month.
(2) All days except the 3rd, 8th, 13th, and 18th.

But this custom appears to be confined to that State, for in the adjacent district of Hoshiárpur any date may be fixed for the betrothal, and at most a *maulavi* is called for the *níyat khair*. In Dasúya tahsíl any date of the lunar month is fixed. This is called *parná*, and on it a party of four at least visits the bride's house with presents, which vary according to the means of the parties. Among the Pathåns, called Wiláyatí and Muhammadans of Kángra generally, betrothal is styled *bale*, or 'assent.' Among the Saddozai and Qizzilbásh Pathåns of Hoshiárpur, for instance, the *bale* simply consists in a visit by the boy's friends to the girl's father and a formal acceptance of the proposed match. The boy himself does not take part in any of ceremonies before his wedding, though these are rather elaborate, and include the *shírint khorí* (sweet-eating) and *rakht-burání* (cloth-cutting). At some date after the *bale* the boy's father, accompanied by some of his family, takes some sweetmeat, pieces of silk and rich cloth, unsewn and uncut, for the bride, but ornaments are not sent till the eve of the wedding. This ceremony is performed with some little *éclat*. The sweetmeat, which is always a mixture of *patásha*, *nuqal*, and *iláichidána* is arranged in trays carried by menials, who form a procession. Before them goes a band. The ladies of the boy's family follow in close carriages. Sometimes fireworks are also used. When this procession arrives at the girl's house the boy's mother or some elderly relative puts a ring on the bride's right-hand finger and says, '*bismilláh*' (by the name of God). She then throws a shawl round her shoulders. After this she cuts the cloth with scissors, repeating '*bismilláh*.' Congratulations to both the parties follow, and sweetmeat is distributed among the women inside the house as well as among the men outside. Finally, the date of the wedding is decided upon and publicly announced.

In Kángra the *bale* is a little more formal, and it is also followed by similar observances. The boy's father, with some respectable elders, goes to the girl's house on the 11th, 17th, 27th or 29th of the month. The girl's father also assembles some men at his house before their arrival, and soon after it he distributes sweetmeats, such as *patáshas*, giving a plateful of sugar with his own hands to the boy's father, and congratulations are exchanged. The giving of the sweetmeats shows that the girl's father has agreed to give his daughter to the boy. This ceremony is called *sharfí khorí*, and females take no part in it. On this day, and sometimes on the next day too, the boy's father sends sweetmeats and fresh fruit to the girl. This sweetmeat is called *majmá rasá*. The fruit is distributed by the girl's parents among their relatives. Thereafter (till the date of betrothal) on each 'Id-ul-Fitr the boy's parents send some *mehndi* and food to the girl, and a he-goat or ram is also sent to her on each 'Id-ul-Zuhá. The animal is painted with *mehndi* and a silver *hansli* put round its neck. It is sacrificed by the girl's parents. On each last Wednesday of the month of Safar, 20 silver rings and a gold ring, with a suit of clothes and some *mehndi*, are sent by the boy's parents to the girl's. The silver rings are meant for her friends and the gold one for the girl herself. On the Shab Barát fireworks are also sent for the girl. These practices are kept up till the *nikáh*, and there is no limit to the period intervening between the betrothal and the wedding.

The date of the *nikáh* is fixed in consultation. First of all the date of the *rakhat bari*, or cutting of the clothes, is settled. The boy's parents take even suits of silk clothes to the girl's house. These clothes are carried by servants on their heads. A pair of laced shoes is also taken. The first cloth for the bride is cut by the oldest and most respected matron of the family. The girl's parents supply the boy's with food for the night at the *rakhat bari*, and the men of his

AAAAA

party depart after taking it. This ceremony is performed ten or eleven days before the wedding.

The auspicious dates for a betrothal are variously given. In the Abbottábad tahsíl of Hazára very few days are unlucky, and auspicious dates are the 1st, 2nd, 4th, 5th, 6th, 7th, 9th, 10th, 11th, 12th, 14th, 15th, 16th, 17th, 19th, 20th, 21st, 22nd, 24th to 27th, 29th, and 30th. But one list from Rájanpur, in Ḍera Gházi Khán, omits the 2nd, 6th, 8th, 9th, 10th, 15th, 16th, 19th, 20th, 22nd, 25th, 26th, and 30th, while in the Leiah tahsíl of Míánwáli the 7th, 11th, 14th, 24th, 25th, or 27th day of the moon is considered really prosperous, though, excepting the ten days of Ashúra, all other days of the year are admissible, whether lucky or not, for performing *mangná.*

In Ferozepore no regard is paid to the date of the month, but the boy's party should reach the girl's house on a Thursday night.

In Lohárn the usages in betrothal are typical of those in vogue in the south-east Panjab. In that State, betrothal (*sagái*) is never solemnised on the 3rd, 13th, 23rd, 8th, 18th, or 28th of a lunar month.

The bridegroom (*bendhá*) only accompanies his father and kinsmen to the house of the bride (*bendhání*) if specially desired to do so by the bride's father. The boy's father then presents Rs. 35 in cash and a cocoanut in a vessel, together with 5½ *sers* of sugar, one *ser* of henna, and a silk cloth, which are put in the bride's lap—an observance called *god bharaná* (literally, 'to fill the lap'). Then the girl's father gives the boy some cloth, a rupee, and a cocoanut, with clothes for himself and his mother. Next follows the *shukaráná*, or thank-offering, a feast of rice, coarse sugar, and *ghí*, given to the boy's party, during which the girl's kinswomen fling insults (*sithinián*) at them.

The betrothal ceremonies in vogue among the Muhammadans of the Lammáṇ tract in Baháwalpur are described below:—

Betrothal is called *mangnán* or *mangewa.* On the date fixed for the betrothal the *putrela* or boy's father party pay a visit to the *dheta* or girl's father, and this visit must be paid at night and on the 1st, 5th, 7th, 11th, 14th, 17th, 19th, 21st, 25th, 27th or 29th of the lunar month. The bridegroom accompanies the party, which takes a quantity of *tapásás* (sugar cakes) with them, and on arriving at the girl's house the *duá-i-fatihá khair* or *níyat khair* is observed, the ceremony being begun by the person who arranged the betrothal. After this the parties exchange congratulations and the bridegroom is given a *lungi.* The boy's father usually distributes the *tapásás*, while the bride's father entertains them with milk. The bridegroom's party returns home the same night. Subsequently a party of women visit the girl's father on behalf of bridegroom's father, taking with them *tapásás* and a *trewar*, comprising a *bochhan*, in which are tied some coins (varying from 4 annas to Rs 25), fruit weighing from 2½ *páos* [1] to 5 seers, a bracelet, a set of bangles and a ring (or *paṭhi mundri*), and these ornaments and clothes are put on the bride by the women.

[1] A *páo*=¼ of a *ser*.

In well-to-do families a woman who makes bangles accompanies the party to the bride's house and puts glass or ivory bangles on her. In other cases the bride is taken next day to a shop and the bangles are bought and put on there. After this the nose of the bride is bored, and as a compensation for the pain she is given 1¼ *chhaṭáks* or 1¼ *páos* of sugar-candy.[1] Finally the visitors are feasted with *choba* (rice or bread with *ghí* and sugar) by the bride's father, but nothing that has been cut with a knife, such as meat, is given them.[2] This ceremony is termed *nath sárá.*

Usages subsequent to betrothal and prior to marriage.

Chandránán.—On the first day on which the new moon is seen in the lunar month following the betrothal the bridegroom visits his father-in-law in order to congratulate him on the new moon, and takes his meals in his house. This is termed *chandránán khâwán.* The bridegroom drops from Re. 1 to Rs. 10, according to his means, in the plate in which food is given him, and his father-in-law in return gives him a ring. This usage is virtually confined to Baháwalpur, being expressly non-existent or obsolete in almost every other part of the Punjab.

After the *chandránán* on both the 'Ids, on the Ashúra (the 10th of Muharram), the Shab Barát, and the last Wednesday in Safar[3] the boy's father sends uncooked food (rice, *ghí,* sugar &c.) to the bride. Here again nothing that has been cut may be sent, and this rule is observed even on the Baqr-'Id day (the festival on which sheep &c. are sacrificed).

But in Ḍera Gházi Khán only a rupee is sent to the bride on the first 'Id. No uncooked food is sent her on the Baqr 'Id, when her home is not far from the boy's.

In Miáwáli, on the first 'Id-ul-Fitr, after the *mangewá* the boy's father sends the bride a *bhochhan* and a silk *kurtá,* some rice, *ghí,* sugar &c. Besides these articles and clothes are sent on each 'Id or festival after the *mangewá.* This is termed *warená* or *sanbhál bhejná,* to send a support or pledge.

After the betrothal various social observances take place, but however costly they may be, few have any religious or ritual significance. For example, among the Jadúns and in the Abbottabad tahsíl of Hazára uncooked food is sent to the girl on each 'Id and Shab Barát after the betrothal This usage is very widespread, but the customs as to what is sent vary considerably. Thus, in Peshάwar, well-to-do people send clothes and ornaments.

[1] Round Miṭhankoṭ, in Ḍera Gházi Khán, the bride's nose is bored by the boy's kinswomen, and they give her the sugar-candy, the one who actually performs the operation giving twice as much as the others.

[2] Round Miṭhankoṭ this restriction is only imposed on the bride.

[3] In the Jámpur tahsíl of Ḍera Gházi Khán uncooked food is sent on the 'Ids, Muharram days, and Shab Barát, by the boy's party, but not on the last Wednesday of the month of Safar.

In Gujránwála on the 'Id day after the *mangní* the boy's party goes to the girl's house with ornaments and clothes, which are put on the girl on that auspicious day. Even poor people take a suit of clothes and silver ornaments worth Rs 20 to 50, while the rich send silk clothes and ornaments costing as much as Rs. 500 to 2,000. Congratulations are exchanged between the parties, and sweets distributed on this occasion. This custom is, however, not in vogue among cultivators. It is confined to the higher castes living in towns.[1]

Kawárá ká sáwaná.—In Hoshiárpur the presents thus sent are called 'Idí and Shab Barátí. In Mandi on any festival day, such as the 'Id or Niáz, and at any marriage in the girl's family after his betrothal, the boy is invited and feasted with rich food. This is called *kawár ká sáwaná*. On the other hand, among respectable families, the girl is supplied with clothes etc. till her *nikáh*.

A similar custom exists in Loháru. In that State *bidri* is a present of sweets etc. (including clothes, if they can be afforded) sent to the girl by the boy's father on every festival between the betrothal and the wedding. If no ornaments or clothes were given to the girl on the day of the *mangní* they are sent with the first *bidri*. In return the girl's parents also send a *bidri* to the boy. If the Tíj festival of the Hindús in Láma happens to fall between the betrothal and the wedding Muhammadans send *sandhárí* to the bride. This consists of *khajúrs* (sweets shaped like dates), made of wheat flour and coarse sugar fried in oil, together with a suit of clothes for the girl.

In the Pindí Gheb tahsíl, on the day after the betrothal, the females on behalf of the boy's father, visit the girl's house, taking with them dried dates, *maulí* thread, and cash for her. This is called *gad*. The boy also visits the girl's house on the second or third day, his mother-in-law gives him a gold or silver finger-ring or some cash. The girl's other relations also give him money.

In Peshâwar city, at an undefined time after the *mangewá*, some of the boy's kinswomen go to the bride's house for the *milní*, as it is called. They take sweetmeats with them, and the bride's parents serve them with boiled rice and sugar, called *chobba*. This ceremony is performed during the day, and the women return home by night. They drop from Re. 1 to Rs. 5 into the vessel from which they are given the rice. At every festival day the boy's parents also send the girl rice and sugar, and in return for this they are given a *chádar* or *dopatta*.

But in Siálkot the *milní* is not carried out by the womenfolk at all. In that district some time after the betrothal and before the wedding,

[1] This usage is subject, of course, to endless variations, not only in different localities, but also in different castes. Thus in Ferozepur, after the *mangnás*, food, clothes, and ornaments are sent to the bride on the 'Id. Among Bodlás the boy's mother goes with these articles herself. The ornaments are a *hansli*, bangles, a *gokhrú* (all of silver), and clothes—a gown and a *kurtá*. Sayyids send 5 *sers* of rice, a rupee, for the price of *ghí*, sugar, shoes, trousers, a laced *kurtá*, and *dopattá*, bangles, and *karyán*. Rájpúts send all the above except the rice, and in return the bride's father sends a *lungí*, *kurtá*, turban, shoes, and a finger-ring for the boy on the last Wednesday. Among Aráíns the boy's father sends two *sers* of rice and one of sugar. Half of this is sent by the bride's father in return.

the fathers of the boy and the girl meet together, and this is called *milni*. The boy's father on this occasion sends the girl some ornaments and clothes, which are put on her. In return her father may give the boy's father valuable clothes and ornaments as well as a she-buffalo or a mare, but this is not generally done.

In Hazára the *milní* appears to be called *pair gela*. Directly after the betrothal, on the return of the boy's party from the girl's house, his kinswomen, with other females of the village, visit the girl's mother, taking with them drums and singing songs on their way. They also take sweetened bread fried in oil. This is called *pair gela*. The bride's kinswomen return the visit in a similar way. By this it is intended that if a birth or death takes place in either of the two families their womenfolk can take part in the marriage festivities or the mourning rites.

The meaning of the term *pair gela* is not very clear. In Attock tahsíl it is thus described: After the conclusion of the betrothal on an 'Id day, the boy's mother, together with thirty or forty other females, the boy, and his *sarbálás*, visit the girl's mother by day. She takes with her clothes, sweetmeats, and parched grain. and presents them to the girl's mother, who distributes them among those present and dismisses her female visitors with present of clothes, but the boys and his *sarbálás* stay on for four or five days. On his departure his father-in-law to be gives him clothes and a ring. Sometimes the *sarbálás* are also given clothes. This is called *pair gela*. On the first 'Id the boy's mother also takes *mehndi*, jaggery, rice and clothes for the girl, and this is repeated on all subsequent 'Ids.

But in the Harípur tahsíl of this district it is said that on the third day, or some time afterwards, the females of the boy's family pay a visit by way of *pair gela* to the girl's mother, taking with them ornaments &c. On their return the girl's parents give them clothes, &c.

In Miánwáli a similar usage is called *pair-á chhorná*. After the betrothal the boy goes to his father-in-law's house, and after taking food there, he drops from Re. 1 to Rs. 5 into the dish in which his dinner was served. His mother-in-law to be then gives him a gold or silver ring in return.

SECTION 8.—MUHAMMADAN MARRIAGE OBSERVANCES.

In the following paper the observances followed, after those connected with betrothal have been completed, just before, at and after the wedding are described. No rigid classification by localities is possible, but speaking very generally the marriage observances of the Muhammadans in the South-East Punjab differ a good deal from those of the centre and north-east districts. In the latter the Muhammadans are few in numbers. The Muhammadans of the Western Punjab, including the North-West Frontier Province, have a good many characteristic usages not found in the centre or east. Roughly speaking then the arrangement in this account follows their territorial differences.

I.—In the South-East Punjab the wedding rites vary among different castes and tribes to a bewildering degree. Those in vogue in the Loháru State may be regarded as typical and are described below, together with those found among the Meos who are Muhammadans with a strong survival of Hindu beliefs and ideas.

Preparations for the wedding.

Ten or fifteen days before the date of the wedding the bride's father sends the *gaṇḍh* (*lit.* a knot).[1] In this observance a piece of silk is knotted as many times as there are days remaining till the wedding day. A *kangná* or bracelet of silk (containing a ring of iron, another of lac and some *rái*) is also made for the bridegroom. The *gaṇḍh*, the *kangná* with a lump of sugar and a rupee, are sent to him by a barber and his sister or his father's sister hangs the *gaṇḍh* on a peg.

Bán butáná then follows.[2] This observance consists in rubbing the bodies of the pair with *baṭná* 3 or 4 days before the wedding.[3]

Among the Meos of Gurgáon *bán* is said to be 'taken out of' the pair from their respective houses thus :—He (or she) is led out of the house, holding a plate on which is a lighted lamp, to a certain distance and is then brought back. This is done seven times. Kinswomen accompany him (or her), singing songs.

The bridegroom is also bathed by the women of his family and oiled. This observance is called *tel charháná*.

A knot in the *gaṇḍh* is untied every day, and when only one remains tied the boy's father sends for his kinsfolk, who are feasted and in return present their *neotá* or *tambol*.

Shortly before the wedding party sets out from the boy's home he is seated on a stool and bathed by the barber. At the same time seven women whose husbands are alive pound up barley in a mortar—an observance called *jau chhare*.[4]

After the boy has been bathed his mother's brother lifts him down from the stool, a custom called *páṭá utárná* [5] or *píṛhá utárná*.

After this four women lead the boy away under a piece of cloth held over him like a canopy, and seat him on a cot. He is then dressed in new clothes and the *kangná* tied on his wrist.

Another observance which takes place a day or two before the wedding is the *nikási*. In this the boy, dressed in his new clothes, with the *kangná* on his wrist and a chaplet of flowers tied round his head, is mounted on a mare (never on a horse) and taken to a mosque, where prayers are said by him and a congregation. On his return he goes round the whole town and is then taken to some house other than his own home until the wedding party sets out at night.

On the day of the *nikáh* when the wedding party reaches the girl's home the *ṭúnṭsá* observance is first held. In this the women assembled jest with one another and hold a mock marriage, one dressed in man's attire and holding a sword in her hand being wedded to another by a third who acts as the Qázi. Another of the women also puts her face into the mouth of a jar and calls all the others ill names.

[1] See Note A on page 836.

[2] See Note B on page 836.

[3] See Note C on page 837.

[4] In the Sangrúr tahsíl of Jínd when a wedding party among the Sayyids sets out the boy is made to cut a branch of a *jand* tree. When his party reaches the bride's house the *mírási* and barber each get from 9 to 15 pies. This fee is called *phera*.

[5] *Paṭ*, a plank or shutter : *Panjabi Dicty.*, p. 882.

While the wedding party is still a mile or so from the bride's home the boy's father sends a bunch of green leaves (called *harí dálí*) by his barber to the father of the girl. The latter receives it seated on a wooden stool and (after giving the barber a rupee as his fee) stains his hands with red and places them on the barber's breast or loins. The latter then returns. Meanwhile the wedding party is nearing the bride's home and is met by the girl's people, being conducted to a suitable place for its stay. Songs are now sung by the girl's kinswomen and the potter's wheel worshipped by them.

At sunset the bridegroom performs the *toran*. Five wooden sparrows are hung up at the bride's house-door and the bridegroom moves them with a stick.

After the *toran* the bridegroom goes to the bride's house, but a barber stops the way and measures him with a thread, receiving for this a fee of Rs. 1-4. Then the bridegroom enters the house of the bride who has taken her stand inside the door. Giving her a rupee, he places his hand over hers—an observance called *hath-lewá* or 'hand-taking.'

The *nikáh* is now solemnised according to Muhammadan Law and the amount of the dower fixed.[1]

Ceremonies after the wedding.

On the morning after the *nikáh* the bridegroom and his *sháhbálá* with their companions are feasted on *khír*, an usage called *kanwar kalewá*.

After this sugar on a plate is set before the bridegroom and he puts some money into the plate—an observance called *sálú artá*.

Next, the pair are seated facing each other with an earthen plate full of water between them, and a silver ring, a nut and two or four coins are put on the bride's head which she inclines, thus throwing the coins etc. into the water. Both then scramble for them in the plate—and the one who first gets the ring wins. This is done thrice. The rite is called *júá khelná*, 'to gamble.'

On the day on which the wedding party is to return home the bridegroom goes to the bride's house and there the pair sit facing each other. Here again the *sháhbálá* accompanies the bridegroom. The pair then come out of the house with their clothes knotted together. The bride's father now gives her clothes etc., a couch and, if he can afford it, a horse, camel or cow. The wedding party departs, with the bride in a cart or on a camel if possible.

On nearing the bridegroom's home the clothes of the pair are again knotted together. At the entrance the bridegroom's sister bars their way till she receives her dues, and further in stand vessels through which the bridegroom must make a way with his sword, the bride

[1] Another usage prior to the *nikáh* consists in the sending of *bari* by the boy's father to the bride. The *bari* consists of clothes, shoes, dried dates, almonds, maize and, if he can afford them, ornaments.

After the *bari* the wedding-party take the boy to the girl's house where her mother places a tray of sugar before him. Into this tray he puts a rupee, called *sásúáná* or the mother-in-law's due.

In Rohtak the *bari* is also called *sáchni* and consists of presents sent to the girl by the boy's maternal relatives.

After the *bari* has been received the women of the bride's family go to see the place where the boy's party is staying—an usage known as *derá jhánkná* or *bhír*. There they are given dried fruits.

accompanying him. Both then seat themselves in the house and the *sháhbálá* says: —

Bhábí, bhábí mujh ghar pahla beṭı ser gur.

Throwing a cocoanut into the air he says also: —

Dahne goḍa dhakní aur bain guḍá súl.
Mujhe ilen laḍḍu aur bhábí ko milen púṭ.

The pair then separate.

Rice is then boiled by women whose husbands are alive and eaten by them and the bride—a rite called *sát* (seven) *suhágan ká kunḍá.*

Two or four days later the bride's brother or other kinsman goes to bring her back to her own home, and he takes with him some sweets. This usage is called *len hárí.*

Mukláwá[1] takes place as a rule one or two years after the wedding. The husband fetches his wife from her home, receiving a present of ornaments from her father, if he can afford to give them.

[1] Or *chálá* in Gurgáon, *e.g.* among the Meos who have several usages. Sometimes the bridegroom accompanies the bride to her home, stays there 3 or 4 days and then returns with her. Sometimes *muklάwá* takes place after one, sometimes after three years, in which cases it is much more formal and costly to the girl's father – and less so to the bridegroom.

Fixing the wedding-day.—In the central districts this is not a very prominent rite, but in some parts it survives. Thus in Gujrát in order to fix a date for the wedding the girl's parents send a barber and *mirási* with Rs. 5 to Rs. 21 or a gold *mohar* for the boy, as well as Rs. 2 to Rs. 11 for the *lágís* which sum is also called 'village expenses' to the bridegroom's house. The boy's father then invites all his kinsmen and friends. The boy is seated in the midst of the assembly and the barber gives him sugarcandy to eat. He also puts in his skirt the cash or the gold *mohar.* Then congratulations are exchanged. This ceremony is called *bhocha.* The date of the marriage is fixed at it and the barber and *mirási* are given from Rs. 1 to Rs. 5 by the boy's party. His parents also dismiss the *lágís* with a *chawnni* and Re. 1 to Rs. 11 together with a *bidh* (bundle) containing dried fruits such as almonds, cocoanuts, dried raisins and *patáshas.*

In Gujránwála to 'tie the knot' or *ganḍ páná,* as it is termed, is the ceremony of fixing a day for the marriage. If any ceremonies connected with the betrothal have not been already performed, they are now observed. The wedding day is fixed by correspondence between the parties or at a personal meeting.

So too in Manḍi some respectable men of the boy's family go to the girl's house with a Qázi and he fixes there the dates of the *nikáh* and *dhám,* and that for applying *mehndi.* These dates are always close to one another. Congratulations are exchanged and sugar sent to relations to notify them of the date of wedding, the *lági* deputed giving each of them sugar while they in return give him from one pice to two annas by way of *waddigí.*

The *mehṇdi* ceremony is performed before the *nikáh.* Women of the boy's party paint his hands with *mehṇdi* at night. Then some *mehṇdi,* a silver ring and Rs. 1-5-9 in cash are sent to the girl through the *lági,* women also going with him. *Mehṇdi* is also applied to the girl. The females of both parties keep awake singing songs all night. On the next day at 4 P.M. *baṭná* is rubbed over the bridegroom's body and he is bathed. Then he is seated in a special room and some of his relatives and friends sit with him. He is dressed in such clothes as are worn by a bridegroom and a *sihrá* is placed round his head. At 8 or 9 P.M. the bridegroom is taken to a mosque in a palanquin or on a horse. He is then made to pass through the bazars and all this time dancing girls dance before his horse and fireworks are let off. He is then taken at a slow pace with the whole of the wedding party to the bride's house, and all are seated then in a specially decorated room. The men of the girl's party and the Qázi also come there. The girl's guardian allows the Qázi to perform the *nikáh.* He first fixes the amount of the bride's dower which depends on the will of her guardian. It is never below Rs. 32-8. If the amount is not fixed according to the demand of the bride's guardian he is entitled to marry her to another. Thereafter two witnesses and a *vakíl* are appointed by each party. They go with the Qázi to the bride and perform the ceremonies of offer and acceptance; she and the bridegroom are told to repeat the sacred *kalma* five times. The *khutbá* ceremony is performed in the presence of all the kin. The dowry, *viz.* wearing apparel, bedding, a couch, household utensils and ornaments are given on this occasion. Dried fruits and sugarcandy are distributed among the people. The Qázi gets Rs. 1-4 for the ceremony while his assistant gets annas 4 for the *duá-i-khair.* All these expenses are borne by the bridegroom. Besides copper coins are distributed among the poor. The bride's guardian feeds the wedding party.

II. Perhaps the best idea of the wedding rites current among the Muhammadans in the Central Punjab may be gathered from the following skeleton account of those prevalent in Gujránwála :—

Sihrá bándhná and Khâre charhná.—One day before the wedding[1] the bridegroom is garlanded with flowers. This ceremony is called *sihrá bándhná.*[2] On this day also *tambol* (presents in money) is offered by the brotherhood and the bridegroom's father gives to his *kamíns* (menials) their *lág* or dues according to his means. Before the *sihrá bándhná* the bridegroom ascends a *khárá* and breaks 5 or 7 *chhunnís.*[3]

When the wedding procession is about to start, the boy is made to ride on a mare. This is called *ghorí charhná,* and his sister aks for *bág pharái*, or a fee for holding the reins. He gives her either a she-buffalo or money according to his means and wishes. Then his mother performs the *sir wárná* or sacrificing over the head, the amount of money offered being a rupee or two which sum is also given to the *kamína.* After this the boy goes to do obeisance at the shrine of an ancestor of the tribe and then the procession leaves at such a time that it may

[1] In Hoshiárpur on the wedding day the bridegroom bathes and a garland of flowers called *sohan sihrá* is hung round his forehead. A coloured cloth is also tied round his head as a turban and saffron sprinkled over his clothes. But Muhammadans who are strict followers of the *shará'* do not observe these usages.

[2] This account says nothing of the *mámi chhak* or articles sent by the maternal relatives of the bridegroom in Siálkot and forming part of the dowry. The *mámí chhak* generally consists of a couch, *pírhá*, 21 large cakes of flour fried in *ghí*, 5 suits of clothes, 5 utensils and some ornaments. The articles given by the parents of the bride generally are an *ársí*, *chhapan* or rings, *phál*, *chaunk* and *mahán* (ornaments worn on the head), *jhumke*, quilt, pillow, 21 suits of clothes, 101 *laddus* and sometime a horse, cow, she-buffalo and a camel. The bridegroom sits on a couch on this occasion.

[3] In Siálkot the wedding party on its arrival at the bride's house is put up in a hut outside the village. The bride's father sends it *hukkas*, *sharbat* etc. by a *lági* who is given annas 8 or Re. 1 as his *lág*. After this the party is called for and the barber on behalf of the bride's father brings with him a basket full of sugar and the fathers of the bride and the bridegroom meet together. The father of the bride gives the other on this occasion some money or a horse. The wedding party is then seated close to the bride's house. The bridegroom's father drops some cash in the basket of sugar. This is followed by a feast to the wedding party. A sieve is suspended in the way and is removed by a female barber on receipt of Re. 0-1-8 as her due. The sweeper also stands in the way of the wedding party and does not allow it to pass without getting his *lág* also. The bride's sisters also exact their *lág* which may amount to Re. 1-4-0. Then the wedding party is served with food. This is followed by the performance of the *bera ghori* ceremony. It may be noted that after the wedding party has taken its food until the next ceremony many *sithnís* (jests) are flung at it. Many obscene songs are sung on this occasion.

In Kángra the *nikáh* is performed after midnight and after it congratulations are exchanged and sweetmeats distributed. The bridegroom is then called inside the house by the women. The bride takes her seat on a *masnad* with females around her. The bridegroom takes his seat at her right and a piece of cloth is thrown over both of them. The Qurán and a looking glass are placed inside this sheet with a cup of sweet water and a spoon. The bridegroom gives a spoonful of the water to the bride and her relations also give her a spoonful to be given to the bridegroom. After this they look at each other's face in the looking glass. This ceremony is called *áína masíf*. The bride is then taken to the house of her father in-law in a palanquin. On the third day the females of the bride's family go to her husband's house to bring her back. The dowry is then exhibited to the kinsfolk. The bride sits on a *masnad* for three days. The bridegroom then comes, takes his wife's arm and leads her to a separate compartment in the presence of the other females. This is called *chauthí*.

reach its destination at nightfall. Some people take with it a band, fireworks and dancing girls, but others do not. When the procession reaches the bride's village, some men come to receive it on behalf of the bride's father. It is then seated at a place where carpets have been spread. *Huqqas* are first smoked and an hour or two later tea is served if it is winter and in the hot season *sharbat* by the bride's party, who then go away. Then the bride's father accompanied by some of his brotherhood enters the house in which the bridegroom's party has been lodged before food is served. As soon as he arrives the ceremony of *milni* is observed. If he is well-to-do he offers a mare as a *milni* present to his *kuram* (the bridegroom's father) and they embrace each other. On this occasion too the *lágis* are given money as their fixed dues. After this the bride's father takes the bridegroom and his party with him to his house and provides a feast for them.

Chhanni turwáná.—Some women of the bride's party now come and take a *chhanni* or sieve which is hanging over the doorway and in which a lamp is burning. After this he and his party sleep, but early in the morning at about 4 A.M. he is awakened by the women of the bride's house and taken to a female apartment where the bride's sister makes him play *berú ghori* and exacts some money from him but the sum taken does not exceed Rs. 11.

Nikáh.—The actual wedding ceremony, the *nikáh*, is performed at 8 or 9 A.M. or at some later hour. On this occasion some people distribute *chhohárás* while others distribute uncooked rice mixed with sugar.

Post-*nikáh ceremonies.*—When the *nikáh* is over the bride is made to ascend a *khárá* and her maternal uncle causes her to descend from it and in return he gives her a she-buffalo or a sum of money which must exceed Rs. 11.

Dowry.—Then the bride's father places on cots whatever dowry he has prepared for his daughter, whereupon the parties meet together and give *lág* to their *kamíns*. This done, the dowry is packed up, the bride seated in a palanquin and the bridegroom's party departs with it and the dowry. When the bride arrives at her father-in-law's village, some women of his household accompanied by singing *mirásans* receive her and bring her to their house.

Ceremonies observed on arrival at the bridegroom's house.—When she reaches the house door, she alights from the dooly and oil is sprinkled on the threshold.

Sacrificing water (suggested to mean drinking health).—After this the bridegroom's mother sacrifices water over his head and attempts to drink it but is dissuaded by her son. The bride is then seated on a carpet or mat or some suitable place in the house.

Múṇh dikhlái or face-showing ceremony.—The bridegroom's mother then gives a sum of money as *múṇh dikhlái* or 'showing the face' to the bride who removes the veil (*ghúnghaṭ*) from her face and is entertained with milk.

Gáná kholná (untying the gáná).—The next morning the bridegroom and bride untie the *gáná.*

The bride returns to her father's on the third day after the arrival at her father-in-law's house.

In Shakargarh—although the *máyán* is said not to be performed—the day before the wedding party starts for the bride's house, drums are beaten and next day the boy is seated on a *khárá* and *baṭná* rubbed on him but the practice of breaking *chapnís* ceased 16 or 17 years ago. His party should reach the bride's house in the first part of the night. Some people take drummers with them. On their arrival the *milní* ceremony is performed.

In the *milní* the men of both the parties stand opposite one another at some distance, and representatives of each embrace. The bride's representative gives a rupee to the boy's. His barber also brings some sugar and rice in a vessel. An *ulma* recites the *níyat khair* and gets Re. 1-4-0 and 4 copper coins from the bride's father as his fee. The barber also gets four annas on this occasion.

In Siálkot the *milní* is thus described :—The girl's father takes his stand on an open site outside the village of the boy's father who comes to meet him there with all his party. Fireworks may be let off at this meeting which is called *milní.* At it too the *mirásís* of the parties recite their genealogies. The parties pass a rupee over one another's head and give it to the *mirásís.* This is called *sir wárná kuram.* Sialkot.

On the arrival of a wedding party in Hoshiárpur the customs of *milní* and *peshkára* are observed and the party is served with *sharbat* It is also supplied with food for one or two days.

III.—In the Western Punjab we are introduced to a number of new rites and to a still greater number of new names for usages already described :—

Preparations for the wedding.

In Hazára preparations for the wedding are made a year or two after the *mangewa.* When the date for it is fixed some money is given to the boy's father to purchase *pará kaun* or provisions, *viz.* wheat-flour or rice, *ghí,* pulse, salt, pepper, turmeric, wood, jaggery, cotton, couches, stools, utensils &c. required for the use of the wedding party. When these things have been procured by the bride's father, he informs the boy's father that the wedding party should reach his house on a certain day and that the *máyán* and *tel* ceremonies are to be performed on such and such days.

In Peshávar city in order to fix a date for the wedding the girl's parents send some respectable members of their kin to the boy's parents. They also send some sweetmeats to the other party. The cash sent to them on this occasion is called *gadh.*

To prepare for the wedding in Attock the boy's father with 10 or 15 men goes to the girl's father and pays him from Rs. 15 to 30. This is called *puchh.* After this a date is fixed for the marriage.

Among the Dhúnds of Hazára after the betrothal a day is fixed for the wedding. On this day the boy's father pays Rs. 10 to 20 to the girl's father. This sum is called *púchh náuká*. The girl's father hands it over to the girl's maternal uncle and he in return gives her utensils, a couch and so on.

Among the Jadúns when some time after the betrothal preparations for the marriage are made the *imám* of a mosque is consulted to fix an auspicious day for the wedding.

Naming the day.—In Attock tahsíl the *naila*, the term applied to the ceremony of fixing a day for the marriage, is thus observed:—The boy's father with 3 or 4 other respectable persons goes to the girl's father and asks him what amount he will accept for the expenses of the wedding. He agrees to take as much grain or cash as he thinks will be consumed and in addition what he will have to spend on the bride's ornaments and clothes.

In Pindi Gheb when the parties are ready to celebrate the marriage two or three men of the boy's party go to the girl's father for the *gandh páwan* and to settle an amount to be paid for the supply of food to the wedding party. One day before the wedding the females assemble in the house of the boy's father and go to the girl's house with drums, *mehndi* &c. to unplait the girl's hair. This is called *mendhí kholná*[1] and *mehndí láná* The wedding party sets out on the wedding day. The number of men in a wedding party depends on the position of the boy's father, and drummers and bandsmen are sometimes engaged. The party reaches the bridegroom's house in the evening and is put up in a separate house. On its arrival the bride's father sends it a pitcher of *sharbat*, a plate of *halwá* and another of mutton. The party is first served with the *sharbat* which is called *haddi sharbat* while the mutton and *halwá* are placed before the bridegroom.

Gandh badhni.—In Leiah allowing a reasonable interval after the *nishání* the boy's party express a wish to have the wedding performed, consult a few near relations and friends and with the consent of the girl's guardians fix a date for it. To satisfy people that this has been done they exhibit a long, slightly twisted thread, coloured white, red and yellow, usually with a knot tied in it and keep it for future use. This thread is called *maulí dá dhágá*. This done they distribute sweetmeats, repeat the *dúa-khair* and withdraw. This ceremony is called *gandh bandhní*. The day thus fixed must be one of the following dates:—4, 5, 7, 11, 14, 17, 21, 24, 25, 26 or 27 of any moon, but the whole months of Kátak and Chet and the 10 days of Asúrá are not allowable for marriage. A wedding during the remaining 20 days of Moharram, though admissible, is unlucky.

About a week or so before the wedding day the boy's father engages a barber or *mirási* and handing him the thread sends him round to notify the date by delivering a bit of it to every relation and friend entitled to join in the ceremony. This is called *gandh pherní*. The

[1] *Mendhí kholná.*—A day or two before the wedding the bride-groom's womenfolk accompanied by his younger brother go to the bride's house and have her hair unplaited. Songs are sung on this occasion (Miánwáli).

preparations then begin. Among the Dhúnds after the arrival of the boy's party the women perform the *bera ghori* at night. In this observance the boy gives the bride's kinswomen Re. 1 to 5 Rs. in a *thál*. This sum is taken by a barber or *mirási*. After this the boy is given *sharbat* to drink and the barber is given another rupee for this service.

In Multán on the wedding day the girl's kinswomen pass the night with the boy, making him walk through the *mohallas* and bazars of the village. This is called *torná*

In Aṭṭock tahsíl before the arrival of the wedding party the boy and his *sarbála* visit his father-in-law by night. He unplaits one lock of the girl's hair and the rest is unplaited by her sisters and brothers' wives. She is made to wash her hands and face and don fresh clothes. All the people sit outside the house on this occasion. A barber then conducts the *beri ghori* ceremony by placing a stool and lighting lamps on a *thál* before the boy. He and his *sarbálá* drop some copper or silver coins into the *thál* and this money is taken by the barber. After this the boy is made to walk through streets for the whole night.

On the wedding day in Bhakkar after levy of the *tambol* the bridegroom is taken to a mosque or shrine. He is then garlanded, a *gáná* tied on his hand and one of his kinsmen is made his *sarbálá* or best man. The garland is generally prepared by an Aráíṇ's wife. The *gáná* is a coloured thread. This is followed by the *dhok* or setting out of the wedding party to the girl's father's house, camels and horses being employed as conveyances. They reach it at nightfall and the girl's father supplies them with food once or twice. The *nikáh* is performed at 10 or 12 P. M.

In Míánwáli however the *gáná* is more elaborate. There the *gáná bandha*, as it is called, is in vogue among all tribes except the Pathána. The boy's womenfolk get a thread from the girl's house and make from it a *gáná*, which consists of an iron ring, a cowry and a bead (*manká*). The *gáná* is knotted 7 times. Then the womenfolk return home and tie a similar *gáná* to the boy.

On the wedding day in Míánwáli or a day before it the females go to a well or river accompanied by the bridegroom's sister and *sarbálá*. The sister carries a pitcher on her head and draws water from the well. Songs are sung on the occasion. On their return home the bridegroom is bathed in this water and seated on a *khárá*, *laṭná* is rubbed on his body. This is also called *ghaṛoli*. After bathing the bridegroom is made to break *dhaknis*

Among Paṭháns in the Abbottábád tahsíl of Hazára the *nikáh* is performed when the bride has been taken to the bridegroom's house. A *mullán* is sent for and seated on a cot with the bridegroom seated beside him. Two trusted persons called the witnesses then go to the bride to ask her consent to the contract. She empowers one of her relations to have the ceremony performed and fix the amount of dower. He is called the *díní bhái*, and the ceremony is performed after obtaining his permission. The amount of dower varies from Rs. 25 to 500. On the

[1] No explanation of this curious usage is given. In Chakwál *mirási* women take the boy through the streets and bazars of the village by night and bring him back home in the morning. They sing songs as they go.

bride's departure her parents give her ornaments and clothes worth from Rs. 20 to 5000. The bridegroom is also given a suit of clothes.

In Chakwál those who are strict observers of Muhammadan Law use a mare instead of a *ḍolí* to take the bride to her husband's house.[1] On reaching its door she will not enter it until she is given some cash by her parents-in-law. On entering the house a child is placed in her lap, and she gives it a rupee. The bride stays in her father-in-law's house for the first time 4 or 5 days. Meanwhile the bridegroom's kinswomen visit her and give her money. This is called *salám karwái*. The kinsmen also feast the bride and bridegroom. After this some relative of the bride comes to fetch her back to the house of her own father, and he brings sweets on behalf of her parents which are distributed among the kinsfolk.

In Leiah the observances are the same as in Baháwalpur, but at the first interview between the newly married couple no sooner has the bridegroom entered the bride's room than a woman ready waiting for the purpose flings a handful of water with all her strength into his face before she will allow him to come further. This is supposed to make him blind with love for the bride. This same woman then leads him close to the right side of the bride who, veiled and dressed in coloured garments, sits bent forward. Here he spreads a clean white cloth and says two *rakats* of *nimáz* and then sits down. Next his father brings a little perfumed oil which he rubs on his son's head and then holding it in his right hand knocks it gently twice or thrice against that of the bride and wishing them prosperity retires. No male save the bridegroom now remains amidst the party of women, who surround the pair singing *sihras* or marriage songs and throwing flowers on their heads. On its conclusion some chosen women sit down and put a round piece of hard dry *guṛ* into the bride's right hand with instructions to hold it fast. The bridegroom is then told to try and open her palm with his right hand and take the *guṛ* without hurting her delicate fingers. It generally takes a few minutes to unfold the palm while the women around joke, laugh, clap hands and cry :—'Take courage, hold fast, don't unloose your palm &c.' This done they put the same piece of *guṛ* into the bridegroom's hand bidding him not to hold it fast but to unfold his palm by-and-by, after the bride has merely touched it once or twice.

Some post-nuptial observances.

Takhat.—In Jullundur on the morning after the *nikáh* the bride and the bridegroom are seated opposite to each other on a cot given to the former on her marriage. Several ceremonies are then performed. The bride puts a cloth round the bridegroom's neck and does not let him go until he promises her to give all that he may earn. This is called *takhat nbelná*. This is followed by the giving of *warí*,[2] a name

[1] In the villages of Baháwalpur the bride is taken to her husband's house on the back of a camel, ox or a mare, while in towns she rides in a *rath* (chariot) or on a mare, the custom of using a *ḍolí* or planquin not being in vogue in this tract.

[2] In Multán the ornaments and clothes put on the bride on the bridegroom's behalf on the wedding day are called *warí* while those given to the bridegroom on her behalf are called *dájh*. Some rich people spend heavy sums on the *dájh*. It consists of clothes, gold and silver ornaments, household utensils as well as a cow, a she-buffalo and sometimes a camel also. In some families *dájh* is given on the *satwára* day. The girl's parents feast the kinsfolk on this day.

applied to those ornaments and clothes which are given to the bride on behalf of the bridegroom. It consists of ornaments, namely, a gold *chaunk*, silver *hanslí*, *báṇk*, *jhánjhar*, *váseh*, a gold *mohur* and a ring called *kawár bir ka chhallá*, as well as 7 *tewars*.[1] Moreover a suit of clothes for the bride and almonds, dried raisins, cocoanut kernel, dried dates, *maulí*, *mehndí* &c. are sent with the *warí*. Then the bride's parents exhibit her dowry, which consists of a gold nosering, ear-rings, 11 *tewars* and 7 *bewars*,[2] 7 turbans, a couch, a stool, a box and some household utensils. Then the wedding party departs. Generally speaking a *ḍolí* is employed for the conveyance of the bride and a horse for the bridegroom. When the bridegroom reaches his house his mother takes a cup full of milk and water mixed, passes it six times over her son's head and drinks it. Fowls are cooked on the bridegroom's arrival at his house. The *kangná* is performed on the third day after marriage. The bride and bridegroom are seated opposite each other in the presence of the women and a vessel full of water is put between them. They then undo each other's *gánás*. Thereafter a barber's wife throws a rupee, a ring and 7 copper coins into the water. This is called *kangná khelná*. On this day or the next boiled rice mixed with sugar called *bhú bhat* is distributed to the kinsfolk.

In Gujránwála after the dowry has been displayed the bridegroom goes inside the bride's house and pays his respects to each member of her family. In return for this each of them gives him a rupee. A *laḍḍú* is also given to each member of the wedding party. This is called *bahi jawárí*. The bride's parting from her parents is always sorrowful. A *ḍolí* is used for her conveyance. It is carried by *kahárs* and a female attendant accompanies her to her father-in-law's house, and on her return she gets a rupee as her *lág*. On the bride's arrival at her new home she is first served with *chúrí*, and her new female relations give her cash and *patáshás* by way of *muṇh dakhální*. Generally speaking she is sent back to her parents' house on the 3rd day. The man who accompanies her is given a suit of clothes on his return. The *mukláwa* ceremony is generally performed a year or two after the marriage and when the husband goes to his father-in-law's house for this ceremony his sister-in-law conceals his shoes. He puts up there for some time and then returns to his own house with his wife.

Bahi jawárí.—In Siálkot on the day after the wedding one *laḍḍú* is sent to each member of the wedding party in the morning. This is called *bahi jawárí* or breakfast. The barber who brings the *laḍḍu* gets Re. 1 as his *lág*. The wedding party is served with food at noon and then they make preparations to return home. The *nikáh* is often performed before the dinner.

Lassi pair and *got kunála*.—In Siálkot after the departure of the wedding party the bridegroom's mother and his uncle's wife put their feet in some *lassí*. This is called *lassí pair páná*. Then milk and rice

[1] A *tewar* consists of three garments, *viz.*, a *kurtá*, trousers and *dopaṭṭa*.

[2] A *bewar* consists of two only, *viz.* a *kurta* and *dopaṭṭa*.

are eaten by all the women together and *mauli* thread is tied to the hair of the bridegroom's mother. This ceremony is called *got kunála.*

Got kunála.—But the *got kunála* has another and more usual form. Thus in Hoshiárpur on the day after the wedding it is thus described :—Rice is boiled and put in a vessel from which all the near kinswomen and the bride eat together. One plateful of rice is also sent to each kinsman. By this ceremony the bride is admitted into the bridegroom's *got.* The *lágís* who come with the bride are given their dues and dismissed after 2 or 3 days. A little while later the near kinsmen of the bride bring some clothes and sweetmeats and take her to their house. This is called *bhora.* Similarly the bridegroom is invited to his father-in-law's house. He takes with him 2 or 4 *lágís* and some sweetmeats. This is called *manḍhá jhukáo.* Thereafter, when the bride's parents are ready to send her to her father-in-law's house, they invite some men of that family and send with her sweetmeats and clothes—half as much as was given in dowry. This is called the *mukláwa.* When the bride is sent for the third time, it is called *tirnoja*

Dhám.—In Mandi an observance called *dhám* is performed on the 3rd day after the wedding. The bride's guardian accompanied by both the parties as well as by the wedded pair goes to the house of the boy's father, and its womenfolk take the pair to a separate room and give the bride milk to drink. The boy's father serves both the parties with rice and mutton. Those of the bride's party who take this food are called the *ladhi tarú,* and it is called *arandal.* As the Muhammadans of Mandi rarely marry outside the State the *muklâwa* is often performed the same night, but those who marry outside it perform this ceremony after the marriage. The date for it is fixed by the Qázi. The boy's father simply sends his son with some relatives to his father-in-law's house where they are feasted and on the following day the girl's father sends her back with his son-in-law after giving them some clothes.

In Siálkot the *muklâwa* ceremony is performed some time after the wedding. The bridegroom accompanied by his barber goes to his father-in-law's house taking with him 101 *laḍḍús* which are given to the bride and *lágs* are distributed among the *lágís.* A *pírhí,* couch, spinning wheel, balls of various colours, spindles, clothes &c. are given on this occasion by way of dowry. The bridegroom's shoes are also hidden and he makes a search for them everywhere, but when convinced that he cannot find them he gives Re. 1-4 to his sisters-in-law as their *lág.* This ceremony ends with the sending of the bride with the bridegroom.

Speaking generally in the Western Punjab the *muklâwa* is replaced by the *satwára* or *sathúra,* which varies in many details. Thus in and around Máchhka in Ḍera Ghází Khán a week after the wedding the bridegroom goes to his father-in-law's house with his bride, and they both stay there for a day or two and then come back. The *gánás* are removed on this day.

About Madgola the *satwára* is also performed 7 days after the marriage, and the bridegroom takes his bride to her parents. Both of them ride a mare. The *gánás* are removed a day or two before the *satwára* and the bridegroom returns home with his wife a day or two afterwards. The bride's parents give her clothes on this occasion also. Round Asri the bridegroom goes to his father-in-law with his wife on the 7th day after marriage.

In Rájanpur too on the 7th day after the wedding the bridegroom goes to his father-in-law's house with his wife, and they put up there for 2, 3 or at most 7 days. They are given a bath and leave off the clothes worn at the wedding. Among the Baloch these clothes are given to a *mirási* woman, but in other tribes they are taken back to the bridegroom's house. He gives the *lungi* which was given him by his father-in-law to the *mirási*. After this the couple return home riding if their village be far off, but if it is very near they return by night on foot. The *gánás* are often removed on the same day, but some people keep them on until they break off themselves. When the bride returns to her father-in-law's house her near relations give her sweets varying from half a *páo* to a *páo*.

In Multán however the girl is sent to her father's house. This is called *sathúra*. The girl remains in their house for as long as he is willing to keep her. After that the bridegroom goes to fetch her back. On this occasion also her parents give her clothes and ornaments. After the marriage the girl's father abstains from eating at the house of his daughter.

Again in Bhakkar the females of the bride's family go 6 or 7 days after the wedding to the bridegroom's house and bring back the bride. She is kept there for some days, and then the bridegroom goes to fetch her and gets some clothes, sweetmeats &c.

In Chakwál tahsíl the bridegroom goes to his father-in-law's house a few days after the wedding, stays there 5 or 6 days, and is given a very warm reception. This is called *sathúra*. Then he takes his wife home.

In Baháwalpur the bride's mother and relations visit her 3 or 6 days after the wedding and in their presence and that of other women of the brotherhood the couple untie each other's *gánás*. This is termed *gáná-chhoran*. The women of the bride's family distribute *tikre* (a kind of sweetmeat) and those of the bridegroom's *chúri*, and the women of the brotherhood put *tapásás* in the bride's lap. This ceremony is called *gadd*. The bride is taken back to her parent's house on the 4th night, and stays there for an hour or two only. (This custom is more general in towns.) On the morning of the 4th day both bride and bridegroom visit the house of the former's parents and there take their supper, after which they return. This ceremony is termed *sattowára*.

Some special local customs in Ferozepore.

A curious rite called *bhatti jhalká*[1] is current in Ferozepur. The boy accompanied by some women and his sister's husband as *sarbála* goes outside the village. There a hearth (*bhatti*) is made and in it the *sarbála* kindles a fire which is put out with the water brought from

[1] *Jhalka*,—a flash, glance, splendour, etc. (*Panjabi Dicty*, p. 491).

the well by the brother's wife of the boy[1]. This is done several times, and then the whole party returns to the boy's home. On his arrival there he is seated on the basket and bathed with the water from the well, for which service the barber is paid Rs. 2. All the kinsmen now contribute *neota,* and the bridegroom dons coloured clothes, saying *salám* to all present and receiving in return something from each of his kinsmen After this the cobbler puts shoes on the boy's feet and the potter brings two *chapnis*. These are placed near the basket with a pice under each, and the boy, jumping from the basket, smashes the *chapnis*. Sandal is then applied to his forehead—an observance called *munh chitarna*, or 'painting the face.' He is also garlanded. Next a plate is put before the boy and into it the *neota* received from the brotherhood is placed. When the *neota* is given the *mirási* proclaims the amount given by each donor and concludes with the *jhukái* which runs :—

Jang par áb re so bhare so dharm.—'If you give your due faithfully 'tis well (otherwise you will be taken to task for not so doing).'

After the *jhukái* the women take the boy to the jungle, singing songs as they go, and there they walk seven times round a *jand* tree, twisting a red thread round its trunk. Then the bridegroom strikes it with a stick, whence this observance is called *jandi waddi (waddhna,* to cut or reap). At this observance also a *mirási* gets Re. 1. After it all the females return home and the wedding party sets out for the bride's house. On reaching her village it halts outside and if it has dancing girls with it they amuse it by dancing. Meanwhile the bride's father together with his *lágis* comes to them and meets the father of the bridegroom. This is called *milni*. Thereafter some girls come to the bridegroom and apply antimony to his eyes. After this the ceremony of *khudaknas* is observed. A short time afterwards the party leaves for the house of the bride. While on their way the bridegroom's father gives the nearest relation of the bride from Rs. 5 to Rs. 100. On entering the village fireworks (if there be any) are let off. The bride's father puts up the party in a separate house and the bridegroom is taken to the females. His mother-in-law takes some curd with his fingers and applies it to his eyebrows. She gives him Re. 1 on this occasion. Thereafter a *mirási* female measures the bridegroom with a thread. The *mirási* and the barber then take the party to the house of the bride. The bridegroom's father on this occasion gives the bride as much money as is asked by him. When this is settled the *nikáh* ceremony is performed. On the occasion of its performance uncooked rice and sugar are distributed among those present. The person performing the *nikáh* ceremony gets Rs. 1-4 as his fee. Thereafter the party is served with boiled rice and sugar. Those who are opulent entertain the party with mutton and rice. Rs. 25 to Rs. 100 are spent on this entertainment. The party puts up from one to three days. At the departure of the wedding party the bride's father assembles all his kinsmen and gives the following articles to the bride :—a couch, stool, antimony pot, plate, *chhanna*, quilt, pillow, clothes,

[1] This water is drawn in a new pitcher by the boy's sister-in-law, on the third day. She goes to the well accompanied by women led by a *mirási* beating a drum. For this the *mirási* gets a fee of a rupee. Apparently the *máchhi* or waterman also helps the sister-in-law, for he gets a fee of two rupees, besides some coarse sugar.

nosering and ear-rings. At this time an empty vessel is placed before the bridegroom's father. He drops from Rs. 5 to Rs. 25 into the vessel. Both the parties give Rs. 12 to each other's *kámíns*. When this is all over the bride is seated in a cart. She is attended by one of the female *lágís*. The party stays for a short time outside the village. The headman of the village is given his fee by the father of the bridegroom. Thereafter the parties meet each other and the wedding party leaves the village. On the third day the bride and bridegroom are seated opposite each other and a plate is placed between them. This plate is always full of a mixture of milk and water. The bride takes off the ornaments of the bridegroom and drops them into the mixture.

Dowry.—The terms for dowry are various and so are the customs connected with the institution itself which is chiefly notable for the disregard paid to the rights of the wife in what is ostentatiously given to her at marriage.

In Hoshiárpur one or two days before the wedding the bride's maternal uncle brings a nose-ring and ivory bangles with some clothes and cash for the bride. The articles are collectively called *nána ke chhak* and are exhibited to the kinsfolk. At or after the *nikáh* the amount of dower is fixed. It is in no case less than Rs. 8-8, but it may exceed Rs. 100 or even Rs. 1000. After this the wedding party is served with food and is supplied with food and is supplied with cots to sleep on. *Wari* is the term applied to the valuable clothes, *suhágpura*[1] and dried fruits, sent by the bridegroom's father to the bride. *Khat* is the term applied to the clothes, ornaments, utensils and all other requisities of a new household supplied by the bride's parents to the bridegroom.[2] The number of clothes &c. is not fixed. Rich folk in order to be well spoken of give 101 clothes, 40 pieces of cloth, Rs. 100 in cash, a palanquin, a box, a small wooden box, utensils, gold and silver ornaments, a mare, a she-camel, a she-buffalo and a suit of clothes for the bridegroom. Some Rájpúts give as much as Rs. 500 or Rs. 1000 in dowry. On such an occasion the members of the wedding party give a horse to the *mirási*, and each member of it is given Re. 1 and a piece of cloth. Thereafter the parties depart. The boy's father passes some silver and copper coins over the *ḍolí*.

In Hazára before the *nikáh* the bride's *vakíl* is sent for and asked by the Qází to fix the amount of dower. Of this there are two kinds, *viz.*, *sharái* or lawful and *riwáji* or customary. The amount of the former is Rs. 125 but that of the latter varies from Rs. 100 to one, two or more thousands of rupees. Some people execute bonds for the amount of dower. This classification is independent of the two

[1] Unlike the Muhammadans in Bahawalpur the amount of dower is fixed in Hoshiárpur according to the bridegroom's pecuniary position at the *nikáh*. Dowry is called *suhágpura* in this district.

[2] In Gujránwála the *khat* or dowry which the bride's parents wish to give their daughter is presented to the bridegroom's father in open assembly. Generally it consists of from 17 to 21 *tewars*, 7 to 11 suits for the boy, utensils, a couch, stool, cattle and ornaments. New clothes are at the same time put on the bridegroom, and he is given a new suit of clothes by the bride's father &c. to put on. The *salámi* ceremony is performed on this occasion, that is the bridegroom pays his respects to his mother-in-law, father-in-law and other near relations. In return for this he gets Re. 1 from each of them.

kinds of legal dower, *viz.* deferred and prompt. In theory deferred dower becomes due by the bridegroom when he cohabits with his wife, but it is never paid on that occasion. After the *nikáh* the dowry is placed in the courtyard of the house and shown to the people. The money presented in the *thál* by the boy's father is spent on ornaments for the girl, and these are put on her at her departure. The clothes exhibited in the dowry are not sent to her father-in-law's house but are kept by her own father, and she fetches them when required.

Among the Jádúns of Pesháwar also the dowry to be given to the girl is spread on a carpet and shown to the people, but it is not given to the bride all at once, out of it only a suit of clothes is given her and a suit is also given to the bridegroom. The remaining clothes are given her when she comes back to her parents' house.

Among the Swátís of Mansehra tahsíl the dowry merely consists of a few clothes, ornaments, a cot and a quilt, and even the cost of the two latter articles is borne by the bridegroom's father.

In Bhakkar the *nikáh-khwán* who appears to be a *maulavi* goes to the bride with two reliable witnesses and tells her that her *nikáh* is to be performed with so and so. She replies that her father or brother is her agent and the *maulavi* then asks his permission. The amount of dower is fixed with the consent of the parties. In general it is 100 copper coins with a gold *mohar* but it may be as high as Rs. 500 and a gold *mohar.*

The boy's father also gives or is supposed to give the bride glass or ivory bangles, a gold nose-ring, a gold *champákali,* silver *tarore,* gold or silver earrings, and a silver *hamail.* Her father also gives her a gold *khatmála,* a gold *basanti,* a silver *losi,* rings for the hands and feet, 10 suits of clothes, a *trewar, bewar,* quilt, curtain, pillow, ladle, antimony pot, pewter plate, couch, *pírha,* &c. A cow, buffalo or mare is also given sometimes.

In Baháwalpur the amount of the dower is fixed. The boy's father usually takes with him some fruit, *gur, til-shakkar* (sesamum and sugar mixed), *hasli* (necklet), ring, *tarore* (an ornament worn on foot); *bohaṭṭe* (armlets), *takhti, dawátin,* or *paṭrida* (square pieces of silver worn round neck), all of silver (a *nath,* good nose-ring, which, however, is more generally given by the townspeople); and a *tarewar,* or *turear,* three garments, *viz.* a *bochhan* or *dopaṭṭa, chola* or *kurtá,* and *ghagrá* (petticoat) or *suththan* (trousers), a *ghagra* being given by the Jáṭ tribes in general and a *suththan* by the Baloch.[1] In villages the bride's father generally gives no feast to the bridegroom's party, and in towns too this custom is practised but rarely.

In the morning a *vakíl* (guardian) and two witnesses go to the bride to ask her consent to the contract, and when she gives it the *nikáh* ceremony is performed according to Muhammadan law. The barber or the *mirási* distributes *til-shakkar* or sesamum and sugar among those present.

[1] In Dera Gházi Khán at the time of departure the bride's father gives her the following articles by way of *dáj*:—*bhochhan* (10 to 15), gowns (5 to 7), earrings, utensils &c. Wealthy men give a cow or she-buffalo for their sons-in-law. The boy's party is not served with food by the bride's party, but on the other hand the bride's party is supplied with food by the bridegroom's party.

Some special tribal customs.

An additional ceremony is performed among the Bhaṭṭí Rájpúts of Ferozepore. When the bride reaches the house of her father-in-law she is seated opposite to the bridegroom. A sword is placed between them, and a *reti* (an instrument used by cobblers for stitching shoes) is also placed near their heads. After this the females commence singing, and keep it up the whole night. The cobbler gets 4 to 8 annas as his reward on this occasion. This is called *rát jága* or waking for the whole night. On the 7th day the bride goes back to her father's house. After this, the bridegroom is sent in company of a *mirási* and a barber with the consent of the bride's father. On this occasion they bring back the bride. This is called *mukláwa*. Nothing is spent on the performance of this ceremony. The marriage expenses vary from Rs. 50 to Rs. 4,000.

In Hissár the Muhammadan Kahárs have some interesting ideas about marriage. To negotiate a betrothal 5 or 10 men of the girl's family visit the boy's home and his father and kinsmen entertain them there for a day. Three days later the boy's father summons his kinsmen and in their presence the girl's father or a near kinsman gives the boy a lump of sugar and a rupee. When the girl's party departs it is given a piece of cloth worth two rupees. This, it is said, makes the betrothal irrevocable. Prior to the wedding the girl's father sends a *tewar*, or gift of three garments, and a *dosára* (two garments, *i.e.* a *phulkári* and a white sheet) by his barber to the boy's father. On his arrival he summons the boy's kinsmen and consults them as to the species of wedding to be performed. Weddings are of three kinds or degrees :—

(*i*) Superior or *ghare ki shádi*, in which the boy's father fills an iron vessel with sweetmeats and then places a silver bangle worth Rs. 15 or 25 on top of it. One *laḍḍu* (sweetmeat) is sent to each man invited. Seven feasts are also given to the boy's party in this kind of wedding. The dower must be not less than Rs. 101.

(*ii*) *Gur ki shádi*, in which 10 or 20 *sers* of coarse sugar are consumed, a little being sent to each invited guest. Five feasts must also be given to the boy's party. The dower fixed is Rs. 80.

(*iii*) *Tage ki shádi*, in which a red thread is sent to each guest, and only four feasts are given. The dower is Rs. 21. When the wedding party reaches the girl's home the eldest representatives of each party meet and the girl's gives the boy's party (or representative) a piece of cloth. This is called *sharbat piláva*. The *nikáh* is then performed. Before leaving with the bride the boy's people send dried fruits to her house and then the girl's father gives her dower. On reaching their home the pair and all their near relatives must sleep on the ground as it would be unlucky to sleep on beds. This observance is known as *thápa*. Next morning the women of the family take the couple outside the village to beat the ground with *jál* sticks, an observance called *chhari*.

The Pachhádas of Hissar have some distinctive wedding customs. In betrothal the barber and two men of the boy's family go to the girl's home and give her father some money. After being feasted there two or three days the barber receives two rupees and each of his companions a piece of silk before they go. *Per contra* the boy's father has to pay the girl's Rs. 12 as menials' dues. This makes the betrothal irrevocable. When the parties have reached maturity the girl's father sends the boys three garments, which become the barber's perquisite. When the boy's party reaches the girl's village it must ride round it (*gáon ká phernú*) before entering it. Meanwhile the girl's people come out to receive them with *sharbat*, for which the boy's father has to pay Rs. 3, together with Rs. 7 for antimony and Rs. 21 for the *chhani* observance. The wedding party is then feasted. At the actual *nikáh* sugar and rice are distributed, but they must be uncooked. This observance is said to be peculiar to the Pachhádas. Rs. 14 are next paid to the girl's party for menials' dues. Among the Pachhádas the gifts of the girl are called *kharwa* (apparently because they include a pair of sabots, *kharáun*). Another distinctive usage is the *bhotani*, the bride's mother-in-law giving her some money on her arrival at her father in-law's house.

Among the Wiláyati Paṭháns in Hissár, *e.g.* at Tohána, the wedding is a simple affair. No observances are usual until both the parties are of age, when a date is fixed for the *nikáh*. The boy's party proceeds to the girl's home and is there feasted. Next morning the girl is made over to them, with her dower, but she returns the very next day to her parents' house for the ordinary *chauthi* observance to be held. On this occasion the boy's party sends her fruit and vegetables. She again goes to her husband's home at night, but visits her parents' house for a year after marriage on every Friday, whence the custom is called *juwa* These customs would obviously be impossible in a tribe which did not closely intermarry.

In Hissár Qassábs effect betrothals by exchange or if that is not feasible by purchase. The boy's father pays the girl's a rupee, or even less if he is poor, and receives from him an equal sum. He also has to pay the barber a fee of one rupee. When the parties are of age the girl's father convenes a meeting of his kinsmen and proposes a date for the wedding. Then he sends the barber to the boy's father, with seven copper coins, a rupee, a lump of sugar and a bit of cloth, to announce the date proposed. The boy's father summons his kinsmen and, accepting the cloth and sugar, remits the other things to the barber. Boiled rice with sugar and *ghi* is then distributed among the kinsmen. This observance is called *gath* by the Qassábs.

The boy's party goes to the girl's home on the day fixed for the wedding and is feasted on *panjíri* (made of coarse sugar and parched flour) in vessels, into which they drop from four annas to a rupee. Women of the boy's family accompany his party in this tribe and sing congratulatory songs at the *nikáh*, those of the girl's side singing in reply. The *milni* is in which the eldest representative of the girl's party formally meets the eldest representative of the boy's and gives him sweetened water to drink together with a sum of money. The boy's party departs on the 3rd day after the wedding, after giving the bride a present of clothes and ornaments called *bari* (a kind of dower), but of these the girl's father only keeps a few, returning the rest, When the bride departs her father also gives her a dowry of ornaments. clothes, utensils &c.

In Lohárú the Qassábs are said to have some different usages. Thus at a betrothal the boy's father gives the girl's a rupee, receiving two in return. This is called *salámí*. Then the boy's father puts some sweets in the girl's lap—the *god bharan*. He also gives her some silver ornaments. If the boy be present the girl's father gives him a rupee, a cocoanut and a suit of clothes. *Bidris* (presents of sweets, clothes and ornaments) are also exchanged on every festival, twixt the betrothal and the wedding *gandh*.

Among Muhammadan Rájpúts in Hissár brides are purchased for cash, the amount being negotiated through a barber. As soon as it is settled the boy's father summons his kinsmen and his son is seated on a chair while the barber places a lump of sugar in his mouth and a rupee in his hand. This is called *ropná*. A date is then fixed for the wedding and the boy's party proceeds to the girl's home. There it is received by representative men of her family bearing two or three vessels full of sweetened water. The eldest representatives of each side then meet formally in the *milni*, the girl's representatives giving a rupee and a piece of cloth called *risá* to the boy's. Gifts are also made to menials. The boy's party is suitably entertained and then the *nikáh* is solemnised according to Muhammadan Law. After the *nikáh* the boy is taken to his bride's house and there his sister-in-law puts questions to him and the *kangná* or bracelet which was tied on the wrist of the pair (*sic*) is unfastened. When the pair return to the boy's house they are given a blanket to sleep on—an observance called *thápná*. Muhammadan Ráwats in Hissár retain two Hindu rites: at betrothal they have the *tilak* marked on the boy's forehead by the barber of the girl's family; and they retain the *ṭewa* or observance in vogue when the date for the wedding is fixed.

Among the Sayyids of Hissár the wedding is a very simple affair and closely resembles that in vogue among Paṭháns.

The few Shaikh Quraishes of Hissár intermarry with those of Patiála. At betrothal the boy's father sends the girl two ornaments, one of silver, the other of gold, through a trusted menial, usually a barber, who goes to her house alone. There he is given from one to five rupees and sent back. The *nikáh* is in accord with Muhammadan Law.

Among the Saddozai and Kizzilbásh Paṭháns of Hoshiárpur several special usages are in vogue. The bridegroom is led into the room where the bride is seated amidst her kinswomen. She stands up to show her respect for him, but as there is a belief that the one who sits down first will yield in influence to the other they each try to persuade the other to sit down first and this contest causes much merriment among the women.

Aína mushaf.—When the pair sit down a covering of silk or shawl is spread over them. First of all an open *Qurán* is put into their hands as a token of blessing. Then the bride gives her husband a spoonful of *sharbat*, and he does the same to her, but as the bride is shy some one holds her hand and puts the spoon into her husband's mouth. Next a looking-glass is given to the pair and for the first time they see each other's faces in it. The bridegroom pays a few rupees for each of these ceremonies. When the *aína mushaf* (showing the *Qurán* and looking-glass) is over the bride's father or guardian puts her hand into that of bridegroom and bids them farewell. This is always a touching scene. The bride is then taken to her husband's house in a palanquin with due pomp. When she reaches it the members of his family pay her some money, termed *rú-numái*, as a fee for seeing her face.

Takht jami.—On the 3rd day after the marriage the bride's mother and relations bring her dowry. She is seated on a cushion called *takht* or bride's 'throne.' Then the bridegroom leads her a few paces by the hand. When this is done they are allowed to become more familiar and they are at liberty to abandon their shyness.[1]

Paṭháns of Peshâwar.

In the Utmán-náma *tappa* of Swábi tahsíl, in Peshâwar, some respectable person goes on the boy's behalf to the girl's parents and proposes the betrothal contract. If they accept a date is fixed. Before that date the boy's party sends some jaggery, rice and wheat flour to the bride's house and goes to her house on the night fixed. The articles referred to above are consumed on this occasion.

Thál ceremony.—After taking their meal at night the heads of both the parties sit in the courtyard of the bride's house and the *mirási* or the barber places a basket containing 4 or 5 *sers* of jaggery in their midst. The head of the boy's party puts some rupees into the basket. The amount is not fixed, but is settled by the head of the bride's party. Generally it varies from Rs. 50 to 1000. Silver ornaments, such as bangles, *kangan* and bracelets, are also placed in the *thál* (plate). After this the basket is removed by the barber or *mirási* who takes it inside the house, and it is returned filled with sugar by the inmates. This concludes the *thál* ceremony. The money and ornaments are afterwards returned. Then the bride's party sends *sharbat* and *mehndí*. Each person present drinks a little *sharbat* and some *mehndí* is placed on their palms. This is called the *ghúnt* ceremony, and it is the binding element in the betrothal contract. After this congratulations are exchanged and the bridegroom's party returns home the same night.

Channa artá.—On the third day of the *koyidan* the bride's kinswomen assemble and take some wheat flour, *ghí* and jaggery to the bridegroom. They remain in his house for 2 or 3 days. *Halwa* and other sweetened articles are consumed as a feast. At departure the bridegroom's parents give his mother-in-law and sister-in-law Re. 1 each by way of *parona* (*dopaṭṭa*). This is called *channa artá*.

Wadh or marriage.—The period between betrothal and marriage in this *tappa* is 1½ years. The date of the wedding is fixed by the eldest representative of the boy's family in consultation with the bride's parent. A suit of clothes is sent her prior to its fixture. Similarly a suit of clothes is sent to the boy by her parents. On the wedding day the boy's party reaches the bride's house at night. It is called *jáúji*, and the bride's party is *máúji*. Both parties pass the time in friendly

[1] There are no customs of *makláwa* and *morní doli* (sending the bride back to her parents' house) among these Paṭháns.

festivity. After the distribution of *lág* among the *lágis* the bride and bridegroom are dressed in new clothes. The bride is put in a *ḍolí*. When it arrives the *nikáh* is performed and the parties retire in the morning. Marriages in this *ṭappa* are made on a low scale. In Peshawár the expenses are very heavy.

Paṭhans of Isa Khel.

Shudnámá.—It is the beating of drums and the playing upon of musical instruments on the occasion.

Walíma.—Both the parties give a feast to their respective relations on the day of marriage. The practice of breaking *dhaknis* is in vogue in some families. When the bridegroom breaks them they say that he is a brave man. On the arrival of the wedding party at the bride's house prayers are recited according to Muhammadan Law. The *nikáh* ceremony is performed through a *vakíl* and *nikáh-khwán*. After this dates and sweetmeats are distributed among those present. The *lágs* are given to the *mírásís* &c. The bride is conveyed on a camel or mare. Sometimes a palanquin is used for the purpose.

Taríja.—On the third day after the marriage the girl's parents send the same articles as were sent by the boy's parents by way of *chan tárá* and *thál karan.*

Satwárá.—The bride returns to her parent's house only a week after her marriage.

Khaṭṭaks of Kohát.

Kwasda or betrothal.—The father of the boy accompanied by 5 or 6 persons and a *mulláh* goes to the girl's father to obtain his consent to the betrothal in private. The *rasmána* or price of the girl is also fixed at this visit. After that, on a Monday, Thursday or Friday, the father of the boy accompanied by 40 or 50 persons and a *mulláh* goes to the girl's father for the betrothal ceremony. The boy also accompanies them. The *nikáh* is performed and the price is also paid. *Gur* supplied by the boy's father is distributed by the barber. Among the *burkhs*, *gur* is not distributed, but instead a goat supplied by the father of the boy is slaughtered. *Niundra,* called in Pashto *achaundi,* is also paid then.

Four or five days after the betrothal a gold or silver finger ring and a suit of new clothes are sent by the boy's father to the girl's father for the girl. The girl is made to wear the finger ring and the *dopaṭṭa* (head dress) at once as a mark of betrothal. After this the father of the girl gives feast to the bridegroom and a few of his relations and gives the bridegroom a finger ring also. On the two 'Ids and Shab Brát a suit of new clothes and cooked food are sent by the bridegroom's father to the bride.

The father of the bridegroom accompanied by a barber and a *mulláh* goes to the bride's father to fix the date of marriage, and the amount of rice, *ghí* &c. to be supplied by him for the feasting of the marriage party is also fixed.

DDDDD

Two days before the marriage a few women on behalf of the bridegroom go in the afternoon to the house of the bride's father. They take off the bride's jewellery and make her sit in a corner of the house and some *gur* is distributed. This ceremony is called *kenawal biṭhána* (in Hindki). Next day in the afternoon many women on behalf of the bridegroom take fried *jawar*, grain or *gur* to the house of the bride's father. This is called *khaunai*.

Before the starting of the marriage the bridegroom and his friends are made to wear a garland, called *seri* in Pashto, which they tie on their turbans. The marriage party usually starts in the afternoon and arrives at the bride's house in the evening. Ornaments and clothes for the bride are taken by the marriage party with them. If the house of the bride is in a different village from the bridegroom's, then the marriage party is fed by the bride's father, but at the expense of the bridegroom. Jewellery and clothes are given to the bride as dowry by her parents. The bride is taken away in the evening. The father of the bridegroom then feeds the whole marriage party in his own house.

On the 3rd day after the marriage the mother or sister of the bride with some other women goes to the bridegroom's house to take the bride back. This is called *orayama* (3rd day). The same day at night, the bride's father gives food to the bridegroom and his relations and after keeping the bride for a day in his house sends her back with the bridegroom. On this occasion the bride's father gives a cow, or clothes or jewellery to the bride which gift is called *brakha*, 'share.'

Paṭhans of Isa Khel.

In Isa Khel tahsíl the terms used for betrothal are the Persian *khulwástgári* and the Arabic *khutba*. Some of the boy's kinsmen go to the girl's father by day or night regardless of the date. They generally take with them a woman's garment with two rupees, one for the barber and one for the *mirási*, from 1¼ *páos* to 1¼ of *sers* of *mehndí*, jaggery, a silver ring, a gold *ḍubbi*, a *kurti*, and an *orhni*. The girl's father serves them with *sharbat* and coloured water is thrown over them. Well-to-do people however take with them various ornaments of gold and silver, cloth and clothes. Some people also send Rs. 1-4 or 2-8 for the barber and *mirási* by way of *chan tárá* or *sehrá*. The girl's father in return gives 1¼ or 2½ *sers* of jaggery.

Munh chhuráwan.—After her betrothal the girl keeps *parda* from the boy's relatives. A few days after the *khulwástgári* the near kinswomen of the boy go to the girl's mother and each gives a rupee and a basketful of sugar to the bride. On receipt of this she discontinues her *parda*. This ceremony is called *munh chhuráwan*.

Thál karan.—After the *mangní* the boy's father's party send *chan tárá*, *i. e.* 25 plates of *halwá*, each also containing 10 *dharáris* or baked loaves. Besides these they send a *sehra* or 30 plates of *halwá*. The *halwá* &c. is distributed by the girl's parents among their relatives.

Warena.—On each festival day after the *mangní*, such as the 'Id-ul-Fitr, 'Id-ul-Zuha, the last Wednesday of Safar and the Shab Barát, the boy's parents send the girl's *ghí*, sugar or sugarcandy, rice, flour or baked loaves, a *kurti* and a silk *orhni*. But respectable families do not accept these things.

Khawání-píwaní.—Some poor parents with a daughter accept wheat or money on account of the price of the he-goat or buffalo for feeding the girls who sing songs and live with the bride. Out of this money they feed the wedding party at the marriage, but respectable families do not accept such gifts as they are not lawful according to religion.

The Wazírs of Bannu.

Among the Wazírs, the preliminary bargain is effected by the father or other near relative of the boy. When this is arranged, 10 or 15 men of the boy's party *with the boy* go at bed-time to the girl's house, having sent beforehand sheep, wheat and other necessities for a feast. Singing and dancing go on all night, a distinctive feature being that the old women of the bride's party come out with a coloured fluid like that used by Hindus at the time of the Holi and throw it on the men of the boy's party. The bride-price is paid in the morning, if it can be managed. The various murders, blood feuds and other wrongs lead sometimes to very young girls being betrothed to the aggrieved party, or else one is betrothed to a man on either side in order that peace may be made.

The price of the girl cannot in all cases be raised at once. For instance an uncle will promise his daughter to his nephew when they are both quite small. One informant stated that he paid nothing at his betrothal, but gave Rs. 100 a year after it, Rs. 200 two years later and that the marriage did not take place for another three years.

At the betrothal, which the Wazírs call *kojhota*, the girl's father gives her a large ring and a silk worked handkerchief.

The bridegroom does not go to the wedding (*shádí*) but only the men and women of his family and acquaintance. Very serious resistance is sometimes offered to his party on their arrival at the other village, which is timed for dark. There is then a feast in the girl's house, after which all the males go to the *chauk* and begin singing and dancing. The women of the bridegroom's party attire the girl, dress her hair like a married woman's, and put *mehndí* on her.

There is next an interchange of small presents, the young boys of the birdegroom's party being given red ropes, and the girl's silken braids by the parents of the girl. Each dancer is presented with a handkerchief. In the early morning the bride is taken away.

The brother or, if there be none, the father of the girl returns with her to her husband's house, but no other member of the girl's party. On arrival most of the villagers disperse, but near relatives remain and are fed at the expense of the bridegroom. The men also get a *pagrí* each and a rupee each is given to the women. At bed-time the orthodox *nikáh* takes place and is followed by consummation. People say that it is a sign of the degeneracy of the times that patience is not observed, and that in the old days modesty used to prevent consummation for a long time. The brother is present during the *nikáh* and leaves next day. Three nights are spent by the girl with her husband and then she goes back to her parents' house with her father or brother, who comes to fetch her. She stops away ten days or so and is again brought back by a relative of the husband. Her father is supposed to give her a second departure. Slight differences may occur in different sections. The points to notice are the presence of the bridegroom at the betrothal, his absence from the wedding, and the accompaniment of the girl by her brother to the husband's house. The *Ḍúm* plays little part except as a musician.

NOTE A.

The full expression is *kápá yá gandhen páka ayyám shádi mugarrar karna* and in Miánwáli it is thus described:—On any date in the daytime the boy's father's party visits the girl's father, and he demands some wheat, a he-goat or heifer, cotton and cash. These articles are however only given by the rich, the poor giving nothing. They simply fix a date for the wedding and return. After this a tailor is sent for to make clothes for the boy who gives him Re. 1. The date is fixed on any day between the 5th and 10th of the lunar month.

NOTE B.

The variations in the observance of *gandh páwán* are of course numerous. Thus in Shakargarh tahsíl, Gurdáspur, a body of 20 or 25 persons of the boy's party goes to the girl's house taking 5¼ to 7¼ *mans* of sugar. On the first night of their visit they are feasted and the boy's father drops from Rs. 1-4 to 11-4 in his dinner plate which the barber takes away, getting 4 annas as his fee. The rest of this money is returned by the girl's parents. Next day the boy's party is feasted again and in the evening the girl's parents invite their kinsfolk. Each party sits separately and then the girl's parents present clothes for the boy, with a ring. All these clothes are sent in a basket, and 5¼ *sers* of sugar go with it. Taking these gifts the boy's parents drop Rs. 30 to Rs. 60 into the basket which is returned to the girl's parents through the barber They pay the *lágis* their dues according to the custom of the village and remit the balance Each *lági* of the boy's party also gets a rupee on this occasion. The females of the girl's party too distribute sugar among their kinsfolk. Then comes the *gandh*, the date for the wedding being fixed between the 11th and 17th of the lunar month as the nights are then moonlit.

In Jullundur where the *gat páná*, as it is called,[1] occurs a month or two before the wedding the date for it is fixed at an assemblage held in the girl's house and care is taken that neither the departure of the wedding party from her house nor the *tel charhána* fall on the 3rd, 8th, 13th, 18th, 23rd or 28th day. The best dates for the wedding are the 10th, 14th, 20th and 25th.

In Siálkot *gandhní páwan* is called *gand parná*. The barber goes to the boy's party with a *trewar* which consists of a *kurta, dopatta* and *suthan*, *i.e. jora* for the *samdhan* (the boy's mother or aunt). A little oil is dropped at the threshold on his arrival and his first meal consists of *khichri*. Then the kinsmen are invited and the girl's father gives the boy a rupee, another to his barber and some copper coins to his *lágis*. The *trewar* is then shown to the kin and given to the boy's party. In return it gives a bundle of *mehndí*, *maulí*, *tapdshas*, dates, dried raisins, cocoanut, 11 *sers* of jaggery and 11 *sers* of sugar besides rice and sugar, for the girl. The date of the wedding is fixed on this day.

Ghanḍ pherná.—Then the parties send *gandá*, i.e. they send jaggery and *maulí* thread to kinsfolk to inform them of the date of the marriage and invite them to give *tambol*.

Gandhin páwan.—The father of the boy, accompanied by his brotherhood and taking with him some *gur* or *tapashás*, visits the bride's father and after consulting him fixes dates for the following ceremonies:—

(1) the *menḍhí kholan dí* or unplaiting the hair;

(2) the *chíkán dí*, the day on which *baṭna* is rubbed on the bodies both of the boy and girl, and on which the *gánás* are tied; and

(3) the *dhoe-dí*, the date of marriage.

These dates are generally fixed at some intervals, thus if the 11th be fixed for the *menḍhí*[2] the 14th and 17th are fixed for the *chíkán* and *dho* respectively.

[1] Another term applied to fixing the date for a marriage is *din dharná*. It is used in Jullundur and on the day when it is held the boy's father summons his kinsfolk, male and female, and songs are sung, sugar and copper coins being also distributed. Apparently this observance is different from and supplementary to the *gath páná*.

[2] Round Mithankot the unplaiting must be done on the 11th, 14th, 17th, 21st or 25th of the month.

In the eastern Punjab, in the valley of the Jumna, the ceremony of fixing the date for the wedding is called *lagan*. Thus in Ambála when the girl's father wishes it to be solemnised he summons his kinsmen to fix the date for the *nikáh* which must not be any date in the lunar month obnoxious to marriage according to Muhammadan Law or custom. As a rule the *nikáh* is never solemnised in the same month as that in which the date of the *lagan* was declared. The girl's father then sends the boy's a letter intimating the date fixed and with it a lump of *gur*, 5 or 7 *sers* of sugar, a handkerchief, ring and a few rupees, from Rs. 2 upwards according to his means. This is the usage known as *lagan*.

On the barber's arrival the boy's father invites his kinsmen to view the presents. The letter is opened and all are informed of the date of the wedding, which is hardly ever changed. Some of the sweetmeat is then eaten by the boy, the rest being distributed among those present. The ring and the handkerchief are taken by him and he puts on the ring while all congratulate the boy's father or guardian. The barber is entertained for 2 or 3 days and then sent away with a gift for himself and an answer to the letter. This done both parties invite their relatives to attend the ceremony.

In Gujránwála when a barber, a *mirási* or both go to the bridegroom's house to fix a date for the marriage on behalf of the bride's father, they take with them a *tewar* which is called the *gandh ká tewar*.

NOTE C.

But in some parts, principally towards the west and centre, other ceremonies precede the *batná*. Thus :—

In the Chakwál tahsíl[1] of Jhelum before the *máyán* a male or female barber takes oil in a vessel and stands by the boy. His kinsmen then put oil on his head with their fingers. They also throw copper coins into the vessel of oil and these are taken by the barber. This ceremony is called *tel lagáná*. The *máyán* is then begun. The boy's party invite the kinsfolk by sending round jaggery, and some mills are set up in the boy's house for grinding flour. Females who have received jaggery go to the boy's house and grind corn on his behalf. This is called *chakkí chúng*. On the *máyán* day the parties distribute the *halwá* to their kinsfolk and if the boy's father be wealthy he proclaims by beat of drum in the village that no one should cook anything in it the day before the wedding. On the wedding day a feast of mutton, bread and *halwá* is given to every one in the village. This is also called *chhak dená*. People incur very heavy expense in connection with this feast and many families have ruined themselves over it.

Similarly in Jullundur *máyán* is preceded by the *tel charháná* which is performed a few days before the wedding. A little oil is rubbed on the girl and boy. Both are seated on *khárás* and *batná* is rubbed on their bodies. *Gánás* are tied to the right hand and foot of each. A *gáná* is also called *kangná*. Henceforth they are considered to be 'in *máyán*' till their wedding. The boy is prohibited from leaving his house from this date. The *batná* is ground by seven females (whose husbands are alive) in a mill. This grinding is called *chakkí chúng*. Both bride and bridegroom wear dirty clothes from this date. On the day of the wedding the bridegroom again sits on a *khárá* and breaks *chapnís*. He is also asked to put curd on his hair and wash his head with it. Thereafter the *niyat-khair* is observed and a garland of flowers hung round the boy's head. The wedding party starts at about 8 P.M., if the bride's house be in the same village, but otherwise it starts at such a time as will enable it to reach her house at or about evening. The bridegroom rides a horse and the party follows him on foot. It is put up on an open site or in a house selected for this purpose. Among some tribes the *nikáh* is performed at 2 A.M. and by others at daybreak. A *vakíl* and two witnesses go to the bride to ask her consent to the contract and she gives it expressly or impliedly. After these formalties the *nikáh* is solemnised in the midst of the assembly as ordained by Muhammadan Law. The barber distributes sweetmeats or dates on this occasion. Ante-*máyán*.

This usage is called elsewhere *chhkún* and it is followed by a period during which the bride is said to be in *máyán*. Thus in the Báhawalpur State from the date of the *chhkún* ceremony till her marriage the bride wears dirty clothes and is said to be in *máyán*, which the bridegroom also observes. The beating of drums, etc., begins from the very date of the *chhkún*. On the day of the *dho* the bridegroom mounts the *khára* (a basket) and breaks some *chhanís* (small earthern covers for pitchers &c).

[1] In Chakwál Muhammadans preserve a curious Hindu custom. One day before te wedding party sets out the bridegroom pretends to be displeased with his family and goes to some relative or friend's house. His father goes to pacify him, accompanied by the womenfolk of the family. He promises to give his son something and the master of the house also gives him sweets and clothes. Thence the father returns with his son. This is called Nadha ruṭhná.

The marriage procession starts in time to enable it to reach its destination at the time of the *zuhr* (the second prayer, recited between 1 and 3 P.M.), or in the first quarter of the night. Villagers prefer to receive the party at the *zuhr* time, while townspeople prefer the night.

Drums, trumpets &c. are carried on the back of a camel along with the marriage procession, and on arriving at the bride's village the bridegroom and his best man (*sábálá* or *sarbálá*) are made to stay apart in a hut (*sahal*) where they remain till the *nikáh*. But this custom is more general in villages than in towns. In Dera Ghází Khán it is, however, not in vogue. In that district the bridegroom is the subject of a common practice. On the *chikán* day a sword or iron of some kind is placed in his hand and one of his kinsmen is told off to accompany him. This man is called a *kasi* or 'iron man' and for his services he gets a handkerchief or a *ritha*. In this district too the rites of *pillá tandhná* and *phul chunna* are observed. In the former the boy's sister ties his shirt to her own and receives a gift of Rs. 1 to 20 for so doing. In the latter a *mirásan* places some cotton in the boy's hand and he puts it in the girl's—this being repeated 4 or 5 times. Then follows the *sirmel* when all the women quit the house leaving the bridal pair inside it. For 2 or 3 days after this the bride keeps her face veiled from her husband's father and brothers, but when they give her a rupee or so she abandons her *parda* before them. This is called *ghund khula di*.

The *mehndi* ceremony is observed to its fullest extent in Kángra. On day before the wedding it is prepared at the girl's house being mixed with water and made into paste, in which wax-candles are stood. Then all the boy's clothes and shoes are put in a plate. Men of the girl's party take these articles to the boy's house in the evening, but females alone take part in this ceremony. The girl's sister goes with them and applies the *mehndi* to the little finger of the boy's right hand, and some is also applied to the *sarbálá's*. A bit of cloth is taken to tie over the *mehndi*. When applying it the girl's sister drops Rs. 3 to 5 into the bridegroom's hands and he returns this sum with the addition of Rs. 2 or 3. The women take their food at the boy's house and return home at night, the bridegroom's mother-in-law or his elder brother's wife accompanying them. *Mehndi* is applied to the girl in the middle of the night by all the women whose husbands are alive. They too drop some money into the girl's hands, and then return home. The *nikáh* is performed next day.

The *máyán* period or condition is closely connected with the tying of the *gánás*, but what the connection is does not appear. Thus in Gujránwálá 3 or 4 days before the wedding the boy and girl are placed under *máyán* and the *gánás* are tied. In this period their bodies are rubbed with *batna* and *mehndi* (myrtle leaves ground and made into a paste) is applied to their hands and feet.

Among the Saddozai and Kizzilbásh Patháns of Hoshiárpur the *máyán* is unknown or has been reduced to a simple observance called *hína* or *mehndi* in which one day before the wedding the bridegroom's father sends dry *hína* for the bride. Some, however, of her party, including her younger sister or any other little girl of her family, go first by night to apply saturated *hína* to his right finger and he pays his sister-in-law-to-be a few rupees for her trouble as an act of courtesy. The remaining *hína* is sent back for the bride to dry her hands and feet with.

In Siálkot this usage is called *máín paṛná*. A few days before the wedding each party distributes *ghunganián*, boiled wheat, to its kinsmen after applying oil to the bride or bridegroom in this wise :—The boy or the girl is seated on a *khárá* (basket), below which a lamp is lit. The womenfolk sing and *suhágan* (women whose husbands are alive) apply oil to the heads of the boy and girl. They also put a little *waṭná* on their hands and rub the remainder on the body. A *gáná* is then tied to their hands and from that day a knife is kept in the boy's hand so that he may not be overtaken by demoniacal influences. He is also precluded from bathing or even going to a lonely place at any distance from his house. The girl's father also puts an iron bangle on her hand. Singing and beating of drums begin from the day of the *máyán* or *máín*, by *mírási* women who sing such songs as the *Jugni challa, Relá, Bugga, Cherewálá nawarang* and *Sassi* as sung by Maulavi Ghulám Rasúl. One day before the relations assemble, *i.e.* on the *wel* day, the bride and bridegroom's hands are painted with *mehndi* which is also distributed to the kinsfolk. All the kinsmen too apply *mehndi* to their hands. After the *máyán gánás* are tied to the mill, sieve, winnowing basket, water-pitchers &c.

Siálkot. In Siálkot a rite called *ghaṛá ghaṛoli bharná* is performed after midday in the following way :—The brother's wife of the boy or some other woman puts a pitcher on her head. Some bread is placed on the pitcher and covered with a piece of red cloth (*sálú*). This woman is accompanied by her husband and their *dopaṭṭas* are tied together. Accompanied by several other women they then go to a well and the boy's sister-in-law takes the

Section 9—Hindu death observances.

Death observances in the Punjab are said to be based on two distinct schemes of ritual, one Vedic, the other based on the *Garúr Purána*.

In the Vedic ceremony the body of the deceased, washed and clothed in new clothes, is taken to the place of cremation on a bier. There in the *shamshán bhúmi* (place of cremation) a *vedi* (a rectangular pit for sacrificial fire) some 2 feet deep is dug, and the funeral pyre, of *dhák*, *pípal* or, in the case of the rich, of sandal wood, is set up in it. On the pyre the body is laid and more wood placed over it. When the flames rise high, four men recite *mantras* from the *Veda*, and at the end of each *mantra*, at the syllable *swáha*, each casts into the fire an oblation of *ghí* mixed with camphor, saffron, and other aromatics. The weight of *ghí*, if thrown into the fire in the oblations, numbering 484 in all, must equal that of the corpse or at least 20 *sers*. When all the oblations have been made, and the dead body is completely consumed, all the deceased's friends and relations bathe in a tank or river, and return home. After expressing their condolence, some return home, others help the survivors to clean and purify their house and perform a great *havan;* which being over, all the members of the household and their friends offer up prayers to the Almighty on behalf of the deceased's soul and themselves. The *havan* may be prolonged a few days, in order to purify the air of the house. On the 3rd or 4th day the ceremony of *asthisanchaya* is performed, and in this the bones of the deceased are picked out of the ashes and thrown into a river. After this nothing is done for the deceased. But if the members of his family are people of means, they give money in alms to the poor or to some charitable movement or start a school, orphanage, *sada barta* etc., at their own expense, to commemorate the memory of the departed. Vedic.

pitcher from her husband's head and places it on the ground. The waterman then draws water from the well in this pitcher and receives a fee varying from 2 annas to 4. Then the husband puts the pitcher full of water on his wife's head and returns to the boy's house. The song sung at the *ghará gharolí* runs as follow:—

Wáh wáh gharolí bhar ayá.
Wáh wáh sir te dhar ayá.
Wáh wáh ní phul jawain dá.
Wáh wáh ní nakhrá Nain dá.
Wáh wáh ní phul torí dá.
Wáh wáh ní nakhrá gorí dá.

When they reach the house the barber's wife takes the pitcher, bread and a *taká* (two copper coins) as her perquisites while the red cloth is kept by the mistress of the house.

After the *ghará gharolí* the boy is made to sit on a *khárá* by the barber's wife, and a lamp is lit beneath it. Then he is washed and a little card thrown on his head. The women all stand round the *khárá* and the barber gets his *wels* of silver and copper coins in the vessel containing the curd. A rupee is also placed under the boy's feet and this too is taken by the barber. All the women contribute *wels* on this occasion. The other menials also gets *wels*. After the boy has bathed the barber covers his head with *salú* and ties a *phúl-kárí* round his loins instead of a *tahband*. He then jumps from the *khárá* and breaks some *chapnís*. The *tambol* is then received and the barber is paid his dues. Thereafter certain persons join the wedding procession. When on his departure to his father-in-law's house the bridegroom mounts the mare, his brother's wife puts antimony into his eyes and his sister seizes the mare's reins to exact their dues. The song sung on this occasion is:—

Kí kujh dená ain wírá wág pharáyí
Wág pharáyí ghorí dáná charáyí.

"Oh brother let me see what thou givest for taking hold of the mare's reins and for feeding her with gram."

The other rites, observed by all the Hindus in general, follow the *Garúr Purána Yagna Valik Smrit* and other *smritis*, which are believed to be based upon old Hindu books, such as the *Grihya Sutras* and *Brahman Granthás*. In this, the popular ritual, the body is washed, clothed and taken to the crematorium as in the Vedic rite, with only this difference that a *panch ratná* (small pieces of gold, silver, brass, coral and pearl) is thrust into its mouth, while it is being washed, and four *pindas* (balls of flour or boiled rice) are offered at four different places, while it is being carried from the house to the crematorium. A son or near kinsman of the deceased is singled out to go through all the death ceremonies, and in common parlance he is called *karmí-dharmí*. He has to go barefoot and sleep on the ground for 11 days. When the body has reached the burning place the pyre is built generally of *dhák* wood, without the *vedí*, and the corpse is burnt without going through the *havan* described above. The *kapál kirya* or breaking of the skull is performed by the *karmí-dharmí*. After it all return, wash their clothes and bodies at a tank or well and offer up *tilanjáli* (an offering of water mixed with sesamum seeds) on behalf of the deceased's soul.

But the *karmí-dharmí* has still to go through many other ceremonies. He places a *ghara* for a male, and a *cháti* for a female, on a *pipal* tree, supported by its trunk and two branches, with a hole in the bottom which is loosely stopped by a few blades of *kusha* grass, so that the water may dribble through. This pot he has to fill with water twice daily for 10 days. Besides this, he has to go through two other daily ceremonies; the *pindu* or offering balls of boiled rice in the morning, and that of lighting an earthen lamp and placing it on a tripod of three small *kanas* or reeds in the evening. On the 4th day the ceremonies of *asthi sanchaya* and the *chaturthik shrádhas* are performed. Food with *dakshna* is given to a Mahá-Brahman and the deceased's bones are picked out of the ashes and sent to Hardwár to be thrown into the sacred Ganges.

The *dasáhi* or shaving of all the members of the family and washing clothes is gone through on the 10th day.

The *kiryá karmá* and *pindí chhed* ceremonies are performed on the 11th day. In the former, *pindás* are offered on behalf of the soul, and food and *shaiya*, which consists of a cot, a pair of shoes, an umbrella, some pots and ornaments, are given to the Mahá-Brahman for the sake of the dead. In the *pindí chhed* the *pindu* or ball representing the deceased's soul is cut into three parts and each is mixed with three other balls representing his father, grandfather and great-grandfather if they are dead. It should not be peformed if he died without male issue or unmarried, but some people do not observe this restriction. The *bárah* is performed on the 12th day. In this ceremony 12 *gharás* or *chátis* (as deceased was a male or a female) filled with water, and each covered with a small piece of cloth, a *mathá* (a large cake of wheat flour cooked in *ghí* or a *ganáorá* (a large cake of sugar) and some pice are given to Brahmans.

The *brahma-bhoja* is performed on the 13th day in the case of a Brahman or Kshatriya and on the 17th in the case of a lower caste. Food with *dakshaná* (two pice at least as a fee or present) is given to 13 or 17 Brahmans. With this ends the ceremony.

If the family of the deceased is well-to-do, it gives a Brahman food every day in the morning only for one year; or else distributes *netaks* or *laddús* 360 in number with some pice as *dakshná* among the Brahmans. Hindus believe that the soul of departed has to walk a long distance for one year to reach the court of Dharma Ráj.

Observances before and at death.

When a person is *in extremis* he should be made to give away some grain, money and a cow in charity,[1] and a *pandit* is sent for to recite verses from the *Bishan Sahansar-nám* and *Bhagwat Gita.*

If the sufferer should recover after all this has been done he is asked what he desires and his wish, whatever it may be, is scrupulously fulfilled, if that be possible. If, however, he shows no signs of improvement, a space of ground near his *chárpái* (cot) or some other place, is smeared with cow-dung and some *dab* grass scattered over it. On this grass a sheet is spread, and the dying person laid on it, with his feet to the east,[2] and his head resting on the lap of his or her eldest son or next-of-kin. Some Ganges water is very commonly dropped into his mouth, together with one or two *tulsí* leaves, and, especially if he is a man of advanced age, a little gold.[3] When death ensues, the corpse is covered with a cloth and its face turned towards the Ganges. It is extremely inauspicious to die on a bed and in Rohtak it is believed that the soul will in that event be re-born as an evil spirit.

In Jínd the dying man is laid on the ground and grain, money, a cow &c. are given away in alms according to his means with his own

[1] The orthodox alms are (*i*) the *gaudán* or gift of a cow, whose horns are ornamented with gold or silver rings, while her neck is garlanded and her body covered with a piece of new cloth—red in the case of a female. Copper coins are placed at her feet, and she is led up to the dying person who gives her to a Vedwá Brahman who prays that she may lead the dying man by the tail to the next world. The donor also pours a few drops of water into the Vedwá's hands. This ceremony is called *gaudán* 'gift of a cow', or *baitarni*, 'viaticum'. Subsequently (*ii*) the *raskha's* gift, of sugar, alkali, soap, cotton and other necessaries of life, is given to the Vedwá. Lastly a *dípa*, earthen lamp, containing a silver or gold coin is placed in the palm of dying person, and after the recital of *mantrás* is given to the Vedwá, but this rite is not observed in all parts of the Punjab. This account comes from Siálkot. In Kángra it is believed that he who dies with the cow's tail in his hand, through the help of the cow (*Baitan*) crosses the deep Baitarní river or Bhanjla *nadi* which is supposed to exist between this world and heaven, and which it is difficult to cross without the aid of a cow. The cow is afterwards given to Brahmans. After this a lamp called *diva dharyará* is lighted and placed by the head of the deceased, with a wick, which must last for 10 days. No new wick may be put in it during that time and if burns out it is considered a bad omen.

[2] In Jínd when a child over 27 months of age, a grown-up person or an old one is dying the ground is first plastered with cow-dung. Then *kusha* grass is spread and on that again a cloth is laid. On to that the dying person is taken down from the cot so that his feet point towards the south, *i.e.* to Lanka or Ceylon. This is called in Urdu *manzil rasánt.*

[3] Or Ganges water, with gold and a tiny pearl, are put in his mouth as passports into Swarga: Karnál. In Multán a little before death a small piece of gold, a pearl and a porcelain bead are put into his mouth *so that the deceased may be* purified. A nut or anything given by *guru* is also placed in his mouth.

Note.—A Hindu must not be allowed to die on a bed or even on a mat, as it is supposed that the soul in separating itself from the body in which it is incorporated, enters into another body which leads it to the abode of bliss destined for it, but if the dying man were to expire on a bed he would be obliged to carry it with him wherever he went, which it may be easily supposed would be very inconvenient.

hands. This is called the *chháya dán* or *akhiri dán* (last gift) and is supposed to avert the agonies of death so that the dying person either recovers or dies without further suffering.

In Kulu, according to a highly idealised account which can only apply to the highest castes, when a man is on his death-bed 7 species of grain, *satnája*, some iron, wool, salt and money are put before him, and he is made to give these articles as his last alms or *ant-dán*: a cow *baitarni* is also given. The scriptures already mentioned are read. If the sick man recovers the alms go to a Brahman, otherwise they are taken by the family *acháraj*, whose office is hereditary. Where it has no *acháraj*, the *dán* is given to a Náth and the cow to the local god. When dead, a *dípak dán* or a gift of lamp is made and a *panch-ratan* (a collection of 5 metals) is put in the mouth, a *saukh* (conch) is blown to make the death known to the neighbours, and the near relations are also informed.

Functions of the chief mourner.

The next of kin or nearest agnate of the deceased is, it may be said, *ex-officio* his chief mourner. In Ambála he is commonly called the *karmí dharmí* or in Siálkot *bhungiwálá*.[1]

After the death he shaves his head, beard and moustache, leaving only the *bodí* or scalp lock, bathes, as already described, puts on a clean loin-cloth and turban, and for a period of 14 days eschews leather shoes but not those of cloth or jute.

In theory the chief mourner is a Brahmácharya until all the rites due to the dead have been completed. It results from this his status that he must avoid several ceremonially impure acts, such as sexual intercourse, eating more than once a day, and taking medicine. He should bathe at least twice daily, and practise other ablutions. He should also avoid sleeping too long and, more especially, sleeping anywhere but on the ground. Lastly he ought to abandon secular business for a time and meditate on God day and night.

If the deceased has left a widow, she loosens her hair. Moreover she is, for a time, ceremonially impure and must not sleep on a bed or touch any household utensil. For 13 days, and until she has bathed in the Ganges or Jamná, she may only eat once a day.

[1] The *bhungiwálá* or chief mourner (a person who is most nearly related to the deceased or who by common usage has the right to perform this function) doffs his clothes, gets his head and face shaved clean and then bathes in order to purify himself from the defilement of the barber's touch. All the younger male relatives of the deceased also get their heads and faces shaved in honour of his death. The *bhungiwálá* then puts on a *dhoti*, *parná* and turban of pure white cloth and a sacred thread, and performs *havan* (a sacrifice to fire) and *samkalpá* giving a few alms to the *achâraj* who appears at the lamentable scene of mourning.

In Multán the body is bathed having its head towards the north and feet to the south. Then it is shrouded in white cloth if a male and in red if a female. A Mansuri coin is tied to the shroud.

The corpse is then washed and wrapped in a piece of ceremonially new cloth, is placed on a kind of state bed called *vimán*. Several other costly coverings of silk and muslin are placed over it in order to show the high social status of the bereaved family. In the case of the death of an elder the *vimán* or litter which is constructed of a plank of wood and several strips of bamboo, is decorated with artificial flowers and birds. Before starting all the women of the household, in particular the daughter-in-law and grand daughter-in-law walk round the litter and do obeisance giving alms to the family barber.

In Ambála 2 copper coins wrapped in red cloth are thrown over her husband's head to indicate that her married life is now over. In Montgomery 2 garments of red cloth (given by her own parents) and 2 of white (given by her parents-in-law) are put on by the widow on the 11th and 13th days respectively.

In Jínd directly after death has ensued the deceased's son sits down on the ground near him and places his knee under his head—an usage called *godá dená*. In some places a lighted lamp is also held by the son. He then 'sits in *kiriá*' (*kiriá baithná*), changes all his clothes and puts on fresh ones which in the case of well-to-do people are of wool.

Before cremation all the sons and grandsons of the deceased get themselves shaved—*bhaddar karwáná*—in Jínd, Bhakkar and elsewhere, but the usage is not universal.[1] Thus in Gurgaon only the eldest or youngest son may shave or one of his kinsmen may do so, but in some villages all the sons shave. In this district the hair shaved off is placed underneath the cloth spread on the *arthí* and taken to the burning ground.

If, in Gurgáon, the deceased's wife is alive she breaks her bangles in token that she has lost her *suhág* on her husband's death. This is called *suhág utárná*. These bangles are also placed on the *arthí*, like the hair. In Karnál she also unties her knot of hair, breaks and throws the pieces of her bangles and her nose-ring on to the corpse, with which they are wrapped up in the shroud. The other females of the household also discard their ornaments.

Soon after the death the body is washed, a man's corpse being washed by men and a woman's by women. The water for washing the dead should be drawn in a particular way: the chief mourner ought to take a pitcher and rope, go to a well and bathe. Then, without drying his body or changing his waist-cloth, he should draw a second pitcher full of water, using only one hand and one foot,[2] and carry it home to wash the corpse. If the deceased was a man of high caste, the *tilák* is applied to his forehead, a *juneo* placed round his neck and a turban tied round his head. The body is invariably clothed: a man being dressed in white, and a married woman, whose husband is alive, in red called *chundrí* A widow is also shrouded in red cloth, but no ornaments are used, whereas a wife whose husband is still living is decked in all her finery,[3] a new set of bangles being put on her wrists, her teeth blackened with *missí*, her eyes darkened with antimony, her nails stained with henna, and a *bindí* fastened on her forehead. The old are dressed with special care. If the death occur too late for the body to be burnt before sunset it is kept in the house for the night, during which some 5 or 10 of the deceased's kinsmen watch the corpse.

[1] So too for example in Bannu before the cremation all the deceased's children and grand-children get their heads, moustaches and foreheads shaved and very often the man who performs the *kirya* gets all the hair of his body shaved. In Isá Khel if a father or a mother dies, all the sons, grandsons and great-grandsons get their moustaches, beard and head shaved, but the eyebrows are not shaved at all. Only the eldest son is allowed to perform the *kirya*. If an elder brother or uncle dies without issue only he who performs his *kirya* gets shaved.

[2] With the right hand alone: Karnál.

[3] With 7 silver ornaments; and the gold nose-ring, if a wife; the latter being removed by the husband at the burning.

In Kulu if the death occurs early in the day so that the cremation can be effected that same day, a bier is made at once and after the corpse has been bathed and the *mritusthán* (death-bed) and *dwárpál* (door) *pinds* have been offered, it is placed on it, and a shroud put on the body. Four of the nearest male relatives carry the bier to the burning-place and midway the bier is put down, a *bisrám* (rest) *pind* being given and the mat on which the man died burnt. All the way grain, fruits and pice are thrown over the corpse, which is then taken to the burning-place where the fourth *pind* is offered. A funeral pyre is then made, and when the corpse is put on it the 5th or *chitá pind* is given. On the corpse are piled big logs of wood to press it down and the pile is then set on fire, first by the *kirm-kartá* or man who gives the *pinds* and then by others. All the near relations and neighbours, especially the brothers, sons etc. of the deceased should go with the *arthi*. When the body is nearly burnt the skull cracks and the *parohit* sprinkles water over the pile: this is called *kapál* (brain) *moksh* or *kapál kirya*. The shroud is given to the *achárajj* and the other white cloth is given to the musicians or Dágís. When burnt to ashes, some on the very day of the burning and others on the third day wash away the ashes and take out the *asthis* (bones of the teeth and fingers) which they keep carefully and send down to Hardwár by one of the family or some reliable person. Some rape-seed and iron nails are spread on the burning place.

As a general rule, death is swiftly followed by cremation among the Sikhs and Hindus, but there are many notable exceptions. Thus, the members of several religious sects and orders are buried, as also are very young children, and in certain cases exposure, especially by floating a body down a stream, is resorted to. But whether destined to be burnt or buried the treatment of the corpse is much the same.

The bier (*pinjri* or *arthi*[1]) is made of the pieces of the bed on which the deceased lay prior to his death, or of bamboo or *farásh* wood. Upon it is laid the hair shaved off by the next of kin, together with the wife's bangles if the deceased leaves a widow. Over the hair is spread a sheet on which the body is laid. For persons of great age or sanctity a *bawán*[2] replaces the *arthi*.

The carrying out of the corpse.

After the body has been tied on to the bier the first *pind*[3] is placed on the deceased's breast, before the bier is lifted up. The bier is then lifted on to the shoulders of four near kinsmen of the deceased, the body being carried feet[4] foremost. As soon as it is taken out of the door of the house, a second *pind* is offered, the third being offered when it has passed the gate of the village or town, and the fourth at the

[1] By metathesis for *rathi* (*Platts*).

[2] Sanskr. *vimána*.

[3] The 5 *pinds* are all made of barley flour, *ghi* and in Jínd they are prepared at the time by the Nain or barber's wife and carried in a dish, *thál*, by the Mahá-Brahman who also carries a *garwá* or basin full of water.

[4] Head foremost in Karnál: in which District, it is said, the bier is merely halted at a tank and *pinds* again placed on it. Then all the *pinds* are flung into the water and the body taken up again *feet* foremost.

ghardban[1] or *adhmárag* or 'half way' between the gate and the burning ground. Before this fourth *pind* is offered water is sprinkled on the ground and the bier is set down, the first *pind* being replaced by this, the fourth. This rite is called *básá dená*, or the 'rest giving,' and the place of the halt is termed *bisrám*, or 'the rest.' Here too the bier is turned round, so that the head of the corpse is now in front, though the same four kinsmen continue to carry it. The fifth *pind* is offered at the burning ground. These offerings are supposed to pacify the *dúts* of *Yáma* (the messengers of the god of death). The bier is set down at the burning-ground, and the eldest son plasters a piece of ground with cow-dung and writes the name of Rám seven times to invoke God's help for the dead. On the same ground the *chita*, funeral pile, is raised and the body being placed on it a *panchratans* (five *metals*) of gold, pearl, copper, silver and coral put in its mouth. In the case of a woman this is done at the house.

Cremation : The pyre.

The purest wood for the funeral pyre is sandal wood, which is, however, rarely used owing to its cost, *pípalí*, *dák* or *jand* being used instead, but a piece of white sandalwood is if possible placed on the pyre. Sometimes the wood is carried by the mourners themselves.

A pyre should be so constructed as to lie due north and south, in a rectangular pit some 2 feet deep, resembling the *vedi* or pit for the sacrificial fire.

When the pyre has been completed the fifth and last *pind* is offered and any valuable shawl or other cloth removed from the corpse, and given to a sweeper or a Mahá-Brahman.

The body is then unfastened, the cords which bind it to the bier being broken with one hand and one foot, and laid on the pyre.

The body is laid supine upon the pyre,[2] its hands being placed behind and so underneath it to prevent its being cruel in the future life.

The shroud is torn near the mouth, and the *panjratni* inserted in it, while chips of sandalwood with some *tulsi* leaves are placed on the deceased's breast.

A man then takes the burning grass in his hands and walks once right round the pyre, keeping it on his right hand, and then turns back until he reaches the feet. Here he halts and throws the burning grass on to the pyre. As soon as it is ablaze all present withdraw out of reach of the smoke until the body is almost consumed when the chief mourner draws near again and pulling a bamboo out of the bier with it smashes the deceased's skull.[3] The smashing of the skull is said to be due to the idea that the life of man is constituted of ten elements, nine of which cease their functions at death, while the action of the tenth (*dhanjiye*) continues for three days after death, causing the body to swell if it remain unhurt. The seat of this, the tenth, element is in the skull, which is accordingly smashed in order to set it free. Finally

[1] In Multán the *ghardban* is considered essential. Midway to the crematorium, the bier is placed on the ground and the deceased's eldest son or the one who is to perform the *kiria karm* walks round it thrice and breaks a pitcher full of water, which he has brought with him from his house. This is done so that if the deceased is in a trance he may regain his senses on hearing the noise.

[2] 'So that it may see the sun' in Multán.

[3] He then throws the stick over the corpse beyond its feet.

he pours over the skull a cup of *ghí,* mixed with sandalwood and camphor. This rite of smashing the skull is called *kapál kiriá* or 'the rite of the skull.'

Kár dená.

After this all the members of the funeral party take a piece of fuel and cast it on to the pyre; and as soon as the body has been completely consumed one of them takes the bamboo which was used to smash the skull, and with it draws a line on the ground from the head of the corpse to its feet, keeping the pyre on his left in so doing.[1]

Mourning.

After this line has been drawn all the deceased's kin stand at his feet with clasped hands and the next of kin raises a loud cry of sorrow—*ḍáh márná.*

Tilánjali.

After the *ḍah* all the men go to a river or well, where they bathe, and wash all their clothes, save those made of wool. The deceased's kinsmen and others now take a handful of water and facing southwards, cast it on the ground, saying his name and *got.* With this water sesame is mixed, whence it is called *tilánjali.* Or a little water mixed with sesame is distributed in the name of the deceased.

In former days a *siápá* or mourning assembly lasted 10 days, but now-a-days it is held only for one day, when the women beat their breasts. But on the death of a full-grown man it lasts for several days and the wife of a *Bháṭ* leads the mourning, and for this she gets a fee which may vary from an *anna* to Re. 1-4-0.[1]

In Siálkot cremation is called *sanskára* and when the corpse is laid on the pyre its face is bared in order that the women of the family may have a last look at it. After pouring *ghí* and *panchratní* into the mouth the face is covered with the shroud. A piece of wood is then thrown over it from west to east and several logs of wood and splinters of sandal wood are placed on it. Before applying fire to the pile, the *bhungíwálá* performs a *havan* under the directions of the *achúraj.* Then a lighted torch is brought to him, but before he takes it, it is customary for him to show his grief by uttering mournful cries, and following his example all the near relatives present also weep. Then taking the torch the *bhungíwálá* sets fire to the four corners of the pile and walks round it four times throwing pieces of wood into it while the *achúraj* recites *mantras.* His example is followed by near relatives of the deceased. The women now leave the scene and collect on the banks of a river or tank to bathe, but the rest of the processionists wait until the skull cracks. This is called the *kirpál kiryá* ceremony. After it they proceed to make their ablutions, but only at a few yards from the burning pile and they sit down again to perform the straw breaking ceremony.

In this the *achúraj* recites aloud a *mantra* ending in the familiar words *yatra áe tatra gachhate* 'whence he came, thither he goes.' At the end of this *mantra* every one takes a straw, breaks it in two and

[1] A somewhat similar rite is found in Multán. There 'they walk round the pyre three times and return home. On their way back at about 30 or 40 paces from the crematory they sit with their backs towards it and each draws a circle before him. Then the *achárai* recites some *mantras* and they break a straw or bid farewell to the deceased for ever.'

throws it backwards over his head. But the *bhungwálá* throws his straw without breaking it, thus showing that some connection still subsists between himself and the deceased.

After purifying themselves of the pollution of having carried a corpse they all return to the door of the deceased's house, though no person may enter it as it is still defiled. Finally everybody taking leave of the relatives of the deceased returns to his own house, where it is usual to sprinkle water upon the clothes in order to completely purify oneself.

It is not until all these funeral rites and formalities have been accomplished that the people of the house are allowed to take any food, for they have neither eaten nor drunk anything since the moment that the deceased expired. All these practices are most rigorously observed.

After the above ceremonies the deceased's relatives spread a carpet or mat on the ground publicly and sit on it the whole day. Friends and acquaintances of the bereaved family come from far and near to sit on the mat in order to express their grief at the death as well as to condole with the relatives. This is called *phaṛí páná* or carpet spreading. The same course is followed by the women of the family, but they spread a carpet in their own house and perform *siápá*, in which a hired woman of some low caste (*siápá ki náin*[1]) sings dirges and the women joining in the chorus, beat their thighs, naked breasts and heads in measured time.

At night several caste-fellows of the deceased sleep on the ground in his house in his honour. Every day for 4 days early in the morning all the males of the family utter loud cries which are followed by the weeping of the women.

If the death takes place late in the evening or at night then all the funeral ceremonies are postponed till the next morning and the corpse is kept indoors. But a stick just as long as the length of the deceased's body is placed beside the dead, in fear, perhaps that the corpse may not get longer.

On returning from the burning ground in Jínd the members of the party bathe at a tank and wash all their cotton clothes to purify themselves, while the Naí gives them *ním* leaves, which they put in their mouths. On arriving at deceased's house they sit in front of it in two rows through which the Naí passes pouring out water, which is also supposed to effect purification. Then they return to their homes.

As a rule no food is cooked in the deceased's house on the day of death. Those who have married sons and daughters receive food from them. But elsewhere, as in Jínd, any relative may supply the family with food, *khichṛi* (rice and pulse), flour and *ghí* in case the deceased was an adult and sugar and rice also in case he was an old man. This provision is called *kaṛwá baṭṭá* or 'bitter food,' and the remains of it are not kept but distributed among the poor. In Gurgáon if the deceased was a Brahman uncooked *khichri* (a mixture of *dhál* and rice), pulse and flour are brought by his *jajmáns* and if he was a Mahájan they are purchased from the bazar. If the deceased was a man of any other tribe this food is sent by some of his relations. When it is cooked a *gaugarás*

[1] Lit., a woman of the Naí or barber caste.

(some loaves of bread given to a young cow) is given. After this the man who has performed the funeral rites takes his food and is followed by other members of the family.

Gurgáon. The man who has to perform funeral rites cannot wear woolen clothes but only a *dhotí* (waist cloth), nor is he allowed to wear leather shoes. He spreads a cloth before his house door and sits there for the whole day. Those who come to pay a visit of condolence stay with him for a short time and then leave him after expressing sympathy with him and the other heirs of the deceased.

A little before sunset this man goes for *ghat bharná* a second time. He fills a pitcher after taking a bath and then returns to his house, but it is not necessary that a *pandit* should accompany him in the evening. In the evening an earthen lamp is lighted on the place where the deceased breathed his last The wick of this lamp is made so long that it may be sufficient to last for ten days.

In Bannu after burying a child or burning a person when the people return home they call a Machhâni or waterman's wife to the door and give her a heap of corn. This ceremony is called *berí bhárá*. By it the right of crossing the river in the lower regions is secured to the deceased.

Nîm ki patti chabáná.

The funeral party now returns to the village, accompanied by the Náí who has plucked a branch of a *nîm* tree. From this every one takes a leave before he enters the village, and this he chews, and then spits out as a token that all contamination has been removed; or to accept another explanation, to invoke a curse on those who wilfully failed to attend the funeral.

The actual funeral ceremonies are closed by a *chaudhrí* or other elderly man saying, after the members of the party have sat for a time close to the deceased's house, *Bháiyo dhoti sakháo*, 'Brothers, change your clothes.'

After the men of the house have returned from the funeral, the women headed by the deceased's wife or mother (in the case of a man, or, in the case of a woman, by her daughter-in law) or by his nearest female relative,[1] go to bathe weeping and singing mournful dirges as they go. After bathing they return in moist clothes to the deceased's house and leaving his heir there go to their own homes. There they take a *shudh ashnán*, bath of purification, and then resume their ordinary duties.

The Náí now obtains from a Kumhár all the articles required for the *g at*, together with those required for burning the lamp at the spot where the deceased died. These articles include some *dab* grass, *jeorán*, sesame, milk, Ganges water, an earthen jar, and *tulsí* leaves. The chief mourner accompanied by a Náí takes these to a well by which he hangs a jar,[2] full of milk and sweet water or simply water, in a *chhinká*

[1] She also takes with her the grass which was spread under the deceased's death-bed and the earthen vessel used in washing the corpse, and casts these away outside the village. This is called *pálá utháná*.

[2] A *ghará* in the case of male, and a *chátí* in that of a female: Ambála. In Kángra this jar is called *chooru* and is hung on a stake of *paláh* wood fixed firmly in the ground in front of the door.

or net on the trunk and two branches of a tree, which the spirits are supposed to haunt. A small hole is made in the bottom of the pitcher and stuffed with *dab* grass so that the water may trickle slowly to the ground. Hence it is called *dhárrá* (from *dhár* a stream) in Jínd. In Gurgáon certain trees are set apart for this rite, which is known as *ghat márná* and for which certain *mantras* are prescribed.

A little before sunset this jar must be refilled, after the chief mourner has bathed, but the *pandit* need not accompany him. The jar has to be filled thus twice daily for 10 days. In the evening too a lamp has to be lighted at the place where the breast[1] of the corpse was or near the spot where the death occurred.[2] This lamp must be furnished with wick enough to last 10 days,[3] and it must be kept burning day and night for that period, to light up the path of the departed spirit through Yáma-Loka. A small fire must also be kept burning there.

At the same time a lamp is lighted and placed on the ground outside the dead man's house. Close to it but on the public road must also be placed a *tikoni* or tripod of reeds, tied together in the middle, on top of which is placed a cup full of water and milk but with a hole in it. All this is done while a *pandit* recites *mantras*. This is repeated on the two following days, a new lamp and *tikoní* being required each day. In Ambála this observance is repeated daily for 10 days.

Next day the *karam-kartá* (one who gives the *pinds*), after bathing, cooks some rice to make three *pinds* on which pieces of betel nut and black wool are placed. A jar containing water, milk and *ghí* is placed on some sand in the compound on a teapoy; and a very minute hole made in the bottom of the jar to let the water out slowly, and *kusha* (sacred grass) is put in the jar. On each of the nine subsequent days only one *pind* is given and more water is poured in the jar to keep it full. A lamp is kept burning for nine days and the *Garur purán* is read by the priest to the audience, who offer money to the lamp, which goes to the priest. On the tenth day the lamp is taken away by a Náth who gets As. 4, and the other things are thrown into a river or stream, everybody has his head shaved and washes his clothes; on the 11th day the *spindí karm* is performed: a bed, umbrella, shoes, a cow, cooking utensils, a suit of clothes and jewelry being given to the *acháraj*.

In Multán on the day after the *kiria* some more wood is thrown on the pyre so that any part of the body unburnt may be completely cremated.

Soharni.

Kanets and other low castes give one *pind* every third day, putting the *pind* in a hollow piece of wood and taking it to the river, where the *karm-kartá* holds it by one end and a carpenter by the other, the latter

[1] Whence it is called *chhati díwá* or 'breast lamp': Jínd.

[2] In Kángra this lamp, called the *díwa dhariara*, is said to be placed by the head of the corpse; and the wick must not be renewed: it is inauspicious if it fail to last the 10 days. Both this lamp and the *choara* are taken, at the expiration of the 10 days to the river side, or to a spring, or placed under a *bar* or *pípal* tree.

[3] Called the *dasdhi* in Jínd.

cutting the wood at the middle and thus the *piṇḍ* is dropped into the water. Water is brought from the river in a pot, with which to knead some flour which is given to cows. Then a goat is killed and relatives and neighbours are fed. This is called *sardhá*.

After the funeral a *paṇḍit* is sent for in Gurgáon to ascertain the *soharní* and *teramí* days.

The *soharní*, also called *astat sanchí*[1] (or in ordinary speech *phúl chugná*) is performed on the third day after the death, provided it does not fall on a Bhadra, *panchak*, a Saturday or a Tuesday, in which case it is observed on an appropriate day.

The deceased's kinsmen go in a body to the pyre and there cook rice and pulse, each in separate vessels. A *piṇḍ* is then placed by the deceased's skull, and eight *balis*[2] set round it in as many different directions.

The bones of the deceased, which are universally called *phúl*,[3] are now picked up with an elaborate ceremonial. First of all the chief mourner picks up three, using only his thumb and little finger. These he places in a platter of leaves and then all those present collect the remaining bones. Secondly, the ashes are collected with a wooden hoe. Then the bones are washed in a *karel* (the lower half of a pitcher) with milk and Ganges water. Lastly eight stakes are driven into the ground on either side of the pyre.

The bag in which the remains are placed should be of red cloth for a woman and of white for a man. But in Jínd only the bones of the hands, toes and the teeth are gathered into a *thelí*, a purse of silk or of deer-skin, and then taken to the Ganges or Pihewa *tírath*. In the Kurukshetra and Devadharti on the Jumna this rite is not observed.

The rest of the ashes are collected into a heap, about which 4 pegs are driven into the ground, and round these cotton thread is tied.

The bones are carried by a kinsman, a Brahman or a Kahár.

But in Montgomery the bones are not picked up until the 4th day and they are then sent to the Ganges, while the ashes are cast into any running water. On the other hand in Rohtak the Jáṭs if well-to-do are said to despatch both bones and ashes to the Ganges while those of people dying of leprosy are cast into the Jamna,[4] while round Tohána in Hissár the ashes are merely piled up in the crematorium.

Hindus dwelling in the Kurukshetar do not send the bones to the Ganges but bury them in an earthen vessel after they have been washed with milk and Ganges water. This is a purely local custom.

[1] *Asthi sanchaya* in some parts.

[2] The *bali* consists of a little rice and pulse put in a *ḍona* or platter of leaves.

[3] The only exception is in Multán where the bones are called *gola*. To 'pick up' the bones is *chugna* in Panjábi.

[4] Distance is not a factor in the matter since in Bhakkar all Hindus send the bones to the Ganges.

In Kulu among the higher classes the *asthi* (bones) should be taken to the Ganges within a year of the death. The man who takes them eats only once a day, because the *pátak* is considered to have been renewed at this time. These bones are taken from the place of cremation and in an earthen pot put in a hollow of a tree or wall. When despatched they are wrapped up in silk cloth and hung round the bearer's neck. If he is not one of the family, he is paid about Rs. 5 as remuneration in addition to the fee for the *dán-pun* at Hardwár and his expenses on the journey. On reaching Hardwár the bones are cast into the river and alms are given. Some water is taken home, where it is called Gangajal and worshipped. Brahmans are fed on his return and some cloth, cash and grain are given to the *parohit*.

The pinds.

In addition to the 5 *pinds* offered during the actual funeral, other *pinds*, which are believed to constitute the body of the dead man, are subsequently offered.

After the bones have been sent to the Ganges all the kinsmen return to the spot where the *ghat* is hanging. Then a patch of ground is plastered over and as many *pinds* offered as days have elapsed since the death. And from this day onwards a Brahman is fed at this same spot, or given 10 days' supply of uncooked food.

After the *phúl chugná* is over in Jínd, the eldest son or he who performs the *kiriá karm* has a *kathá* (reading) of the *Garúr Purána* recited by a Brahman at the deceased's house for 10 days among Vaisyas and for 13 among Brahmans, Káyasths and Játs; and some money is spent on this *kathá* by the members of the family and kin.

Of pátak or impurity.

Corresponding to the *sútak* or ceremonial impurity which ensues on birth is the *pátak* or *bhit*, sometimes erroneously called *sútak* which ensues on a death. In theory the period of this impurity is 10 days among Brahmans, 12 among Khatrís, 15 among Vaisyas and a month for Sudras, but it is now in practice 13 days among all classes, or less according to the degree of relationship: *e.g.* the death of a kinsman in the 4th degree involves *pátak* for 10 days, and that of one in the 10th degree for 1 day only.

Pátak extends in theory always to kinsmen of the 7th degree.

These rules are, however, subject to many variations. For instance in Siálkot the *bhit* lasts only from the day of death to the 11th day and no outsider ventures to eat or drink in the deceased's house during this period.

But in Bahàwalpur the family in which a death has taken place is held to be impure for 13 days, and other Hindus do not eat or drink with any of its members. The impurity extends to all the descendants of the common ancestor for five generations: thus if F dies all the descendants of—

are ceremonially impure. After the 13 days the members of the family remove this impurity by bathing, washing their clothes or putting on new ones, and by re-plastering their houses. A person affected by the *bhiṭ* or impurity is called *bhiṭṭal.*

In Bhakkar tahsíl the rules are the same, but the period is only one day on the death of a child of 6 months, 3 days on that of one of 5 years, 6 days if he was 10 years old and 13 days in the case of all persons whose age exceeded 10 years.[1] It is removed by breaking old earthenware, as well as by washing clothes &c. On the last day an *achâraj* is fed and after taking his meal he recites *mantras* whereby the house is purified. But in other parts of Míánwálí a family in which a child dies is impure for 3 days; and in all other cases for 11 days among Brahmans, 12 among Khatrís and 13 days among other Hindus.

In Bannu the rule is that the pollution lasts for as many days as there were years in the dead-child's age. If one more than seven years dies the pollution lasts for 13 days, and affects the descendants of the four higher generations.

The *kiriá karm* is performed, at least in theory, on the close of the period of pollution. Thus in Gujránwála it is performed by the eldest or youngest son on the 13th day, as the family is deemed to be in *sútak* (state of impurity) for 13 days. This impurity affects the kin to the 3rd or 4th generation. So too in Kapúrthala the *kiriá karm* is performed among Brahmans on the 11th day after death, among Khatrís on the 13th, while Vaish observe it on the 17th and Sudras on the 31st day after death.

In Sháhpur, however, the family is considered impure for only 12 days. This impurity affects all relations up to the 7th degree. On the 13th day it is removed by donning new clothes and plastering the house. A person affected with impurity is called *marutak.*

In Rohtak the sect of the Sat-Námi *sádhús* does not mourn or perform any *kiriá karm* after death.

[1] But the period of *bhiṭ* is also said to be as follows:—

Age of deceased.	*Duration of* bhiṭ.
Six months.	Immediately after burial or throwing into water.
Over 6 months, up to 3 years	1 day.
Over 3 years, up to 5 years	3 days.
Over 5 years, up to 10 years	6 days.
Over 10 years	11, 12, 13 days according to the caste.

There is in some parts a tendency to simplify the full rites. Thus in Kohát after the body has been washed and five valuables put in its mouth it is carried on a bier by 4 men who are relieved from time to time on the way. There appears to be no *adhmarg* and the *pinḍ karáná* (as it is termed) is only performed thrice, once at the place of death, once at the outer door of the house and lastly at the burning ground. After this the man who has offered the *pinḍs* carries a pitcher full of water round the body, breaks it and spills the water. The body is carried out with its feet towards the burning ground, but on reaching it is turned round so that its feet are towards its house. On the way raisins, dates and pice are thrown over the coffin, and if the deceased was a very old man flowers too are cast upon it.

At the burning ground the body is washed a second time and *ghí* is put in its mouth. After the *kapál kiriá* the man who is to perform the *kiriá karm* circumambulates the fire 6 times, being joined by all the other members of the deceased's clan in the 7th round. Then all those attending the funeral withdraw. A short distance from the pyre on their way back all collect and each picks a few blades of grass while the *acháraj panḍit* (*sic*) recites some *mantras*, and on their completion all men except the one who is to do the *kiriá karm* cut the blades into pieces and when they come to some water bathe and wash their clothes. Then all the clansmen take water in their hands and putting sesame in it while the *achárj* recites *mantras*, throw it on the ground. The deceased's family then gives the *achárаj* sweetmeats and 1¼ yards of cloth are given to the man who is to perform the *kiriá karm* for his turban or *bhungí*. After prayers all may now depart or accompany the deceased's family to their house which the *kiriá karm* man enters, but he or some other relation presently comes out and bids them adieu. When they reach their own houses they stand at the door while some one from inside sprinkles water over them before they enter.

A lamp placed in a small pit dug at the place of the death is kept burning for 10 days during which the *panḍit* recites the *Garúr Purán* by night or day. In the morning a *pinḍ* and in the evening *tarkashta* is offered during these 10 days outside the door of the house. The *kiriá* man bathes twice daily, but eats only once, though he is given good food. Very early on the morning of the 10th day the lamp is taken to a spring or river where the *pinḍ karm* (*sic*) was done on the first day and put into the water with its face to the south. While so doing a naked weapon is placed on the *kiriá* man's head and the same day all the deceased's clansmen bathe and the boys get shaved. The *kathá* or reading ends on this day and the *panḍit* is given some cloth and cash. The relations give turbans to the *kiriá* man, who is thus recognised as the deceased's representative. Some cash is also given him and his kinsmen console and encourage him to do his work. Brahmans perform the *kiriá* on the 11th day, Khatrís on the 13th and Aroras on the 15th. At this rite the *achárаj* makes figures of the *deotás* (gods) on the ground with dry flour and then reads *mantras*. After he has finished a bed with bedding, ornaments, grain, a cow, some cash &c. are given away in charity in the deceased's name. Another rite called *khorsha* very like the *kiriá* is held on the 16th day when Brahmans are fed. Until the *khorsha* is done, the deceased's clansmen are considered impure (*sutki*) and other people will not eat or drink from their hands.

On the 4th day after death the bones are picked up to be thrown into the Ganges, but the ashes are collected and cast into the nearest river. On the 10th day *khichri* (rice mixed with pulse) is cooked by a man not belonging to the family and distributed among the kinsfolk.

For 10 days the females assemble together and mourn.

Children dying under 5 are said to be affected by *athráh*, a kind of disease.

In Gurgáon from the time the bier is taken up until it reaches the burning ground all the mourners keep saying in a loud voice *Rám nám sat hai—sat bole gat hai* 'The name of *Rám* (God) is true and will last till eternity. He who meditates on His name will get salvation.'

Káraj or *Káj*.

The *káj* or *din* ceremony is not performed on any particular day in Gurgáon but care is taken to perform it as soon as possible. In villages the people cook rice with *ghí* and sugar, while Bániás and Brahmans in the town fry *laddus* and *kachauris*. All kinsfolk whether living near or at a distance are invited and the people of the village, as well as Brahmans, Jogís and beggars are fed with sweetmeats. Some only entertain people of 36 castes on this occasion, while others invite men of every caste. The relations who are precluded by kinship from eating from the bereaved house are given *pattal* or a separate share, and travellers visiting the village are treated in the same way. Others in addition to inviting kinsfolk in this way give Re. 1 and a *laddu* weighing a *ser* to each man of the tribe which does not disdain to receive alms. Some people have been known to spend about a *lákh* of rupees on an ancestor's *káj*. Relations invited on the occasion are on their departure given cash as well as sweetmeats. Those who are bound by relationship to pay something give money when the deceased's heir binds his turban.

Among the Bishnois the dead are buried at a place called *ogárá* where cattle are tethered. It is believed that the deceased will not turn into an evil spirit by reason of cows' urine always falling on it. In the absence of such a place they bury the dead in a burial-ground or crematory. No ceremony is performed in the case of a child. But in that of a young or old person they perform the *tíju* or *káj* ceremony on the 3rd day after death. The ceremonies connected with the 13th and 17th day are not performed. The *káj* of a youthful person is on an ordinary scale, *i. e.* only 20 or 22 kinsmen and 5 or 6 Brahmans are served with food. Recitations from the sacred books are continued for three days. The *káj* of an old person is celebrated with great *éclat*, large sums of money being spent on it. An ordinary Bishnoi only feasts all his villagers but rich folk spend thousands of rupees. A cow and the clothes of the deceased are given to a Brahman in charity.

Purián bharná.

The food prepared on the *káj* day is at first placed on the deceased's tomb in the leaf of an *ak* plant together with a cup of water. It is believed that it is more auspicious if this food is eaten by crows than by any other bird. The period of impurity of *pátak* is limited to three days. The actual members of the family are alone considered to be impure. An observance peculiar to this sect is that the marriage of a daughter or granddaughter or great-grand-daughter of the deceased is celebrated on the *káj* day.

Barni baṭhání in *Gurgáon.*

This observance depends on the pecuniary means of the deceased's heir. On the *soharní paṇḍits* are sent for and made to recite the *Gáyatri mantra* about 125,000 times for the deceased's benefit at a place fixed by the owner of the house. All the *paṇḍits* rise early and after bathing recite the *mantra* till 2 P.M. when they take food. If one of them has to make water while reciting the sacred verse, he may do so but cannot resume his place without washing. Smoking is also forbidden during this time. On the 11th day all the *paṇḍits* assemble at the *ghát* to perform a *havan*. After this they are dismissed with some *dakkshná* or remuneration.

Banjúr chhorná.

This rite is performed on the *ekádshi* or 11th day after death if the heirs are men of wealth and position. It consists in marrying a cow with a bull. The dues on this wedding are as usual given to the menials concerned, and after it the cow and bull are spotted with *mehndí* and let loose, to run wild, but the cow is generally given to a Mahá-Brahman, while the bull is branded so that it may not be put to work. Agriculturists will not harass a bull so branded. It is fed by the deceased's heir until full grown. Further it is never tethered with a rope or confined in any house. This rite is also called *barkhotsar chhorná* or *akal chhoná*. It is not necessary that it should be performed on the death of an old man, but it may be performed on the death of a young one, and generally speaking it is done in the former case also.

Gankhas járná.

This is only performed when the *banjúr chhorná* has been duly observed. It consists in planting a long bamboo (about the height of a man) in the ground outside the village with a human head dyed red on its top.

The erection of chhatrís.

Rich men and those of good position often raise a fine building to the memory of a deceased ancestor at the place where his body was burnt. In the middle of it they erect a structure of the shape of an umbrella. Beneath this in the second storey they have the deceased's foot-print carved. These are always marked on hard ground whatever be the height of the building. Some *chhatrís* in Gurgáon have cost Rs. 10,000 or Rs. 12,000 each. They are handsome buildings containing decorated staircases &c. They serve as shelters for travellers. Some people raise these *chhatrís* to a considerable height so that they may be seen from the roofs of their houses.

The following superstitions are current in Gurgáon :—

(1) One who joins in funeral procession to the burial or burning ground abstains from eating sweetmeats or drinking milk for that day.

(2) Those who raise a funeral pyre for the first time do not drink milk or eat sweetmeats for three days.

(3) If any one dies in the *panchak*, his death will be followed by another and so a *panchak shánti* is performed.

(4) The man who takes the remains of a deceased to the Ganges does not re-enter his house without going to the deceased's burning place and sprinkling Ganges water on it.

(5) If the death of a young person occurs on some festival it is never celebrated until a male child has been born in the family on the same festival.

(6) A man is considered to be very lucky if he has a great-grandson at his death, and it is believed that he will go straight to the Paradise. But it is considered unfortunate if he leaves a great-great-grandson at his death as he will then go to hell. A body is watched till the *sokarní* so that no one may take wood or coal from its pyre as it is believed that if this be done the spirit will fall under the control of some evil person.

Fruit of some kind is given to a husband and wife in halves on the death of a child so that they may soon be blessed with an another one.

The shroud of a child dying of *másan* (a wasting disease) is brought back to the house and carefully kept after being washed. On the birth of a second child it is laid on that shroud, the main object being that it may not die of that disorder.

A death is considered auspicious if it occurs during the *amáwas* and *kanagat* days, and it is believed that a man dying during those days will get an exalted place in Heaven.

If a man dies at a place of pilgrimage or while on his way to it intending to pass the rest of his life in meditation he is believed to have secured a place in Heaven.

In theory Hindu mourning lasts a year, during which period many rites have to be observed. The principal ones in Siálkot are : (*i*) the *pinda* offering :—On the day after the funeral, the *bhungiwálá* rises early and bathes, puts on a *pavitram* (a straw ring), performs a *havan*, offers one *pinda* (a ball of boiled rice) and goes out to water a sacred *pípal*. All these practices are repeated every morning and evening up to the 10th day under the directions of the *acháraj*. The number of *pindas*, which are regularly placed side by side in water at a fixed locality, is increased until it reaches 10 on the 10th day. (*ii*) *The chautha* :—On the 4th day, after performing these rites in the morning, as usual, the *bhungiwálá* with his friends and relatives goes to the cremation ground for the bone gathering (*phúl chunná*). The bones are generally picked up on the 4th day, but if it falls on an ill-omened day the rite is performed on the 3rd. Provided with *panch saviya* and other viands, he performs a *havan* there, and taking an earthen pot full of water and milk, sprinkles it over the ashes. He sits on his heels with his face to the east, performs the *sankalp* once more, stirs the ashes with a small wooden spade, looking for any bones that may have escaped the flames, and puts them into an earthern pot reciting a *mantra* meanwhile. Taking up a portion of the ashes he throws them into any river near by.

The remainder he collects into a heap covering it with a piece of cloth supported on 4 sticks, like a canopy. Then he offers a sacrifice to it. These mementoes of the deceased he brings home and they are buried in a corner of the house to be thrown one day into the sacred waters of the Ganges.

In Sháhpur on the 4th day after the death *all* the bones and ashes of the deceased are thrown into the Ganges in the case of a rich person. But in that of a poor one only one bone from each limb is thrown into that river. The ashes however are always thrown in a stream.[1]

In Miánwáli the remains are also collected on the 4th day. The bones washed with milk and Ganges water are put in a bag made of deer skin and thrown into the Ganges with some gold or silver while the ashes are thrown into any running channel.

In Isá Khel some kinsmen accompanied by an *achárај* visit the crematory on this day to pick up bones which are put into a new earthen vessel while the ashes are thrown into a stream. The vessel is sent to the river Ganges. But if a stranger die on a journey both ashes and bones are thrown into the river. In this tahsíl *Garúr Purán* is also recited on the 4th day.

The tenth day after death.

This day is known by various names. In the eastern districts it is called the *dasáhi* and in Jínd two rites are observed on it: (1) all the kinsfolk (both men and women) of the deceased go to a tank and bathe there, but only the members of his family have their heads shaved as well; (2) his eldest son distributes 10 *chhahnás* (pieces of cloth) with 10 pice and 10 *laḍḍús* of rice, each wrapped in a *chhahná*, and cooked gram among the Náí, Jhíwar, Brahman and relatives of his family. This observance is called *dasáhi ke laḍḍú bánṭná*. The kinsfolk do not take those things home, but give them to the poor, merely tasting the gram and throwing the rest away. This is said *pátak nikálna*, 'to avert the impurity,' or evil influences of the death.

The dasgátar.

The 10th day after death is theoretically one of ceremonial importance. In Gurgáon it is known as the *dasgátar*, and upon it the first *seja* is offered. During the 9 preceding days the *ghat* has been kept filled and a single *pinḍ* offered daily, but on the 10th day all the deceased's kinsmen go to the place where the jar hangs and there the next of kin, with some other (near) relatives, is shaved; and after bathing they give to a Mahá-Brahman all the necessaries of life.

This ceremony takes fully six hours, and is concluded by giving away 360 *pinḍs*, and lighting 360 lamps. In addition 16 special or *khorsi pinḍs* are given and *tilánjali* is also distributed 360 times. After this the *ghat* is untied, and the spot where the deceased died is plastered with cow-dung, mixed with cow's urine and Ganges water, and is thus purified.

[1] In Sháhpur on the 4th day an effigy of the deceased is made and sweetmeats and copper coins distributed

In Kulu on the 10th day after death a goat is killed and relations feasted. This is called *sondha.* The ceremonies of *jowásha* etc. are not observed. The higher classes perform the *shudhi* or purificatory rites on some auspicious day, and the lower on the 3rd, 5th or 7th day after the death. In this rite Brahmans, neighbours and relatives are feasted and sometimes a sheep is killed. The Kanets of Lag drink *lugri* or *sur* (hill beers) on this occasion, while the Dágís kill a sheep or goat on the 3rd day. The following table shows after how many days the various tribes are considered to become purified after a death in the family:—

Lower castes, Dágís, etc., 3 days.

Kanets, 3, 5, 7, 11, or 13 days.

Brahmans, 11 days.

Rájpúts, 13 days.

Khatrís, 15 days.

Mahájans, Bohrás, Súds and goldsmiths, 16 days.

In Siálkot the 10th day or its ceremonial is called the *dasahra.* And after the ceremonies usual on it, the friends and caste-fellows of the chief mourner meet on the banks of a tank or river for the final ablutions. He and his near relatives are shaved on this day, shaving not having been allowed during the preceding 10 days. Having finally purified themselves the deceased's relatives hold a funeral feast to which all kinsfolk from far and near are invited. They stay two days in his house and then the women wash their clothes and hair with curds and soap. The earthen pot of water and the lamp which was kept burning day and night are also cast into water. But according to another account the purification is not attained or complete until the day of the *kiriá karm,* the date of which varies.

The rites in Isa Khel are much the same, but in addition a few members of the community put a burning lamp before sunrise on a bundle of *khas* or *kháshak* and set it afloat on a river or pond. All the members of the family shave the head, moustaches and beard, and bathe after their return home. They also pour 360 pitchers of water at the root of a *pípal* tree with the aid of the *acháraj* who recites *mantras* all the time. The women also wash their heads and all the clothes worn in performing the above ceremonies. In the afternoon all the members of the community gather together, and the Brahman finishes reading the *Garúr Purán* the same day, receiving some cloth and a little money as his fee. But of late in the towns the Brahmans have not completed the *Garúr Purán* till the 14th day instead of the 10th, because the pollution is absolutely removed on the 14th and also because almsgiving to Brahmans is most proper when no impurity remains. On the day when the *kirya* ceremony is finished, the *acháraj* is offered a bedstead, a quilt, a coverlet, a few ornaments and a sum of money and is then dismissed.

After-death ceremonies.

Karnal. On the third day some of the relations of the deceased go to the crematory for the purpose of what is known as *phúl chugná* (collection of fragments of bones of the deceased) which without being brought over to the town are despatched to be thrown into the Ganges through a relation, a Brahman or a Kahár. The house is impure (*pátak*) for 13 days. On the 10th day the household perform *dasáhi*, *i.e.* they go to the tank, wash their clothes, shave and offer *pinds*. On the 13th day a number of Brahmans are fed; the walls and the floor are besmeared with cow-dung; the earthen vessels are changed; the clothes are washed and thus the house is purified.

If the deceased left sons the eldest performs the *kirya karm*. This ceremony is performed on the 11th day among Brahmans, on the 13th among Khatrís, and among Vaishas on the 16th. Among Brahmans the ceremony is observed by the eldest son, among Khatrís by the eldest or youngest son and among Vaishyas by the agent of the deceased. A family in which a death occurs is considered to be impure until the *kirya karm* has been performed. Siálkot

The *bhungíwálá* rises early to make his ablutions. The *acháraj* draws a *chauk* (square) showing therein the symbols of various gods and goddesses on the ground and constructs a *pandál* over it in his courtyard. Rice is boiled and several kinds of flowers, vegetables and scents provided. Indeed many other things are prepared which are indispensable for the sacrifices and offerings which he is to make. The *kirya karm* lasts for several hours and the ceremonies connected with it are too complicated and numerous to be detailed here. It is supposed that from this moment the departed is divested of his hideous form and assumes that of his forefathers to live among them in the abodes of bliss. This ceremony is observed by Khshatriás and other castes excepting Brahmans on the 13th day. On this day, too, many Brahmans are summoned to a feast to be eaten by proxy for the deceased. Popularly the day is called *Burá din* or the evil day and on it a widow's parents send her clothes, ornaments and cash according to their means in order that she may pass her widowhood in comfort.

Randepa *or widowhood.*—The same afternoon at the conclusion of the *kirya karm*, the *randepa* ceremony is observed. The deceased's widow, after performing ablutions, decorates her body, puts on her richest garments and bedecks herself with all her jewels. Married women surround her, clasp her in their arms, and weep with her beating their heads and breasts in measured times crying and sobbing as loud as they can. Now too it is customary for the deceased's relatives to give his widow valuable clothes and ornaments in token of their sympathy with her. But she then divests herself of all her jewels and rich garments which are never to be donned again in her afterlife, thus showing her fidelity and devotion to her departed husband.

On this day at the death of an elder splendid feasts are given to his daughters and grand-daughters' husbands and their relatives. *Ghí* and turmeric, the use of which is strictly prohibited during the preceding 10 days of mourning, are now used in the preparation of diverse dainties for the entertainment of the guests. The *bhungíwálá* puts on new clothes and turban bestowed on him, if married, by his father-in-law.

The eleventh day after death.

The rites on this day appear to be either the *kirya karm* or survivals of the full *kirya* rite. Thus in Jínd on the 11th day after death a Brahman performs the *pinḍ-dán*. The *pinḍs* consist of rice, flour, *ghí* and sugar, and *mantras* are read by the Brahman. A bedstead, clothes, utensils and grain are given in the deceased's name according to his means in alms to an *acháraj*, who is supposed to satisfy the desires of the *bhúta* or ghost-body by means of his *mantras* &c. This observance is called the *kirya of Gyárah* or ceremony of 11th day. The eldest son who has performed the *kirya karm* now changes his clothes and puts on a coloured turban.

In Bhiwáni the *gyárwín* is solemnised on the 11th or 12th night after death. Sweet-scented things are burnt in fire to the recitation of verses from the *Vedas*, and all tribes except the Sarságís give the *acháraj* clothes, cash and utensils on this day.

The twelfth day after death.

Bárah.—In Ambála and Karnál the 12th day after death is observed as follows:—Twelve *gharás* (or *chátís* in the case of a female) are filled with water, covered with a small piece of cloth, and with a *mathu* (a large cake of wheat flour fried in *ghí*) or a *gandora* (a large cake of sugar) and some pice, given to Brahmans.

Dwalsha.—Four *pinḍs*, one for the deceased, and one each for his father, grandfather and great-grandfather are prepared on the 12th day at the place where the death occurred. The deceased's own *pinḍ*[1] is cut into 3 parts, with a piece of silver or a blade of *dab* grass, and each part kneaded to one of the other three *pinds*, to typify the dead man's re-union with his forefathers. At this rite a Gujráti Brahman is feasted and fed. A gift of at least two utensils, a cup and a jar (*tilia*) is also made to him.

In Jínd this rite is called the *spinḍí karm*. It is observed on the 12th day by a Brahman, and four *pinḍs*, money and food are given to a Biás Brahman.

Hawan.—In Gurgáon a *hawan* is peformed at the spot where the death occurred, and at night a fire of *dhák* wood is lighted and on it is thrown a mixture of *ghí*, barley, sesame, dried fruit and sugar, by means of a stick. The deceased's house is now deemed purified.

The thirteenth day after death.

Brahmabhoja. Brahmans and Khatrís celebrate the Brahmabhoja on the 13th day, other castes on the 17th. Food, with a fee of at least 2 pice, is given to 13 or 17 Brahmans.

Terawín.—On the 13th day at least 13 Brahmans (one of whom must be a female, if the deceased was a female) are fed. The second *seja dán*, which is precisely like the first, is also offered on this day, but it is the perquisite of the *parohit*, the other 12 Brahmans each receiving a vessel of water covered with a bit of cloth, a cup full of sweetmeat, a nut, *kanwal gatta*, and a pice.

This ceremony is sometimes held on the 12th day or, in Delhi, postponed to the 17th day after the death.

But in Bhiwáni on the 13th day only one Brahman is fed, the

[1] Hence this rite is known as the *pinḍ chhedan karam*. In Karnál it is said to be observed on the 11th day and as a rule only to be observed if the deceased left male issue, a condition not always adhered to.

house plastered and cow's urine and Ganges water sprinkled in it. It is then considered purified.

Dastár Bandi.—The ceremony of installing the heir, of which the *dastár bandi* or tying on of the *pagri* is emblematical,[1] is held in the afternoon of the 13th day after death. In Montgomery if the deceased had a shop his heir is made to open it.

The 13th is in a sense an auspicious day, auspicious that is for the performance of rites designed to secure future happiness. Thus in Gujrát a widow is made to don fine clothes and ornaments on the 13th or *kirya* day after her husband's death and clothes and money are given her for her support in the hope that she will pass the rest of her life in resignation. Nevertheless the donors weep over her on this date. In order too to secure future fertility to the bereaved family some vegetables and water in a new pot are brought into the house on this date.

In Jínd on the 13th or 17th day after death, the whole house is plastered and a *hawan* performed, so that the house is purified. In the case of a wealthy man 12 bronze *gaṛwas* (small pots) with covers filled with the water are upset and in the case of a poor one as many earthen ones are filled and upset. 13 or 17 Brahmans are feasted and the *parohit* given a bed, utensils, clothes and money according to the donor's means. In the case of an old man, the family if wealthy of the deceased perform a *jag*, called the *bara karna* or 'making known' rite. A man of average wealth gives food to all the Brahmans of his town, and a rupee to each with a feast to his brotherhood.[2] A very wealthy person gives a *jag* to 20 or 30 villages in the neighbourhood. This custom, still prevalent in the villages of Jínd tahsíl, is also called *káj karna* or *hangama karna*. The *Neota* ceremony is also practised at this time.

After this some wealthy men feast a Brahman daily in the deceased's name, while others give him two loaves and an earthen pot filled with water every month.

Satáriṇ.—On the 17th day some food, clothes and utensils are often given to a Brahman, as in Montgomery.

The *s tárwáṇ* or 17th day in Siálkot is the occasion for just as many elaborate ceremonies as are performed in the *kirya karm*, but the gifts offered now go to the family *parohit*. In this district it is also called *satárhwiṇ* and on it the period of impurity ends although the *kirya karm* is performed some days earlier according to the deceased's caste.

On or after the seventeenth day the ceremony of *dhárm shánta* is observed in Isa Khel and the Brahman is again offered clothes and little money. The family also invites not less than 17 Brahman guests and offers them food of all kinds but especially *khír* and *halwa* or sweetmeat.

Some ceremonies are also observed on the 28th day or *masak* but it is needless to detail them here. (Siálkot.)

[1] *Cf.* the exchange of *pagris* or *pagwat*.

[2] The number of villages varies from 1 to 101.

Monthly commemoration.

The dead are commemorated by Hindus every month during the first year and thereafter annually. This monthly commemoration consists in feeding a Brahman (or a Brahmani if the deceased was a female) on the day *tithi* in each lunar month corresponding to the date of the death. In Kángra this is called *másak*, and consists in giving some flour and *dál* to a Gujráti Brahman, hence called Máhku or 'he who receives the monthly offerings.' Elsewhere the monthly gift consists of a pitcher of water and some food, or of necessaries of all kinds. The subsequent commemorations are really a continuation of the observances on the lunar date of the death.

Thus in Kulu the death of a man is commemorated by performing the yearly *sharádhs* during the *kaniagats*. In these *sharádhs* priests and Brahmans are fed according to the position of the performer. Some also observe the *sambatsari shrádhs*, which are not confined to the *kaniagats*, but on the contrary are performed on the lunar date of the death.

Annual commemorations.

The annual commemorations are the *barsodhi* or *barsi* or first anniversary, the *khiabi* or recurring anniversary, and the *chaubarsi* or fourth anniversary of the death. The *barsi* and *chaubarsi*[1] consist in the offering of a *sejadán*, and in feeding Brahmans and the poor. After the *chaubarsi* the annual commemoration may be said to be merged in the general commemoration of the dead ensured by the observance of the *ganagat*, but the *khiabi* is said to be observed every year until the heir goes to Gya and celebrates the rite there. The *khiabi*, as the term implies, merely consists in feeding a Brahman or his wife.

Generally speaking all the ceremonies hitherto described are modified or liable to modification to meet various contingencies. For instance in the event of a death occurring just before the dates fixed for a wedding all the funeral and other rites which are usually spread over 13 days can be completed in 3 days or even 3 *pahrs* of 3 hours each.

But still more important are the modifications due to the age of the deceased, the circumstances under which death occurred, such as its cause or the time at which it happened.

The death-rites of children.

Very common are the customs in vogue in Baháwalpur in which State if a child of less than six months dies it is buried under a tree, and a cup of water is put beside the grave at its head. But in Shahpur if a child of six months dies the body is thrown into a river or running channel and in some cases it is buried, but no cup of water is placed near the grave. A child over six months but under five years of age is buried or thrown into a river But these rules are subject to endless variations. Thus in the towns of Jínd children dying when under 27 months of age are merely taken down on to the ground and then buried There is no *mansil raváni*. Children in villages dying under the age of 6 years are similarly treated.

[1] In Kángra the offerings at the *barkhi* still go to the *achárj*: those of the *chaubarkhi* to the *parohit* of the family.

As a general rule children are buried and not burnt, if they die before attaining a certain age, which is very variously stated as being 6 months or a year in Gujránwála; 2½ years or even 8 years in Hissár[1]; before the 1st tonsure at 22 months in Kángra; 2 years generally in Siálkot,[2] Gujránwála,[3] Montgomery; 3 in Gújrát and in the Zafarwál tahsíl of Siálkot; 5 years among Hindu Rájpúts, Jaṭs and Mahájans in Rohtak; 2½ years in towns among the higher castes, but 6 years in villages among all castes in Jínd; up to 10 years, if unmarried in Guṛgáon; after cutting the teeth in Kapúrthala.

It is impossible in the present state of our knowledge to say why the ages reported are so discrepant and what the causes of the discrepancies are. In Kángṛa stress is laid on the *mundan sanskár* or tonsure. If a child dies before that rite it is buried under a tree or behind the house; but if it dies after it it is burnt. It is generally performed before the child is 22 months old, and only in the case of a male, but a girl child is also buried up to the age of 22 months. *All* persons more than 22 months old are said to be cremated in this district. So too in Multán children exceeding the age of 5 in general and those whose hair-shaving rite has been performed in particular are cremated. Elsewhere no such rule is known or at any rate reported. Thus in Rohtak among Mahájans, whose children are generally buried if under 5, those under 2 are carried to the burial-ground in the arms but those over 2 are borne on a bier. A child over 5 is cremated.[4] If a child die of small-pox it is set afloat on the Ganges or Jamna. Hindus are especially careful that a child does not die on a cot as it is believed that one who dies on a bed transmigrates into an evil spirit. A dying person is therefore laid on the ground a little before death.

In Siálkot although children over 2 are cremated no *kirya karm* is performed for those under 10 and both the bones and ashes of such children are set afloat or buried. In Zafarwál tahsíl they are interred in burial-grounds. Children who die after these periods are usually burnt in Hissár, though sometimes the body is set afloat on a canal or river—in Rohtak this is done only if the death was due to small-pox, and in Guṛgáon victims to that disorder are not burnt even up to the age of 12, but are set afloat on the Jamna or the Ganges, because Sítla

[1] In Hissár the custom seems to depend on the parents' position or caste. As a rule a child under 2½ years is buried with a cup of milk at its pillow. But around Tohána children are buried in burial-grounds up to the age of 8, except in the case of *pandit* families when they are cremated after the age of 5. As a rule only well-to do people send the remains to the Ganges, but it is indispensable that those of a married person should be cast into that river.

[2] But another account says that if a child of less than 6 months dies it is buried but not under a tree and no cup of water is placed beside its grave except in the Duggar where the custom of placing the cup beside the grave does prevail.

[3] But in the Khángáh Dográn tahsíl of this district it is said that a child dying under one year is buried near a bush, while children over that age are cremated and both bones and ashes thrown into a river or canal. Only the bones of those dying when over 11 years of age are sent to the Ganges.

[4] But another account from this same district says that among Hindu Jaṭs children under the age of five are generally buried. If a Hindu boy between five and ten years die, townsmen as well as rich people in villages set the body afloat in the Jamna, while ordinary villagers bury it in the burial-ground. Persons *above* the age of 10 are cremated. Jaṭs are not townsmen and the account is not easily reconciliable with the one given in the text.

would be displeased if they were cremated and the disease would spread.[1] In Amritsar all children dying under 5 are said to be cast into a river or tank, or if that is not possible buried, and if less than one year old buried under a *jand* tree. Further, it is said, those exceeding 5 years of age are cremated and their *kirya karm* is performed on the 4th, 7th or 13th day, 'with reference to their age.' In such cases the funeral pile is made of the reeds or sticks on which the body is carried to the crematory.

In Isa Khel children under 1 are buried near the banks of a stream or watercourse, but those who die between 1 and 5 are set afloat on a stream, with a jar of sand tied to the neck so that they may be eaten by fishes. And in Gujrát this is also done, but a second jar, filled with rice and sweetstuff, is also tied round the child's neck.

Townspeople, and in villages the well-to-do, prefer to set the body of a child afloat on a stream, but villagers as a rule bury their children up to the age of about 10 in Rohtak: but in Montgomery children over 2 but under 5 (or even under 10 among the poor) are set afloat on a stream, those under 2 being buried in pits in a grove of trees. Similarly in Miánwáli children under 6 months are buried in pits near the bank of a stream or under the shade of a tree and on the following day a cup of milk is placed near the grave.

Though cremation of children is not unusual, it is not the rule to vouchsafe them all the rites if they die before the age of 10, or even 14. But in Siálkot the rule is that up to 2 or 3 children are buried, from 3-5 they are burned and their ashes cast into a running stream, but their bones are not taken to the Ganges unless their age exceeds 5. In Kapúrthala the body of a child which has cut its teeth but not reached puberty is cremated, but instead of the *kirya karm* only the *dasgátri* is performed. This merely consists in both men and women bathing at a well or river.[2]

In Dera Ghází Khán the *kirya karm* rites of a boy of 10 are brief and only extend over 4 days, and it suffices to cast his bones and ashes into the Indus.

After marriage or attaining puberty the rule is that the body of a child, at whatever its age it may have died, should be cremated.

Children are buried in a place specially set apart for that purpose (called the *chhur gada*[3] in Gurgáon), and *masán*[4] in Jámpur.

In Gurdáspur an infant under one year of age is buried under the bed of a stream, if there be one within reach; and a child under two is buried in a lonely spot far from the village and all paths, among bushes and preferably near water.

[1] But in Dera Ghází Khán only men and boys, young or old, who die before the *Sútla puiná* is performed, are said to be thrown into a river.

[2] In Gujrát it is said to consist in giving an *achárya* a suit of clothes, which would fit the dead child, on the 4th day when its bones and ashes are cast into a stream. Though observed on that day it is called the *dasgátar*.

[3] Not traceable in dictionaries.

[4] *Cf. Pb. Dicty.*, p. 787: *maswána*—*masán*—burning-ground.

In Baháwalpur the body of a child under 6 months is buried under a tree.

The rites at the burial of a child are very simple and have already been noticed incidentally.

A cup of water is often put beside the grave at its head, and in Hissár a cup of sweet water is put by the head of a male child which was not being suckled at the time of its death. Sometimes a cup of milk and some sweetmeats are so placed.

It is a common custom for the relations[1] to bring back on their return from the burial the leaves of a tree or vegetables and cast them into the mother's lap, [2] in order that she may continue to be fertile. A similar idea underlies the custom in Gujrát, where on the 13th day some vegetables and water are brought into the house in a new earthen jar, to ensure the continuance of the family's fertility.

In Kapúrthala one of the ornaments belonging to a dead child is re-made into a foot-ornament which the mother puts on in order that she may bear another child.

When a child is buried and its body disinterred by jackals,[3] there is a widespread belief that the parents will soon have another child, if the marks show that it was dragged towards their home: otherwise, their next child will be long in coming.

Another widespread superstition is that when a child dies its mother should take hold of its shroud and pull it towards her, in order that she may have another child; sometimes too a small piece of the shroud is torn off and sewn on to her head-cloth. After burying a child the relations bring leaves of vegetables (*ság*) and put them in the lap of the mother, in hope that she may get another child. These beliefs are found in Baháwalpur and in Kángra and with variations elsewhere. Thus in Tohána the father or some other relative of the dead child brings green *dabh* grass and casts it into the mother's lap. In Isa Khel the mother is forbidden to walk openly in the streets after the death of her child until she has menstruated a second time.

If a child aged between 4 and 6 die leaving a younger brother the parents take a black thread or a red thread equal to its height in length, and tie it round the younger boy's leg where it remains until he has passed the age at which the elder child died. It is then thrown, with some sugar, into a river. This thread is called *lákh*.

In Baháwalpur if a child aged 4 to 6 years who has a younger brother dies the parents take a red thread, touch the body with it and then fasten it round the leg of the younger boy, and it is not removed

[1] In parts of Míánwáli this is done by an Aráín.

[2] In Dera Ghází Khán they are put into the father's lap, and he places them in the child's cradle. If a Hindu child dies in Shahpur the mother gets one of its ornaments re-made into one for her own feet, but the custom of dragging the shroud is extinct. Instead of putting greens into the mother's skirt something such as sweetmeat is put into it.

[3] To prevent this fire is kept burning at the grave for 3 days: Karnál. But in Gujrát just the opposite occurs, for the mother places bread on the grave in the hope that it will attract dogs to it and that they will disinter the corpse.

HHHHH

until he has passed the age at which his elder brother died. This thread is called *lákh*. In Amritsar a child dying in such case is not buried until one of its ornaments has been put on the younger brother and a thread touched by the dead body tied on his right foot. When the younger brother has passed the age on which the child died these are both removed.

Effects of death on the mother.

Care is taken that the shadow of the dead child's mother does not fall on any other woman until the milk disappears from her breasts, lest the other's child pine away and die. When the milk has disappeared from the mother's breasts she is taken to a place outside the town, and there made to bathe and put on new clothes. On her return some green vegetable is put in her skirt.

Effects on subsequent children.

If an infant whose parents are greatly attached to him dies and another child is subsequently born to them they are careful not to make any show of affection for it. Thus if on the occasion of the deceased child's birth they distributed *gur* or sweetmeats they now distribute onions instead. So too in Bannu tahsíl those whose children die one after the other distribute *gur* instead of *batáshas* or sugarcandy on the birth of another child.

This custom is widely spread and the idea on which it is based gives rise to many similar customs Thus in Hissár the second child is dressed in clothes begged from another house. In and about Tohána blue woollen threads with cowries on them are tied to both his feet and not removed until he has passed the age at which the deceased child died. In Karnál the father bores the nose of the son born afterwards and often gives it a girlish or worthless name, with a view to scare away death from it; it being considered that the Death-god (*Yáma*) strangles in his nose more male infants than female. In Kángra nothing is distributed at the birth of such a son and in Montgomery no ceremony is observed on his birth or it is observed with some alterations; *e.g.* the kinsmen are not feasted at the observance of the *chola* ceremony. In Sháhpur a child born after 3 or 4 children have died is given iron bangles made of the nails of a boat to put on its feet. In Gujrát if a man's children do not live, he adopts the birth ceremonies of another caste avoiding those of his own.

A similar idea underlies the following custom:—

If a man's children do not live, he gives opprobrious names to those born afterwards. Such names are Khotá Rám (*khotá*, an ass), Tíndan (worm), Lotá (an earthen vessel), Ledan (camel-dung), Chúhrá (a sweeper), Chúhá (rat), Giddar Mal (jackal), Lála-Lela (kid) and Daḍḍú Mal (frog) for boys: and Hirni (a doe), Ralí (one mixed with others), Chúhrí (a sweepress), Chúhí (she-rat), Chiṛí (sparrow), and Billo (cat), for girls.[1]

[1] Similar names are given in Montgomery if a man has several daughters successively, the third or fourth being given such names as Akki or Nauri.

Effects on subsequent wives.

*The páháj**rí*.—If a man in Bhakkar lose his first wife and marry again he places a *páhájrí* [1] or silver effigy of his first wife round the neck of the second, distributing, in memory of the former, sweetmeats among young girls. And for the first three nights he and his wife sleep with a naked sword between them.

If he lose his second wife also he is married the third time to an *ak* plant, or a sheep, so that the marriage to his third wife may be his fourth, not his third. His third wife wears the *páhájrís* of the first two, and the other rites are also observed.

In Multán if a betrothed child is dying, members of the opposite party take some sweetmeats to him a little before his death. Of this a small quantity is kept and the rest sent back. By this the connection between them is considered to be severed for good.

Effects on a betrothed girl.

If a girl lose her fiancé she is made to stand in the way of the funeral cortége and pass under the bier in order to avert all evil in the future from her own life. In the south-west especially the fiancé's death is kept a secret from the girl's relatives, and rejoicings are actually held by his kinsmen, who go about their business as usual by day, and at night secretly carry out the corpse, wrapped in a blanket, to the burning ground. The fiancé's parents attribute his death to the girl, and her relatives perform rites to avert evil to her.

In Amritsar if either of two affianced parties die the survivor comes to the deceased's house and tries to knock his or her head against the wall. This clashing of head is considered by the deceased's heirs an unlucky omen. If the other party cannot find an opportunity to effect it, he tries to get a chance to touch a piece of cloth with one worn by the deceased. In former times the attempts to get access to the house or possession of such a piece of cloth even led to blows. Even in recent years the belief has led to trouble. Thus in 1903 a betrothed boy died of cholera at Lahore. So closely was the secret of his illness kept that the most essential sanitary precautions were ignored and he was carried out stealthily to be burnt, lest his fiancée should succeed in striking her head on the *thará* or raised platform of his house, which was kept shut up. Failing in this the girl's father got his daughter's forehead marked with small stars and placed her, clad in a red cloth, in a hackney carriage. Accompanied by 3 or 4 persons he stopped it before the boy's house and made the girl alight from the carriage in order to strike her head on the *thará* but she was prevented from doing so by the police posted there at the instance of the boy's father. He next tried to bribe the police but without success : then in desperation he tried to throw his daughter headlong across the *thará* from the roof of the house, but he was prevented from doing this either by the police, and a free fight resulted between his party and them. Unsuccessful in all these attempts, he then went to the *shamshán*, but its gates had already been locked by the boy's father. The girl's partizans next tried to scale the walls, but those inside threw

[1] *Páháj*=co-wife? : in Multáni=country-woman.

bricks at them, the besiegers retaliated and a hotly contested fight ensued, but at last the boy's body was burnt and his ashes together with below them 6 inches of the earth were put in a cart and taken by another route to the river into which they were thrown.[1]

Effects on a girl widow.

If the husband of a young girl dies his ashes are wrapped in a cloth which is put round the widow's neck in the belief that she will pass the remainder of her life in patience and resignation.

In Montgomery if a young girl becomes a widow, two pieces of red cloth and two of white are put on her on the 11th and 13th days. The red cloth is given her by her own parents and the white by her husband's.

Death rites of the old.

When in Jínd an old man is dying the womenfolk of the family prostrate themselves before him and make an offering of money which is the barber's perquisite. If an old man die, leaving grandsons and great-grandsons, his relatives throw silver flowers, shaped like *chamba* flowers, and silver coins (or if poor, copper coins) over his bier. In Miánwáli only Muhammadans[2] and Acháryas will take these flowers and coins, but towards Multán and generally elsewhere people pick them up and place them round their children's necks, in hopes that they will thus live as long as the deceased. But in some places, such as Hissár, they are taken by the poor. This is the case too in Bhakkar where the same usage prevails in the case of a 'perfect devotee' of an unspecified sect or order who is further honoured by being cast into a river.

In Amritsar much joy is displayed on the death of an old person with living grandsons and great-grandsons and his kinsmen send pitchers full of water for a bath to his eldest son. These are broken and the wood purchased for cremating the body is pilfered. Flowers of gold and silver, almonds and dried dates passed over the funeral pyre are considered auspicious and the women strive their utmost to pick them up. The pyre is built of wood, wrapped in a silk cloth, which is taken by the Acháraj.

Death from disease or violence.

As we have already seen children who die of small-pox are often thrown into water. And in Multán children dying of that disorder, measles or whooping cough are in general thrown into a river, the idea being that the goddess of small-pox must not be burnt or cast into fire. When thrown into a river the body is put in a big earthen vessel full of earth and sand to sink it.

All who die of leprosy are cast into the Jumna. If a man be drowned and his body cannot be found his relatives go to Thánesar,

[1] The *Hitkari*, Lahore, of July 19th, 1903.

[2] In Bannu when a young man or an old one dies, the kinsfolk throw copper coins and resin over his bier, and the coins are given to a Muhammadan beggar, but no Hindu beggar will take them.

and then make an effigy of him which is duly cremated on the banks of the Saraswati.

In Kulu in such a case a *Narain-bal* is performed at a sacred place, such as Kuruschhetar in the manner prescribed in the *Shástras*. A lighted lamp is placed on the breast of the corpse, if it has been found: otherwise an image of flour or *kusha* is made and the lamp is put on its breast. It is then cremated in the usual manner.

The lower castes take water in a pot and pour some rape-seed into it. A bee is also put in, and the *chela* buries the pot on the spot where the death occurred. A fowl is sacrificed there and then all the other performances are observed. The people say that if the *Narain-bal* be not performed the dead man goes to hell.

If in Multán a person dies so suddenly that the lamp cannot be lit before his death it is believed that he will become an evil spirit and to prevent this the person performing the *kirya karm* goes to the Ganges and performs the *Narain-bal*.

Death at certain times &c.

When a man dies in the *panchak*, idols of *kusha* grass are made, one for each of the remaining days of the *panchak* and burnt with the dead; some perform the ceremony of *panchak shánti* on the *spindi* day.

A death during a solar or lunar eclipse is considered inauspicious and in such cases *grahan shánti* is performed on the *spindi* day, but the other matters of *ras* and *nakchhattar* are not observed.

In Kulu when a man dies without issue or at enmity with his family, an image is made to represent him and worshipped by his survivors and their descendants as an *autar deota* (sonless deity). This image is worshipped before beginning to consume a new crop and at every festival it is kept at the village spring or at home. Non-performance of this ceremony is believed to cause illness or some other evil. The worship is continued indefinitely, as it is believed to do good to the survivors' descendants for ever.

Other beliefs.

The Kulu people believe in the predictions made by the *chelas* of a *deota* when at a burning place they see some one who was really elsewhere. To avert the danger they sacrifice a sheep, a goat or a fowl and recite certain *mantras*. Some cooked rice and meat are also put in a broken earthen jar and thrown away far from home. A priest or *jotshi* is sometimes consulted and advises charity.

It is unlucky to carry a corpse through a gate or door—lest death subsequently find its way through it. Thus if a death occur in one of the palaces of the Nawábs of Baháwalpur the body is carried out through a hole in the wall. So too in Máler Kotla it is, or used to be, forbidden to bring a body into the town unless permission be obtained to break through the town wall, in which case the body must be brought in and taken out again by that gap.

Death customs.

According to the older astrology the sky was divided into 27[1] lunar mansions (*nakshatras*), of which 2¼ thus lay in each of the 12 zodiacal signs (*burj* or *ras*); and of these *nakshatras* the last 5, *viz.* the second half of Dhanishta, Sat Bikka, Purba-bhadrapad, Utara-bhadrapad and Reoti, occupy the signs of Aquarius (Kumb) and Pisces (Min). This period of 4½ *nakshatras* is counted as 5 days and thence called *panchak*, or, dialectically, *panjak*.

This period is uncanny in several ways, and it is especially inauspicious for a death or, to recall the original idea, for a cremation, to occur in it. Any one so dying can only obtain salvation if a *shánti* or expiatory ceremony be performed on his behalf. This consists in employing 5 Brahmans to recite verses, and on the 27th day after the death, on which the moon is again in the asterism in which the deceased died, the *shánti* is performed, various things such as clothes, flowers and furniture being given away.

The chief superstitions appertaining to the *panchak* related, however, to the surviving kin, for the Hindus believe that a death in this period will involve the deaths of as many others of the family as there are days remaining in the *panchak*. To avert this the corpse should not be burnt until the *panchak* is over, or if this cannot be avoided as many dolls are made of cloth of the *darabh* or *dabh* grass (or among the well-to-do of copper or even gold) as there are days remaining. The dolls may also be made of cloth or cowdung, and in some places a branch of a mango tree is carried with the corpse and is burnt with it, as in Sirmúr. In Ḍera Ghází Khán wooden dolls are made. These are placed on the bier along with the dead body, and burnt with it. For instance, if a person dies on the 2nd day of the *panchak*, 3 dolls, and if on the 3rd, 2 dolls are made, and burnt with the corpse.[2]

As always various additions to or variations of the rite occur locally. Thus in the Simla Hills, at least among the higher castes, 5 dolls are made and placed with the body, which is then carried out by the door, but 5 arrows are placed on the threshold. These arrows must each be cut in twain by a single sword-cut, otherwise as many persons will die as there are arrows remaining uncut, while the swords-man himself will die within the year. Great care is taken lest an enemy possess himself of the dolls. After the corpse has been burnt *tiranjali* is given 5 times in the name of the 5 dolls. Then 5 Brah-mans recite *mantras*, and make, usually in a *ṭhákurdwára*, a *chauk* on which they arrange 5 jars, one in the centre and one at each corner. Into these are poured water and *panj-amrit*, and they are then closed with bits of red silk on top of which are put copper plates with images of Vishnu, Shiva, Indra, Jám and Bhairoṇ, one god engraved on each. The appropriate *mantras* are recited at least 1250, but not more than 125,000, times for each god and *mantras* are then recited in honour of

[1] Note the custom of not *burning* children under 27 months of age. It is apparently inauspicious to associate 27 with burning.

[2] But one account says that 5 dolls are always burnt, irrespective of the number of days remaining. These are named Pret-bah,—mukh-ap, bhumip and barta, and, after being worshipped with flowers etc. are placed on the pyre, at the head, eyelids, left armpit, abdomen and feet of the corpse: Kalsia.

Gatri and Trikal (?). After the recitations are finished a *hawan* is performed. The Brahmans are fee'd and fed, and then take water from each jar and sprinkle it over the members of the deceased's family. This removes the evil effects of the death in the *panchak*. The head of the family also performs a *chhaya-dán*.

In the Pachhád tahsíl some people fill a new earthen pot with water from 5 different tanks or rivers and hang it from the door of the house by a rope made of 5 kinds of twine. The water of the Giri, or of large tanks which never run dry, is preferred. In the cis-Giri country a *panjak shánti* is performed by a Brahman who recites *mantras*. The corpse is not burnt on the ordinary burning ground but in some other place and, if practicable, in the lands of another village; and Brahmans are feasted one day before the ordinary time. People do not venture to wear new clothes or jewels, buy or sell cattle, lay the foundation of a house or take any new work in the hand during the *panchak* days.

Some of the Muhammadan peasantry in Baháwalpur believe in the *panjak*, but according to them any one dying in the first or last 5 days of a lunar month is said to have died in the *panjakan*; and the belief is that 5 or 7 members of the family must then die. The following measures are taken:—

(*i*) While carrying the coffin they sprinkle mustard seed on the road to the graveyard. (*ii*) Blue *pothas* (small beads used by girls for decorating dolls) are put into the mouth of the corpse. (*iii*) A piece of *ak* plant is buried with the body. (*iv*) After the body has been buried, an iron peg is driven into the ground outside the grave, towards the deceased's head.

If a person dies during the *panjak* and his relations knowingly omit these ceremonies at his funeral, and deaths ensue in the family, they exhume the body, and ignorant people believe that it will by then have grown long teeth and eaten its shroud. Some sever the head from the corpse: others think it sufficient to drive a nail into the skull.

The occurrence of a death in the *panchak* also modifies the rites observed after the cremation. Thus on the 7th or 8th day after such a death orthodox Hindus of Ḍera Gházi Khán sometimes make an image of 360 pieces of wood or of *drabh* grass and burn it, with full rites; and on the 27th a special *panjak shánt* is performed.

In Gujrát on the 13th or 27th day after death the Hindus fill 5 jars with grain of various kinds and make 5 dolls of metal—gold, silver or copper according to their means. These images are then worshipped and fed with butter, curds etc., and 5 Brahmans recite *mantras*, receiving Rs. 1-4 (5 4-anna pieces) for their services.

In Sirmúr, on the corresponding day of the *panjak* in the following month, a door frame, made of *thimbu* wood, is erected beside the house-door through which the corpse was taken out; and in this 7 different kinds of grain are stuck with cowdung. A special *mantra* is recited on these before they are stuck to the door. A he-goat's ear is also cut off and the blood sprinkled upon the frame. If these ceremonies are not performed as many people of the family or the village will die as there are days of the *panjak* remaining

It is not easy to say what are the precise ideas originally underlying the *panchak* observances, but it would appear as if the leading idea was that anything which occurs during this period is liable to recur. For this reason it is unwise to provide anything likely to catch fire—lest it get burnt and a funeral pyre ensue—during the *panchak*. Accordingly fuel should not be bought, cloth purchased or even sewn, beds be bought or houses thatched; nor should a pilgrimage be undertaken towards the south, or indeed at all: nor should one sleep with one's head towards the south. It is indeed unlucky to commence any new work, but as a set-off to the prevailing gloom of the period it is peculiarly auspicious, at least in the south-west Punjab, for Hindu women to wear ornaments during the *panchak* days, the idea being that they will get as many more ornaments as there remain days before the period expires.

If in Sirmúr a corpse has to be burnt on a Wednesday an iron nail or peg is fixed at the spot where the death occurred, near the head, before the body is removed. Otherwise another death will occur in the house within a year. Generally speaking this superstition is only common among Hindus, Muhammadans disregarding it.

In the Simla Hills it is believed that if a corpse be burnt on a Sunday or a Tuesday, another will soon be burnt on the same ground.

If a person dies in the Swáti *nakshatra* the following ceremony is performed, lest many deaths occur among the brotherhood and the villagers. After the body has been burnt 5 wooden pegs are driven into the ground, at the spot where it was burnt, in a peculiar shape, and round these an untwisted cotton thread is tied. As the mourners go back a hole is made in the road, at a short distance from the pyre, and in this a he-goat's head is buried with a loaf made of 7 kinds of grain, and a *patka*[1] in which are fixed 7 iron nails besmeared with goat's blood and over which a special *mantra* is recited.

In the trans-Giri country if a person dies during the Swáti or Múl *nakshatras*, or on the 1st or 7th day of either half of the lunar month 4 pegs of *thimbu* wood are fixed to the door of the house in which the death occurred, and a white woollen thread is tied round them, while *mantras* are recited. Seven kinds of grain are also stuck with cowdung on to the upper part of the door. Six more deaths will take place among the relations or villagers if this ceremony is not performed for a death occurring in the Swáti or on the *saptami* (7th) day of either half of the month, and an indefinite number will ensue on a death in the Mula or on the Purima (first day of either half).

In the Simla Hills, in the country beyond Phágu, a death in Makar (Capricorn) portends the deaths of 7 kinsmen, and to avert its consequences 7 dolls are made and 7 arrows cut in precisely the same way as in the *panchak* rite. This superstition is called *satak* (from *sát* 7). In the same part of the hills it is also believed that if *A* die in

[1] A wooden tube through which seed is poured on to ploughed land.

the *nakshatra* of *B's* birth, *B* will die within the year, or fall victim to a dire disease. To avert this a rite is held in honour of Mahámúrti jí, when the *nakshatra* recurs. *B* is covered with a white cloth and the Brahman, after performing a *chhaya-dán*, worships with offerings of 7 kinds of grain. In some places a he-goat is killed over *B's* head; but elsewhere the following is the ritual :—By night a large loaf of wheat-flour is baked, and round it lamps are lighted, a flour image of Jogni Deví being placed on its centre. About midnight a Brahman puts this loaf etc. before *B* and mutters *mantrás*, offering 7 kinds of grain over his head and putting them also on the loaf. Then he sacrifices it over his head and takes it with 5 *balis* (victims, ordinarily he-goats) to the burning-ground, a few men following him. As he goes he signals for the sacrifices to be offered at various spots along the road, and those who follow him observe perfect silence, under pain of death, and do not look back, as that would vitiate the ceremony. The party, moreover, must not return to their homes that night but spend it in the forest or another village. At the burning-ground the Brahman deposits the loaf there and a he-goat is sacrificed, its flesh being consumed by the party on the spot, anything left being the Brahman's perquisite.

In the Simla Hills if the drum beaten at a Kanet funeral emit a loud sharp note, it is believed to portend another death in the village, and the rites in vogue are ineffective to prevent it.

In the Simla Hills the Kanets and lower castes, especially, after collecting the bones to take to Hardwár, drive two wooden pegs into the ground and place a mill-stone on the site of the pyre, enclosing it with thorns, in order to weigh down Jam, the god of burning-grounds, for several days. Otherwise he would devour people.

In the Simla Hills the musicians and the makers of the *bamán* or hearse go to the burning-ground and kindle fire in a large stove for warmth, but if any one's shadow fall on the stove he will, it is believed, die within the year : or if part of his shadow fall on it, he will suffer sickness. Sitting round the stove these men profess to see a spirit flying through the air, as if impelled by some force into the stove. This spirit they identify as that of some one still living and to avert the omen he worships *nakshatrás* and offers sacrifices.

It is usual in the Simla Hills, especially among Kanets, to drive two pegs, one at the head, the other at the feet, of the corpse, in order to prevent a demon's entering into it. If a demon does so, the body will grow to a great height and, standing erect, devour the survivors of its family. With the same object a lamp is also lit close by the corpse, and a weapon placed near it. If, when the pyre is lighted, the corpse fold a piece of the wood in its arms, it is taken as an omen that another of the family will soon die. This belief is held by the Kanets and lower castes of the Simla Hills, who in some parts think that if the ghostly effigy of the dead be seen wandering round the house, or if his voice be heard calling any one by name, he who is called or sees the ghost will die. It is believed that the spirit can find no home. In such cases *Narain-bal* or *Gaya-pind* is also performed.

If within 4 years of a death in the Simla Hills any one of the deceased's family be attacked by *dadra*[1] it is supposed that the dead man's funeral rites were not duly performed. So a Brahman is called in to ascertain all details by astrology: and a *chela* is sent into an ecstasy (*khelná*) until he reveals who it is that has become *pitar*. An image of the *pitar* must then be made, lest the sufferer become a leper, and a rupee placed before the *chela* by the members of the family, who give the *pitar* a certain period—6 months or a year—in which to cure the patient, if he desires to be worshipped as a true *deota*, otherwise they will have recourse to a doctor. For this period the patient is left without treatment of any kind. If he recovers, a temple is built to the *pitar*: otherwise he gets nothing. Such diseases are attributed to those dead whose *gati* or funeral rites were not performed, or who died a violent death, or who when *in extremis* felt a longing not to quit their family or yearned for wealth and so on; or who sacrificed their lives to their devotion to their families.

Section 10.—Muhammadan death observances.

Occasionally, for instance in Gujrát, old people who see their end drawing nigh build their own tombs, while still alive. And if they feel misgivings that their death rites will not be properly performed they feast their kinsfolk and the poor in anticipation of death. In Gurgáon a good many men get their graves constructed of masonry and filled with grain before death. The grain remains there till their death and is given away in alms at their burial.

Amulets &c. are used to escape death. The *Imám zamán ká rupya* is also protective, and as many as seven goats are sacrificed. Sometimes a disease is taken for the influence of an evil spirit. By others it is ascribed to the displeasure of Mírán Sáhib, Madár Sáhib and Khwája Sáhib. The remedy is the sacrifice of a he-goat in the saint's name. Sometimes unmarried girls are feasted to secure recovery from sickness.

As soon as the shadow of the Angel of Death falls on a dying person, the first duty of his (or her) kinsfolk is to straighten the limbs, close the eyes and mouth of the deceased, place his hands one over the other on the breast and set his cot north and south so that his soul may depart with its face towards Mecca.[2] Members of his family mourn and preparations are begun by his kinsfolk for digging the grave.

On the death of her husband a wife breaks her bangles and takes off all her jewellery in sign of widowhood.

Strict followers of the Muhammadan law recite the *Sura-i-yasín* or other verses relating to pardon for sins near one who is at the point of death. They also ask him to recite them himself. It is believed that this recital will draw his attention to one direction only and that if he dies he will not suffer any difficulty at the time of death.

In Ludhiána when the case is seen to be hopeless verses from the *Qurán* are recited, and just before death the medicines are stopped and

[1] A disease in which blisters appear all over the body while the extremities are inflamed. (Not in *P. Dicty.*)

[2] This is called *rakh sir karná* in Ambála.

pure honey with sweet water is given to the dying person in a spoon. The *kalima* is whispered to him and he is also bidden to recite it himself. He is now made to look towards the north.

In Gujrát something sweet, honey as a rule, or if that is not procurable, *sharbat* is poured into the dying person's mouth.

In Kapúrthala it is explained that the *kalima* literally means that God alone is worthy to accept devotion and that Muhammad is His Prophet, and that it is intended that the dying man may carry with him the idea of the unity of God. It is only when he is unable to speak that the *Sura-i-yasín* is recited to him. When he breathes his last the people burst into cries of mourning and females begin to beat their breasts, but in cultured circles the shock is borne with resignation and the bereaved repeat:—*Inna-lilláhe-wa inná ilahie rajiun*, 'we have come from God and to Him we will return.'

But in Gujrát when the end is seen to be near the *mulláh* is sent for to recite the *Sura-i-yasín* or other passages from the *Qurán* and this is called *Husaini paṛhná* although the Muhammadans in this district are Sunnís. If a *mulláh* is not available a relative or friend can officiate. Great importance is also attached to the repetition of the *kalima*. All those standing round the death-bed repeat it and the dying person is required to do so too until the end approaches. A person dying with its words on his or her lips is considered to have had a happy end. In the ordinary affairs of life, a Muhammadan will take an oath:—'Be it my lot not to be able to repeat the *kalima* on my death-bed, should I fail to do such and such a thing.'

In the Leiah tahsíl of Miánwáli a form of death-bed confession is found. It is called *hadia Qurán*. If the dying person is in his senses he takes the *Qurán* in his hands and confesses all his sins, saying that he has brought God's own words (in the *Qurán*) as a claim to forgiveness. At the same time alms of different kinds equal in value to the *Qurán* or the book itself is given to a poor orphan or a *mulláh* who places it in the mosque where the village boys read. If however the dying man is not in his senses his rightful heir performs this rite.

When the bier has been carried out of the house, the people stand in one or two rows or as many as the space permits or as there may be present, with a *mulláh* in front of them to pray for the deceased. This is called *nimáz janázah*. After this another *hadya* is given and then those not closely connected with the bereaved family return while those of the brotherhood generally accompany the funeral to the burial ground where again when the grave is ready and it is time to bury the body a similar *hadya* is made by the heir.

When the body is buried, the *mulláh* standing at the tomb calls out the *báng*, the belief being that when the deceased who, by the departure of the soul, lives in a sleeping posture hears the call, he being a Muslim pronounces the *Lá Iláha Illá'lláh-o-Muhammad-ur-rasúl-Alláhe*; and the two angels Munkir and Nakír, who recorded all his sins during life, go away thinking him a Muslim who according to Islám is free from all pain when he repeats the above verse.

If the deceased was one of a well-to-do family and died a day or two before Friday eve, his heirs engage some *háfis* or *mulláh* to sit day and night at his tomb and repeat verses until that night, it being thought that on that auspicious night he will not be called to account for his sins and that afterwards too God will also show him mercy.

The brotherhood on the night after the death raise money by subscription and manage somehow to provide food for those who accompanied the funeral to the burial-ground. This is called *kaurí wate dí roṭí* or *kaurí roṭí* which must not be confounded with *mun-lr-chhor* or *munh-chhor* which is the food supplied to the bereaved family by its nearest relation.

In Kángṛa the face of the dying person is turned towards Mecca. If possible the corpse is buried on the day of death but when this cannot be done the *Qurán* is recited and a knife placed upon the body to keep off evil spirits.

In Gurgáon two classes of Muhammadans must be distinguished. The first includes the immigrant Shaikh, Sayid, Mughal, Paṭhán and Baloch and the second the indigenous Meo, Khánzáda and Rájpúts converted to Islám by the former. But a large number of these converts have now become assimilated to the former class, and owing to this many Hindu customs have been adopted even by the immigrant classes though in a somewhat altered form, and they are of course still observed by Muhammadans who embraced Islam recently. Other Muhammadans of inferior rank found as tenants in villages are the Qasái, Kunjṛa, Bhaṭiára, Manhiár, Saqqa, Nái, Mírási, Dhunna, Teli and Rangrez, who are dependants of the two groups mentioned above and being affected by their influence observe the same rites and ceremonies as they do. When a body is taken to the graveyard the bier is set down at least once on the way. This is called *muqám dena*. At this spot the head is always kept to the north. After the burial some grain and copper coins are given there in alms.

The place where a person breathed his last and was washed is called *lahad* and a lamp is kept burning there for 40 or at least 10 days. A man always remains sitting on the *lahad*.

Washing the body.

The body is washed with various rites and by various agents. For example in Gurgáon some of those present at the death who are acquainted with the doctrines of Islám wash the body with the heirs' permission. If it be washed in a river or tank it will not require *lahad*, but if washed inside the house a rectangular pit of the height of a man and 4 or 5 feet deep called *lahad* must be made for it. A flat board prepared from a public fund raised for this purpose is then put up over the *lahad*. Then the body is laid on the board, with its face to the east and feet to the west. The clothes are removed and the private parts covered with a piece of cloth. The garments of the deceased as well as the clothes of the bed on which he died are given to beggars. After this the washing is begun. First the dirt on the body is removed with gram flour &c. A first bath is given with sandal water, the second with camphor water and the third with pure water. But Sunnís bathe the body with hot water The body of a male is washed by males and that of a female by females. Those who are to wash the body are chosen at the will of the family. One of them supplies the water, another pours it on the body and the third rubs it on. The private parts are not touched. Meanwhile the people assembled in the deceased's house recite prayers for the benefit of the departed soul. Rich people have the *Qurán* recited over the deceased person from his demise till the 3rd day, and sometimes the recitations are prolonged for a full year or more These customs are in vogue among those who are to some extent educated or well-to-do. New converts observe them in a much simpler way.

In Gujrát the body is washed on a wooden board (*patra*) kept expressly for this purpose by the *mulláh*, with water drawn fresh from a well and mixed with green leaves from a *ber* tree. Only if the weather is cold is the water moderately warmed. If the deceased was a woman 3 or 4 of her silver ear-rings are given to the woman who washes her body. In other parts of the province, however, the *mulláhs* proper perform other functions. For example in Jullundur 'a special class of *mulláhs* called *murda-sho'* washes the body of the deceased Moslem.[1] But elsewhere such a duty does not appear to be performed by any special class. Thus in Sháhpur each mosque is in charge of an *imám* or *ulmá* who teaches the boys to repeat the *Qurán* and officiates at weddings and funerals.[2] But, it is also said, the *mulláh* recites the burial service (*janáza*) accompanied by the mourners. He gets as his fee a copy of the *Qurán* and a rupee or two, and he is also feasted with the guests.[3]

In Ludhiána immediately after the death the kinsfolk are notified through the barber and the *ghussál* (washer of the body) is sent for. Meanwhile the Qázi prepares the shroud. The body is washed in hot water being kept covered down to the knees. Rose water and camphor are also sprinkled over it. After this it is laid on a couch which is then carried to the grave-yard.[4]

For the bath hot water with *ber* leaves boiled in it, soap and sweet- Kaya.
scented things such as rose water, camphor, sandal &c. are required.

The bath being prepared the body is laid on a wooden board with its feet facing west and veiled from sight with sheets, only the washerman (or woman as the case may be) and the nearest of kin remaining inside. The deceased's clothes are removed, the waist-cloth being used to cover the body from the navel to the knees. The washerman then rubs it with soap and water, towels being used to dry it and sandalwood burnt to give it fragrance. Then the shroud, cut in two, is spread over the bed and the body is laid on one half and covered with the other down to the knees. Verses from the *Qurán* are written on the shroud with burnt charcoal or clay. Camphor dissolved in rose-water is painted

[1] Purser, *Jull. S. R.*, p. 68.

[2] Sháhpur *Gazetteer*, 1897, p. 85.

[3] *Ib.*, p. 3.

[4] Sometimes the *kalima* or *aiyat-ul-kursi* is written on the coffin.

on every joint, the higher classes using scents instead. The lower sheet is then wrapped round the corpse, and knotted in three places, on the head, on the waist and over the feet. A copy of the *Qurán* is placed at the head of the body, and the nearest of kin, friends and others are shown the face of the deceased for the last time, accompanied with weeping. A red cloth is thrown over the corpse, if the deceased is an aged person.

Amb Sometimes the toes of the hands and feet are tied together with a piece of cloth. This is called *sarakh*. Similarly a piece of cloth is tied round the head across the chain to shut the mouth. This is called *taht-ul-hanak*.

Ceremonies regarding the shroud.

After washing the body it is dried with white napkins and is laid on the cot on which it is to be carried to the graveyard and on which the shroud has been already spread. Before it is shrouded camphor is rubbed on the body as ordained by the *shará* on all the points which touch the ground when the head is bowed in prayer. Then the shroud is wrapped round the body.

In Gurgáon Shía Muhammadans use the shroud on which verses from the *Qurán* are stamped with earth from Mecca or if it be not obtainable they use white cloth as shroud and print the verses on it. As regards this the Shías believe that followers of Hazrat Ali are exempted from the sorrows of the tomb and the fires of Hell and so they print verses on the shroud to let the angels know that the deceased was a Shía and to prevent their troubling him. It is considered essential by some tribes to shroud the body of a female in red cloth.

Raya. The Chhímba (tailor or washerman) comes to the house without being called to supply cloth for the shroud &c. Country cloth is preferred for this as more durable. About 30 yards are required as the grave clothes consist of two sheets, a shroud, a prayer-cloth, four towels and a waist-band.

Among the agricultural tribes such as the Rájpút, Awán, Ját, Gujar, Dogar and Aráín of Ludhiána women spin cotton with folded feet in the month of Ramzán and make cloth which is kept in boxes for use as shrouds exclusively. It is always 40 yards in length. In towns the cloth is purchased from the bazar.

In tahsíl Jámpur, Dera Gházi Khán, when the body is dressed in the shroud (*kafan*) a piece of cloth called *kafin*, wetted with *áb-i-zam-zam* or water from the well at Mecca and inscribed with the words *bismilláh-ul-rahmán-ul-rahím* and the *kalima*, together with some *khák-i-shafa* or earth from Mecca, is placed on the breast. If these articles are not procurable the *kafin* is wetted with ordinary water and a clean clod of earth used.

In Gujrát the *mulláh* merely writes the *kalima* on the shroud in *geri* (?)

In Gurgáon if a woman die in child-birth some superstitious females tie an *atti* (skein) of cotton thread on her legs as she is believed to have died in impurity and it is feared she may become an evil spirit and injure the family. As a further precaution a man throws mustard seed behind her bier from the place of her death all the way to the grave-yard and on reaching it he drives in 4 nails, one at each corner, and the 5th in the middle of the grave. By doing this, it is believed, the departed soul will not return.

The husband may not touch the body of his dead wife or even help to carry her coffin though comparative strangers may do so. If the deceased was old and his heirs are in easy circumstances and disposed to pomp, singers are engaged to lead the procession singing the *maulúd* verses, a narration of Muhammad's birth, loudly in chorus. Every Muhammadan seeing a procession on its way to the grave-yard is religiously bound to join it. On arrival there ablutions are performed by the funeral party, preparatory to prayer. The coffin being placed in front, those who are to join in prayer arrange themselves into 3 or 5 rows, the *mulláh* leading the service. This over, permission is given to all present to depart, but as a rule very few leave at this stage. All present sit on the ground and the ceremony of *askát* is performed, but only in the case of adults, minors being regarded as innocent and not answerable for their doings. The *askát* is thus performed.

Some cooked meal and cash, varying in amount according to the means of the parties, with a copy of the *Qurán*, are placed before the *mulláh* in a basket. Another man sits in front of him so that it lies between them. The *mulláh* then says solemnly:—" The deceased failed to obey certain commandments and to refrain from certain acts on Saturdays during his or her life. This meal, cash and *Qurán* are given in alms to atone for those sins" : and so saying he passes the basket with its contents to the other man who gives it back again. The *mulláh* again hands it over to him with the same words, but refers to the deceased's sins on the Sundays in his life. This is repeated for each day of the week. The *mulláh* is then paid Re. 1 with the copy of the *Qurán*, and the body is interred.[1] The sheet spread over the coffin is now given to the Nái (barber). After the interment the cash and meal in the basket are distributed in alms. Informal prayers are again said for the benefit of the deceased and the funeral procession returns to the house of the deceased.

In Siálkot the *askát* is performed *before* the burial. Several *mulláhs* sit in a circle, the leader being given a copy of the *Qurán* ; a rupee and some copper coins, grain, salt, sweetmeat &c. are also placed before him. Then one of the *mulláhs* makes over the sins of the deceased to another, he to a third and so on till the circle is completed. By this it is believed that the deceased's soul is freed from the penalty of sin. Lastly the head *mulláh* distributes the cash &c. among the poor and the other *mulláhs*. If the deceased was old, clothes are distributed among the poor. The *Qurán* and a rupee are taken by the *mulláh* himself.

In Sháhpur poor people only borrow a copy of the *Qurán* which changes hand for seven days simply as a matter of form. It is borrowed from a *mulláh* who is given Rs. 1-4.

[1] The *ahl-i-hadís* regard *askát* as an innovation and do not observe it.

Raya. Some of the deceased's relatives sit near the cot with the Qázi who takes the *Qurán* in his hands, and offers it on the part of the deceased, as a sacrifice for his sins. The book then changes hands, the Qázi is paid a rupee or more according to the position of the parties, and the *Qurán* is thus redeemed.

The followers and mourners in the meantime have washed their hands &c. for prayer. The Qázi having spread the carpet stands forward, with his face towards the corpse, which is placed with its head to the north. Behind him the followers stand in odd lines and pray after which the corpse is taken to the grave into which it is lowered to two men who descend and place it in the *lahd* (burial niche). In sandy tracts, the knots tying the corpse are undone to admit of this being done. If the *lahd* is in one of the sides, the opening is closed with clods or earthen vessels, if in the centre, with fuel wood. All the by-standers take a little earth in their hands, repeat some verses over it, and drop it at the head of the corpse. The cot is turned on its side as soon as the body has been taken off and in the case of an aged person the red cloth is given to the barber or *mírási*. While the grave is being filled in the Qázi recites the *khatm* or final prayer and then all present raise their hands to supplicate forgiveness for the deceased. The *tosha* is next distributed among the poor. When a corpse is carried out a cup of water is emptied to ensure the family's future safety. The cot brought back after the burial is not allowed to stand lengthwise.

Ambála. When the body has been washed and is being placed in the coffin 7 cakes are cooked in the house and with some grain carried out with the corpse to the burial-ground. These cakes are called *toshe ki roti* or 'bread for the journey' as it is believed that this food will be needed by the dead person on his road to the other world. While the body is being carried to the burial-ground all who accompany it recite the *kalima*. At the ground all recite the prayer for the dead, standing in a circle round the body, and then lower it into the grave. The *toshe ki roti* and grain are then given to the poor. In some places after the burial a call to prayer (*ázán*) is made and a prayer offered for the soul of the departed. All then return and after expressing their sorrow and sympathy with the relations of the deceased go home. In some places the women of the family cause *fatihas* to be recited in the name of the brown worms of the tomb in the belief that they will dictate to the dead person the correct answers to the questions put by Munkir and Nakír.

So too in Raya while the body is being washed *tosha* (food for charitable purposes) consisting of *halwá*, boiled rice with sugar, and loaves is made ready in the house. The cot is lifted up, the towels and the waist-cloth going to the washerman (or woman as the case may be). Four men lift up the four legs of the cot, but as many men as can do so relieve them on the way, reciting verses from the *Qurán* all the while, regarding this as an act of piety.[1] The cot and *tosha* are set down outside the cemetery.

[1] So too in Kángra the carrying of the body is considered good for the soul of the carrier and for this reason the corpse is carried by the attendants turn by turn.

But in Isa Khel when a body is carried to the graveyard all except the near relatives are given two annas each, so that the deceased's soul may not be indebted to them for their toil. Poor people however only give the bearers sweetened rice on a Thursday. The food given in this way is called *khattes*. The body before being taken to the burial-ground is shrouded in a cloth which is taken by the carpenter or ironsmith.

Ceremonies at the burial of the dead.

After washing and shrouding the body it is taken to the graveyard, the cot on which it is laid being carried by all the collaterals in turn but not by the nearest kinsmen such as the father, son &c. On the way to the graveyard they recite sacred verses, the *kalima* and prayers for the deceased. At a short distance from the graveyard the bier is set down north and south at a spot swept clean and all those present recite the funeral prayers. But they do not bow the head at this rite and only invoke blessings for the departed soul. Then the bier is carried on to the graveyard. The grave is always dug from north to south, and has two chambers, the lower, called *lahad*, in which the body is placed being as long as a man's height. The face of the body is kept towards the Qibla, that of a man being laid by men while that of a female is laid by her husband and other near relatives. Then the *lahad* is filled up with stones and bricks in such a way that earth from the upper walls may not fall on it. The upper part of the grave is then filled in with earth by all the mourners except the deceased's heirs. When filled in water is sprinkled over it and the *chádar* in which the dead body was wrapped is spread over it. The members of the funeral party now recite the *fátiha* or verses from the *Qurán* for the benefit of the departed soul and on their return condole with the heirs. They then depart to their homes. Food and *halwá* which are called *tosha* as well as grain and cash are carried in some quantities to the graveyard and distributed among beggars after the burial.

When the *janása* of the corpse is being carried out in Dera Gházi Khán the *Qurán* is placed on the cot near the body and sweet-scented flowers, rose-water, otto of roses &c. are put on the shroud. Both the flowers and *Qurán* are removed when it is lowered into the grave. Dera Gházi Khán.

When the body is taken out for burial some of those accompanying it recite the *maulúd sharíf*, others the *kalima sharíf*, slowly, until they reach the place where prayers called *namáz-i-janása* are said. After the prayers the *mulláh* who read the *janása* stands close to the head of the deceased and calls on the assembly to give the benefit of the words, *i.e.* the *kalám darúd, khatm Qurán* or whatever they may have read before and then raises his hands, forgives the words read in favour of the deceased and prays for the forgiveness of his sins. After the prayer is finished the heir stands up and permits the people to go by calling out aloud, *rukhsat ám*, thrice. Then all who congregated for the sake of prayer return home while members of brotherhood carry the corpse to the tomb.

Gurgáon.

In Gurgáon while the body is being carried to the grave-yard some water is thrown behind the bier on the way as it is believed that it will bring resignation to the deceased's heirs. The women of houses on the route taken by the bier also cast the water out of their vessels, chew *ním* leaves and spit on the ground. The water is thrown out so that the departed soul may not stay in any vessel containing water and the *ním* leaves are chewed as a token that the shock is unbearable.

ra Ghási hán.

When the body is lowered into the grave the *mullóh* is asked to write the *kalima sharíf* with a stick on a mud brick which is put in the grave near the deceased's head. When the body is in the grave the *mullóh* calls on each of those present to recite the *surat ikhlás* over 7 clods of earth and puts them together near the head of the deceased. Then all join in filling the tomb with earth.[1]

Gurgáon.

Most of the Shíás and some Sunnís place a written paper called *ahdnáma* in the deceased's mouth in the grave. This 'agreement' contains a declaration by him of the principles and doctrines of Islám and it is placed on him with the idea that he may not be terrified at the questions put to him by Munkir and Nakír when they appear before him with dreadful looks, but may answer them with the aid of the agreement.

In Gurgáon two loaves with *ghí* and sugar spread over them are tied in a handkerchief and are sent to the graveyard through a *faqír* with a pitcher full of cold water and a goblet, placed one over the other. After the burial the *faqír* recites the *fatiha* over the bread and takes it to his house. These breads are called *tosha* (provisions for the journey). As in life a man requires provisions for a journey so a dead person requires *tosha* on his last journey from his house to the grave.

[1]In Kohát the female neighbours assemble at the house and standing round the body continue to wail, beat their breasts and slap their faces. A matron leads the mourning and the rest wail in chorus after her.

Meanwhile the deceased's friends and relations assemble for the funeral procession (*janáza*) which is preceded by *mulláhs* carrying from 3 to 21 *Qapuráns* according to his rank. Women take no part in the assembly. At a short distance from the grave the corpse is set down, while the prayers for the dead (Arabic *janáza*) are recited, the mourners ranging themselves behind the leading *mulláh* (as *imám*) in lines of odd numbers varying from three to seven.

After the prayers money is distributed to the *mulláhs* present, with grain and salt and a few copies of the *Qurán*. Cash and grain are also given to the poor there present. At a child's funeral the grain and salt are replaced by sweetmeats. The body is then taken to the grave which is dug north and south and after it has been let down and laid with the face to the west, stones are placed over it and the earth filled in. In the case of a man two tombstones are erected, one at the head, the other at the feet. For a woman a third stone is set up in the centre.

There are two kinds of graves—one on the *lahad* system containing a side sepulchre for the body, and the other a pit (*chirwan*) dug deep in the ground with an enclosing wall of stone or brick about 4 feet high. After the body has been returned to the dust the *mulláh* recites the law of inheritance (*mirás ká masla*) and then all present offer prayers, invoking blessings on the deceased.

Some of the mourners then accompany his heirs home and they give them cooked rice &c. (some is also given to the poor) and then dismiss them. Next day kinsfolk assemble in a mosque and offer prayers for the deceased. On the 3rd day 30 *sipárás* of the *Qurán* are handed in separate parts to *mulláhs* and others who can read so that the

Only two loaves are given because, it is said, Noah satisfied the hunger of Anak, who was of a great stature and whose hunger was never appeased, with only two loaves. Moreover it is often related in the miracles of saints and *pírs* who passed their lives in forests that they received two loaves and a goblet of water from God. So it is believed that a man's daily food as fixed by the Almighty is two loaves and a goblet of water. Dárá Shikoh also, when imprisoned by Alamgír, wrote to him that he only required two loaves and a cup of water.

It is essential that no flesh should be used in the *tosha* and so sugar and *ghí* are used instead, because the food of people in Heaven generally consists of sweet things as is evident from the fact that there canals of milk and honey are believed to flow. The water of Kausar, a stream in heaven, is sweeter than honey and whiter than milk or ice. In the time of Moses, *manna* and *salwa* (a savoury food) were received by the Israelties in the wilderness. As to this tradition the people, contrary to what is written in the religious books, believe that these things were received from the sky in large plates and were softer and whiter than carded cotton and sweeter than anything on earth.

A dying person is laid with his face towards the Qibla and Gurdáspur.
verses of the *Qurán*, especially the *Sura-i-yasín*, are recited. A copy of the *Qurán* and a little money are caused to be given by his hand in charity to a *mulláh*. Kinsmen and relatives repeat the *kalima* aloud so that on hearing it he may do the same. In villages grain &c. is distributed to the poor in alms. When life is extinct, the face is wrapped in a cloth and a shroud and a bath are prepared. The shroud consists of 3 clothes in the case of a male and 5 in the case of a female. There must be one red cloth in the latter case. If the deceased was a young female a *gahwara* (cradle) is also made of white cloth. Moreover a *dhodna*, consisting of a *dopatta* or sheet of white muslin (*malmal*) or striped (*doruja*) and a red *dopatta*, is put on the body and after burial one is given to the barber and the other to the washerman. This *dhodna* is given simply as a social usage. After the bath one ear-ring is given to the woman who washed the corpse and the other to the washerman. If the deceased be an old woman a coloured shawl (*doshála*) is put on her and given to the barber after the burial.

When the bier is carried out to the graveyard some grain, *halwá* (a kind of pudding made of flour, *ghí* and sugar) and bread are taken with it and when the recital of the funeral prayers is over a rupee is given to the person who gave the bath and a rupee or a copy of the *Qurán* to the

whole recitation may be finished in a short time. After its conclusion sweetmeats are distributed by the deceased's heirs and then one of the *mulláhs* observes the *kúl khwání* (a recitation of certain *Suras* of the *Qurán* called *Kúl*) and is given some cash as his fee. Then follows the *dastárbandi* or formal recognition of the heir.

Every evening for 40 days the heirs supply food to the *mulláh* and every night a lamp is lit at the place where the body was washed. For some weeks too food is distributed every Thursday to the poor in his name, and on the last Thursday clothing, sweetmeats &c. are given to the *mulláh* and a general feast to the kinsfolk. For 2 or 3 years on the anniversary of the death the heirs distribute food and alms to the poor.

The cost of a funeral of an average agriculturist including food and alms may vary from Rs. 5 to Rs. 50 according to his position.

imám of the mosque. If the deceased was an old man or woman, people generally distribute pice in charity to such *faqírs* and blind men as may be present at the grave. The bread, *halwá* &c. mentioned above are also given in alms. Some people also appoint *háfis* or readers of the *Qurán* to recite verses from it at the grave till the following Thursday. In the case of an old man's death *kamíns* of his family are also given a rupee or 8 annas each. This custom is not in force among the followers of Muhammad. When after the funeral they come back to the house any near kinsman or neighbour gives a meal to the bereaved family. One meal is always considered essential, but if there are more houses of brotherhood 3 meals at the outside are given. Immediately on the return from the funeral, rice and 4 loaves are sent to the person who bathed the body or to the mosque in the name of the deceased. But this custom is not observed by the *ahl-i-hadís*.

The deceased's heirs do no business for 3 days but stay in the *deorhi* (entrance hall) or *baiṭhak* (sitting place) for the *fatíha-khwání*, and the kinsfolk come for that purpose. On the 3rd day the ceremony of *qul-khwáni* is performed, verses of the *Qurán* being recited for the benefit of the deceased's soul. Condolences are offered to the bereaved family with a request to recommence business. On the following Thursday the ceremony of *khatam* is performed and the deceased's clothes are given to the person who washed his corpse. Kinsmen are invited on this occasion also.

In the same way, *khatam* is performed on every Thursday or on the 10th, 21st or 30th day after death. On the 40th day (*chihlam*) a feast is given to *ulmá* (learned men) and *faqírs*, and clothes, copies of the *Qurán* and cash are also distributed. Kinsmen are also invited if the deceased was an aged person. This custom is called *roṭi karna*. These customs are not observed by the *ahl-i-hadís*. One loaf or a man's meal (according to their means) is given daily for 40 days to the man who bathed the body or is sent to a mosque.

On the morning after the *chihlam*, *i.e.* early in the morning before the morning prayer, they bid farewell to the soul. The females cook rice and send it to the *mulláh* in the mosque and thus bid farewell to the soul. On this the women believe that the soul leaves the house. For a year food is given to *faqírs* at festivals and again after a year food is distributed among the poor.

The rites in Míánwáli are peculiarly interesting because of the part played in them by the *mulláh* who is styled the *dínidár*. After the *isqát* the deceased's body is washed by him and his old clothes are kept to be given away in alms on the 3rd day. After this it is shrouded, and also wrapped by the near relatives in sheets called *uchhar*. They may be of ordinary longcloth or of a valuable silk and, before the body is placed in the grave, they are removed and distributed among the potters, ironsmiths and carpenters who dug the grave, and on hearing of the death went to the graveyard of their own accord for that purpose. After burial the surface of the grave is raised a little and the coffin is buried with the body.

The bereaved family is supplied with *kauri roti* by a brother or relative of the deceased. Fire is not kindled in their house for three days. Relatives and friends at once join in the mourning and are served with *kauri roti*. Though the mourning mat is burnt all the mourners sleep on the ground or on cots turned upside down. This state of affairs lasts for 3 days, during which the *díndár* (or washer of the dead) gets some of *kauri roti*. Contrary to the usage elsewhere the *díndár* leads the funeral prayers. On the 3rd day *qul khwáni* is performed in the following manner :—

The *díndár* has a basket of grain put before him with a vessel of water containing leaves of a plum tree, recites verses from *Qurán* and blows them on to the water, which is then spilt at the place where the body was washed. It is believed that the deceased's soul is benefited by this. The grain etc. is taken by the *díndár*.

The old clothes are now cast down at the place where the body was washed and are removed on the third day when the water is spilt. After the *qul* the mourners bathe, wash their own and the deceased's clothes which are given to the *díndár*. Rich folk give him a new suit and if the deceased's widow survives some ornaments also. The eldest member of the family is next made to don a *dastár* which is given him by the relatives, to signify that he has become the deceased's representative. They also give him one or two rupees.

At the *fatah-khwáni* ceremony held immediately after the burial the relatives also contribute a rupee each. A little before death the whole of the *Qurán* is recited and the reciters given a *Qurán* or cash. On the second day after death the relatives visit the grave and recite the whole *Qurán* there. On the first Thursday after death sweetened rice or *halwá* is prepared, but before the relatives are served with it, it is given to the *díndár*. This practice is continued for seven days, except by the poor who can only afford it for the first Thursday, the *díndár* is also fed daily for 40 days, and it is essential that his food should be sent him before sunset. It is called *arwáh* and is intended for the deceased's benefit. The *díndár* is also fed and given an ornament on the first 'Id after death. The couch on which the deceased lay before death is broken to pieces and its strings are buried with the body. In the month of Shehbán *halwá* or some other sweetmeat is prepared and is sent to the *mulláh* and *díndár*. This is called *ruh-rilána*. Every year in Muharram the relatives visit the grave and pour a little water over it. **Miánwáli.**

For the benefit of the soul of any ancestor who died an accidental or unnatural death, and for a childless ancestor, Qassábs feed the poor in their names every Thursday, or at least twice a year.

The *qul-khwáni* ceremony is performed on the third day. The old clothes of the deceased are given to the *mulláh*. Sometimes new ones are also made and given away in charity for the benefit of his soul. On this day too the lawful heir is made to put on a *dastár* by his *pír* or a Sayyid. Sometimes on the 7th day food is given to the poor, but this is not common.

On the 10th, 20th and 40th days after death relations and friends may collect and eat together and also distribute food to the poor but this also is not usual.

From the 3rd day to the 40th, two loaves (*i. e.* food sufficient for one man) generally flavoured with sugar and *ghi* are sent to a *faqír* daily before nightfall. These loaves are called *ubhá ki rotián*. *Ubha* means inauspicious. On each Thursday in the first 40 days *niás* is given for the deceased's benefit as on the 3rd day.

The *chalíswán* ceremony in connection with a female's death is generally performed on the 28th and in the case of a male on the 30th day or in special cases on the 39th. On this day the deceased's heirs feast their kinsfolk according to their means, and they in return give them a turban and some money. The expenses of this ceremony generally depend on one's means. On this occasion too *niás* is given and the *fatiha* recited as on the *soyam*, but no cup of water is sent to the *faqír* with the bread. It is not necessary that the bread should be cooked by the same person who did so on the first day. On the 40th day a new suit of clothes is given away in the deceased's name, but the custom of giving away ornaments does not exist. On the same day his soul is dismissed in the following manner :—

In the evening a vessel full of water is placed near the *lahad* (where the dead body was washed). In it are put two copper coins and a few plates of rice, bread and *halwá* are set by it. The near female relatives light a lamp and wake for the whole night. In the morning a *faqír* comes, takes the vessel of water with the plate and backs to the door with his face towards the females. On reaching the door he turns round and goes to his own house. As he quits the deceased's house the females weep as bitterly as if his bier were being carried out. The people believe that the soul after leaving the body remains in two places, Allain and Sajjain, and maintains its connection with the grave and *lahad* for 40 days. It is also believed that the soul is allowed a walk at the time of *maghrab* prayers, and that it continues anxious to receive the *niás* &c. given for its benefit. Hence the *chálíswán* or 40th day rite is performed 10 days before the actual day. After the 40th day the soul is believed to be set free every Thursday and for this reason on each Thursday the *fatiha* is recited for its benefit. It is also believed to receive food given to *faqírs* and so several kinds of food are given them at the *fatiha*. The *tamáhi*, *chhamáhí* and *barsi* ceremonies are performed after 3 and 6 months and a year respectively. One day before the 'Id, Bakar 'Id, Muharram and Shab Barát as also on the 14th of Rajab *halwá* and bread are given as *niás*. This is usually done for one year only, but some people observe these ceremonies always. Nothing is given by way of *niás* before the 3rd day because the soul is not set free from Allain and Sajjain before that day. The reason assigned for the 10 days' interval between the *daswán*, *bíswán* and *chálíswán*, which last is generally performed on the 30th day, is that mourning lasts 10 days just as the first 10 days of Muharram are observed as days of mourning for the death of Hussain.

A widow does not wear glass bangles or coloured clothes. If a woman dies married, her hands are stained with *mehndi* and antimony is applied to her eyes after her body has been washed. On a man's death his widow's parents give their daughter bangles, called the bangles of widowhood. If her parents be well off they also give her ornaments and cash by way of *khichri*. On the death of a female also her parents give some cash by way of *khichri*. When a saint dies his *urs* is celebrated annually on the day of his death. All his followers and believers gather together on that day and cook food, they also offer *niáz*, recite the *fátiha* and light an earthen lamp on his grave every Thursday. Fruit and sweets are also offered at his grave. In Qádaria and Naqshbandia families the members sit near a grave, sing hymns in praise of the Almighty and recite eulogies of the saint. They also repeat verses from the *Qurán*, but use no musical instruments, a prohibition not observed in Chishti circles. Singers and prostitutes dance at their tombs on the *urs*.

On the 7th or 10th day after death a *khatam* is given, *i.e.* food is cooked and offered to the *qázi*, *faqírs*, the tomb-digger, and bier-bearers of the deceased. It consists of milk, *halwá*, vegetables, meat, pulse, fruit, rice and dry bread. Some people do this on four Thursdays after the death within 40 days, give the deceased's clothes to the *qázi*, with some cash and a *Qurán*. Rayn.

From the *tíjá* to the 40th day the deceased's heirs feed a needy person once a day for the good of his soul. The *daswán* and *bíswán* ceremonies are performed in different ways by different sects of Muhammadans. *Nán* (bread) and *halwá* or other food is distributed by them to their kinsfolk as well as to the poor.

The followers of the *Imámia* sect also hold another assembly in honour of their martyrs in addition to those already named. After it has dispersed they recite the *fatiha* prayers first in honour of the martyrs on the field of Karbala and then for the benefit of the departed soul.

On the 3rd day, after the *kul-khwáni* the deceased's heirs place some palm leaves, sweet scented flowers, and green leaves of a fruit tree on his tomb. These are called *phul-patri*. It is believed that these reduce or alleviate his sufferings. Dera Ghází Khán.

After the *tíjá* the parents-in-law of a deceased husband give his widow some cash, clothes and ornaments which are called *joṛu ranḍsála* or garb of widowhood.

The custom of giving *kaura watta* for 3 days after death is in vogue among the Muhammadan Telís of Pesháwar city and for those days no one eats anything from the deceased's house, nor is any food cooked by his family. Each of his relatives sends it food in turn. After the three days food is again cooked by the deceased's family. The *qul-khwáni* and *dastárbandi* ceremonies are also performed on Pesháwar.

that day. Other Muhammadans, *viz.* the Shi'a Qizilbásh and Kashmíri communities living in Peshâwar, eat nothing from the deceased's house for 40 days after a death but they send nothing to it. The Parácha, Wastir and Qázi residents of the city do not eat or drink from the house for 3 days. With these exceptions there are no restrictions on eating or drinking from the deceased's family at a death. All others eat and drink from the bereaved family's house during the 40 days.

The menial tribes living in the city give Re. 1 on the day of the *qulk-hwáni* by way of *kaura watta*. This custom is not in vogue among the high castes.

Raya. On their return from the cemetery all those taking part in the funeral turn their faces towards it when some way from it and recite the *fatiha*. The cot is carried by a menial, but not on his head in the usual way until he reaches the village.

All men assemble at the *takia* and repeat the *fátiha*. Then all but the heirs depart and they must stay there 3 days at least.

The practice of sitting for prayer between the grave and the deceased's house is termed *goda-diwána*, 'knee-resting.'

Bannu. In Bannu tahsîl on the evening of the funeral the deceased's heirs feast people who come to pay them a visit of condolence. This feast is called *shuma*. All those assembled recite the *kalima* about 100,000 times for the benefit of the deceased's soul. Food is sent to the *mullâh* every evening for 40 days in succession. But no other ceremony is performed in this district. Even the *qul-khwáni* is not performed on the 3rd day. The deceased's heirs merely sit in *chauk* from the 1st day to the 3rd to receive the visits of condolence from people who pray for the deceased and then depart. Quraishís, Sayyids and Ulmá sit in a mosque.

But in Marwat after the burial the deceased's brother or some other near kinsman supplies the bereaved family with food for the night and this is called *kauri roti*. The mourning (*tiddi*) lasts for 3 days, and on the 3rd the family bathes and washes its clothes. The deceased's clothes are given away in charity. The *qul-khwáni* ceremony is performed and the whole of the *Qurán* recited for the benefit of his soul. His clothes are washed and given to the *imám* of a mosque with some cash. The custom of giving ornaments is extinct. The deceased's heir is invested with a *dastár* on the 3rd day, but his kinsmen contribute no cash. Rice, *halwá* and *roti* are given in charity for 5 or 6 Thursdays, but during this time no *khatam* prayers are recited. Alms are also given for the benefit of the departed soul on the 20th day, and for 40 days a loaf with *ghí* and sugar is sent to the *imám* who washed the corpse. It is always sent in the evening and is called the *zimáshan da gogi*. There is no rule that it should be cooked by the woman who did so on the first day. The custom of giving a goblet of sweet water is extinct. On the 40th day alms are also given according to one's means. A year or two after death the heir gives a feast called *shuma* to his kinsmen.

During the day the kinsmen sit with the men but after the evening meal it is essential for each sex to sit with the mourners of that sex for 3 or 4 days, obviously in order to soothe their grief. Bays.

On the 3rd day (*tíja*) friends and relatives collect at the deceased's house or at the mosque and recite the *kalima* once over each grain in a heap of gram, so that the total recitations number 125,000. This gram is then distributed. This rite is called the *kul panchdyat* in Ambála.

After this a new turban is put on the head of the heir and he is thus recognised the legal and religious heir of the deceased.

The ceremony known as *tíjá* or *soyam* or of picking up the bones is performed on the 3rd day after a burial by strict Muhammadans in the following way:—All the heirs and relatives of the deceased rise early and assemble at his house. Those who are literate recite the *Qurán*, those who are not the *kalima* over each grain of the parched gram which stands there in a heap. Sunnís close this ceremony by reciting the five verses called *Panjat* from the *Qurán*, while Shia's close it by reciting the *fatiha* prayers in the names of deceased ancestors and prophets slain at Karbala. Those who embraced Islám recently such as the Rájpúts, Khánzádas, Gujars, Meos &c., excepting a few persons who are well versed in their religious principles, do not observe this rite.

In Gurgáon the *daswán* ceremony is performed on the evening of the 9th and the *bíswán* on the evening of the 19th day. On these days also the *fatiha* is recited and food is distributed as on the 3rd day. These ceremonies are performed one day before the actual day because among Muhammadans a day includes the day and subsequent night and begins at sunrise.

In Gurgáon on the morning of the 3rd day, *soyam*, the *qul khwáni* or *phúl* ceremony is performed. The Muhammadan custom is that all assemble and some parched gram weighing 12¼ *sers* is placed before each. Each then recites the first half of the *kalima* (*La illa illilláh* only) on the first 10 grains, and the whole of it on the 11th, keeping all the grain by their side. The whole *kalima* is not recited on each grain so as to maintain the distinction between the Prophet and the Almighty. After this all the grain is made into a heap and sweetened *iláchi dána* of the same weight is mixed with it. Then incense *lobán* and *aggar* are burnt and verses from the *Qurán* &c. are recited for the benefit of the departed soul. Lastly the grain is distributed among all present. The incense is burnt to purify the air.

Camphorated water is also sprinkled on the bier and coffin. The *fátiha* is also recited on reaching the grave, and flowers are thrown on it, for which reason the *soyam* ceremony is called *phúl*. On the same evening *niás* or *fátiha* is offered for the benefit of the deceased. Seven kinds of food, *halwá*, *khír*, flesh, bread, rice &c. are cooked and distributed among the poor after recitation of the *fátiha*.

Ceremonies regarding Karwi khichri.

At meal times remote relations of the deceased send cooked *khichri* for his family and any guests who have come for the occasion, the relatives supplying the bereaved family by turns.

Early in the morning after the interment the head of the family repairs to the graveyard and sits by the grave, others following him as they come. Prayers are said for the benefit of the deceased till sunrise when all return to his house. This is done for three days. But this custom is not general, being confined to certain tribes such as Kashmírís.

The day after the death, food-offering to the Qází commences, and he is given one meal every day for 40 days, the earthen vessels and the cloths used being also presented to him.

About two *sers* of gram, maize or some other grain is taken and the *qul* verse is read over it grain by grain 125,000 times. It is then boiled and distributed among children.

In some places this custom is observed differently. Early in the morning Qázís are invited to meet in a mosque and read the *Qurán*. At about midday the community collects, the Qázís receive offerings from the heirs, and the whole community then bestow the spiritual benefit of the *Qurán* reading on the departed spirit.

Leiah.

The *kul-khwáni* for children is observed both in towns and the villages. The Chandias of Leiah town observe it at the tombs of the aged, but others perform it on the 3rd day after death, at the deceased's house or a mosque. All the *mulláhs* recite in turn, one *sipáráh* each, for the benefit of the deceased's soul. *Hadia*, money varying from Rs. 1-4-0 to 10 or more, is given by the kinsfolk either at death after the *janása* or at the burial. Trusting in the *Qurán* as their mediator, they begin their prayers thus: 'O God! Forgive this man all his sins.' The price of the *Qurán* is taken and out of the money the cost of the paper and ink used as *hadia* is paid and annas 2 or more given to each *kúl-khwán*, the remainder being distributed among the poor who are present. In villages grain is distributed instead. Besides this *hadia* wealthy people also distribute alms in cash and in grain When the *kul-khwáni* is celebrated on the 3rd day the clothes worn by the deceased's heirs and some new ones are given to the person who washed the body and to relatives and friends.

On the day of the *kul-khwáni* the near kinsmen let the deceased's heir put on a turban (*dastár*) and also give him a cloth for a turban and cash from 4 annas to Re. 1 as *bháji*. The kinsfolk pay Re. 1 or flour according to their means. In villages, those who give *bháji* are feasted; but this custom does not exist in towns. Wealthy people both in villages and towns appoint *mulláhs* to recite verses from the *Qurán* at the tomb for 3 or 4 days and even till the evening of the first Thursday after death. Whatever part of the *Qurán* they recite, they bestow it for the benefit of the deceased's soul. Members of the bereaved family give a meal, at their own cost, to the *mulláhs*, who get besides a fee of 4 annas per day.

Wealthy people distribute sweet rice, meat or meals to the kinsfolk and friends every Thursday for 7 weeks. They give in charity sweet rice, and pudding made of half-ground grain. There is no custom of appointing *mulláhs*, at the tombs of infants, because they are innocent. Food consisting of bread with *ghí* and sugar on it and some milk or *sharbat* is sent every day before sunset to the *mulláh* for 20 or sometimes 40 days. This is called the soul's spiritual food. It need not necessarily be prepared by the same woman.

Various usages prevail regarding the reading of the *Qurán* at the grave after death. Thus in Ambála some well-to-do people engage *maulavís* versed in the *Qurán* to recite from it at the grave for a period.

In some cases the *mulláhs* are asked to recite the *Qurán* on the grave till the following Thursday. This ceremony is in vogue among followers of the Hadís sect, but elsewhere it is said that the followers of the Hadís sect do not perform any ceremony.

If the heirs are well-to-do they build a hut near the grave and engage four *mulláhs* to sit in it, and recite the *Qurán* through from end to end day and night. These four *mulláhs* may take it in turns to recite the *Qurán*, but the recital must be continuous and not stopped even for a moment till the following Thursday evening when they are dismissed with a fee ranging from Rs. 20 to Rs. 10. The deceased's heirs have to feed the *mulláhs* during these days.

In Raya also from the moment of burial, *Qurán* readers are employed to recite the Holy Book at the tomb which they do unintermittently day and night to the close of the following Thursday. The belief is that so long as the reading continues the deceased escapes the torments of the tomb. But this is not done for one who dies on a Thursday, as the belief is that by virtue of that day, he will escape the torments. The reciters of course receive offerings.

In Ḍera Gházi Khán wealthy people arrange for *háfis* to sit at the tomb after burial and recite the *Qurán* day and night and supply them with food there. They continue this recitation till the following Thursday and when it is completed each is paid Rs. 2 or Rs. 2-8-0 as *hadya Qurán Sharíf*. The object of this is that when the angels Munkir and Nakír come to ask questions from the deceased about his deeds he may find it easy to answer them by the blessing of the *Qurán*.

After burial the deceased's heirs distribute sweetmeat at the tomb or give some cash to *faqírs* by way of *hadya Qurán Sharíf*.

The custom of visiting the graves of dead relatives and throwing fresh earth over them at festivals, particularly in Muharram, is fast dying out, men of the new light as the phrase goes, being very indifferent to it.

Section 11.—Domestic Observances in the South-East Punjab.

The following account of domestic observances in Karnál is reproduced from the *Settlement Report* of that District written in 1893 by the late Sir Denzil Ibbetson :—

When a woman is about to be delivered she is taken off the bed and put on the ground. If a boy is born, a brass tray is beaten to Karnal. Ibbetson S. R.— § 316.

spread the news. A net is hung up in the doorway, and a garland (*tandarwál*) of mango leaves; and a branch of *nim* is stuck into the wall by the doorway, and a fire lighted in the threshold, which is kept up night and day. Thus no evil spirits can pass. The swadling clothes should be got from another person's house. They are called *potra;* thus *potron ká amír* is equivalent to 'a gentleman from his cradle.' For 3 days the child is not suckled. For 5 days no one from outside, except the midwife, goes into the house. On the night of the 6th day (natives always count the night *preceding* the day as belonging to it) the whole household sits up and watches over the child; for on the 6th day (*chhata*) the child's destiny (*lekh*) is written down, especially as to his immunity from small-pox. If the child goes hungry on this day, he will be stingy all his life; and a miser is accordingly called *chhate ka bhúkha;* so a prosperous man is called *chhate ka rája*. On the 6th day the female relations come on visits of congratulation, but they must not go into the room where the woman is lying in The father's sister, too, comes and washes the mother's nipple and puts it into the child's mouth, and the mother takes off her necklace and gives it to her sister-in-law; *gur* is divided to the brotherhood. On the 7th day the female Dúm or bard comes and sings Till the 10th day the house is impure (*sútak*); and no one can eat or drink from it, and no man can go into it unless belonging to the household. On the 10th day (*dasútan*) the net is taken down, the fire let out, all the clothes washed, all the earthen vessels renewed, and the house new plastered; the Brahmans come and do *hom* to purify the house, and tie a *tágri* of yellow string round the boy's waist; and the Brahmans and assembled brotherhood are feasted. The child is often named on this day; the Brahman casting the horoscope and fixing the name. But the parents sometimes change the name if they do not approve of the Brahman's selection At the birth of a girl the tray is not beaten, no feasting takes place, and no net is hung up or fire lighted. The mother remains impure for five weeks; no one can eat or drink from her hands; and she takes her food separately. As soon as there is hair enough the boy's head is shaved and his *choti* (scalplock) made; but there are no further ceremonies till his betrothal.

Ibid., § 317. Betrothal is called *sáta;* the ceremony *sagái*. It generally takes place in infancy. When the father of a girl wishes to betrothe her he makes inquiry for a marriageable boy of good family, the village barber acting the part of go-between. If matters are satisfactory he sends the barber to the boy's village, who puts either a ring or one rupee into the boy's hand. This is called *ropna* (fr. *rokna* to restrain); and if the boy's father returns Re. 1-4, called *biddigi,* to the barber to take to the girl's father, he hereby accepts the offer and clenches the engagement. This engagement is not a necessary preliminary of betrothal; and is most customary among castes, such as the Rájpúts, who marry at a comparatively late age, and who do not wish to go to the expense of a formal betrothal so long beforehand, for fear one of the children should die and the money be wasted. Among the Gujars, on the other hand, the above ceremony constitutes betrothal; but the *tika* is affixed at the time by the Brahman as described below. It is possible for the proposal to come from the boy's side, in which case he sends his sister's necklace; and if the girl keeps it his proposal is accepted. But this is only done when the families are already acquainted.

When it is decided to proceed to the betrothal (*sagái*), the barber and Brahman are sent with the *pích-narial*; or one rupee which has been all night in the milk which is set for butter, a loin-cloth (*pích*) and a cocoanut (*narial*) The boy is seated in a chair before the brotherhood, the Brahman puts the *tíka* or mark on the boy's forehead and the other things into his lap, and *gur* is divided by the boy's father, who takes hold of the hand of each near relation in turn and puts some *gur* into it. The boy's father then gives Re. 1-4[1] to the Brahman and double that to the barber. This is called *neg* or *lág*, and must be brought back to the girl's father; and when so brought back completes the betrothal. Ordinarily *no* relation of the girl *may* take any part in the embassy (*lágs*) of betrothal; but Brahmans send the girl's brother-in-law or relation by marriage. Exchange of betrothals between two families ((*sánta náta*) is considered very disgraceful; and if done at all, is done by a tripartite betrothal, *A* betrothing with *B*, *B* with *C*, and *C* with *A*. Among the Jáṭs, if the boy dies his father has a right to claim the girl for his other son; or, in default of another any male relation in that degree. If the girl dies her family has no claim. *Ibid.*, § 318.

Jáṭs marry at about 5 or 7 years old; Rors and Gujars at 12 to 14; Rájpúts at 15, 16, or even older. The prohibited degrees are thus described:—Every *gens* (*got*) is exogamous; that is, that while every man *must* marry into his own tribe, no man *can* marry into his own *gens*. But this is by no means the only limitation imposed upon inter-marriage. In the first place, no man can marry into a family, of *whatever gens* it may be, that is settled in his own village or in any village immediately adjoining his own. The strength of this custom is shown by an answer given me, to the effect that the speaker could not marry into a 'family of his own *gens*, even if it lived 100 miles off.' The prohibition is based upon *simjor kí birádri*, or the relationship founded upon a common boundary; and is clearly a survival from marriage by capture. This limitation is further extended by the Rájpúts, so that no man of them can marry into any family living in the *thapa* into any family of which his father, grandfather, or great-grandfather married. Thus if a Mandhár Rájpút married a Chauhán Rájpút of *thapa* Jundla, his son, grandson, and great-grandson would not be able to marry any Chauhán of any village in the Jundla *thapa*. But beyond this, and the prohibition against marrying within the *gens*, the Rájpúts have no further limitations on inter-marriage. Among the other castes the *thapa* is not excluded; but no man can marry into any family of the *gens* to which his mother or his father's mother belongs, wherever these *gentes* may be found. The Gujars, however, who are generally lax in their rules, often only exclude such persons of these *gentes* as live in the individual village from which the relation in question came. In some parts of Ambála the people are beginning to add the mother's mother's *gens*, or even to *substitute* it for the father's mother's *gens*; and this may perhaps be a last stage of the change from relationship through women to relationship through men. *Ibid*, § 319.

[1] Wherever other people give Re. 1-4, the Jáṭs pay Re. 1 and 4 *ṭakas*, that is 8 country pice at 5 to the *ánd*.

Foster relationship is equivalent to blood relationship as a bar to marriage. Any number of wives may be married, but a second wife is seldom taken unless the first is childless. A sister of a first wife may be married, or any relation in the same degree; but not above or below.

Ibid., § 320 The boy's Brahman fixes an auspicious day, and decides how many ceremonial oilings (*bán*) the boy is to undergo. It must be 5, 7, 9, or 11; and the girl will undergo *two* fewer than the boy. The boy's father then sends a *lagan* or *tewá*, generally 9, 11, or 15 days before the wedding, which is a letter communicating the number of *bán* and the number of guests to be expected, and is accompanied by a loin-cloth or a complete suit of female clothes (*twal*) and a pair of shoes. In all these communications the Brahman who takes the letters always gets Re. 1-4.

Ibid., § 321 The boy and girl then undergo their *báns* in their respective homes. The women collect and bathe them while singing, and rub them from head to foot with oil and turmeric and peameal. The *báns* are given one each night, and are so arranged that the boy's will end the night before the procession starts, and the girl's the night before the wedding. After each *bán* the mother performs the ceremonies of *árata* and *sewal* described below to the boy. The girl has only *sewal* performed, as *árata* can under no circumstances be performed over a female. The day of the first *bán* is called *huladhát*, or 'red hand.' Seven women with living husbands husk 5¼ seers of rice and make sweets with it. The Brahman comes and sticks up two small round saucers, bottom outwards, against the wall with flour, and in front of them a flour lamp is kept alight in honour of ancestors. On either side he makes five marks of a bloody hand on the wall. This is done in each house. In the girl's village the street turnings all the way from the village gate to the bride's house, and the house itself, are also marked with red or red and white marks. After the first *bán* the boy has the *rákrí* or black woollen thread, with a small iron ring (*chhalla*) and some yellow cloth and betel-nut, tied round his left ankle. The girl has her small gold nosering put on; for up to that time she can only wear a silver one; and she must not wear a large one till she goes to live with her husband. She also takes off her silver wristlets (*chúrá*) which no married woman may wear; and substitutes for them at least five of glass on each arm. These glass wristlets and her nosering form her *sohág*, and a woman who has a husband living (*s há an*) must always wear them. When her husband dies she breaks the wristlets off her arm, and throws the pieces and nosering on to the corpse, and they are wrapped up with it in the shroud. After that she may wear silver wristlets again. And occasionally, if a widow has plenty of grown-up sons, she will continue to wear the *sohág*.

Ibid., § 322. The day before the procession is to start or arrive, as the case may be, the *manda* or *mandab* is erected. At the boy's house they take five seed-stems of the long *sarkara* grass and tie them over the lintel. They dig a hole in front and to the right of the threshold, put money in it, and stand a plough beam straight up in it. To this they hang two small cakes fried in *ghi*, with three little saucers under and two above this, and two pie, all tied on a thread. Finally, some five *beran* culms, and a *dogar*, or two vessels of water one on top of the other, are brought by the mother, attended by singing women, and after worship of the potter wheel (*chak*) are put by the door as a good omen. At the girl's house the same is done; but instead of burying the plough beam, they erect a sort of tent with one central pole, and four cross sticks, or a stool with its four legs upwards, at the top, and on each is hung a brass water pot upside down surrounding a full one in the middle; or a curtained enclosure is formed, open to the sky, with at each corner a *lichi* or 'nest' of five earthen vessels, one on top of the other, with a tripod of bamboos over each.

On the same day the mother's brother of the boy or girl brings *Ibid.*, § 323.
the *bhát*. This is provided by the mother's father, and consists of a presents of clothes; and necessarily includes the wedding suit for the bride or bridegroom, and in the case of the boy, the loin-cloth and head-dress he is to wear at the marriage; for all that either party then wears must always be provided by his or her mother's brother. The boy's maternal uncle also brings a girl's suit of clothes and a wedding ring, and the girl wears *both* suits of clothes at the wedding. When the *bhát* is given, the boy's or girl's mother performs the ceremony of *árata* or *minna*. She takes a 5-wicked lamp made of flour, places it on a tray, and while her brother stands on a stool, waves it up and down his body from head to foot. She also performs *sewal*, which consists in picking up her petticoat and touching his body all over with it. They then take the brother in-doors and feed him on *laddús* or sweetmeat balls. The people then at the boy's village collect in the village common room and the *neota* (§ 337 *infra*) is collected the *bháti* (giver of the *bhát*) putting in his money first, which is a free gift and not entered in the account.

On the day when the marriage procession (*janet, barát*) is to *Ibid.*, § 324.
start, the boy receives his last *bán* and is dressed in his wedding suits, the *kangna* or seven-knotted sacred thread is tied on his wrist, and his head-dress is tied on, consisting of a crown (called *mor*) of mica and tinsel, a *pechi* or band of silver tinsel over the turban, and a *sera* or fringed vizor of gold tinsel.

He then performs the ceremony of *ghurchari*. The barber leads him, while singing women follow, and the mother with a vessel of water; and his sister puts her wrap over her right hand, and on it places rice which she flings at his crown as the boy goes along. He then gives her Re. 1, worships the gods of the homestead, and gives Re. 1 to the Bairági. He is then put into a palanquin, and the procession, to which every house nearly related must contribute a representative, and which consists of males only, starts, as much as possible on horseback, with music of sorts. At each village they pass through they are met by the barber, the Ḍúm, and the Brahmans, whom they pay money to, and who put *dúbh* grass on the father's head and pray that he may flourish like it. The procession must reach the girl's village after the midday meal.

A place, rigorously outside the village, has been appointed for *Ibid.*, § 325.
them called *bág* or *goira*. The girl's relations come to meet them, bring in a loin-cloth and 11 *takas* and a little rice and sweetmeats in a tray. The two parties sit down, the Brahmans read sacred texts, the girl's Brahman affixes the *tika* on the boy's forehead, and gives a loin-cloth and 11 *takas*, taking a loin-cloth and 21 *takas* in exchange. The two

fathers then embrace, and the girl's father takes Re. 1 from his turban and gives it to the boy's father, who gives him in exchange the cloth which is to form the *patka* at the wedding. The girl's father then asks the boy's father for either 11 or 14 pice, the *goira ká kharch* or expenses of the *gora*; and these he distributes to the menial bystanders, and makes the boy's father pay something to the barber and Brahman. The procession then proceeds to the girl's house, the boy being put on a horse, and pice being thrown over his head as a scramble (*bakher*) for the menials. They do not go into the house; but at the door stand women singing and holding flour lamps. The boy is stood on a stool, and the girl's elder married sister, or if she has no married sister her brother's married daughter, performs to him the ceremonies of *árata* and *sewal* already described, and the boy's father gives her Rs. 1-4. She also performs the ceremony of *wárpher* by waving a pot of water over the boy's head and then drinking a little of it, and waving a rupee round his head. The girl's and boy's relations then fight for the stool on which the boy stood, and the boy's relations win, and carry it off in triumph to the *jandalwása* or *dandalwása*, which is the place fixed for the residence of the guests. This *should*, in theory, be outside the village; but for the convenience sake it is generally in the *chopál*. Presently the guests are bidden to the girl's house, where they eat; but the boy stays in the *jandalwása*, as he must not enter the girl's house till the wedding itself. So, too, the girl's relations do not eat; for they cannot eat that day till the wedding ceremony is over. This ends the first day called *dhakáo*.

Ibid., § 396. That night, at some time after sunset, the wedding ceremony (*phera*) takes place. Shortly before it the girl's barber goes to the *jandalwása*, where the boy's father gives him a complete suit of clothes for the girl, some jewels, sacred coloured strings to tie her hair up (*nála*), some henna for her hands, and a ring called the yoke-ring (*júa ki angúthi*). The girl wears nothing at all of her own unless it be a pair of scanty drawers (*dhola*); and she is dressed up in the above things, and *also* in the clothes brought in the *bhát* by her maternal uncle, one on top of the other. The ring she wears on the first finger; and on her head she wears the *choláop*, or an unsewn and unhemmed reddish yellow cloth provided by her maternal grandfather, used only at weddings, but worn after the ceremony till it wears out. Meanwhile her relations sit down with their Brahman under the *manda*.

There a place on the ground (*chauri, bedi*) has been fresh plastered, and the Brahman makes a square enclosure (*mandal* or *púrat*) of flour, and on it puts sand and sacred fire (*hawan*) of *dhak* wood, and *ghi*, and sugar, and sesame. Meanwhile the other party has been sent for; and the boy, dressed in the clothes brought by his maternal uncle, comes attended by his father and nearest relations only. They sit down to the north, the girl's people to the south, and two stools are placed facing the east, on which the boy and girl, who are fetched, after all have sat down by her mother's brother, are seated each next his or her people, so that she is on his right hand. When the ceremony commences the girl's people hold up a cloth for a minute so as to hide the boy and girl from the boy's people, 'just as a matter of form.' The Brahman puts five little earthen pots (*kulia*) in the sacred enclosure, and makes the boy and girl dip their third fingers into turmeric and touch pice, which he then puts into the pots, the boy offering twice as many as the girl. Sacred texts are then recited. The girl then turns her hand-palm upwards, her father puts one rupee and a little water into it, and takes the hand and the rupee and solemnly places them in the boy's hand, saying *main apni larkí dán, kanya dán*: 'I give you my daughter; I give her virgin.' This is called *kanya dán*. Then the sacred fire is stirred up, the Brahman ties the hem (*palla*) of the girl's wrap to a piece of cloth called the *patká*, and the boy takes the latter over his shoulder and leads her round the fire counter clockwise four times, and then she goes in front and leads him round three times. Meanwhile the family priests recite the tribe and *gens* of each, and the names of their ancestors for four generations. This is the *pherá*, and constitutes the real marriage. After this the Brahmans formally ask each whether he or she accepts the other, and is ready to perform duties which are set forth in time-honoured and very impressive and beautiful language. The boy and girl then sit down, each where the other sat before; and this completes the ceremony. The bride and bridegroom are then taken into the girl's house, where the girl's mother unties the boy's head-dress and gives him a little *ghí* and *gur* mixed up. There two small earthen saucers have been fixed with flour against the wall, bottom outwards, and a lamp lighted in front of them. This they worship; the boy returns to the *jandalwása* after redeeming his shoes, which the women have stolen, by paying Rs. 1-4; while the girl stays with her people.

On the second day (*badhár*) the boy's people must not eat food of the girl's people; and they get it from their relations and friends in the village. Various ceremonies involving payment to Brahmans and barbers are performed. *Ibid.*, § 328.

At night the girl's father and friends go to the *jandalwása*; the two fathers, who are now each other's *simdís*, embrace; the girl's father gives his *simdí* one rupee and invites the whole *barát*, including the boy, to eat at the girl's house. But when, after eating, they have returned to the *jandalwása*, the girl's friends follow them and make them give a nominal payment for it, called *roṭí ká kharch*, which is given to the menials.

On the third day, called *bida*, the *neota* is collected in the girl's house just as it was in the boy's house before the *barát* started. *Ibid.*, § 329. The boy's people then eat at the girl's house, and return to the *jandalwása*, whence they are presently summoned to take leave (*bida hona*). The boy's father then presents a *bari*, which is a gift of sugar, almonds, sacred threads, fruits &c. to the girl's people. The ceremony of *patta* is then performed. The girl's relations form a *panchâyat* or council, and demand a certain sum from the boy's father from which the village menials then and there receive their fixed dues. The money is called *patta*. The girl's *panch* having ascertained that all have been paid, formally asks the boy's father whether any one in the village has taken or demanded ought of him save this money; and he replies in the negative. During this ceremony the girl's father sits quite apart, as he must have nothing whatever to do with taking money from the boy's people, and in fact often insists upon paying the *patta* himself. While the *patta* is being distributed, the girl's mother makes the boy perform the ceremony of *band khulái*, which consists in untying one knot of the *manda*. She then puts the *tíka* on his forehead and gives one rupee and two *laddús* (a sweetmeat made into a ball), and the other women also feed him. This is called *joh ári*. Then the girl's father presents the *dán* or dower, which includes money, clothes, vessels &c., but no female jewels; and the *barát* returns to the *jandalwása*. The boy's father then visits all the women (*gotán*) of his own gens who live in the village, and gives each one rupee. The horses and bullocks are then got out, and should assemble at the outer gate of the village, though they sometimes go to the door of the house for convenience. Her maternal uncle takes the girl, and, followed by women singing, places her in the ox-cart in which she is to travel. She is accompanied by a female barber called the *larambi*, and the boy is kept apart. When they are just starting the two fathers embrace, and the girl's father gives the other one rupee and his blessing; but the girl's mother comes up, and having dipped her hand in henna, claps the boy's father on the back so as to leave a bloody mark of a hand (*thapa*) on his clothes. A few pice are scrambled over the heads of the happy pair; and the procession starts for home, the girl screaming and crying as a most essential form.

Ibid. § 330. When the *barát* reaches the boy's village, the friends are collected at the boy's door, which has five red marks of a hand on the wall on either side. The boy and girl are stood on the stool which the *barát* have brought from the other village and the boy's mother measures them both with a *sela* or string made of the hair of a bullock's tail, which is then thrown away. She also performs the ceremony of *sewal* and waves a vessel of water over their heads and drinks a little of it. The boy's sister stands in the doorway, and will not admit them till the boy pays her one rupee. That night the boy and girl sleep on the floor, and above where they sleep are two mud saucers stuck, bottom outwards, against the wall, and a lighted lamp before them.

Ibid, § 331. On the next auspicious day the girl puts on the wrap with the *paṭka* still knotted to it; the boy takes it over his shoulder and leads her off, attended by women only and music, to worship the god of the homestead, the sacred *tulsi* tree, the small pox goddess, and all the village deities and the wheel of the potter, who gives them a nest of vessels for good luck. They go outside the village and perform *kesora*, which consists in the boy and girl taking each a stick and fighting together by striking seven blows or more. Then comes the ceremony of *kangna khelna*. The girl unties the *kangna* or 7-knotted sacred thread which the Brahman tied round the boy's wrist before he started, and he undoes hers. The *kangnás* are then tied to the girl's yoke-ring; and it is flung by the boy's brother's wife into a vessel of milk and water with *dúbh* grass in it. The two then dip for it several times with their hands, the finder being rewarded with cheers.[1] Till this ceremony is performed the boy and girl must sleep on the ground and not on bedsteads. Then the boy's elder brother's wife (his *bhábi*) sits down, opens her legs, and takes the boy between her

[1] Among the Rájpúts there are two *kangnás*, one with a rupee and the other with betelnut tied to it. This ceremony is performed with the former *kangná* at the girl's village the day after the *phera*, and with the latter as described above.

thighs. The girl sits similarly between the boy's thighs, and takes a little boy into her lap. The girl or his mother gives him two *laḍḍús*; and he says, 'a son for my sister-in-law, and two *laḍḍús* for me.' Some few days after a barber comes from the girl's village, and takes her back to her home.

So far the bride and bridegroom are infants, and of course the marriage has not been consummated; in fact, a child conceived at this stage would be illegitimate. The consummation takes place after the return of the girl to her husband's house, called *challa* or *mukláwa*. This takes place when the girl is pubert; but must be in either the 3rd, 5th, 7th, 9th, or 11th year after the wedding. The girl's people fix the day; and the boy with some male friends, but without his father, goes to fetch her. The girl then for the first time wears a large nosering, an armlet (*ṭadia*), and a boddice or *angi*. The girl's father gives her some clothes and jewels, and they go off home. As they start the girl must scream and cry bitterly, and bewail some near male relation who has lately died, saying, 'oh! my father is dead,' or 'oh! my brother is dead.' After reaching home they live together as man and wife. *Ibid.*, § 332

The girl stays with her husband a few weeks only; and must then return to her father's home and stay there some six months or a year. She is then brought back for good by her husband, her father presenting her with her trousseau (*piṭár*) of clothes and jewels. This she retains; but all clothes given by her father to the boy's father previous to this, at marriage or *challa*, must be divided among the female relations of the boy's father and not retained by him. *Ibid.*, § 333

This is the course of affairs when the parties marry in infancy. But among Rájpúts who always marry late, and generally when the marriage has from any cause been delayed till puberty, there is no *muklávwa*, but on the third day before the *barát* starts the ceremony of *patra pherna* or changing the stools is performed. The girl changes all her clothes, putting on clothes provided by her father, and also a large nosering, armlets, and boddice. The boy and girl are then seated on stools and exchange places, each sitting where the other was, and the *paṭka* is tied up. The girl's father presents both the dower and the trousseau at the same time; and the pair, on reaching home, live as man and wife. *Ibid.*, § 334.

Among Musalmáns there is no *phera*; the *nikáh* or Musalmán marriage ceremony being substituted for it, which the *qázi* reads in presence of witnesses. Envoys (*wakíls*) go into the girl's house to take her consent and come out and announce it; the boy consents himself three times, and the ceremony is complete. But among converts to Islám, at any rate, the other customs and ceremonies are almost *exactly* the same. Of late years the Musalmáns have begun to leave off the *sewal* and *árata* and they often use no *pechi*, though they retain the *sera*. *Ibid.*, § 335.

Local and tribal variations are numerous, but quite unimportant. There are innumerable *minutiæ* which I have not detailed, and which vary greatly, though quite constant for each tribe or locality. The Rájpúts never use a *mor*, nor have the customs of *thápa*; and the tent is often omitted from the *manda* in the Khádir.

Ibid., § 336. The wife has to hide her face before all the elder brothers and other elder relations of her husband; not so before the younger ones, elder and younger being, of course, a matter of genealogical degree, and not of age. Nor may she ever mention the name of any of the elder ones, or even of her husband himself.[1]

When once the ceremonial goings and comings are over—among Rájpúts, for instance, where there is no *muklâwa,* directly the wedding is over—she may never return to her father's house except with his special leave; and if he sends for her, he has to give her a fresh dower.

The village into which his daughter is married is utterly tabooed for the father, and her elder brother, and all near elder relations. They may not go to it, even drink water from a well in that village; for it is shameful to take anything from one's daughter or her belongings. On the other hand, the father is continually giving things to his daughter and her husband as long as he lives. Even the more distant elder relations will not eat or drink from the house into which the girl is married, though they do not taboo the whole village. The boy's father can go to the girl's village by leave of her father, but not without

Ibid., § 337. There is a curious custom called *neota* by which all the branches of a family contribute towards the expenses of a marriage in any of its component households. If *A* and *B* are relations, and *A* first marries his daughter, *B* will contribute, say, Rs. 10. If *B* then marries his daughter, *A* must contribute more than this, or say Rs. 12. At further marriages, so long as the *neota* consists between them, the contribution will always be Rs. 10, so that *B* will always owe *A* Rs. 2; but if either wishes to put an end to the *neota*, he will contribute, if *A*, only Rs. 8, if *B* Rs. 12. This clears the account, and, *ipso facto*, closes the *neota*. The *neota* is always headed by the *bhâti* or mother's brother; but his contribution is a free gift, and does not enter into the account, which is confined to the relations of the male line. These contribute even when the relationship is very distant indeed.

Ibid., § 338. This is the real *neota*; and is only called into play on the occasion of the marriage of a daughter or son of the house. But in a somewhat similar manner, when the *bhát* is to be provided by the mother's father, he sends a little *gur* to each *neotára*, or person between whom and himself *neota* exists; and they make small contributions, generally Re. 1 each. So, too, when the boy's father gives *gur* to his relations at his son's betrothal they each return him Re. 1.

The Rájpúts call the custom *bel* instead of *neota*, and take it, in the case of the *bhát*, only from descendants of a common great-grandfather.

Ibid., § 339. As I have said, a man may marry as often as he pleases If he marries again on the death of his wife, he is called *dheju*. The ceremonies are exactly the same for a man's different marriages. But under no circumstances can a woman perform the *phera* twice in her life. Thus, among the Rájpúts, Brahmans and Tagás, who do not allow *karewa* or *karáo*, a widow cannot under any circumstances

[1] In one village there is a shrine to an ancestor who had died childless. It is known by his nickname, and not by his proper name, because the women of the family do not like to pronounce the latter.

remarry. But among other castes a remarriage is allowed under the above name. It is, in its essence, the Jewish levirate; that is to say, on the death of a man his younger brother has first claim to the widow, then his elder brother, and after them other relations in the same degree; though *karewa* cannot be performed while the girl is a minor, and her consent is necessary. But it has been extended so that a man may marry a widow whom he could not have married as a virgin, the only restriction being that she is not of his own gens. Thus, a Gujar may marry a Jáṭ or Roṛ widow of any gens but his own. I need hardly say that neither marriage, nor adoption, nor any other ceremony, can change the gens of a man or woman; that being, under all circumstances, the gens of the original father. Even women of menial castes can be so married; but the woman is then called *heri húi*, though it is still a real marriage. At the same time any marriage out of one's own caste, even if with a higher one, is thought disgraceful.

The marriage must not take place within a year of the husband's death. It is effected by the man throwing a red wrap over the woman's head and putting wrislets (*chúra*) on her arm in presence of male and female members of the brotherhood. There is no *seota* in *karewa*, because there are no expenses.

When a Hindu is on the point of death, he is taken off the bed and put with his feet to the east on the ground, on a fresh plastered spot strewn with the sacred *dúbh* grass and sesame. Ganges water and milk, and a tiny pearl (they can be bought for a few pice), and gold, are put into his mouth. The friends are called in and the son or nearest heir shaves completely in public, draws water with his right hand alone, bathes and puts on a clean lion-cloth, turban, and handkerchief, and no other clothes. Meanwhile the widow has broken her *sohág*, and throws it on the corpse, which the men or women of the family, according to its sex, bathe with the water the son has drawn, put on it a loin-cloth, and sew it up in a shroud (*guji* or *ghúgi*). They then place it on the bier (*arti* or *pinjri*) and bear it out head foremost. At the door a Brahman meets it with *pinḍs* (balls of dough) and water which the son places on the bier by the head of the corpse. On the road they stop by a tank or some water, and *pinḍs* are again put on the bier. Then all the *pinḍs* are flung into the water, and the bier is taken up the reverse way with the feet foremost. When they reach the burning place (*chhalla*), the corpse is placed on the pyre (*chita*), and the son taking sacred fire, lit by the Brahman, lights the wood (*dág dena*) and fans it. This is the *kiria karm* so often mentioned. When the bone of the skull is exposed, the son takes one of the sticks of which the bier was made, drives it through the skull (*kapál kiria*) and throws it over the corpse beyond the feet. When the corpse is completely burnt, all bathe and return together to the house, and then go off to their homes. The burning should be on the day of death, if possible; but it should always be before sunset. *Ibid.*, § 840.

If the burning was performed on the bank of the Jumna, water is thrown on the ashes; if in the Kurukshetr, the bones are thrown into one of the sacred tanks, and all is over. Otherwise, on the third day the knuckle-bones and other small fragments of bones (*phúl*) are collected. If they can be taken to the Ganges at once, well and good; *Ibid*, § 841.

if not they are buried in the jungle. But they must not be brought into the village in any case; and when once ready to be taken to the Ganges, they must not be put down anywhere, but must always be hung up till finally thrown by a Brahman into the stream. Their bearer, who must be either a relation, or a Brahman, or Jhíwar, must sleep on the ground, and not on a bed, on his way to the Ganges. After the death a *ghara* of water with a hole in the bottom, stuffed with *dúbh* grass so that water will drip from it, is hung in a *pípal* tree; and the water is filled, and a lamp lighted daily for 11 days.

Ibid., § 342. The house is impure (*pátak*) till the 13th day after death. On the 10th day the Mába Brahman or Achárj comes. The household perform *dasáhi*; that is, they go to the tank, wash their clothes, shave, offer 10 *pinds*, and give the Achárj grain enough for 10 meals. On the 11th or day of *sapinda*, a bull calf is let loose, with a trident (*tarsúl*) branded on his shoulder or quarter, to become a pest. The Achárj is seated on the dead man's bedstead, and they make obeisance to him and lift him up, bedstead and all. He then takes the bedstead and all the wearing apparel of the dead man, and goes off on his donkey. But he is held to be so utterly impure that in many villages they will not allow him to come inside, but take the things out to him. On the 12th day the Gújráti Brahman is fed, being given *sidha* or the uncooked materials for dinner only, as he will not eat food cooked even by Gaur Brahmans. On the 13th day the Gaur Brahmans are fed, and then the whole brotherhood; the walls are plastered, the earthen vessels changed, all clothes washed, and the house becomes pure. If the man died on his bed instead of on the ground, the house is impure for 45 days; and after the 11th day special ceremonies called *jap* have to be performed to purify it. Again, if he has died on certain inauspicious days of the month, called *panchak*, 5 or 7 Brahmans have to perform *barni* in order to ease his spirit.

Ibid., § 343. The same ceremonies are observed on the death of a woman. Children under 8 years of age are buried without ceremony.

There are no particular ceremonies observed at the death of a Musalman, who is, of course, buried with his feet to the south. Gosains and Jogís are buried sitting up in salt; and used to be so buried alive before our rule. Their graves are called *samáds*. Bairágís are burnt, and in the case of an abbott a *samád* erected over some of the bones. Chamárs are burnt; while sweepers are buried upside down (*múndha*).

Ibid., § 344. The disembodied spirit while on its travels is called *parct*; and remains in this state for one year, making 12 monthly stages. For the first 12 days after death a lamp is kept lit, and a bowl of water with a hole in the bottom for it to drip from kept full in a *pípal* tree for the use of the spirit. At the end of each month the son gives his family priest the 'monthly *ghara*' which consists of a *sidha* or uncooked food for two meals, a *ghara* of water, a towel, an umbrella, and a pair of the wooden shoes (*khardun*) used where the impure leather is objectionable. At the first anniversary of the death (*barsaundi*) he gives the Brahman a bedstead and bedding, a complete suit of clothes, some vessels, and such other parts of a complete outfit as he can afford. This is called *sajja*. He also gives him a cow with a calf at foot and some rupees in water.

SECTION 12—FICTITIOUS KINSHIP IN THE PUNJAB.

The ideas underlying the formation of the ties of fictitious kinship and the effects of those ties, when formed, are not only of importance from a practical point of view, as illustrating such practices as adoption, rules of succession, and the like, but they are also of considerable interest as illustrating the possibilities of castes, or even tribes, having been formed by processes of accretion. Among the most primitive races on the North-West Frontier of India the ties of fosterage are very strong, more stringent even than those of blood kinship[1]; and throughout India, at least among the non-Muhammadans, adoption plays a very important *rôle* in the law of inheritance.[2] The following notes on these ideas and customs have been collected in an attempt to ascertain how far fictitious kinship is now formed in the Punjab.

Gangá-bháís.—A fraternal relationship entailing the consequences of natural kinship and thus operating as a bar to marriage between the parties, who become Gangá-bháís each to the other, is established by making a pilgrimage to the Ganges together and there drinking the waters of the sacred river from each other's hands.[3] This relationship is also established between two women (or even between a man and a woman),[4] irrespective of caste, and the parties should drink thrice,[5] or seven times, while lasting friendship and sisterhood are vowed. In Gurgáon women who exchange *dopattas* (shawls) at a sacred place, or on a pilgrimage, become Gangá-bahin, Jamná bahin (if that river is the place of pilgrimage), or, generally, *tirath-bahin*. Such women each treat the other's husband as a *jíja*, *i.e.* as a sister's husband, and it is said that the custom of making these alliances is more prevalent among women than among men, and more binding also. With the extension of facilities for making pilgrimages this custom is becoming rarer, but when a pilgrimage involved journeying and living together the tie was often contracted, and it is still not rare in cases where some service or aid was rendered. A Sanskrit adage declares that no wrong should be done to a person with whom one has walked seven paces, an idea to which the seven steps at a wedding owe their significance.

The *pahul.*—Among Sikhs the taking of the *pahul* together creates a similar tie, and those bound by it are called *gurbháís*. Here again caste is disregarded and the relationship created operates as an absolute bar to marriage.

Adoption.—Adoption, as a religious rite, is not very common in the Punjab, even among Hindus. It is solemnized with few rites, and is usually called *god lená*, or 'taking in the lap.' An adopted son is

[1] *E.g.*, among the so-called Dards; *see* Biddulph's *Tribes of the Hindoo Koosh*, pp. 82-3.

[2] *E.g.*, among the Nambudri Brahmans of Kerala, on the Malabar coast (*see Calcutta Review*, 1901, pp. 121 *et seqq.*), we find two kinds of religious and one of secular adoption. All three forms have remarkable effects on the laws of succession.

[3] It is said that the exchange of *pagris* at Hardwár merely cements a long and intimate friendship without creating any bond of artificial kinship.

[4] It is, however, said that this tie is *only* contracted between women. It is apparently rare between a man and a woman, but not unknown. In Multán the tie is called *bhirappí* and does exist between men and women. In *Wide-Awake Stories* (Mrs. F. A. Steel and Sir R. C. Temple) Princess Ambergine exchanges veils with the Queen and drinks milk out of the same cup with her—'as is the custom when two people say they will be sisters': p. 81.

[5] This is called in Panjábí *chulián lena* [literally 'to take handfuls' (of water)]. Women thus become *dharm-bahin*, if Hindus.

termed *putrela* by Hindus.[1] But besides the custom of formal adoption a kind of informal adoption of a man or woman as father or mother is not unusual. The adoptive parent is thenceforth treated as a natural parent, but apparently no legal results ensue.

Exchanging *gánáṇs*.—An analogous tie can be created between two youths by exchanging *gánáṇs*[2] or wedding wristlets, and eating rice and milk together. The youth who is to be married puts on a *gánáṇ*, and his would-be friend unties it, while a Brahman repeats the following *mantrá* :—

TRANSLITERATION.

Maṅglaṅg[3] *Bhagwán-Vishnu*[4]
Maṅglaṅg Garaṛ-dhwijá ![5]
Manglang Púnri-kákhiyó[6]
Maṅglá yatṇo[7] *Hari.*[8]

TRANSLATION.

Bhagwán Vishnu }
Garar-dhwij } is the embodiment of bliss.
Punri-kakhiyá }
Harí is the abode of happiness.

God is the centre of all bliss, happiness emanates from Him.

This is a benediction (*ashir wád*) which a Brahman gives to other men. The idea being 'May God, the embodiment of all bliss, give you happiness.'

Another *mantrá* :—

Yen badhdho Pali-rája dán-vaṇdro, Mahá-bala !!
Te-natwáṇg prit-badhnámi rakshe má-chal má-chal !!

"In the name of Him who killed Rájá Bali, the mighty leader of the Daits, I fasten this *rakhri* thread round your wrist and protect you, may you persevere, cleave to it, and never deviate from it."

Generally this *mantrá* is recited when a *rakhri* (amulet) is tied by a Brahman at the Rakhṛí festival (on the full-moon day in the month of Sáwan).

Various other means are adopted to create or cement enduring friendships, hardly amounting to fictitious relationship. Thus the *muṇḍan* ceremony affords an opportunity to swear lasting friendships,

[1] The subject of adoption is fully treated in the present writer's *Compendium of the Punjab Customary Law*.

[2] *Gánáṇ*, M., a string of coloured cords or of goat's hair. The man or youth who unfastens the *gáná* of a bridegroom at his wedding is also bound to him by special ties of friendship.

[3] Happiness, fortune, bliss, felicity.

[4] The second deity of the sacred triad, entrusted with the preservation of the world.

[5] An epithet of Vishnu. *Garaṛ* is represented as the vehicle of Vishnu and as having a white face, an aquiline nose, red wings and a golden body. *Dhwij* means a banner, flag. It generally bears a picture of the deity's vehicle.

[6] An epithet of Vishnu. Lit., having eyes like a white lotus flower (*punrak*=white lotus, *kakhiyá*=eyes).

[7] Lit., house, residence.

[8] An epithet of Vishnu.

batáshas being distributed among those present, or a child of the same age being made to catch the boy's hair as it falls, and thus form a tie of kinship with him. Simultaneous circumcision forms a similar bond.

Among the Sánsís friendship is sworn by one man's placing a sword between himself and his friend. The latter removes it, and the tie is complete.

Pagwaṭ.—But far commoner than the solemn religious bond created by the foregoing fictions is the looser social bond created by the exchange of *pugrís*, or *pagwaṭ*, as it is called in Gujrát. As a rule this exchange creates a bond like that of kinship,[1] though it is said that only among Hindus is its existence a bar to intermarriage, and that among Muhammadans this is not the case. The *pagṛí* or turban[2] is typical of a man's honour, so that the exchange means that the honour of the one party becomes that of the other.

Such 'brothers' are ordinarily termed *pag-bhái* or *dharam-bhái*, the latter term being ordinarily used to denote a brother artificially created as opposed to a natural brother.

Chádar or *orhná-badal.*—Women in the same way exchange *chádars* or *orhnás*, and among Muhammadans become *dharm-bahin* or *imán-bahin* to each other. But these customs are more prevalent among Hindus than among Muhammadans.

A custom prevalent among *children* is noted in Ambála; friendship is made or broken off by placing the finger on the chin and moving it backwards and forwards, saying *merí terí yárí hodí*, 'There is friendship twixt thee and me,' or *merí terí yárí kuṭ*, 'Our friendship is broken.' In Multán children hold their thumbs in their mouths and lock their little fingers together, one saying, 'Is thy friendship like a sieve, or a river?' If the other reply, 'like a river,' the friendship is cemented. Occasionally instead of a sieve and a river, a brass vessel and a grinding-stone are the simile. But the friendship may be broken off by taking a little dust in the palm and blowing it away, or, in Jhang, by breaking a straw.

These modes of creating fictitious relationship, or the ideas which underlie them, appear to be the basis of certain practices which exist in various parts of the Punjab.

These practices on the one hand find analogies in the custom of seeking asylum, while on the other they merge in certain forms of oaths.

The *pagwaṭ* finds a curious application among cattle-lifters and other criminals. Finding himself suspected, the chief offers to restore the stolen property, on condition that the owner exchanges *pagrís* with him as a pledge that he will not lodge a complaint.

An apparent extension of this practice is the custom of *ṭallí páná*,[3]

[1] But in Ambála, for instance, it is said that no such tie is created, because *pagwaṭ* sometimes takes place between persons of different religions (and between them no such tie *could* be created). In Jhang and Multán it creates no such tie.

[2] *Cf.* the adage, *Wair Barárán Bhaṭṭián, Ki honda paggán-waṭián?* When Barárs and Bhaṭṭís are at enmity, of what avail is it to exchange *pagrís*?"

[3] *Talli*, a small piece of cloth, a patch; *tikr* and *tigra* are not given in Maya Singh's, *Panjabi Dictionary*, but both are said to have the same meaning as *ṭalli*. In the Jhang district at a wedding the bridegroom's friend casts a piece of cloth over the bride's head in precisely the same way.

ṭallá páná, tiári páná or *tigrá satná*, as it is variously called. This custom may be thus described. The supplicant casts a piece of clothing over the head of his enemy's daughter or sister, whether he be the person whom he has actually wronged, or a witness against him, or his would-be captor. If he cannot get access to the girl herself he employs a Mirásan or a Machhiáni to go to her father's house and throw the cloth over her head in his name. It suffices to give the girl a small ornament instead of casting a cloth over her. By this means a complainant or a hostile witness may be compelled to assist a thief or any wrong-doer instead of pressing the charge against him; or a loan may be extorted from a money-lender.[1]

Among Muhammadans in the Western Punjab the relatives of a man in trouble with the police approach the complainant with a Quran which they place in his hands and thus constrain him to abandon the prosecution. In former times, it is said, if a man who had a feud died, and his kinsman could not, or would not, continue the feud they took his corpse to his enemy and thus compelled him to friendship. This is called *pallo páná*,[2] or *niyat khair*.[3] Refusal involves divine displeasure. In the Miánwáli district it is customary for one side to send Sayyids, Brahmans, or daughters[4] as envoys to the rival faction in order to induce it to give up its claims. If this request is refused and the rival party meets with misfortune, it is attributed to its rejection of the terms proposed by the Sayyids, or the other envoys. In the same district it is customary for a thief to send a widow (called *káli siri*)[5] to beg for mercy from the complainant. Such an envoy refuses to sit until her request is granted.

The custom of casting one's garment over an enemy's daughter is found as far west as Kohát, but in that district another method is also in vogue. The thief, or one of his relatives, goes to the complainant's house, places his hands on his *chulha* (hearth or oven) and says: *ta angh-are ma wauiwale da*, 'I have grasped your oven'; thus claiming his hospitality.

Compurgation is also not unknown. Thus in Gujrát if *A* is suspected of stealing *B's* cattle, but denies his guilt, the parties nominate an arbitrator and agree to abide by his word. This is called *sugh laina*, or taking an oath, but it is termed *ra . dena* in Jhang, Multán &c.

[1] In Gujrát the suppliant party assembles all the respectable men of the locality, and they go in a body to the house of him whose favour is sought. This is called *meta* (? surely *mela*) *páná*. In Dera Gházi Khán the deputation is formed in a very similar way, and is called *merh* (? *mehar*, ? ., a crowd). Both Hindus and Muhammadans have this custom but only the latter take a Qurán with them.

[2] *Pallo*, the border of a shawl; *pawan*, to spread out the end of one's shawl, to invoke a blessing; so called because *Hindus* spread out the end of their shawls on the ground before them when invoking a blessing.

[3] If the complainant violate his solemn promise on the Qurán to take no action he is said to be *niyat khair khota*, and is cut off from all social intercourse with his fellows, being only received again into fellowship after he has given them presents and feasted the whole brotherhood. The surrender of the corpse reminds one of the attachment of the dead for debt. See *The Grateful Dead*.

[4] Among some of the low castes daughters act as priests, *vice* Brahmans.

[5] *Káli siri*, lit. 'black-head' apparently. A widow would seem to be sent because she is the most deserving or pitiable of all suppliants.

Nanwati.—Very similar in idea is the Paṭhán custom of *nanwati*, or *nahaura*. If a man seeks mercy, or the protection of a powerful patron, he or his relative goes to his house with a *posse* of leading men of the village and there kills a goat or a sheep by way of peace-offering.

Sayyid Ahmad Dehlari furnishes some curious information on the customs among women in Delhi. He informs me that the princesses of the old Mughal dynasty, when resident in the palace, used to effect a tie of sisterhood, called *sanákhi*. *Zanákh*[1] is the breast-bone of a fowl or pigeon, and two ladies used to break it, as we break a wishing bone. They then became *sanákhi*, each to the other, and the tie thus created was a very strong one. The custom is said to have been brought with them from Turkestán. Similar ties were formed by women of the palace who were known as *dilján*, 'heart's life,' *jan-i-man*,[2] *dilmila*, *dushman* (lit, 'enemy'), *dúgána*, *chhagána*, &c, but these ties were less binding. *Dilmila* may be taken to mean 'confidante.' *Dúgána* is applied to two ladies of equal age whose friendship is strengthened by eating phillipine almonds, 'as if they were sisters, born of one mother.' *Chhagána* would appear to be derived from *chhe*, 6, and to mean one who is six times dearer than a sister. *Dushman* is used, curiously enough, to imply that the enemy of either is also the enemy of the other.[3]

Among the women of Delhi generally, the terms applied to such adoptive sisters are *súhelí* (companion),[4] *bahneli*,[5] and *sakhí*,[6] or *sakhelí*, but the latter term is seldom used except in poetry. Another term for adopted sister is *múṇh-ḅoli*, or 'adopted by word of mouth.' Other terms remind one of the *pagri-badal* or *ṭopi-badal* brotherhoods formed among men and include the *challa-badal-bahin*, or sister by exchange of rings, and *dopaṭṭa-badal-bahin*, or sister by exchange of scarves. The latter tie is formed ceremoniously, each 'sister' sending the other an embroidered scarf (*dopaṭṭa*) in a tray and putting on the one received from her, after which a number of invited guests are feasted. Religious sisterhood is formed by following the same faith and becoming *chíni-bahin*; by affecting the same spiritual teacher (*pír*) and becoming *pír-bahin*; or by drinking the water from the Jumna or Ganges from each other's hands while bathing in one of those rivers, and thus becoming Jamna or Ganga-*bahin*. The latter is the stronger tie. Foster sisters are styled *dudh-sharík-bahin*.[7]

[1] *Zanákh*, Pers., means 'chin'; Platts' *Hindustani Dictionary*, p. 618, but it does not give *sanákh*.

[2] *Ján-i-man*, 'life of mine,' or possibly 'life of my heart.' I can trace none of these Palace terms in Platts.

[3] These palace terms have been somewhat disregarded, or have at least lost much of their original force, in *rekhti*, the doggerel verses written in women's language and expressing their sentiments (Platts, p 611). *Chhagána*, however, occurs in the verse: *Mui na gaie s'ashiq ko tinke chunwáe, Qurbán ki thí chhagána woh kahmúí Latíf* in the *Taskira-i-Gulistán-i-Sakhun* of Mirza Fakhr-ud-Muhk. With the exception of *dugána* and *chhagána* they are also said to occur in three books, the *Chata-bhanchi*, *Sugharsaheli*, and *Bas-i-akhir*, written by a gentleman who had been brought up in the Delhi Palace, and describing the colloquial language used therein.

[4] Platts, pp. 707-8.

[5] An adopted visitor, or female friend: Platts, p 194.

[6] A female friend etc., *see* Platts, p. 666.

[7] In Northern India, from Agra as far south as Bihár, the term *guiyan* is much in use among women and in poetry. In Márwár and Upper India the corresponding term is *sajní*, which Platts (p. 648) gives as a synonym of *sahelí*. *See* p. 928 for *gúinán*, 'a partner,' or 'female companion.'

CHAPTER III.

CASTE AND SECTARIAL MARKS IN THE PANJAB.

SECTION I.—CASTE MARKS.

Caste marks, like sectarial marks, probably had a religious origin, but they should nevertheless be carefully distinguished from the latter. They are in themselves only a part of the symbolism of caste, and find counterparts in various other outward signs and observances, which distinguish one caste from another.

According to the commonly-accepted theoretical division of Hindu society, the outward and visible signs of the castes were as follows:—

	Brahmana.	Kshatriya.	Vaisya.
Clothing in skins ...	black deer.	red deer.	goat.
Sacred thread ...	cotton.	hemp.	wool.
Staff[1] ...	*dhák.*	*bar.*	*jál.*

The Brahmácháryas of each of the above castes are said to have been distinguished by more elaborate differences in the matters of clothing and staff. Thus:—

	Brahmana.	Kshatriya.	Vaisya.
Under garment ...	hemp.	silk.	sheep-skin.
Upper garment of skin. ...	black-buck.	*rúrú*, a deer.	goat.
Staff	*dhak.*[2]	*bilva.*[3]	*gúlar.*[4]
Height of staff[5]	to the head.	to the forehead.	to the nostrils.
Girdle ...	*múnj.*[6]	*murba.*[7]	hemp.

There was a difference also, according to caste, in the forms of the words used by the Brahmácháryas in asking alms[8]:—

Brahmana.	Kshatriya.	Vaisya.
Bhavti bhikhyam. Dehi.	*bhikhyam bhavti. dehi.*	*bhikhyam dehi. bhavti.*

In connection with the above distributions of clothing and accoutrements, each of the four chief castes wore, on the forehead between the eyebrows, a distinctive caste mark of coloured sandal-wood paste[9]

[1] *I. e.* of the wood of the *butea frondosa, ficus Indica* and *acacia Arabica*, respectively.

[2] Called the *chhichhrá*.

[3] *Aegle marmelos*, or wood-apple.

[4] *Ficus glomerata.*

[5] According to Manu, *sloka* 45. The varieties of the Brahmácharya staff above given are arranged according to the *Grihyasutra*. Manu, *sloka* 45, gives a wider range of choice: *e. g.* Brahmana, *dhák* or *bilva*; Kshatriya, *bar* or *khairsál* (*acacia catechu*); Vaisya, *jál* or *gular*.

[6] A vetch.

[7] A creeper.

[8] See Páraskara, *Grihyasutra*, ed. Kasíji Med. Hall, under the authority of the Mahárájá of Hathwá, *St.* 1952: *Khandá* II, pp. 300 ff.: *sutras* 16 to 28. Manu, *Dhagá* 2, *sl.* 41, 45, 46 etc.

[9] Bráhmanas also used *bhabhúti*, ashes, for this purpose.

CASTE AND SECTARIAL MARKS.

Caste Marks: Manu, Gṛihyasûtra, etc.

1 2 3 4

Caste Marks: Meru Tantra.

5 6 6a 7 8

Vaishṇava Sectarial Marks.

9 10 11 12 13a 13b 14 15

Saiva Sectarial Marks.

16 17 17a

Shâktaka.

18

Jains.

19 20 21

Marks of Hindu Religious Orders.

22 23 24

January, 1917.—No.5786-1 656.

(*vide* Plate, figs. 1, 2, 3 and 4). The colour, as well as the form, of the caste-mark was distinctive for each caste, as under :—

Brahmana.	Kshatriya.	Vaisya.	Súdra.
White.	red.	pale yellow.	black.

According to a *sloka* in the *Padma Purán*, the colours abovementioned correspond with the complexion of each caste, which was assumed to convey its general mental qualities :—

Brahmana.	Kshatriya.	Vaisya.	Súdra.
Venerable.	merciless.	merciful.	vain.

The *Meru Tantra*, however, prescribes quite a different set of marks (*vide* Plate, figs. 5, 6 and 6*a*, 7 and 8) :—

Brahmana.	Kshatriya.	Vaisya.	Súdra.
Vardhapundra.	*tripundra.*[1]	*ardhachandraká.*	*chauká.*

Other authorities again permit Brahmanas to wear the *tripundra* in its straight form, though Shâktakas might wear both, while the *vardhapundra* is prescribed for Kshatriyas.

The materials for the *vardhapundra* wear also varied to saffron, clay, turmeric and earth from sacred places. In modern practice the colour is rarely pure white.

Historically the discrepancies to be observed in the authorities more than probably represent local feeling at various epochs and show that at no time was there any hard and fast general rule. Nowadays, in practice, the distinctions noted in the books do not exist, and customs that are not to be found in them are observed. *E. g.*, the sacred thread is usually of cotton, and caste distinction is shown by the knots used; the castes assumed to represent the old Brâhmana and Kshatriya divisions employing the *brahm-ganth*, and those representing the old Vaisyas, the *vishn-ganth*.

SECTION II.—SECTARIAL MARKS.

1. Vaishnava.

Sectarial marks as now used are probably of comparatively modern form. That of the Vaishnavas is the *urdhpund*, representing the *bishnpad* or footprint of Vishnu : (Plate, fig. 9).

It is also described as consisting of two upright lines with a point between them (see Plate, fig. 5), and as a simple vertical line. This last statement is, however, expressly contradicted by another account, which says that Vaishnavas are forbidden to use the single vertical line, and proceeds to prescribe marks for each of the great Vaishnava sects and their offshoots as understood in the Punjab.

This account leads us into an extremely instructive presentation of sect development among Vaishnavas in the Northern parts of India. These sects are given as follows, employing the terms for them used by the modern Punjábís :—

[1] In two forms; three straight lines or three lines curved upwards.

CHAPTER IV.

SUPERSTITIONS AND CEREMONIES RELATING TO DWELLINGS IN THE PANJAB.

SECTION I.—THE ASPECT OF THE HOUSE.

1. The south.

A southern aspect is unlucky.

In Jullundur (Jálandhar) it means that it will generally remain empty. In Lahore a house facing south, or a site on which a house facing south, can only be built, has a markedly lower selling value than one with any other aspect. Builders make every effort to avoid a southern aspect. In Gurgáon a house should, if possible, face towards the Ganges, never south. In Dera Ghází Khán this aspects is specially unlucky.

2. The astrological aspect.

In Trans-Girí Sirmúr the *nám rás*[1] of the village settles the aspect in the first instance. If it is Kumbh, Tulá or Brichhak, the house must face west : if in Brikh, Kunyá or Makar, south : if in Mín, Kirkh or Mithan, north.

The house must never face east. But north and south are also unlucky,[2] as the north aspect brings poverty and the south admits demons. Therefore when a house, according to the *nám rás* rule ought to face north, south or east, it is made to face north-east or north-west, south-east or south-west.

3. Other aspects.

In Amritsar a house built in front of a tree, or facing a tank or river, is unlucky.[3]

SECTION II.—TIMES FOR BUILDING.

1. The auspicious moment.

In Sirmúr a handful of earth from the site selected is taken to a Brahman, who predicts the auspicious moment for laying the foundations, by declaring that a leopard, cow, fox or other animal or drum will be heard at the appointed time. The prophecy usually comes off, because it is made with due regard to local circumstances at the time, but if it fails, the time is postponed and another day fixed.

[1] The Hindí alphabet is divided among the twelve zodiacal signs, each of which affects the letters allotted to it. The *nám rás* is the sign to which the initial letter of the name of the village (as also of a person) belongs.

[2] Also among Muhammadans in Dera Ghází Khán.

[3] In this District, if a *pípal* tree grows within the house precincts, it is unlucky. But in Lahore symmetry and even safety are sacrificed in order to preserve a *pípal* tree growing on the site of a house, or within its precincts, unless the tree can be easily transplanted.

2. Months for building.

Baisákh, Bhádoṇ, Mágh and Phágun are lucky, unless the builder's *nám rás* is in Saturn, Mars, Ketu or Ráhu.

In Kángṛá, the only lucky months are those between Mágh and Háṛ.

In Dera Gházi Khán, the lucky months are Sáwan, Kátik, Poh, Phágun and Baisákh.

Phágun and Baisákh are the lucky months. (Sáwan provides sons: Kátik brings gold and silver: Poh finds worship acceptable to God.) The unlucky months are Háṛ, Bhádoṇ, Asauj, Maghar, Mágh, Chet and Jéṭh. Háṛ breeds mice: Bhádon makes the owner ill: Asauj produces family quarrels: Maghar produces debt: Mágh creates danger of fire: Chet brings ill-luck, and Jeṭh loss of the money spent in building.

SECTION III.—FOUNDATION CEREMONIES.

1. Sirmur.

In Trans-Girí Sirmúr a betel-nut, for fertility, and a *pirindá*[1] for longevity, are always, and a hair from a tiger's or a leopard's moustache for courage is often placed beneath the foundation stone.

Elsewhere in Sirmúr four jars containing articles, brought from Hardwár or other sacred place, are set at the four corners of the house, and on these are laid the foundation stones.

2. Kangra.

In Kángṛa tahsíl the foundations are laid at an auspicious moment, when a stone *chakki* (grindstone), called *vastá*, is placed in them and worshipped, a goat being sacrificed and *karáh parshád* offered to it.

3. Ambala.

In Ambála, the foundation is laid at the time fixed by a Brahman, and oil is poured on the spot, *gur* being distributed to those present.

4. Amritsar.

In Amritsar, the foundation rites are called *shilá asthápan*, 'setting up of the stone.'

A pit is dug at an auspicious moment, and mangoes, betel leaves with an iron peg driven through them into the earth, curds, *bari* (a mess of pulse), and *guṛ* are placed in it as offerings. White rape-seed and asafœtida are then sprinkled over the pit. Next a new jar, covered with a spotted red and yellow cloth and containing a cocoanut, seven kinds of grain, a gold or silver coin and a paper, recording the year, day and hour of laying the foundation, is placed in it. Lastly, oil is sprinkled over the jar, the gods and serpents are worshipped, and the pit is closed with five or seven flat bricks.

[1] A silk cord for tying a woman's hair. Usually it denotes a wife's good fortune, but here long life to the men of the family.

The object of the various articles used in this ceremony is as follows:—Mangoes for fertility: betel leaves for a gentle temper: the iron peg for strength to the foundations: the cocoanut for riches in fruit grain and money. The curds and *gur* are offerings to the gods, and the rape seed and asafœtida ward off evil spirits.

SECTION IV.—THE ARCHITRAVE.

1. Ambala.

When the door frame is set up, a *gaṇḍá* of wool, with a small bag of madder tied to it, is fastened to the lintel, to avert calamity and for the prosperity of the inhabitants.

2. Amritsar.

The door frame is set up at an auspicious moment, and a *maulí* thread, with a bag containing rice, rape-seed, a bit of red silk cloth, a *kauṛí*, a ring of iron and of glass, is tied to it to the northward. *Gur* is distributed and the gods worshipped. Five or seven impressions of the hand in red are then made on the frame, to signify the completion of the rites.

The door frame is guarded until the walls reach the top of it, lest a woman should bewitch the frame and cause death or injury to the owner.

The 'Five Gods' are often carved on the lintel for the protection of the inmates.

3. Gurgaon.

A *kángni* of red thread, an iron ring, a betel nut and mustard seed are all tied to the lintel to keep off the evil spirits.

SECTION V.—COMPLETION CEREMONIES.

1. Sirmur.

As the house approaches completion a *pirindá*, a betel nut, and an iron ring, called the three *shákhs*, are tied to a beam and to the lintel of the door. The iron ring is a protection against evil spirits.

2. Kangra.

The completion rite is called *pataishtá*, when Brahmans and the kinsmen are feasted and a goat is sacrified. An image of Ganesh carved in stone, called *wástá* or *jagjúp*, is also set up in a niche in the hall.

3. Ambala.

When the building is finished a black *hanḍiá* (pot) is hung inside it and a black hand is painted on the wall to avert the evil eye.

4. Amritsar.

A house should not be roofed during the *parjá* in any month, but at a fixed auspicious time. The roof should have an odd number of beams.

A staircase should always be to the left of the entrance and contain an odd number of steps.

SECTION VI.—OCCUPATION CEREMONIES.

1. Ambala.

Before occupation a Brahman is asked to fix the *mahúrat*, or lucky time for entrance. Seven or eleven days previously a *pandit* performs a *hawan* inside the house. On the day fixed for the occupation *pandits* also recite *mantras* to avert evil spirits and the owner feeds Brahmans and gives alms.

2. Amritsar.

A Brahman fixes a lucky day for the occupation when the ceremony of *chaṭh* is performed. As a preliminary, green leaves from seven trees are tied to a *mauli* on the outer door. The gods are worshipped, *hawan* is performed and figures of five or seven gods are drawn on the ground, together with that of Wástá, the house god.[1]

After first throwing a little oil on the threshold, the master and his family enter at an auspicious moment, carrying a new jar full of water, flowers, *guṛ*, yellow thread, fruit, nuts, etc., while the house wife carries a jug of curds. The master wears new clothes and a turban. Both man and wife, together with a quiet milch cow, are led by a girl, wearing a red cloth on her head and a nose-ring. Sometimes a sacred book is carried in also. A Brahman recites *mantras*, and then all the articles brought in are placed north and south of a *bedí*, in which are stuck flags of ten various colours. These are afterwards removed and affixed to the outer wall of the house on either side of the door. Brahmans and kinsmen are fed and the ceremonies are ended

3. Gujrat.

The *chaṭh*,[2] or occupation ceremony, simply consists here of the worship of a figure of Ganesh painted in red or smeared with flour on the house-wall by the owner.

4. Gurgaon.

Before occupation *hawan* is performed, the *kathá* of Sat Nárain is recited and food given to the Brahmans.

5. Ludhiana.

Before occupying a new house the ceremony of *griha pratishta* is performed.

Before reoccupying a house that has not been lived in for some time, the ceremony of *bhástá pújá* is performed.

SECTION VII.—THE FORM OF THE HOUSE.

1. General.

It is unlucky to build a house broader in front than at the back. Such a house is called *sher-dahan*, lion-mouthed, or *bágh-mahan*, tiger-mouthed.

[1] See above section III, 2; and section V, 2.

[2] See preceding paragraph.

00000

A house, to be lucky, should be *gau-mukhá*, cow-mouthed, or broader behind than in front.

Houses, also, to be lucky, should have an equal number of sides, preferably four, six or twelve sides.

2. Amritsar.

In Amritsar, a house that is *kushák-dahan*, open-mouthed, or wider in front than behind, will make the tenant spend more than his income.

A house with its front higher than its back is unlucky.

SECTION VIII.—THE ROOF.

1. Ceilings.

The beams of the upper storey[1] must not cross the rafter of the lower storey, but lie parallel with them. If they do cross it is a bad omen, and the condition is called *gul*. This does not apply to the ceilings of different rooms on the same floor.

2. Rafters.

Rafters are counted in sets of three, the first of each set being called respectively *bhastúráj* (lord of the dwelling), Ind (for Indar, the rain-god), Yám (for Yáma, the god of death), or simply *ráj*. Endeavour is always made to so arrange the rafters that the last may be counted as *ráj*[2] as that brings luck. If the counting ends in Ind, the roof will leak, which is tolerated: but on no account must the last rafter be counted as Yám, as that would bring death or adversity.

3. Thatch.

Some Gújars of the Palwal tahsíl of Gurgáon affect thatched roofs, as any other kind will bring down on them the wrath of their Pír, or patron saint.

SECTION IX.—STRUCTURAL ALTERATIONS.

Between the months of Háṛ and Kátik the gods are asleep and no structural alteration should then be made.

SECTION X.—CEREMONIAL DECORATIONS.

1. General.

On numerous specified occasions, the house is decorated or marked with figures and designs, everyone of which has, or originally had, a meaning of its own. They are always drawn by the women, never by men.

[1] Upper storeys are sometimes tabu'd; *e. g.* the Najar Jáṭs of the Samrála tahsíl of Ludhiána think an upper storey brings bad luck.

[2] Thus with four rafters, the last counts as Ind: with seven rafters, the last would count as Yám: with ten rafters the last would count as *ráj*, the lucky number.

SUPERSTITIOUS DECORATION OF BUILDINGS.

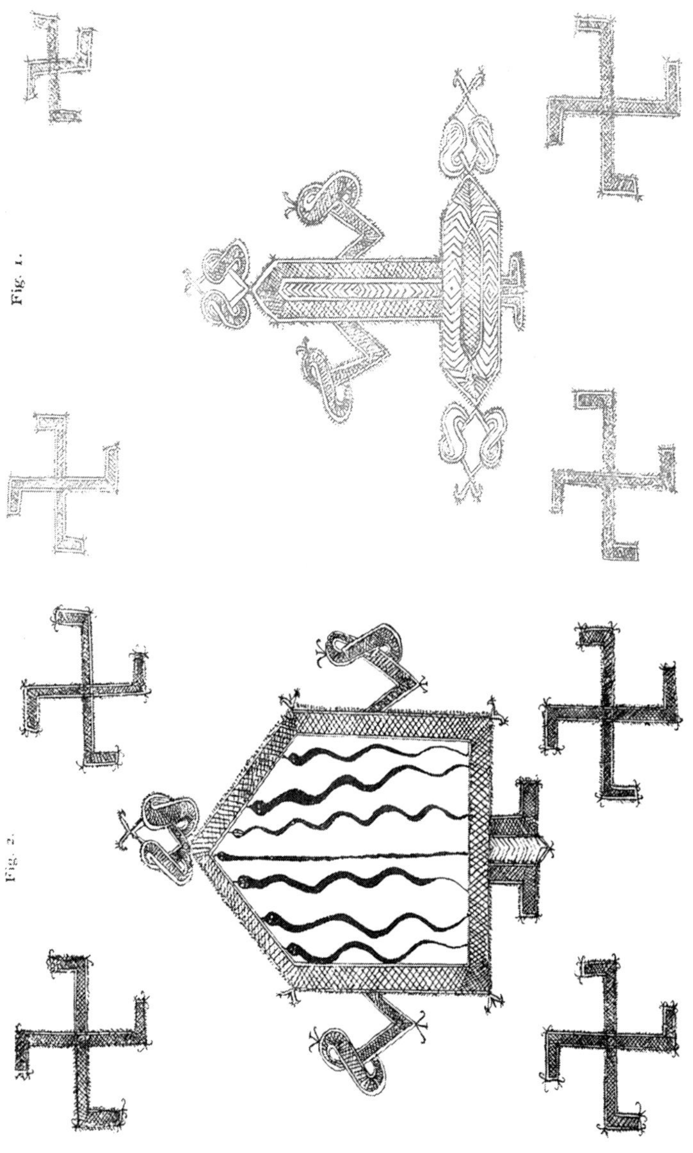

January, 1917.—No. 5786-656.

2. Figures used on religious festivals in Gurgaon.

(*a*) *Solono.*

On the Solono day a figure, called *son i* (Plate I, fig. 2), is drawn in red on the house-wall. It is said to represent the asterism Srávana, and is worshipped by placing sweetmeats before it, which are afterwards given to Brahmans.

(*b*) *Nág Panchamí.*

On the Nág Panchamí, 5th of lunar Bhádoṇ, the figure shown on Plate I, fig. 1, is drawn in black on the house-wall. It represents the snake-god in his dwelling and is believed to prevent the house from being infested with snakes.

(*c*) *Kátik and Díwálí.*

In Guṛgáon, Bániás and Brahmans draw the figure on Plate II, on the house-wall. It must be begun on the 4th and finished on the 8th of lunar Kátik.

The first part (*a*) is called *siáṇ* and represents Rádhikí (Rádhá) spouse of Krishna. This is worshipped on the 8th of lunar Kátik by placing sweetmeats before it.

The second part (*b*) represents the goddess Amanashyá and is worshipped at noon on the Díwálí by placing before it rice and milk, which are afterwards given to Brahmans.

The third part (*c*) represents Lakshmí as the goddess of wealth, and is worshipped at midnight on the Díwálí by placing money before it. An all-night vigil is kept on this occasion.

(*d*) *Deo-uthán.*

On the Deo-uthán day in Kátik when the gods awake from their sleep the figure in Plate III is drawn in the courtyard of the house and worshipped by placing before it fruit and vegetables in season. The women of the household call in a Brahmaní, and with her they sing songs and beat the mat with which the figures are covered, and then, it is believed, the gods are awakened from their sleep. The male representation to the right is of Náráyan.

(*e*) *Náráyan.*

On Náráyan's day white dots are made on the tops of the figures, in parallel rows on the house-wall; and figures of birds and animals, all in white dots, are also drawn.

(3) Figures of deotas.

In Sirmúr a house is at once abandoned if the sign or image of a *deota* is painted on it, in the belief that it was thereby become sacred.

(4) Weddings.

Chariots, peafowl and many other objects are drawn on the house-walls at a wedding. In Guṛgáon, in addition, a picture of the god Binnáik or Bindáik,[1] covered over with an earthen jar fastened to the

[1] Sanskr. Vinnáyaká or Vinnáyiká (?).

wall, is drawn several days before the wedding of a male member of the family, and is worshipped daily to avert calamity.

(5) The Dehra.

In Kángṛa, every house should possess a *ḍehrá*, upon which a ball of clay, made by an elderly woman of the family, is placed on the birth of a child. This ball is called Bhaín or Atam Deví.

At the wedding of a boy or girl the enclosure of the *ḍehrá* is plastered over with cowdung and the figure of the *ḍehrá* drawn anew with ground rice in red and yellow. See Plate I, fig. 1.

The enclosure in which the *ḍehrá* is drawn is decorated with pictures of Ganesh, Deví, Shib and Párbatí adorned with flowers, and so are both sides of the door. In the courtyard of the house a chariot is drawn with wheat flour on a portion of the yard plastered with cowdung.

SECTION 11.—CEREMONIAL MARKS AND SIGNS.

1. Swastika.

(*a*) *Form.*

The usual form of the sátiá or satiá is 卐 but in Dera Gházi Khán District a curious arm is added. See Plate I, fig. 1.

(*b*) *Meaning.*

The *satiá* is divided into four main lines + which represents the gods of the Four Quarters:—Kuber, north; Yám ráj, south; Indar, east; Varun, west. The four additions 卐 represent the gods of the 'half quarters':—Isar, north-east; Agni, south-east; Vayu, north-west; Nainit, south-west. In the centre sits Ganpati, lord of divine hosts.

(*c*) *Uses.*

To bring luck; it is drawn on the doors of and inside houses and shops in Gurgáon.

To avert the evil eye; it is drawn in black on newly-built houses.

To avert evil spirits; after the Holi or festival of the harvest god, by matrons in red or yellow on either side of the house door; and after the birth of a boy, by a girl of the family or by a Brahmaní on the seventh day after the birth with seven twigs inserted in it.

2. Bandarwal.

(*a*) *Form.*

A *bandarwál* is properly a string of *siras* or mango leaves tied across the door as a sign of rejoicing.

SUPERSTITIOUS DECORATION OF BUILDINGS.

Plate II.

No. 3669.

(*b*) *Variants.*

In Ludhiána it is termed *kainknáwál.*

In Sirmúr a *bandarwál* of red flowers is tied all around the houses on the first of Baisákh to invoke the blessing of Srí Gul.

In Sirmúr, in Bhádoṇ a branch of *tejbal* is kept at the door to avert evil spirits and *dágs.*

A common variant is a row of (probably seven) cyphers under a line.

In Kángṛa, at a wedding or birthday, seven cyphers are drawn on the house-wall in saffron, and *ghí* is poured on them seven times. This mark is termed *bisú-dhárá*, and is a symbol of Lakshmí as goddess of wealth.

In Firozpur,[1] the Bhábṛás carve in wood over their doors during a wedding the following figure :

3. Thaps.

(*a*) *Meaning.*

A *thápá* is an impression of a hand, and popularly represents the hand of an ancestor raised in blessing on those who do them homage. In the *Shástrás*, *thápás* represent the hands of Asvi, god of wealth, and Púshá, god of intelligence

(*b*) *Use.*

A *thápá* is always a sign of rejoicing.

(*c*) *Gurgáon.*

In Gurgáon, five or seven *thápás* in red beside the house door denote the birth of a boy or a wedding in the family : a single *thápá* in yellow, with another drawn in *ghí*, denotes that a vigil (*jugrátá*) is being kept in honour of the house goddess.

(*d*) *Ludhiána.*

Thápás stamped with turmeric, *rolí* or *ghí* denote rejoicing. At weddings they are placed on both the bride's and bridegroom's house. In the former they are worshipped by the newly-married couple immediately after the *pherá*, and in the former after the bride enters it.

SECTION XII.—SHOPS AND OUT-HOUSES.

1. Shops.

In Gujrát the *thara* is a large, raised, circular mark on shop walls. It begins by being a circle, nine inches in diameter, to the right of the door. Every Sunday it is rubbed over with wet cowdung, and incense (*dhúp*) is burnt before it. In time the layers of cowdung form a considerable incrustation on the wall. (*Thara* literally means a platform).

[1]Vide *Punjab Notes and Queries*, 1886, § 771.

2. Out-houses

The *kothá*, if meant for treasure, is invariably ornamented, and if built into the wall of the dwelling house, the style of decoration suggests that the aid of some protecting power is invoked. The outer edge is enclosed with a square beading of notches in three longitudinal and five transverse lines alternately, making a continuous chain. The corners are furnished with a pentagonal lozenge with a dot in the centre, an adaptation of the circle with a dot. This chain of three and five ///// ≡ ///// ≡ is continued all round the *kothá*, but occasionally in the upper centre, for five consecutive times, the five transverse notches are left out, and the three longitudinal ones are made into figures of three tongues turned about alternately, by inclining two notches to an angle and making the third spring out of it, thus, ⋲⋺⋲⋺⋲. Beneath the beading at the four corners is added a *swástika* without the usual regular additions, but with four dots suggestive of the modern Vaishnava innovations of the four elements. The door is surrounded by a double beading of a square, topped by a larger one with trefoils in the corners, and two serpents with their heads back to back in the centre. Their eyes are dots, but the symbol being incomplete without the mystic three, a dot is placed between the two heads so as to form the apex of a triangle. The trefoils are double, the lower being the larger of the two showing a dot on each leaflet, while the upper one has only two dots, one in the centre and one in the stalk.

If the *kothá* be for storing grain, it has a hole in the bottom for taking the grain out of it, and this is ornamented with the sun symbol,[1] a circle with curved radii or spokes.

SECTION 13.—MUHAMMADAN USAGES.

All the foregoing observances are, as a rule, confined to Hindus, and then chiefly to the higher castes. The Muhammadan observances are much more simple.

1. Gujrat.

In occupying a new house, friends and kinsmen are feasted and some alms distributed.

2. Dera Ghazi Khan.

On laying the foundation, *gur* is distributed as alms. On completion alms are distributed and a sacrifice (*ratwál*) of a living animal is made to avert evil. The formal entry is made at an auspicious time fixed by the *ulama*, the owner carrying a *Qurán*, with some salt and a jar of water as emblems of fertility.

[1] *Punjab Notes and Queries*, Series II, § 75.

CHAPTER V.

DANCING.

In Baháwalpur there are several kinds of dances :—

Jhumar[1] { 1. *Jhumar khás or sádá.*
2. „ *dakkhanwál* or *chhej.*

Of these the former is in general use among Muhammadans, and the latter among Hindus (Kirárs), especially among the Pushkarn Brahmans.

The *sádá jhumar* is further sub-divided into 3 varieties, called *sidhi*, *Balochki* and *tretari*.

In the *sidhi* the performers stand erect, moving in a circle both feet and hands moving in time to a drum,[2] the hands not being raised above the breast. In the Balochki the movements are the same, but the hands are raised above the head. *Tretari* simply means 'accompanied[3] by three claps of the hands' to each beat of the drum.

The *jhumar* is performed to the accompaniment of songs both secular (*e.g.* in praise of the Nawáb) and religious.

It is also performed by Muhammadans, when they visit a shrine to offer a *nazr* or *mannati* such as *áta-ghála* (or flour and a he-goat). That is to say it has sometimes a religious character.

The *sádá jhumar* is also called *salámin* if performed by women, and *mardáwin* if danced by men. The *saláwin* is danced by village women, or by Mirásans, in a spot which is somewhat secluded, and men may take part in it, if nearly related to the women who dance it. There is no difference in the manner in which *saláwin* and *mardáwin* are performed.

The *chhej* of the Hindus is also of three kinds :—(i) *sidhi*, (ii) *phirwi* and (iii) *bithawin*. In the *sidhi* the dancers also circle round a drum, keeping time with their feet and turning now to the right, now to the left. Sticks *(daka)* are carried. The Pushkarn also perform this dance individually. The following are the songs :—

Subh sadiq sahabian manen.
Panwen putran kon gane gehne.

[1] *Jhumar*, on the Indus, } s. f.
Jhumir, on the Chenab }

A circular dance of the Jáṭs at weddings and other occasions. There are three kinds :—

1. *Lammochar* or southern.
2. *Trai tari* or 'with three claps of the hands.'
3. *Tirkhi*, or quick-time.

Jhomri=dancer. (*Multani Glossary*, p. 87.)

In Shahpur :—

Ghumbar, s. m. } circular dance of men
Dhris, s. f. }
Sammi, s. m. ... „ „ women.

Bagha, s. m. (*mar* or *vaga*) a circular dance, beating with feet, and raising arms alternately. *Grammar and Dictionary of Western Punjabi*, p. 60.

[2] HIBO, S. F.—A circular dance danced by Jáṭs at weddings and wherever they happen to collect in large numbers. They form a ring and dance round ; their arms stretched out on a level with the head, are moved round with a wavy motion. The other circular dance in vogue is 'jhumir,' which differs from HIBO only in that the dancers keep the hands low and clap them together as they move.

[3] The rhythm is *tan na na, tan na na tan, tan, tan.*

Or the following *dokra* :—

Miṭhí Rám nám dí bolí,
Jihá ján tosaṇ te gholí.
Jehre Rám nám dhiyáwan,
Wai Kunṭh wich wása páwan.
Miṭhí Rám nám, etc.

'Rám's name is sweet; let one devote his life to him who contemplates God, because thus he will be rewarded with heaven.'

The *sidhi* then is distinctly a religious dance.

(ii) The *phirwi* or *chinan jhumar* is performed thus :—

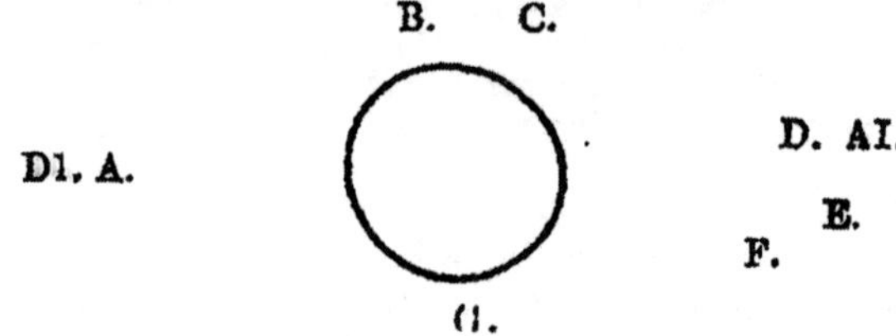

The dancers, who may number 100, carry sticks (*dakas*) and dance in a circle, and from time to time dancers change places. Thus A goes to A1, and, still keeping time with hands, feet, and stick to the music, fence with C. and E. Similarly D. move to D1. and fence with B and G and so on.

(iii) The *biṭhdwin* is performed sitting, the players swaying their bodies, otherwise it is like the *sidhi*.

The two latter dances are not much in vogue.

Kirárs who are expert in the *chhej* are in great request for the *chandráta, i.e.* the Wednesday, Sunday or Friday, preceding the day fixed for a wedding.

There is also a dance called *dhamal,* performed by Jáṭs in the Minchinábád *iláqa*. They dance round a drum singing :—

'Alláh Muhammad Chár-Yár, Háji Qutb Faríd'; (*i e*, God, Muhammad, his four Caliphs, and Qutb Faríd.)

While uttering the word 'Faríd' the Jáṭs dance enthusiastically. Here the dance has distinctly a religious character.

There are one or two points to notice about dancing. In the first place it is, as a popular pastime, confined almost entirely to the hills and the Indus valley. Elsewhere it is a profession, and confined to certain castes. Further where it is allowable for people to do their own dancing, without calling in the professionals, it is more or less confined to religious or ceremonial occasions. For example, the Wazíris hold public dances at certain fixed places upon the 'Id.[1] It would be of interest to know if the Khaṭṭaks have special occasions on which dances are held.

[1] (Lorimer's *Waziri Pashto*, p. 326).

377 CS—656—12-7-18—SGPP Lahore.

(*a*) Lakhmíji or Sri,

founded by Rámánúj Achárya.

The Panjábi followers of Rámánúj are divided into two sects, using the same sectarial mark, but of different colours (see Plate, fig. 10). That is, the inner part of the mark is called *sri*, and is coloured yellow by the Rámánúj Sect, and red by the Rámánand Sect, who are *bairágis*.

(*b*) Seshji,

founded by Mádhev Achárya.

This sect also has two divisions, and they use quite separate marks. That of the Seshji Sect is a *tulsi* leaf and is called *sri gunjan mali* (Plate, fig. 11), and that of the Gopálji Sect has a peculiar elongation down the nose (Plate, fig. 12).

(*c*) Mahádevji or Rudra,

founded by Balabh Achárya.

This sect has seven *gaddis* or seats, six of which use the *urdhpuṇḍ* mark, some with a dot below it (Plate, figs. 13*a* and 13*b*). The seventh *gaddi*, at Gokalnáth near Mathura, uses two vertical lines (Plate, fig. 14).

(*d*) Sankádika,

founded by Nimbark Achárya.

This sect uses a modification of the *urdhpuṇḍ* with the *sri* (Plate, fig. 15)[1].

2. Saivas.

The Saivas commonly use the curved *tripuṇḍ* (see Plate, fig. 6*a*), representing a half-moon, the symbol of Siva. The *tripuṇḍ* is, however, not of a constant character, being also described as three oblique lines with a point under them or simply as three parallel lines (Plate, fig. 6). It also takes the form shown in Plate I, fig. 16.

The parallel or curved form of the *tripuṇḍ* with a dot on the central line (Plate, figs. 17 and 17*a*) is utilized to show the particular form of worship affected by the Saiva devotee. The worshipper of Siva wears the *tripuṇḍ* made of ashes, saffron or sandal. The worshipper of his consort Devi has the central dot made of sandal coloured red. The worshipper of Ganesh has the central dot of *sindúr* (vermilion). The worshipper of Súrya wears no special colour, but his *tripuṇḍ* mark is sometimes red.

---

[1] Vaishnavas have of course other insignia, as the necklace of *tulsi* beads, in contradistinction to the *rudráksha* of the Saivas. The Vaishnava sectarial marks in Southern India differ altogether,—*vide* Dubois, *Hindu Manners, Customs and Ceremonies*, 3rd ed., p. 113,

3. Other Hindus.

The Sháktaks are distinguished by a single dot of vermilion[1] (Plate, fig. 18).

The Samarts, the Sanos and the Shankars are said to use the *urdhpunḍ* and the *tripunḍ* indifferently, and the Ganpatís to use the *tripunḍ* only.

4. Jains.

The mark of the Jains is said to be a vertically elongated dot of saffron. The Indian Buddhists are said to distinguish themselves by the same mark (Plate, fig. 19).

Another account however says that the Sitambri Jains use a round saffron dot (Plate, fig. 20), while the Digambri Jains wear a thick vertical line of saffron (Plate, fig. 21).

5. Hindu Religious Orders.

The Religious Orders of the Hindus wear certain marks which may be regarded as sectarial. Thus the Bairagís and some Udásís paint a curious mark (Plate, fig. 22) on the forehead, and also wear their hair long (*jaṭa*).

Jogís, both of the Aughar and Kanphatta degrees, as Saivas wear the *tripunḍ* without any special embellishments.

Suthrá-sháhís paint the forehead black.[2]

The Achári Bráhmaṇ in the first stage of his career wears a red vertical line with a white one on either side. [3] (Plate, fig. 23.)

Some minor religious orders have sectarial marks of their own, such as the mystic word *om*, painted on the forehead. Others wear the *tripunḍ* with two lines added above (Plate fig. 24). Others have a *tulsí-patra* inside a *tripunḍ*, a complicated combination (Plate, figs. 3 and 11).

Section III.—PILGRIMAGE STAMPS.

Hindus generally, it is said, are required by their religion to tatoo the hands in blue when going on a pilgrimage. Saniásís who visit Hingláj in Balúchistán are also said to tatoo an emblem of Mahádev under the sleeve.

Branding is, however, a much more common device, at least when the pilgrim belongs to a religious order. Thus, Bairágís who visit Rámár, sixty miles from Dwárka, have the seal of Rámár seared on the

---

[1] "A single mark of red-lead" is worn in Kohát by the Teri Shoit, a class of Musalmán *faqírs*, who wear a long cloak, often carry a trident tied to the shoulder, and "revolve a metal plate."

[2] Sikhs do not use any mark as a rule, though some wear a dot, and their sectaries appear to have no distinguishing marks other than those used by the Udásís and Suthrá-sháhís.

[3] This appears to resemble the Vaishṇava *namam* of Southern India.

wrist so as to leave a black brand. Those who visit Dwárka itself have a *tapt mudra*, or brand of a conch, discus, mace, or lotus, as emblems of Vishṇu, or a name of Vishṇu, burnt on the arms.[1] Those again who visit Rámeshwar have the right shoulder branded thus.[2]

Section IV.—FEMALE CASTE MARKS.

I add here a cutting from the *Pioneer* of the 26th May 1907, reproducing a note from the *Madras Mail* as to the custom of wearing caste marks by women in Southern India. I have not heard that there is a similar custom in the Punjab :—

" The caste-marks worn by women are confined to the forehead and are, says a writer on caste-marks in Southern India in the *Madras Mail*, more uniform than those affected by the men. The orthodox mark invariably worn on religious and ceremonial occasions is a small saffron spot in the centre of the forehead. But the more popular and fashionable mark is a tiny one made with a glue-like substance, usually jet black in colour, called in Tamil *sandhu*, which is obtained by frying sago till it gets charred and then boiling it in water. *Sandhu* is also prepared in various fancy colours. Women who have not reached their twenties are sometimes partial to the use of *kuchchilipottus*, or small tinsel discs, available in the bazar at the rate of about half-a-dozen for a pie. To attach these to the skin, the commonest material used is the gum of the jack-fruit, quantities of which will be found sticking to a wall or pillar in the house, ready for immediate use. The vogue of the *kuchchilipottus* is on the wane, however.

In the more orthodox families, it is considered objectionable that the forehead of a woman should remain blank even for a moment, and accordingly it is permanently marked with a tatooed vertical line, the operation being performed generally by women of the Korava tribe. The blister takes sometimes a fortnight to heal, but the Hindu woman, who is nothing if not a martyr by temperament and training, suffers the pain uncomplainingly."

---

[1] The *tapt mudra* is a 'burnt impression' as opposed to the *sital mudra* or 'cold impression,' which means the painting of emblems daily on the forehead, chest or arms with *gopi chandan* or clay, while worshipping a god.

[2] [During my wanderings in bazars in India, I frequently collected pilgrimage stamps of brass of the kind above mentioned. They were not at all difficult to procure twenty years ago in such places as Hardwár, Gaya, Mirzápur, Bareli, and so on. But I have never reproduced or used them, as I could not ascertain to which shrines they belonged. When the stamp contained a name it was usually Rám-nám, Rám Náráyan or some such Vaishnava term.—ED., INDIAN ANTIQUARY.]

INDEX TO VOL. I.

A.

Abandonment of property, 437.
Abbās, house of, 490.
Abbās, Hazrat, 578.
Abbaside, Māman Pir an, 591.
Abdāl, 503, 779.
Abdāl, chihil, 243.
Abdāli, 243, 703.
Abdul Bāqi, 581.
Abdul Hākim. 497–8.
Abdul Jalīl, Shaikh Chuhar, 546.
Abdul Qādir Jilāni, 538.
Abdul Razzāk Makāi, 616.
Abdul-Samad Daler-Jang, 701.
Abdul Wahāb Ghāzi, Miān, 593.
Abd-un-Nabī, Shaikh, 499.
Abd-ur-Rahim(-Karīm,or-Razāk), 626.
Abd-us-Salām Chishti, 538.
Abhīraphalli, 368.
Abisares, of Darva-Abhisāra, 27.
Ablutions, Sikh, "washing of 5," 697.
Abortion, precautions against, 738, 759.
Abu Hanīfa, 505.
Abu Ishāq Shāmi Chishti, 529.
Abu Shakūr Silmi, 536.
Achar, character, 716.
Achāraj, 120, 709, 842.
Achārya, 111.
Achaunai, P = neota, 833.
Achhrān, Rāni, 125.
Achhwāni, candle, 765.
Achleswar, 121.
Achhwānī, 765.
Adage, Sanskrit, on betrothal, 785.
Adam Banūri, Shaikh, 597.
Adhami, 529.
Adharma, 107.
Adh-gabh, mid-pregnancy, 733.
Adhivāsa, 367.
Adhmarg, 853
Adi Brahma, 118.
Adi-Granth, 682, *see* Granth.
Adīl, judge, 504.
Adīna Beg, 702.
Adoption, 903.
Adraistai, 28 = Aratta (?), 50.
Adshakti, 334, 354.
Advaita, system, 373.
Afghān, 58.
Afrasiāb, 22.
Afshār, 799.
After-birth, 747.
After-birth, disposal of, 763.
Agarwāl, 105.
Agwāni, Devi, 350.
Agnikula, 43.
Ahangar, saint, 543.
Ahangkara, vanity, 716.
Ahd-nāma, agreement, 882.
Ahichhatra = Arura or Hatūr, 48.
Ahinsa, 63, 368.
Ahīr, 10, 13, 45, 359, 369, 370.
Ahirwati, 52.
Ahl-i-hadīs, 505–6.
Ahluwālia, 701, 702, 706.
Ahmad ibn Hanbal, 505.
Ahmad Kabīr, Sayyid, Jahāniān Jahāngasht, 605.
Ahmad Khān, Miān, 627.
Ahmad, Khwāja, Naqshband, 547.
Ahmad Qattāl, Sultān, 605.
Aīna masūf, 817, 831–2.
Airapati Naik, 687.
Ajīt Nāth, 114.
Ajia Pāl, 186, 428.
Ajīt Singh, 690.
Ajīvaka, 367.
Ajmal, a *deota*, 430.
Ajnāla, 734.
Akāl, 702; —chhornā, 855.
Akālī, 704, 708–9.
Akar, 64.
Akās Devi, 330.
Akās Ganga, 133.
Akās-bel, 254.
Akbar, 499 ff, 682–3.
Akbar Ali, 536–7.
Akchobhya, 70, 78.
Akhīri dān "final gift" = chhāya dān, 842.
Akhūnd of Swāt, 631.
Ala Singh, of Patiāla, 701, 703.

Alam Pīr, 604.
Alā-ud-Dīn, 493.
Ali, 504, 579; "Mushkil-kushā," 763.
Ali Ashāb, 627.
Ali Hamdān Bābā, Sayyid, 594.
Ali Jalāli, 532.
Ali Makhdūm Hujweri, 532.
Ali Rangrez, 543.
Alif Khan, 690.
Alladād, Shaikh, 598.
Allāh Dād Quraishi, 605.
Allāh Dād Sāhib, 536.
Al-mast, Udāsi, 684.
Alms-giving, 742 Note 1, 751, 754, 755, 758, 761, 768, 839, 841. 853, 884.
Alochana, 110.
Altamsh, 490 f.
Alterations in structures, times tor, 914.
Amal, a *deota*, 430, 432.
Amanashya, Devi, 915.
Amar Dās, Gurū, 681, 705, 719.
Amar Singh, 176, 177.
Amar Singh, rājā of Patiālā, 692.
Amāwas, 245.
Amba, 124.
Ambala, saints at, 616–7.
Ambashthana, a tribe, 54.
Ambastha. a tribe, 55.
Ambkā Devi, 322, 325, 345.
Amho samhanā, 788.
Amīr Shāh Sayyid, 585.
Amīrān Sāhibā, Māi, 608.
Amitābha, Amitāyus, 78.
Amitābha, 75; Buddha Odpagmed, 76.
Amrāoti, 688.
Amrit, 709; —chhaknā, 696.
Amrit sanskār = pahul, 720.
Amritsar, 699; (Rāmdāspur), 680, 682, 685, 687, 691, 703–4, 733–4.
Amulets, 237.
Anandgarh, 690.
Anandpur, 686, 687–8, 690.
Ancestor-worship, 195 *et seq*.
Anchela, 113.
Andla, Devi, 316.
Andrāo, 349.
Angad (Lahna), Guru, 705, meaning of, 680, *mat* of, 713, 719.
Angel of Death, 894.
Angels Munkir and Nakir, 875.
Angint, 222.
Angirasa, 367.
Animal sacrifice, 402.
Animal worship, 135.
Anjana, -eya, 120.
Anjani Devi, 322.
Ant-dān, 842.
Ankh salāi, 731.
Antidotes to planetary influence, 739.
Anuloma marriage, defined, 43.
Apalāla, Nāga, 171.
Apapanthī, 134, 394.
Aphar, 799.,
Apollonius, of Tyana, 33.
Apsara Kund, 428.
Aqīqa, tonsure, 768.
Aql, 507.
Arab. 59; conquest, 489.
Arāīn, flower woman, the, 774.
Arandal, 824.
Arata, = minnā, lustration with a 5-wick lamp, 899.
Aratta, a tribe, 54.
Ardhachandraka, 909.
Ardhapālaka, 113.
Ardhnareshwara, 420.
Arghya, 800.
Arhat, Buddhist, 77, 82.
Arhats = Tirthankars, among Jains, 101.
Arishtanemi, 107.
Arjan, 121, 175–182, 184, 188.
Arjan, Dev, 705; Guru, 682, 719.
Arjan Gophar, 430.
Arjuna, 368.
Arorā, 388, 390; 710; enterprise of, 687, 786, n. 2.
Arsakes, of Urasha, 29.
Arsh, 795.
Art, Sikhism in, 708.
Arwāh, 885.
Aryadeva, 82.
Aryan, 57, 68.
Aryans, 800.
Asā Harā, 212.
Ashāb, 589.
Ash-Shafi'i, 505.
Ashtami, 245.
Asht-bans Brahmans, 41.
Ashūra, 811, 820.
Askāt, 879.
Asoka, 67.
Asrava, 107, 111.
Asri, 825.
Assassin, 507, 518, 583.

Asthal, 285, 288.
Asthīpanchaya, 839, 840.
Astik, 180.
Astisanchaya, 839, 840.
Astihis, 844.
Astrological signs, 870 (death customs).
Astrology, 127, 247, 870; —natal, 739f, 741; —in Hindu betrothal, 784.
Asur Dānūn, 292.
Asura, marriage, 795.
Asūra(s), 83.
Asvi, 917.
Atal Rai, tomb of, 685.
Atam Devi, 916.
Athāran Imām, 600.
Ath-bhoja, Devi, 361.
Athra (? lit. a head), an infection causing a woman's children to die in infancy: hence -wāli, a woman so afflicted:—kā mankā, 760.
Athrāb, 854.
Athwā, 738.
Athwāhā, a child born in 8th month, 739.
Athwahān, a rite in 8th month of pregnancy, 736.
Athwān, a rite in 8th (or 9th) month of pregnancy, 736.
Athwānsa, a rite in 8th month of pregnancy, 737.
Attock, charms in, 629.
Audayika, 109.
Aulia, 507, 601.
Aunla, 137.
Aurangzeb, 504, 635, 685, 688; —death of, 698.
Autar, 200.
Autar = aputra, 212.
Autar deota, sonless spirit, 869.
Avalokitesvara, meaning of, 71 =Padmapāni, 80-1: Saktis of, 82, 88.
Avatāra, 372f.
Avicenna, 518.
Awān, 49; —ancestor of, 519.
Awānkāri, 50.
Axe, double—, 554.
Ayāzi, 529.
Azān, Note 5, 764, 880.

B.

Bāba, 543-4; —s, descendants of Nānak, 693.
Bābā Adam, 260.
Bāba, ziārat, 590.
Bāba, Farīd, 532, a grandson of, 533, 534.
Bāba Lāl, 502.
Bāba Rām Thamman, 676.
Babar, 677, 678-9.
Bābū Shahīd (lock of hair), 781.
Bāchila, 183–4, 186.
Bāchla, Bāchhal, 172, 173–182.
Bachrā, 177.
Badakharah, a fair, 532.
Bādhā, a (disparity) fine, 788.
Badhār, 2nd day of wedding rites, 897.
Badhāwa, increase (in vow), —— Pir Sāhib, 780.
Bādi, 120.
Badranjo, 472.
Badrinārāin, 366.
Badr-ud-Dīn, Imām, 618.
Bāg, = goira, q.v., 895.
Bāg pharāī, seizing the bridle, 817.
Bāgari, Jats, 171.
Bagga Sher, 604.
Bagh-mahan, 913.
Bagha, a dance, 919.
Bagla, 253.
Baglā Mukhi, 319–20, 329.
Bāgrīs, 739.
Bahādur Sāhib, Hāji, 590, 597.
Bahādur Shāh, 699.
Bāhan, 433.
Bahā-ud-Dīn, 617.
Bahā-ud-Dīn, Khwāja, 547.
Bahā-ud-Dīn Zakarīa, Shaikh, 491; Multāni, 544.
Bahā-ul-Haqq, Bahāwal Sher, 534.
Bahī jawārī, breakfast, 823.
Bāhīkā, Bāhlīka, 30, 50; fr. Balkh, 54.
Bahlolpur, 699.
Bahāwalpur, 733, 787, 822, 825, 828.
Bahore, 735.
Bahneli, 907.
Bahrām, Sultan of Pīch and Lamghān.
Bahro, 212.

Bahū, 803.
Bahut, 222.
Bai, *bai'at*, sale, 645.
Bai'at, 539.
Baib, 244.
Bāīgrām, 50.
Baij Nāth, 265.
Baijnāth, 424.
Baindra, a *deota*, 466.
Baindri, 438.
Bairāg Lok, 264.
Bairāgi, 227, 284–5, 388, 393f, 676.
Baisākh, 128, 241.
Baitarni, "viaticum", 841.
Baitul, 205.
Baithak, 203, 376.
Bāj, Bāz, Bāba, 281.
Bajendri batāi, 438.
Bajr Danshan, 155.
Bāju Rajputs, 51.
Bājwa, 281.
Bajwāt, 51.
Bakāla, 686.
Bakher, scramble, 896.
Bāl Gurū, 393.
Bal Nāth, Jogī, 289.
Bāla, Sindhu Jāt, 681.
Bala Durga, Devi, 422, 341, 426.
Bāla Gheb, a tribal tract, 49.
Bala Rāja, 128.
Bāla Rāma, 397.
Bāla Sundari, 319–20, 329, 337.
Bālak Nāth, 264; Bāba, 279.
Baladeva, 367.
Bālak Rūpī, 261.
Bālaknāth, 420.
Bālamarana, 112.
Balarāma, 369.
Balbir Sain, Rāja, 358.
Baldeo, 370.
Baldeo Chhat, fair at, 394.
Baldeoji, 394.
Baldeva, 191.
Bale, assent, 808.
Bali, 850.
Balkh, 687.
Ballad of Hari Singh Nalwa, 720.
Baloch, Chandia, 388–89; Omens, 226, 236.
Balochki, a dance, 919.
Balrama, 697.
Balti, fair, 464.
Balū Nāg, 166, 168.
Bām-mārgi, 329.
Bān, oiling, 814, 894–5.
Bān butānā, 814.
Bana Banoi, Pir, 640.
Banār, a god, 407 ff.
Banāsat, 212, 214.
Banbīr(s), 212.
Band khulāī, 898.
Banda Bairagi, 676ff; 691: accession, 698; edict against, 700.
Banda Sāhib, Legend of, 722.
Banda-bhara, 680.
Bandagi, Muhammad Ghaus, 605.
Bandāī Sikhs, the, 698ff.
Banda-panthi, 700.
Bandarwāl, 916, 917.
Bandha, 107; an ornament —āna, a form of marriage, 796.
Bāndhnā, 217.
Bandichhor, 702.
Baneshwar, 466.
Bāng, 875.
Bangash, 574–5.
Bānia, 352, 370; —s, 132.
Banjūr chhornā, 855.
Banka, 457.
Banshera, -īra, 212, 217, 377, 470.
Bansi Dhar, 389.
Bantari, 221.
Banūr, in Patiala, 48.
Bāptism, Sikh, 696–7.
Bāqi-billāh, Naqshbandi, 534.
Barā Bhāi, 538.
Barā karnā, to make known, 861.
Bāra Deo, 468.
Bārah, or 12th day after a death, 840, 860.
Barānwīn, 736.
Barāpindiān, 707.
Barāt, 801.
Barat Shāh, 627.
Barbata, Sikh fair at, 712.
Bargūjar, 15.
Barī, a present of clothes, &c., 815, 830; a gift of sugar, almonds, &c. to girl's people, 897.
Bari, Devi, 340, 341.
Barkat, among Sikhs, 682.
Barkhotsar chhornā, 855.
Barnāg, 170.
Barni, 902; bathāna, 855.
Baroch, 703.
Barri Latīf, Shāh, 595–6.
Barri Sultān, 130.
Barsandi, 902.
Barsi, 1st anniversary of a death, 862, 886.
Barsodhi, 862.

Bāsak Nāg, 185.
Basanti, 350.
Basauli, rāj of, 690.
Bāsdeo, Brahman, 367.
Bashahr, 403, 419; Rāja of, 98; State, divine child in, 475 ff.
Bāshak, 408.
Basheru, 146.
Basheshar, Mahādeo, 274; Nāth, 430.
Bashgali language, 25.
Bāshik, 304.
Bashist, *rikhi*, 421.
Basohli, 692–3.
Basri, 699.
Bastal (Shaikh Abd-us-Sabur Qādiri), 596.
Bāsu Nāg, distinct from Bāski (*see* Vāsuki), 170.
Batāla, 700–1; *madrasa* at, 497.
Batāli = churel, 146.
Bātānā, bat-jānā, 804.
Bateri, 790.
Bathindlu, 155.
Bathu, minor godlings, 433.
Bātinia, 518.
Batuā, 837.
Batto kā biyah, 788.
Bauria, 330.
Bāwā Fathū's shrine, 692.
Bazars, custom of taking boy through, 821.
Beāi *jag*, 347.
Beas, 134.
Beda, caste, 345.
Bedi, a Khatri section, 676 f; descendants of, 693.
Bedi = chauri, 896.
Behmātā, 330.
Bejindri, 438.
Bejisari Devi, 319.
Bektāsh, 553 ff.
Bel, 267, 900.
Belema = Bahlīm, 48.
Belief in metempsychosis (karma), 697.
Bendha, bridegroom, 803.
Benu, a *deota*, 462 f.
Ber Baba Nanak, 678.
Bera ghori, "boat and mare" ceremony, 817; beri, or -ū, 818, 821.
Beri (bandhnā) (to tie a blue cotton) thread, 769.
Berruthan, 429.
Beshi, demon, 404.
Betha = Hensi, in Spiti, 69.
Betrothal, Shastric ideas on, 782 ff; by purchase, 789; observances, 784; pre-natal, 791, 804; terminology, Moslem, 803.
Bhabbar, 700.
Bhabra, custom, 200; usage at wedding, 917; —s, history of, 99.
Bhadarpadān, 784.
Bhaddan = jhand, 755.
Bhaddani, 697.
Bhaddar, shaving:—karwānā, to get oneself shaved, 843.
Bhaddar Kāli, 323, 379.
Bhādon, 211, 215; lucky for human births, 740: 4th patharchauth, 126; Nāgpanchmi, 144.
Bhadrawāh, 693.
Bhāg Singh, Guru, 711.
Bhagat, 236, 329.
Bhagat sāis, 256.
Bhagat-panthi, 222.
Bhāgavata, 191, 367, 372 ff.
Bhāgbati, 170.
Bhagirathi = Ganges, 134.
Bhāgsu, 131; — Nāth, Mahādeo, 272.
Bhagti, 393.
Bhagwa, ochre-coloured, 709.
Bhagwān, 177, 192; —ji, 393.
Bhagwat Gīta, 841.
Bhagwati, 158, 159, 321, 329, 337, 453, 479.
Bhāi, a title, 583, 695; —dīnī = vakīl, 821.
Bhāi Bālā (Sikh fair, Ludhiāna), 715.
Bhai Budha, 680.
Bhāi Khel, 710.
Bhai Rāja, 22.
Bhaiduj, 472 f.
Bhaīn = Atam Devi, 916.
Bhairon, 119, 120, 211, 317, 420, 568, 571, 870; —Jati, 318.
Bhaiyon, 194.
Bhajū, 179.
Bhaker, 687.
Bhakhant, 65.
Bhakti, 371 ff.
Bhalla, 58.
Bhalogu Nāg, 170.
Bhambu Rao, a *daint*, 454.
Bhanāh Mahādeo, 274–5.
Bhandli, Bhādli, 127.

Bhangain Devi, 335.
Bhangan, 227.
Bhangewāla, 393.
Bhangi, 217; —misl, 673, 693; 706.
Bhaniār Shivji, 265.
Bhār, 158.
Bharai, 570.
Bharāri, Devi, 319–20.
Bharmaur, in Chamba (Brahmapura), 53.
Bhartari, Rāja, 155.
Bhārti, Devi, 335.
Bhartpur, Raja of, 13.
Bhāstā pāya, 913.
Bhastūrāj, 914.
Bhāt, 267.
Bhāt, a wedding-present; hence —ī, mother's brother, 900.
Bhāt Deo, 468.
Bhāt *deota*, 453.
Bhatak Bhairon, 317.
Bhatner, 52.
Bhatti customs, 829; —Dulla, Legend of, 646 ff.
Bhattī jhalkā, 825.
Bhattiāna, 52.
Bhattiora, 52.
Bhattiyāt, 52.
Bhavanapati, 112.
Bherī bhārā, 848.
Bhīkha Shāh, 625.
Bhikshu, 86, 87.
Bhilowāl, 701.
Bhīm, a Pāndava, 466.
Bhīma Kāli, 483 f.
Bhir, 815.
Bhit, impurity, 851.
Bhocha, 816.
Bhochhan, sheet, 806.
Bhog, 712; —bharne kī, 732.
Bhojan, 712.
Bhojkī, 319, 320, 359–60, 435; = Maga or Bhojaka, 45.
Bholā Singh, 709.
Bhondar village (Sikh fair), 715.
Bhonpāl, 195.
Bhopat, Bāba, 403.
Bhor, subordinate to god, 456 f.
Bhorā, bahore, a rite in pregnancy, 735.
Bhorewāli, ziārat, 593.
Bhotanī, 830.
Bhotanti, Devi, 170, 345.
Bhotu, 304.
Bhrigu, 369.
Bhrikhūngpa, sub-order of Nyigmapa, 74.
Bhulla Shāh, 542.
Bhūltai, of Chilās, 59.
Bhūm bhāī, 176.
Bhumar Nāth, Jogi, 625.
Bhūmi, 64.
Bhūmia, 193, 194, 401.
Bhunda, fair, 345.
Bhungiwāla, chief mourner, 842, 856, 859.
Bhūpat, Bāba, 427.
Bhur, a gift in cash, 798.
Bhur Singh, 301.
Bhūra, Sayyid, 318.
Bhūri Singh, 188.
Bhūt, 200, 204, 205, 206, 208; (ghost) 470.
Bhūt Bhairon, 317; —Nath, 420.
Biāh, asur biāh (marriage ritual), 795, 796.
Biāh, brahm, 795.
Biāh, Bedi, 795.
Biās, *rikhi*, 421.
Biāsji, 120.
Bibeki (Akāli)), 708–9.
Bībī, spirit, —*ān kā bhojān bharnā*, to make offering to the spirits, 732.
Bibi, Parāniwāli, 593.
Bida, "leave"-taking; so third day of wedding rites, 897.
Bidāigī, return. The boy's father returns Rs. 1. 4 to clinch the betrothal, 892.
Bidh, a bundle, 816.
Bidhimātā, 142, 330.
Bidh-māta, 750, 754.
Bidri, a present of sweets, &c., 812, 831.
Bidya, 218.
Bier, the, 844.
Bīghanta, a tract, 52.
Bigīr-bachcha, a birth custom in Delhi, 773.
Biha bhat, 801.
Bihāī, or Beh Mātā, Hindu goddess, 778.
Bijāi, 299.
Bijat, 299 f.
Bijli Mahādeo, 275.
Bīju, *deota*, 448. 469.
Biland Khel, 586–7.
Bilāsa Devi, 319.
Bilāspur, 689 ff, 699: Bhim Chand, rājā of, 689, 690.

Bil-patri, 267.
Bināyāk, Sidhi, 420, 915.
Bindi Jur, Mahadeo, 271.
Bindeshwar Mahādeo, 277.
Bindū, silver wire, 769.
Bini Mahādeo, 273.
Binnāik, 915. *See* Bināyāk.
Bir = hero, 171; —s, 186.
Bir, Barmdhī, 427; —Batāl, 213, 563; —Bhadar Shūr, 267.
Bīrbal-panthi, 392.
Birth observances, Hindu, 738 ff; —observances (Moslem), 763; —Moslem, announcement of, 768.
Birth, symbolical. from a cow (goparsab), 740.
Birthplace of Nānak. 676.
Bisūdo, 126.
Bisā-dhāra, 917.
Bisāh, fair, 394.
Bishan Sahansar-nām, 841.
Bishn-i, -puj, 366.
Bishnoi, 10, 136.
Bishu, festival, 474.
Bis-panthi, 103. 104.
Bisrām, 845.
Biswān, 886.
Bithāwin, a dance, 920.
Biyāhi. a ball, 750–1.
Blāj, Valirāja, 474.
Blue, 697; —indigo, 239.
Bouli. *See* Bu Ali.
Bodhi, 63.
Bodhisattva, Manjūsri, 75;—Chanresi, 76; —s, 77, 80, 87, 280.
Bodi, scalp-lock, 366.
Bodlās, 812.
Boh Bin, 357.
Bohali, 218.
Bola, exchange betrothal, 788.
Bolaji Tripathi, 688.
Bombay, 688.
Bon-chos, religion, 61, 62, 63, 64, 72.
Bougru Mahādeo, 274.
Bot, = Tibetan, 70.
Botha, 408.
Botia, = Mongolian, 43.
Bragu Deo, 389.
Brahm, 391; —ana, form of marriage, 795.
Brahm(a) bhoj(a), 437, 797, 840–1, 860.
Brahma, 118, 119, 183, 267, 368, 745.
Brahmāchāryas, 842, 908.
Brahman, 117, 171; —*devta*, 118; of original settlers, 193; position of, in Hills, 0; *tabus*, 230; Ashtbans, 41; status of *gurus* (Brahmans) in Lahul, 42; Harichandra, 43; Bāsdeo, 367; Dakaut, 745; Genhdar, 391.
Brahmana, 908, 909 (caste marks and clothing of).
Brahman-hood, attainment of, 41.
Brahmani Devi, 334.
Brahmanism, 79, 116; in Lahul, 89.
Brahmans, 283 ff, 709, 757, 784, 785, 788, 795, 797, 805; nāchuhan, 403; tabus among, 230; Pushkarn, dances of, 919.
Brahm-ganth, 909.
Brahmbhatīyā, 204, 364.
Brahm-panthi, 119.
Brahm rākhas, 205.
Brakha, 834.
Brāri, 645.
Bride's parting song, 794.
Bridegroom's absence from wedding, 835.
Brij Rai, Thākur, temple of, 374.
Brijrāj Deo, 693.
Bronze Age, 19.
Brua, snakes of, 164.
Bū Ali Qalandar, 531, 619; *see also* under Qalandar.
Buda Mahādeo, 274.
Budāni, 55.
Buddar, 409.
Buddha, 369.
Buddhas, Pancha Dhyāni, 68, 77; of Confession, 77, 79.
Buddhism, influence on Sikhism, 66; primitive, 70; dominant in Tibet, 71; in Lahul, 89, 400.
Budh, Wednesday, 769.
Budha, Bhai, 680.
Budhi Nāgan, 400.
Budho, 127; —mātā, 853.
Budhu Shāh, 690.
Budki, 805.
Budhwār, 127.
Budh-worshippers, 127.
Budni, Budli, 48, 49.
Bugiāl, 50.
Buba, a present after betrothal, 791.
Building ceremonies (Hindu), 911.
Bukhal, a lucky child, 744.

Bukhāra, 687.
Bullan Shāh, 640, 641.
Būm, 64.
Bunan, a dialect of Lahul, 90–91.
Būndela, 195.
Būndī, 177.
Burail, 699.
Būre Shāh, Miān,, I., 623.
Būre Singh, 301.
Burhanpur, 687.
Burial among Sikhs and Hindus, 844.
Burial of Moslem dead, 881.
Burkhs, 833.
Burqa'i, 584.
Burqa-posh, *ziarat*, 578, 584.
Burra, 600.
Bustām, 21.

C.

Caliph, 489; *see also* Khalīfa.
Caste clothing, 908; marks, 908; mutability of, 41.
Castes, among trees and diseases, 256; in Sikhism, 681; twice-born, 797.
Cat(nakti) "noseless one," 767.
Cats, beliefs about, 738, 749, 767.
Candle (achhwāni), 765.
Celibacy, 391.
Central Punjab, 732, 817, 837.
Ceremonial impurity (pātak), 842, 851, 858; marks and signs, 916.
Ceylon, Sikhism in, 678, 687–8.
Chabel Dāsi, 389.
Chādar or orhnā-badal, 905.
Chadei, *deota*, 447.
Chāhil, 281.
Chāhri, 316.
Chāhzang, a class in Spiti, 69.
Chakabu, 211.
Chakar Kund, 267.
Chakki chung, a wedding rite, 798, 837.
Chakwāl, 50.
Chālā, = muklāwa, 816.
Chaldu, 305.
Chālīswān, 40th day rite, after a death, 886.
Challa = muklawa, 899, wife's return to husband's house.
Challa-badal bahin, 907.
Chalya, wife of Gautama, 126.
Chamār, 125, 183, 348, 398; —s, 257.
Chamba, 400; Sikh attacks on, 692; Sikh influence in, 693.
Chambhu, deota, 438, 441.
Chambi, 466.
Chamda, 319.
Champions, as saints, 622.
Chamunda, 325, 326, 334.
Chamundri Devi, 321.
Chanana, *deota*, 448.
Chandāla, 41, 57.
Chandkosia, 191.
Chandra-Bhāga valley, 89.
Chandrāta, 920.
Chandu Lal, dīwān, 683.
Chandrānān, 811.
Chandrāta, 920.
Chang Mangal, *ziārat*, 591.
Changhūl, P., bridegroom: fem. —alā, 803.
Channa arta, 832.
Chānnī jornā, 799.
Chanresi, 71, 76, 87.
Chan tārā, 833.
Chanwand, 193, 194.
Chār, 471 f.
Chāran, 267, 741.
Charan, foot, 695.
Charan pahul, 700; Note 7, 695.
Charas and bhog, 715.
Charms, 208, 629; —and prayers during confinement, (Moslem) 763; harvest and cattle, 220.
Chasrālu, 38, 305, 476 ff.
Chath, 913.
Chatti, sixth day after a birth, 768, 769, 770, 778–9.
Chatri Nāg, 169.
Chatur Mukh, 460 ff.
Chaturthīk shrādha, 840.
Chaubarsi, fourth anniversary of a death, 862.
Chaubea = Joiya?, 22.
Chauhān, Rāja Shāmji, 120.
Chauhāns, 15, 21; = Chahāmāna, 36, 47.
Chauka, 909.
Chauki, 202, 203, 569, 644.
Chaulakya, Chālukya, 47.
Chaumak, -mukh, a four-mouthed lamp, 772.
Chaunk (chonk) ulanga, 798.
Chaurangi Nāth, 125, 126.
Chaurāsi Sidh, 440.
Chauthī, 817.

Chāwala, Aroras, 710.
Chawali Mashaikh, 677.
Chāwal-shāhi, 709.
Chebri, Devi, 340.
Chela, 147, 148–9, 214;—sept. 503.
Chenab, the, 700; saints on, 389.
Cheochak, a gift of clothes, 770.
Chet, 239, 350 ff, 820; 1st of, 396.
Chhabala, 389.
Chhabilwala, 389.
Chhagāna, 907.
Chhajka, *ziārat*, 593.
Chhak denā, to give a feast—to a village, 837.
Chhalla, 901.
Chhamāhi, rite observed six months after a death, 886.
Chhanchan, 126.
Chhand, hymns, 355.
Chhanni turwānā, to make the bridegroom break the sieve. 818.
Chhapi, sinister, 226.
Chharī, 829.
Chhata, 6th (day after birth) 892: — e kā bhūkhā, a miser, — e kā rājā, a prosperous man.
Chhatar Mukh, 465.
Chhaṭi (gontar), a rite held originally on the 6th day after a birth, 751, ff.: syn. *dhamān*.
Chhatrāb(a)ri, 316, 334.
Chhatri, canopy, 855.
Chhatt, and Banūr, 48.
Chhatwān Bādshāh, 685.
Chhawāni, 765.
Chhāya dān, 842, = akhīri dān.
Chhej, a dance, 919–20.
Chheringma, = Tarema *q.v.*, 192.
Chhidra, 216, 217; —rite, 433, 436: —spirit, 470.
Chhil(l)a, bath on 40th day after a birth, 771, 772.
Chhochho, a washing girl, 775.
Chhog-dak, = Ganesha, 92.
Chhota Ghallughara, 702.
Chhūchhak, gift, 770, 775.
Chhur gada, 864.
Chhūt, period of impurity after a birth, 748.
Chihil abdāl, 243.
Chihl Hāfiz, 536.
Chihlam, 884.
Chikūn, 837.
Chila, 536.
Chila Shah Barri Latif, 595.
Chilās, people of, 59.
Child-bed, death in, 747, 748.
Child-birth, death in, 878.
Children, death-rites of (Hindu), 862 ff; lucky, 742; unlucky, 743 ff.
Chilla, 592.
Chilwān, fr. *chihl*, "loin," 733.
China Des, a tribal area, 51.
Chiman, rikhi, 421.
Chin-chang, 483.
Chīni-bahin, 907
Chintpurni, 318.
Chirāgh Shāh, 626.
Chirāgh-i-Delhi, 491.
Chirkhu-masān, 215.
Chirwan, type of grave, 882.
Chishti, 529; shrines, 533 ff; —tradition, 491; —Qutb, 534.
Chita, pyre, 901.
Chitarni, 984.
Chithri Pīr, 628.
Chitrāli, festival, 471 f.
Chittagong, 687.
Chobanj, 788.
Choi-chong, 83, 85
Choi-je, 85.
Chola, clothing a child for first time, 754–5.
Chola Sāhib, 710.
Cholasop, an unsewn and unhemmed reddish-yellow head-dress provided by the bride's maternal grandfather and worn by her till it wears out, 896.
Cholera, 140.
Choti, 391.
Chrewal, 1st Bhādon, 473.
Christian, creed, 256.
Chūda, Bāba, 326.
Chughattai, 58.
Chūhās, 630.
Chūhewāla, 393.
Chūhrā, 217, 226.
Chuhri-saresh, —saroj, 145.
Chuhru, 297–8.
Chuliān lenā, 903.
Chundri, red (? cloth), 843.
Chungru, 433.
Chungu, 213.
Churāh, *wizārat* of Chamba, 693.
Churel, 202, 204, 206, 207.
Chūrīshwar, 416.
Ch'yi-dar, later Buddhism, 72.

Circumcision, 778 ff; rites in Kāngra, Western Punjab, Lahore, Māler Kotla, 779; Bahāwalpur, 779; Rāwalpindi, 779.
Cocoanut, 680.
Coins, Sikh, 702.
Colombo, 687–8.
Comet, 129.
Compurgation, 907.
Confession, 552.
Cord, umbilical, 747, 764.
Coronation mark (*tilak*), 680.
Cosmogony, Moslem, 560.
Convale, 761; —in Mandi, 742.
Cow, worship of, 139, 140.
Cremation, 845.
Crown, at weddings, 798.
Crows, omens from, 228.
Cults, Vedic, 118.
Cup-marks, 626.
Cure, of disease, 254 ff.

D.

Dābistan, 685.
Dacca, 684, 686–7.
Dadra, a disease, 874.
Dadru, a *deota*, 155.
Dāduji, 394.
Dāg, -ni, demon, 211, 217, 470.
Dāgi, 348–9, 435.
Dagiali, festival, 472 f.
Dahla, founder of Dehli, 23.
Dāhmārnā, 846.
Dahomey, Note 4, 743.
Dain(s), 182, 206.
Dākhila, 802.
Dakshanā, 841.
Dājh, presents from bride's side to bridegroom, 822.
Daka, rishi, 43.
Dākan, 211.
Dakaut, Brahmans, 43, 126, 127.
Dākhila, entrance, 802.
Dakhnashūri, 439.
Dākkini, 77, 82.
Dakni, 377.
Dal, army, 701, 702.
Dala, god of war, 83.
Dalai-Lama, 82, 84, 85; Rāja of Bashahr, incarnated as, 98.
Dalāla, go-between, 806.
Dāli hālnā, 145.
Dallawālia, 706.
Dallewālia, 701.
Dāmara, 53.
Dambah, ? bride-price, 786.
Damdama, 685; Sāhib, 711.
Dammar, 53.
Damodri, 801.
Damohal, a *deota*, 430.
Dan, charity, 716.
Dāna Sher, shrine of, 769.
Dancing, in Shāhpur, Balochki, 919; religious, 920; as a pastime, 920.
Danda, 801.
Dandalwāsa, jan, 896.
Dandāsa, toothstick, 760.
Dandigars, saint of, 543.
Dangar Khel, 591.
Dangar Pīr, 589–90, 591.
Dani, a godling, 432.
Daniāl, 357.
Danigheb Singh (Sikhs of Sindh Sāgar Doāb), 707.
Dānu, Sarsahan, 400.
Danwi Nāg, 167.
Darā Devi, 340.
Dāra Shikoh, 394, 502, 615–6, 635, 685, 883.
Darada, Dard, 53, 60.
Darbār Sāhib, 711, 712.
Dardhak, Dār–, 51.
Dards, cannibalism among, 25; influence of, 35.
Dareoti, shrine, 471.
Dāri, *ziārat*, 593.
Darohi, oath, 482 f.
Darrial, 60.
Darshana, 63, 108.
Dart denā, to give the thread, 751.
Daruna, 120.
Darweshes (feeding), 760.
Dasāhī, 10th day after a death, 857, 859, 902; shaving on, 840.
Dasahra, 10th day after a death, 858.
Dasaundh, —wandh, 683; a tithe, 780.
Daselira, 706.
Dasgātar, 10th day after a death, 857.
Dastār bandī, 861.
Dastgīr, 542.
Dast-i-ghaib, 493, 507.
Dasūni, 471.
Dasūt(h)an, bathing on 10th day after child-birth, 752, 892.

Daswān, 886.
Dāta Ganj Bakhsh, 532.
Dāta Sher Baklol, 535.
Dāūd Jahāniān, 605.
Dāūd-az-Zāhiri, 505.
Daulat Khān, Nawab, Lodi, 677.
Daya, mercy, 916.
Daya Gir, Bāba, 427.
Dayā-kalbi, 244.
Daya Rām Gujar, Story of, 654 ff.
Days, unlucky, &c., 240, 241; for fairs, 397.
Dead, malevolent, worship of, 202; propitiated, 198-9.
Death ceremonies, Hindu, 839.
Death customs (Moslem) in Gujrāt, 874, 875, 877; Gurgāon, 874, 882, 889; Ludhiāna, 874, 877; Kapūrthala, 875; Leiah tahsīl, Miānwali, 875, 890; Jullundur, 877; Shāhpur, 877, 879; Raya, 878, 880, 887, 888, 889; Siālkot, 879; Ambāla, 880, 891; Isa Khel, 881; Dera Ghāzi Khān, 881, 882, 887, 891; Kohāt, Note I, 882; Gurdāspur, 883; Miānwāli, 884, 885; Peshāwar, 887; Bannu, 888.
Death customs (Moslem) among the Shiāh Muhammadans of Gurgāon, 878; Rajputs, Awāns, Jāts, Gujars, Dogars and Arāīns of Ludhiāna, 878; Shiāhs and Sunnīs of Gurgāon, 882; Sunnīs and Shiāhs, 889.
Death customs (special) in Sirmūr, 870, 871, 872; Dera Ghāzi Khān, 870, 871; the Simla Hills, 870, 871, 872, 873; Pachhād tahsīl, 871; Gujrāt, 871; the Cis-Giri country, 871; the Trans-Giri country, 872; among Kanets.
Death superstitions, various, 868.
Death, effects of, on the living, 866.
Death-bed confession, Moslem, 875.
Death observances, Moslem, 874.
Death Ritual (Vedic), 839; Garūr Purāna, 840.
Death rites of the old (Hindu), 868.
Death superstitions (Hindu), 868.
Death in childbed, 747, 878.
Death observances (Hindu), 839.
Death commemorations, Hindu, 862.
Death, sickness and, 209.
Dedhu Lāl, 604.
Deg, bowl, 703.
Dehia, a Jāt faction, 14.
Dehra, 706, 916.
Dehra, the, 916.
Dehra Bābā Nānak, Kangra, Sikh temple and tomb, 716.
Dehra Bābā Nānak, mandir containing tomb of Guru Nānak at Gurdaspur, 710.
Dehra Dūn, 686.
Del, a share, 797.
Delhi, 490, 678, 685, 690, 774, 779, 860; Moslem Colleges at, 496 f.
Demchog, Samvara, 77.
Deo, aborigine, 55.
Deo, dynasty of Jammu, 693.
Deo Chand, *deota*, 447.
Deo Ghurka, 465.
Deo Junga, 467.
Deo Māta, 407.
Deo Sūr, 469.
Deodār, 403, 466.
Deoki, 369; — Nandan, 370.
Deokiji's Paean of Joy, 767.
Deothan, 472 f.
Depa-rāja, *see* Dev.
Depūng, 85.
Dera jhānknā, 815.
Dev, Depa-raja, of Bhutan, 85.
Dev = *pari*, 559.
Deva, 113.
Devi, 132, 137, 147, 149, 233, 259, 314, 318 ff, 419; cult of, 694-5, 916; as small-pox goddess, 350 ff; in Suket and Mandi, 426 f.
Devi Chand, 184.
Devi Hawrā, 274.
Devi Mātā, 355.
Devi Shimlāsan, 302.
Devi Tāra, 357.
Devi Thal, 321.
Devki, 129.
Devuthni, 238.
Dewa, 293 ff.
Dewa-dhāmi, 735.
Dewal, 287.
Dewat, Siddh, 278.
Dhāi-sira, meanings of, 746.
Dhaji, monolith, 175.
Dhakāo, first day of wedding rites, 896.

B 2

Dhām, 816, 824.
Dhamal, a dance, 920.
Dhamān (period of child-birth), = chhati, 751–2.
Dhamān. karnā, 775.
Dhamtal, 393.
Dhanah Devi, 340.
Dhānak, 352.
Dhāndi Deo, 467.
Dhang ceremony, 793.
Dhani, a tribal tract, 50.
Dhaniāl, a Rajput tribe, 50.
Dhanigheb Singh, 707.
Dhanjiye, 845.
Dhānu Deo, 468.
Dhānūn, *deota*, 448.
Dhanvantari, 369.
Dhanwantar, -wānn, 120.
Dharch, 469.
Dharm = pun, betrothal, 785–6.
Dharma, 107, 368; faith in divine existence, 716.
Dharmapāla, 77.
Dharma-puna, 789.
Dharma Rāj, 841.
Dharm-bhai, 905.
Dhārm shānta, 861.
Dharpi Singh (Sikhs of the Rachna Doāb), 707.
Dharti Māta, 123, 129, 193.
Dhaulu, a god, 416.
Dhe, a Jāt class, 14.
Dheju, a widower who re-marries, 900.
Dhenuka, 369.
Dheta, bride's father or kin, 787, 803.
Dhiāna, 110.
Dhiāni, a girl born in the tribe, 750.
Dhiāni-Boddhisattva, 78, 80, 81.
Dhiānpur, in Gurdāspur, 394.
Dhīnwar girls, 317.
Dhir Mal, 686.
Dhīraj, toleration, 716.
Dhobi, 356.
Dhodua, 883.
Dhok, setting out, 821.
Dhola, scanty drawers worn by a bride, 896.
Dholi Devi, 323.
Dhris, a dance, 919.
Dhudhu, 605.
Dhuj, 148.
Dhuk, request, 804, -nā, 805.
Dhumbal Nāg (Dhum Rikhi), 169.
Dhunds, 820.
Dhundia, 103.
Dhūru, *deota*, 447.
Dhyāna, 63; Dhiāni-Buddha, 77, 78.
Diāl-Bhāwan-panth, 393.
Diāli, ? *diwāli*, 347.
Digambara, 103, 104, 105, = Botika or Digvasana, 113.
Dīksha, 111.
Dikshūl, 246.
Dilāwar Khān, 606.
Dil-jān, -mila, 907.
Dīndār, a mullāh, 884–5.
Din dharnā, to fix the day—for a wedding, 836.
Dini-bhai, 821.
Dīn Panāh, 603.
Dionysos, 371.
Disāsul, 239.
Disease, transfer of, 257; wasting, 252 f.
Distinction of castes (kelnas) prohibited among Sikhs, 698.
Dithu, *deota* family, 454.
Diva dharyarā, 841.
Divination, in Kanaur, 94.
Divine Faith, of Akbar, 501.
Divinity, Sikh conception of, 720.
Dīwa dhariara, 849.
Diwāli, 145, 238, 325, 755, 915.
Diwāna Malang, 579.
Doāba Singhs (Sikhs of the Jullundur Doāb), 707.
Dog, 225.
Dogar, 221.
Dohangnu, 433.
Doll, fair, 897.
Dolma, 71, 81; described, 93.
Domestic observances in Karnal 891.
Domūuha, 145, 400.
Donkhru, a *deota*, 430.
Dorje = vajra, 77.
Dorjedak, monastery at, 74; Dorjechang, Vajradhara, 77.
Dorje'chang = Vajradhara, 74.
Dorjechigje, Vajrabhairava, 77.
rDorjep'ag-mo, 82 = Vajravāhāri, 88.
Dorjesempa, Vajrasattva, 77.
Dormāi, 379.
Dothainya, 157.
Dowry, Hindu, 801, 818; Muhammadan, sharāi (lawful), riwāji (customary), 827, 828.

Doyān, a ceremony on 6th or 7th day after birth, 770.
Drama, sacred, 52.
Dravidians in N. India ?, 20.
Dravya, 107.
Dreams, 235, 506.
Drewandi, 585.
Drona Acharya, 131, 353.
Druze, 489.
Duā-i-khair, 804.
Dūbaut, 65.
Dūdadhāri, 217, 470.
Dudalin, Shiv, 265.
Dūd-po, phantoms, 83.
Dūgāma, 907.
Dughli, *deota*, 694.
Dūgpa, sub-order of Nyigmapa, 74.
Dukar, 93.
Dalhā, dūlo, bridegroom, 803.
Dulla Bhatti, Legend of, 646 ff.
Dulo or Dulha, 803.
Dūm, 161, 231; cult of, 448 ff; descent of, 55; a class in Chilās, 59; at weddings, 836.
Dumbāla, 709.
Dumindo, 563.
Dūmni, 760, 779.
Durbha Sharshi, 430.
Durga, 318, 325, 337, 339, 354 ashtami, 359.
Durminda, 563.
Dushman, 907.
Dwadsha, 12th day after a death, 860.

E.

Earth, sleeps, 252.
Earthquake, 134.
Earth-worship, 130.
Eastern Punjab, Note 3, 786.
Eclipse, in pregnancy, 127, 738; death during, 869.
Education, Moslem, 495.
Effects of death on living, 866.
Egyptian mummies, 688.
Eighth child, 745.
Elements of life, 845.
Eminabad, 679, 701.
Eunuchs, 396.
Evil eye, 209; precautions against, 766.
Exchange betrothal and marriage, 788.
Excommunication of Banda, 700.
Expiatory ceremony (Hindu), 870.

F.

Fairies, 211.
Fairs, in Kulu, 435.
Faizullapuria, *misl*, 700.
Fakhr Alam, Sayyid, 580.
Fakhr-ud Din, 491.
Fakhr-ud-Din Muhīb-un-Nabi, Maulāna, 533.
Faqīr Sar, Sikh temple and fair, 715.
Fārābi, al-, 507.
Farīd-ud-Din Shakarganj, 491 f, 495; a disciple of, 534, 535–6.
Farīdūn, 21.
Farrukhsiār, 700.
Fasts, 237.
Fatāwa, -i-Alamgīri, 503 f.
Fateh Gul Bāba, 598.
Fateh Shāh Sāhib, Pir, 598.
Fatehgarh, 690.
Fathū, Bāwā, shrine at Rāniwal, 692.
Fathullāh Shīrāzi, Amīr, 500.
Fatiha, 886; -khwāni, 884.
Fatima, daughter of Muhammad, 177, 778.
Fatimid movement, 507.
Fatu, Bāba, 403.
Fazl Shāh, 551.
Feeding Brahmans, 733, 734, 742, 745, 750, 753, 754, 756, 851, 853, 854, 859, 860, 861, 871.
Feeding the brotherhood or kinsfolk, 732, 733, 734, 735, 737, 742, 750, 751, 752, 753, 754, 755, 760, 775, 854, 859, 883.
Fees to Brahmans and priests, 753, 754, 765, 841, 849, 871, 879.
Female infanticide, 696, 697.
Ferozepur, Sikh shrines in, 712 ff.
Festivals, 237.
Feudalism, in hills, 401.
Fictitious kinship, 903.
Firdūsi, 540.
Fire-worship, 46.
Firoz Shāh I., 543.
Firoz Shāh II., 492.
Firoz (Shāh) III., 490, 494–5.
First fruits, 437.
First tonsure, 755.

First-born, 742 : son (*jeth*), 743.
Firūzi College, at Uch, 495.
Footprint of Vishnu, 909.
Forms of houses, 915.
Fosterage (Hindu), 754 ; (Moslem), 775.
Freemasonry, 554.
Friday, 240.

G.

Gachcha, 113
Gad (? gadh), a visit, 812, 819, 830.
Gadd. 825.
Gadderan, a tribal tract, 51.
Gaddi, 130, 216 ; -s, betrothal among, 788.
Gadāī Shaikh, 499.
Gadh, a present of cash, 819.
Gajju, Bābā, 200.
Gakhar, 49 ; Turki origin of, 58.
Gāl, 438.
Galdan, centre of the Gelukpa, 75, 76 ; University, 85.
Gambhīr Deo, 467.
Gambling, at wedding, 815.
Gāmi, musk, 471.
Gānā, a wristlet of coloured thread, 821 ; = kangnā, 837.
Gānā kholnā, "loosing the zone," 819 ; chhoran, 825.
Ganas, 113.
Gānās, exchange of, 904.
Gand, knot, — chitrāwa, knotting of married pair's clothes in pregnancy of wife, 735.
Gandaria, 58.
Gandh, knot, 814, 836–7 ; —bandhi, 820 ; — pāwan, 820.
Gandhāra, boundaries of, 26.
Gandharb, marriage, 795.
Gandhāri, type of *sati*, 200.
Gandmūl, inauspicious time, 741.
Gandorā, large cake of sugar, 840.
Gands, the, 742.
Ganer, a festival, 348 f.
Ganesh, 119 ; —pūja (form of marriage, 795 ; worship of, 375, 420, 784–5, 787, 788, 789, 795, 916.
Gang Bhairo, Mahādeo, 269.
Ganga, 131.
Ganga-bahin, 907 ; -bhais, 903.
Gangajal, 851.
Ganges, 132, 840, 841, 842, 850, 856, 863.
Gangor, 327.
Gangūshāhī, sect, 692.
Ganin, 111.
Ganjamali, shrine, 388.
Gankhas jārnā, 855.
Ganpati, worship of, 731, 736, 737.
Ganwali, 350.
Gārā Durgā Devi, 339.
Garni Patan, 357.
Garbh sanskār, 732.
Garmakhya, 85.
Gartlok, Kartlok, 74.
Garūr, 225.
Garūr Purāna, influence on death rites, 839–40.
Garūr Sain (Chand), 403.
Gash, *deota*, 433
Gāsi, fairy, 217.
Gaterir, 470.
Gateru, 217.
Gat(h)pāna, 836.
Gati, funeral rites, 874.
Gau-dān, gift of a cow, 841.
Gauhri, = Bīr Nāth, 429, 430.
Gau-mukha, 914.
Gaun, *deota*, 418.
Gaurā (-i), 420.
Gautama, 66, 67, 119 ; rishi, 126, 169, 421.
Gayāshin, Devi, 339.
Gayathri mantra, Note 2, 748
Gazrūni, 540
Geg, demon, 83.
Gelong, 84.
Gelukpa, 73, 75, 77, 85.
Gen-yen, 64, 84.
George Thomas, 703, 707.
Geses, 85.
Getsūl, 84.
Ghaib, al, 506.
Ghaibi Pīr, 627.
Ghalla-ghara, "defeat," 702–3.
Ghania, Kanhia, 706.
Gharāban (adhmārag), 845.
Gharāsni, jag, 436.
Gharastni, a wedding custom, 796.
Gharbiāh, marriage, 795.
Ghare Bhan, Pīr, 628.
Gharolī, 821.
Ghat, 857 ; —mārnā, 849.
Ghatak, inauspicious, 742.
Ghatiāla, 217, 470.

Ghati-chandarmān, when moon is inauspicious, cf. ghatak, 740.
Ghatriāli, 800.
Ghāzi, 140, 622.
Ghāzi Sultan Muhammad, 631.
Ghāzi Walipuri, 626.
Ghela, 124; birth-customs of, 764, 782.
Ghirth, -ni, hypergamy among, 42.
Ghorda, 416.
Ghore Shāh, 617.
Ghori charhnā, mounting the mare, 799, 817.
Ghorian, 794.
Ghosa, 368.
Ghosts, 197–8; precautions against, 747, 879.
Ghot, bridegroom, 803.
Ghrankā, 354.
Ghulām, 508.
Ghulām Husain Khān, 690.
Ghumbar, a dance of men, 919.
Ghundakai, ziārat, 589.
Ghūnt, 807, 832.
Ghurchari, 895.
Ghussāl, washer, 877.
Ghutti, 765, 804.
Giāna, 716, 717.
Giāri, 438.
Giāru, family, 277.
Gifts "in extremis" (Hindu), 841; to bride (Hindu), 800–2.
Gil, 281.
Gil, festival, 471 f.
Gilgit, 127.
Gilhru Thān, 432.
Girah-pūja, 739.
Giri, 871.
Gnostics, 516.
Goat, 134.
Gobind Singh, Gurū, 391.
God bharnā, to fill the lap, 810; —lenā, to adopt, 802.
Godā denā, to place one's knee (under head of deceased), 848.
Goda-diwāna, knee-resting, 888.
Godar Shāh, 625.
Godlings, minor, 433.
Gods' awakening, the, 915.
Gogo, the cow of Brahma, 183.
Goira, = bāg, 895, 896.
Gola, bones, 850.
Golden Temple, 719.
Goler, rājā of, 689.
Goli, Nāg, 163–4.
Gom, "meditation," 63.
Gondal Bār, 53.
Gondal Jāts, 58.
Gonkar-chhāg-dugba, Tārā-Devi, 94.
Gopāl, Thākur, 261.
Gopāla Krishna, 368.
Goparsab, symbolical birth from a cow, 740.
Gor Sultān, Pīr, 622.
Gorakh-hatri, 679.
Gorakhmātā, 679.
Gorakhnāth, 125–6, 172, 178–81, 184, 191, 264.
Gorāya, 282.
Goriya, Sidh, 427.
Gor-khatri, at Peshawar, 679.
Gosain, 261–2, 264, 319, 388 f, 391 f, 420; —s, Gir, 285.
Goshāli Nāg, 169.
Got kunāla, 802, 833–4.
Gotrachār (recitation of), 787.
Govind (Rai) Singh, Gurū, 369, 688 ff, 694, 704, 714–5.
Govindwāl, 681.
Grāhin denā, to give a morsel of bread, 785.
Grahn, 127.
Gramang, a *deota*, 432.
Granth, the, manuscripts of, 688; Sikh, 676; Rāg Asā, 677, 681, 682, 688; —Gurus' heir, 705, 710, 711–2, 713.
Granthi, 704.
Greek thought, and Islām, 507.
Griha, pratishta, 918.
Grihya Sutras, 840.
Grūb-chen = *rishi*, 82.
Gudd, denā, 734.
Gūga, 121, 143–4, 171, 200, 317, 377; *see* "Gugga."
Gūga Mahādeo, 271.
Gūgat, 179.
Gugerī, 186.
Gugga, 262, 301.
Guggnaih, 188.
Gugri, 182.
Guilds, patron saints of, 398, 543.
Gujar, 13; fr. Gurjara, 36; intermarriage with Rajputs, 44; Dāya Rām, story of, 654 ff.
Gujarāt Singh (Sikhs of the Chinhat Doāb), 707.
Gujrāt, Gurjara, 31; = Mewāt, in Alberuni, 36.
Gul, 914.
Gul Muhammad, 596.

Gulia ritha, 679.
Guna, instinct, *asuri*, "lower," 716, *daivi*, "higher."
Gunds, factions in Kurram, 586–7.
Gunga, 146–7, 214.
Gupt Ganga, 130, 266.
Gupt Sar, 714.
Gupta ascendancy, 31.
Gupti, 110.
Guptushar, Thākur, 428.
Gur, sorcerer, 437; a rite, 792.
Gurbaksh Singh, S. 679.
Gur-bhai, 903.
Gurchara, Sikh horse, 708.
Gurdāspur, 700; Moslem shrines in, 624–5; Sikh shrines in, 710–11.
Gurditta, Bāba, 685–6, 705.
Gurgāon, death superstitions, 855; Moslem shrines in, 624; Muhammadans, 876.
Gürgon, 73.
Gurj, sword, 147.
Gurmukhi, origin of, 677, 681.
Gurohāch, 470.
Gurū, the, first initiates of, 697.
Guru Amar Das's teaching, 682.
Guru, Ram Das, 682; Arjan, 682; Har Govind, 684; Har Rai, 685; Har Kishan, 685; Teg Bahadur, 686; Govind Rai, 688; Nanak, 676; Angad, 680; Amar Das, 681; Har Sahāi, 705, 710, 714.
Gurudwāra in Ropana (Sikh temple), 714.
Gurumatta (Council of the Guru), 704.
Guru's authority, 684; office becomes hereditary, 682.
Gurus' succession rites, 680.
Gurū Sar, 712, 715.
Gurū, Mahārāja, 704; —matta, *ib.*
Gurya Siddh, 184.
Gurzmār, 559.
Gwāla, 214.
Gwalior, 684.
Gwālji, 370.
Gya, 862.
Gyāl, 202.
Gyānsarūpa, 125.
Gyārah, kirya on 11th day after a death, 860.
Gyārwin.
Gyāsi, Devi, 330.
Gyephan, 403.
Gyūr-Bon, 61.

H.

Habibi, 540.
Haddi, sharbat, 820.
Hādi, Pir, Rāhnumā, 543.
Hadia Qurān, 875.
Hadīs, 505; of Umm-i-Khālid, 519.
Haiāt-u'l-Mīr, 620.
Hāji Muhammad, 550.
Hāji Ratan, 551.
Hāl, 130.
Haldhāt, "red hand," the day of the 1st *ban* [from *haldi hāth*].
Half-head, 780.
Hāli, 150.
Hamāil, 780.
Hamīd-ud-Dīn Abulgais, 547.
Hamsa, 369.
Hamza Ghaus, of Sialkot, 678.
Hamza Sultān, 602.
Hanafi, 502 f.
Hanbal, Ahmad ibn, 505.
Handāl, 571.
Hangama karnā, 801.
Hanīf, 517.
Hansi I. Note 4, 786, 791.
Hanūmān, 119, 120, 129, 211, 253, 317; Bir, 185.
Haqāni Shāh, *ziārat*, 593.
Har Govind, 683–4, 704–5; masjid of, 710, 711.
Har Kishan, Gurū, 685, 705.
Har Rai, Gurū, 685, 705.
Har Sang Deo, 468.
Harda Lāla, 203.
Hardaul Lāla, 195.
Hardwār, 840, 844, 851.
Hari, 367, 368, 677, 682.
Harī dālī, 815.
Hari Rānji, Baba, 393.
Hari Singh Nalwā, Ballad of, 720.
Haridās, 390.
Haridwār, 680.
Hari mandar, 709, 682–3.
Harimbha, *rākshani*, 466
Haripur, rājā of, 688; Sikh mandir and two fairs at, 715; —in Mahlog, 692
Harwā, Devi, 274
Harmal, 355.
Harnākas, 366.
Harsha, 39.
Harshu, 204.
Hasan Abdal, 678.

Hasan, al-Basri, 506.
Hasani, 559.
Hāshim Shāh, 624.
Hasan Abdāl, 678.
Hasu Teli, 543.
Hastinapur (Delhi), 697.
Hastni, 784.
Hāt Koti, 338; Māta, 405.
Hatārh, 788; exchange betrothal, 788.
Hāteshwari, Durga, 405.
Hath bhra, 798; =chauuk ulanga.
Hathlewan, "hand-taking," in marriage, 797, 815.
Hathūr, 703.
Hatiyā, 364.
Haulānia, a Jāt faction, 14.
Hawan (or hom), a (purification by fire), 740, Note 5, 741, 742, 839, 860, 871.
Hayāt-ul-Mīr, 130.
Hayāt-ul-Mīr, Sakhi, 594.
Hazāra (Dist.), shrines in, 593 ff.
Hazrat, 208.
Hazūri, 541.
Head compression, 754
Hele Jāts, 14.
Hem Rāj, 394.
Hensi, in Spiti, 69.
Herāt, a tract in Gujrāt, 50.
Herī huī, married (used of a woman of lower caste than her husband), 901.
Hibo, a dance, 919.
Hidāyatullah, 532.
Hill rajas' confederacy against Sikhs, 690.
Hills, Eastern, Ethnography of the, 5.
Himalaya, Hinduism in, 400 ff.
Himalayan Tract, The, 4.
Himalayas, shrines in, 197.
Hindu betrothal, 782; kinds and terms for, 785; by exchange, 788; annulment of (pānī pilāwan, mathe lagāwan or sawan), 787; contract, times for, 784; contract, validity of, 790; ages for, 791; observances, 784; repudiation of, 790; observances in Gurgāon, 786; South-east Punjab, 786; Gurdāspur, 791; Western Punjab, Note 2, 786, 791; Bahawalpur, 787; Muzaffargarh, 788–91, 792; North-east of Punjab, 789; Kulu, 789; Shahpur District, 790–1; Jhelum, 791; Siālkot, 791; Dera Ghazi Khan, 791; Hansi, 791; Jhang, 792; observances among the Gaddis of Chamba, 788; Kanets, 789; Chūhrās of Siālkot, 789; Gujars, Rors and Jāts of Kaithal, 790.
Hindu bride's return home, 802.
Hindu children's participation in Tazia procession, 742.
Hindu birth observances in Dehra tahsīl of Kāngra, 739; Bahāwalpur, 739; Ferozepur, 739–747; Mandi, 739–747, 750; Nūrpur tahsīl of Kāngra, Note 1, 741; Ambāla, Note 6, 741, the Simla Hills, 742; Kāngra, 742; Sarāj, 742; Hamirpur, 742; Jāmpur tahsīl, 743; Kasūr, 744; Hoshiārpur, 745–747, 748; Karnāl, 745; Rohtak, 745; Ludhiāna, 747; Siālkot, 747; Gūjrānwala, 747.
Hindu children, death rites of, in Bahāwalpur, 862, 865; Shāhpur, 862, Note 2, 865; Jind, 862, 863; Zafarwal tahsīl, Siālkot, 863; Gurgāon, 863, 864; Kapūrthala, 863, 864, 865; Multān, 863; Dera Ghāzi Khān, 864, Note 2, 865; Jāmpur, 864; Gurdāspur, 864; Tohāna, 865; Karnāl, Note 3, 865; Khāngāh Dogran tahsīl, Note 3, 863; Gujrānwāla District, 863; Hissār, 863; Kāngra, 863, 865; Siālkot, 863, 864; Gujrāt, 863, 864, Note 3, 865; Rohtak, 863, 864; Amritsar, 864, 866; Isa Khel, 864, 865; Montgomery, 864; Miānwāli, 864.
Hindu children, death rites of, among the Rājpūts, Jāts, and Mahājans, in Rohtak, 863.
Hindu Jāts, Note 4, 863.
Hindu death observances in Jīnd, 841, 843, 849, 850, 851, 860, 861, 868; Rohtak, 841, 852; Siālkot, 841, 851, 856, 858, 859, 861; Kāngra, 841, 849; Kulu, 842, 851, 858, 869; Ambāla, 843; Montgomery, 843, 861; Gurgāon, 843, 848–850, 853, 857; Multān, 849, 868, 869;

Tohana in Hissār, 850; Bahāwalpur, 851, 869; Bhakkar Tahsīl, 852; Miānwāli, 852, 857, 868; Bannu, 852, Note 2, 868; Shāhpur, 852, 857; Kohāt, 853; Isa Khel, 857, 858, 861; Gujrāt, 861; Hissār, 868; Maler Kotla, 869.

Hindu death observances in the Kurukshetr, 850; among Brahmans, Khatrīs, Vaisyas and Sudras, 851, 852, 853–858, 859; the Aroras, 853; the Bishnois, 854; the Dāgis, 858; the Kanets, 858; the Rajputs, 858; the Mahajans, Bohrās, Sūds, and goldsmiths, 858; Kshatriyas, 859; at Bhiwāni, 860.

Hindu marriage observances among the Brahmans and Khatris, Gurdāspur, Note 1, 795–797; Jāts Gurdāspur, 795.

Hindu marriage observances in Gurdāspur, 798, 799; Bahāwalpur, 795; Kulu, 795, 796; Churāh wizārat, Chamba, 796; Kāngra, 796; Kalāls, 798.

Hindu marriage observances among the Brahmans, Khatris and Jāts of Gurdāspur, 795, and Note 1, 798; Gaddis of Chamba, 796.

Hindu Post-natal rites and precautions among the Brahmans, 748; Khatrīs, 748–754; Vaisyas, 748; Sudras, 748; Jats of Hoshiārpur, 748, 749; Jhinwars, Note 2, 748; Nais, Note 2, 748; Aroras, 754; Sikhs, 756.

Hindu post-natal precautions and rites in Rāwalpindi, 748–751; Rohtak, Note 2, 748–750, 755; Lohāru, Note 2, 748; Patiāla, Note 2, 748; Sangrur, Note 2, 748; Sirmūr, 750; Dasūya tahsīl of Hoshiārpur, 751; Jhelum, 751; Hazro tahsīl, Attock, 752; Mandi, 753; Ferozepur, 754, 756; Montgomery, 755, 756; Gujrānwāla, 755; Hoshiārpur, 755; Ludhiāna, 755.

Hindu post-natal rites, 748.

Hindu pregnancy rites among the Lahoria Khatrīs, Note 4, 732; Bunjahi Khatrīs, Note 4, 732.

Hindu pregnancy rites in Fāsilka, 731; Siālkot, 731–733, 735; Hoshiārpur, 731–733, 734; Hissār, 731–734; Patiāla, 731; Gurdāspur, 731, 734; Jind, 732; Ferozepur, 732; Central Punjab, 732; Amritsār, 733, 734; Gujrānwāla, 733, 734; Bahāwalpur, 733, 734; State of Suket, Note 1, 736.

Hindu pregnancy rites in the third month, aukh salai, 731; third month, thakni, 731; third month, mitha bohia, 732; fifth month Sādh (religious), 732; fifth month, chhotī rītan (religious), 732; sixth month-chilwan, 733; seventh month; barī rītan, religious, 732; kanji or rīt, 734; mid-pregnancy (adh-gabh), 733; seventh month, Dewā-Dhāmī, 735; eighth month, Athwahān, 736; eighth month, Athwanss, 737.

Hindu observances; birth, 738 ff; pregnancy, 731 ff.

Hinduism, 115.

Hinglaj, 327.

Hirma, Devi, 342, 347.

Hisba, 504.

Hoi, 326

Hoja, Aroras, 710.

Holkar, 704.

Homa, 695.

Horoscopes, 783, 786.

Horse, 140; "points" of a, 223–4.

Hosain Khan, Note 4, 683.

Hours, lucky, 251.

Houses, superstitions and ceremonies relating to, 910 ff.

Hubairi, 529.

Huda, Jāts, 356.

Hujaj, 581.

Hujat-ul-Aulia · Shaikh Dāūd Gangū, 539.

Hujra Shāh Mohkam, 533; meaning of, 534.

Human sacrifice, 694–5.

Humāyūn, 534.

Hun, first recorded—invasion, 39.

Huns, meaning of, 39.

Hūnā, Brahman, 404.

Huns, White, 31; Ephthalites, 35.

Hūri Devi, 320.

Husaini. 559; Sayyids, 586.

Hust, 784.

I.

Ibādite, laws, 506.
Ibrahīm, Hāji, 502.
Ichhrān, 124.
Iconography, Jaina, 113.
Id, 806, 807, 809, 811, 812, 813, 834, 885, 886.
Ideal Hīndu bride, the, and bridegroom, 783.
Ifrīt, 560.
Ijmā, 505.
Ikhtilāf, 506.
Ikhwān-us-Safā, 507.
Ilāhi, sect, 502.
Ilhām, 393.
Ilm-i-bātin, 517.
Ilm-i-zāhir, 517.
Ilyas, Mihtar, 563.
Images, positions of, 434.
Imām, 600, 601; —s, the four, 517.
Imām Mahdi, 495, 502.
Imām Razāi, 579.
Imām Shāh, 607.
Imām, the, 807, 888.
Imām Zāmān kā rupiya, 874.
Imāmia, a sect, 887.
Imām-i-ādil, 501.
Imāmon-kā-paik, 780.
Imāms, the 12, 554.
Imāms, of Pānipat, 618.
Incarnations, of Vishnu, 369 f.
Indar, 745, 870.
Indar Shūr Mahādeo, 270.
Indeshar, 271.
Indigo, 137.
Indo-Scythian, 33.
Indr, 801.
Indra, 80, 101, 126; = Govid, 369, 371.
Indru Nāg, 151, 154.
Indus, 864.
Infanticide, female, 635.
Invasions, two Aryan, 57.
Investiture with the sacred thread, 797.
Invisibility —of tombs and saints, 627.
Invisible saints, 627.
Iqrār Husain, 608.
Iranian dominion, 20; elements, 25; Kambojas, Iranians, 25.
Iron, first use of, 19.
Ishan, 244.
Ishāq Ashāb, 600.
Ishar, 401.
Ishatprāgbhāra, 112.
Islam, religious history of, 489; Nānak's attitude to, 681.
Islamic theology, 504.
Ismāīl, Sāmāni, 489.
Ismail Shāh, 535.
Ismailian, 507.
Isqāt, 884.
Istihsān, 505.
Istislāh, 505.
Istisqā, 533.

J.

Jabha, 579.
Jackal, 227.
Jādu, 15.
Jadun, 161.
Jaffna, 687.
Jāga, vigil, 293.
Jagadgauri, 318.
Jagādhri, 680.
Jagannāth, 680.
Jagatipnt, 349.
Jagatsukh, in Kulu, 420.
Jagesar Mahādeo, 273.
Jagitam, 430.
Jagmātā, 430.
Jagitpat, 430.
Jag-jūp, 420, 912.
Jāgra, vigil, 147; defined, 474.
Jagrātā, 917.
Jagru, 439.
Jagru jag, 437.
Jahangir, 393, 501, 683–4, 689.
Jahāz Mahāl, 546.
Jain, 99.
Jain Sayyid, 203.
Jainism and Buddhism, 99.
Jairāmi, 393.
Jajmān, 259.
Jakh, 214, 233.
Jal-mātri, -pāri, water-sprites, 470.
Jalāl Bābā, Sayyid, 595.
Jalāl-ud-Dīn, Shāh, 619.
Jalālābad, 699.
Jalāli, 552.
Jalāl-ud-Dīn Rūmi, 544–5.
Jalandhar, in Kulu, 459.
Jālandhar, 131, 132, 495.
Jalāndi, deota, 440.

Jaljogan, 215.
Jal jogni, 216.
Jal-mātri, 216.
Jalpā, Devi, 319, 423.
Jalpari, 216, 217.
Jalsū Nāg, 170.
Jalūs, accession, 499.
Jām (god of burning grounds), 870. 873.
Jamādi-us-Sani, 808.
Jamāl Ghāzi, 596.
Jamāl Shāh, Sayyid, 390.
Jamāl-ud-Dīn, Sayyid, 532.
Jamāl-ud-Dīn, Shaikh, of Uch, 495.
Jamāli, 113.
Jamawana, a gift made to a mother by her parents, 771.
Jambu, 113, 227.
Jambūsvāmin, 111.
Jāmdaggan, *rishi*, 379.
Jamlu, 347, 422, 423, 424.
Jamme Shāh, 623.
Jammu, 22, 23; Deo kings of, 693.
Jamna-bahin, 907.
Jamna-ji, 123, 193.
Jāmpāl Nying-po, 75
Jampuri, 132.
Jamun Nāg, 149.
Jāmwālan, Nāg, 154.
Jamwālu, 263.
Jan, 49.
Jān Muhammad, 504.
Jana, divine child, 475 ff.
Janāi, marriage, 796.
Janāza, funeral procession, burial service, 877, 881, 882.
Jand, 136, 137.
Jandalwāsa, 898.
Jandi puja, 351.
Jandi waddi, 826.
Jandiāla, 702.
Janeo, 393, 697, 756; or sacred thread ceremonies among the "Twice-born" castes, 756; Sudras, 756; Brahmans, 756, 757; Khatrīs, 756; Vaisyas, 756; Kshatriya, 756; Gaddis of Kāngra, 757; in Benares, 757; in Sirmūr, 757; usual ceremony of initiation, 758; mode of wearing, 758; mode of wearing while worshipping the gods, 758; among the Jogis, 758; addition to, of the Kalli sutar, among the Acharj Brahmans, Vaishnav and Bairāgi Sādhūs, 758; or sacred thread, length of, 756; agras (strands of), 756; Kath, tool used, 756; Granthis, knots in a janeo, 757; length, material and age for wearing for Brahman, Chhatri, and Vaisya, 757; kinds of, viz., Brahmgandh, Vishnugandh, 757; in betrothal, 785.
Janera, a *deota*, 462.
Janet, = barāt, 895.
Jangal Des, 178.
Janiāri Devi, 319.
Jān-i-man, 907.
Janmashtami, 472.
Janti Dās, Bāba, 428.
Jap, 717; Japp, *ib.*
Jār, 732; —bharne kī.
Jār-, jind-phuka, marriage, 796.
Jareta, 182.
Jarolan = chūrā karm, 753.
Jārtika, meaning of, 59.
Jāru Nāg, 167.
Jasrae, Lāla, 393.
Jasrota, 701.
Jassa Singh, Kalāl, 702.
Jaswāl, rājā of, 689.
Jaswān Dūn, 51, 689.
Jāt, 136, 351, 352; Jats, dances of, 919; —Gandia, 389; fair, 363 f.
Jatanti Devi, 322.
Jatāsura, 53.
Jatātar, 50, 51, 53.
Jather, ancestor, 200.
Jathera, 193, 194.
Jathiāli, 348, 435.
Jati, 104.
Jati Abdāl, 503.
Jatiyāt, 52.
Jatki, a dialect, 17.
Jātra, 149.
Jātri, 262.
Jāts, 201; omens, 226, 236; in plains, 7; customs of, 8; distinguished from Rajputs, 12; factions of in S.E., 13; meanings of, 57–9.
Jattha, company, 701.
Jatti Pind, *ziārat* at, 593.
Jātu, 15.
Jau chhare, pounding up of barley, 814.
Jāu, *deota*, 447.
Jaur, 182.
Jaur Singh, 188, 301.

Jawahir Singh, 692.
Jawalaji, -mukhi Devi, 319, 335.
Jawālamukhi, 694.
Jawatra, 787.
Jawāya Shāh, 534.
Jazya, 494.
Jeshar, 461.
Jesth, marriage of a first-born son in, 743.
Jeth, 128, 241.
Jetha, first, —hamal, first pregnancy, 732.
Jethā Bhutta, 220.
Jewar, 172, 173–180, 188.
Jhajra, 796—
(1) Putting the ring in the bride's nose;
(2) "Regular" marriage in Sirmūr.
Jhand, tonsure, 755; syns. mūndan, bhaddan; hair, 768, 603, 781; —(utārnā), 390.
Jhandūla, "hairy," 762.
Jhanjarira, re-marriage, 796.
Jhanjhoti, 424.
Jhānknā, dera—, to visit, 815.
Jhatak, 456.
Jhilri, 799.
Jhīnwar, 563.
Jholi (pilgrim's wallet), 758.
Jhomri, 919.
Jhumar, dance, kinds of, 919.
Jhūn, 49.
Jibrā'īl, 522.
Jīna, Dhiani-Buddha, 757.
Jinda Kaliāna, 390, 391 f.
Jinda Sāhib, 390.
Jindphuka, 796.
Jinn, 207, 604; —s, 561.
Jīpūr, *deota*, 443.
Jirga kī rotī, 806.
Jīt Dānon, 465.
Jiva, "soul," 107.
Jiwar, a Chauhān, 178.
Jizya, 503.
Jnāna (gyān), perfect wisdom, 63, 108.
Jodha Rām, 393.
Jog, 247.
Jogan, 437.
Jogeshri, 247.
Jogi, 126, 139, 171, 329, 366, 625.
Jogini, 212, 214, 244–5.
Jogis, the, 684, 679, 698; (or yogis) 717, 758–854.
Jogis, Kanphata, 125, 238.
Jogni, 401; —feast, 436.
Johāri, feeding of bridegroom by women, 898.
Jola-Bon, 61.
Joiya = Chaubea, 22; = Yaudheya, 31, 55.
Jora, a gift, 807.
Jora, twin, 301.
Jora, randsala, garb of widowhood, 887.
Jowsha, 858.
Jūā khelnā, 815.
Julāha, 399.
Juth. 789.
Jūthā tikka, 799.
Jyotiskas, 112.
Jumāshāh fair, 604.
Jūme Shāh, 625.
Jūn = Kātbi ?, 49.
Jūna, King of Kanauj, 23.
Junaidi, 540.
Junga, *deota*, 443.
Jupiter, offerings to, 739.
Jutha tikka, 799.
Juthlawnā, to defile, 805.

K.

Kabīr, 682; —bansi, 398.
Kābul, 687, 709.
Kachh, short drawers, 695; signification of. 717.
Kāchila, 184.
Kāchla, Kachhal, 172, 173–181.
Kachwāhā, 22, 23.
Kādampa, order, 72.
Kadphises, 33, 34, 57.
Kafan, shroud, kafin, 878.
Kahārs, Muhammadan, customs of, 829.
Kahlur, 689.
Kahnuwān, in Gurdāspur, 393, 702.
Kahūt, 50.
Kahutāni, a tribal tract, 49, 50.
Kaikeya, a tribe, 54, 55.
Kainkniwal = bandarwāl, 917.
Kaila, *bir*, 180.
Kailās, 129, 130.
Kailu, 183; —Bir, 185, 215.
Kailung Nāg, 154, 215.
Kaithal, 790–1.
Kāj, karāj, 854; —karnā = hangama karnā, 861.

Kajarawal, 681.
Kāl Bhairon, 317.
Kala Bhairon, Bīra or Bāhan, 377.
Kāla Bir, 212, 402.
Kāla Mahar, 193.
Kala Pīr, 283.
Kāla Singh, 301.
Kalāls, 798.
Kalānaur, 701.
Kalaur, a *deota*, 445.
Kāli, 68, 158-9, 217, 237, 317, 416, 419, 700; Devi, 401; Great and Lesser, 469; Lonkra, a *bir* of, 478, 479; sacrifice to, 470; —of Tuna, 317, 318, 325, 339; —ri-diāli, 347.
Kāli Auri, 342.
Kāli Bīr, 186.
Kāli Nāg, 155, 169, 170.
Kāli Singh, 188, 301.
Kalia Bīr, 377.
Kalihār Nāg, = Kelang, 151, 185.
Kalima, the, 875, 879.
Kāli-siri, = widow, 906.
Kalkin, 369.
Kalli-sutar, 758.
Kalpi, 124.
Kalsā Jal, 114.
Kalsia, dehra, 707.
Kalsia, State, 6: —Sikh *misl*, 7.
Kālu, Kallu, 676.
Kālū Chand, father of Guru Nanak, 676.
Kalwa Nāg, 157, 162.
Kamāngar, offering by, 775.
Kamardan, a *deota*, 430.
Kamboh, a title, 499.
Kamboja, an Iranian tribe, 25; — desa= Tibet, 26.
Kāmdhan, 379.
Kamīn, a class in Chilās, 59.
Kamlāgarh, 691.
Kamli, 379.
Kamteshar, 208.
Kāna, a *deota*, 460 f.
Kāna kachha, 676.
Kānākāmuni, 78.
Kanaur, 129; —Upper, Buddhism in, 90.
Kanauri, 488:
Kandahar, 687.
Kandelwāl Bānias, 105; *cf.* Khandilwāl.
Kandi Māta, 352.
Kandūri, 177.
Kanehti, State, 460.
Kanet, 231; —betrothals, 789.
Kanets, 37; hypergamous, 42; Mongolians in Gāra and Rangloi valleys, 44; etymology of, 53; tabus on milk, 231; 789-95.
Kaneti, *deota*, 446.
Kangha, comb, 695; significance of, 717.
Kangna khelnā, 802, 823.
Kāngra, 401, 700; doll fair in, 397; Moslem shrines in, 626.
Kanhya, a Sikh *misl*, 7, 706.
Kani Pawā, 176, 177.
Kaniagut, 862.
Kaniya Devi, 320, 330-1.
Kanjars, 785.
Kanjesar Mahādeo, 270.
Kanji, rite in pregnancy, 731; described, 734-5.
Kanjūr, 72, 73, 76.
Kanka, a tribe, 54.
Kankarīān, fair, 319.
Kansa, 129, 369.
Kanthar Nāth, Jogi, 262.
Kapāl (kirpāl) kirya, breaking of the skull, 840.
Kapal Muni, 421.
Kapāla, a caste, 48.
Kapāli, Bhairon, 266.
Kāpi, 124.
Kapila, 369.
Kapp, a *rishi*, 192.
Kapūr Singh of Faizullapur, 701.
Kapūrthala State, 677.
Kār, circle, 258; denā, to draw a line, 846.
Kara, iron bangle, 695; significance of, 717.
Karaj or tiju, 854.
Karam-kartā, 849.
Karangla, 460.
Karani, 433.
Kāranrūp = Kararu Des, 172.
Karewa, 13.
Kargyūt-pa, 74.
Karī, 737.
Karkhi, 540.
Karm Singh, of Patiala, 714.
Karma, 63, 76, 697; in Jainism, 107, 108, 109, 113.
Karmakāra, a smith (caste), 43.
Karmakhya, Nyigmapa monastery at, 74.
Karmapa, sub-order, 74.
Karmanasharīra, 107, 109.

Karmīdharmī, kinsman of deceased, 840.
Karnal, Moslem shrines in, 618 ff.
Karodh, anger, 716.
Karrāls, 124.
Kārshnāyana, *gotra*, 367.
Kārtak Swāmi, 421.
Kartārpur, 680, 711; foundation of, 31.
Karuwa Chauth, 473.
Karwā batta, bitter food, 847.
Karwī khichri, 889.
Kasb, 519.
Kashāya, 107.
Kasha-bāhana, 419.
Kashmir, 679, 698.
Kashtwār, 693.
Kasumbha, Sikh avoidance of, 697.
Kasumbha, Devi, 339, 340.
Kāsyapa, 78.
Kātak, unlucky for birth, 740, 745.
Katās, 289.
Katāsan, Devi, 337.
Kathān, a Kane sept, 450.
Kathar, 49.
Kāthgarh, 689.
Kāthi = Jūn, 49.
Kāthias = Kathaioi ?, 28; tribal confederacy of, 29.
Kathura Nāg, 154.
Katik, 915.
Kātil Rajputs, 317.
Katoch, 701; rājā of, 689; = Kathaioi, ? 28.
Kaundinia, a Rājput *got*, 41.
Kaura watta, 887.
Kaurī roti, 876, 885.
Kausar, a stream in Heaven, 883.
Kawārā ka sāwanā, 812.
Kayasth, 120.
Kehal, tribe, 505.
Kelang, 151-2.
Kenuwal bithāna, 834.
Keonthal, State of, 443.
Kes, long hair (keshas), 695; significance of, 717.
Kesar, king, 61.
Kesar Shāh, 393.
Kesgarh, 690.
Keshi, a demon, 409 f.
Kesora, fighting with sticks, of bride and bridegroom, 898.
Kesu Rai, 21.
Kevala, 107.
Kevalin, 111, 112, 113.
Kewal Rām, 290.
Khadur, 681.
Khajūria Pir, 623.
Khakhai, Khashai, Pathāns, 37.
Khakhas, 37.
Khāki Sāhib, Mīān, 594.
Khalīd, son of Walīd, 600.
Khalīfa, 490, 504, 520, 539.
Khalīfa Nika, *ziārat*, 589.
Khālsa, 695, 705, 706; defined, 720; community, growth of, 718.
Khāman, 438.
Khamani, a ring of thread, 779.
Khammār, vintner, 522.
Khamtathag, monastery at, 74.
Khand, 49.
Khand, *ziārat*, 589.
Khanda, steel knife, 495; pahul (initiation of the dagger), Note 7, 695-6, 700.
Khandwāla Pīr Sāhib, 596.
Khanpo, 84-85.
Khānqāh, 518.
Khanwada, 579.
Khapar (skull), sacred cup, 700.
Khārān, 784.
Kharar, 699.
Kharatara, 113.
Khāre charhnā, to mount on a basket, 817.
Kharwa, 830.
Khash, Khasha, Khasia, 37; in Kashmir, 53.
Khat, dower, 801, 827.
Khateshwar, 447.
Khatm, 521, 880, 884, 887.
Khatpujnā, 793.
Khatri, fr. Kshatriya, 59, 370, 388-9, 676 ff; *tabus*, 230.
Khatris, 230, 676, 679, 681, 687, 701, 757, 786, 795; 797; enterprise of, 687-8; of Burhānpur, 688.
Khattak, 586.
Khattār, a tribal tract, 49.
Khattara, birth-custom of, 764.
Khatten, 881.
Khaunai, 834.
Khāwand, P., bridegroom, 803.
Khawāni-piwānī, 835.
Khawās Khān, 631 f.
Khazar, = Gujar, 46.
Khelnā (of possession), 874.
Khera Deota, 193, 194.

Kherādis, saint of, 543.
Kheshgi, Pathans, 130.
Khetrpāl, 194, 217, 317.
Khiabi, recurring anniversary of a death, 802.
Khilāfat, 489, 533.
Khilwat, 521.
Khirqa, 520.
Khitāb Shāh, *ziārat*, 595.
Khizar Khan, 618.
Khizr, 135, 175, 213, 218, 539; Khwāja, 193, 562 ff.
Khizri, script, 563.
Khojaki, *ziārat*, 592.
Khojal Khel, 589.
Khojas, saint of the, 543.
Khokhar, tribe, 22, 489.
Khokharain, a tribal tract, 51, 786.
Khol, see *ol*, 438; circumcision, 779.
Khoru, a *deota*, 462.
Khrain, a festival, 472, 474.
Khūbilgan, 84, 85.
Khudaknas, 826.
Khudījal, Mandir, 440.
Khulāi, *ziārat*, 598.
Khulāsa, 706.
Khulwāstgāri, 834.
Khurli, 801.
Khusru, Prince, 684.
Khutba, at weddings, 816, 834.
Khūtūktū, 84, 85.
Khwāb, defined, 576.
Khwāja, Abdul Ahad, 529.
Khwaja Fuzail, 529.
Khwājā Khizr, 681.
Khwāja Sāhib, 874.
Khwājas, 549.
Khwāsi, 196.
Kiāni Nāg, 170.
Kidār Nāth, 375, 402–3.
Kidār Raja, 22.
Kīkar, 138, 139.
Kinship, fictitious, 903 ff.
Kīoka (i) a present, 759; (ii) drugs, 762.
Kīra tribe, 35, 53.
Kirār, 788.
Kīrat Parkāsh, Raja of Sirmur, 691.
Kiratpur, 684, 685, 689, 690.
Kiri, 699.
Kiria karm, 901; karmā, 840, 858–9, 864; baithnā, to sit in *kiriā*, 843; of gyārah, 860.
Kirmān, legend of, 56.
Kirmar, demon, 404, 409 f.
Kirmat dānu, 304.
Kirpāl Chand, 202.
Kirtakā, 404 f.
Kirtnā Nāg, 167, 168.
Kiyāla, a god, 407 ff.
Klainū, *deota*, 467.
Kohla, Devi, 340.
Koil, 221.
Koilo, 215.
Kojhota, betrothal, Wasīr P., 835.
Kokal, 433.
Kokilan, 124.
Kola-chāri, 329.
Koli, 158, 231ff.
Koneri, *deota*, 441.
Korgan Deo, 468.
Kot Ishwar, 454; Mahādeo, 276, 485.
Kot Khāi, State, 460, 466.
Kotā, 918.
Koteshar, deota, 452.
Koti State, 41.
Kotlehr Rājas, 41.
Koyidān P., betrothal, 803.
Krākuchanda, 78.
Kret, offerings to, 739.
Kripān, small knife, 695; significance of, 717.
Krishn, Krishna, 388 f, 367, 370, 377, 397, 801; Lālji, 389.
Kritkan, 784.
Krora-Singhia, 707.
Kshapita, 109.
Kshatrapa, = satrap, 45.
Kshatriya, 797, 908.
Kshāyika, 109.
Kuchi, 53.
Kuchika, 53.
Kudīn, Devi, 336.
Kudrāsi, Narain, 432.
Kui Kandha, Nāg, 168.
Kūka, 707.
Kul panchayat, 889.
Kūlachar, family usage, 782.
Kulchhetar Mahādeo, 274.
Kulia, pots, 896.
Kulīnza, demon, 471.
Kul-khwāni; *see* qul.
Kūlthi, *deota*, 447.
Kulu, 88, 89, 401, 419, 789, 795–6, 842–44; beliefs in, 474 ff; historical notes on, 486 ff; rājās of, 690, 197; *rishis* in, 420.
Kuluta, 53.

Kumant, 205.
Kumaru, Nāg, 170.
Kundā- marg, -panthi, 329.
Kunds, 266.
Kunisht, a custom, 775.
Kunjhain, 217, 470.
Kunti, 121.
Kūntū-bzang-po, = Brahma, 61, 62; = Samanta-bhadra, 73.
Kunwāri, 131.
Kuram, 818.
Kuran Kanets, 38, 480.
Kūrewāla, 393.
Kuri, 803.
Kurimār, 697.
Kurīna, 369.
KurmāI, 786, 803.
Kurram, 783; Islām in, 574; legends of, 55.
Kurū, a tribe, 26.
Kurukshetr, 680, 686.
Kushāk-dahan, 914.
Kushān, 31.
Kutān, 784.
Kuvera, 83.
K(a)wāru kā sāwanā, a feast, fr. kwār, bridegroom, 812.
Kwazla, P., betrothal, 833.
Kyad-par, 64.
Kyar-Bon, 61.
Kyūng, 62.

L.

Lā Devi, 336, 379.
Labrang, monastery at, 71.
Lachhman, 370; = Gūga, 191.
Lachhmi Narain, 375, 386 f.
Ladhar Bāba, 564.
Ladhi taru, 824.
Ladwa, 699.
Lāg, a due or vail, 893.
Lagan, 797, 837, 894.
Lagāsan Devi, 337.
Lāgi, a priest, a barber, or a bard, 786, 805, 818.
Lagoi, 86.
Lahd, 876, 880, 881–2.
Lahl, in Gurdāspur, 393.
Lahore, 504, 685, 690, 700, 702; Moslem college at, 497.
Lāhul, 88, 89, 90, 91, 401.
Lai Devi, 335.
Laila Majnūn, 579.
Lakaria, Devi, 351.
Lākh a thread, 855.
Lakha Lahri, 601.
Lakhdāta 182, 566, 571.
Lakhnaur, 688.
Lakhnotari, programme, 797.
Lakho, Bībī, 676.
Lakhpat Rai, 702.
Lakhshana Devi, 331.
Lakhwera Joīyas, 533.
Lakkhe Shāh, Darvesh, 617
Lakshmi, 915, 917.
Lāl Hussain, 616.
Lāl Isān, 561.
Lāl Mūsān, 607.
Lāl Parwāna, 600.
Lāl Pūri, Jogi, 262, 268.
Lāla Gul, 582; Sayyid, 584.
Lala Sohan Lal, 685.
Lālgīr, Bābā, 601.
Lālji, 387, 394.
Lāma, 62, 63; red, 64, 75, 76; = *guru*, 82; clergy of Tibet, 84, 85; functions of, 87, 88; in Lahul, 90, 812.
Lāmaism, of Tibet, 67, 70; schools of, 72; no theology of, 77.
Lankariā, Devi, 350, 351.
Lammnochar, 919.
Lamp of Life, 735.
Langan-darze, *see* Chhog-dak, 92.
Langar, refectory, 681.
Langri, 205.
Lārā, a bridegroom, 803.
Larain Mahādeo, 275.
Lāri Māi, Deo, 409.
Larumbi, female barber, 898.
Lashkar, 687.
Lassi pair, 801, 823.
Last rite of Hindu marriage, 802.
Lata, 456.
Lāth Bhairon, 317.
Laudpindīān, 707.
Ledar, festival, 471 f.
Legend of Banda Sahib, 722.
Legitimacy, degrees in, 795.
Lehna, Gurū Angad, 705.
Lekh, destiny, 892.
Len hārī, 816.
Leshya, 109.
Lha, 90, 401.
Lha-chos, "spirit-cult," 61.
Lhag-lha, 77.
Lha-ma-yin = *asūras*, 83.
Lha-mo, Mahā-kāli, 83.
Lharampa, 85.
Lhāsa, 70.

Līchi, a nest of five earthen vessels, 495.
Lightning, 129, 143.
Līk, dues, 786.
Līlā Dhar, 389.
Ling, 259, 260.
Lingam, 101, 419.
gLing-chos, 61.
Lingti, festival, 471.
Lishkmār, 127.
Lobh, vanity, 716.
Logu, a deota, 362.
Lohār, in Spiti, 69.
Lohgarh, 690, note 3, 699, 700.
Lohri, festival, 755, 794.
Lokākāsa, 107.
Lomasha, *rishi*, 420.
Lonkra, Launkra, 479; younger, 325.
Lotsava Rinchen-bzango, 92.
Lucky children, 742; —days for marriage, 820; —times for birth, 740.
Ludhiāna, 703.
Lūli, Lūri, musicians of modern Persia, 22.
Lullabies, 779.
Lūnān, Lundan, 125, 200.
Luther, 676.

M.

Māchhi, offering by, 774.
Māchhka, 824.
Madan Mohan, Thākur, temple, 374.
Madār Bāba, *ziārat*, 592.
Madār Sāhib, 874.
Madār, Shāh, 399, 428, 637, 640.
Madāri, 551.
Madda Khel, 589.
Madgola, 824.
Mādho Lāl Hussain, 616.
Madhor Deo, 469.
Mādhu Rai, 420, 475
Madkhūia, concubinage, 795.
Mādhyamika, 71, 74.
Madra, Madda, Madraka, 30, 50; akin to the Ambashthana, 54; cf. 55.
Madras, 687.
Madrasa, 496.
Mādreya, = Madra Des, 48.
Mādri, 121.
Maga, = Bhojaka, 45, 46.
Magar, 473.
Māgh, 239.
Maghhān, 784.
Magic, 402; —white, 236; —black, 237.
Magneshwar, 177; —Mahādeo, 451.
Mahā Lakshmi, 190–1.
Mahā Māi, Devi, 350, 355.
Mahābidia, 354.
Mahābīr, = Hanūmān, 119.
Mahābīr Swāmi, 191.
Mahādeo, -dev, 135, 267 ff, 686.
Mahādeva, 267 ff.
Mahādevi, 356.
Mahal Nāg, 140.
Mahān Chand, rājā of Bilaspur, 692.
Mahān Kāl, 272.
Mahān Prabhū, 389.
Mahānbīr, 211.
Mahānpha, *deota*, 447.
Mahant, 392.
Mahārāja Sher Singh, 691.
Mahārāja — in Kulu, 420.
Mahāsu (Shiva), 38, 165, 302 ff, 404, 462.
Mahāvīr, 101, 113; —bīri, 114.
Mahāyāna, 72, 76, 80, 81, 82.
Mahāyana, "Great Vehicle" Buddhism, 30.
Mahdi, 502.
Mahesh Dāsji, 393.
Mahesri, Jains ?, 105.
Māhku, a Gujrāti Brahman in receipt of monthly offerings, 862.
Mahmūd, of Ghazni, 489.
Mahrāja, eldest son of Krishna, 20, 21–2.
Mahrāja II., 22.
Mahsūd, 592.
Mahti, 433.
Mahton, 201.
Māhu Nāg, 170.
Mahūrat, 913.
Māiān, 798–819.
Māīn parnā, 838.
Maitraka, 46, = Mer, Mair, 47.
Maitreya, 80, 82.
Mājū, widower, 792.
Makal, 433.
Makāl, 219.
Makarāha, —āsa, 486 f.
Makarāsa, 486.
Makol, a circle, 750.

Malāhidah, 489.
Malāna, 424.
Malang, 586.
Malānshar, 155.
Malenda, 455.
Māler Kotla, 699, 703.
Mallhwan, 734.
Māli caste, 13.
Mālik ibn Anas, 505.
Mallāh, 563; —in Sufiism, 522.
Mallhi, 282.
Malloi, 28:—tribal confederacy of, 29.
Mālpunya, 472.
Mālwa, 686.
Mālwāī, 707.
Mālwa Singh (Sikhs of the country south of the Sutlej), 707.
Māma-Bhānja, 129, 621.
Māman, Pīr, 591.
Māmi chhak, 817.
Māmin *ziārat*, 592.
Manas, 108.
Mānashāri, 217, 470.
Manaut, a vow, 780.
Manchat, a dialect of Lahal, 90, 91.
Mand, 353.
Manda, mandab, 899.
Mandahārs, 15.
Mandasan, a *deota*, 430.
Mandehi, 124.
Mandhi, 354.
Mandī, 404, 420, 690 ff, 731.
Mandirpanthi, 103.
Mandlā, 354.
Manduri Sayyid, 588.
Mangal, Tuesday, 127.
Māngal, a tribal tract, 51.
Mangedar, —tar, bridegroom, 803.
Mangewa or Mangni, 786, 807–8, 810.
Mangleshar Deo, 421.
Manglishwar Mahādeo, 275.
Mangula, hand-mark, 577.
Mani, 69.
Manikarn, 420.
Manipadma, 88.
Manīr Rai, 21, 22.
Manja, = diocese, 681, 683.
Mānjhī, 707.
Manji Mātā Sāhib, Sikh *mandir*, 711.
Manjki, 51.
Manjusri, 81.
Manka, 253.
Man-marzi, 796.
Mansa Devi, 203, 318.
Mansehra, 828.
Manu, 326; position assigned to Brahman and Kshatriya by, 6.
Manūni, = Mahādeo, 445.
Mānūshi-Buddha, 98.
Manzil rasāni, setting in the way, 841.
Mara Panga Shahīd, 590–1.
Mardān Sāhib, Miān, 593.
Mardana, Dūm, 677, 678.
Mardāwin, 919.
Marechh, family of, 454, see Dithu.
Māri, 188.
Mari Māī, 356.
Mariam kā panja, Bībī, 763.
Marīd, 560.
Mārkanda, 421, 422.
Marnāth, Jogi, 395.
Marriage, Hindu, 793; civil, 794; with woman purchased from former husband, 796; expenses, Hindu, 797; rites in Kulu, 795–7; observances (Moslem), 814; ancient forms of Hindu, 795; Moslem ceremonies after a wedding, 815; observances, Hindu, 793; songs, Hindu, 794.
Mars, house of, 783; offerings to, 739.
Marsia, 575.
Martani, 79, 393.
Martyrdom of Teg Bahadur, 688.
Māru-desa, = Bāgar, 176.
Marūnda, a ball of sugar, —on ki rasm, 782.
Marwāha Sarīn Khatris, 697.
Marwat, a tribal area, 53.
Māsak (one month) 28th day after a death, 861–2.
Masān, 252; = Mashān, 215, 352; 856; burning-ground, 864.
Masands, Sikh collectors, 682; 683, 686–7.
Masandia, 697.
Masāni, Devi, 350, 352 f.
Mā-sati, 201.
Mashhadi, 579.
Māshshātā, 803.
Mat or monastery of Gurū Angad, 713.
Mata Devi, 321.
Mātā Damodari, Sikh fair and shrine, Moga, Ferozepur, 712.

Mātā Sāhib Devi, Mother of the Khalsa Sikhs, Note 2, 696.
Mātangi, Devi, 354.
Matas, 485.
Maternal uncle, beliefs about, 741. 746.
Mathe lagāwan, to cancel a betrothal, 787–8.
Maths or Yogi temples, 688.
Mati Dās Chhibra, 688.
Matrī, 286.
Matsya, 369.
Mattri, a small shrine, 912.
Mauli dā dhāgā, 820.
Maulūd, 879; — sharīf, 881.
Mauni, *see* Magneshar Mahādeo.
Mauryan dynasty, 30.
Māwali, a god, 737.
Māwi, 466.
Māyān, 819, 837–8.
Mazhabi Singh, 701.
Mecca, 874.
Mecha, a measure, 797.
Med, ? fr. me*th*a, boatman, 47.
Medium, 198.
Meeting, omens, 226–7.
Megarsus, Sutlej, 487.
Mehndī, 816, 887; kholnā and lānā, 820, 838.
Mehr Dās, 393.
Mela, Devi, 354.
Melan, *deota*, 460.
Me-lha, god of fire, 83.
Memorial tablets, 403; — stones, 404.
Menials' offerings to young child, 774.
Meo, 624 f; = Matsya or Maccha, 26.
Meoras or Mewatis, 683.
Merelu, 462 f.
Mercury, offerings to, 739.
Messengers of the Imāms, 780; of the god of death, 845.
Metempsychosis, 98; Sikh view of,
Meteor, 129.
Metla, Jāts, 605.
Mewāt, 52.
Mewāti, 683.
Mezmi, mask, 471.
Miān, 162.
Miān Ahmad Sāhib, 603.
Miān Ala Bakhsh Gangohi, 640.
Miān Bībi, 637.
Miān Hayāt, 604.
Miān Mīr, 615, 683–4.
Miān Mitthu, 627.
Miān-Murīd, 575, 585–6.
Miān Wadda, 616.
Michan Bāba, 592; — Khel, 592.
Mihar Shah Singh, 709.
Mihiragula, 39.
Mihrāb, 708.
Mihtar, 256.
Milāp, 804.
Milk, *tabus* on, 231–3.
Milky Way, 133.
Milnī, meeting, 499; 798–799, 819, 826, 830; return visit, 806, 813.
Mīnā, 682, 705.
Mīna-Dhirmallia, sect, 697.
Mindhal Devi, 331, 334.
Mindoling, monastery at, 74.
Minna, = ārata, 895.
Mīr Ahmad Khel, 597.
Mīr Habīb Shāh, 597.
Mīr Ibrahīm, 580.
Mīr Kāsim, Mast, 578.
Mirāj-ud-Dīn, S., 609.
Miran Bai, 392–3.
Mīrān Nau-Bahār, 535.
Mīran Sahib, 179, 621–2, 874.
Mīrān Sayyid Husain, Song of, 666 ff.
Mīrān Shāh Nūr, 608.
Mirās kā masla, "law of Inheritance," 882.
Mīrāsan, 203, 644; —s, as dancers, 919.
Mirg mārnā, a custom at birth, 772.
Mirkula, 331.
Mirza and Sāhibān, a version of, 659 ff.
Misl, 12 Sikh, 706.
Misls, history of Sikh, 693.
Misra Jawāla Parshād, 688.
Mitha, 628.
Mitha bhat, 801.
Mitra, a *sharma* or name-ending, 47.
Moh, attachment, infatuation, 716.
Mohkam-ud-Dīn, Miān, 623.
Mo'mīn, 506.
Mon, Molān, 49.
Mon, origins of the, 35.
Monday, 242; unlucky for birth, 739.
Mongolia, 85.
Monoliths, 195, 196.
Montha-Makan, 433.

Months, 239.
Moon, 249; offerings to, 739; worship of, 126.
Moravian missionaries, 89.
Moru, monastery of Nyigumpa at, 73; University, 85.
Moslem, betrothal by exchange, 808.
Moslem, special betrothal observances in Kangra. 809; Bahawalpur, 810; Loharu, 812; Pindi Gheb, 812; Peshāwar, 812; Sialkot, 812; Attock, 813; Dera Ghazi Khan, 811; Mianwali, 811, 813; Hazāra, 811, 813; Gujranwāla, 812; Hoshiarpur, 812.
Moslem birth observances in Kāngra, 763; Amritsār, 764; Gujrāt, 764; South-East Punjab, 764; Hissār, 764; Delhi, 764.
Moslem burial fees, 879.
Moslem converts from Hinduism, 804.
Moslem marriage observances among the Muhammadan Meos, Lohāru State, 813; Meos of Gurgāon, 813; Muhammadans in Central Punjab, 817; Dhunds of Hazāra, 820; Jadūns, 820, 828; Dhunds, 821; Pathans of Abbottabad, 821.
Moslem marriage observances in Sangrūr Tahsīl, Jīnd, 814; Gujrāt, Note 1, 816; Gujrānwāla, Note 1, 816, 817, 823, Note B, 837; Mandi, Note 1, 816, 824; Multān, 821, Note 2, 822, 825; Bhakkar, 821, 825; Miānwāli, 821, Note A, 836; Chakwāl, Note 1, 821, 822; Leiah. 822; Western Punjab, 819; Hazāra, 819, 827; Peshawar, 819; Attock, 819, 821; Attock Tahsīl, 820; Pindi Gheb, 820; Jullundur, 822, Note B, 836, 837; Bahāwālpur, Note 1. 822, 825; Māchhka (Dera Ghāzi Khān), 824; Madgola, 824; Rājanpur, 825; Chakwāl Tahsīl, 825, Note C, 827; Ferozepur, 825; Siālkot, Note 3, 817, 819, 823, 824, 826, 838; Kāngra, Note 3, 817, 838; Shakargarh, 819, Note B. 836; Hoshiārpur, 819, 824, 827.
Moslem pregnancy rites in the seventh month, Satwāhin, 759; Rīt, 760; Satwānsa, 761.
Moslem pregnancy rites in Ambāla, 759; Sirmūr, 759; Kāngra, 759; Ludhiāna, 759; Rāwalpīndi, 760; Māler Kotla, 759; Lahore, 760; Fatehjang, 760; Hānsi, 761; Sirsa, 761; Rohtak, 761; City of Delhi, 762; Dera Ghāzi Khān, 762.
Moslem nursery songs, 775; — sacrifice for sins, 879; — vigils, 778; — vows, 780-1; — Rawats, 831; — Rajputs in Hissar, 831; — of Delhi, 804; — law on marriage, 804.
Moslem building usages, 918.
Mosque, of Guru Hargovind, 700.
Mother's brother, 746.
Mourner, functions of the chief Hindu, 842.
Mourning, Hindu, 846.
Mrichh, 487.
Mrig Satāi, 471 f.
Mrigshār, 784.
Mubāriz Khān, 532.
Mubtadi, 521.
Mufti, 501.
Mugān dena, 876.
Mughal, 58; customs, 773, 774; inroads, 493 f; palace terms, 907; province of Sirhind, 703; —s, 683, 685, 688, 699, 701, 703.
Mughal Sāhib, Sultan, 594.
Muhammad Akbar, 533.
Muhammad Akram, 502.
Muhammad Aqil, Qāzi, 533.
Muhammad Aqil Sāhib, 599.
Muhammad Azam Shāh, 504.
Muhammad Ghaus, Bandagi, 605.
Muhammad of Ghor, 489 f.
Muhammad Hamīd-ud-Dīn Nāgauri, Qāzi, 491.
Muhammad Ismāīl, Maulavi, 616.
Muhammad Jamāl, Hāfiz, 533.
Muhammad Sālih, 499.
Muhammad Sharīf Sāhib, 599.
Muhammad Sulaimān Khān, Khwāja, 533.
Muhammad Sulaimān Khan, Khwāja, of Tzaunsa, 602.
Muhammadan betrothal, 802; lucky dates for, 810.
Muhāra, 220.

Muharram, 742, 808, 811, 820, 885, 886.
Muhibb-i-Jahāniān, 533.
Muhīb Jahāniān, 605.
Muhi-ud-Dīn, Khwāja, 179.
Muhtadi, 521.
Muhtasib, 504.
Muin-ud-Din Chishti, shrine of, 769.
Muizzi College, at Dehli, 495.
Mujtahid, 501; office of, 506.
Mukanna', 583.
Mukat, crown, 798.
Mukeshwar, 121.
Mukhlasgarh, 699.
Mukh-manjan, 713.
Muklāwā, 802, 816, 823, 824, 829, 832, 900.
Mukt, salvation: — sar. 713.
Mukta, 107.
Mul, = Padoi, 157.
Mul Padoi, 457.
Mūl Nāg, 156.
Mūla, blight, 258.
Mula, a child whose head has not been properly shaped, 746.
Mula Jats, 13.
Mūlasangha, 113.
Mūla Sant, 390.
Mūlasanti, 390.
Mūlisthān, Multan, old names of, 45.
Mullāh, 501, 574 f, 764, 765, 875, 877, 878, 879, 882, 884, 891; at betrothal, 808; —'s whisper to new-born child, 765.
Multān. 489.
Mulwāna, 219.
Munda, 124.
Mūndan, sanskār, tonsure, = jhand, 755, 904.
Mundlīkh, 183.
Mundr-chhor, munh-chhor, 876.
Mūnh chhurāwan, 834; chitarna, 826; juthlāwnā, 805; dikhlai, showing her (bride's) face, 818.
Munh Mahesh, 130.
Munh boli, 907.
Muni, 104, 401.
Munkir, 875.
Muqām, defined, 576; denā, 876.
Murād Ali Shāh, 551.
Murda-sho, a class of *mullahs*, 877.
Murīd, 520, 539, 591.
Murji'ite, 506.
Murlidhar, 370.
Murshid, 521, 544.
Murtaza-Shāhi, 522.
Mūsā Chishti, 536.
Mūsa Nikka, 591-2.
Musalli, 553; offering by. 774-5.
Mūsān Shāh, 605.
Musavi, Sayyid, 546.
Mūsha Varma, Rāja, 149, 278.
Mu'tazila, 506.
Mutsaddi, 687.
Mythology, 112.

N.

Nābha, 703.
Nād, 200, 212.
Nāda, 368.
Nādaun, 690.
Nādaunti, a tract, 51.
Nadha, 803; rasnā, 837.
Nādir Shāh's Invasion, 701.
Nāg, 137, 145, 215, 233-4, 306. 400-1, 419, 459, 461; Bāsak, 132, 144; cult, 66; at Lahore, 712; of Pekha, 475; —s, ? water spirits, 147-71; not connected with funerals, 197.
Nāg Chauth, 407.
Nāg Panchami, 915.
Nāg-worship, 400.
Nāga, 367.
Naga Bari, 155.
Nāgan, Badi, 166, 168.
Naga-worship, 66.
Nāgar. Brahmans, 47.
Nagaria. 707.
Nāgarji, a shrine, 389.
Nāgārjuna, 82.
Nagarkoti Devi, 335.
Nagarkotia —*see* Dūm.
Nagdi, 205.
Nāgi, Suchemi, 170-1.
Nagni, 147, 169.
Nāgrā Jāts, 48.
Nahas pari, 216.
Nahaura, 907.
Nai, 398.
Naina Devi, 318, 319, 336, 341, 694-5, 720.
Nairrit, 244.
Naita, "naming the day," 820.
Nakkāi, 707.
Nakshatras, lunar mansions in astrology, 249 f, 741, 784, 870.

Nakti, cat, 768.
Nāla, hydropathy, 256.
Nālagarh, 683, 684; raja of, 689, 699.
Nām, -i, -a-nāmika, 395–6.
Nām-chhrn, Nāmin, 92.
Nāmdeo, 682–3; -deo, -devi, 398.
Name, of God, worshipped, 395 f.
Names, of places, 252; opprobrious, 866.
Nām-rakhā, 354.
Nām-rās, 910.
Nāna, 676; ke chhak, 827.
Nānak, Bāba, 536, 705–715; Guru, 676 ff, 713, 718–9; birthplace of, life of, 676; his descendants, 680, 693; attitude towards Islam, 681; attitude toward-Hinduism, 681; as controller of an infectious fever, 694; derivation of name, 676; character 676, 677; miracles, 678–9; his 5 pilgrimages, 678; his fictitious pilgrimages, 680; cloak, 679; teachings, 679; origin of name, 747.
Nānaki, 676.
Nānakmāta, 679; -mata, 684.
Nānakpanthi, 707.
Nānak-putra, 680.
Nānakshāhi, rupee struck, 703.
Nand Lal, 370.
Nanda, 369.
Nandhrāri, 466.
Nandi, 113; —Kashūr Mahādeo, 271.
Nanhda, 433.
Nankāna Sahib, 676, 679.
Nanwati, 907.
Nao Nihāl Singh, 691.
Nāpita, barber (caste), 43.
Naql, 507.
Naqshbandi, Order, 547 ff.
Nar, a caste, 433, 436.
Nār, katai, 764.
Nār Singh, 176, 188, 402;—*see* Nārsingh.
Nārada, 369.
Nārāin, 366 f, 380, 382 f, 348, 484; = Nāg, 169; —Bairāgi, 393.
Narain-bal, 869.
Narains, lesser, 432.
Naranjan, 376.
Narathe, *naurātra*, 471.
Narāyan, 348, 368, 915;—Lachhmi, 360.
Nāro'chorug, doctrine of Nāro, 74.
Narolia, *deota*, 458.
Nārsingh, 179, 212, 301, 366; —Bīr, 469; —cult of, 376 ff; —image of, 715.
Nārwa Sārwa Devi, 323.
Nāzim'ullāh, *ziārat*, 588.
Nāsir-ud-Dīn Shīrāni, Imām, 496.
Nāsiria College, at Delhi, 496.
Nat, 120.
Nata, caste, 43.
Nātā, betrothal, 803, 806; = betrothal: the ceremony is *sagāi*, 892.
Natal Astrology, 741.
Nātaputta, 106.
Nāth, 401, 842; —sūrā, 811.
Natha Sahib, 684.
Nationality, Sikh, appeal to sentiment of, 697.
Natta or nātā, 803.
Nature, 115; —worship of, 121.
Nau-gazā, 209, 605, 622–3.
Naumāsa, a rite in ninth month of pregnancy, 762.
Naumi, festival, 471.
Naun, 199.
Nauni, a *jogini*, 432.
Naur, 199.
Naushah or Naudho bridegroom, 803.
Naushāhi, order, 550.
Nawab Daulat Khan, 677.
Nawahi, 426.
Nawani, a *deota*, 431.
Nāwī, 803.
Naya, 107.
Nazar, 209; —wattu, 210.
Nazrānā, 709.
Neg = lāg, 893.
Negi, 786.
Neota, -āra, 900–1, 814; —after a death, 801.
Nestorian, a monk, instructor of Sumatikirti, 75.
Newa = *pāp*, 156, 172, 173 f; —spirit, 470.
Newar, 172–3.
Next of kin, 842.
Ngadar, primitive Buddhist period, 70.
Niāmat-ullāh Shahīd, 535.
Niaz, 812, 886.
Nichla Kalān Darbār Sāhib, Batāla, gurdwara at which four fairs are held, 711.

Nicknames, 557.
Nigāha, 678.
Nigāhia, 566.
Nigantha, old name of Jainism, 106.
Nigoda, 108.
Nihang, 708.
Nihāsa, 433.
Nikāh, 808, 814, 818; -khwān, 828, 830-1.
Nikāsi, 814.
Nila-rath, 187.
Nīm, 882; —ki patti chabānā, 848.
Nimāwat, 372.
Nimāz janāzah, 875.
Nimbārka, 372.
Nimbulla, fairy king, 56.
Ningmat chebe, 98.
Nirbhav, 366
Nirjara, 108.
Nirmal (Nizam's dominions), 688.
Nirmalas, 709.
Nirvāna, 76; = nirvriti or mukti, 107-8.
Nisbat, 803.
Nishādi, a mixed caste, 41.
Nishān, 624.
Nishānī, token, 806-7; —rakhna.
Nishānia, 706.
Niundra = neota, 833.
Niyat khair, 808, 819.
Nizām Dīn, Maulavi, 616.
Nizām ud-Dīn, Aulia, 491, 492 f.
Nizāmia, 529.
Nnāl Deo, 468.
Noah, 883.
Nodh, daughter-in-law or bride, 808.
Nogi, 357.
Nolar, 762.
North, 132.
North-eastern Punjab, 789.
Numāna Shāhwāli, 596.
Number five in Sikhism, 696; —s, lucky and unlucky, 222, 223.
Nuptial fire, the, 797.
Nūr Muhammad Mahārwi, 533.
Nūr Muhammad Sāhib Noruwāla, Khwaja, 600.
Nūr Shāh, 622.
Nūr Shāh Wali, 605.
Nurya Siddh, 184.
Nyāyak, Granth, 119.
Nyigma-pa, red *lāmas*, 64, 73, 86.
Nyūngpar, 86.

O.

Od, 134.
Ol, a crack, 438.
Om mani padme hūm, explained, 88.
Omens, 223-29; agricultural, 234; from meeting, 226-7; in children, 746.
Omes Karīm, 399.
Omphis=Ambi, 27; of Taxila, 29.
Orayana, 834.
Orhnā-badal, 905.
Orra, 205.
Ossadioi, 29.
Oswāl, 105.
Out-houses, 918.
Owl, 221.
Oxythroi, Xathroi = Kshatriya, 29.

P.

Pabasi, 304.
Puchār, betrothal, dharm di, 785; takkiān di, 786, 787.
Pachhāda, wedding customs of, 829.
Pachhwā, west wind, 129.
Pachlā Devi, 340.
Padihār, Parihār, 47.
Padmani, 784.
Padma Sambhava, 71, 72, 73.
Padmapāni, 80, 81 = Manipadma or Avalokiteswara, 88.
Padoi, 161.
Padoi, Mul, 457.
Pādshāh, 702.
Pāel, 699.
Pa'el, a child born feet foremost, 763.
Pagal Panth, 126.
Pag-bhāi, 905.
Pagwat, 905.
Pahāj, ? co-wife, pāhājri, effigy of a, 867.
Pahlaunthi, first-born, 764.
Pahul, rite, 695-6.
Pahul, 903.
Pahul = amrit sanskār, 720.
Pahulia, 706.
Pair pānā, 792; —gela, 813=milnī; —ā chhornā, 813.

Pairā chhornā, 813, cf. pair gela.
Paithān = Pimprana, 28.
Pāk-damanān (chaste wives), 778.
Pākhān, 377.
Paktyes, 27.
Pakwān, sweetmeat, 806.
Pāl dynasty, 349.
Pāldan-lāmo = Mahā-Kāli, 93.
Palmistry, 783.
Panch, -āyat, 704–5.
Panch Nāg, 145.
Panch ratnā, 840–2.
Panchak, 850, 856, 869–70, 902.
Panch-kaliān, 225, —i, 186.
Panchpir, 195.
Panchen Rinpoche, 84, 85.
Pāndava, 131, 404.
Pandit Shib Ram Das, Note 2, 782.
Panditamarana, 112.
Pāndo, Bhīm, a, 466.
Pandru, 15th Poh, 473.
Pāndu, 121, 353.
Pandava, 120, 121; —ūān ka Sthān, 120.
Pane Nāg, 167, 168.
Pāngi, Buddhism in, 67.
Pāngwāl, 216.
Pāni pilāwan, giving water to drink, to cancel a betrothal, 787.
Panihār, 198.
Panhiyār, 199.
Pānīpat, 502; battle of, 702; Imāms of, 618.
Panj Bir, 429, 441.
Panj ishnānā (washing of 5), 697.
Panj Pīr, 573.
Panjāb, rite of alms-giving, 742.
Pānjag, festival, 474.
Panjgarhia, 707.
Panjuanish, 697.
Panjpiri, 121.
Pantheon, Hindu, 115–16.
Pāon bhārī, "heavy feet," a rite of mid-pregnancy, 738; phernā, turning the feet, 762.
Pāonta, 689.
Pāp, 156, 470 f.
Pāpa, sin, 107.
Pāpra, curse, 199.
Pāpujī, 370.
Para kaun, provisions, 819.
Pārada, a tribe, 54.
Parama, dharma, 108.
Pāras Nāth, 101, 114.
Paras Rām, 345, 366; cult of, 379 ff.
Parāsar, rishi, 421.
Parāshari Brahmans, 46.
Pārbati, 121, 916.
Parchāva, 209.
Parchhāwān, a woman whose child has died within 40 days of birth, lit. shadow, 748, 593–4 f.
Paret, 204; pūjan, feast, 436.
Parhan, 784.
Pari, 470; = dev, 559.
Pari Devi, 324.
Parihār = Pratihāra, 36.
Parind, 204.
Parinirvāna, 82.
Parjā, 912.
Parjāpat, 326.
Pārjapati, Bāwā, 692.
Parkarmān, circumambulation, 711.
Parona, P., a shawl, 807, 832.
Parrewi, 472.
Pārshva, 107, 114.
Parthian influence, 33.
Parthivapūja, 472–3.
Pārvati, 325, 373 f.
Pashāj, in Bahāwalpur, 217.
Pashto, 803.
Pasrūr, 701.
Pātā utārnā, 814; or pīrhā utārnā, 814.
Pataishtā, 912.
Pātak, 851.
Patān, ziārat, 592.
Pathānkot, battle of, 699, 700.
Pathans at Pāonta, 689; of Māler Kotla, 703; Saddozai and Kizzilbāsh, 831; — of Peshāwar, Isa Khel and Kohat, 832 ff; Wilāyati, weddings among, 830.
Pathānti, a tract, 51.
Paths, seven, 539.
Paththarwāli, Devi shrine, 331.
Patiala, 731, 831.
Patkā, 899.
Patna, 686–7.
Patnos, 807.
Patrā phernā, to change the stools, 899.
Patta, money paid by boy's father for menials' dues, 897.
Patti, 701; Sāhib, Sikh shrine, Lahore, 712.

Paurava = Poros, 28.
Pavana, 120.
Pecha, turban, 696.
Pechi, a band of silver tinsel over the turban, 899.
Pera, a mess of *pīthi*, 797.
Persian invasion, unrecorded, 25. *See* Iranian.
Peshāwar, 679.
Peshkāra, 819.
Petā, intestine, 769.
Phāgali, 326.
Phāgli, place of origin, 433.
Phāl Nāg, 169.
Phalgani, 784.
Phangi. 433.
Phangni, 214.
Pharaknā, 258.
Phera, a fee, 814.
Pheru, Bhai, 129, 568.
Philosophy, of Jainism, 106.
Phirwi, a dance, 919.
Phugni, 215; Devi, 426.
Phūl, "flower," 889; bones, 850; chunna, 838.
Phūlan Devi, 352.
Phulkian States, 703; dehra, 707.
Phul-patri, fruit and leaves, 887.
Phūlsak, 127.
Phungāni, Devi, 341–2.
Phungni, Devi, 342.
Phungni, feast, 436.
P'hūr, 23.
Phūrī pānā, carpet spreading, 847.
Piāra, 698.
Pīch, loin-cloth, 893.
Pichch (?), rice water, 750.
Pichhāwān, shadow, 775.
Pichhlagra, a dish of rice mixed with salt, 750.
Pihar, or Behar, god of monasteries, 83.
Pilpa. *See* Pīpnākh.
Pimprama, 28.
Pindas, 840–44.
Pindi, 387 f; —chhed, cutting up the pinda, 840.
Pindori, in Gurdāspur, 393.
Pinds, 856–7; —offering of, 844 ff.
Pipa Bhagat, 124, 125.
Pīpal, 136, 138, 910.
Pīpnākh, 200.
Pir, 221, 507, 590–1.
Pīr Adil, 599.
Pir Aulia Ghori, 534.
Pīr Balāwal Shāh, 606.
Pir Daulat Shāh, 539.
Pīr Ghāzi Shāh, *ziarāt*, 595.
Pīr Mohka, 616.
Pir Muhammad Rājan, 501.
Pīr Rāmdīn, 586–7.
Pīr Sabiq, 586.
Pīr Salohi, 626.
Pir Sampounwāla, 533.
Pīr Shāh, 551.
Pir Zaki, 617.
Pīrān-i-Pīr, 538.
Pir-bahin, 907.
Pirhain, the, 779.
Piridai, 792.
Pirinda, 911–2.
Pir-murīdi, 522.
Pīrs, the five, 572–3.
Pirthi Chand, 682, 705.
Pita, spirit, 199–200.
Pitar, 874.
Pitār, trousseau, 899.
Pīth, a *deota*, 431.
Pithā tandhnā, 838.
Pīthi, finely ground *māsh*, 797.
Pitr, 132, 195, 200.
Piūli (Pīli) Nāg, 169, 170.
Plague, cattle, 218.
Plains, Eastern, 8, Physical divisions of, 9; Ethnography of, 10–12; —Western, 15; Ethnography of, 17.
Planet-worship, 126.
Poh, 239.
Polamde, 350.
Poros = Paurava, 28.
Portents, travel, 225.
Possession, demoniacal, 561.
Pothi, 48.
Pothi-Māla, shrine, 714.
Pothwār, 48.
Potra, swaddling clothes, —ron ka amīr, a gentleman from his cradle, 892.
Potter's wheel worship, 815.
Prahlād, 366.
Prajāpati, 120.
Prasthala, an extinct tribe, 54.
Pratihāra, 36; Brahman and Kshatriya, 43.
Pratiloma marriage, 43.
Pratima, 112.
Pratyeka, Buddha, 79.
Pravajya, 84.
Prayers, benedictory, 784.

Pregnancy observances, Muhammadan 759; rites (Hindu), 3rd month, sukh salai, 731; thakui, 731; mita bohia, 732; 5th month sādh (religious), 732; chhoti rītān (religious), 732; 6th month, chilwan, 733; 7th month, barī rītān, 733; kunji or rīt, 734; mid-pregnancy (adh gabh). 733; 7th month, dewā dhāmī, 735; 8th month, Athwahān, 736; 8th month, Athwānsā, 737; rites among the Kakezais (distillers), 760; Qasābs (butchers), 760; Arāīns (market gardeners), 760; Dhobīs (washermen), 760; Māshkis (watermen), 760; Moslem castes in the North Punjab, 760; Lahoria Khatris, Note 4, 732; Bunjahi Khatris, Note 4, 732; Muhammadan Saqqās, 734.

Pregnancy rites (Hindu) in Patiāla, 731; in Gurdaspur, 731–34; in Jind, 732; in Ferozepur, 732; in Central Punjab, 732; in Suket, State of, Note 1, 736; in Jhelum, 733; in Rajanpur, Tahsīl, 733; in Ramnāgar, 734; in Lahore, 735; in Montgomery, 735; in Jammu, 735; in Amritsār, 733–34; in Gujrānwāla, 733–34; in Bahawalpur, 733–34; in Fāzilka, 731; in Sialkot, 731–33–35; in Hoshiarpur, 731–33–34; in Hissār, 731–34; in Talagang, 735; in Hazro, 735–36; in Mandi, 736; in Chamba, 738; in Kangra, Note 1, 738.

Post-cremation observances, 846.

Post-natal festivals, 755; precautions, 749.

Post-*nikāh* ceremonies, 818; nuptial observances, 822.

Prem Tot (?), 399.

Premature birth, Hindu, 738.

Preparations for death, Moslem, 874.

Priest's wife or priestess, rites performed by, 735, 736, 752.

Prikamma, 238.

Prikrati = kūlachar, family usage, 782.

Prince Khusru, 683.

Prince Rafi-us-shān, 699.

Pritha, 121.

Prithema, 245.

Prithi, earth, 193.

Prithivishwara, 323, 324.

Priyugi, Rāja, 128.

Proposal ceremonies, Moslem, 806.

Proverb on treatment of girls, 785.

P'ro-Yidam, 73.

Pseudo-science, 241.

Pubhāri, *deota*, 441.

Puchh, demand, 819; —nānkā, 820.

Pudgala, 107.

Pugwat, 905.

Puj, pujāri, pujera, 108.

Pujāra, 148.

Pujāri, 293 ff; castes of, 435.

Pujārli, Devi, 340.

Pun, 785–9; —san (?), 736.

Pun-savan, causing a male birth, 731, Note 2.

Pundīr, 15.

Pūnya, 107.

Punwār, 15, 21; = Paramāra, 36.

Punwārwati, 51.

Purakh Siddh Chauraujwo-nāth, 125.

Pūran Bhagat, 124.

Puran Mal, 394.

Pūranmāsi, 245.

Puriān bharnā, 854.

Purification after child-birth, 753, 772.

Purification after a death, 846, 860, 885.

Purwā, East wind, 129.

Putrela, 904.

Putreta, boy's father or kinsman, 787, 803.

Pyre, the (chita), 845.

Q.

Qadr, -ites, 506.

Qādiri, 502; shrines, 540 ff.

Qādiri, Sh. Abd-us-Sabūr, 596.

Qādiria, Order, 538 ff.

Qaisar Shāh, 551.

Qaisarshāhi, Order, 550.

Qalandar, 494, 531, 543 ff, 619; —Shāh Sharif, 595.

Qānūn, 506.

Qarmatian, 489, 507.

Qarramite, 507.

Qāsim, Imām, 621.

Qassāb, 399; betrothals among, 830–1:
Qāzī, 504, 808, 816, 824, 827, 880, 887, 890; post of, 490 f.
Qibla, the, 881, 883; -i-Alam, 533.
Qirāmita, 491; *see* "Qarmatian."
Qiyās, 505.
Qizzil-bāsh, 553; Pathāns, 808–31.
Qul-khwānī, 885, 888, 889, 890.
Qurān, 778, 830, 874, 875, 876, 877, 878, 879, 880, 881, 883, 885, 891, 918.
Qutbs, four, at Hissar, 534, 559.
Qutb-ud-Din Bakhtyār, of Ush, 491, 492.

R.

Rabābi, 677.
Rabjampa, 85.
Rachhpāl, a godling, 432.
Rādhā, 370.
Rādhaswāmi, 370.
Rafāi, 555, 557.
Rafī-ush-Shan, Prince, 699.
Raghunāth, 379, 420, 433, 474, 485.
Raghu Rām, 370.
Rāh, offerings to, 739.
Rahbari, 46.
Rah-denā, 906.
Rāhib, Christian, 517.
Rahirās, 717.
Rahit, 717.
Rahmān Shāh, 551.
Rahtor, Ramdeo, 23.
Rāhu, 127; worship of, 740.
Rahu (Rao), Kanet, 37.
Rai-Bhāt, 360.
Rai Boe, 676.
Rai Bulār, 677; Talwandi, 676.
Rai Thamman, Bairāgi, 670.
Raikot, 699.
Raimal, a *deota*, 431.
Rain, 132, 133; a —god, 146; charms for, 629; feast to obtain, 436.
Rainbow, 133.
Rainka, 379.
Raīs Sāhib, Shaikh, 600.
Rāīta, *deota*, 448.
Raj Singh of Chamba, 693.
Rāja, *asārband* of, 256.
Rāja Bābā, Dīwān, 594.
Rāja Bhim Chand, 689.
Rajaka (? mason), 43.
Rajal-ul-ghaib, 246.
Rājeshwari, 426.
Rājput, 131, 201, 230, 692–3, 701; Bhatti, special customs of, 829; Chibh, 781; Hindu, 7; and Jats, 12, 57; Muhammadan, bride-price among, 831.
Rākas, 215.
Rakhāli, 196.
Rakharpunia, festival, 471.
Rākhi (price of) - "protection," 707.
Rakhri, 904.
Rakht-bari, -burāni, clothes-cutting, 809.
Raksha, 841.
Rākshasa, 139, 216.
Rākshini, 214.
Raktavija, 325.
Rali worship, 327–8.
Rām, 119, 221; name of, worshipped, 395 f.
Rām Chandra, 133; kā-bhagat, 142.
Rām Piāra, 390.
Rām Rai, 685, 705.
Rām Rāiā, sect, 697.
Rām sat, 792.
Rām Thamman, 679, 698.
Rāma, 801.
Rāma Chandra, 396–7.
Rāmānanda, 374, 392 f.
Rāmanandi, 394.
Rāmānuja, 374.
Rāmchandra, 367, 370 f.
Rāmdās, Guru, 682, 705, 719.
Rāmdāsia, 398, 701.
Rāmdāspur (Amritsar), 682.
Rameshwar, 687.
Rāmgarhia, 706; a Sikh *misl*, 7, 693.
Rām-ki-gao, 142.
Rām-kund, 130.
Ramoche, monastery at, 71; of the Nyigmapa, 73.
Rāna, 196; = Shīn, 59.
Randepa, or Hindu widowhood, 859.
Randol, re-marriage —of a widow, 795.
Rang Rangita, 389.
Rāni, 196.
Rāniwāl, 692.
Rānja Des, 51.
Ranjit Deo of Jammu, 693.

Ranjit Singh, 691, 692–3, 703.
Rankā, 354.
Ranpal, a *deota*, 431.
Rāri, 645.
Rasālu, 123, 130.
Rasmāna, bride-price, 833.
Rasūlwāhi, 219.
Rāth, a tract, 52.
Rāthi, 149; status of, 42; —s, 757.
Rāt-jāgā, vigil, 778, 829.
Ratn, Bāba, — Shāh, 552.
Rattau (Ratn), Hāji, 175, 179.
Ratn Nath, 181.
Ratn Pāl, 551.
Ratnapāni, 80,
Ratna-Sāmbhava, 78.
Ratu Sāhib, 609.
Ratwāl, sacrifice, 918.
Rāvi, river, 680.
Rāvi Dās, 682.
Rawal, a *deota*, 431.
Rāwan, 801.
Rāwandi, 583.
Rawin, a tribal tract, 51.
Razāqia, 540.
Razzar, a tribal area, 53.
Rehāru, 212.
Relics, worship of, 102.
Religious house decorations, 915.
Reota, 784.
Republics, in Buddhist times, 26.
Resha, a *deota*, 431.
Rewal, a Gheba sept, 49.
Rhyāli, 474.
Rikhi, 401.
Rirku, *deota*, 458.
Risabha, 369.
Rishabnāth, 101.
Rishet, 217.
Rishi, 82; —s, in Kulu, 420.
Rīt, marriage, 796; rite, 731; pl. —ān, 732 ff: = *kanji*, 734.
Ritual marriage in the hills, 797.
Rizā, 831.
Rode Shāh, 608.
Rohat, 22.
Rohni, 784.
Ropnā, ratification (? fr. *roknā*, to restrain, so to clinch): the girl's father sends a barber to the boy's village, and if matters are satisfactory he puts a ring or a rupee into the boy's hand, 892.
Ropnā, defined, 786, 803.
Ror, 13; —s, 790.
Rori Sahib, 679.
Rosaries, Hindu, 280–1; Moslem, 629; Sikh, 708.
Roshani, fair, 538.
Roshanīa, sect, 496, 516.
Roshan-ud-Daula, 529.
Rudar, 745.
Rudra, *sampradāya*. 373.
Ruh rilāna, 885.
Rukmani, 801.
Ruku-i Alam, of Multan, 493.
Rukn-ud-Dīn, Imām Mahdi, 495; Qazi, 679.
Rūmi Khel, 579.
Ru-numāī, 832.
Rupar, 699; Nawab of, 689.
Russia, 678–87.
Rustam, 21, 22.
Ruti manāi, 795.

S.

Sa'ādat, Bāra, 557.
Sa'ad-ud-Dīn, Akhūnd, 595.
Sa-bdag, local deities, 77, 83.
Sābir, 529.
Sābiria, 529.
Sacha sauda, 719.
Sachi, 801.
Sāchui = barī, *q.v.*, 815.
Sacramental character of Hindu marriage, 793.
Sacrifice, 209; of first-born, 743; of a fowl, 869; of goat, 742, 769, 781, 850; human, in Lahul, 91.
Sacrificing water, 818.
Sada Nand, 179.
Saddozai, 808.
Sādh ("half"), a rite in mid-pregnancy, 732.
Sadhar, "seven things," in the seventh month of pregnancy, 766; a present of vegetables, &c., 762.
Sādhaura, 690, 699.
Sādh-margi, 103.
Sādh-sangat, good companionship, 716.
Sādhu, Jain, 104.
Sadr, 501; —s, of Akbar, 499.
Sadr Jahān, 501, 644.
Sadr-ud-Din Maleri, 547, 644.
Sadrel, *deota*, 458.
Sāer, fair, 360 f; suji, 472 f.

Safar, 809–11
Saffron, 700.
Sāg = wat, walawan, vegetables, 792.
Sagāi, betrothal, 786, 801, 803; the ceremony of betrothal, *cf.* *nata*, 892.
Sāhā chitthi, 797.
Sahāranpur-Buria, 699.
Sahdeo, 127, 128.
Sāhib Singh, Bedi, 703, Note 3, 695.
Sāhib-i-Zamān, 502.
Sahu, "gentle," 57.
Sa'id Halim, Bukhāri, Shāh, 598.
Sāīd Karam, 577.
Saidpur, sack of, 679.
Saif Ali, *ziārat*, 589.
Saifābād, 688.
Sain dynasty, 361.
Sainbhagti, 398.
Saints, Chishti. 529, 530–1.
Sairi, principality of, 401.
Sairindhras, 53.
Saiyid, 195.
Saiyad-kā-than, 195.
Sāja, first day, 471.
Sajalif, Bāba, 594.
Sajan, Shaikh, 678.
Sajja, 902.
Saka, 34, 45.
Sakhī, -eli, 907.
Sakhi Habīb, 593.
Sakhi Sarwar, 129, 133, 284, 678; cult of, 566 ff.
Sakti, 61, 62; Buddha, 68 = *yūm*, 73; Dorje-p'agmo, 75, 79; *cf.* Avalokiteswara, 82.
Sakulya, 782.
Sakya, 85.
Sākyamūni, 70, 78, 80.
Sakya-pa, 74.
Salām karwāī, 822.
Sālār Ma'sūd Ghāzi, 624.
Sālār Qamar-ud-Dīn of Irāq, 620.
Sālbāhan, 200.
Salhor, a feast, 438, 471 f.
Salig Rām, 377.
Sāligrām, 390.
Sālivāhana, 124.
Salono, a fair, 362.
Salt Range, 18 = Singhapura, 32.
Sālū artā, 815.
Salur, 687.
Sām, 21, 22.
Samādhs, 286 f.
Samāna, 688.
Samanta-bhadra, 80.
Samavasarana, 112.
Sambatsari shrādhs, 862.
Sambegi, Samegi, 104.
Sanbhal bhejna, 811.
Samiti, 110.
Samjnin, 108.
Sammi, a dance of women, 919.
Samosa, sweetmeat, 739.
Samsārin, 107.
Samudghāta, 110.
Samvara, 111.
Samye, monastery at, 71; of the Nyigmapa, 73.
Sanaka, 373.
Sanbhāl, support or pledge, 811.
Sanctuary and fair of Gurū Har Gobind at Sanir, Ferozepur, 712.
Sanda, 760.
Sandal, 182.
Sāndal, rikhi, 421.
Sandeo, *deota*, 442.
Sandhārī, 812.
Sandhola Nāg, 154.
Sāndilya, 113.
Sandla, 316.
Sang, 569.
Sangal, 149.
Sangaldīp, Sialkot, 125.
Sangat, 686–7; (Sikh congregation), 678.
Sangdus, 77.
Sangha, 86.
Sangtia, 683.
Sankhani, 784.
Saniāsi, 329, 366.
Sanīchar, 126, 127.
Sank, 223.
Sankal Rājā, 22.
Sankarachārya, 373.
Sankhani, 784.
Sankhya, 106.
Sansār Chand = Chandra Gupta, 23.
Sansār Sain, 364.
Sansāra, 108.
Sānsi, rite of friendship, 905.
Sanskāra, cremation, 846; —s, 102.
Santokh, contentment, 716.
Sanwal-shāhi, 709, 380.
Sanyāsi, 69.
Sapādalaksha = Siwālik, *q.v.*
Sāqi, cup-bearer, 522.
Sar Prikarai Faqīr, 587.

Sarad, Saraswatī, 172.
Sāradā, 418.
Sarāj (Seorāj), 88; (Kulu), 422; Inner, land worship in, 437.
Saraogi (Sewak), 46; = sikh(s), 99; among Jains, 104, 105, 114.
Saraswati, 216, 323, 325, 869.
Sarbālā, bridegroom, 793, 799, 813; Shāhbala, 815, 821.
Sarbokhadi, 740.
Sardān, shīrdān, 774.
Sardha, 850.
Sardkā, 850.
Sareli, dragon, 156.
Sarma, School of Nyigmapa, 74.
Sarmkaul, 433.
Sarsahan, 400.
Sarsut, Brahmans, 119.
Sarsuti, 135.
Sarūp Das, Bhāi, 714.
Sarwardīn, ziarāt, 588.
Sarwaria, 566.
Sarwat Khālsa, 706.
Sat, 258.
Sat Nārāins, 366.
Sat sang, company of holy men, 716.
Sāt Suhāgan kā kundā, 816.
Satārīn, 17th day after a death, 801.
Satārwān; —hwīn.
Sathī = chhathī, 752.
Sathorā, 802.
Sathūra, 824–5.
Satī, fem.; satū, m., 200, 201, 404, 682; "faithful," 325; (Gujari), 534; pillars, 196; wife of Sankara, 373.
Satiā, sātiā = swāstika, 916.
Sat-nami, sect, 852.
Satsaroch, 800.
Sat-sira = mula, q.v., 746.
Sattār Shāh Ghāzi, Pīr, 596.
Sattowāra, 825.
Sattvam, 64.
Saturday, 257.
Saturn, 240, 739.
Satvata, 367.
Satwāhin, 759.
Satwān, seventh day observance after a birth, 752.
Satwānsa, —ī, 761.
Satwāra, sathūra, = muklāwā, 824–5, 833.
Saukan mora, 202.
Saura, —patia, 123.
Sanvīra, an extinct tribe, 54.
Sawāl, request, 804.
Sāwan, 149, 233, 240, 788; swinging in, 397.
Sawan = mathe lagāwan, 787.
Sawānī, 735.
Sawant, 221.
Sawerni, 180.
Sāyā, 252.
Sayyid, 203, 399, 579 ff; 805, 812–831; = Shahīd, 327; —Ishāq, 585; —Kabīr, 621; —Mahmūd, 620; —Muhammad, 538–9.
Sayyids, 256.
Sāzindah-i-Māh, moon-maker, 583.
Scarcity, 132, 133.
Science of unlucky times, 243.
Sectarial marks, 909.
Sects, Jain, 113; 72, of Islām, 502.
Seja, 857, 860, 862.
Sela, 898.
Seli, 391.
Sen Devi, 331.
Sena, 113.
Sengi, demon, 404.
Seur or Sain, 787.
Sera, 85, 899.
Ses (Shesh?) Nāg, 166.
Seven paths, the, 539.
Sewak, 46, 389.
Sewal, 898, 899. The boy's or girl's mother picks up her petticoat and touches his body all over with it.
Sex, determination of, 761; in trees, 741.
Sgoh, festival, 472.
Shab Barāt-i, 806, 809–811, 812–833, 886.
Shādi = circumcision, 779; Ghare ki, Gurki, Tage ki, 829.
Shādi Khān, 618.
Shadi, martyr, shrine of, 781.
Shāfian tenets, 503.
Shagūn, 786, 787–92, 803.
Shāh, a title, 709–10; Abdul Azīz, 627; Abulla Namāzi, 598; Ahmad Chishti, 537; Ali Muhammad Husain, 605: Badr Dīwān, 624; Bhīk, Rosāi, 529, 530; Bilāwal, 542; Chand, 551; Chirāgh, 543; Chokha, Sayyid Akbar Ali, 536–7; Daula, 630 ff.; Dujan, 547; Ibrahīm,

ziārat, 579; Ismāīl Sāhib, 597; Jahān, 498, 501, 542, 635; Jamāl, 542; Qadiri, 543; Junaid, 535; Maqbūl, 593; Maqsūd, 593; Mohkam, *hujra* of, 533; Muhammad Ghaus, 542–3; Niāz Ahmad, 491; Qumes, 542; Rahma, 623; Rahmatullah Shāh, 533; Razā, 542; Sadr-ud-Dīn, 602; Shams, 603; Sharīf, Qalandar, 595; Sondha, 532; Sulaimān, Khwāja, 491; Walayat, 532; Wilayat, 624.

Shāhābād, 699.

Shāh-i-Latīf Barri, 130.

Shahāna, Bāba, 390.

Shāhbāla. *See* sarbālā.

Shāhbāz-i-Qalandari, 543.

Shahīd, 203, 327, 622, 624, 701, 707; Ganj, 713; Mard, 601.

Shāhpuri, 204.

Shaikh, 520–2; a grade, 539, 549, 555, *cf.* 590; Abdulla, Miān, 504; Chilli, 626; Faizi, 501; Hākim, 547; Mahmūd, 532; Muhammad, 504; —Bakā, *ib.*; Mūsa, 543; Nizam, 503; Quraishes, 831; Sadr Jahān, 759; Sajan, Thag, 678.

Shaikh-ul-Ahmad, family of, 701.

Shaikh-ul-Islām, 492.

Shaikh Yūsuf, 596; Zakariā, 502; Zamān, 502.

Shaikhsha, 111.

Shail, a stone temple, 434.

Shaitān, 559.

Shaiva, and Vaishnava, 259.

Shaivism, 283 ff; Tantric, 82.

Shaiya, 840.

Shākadvīpi Brahmans, 45, 46.

Shākan, 217.

Shākhs, 912.

Shakti, 259, 372; Devi, 331.

Shāli, a Jāt *got*, 351.

Shālu, 311.

Shām Das, —ji, 388 f.

Shamanism, 61, 62.

Shāmji, 120.

Shams Khan, Mughal faujdār, 699.

Shamshān, 867; *bhūt*, 377.

Shamsheri Mahādeo, 273.

Shamsi Tālāb, 546.

Shams-ud-Dīn, 542; Tabrīzī, 544, 545–6; Turk, 620.

Shān, 798.

Shānd, 435; *jag*, 345.

Shanei, *deota*, 447.

Shaneti, *deota*, 447.

Shang Chūl, *deota*, 442.

Shanghari, 433.

Shankara Devi, 354.

Shankhū Nāg, 168–9.

Shānti, 744, 747, 870; —hawan, 436.

Sharaf-ud-Dīn, Bū Ali Qalandar, 619; Shāh, 618.

Sharālī Deo, 467.

Sharfī khorī, 809.

Shargan, a *deota*, 431.

Sharshāi, a Nāg, 167, 168.

Sharvan Nāg, 162.

Shastras, 745, 784–5, 799–801, 917.

Shattaria, Qadiria, 542.

Sheep, wild, in Lahul, 96.

Sheo Narain, R. B. Pandit, 696.

Sher—Muhammad Ghāzi, 593; Shāh, 605; Shāh Sūr, 626; -dahan, 913.

Sheri = saer, *q.v.*, 474.

Sherkot, Mahādeo, 277.

Shesh Nāg, 154, 191, 317–8.

Shi'a, 143, 574 ff, 586; rosaries of, 629.

Shi'ite, Laws, 506.

Shib, 916.

Shikāri Devi, 426.

Shila asthāpan, 911.

Shimlāsan, Devi, 302.

Shīn(s), cannibalism among, 25, = Chīna ?, 53; = Rāna, 59.

Shir, *deota*, 458.

Shirgan (Sargun) Nāg, 169, 170.

Shīrīnī khorī, sweet-eating, 809.

Shiv Nāth, 687.

Shiva, 80, 119, 132, 259, 260 ff, 273 f, 358, 373 f, 401, 419, 420, 740, 870; bhūmi, 130; worship of, 31.

Shivāla, 259, 283 ff; in Karnāl, 286.

Shivanāth, 687–8.

Shivi, 55.

Shivkanji, 687.

Shogu, *deota*, 469.

Shop and out-houses, 917.

Shor, Shorkot, Shibipura, 29.

Shri Badat, 357.

Shri Bai, goddess, 357.

Shrigul, 290 ff.

Shrine, in memory of Gurū Nanak's marriage, 711; —s, 197–8; aspects of, 193; Chishti, 530–1; hypaethral, 534.
Shringa, *rishi*, 422, 423, 424.
Shroud ceremonies, 878.
Shubh, a *deota*, 431.
Shudāni, 55.
Shudhi, purification, 858.
Shudnāmā, 833.
Shujātpur, near Dacca, 684.
Shukar, dūsri, 354.
Shukar, Venus, 128.
Shukarāna, 810.
Shuma, a feast, 888.
Shumshān bhūmi, 839.
Shyāni Deo, 468.
Siāl, 124; Chela sept of, 503.
Siāl sing, 253.
Sialkot, 125, 127, 504; schoo a 497.
Siān figure (Rādhiki), 915.
Siāna, "cunning," a wizard, 738.
Siāpa, mourning, 846–7.
Siar, 48.
Sich'en-tsogch'en, monastery at, 74.
Sidala, Devi, 354.
Siddh. Sidh, 278 ff, 401; Chaurāsi 440.
Sidh Anūnia, a book, 698, Note 4.
Siddh, Bairāg Lok, 264.
Sidha, 902.
Sīdhi, a dance, 919, 920.
Sīdi Maula, 492.
Sihra, a marriage song, 822.
Sihrā bandhnā, to tie on the chaplet of flowers, 817.
Sika Rām, 577.
Sikh, 389; a belief, 258; Initiates (first five), 697; temple in Lahore (Chūnīān), 714; watermen, 317; war with Mughal court, 683–701; —s in Mandi, 691; —s in Kangra and Chamba, 692; later incursions into the hills, 692; fiscal system, 682; Note 2, 683, 693; the five K's, 695; attitude to Hindu cults, 694; Khalsa sect instituted, 695; Pahul rite, 696; women, Note 2, 696, 697; Expiation of infanticide, 696; development of warlike character, 684; schisms, 686; relations with Hill states, 688; watchwords, 698; coinage, 702; inscriptions on, 703; régime, 704; and government, 704; —s, disruption of, 700; transition from theocracy to monarchy, 678; sects (1) the Tat Khalsa, (2) the Bandai; confederacies, 706; Dehras or camps, 707; misls, 706; territorial divisions, 707; taxation, 707; military resources, 707; quoits, 708; rosaries, 708; Art. I., 708; blue dress, 709; shrines, 710; shrines in hills, 692; shrines in Gurdaspur, 711; shrines in Ferozepur, 712; ideals, 716; philosophy, 717; military character, origin of, 719; Dals or armies (1) Budha (or veteran), (2) Taru, or Young, 701; view of Transmigration, 720; Conception of Divinity, 720; definition of Khalsa, 720; —s in Chamba, 693; pilgrim's itinerary to S. India and Ceylon, 687; rule in Kulu, 692; temples in S. India, 687; Bhatra, 687; Mānjhi, 707; Mālwāi, 707; —s as mercenaries, 693; 844; ism, extension of, 686; recluses, 681; beliefs, 682; reformers, 682; Decalogue discovered, 682; Buddhist predecessors of —*gurus*, 66.
Sikhi, 709; a tithe, 683.
Sikhin, 78.
Sikhism, 676 ff.
Sil, essence, 716.
Sīmanat (?), 735.
Simdi, = kurram, 897.
Simha, 113.
Simjor, contiguity (?), —*kī birādrī*, kinship founded on a common boundary, 893.
Simla Hills, 197.
Simlāsan, 336.
Simuk, 258.
Sindha, 181.
Sindhū, 54, 283.
Sīndhu Bīr, 316 ff, 645.
Sindhu, Jāts, 193.
Sin-dje, 83.
Singa, *rishi*, 422.
Singh (lion) adoption of title by Sikhs, 695, 709–10; = snake god, 143; 698–9.
Singha, 172.

Singhapura, = Salt Range, 32.
Singhāsan Devi, 334.
Singhpuria, 706.
Singi, *rākshasa*, 410 f.
Sīp Deo, 467.
Sīpi, fair at, 401.
Sīpur, *devata*, 401.
Siqti, 540.
Sir guddi, marriage, 796.
Sir jori, head touching, 801.
Sir wārnā kuram, 817, 819.
Sirāi Mangha (Sikh temple and fair), 713.
Sirhind, 504, 699–707; battle of, 703.
Siriāl, 175; Chhariyāl.
Sir-kap, 124; Raja, 131.
Sirkap Shāh, 622.
Sirmūr, 691, 699, 792–96.
Sirmūri, 302.
Sir-sukh, 124.
Sisant, rite in sixth month of pregnancy, 731.
Sister's son, 129.
Sīta, 370, 801.
Sītala, 318; Devi, 350 ff.
Sithnī, insult, 810.
Sitla, 863.
Sītlū Mahādeo, 322.
Siva, 404 ff.
Siwālik = Sapādalaksha, 22, 47; rājās of, 23; Gurjaras of, 37.
Si- Yidam, Vajra-pūrba, 73.
Sīyar, = Sītalaghar, 351.
Skandila, 113.
Snake, worship, 143.
Sneezing, omens, 221.
Sodhi Khatris, 682; —s of Anandpur, 692.
Sodhi Sultan, 683.
Sogu Nāg, 169.
Sohāg, 901, 794; — utārnā, 843; glass wristlets and a nose-ring, 894.
Sohāla, 717.
Sohan sihrā, a garland of flowers, 817.
Soharni, 850, 855–6.
Sohla, eulogy, 759.
Sohra, 787.
Solanki=Chalukya, 36.
Solono, day, 915.
Somān, 709.
Sona, figure, 915.
Sondha, 858.
Sondhia, = dasūthan, 752.
Sondip, 687.
Sophytes, Saubhūti, 28.
Sotar, = snake, 400.
South-eastern Punjab, 786, 803, 810.
South-west Punjab, 787–803.
Soyam, = *tija*, 889, and *phūl*, 886, 888.
Spatik, white crystal, 708.
Spīn Gund, 586.
Spirit, after death, 204; —s, 205; and witches, 206; on earth, 207.
Spirits, 65, 199; Moslem beliefs in, 560.
Spiti, Buddhism in, 67, 88.
Sri Chālda, 408 ff.
Sri Chand, Bāba, 710, 712.
Sri Chola Sāhib, mandir, Gurdāspur, 710.
Sri Darbar Sāhib, Sikh mandir, tank and fair at Ferozepur, 713.
Sri Girdhāri Ji, shrine, 389.
Sri Khand Mahādeva, 261.
Sri Kun, 171.
Sri Soba Nāth, 269.
Srividya, 426.
Sthān, of Guru Hargovind, 712.
Sthānakwāsi, 103.
Stars, seeing the, after a birth, 773–4.
Status of hostages, Note 6, 685.
Sthavira, 82.
Stone Age, 19
Structure of house, 914.
Sūbal, 501.
Subha, exchange of presents, 792.
Subhadra, 397.
Submontane, Eastern, Ethnography of, 37; Western, Ethnography of, 8.
Such, purity, 716.
Sucha Singh, Note 1, 707.
Sudak kā khānā, 770.
Sudharman, 111.
Sūdrā, occupations, 43; caste marks for, 909.
Sūf, "wool," 517.
Sufaidāhwāla Bābā, *ziārat*, 595.
Sufed Koh, 577.
Sūfi, 502; literature, 522–3; orders, 540 ff, 542.
Sufiism, 502.
Suhāg-pattāri, 800; utārnā, 843.
Suhāgpura, 827.
Suharwardi, 540; Qādiri, 542; Order, 544 ff.

Suhbat, 518.
Sūheli, 907.
Sukarchakia misl, 693.
Sulaimān, 129.
Sultān Ghāzi, Mīān, 595.
Sultān Ibrahim, 529.
Sultāni, 566.
Sumbha, 325.
Sun, offerings to, 739; symbol, 918; temple of, 489; worship, 123.
Sunar, 795.
Sundar-Shāhia, 710.
Sunday, 218, 240, 241, 257, 258, 352.
Sundrān, Rāni, 125.
Sunh-lainā, 906.
Sunnat, 521, 778.
Sunni, 586; doctrines, 575; rosaries, 629.
Sunyata, 63.
Superstitions, agricultural, 218 *et seqq.*; minor, 221; about dwellings, 910.
Sūtak, 892.
Surail, 177, 178.
Suraj, 765; Deota, 193; Kūnd, 403; Narain, 123.
Sūraj, Bāba, 393.
Surajpāl, 431.
Suranjīt, 220.
Sūrasena, 26.
Sūrat, 687.
Suril, Seral, 192.
Sūrjan, 175.
Surjila, 185.
Sust Gund, 585.
Sutarbandh, 435–6.
Suthankal, 433.
Sūtra, thread, 753.
Svetadvīpa, 367, 368.
Swabi Tahsil, 832.
Swāmi Dyāl, fair, 277.
Swāmi-Kārttika, 323.
Swarga, 841.
Swastika, 65; —bon, 61; on houses, 916, 918.
Swāt, 56.
Swāti, 594, 595, 784.
Swayas, 717.
Swearing friendship, 904.
Swetambara, 103, 104, 105, 113.
Swinging, at fêtes, 397.
Syādvāda, 107.
Syāna, 236; —s, or wizards, 738.
Sylhet, 687.
Symbolism, in building rites, 912.

T.

Tabus, 230 ff.
Tadia, armlet, 899.
Tafūri, 540.
Tagādhri, a thread, 753, 756.
Tāhir Bandagi, 541.
Tahli Sāhib, mandir at Ferozepur, 710.
Tahur, tahūr = circumcision, 778.
Taht-ul-hanak, 878.
Tāj-ud-Dīn, Shaikh, 502, 533.
Tāj-al-Arifīn, 502.
Takan, Tukan, a province of Vāsdeo, 40.
Takbir, 764.
Takht, 494; "throne," 822; —ubelnā: —jami, 832.
Takia Mahāndri, and — wāli shrine, 595.
Takka, 47.
Takke or Takhiān di pachar, 786.
Takolak, Nāg, 154.
Takrasi Nāg, 168–9.
Tala, rite, the, 435.
Talikot, battle of, 687.
Talli, pānā, 905.
Talwandi, birth-place of Gurū Nanak, 676.
Tamāhi, rite observed three months after a death, 886.
Tambol = neota, 814.
Tambū Sāhib, 713.
Tamdin, Hayagriva, 77.
Tanāwali, 595.
Tānk, 40.
"Tank of the Gurū" fair at Khosa Kotla, 712.
Tāntra, Yogachāra, 71, 73.
Tantrism, 79, 82.
Tāntrists, 68.
Tanjūr, 72.
Tao-ism, 61, 62.
Tapā, 113.
Tapas, 109, 110, 184.
Tapteshar Mahādeo, 269.
Tāra, 71, 329, 325; the helper, 81; the 21 Taras, 82 = Ganbo-chhāg-du gba, &c., 93; Devi, 426; Devi, of Tārab, 357.
Tāra Nāth, 358.
Taragga, a thread, 753.
Tarain sāja, first Māgh, 474.

Taran Imām, 601.
Tārar, a tribal area, 51.
Tarema = Lakshmi, 92.
Tarer, 131.
Tarīja, 833.
Tarkhān, 366.
Tarn Tāran, 683.
Tarslān, fair, 341.
Tarūna-Dal, 701.
Tasawwaf, 548.
Tasbīh, 629.
Tat Khālsa, 700–1.
Tathagata, 77, 78, 79.
Tātig Nāg, 175.
Tatiri, plover, 241.
Taxiles, 27.
Tazia, 742.
Teething, omens from, 746.
Teg, sword, 703; Bahādur, 686.
Tej Chand, Raja of Mandi, 429.
Teja, 203.
Tejbal, averts evil spirits, 917.
Tel, 819; —lagāna, 837; charhānā, 814.
Telar, Telu Rām, a son born after three girls, 745.
Telirāja, 319.
Telu Rām, 745.
Temples, form of, 434.
Teramī, 850.
Tera-panthi, 103, 104.
Terminology of Moslem betrothal observances, 803.
Tewa = lagan, 894.
Tewar, teur, trousseau, 732; *trewar* in S.W.
Thadairi, archery, 363.
Thaknā, charm, *danton ka*—, charm of the teeth, 746.
Thākni, thanknī, rite in pregnancy, 731.
Thakur, 42; (Bain), 155; = Mahādeo, 68.
Thākurain, 51.
Thākurdwāra, 259.
Thāl ceremony, 807, 832–834.
Thāma, a wedding rite, 797–8.
Thān, 431.
Thānakwāsi, 103.
Thānesar, 31, 868.
Thankni, Note 2, 731.
Thāpa, 829, 893, 917.
Thapna, 831.
Tharā, circle, 917.
Thāran Imām, 600.
Tharu, Rājā, of Habri, 621.
Thaska Mirānji, 529, 688.
Thathlu, *deota*, 458.
Tharapere, 433.
Tharu-bateri, 433.
Theocracy, Sikh, 704.
Thīkri, sherd, —kī sagāi, betrothal at birth, 768; kī māng, pre-natal, 804.
Thir Mal, *deota*, 431.
Thobar, Euphorbia Royleana, 750.
Thomas, George, 703.
Thombar, 433.
Three, unlucky, 222.
Threshing-floor, 219.
Thumbardevi, 433.
Thunder, 134.
Thursday, 241.
Tiāri pānā, 906.
Tibet, Western, 35.
Tibetan race, in Spiti, &c., 6; invasion, 35.
Tiddi, mourning, 888.
Tigra satnā, 906.
Tij festival, 812.
Tījā = *soyam*. 887, 889.
Tijon, fair, 395.
Tīka, 684; or sikka, 786; *cf.* tilak.
Tīkās, 22, of Junga, 444 f.
Tikar-jag, feast, 436.
Tikka bhejnā, 805.
Til chāwali, rice and *til* mixed, 761.
Til khelnā, 802.
Tilak, 259, 376, 680; Note 7, 786; *cf.* tika.
Tilanjali, offering of water and sesamum seeds, 840, 846, 857.
Tilla Jogian, 289.
Tilli = Chilli, 626.
Timbulla, 56.
Times, unlucky, 239 f.
Tinan, a dialect of Lāhul, 90.
Ting Gund, 585.
Tingri, Pīr, 628.
Tīrath-bahin, 903.
Tiraths, 288 f.; —Parālsar, 288.
Tirauri, 699.
Tirkhi, quick time, 919.
Tirmalkheri (Madras town), 688.
Tirphal kā gontar, a rite observed on the third day after a birth, 750.
Tirphalla, 751.
Tirsūl, trident, 147.

Tiru, 447.
Tith, lunar day, 740.
Timāna, 124.
Tohāna, 830,
Toleration, Moslem, 495.
Tonchara, inoculator, 356.
Tong-srūng, 64.
Tor Gund, 586.
Tor Kamāl, *ziārat*, 597.
Toramāna, 39.
Toran, 815.
Tornā, 821.
Tosha, food given in alms, toshe kī rotī, food "for the journey," 880, 881, 882.
Trāga, 204.
Transmigration. *See* Metempsychosis, 720.
Travel, portents, 225.
Treabanj, 788.
Tree, worship, 135, 136–7.
Trees, castes among, 256.
Tretari, dance, 919.
Tribes of Sirsa, 790; Rajputs of Kaithal, 791; Gujars of Rupar, 791: Jats of Lahore, 791; Rajputs of Lahore, 791.
Trigartta, 131.
Trikhā Tīrath, 288.
Trikhals, beliefs about, 745.
Trikhal, (1) third (conception): (2) a child of one sex born after three of the other, 743; —*shānti*, 744.
Triloknāth, 420.
Triplets, 742.
Tripundra, 909.
Tsanit, 85.
Tuesday, 217, 218, 242, 253.
Tughlaq Shāh, 493.
Tukhāra, a tribe, 54.
Tulādān, 256.
Tulamba, 678.
Tulsi ki minjarān, 267.
Tulsi, 138, 259.
Tuna, *tona*, 258.
Tunda *rākshasa*, 325–6.
Tundi Bhūt, 326.
Tunga, 426.
Tūntiā, 814.
Tūnwar, 15: = Tomara, 36.
Tūri, 506.
Tūri, 576.
Turi, Malli Khel, 588.
Turk, Turki, 34.
Turu Nāg, 170.
Tūsi, 540.
Twelve, 222.
Twins, 746.
Typhus, 694.

U.

Uba achwal, 807.
Ubhā ki rotiān, 886.
Uboh, 124.
Uch, college at, 490.
Uch, 495.
Uch Sharīf, 605.
Uchhar, 884.
Udah, Devi, 428–9.
Udāsi, 399, 710, 711, 714;—Sikhs, 681, 684, 685, 694.
Ugdi-Gūga, 178.
Ugga, 254.
Ujlā, white, 762.
Ulma, 501–2.
Uma, 325.
Umar Aga, 592.
Umbilical cord observances, 747, 764.
Umdatul-Tawarikh, 685.
Umm-us-sabiān, 217.
Unlucky children, 743.
Upādhyāya, 111.
Upakesa, 113.
Upashamita, 109.
Upāshraya, 111.
Upendra, 371.
Urdhpund, 909.
Urna, "wool," 517.
Ushīnara, 55.
Utmānnāma Tappa, 807, 832.
Utmanzais, 806.
Utrahān, 784.
Utrān, 784.

V.

Vaccination, 257.
Vachā Chauhan, 178, 188.
Vāchaka, 111.
Vaimānika, 112.
Vairochana, 78.
Vaishnava, 259, 390, 391, 681, 909.
Vaishnava, innovations of, 4; elements, 918.
Vaishnava sect, 909–10.

Vaishno Devi, 329.
Vajrapani, 80, 81.
Validity of Hindu betrothal, 790.
Vāmana, 369.
Varā sūi, 801.
Varāha, 369.
Vardhamāna Mahāvira, 106.
Vardhapundra, 909.
Vasāti, an extinct tribe, 54.
Vāsdev, Vāsudeva, 23; the Kushān king, 31; his nationality, 47.
Vassa, rains, 86.
Vāsudeva, 367, 368 f, 377.
Vāsuki, 132, 169.
Vāyu, 120.
Veda, 118.
Vedic culture, antiquity of, 20.
Vedic death rītual, 840.
Vedic scheme of death ritual, 839.
Vedwā, gifts to, 841.
Veiled prophet, 582–3.
Ventura, General, 691.
Venus, offerings to, 739.
Vīaticum (baitarni), 841.
Vichār, thoughtfulness, 716.
Vidhāta Mata, worship of, 750, 754.
Vidya, 63.
Viewing the stars, 772.
Vigils, 778.
Vikramaditya, 131.
Vimān, bier, 842.
Vimānas, 112.
Vipāsyin, 78.
Vishn-ganth, 909.
Vishn-pad (Bishn-), 909.
Vishnu, 80, 119, 259, 366 ff, 377, 396, 401, 870, 905.
Vishnu, incarnate in Rishabnāth, 101.
Visvābhu, 78.
Visvakarma, 366, 398.
Vitunda, 325.
Vows, 769, 780 f, 782.
Vrata, 109.
Vrishni, 367, 368.
Vūgūpa, a demon, 62.
Vyāsa, 120, 134–5.

W.

Wadh, marriage, 832.
Wahābia, 540.
Wajūd-i-zilli, 533.
Wākdān, irrevocable Hindu betrothal contract, 785.
Wali Abdāli, Shāh, 628.
Wali Qandhāri, Moslem Saint, 678.
Wali Qandahāri, Bāba, 628.
Walīma, 833.
Waliyati = bejindri, 438.
Waq, 790.
Warenā, support: *cf.* saubhāl, 811, 834.
Wari, 822, Note 2, 827.
Warī, clothes, &c., given to the bride on the boy's behalf, 822.
Wārpher, 896.
Warweshwar Mahādeo, 272.
Washing corpse, 876.
Wasi Karam, Khwāja, 577.
Wāsil, ibn-i-'Ata, 506.
Wāslia, 517.
Wāstā (house-god), 913.
Wāstā, 912, 913.
Wat = sāg, 792.
Watta-satta, 786.
Watr sākh, 792.
Wazīr, ancestor of, 592.
Wazīrs, 835.
Wazīr, Kābul Khel, 586–7, 589.
Wazīr, Karmandi Khel, 589.
Wazīr, Madd Khel, and Ahmadzai, 589.
Wazīrs' dances at 'Id, 920.
Wednesday, 218, 240, 241, 353.
Weham, gifts, after a birth, 771.
Well at Govindwal, beliefs about, 682.
Well worship, 754.
Wells, 133, 134.
Widow re-marriage in Kāngra and Kulu (jhajra), 796.
Widow's mourning (Hindu), 843.
Wilāyat Shāh, 624.
Wilāyatī Pathans, 808, 830.
Witchcraft, 208, 213.

Y.

Yahar (Yeer), 49.
Yakkha, 367.
Yāma, 83, 134, 470.
Yāma. the Death-god, 866.
Yāma-Loka, 849.
Yamarāj, 205.
Yāna, 64.
Yār Muhammad, Hāji, 504.

Yashkun, 59.
Yāth, f-ini, 357.
Yatīm, Shāh, 536.
Yaudheyas = Joiyas?, 31, 55.
Ye'sen, 64.
Yidam, tutelary deities, 77, 79; — Chakdor, 79, 80, 82, 87.
Yoga, 63, 74.
Yogachāra, 71.
Yogni, 249.
Yoni, 68.
Yueh-chi, 34.
Yul-lha = Dewa, 77, 83.
Yūm, 79.
Yung-drung-bon, 61.
Yūsufzai, tribal tract, 53.

Z.

Zābul, 22.
Zābulistan, 40, 47.
Zacha, 766; — giri, rāni, "queen mother," 773.
Zāhir Dīwān, 178.
Zahir Pir, 121.
Zāhir Pir, 171, 182.
Zaidi, 529.
Zaimusht, 575.
Zain-ul-abidain, 566.
Zakaria Khān, 702.
Zalāwin, 919.
Zamān Shāh, 709.
Zamīndār = Jāt, 13.
Zanakh, 878.
Zanākhi, 907.
Zar-i-zimmīya, 495.
Zat fair, 362.
Ziārat, defined, 576.
Ziārats, in Kurram, 577 ff.
Zikr, 520–1.
Zikr, 539, 549, 553.
Zinda, 391.
Zinda Pir, 562, 563.
Zinda Pir, 601.
Zoho, a class in Spiti = Lohār, 69.
Zoroastrians, 25; deities on Kushān coins, 34; *cf.* 45.
Zuhāk, 21, 22.
Zuhr prayer, 805.
Zunnār, 521.